June 6–9, 2016
New York, NY, USA

Association for Computing Machinery

Advancing Computing as a Science & Profession

ICMR'16

Proceedings of the 2016 ACM International Conference on Multimedia Retrieval

Sponsored by:

ACM SIGMM

Supported by:

IBM Research, Columbia University, and Google

Association for
Computing Machinery

Advancing Computing as a Science & Profession

The Association for Computing Machinery
2 Penn Plaza, Suite 701
New York, New York 10121-0701

Notice to Past Authors of ACM-Published Articles
ACM intends to create a complete electronic archive of all articles and/or other material previously published by ACM. If you have written a work that has been previously published by ACM in any journal or conference proceedings prior to 1978, or any SIG Newsletter at any time, and you do NOT want this work to appear in the ACM Digital Library, please inform permissions@acm.org, stating the title of the work, the author(s), and where and when published.

ISBN: 978-1-4503-4359-6 (Digital)

ISBN: 978-1-4503-4599-6 (Print)

Additional copies may be ordered prepaid from:

ACM Order Department
PO Box 30777
New York, NY 10087-0777, USA

Phone: 1-800-342-6626 (USA and Canada)
+1-212-626-0500 (Global)
Fax: +1-212-944-1318
E-mail: acmhelp@acm.org
Hours of Operation: 8:30 am – 4:30 pm ET

Printed in the USA

ICMR 2016 Chairs' Welcome

It is our pleasure to welcome you to the *2016 ACM International Conference on Multimedia Retrieval – ICMR'16.* This year's conference continues a 17-year tradition of being the premier forum for presentation of research results and experience reports on multimedia retrieval research, systems, and users. This annual international conference, started in 2011, continues the leadership of the two former ACM CIVR (from 2002) and ACM MIR (from 2000) series in state-of-the-art developments in the analysis, storage, comparison, retrieval, and presentation of image, video, audio, and text working together on diverse platforms.

The call for papers attracted over 230 submissions from across the world. The program committee reviewed and accepted the following:

Track	*Reviewed*	*Accepted*	
Long Papers	120	20	16%
Short Papers	72	36	50%
Special Session Papers	6	3	50%
Brave New Ideas Papers	6	4	66%
Student Showcase Papers	4	3	75%
Demonstrations	15	10	66%

We also encourage attendees to attend the keynote talk and industry presentations.

Putting together *ICMR'16* was a large distributed effort. We thank the many authors for providing the technical and interactive content of the program. We are grateful to the many program committee members (for papers, panels, demonstrations, tutorials, and workshops) who worked hard in recruiting, reviewing, and organizing their sessions. We are especially grateful to our webmaster for his inventive http://www.icmr2016.com/. We thank IBM Research and Columbia University for their logistical support, and our sponsor, ACM for all things organizational. We are particularly thankful for the financial support of Google Research and IBM Research.

We hope that you will find the conference to be informative and stimulating, and the venue—the greatest city in the world—to be an exciting place to interact with your fellow researchers and practitioners from around the world.

John R. Smith
ICMR'16 Co-General Chair
IBM Research, USA

John R. Kender
ICMR'16 Co-General Chair
Columbia University, USA

Table of Contents

ICMR 2016 Organization xi

ICMR 2016 Sponsors & Supporters xv

Tutorials

- **Situation Recognition from Multimodal Data** 1
  Vivek K. Singh *(Rutgers University)*, Siripen Pongpaichet, Ramesh Jain *(University of California, Irvine)*
- **On the "Face of Things"** 3
  Ranran Feng, Balakrishnan Prabhakaran *(University of Texas at Dallas)*

Keynote

- **New Frontiers of Large Scale Multimedia Information Retrieval** 5
  Shih-Fu Chang *(Columbia University)*

Oral: Deep Learning and Applications

- **Matching User Photos to Online Products with Robust Deep Features** 7
  Xi Wang, Zhenfeng Sun, Wenqiang Zhang *(Fudan University)*, Yu Zhou *(Chinese Academy of Sciences)*, Yu-Gang Jiang *(Fudan University)*
- **Video Emotion Recognition with Transferred Deep Feature Encodings** 15
  Baohan Xu *(Fudan University)*, Yanwei Fu *(Disney Research)*, Yu-Gang Jiang *(Fudan University)*, Boyang Li, Leonid Sigal *(Disney Research)*
- **Scene-driven Retrieval in Edited Videos using Aesthetic and Semantic Deep Features** 23
  Lorenzo Baraldi, Costantino Grana, Rita Cucchiara *(Università degli Studi di Modena e Reggio Emilia)*
- **ACD: Action Concept Discovery from Image-Sentence Corpora** 31
  Jiyang Gao, Chen Sun, Ram Nevatia *(University of Southern California)*

Oral: Image and Video Content Analysis

- **GPU-FV: Realtime Fisher Vector and Its Applications in Video Monitoring** 39
  Wenjing Ma *(Chinese Academy of Sciences)*, Liangliang Cao *(Yahoo)*, Lei Yu, Guoping Long, Yucheng Li *(Chinese Academy of Sciences)*
- **Mouse Activity as an Indicator of Interestingness in Video** 47
  Gloria Zen *(University of Trento)*, Paloma de Juan, Yale Song *(Yahoo Research)*, Alejandro Jaimes *(AiCure)*
- **Automatic Identification of Sports Video Highlights using Viewer Interest Features** 55
  Prithwi Raj Chakraborty, Ligang Zhang, Dian Tjondronegoro, Vinod Chandran *(Queensland University of Technology)*
- **Diverse Concept-Level Features for Multi-Object Classification** 63
  Youssef Tamaazousti *(CEA LIST & University of Paris-Saclay)*, Hervé Le Borgne *(CEA LIST)*, Céline Hudelot *(University of Paris-Saclay)*

Oral: Brave New Ideas

- **Personalized Privacy-aware Image Classification** 71
  Eleftherios Spyromitros-Xioufis, Symeon Papadopoulos *(CERTH-ITI)*, Adrian Popescu *(CEA, LIST)*, Yiannis Kompatsiaris *(CERTH-ITI)*

- **The Science and Detection of Tilting** ... 79
  Xingjie Wei *(University of Cambridge)*, Jussi Palomaki *(University of Helsinki)*,
  Jeff Yan *(University of Lancaster)*, Peter Robinson *(University of Cambridge)*
- **Using Photos as Micro-Reports of Events** ... 87
  Siripen Pongpaichet, Mengfan Tang, Laleh Jalali, Ramesh Jain *(University of California, Irvine)*
- **Searching for Audio by Sketching Mental Images of Sound: A Brave New Idea for Audio Retrieval in Creative Music Production** ... 95
  Peter Knees *(Johannes Kepler University)*, Kristina Andersen *(Studio for Electro Instrumental Music (STEIM))*

Oral: Multimedia Datasets and Applications

- **The LFM-1b Dataset for Music Retrieval and Recommendation** ... 103
  Markus Schedl *(Johannes Kepler University)*
- **Foreground Object Sensing for Saliency Detection** ... 111
  Hengliang Zhu, Bin Sheng *(Shanghai Jiao Tong University)*,
  Xiao Lin *(University of Shanghai for Science and Technology)*,
  Yangyang Hao, Lizhuang Ma *(Shanghai Jiao Tong University)*
- **Constrained Local Enhancement of Semantic Features by Content-Based Sparsity** ... 119
  Youssef Tamaazousti *(CEA LIST & University of Paris-Saclay)*, Hervé Le Borgne, Adrian Popescu *(CEA LIST)*
- **Event Detection with Zero Example: Select the Right and Suppress the Wrong Concepts** ... 127
  Yi-Jie Lu, Hao Zhang *(City University of Hong Kong)*,
  Maaike de Boer *(Netherlands Organization for Applied Scientific Research (TNO) & Radboud University)*,
  Chong-Wah Ngo *(City University of Hong Kong)*

Oral: Best Paper Candidates

- **Homemade TS-Net for Automatic Face Recognition** ... 135
  Shilun Lin, Zhicheng Zhao, Fei Su *(Beijing University of Posts and Telecommunications)*
- **Pooling Objects for Recognizing Scenes without Examples** ... 143
  Svetlana Kordumova, Thomas Mensink, Cees G. M. Snoek *(University of Amsterdam)*
- **Multilingual Visual Sentiment Concept Matching** ... 151
  Nikolaos Pappas *(Idiap Research Institute)*, Miriam Redi *(Yahoo Inc.)*, Mercan Topkara *(JW Player)*,
  Brendan Jou, Hongyi Liu, Tao Chen, Shih-Fu Chang *(Columbia University)*
- **Action Recognition by Learning Deep Multi-Granular Spatio-Temporal Video Representation** ... 159
  Qing Li, Zhaofan Qiu *(University of Science and Technology of China)*,
  Ting Yao, Tao Mei, Yong Rui *(Microsoft Research)*, Jiebo Luo *(University of Rochester)*

Special: Learning with Semantic Information for Large Scale Multimedia Understanding

- **A Short Survey of Recent Advances in Graph Matching** ... 167
  Junchi Yan *(East China Normal University)*, Xu-Cheng Yin *(University of Science and Technology Beijing)*,
  Weiyao Lin *(Shanghai Jiao Tong University)*, Cheng Deng *(Xidian University)*,
  Hongyuan Zha *(Georgia Institute of Technology)*, Xiaokang Yang *(Shanghai Jiao Tong University)*
- **The ImageNet Shuffle: Reorganized Pre-training for Video Event Detection** ... 175
  Pascal Mettes, Dennis C. Koelma, Cees G. M. Snoek *(University of Amsterdam)*,
- **Learning for Traffic State Estimation on Large Scale of Incomplete Data** ... 183
  Yiyang Yao *(State Grid Zhejiang Company)*, Yingjie Xia *(Zhejiang University)*,
  Zhenyu Shan *(Hangzhou Normal University)*, Zhengguang Liu *(National University of Singapore)*

Oral: Image and Video Search

- **Diverse Yet Efficient Retrieval using Locality Sensitive Hashing** 189
  Vidyadhar Rao *(IIIT Hyderabad)*, Prateek Jain *(Microsoft Research India)*, C. V. Jawahar *(IIIT Hyderabad)*
- **Correlation Autoencoder Hashing for Supervised Cross-Modal Search** 197
  Yue Cao, Mingsheng Long, Jianmin Wang, Han Zhu *(Tsinghua University)*
- **Regional Subspace Projection Coding for Image Retrieval** 205
  Mingmin Zhen, Wenmin Wang, Ronggang Wang *(Peking University)*
- **Scaling Group Testing Similarity Search** 213
  Ahmet Iscen *(Inria)*, Laurent Amsaleg *(CNRS-IRISA)*, Teddy Furon *(Inria)*

Posters

- **Vinereactor: Crowdsourced Spontaneous Facial Expression Data** 221
  Edward Kim, Shruthika Vangala *(Villanova University)*
- **Mirroring Facial Expressions: Evidence from Visual Analysis of Dyadic Interactions** 225
  Yuchi Huang, Saad Khan *(Educational Testing Service)*
- **Sequential Correspondence Hierarchical Dirichlet Processes for Video Data Analysis** 229
  Jianfei Xue, Koji Eguchi *(Kobe University)*
- **A Computational Approach to Finding Facial Patterns of a Babyface** 235
  Zi-Yi Ke, Mei-Chen Yeh *(National Taiwan Normal University)*
- **Video Description Generation using Audio and Visual Cues** 239
  Qin Jin *(Renmin University of China)*, Junwei Liang *(Carnegie Mellon University)*
- **Xplore-M-Ego: Contextual Media Retrieval Using Natural Language Queries** 243
  Sreyasi Nag Chowdhury, Mateusz Malinowski , Andreas Bulling, Mario Fritz *(Max Planck Institute for Informatics)*
- **Learning Music Embedding with Metadata for Context Aware Recommendation** 249
  Dongjing Wang *(Zhejiang University & University of Technology Sydney)*, Shuiguang Deng *(Zhejiang University)*, Xin Zhang *(Shandong University)*, Guandong Xu *(University of Technology Sydney)*
- **Region Trajectories for Video Semantic Concept Detection** 255
  Yuancheng Ye *(The Graduate Center, CUNY)*, Xuejian Rong *(The City College, City University of New York)*, Xiaodong Yang *(NVIDIA Research)*, YIngli Tian *(The City College, City University of New York)*
- **Audiovisual Summarization of Lectures and Meetings Using a Segment Similarity Graph** 261
  Chidansh Bhatt *(FX Palo Alto Laboratory Inc)*, Andrei Popescu-Belis *(Idiap Research Institute)*, Matthew Cooper *(FX Palo Alto Laboratory Inc)*
- **Recurrent Support Vector Machines for Audio-Based Multimedia Event Detection** 265
  Yun Wang, Florian Metze *(Carnegie Mellon University)*
- **Adding Chinese Captions to Images** 271
  Xirong Li, Weiyu Lan *(Renmin University of China)*, Jianfeng Dong *(Zhejiang University)*, Hailong Liu *(Tencent)*
- **Emotion Recognition from EEG Signals Enhanced by User's Profile** 277
  Tanfang Chen, Shangfei Wang, Zhen Gao, Chongliang Wu *(University of Science and Technology of China)*
- **Multimodal Deep Convolutional Neural Network for Audio-Visual Emotion Recognition** 281
  Shiqing Zhang *(Peking University & Taizhou University)*, Shiliang Zhang, Tiejun Huang, Wen Gao *(Peking University)*

- **Large-Scale E-Commerce Image Retrieval with Top-Weighted Convolutional Neural Networks** 285
  Shichao Zhao, Youjiang Xu, Yahong Han *(Tianjin University)*
- **Web Video Popularity Prediction using Sentiment and Content Visual Features** 289
  Giulia Fontanini, Marco Bertini, Alberto Del Bimbo *(Università di Firenze)*
- **Accurate Aggregation of Local Features by using K-sparse Autoencoder for 3D Model Retrieval** 293
  Takahiko Furuya, Ryutarou Ohbuchi *(University of Yamanashi)*
- **Image Annotation using Multi-scale Hypergraph Heat Diffusion Framework** 299
  Venkatesh N. Murthy *(University of Massachusetts, Amherst)*, Avinash Sharma, Visesh Chari *(IIIT Hyderabad)*, R. Manmatha *(University of Massachusetts, Amherst)*
- **Discriminant Cross-modal Hashing** 305
  Xing Xu, Fumin Shen, Yang Yang *(University of Electronic Science and Technology of China)*, Heng Tao Shen *(University of Electronic Science and Technology of China & The University of Queensland)*
- **CNN-based Style Vector for Style Image Retrieval** 309
  Shin Matsuo, Keiji Yanai *(The University of Electro-Communications)*
- **MVC: A Dataset for View-Invariant Clothing Retrieval and Attribute Prediction** 313
  Kuan-Hsien Liu, Ting-Yen Chen, Chu-Song Chen *(Academia Sinica)*
- **A Quality Adaptive Multimodal Affect Recognition System for User-Centric Multimedia Indexing** 317
  Rishabh Gupta *(Sensaura Inc. & University of Quebec)*, Mojtaba Khomami Abadi *(University of Trento)*, Jesús Alejandro Cárdenes Cabré *(Sensaura Inc.)*, Fabio Morreale *(University of Trento)*, Tiago H. Falk *(University of Quebec)*, Nicu Sebs *(University of Trento)*
- **Rank Diffusion for Context-Based Image Retrieval** 321
  Daniel Carlos Guimarães Pedronette *(Universidade Estadual Paulista (UNESP))*, Ricardo da S. Torres *(University of Campinas (UNICAMP))*
- **Bags of Local Convolutional Features for Scalable Instance Search** 327
  Eva Mohedano, Kevin McGuinness, Noel E. O'Connor *(Dublin City University)*, Amaia Salvador, Ferran Marqués, Xavier Giró-i-Nieto *(Universitat Politecnica de Catalunya)*
- **Interactive Multimodal Learning on 100 Million Images** 333
  Jan Zahálka, Stevan Rudinac *(University of Amsterdam)*, Björn Þór Jónsson *(Reykjavik University & University of Amsterdam)*, Dennis C. Koelma, Marcel Worring *(University of Amsterdam)*
- **Combining Holistic and Part-based Deep Representations for Computational Painting Categorization** 339
  Rao Muhammad Anwer *(Aalto University)*, Fahad Shahbaz Khan *(Linköping University)*, Joost van de Weijer *(Universitat Autonoma de Barcelona)*, Jorma Laaksonen *(Aalto University)*
- **Bidirectional Joint Representation Learning with Symmetrical Deep Neural Networks for Multimodal and Crossmodal Applications** 343
  Vedran Vukotić *(INSA Rennes)*, Christian Raymond *(INSA Rennes)*, Guillaume Gravier *(CNRS)*
- **SSD Technology Enables Dynamic Maintenance of Persistent High-Dimensional Indexes** 347
  Björn Þór Jónsson *(Reykjavik University)*, Laurent Amsaleg *(CNRS-IRISA)*, Herwig Lejsek *(Videntifier Technologies)*
- **Item-Based Video Recommendation: An Hybrid Approach Considering Human Factors** 351
  Andrea Ferracani, Daniele Pezzatini, Marco Bertini, Alberto Del Bimbo *(Università degli Studi di Firenze)*
- **Human's Scene Sketch Understanding** 355
  Yuxiang Ye, Yijuan Lu *(Texas State University)*, Hao Jiang *(Boston College)*
- **Retrieval of Multimedia Objects by Fusing Multiple Modalities** 359
  Ilias Gialampoukidis, Anastasia Moumtzidou, Theodora Tsikrika, Stefanos Vrochidis, Ioannis Kompatsiaris *(ITI-CERTH)*

- **Incremental Learning for Fine-Grained Image Recognition** 363
  Liangliang Cao *(Yahoo Labs)*, Jenhao Hsiao *(Yahoo Taiwan)*, Paloma de Juan *(Yahoo Labs)*, Yuncheng Li *(University of Rochester)*, Bart Thomee *(Yahoo Labs)*
- **Spatially Localized Visual Dictionary Learning** 367
  Valentin Leveau, Alexis Joly *(INRIA Zenith & INA)*, Olivier Buisson *(INA)*, Patrick Valduriez *(INRIA Zenith & INA)*
- **Semantic Binary Codes** 371
  Sravanthi Bondugula, Larry S. Davis *(University of Maryland, College Park)*
- **On the Effects of Spam Filtering and Incremental Learning for Web-Supervised Visual Concept Classification** 377
  Matthias Springstein *(German National Library of Science and Technology)*, Ralph Ewerth *(German National Library of Science and Technology & Leibniz Universität Hannover)*
- **Semi-supervised Identification of Rarely Appearing Persons in Video by Correcting Weak Labels** 381
  Eric Müller *(German National Library of Science and Technology & University of Applied Sciences Jena)*, Christian Otto *(University of Applied Sciences Jena)*, Ralph Ewerth *(German National Library of Science and Technology & Leibniz Universität Hannover)*
- **Introducing Concept And Syntax Transition Networks for Image Captioning** 385
  Philipp Blandfort, Tushar Karayil *(University of Kaiserslautern)*, Damian Borth, Andreas Dengel *(German Institute of Artificial Intelligence (DFKI))*

Demos

- **SentiCart: Cartography and Geo-contextualization for Multilingual Visual Sentiment** 389
  Brendan Jou, Margaret Yuying Qian, Shih-Fu Chang *(Columbia University)*
- **Personalized Retrieval and Browsing of Classical Music and Supporting Multimedia Material** 393
  Marko Tkalčič *(Free University of Bolzano)*, Markus Schedl *(Johannes Kepler University)*, Cynthia C. S. Liem, Mark S. Melenhorst *(Delft University of Technology)*
- **The Social Picture** 397
  Sebastiano Battiato, Giovanni M. Farinella, Filippo L. M. Milotta, Alessandro Ortis *(University of Catania)*, Luca Addesso, Antonino Casella, Valeria D'Amico, Giovanni Torrisi *(JOL WAVE Telecom Italia)*
- **Watching What and How Politicians Discuss Various Topics - A Large-Scale Video Analytics UI** 401
  Emily Song, Joseph G. Ellis, Hongzhi Li, Shih-Fu Chang *(Columbia University)*
- **Object-aware Deep Network for Commodity Image Retrieval** 405
  Zhiwei Fang, Jing Liu, Yuhang Wang, Yong Li, Song Hang *(CASIA)*, Jinhui Tang *(Nanjing University of Science and Technology)*, Hanqing Lu *(CASIA)*
- **An Automated End-To-End Pipeline for Fine-Grained Video Annotation using Deep Neural Networks** 409
  Baptist Vandersmissen, Lucas Sterckx, Thomas Demeester, Azarakhsh Jalalvand *(Ghent University - iMinds)*, Wesley De Neve *(Ghent University - iMinds & KAIST)*, Rik Van de Walle *(Ghent University - iMinds)*
- **Serendipity-driven Celebrity Video Hyperlinking** 413
  Shujun Yang, Lei Pang, Chong-Wah Ngo *(City University of Hong Kong)*, Benoit Huet *(EURECOM)*
- **Complura: Exploring and Leveraging a Large-scale Multilingual Visual Sentiment Ontology** 417
  Hongyi Liu, Brendan Jou, Tao Chen *(Columbia University)*, Mercan Topkara *(JW Player)*, Nikolaos Pappas *(Idiap Research Institute & EPFL)*, Miriam Redi *(Yahoo)*, Shih-Fu Chang *(Columbia University)*
- **Multimodal Event Detection and Summarization in Large Scale Image Collections** 421
  Manos Schinas, Symeon Papadopoulos, Georgios Petkos, Yiannis Kompatsiaris *(Centre of Research & Technology - Hellas)*, Pericles A. Mitkas *(Aristotle University of Thessaloniki)*

Oral: Student Symposium

- **Multimodal Analysis of User-Generated Content in Support of Social Media Applications** 423
  Rajiv Ratn Shah *(National University of Singapore)*
- **Multimodal Visual Pattern Mining with Convolutional Neural Networks** 427
  Hongzhi Li *(Columbia University)*
- **Facial Landmark Detection and Tracking for Facial Behavior Analysis** 431
  Yue Wu *(Rensselaer Polytechnic Institute)*

Author Index 435

2016 International Conference on Multimedia Retrieval Organization

General Chairs:	John R. Kender *(Columbia University, USA)* John R. Smith *(IBM Research, USA)*
Honorary Chair:	Shih-Fu Chang *(Columbia University, USA)*
Technical Program Chairs:	Jiebo Luo *(University of Rochester, USA)* Susanne Boll *(University of Oldenburg, Germany)* Winston Hsu *(National Taiwan University, Taiwan)*
Industry and Practitioners Chairs:	Paul Natsev *(Google Research, USA)* Rogerio Feris *(IBM Research, USA)* Yong Rui *(Microsoft Research Asia, China)*
Grand Challenge Chairs:	Lexing Xie *(Australian National University, Australia)* Nicu Sebe *(University of Trento, Italy)*
Demonstration Chairs:	Cees Snoek *(University of Amsterdam, Netherlands)* YingLi Tian *(City University of Hong Kong, USA)*
Special Sessions Chairs:	Alex Hauptmann *(Carnegie Mellon University, USA)* Shin'ichi Satoh *(National Institute of Informatics Tokyo, Japan)*
Brave New Ideas Chairs:	Gerald Friedland *(International Computer Science Institute, USA)* Hari Sundaram *(University of Illinois at Urbana Champaign, USA)*
Tutorials Chairs:	Chong-Wah Ngo *(City University of Hong Kong, China)* Selcuk Candan *(Arizona State University, USA)*
Workshop Chairs:	Liangliang Cao *(Yahoo! Research, USA)* Yu-Gang Jiang *(Fudan University, China)*
Student Showcase Chairs:	Rainer Lienhart *(University of Augsburg, Germany)* Yao Wang *(New York University, USA)*
Panel Chairs:	Alejandro Jaimes *(Aicure, USA)* Vincent Oria *(New Jersey Institute of Technology, USA)*
Publicity Chairs:	Benoit Huet *(Eurecom, France)* Kiyoharu Aizawa *(University of Tokyo, Japan)* Balakrishnan Prabhakaran *(University of Texas at Dallas, USA)*
Sponsorship Chair:	Gang Hua *(Microsoft Research Asia, China)*

Proceedings Chair: Quoc-Bao Nguyen *(IBM Research, USA)*

Local Organization Chairs: Matthew Hill *(IBM Research, USA)*
Felix Yu *(Google Research, USA)*
Michele Merler *(IBM Research, USA)*

Program Committee:

Kiyoharu Aizawa
Laurent Amsaleg
Noboru Babaguchi
Werner Bailer
Lamberto Ballan
Marco Bertini
Bishwaranjan Bhattacharjee
Subhabrata Bhattacharya
Susanne Boll
Damian Borth
Lisa Brown
Dick Bulterman
Selcuk Candan
Liangliang Cao
Andrea Cavallaro
Lekha Chaisorn
Vijay Chandrasekhar
Vincent Charvillat
Aaron Chavez
Kuan-Ting Chen
Yan-Ying Chen
Wen-Huang Cheng
Wei-Ta Chu
Tat-Seng Chua
Yung-Yu Chuang
Noel Codella
John Collomosse
Noel E. O Connor
Matthew Cooper
Ingemar Cox
Peng Cui
Hamdi Dibeklioglu
Ajay Divakaran
Mario Doeller
Matthijs Douze
Lingyu Duan
Pinar Duygulu
Wolfgang Effelsberg
Dan Ellis
Ralph Ewerth
Jianping Fan
Quanfu Fan
Rogerio Feris
Gerald Friedland
Yun Fu
Chuang Gan
Mingyan Gao
Pierre Garrigues
Efstratios Gavves
Jan van Gemert
Bernard Ghanem
Nikolaos Gkalelis
William Grosky
Cathal Gurrin
Martin Halvey
Mei Han
Allan Hanbury
Devin Harper
Richard Harvey
Alex Hauptmann
Andreas Henrich
Matthew Hill
Steven C.H. Hoi
Richang Hong
Frank Hopfgartner
Winston Hsu
Xian-Sheng Hua
Qingming Huang
Tiejun Huang
Benoit Huet
Tan Hung-Khoon
Ichiro Ide
Bogdan Ionescu
Alejandro Jaimes
Mihir Jain
Ramesh Jain
C.V. Jawahar
Yu-Gang Jiang

Program Committee *(continued)*:

Alexis Joly
Joemon Jose
Carlos Silla Jr
Herve Jegou
Mohan Kankanhalli
Marie Katsurai
John Kender
Lyndon Kennedy
Yiannis Kompatsiaris
Martha Larson
Hyowon Lee
Paul Lewis
Kai Li
Xirong Li
Xuelong Li
Mark Liao
Rainer Lienhart
Chung-Ching Lin
Qian Lin
Yen-Liang Lin
Suzanne Little
Dong Liu
Haiming Liu
Guojun Lu
Jiebo Luo
Zhigang Ma
Joao Magalhaes
Yasushi Makihara
Raghavan Manmatha
Tao Mei
Thomas Mensink
Bernard Merialdo
Michele Merler
Vasileios Mezaris
Xavier Anguera Miro
Jayanta Mukhopadhyay
Venkatesh Narasimha Murthy
Apostol Natsev
Chang-Wah Ngo
Quoc-Bao Nguyen
Liqiang Nie
Claudia Niederée
Naoko Nitta
Vincent Oria
Pietro Pala
Sharath Pankanti
Ioannis Patras
Yuxin Peng
Guo-Jun Qi
Georges Quénot
Nalini Ratha
Carlo Busso Recabarren
Miriam Redi
Yansong Ren
Matthew Rowe
Stevan Rudinac
Stefan Rueger
Yong Rui
Harald Sack
Mohammed Abdel-Megeed Salem
Paulo Sampaio
Maria Luisa Sapino
Shin'ichi Satoh
Ansgar Scherp
Klaus Schöffmann
Nicu Sebe
Fumin Shen
Heng Tao Shen
Koichi Shinoda
Lidan Shou
Chiao-Fe Shu
Mei-Ling Shyu
Vivek Singh
Malcolm Slaney
Alan Smeaton
John Smith
Cees Snoek
Thomas Steiner
Chen Sun
Hari Sundaram
Jinhui Tang
Mengfan Tang
Bart Thomee
Qi Tian
Yingli Tian
Yonghong Tian
Christian Timmerer
Raphael Troncy

Program Committee *(continued)*:

Theodora Tsikrika
Rosario Uceda-Sosa
Jasper Uijlings
Raphael Viguier
Robert Villa
Stefanos Vrochidis
Changhu Wang
Jian Wang
Jun Wang
Meng Wang
Xiangyu Wang
Yan Wang
Yao Wang
Xiaoyong Wei
Marcel Worring
Fei Wu
Hui Wu
Xiao Wu
Lexing Xie
Changsheng Xu
Shuicheng Yan
Yan Yan
Keiji Yanai
Yi Yang
Yi-Hsuan Yang
Guangnan Ye
Felix Yu
Yun Yu
Zheng-Jun Zha
Luming Zhang
Yan-Tao Zheng
Xiangdong Zhou
Roger Zimmerman

ICMR 2016 Sponsors & Supporters

Sponsors:

Association for Computing Machinery

SIGMM

Supporters:

IBM Research

Columbia University in the City of New York

Google

Situation Recognition from Multimodal Data

Vivek K. Singh
Rutgers University
New Brunswick, NJ, USA
v.singh@rutgers.edu

Siripen Pongpaichet
University of California
Irvine, CA, USA
spongpai@ics.uci.edu

Ramesh Jain
University of California
Irvine, CA, USA
jain@ics.uci.edu

Keywords
Events; Situation Recognition; Concept Detection; Event Detection; Multimedia Data Fusion

1. EXTENDED ABSTRACT

Situation recognition is the problem of deriving actionable insights from heterogeneous, real-time, big multimedia data to benefit human lives and resources in different applications. This tutorial will discuss the recent developments towards converting multitudes of data streams including weather patterns, stock prices, social media, traffic information, and disease incidents into actionable insights.

For multiple decades, multimedia researchers have been building approaches like entity resolution, object detection, and scene recognition, to understand different aspects of the observed world. Unlike the past though, now we do not need to undertake sense-making based on data coming from a single media element, modality, time-frame, or location of media capture. Real world phenomena are now being observed by multiple media streams, each complementing the other in terms of data characteristics, observed features, perspectives, and vantage points. Each of these multimedia streams can now be assumed to be available in real-time and increasingly larger portion of these come inscribed with space and time semantics. The number of such media elements available (e.g. Tweets, Flickr posts, sensor updates) is already in the order of trillions, and computing resources required for analyzing them are becoming increasingly available. We expect these trends to continue and one of the biggest challenges in multimedia computing in the near term to be that of concept recognition from such multimodal data. As shown in Figure 1, the challenges in situation recognition are fundamentally different from those in object or event recognition. They involve dealing with multiple media, each capturing real world phenomena from multiple vantage locations spread over time.

Detecting situations in time to take appropriate actions for saving lives and resources can transform multiple aspects of human life including health, natural disaster, traffic, economy, social reforms, business decisions and so on. Examples of such relevant situations include beautiful-days/ hurricanes/ wildfires, traffic (jams / smooth/ normal), economic recessions/ booms, block-busters, droughts/ great-monsoons, seasons (early-fall/ fall/ late-fall), demonstrations/ celebrations, social uprisings/ happiness-index, flash-mobs, flocking and so on.

This tutorial will provide the audience with a thorough theoretical and practical grounding on the field of situation recognition. It will bring together the work by multiple scholars working in the area of situation recognition both within and outside the multimedia research community. The attendees would be introduced to the different interpretations of situations across multiple fields, and how it builds upon and extends the efforts on object detection, event detection, scene recognition and so on. The tutorial will provide a review of recent efforts within the multimedia community towards detecting real-time situations, and the attendees will be introduced to multiple practical situation recognition approaches and applications. Specific attention will be paid to discussing the relevant open research challenges for the community to extensively advance the state of the art in situation recognition.

ICMR'16, June 06-09, 2016, New York, NY, USA.
ACM 978-1-4503-4359-6/16/06.
http://dx.doi.org/10.1145/2911996.2930061

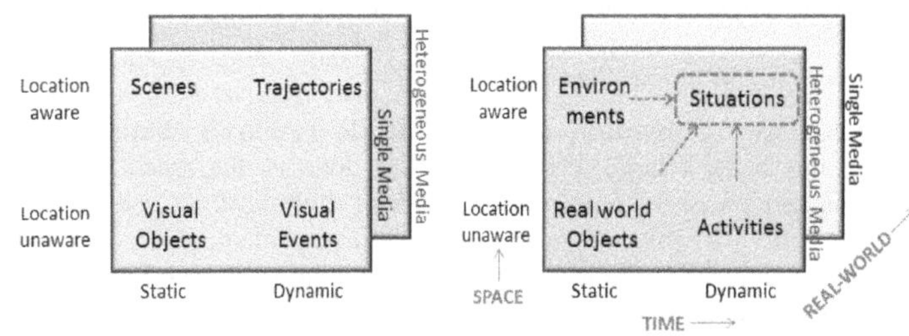

Figure 1: Different Types of Concepts can be detected in different data availability settings. Single media, such as images, results in concepts more in images than in the real world, but using different media it is possible to detect concepts in the real world

Learning objectives

At the end of the tutorial the attendees should be able to:

1. Describe the problem of situation recognition and how it is different from object detection, event recognition, scene understanding etc.
2. Outline the different interpretations of situations across different fields e.g. multimedia, ubiquitous computing, robotics, aviation etc.
3. Articulate a computational definition for the concept of "situation" and the problem of situation recognition.
4. Identify the important categories of operators needed for the task of situation recognition.
5. Relate to the practical experience of creating at least one practical situation recognition application using an open-source situation recognition toolkit.
6. Articulate the emerging trends in situation-based computing and identify the open challenges in the field of situation recognition.

2. MODULES OF THE TUTORIAL

1) Concept recognition from Multimedia data

As shown in Figure 1, ***Situation recognition*** builds on and extends object recognition, scene recognition, activity and event recognition, and complex event processing. It pushes the envelope beyond detecting ***intra-media concepts*** (i.e. those which manifest themselves, and can be detected within a single media object e.g.

a tree, or a chair *in* an image), to define and making quick progress on detecting ***real-world concepts*** (i.e. those which occur in real world, are constantly evolving, and inherently manifest themselves over heterogeneous multimedia streams from numerous sources). As a simple example, we may now look beyond the problem of creating a *tree* detector and/or testing it over Millions of Flickr images; to that of using a stream of Billions of such images and other available data to detect seasonal patterns, plant disease spreads, deforestation trends, or global warming. These are the problems which could not be tackled earlier because of the lack of data and computational resources; but those are no longer the bottlenecks.

2) Situation recognition across multiple research domains
There has been a large amount of work done in the areas like ubiquitous/pervasive computing building automation, mobile application software, aviation/air traffic control, robotics, industrial control, military command and control, surveillance, linguistics, stock market databases, multimodal presentation, about situation modeling, situation awareness, situation calculus, situation control, and situation semantics (*c.f.* [1, 2]). The interpretation of *situation* however is different across different areas and even across different works within the same area. Multiple such interpretations will be discussed and the differences as well as the commonalities in these interpretations will be identified.

3) Situation recognition

To combine heterogeneous real-time data streams into actionable situations, one may focus on the spatio-temporal commonality across streams to integrate them. A recent approach proposed in the multimedia community focuses on using a simple unified representation (called *Emage – Event-based-image*), that indexes and organizes all data into a common representation. Similarly, for going from individual data nuggets (micro-events) to macro-situations it uses a set of generic spatio-temporal analysis operators [3, 4]. Other researchers have identified variants of this representation called *Cmages (Concept-based-images)* to allow for concept-based-images that can be created using heterogeneous data and allow for information fusion and situation recognition [5]. Yet other set of researchers have defined a *FraPPE (Frame, Pixel, People, Events)* ontology for combining heterogeneous spatio-temporal data into actionable insights [6]. A common thread in all these approaches is the unified representation of heterogeneous data as pixels and defining analytics operators on them. The salient points of these approaches and the application of the defined operators for situation recognition will be discussed.

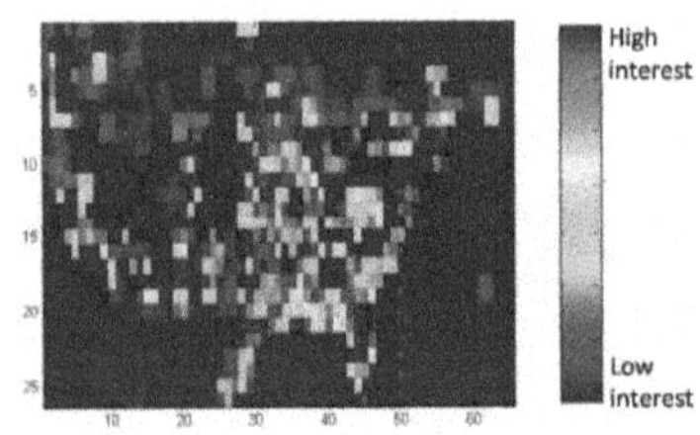

Figure 2: An Emage Showing User Interest across Mainland US in Terms of Number of Tweets Containing the Term 'iPhone' on 11th June 2009

4) Designing situation based applications

Participants will be exposed to multiple platforms that support integration of heterogeneous multimedia data for situation recognition. The open-source framework of EventShop focuses on declarative operators that work on top of the Emage representation [3]. The FraPPE model works on an ontology model and employ a human in the loop to undertake Visual Analytics [6]. The tutorial will discuss multiple examples, and the participants will get hands-on experience with creating one practical application – asthma risk score for any location.

5) Future trends and open problems

There exist multiple open problems in situation recognition. These include issues of scalability, network based models for situations, data discovery, dealing with data uncertainty, and spatio-tempoal concept detection. Consequently there lie tremendous opportunities in leveraging and repurposing multimedia processing techniques (e.g. convolution, vector representation, optical flow) for analysis of spatio-temporal gridded data and spatio-temporal situation recognition. Further, newer trends in computational crowd-sourcing and human-in-the-loop methods for multimedia processing tasks can be used for distributed multimedia data generation and processing. This tutorial will encourage multimedia researchers to tackle these problems.

3. IMPORTANCE AND RELEVANCE TO MULTIMEDIA RESEARCH COMMUNITY

Multimedia research community is particularly well positioned to take on the challenge of situation recognition. First, the community's core competence lies in handling heterogeneous media (audio, video, text, phone logs, micro-blogs, sensors etc.). Equally importantly, it is the only research community which has studied concept detection across both time (event detection), and space (like spatial organization of pixels in images). The tools for raster image processing translate directly onto spatial data layouts and notions of neighborhood, regions, boundaries, and motion vectors translate seamlessly across to spatio-temporal analysis.

Recognizing situations in the right place at the right moment to take appropriate actions can save lives and resources in various aspects of human life. For instance, approximately 250,000 people die prematurely each year from asthma attacks, and almost all of these deaths are avoidable. Asthma patients can be notified to avoid the places that can cause their asthma attacks when they are in critical situation. Similar applications of situation recognition lie in areas including emergency evacuations, business analytics, and epidemic detection.

4. REFERENCES

[1] V.K. Singh, "Personalized Situation Recognition", Advisor-Ramesh Jain, Ph.D. Thesis, University of California, Irvine. 2012.

[2] Dousson, C., Gaborit, P., & Ghallab, M. (1993, August). Situation recognition: representation and algorithms. In IJCAI (Vol. 93, pp. 166-172).

[3] V. K. Singh, M. Gao and R. Jain, "Social pixels: Genesis and evaluation," in Proceedings of the International Conference on Multimedia, 2010, pp. 481-490.

[4] V. K. Singh, M. Gao and R. Jain, "Situation recognition: an evolving problem for heterogeneous dynamic big multimedia data." Proc. Int. Conf. on Multimedia, 2012

[5] Wang, Y., & Kankanhalli, M. S. (2015, May). Tweeting Cameras for Event Detection. In *Proceedings of the 24th International Conference on World Wide Web* (pp. 1231-1241). International World Wide Web Conferences Steering Committee.

[6] Balduini, M., Della Valle, E., Azzi, M., Larcher, R., Antonelli, F., & Ciuccarelli, P. (2015). Citysensing: visual story telling of city-scale events by fusing social media streams and call data records captured at places and events. *IEEE MultiMedia*, *22*(3)

On the "Face of Things"

Ranran Feng
University of Texas at Dallas
800 W. Campbell Rd
Richardson, TX 75080
rrfeng@utdallas.edu

B. Prabhakaran
University of Texas at Dallas
800 W. Campbell Rd
Richardson, TX 75080
bprabhakaran@utdallas.edu

ABSTRACT

Face is crucial for human identity, while face identification has become crucial to information security. It is important to understand and work with the problems and challenges for all different aspects of facial feature extraction and face identification. In this tutorial, we identify and discuss four research challenges in current Face Detection/Recognition research and related research areas: (1) Unavoidable Facial Feature Alterations, (2) Voluntary Facial Feature Alterations, (3) Uncontrolled Environments, and (4) Accuracy Control on Large-scale Dataset. We also direct several different applications (spin-offs) of facial feature studies in the tutorial.

Keywords

Face Detection; Face Recognition; Uncontrolled Environment

1. INTRODUCTION

Our face describes our identity, carries our emotions, reflects our minds, conveys much more information, and yet is constantly changing over time. For instance, by looking at the face shape or wrinkles, we can tell age; by looking at different expressions, we can tell someone is happy or sad; by checking facial features, we can infer someoneŠs race etc. In fact so much more information can be deduced (as if by Sherlock Holmes) from just a face, and yet a face can also be very deceiving at times.

In this tutorial, we identify and discuss the following research challenges in current Face Detection/Recognition research and related research areas:

- Unavoidable Facial Feature Alterations – our age, health status, living habits, environment, etc all play important roles in facial feature changes (e.g., wrinkles, cloudy eye). How do we identify faces with these unavoidable feature changes?
- Voluntary Facial Feature Alterations – the pursuit of beauty drives people to all kinds of facial variations: change of hair style, make-up, etc. How do we identify faces with these voluntary feature changes?
- Uncontrolled Environments – other than the face itself, the quality of the media also plays a crucial rule to the accuracy of face identification. How do we take account of uncontrolled environment variables?
- Accuracy Control on Large-scale Dataset – the extracted facial features or facial identification algorithms should be scalable when applied to large-scale dataset.

2. DETAILED TUTORIAL MODULES

2.1 Fundamentals of Facial Features and Face Identification

There are many face detection and face recognition techniques to locate and identify a human face - easier and harder ones, faster and slower ones, etc. Given an image, these techniques locate/identifies a face based on a set of features, for example, skin color, edge, classifier cascade. We will walk through a number of most common facial features/models that are used in face detection or recognition, as well as a number of most common face detection and face recognition techniques.

2.2 Unavoidable Face Alterations

The human face is not constant: it keeps changing as time passes by. Some changes are unavoidable, such as aging, mole growing. And these types of unavoidable facial alterations challenge the accuracy of face recognition algorithms. In this tutorial, we will discuss one most common unavoidable facial alteration: aging - How aging changes facial features? What facial features are changed? How aging affects the accuracy of face recognition? How to factor aging impacts when identifying a face? We will also discuss several common methods to handle unavoidable facial alterations and discuss a number of applications.

2.3 Voluntary Face Alterations

Unlike discussed above, some facial changes are voluntary, such as camouflage, plastic surgery, make-up, etc. Unfortunately, these types of voluntary facial alterations challenge the accuracy of face detection and recognition algorithm too. In order to handle these types of facial alterations, we need to study the nature of these alterations, find an efficient way to detect the alterations, and then handle the face detection

ICMR'16 June 06-09, 2016, New York, NY, USA

ACM ISBN 978-1-4503-4359-6/16/06.
DOI: http://dx.doi.org/10.1145/2911996.2930062

or face recognition in the traditional way. We will discuss three most common voluntary face alterations: make-up, plastic surgery, and camouflage in this tutorials, and discuss several ways to handle voluntary face alterations.

2.4 Uncontrolled Environments

Given the same face detection or face recognition solution, the results (accuracy) can be very different when running against image sets with controlled environment (e.g. a plain monocolour background with standard lighting) or image sets with uncontrolled environment. In this tutorial, we will discuss common environmental variables and discuss how these variables affect the accuracy of the algorithms; and different ways to reduce impacts of these environmental variables.

2.5 Accuracy Control in Large-scaled Dataset

We have progressed significantly within last decades and achieved high accuracy on a number of standard test sets. However, these test sets are relatively small (e.g. thousands of sample images), compare with what we have nowadats on the large scale social media or cloud (e.g. millions of images on a daily basis). Thus, it is important to explore the need and importance of accuracy control of any face identification application in large-scaled dataset. In this tutorial, we will discuss current issues within applications on large-scale social media data and strategies that we can use to help improve accuracy, or the fit specific requirements.

3. APPLICATIONS AND CONCLUSIONS

The challenges discussed in this tutorial can all be extended and branched into more research topics and applications. For example, analysis of common False Positives on large scale social media dataset direct us to a significant percentage of emoji images and pet images - which leads to investigation distinguish human faces vs. synthetic faces or animal faces. In this tutorial, we will describe different application areas (spin-offs) of facial feature studies and the associated challenges.

In summary, due to the nature of human face (not a constant), it is always challenging for computer algorithms to account the variances of facial features when detection or identifying a human face. We briefly introduced common facial features, face detection/recognition techniques, and common methods to handle the variance. We hope our viewing of the tip of the iceberg in this tutorial can inspire our audience to explore further in this topic.

BIO

B. Prabhakaran is a Professor in the faculty of Computer Science Department, University of Texas at Dallas. Dr. Prabhakaran received the prestigious NSF CAREER Award FY 2003 for his proposal on Animation Databases. He was selected as an ACM Distinguished Scientist in 2011 and is currently a IEEE Senior Member. He received the Best Associate Editor for 2015, from SpringerŠs Multimedia Systems Journal. Dr Prabhakaran is a Member of the Executive Council of the ACM Special Interest Group on Multimedia (SIGMM) and is the Co-Chair of IEEE Technical Committee on Multimedia Computing (TCMC) Special Interest Group on Video Analytics (SIGVA). Dr. Prabhakaran is the General Co-Chair of the IEEE International Conference on Health Informatics (ICHI) 2015. He was also a General Co-Chair of ACM International Conference on Multimedia Retrieval 2013 (ICMR 2013), IEEE Haptic, Audio, and Visual Environments (HAVE) 2014, a General Co-chair of ACM Multimedia 2011, and ACM Multimedia and Security (MMSec) 2007. Prof Prabhakaran's research has been funded by Federal Agencies such as the National Science Foundation (NSF), USA Army Research Office (ARO), and the US-IGNITE Program.

BIO

Dr. Ranran Feng received the B.E degree in Computer Science and Engineering from Harbin Institute of Technology (Harbin, China) in 2007, the M.S. degree in Computer Science from Sam Houston State University (Huntsville, TX) in 2009, and a PhD. in Computer Science from the University of Texas at Dallas (Richardson, TX) in 2014. Dr. Feng is now back at UTD as a proud member of the faculty in the Department of Computer Science. Prior to earning her doctorate, Dr. Feng served as a Research Scientist at Image Vision Labs, Inc., where her research focused mainly on Multimedia Fraud Detection, Multimedia Content Analysis, and Pattern Recognition. Dr. Feng serves as Peer Reviewer for multiple domestic and international conferences (e.g. SIGMAP 2015), as well as Journals (e.g. IEEE Transactions on Multimedia). Dr. Feng is also interested in inter-disciplinary research, and has helped in planning and launching a number of collaborative proposals between the department of Computer Science and other departments within the University.

New Frontiers of Large Scale Multimedia Information Retrieval

Shih-Fu Chang
Columbia University
shih.fu.chang@columbia.edu

ABSTRACT
Multimedia information retrieval aims to automatically extract useful information from large collection of images, videos, and combinations with other data like text and speech. As reported in recent news, it's now possible to search information over millions or more of products with just an example image on the mobile phone. Intelligent apps are being deployed by major companies to automatically generate keywords or even captions of an image at a sophistication level that could not be imagined before. In this talk, I will review core technologies involved and discuss challenges and opportunities ahead. First, to address the complexity bottleneck when scaling up the data size, I will present extremely compact hash codes and deep learning image classification models that can reduce complexity by orders of magnitude while preserving approximate accuracy. Second, to support easy extension of recognition systems to new domains, instead of relying on fixed image categories, we introduce a new paradigm to automatically discover unique multimodal concepts and structures using large amounts of multimedia data available. Last, to support emerging applications beyond basic image categorization, I will discuss on-going efforts in understanding how images are used in expressing sentiments and emotions in online social media and how languages/cultures may influence such online multimedia communication.

Keywords
Multimedia Information Retrieval

Bio
Shih-Fu Chang is the Sr. Executive Vice Dean and the Richard Dicker Professor of Columbia Engineering. His research is focused on multimedia information retrieval, computer vision, machine learning, and signal processing, with the goal to turn unstructured multimedia data into searchable information.

His work on content-based visual search in the early 90's, VisualSEEk and VideoQ, set the foundation of this vibrant area. Over the years, he continued to create innovative techniques for image/video recognition, multimodal analysis, visual information ontology, image authentication, and compact hashing for large-scale image databases. For his long-term pioneering contributions, he has been awarded the IEEE Signal Processing Society Technical Achievement Award, ACM Multimedia SIG Technical Achievement Award, Honorary Doctorate from the University of Amsterdam, the IEEE Kiyo Tomiyasu Award, and IBM Faculty Award. For his dedicated contributions to education, he received the Great Teacher Award from the Society of Columbia Graduates. He served as Chair of Columbia Electrical Engineering Department (2007-2010), the Editor-in-Chief of the IEEE Signal Processing Magazine (2006-8), and advisor for several research institutions and companies. In his current capacity in Columbia Engineering, he plays a key role in the School's strategic planning, special research initiatives, international collaboration, and faculty development. He is a Fellow of the American Association for the Advancement of Science (AAAS) and IEEE.

ICMR'16, June 06-09, 2016, New York, NY, USA
ACM 978-1-4503-4359-6/16/06.
http://dx.doi.org/10.1145/2911996.2930063

Matching User Photos to Online Products with Robust Deep Features

Xi Wang†, Zhenfeng Sun†, Wenqiang Zhang†, Yu Zhou‡, Yu-Gang Jiang†
†School of Computer Science, Fudan University, Shanghai, China
‡Institute of Information Engineering, Chinese Academy of Sciences, Beijing, China
†{xwang10, 14110240031, wqzhang, ygj}@fudan.edu.cn
‡zhouyu@iie.ac.cn

ABSTRACT

This paper focuses on a practically very important problem of matching a real-world product photo to exactly the same item(s) in online shopping sites. The task is extremely challenging because the user photos (i.e., the queries in this scenario) are often captured in uncontrolled environments, while the product images in online shops are mostly taken by professionals with clean backgrounds and perfect lighting conditions. To tackle the problem, we study deep network architectures and training schemes, with the goal of learning a robust deep feature representation that is able to bridge the domain gap between the user photos and the online product images. Our contributions are two-fold. First, we propose an alternative of the popular contrastive loss used in siamese deep networks, namely *robust contrastive loss*, where we "relax" the penalty on positive pairs to alleviate over-fitting. Second, a multi-task fine-tuning approach is introduced to learn a better feature representation, which not only incorporates knowledge from the provided training photo pairs, but also explores additional information from the large ImageNet dataset to regularize the fine-tuning procedure. Experiments on two challenging real-world datasets demonstrate that both the robust contrastive loss and the multi-task fine-tuning approach are effective, leading to very promising results with a time cost suitable for real-time retrieval.

Keywords

Visual Similarity, Image Retrieval, Deep Learning.

1. INTRODUCTION

Online shopping is extremely popular nowadays, where consumers normally use keywords to find their interested products on online shopping sites. However, textual keywords are not always sufficient. For instance, one may see a product with brand unknown and be interested in buying it. It would be very helpful if a shopping site supports visual search in this case, so that the user can take a photo and search visually the same products online.

Although we have seen such functions provided by companies like Amazon, Google and Alibaba, automatically matching user photos to online product images is still not easy and the room for improvement is huge. User photos used as search queries are usually captured by consumers with their mobile phones under uncontrolled settings, while the product images in online shops are often professionally photographed. On the one hand, products in user photos often have cluttered backgrounds or even partial occlusions. On the other hand, some online product images only contain a part of the products in order to show some details to the consumers. This extremely large domain gap makes the task highly challenging.

Key to the development of an effective product image retrieval system is the extraction of good feature representations. In contrast to hand-engineered descriptors like the SIFT, using deep neural networks to directly learn feature representations from raw data has recently demonstrated very impressive results in many areas. In particular, the convolutional neural networks (CNN) have produced strong performance on various vision tasks like object detection [9, 20], image segmentation [6] and video classification [26]. Different from visual recognition where a conventional deep CNN is normally sufficient, the problem to be tackled in this paper is a typical image matching setup where training images are normally provided in pairs (same/different product), not in classes (which can be converted to training pairs, but not vice versa). To deal with this issue, the siamese network architecture [7, 1, 12] provides a unique capability that can naturally rank the similarity between input image pairs by a contrastive loss function, which has been successfully used in several problems like face image matching [3].

In this paper, we adopt the siamese network (cf. Figure 3) for product image search. To bridge the large domain gap between user photos and online images, we propose a simple alternative optimization target called *robust contrastive loss*. A key difference is that in the training process we do not consider positive image pairs (containing the same product) that are visually too different. We underline that this is critical in our problem setting as penalizing too much on such pairs may incur over-fitting and poor generalization capability of the learned network. In addition, we propose a multi-task fine-tuning method to tune the parameters of the siamese network, which uses not only product images but also general images from the ImageNet corpus. We show that optimizing the network with multiple tasks, i.e., match-

ICMR'16, June 06-09, 2016, New York, NY, USA
© 2016 ACM. ISBN 978-1-4503-4359-6/16/06...$15.00
DOI: http://dx.doi.org/10.1145/2911996.2912002

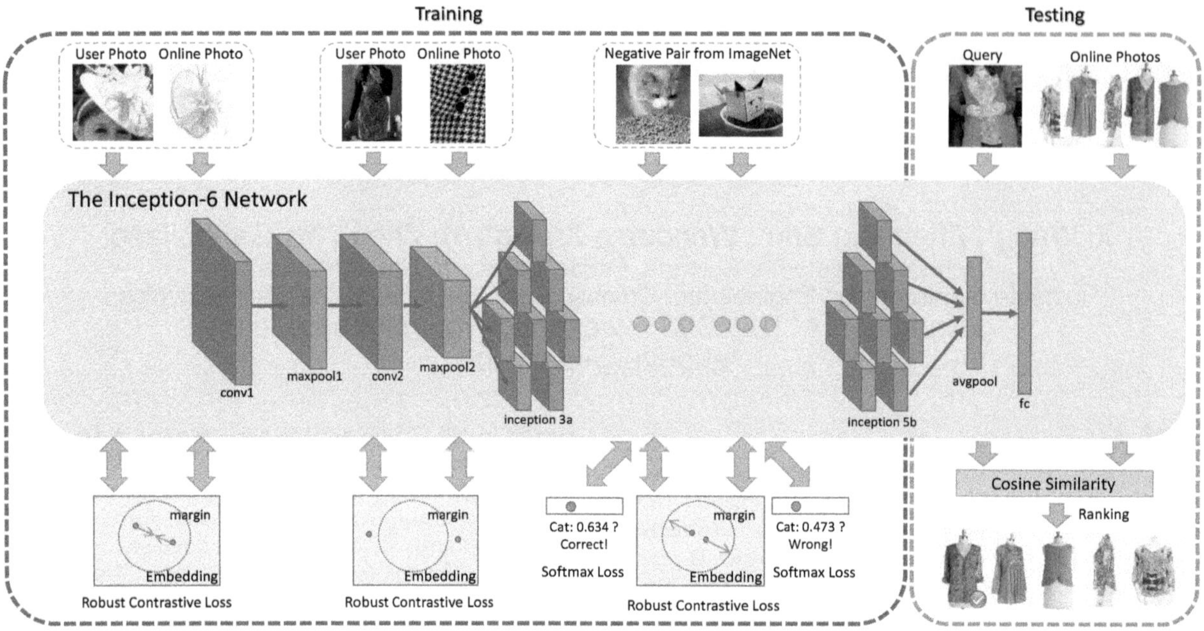

Figure 1: Illustration of the proposed product image retrieval approach. See texts for more discussions.

ing (both product and ImageNet images) and recognition (ImageNet images), can also help improve the performance of product retrieval.

Figure 1 illustrates the proposed approach. The core component of the framework is a deep neural network called Inception-6 [11]. In the training process (the left blue dashed box), each time a pair of images are given as input, each go through the Inception-6 network, and optimization is performed based on the robust contrastive loss. Positive pairs with distance larger than a pre-defined margin (e.g., the second pair in the figure) are not considered in the training process to avoid over-fitting. In addition, for image pairs from ImageNet (the third pair), we employ the proposed multi-task fine-tuning method, which not only optimizes the network parameters based on contrastive loss between the image pairs, but also tunes the network based on recognition outputs of each individual image, namely softmax loss. After training, in the online retrieval process (the right green dashed box), a feature representation can be quickly computed for a query image using the learned network, and retrieval results can be obtained by simply computing its similarity to the online product images. More details will be explained in Section 3.

With the proposed robust contrastive loss and multi-task fine-tuning, the learned network is able to produce superior retrieval accuracy on the challenging Exact Street2Shop Dataset [14] and the Alibaba Large-scale Product Image Dataset[1]. In the following, we first review related works, and then elaborate the proposed approach and discuss experimental results.

2. RELATED WORKS

Product Image Retrieval: There has been growing interests in developing product image retrieval systems in both research and industry. For instance, He et al. [8] proposed a visual search system for mobile devices using various features and indexing methods. Liu et al. [18] focused on a street-to-shop photo retrieval problem using a part alignment approach. Kalantidis et al. [13] proposed an approach to suggest multiple relevant clothing products based on some given images, using clothing recognition and segmentation techniques. In [1], Bell et al. adopted a similar pipeline to ours for similar product retrieval, but used the standard contrastive loss.

Instead of looking for similar items, Kiapour et al. [14] focused on a more challenging task called exact street-to-shop retrieval, in order to find exactly the same item in online shopping sites, which is very useful in practical applications. The same problem has also been investigated by Huang et al. [10] using ideas of visual attributes. This paper addresses the same problem of exact product retrieval with technical extensions tailored for tackling this specific problem.

Feature Representations: Extracting discriminative feature representations is critical to product image retrieval. For instance, Kuo et al. [16] proposed a semantic feature discovery approach through visual and textual clusters to derive semantically related feature representations. In contrast to the hand-engineered features, learning feature representations from raw data using the CNNs has demonstrated very impressive performance on many problems. Recent works in [5, 19] showed that a deep feature embedding trained to perform a specific task like object classification [21] can also generate competitive performance on a wide range of related tasks like fine-grained visual recognition, attribute detection, scene recognition and general image retrieval. Based on this fact, we choose to use the effective Inception-6 network [11] pre-trained on the ImageNet dataset [4] in our proposed approach.

Similarity Learning: Learning features using a siamese network [7] with contrastive loss is related to similarity or metric learning. In this category, the Online Algorithm for Scalable Image Similarity (OASIS) [2], which learns a bilinear similarity measure over hand-engineered descriptors, is one of the most successful approaches. More recently, Ki-

[1] https://tianchi.aliyun.com/competition/introduction.htm?raceId=231510

apour et al. [14] used a two-layer neural network to predict whether two features represent the same item. Using the conventional contrastive loss function, the authors designed an end-to-end neural network for metric learning [1]. Also based on the siamese network, Huang et al. [10] proposed a Dual Attribute-aware Ranking Network (DARN) for feature learning. Wu et al. [25] introduced a deep similarity learning approach for image retrieval called Online Multimodal Deep Similarity Learning (OMDSL) algorithm.

As label errors often exist in the training data, distance metric learning approaches that are more robust to training noise have been investigated (e.g., [17]). Different from [17], our work in this paper is based on the siamese network, using a novel loss function and a multi-task network fine-tuning scheme.

3. THE PROPOSED APPROACH

In this section, we first describe the siamese network and then introduce our proposed robust contrastive loss function, followed by the multi-task fine-tuning method with implementation details.

3.1 Siamese Network

Using the CNN to extract features from an image can be expressed as $\vec{X} = f(I, \theta)$, where the function f indicates the CNN structure, which computes a feature representation $\vec{X}$ for an input image I based on network parameters θ. Pre-training a CNN on a general image dataset such as the ImageNet can provide a reasonably good θ for the product retrieval problem, which has been verified in a recent work [14]. However, as the network is trained for general image classification tasks, the feature distance between two photos of the same product can be larger than that between photos of different products with certain visual similarity, which is undesirable for tackling the product image retrieval problem.

In order to extract a better feature representation that can correctly map the product image proximity to feature distance, we adopt a siamese network that contains two copies of the Inception-6 network with shared weights θ, as shown in Figure 2. The siamese network is often optimized with the conventional contrastive loss function [7]. Given a pair of input features $\vec{X}_p, \vec{X}_q$ and a binary label Y indicating whether the given pair is similar, the contrastive loss function can be written as:

$$L_{Y=1}(\vec{X}_p, \vec{X}_q) = ||\vec{X}_p - \vec{X}_q||_2^2,$$
$$L_{Y=0}(\vec{X}_p, \vec{X}_q) = \max(0, m^2 - ||\vec{X}_p - \vec{X}_q||_2^2),$$

where $Y = 1$ indicates that the input pair is similar (i.e., a positive pair containing the same product), otherwise $Y = 0$. The parameter m denotes a margin. If a negative pair can already be separated, i.e., with distance larger than the margin, the loss function should not give any further penalty. In the learning process, the shared network parameters θ are optimized to minimize the contrastive loss function.

3.2 Robust Contrastive Loss

Similar to the original contrastive loss function, the robust contrastive loss also runs over pairs of inputs. Given a pair of features $\vec{X}_p, \vec{X}_q$ and a binary label Y, the robust contrastive loss function is written as:

$$L_{Y=1}(\vec{X}_p, \vec{X}_q) = \min(m^2, ||\vec{X}_p - \vec{X}_q||_2^2),$$
$$L_{Y=0}(\vec{X}_p, \vec{X}_q) = \max(0, m^2 - ||\vec{X}_p - \vec{X}_q||_2^2).$$

Different from the conventional contrastive loss, not only sufficiently separated negative pairs are not further penalized, the penalty of positive pairs which have large feature distances are also *constrained* in the robust contrastive loss function.

The major reason behind this extension is that positive pairs with little visual similarity often exist in real-world situations. As shown in Figure 3, such pairs create large gradients via the original contrastive loss function, which may incur over-fitting (and much lower testing performance) of the learned network model.

The original siamese network was extended in a recent work [1], where, as shown in Figure 2, the softmax loss functions are also incorporated to predict the object categories of the input images. The authors of [1] showed that using the additional softmax loss can also help prevent undesirable overfitting that may be caused by using only the contrastive loss function. In this work, we adopt the same pipeline with our robust contrastive loss. We show that, by combining our robust contrastive loss with the softmax loss, the generalization capability of the learned network can be greatly enhanced.

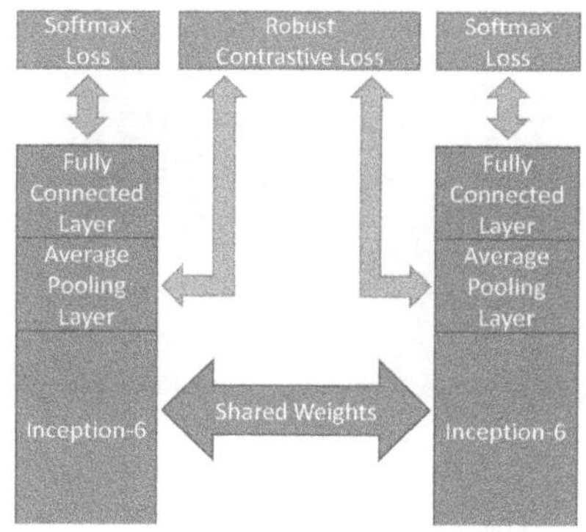

Figure 2: Siamese network architecture. In our experiments, the output of the average pooling layer is 1,024 dimensions, and the output of the fully connected layer is 21,841 dimensions.

3.3 Multi-task Fine-tuning

Different from the improved siamese network described in [1], which uses the category information of product images in the softmax loss to regularize the fine-tuning procedure, we introduce another multi-task fine-tuning scheme here to incorporate additional training samples.

As aforementioned in Section 1, we employ the recently released Inception-6 [11] (a.k.a. BN-Inception) network structure. Compared with traditional network structures like AlexNet [15] and GoogLeNet [22], the batch normalization layers are added to the Inception-6 network, which can help the network achieve similar or even better accuracy with much fewer training steps. These extra layers can be viewed as a regularizer, eliminating the need of dropout layers in some cases. The ImageNet dataset[2] [4] which has 21,841 ob-

[2]ImageNet Fall 2011 release:
http://www.image-net.org/archive/stanford/fall11_whole.tar

Figure 3: Positive image pairs with small visual similarity values incur "unwanted" large gradient via the original contrastive loss function, which may result in over-fitting.

ject categories is used to pre-train the Inception-6 network. Our pre-trained network achieves 0.315 top-1 accuracy over a randomly sampled validation dataset.

With the pre-trained model, a siamese network is created by simply making a copy of the Inception-6 and connecting both models with the robust contrastive loss. As shown in Figure 2, the robust contrastive loss function is placed after the 1,024-d average pooling layers. Two softmax loss functions are further adopted after the 21,841-d fully connected layers, measuring the recognition/classification errors of each individual input image.

The main difference between our multi-task fine-tuning scheme and the previous methods is that we use the images from ImageNet and their category labels to "regularize" the fine-tuning procedure. The benefits are two-fold. On the one hand, our proposed approach no longer requires annotated category labels for product images. On the other hand, existing product image datasets are often domain specific, and the product category number is usually much smaller than that of the ImageNet categories. Although ImageNet data is different from product images, we emphasize that using sufficient training data is more important when the softmax loss serves as an auxiliary regularizer to prevent over-fitting. As will be shown later, our scheme produces clearly better results than [1], which uses only the product images for the softmax loss.

More specifically, in order to form the training and validation sets for the proposed multi-task fine-tuning, we construct three kinds of input image pairs. The *positive pairs* can be created using the training product images based on the ground-truth labels. In addition, for each user photo in the training set, using the pre-trained Inception-6 network and cosine similarity, we can retrieve a set of online product images from the training set. *Hard negative pairs* can then be constructed based on the false positives in the top-retrieved results. Finally, the last part is *background negative pairs*. For this, we randomly sample images from different ImageNet categories to ensure that each pair contains two different objects. As only the images from the background negative pairs have category labels, we simply set the gradient from softmax loss to 0 for the other two types of training pairs. With a ratio of approximately $1:1:4$, the three kinds of image pairs are merged to construct the training and validation sets.

To fine-tune the siamese network, we set the learning rate to 5×10^{-5}, the momentum to 0.9 and the weight decay to 10^{-4} initially. The margin m in the robust contrastive loss function is set to 40.0 in our following experiments if there is no additional description. The size of each mini-batch is 128, which means 128 pairs of product images are processed by the network simultaneously. The training procedure lasts $12,000$ iterations maximally, and early stopping is used based on results on the validation set.

In addition, for the user photos, after resizing the smaller dimension to 256, we use the 224×224 center-cropped regions as the inputs. For the online product images, assuming we have a $w \times h$ bounding box in a $W \times H$ image, the edge length of the selected area is $min(max(w, h), min(W, H))$. After fine-tuning, given a new image, the outputs of the last average-pooling layer (1,024-d) of the trained Inception-6 network are used as its feature representation. With the features, we adopt Cosine similarity to measure the proximity of two images, because we found it can produce better results than Euclidean distance (about 3 absolute percentages higher). Notice that other similarity measures or advanced fast similarity search approaches (e.g., hashing) are all applicable on top of our features, which is beyond the scope of this work.

The proposed approach is named as *R. Contrastive & Softmax* in the following experiments. We also evaluate the performance of a network fine-tuned by robust contrastive loss function but without the softmax loss, which is named as *R. Contrastive*.

4. EXPERIMENTS

4.1 Experimental Setup

4.1.1 Dataset and Evaluation Measure

In most of the experiments, we adopt the newly released *Exact Street2Shop Dataset* [14], which focuses on the matching between real-world user (street) photos and product images of clothing items in online shopping sites. The dataset has two types of images: 1) *street photos*, which are usually captured by end-users under everyday uncontrolled settings, and 2) *shop photos*, which are photos of clothing items from online shopping sites, mostly taken under more professional settings.

Specifically, the Street2Shop dataset contains 20,357 street photos and 404,683 shop photos containing 204,795 distinct clothing items from 11 large categories. It also provides 39,479 pairs of exact matching items between the street and the shop photos. This makes the dataset an ideal testbed for our work. Following [14], the street-to-shop pairs are divided into training and testing sets with a ratio of approximately 4:1 in each category. In the experiments, a search query consists of a street photo with a bounding box indicating the location of the target item and its category label. Retrieval is then performed within the corresponding category, according to [14].

In addition, we adopt the *Alibaba Large-scale Product Image Dataset* (see footnote 1 for its URL) as the second dataset to evaluate the generalization capability of our proposed approach. As the official testing labels of this dataset are not publicly available, we randomly divide the street-to-

Category	#Queries	#Testing Images	AlexNet [14]	F. T. Similarity [14]	Inception-6	Contrastive & Softmax	R. Contrastive	R. Contrastive & Softmax
Dresses	3,292	169,733	22.2	37.1	31.0	44.0	55.7	**56.9**
Footwear	2,178	75,836	5.9	9.6	10.9	11.2	10.8	**13.1**
Tops	763	68,418	14.4	38.1	30.7	41.5	46.4	**48.0**
Outerwear	666	34,695	9.3	21.0	16.4	**21.5**	19.1	20.3
Skirts	604	18,281	11.6	**54.6**	39.1	40.6	49.7	50.8
Leggings	517	8,219	14.5	**22.1**	17.0	15.3	15.9	15.9
Bags	174	16,308	23.6	37.4	30.5	**46.6**	42.5	**46.6**
Eyewear	138	1,595	10.1	35.5	34.8	**39.1**	17.4	13.8
Pants	130	7,640	14.6	**29.2**	22.3	17.7	22.3	22.3
Belts	89	1,252	6.7	13.5	**24.7**	19.1	22.5	20.2
Hats	86	2,551	11.6	**38.4**	30.2	23.3	25.6	24.4
Overall	8637	404,528	14.66	28.97	24.37	30.86	35.88	**37.24**

Table 1: Top-20 retrieval accuracy (%) of our proposed approach and the alternative methods on the Exact Street2Shop Dataset. Notice that the F. T. Similarity method uses category-specific models and selective object proposals, while others use unified category-independent model and simple center crop of the images.

shop pairs (1,417 products and 92,572 manually annotated positive pairs) with a ratio of 2:1 (training vs. testing) without product overlap and report the top-20 retrieval accuracy. Different from the Street2Shop dataset where retrieval is performed within a category, we do not impose any category constraint on this dataset and each query is searched against all the online product images.

The retrieval performance is evaluated by top-k accuracy—a search is considered successful if at least one correct match can be found within the top-k returned results. Notice that only exactly the same product with the query is viewed as a correct match in our setup.

4.1.2 *Alternative Methods for Comparison*

To validate the effectiveness of our proposed approach, we compare with the following alternatives: 1) *AlexNet* network, which was used in [14], where the activations of the fully-connected layer FC6 (4,096-d) are used to form the feature representation. The network is trained on a subset of the ImageNet dataset [21] (1,000 categories). 2) *F. T. Similarity* [14], where category-specific two-layer neural networks are trained to predict whether two features extracted by the AlexNet represent the same product item. The method also uses the selective search algorithm [23] to extend the training and testing sets. 3) *Inception-6*, where the activations of the last average-pooling layer (1,024-d) of the pre-trained Inception-6 network are used to represent each image. 4) *Contrastive & Softmax*, which is based on the siamese network, where the traditional contrastive loss function and softmax loss function are used like [1]. Our proposed multi-task fine-tuning is also adopted. We compare with this alternative to demonstrate the effectiveness of our robust contrastive loss. Similarly, the outputs of the last average-pooling layer (1,024-d) are used as the feature representation. The cosine similarity is used in all these methods except 2, which uses pre-trained neural networks to predict whether two features represent the same product item.

4.2 Results on Street2Shop Dataset

Table 1 summarizes the results of both our approach and the compared methods on the *Exact Street2Shop Dataset*. Overall, our proposed approach achieves the highest average retrieval accuracy on the dataset, significantly outperforming F. T. Similarity by over 8 absolute percentages. Compared with the per-category results of F. T. Similarity, our proposed approach shows lower accuracy on a few product categories with less photos. This is mainly because our approach does not use category-specific models, and a unified model tends to bias towards the categories with more training data. Because our approach only uses the center crops of user photos for speed consideration, it shows better performance on categories with larger object, like dresses, tops and bags. We also observe that Inception-6 is clearly better than AlexNet, based on which we conjecture that the ideas of F. T. Similarity can be used in conjunction with Inception-6 for further improvements. However, we refrain from doing this, because training category-specific models requires more cost and is hard to be applied in practice as the category of the query is often unknown.

Comparing the results in the last three columns of Table 1, we can observe clear contributions from both robust contrastive loss (6.3 absolute percentages) and softmax loss (1.3 absolute percentages). In the following we discuss the results in detail under more experimental settings.

Figure 4 shows the top-20 retrieval accuracy of the last three approaches in Table 1, under different numbers of training iterations. The R. Contrastive approach achieves consistently worse performance than the R. Contrastive & Softmax approach, indicating that the softmax loss function is helpful. Compared with the Contrastive & Softmax approach, we see that using the proposed robust contrastive loss is very important. The main reason is that, as discussed earlier, some positive pairs with small visual similarities may incur over-fitting of the Contrastive & Softmax approach, which also explains its performance trend shown in the figure (increases at a faster pace earlier and then decreases). In addition, as shown in the figure, the performance of all the approaches saturates at some time points and then decreases, indicating that the early stopping strategy is also necessary to avoiding over-fitting.

Figure 5 further shows the top-20 accuracy under different margin parameters and training iterations, using the R. Contrastive & Softmax approach. Results indicate that an appropriate margin parameter is critical to retrieval performance. A small margin cannot incorporate sufficient training information, while a large margin may introduce "noises" that result in over-fitting. In our experiments, 40 is correctly predicted as a good option on a validation set.

Finally, we plot the top-k accuracy at different k in Fig-

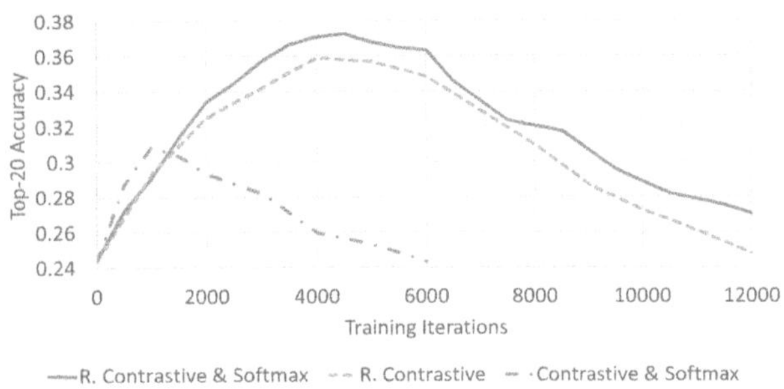

Figure 4: Top-20 accuracy on Street2Shop dataset under different loss functions and training iterations.

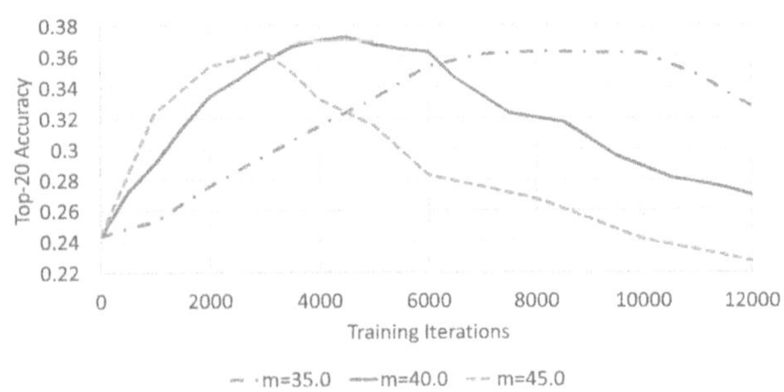

Figure 5: Top-20 accuracy on Street2Shop dataset under different margin parameters and training iterations.

ure 6. As expected, the retrieval accuracy of all the approaches increases with k. Nearly 60% of the queries can find their correct matches in the top-200 returned images.

Figure 7 shows some example retrieval results. Successful retrieval examples are shown in the top three rows, and the bottom three rows are failure cases. From the figure, we observe that the reasons behind a failure case include poor lighting environment and defocused image (e.g., the shoe example in the 4th row), highly occluded target (e.g., the yellow shirt in the 5th row), or simply the lack of visual characteristics of the specific product (e.g., the 6th row). We also find that sophisticated patterns on the products are helpful as they are visually distinctive. For example, the query photo in the 3rd row is visually very different from the shop photos in viewpoints, color and lighting, but can be correctly identified due to its unique pattern.

4.3 Results on Alibaba Dataset

We also report results on the *Alibaba Large-scale Product Image Dataset* to verify the generalization capability of the learned network. As shown in Table 2, we observe similar performance trend to that on the Street2Shop dataset. Both robust contrastive loss and softmax can improve around 2%, which again confirms the effectiveness of our approach. To evaluate the benefit from using the ImageNet samples, we also run the same R. Contrastive & Softmax approach with only samples from this dataset, where the softmax loss is evaluated using the class labels (604 classes) of the Alibaba images. An accuracy of 69.2% is achieved, which is nearly 3% lower than that using the ImageNet data (71.9%).

The improvement of robust contrastive loss is relatively

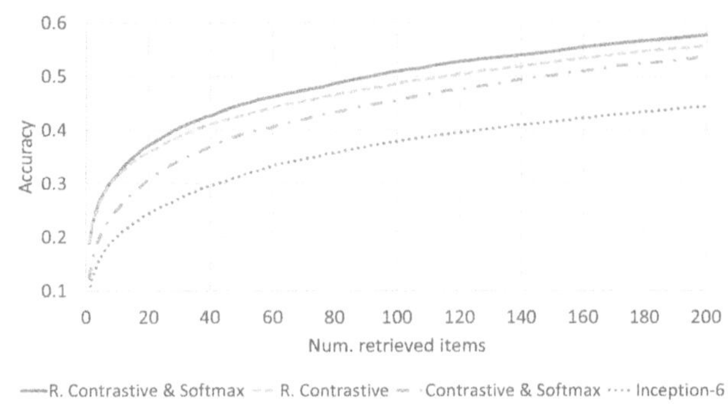

Figure 6: Top-k accuracy on Street2Shop dataset under different fine-tuning approaches and numbers of retrieved items.

Approach	Top-20 Accuracy
AlexNet	62.0
Inception-6	65.7
Contrastive & Softmax	69.5
R. Contrasive	69.3
R. Contrasive & Softmax	**71.9**

Table 2: Top-20 retrieval accuracy (%) of our proposed method and the state-of-the-art results on the Alibaba Large-scale Product Image Dataset.

smaller (but is still fairly significant) on this dataset because the labels are cleaner with less errors. In other words, for the Street2Shop dataset, in addition to the dissimilar positive pairs, wrongly labeled "false" positive pairs can also be excluded by our robust contrastive loss for improved results. Figure 8 further shows several example retrieval results.

4.4 Visualizing the Feature Embedding Space

To get a visual impression of the learned features, we use the t-SNE algorithm [24] to visualize the feature embedding space. First, the learned features extracted from the average pooling layer of the Inception-6 network are projected to 50 dimensions using the PCA algorithm to reduce the calculation cost. The t-SNE algorithm is then applied to further project the 50-d features to a 2-d space. To visualize the 2-d embedding space, we randomly select 5,000 images from both the street photos and the shop photos in the Street2Shop dataset and then place these photos to their corresponding 2-d locations.

As shown in Figure 9, the embedding space of the ImageNet-trained Inception-6 network tends to group the photos with similar view-angles together. In contrast, our approach based on robust contrastive loss of a siamese network tends to place the photos of the same products in close proximity, no matter they are street photos or shop photos, which is critical in real-world applications.

4.5 Efficiency

All the experiments are conducted on a server with an Intel i7-5820K CPU and two Nvidia GTX Titan X GPUs. Training a siamese network with the proposed loss function normally requires 4 to 8 hours, depending on the complexity of the dataset. Compared with model training that can be executed off-line, feature extraction time (model testing

Figure 7: Example retrieval results of our proposed approach in the Exact Street2Shop Dataset. Top three rows are successful queries (at least one correct match is found within top-20 returned images, marked by the green icon) and retrieval results, while the bottom three rows are failure queries with ground-truth matches and top retrieval results.

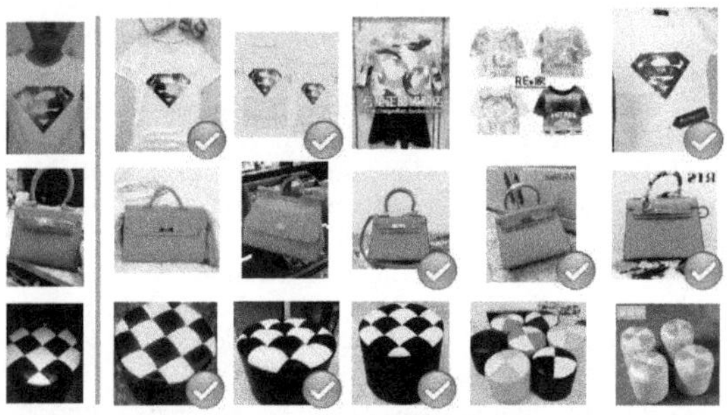

Figure 8: Example retrieval results of our proposed approach in the Alibaba Large-scale Product Image Dataset.

time) is way more important in real-time online search scenario. Using the Inception-6 network structure, the feature extraction process only costs 3.1 seconds per 1,000 images, which is sufficient for online search.

As aforementioned, once the features are extracted, many approaches like hashing can be adopted to accelerate the search process, which are not investigated in this work. With the brute-force exhaustive search, it costs around 150 ms for both feature extraction and retrieval of a query in the Street2Shop dataset.

5. CONCLUSION

We have presented a neural network based approach for the problem of matching a user photo to exactly the same product in online shopping sites. To alleviate the effect of label noise and prevent over-fitting caused by some positive pairs (that are visually different), we proposed a robust contrastive loss that automatically excludes such training samples in the network training process. A multi-task fine-tuning method was also proposed to harness extra data from the ImageNet with a softmax loss for improved results. Experiments on two real-world datasets have clearly demonstrated the effectiveness of our approach.

6. ACKNOWLEDGEMENT

This work was supported by China's National 863 Program (#2014AA015101), a grant from NSF China (#61572134) and a grant from STCSM (#16QA1400500). The *Alibaba Large-scale Product Image Dataset* was constructed and provided by Alibaba Group.

7. REFERENCES

[1] S. Bell and K. Bala. Learning visual similarity for product design with convolutional neural networks. *ACM Transactions on Graphics*, 34(4):98, 2015.

[2] G. Chechik, V. Sharma, U. Shalit, and S. Bengio. Large scale online learning of image similarity through ranking.

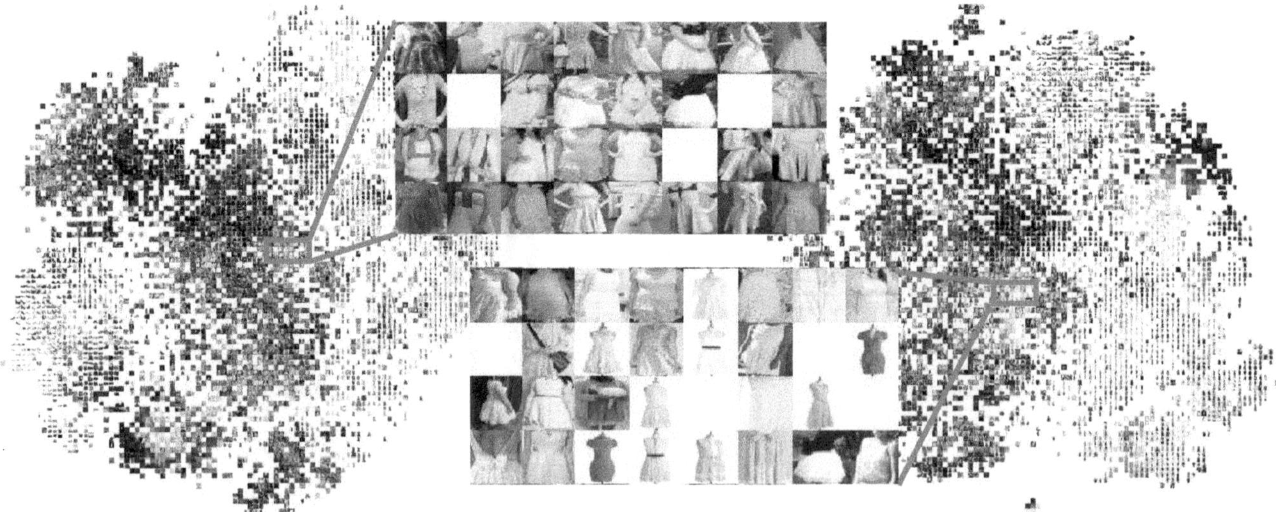

Figure 9: Visualization of image proximity using features from the ImageNet-trained Inception-6 network (left) and our proposed approach with the siamese network (right). See texts for more discussions.

The Journal of Machine Learning Research, 11:1109–1135, 2010.

[3] S. Chopra, R. Hadsell, and Y. LeCun. Learning a similarity metric discriminatively, with application to face verification. In *Computer Vision and Pattern Recognition, 2005. CVPR 2005. IEEE Computer Society Conference on*, volume 1, pages 539–546. IEEE, 2005.

[4] J. Deng, W. Dong, R. Socher, L.-J. Li, K. Li, and L. Fei-Fei. Imagenet: A large-scale hierarchical image database. In *Computer Vision and Pattern Recognition*, 2009.

[5] J. Donahue, Y. Jia, O. Vinyals, J. Hoffman, N. Zhang, E. Tzeng, and T. Darrell. Decaf: A deep convolutional activation feature for generic visual recognition. *arXiv preprint arXiv:1310.1531*, 2013.

[6] C. Farabet, C. Couprie, L. Najman, and Y. LeCun. Learning hierarchical features for scene labeling. *IEEE Transactions on Pattern Analysis and Machine Intelligence*, 35(8):1915–1929, 2013.

[7] R. Hadsell, S. Chopra, and Y. LeCun. Dimensionality reduction by learning an invariant mapping. In *Computer Vision and Pattern Recognition*, 2006.

[8] J. He, J. Feng, X. Liu, T. Cheng, T.-H. Lin, H. Chung, and S.-F. Chang. Mobile product search with bag of hash bits and boundary reranking. In *Computer Vision and Pattern Recognition*, 2012.

[9] K. He, X. Zhang, S. Ren, and J. Sun. Deep residual learning for image recognition. *arXiv preprint arXiv:1512.03385*, 2015.

[10] J. Huang, R. S. Feris, Q. Chen, and S. Yan. Cross-domain image retrieval with a dual attribute-aware ranking network. In *International Conference on Computer Vision*, 2015.

[11] S. Ioffe and C. Szegedy. Batch normalization: Accelerating deep network training by reducing internal covariate shift. *arXiv preprint arXiv;1502.03167*, 2015.

[12] Y.-G. Jiang and J. Wang. Partial copy detection in videos: A benchmark and an evaluation of popular methods. *IEEE Transactions on Big Data*, PP(99), 2016.

[13] Y. Kalantidis, L. Kennedy, and L.-J. Li. Getting the look: clothing recognition and segmentation for automatic product suggestions in everyday photos. In *ACM International Conference on Multimedia Retrieval*, 2013.

[14] M. H. Kiapour, X. Han, S. Lazebnik, A. C. Berg, and T. L. Berg. Where to buy it:matching street clothing photos in online shops. In *International Conference on Computer Vision*, 2015.

[15] A. Krizhevsky, I. Sutskever, and G. E. Hinton. Imagenet classification with deep convolutional neural networks. In *Advances in Neural Information Processing Systems*, 2012.

[16] Y.-H. Kuo, W.-H. Cheng, H.-T. Lin, and W. H. Hsu. Unsupervised semantic feature discovery for image object retrieval and tag refinement. *Multimedia, IEEE Transactions on*, 14(4):1079–1090, 2012.

[17] D. Lim, G. Lanckriet, and B. McFee. Robust structural metric learning. In *International Conference on Machine Learning*, 2013.

[18] S. Liu, Z. Song, G. Liu, C. Xu, H. Lu, and S. Yan. Street-to-shop: Cross-scenario clothing retrieval via parts alignment and auxiliary set. In *Computer Vision and Pattern Recognition*, 2012.

[19] A. S. Razavian, H. Azizpour, J. Sullivan, and S. Carlsson. Cnn features off-the-shelf: an astounding baseline for recognition. In *Computer Vision and Pattern Recognition Workshops*, 2014.

[20] S. Ren, K. He, R. Girshick, and J. Sun. Faster r-cnn: Towards real-time object detection with region proposal networks. In *Advances in Neural Information Processing Systems*, 2015.

[21] O. Russakovsky, J. Deng, H. Su, J. Krause, S. Satheesh, S. Ma, Z. Huang, A. Karpathy, A. Khosla, M. Bernstein, A. C. Berg, and L. Fei-Fei. ImageNet Large Scale Visual Recognition Challenge. *International Journal of Computer Vision*, 115(3):211–252, 2015.

[22] C. Szegedy, W. Liu, Y. Jia, P. Sermanet, S. Reed, D. Anguelov, D. Erhan, V. Vanhoucke, and A. Rabinovich. Going deeper with convolutions. In *Computer Vision and Pattern Recognition*, 2015.

[23] K. E. Van de Sande, J. R. Uijlings, T. Gevers, and A. W. Smeulders. Segmentation as selective search for object recognition. In *International Conference on Computer Vision*. IEEE, 2011.

[24] L. Van der Maaten and G. Hinton. Visualizing data using t-sne. *Journal of Machine Learning Research*, 9(2579-2605):85, 2008.

[25] P. Wu, S. C. Hoi, H. Xia, P. Zhao, D. Wang, and C. Miao. Online multimodal deep similarity learning with application to image retrieval. In *ACM International Conference on Multimedia*, 2013.

[26] Z. Wu, X. Wang, Y.-G. Jiang, H. Ye, and X. Xue. Modeling spatial-temporal clues in a hybrid deep learning framework for video classification. In *ACM International Conference on Multimedia*, 2015.

Video Emotion Recognition with Transferred Deep Feature Encodings

Baohan Xu[1], Yanwei Fu*[23], Yu-Gang Jiang[1], Boyang Li[3] and Leonid Sigal[3]
[1]School of Computer Science, Shanghai Key Laboratory of Intelligent Information Processing, Fudan University, China
[2]School of Data Science, Fudan University, China
[3]Disney Research, USA
{bhxu14, ygj}@fudan.edu.cn, y.fu@qmul.ac.uk, {albert.li, lsigal}@disneyresearch.com

ABSTRACT

Despite growing research interest, emotion understanding for user-generated videos remains a challenging problem. Major obstacles include the diversity and complexity of video content, as well as the sparsity of expressed emotions. For the first time, we systematically study large-scale video emotion recognition by transferring deep feature encodings. In addition to the traditional, supervised recognition, we study the problem of zero-shot emotion recognition, where emotions in the test set are unseen during training. To cope with this task, we utilize knowledge transferred from auxiliary image and text corpora. A novel auxiliary Image Transfer Encoding (ITE) process is proposed to efficiently encode and generate video representation. We also thoroughly investigate different configurations of convolutional neural networks. Comprehensive experiments on multiple datasets demonstrate the effectiveness of our framework.

1. INTRODUCTION

Recognizing implicitly conveyed emotions in user-generated videos is an important yet often overlooked dimension of dimension of video understanding. Computational understanding of such emotions has many applications. For example, video recommendation services can benefit from matching users' interests with video emotion. An accurate understanding of video emotion can maintain consistency between emotions expressed in the main video and advertisements accompanying it, avoid social inappropriateness such as placing a funny advertisement alongside a funeral video.

Recognizing emotion from video, especially user-generated video, is challenging for the following reasons. First, due to close interaction between cognitive processes and emotional appraisals [29, 13, 14], human emotions are rich and complex. Recent research [2, 25] suggests that basic emotion categories, such as proposed by Ekman [11] and Plutchik [34], are merely modal responses, which cannot capture the full range of human emotion. Second, emotional expressions are sparse in videos. Of all frames in a video, only a small subset directly depict emotions. The rest of frames are needed, for instance, to set up the situation and introduce the context. Finally, user-generated videos are highly diverse. Compared to commercial content like movies and sports, user-generated videos cover a broader set of content and exhibit highly variable quality. Such intra-class variability creates difficulties for emotion recognition.

For the first time, we systematically study emotion recognition in user-generated video, specifically *supervised* [20] and *zero-shot* emotion recognition [42]. The zero-shot emotion recognition, where emotions in the test set are completely unseen during training time, is directly motivated by the variability of real-world emotions and insufficiency of basic emotion categories [2, 25]. To solve these tasks, a unified deep convolutional neural network (CNN) architecture is introduced to enable our encoding-based multi-instance learning framework, which transfers knowledge from auxiliary image and text data to better understand testing video data.

Our contributions are three-fold: (1) a novel auxiliary Image Transfer Encoding (ITE) process is proposed to efficiently encode and generate video representations; (2) we, for the first time, systematically and comprehensively investigate the effectiveness of features from different CNN architectures and layers in the task of video emotion recognition and knowledge transfer; and (3) we also explore the complementarity of deep features with the existing visual and audio hand-crafted features. The results show that our framework can significantly improve upon the previous state-of-the-art results [20] by 7.7% absolute percentage points on YouTube dataset. To our best knowledge, this is the first large-scale systematic study of video emotion recognition conducted by transferring deep feature encodings.

2. RELATED WORK

2.1 Psychological Theories of Emotion

Basic emotion theories claim existence of few universal emotion categories, each of which is associated with a set of prototypical facial expressions, physiological measurements, behaviors, and external causes. Ekman [11], for example, proposed six basic emotions including happiness, sadness, disgust, surprise, anger, and fear. However, recent find-

*Corresponding Author.

ICMR'16, June 06 - 09, 2016, New York, NY, USA

ISBN 978-1-4503-4359-6/16/06...$15.00
DOI: http://dx.doi.org/10.1145/2911996.2912006

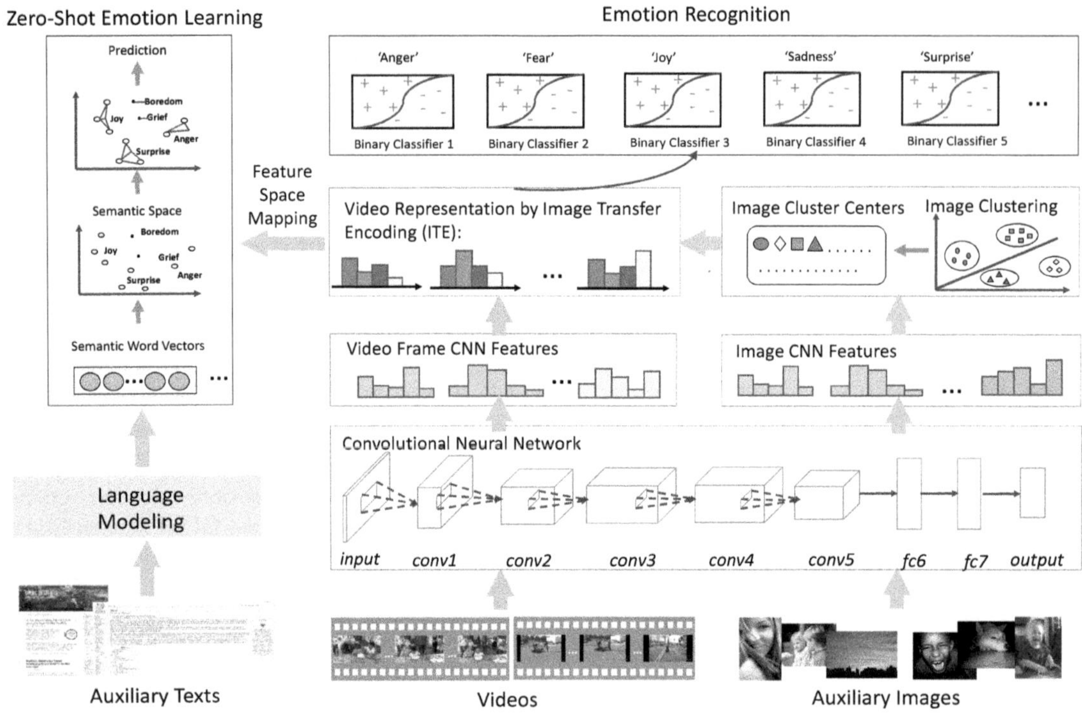

Figure 1: An overview of our framework. Information from a large text corpus is utilized for zero-shot emotion recognition as illustrated on the left. Auxiliary images (bottom right) are used to extract an emotion-centric dictionary, which help subsequently encode video (bottom middle) and recognize supervised emotion recognition (top right) and also enable zero-shot emotion recognition (top left).

ings [5, 2, 25] dispute whether these emotion categories are exhaustive, and suggest that among the diverse emotional landscape, the basic emotions are merely prototypical responses. Cognitive processes (which are needed for processing context) and emotional appraisal closely interact to create a diverse sets of emotions and affects [13, 14, 29], potentially leading to difficulties in labeling non-protypical emotions. Besides the traditional supervised recognition, we consider zero-shot emotion recognition, which allows us to recognize a large variety of emotion categories at test time without training examples.

2.2 Deep Visual Sentiment Analysis

In recent years, features from deep neural networks have been widely used for variety of tasks in computer vision and multimedia, *e.g.*, image categorization [6, 23] and object detection [35]. Promising results of such architectures in other domains inspired us to evaluate deep feature representations for video emotion recognition task. Further, we utilize auxiliary image information to the improve the effectiveness of the resulting recognition model.

Existing works explored emotion recognition from commercial movies [22, 39], animated images [21] and, to a lesser extent, user-generated videos [20]. Recently, several works on emotion recognition [7, 43, 47] also explored deep features extracted from CNNs, such as AlexNet [23]. Such deep features were shown to outperform hand-crafted low-level features and features from SentiBank [3]. In this paper, we perform a systematic layer-wise study of features from deep CNN architecture, and complementarity of such representations with hand-crafted features, in the setting of knowledge transfer and zero-shot learning.

2.3 Multi-Instance Learning

Multi-instance learning (MIL) is a particular form of learning where each input is a bag of multiple data vectors and only one class label is observable for all vectors. Most of early MIL approaches adapt single-instance supervised learning algorithms directly to multi-instance bags; examples include miSVM [1], MIBoosting [44], Citation-kNN [40], and MI-Kernel [15, 36]. Such approaches achieve satisfactory results in small or moderate-sized datasets but have difficulties with large-scale video data-sets due to the high computational cost. More recent algorithms (*e.g.*, CCE [48], Mi-FV [41], and MILES [8]) explore encoding multi-instance bags into single-instance representations to cluster the instances of all the bags to several groups. Inspired by these works, we encode multi-instance bags into video-level emotion-related representations. Different from the other methods we employ auxiliary sentiment image data to help the encoding procedure. Particularly, we study the role of various deep feature representations in such a MIL framework, as well as combination of such representations with other features (*e.g.*, audio) to improve performance.

3. PROBLEM FORMULATION

Figure 1 shows an overview of our framework. In this section, we formally define the video emotion recognition problem. We define a training video dataset as

$$Tr = \{(V_i, X_i, \boldsymbol{s}_i, z_i)\}_{i=1,\cdots,n_{Tr}},$$

where the ith video V_i is a set of n_i frames $\{\mathbf{f}_{i,1}, \cdots, \mathbf{f}_{i,n_i}\}$, and each frame $\mathbf{f}_{i,j}$ has a feature vector $\mathbf{x}_{i,j}$. X_i is the set $\{\mathbf{x}_{i,1}, \cdots, \mathbf{x}_{i,n_i}\}$. $\boldsymbol{s}_i$ denotes a video-level feature of video V_i, obtained using auxiliary image transfer encoding, which is introduced in Sec. 3.1. $z_i \in Z_{Tr}$ is the class label from the set of training labels Z_{Tr} and n_{Tr} is the total number of training videos. The testing data set is likewise defined as

$$Te = \{(V_i, X_i, \boldsymbol{s}_i, \tilde{z}_i)\}_{i=1,\cdots,n_{Te}},$$

where n_{Te} is the total number of testing videos. For the purpose of knowledge transfer, we introduce a large-scale auxiliary image set, denoted as $A = \{(a_i, \boldsymbol{\phi}_i)\}_{i=1,\cdots,|A|}$, where $\boldsymbol{\phi}_i$ is the feature vector for an image a_i. Deep CNNs are used to extract both $\mathbf{x}_{i,j}$ and $\boldsymbol{\phi}_i$ from video frames and images.

An auxiliary text sentiment dataset is introduced here for zero-shot emotion recognition; particularly, textual data are represented as a sequence of words $W = (w_0, \ldots, w_{|W|})$, $w_j \in \mathcal{V}$ where the vocabulary $\mathcal{V}$ is the set of unique words. A $\mathcal{K}$-dimensional distributed word embedding $\boldsymbol{\psi}_w$ is learned for each $w \in \mathcal{V}$ by the skip-gram model [30].

3.1 Auxiliary Image Transfer Encoding (ITE)

We treat a video as a bag of video frames (in the MIL sense) and introduce Image Transfer Encoding for encoding videos as a BoW representation obtained using auxiliary image sentiment data. Note we do not use the clustering of instances from all training bags, since the video emotions are typically very sparsely expressed in only a few key frames.

We first compute D clusters from the auxiliary images by performing a spherical k-means clustering [18] on the auxiliary image dataset, which amounts to solving:

$$\min \sum_{i=1}^{|A|} (1 - \gamma_{i,d} \cos(\boldsymbol{\phi}_i, \boldsymbol{c}_d)), \tag{1}$$

where $\cos(\boldsymbol{\phi}_i, \boldsymbol{c}_d)$ is the cosine similarity between $\boldsymbol{\phi}_i$ and $\boldsymbol{c}_d$. The goal is to find D spherical cluster centers $\boldsymbol{c}_1 \ldots, \boldsymbol{c}_D$. The *responsibility* $\gamma_{i,d} = 1$, if an image a_i is assigned to the closet cluster center d (*i.e.*, $d = \text{argmax}_j \cos(\boldsymbol{\phi}_i, \boldsymbol{c}_j)$).

The cluster centers are then used to encode each video V_i into a single vector. Our BoW scheme translates the feature set X_i into a D-dimensional vector $\boldsymbol{s}_i = (s_{i,1}, \ldots, s_{i,d}, \ldots s_{i,D})$. Given the cluster centers $\{\boldsymbol{c}_1, ..., \boldsymbol{c}_D\}$, we identify K nearest cluster centers for each frame $\mathbf{f}_{i,j}$. The assignments $\nu_{i,j,d}$ are thus defined as

$$\nu_{i,j,d} = \begin{cases} 1 & if\, \boldsymbol{c}_d \in \text{KNN}(\mathbf{x}_{i,j}), \\ 0 & otherwise, \end{cases} \tag{2}$$

where $\text{KNN}(\mathbf{x}_{i,j})$ denotes the spherical K nearest neighbours[1] to $\mathbf{x}_{i,j}$ from the cluster centers. The feature vector $\boldsymbol{s}_i$ is computed as $s_{i,d} = \sum_{j=1}^{n_i} \nu_{i,j,d} \cdot \cos(\mathbf{x}_{i,j}, \boldsymbol{c}_d)$.

3.2 Supervised Emotion Recognition

The encoding scheme from the frame-level deep features to the video-level emotional representation helps the standard video emotion recognition task. Given a test video $V_k \in Te$, its class label can be estimated using

$$\hat{z}_k = \text{argmax}_z \mathcal{L}(\boldsymbol{s}_k \mid \boldsymbol{s}_{Tr}, z_{Tr}), \tag{3}$$

where $\mathcal{L}(\cdot)$ is the predictor trained from the video-level feature set S_{Tr} of the training video set Tr. We use the support vector machines (SVM) [10] classifier with chi-square kernel as the predictor $\mathcal{L}(\cdot)$.

3.3 Zero-Shot Emotion Recognition

Old emotion theories (*e.g.*, of Ekman [12]) only analyze a fixed number of prototypical emotions with relatively detailed textual explanations. In contrast, some very recent research [2, 25] questioned the validity of basic emotional categories and implied high variances of emotions far beyond several fixed basic categories. This naturally raises an interesting question: when the variances of emotions are big enough to be separated into a sub-emotion class, whether we can identify those emotions purely from their definitions.

Zero-shot emotion recognition predicts the emotions not observed in the training set. We relate the class labels in the training set, w_{Tr}, and those in the test set, w_{Te}, through an embedding space that (partially) captures the meaning of the label words. The embedding space maps a label word to a feature vector, and is obtained by training the *word2vec* model [30] on a large-scale textural corpus with significant emotion descriptions. Thus the emotion class z can be represented by a word vector $\boldsymbol{\psi}_z$. We use the embedding space as an intermediary between video features and emotion classes by training a regressor from the video feature space to the word embedding space:

$$g : \boldsymbol{s}_{Tr} \to \boldsymbol{\psi}_{w_{Tr}}, \tag{4}$$

where g is a support vector regressor with a linear kernel for each dimension of the word vector $\boldsymbol{\psi}_{w_{Tr}}$, similar to [24].

Given test video V_j, its class label $\tilde{z}_j$ can be estimated as

$$\hat{\tilde{z}}_j = \text{argmax}_{z \in Z_{Te}} \cos(g(\boldsymbol{s}_j), \boldsymbol{\psi}_z). \tag{5}$$

Note that Eq (5) intrinsically solves the problem of vector space classification; and $\boldsymbol{\psi}_z$ ($z \in Z_{Te}$) is the only available information for recognition. Thus to further improve the results, we propose Transductive 1-Step Self-Training (T1S) to adjust the word vector of new emotion classes. This strategy is a variant of Rocchio algorithm in information retrieval [28], which is a method for relevance feedback that works by using more relevant instances to update the query instances for better recall and possibly precision in vector space. Specifically, for a class $z \in Z_{Te}$ and the corresponding word vector $\boldsymbol{\psi}_z$, we compute a smoothed version $\bar{\boldsymbol{\psi}}_z$:

$$\bar{\boldsymbol{\psi}}_z = \frac{1}{K} \sum_{g(\boldsymbol{s}_i) \in \text{KNN}(\boldsymbol{\psi}_z), V_i \in Te}^{K} g(\boldsymbol{s}_i), \tag{6}$$

using a set of spherical K nearest neighbors to $\boldsymbol{\psi}_z$.

We empirically verify the semantic word vectors using emotion-based vector-oriented reasoning. Interestingly, we find that such reasoning is compatible with emotion theories such as [32]. For example, Vec("surprise") +Vec("sadness") is closest to Vec("disappointment"); Vec("joy") is very far from Vec("sadness").

4. FEATURES FROM DEEP NETWORKS

While convolutional neural networks gained popularity in emotion recognition, existing studies do not attempt to quantify or systematically study how CNN features affect the performance. For the problem of image categorization,

[1] Generally, we require that $K \gg 1$, since video frames can express much more 'versatile' emotions compared to images.

on the other hand, several works studied architecture design [23] and how to combine features across CNN layers [6]. Findings suggest that for image categorization deeper architectures tend to perform better [6] and that combining features across layers further improves the performance [17]. Yet, for some tasks, like texture recognition, deep learning features are not as effective and custom designed features or combinations are more effective [9]; for pose estimation [16] the $5th$ layer features tend to be more invariant to pose. These results indicate that studying the architectures and features within specific vision problem is important. In this section we conduct exhaustive and comprehensive study of various CNN architectures, feature combinations from various levels and combination of CNN features with hand constructed counterparts for the problems of supervised and zero-shot video emotion recognition.

4.1 Different Deep Architectures

Several popular deep convolutional architectures have been proposed for large-scale image classification tasks, including AlexNet [23], VGG-16, VGG-19 [6], and GooLeNet-22 [38]. **AlexNet** has seven layers where the first five are convolutional ($conv1 - conv5$) followed by 2 fully connected layers ($fc6 - fc7$). The fully connected layers can be represented by 4096 dimension features after ReLU, while convolutional layers ($conv1 - conv5$) are multidimensional arrays that represent convolution of the image with a learned filter; in practice they can be flattened in to d-dimensional feature vectors. Since filter sizes change with the layer, the dimensions of the feature representations at ($conv1 - conv5$) change as well. **VGG-16 and VGG-19** models [6] extend the AlexNet by expanding convolutional layers and have 16 and 19 layers respectively. **GoogleLeNet-22** is inspired by Hebbian principle with multi-scale processing and it has 22 layers. Nevertheless, these layers are still designed and optimized for image (esp. ImageNet) classification tasks; but not necessarily good for video emotion recognition tasks.

In the experimental section, we study the results of using these different deep convolutional architectures for video emotion recognition. Interestingly, while GoogleLeNet-22 is shown to be very effective for image recognition [38] and store-front classification [31], we find that it performs poorly on the emotion recognition problem.

4.2 Layer-wise Features of Deep Architecture

Rather than giving us a single feature representation, deep neural network is inherently a stacked structure which gives us a feature representation from each layer. One interesting phenomenon is that, from bottom to top layers of deep architectures, the features learned are from *general* to *specific*. For example, the first layer is known to learn the features that are similar to Gabor filters and color blobs. Such types of features are shown to be agnostic to the task, *i.e.*, they are *general*. In contrast, the higher-level layers are usually well trained for *specific* tasks, *e.g.*, image classification [46].

Most previous work on image sentiment analysis [7], [47] and [43] by default directly use the feature outputs of high-level layers, since the high-level semantics expressed in these high-level layers potentially are more related to image sentiment. Recently, [4] explored the layer-wise features on image sentiment dataset. However, video emotion is different from image sentiment analysis due to more diverse video content and more sparsely expressed video emotions. No previous work discussed how deep features should be used for video emotion recognition; not to mention the effects of layer-wise features and combinations.

We explore these questions in this paper. Particularly, we evaluate using $conv1 - conv5$ and $fc6 - fc7$ features from AlexNet [23]. The output of each layer is considered as visual descriptor of each frame. These experiments enable us to measure the difference in accuracy between layers and get intuition on their suitability for video emotion analysis.

4.3 Complementarity of Deep Features

As mentioned above, the deep architecture (from bottom to top) learns the features from *general* to *specific* with respect to a supervised classification objective. This notion raises another important question: the complementarity of deep features from various layers. To simplify discussion and isolate confounding factors, we evaluate these properties by using the direct concatenation of different layer features for video emotion recognition.

We also discuss complementarity of CNN with hand-crafted features. This is inspired by the recent study of using hand-crafted features for video emotion understanding [20]. Particularly, we use denseSIFT [27] as visual hand-crafted features. DenseSIFT method densely samples local frame patches rather than only use interest points in original SIFT. Then dense extracted SIFT descriptors are further encoded into a bag-of-words representation.

Audio hand-crafted features are also investigated, since human perception often relies on the use of multiple senses [37]: for example, videos that convey "joy" mostly contain laughter and "fear" may co-occur with screaming in the audio track. We utilize the well-known Mel-frequency cepstral coefficients (MFCC) as audio representation. An MFCC descriptor is computed over every 32 *ms* time-window with 50% overlap. The descriptors from the entire soundtrack of a video are converted to a bag-of-words representation using vector quantization.

5. EXPERIMENTS

In this section, we first introduce the experimental settings in Section 5.1, and then validate the effectiveness of our framework on supervised and zero-shot emotion recognition using the features from $fc7 - 7^{th}$ fully-connected layer in Section 5.2. Finally, the details of different deep architectures as well as the complementarity with hand-crafted features are investigated and compared for supervised video emotion recognition in Section 5.3.

5.1 Datasets and Settings

We utilize two video emotion datasets for evaluation: YouTube and Ekman. The Ekman dataset was collected from social mediate platform by us and will be made available to the community.

5.1.1 The YouTube emotion dataset

YouTube emotion dataset contains 1101 videos annotated with 8 basic emotions from the Plutchik's Wheel of Emotions [20]. To validate the zero-shot emotion recognition, we re-annotate the dataset with 'fine-grained' emotions. We create these more diverse emotion categories by adding 3 variations to each original emotion (24 emotions in total). For example, *anger* class is split into *annoyance*, *anger*, and *rage* along the arousal dimension according to Plutchik's wheel of emotions

dataset	MaxP	AvgP	Mi-FV	CCE	ITE($fc7$)
Y	34.5	41.1	38.4	30.2	**43.8**
E	39.0	48.4	36.4	31.5	**50.9**

Table 1: Supervised learning results reported on emotion recognition datasets. We use 2000 bins and $fc7$ features for our method. The two baselines use both linear and chi-square kernels.

[33]. We use **Y-8** (or just **Y**) and **Y-24** to indicate the original and re-annotated datasets respectively. Specifically, **Y-24** has 36 *anger*, 33 *annoyance*, 32 *rage*, 44 *anticipation*, 32 *interest*, 25 *vigilance*, 42 *boredom*, 64 *disgust*, 9 *loathing*, 12 *apprehension*, 79 *feat*, 76 *terror*, 23 *ecstasy*, 76 *joy*, 81 *serenity*, 27 *grief*, 11 *pensiveness*, 63 *sadness*, 29 *amazement*, 59 *distraction*, 148 *surprise*, 39 *acceptance*, 26 *admiration*, and 35 *trust* videos.

5.1.2 The Ekman-6 emotion dataset

According to Ekman's there are 6 basic emotions. The dataset is collected from social video-sharing websites (*e.g.*, YouTube and Flickr), resulting in 1637 videos for which those 6 emotions are annotated, with a minimum of 221 videos per class. The labels are annotated by 10 different volunteers who are unaware of the goals of the project. Each video was labelled by the majority voting result from at least 3 annotators.

5.1.3 Auxiliary images and texts

We use an auxiliary image dataset, a subset of $110K$ images of Adjective-Noun Pairs (ANPs) in Flickr image dataset [3] that have the top ranks (440 ANPs) with respect to the emotions[2]. The auxiliary text data has 7 billion words[3]. Most of the documents are about scientific articles and professional reports which have very strict definitions, descriptions and usage of the emotion and sentiment related words. To facilitate the efficient training of such large-scale corpus, we employ the *word2vec* model [30] which results in 4 million element vocabulary semantic space.

5.1.4 Experimental settings

Each video is uniformly sampled every 5 frame to reduce the computational cost. Our AlexNet model [23] is trained using 2600 ImageNet classes with the Caffe toolkit [19]. The auxiliary image data are clustered into 2000 clusters ($D = 2000$). The number of nearest neighbors K in Eq (2) is empirically set to 10% of the image clusters, which balances the computational cost with a good representation. For presentation simplicity, we use **Y**, **E** to represent the YouTube and Ekman-6 datasets respectively.

5.2 Video emotion recognition by $fc7$

In this subsection, we use the $fc7$ features of AlexNet for video emotion recognition, since $fc7$ is the most widely used deep feature (*e.g.*, the top layer feature) in most of the other computer vision tasks [23, 35].

[2]Please refer to Table 2 in [3].

[3]Composed of the UMBC WebBase data (3 billion words), the latest Wikipedia articles (3 billion words) and some other documents (1 billion words).

	VGG-16	VGG-19	GoogLeNet-22	AleNet
Y	44.7	44.0	35.6	41.1
E	49.3	48.8	38.3	48.4

Table 3: VGG and GoogLeNet architecture comparisons. The AvgP is used for reported results here.

5.2.1 Supervised emotion recognition

To evaluate our encoding algorithm, we compare different video emotion recognition methods by using $fc7$ with the following baselines. **(1) MaxP.** Instance-level classifiers are trained to recognize instance labels of every testing video. The video class label is majority-voted by predicted instance labels [26]. **(2) AvgP.** It is a standard approach of aggregating, using an average, frame-level features into video-level descriptions (*e.g.*, [45]). **(3) Mi-FV.** It maps MIL bags of training videos into a new bag-level Fisher Vector (FV) representation, which efficiently deals with large-scale of data such as emotion datasets[41]. **(4) CCE.** [48] clustered the instances of all training videos into b groups. Each bag is re-represented by b binary features: assigning 1 to the ith feature if one bag has instances falling into the ith group and 0 otherwise. Linear kernel is used for Mi-FV and MaxP due to the large number of samples/dimensions, and the Chi-square kernel is used for others. We use 1-Vs-All strategy for multi-class classification.

ITE > MaxP/AvgP/Mi-FV/CCE. The result is reported in Table 1, which shows that the ITE method significantly outperforms the four methods on both datasets. The improvement of ITE over CCE and Mi-FV shows that using auxiliary image dataset to achieve knowledge transfer can create better video-level feature representations. This also support our hypothesis that most of frames are not closely related to video emotions. The worst performance comes from CCE. This might be because re-encoding process of CCE loses discriminative information gained from the deep learning network. The same training/testing split are used as in [20] on YouTube dataset. AvgP and ITE have much better results than Mi-FV and MaxP and thus we employ AvgP and ITE as the main comparison methods in following experiments. The AvgP result is comparable with the 41.9% reported in [20] of using all visual features, while our ITE results are much better. Note that the result of 41.9%±2.2% combines different types of hand-crafted visual features with the state-of-the-art multi-kernel strategy. In contrast, AvgP simply averages frame-level image features. This means that the performance of the $fc7$ features is comparable to those of multi-kernel combination of visual hand-crafted features.

Some qualitative results of supervised emotion predictions are shown in Figure 2. In the successful cases, testing videos share the common visual characteristics with auxiliary image dataset like the *bright light* and *smile face* in the "joy" category. The "anger" videos are wrongly classified as "fear". Comparing with "anger", the "fear" category is more highly correlated with *dark lightning* and *screaming faces* which are visually dominated in the failed case.

5.2.2 Zero-shot emotion recognition

Since Ekman dataset lacks sufficient variants (only 6 classes) of emotions, we conducted zero-shot emotion recognition on **Y-8** and **Y-24** dataset, which has more diverse emotion

	Chance	DAP $fc7/fc6/conv5/conv4$	Ours $fc7/fc6/conv5/conv4$
Y-8	50	51.5/ 53.04 / 48.05 /50.37	56.3 / **56.44** / 43.32 /53.55
Y-24	16.7	23.3 / 27.59 / 21.45 / 22.28	**32.6** /32.14 / 16.22 /27.76

Table 2: Zero-shot Learning on emotion dataset analysis. Video are only encoded by ITE since AvgP method can get very weak results which are slightly higher than chance and thus not considered here.

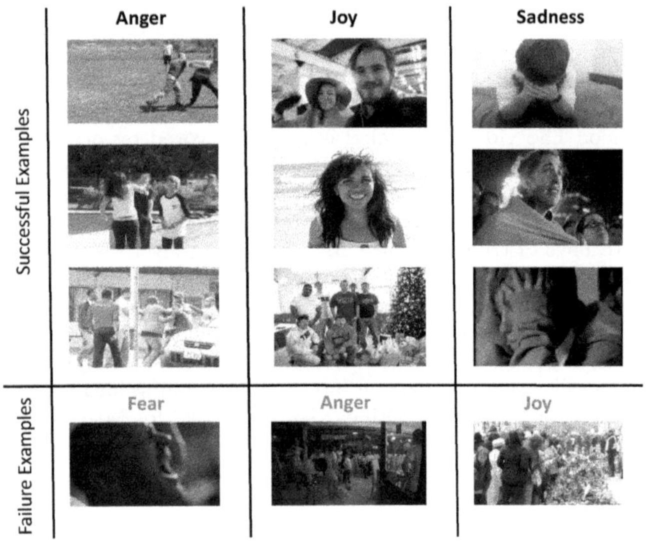

Figure 2: Qualitative results on supervised emotion prediction. The experiment uses $fc7$ features on Ekman dataset. The ground truth categories are at the top of each column; red labels indicate wrong predictions.

categories. **Y-8** uses *fear* and *sadness* as the testing classes. For **Y-24**, we randomly split dataset into 18 training and 6 testing classes with 5-fold repeated experiments. No testing class video instances are seen during training in zero-shot recognition tasks.

T1S > DAP. As a baseline for zero-shot recognition, we compare with Direct Attribution Prediction (DAP) which is proposed in [24] and is the most canonical algorithm used for zero-shot learning. For DAP, at test time each dimension of the word vectors of each test sample is predicted, from which the test class labels are inferred. DAP can be formulated as directly using Eq (5) without the word vector smoothing. Table 2 shows the results of each layer of deep architecture. We find that our method is much better than DAP when using the features of fully connected layers. The results improve DAP baseline by 4.9 and 9.3 absolute percentage points on $fc7$, which validate the effectiveness of our method.

$fc6/fc7$ > $conv5/conv4$. We further validate the zero-shot emotion prediction by using different types of features (*e.g.*, $fc6$, $conv5$ and $conv4$) as compared in Tab. 2. The results show that the features of fully connected layers ($fc6$ and $fc7$) are generally more favorable for zero-shot emotion recognition than those of convolutional layers ($conv4$, $conv5$). And the results of using convolutional features are only slightly higher than chance. If we compare the results

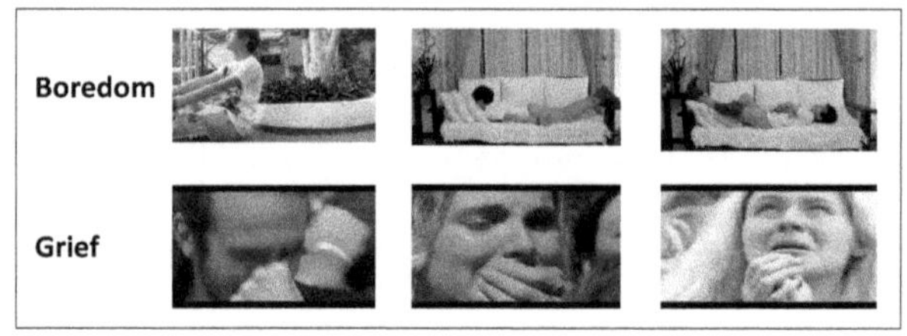

Figure 3: Key frames of two successful cases of zero-shot emotion recognition ($fc7$ features on Y-24): top row is a video about a bored boy walking and lying on the couch; the bottom row illustrated video of grief fans feel when their football team loses a game.

of the two dataset, we find that the results on Y-24 have a larger margin improvement than those on Y-8 for the same type of features. This means that finer-grained variant set of auxiliary emotions can enable better zero-shot learning.

In Figure 3, we show some successful examples of zero-shot emotion prediction. We highlight that even without any training examples of these categories, our method can still classify these video successfully using the encoded features. Considering the difficulty of zero-shot emotion prediction, our results are very promising.

5.3 Results of Validating Deep Architecture

5.3.1 *Different deep architecture*

VGG-16/VGG-19/AlexNet > GoogLeNet. While previous experiments showed satisfactory results on emotion analysis task by using AlexNet architecture, we want to compare different architectures to better understand deep feature encodings. VGG-16 and VGG-19 [6] and GoogLeNet-22 [38] achieved state-of-the-art performance for image classification on ImageNet challenge. Thus we conducted video emotion recognition using high layer features extracted from the two architecture as descriptors. Table 3 illustrates experimental results. We use $fc7$ of 16 and 19 layers VGG and $inception-5b$ of GoogLeNet. AvgP is used for all the deep architectures. The results of VGG-16 and VGG-19 are comparable to AlexNet, and outperform that of GoogLeNet-22. The result of VGG-19 is a little lower than VGG-16, which demonstrates that deeper networks may not be appropriate for the emotion recognition task. Although GoogLeNet gets promising results on image classification task, the lower results in Table 3 imply that GoogLeNet may not be the best choice for video emotion recognition.

5.3.2 *Layer-wise features of deep architecture*

$fc6/fc7$ > $conv4/conv5$. The results of the experiments on layer-wise features are reported in Table 5. Clearly features of fully connected layers significantly outperform those

	denseSIFT	MFCC	ITE($fc7$)	[ITE($fc7$), denseSIFT]	[ITE($fc7$), MFCC]	[ITE($fc7$), denseSIFT, MFCC]
Y	35.6	44.0	43.8	43.8	**52.6**	46.7
E	38.6	39.0	50.9	48.8	**51.2**	50.4

Table 4: Concatenated results of hand-crafted feature and deep features. ITE is computed from $fc7$.

Methods	ITE		AvgP	
Features	$fc7$	$fc6$	$fc7$	$fc6$
Y	43.8	**45.6**	41.1	42.0
E	**50.9**	49.4	48.4	48.7

Table 5: Layer by layer analysis results on emotion datasets. We use AvgP as the default video emotion recognition method. The results for convolutional layers $conv5 - conv1$ are $22.5 \pm 2\%$ which are significant lower than those of fully connected layers.

of convolutional layers (which is $22.5 \pm 2\%$) by a large margin. This means that the features of convolutional layers ($conv5 - conv1$) are too general to be discriminative enough for video emotion recognition; at the same time indicating that features of high-level layers contain more semantic information which can benefit video emotion understanding.

ITE>AvgP and $fc6 \sim fc7$. Inspired by the good performance of fully connected layers, we further report the results of using ITE encoding on $fc6$ and $fc7$ layers. And it also clearly shows that the ITE results are better than the AvgP of corresponding layer, which also validate the effectiveness of our framework. Nevertheless, the results of using $fc6$ features are generally comparable to those of using $fc7$ features in our experiments: the results of YouTube dataset are more favorable on $fc6$ features, while those results of Ekman dataset have better performance on $fc7$.

5.3.3 Feature Complementarity

We investigate the concatenation of different layer features in the deep architecture in Table 6. Specifically, we notice that (1) fully connected layers ($fc6$ and $fc7$) are generally complementary to each other. Both the concatenated features of $[fc6, fc7]$ for AvgP and ITE methods have better performance than those of only $fc6$ and $fc7$ respectively. (2) Fully connected layers are complementary to convolutional layers. This is shown by the results of $[conv5, fc6, fc7]$ of AvgP and ITE methods, which are better than those of $[fc6, fc7]$. (3) The results of convolutional layers are comparatively less complementary to each other. There is no significant improvement in accuracy when adding the features of $conv4$: the ITE result of $[conv4, conv5, fc6, fc7]$ is slightly worse than that of $[conv5, fc6, fc7]$ on YouTube dataset, due to the increased dimensionality (from less complementary $conv4$ layer features).

Table 4 reports concatenated results using ITE encoding and hand-crafted features. We normalized the different sets of features before concatenation. We find that (1) the concatenated results of visual features (denseSIFT) are still comparable to those of ITE on two dataset. This shows that deep features are less complementary to visual hand-crafted features. (2) The methods of using audio features can achieve very high accuracy for video emotion analysis. This means that audio track is very useful for video emotion recognition; (3) The audio hand-crafted features (MFCC) are very complementary to deep video features, since they come from different "sensors". (4) Concatenating all features has worse results than that of $[ITE(fc7), \text{MFCC}]$ due to the increased dimensions from weaker visual hand-crafted features.

Methods	ITE		AvgP	
Dataset	Y	E	Y	E
$[fc6, fc7]$	44.7	49.1	42.2	48.7
$[conv5, fc6, fc7]$	**45.1**	50.2	42.4	48.8
$[conv4, conv5, fc6, fc7]$	44.9	**51.2**	42.0	48.9

Table 6: Concatenation results of different layers of deep features in supervised learning setting.

5.3.4 Fine-tuning

We tried to fine-tune the networks to further improve results of video emotion recognition. The tuning data came from both training video frames or auxiliary image dataset. However, our experimental results suggested fine-tuning does not work well for video emotion recognition tasks. Even after 1 million iterations, the loss function still did not significantly decrease, and the deep features only marginally improve the final results ($\pm 0.5\%$). Our fine-tuning does not work due to (1) The images of the same category may be in different emotion class, *e.g.*, we have 'adorable cat', 'crazy cat', 'lonely cat', 'ugly cat', *etc.*, which will confuse deep network which is trained from ImageNet classification data. (2) The noisy images further confuse the deep network. For example, 'terrible fire' class has both images of fierce fire and images of some fire trucks.

6. CONCLUSIONS

This paper, for the first time, provides the study of knowledge transfer for both supervised and zero-shot emotion recognition. Image Transfer Encoding (ITE) framework facilitates the creation of a representation conducive to the tasks of video emotion understanding. Deep architectures are also systematically explored for video emotion recognition tasks. We validate how different CNN architectures and layers are related to video emotion understanding, which can set the foundation for future research on video emotion analysis using deep features. Furthermore, we investigate the concatenation of CNN feature encodings and other hand-crafted features. Comprehensive set of experiments shows the effectiveness of deep features and their complementarity among layers and with audio features. Future work will address advanced fusion strategies on different deep features to further improve the recognition results.

7. ACKNOWLEDGEMENT

This work was supported in part by a National 863 Program (#2014AA015101) and a grant from the NSF China (#61572134).

8. REFERENCES

[1] S. Andrews, I. Tsochantaridis, and T. Hofmann. Support vector machines for multiple-instance learning. In *NIPS*, 2003.

[2] L. F. Barrett. Are emotions natural kinds? *Perspectives on Psychological Science*, 1(1):28–58, 2006.

[3] D. Borth, R. Ji, T. Chen, T. M. Breuel, and S.-F. Chang. Large-scale visual sentiment ontology and detectors using adjective noun pairs. In *ACM MM*, 2013.

[4] V. Campos, A. Salvador, X. Giro-i Nieto, and B. Jou. Diving deep into sentiment: Understanding fine-tuned cnns for visual sentiment prediction. In *ACM ASM*, 2015.

[5] J. M. Carroll and J. A. Russell. Do facial expressions signal specific emotions? Judging emotion from the face in context. *Journal of Personality and Social Psychology*, 70(2):205–218, 1996.

[6] K. Chatfield, K. Simonyan, A. Vedaldi, and A. Zisserman. Return of the devil in the details: Delving deep into convolutional nets. In *BMVC*, 2014.

[7] T. Chen, D. Borth, Darrell, and S.-F. Chang. Deepsentibank: Visual sentiment concept classification with deep convolutional neural networks. *CoRR*, 2014.

[8] Y. Chen, J. Bi, and J. Z. Wang. Miles: Multiple-instance learning via embedded instance selection. *IEEE TPAMI*, 28(1):1931–1947, 2006.

[9] M. Cimpoi, S. Maji, I. Kokkinos, S. Mohamed, and A. Vedaldi. Describing textures in the wild. In *CVPR*, 2014.

[10] C. Cortes and V. Vapnik. Support-vector networks. *Machine learning*, 20(3):273–297, 1995.

[11] P. Ekman. Universals and cultural differences in facial expressions of emotion. *Nebrasak Symposium on Motivation*, 19:207–284, 1972.

[12] P. Ekman. An argument for basic emotions. *Cognition & emotion*, 6(3-4):169–200, 1992.

[13] Y. Fu, T. M. Hospedales, T. Xiang, and S. Gong. Learning multimodal latent attributes. *IEEE TPAMI*, 36(2):303–316, 2014.

[14] Y. Fu, T. M. Hospedales, T. Xiang, and S. Gong. Transductive multi-view zero-shot learning. *IEEE TPAMI*, 37(11):2332–2345, 2015.

[15] T. Gärtner, P. A. Flach, A. Kowalczyk, and A. J. Smola. Multi-instance kernels. In *ICML*. Morgan Kaufmann, 2002.

[16] A. Ghodrati, M. Pedersoli, and T. Tuytelaars. Is 2d information enough for viewpoint estimation? In *BMVC*, 2014.

[17] B. Hariharan, P. Arbelaez, R. Girshick, and J. Malik. Hypercolumns for object segmentation and fine-grained localization. In *CVPR*, 2015.

[18] J. A. Hartigan and M. A. Wong. Algorithm as 136: A k-means clustering algorithm. *Journal of the Royal Statistical Society. Series C (Applied Statistics)*, 28(1):100–108, 1979.

[19] Y. Jia, E. Shelhamer, J. Donahue, S. Karayev, J. Long, R. Girshick, S. Guadarrama, and T. Darrell. Caffe: Convolutional architecture for fast feature embedding. *CoRR*, 2014.

[20] Y.-G. Jiang, B. Xu, and X. Xue. Predicting emotions in user-generated videos. In *AAAI*, 2014.

[21] B. Jou, S. Bhattacharya, and S.-F. Chang. Predicting viewer perceived emotions in animated gifs. In *ACM MM*, 2014.

[22] H.-B. Kang. Affective content detection using hmms. In *ACM MM*, 2003.

[23] A. Krizhevsky, I. Sutskever, and G. E. Hinton. Imagenet classification with deep convolutional neural networks. In *NIPS*, 2012.

[24] C. H. Lampert, H. Nickisch, and S. Harmeling. Attribute-based classification for zero-shot visual object categorization. *IEEE TPAMI*, 36(3):453–465, 2013.

[25] K. A. Lindquist, T. D. Wager, H. Kober, E. Bliss-Moreau, and L. F. Barrett. The brain basis of emotion: a meta-analytic review. *Trends in cognitive sciences*, 35(3):121–143, 2012.

[26] G. Liu, J. Wu, and Z. Zhou. Key instance detection in multi-instance learning. In *ACML*, 2012.

[27] D. G. Lowe. Distinctive image features from scale-invariant keypoints. *International journal of computer vision*, 60(2):91–110, 2004.

[28] C. D. Manning, P. Raghavan, and H. Schutze. *Introduction to Information Retrieval*. Cambridge University Press, 2009.

[29] S. Marsella and J. Gratch. EMA: A process model of appraisal dynamics. *Journal of Cognitive Systems Research*, 10(1):70–90, 2009.

[30] T. Mikolov, I. Sutskever, K. Chen, G. Corrado, and J. Dean. Distributed representations of words and phrases and their compositionality. In *NIPS*, 2013.

[31] Y. Movshovitz-Attias, Q. Yu, M. C. Stumpe, V. Shet, S. Arnoud, and L. Yatziv. Ontological supervision for fine grained classification of street view storefronts. In *CVPR*, 2015.

[32] A. Ortony, G. Clore, and A. Collins. *The Cognitive Structure of Emotions*. Cambridge University Press, 1988.

[33] R. Plutchik and H. Kellerman. *Emotion: Theory, research and experience. Vol. 1, Theories of emotion*. 1980.

[34] P. R., editor. *The emotions*. University Press of America, 1991.

[35] P. Sermanet, D. Eigen, X. Zhang, M. Mathieu, R. Fergus, and Y. LeCun. Overfeat: Integrated recognition, localization and detection using convolutional networks. In *ICLR*, 2014.

[36] B. M. Sikka K, Dhall A. Weakly supervised pain localization using multiple instance learning. In *IEEE FG*, 2013.

[37] S. T. R. Stein B E. Multisensory integration: current issues from the perspective of the single neuron. *Nature Reviews Neuroscience*, 9(4):255–266, 2008.

[38] C. Szegedy, W. Liu, Y. Jia, P. Sermanet, S. Reed, D. Anguelov, D. Erhan, V. Vanhoucke, and A. Rabinovich. Going deeper with convolutions. *CoRR*, 2014.

[39] H.-L. Wang and L.-F. Cheong. Affective understanding in film. *IEEE TCSVT*, 16(6):689–704, 2006.

[40] J. Wang and J.-D. Zucker. Solving the multiple-instance problem: A lazy learning approach. In *ICML*, 2000.

[41] X.-S. Wei, J. Wu, and Z.-H. Zhou. Scalable multi-instance learning. In *ICDM*, 2014.

[42] B. Xu, Y. Fu, Y.-G. Jiang, B. Li, and L. Sigal. Heterogeneous knowledge transfer in video emotion recognition, attribution and summarization. *CoRR*, 2015.

[43] C. Xu, S. Cetintas, K.-C. Lee, and L.-J. Li. Visual sentiment prediction with deep convolutional neural networks. *CoRR*, 2014.

[44] X. Xu and E. Frank. Logistic regression and boosting for labeled bags of instances. In *PAKDD*, 2004.

[45] Z. Xu, Y. Yang, and A. G. Hauptmann. A discriminative CNN video representation for event detection. *CoRR*, 2014.

[46] J. Yosinski, J. Clune, Y. Bengio, and H. Lipson. How transferable are features in deep neural networks? In *NIPS*, 2014.

[47] Q. You, J. Luo, H. Jin, and J. Yang. Robust image sentiment analysis using progressively trained and domain transferred deep networks. In *AAAI*, 2015.

[48] Z.-H. Zhou and M.-L. Zhang. Solving multi-instance problems with classifier ensemble based on constructive clustering. *Knowledge and Information Systems*, 11(2):155–170, 2007.

Scene-driven Retrieval in Edited Videos using Aesthetic and Semantic Deep Features

Lorenzo Baraldi, Costantino Grana and Rita Cucchiara
Dipartimento di Ingegneria "Enzo Ferrari", Università degli Studi di Modena e Reggio Emilia
Via P. Vivarelli, 10, Modena MO 41125, Italy
name.surname@unimore.it

ABSTRACT

This paper presents a novel retrieval pipeline for video collections, which aims to retrieve the most significant parts of an edited video for a given query, and represent them with thumbnails which are at the same time semantically meaningful and aesthetically remarkable. Videos are first segmented into coherent and story-telling scenes, then a retrieval algorithm based on deep learning is proposed to retrieve the most significant scenes for a textual query. A ranking strategy based on deep features is finally used to tackle the problem of visualizing the best thumbnail. Qualitative and quantitative experiments are conducted on a collection of edited videos to demonstrate the effectiveness of our approach.

Keywords

Video retrieval; Thumbnail selection; Ranking

1. INTRODUCTION

Suppose to search for a given content in a large video collection, which contains long edited videos with different subjects and heterogeneous content, like a collection of documentaries or movies. In this context, users would like to have a quick overview of results, even with a low precision, but capable to give a glance of what can be associated with a query for a further manual refining. Examples are in advertisement where video are re-used to find interesting sequences, in education and edutainment to enrich textual explanations with visual suggestions, in magazine editing, in broadcast-to-web presentations, and also in web search engines.

Nowadays, retrieval is changing towards a greater focus on *aesthetic quality*, a subjective aspect difficult to quantify. Datta *et al.* [5] assessed that modeling aesthetics of images is an important open problem, and it is still not solved. It concerns in general with the kind of emotions a picture arises in people, or more simply in beauty-related of images or videos.

ICMR'16, June 06-09, 2016, New York, NY, USA
© 2016 ACM. ISBN 978-1-4503-4359-6/16/06... $15.00
DOI: http://dx.doi.org/10.1145/2911996.2912012

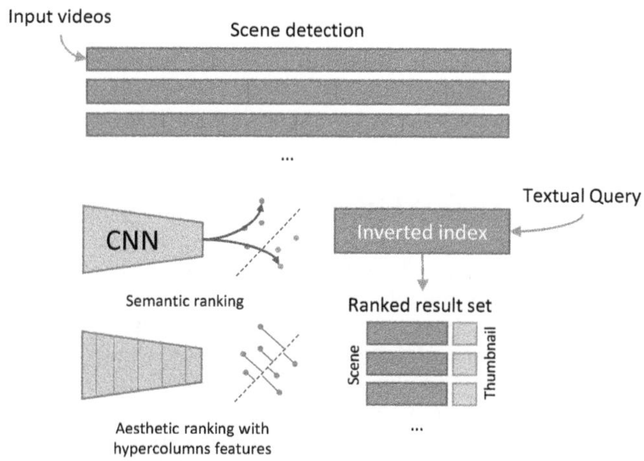

Figure 1: Overview of the proposed method. Given a collection of videos and a textual query, we retrieve a ranked list of the most significant parts (*scenes*) according to both semantics and aesthetic quality. Each retrieved scene is presented with an appropriate thumbnail.

This is an old story: Plato, in *Symposium*, discusses his idea of beauty, that comes from the perception of objects, their proportions, their harmony or unity among the parts, in the evenness of the line and purity of color. This Greek ideal permeates most of the occidental concepts of beauty and the current aesthetic theories, and affects as well theories on user interface designs and, recently, on retrieval too. Google, for instance, spent a large effort in changing the image search interface and the ranking, in order to convey not only the most relevant, abut also the most beautiful or fine results. Hongyi Li, associate product manager at Google, said that Google Images has been redesigned to provide "a better search experience, faster, more beautiful and more reliable"[1]. If image retrieval results are generally not only concerning the query but also ranked to have the more aesthetically valuable, this can be done also in video retrieval, where the complexity is higher. Moreover, also the granularity level could be changed: it is often the case, indeed, that long videos contain different parts and topics, hence an effective retrieval strategy should be able to recover the exact portion of the video the user is looking for.

In this paper we address the problem to provide both se-

[1]https://googlewebmastercentral.blogspot.co.uk/2013/01/faster-image-search.html

mantically and aesthetically valuable results of a query-by-text-retrieval in collections of long and heterogeneous video. Results are presented by thumbnails which recall the content of a video part associated with the specific search concept. Our proposal addresses three common drawbacks of the existing video retrieval pipelines. First, we do not rely on manually provided annotations, like descriptions or tags, which are expensive and not always available, and exploit solely the visual and audio content of the video. Secondly, we let the user search inside a video with a finer granularity level. Lastly, once a set of candidate results has been collected, each should be presented to the user with a thumbnail which is coherent with the query and aesthetically pleasant. To lower the granularity level of searches, we temporally segment each video into a set of semantically meaningful sequences. This task, which is known in literature as *scene detection*, results in a collection of scenes which have the property to be almost constant from a semantic point of view, and therefore constitute the ideal unit for video retrieval.

2. RELATED WORK

The process of producing thumbnails to represent video content has been widely studied. Most conventional methods for video thumbnail selection have focused on learning visual representativeness purely from visual content [10, 18]; however, more recent researches have focused on choosing query-dependent thumbnails to supply specific thumbnails for different queries. Craggs *et al.* [4] introduced the concept that thumbnails are surrogates for videos, as they take the place of a video in search results. Therefore, they may not accurately represent the content of the video, and create an *intention gap*, i.e. a discrepancy between the information sought by the user and the actual content of the video. To reduce the intention gap, they propose a new kind of animated preview, constructed of frames taken from a full video, and a crowdsourced tagging process which enables the matching between query terms and videos. Their system, while going in the right direction, suffers from the need of manual annotations, which are expensive and difficult to obtain.

In [13], instead, authors proposed a method to enforce the representativeness of a selected thumbnail given a user query, by using a reinforcement algorithm to rank frames in each video and a relevance model to calculate the similarity between the video frames and the query keywords. Recently, Liu *et al.* [14] trained a deep visual-semantic embedding to retrieve query-dependent video thumbnails. Their method employs a deeply-learned model to directly compute the similarity between a query and video thumbnails, by mapping them into a common latent semantic space.

On a different note, lot of work has also been proposed for video retrieval: with the explosive growth of online videos, this has become a hot topic in computer vision. In their seminal work, Sivic *et al.* proposed *Video Google* [21], a system that retrieves videos from a database via bag-of-words matching. Lew *et al.* [12] reviewed earlier efforts in video retrieval, which mostly relied on feature-based relevance feedback or similar methods.

Recently, concept-based methods have emerged as a popular approach to video retrieval. Snoek *et al.* [22] proposed a method based on a set of concept detectors, with the aim to bridge the semantic gap between visual features and high level concepts. In [2], authors proposed a video retrieval approach based on tag propagation: given an input video with user-defined tags, Flickr, Google Images and Bing are mined to collect images with similar tags: these are used to label each temporal segment of the video, so that the method increases the number of tags originally proposed by the users, and localizes them temporally. Our method, in contrast, does not need any kind of manual annotation, but is applicable to edited video only.

3. VISUAL-SEMANTIC RETRIEVAL

Given a set of videos $\mathcal{V}$, each decomposed into a set of scenes, and a query term q, we aim at building a function $r(q)$ which returns an ordered set of (video, scene, thumbnail) triplets. The retrieved scene must belong to the retrieved video, and should be as consistent as possible with the given query. Moreover, the returned thumbnail must belong to the given scene, and should be representative of the query as well as aesthetically remarkable.

To detect whether a (video, scene, thumbnail) triplet should correspond to a query, we exploit visually confirmed concepts found in the transcript, as well as a measure of aesthetic quality. We parse the transcript of a video to identify candidate concepts, like objects, animal or people. Then, for each concept a visual classifier is created *on-the-fly* to confirm its presence inside the video, by means of an external corpus of images. Notice that when the transcript of video is not given, it can be easily replaced with the output of a standard speech-to-text software.

Scene detection To segment an input video into a set of coherent scenes, we apply the state-of-the-art algorithm described in [3]. Given a ground-truth temporal segmentation of a set of videos, [3] first runs a shot detector, then trains a Siamese Deep network to predict whether two shots should belong to the same temporal segment. Each branch of the Siamese network is composed by a Convolutional Neural Network (CNN) which follows the AlexNet architecture [11], and whose penultimate layer is concatenated with features extracted from the transcript of the video. The overall network is trained using a contrastive loss function, which computes the distance between two input shots. In test phase, distances between shots provided by the Siamese network are arranged into a similarity matrix, wich is then used together with Spectral Clustering to obtain the final scene boundaries.

Semantic concept detection Sentences in the corpus are parsed and words annotated as *noun*, *proper noun* and *foreign word* are collected with the Stanford CoreNLP part of speech tagger [6]. Each term is converted into its *lemmatized* form, so that nouns in singular and plural form are grouped together. Due to the huge variety of concepts which can be found in the video collection, the video corpus itself may not be sufficient to train detectors for the visual concepts. Therefore, we mine images from the Imagenet database [7], which contains images from more than 40.000 categories from the WordNet [17] hierarchy. Notice that our method, in principle, is applicable to any visual corpus, provided that it contains a sufficient large number of categories.

Each concept in WordNet is described by a set of words or word phrases (called *synonim set*, or *synset*). We match each unigram extracted from the text with the most semantic similar synset in a semantic space. In particular, we

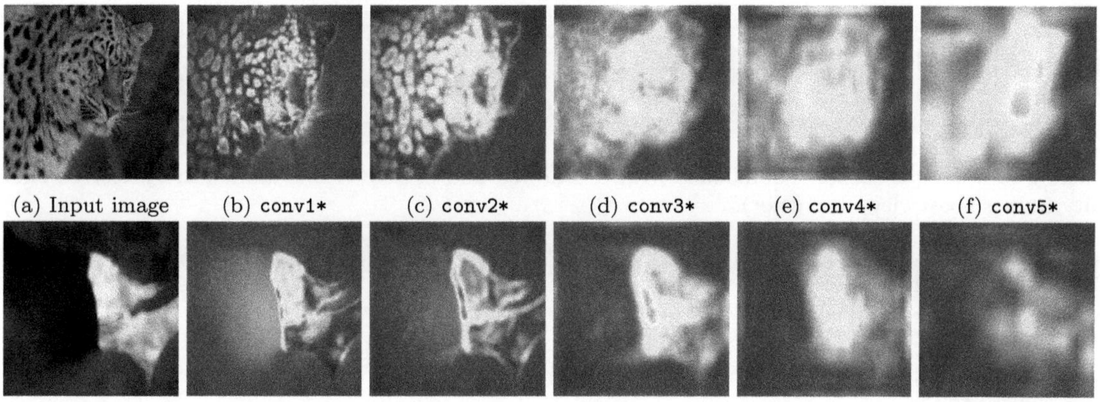

(a) Input image (b) conv1* (c) conv2* (d) conv3* (e) conv4* (f) conv5*

(g) Input image (h) conv1* (i) conv2* (j) conv3* (k) conv4* (l) conv5*

Figure 2: Hypercolumn features extracted from two sample images. Each map represents the mean activation map over a set of layers: (b) and (h) are built using layers conv1_1 and conv1_2, (c) and (i) with layers conv2_1 and conv2_2; (d) and (j) with conv3_1, conv3_2 and conv3_3; (e) and (k) with conv4_1, conv4_2, and conv4_3. Finally, (f) and (i) are built using layers conv5_1, conv5_2 and conv5_3. Best viewed in color.

train a skip-gram model [16] on the dump of the English Wikipedia. The basic idea of skip-gram models is to fit the word embeddings such that the words in corpus can predict their context with high probability. Semantically similar words lie close to each other in the embedded space.

Word embedding algorithms assign each word to a vector in the semantic space, and the semantic similarity $S(u_1, u_2)$ of two concept terms u_1 and u_2 is defined as the cosine similarity between their word embeddings. For synsets, which do not have an explicit embedding, we take the average of the vectors from each word in the synset and L_2-normalize the average vector. The resulting similarity is used to match each concept with the nearest Imagenet category: given a unigram u found in text, the mapping function to the external corpus is as follows:

$$M(u) = \arg\max_{c \in \mathcal{C}} S(u, c) \quad (1)$$

where $\mathcal{C}$ is the set of all concepts in the corpus.

Having mapped each concept from the video collection to an external corpus, a classifier can be built to detect the presence of a visual concept in a shot. Since the number of terms mined from the text data is large, the classification step needs to be efficient, so instead of running the classifier on each frame of the video, we take the middle frame of each shot, using the shot detector in [1]. At the same time, given the temporal coherency of a video, it is unlikely for a visual concept to appear in a shot which is far from the point in which the concept found in the transcript. For this reason, we run a classifier only on shots which are temporally near to its corresponding term, and apply a Gaussian weight to each term based on the temporal distance.

Images from the external corpus are represented using feature activations from pre-trained CNNs. In particular, we employ the 16-layers model from VGG [20], pretrained on the ILSVRC-2012 [19] dataset, and use the activations from layer fc6. Then, a linear probabilistic SVM is trained for each concept, using randomly sampled negative images from other classes; the probability output of each classifier is then used as an indicator of the presence of a concept in a shot.

Formally, given a shot s which appears in the video at time t_s, and a unigram u found in transcript at time t_u, the probability that u is visually confirmed in s is computed as:

$$P(s, u) = f_{M(u)}(s) e^{-\frac{(t_u - t_s)^2}{2\sigma_a^2}} \quad (2)$$

where $f_{M(t)}(s)$ is the probability given by the SVM classifier trained on concept $M(t)$ and tested on shot s.

Aesthetic ranking The probability function defined above accounts for the presence of a particular visual concept in one shot, and is therefore useful to rank scenes given a user query. However, the thumbnail returned to the user should be visually representative as well. This requires a thumbnail selection step, which should account for low level characteristics, like color, edges and sharpness, as well as high level features, such as the presence of a clearly visible object in the center.

We claim that the need of low and high level features is an excellent match with the hierarchical nature of CNNs: convolutional filters, indeed, are known to capture low level as well as high level characteristics of the input image. This has been proved by visualization and inversion techniques, like [23] and [15], which can visualize the role of each filter.

Being activations from convolutional filters discriminative for visual representativeness, a ranking strategy could be set up to learn their relative importance given a dataset of user preferences. However, medium sized CNNs, like the VGG-16 model [20], contain more than 4000 convolutional filters, which produce as much activation maps. This makes the use of raw activations infeasible with small datasets: moreover, maps from different layers have different sizes, due to the presence of pooling layers. To get around with this, we resize each activation map to fixed size with bilinear interpolation, and average feature maps coming from the different layers, inspired by the Hypercolumn approach presented in [8]. Moreover, since the the user usually focuses on the center of the thumbnail rather than its exterior, each maps is multiplied by a normalized gaussian density map, centered on the center of the image and with standard deviation $\sigma_b \cdot l$, where $l \times l$ is the size of the CNN input.

Following the VGG-16 architecture, we build five hypercolumn maps, each one summarizing convolutional layers

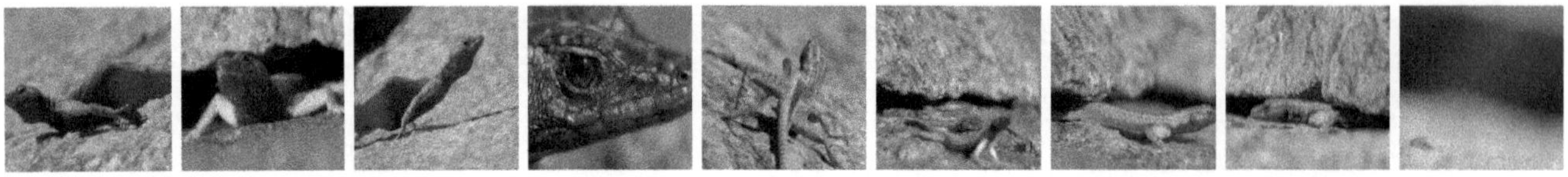

Figure 3: Ranking of a sample scene. Thumbnails with a centered and clearly visible animal are preferred against blurred and low-quality frames (best viewed in color).

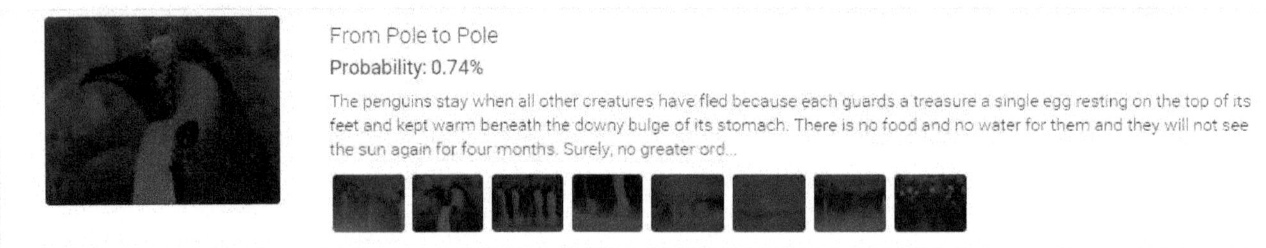

(a) Result for query *penguin*.

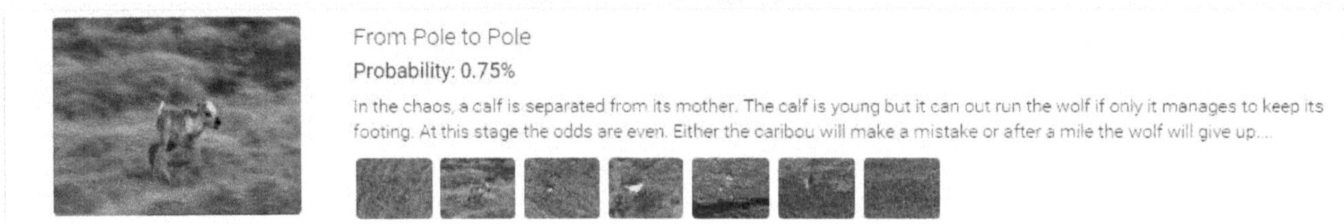

(b) Result for query *calf*.

Figure 4: Retrieval results. The same video is retrieved when searching for *penguin* and for *calf*, however, two different scenes are selected. Reported probability values correspond to $R_{scene}(q)$ in the paper.

before each pooling layer: the first one is computed with activation maps from layers `conv1_1` and `conv1_2`; the second one with `conv2_1` and `conv2_2`; the third with `conv3_1`, `conv3_2` and `conv3_3`; the fourth with `conv4_1`, `conv4_2` and `conv4_3`; the last with `conv5_1`, `conv5_2` and `conv5_3`. An example of the resulting activation maps is presented in Fig. 2: as it can be seen, both low level and high level layers are useful to distinguish between a significant and non significant thumbnail.

To learn the relative contribution of each hypercolumn map, we rank thumbnails from each scene according to their visual representativeness, and learn a linear ranking model. Given a dataset of scenes $\{s_i\}_{k=0}^{n}$, each with a ranking r_k^*, expressed as a set of pairs (d_i, d_j), where thumbnail d_i is annotated as more relevant than thumbnail d_j, we minimize the following function:

$$\begin{aligned} \underset{\mathbf{w},\epsilon}{\text{minimize}} \quad & \frac{1}{2}\|\mathbf{w}\|^2 + C\sum_{i,j,k}\epsilon_{i,j,k} \\ \text{subject to} \quad & \forall(d_i,d_j)\in r_1^* : \mathbf{w}\phi(d_i) \geq \mathbf{w}\phi(d_j) + 1 - \epsilon_{i,j,1} \\ & \dots \\ & \forall(d_i,d_j)\in r_n^* : \quad \mathbf{w}\phi(d_i) \geq \mathbf{w}\phi(d_j) + 1 - \epsilon_{i,j,n} \\ & \forall i,j,k : \epsilon_{i,j,k} \geq 0 \end{aligned} \tag{3}$$

where $\phi(d_i)$ is the feature vector of thumbnail d_i, which is composed by the mean and standard deviation of each hypercolumn map extracted from the thumbnail itself. C allows trading-off the margin size with respect to the training error. The objective stated in Eq. 3 is convex and equivalent to that of a linear SVM on pairwise difference vectors $\phi(d_i) - \phi(d_j)$ [9].

Retrieval Given a query q, we first match q with the most similar detected concept u, using the Word2Vec embedding. If the query q is composed by more than one words, the mean of the embedded vectors is used. Each scene inside the video collection is then assigned a score according to the following function:

$$R_{scene}(q) = \max_{s \in scene}\left(\alpha P(s,u) + (1-\alpha)\max_{d \in s}\mathbf{w}\phi(d)\right) \tag{4}$$

where s is a shot inside the given scene, and d represent all keyframes extracted from a given shot. Parameter α tunes the relative importance of semantic representativeness and aesthetic beauty. The final retrieval results is a collection of scenes, ranked according to $R_{scene}(q)$, each one represented with the keyframe that maximizes the second term of the score.

From an implementation point of view, $P(s,u)$ can be computed offline for each unigram u found in the transcript, for example with an inverted index. $\mathbf{w}\phi(d)$, as well, can be computed in advance for each key-frame, thus greatly reducing the computational needs in the on-line stage.

4. EXPERIMENTAL RESULTS

We evaluate the proposed method on a collection of 11 episodes from the *BBC Planet Earth*[2] series. Each video

[2]http://www.bbc.co.uk/programmes/b006mywy

Episode	Shots	Scenes	Unigrams
From Pole to Pole	450	66	337
Mountains	395	53	339
Fresh Water	425	62	342
Caves	473	71	308
Deserts	461	65	392
Ice Worlds	529	65	343
Great Plains	534	63	336
Jungles	418	53	346
Shallow Seas	368	62	370
Seasonal Forests	393	57	356
Ocean Deep	470	55	333

Table 1: Statistics on the *BBC Planet Earth* dataset.

is approximately 50 minutes long, and the whole dataset contains around 4900 shots and 670 scenes. Each video is also provided with the transcript, and on the whole dataset a total of 3802 terms was extracted using the CoreNLP parser. Table 1 reports some statistics on the dataset. Parameters σ_a and σ_b were set to 5 and 4.5 respectively, while C was set to 3.

4.1 Thumbnail selection evaluation

Since aesthetic quality is subjective, three different users were asked to mark all keyframes either as aesthetically relevant or non relevant for the scene they belong to. For each shot, the middle frame was selected as keyframe. Annotators were instructed to consider the relevance of the visual content as well as the quality of the keyframe in terms of color, sharpness and blurriness. Each keyframe was then labeled with the number of times it was selected, and a set of (d_i, d_j) training pairs was built according to the given ranking, to train our aesthetic ranking model.

For comparison, an end-to-end deep learning approach (*Ranking CNN*) was also tested. In this case the last layer of a pre-trained VGG-16 network was replaced with just one neuron, and the network was trained to predict the score of each shot, with a Mean Square Error loss. Both the Ranking CNN model and the proposed Hypercolumn-based ranking were trained in a leave-one-out setup, using ten videos for training and one for test.

Table 2 reports the average percent of swapped pairs: as it can be seen, our ranking strategy is able to overcome the Ranking CNN baseline and features a considerably reduced error percentage. This confirms that low and high level features can be successfully combined together, and that high features alone, such as the ones the Ranking CNN is able to extract from its final layers, are not sufficient. Figure 3 shows the ranking results of a sample scene: as requested in the annotation, the SVM model preferred thumbnails with good quality and a clearly visible object in the middle.

4.2 Retrieval results evaluation

On a different note, we present some qualitative results of the retrieval pipeline. Figure 4 shows the first retrieved result when searching for *penguin* and *calf*, using $\alpha = 0.5$. As it can be seen, our method retrieves two different scenes for the same video, based on the visually confirmed concepts extracted from the transcript. The same video, therefore, is presented with different scenes depending on the query. Moreover, selected thumbnails are actually representative of

Episode	Ranking CNN	Hypercolumns Ranking
From Pole to Pole	8.23	4.10
Mountains	12.08	7.94
Fresh Water	12.36	8.11
Caves	9.98	8.76
Deserts	13.90	9.35
Ice Worlds	6.62	4.33
Great Plains	10.92	9.63
Jungles	12.28	7.43
Shallow Seas	10.91	6.22
Seasonal Forests	9.47	4.82
Ocean Deep	10.73	5.75
Average	**10.68**	**6.95**

Table 2: Aesthetic ranking: average percent of swapped pairs on the *BBC Planet Earth* dataset (lower is better).

the query and aesthetically pleasant, when compared to the others available keyframes for those scenes. Depending on the query, it may also happen that the same scene is presented with two different thumbnails, as depicted in Fig. 5: in this case the same scene was retrieved with query *ant* and *spider*; however, in the first case the selected thumbnail actually represents an ant, while in the second case a spider is selected, thus enhancing the user experience.

4.3 User evaluation

To quantitatively evaluate the ranking results and their effect on user experience, we conducted a user study with 12 undergraduate students. A demonstration and evaluation interface was built, in which the first three results returned by our method could be directly compared with three scenes retrieved with a full-text search inside the transcript, and presented with a random thumbnail different from the one selected by our system. As in Fig. 4 and 5, each retrieved scene was presented with the selected thumbnail, the corresponding transcription and with all the key-frames extracted from the scene. Users could also click on the thumbnail to watch the corresponding scene.

Evaluators were asked to compare the provided result sets and vote the one they liked most, for a set of 20 queries. Results from our method were preferred to those provided by the baseline in the 82% of cases, in the 15% of evaluations they were said to be equivalent, while in the remaining 3% of cases the baseline was preferred. The same queries were presented again replacing the thumbnails selected by our method with random ones. In this case the preferences were 12% for the baseline and 57% for our proposal, while in the 31% of cases results were evaluated as equivalent.

This confirms the role of selecting appropriate thumbnails when dealing with casual users (the students didn't have any real goal, nor were particularly interested in the queries we provided). One of the conclusions we can draw from this tests is that the presentation of the results may strongly influence the feeling of "correctness" of the retrieved results.

5. CONCLUSIONS

We presented a novel video retrieval pipeline, in which videos are decomposed into short parts (namely scenes), that are used as the basic unit for retrieval. A score function was

(a) Result for query *ant*.

(b) Result for query *spider*.

Figure 5: Retrieval results. In this case the same scene from the same video is retrieved with two different queries (*ant* and *spider*), however, two different (and significant) thumbnails are selected. Reported probability values correspond to $R_{scene}(q)$ in the paper.

proposed to rank scenes according to a given textual query, taking into account the visual content of a thumbnail as well as its aesthetic quality, so that each result is presented with an appropriate keyframe. Both the semantics and the aesthetics were assessed using features extracted from Convolutional Neural Networks, and by building on-the-fly classifiers for unseen concepts. Our work has been evaluated both in qualitative and quantitative terms, and results in enhanced retrieval results and user experience.

Acknowledgments We gratefully acknowledge the support of NVIDIA Corporation with the donation of the GPUs used for this research. This work was carried out within the project "Città educante" (CTN01_00034_393801) of the National Technological Cluster on Smart Communities cofunded by the Italian Ministry of Education, University and Research - MIUR.

6. REFERENCES

[1] E. Apostolidis and V. Mezaris. Fast Shot Segmentation Combining Global and Local Visual Descriptors. In *IEEE International Conference on Acoustics, Speech and Signal Processing*, pages 6583–6587, 2014.

[2] L. Ballan, M. Bertini, G. Serra, and A. Del Bimbo. A data-driven approach for tag refinement and localization in web videos. *Computer Vision and Image Understanding*, 140:58–67, 2015.

[3] L. Baraldi, C. Grana, and R. Cucchiara. A deep siamese network for scene detection in broadcast videos. In *Proceedings of the 23rd Annual ACM Conference on Multimedia Conference*, MM '15, pages 1199–1202, New York, NY, USA, 2015. ACM.

[4] B. Craggs, M. Kilgallon Scott, and J. Alexander. Thumbreels: query sensitive web video previews based on temporal, crowdsourced, semantic tagging. In *Proceedings of the SIGCHI Conference on Human Factors in Computing Systems*, pages 1217–1220. ACM, 2014.

[5] R. Datta, D. Joshi, J. Li, and J. Z. Wang. Image retrieval: Ideas, influences, and trends of the new age. *ACM Computing Surveys (CSUR)*, 40(2):5, 2008.

[6] M.-C. De Marneffe, B. MacCartney, C. D. Manning, et al. Generating typed dependency parses from phrase structure parses. In *Proceedings of LREC*, volume 6, pages 449–454, 2006.

[7] J. Deng, W. Dong, R. Socher, L.-J. Li, K. Li, and L. Fei-Fei. Imagenet: A large-scale hierarchical image database. In *IEEE International Conference on Computer Vision and Pattern Recognition*, pages 248–255. IEEE, 2009.

[8] B. Hariharan, P. Arbeláez, R. Girshick, and J. Malik. Hypercolumns for object segmentation and fine-grained localization. In *Proceedings of the IEEE Conference on Computer Vision and Pattern Recognition*, pages 447–456, 2015.

[9] T. Joachims. Optimizing search engines using clickthrough data. In *Proceedings of the eighth ACM SIGKDD international conference on Knowledge discovery and data mining*, pages 133–142. ACM, 2002.

[10] H.-W. Kang and X.-S. Hua. To learn representativeness of video frames. In *Proceedings of the 13th annual ACM international conference on Multimedia*, pages 423–426. ACM, 2005.

[11] A. Krizhevsky, I. Sutskever, and G. E. Hinton. Imagenet classification with deep convolutional neural networks. In *Advances in Neural Information Processing Systems*, pages 1097–1105, 2012.

[12] M. S. Lew, N. Sebe, C. Djeraba, and R. Jain. Content-based multimedia information retrieval: State of the art and challenges. *ACM Transactions on Multimedia Computing, Communications, and Applications (TOMM)*, 2(1):1–19, 2006.

[13] C. Liu, Q. Huang, and S. Jiang. Query sensitive dynamic web video thumbnail generation. In *Image Processing (ICIP), 2011 18th IEEE International Conference on*, pages 2449–2452. IEEE, 2011.

[14] W. Liu, T. Mei, Y. Zhang, C. Che, and J. Luo. Multi-task deep visual-semantic embedding for video thumbnail selection. In *Proceedings of the IEEE Conference on Computer Vision and Pattern Recognition*, pages 3707–3715, 2015.

[15] A. Mahendran and A. Vedaldi. Understanding deep image representations by inverting them. In *Computer Vision and Pattern Recognition (CVPR), 2015 IEEE Conference on*, pages 5188–5196. IEEE, 2015.

[16] T. Mikolov, I. Sutskever, K. Chen, G. S. Corrado, and J. Dean. Distributed representations of words and phrases and their compositionality. In *Advances in Neural Information Processing Systems*, pages 3111–3119, 2013.

[17] G. A. Miller. Wordnet: a lexical database for english. *Communications of the ACM*, 38(11):39–41, 1995.

[18] A. Rav-Acha, Y. Pritch, and S. Peleg. Making a long video short: Dynamic video synopsis. In *Computer Vision and Pattern Recognition, 2006 IEEE Computer Society Conference on*, volume 1, pages 435–441. IEEE, 2006.

[19] O. Russakovsky, J. Deng, H. Su, J. Krause, S. Satheesh, S. Ma, Z. Huang, A. Karpathy, A. Khosla, M. Bernstein, A. C. Berg, and L. Fei-Fei. ImageNet Large Scale Visual Recognition Challenge. *International Journal of Computer Vision*, pages 1–42, April 2015.

[20] K. Simonyan and A. Zisserman. Very deep convolutional networks for large-scale image recognition. *arXiv preprint arXiv:1409.1556*, 2014.

[21] J. Sivic and A. Zisserman. Video google: A text retrieval approach to object matching in videos. In *Computer Vision, 2003. Proceedings. Ninth IEEE International Conference on*, pages 1470–1477. IEEE, 2003.

[22] C. G. Snoek, B. Huurnink, L. Hollink, M. De Rijke, G. Schreiber, and M. Worring. Adding semantics to detectors for video retrieval. *Multimedia, IEEE Transactions on*, 9(5):975–986, 2007.

[23] M. D. Zeiler and R. Fergus. Visualizing and understanding convolutional networks. In *Computer vision–ECCV 2014*, pages 818–833. Springer, 2014.

ACD: Action Concept Discovery from Image-Sentence Corpora

Jiyang Gao
Univ. of Southern California
jiyangga@usc.edu

Chen Sun
Univ. of Southern California
chensun@usc.edu

Ram Nevatia
Univ. of Southern California
nevatia@usc.edu

ABSTRACT

Action classification in still images is an important task in computer vision. It is challenging as the appearances of actions may vary depending on their context (*e.g.* associated objects). Manually labeling of context information would be time consuming and difficult to scale up. To address this challenge, we propose a method to automatically discover and cluster action concepts, and learn their classifiers from weakly supervised image-sentence corpora. The proposed method obtains candidate action concepts by extracting verb-object pairs from sentences and verifies their visualness with the associated images via two fold cross-validation. Candidate action concepts are then clustered by using a multi-modal representation with image embeddings from deep convolutional networks and text embeddings from word2vec. More than one hundred human action concept classifiers are learned from the Flickr 30k dataset with no additional human effort and these action concepts are clustered into 81 action clusters. We train a SVM classifier for each of them and we show promising classification results on Flickr30k. We further apply the AdaBoost algorithm to automatically select and combine relevant action concepts given an action query. Promising results have been shown on the PASCAL VOC 2012 action classification benchmark, which has zero overlap with Flickr30k.

Keywords

Concept Discovery, Multi-modal Representation, Action Classification, Domain Transfer

1. INTRODUCTION

Action classification in still images is an important computer vision task with wide applications. One major difficulty for this task is that the appearances of actions usually depend not only on the action itself but also on the objects that they are applied to. For example, the action *play musical instruments* is general, its appearance varies significantly when the object is different (*e.g. play violin* and *play piano*); varying objects is sometimes also termed as varying context. To make the situation worse, the potential space of action and context combinations is very large.

ICMR'16, June 06 - 09, 2016, New York, NY, USA

ISBN 978-1-4503-4359-6/16/06. . . $15.00

DOI: http://dx.doi.org/10.1145/2911996.2912014

Figure 1: Top 3 action recognition outputs on PASCAL VOC 2012 using our discovered action concept classifiers from Flickr30k

Most previous methods in action classification [28, 22, 10, 8, 19, 12] focus on learning action classifiers from fully annotated datasets with limited categories [1, 6, 29]. To extend the action vocabulary and allow context awareness, such methods require labeling actions in images manually, which is time-consuming and difficult to scale up. On the other hand, there are many large-scale datasets with image and sentence descriptions [23, 4, 30, 11, 18, 15] readily available. Many of the verb-object (VO) pairs in these sentence descriptions can be treated as actions with context. However, there are two major challenges of learning action classifiers from such image-sentence corpora:

- **Annotation noise:** a sentence description may contain several VO pairs, many of which may not correspond to actual actions in the image.

- **Language diversity:** humans might refer the same action category by different terms. For example, the actions of jump, leap and flip are visually similar, but there is only one tag for this kind of action, *jump*, in PASCAL VOC 2012 action classification dataset.

To address these challenges, we propose a method to automatically discover *action concepts*, cluster them and learn classifiers for them from image-sentence corpora (ACD). Some action recognition results are shown in Figure 1. To cope with annotation noise, the ACD framework filters action concepts based on a visually discriminative criterion: each action concept classifier must perform reliably on validation data. For the language diversity problem, ACD merges different VO pairs referring to the same actions together.

The overall pipeline proceeds as follows: we first extract subject, verb and object triples from the sentences in image-sentence corpora with an off-the-shelf NLP parser, and filter out the ones whose subjects are non-human. We then extract a 4096-dimensional feature vector for each image by passing it through pre-trained (on ImageNet) convolutional neural networks (CNN). Two-fold cross validation is applied to verify the visual discriminative power of action concepts. For each action concept, we construct a multi-modal representation by concatenating CNN feature vectors of its associated images and its word2vec [21] embedding features. The similarity between two action concepts is defined as the cosine similarity of the multi-modal representations. To merge different concepts referring to the same action, we cluster the discovered action concepts with a nearest neighbor (NN) clustering algorithm based on the multi-modal similarity metric. Finally, for each cluster, we train a linear SVM classifier on all the associated images.

For our experiments, we learned action concepts from the Flickr30k [30] dataset which contains 30 thousand images and each image is associated with 5 sentences to describe it. The sentences are generated by Amazon Mechanical Turk. An image-sentence example is shown in Figure 2. Besides testing the classifiers on subsets of the Flickr30k dataset, to compare with other weakly supervised methods, we also test the classifiers on an independent and widely used PASCAL VOC 2012 action classification dataset, which has 10 pre-defined categories. Note that this amounts to a transfer learning task with Flickr30K as the *source domain* and PASCAL as the *transfer domain.* Since a certain action tag in the transfer domain could be related to multiple concept clusters, we use the action tag as search keywords to find related clusters in the cluster pool and combine all the related cluster classifiers using AdaBoost [27] for this action tag to build a stronger classifier.

The key contributions of this paper are:

1. A methodology to discover, filter and cluster action concepts from image-sentence corpora automatically.

2. A multimodal representation for actions by combining the convolutional neural networks feature of related images and word2vec feature of the concept terms (verb+object).

3. A method for building a stronger classifier for transfer domain by using an ensemble of learned action classifiers from source domain.

2. RELATED WORK

Visual Concept Learning: There have been two trends in learning visual concept automatically. One relies on Internet search engines [3, 5] to collect images and train concept classifiers on those images. In particular, NEIL [3] uses a never-ending-learning algorithm to gather visual data from internet and build relationships between these concepts. However, the vocabulary dataset is fixed. LEVAN [5] discovers comprehensive vocabulary from Internet data and trains detectors for them using the images collected by search engine.

The second trend discovers concepts from weakly labelled data. Specifically, VCD [26] proposes a concept mining and clustering algorithm based on visual and semantic similarity. However, it mainly focuses on general object concept learning. ConceptLearner [31] designs a scalable max-margin algorithm to discover and to learn visual concepts from weakly labeled image dataset [23, 4]. However, it lacks concept clustering.

Multimodal Integration: There is large literature on multimodal representation models. We only select a few representative systems to describe here. [13] adopts a concatenation strategy and use a convolutional neural network to extract features from images and skip-gram model for text. [2] constructs text feature vectors and image feature vectors separately and then mixes them by Singular Value Decomposition on their concatenation. [17] extends skip-gram model by taking visual information into account, which is called multimodal skip-gram. Image dispersion-based filtering in [14] improves multi-modal representations by approximating conceptual concreteness from images and filtering model input.

Action Classification in Still Images: The use of convolutional neural network (CNN) has brought huge improvement in action classification. [22] finetunes the CNN pre-trained on ImageNet and shows improvement over traditional methods. [10] designs a multi-task (person-detection, pose-estimation and action classification) model based on R-CNN. [8] develops a part-based approach by leveraging convolutional network features for action and attribute classification. They show top performance on PASCAL VOC human attribute and action classification. [9] develops an end-to-end deep convolutional neural network that utilizes contextual information of actions. Most previously leading methods in action classification for 2D images are based on part detectors. In particular, [19] trains action specific poselets and for each instance creates a poselet activation vector which is being classified using SVMs. In [12], image regions are identified in different classes by using a dense sampling space and a random forest algorithm with discriminative classifiers. These works are all based on fully-supervised learning method and trained on fully-labeled data.

3. ACTION CONCEPT LEARNING

In this section, we first present our method to extract action concepts from sentences in the source domain (Flickr30k) and verify the visualness of concepts. Secondly, our multimodal representation for action concepts and NN-clustering algorithm are demonstrated. Finally, we present the method using AdaBoost to combine multiple related action classifiers.

3.1 Action Concept Extraction

We use grammatical relations called *dependencies* to discover action concepts from sentences. Specifically, the sentences are parsed by the Stanford CoreNLP parser [20], and then verb-object(VO) pairs are extracted from the parsed sentences with only human subjects. A VO pair, such as play basketball, is used as action, for example "play basketball", "ride horse". For the actions that have no object, we use a word "none" as their object, such as "run none" and "walk none". We remove the terms that occur fewer than k times (we set k=30 in our experiments). Remaining VOs are action concept candidates. Now each image may contain several VOs (*i.e.* action concepts) and each VO may be associated with several images.

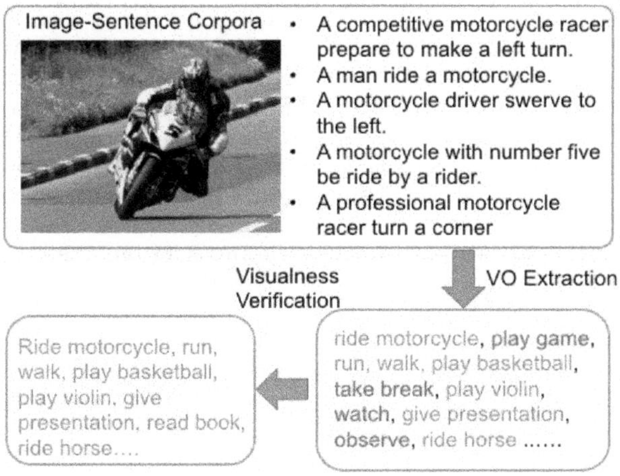

Figure 2: VO pairs extraction and verification

3.2 Concept Visualness Verification

After filtering VO pairs from the corpus, the remaining ones are meaningful action concept candidates, as shown in Figure 2. However, some of them may not be visually distinct. For example, there are no obvious visual patterns for the action "take break". Concept visualness verification is used to eliminate the visually non-distinct action concepts. We collect positive samples from the images associated with a concept and randomly choose equal number of negative samples from other images. Each image is processed by an ImageNet pre-trained VGG-16 [25]. The network takes in a 224*224 pixel RGB image and generate a 4096-dimensional vector as the image feature. Linear-SVM classifiers are trained for each action concept candidate and their performance is evaluated by two fold cross-validation. We prune the action concepts whose average precision (AP) is lower then 70%.

3.3 Concept Multimodal Representation

For visual representation, similar to [13], our approach makes use of the collection of images associated with the action concept. After we extract image-level holistic features from a pre-trained deep CNN for each image, two approaches are considered to aggregate the image features for each action concept, as shown in Figure 3:

1. Compute the average for all feature vectors (CNN-Mean).
2. Compute dimension-wise maximum for all feature vectors (CNN-Max).

For linguistic representation, we extract 200-dimensional word embedding for each word. In particular, we train a skip-gram [21] model using the English Wikipedia dump. The feature vector for the fake object "none" is an all-zero vector. The semantic representation for an action concept is 400-dimensional (200d for the verb part and 200d for the object part). We construct our multimodal representation for action concept by concatenating the visual representation and linguistic representation. Note that the visual feature vector and the linguistic feature vector are both L2-normalized.

$$V_{concept} = \alpha V_{visual} \oplus (1 - \alpha) V_{linguistic}$$

where $\oplus$ is the concatenation operator and α is a parameter balancing the weights given to the visual and linguistic

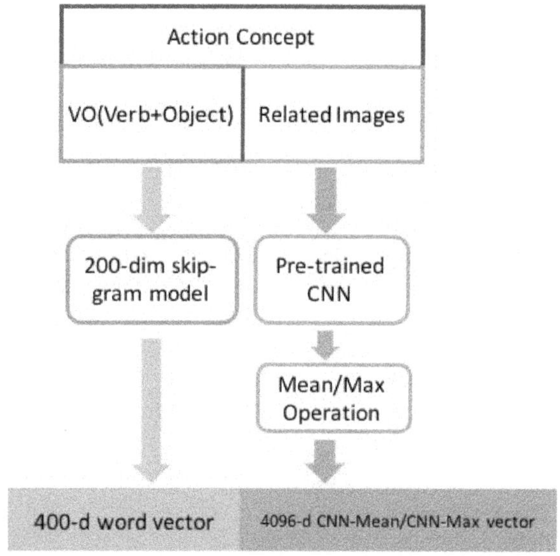

Figure 3: Multimodal representation by concatenating the visual feature and linguistic feature. For the visual part, we use pre-trained CNN to extract image-level features and combine them by computing the average or component-maximum. For the linguistic part, we use word2vec to extract a 200-dimensional semantic feature vectors for "verb" part and "object" part and concatenate them together.

representations. Similarity between two concepts, c_i and c_j, can be calculated by cosine similarity:

$$S(c_i, c_j) = \frac{V_{c_i} V_{c_j}}{\|V_{c_i}\| \|V_{c_j}\|}$$

3.4 NN Clustering

The total number of the action concepts is smaller then the number of general concepts, so there may be more differences and less general patterns between different datasets. To be adaptive to different situations, we make use of the patterns within the dataset to cluster the action concepts. For example, if the whole concept set is {play basketball, play sport, play instrument}, then there should be two clusters {play basketball, play sport} and {play instrument}. In another situation, the whole concept set is {run, play sport, play instrument}, then there should be three clusters. So the intuition of the solution is that the compactness of cluster should be determined by the dataset itself.

We design a clustering algorithm based on the nearest neighbors (NN) of each concept, called NN-clustering. It's a non-parametric clustering algorithm, unlike K-means or spectral clustering which specifies the number of clusters explicitly. Suppose that the size of a cluster is k, *i.e.* the number of concepts in that cluster, then this cluster meet two conditions:

1. For any two concepts, c_i and c_j, in this cluster, suppose c_i is the nearest n neighbor of c_j and c_j is the m nearest neighbor of c_i, then $m <= k + C, n <= k + C$, C is a constant.
2. For any two concepts c_i and c_j in the cluster, the similarity between c_i and c_j, $S(c_i, c_j)$ must be larger then the av-

erage concept similarity S_{avg}. $S_{avg} = \frac{1}{n^2}\sum_{i=1}^{n}\sum_{j=1}^{n} S(c_i, c_j)$, where n is the size of the whole concept set.

```
Data: concept similarity matrix of size l × l and
      concept list of size l
Result: cluster list
// initialization process:
for i ← 0 to l do
    for j ← i + 1 to l do
        if concepts[i] and concepts[j] are mutually the
          nearest neighbour then
            clusters.add(cluster(concepts[i],concepts[j]));
        end
    end
end
// iteratively clustering:
while unclustered concept ≠ ∅ do
    change ← True;
    while change == True do
        change ← False;
        for i ← 0 to l do
            for k ← 0 to length(clusters) do
                if checkClustered(clusters[k],concepts[i])
                 then
                    // if concept could be added
                    into cluster
                    clusters[k].add(concepts[i]);
                    change ← True
                end
            end
        end
    end
    index=randint(length(unclustered concepts));
    clusters.add(cluster(concepts[index]));
end
```

Algorithm 1: NN-Clustering Algorithm

The first condition causes mutually similar concepts to be clustered together. The constant C controls the compactness of the cluster. The larger is C, the looser is the cluster. Note that mutual similarity is a very important constraint. Suppose that we have an action concept which is not similar to any other concepts, but there is still a ranking list of its similar concepts. If we only use unilateral similarity, then it would be clustered with its most similar concept. Only the first condition would tend to make the cluster as large as possible. If we regard the whole action concept set as a cluster, then it will still satisfy the first condition. So we must use the second condition as an additional constraint. We implement this algorithm in an iterative way, as shown in Algorithm 1.

3.5 Training Action Classifier with SVM and AdaBoost

After clustering concepts, we train a linear-SVM classifier for each cluster using CNN image features. We notice that action tags in traditional action classification dataset can relate to multiple concept clusters. For example, the action tag "jump" (in PASCAL VOC 2012 action classification) relates to{*do jump, do flip*}, {*leap none, jump none*} and {*midair none, do jump, fly none*}. Each related cluster can be trained as a weak classifier to the action tag and these weak classifiers can be combined to a single strong classifier using ensemble learning methods, such as AdaBoost. We search all the related clusters automatically for a specific action tag. Specifically, we use the action tag as a keyword to search in our cluster pool. If there is a concept of the cluster that matches with the action tag, then this cluster is picked out as a related action cluster. The pipeline is shown in Figure 4.

AdaBoost generates a new hypothesis by applying the weak learning algorithms to a sample of the training data.The key idea is to set weights to the training data so that wrongly classified data points are more likely to be considered by the new hypothesis. The output is given by

$$f_T(x) = \sum_{i=1}^{T} \beta_i h_i(x)$$

where x is the input feature, $f_T(x)$ is the AdaBoost classifier, $h_i(x)$ are the linear-SVM classifier of the related clusters and β_i is the learned goodness weight for each weak classifier.

4. EVALUATION

In this section, we evaluate our multimodal representation with different α values. NN-Clustering algorithm is applied with different C values. We also evaluate our action classifiers on the *transfer domain* (PASCAL VOC 2012 action classification dataset) and *source domain* (Flickr30k).

4.1 Multimodal Representation

We use all images and associated sentences in the source domain (Flickr30k) to discover action concepts. After parsing each sentence with Stanford CoreNLP and extracting VO from the whole corpus, we get 327 action concept candidates. 171 VOs pass the visualness verification step and are action concepts.

We calculate two versions of multimodal representation (CNN-Mean and CNN-Max) for each action concept with $\alpha \in \{0, 0.1, 0.2, ..., 0.9, 1.0\}$ and cluster these action concepts with $C = 4$. Given the clustering results, we train linear-SVM classifiers using LIBLINEAR [ ] for each cluster. A typical objective of clustering algorithm is to attain high intra-cluster similarity and low inter-cluster similarity, which implies that if we train classifiers for each cluster, then the performance of those classifiers should depend on the quality of the clustering results. If we fix the clustering algorithm itself, then a more powerful representation of the action concepts should yield a better clustering results, hence better classification performance. We define the average classification accuracy as the mean of accuracies of all action classifiers and use it as our metric to evaluate the multimodal representation.

From the experimental results shown in Figure 5, we can see the following: a) the performance of CNN-Mean is generally better than that of CNN-Max. The reason could be that the maximum operation is more subject to noise. b) When $\alpha = 0.6$, both method achieve the highest average classification accuracy. The parameter α weights the relative contribution of the linguistic part and the visual part. The larger the tuning parameter α is, the larger contribution the visual part will make. This observation shows that the visual part and the linguistic part are almost equally important to construct a good representation.

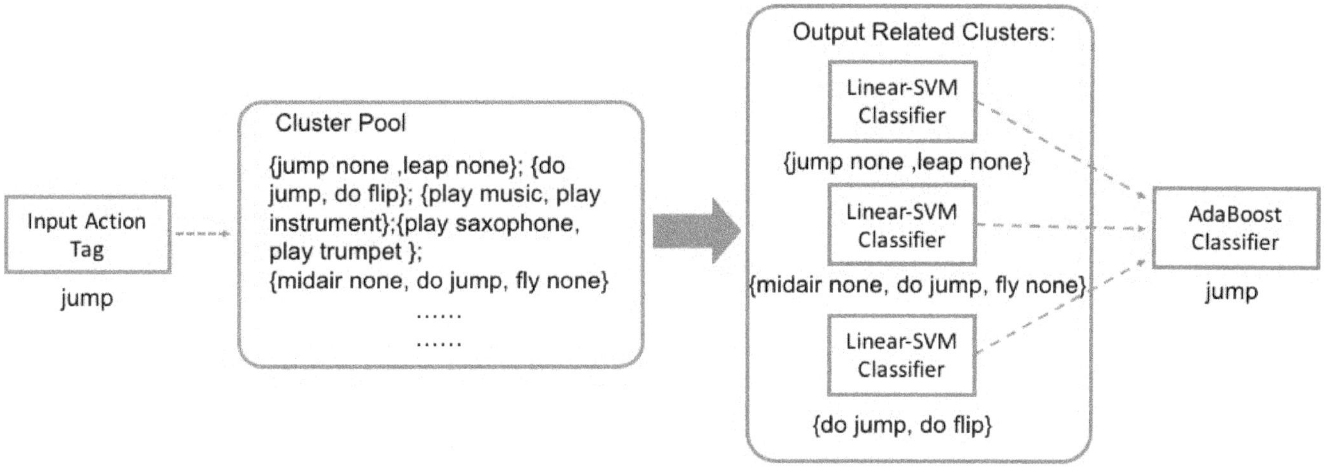

Figure 4: Combining multiple classifiers of related clusters. For example, if the input action tag is "jump", we first search for the related clusters in the concept cluster pool. The classifiers of related clusters are regarded as weak classifiers to the action tag. Then we train an AdaBoost classifier to combine all the weak classifiers to a stronger classifier for the input action tag, *i.e.* jump.

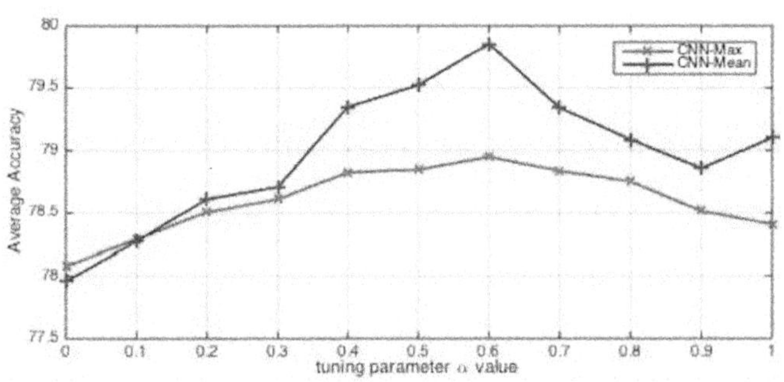

Figure 5: Evaluation of the multimodal representation (CNN-Mean and CNN-Max) with different α values on average accuracy

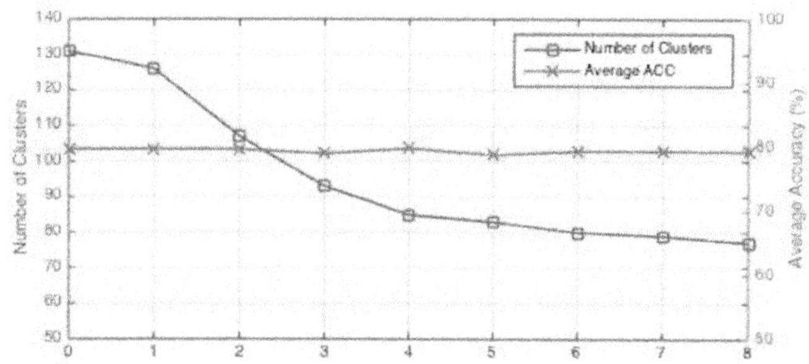

Figure 6: NN-clustering evaluation by changing the value of the constant C.

We discuss the influence of tuning parameter α in more specific examples and see the obvious differences of large α and small α. When $\alpha = 0.9$ (almost all visual features), some good results include {*ride bike, ride bicycle, bike none, biking none*}, {*ride skateboard, skateboarding none, skate none*}, {*throw ball, play baseball*}. Apparently, "throw ball" and "play baseball" are semantically-unrelated, at least not as similar as "throw ball" and "hit ball", but they are very similar visually (Baseball game is about throwing ball and catching ball, so when we use a large α value, these two action concepts are clustered together. If we adopt a small α value, "throw ball" would be clustered with "hit ball" and "kick ball".) On the other hand, large α also generates some "bad" results: {*play trumpet, play saxophone*}, {*play instrument, play music*} and {*play accordion*}. Perhaps all these three clusters should be in one cluster, because they are all related to "play instrument". When $\alpha = 0.1$, the algorithm indeed clusters all these together: {*play trumpet, play saxophone, play violin, play keyboard, play drum, play guitar, play music, play accordion, play instrument*}. However, small α also produces poor clustering results in other cases, for example, {*ride bike, ride bicycle, ride motorcycle, ride skateboard, ride horse, ride scooter*}; all these actions are about riding something. According to the discussion above, both small α and large α could produce good clustering results depending on our desired goodness criterion.

We use multiple α values to clustering concepts to get a comprehensive cluster set. Specifically, we calculate the CNN-Mean action representations and cluster the action concepts with $\alpha \in \{0, 0.1, 0.2, ..., 0.9, 1.0\}$. The union of all these clusters from different α values make a comprehensive cluster pool.

4.2 Clustering Algorithm

We evaluate the NN-clustering algorithm with different value of constant C, where C controls the compactness of the cluster. The larger the value of C, the looser the cluster will be, that is the concepts in the same cluster will be less similar. We test the algorithm with $C \in \{0, 1, 2, 3, 4, 5, 6, 7, 8\}$ on average classification accuracy and the number of clusters, as shown in Figure 6. The average classification accuracy is the same as shown in Section 4.1.

According to the experimental results, we make two observations: a) the average accuracy doesn't change much with constant C; b) the number of the clusters is stable around 80 when $C > 4$. Based on these observations, we fix $C = 4$ and $\alpha = 0.6$. Some cluster examples are shown in Table 1.

Index	Cluster Terms	AP(%)
1	{play trumpet, play saxophone, play violin, play guitar, play accordion, play instrument, hold guitar, play keyboard, play drum}	68.13
2	{play soccer, play hockey, play football, play sport, play basketball, play baseball, play tennis, play volleyball, compete none}	71.38
3	{climb mountain, climb face, climb wall, climb rock, climbing none}	80.05
4	{bike none, biking none}	69.55
5	{ride bike, ride bicycle, ride motorcycle, ride scooter}	86.92
6	{read book, read newspaper}	75.71
7	{cooking none, cook none, kitchen none}	84.51
8	{prepare food, prepare meal, eat food, drink beer, have drink}	52.24
9	{give presentation, give speech}	67.28
10	{walk sidewalk, walk street, cross street}	52.62
11	{swim trunk, swim none, pool none, diving none}	65.78
12	{kayake none, paddle none}	71.85
13	{surf none, surf wave}	90.33
14	{hold baby, hold boy, hold infant}	62.46
15	{kick ball, throw ball, hit ball}	58.91
16	{perform trick, do trick}	58.56
17	{sing none, singing none}	73.32
18	{ski none}	87.60
19	{leap none, jump none}	58.65
20	{take photo, take photograph, take picture, hold camera}	66.82
	Average of all 84 clusters	65.48

Table 1: Concept cluster examples are selected based on the number of positive samples in each and sorted in descending order. The AP of random guess is 10%

4.3 Action Classification

Data: ACD discovers and learns action concepts from *source domain*, which is Flickr30k. Flickr30k contains 30 thousand images and each image is associated with 5 sentences to describe it. The sentences are generated by Amazon Mechanical Turk. PASCAL VOC 2012 action classification is used as *transfer domain* to test the discovered action concepts. It's a standard benchmark for action classification in still images and there are 10 action tags in it: {jump, phone, play instrument, read, ride bike, ride horse, run, take photo, use computer, walk}.

Metric: Average precision (AP) and mean average precision (mAP) are used as evaluation metric in the action classification task.

First we evaluate the classification performance on the source domain. The associated images of each cluster are split into two halves: one half is used for training and the other half is used for testing. The negative samples are randomly selected from other clusters and the ratio of negative samples and positive samples is 10:1. There are 84 clusters in total; 20 of them are shown in Table 1. Concept cluster examples in Table 1 are selected based on the number of positive samples in each and sorted in descending order. The mAP of all 84 cluster classifiers is 65.48%. The random mAP is 10%. Note that the mAP can be boosted by reducing the number of concept clusters but at the cost of losing specificity. The AP is lower on some clusters, such as {prepare food...} and {walk...}, because they have larger intra-class variance and don't have particular patterns. For example, "walk" is a similar action to "run". On the other hand, "walk" contains many different varieties, such as "walk on the street" and "walk on the grass", and those varieties have different scenes.

We further evaluate our action classifiers on PASCAL VOC 2012 test server and results are shown in Table 2. Note that we don't use any data from PASCAL to finetune the action classifiers learned from the source domain (Flickr30k). The baseline method (denoted as **NO-ACD**) is trained as follows: use pre-defined vocabularies (*i.e.* action tags in PASCAL VOC 2012 action classification dataset) as search keywords, collect image data in Flickr30k that associated sentences contain those tags and train linear-SVM classifiers for each action tag using the associated images. For the method **ACD-A**, we search in the classifier pool to find all the related action clusters and train an AdaBoost classifier for each action tag. The training data for the AdaBoost classifier is the union of images of each related cluster from Flickr30k (no PASCAL data is used). We also train a linear SVM classifier on the *trainval* set of PASCAL VOC 2012 action classification as a reference (denoted as **VGG-SVM** in Table 2). Oquab *et al* [22] finetunes the pre-trained CNN [16] on PASCAL VOC 2012 action classification dataset.

The item "box" list in Table 2 denotes whether the method makes use of the persons' bounding boxes in PASCAL VOC 2012. The item "supv." in Table 2 provides the kind of supervision adopted by the method. The item "domain" in Table 2 provides whether there is domain transfer between training set and testing set. Some action recognition results on PASCAL VOC are shown in Figure 7.

Weak Supervision and Domain Transfer: Our action concepts are discovered and learned from image-sentence corpora, which is a weakly-labelled dataset. We denote this kind of learning as *weak supervision*. We evaluate our discovered action classifiers on PASCAL VOC 2012 action classification dataset. As the training and test data are from two different domains (*i.e. domain transfer*), the differences may lead to dataset bias [27].

Discussion: The naive baseline is worse than our methods for two reasons: a) Humans might term the same action with different words, for example "do flip" and "jump". Searching keywords ignores all the other terms and their related images; b) An action might have multiple sub-categories: For example, "play guitar" and "play" piano are sub-categories of "play instrument". The problems of the naive approach highlights the value for our ACD method. Oquab *et al* [22] outperform our method (ACD-A) in mAP for 2 reasons: a) They use fully-labelled data and don't encounter domain differences: they finetune CNN on *trainval* set of PASCAL VOC 2012 action classification. But we don't use any data from PASCAL VOC. b) They use person's bounding box in training and testing, but we don't. However, ACD-A still

method	supv.	domain	box	jump	phone	instr.	read	bike	horse	run	photo	comp.	walk	mAP
NO-ACD	weak	transfer	no	38.1	12.2	76.2	12.9	83.5	83.5	24.9	22.4	68.9	19.6	44.2
ACD($\alpha = 0.6$)	weak	transfer	no	**63.4**	15.4	71.7	28.9	66.9	69.7	53.5	13.9	69.2	30.9	48.3
ACD-A	weak	transfer	no	62.2	**15.4**	**78.8**	**29.6**	**84.5**	**85.9**	**60.8**	**24.0**	**69.2**	**32.4**	**54.3**
VGG-SVM	full	same	no	73.1	43.1	84.8	45.4	86.7	92.0	73.1	34.5	76.0	30.7	63.9
Oquab *et al* [22]	full	same	yes	74.8	46.0	75.6	45.3	93.5	95.0	86.5	49.3	66.7	69.5	70.2

Table 2: Comparison of different methods on the PASCAL VOC 2012 action classification test set (AP%). "Box" denotes the bounding box in the training data of PASCAL VOC 2012. Except Oquab *et al.*[22], other methods don't use any bounding box information to train. The abbreviations in table: "instr."= "play instrument", "bike"="ride bike", "horse"="ride horse", "photo"="take photo", "comp."="use computer". The AP of "use computer" and "phone" are the same among our three methods, that's because only one cluster for this action is discovered by our algorithm.

Figure 7: Some examples of the top 3 prediction results on PASCAL VOC 2012 using the discovered action classifiers in ACD($\alpha = 0.6$). Green represents correct prediction, red represent wrong prediction and black stands between correct and wrong prediction. {ride bike...} stands for {ride bike, ride bicycle, bike none, biking none}; {walk none...} stands for {walk none, walk street, walk dog, walk sidewalk, walk past}; {paddle none...} stands for {paddle none; paddle boat; boat none; fishing none}; {play instrument...} stands for{play keyboard, play guitar, play instrument, play violin, play drum, play music, play accordion}.

outperforms Oquab *et al.*[22] in "play instrument" and "use computer".

5. CONCLUSIONS

We presented a system to automatically discover, cluster and learn the action concepts from image-sentence corpora. Verb-Object pairs were extracted from sentences as action concept candidates. We used VGG features and 2 fold cross-validation to verify these candidates. Multimodal representation, which combines the visual and linguistic information, was adopted to represent and cluster the action concepts. More than 100 human action concepts and 81 action clusters were learned from source domain (Flickr30k). We applied the learned classifiers of action concept clusters to action recognition task. We also quantitatively evaluated the learned classifiers on a different transfer domain (PASCAL VOC 2012 action classification). To further improve the performance, AdaBoost was applied to combine multiple related concept classifiers for a single action tag. Finally, we showed promising results compared to previous fully supervised method.

6. ACKNOWLEDGMENTS

This research was supported, in part, by the Office of Naval Research under grant N00014-13-1-0493.

7. REFERENCES

[1] M. Andriluka, L. Pishchulin, P. Gehler, and B. Schiele. 2d human pose estimation: New benchmark and state of the art analysis. In *CVPR*, 2014.

[2] E. Bruni, N.-K. Tran, and M. Baroni. Multimodal distributional semantics. *JAIR*, 2014.

[3] X. Chen, A. Shrivastava, and A. Gupta. Neil: Extracting visual knowledge from web data. In *ICCV*, 2013.

[4] T.-S. Chua, J. Tang, R. Hong, H. Li, Z. Luo, and Y. Zheng. Nus-wide: a real-world web image database from national university of singapore. In *CIVR*, 2009.

[5] S. K. Divvala, A. Farhadi, and C. Guestrin. Learning everything about anything: Webly-supervised visual concept learning. In *CVPR*, 2014.

[6] M. Everingham, S. A. Eslami, L. Van Gool, C. K. Williams, J. Winn, and A. Zisserman. The pascal visual object classes challenge: A retrospective. *IJCV*, 2014.

[7] R.-E. Fan, K.-W. Chang, C.-J. Hsieh, X.-R. Wang, and C.-J. Lin. Liblinear: A library for large linear classification. *JMLR*, 2008.

[8] G. Gkioxari, R. Girshick, and J. Malik. Actions and attributes from wholes and parts. In *ICCV*, 2015.

[9] G. Gkioxari, R. Girshick, and J. Malik. Contextual action recognition with r* cnn. In *ICCV*, 2015.

[10] G. Gkioxari, B. Hariharan, R. Girshick, and J. Malik. R-cnns for pose estimation and action detection. *arXiv preprint arXiv:1406.5212*, 2014.

[11] M. Hodosh, P. Young, and J. Hockenmaier. Framing image description as a ranking task: Data, models and evaluation metrics. *JAIR*, 2013.

[12] A. Khosla, B. Yao, and L. Fei-Fei. Integrating randomization and discrimination for classifying human-object interaction activities. In *Human-Centered Social Media Analytics*. 2014.

[13] D. Kiela and L. Bottou. Learning image embeddings using convolutional neural networks for improved multi-modal semantics. In *EMNLP*, 2014.

[14] D. Kiela, F. Hill, A. Korhonen, and S. Clark. Improving multi-modal representations using image dispersion: Why less is sometimes more. In *ACL*, 2014.

[15] R. Krishna, Y. Zhu, O. Groth, J. Johnson, K. Hata, J. Kravitz, S. Chen, Y. Kalantidis, L.-J. Li, D. A. Shamma, M. Bernstein, and L. Fei-Fei. Visual genome: Connecting language and vision using crowdsourced dense image annotations. 2016.

[16] A. Krizhevsky, I. Sutskever, and G. E. Hinton. Imagenet classification with deep convolutional neural networks. In *NIPS*, 2012.

[17] A. Lazaridou, N. T. Pham, and M. Baroni. Combining language and vision with a multimodal skip-gram model. In *NAACL*, 2015.

[18] T.-Y. Lin, M. Maire, S. Belongie, J. Hays, P. Perona, D. Ramanan, P. Dollár, and C. L. Zitnick. Microsoft coco: Common objects in context. In *ECCV*, 2014.

[19] S. Maji, L. Bourdev, and J. Malik. Action recognition from a distributed representation of pose and appearance. In *CVPR*, 2011.

[20] C. D. Manning, M. Surdeanu, J. Bauer, J. Finkel, S. J. Bethard, and D. McClosky. The stanford corenlp natural language processing toolkit. In *ACL*, 2014.

[21] T. Mikolov, I. Sutskever, K. Chen, G. S. Corrado, and J. Dean. Distributed representations of words and phrases and their compositionality. In *NIPS*, 2013.

[22] M. Oquab, L. Bottou, I. Laptev, and J. Sivic. Learning and transferring mid-level image representations using convolutional neural networks. In *CVPR*, 2014.

[23] V. Ordonez, G. Kulkarni, and T. L. Berg. Im2text: Describing images using 1 million captioned photographs. In *NIPS*, 2011.

[24] R. Schapire. A short introduction to boosting. In *IJCAI*, 1999.

[25] K. Simonyan and A. Zisserman. Very deep convolutional networks for large-scale image recognition. In *ICLR*, 2015.

[26] C. Sun, C. Gan, and R. Nevatia. Automatic concept discovery from parallel text and visual corpora. In *ICCV*, 2015.

[27] A. Torralba, A. Efros, et al. Unbiased look at dataset bias. In *CVPR*, 2011.

[28] W. Yang, Y. Wang, and G. Mori. Recognizing human actions from still images with latent poses. In *CVPR*, 2010.

[29] B. Yao, X. Jiang, A. Khosla, A. L. Lin, L. Guibas, and L. Fei-Fei. Human action recognition by learning bases of action attributes and parts. In *ICCV*, 2011.

[30] P. Young, A. Lai, M. Hodosh, and J. Hockenmaier. From image descriptions to visual denotations: New similarity metrics for semantic inference over event descriptions. *TACL*, 2014.

[31] B. Zhou, V. Jagadeesh, and R. Piramuthu. Conceptlearner: Discovering visual concepts from weakly labeled image collections. In *CVPR*, 2015.

GPU-FV: Realtime Fisher Vector and Its Applications in Video Monitoring

Wenjing Ma
State Key Laboratory of Computer Science,
Laboratory of Parallel Software and Computational science,
Institute of Software, Chinese Academy of Sciences
wenjing@iscas.ac.cn

Liangliang Cao
Yahoo
liangliang@yahoo-inc.com

Lei Yu
Laboratory of Parallel Software and Computational science,
Institute of Software, Chinese Academy of Sciences
yulei@iscas.ac.cn

Guoping Long
Laboratory of Parallel Software and Computational science,
Institute of Software, Chinese Academy of Sciences
guoping@iscas.ac.cn

Yucheng Li
Laboratory of Parallel Software and Computational science,
Institute of Software, Chinese Academy of Sciences
yucheng@iscas.ac.cn

ABSTRACT

Fisher vector has been widely used in many multimedia retrieval and visual recognition applications with good performance. However, the computation complexity prevents its usage in real-time video monitoring. In this work, we proposed and implemented GPU-FV, a fast Fisher vector extraction method with the help of modern GPUs. The challenge of implementing Fisher vector on GPUs lies in the data dependency in feature extraction and expensive memory access in Fisher vector computing. To handle these challenges, we carefully designed GPU-FV in a way that utilizes the computing power of GPU as much as possible, and applied optimizations such as loop tiling to boost the performance. GPU-FV is about 12 times faster than the CPU version, and 50% faster than a non-optimized GPU implementation. For standard video input (320*240), GPU-FV can process each frame within 34ms on a model GPU. Our experiments show that GPU-FV obtains a similar recognition accuracy as traditional FV on VOC 2007 and Caltech 256 image sets. We also applied GPU-FV for realtime video monitoring tasks and found that GPU-FV outperforms a number of previous works. Especially, when the number of training examples are small, GPU-FV outperforms the recent popular deep CNN features borrowed from ImageNet.

CCS Concepts

•Computing methodologies → Activity recognition and understanding; Image representations;

ICMR'16, June 06-09, 2016, New York, NY, USA

© 2016 ACM. ISBN 978-1-4503-4359-6/16/06...$15.00

DOI: http://dx.doi.org/10.1145/2911996.2911997

Keywords

Fisher vector; image classification; real-time; event detection; GPGPU; CUDA

1. INTRODUCTION

Many recent research show that Fisher vector [30] is a very useful representation of images, which obtains state-of-the-art results in a number of applications, including image retrieval [22, 10], art classification [19], relevance feedback of videos [13], event recounting in videos [29], texture recognition [6], face verification [26], object detection [5, 33], and fine grained image recognition[12, 23]. Although the recent deep convolutional neural network [16] outperforms Fisher vector in large scale visual recognition challenges such as ImageNet LSVRC [9], the training process of deep CNN usually requires a lot of training examples. In scenarios where the training set is in small or middle scale, Fisher vector is still a very attractive choice, especially when the problem lies in a different domain from the existing large scale dataset.

However, Fisher vectors pose an even heavier computational demand, which limits its usage in real world applications. It takes about 2-5 seconds for a typical implementation of Fisher vector to classify a normal sized image. Such a slowness prevents Fisher vectors from many real applications. To bridge the gap, this paper proposes GPU-FV, an efficient implementation of Fisher vector with the help of GPUs [1].

It is not trivial to write efficient GPU code for Fisher vector, because of the data dependency in dense SIFT, and the complicated memory access patterns in GMM estimation. To overcome this challenge, we not only design efficient kernels to explore the parallel nature in SIFT extraction, but also formulate GMM estimation in a way that can utilize the limited bandwidth and memory in modern GPUs. We propose several techniques to optimize the feature extraction speed: (1) Loop tiling, (2) early termination, and (3) vec-

[1] The code can be downloaded from the following link https://bitbucket.org/mawenjing/gpu-fv

torization, and (4) using 8 scales for dense SIFT exatraction. We demonstrate that our optimization technique can speed up a naive Fisher vector implementation on GPUs by more than 20 times.

Some techniques in optimizing the GPU computation bring approximation of the computation. To evaluate the effects of these approximations, we compare our GPU implementation with the original Fisher vector on two standard datasets: PASCAL VOC 2007 and Caltech 256. The results show that our approximate obtain a similar accuracy but with a much higher speed. We believe such evaluation provides strong evidence that our GPU based Fisher vector can be used for many applications.

Our GPU-FV system can process a 320 * 240 image in 34ms. Such an efficiency makes it possible to employ Fisher vector to realtime applications. To demonstrate it, this paper shows an example of applying an abnormal event detector in realtime surveillance videos, and an example of detecting baby's laugh in a video. In surveillance and video recognition, existing solutions are very slow and it is difficult to apply them to online processing scenarios. However, this paper demonstrates that our new GPU based Fisher vector can model complicated subjects and obtain an accuracy comparable with the the state-of-the-art.

2. RELATED WORKS

GPUs have been evolving fast, and have been applied in high performance computing successfully. However, it remains unclear what are the bottlenecks in accurate visual categorization with the Fisher vector model on GPU.

SURF is an optimized robust feature extraction system for images [1]. Cornelis and Van Gool [8] implemented SURF on the GPU (Graphics Processing Unit) and obtained an order of magnitude speedup compared to a CPU implementation. Extracting SIFT descriptors on GPU has been studied by other researchers [28, 35]. Recent efforts were also made on accelerating Dense SIFT computation [21]. SVM model training, have been independently studied on the GPU before [3]. To address the bottlenecks in accurate visual categorization systems, Sande et.al [32] did a detailed analysis, and proposed two GPU-accelerated algorithms, GPU vector quantization and GPU kernel value precomputation, which results in a substantial acceleration of the complete visual categorization pipeline. However, their method does not involve Fisher vector encoding.

Efforts have been made to reduce the storage and computation overhead of Fisher vector [22], by compressing the Fisher vector, with some loss of precision. The widely used Vlfeat package [34] provides a wonderful implementation of the Fisher vector, along with other popular computer vision algorithms. However, there was no GPU-based implementation in this package. A few years back, some researchers implemented Fisher vector on GPU [2], but it is on a modified algorithm with hierarchical GMM model, and the accuracy is lower than the state-of-the-art.

The problem of abnormal event recognition in videos has attracted many attentions [37] [15] [17]. However, the approaches listed above did not use Fisher Vector due to its slowness. Chen et al. [4] used MoSIFT and Fisher Vector for event detection, and obtained good performance on TRECVID data. However, their work did not consider how to speed up local feature extraction or Fisher vector encoding. As a result, their method relies on significant subsampling of one from 30/60/120 frames and the time of encoding such a frame is about 0.4 second (with feature extraction it will be longer). We believe our work in this paper can be easily employed by the framework [4] and provide similar speed up. Oneata et al. also used Fisher Vector in action localization and event recognition [20], at a speed 2.4 times slower than real-time. In this paper, we demonstrate that with GPU based Fisher Vector, we can handle some abnormal event recognition very well at a realtime speed.

In recent years, deep neural network have enjoyed a remarkable success as efficient and effective in a number of visual recognition tasks [27, 31]. Especially, Razavian et al. [24] showed that by simply borrowing the CNN-based AlexNet model [16] trained for ImageNet, a SVM model using CNN features can obtain the state-of-the-art in many applications. The deep CNN features could be sped up significantly by GPUs. We believe Fisher vector can be sped up with the same hardware, and in this paper we show that GPU-FV can outperform deep CNN features in some applications with limited amount of training samples.

3. GPU-FV

In this section, we will first introduce the Fisher vector algorithm and then explain our GPU-based implementation in detail.

3.1 Overview of Fisher Vector

There are two main computation components when generating Fisher vector for a picture. The first component is extracting the dense SIFT descriptors. An image is scaled to different sizes. Descriptors are extracted for all the scales. For each scale, the gradients of the pixels fall into 8 orientation bins. Then, the convolution kernels are applied. After that, each value in the 8 orientation bins is multiplied with the weights computed for each of the 16 spatial bin (4 on X and 4 on Y dimension). Therefore, a 128 dimension descriptor(8*4*4) is generated for each pixel. Then, by lowering the dimension to m (m <128) with PCA and adding the normalized X and Y axis, a descriptor with dimension M=m+2 is generated for a pixel. The descriptors are extracted with a stride of S on X and Y dimension, which means we get a descriptor in every S^2 pixels.

The second component is using the descriptors to generate the Fisher vectors with the GMM components trained beforehand. With the $means$, $covariances$, and $priors$ values of GMM, the dense SIFT descriptors are used to generate a Fisher vector for an image. The algorithm is described in Algorithm 1 [30]. Generating the Fisher vector includes two phases. In the first phase, we get the posteriors for each descriptor regarding the GMM components. In the second phse, the Fisher vector for the image is generated, represented as the concatenation of vectors V and U in Algorithm 1. V and U are of size $M*N$, where M is the dimension of a descriptor, and N is the number of GMM components.

3.2 The Parallelization Scheme on GPU

In this section, we describe the implementation details of the GPU-FV system.

Terminology First, we introduce some terminology to be used when describing GPU programs. A GPU kernel is a function launched by the CPU and run on the GPU. A kernel is run by a $thread\ grid$, which consists of a bunch of $thread\ blocks$. Each $block$ is comprised with a certain number of threads. Threads in the same block run on the same multiprocessor in a GPU, and share a piece of scratchpad memory, called $shared\ memory$, which could be read and written by the program, and is much faster than the GPU device memory. Threads are scheduled as $warps$, which is a bunch of threads that run in a SIMD fashion. With conditional branches such as "if...else...", if the condition varies among threads in the same warp, the whole warp must go through both branches.

Dense SIFT on GPU There are two types of dense SIFT extracting methods: flat window and Gaussian window. In flat window dense SIFT, the triangular convolution kernels are used, and the convolution routine need to be called only twice (once on each dimension) for the 8 gradient bin, therefore reducing the amount of

Algorithm 1 Fisher Vector Encoding Algorithm

Input: Dense SIFT descriptors $data$
Input: GMM model: $means, covariances, priors$
Output: Fisher Vector: V,U

Compute $\sqrt{\sigma^{-1}}$
for $i = 0$ to $num\_descriptors$ **do**
  for $j = 0$ to $num\_components$ **do**
    t=distance($data[i], means_j, covariances_j$);
    Compute $posteriors_{i,j}$ with $temp$;
    $maxPost$ = max$\{maxPost, posteriors_{i,j}\}$;
  end for
  for $j = 0$ to $num\_components$ **do**
    $posterior_{i,j} = e^{posterior_{i,j} - maxPost}$;
    sum += $posterior_{i,j}$;
  end for
  for $j = 0$ to $num\_components$ **do**
    $posterior_{i,j} = posterior_{i,j} / sum$;
  end for
end for
for $i = 0$ to $num\_descriptors$ **do**
  for $j = 0$ to $num\_components$ **do**
    if $posterior_{i,j}$ >threshold **then**
      for $k = 0$ to $DIMENSION$ **do**
        $U_{j,k}$+=$(data[i][k] - means_{j,k}) * \sqrt{\sigma^{-1}} * posteriors_{i,j}$;
        $V_{j,k}$+=$(((data[i][k] - means_{j,k}) * \sqrt{\sigma^{-1}})^2 - 1) * posteriors_{i,j}$;
      end for
    end if
  end for
end for

computation. To leverage this optimization, we implemented our GPU code based on the flat window dense SIFT algorithm. However, the original CPU implementation cannot be changed to GPU code directly because of its sequential nature. The triangular convolution involves 4 steps: (1) integrate backward the column, (2) compute the filter forward, (3) integrate forward the column, and (4) compute the filter backward. The first and third steps are accumulations, while the second and the fourth steps are subtraction operations. Each step is a *scan* operation in nature, as shown in Step 1 in Figure 1. Because the computation of $b[i]$ depends on the result of $[i-1]$ computed in the last iteration, the computation of $b[i]$ and $b[i-1]$ cannot be done in parallel. *Scan* operation need aggressive optimization when implemented on GPU to gain performance benefits [36], and *scan* with subtraction is even harder to be implemented on GPU.

With careful examination, we found that there is useless computation in this process, because some data are added (in step 1 or 3), then subtracted (in step 2 or 4). Therefore, we revised the algorithm into a 2-step procedure, by combining the first two steps, and the last two steps. In each of the two steps, GPU threads sum up only the needed f data for each output point, where f is the filter size. Figure 1 shows this combination. The red squares are inputs to the first step. The green squares are the results after the adding operation in Step 1. The yellow squares are the results after two steps, which is the *scan* operation with subtraction. The window size is 2. By combining Step 1 and Step 2, we got a simplified computation pattern, as shown in the "Combined Step". Now the subtraction operation is not required any more. This algorithm could run efficiently on GPU. We spread the threads in each thread block on the columns of an image, and let each thread block process one column of the image. Thus, each thread does the convolution for a pixel by doing two rounds of adding operations, with f adding operations in a round. Threads in the same block use the shared memory to buffer the data in the same column of the image, to accelerate data access.

We also optimized the GPU computation by removing computation for unused pixels. As mentioned in Section 3.1, the descriptors are extracted with a step of 4 on X and Y dimension, which means we need only 1 descriptor in every 16 pixels. In the original code, all the pixels are processed with both of the two convolution operations. In the GPU code, we reduced computation time by computing only the required data in the second convolution.

Generating the dense SIFT descriptors need preprocessing of images, such as image resizing, computation of gradients, normalization, etc. These steps are easy to be implemented as GPU kernels. With the preprocessing done on GPU, we were able to avoid extra data copy from host memory to GPU memory.

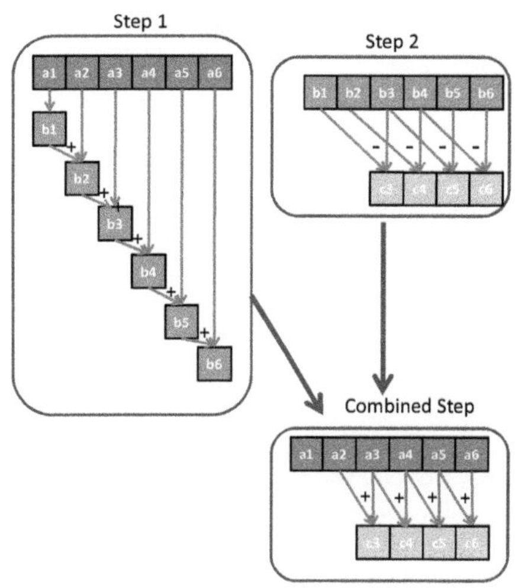

Figure 1: Combining two steps in Dense SIFT

Generating Fisher Vector on GPU

The GPU implementation of the two phases is shown in Algorithm 2 and 3 respectively. In Phase 1, the posterior values are calculated for each descriptor. Phase 2 generates Fisher vector based on the posteriors. Therefore, both phases involve an outer loop on the number of descriptors. So it is natural to parallelize the outer loop (the loop on the number of descriptors) at block level on GPU. It means thread block i processes $data[i * CHUNK]$ to $data[(i+1) * CHUNK]$ by looping through the $CHUNK$ descriptors. An important factor affecting performance is the choice of $CHUNK$. We will explain how we choose this value later in this section. Now let us look at the implementation of Phase 1 first. Algorithm 2 describes the implementation of the main kernel on GPU, and before this function starts, $\sqrt{\sigma^{-1}}$ has been computed with a simple GPU kernel. In this phase, the most time consuming computation is calculating the distances between the descriptor and each GMM component. We parallelized this computation at thread level. For each GMM component, every thread processes one dimension of the descriptor, and obtain the distance value in that dimension. The results of all the threads are summed up by a tree structured reduction operation, to obtain the final distance value

Algorithm 2 GPU code for Phase 1

Input: Dense SIFT descriptors $data$
Input: GMM model: $means, covariances, priors$
1: //Each block processes one descriptor at a time
2: **for** $i = 0$ to $num\_descriptors$ **do**
3: Load all dimensions of $data[i]$ to shared memory;
4: Synchronize();
5: **for** $j = 0$ to $num\_components$ **do**
6: //Thread k processes $data[i][k]$
7: t=distance($data[i][k], means_{j,k}, covariances_{j,k}$);
8: Sum up t from all the threads in the block in a tree structure;
9: Synchronize();
10: **if** ThreadID==0 **then**
11: Compute $posteriors_{i,j}$ with t;
12: $maxPost$ = max$\{maxPost, posteriors_{i,j}\}$;
13: **end if**
14: Synchronize();
15: **end for**
16: //Each thread processes one component at a time
17: **for** $j = 0$ to $num\_components$ **do**
18: $posterior_{i,j} = e^{posterior_{i,j} - maxPost}$;
19: sum += $posterior_{i,j}$;
20: **end for**
21: Synchronize();
22: Sum up sum with all the threads in the block in a tree structure;
23: Synchronize();
24: //Each thread processes one component at a time
25: **for** $j = 0$ to $num\_components$ **do**
26: $posterior_{i,j} = posterior_{i,j}/sum$;
27: **end for**
28: **end for**

of this descriptor.(Intuitively, we could let each thread process all the dimensions for each GMM component, therefore avoiding the need for reduction on the computation of distances. However, we found that the parallelization on the inner loops is more beneficial, because it enables coalesced access to global memory, and avoids bank conflicts when accessing shared memory.)

At the end of the reduction process, Thread 0 would have the distance value for the descriptor. Then Thread 0 computes the posterior value for the descriptor, and updates $maxPost$.

After that, the posteriors are updated with the exponential operation, as in Line 17 in Algorithm 2. Then, to get the summation of the posteriors for all the components, a new round of reduction is conducted. Finally, we are able to get the normalized posterior values by dividing the posteriors with the sum.

In the second phase, we compute the Fisher vector (concatenation of U and V) with the posteriors obtained from the first phase. Similar to the first phase, each thread block processes $CHUNK$ descriptors assigned to it in a loop. Every thread computes one dimension in *U[j]* and *V[j]* at a time. As shown in Line 7 and 8 in Algorithm 3, the calculated values are used to update U and V. The descriptor and the posterior values are buffered in shared memory, since they can be reused when processing each component, as Line 3 in Algorithm 3. A challenge in updating U and V values on GPU is that all the thread blocks are updating the same elements in U and V. To solve this problem, we keep one copy of U and V for each block, and every block only updates its own copy. When this kernel finishes, each block has computed the values of U and V regarding the posteriors that it process. Then, we launch a new kernel to sum

Algorithm 3 GPU code for Phase 2

1: //Each block processes one descriptor at a time
2: **for** $i = 0$ to $num\_descriptors$ **do**
3: Load all dimensions of $data[i]$ and $posterior_i$ to shared memory;
4: **for** $j = 0$ to $num\_components$ **do**
5: //Thread k processes $data[i][k]$
6: **if** $posterior_{i,j} > threshold$ **then**
7: $U_{j,k}$+=$(data[i][k] - means_{j,k}) * \sqrt{\sigma^{-1}} * posterior_{i,j}$;
8: $V_{j,k}$+=$(((data[i][k] - means_{j,k}) * \sqrt{\sigma^{-1}})^2 - 1) * posterior_{i,j}$;
9: **end if**
10: **end for**
11: **end for**
12: //Start a new kernel for accumulation of U and V
13: //Each block processes U and V for one GMM component
14: **for** $i = 1$ to num_blocks **do**
15: //Thread k processes $U_{j,k}$ and $V_{j,k}$
16: $U_{j,k}$+=the ith copy of $U_{j,k}$
17: $V_{j,k}$+=the ith copy of $V_{j,k}$
18: **end for**

up the U and V copies updated by each block, to obtain the final Fisher vector.

Now let us revisit the problem of choosing the values of $CHUNK$. We used different $CHUNK$ values for the two phases. This is because Phase 2 needs to accumulate the U and V values calculated from each descriptor. Having a large $CHUNK$ implies fewer thread blocks, because each block processes more data. Therefore, we will have less copies of U and V, reducing the overhead of summing up values from different blocks. On the other hand, using small $CHUNK$ number for Phase 1 will enable better load balance and higher level of parallelism, so we chose a smaller $CHUNK$ size for Phase 1. Different $CHUNK$ values imply different thread block numbers, therefore we launch a separate kernel for each phase. By testing with different values, we chose $CHUNK$=4 in Phase 1, and $CHUNK$=192 in Phase 2 in our experiments.

3.3 Optimizing GPU Implementation

Loop tiling As a common optimization in CPU code, loop tiling turned out to be an effective optimization for GPU code also. Normally, loop tiling improves performance by reducing the number of conditional checking. In our case, this technique provides more benefit by avoiding a number of synchronizations among threads in a block. As shown in Algorithm 2, we need synchronizations before and after thread 0 computes the posteriors. Besides, there is a synchronization operation after reduction on every level. Suppose there are 10 synchronizations in the loop body. If we tile the loop by 4, the total number of synchronizations in 4 iterations is still 10, therefore the number of synchronizations is reduced by 75%.

In the first phase, we tiled the outer loop by 4, which means each block processes 4 descriptors at a time. The inner loop, which is on the number of components, is tiled by 2. The loops in the second phase are also tiled. The outer loop (on the number of descriptors) is tiled by 2, and the inner loop (on the number of components) is tiled by 4.

Early termination of an iteration In the second phase, we were able to apply early termination of an iteration by checking conditions in a clustered way. In the original algorithm, if the posterior of a certain point is less than a threshold, the value does not need to be added, as Line 18 in Algorithm 1. In the tiled GPU code, each block processes 8 posteriors in one iteration, so we load the *means* value to shared memory for computation before processing the descriptors, since the *means* values could be reused. However, we noticed that the posterior values are very sparse, therefore, if all the 8 values in an iteration are below the threshold, we can simply skip the iteration, as shown in Algorithm 5. In this case, we avoided the loading of *means* for this iteration, and we combined the 8 branches into one branch, which is beneficial to GPU code because of its SIMD nature.

Vectorization Vectorization is an importation optimization for modern GPU. With loop unrolling, each thread is processing multiple data elements, therefore we pack the operation on multiple data elements into a vector operation. For example, when computing the distance between a data point and a component, the loop is unrolled with a factor of 4. Therefore we use vector operations on vectors with 4 float point data. By applying vectorization to the computation of posteriors on GPU, we were able to further improve the performance.

Figure 2 shows the effectiveness of the optimization. The bars with "no optimization" means the code without optimization. The bars labeled "Loop tiling" are running time with loop tiling. Bars with "Early termination" represents timing with both loop tiling and early termination, and those labeled with "Vectorization" are timing with all the three optimization methods. Since there are many synchronizations in Phase 1, it gains a good deal of performance improvement from loop tiling. Early termination applies only to Phase 2. Because there are many small posterior values, the early termination is very effective in reducing the time of Phase 2. Vectorization gave a further improvement for Phase 1, which has a good amount of dense computation.

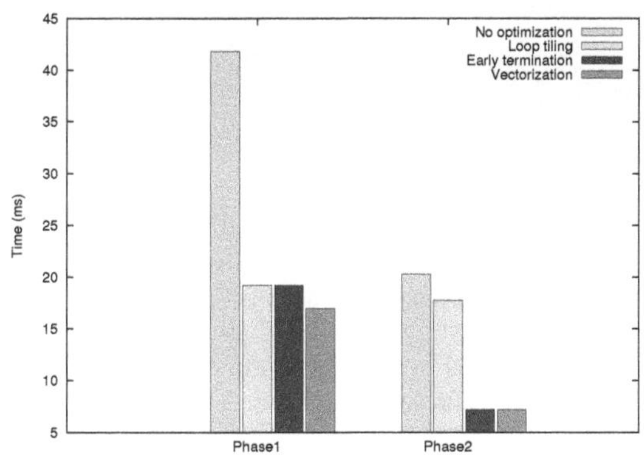

Figure 2: Performance improvement with the optimization

Algorithm 4 Basic loop structure of Phase 2 on GPU

for $i = 0$ to $num\_descriptors$, $step = 2$ **do**
  for $j = 0$ to $num\_components$, $step = 4$ **do**
    if $posterior_{i,j} > threshold$ **then**
      Compute U and V values
    end if
    if $posterior_{i,j+1} > threshold$ **then**
      Compute U and V values
    end if
    ...
  end for
end for

Algorithm 5 Optimized loop structure of Phase 2 on GPU

for $i = 0$ to $num\_descriptors$, $step = 2$ **do**
  for $j = 0$ to $num\_components$, $step = 4$ **do**
    bool $b1 = posterior_{i,j} < 1e-6$;
    bool $b2 = posterior_{i,j+1} < 1e-6$;
    ...
    bool $TotalB = b1\&b2\&b3...b8$;
    if $TotalB > 0$ **then**
      continue;
    end if
    if $posterior_{i,j} > threshold$ **then**
      Compute U and V values
    end if
    if $posterior_{i,j+1} > threshold$ **then**
      Compute U and V values
    end if
    ...
  end for
end for

4. EXPERIMENTS

We evaluated our GPU-FV system in two scenarios. The first scenario is image classification with Fisher vector. The second part is event/expression detection in video, using Fisher vector generated for each frame. The testing platform is a dual CPU computer, which has two Intel Xeon E5-2630 v3 CPUs at clock rate of 2.40GHz, with 8 cores on each. It has an NVIDIA Tesla K40 card, with CUDA 7.0 installed. We used the same encoding scheme as VLFeat, with 256 GMM components, and 82 dimension dense SIFT descriptors at a stride of 4 on each dimension of the original image. The 9 scales of an image are selected from 2 to 1/8, with a decreasing factor of $\sqrt{2}$.

4.1 Comparing GPU-FV with Fisher vectors on CPUs

We tested our GPU code on the PASCAL VOC2007 and Caltech256 image sets. We compare GPU-FV with the MATLAB CPU code in VLFeat. The same encoding and classification algorithms are used in all the versions. The average encoding time for each image is plotted in Figure 3, and the accuracy values in mAP are listed in Table 2. For the CPU code, since VLFeat provided OPENMP implementation, we tested it on 1 thread and 16 threads, shown as the first two bars in each cluster of Figure 3. To show the effectiveness of the optimization to the GPU code, we included tests on GPU with and without the optimizations mentioned in Section 3.3, plotted as the two bars labeled "GPU 9 scales no optimization" and "GPU 9 scales". By "9 scales", we mean that dense SIFT is extracted from 9 scales of an image, which is the original setting in VLFeat. For the GPU code, we also tested the version with 8 scales in dense SIFT by removing the largest scale (resized to 2 times of the image), shown as the last bar in each cluster of the figure. Using 8 scales and with all the optimization strategies, the average encoding time for each image is 77.58ms for the VOC2007 set, and 53.99ms for the CalTech256 set. We did this test to show that this approximation (removing one scale) could improve performance dramatically, while maintaining about the same accuracy.

The tests on VOC2007 used 5011 images for training the svm classifier, and used another 4952 images as testing set. The average encoding time for each picture is shown in the left cluster of bars in Figure 3. Our optimized GPU code got a speedup of 12.68 over the 1 thread CPU code, and 4.53 over the 16 thread CPU code. The optimization of GPU code improves performance by 53.5% over the unoptimized version. The tests on 8 scales further reduced the running time by 48%, but the accuracy is not affected by removing one scale. The accuracy of each class is shown in Table 1.

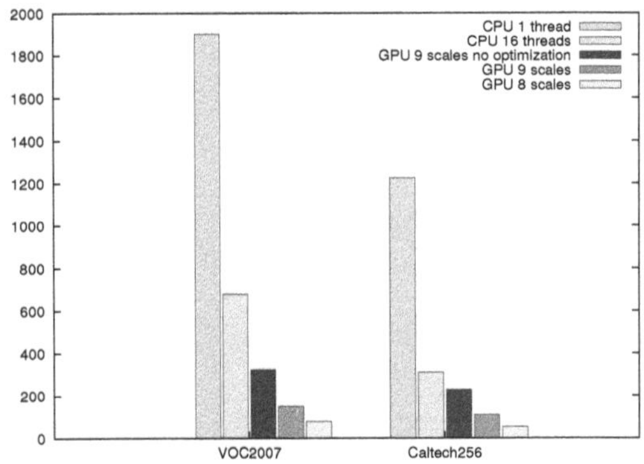

Figure 3: Average encoding time for each image

Table 1: The accuracy of each class in VOC2007

class	CPU 9scales (%)	GPU 8scales (%)
aeroplane	82.90	81.75
bicycle	65.44	65.52
bird	57.40	52.93
boat	72.94	72.60
bottle	27.12	28.03
bus	65.32	67.01
car	81.51	81.45
cat	57.56	55.97
chair	50.92	45.89
cow	43.60	43.45
diningtable	58.00	55.51
dog	41.84	41.05
horse	81.84	81.07
motorbike	66.64	68.67
person	84.97	84.51
pottedplant	30.19	27.88
sheep	48.30	46.33
sofa	56.70	53.56
train	82.07	81.63
tvmonitor	52.98	51.16

Table 2: The accuracy of different versions

Data set	CPU	GPU 9scales	GPU 8scales
VOC2007 (mAP)	59.93%	59.03%	59.3%
Caltech256 (accuracy)	42.08%	42.88%	39.48%

The test on Caltech256 uses 7680 images for training, and 6400 images for testing, with more diversity in image size and shape. The performance is shown in the 5 bars on the right in Figure 3. The GPU code got a speedup of 21.8 over the 1 thread version, and 5.53 over the 16 thread version. The optimization reduced average running time on 9 scales GPU code by 52.5%. The accuracy on 8 scales is still acceptable, while the time is reduced by 50%.

4.2 Applications for Real Time Video Monitoring

In our tests with Caltech256 set, we found that the encoding time on GPU is a few dozens of milli-seconds for small pictures. Therefore, we try to apply GPU-FV to real-time video processing scenarios. By encoding each frame in a video, various classification and detection jobs could be conducted. We show two experiments on video processing in this paper. In detecting abnormal events, we used the GMM components trained in the Caltech256 experiment to generate Fisher vectors for the frames. For baby laughing detection, we used GMM components trained from random samples in pubfig, which is a data set with pictures of human faces.

In the first experiment, we tried to detect abnormal events from the UMN crowd activity video[2]. The video consists of 3 scenes. In each scene, people are walking casually or standing. At a certain time, all the people are running away in various directions. The three scenes are in different places, with different light conditions. Each frame has a label to denote whether it is in the abnormal event. The frames with people running are labeled as "abnormal events". Figure 4 shows a frame without any abnormal event on the left, and a scene with abnormal event on the right. The resolution of the video is 320*240 pixels.

In each scene, we used the first 700 frames to train a classification model with liblinear [11]. Then we use the model to predict abnormal events in the scene.

Figure 4: Example frames for UMN abnormal event dataset.

In the experiments, we used 8 scales for dense SIFT descriptors, and the total encoding time for each frame is 34ms on average. It means that we can process about 29 frames in a second, implying that we can apply the classification to real-time usage. We compare the performance of our GPU-FV with some well-known event detection methods in Table 3. The second column shows the accuracy of prediction in AUC, and the last column lists the time for generating feature for each frame (or for each segment for C3D). C3D generates feature for every segment of 16 frames, so we evaluated its AUC with prediction for both segment level and frame level. It can be seen that our GPU-FV is much faster than the traditional event detection methods.

Deep CNN features with Caffe is the only one that outperforms GPU-FV in encoding time, but at a lower AUC value. Figure 5 compares the prediction values using GPU-FV and deep CNN features [24] on the three scenes. We presented the prediction values from liblinear with the red star lines. The blue lines depict the ground truth, in which a value "1" represents an abnormal event. In the 3 graphs on the left, which are results using GPU-FV, it can be seen that the bursts with high value in the red start lines are consistent with the periods in which the blue lines are with value "1". And it is clear that GPU-FV outperforms deep CNN features by providing clearer distinction between normal scenes and abnormal scenes. The average AUC (area under ROC curve) for GPU-FV is 0.984, while the average AUC for deep features is 0.930. The

[2]http://mha.cs.umn.edu/

Table 3: The performance on UMN dataset (three scenes together).

Method	AUC	Encoding Time
Our GPU-FV	0.984	0.034s
Deep CNN feature [14]	0.930	0.020s
sparse reconstruction cost [7]	0.978	0.8s
local statistical aggregates [25]	0.985	1.1s
social force [18]	0.960	5s
C3D [31]	0.945(segment)	0.053s
C3D [31]	0.946(frame)	0.053s

reason why deep feature does not work well for this problem is because the number of training examples in the classification of frames in a video is too small. In addition, the scenario of abnormal event detection is very different from ImageNet objects, where the deep CNN features are trained from.

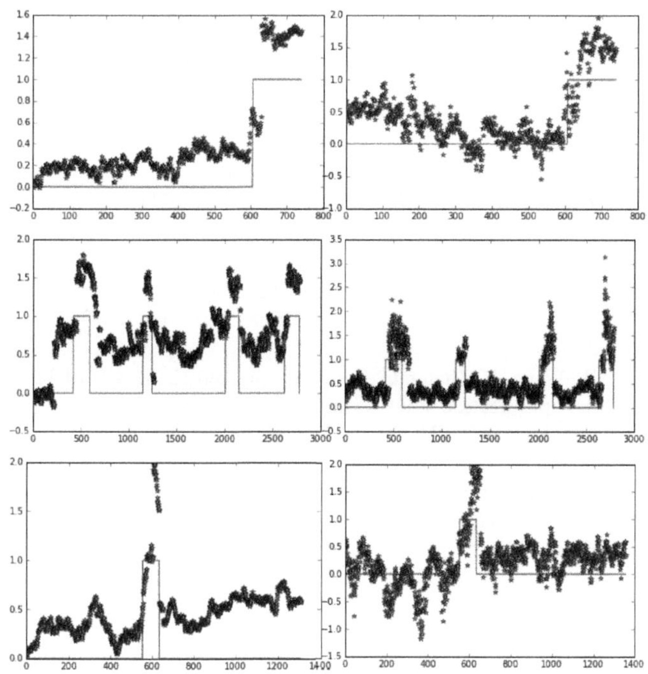

Figure 5: Comparing the prediction values using GPU-FV (left) and deep CNN feature (trained from ImageNet using AlexNet).

Another experiment we did is detecting baby's laugh from a video. The video is also of resolution 320*240. We labeled the frames when a baby is laughing as 1, and the other frames as 0. The left picture in Figure 6 shows a frame when the baby is laughing, the one on the right is a frame when the baby is not laughing. Similar to the first experiment, we used the first 700 frames as training set, and used the following frames as testing set. We also tested this video using CNN from Caffe [14] and C3D [31], with performance comparison listed in Table 4. It shows that though encoding on Caffe is faster, our method obtained a much higher accuracy than CNN features (0.935 compared to 0.655). And because we extracted features for each frame, we got a much higher AUC than C3D when evaluated at frame level.

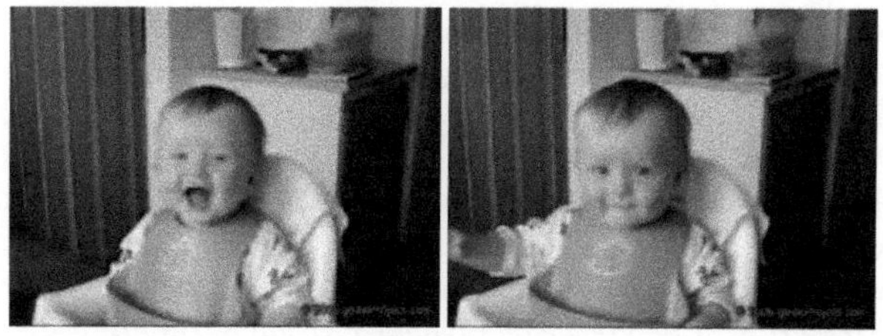

Figure 6: Example frames of baby expression video.

Table 4: The performance on detecting baby's laugh.

Method	AUC	Encoding time
Our GPU-FV	0.935	0.034 s
Deep CNN feature [14]	0.655	0.020 s
C3D [31]	0.914(segment)	0.083 s
C3D [31]	0.593(frame)	0.083 s

5. CONCLUSION

In this paper, we introduced an optimized implementation of Fisher vector on GPU (GPU-FV), and showed its application to image classification and events detection in videos. Our method demonstrated a promising approach to using Fisher vector for real-time video processing. In future, we plan to expand the algorithm to more applications in video processing, to provide support for real-time situations.

6. ACKNOWLEDGMENTS

This work is supported by the National High-tech R&D Program of China (No. 2012AA010902), and the National Natural Science Foundation of China (No. 61303059).

7. REFERENCES

[1] H. Bay, A. Ess, T. Tuytelaars, and L. V. Gool. SURF: Speeded up robust features. In *Computer Vision and Image Understanding (CVIU)*, 2008.

[2] E. Bodzsar, B. Daroczy, I. Petras, and A. A. Benczur. GMM based fisher vector calculation on GPGPU. 2011.

[3] B. Catanzaro, N. Sundaram, and K. Keutzer. Fast support vector machine training and classification on graphics processors. In *ICML*, 2008.

[4] Q. Chen, Y. Cai, L. Brown, A. Datta, Q. Fan, R. Feris, S. Yan, A. Hauptmann, and S. Pankanti. Spatio-temporal fisher vector coding for surveillance event detection. In *Proceedings of the 21st ACM International Conference on Multimedia*, MM '13, pages 589–592, New York, NY, USA, 2013. ACM.

[5] Q. Chen, Z. Song, R. Feris, A. Datta, L. Cao, Z. Huang, and S. Yan. Efficient maximum appearance search for large-scale object detection. In *IEEE Conference on Computer Vision and Pattern Recognition*, pages 3190–3197, 2013.

[6] M. Cimpoi, S. Maji, I. Kokkinos, S. Mohamed, and A. Vedaldi. Describing textures in the wild. In *IEEE Conference on Computer Vision and Pattern Recognition*, 2014.

[7] Y. Cong, J. Yuan, and J. Liu. Sparse reconstruction cost for abnormal event detection. In *IEEE Conference on Computer Vision and Pattern Recognition*, pages 3449–3456, 2011.

[8] N. Cornelis and L. V. Gool. Fast scale invariant feature detection and matching on programmable graphics hardware. In *CVPR workshop*, 2008.

[9] J. Deng, W. Dong, and et al. ImageNet: A Large-Scale Hierarchical Image Database. In *CVPR*, 2009.

[10] M. Douze, A. Ramisa, and C. Schmid. Combining attributes and Fisher vectors for efficient image retrieval. In *CVPR 2011 - IEEE Conference on Computer Vision & Pattern Recognition*, pages 745–752, Colorado Springs, United States, June 2011. IEEE.

[11] R.-E. Fan, K.-W. Chang, C.-J. Hsieh, X.-R. Wang, and C.-J. Lin. LIBLINEAR: A library for large linear classification. In *Journal of Machine Learning Research*, 2008.

[12] E. Gavves, B. Fernando, C. G. Snoek, A. W. Smeulders, and T. Tuytelaars. Fine-grained categorization by alignments. In *Computer Vision (ICCV), 2013 IEEE International Conference on*, pages 1713–1720. IEEE, 2013.

[13] J. U. N. S. IonuÅč MironicÄČ, Bogdan Ionescua. Fisher kernel based relevance feedback for multimodal video retrieval. In *Computer Vision and Image Understanding*, Feb 2016.

[14] Y. Jia, E. Shelhamer, J. Donahue, S. Karayev, J. Long, R. Girshick, S. Guadarrama, and T. Darrell. Caffe: Convolutional architecture for fast feature embedding. *arXiv preprint arXiv:1408.5093*, 2014.

[15] L. Kratz and K. Nishino. Anomaly detection in extremely crowded scenes using spatio-temporal motion pattern models. In *CVPR*, pages 1446–1453, 2009.

[16] A. Krizhevsky, I. Sutskever, and G. E. Hinton. ImageNet classification with deep convolutional neural networks. In *NIPS*, pages 1106–1114, 2012.

[17] C. Lu, J. Shi, and J. Jia. Abnormal event detection at 150 fps in matlab. In *ICCV*, pages 2720–2727, 2013.

[18] R. Mehran, A. Oyama, and M. Shah. Abnormal crowd behavior detection using social force model. In *IEEE Conference on Computer Vision and Pattern Recognition*, pages 935–942, 2009.

[19] T. E. J. Mensink and J. C. van Gemert. The rijksmuseum challenge: Museum-centered visual recognition. In *ACM International Conference on Multimedia Retrieval*, 2014.

[20] D. Oneata, J. Verbeek, and C. Schmid. Action and Event Recognition with Fisher Vectors on a Compact Feature Set. In *ICCV 2013 - IEEE International Conference on Computer Vision*, pages 1817–1824, Sydney, Australia, Dec. 2013. IEEE.

[21] D. Patlolla, S. Voisin, H. Sridharan, and A. Cheriyadat. GPU accelerated textons and dense sift features for human settlement detection from high-resolution satellite imagery. In *GeoComp*, 2015.

[22] F. Perronnin, Y. Liu, J. Sánchez, and H. Poirier. Large-scale image retrieval with compressed fisher vectors. In *Computer Vision and Pattern Recognition (CVPR), 2010 IEEE Conference on*, pages 3384–3391. IEEE, 2010.

[23] H. J. F. P. Philippe-Henri Gosselina, Naila Murrayc. Revisiting the fisher vector for fine-grained classification. In *Pattern Recognition Letters*, Nov 2014.

[24] A. S. Razavian, H. Azizpour, J. Sullivan, and S. Carlsson. CNN features off-the-shelf: an astounding baseline for recognition. *CVPRW DeepVision workshop*, 2014.

[25] V. Saligrama and Z. Chen. Video anomaly detection based on local statistical aggregates. In *IEEE Conference on Computer Vision and Pattern Recognition*, pages 2112–2119, 2012.

[26] K. Simonyan, O. M. Parkhi, A. Vedaldi, and A. Zisserman. Fisher vector faces in the wild. In *Proc. BMVC*, volume 1, page 7, 2013.

[27] K. Simonyan and A. Zisserman. Two-stream convolutional networks for action recognition in videos. In *NIPS*, 2014.

[28] S. Sinha, J.-M. Frahm, M. Pollefeys, and Y. Genc. Feature tracking and matching in video using programmable graphics hardware. *Machine Vision and Applications*, 22(1):207–217, 2011.

[29] C. Sun, B. Burns, R. Nevatia, C. Snoek, B. Bolles, G. Myers, W. Wang, and E. Yeh. ISOMER: Informative segment observations for multimedia event recounting. In *Proceedings of International Conference on Multimedia Retrieval*, ICMR '14, pages 241:241–241:248, New York, NY, USA, 2014. ACM.

[30] J. SÃąnchez, F. Perronnin, T. Mensink, and J. Verbeek. Image Classification with the Fisher Vector: Theory and Practice. In *International Journal of Computer Vision*, 2013.

[31] D. Tran, L. Bourdev, R. Fergus, L. Torresani, and M. Paluri. Learning spatiotemporal features with 3D convolutional networks. In *ICCV*, 2015.

[32] K. E. A. van de Sande, T. Gevers, and C. G. M. Snoek. Empowering visual categorization with the GPU. *IEEE Transactions on Multimedia*, 13(1):60–70, 2011.

[33] K. E. A. van de Sande, C. G. M. Snoek, and A. W. M. Smeulders. Fisher and VLAD with FLAIR. In *CVPR*, 2014.

[34] A. Vedaldi and B. Fulkerson. VLFeat: An open and portable library of computer vision algorithms. http://www.vlfeat.org, 2008.

[35] W. Wang, Y. Zhang, G. Long, S. Yan, and H. Jia. CLSIFT: An optimization study of the scale invariance feature transform on GPUs. In *HPCC 2013*.

[36] S. Yan, G. Long, and Y. Zhang. StreamScan: fast scan algorithms for GPUs without global barrier synchronization. In *ACM SIGPLAN Symposium on Principles and Practice of Parallel Programming, PPoPP '13, Shenzhen, China, February 23-27, 2013*, pages 229–238, 2013.

[37] B. Zhao, L. Fei-Fei, and E. P. Xing. Online detection of unusual events in videos via dynamic sparse coding. In *CVPR*, pages 3313–3320, 2011.

Mouse Activity as an Indicator of Interestingness in Video

Gloria Zen
DISI, University of Trento
gloria.zen@unitn.it

Paloma de Juan and Yale Song
Yahoo Research
{pdjuan,yalesong}@yahoo-inc.com

Alejandro Jaimes
Ai Cure
aj27@caa.columbia.dot.edu

ABSTRACT

Automatic detection of interesting moments in video has many real-world applications such as video summarization and efficient online video browsing. In this paper, we present a lightweight and scalable solution to this problem based on user mouse activity while watching video. Unlike previous approaches that analyze video content to infer the interestingness, we leverage the implicit user feedback obtained from thousands of online video watching sessions. This makes our method computationally efficient and scalable to billions of videos. Most importantly, our approach can handle a variety of video genres because we make no assumption on what constitutes interestingness: we let the crowd tell us through their mouse activity. By analyzing 106,212 user sessions collected from a popular online video website, we show that mouse activity is highly indicative of interestingness, and that our approach has competitive performance to several state-of-the-art methods.

1. INTRODUCTION

Over the last five years, the average time US adults spend per day watching online video has grown from 21 minutes to 76 minutes, with an average annual growth rate of 38.4%.[1] Prediction estimates reveal that, by 2019, online video will be responsible for four-fifths of global Internet traffic.[2] Now more than ever, it is crucial to have an automatic method able to analyze video content and produce various types of metadata, such as time-stamped tags and highlights. This information can help improve user experience by generating high quality video previews [26] and efficient online video browsing [6], and bring more revenue to the service providers by, e.g., inserting relevant ads within a video [25]

In this paper, we investigate the usefulness of mouse activity in detecting interesting moments in videos by analyzing user data collected from thousands of online video watching sessions. Our work is motivated by recent works that analyze user feedback while watching online video [8, 22, 29, 34, 39] and those that analyze mouse cursor activities [1, 7, 15, 16, 23, 31]. Previous research has mainly focused on using mouse activity to estimate gaze density while browsing websites [7, 23], performing web search [15, 16, 31], and reading news articles [1]. We contribute to this line of research by showing that this implicit form of user feedback is highly indicative of interesting moments in video. To the best of our knowledge, our work is the first to study the relationship between mouse activity and user attention while watching online video.

There are four main advantages of using mouse activity for our task: It is efficient, scalable, non-intrusive, and generalizable. Most existing approaches to detecting interesting moments from video are content-based, extracting expensive audio and visual features

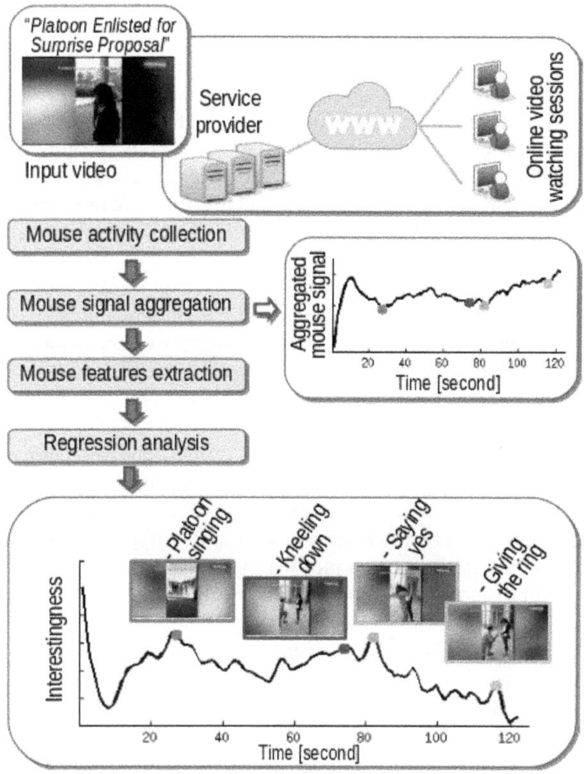

Figure 1: An overview of our approach. Shown here are the main phases of our approach for a video from our dataset, "*Platoon enlisted for surprise proposal*", for which we collected mouse activity from over 2,600 online video watching sessions. We derive several mouse features from the aggregated mouse signal, then perform regression analysis to estimate the degree of interestingness for each second.

[1]eMarketer, April 2015: "US Adults Spend 5.5 Hours with Video Content Each Day."
[2]Reelseo, June 2015: "By 2019, 80% of the world's internet traffic will be video."

ICMR'16, June 06-09, 2016, New York, NY, USA
© 2016 ACM. ISBN 978-1-4503-4359-6/16/06...$15.00
DOI: http://dx.doi.org/10.1145/2911996.2912005

and using advanced machine learning techniques to estimate the level of interestingness [11, 13, 17, 36, 37]. Compared to those approaches, our method is computationally efficient because the mouse activity signal is low-dimensional and fast to compute. Also, our method analyzes mouse activity per video, and thus is scalable to billions of online videos by processing them in parallel. Further, our signal collection is passive and non-intrusive (mouse events are collected using JavaScript), so users can remain in their natural setting and their behavior is not affected by the data collection process, a crucial factor in designing online experiments. Finally, and most importantly, unlike most previous works [22, 24, 30, 37, 38], our approach can be applied regardless of a video genre, since we make no assumptions on what makes a video interesting.

To study the relationship between mouse activity and interestingness at a large scale, we collected mouse events that happened within the web browser from 106,212 video watching sessions on a popular online video website. We also collected a total of 1,800 responses from Amazon Mechanical Turk (AMT) to generate the timeline annotation of interestingness levels for these videos. We then extracted several features from the mouse activity signals and performed a regression analysis with the degree of interestingness obtained via crowdsourcing as the target variable. We evaluated the effectiveness of our approach by automatically detecting interesting moments in video and comparing this to the output of some of the recent content-based approaches [11, 13]. Our results show that mouse activity is more effective at predicting interesting moments than methods based on visual features, suggesting that mouse activity is indicative of interestingness in video.

Figure 1 shows the close relationship between the video's storyline and the aggregated mouse activities of over 2,600 users. The video is a news story about a man proposing to his girlfriend with help from his platoon. The mouse signal (middle plot) represents the level of mouse activity aggregated over all users. We see the inverse relationship between the mouse signal (y-axis) and the highlights (shown in the bottom plot with keyframes). For instance, a high level of mouse movement is observed after about 10 seconds as the news anchor introduces the story, which we interpret as a drop of interest. The mouse movement level sharply decreases and negatively peaks at around the 30th second when the platoon starts singing a song to the woman, representing one of the most interesting moments in this video. Later, around the 80th second, the movement decreases again as the man kneels down to propose to his girlfriend – another interesting moment in this video. Towards the end of the video, around the 118th second, another peak of interest can be observed when the man gives an engagement ring to his girlfriend. As we will show later in this paper (Table 2), the aggregated mouse activity shows higher correlation to interestingness than various other content-based features.

The main contributions of our work are: (i) we investigate the relationship between mouse activity and user attention in video, which, to the best of our knowledge, has never been explored before; (ii) we propose an efficient framework to predict interestingness in video based on user mouse activity during online video watching sessions.

2. RELATED WORK

Our work is related to three lines of research. The first includes works that use mouse movement while interacting with web pages in order to infer user intention or to evaluate the interestingness of web pages. The second includes works that focus on determining interestingness in video, either based on user responses (e.g., physiological signals, click interactions with video player), or on video content analysis (e.g., visual cues). The third includes works that can benefit from estimating video timeline interestingness for building applications for users (e.g., more positive video browsing user experience) or service providers (e.g., higher efficiency on video transmission).

Mouse Movement Analysis. Mouse movement has been used as proxy for gaze location in the context of interaction with web pages. Rodden et al. [31] found that the distance between cursor and gaze position is larger along the x-axis than the y-axis of screen, and is generally shorter when the cursor is placed over the search results. They also observed four types of mouse cursor behaviors: neglecting the cursor while reading, using the cursor as a reading aid to follow text (either horizontally or vertically), and using the cursor to mark interesting results. Huang et al [15] proposed a technique to predict the gaze position from the cursor position with high accuracy. Hauger et al. [14] found a higher correlation between gaze and cursor positions when the cursor is in motion. Arapakis et al. [1] predict the outcome of online news reading experience by analyzing mouse activity while reading the article. Huang et al. [16] use mouse movement to analyze the user behavior when interacting with search engine result pages, and show that this signal is more informative than one obtained by collecting user click interactions.

User Response Analysis. The works in this category collect implicit user feedback, such as Twitter feeds [32, 38] and video player interaction patterns (e.g., play, pause, skip, etc.) [2, 20, 21, 27, 40]. Similar to our approach, this type of user responses can be collected passively and remotely, in a scalable and efficient manner. Promising results have been reported on various video categories, such as live events [32, 38], online lectures [2, 20, 21] and sport games [27, 40], suggesting a strong correlation between the *replay* action and important video segments. However, some of the user responses are mostly found in very specific video categories (e.g., the replay action is less likely to occur in news videos compared to online lectures or sport games), making this kind of approaches not particularly suited to generic video categories.

Recent works explored crowdsourcing user responses while watching video, developing efficient annotation tools [22, 33, 39] or collecting physiological signals (e.g., brain activities, facial expressions, eye blinking, head motion, heart rate) [3, 4, 8, 29]. This line of work has no category-specific assumption and thus can generalize well to many types of videos. Bao et al. [3] infer within-content ratings by collecting reactions from users watching movies on tablet devices. Similarly, Shirazi et al. [34] annotate a video timeline based on excitement information acquired using an EEG headset, and show that this information correlates well with important scenes of a video. Wu et al. [39] propose a framework for generating video abstracts based on explicit user feedback. These approaches, however, do not translate well into the online video realm, due to the cost of recruiting annotators, and the difficulty of obtaining user consent (e.g., facial expressions) or setting up expensive laboratory devices (e.g., brain signal sensors).

Compared to the two sets of user responses described above, mouse signal has the advantages of scalability (i.e., it can be collected passively from a large sets of users) and of being generalizable to a variety of video categories.

Video Content Analysis. The works in this category focus on analyzing content of video, such as audio and visual features, and use advanced machine learning techniques to detect interesting moments in video. The main challenges include defining what is interesting in a video without an a priori knowledge about its main topic. Potapov et al. [30] use category-specific prior information based on a predefined semantic taxonomy, e.g. weighing higher on scenes that contain "blowing on a candle" for the videos in a category "birthday party." Other works crawl images and videos from the web to learn a prior information on important moments in videos on a specific topic [37, 24, 9]. While promising results have been reported, the need for building a complete taxonomy makes these approaches difficult to scale to online videos. Song et al. [36] determine the visual importance of shots based on their visual similarity to topical images, crawled from the web using query terms derived from the video title. This approach has the advantage of being category-independent, assuming that the title describes the main subject of the video. However, its performance is largely influenced by the descriptiveness of a title.

A different thread of work specifically focuses on determining a general measure of interestingness, based on emotional and psychological studies. Grabner et al. [11] focus on predicting interestingness in webcam image sequences; Gygli et al. [13] use the predicted interestingness for generating summaries of user generated videos and egocentric videos. Other work focus on detecting interestingness of images [12, 35] and videos [18].

Improving User Experience. Recently, a growing interest has been shown on methods for improving user experience by providing easier access to video content [22] or by allowing more efficient video browsing [5, 6, 19]. Kamvar et al. [19] propose a method for browsing multimedia collection of videos on mobile devices. The instructional videos are segmented into informational chunks (manually or automatically via a video segmentation algorithm) and a list of relevance segments is produced through a keyword query. Chen et al. consider seeking (i.e., jumping to a new position of the video) as a special form of browsing [5, 6]. They propose a smart video streaming approach to avoid user early departure due to excessive buffering time and to reduce the bandwidth wastage (i.e., downloaded video content that is never watched) [6]. Their analysis leads to a user behavior model in which a user transitions through a random number of short views before a longer view. A method for detecting the interesting segments of a video would be highly beneficial for these approaches. For example, providing the most relevant information first may allow the user to reduce the time needed to find the desired information, thus improving the experience and reducing the risk of early departure.

3. FROM MOUSE ACTIVITY TO INTERESTINGNESS

Our method collects mouse activities from online video watching sessions and extracts several features from the aggregated mouse signals. We then perform a regression analysis with the level of interestingness as the target variable. This section describes our method in detail. In the next section we present the collected dataset.

3.1 Hypothesis on Mouse Activity

We formulate the following hypothesis on user mouse activity: When a user is focused on the video content, no mouse movement will occur (but the inverse may not hold). On the other hand, when a user starts to lose focus on the video, mouse movement is the first indication of the loss of attention. Note that having no mouse movement does not guarantee that a user is focused on the video (e.g., in case when the user has switched to another tab, or minimized the window). We consider those edge cases when collecting mouse activity signals, which we describe below.

3.2 Mouse Activity Collection

To record mouse activities of a user within a video page, we set up a script that runs in the background on the browser and records the position of the mouse every 100 ms throughout the video session. A session starts when the user enters the video page, either by typing an URL in the address bar, or by clicking on a link to another page. A session can also start if the video is part of a playlist. In that case, the session starts automatically when the previous video finishes and the new one is automatically loaded. The session ends when the user leaves the video page either by closing the tab or the browser, or navigating away from the page (i.e., loading a different page in the same tab).

The mouse coordinates are buffered and sent back to the server, along with the playback status (play or pause) of the video player at each instant. This data is processed as follows:

- If a video is playing, the current mouse position is compared to the previous one: (i) if the position has changed, the event is registered as "mouse movement;" (ii) otherwise, the event is registered as "no mouse movement."
- If the video is not playing at that instant, the data is discarded.

It is important to note that mouse movement can only be tracked within the limits of the browser. Any mouse movement occurring outside the page where the video is displayed is not detected. As a consequence, if the video is playing and the mouse is moving beyond the limits of the browser, this can be misinterpreted as "no mouse movement."

To handle this case, we process two additional browser events: "blur" and "focus." The former occurs when the page loses focus, i.e., if the user switches to a different tab or window (by clicking on it or using keyword shortcuts), or minimizes the window; the latter occurs when the page gains focus again. When the page where the video is playing loses focus, the playback status is not affected (i.e., video keeps playing), but the mouse movement can not be tracked anymore.

As we do not know whether the video player is still visible to the user or not, we mark the whole period between the "blur" and the "focus" events as "mouse movement." If the user does not return to the page within the video session (i.e., there is no "focus" event), the "blur" event is interpreted as the end of the session. For each user session, our procedure leads to the collection of a binary vector, where each bin encodes the mouse activity observed during a time interval of 100 ms. We set the value to 1 for the event "mouse movement" and to 0 for the event "no mouse movement."

The collected binary signal is process through three steps: First, in order to make it easier to align and aggregate mouse signals for all users watching the same video, we rescale the signal to a 1 second temporal resolution. This length is assumed to be small enough to keep a fine granularity that allows us to clearly separate the highlights from the subsequent attention decays. Second, we binarize the signal in order to filter out small mouse movements. Finally, we smooth the obtained binary signal using a gaussian filter, in order to take into account short temporal delays and eventual sparsity of data. To this aim, we use a temporal window of length 3 seconds.

3.3 Mouse Signal Aggregation

We define the *user mouse signal* as $x_i \in \mathbb{R}^L$ associated with the i-th user session for a specific video, where L is the video length (expressed in seconds). This signal is obtained by -1 padding the smoothed mouse signal previously obtained, thus setting to -1 the user mouse signal for the time intervals ℓ during which no mouse activity was recorded (e.g. the user session was terminated).

By combining mouse signals x_i over the N users who watched the video, we obtain a matrix $\mathcal{M} \in \mathbb{R}^{N \times L}$. Based on this matrix, the *aggregated mouse signal* $\mu \in \mathbb{R}^L$ is computed as:

$$\mu = \left\{ \frac{1}{N^\ell} \sum_{j=1}^{N^\ell} y_j^\ell \right\}, \quad \ell = 1, \cdots, L \tag{1}$$

where $N^\ell = |y^\ell|$ and $y^\ell = \{\mathscr{M}(i,\ell) \neq -1\}\, i = 1 \ldots N$. In practice, for each time interval ℓ the collected mouse signal μ indicates the percentage of mouse events observed, computed over the current active user sessions N^ℓ.

3.4 Mouse Feature Extraction

Intuitively, frames with the same value of the aggregated mouse signal μ can indicate different levels of interestingness, depending on whether they are located on a descending or an ascending slope, or on slopes with different degrees of steepness. We define a set of mouse features designed to capture the shape and the temporal variations of the aggregated mouse signal.

Global features. Some videos may *globally* have more active mouse movements than other videos; one level of mouse activity in a video should not be treated as equal in another video. In order to obtain a global representation of mouse movement signals that does not depend on the type of a video, we convert all instances of the aggregated mouse signal from each video into their percentile ranks within that video.

Local features. In order to capture the local pattern of a signal (e.g., ascending, flat, or descending slope), we concatenate the values within a local temporal window of 3 seconds of length.

Local variation features. We consider the variation of μ in its local range, by computing the distance between the values of μ within $[\ell-1, \ell+2]$. We consider first-order and second-order variations. For the latter, we take as input the first-order local variation instead of the original signal μ.

Spectral Features. The mouse signal temporal variations can have different time periods. To take into account the duration of local variation of μ, we compute the Discrete Cosine Transform (DCT) [28] for the local range of a 3 second temporal window.

3.5 Interestingness Estimation via Regression Analysis

The final interestingness score is computed by combining scores obtained by the mouse features presented in the previous section.

In order to determine the importance of each feature for predicting interestingness, we follow the same procedure presented by Grabner et al [11], who focus on predicting interestingness based on a combination of various cues extracted from visual content. As in [11], features are firstly normalized to their mean and variance, and then mapped into the interval [0,1] using a sigmoid function $s = \frac{1}{(1+exp(-az+b))}$.

Secondly, the final interestingness score is obtained as a linear combination of the considered features. This is formalized as: $\hat{s} = w^T \hat{s}$, where $\hat{s} = [s^{(f1)}; \ldots; s^{(fN)}]$ and $\{s^{(f1)}, \ldots, s^{(fN)}\}$ is the set of considered features. The optimal values of the parameters of the sigmoid function (a,b) and the weights w are estimated through a regression analysis using least square minimization and leave-one-video-out cross validation.

4. MOUSE ACTIVITY DATASET

4.1 Collection Setting

We deployed a *bucket* in an online video website, Yahoo Screen[3], where the mouse movement tracking script is integrated into the regular data logging process. Having a bucket is a typical setup in large companies; it guarantees that only a small percentage of users, chosen at random, will be exposed to the script. The script collects user mouse movements non-intrusively. We recorded mouse activity only within the limits of the browser and for the specific video website; all the recorded events were completely anonymized. We recorded the mouse activities for all videos watched in the bucket during a collection period of few weeks.

The final Mouse Activity Dataset consists of a total of 45 videos and 106,212 user sessions. The videos collected belong to a variety of categories such as News, Interviews, Comedy, Slideshow, User Generated, etc., and cover a variety of topics such as "food," "nature," "fashion" or "science." Also, the videos have the following properties: (1) the video is in English, and understanding its content does not require domain-specific or prior knowledge; (2) the video is no longer than 5 minutes; (3) the mouse activity is collected from more than 100 users and the associated inter-user agreement is positive (Cronbach's alpha $\alpha_u > 0$). The first two criteria garantee that the collection of human judgment can be fairly conducted with the same AMT task developed for our study. The third criterion ensures that the collected mouse signal for the video is significant enough, considering the instrisic noisy nature of the individual mouse signal. A discussion regarding the effect of N and α_u on the validity of mouse signal as an indicator of interestingness in video is reported in the result section. We provide details of our dataset (i.e., title, length, category, number of users from whom we collected mouse activity, Cronbach's alpha values, etc.) in the supplementary material online.[4]

4.2 Inter-User Agreement

We measure the agreement of the collected mouse signals for each video using Cronbach's alpha coefficient α. Our hypothesis is that when this agreement is sufficiently high, the aggregated mouse signal is not simply noise and we can rely on this signal to discover interesting moments in video.

Since the number of users N^ℓ who have not stopped playing the video decreases as the video advances, we compute α_ℓ at each instant of the video ℓ by considering only the user sessions that are not finished by time ℓ. In detail, we compute α_ℓ over the matrix $\mathscr{M}_\ell = \mathscr{M}(i,\bar{\ell})$, where $\bar{\ell} = \{1, \ldots, \ell\}$ and i is the index set of the user sessions N^ℓ. The final inter-user agreement is computed as $\alpha_u = \text{median}(\alpha_2, \cdots, \alpha_L)$.

4.3 Annotation Settings

We set up an annotation task that consists of watching a video and providing an explicit response regarding the interestingness of the given content. The feedback was provided through two buttons – *thumb up* and *thumb down* – next to the video player. The participants were asked to click either button whenever they thought something interesting or uninteresting was being shown. Every time the worker clicked one of the two buttons, an event *up* or *down* was recorded. The video was played from the beginning to the end without interruption. The workers were not allowed to pause or skip the video, but they were allowed to replay it from the beginning at any time, if they needed so.

By default, each annotation m was initialized as a zero vector of length L. Each element covered a time interval of 1 second. We set $m_\ell = 1$ or $m_\ell = -1$ every time an *interesting* or *uninteresting* event was recorded within the time interval ℓ.

For quality control, we asked the participants to answer a questionnaire after having finished the video. In order to ensure they had genuinely watched the video while performing the task, we asked two objective fact-check questions about the content of video. Also, in order to ensure that the participants used their best criteria to per-

[3]As of January 2016, Yahoo Screen has been sunset. All video content is available on digital magazine properties instead.

[4]https://disi.unitn.it/~zen/data/mouse-track-dataset.pdf

form the task, we asked them to provide at least three keywords or keyphrases explaining their choices. We collected a total of 1,800 annotations, 40 per video. The workers were free to choose how many videos to annotate (between 1 and 45), but were not allowed to annotate the same video more than once.

4.4 Inter-rater Agreement

For the sake of coherece with the pre-processing applied to mouse signals, we smoothed the collected annotations using Kernel Regression and a temporal window of 3 seconds of length, and we computed Cronbach's alpha $\hat{\alpha}_r$ to assess the inter-rater agreement.

We obtained an average value of $\bar{\alpha}_r$=0.53. As there is no objective way to evaluate the correctness of a subjective annotation (i.e., it is difficult to tell whether an annotation is an outlier because it was done at random or because of a different opinion), we decided to discard those that greatly differed from the rest of the annotations based on a measure of internal consistency. For that, we filtered out up to 10 annotations for each video, by greedily leaving out the annotations that were lowering the inter-user agreement. The resulting average Cronbach's alpha of the reduced set is $\bar{\alpha}_r = 0.71$.

In the following phases of this work, we considered both the original and the reduced sets of annotations, and we did not observe significant changes in the final results. Results obtained with these two sets are reported and discussed in the Section 5.3.

4.5 Interestingness Scores

We denote as *real-valued interestingness score* the signal obtained by averaging the annotations collected via AMT. In order to evaluate the efficiency of our method in detecting interesting moments in video, we binarize the real-valued scores into "interesting" and "not interesting" and denote the obtained signal as *binarized interestingness score*. We do this by first normalizing the real-valued score distribution to have zero mean and one standard deviation, then threshold the normalized scores using value one.

5. EVALUATION

We conduct two sets of experiments to assess the validity of using mouse signal as an indicator of interestingness in video.

In the first experiment, we select videos based on different numbers of user sessions N and Cronbach's alpha α_u. This analysis aims to investigate the conditions in which the collected mouse signal can be considered a trustworthy measure of interestingness in video. In particular, we validate α as an indicator of the trustworthiness of the mouse signal, and we empirically find the optimal value of N required for collecting a trustworthy mouse signal.

In the second experiment, we validate our approach only on the set of videos for which the collected mouse signal is considered reliable. To this aim, we select videos with $\alpha > 0.7$, which is indicated in literature as the desirable minimum value of α for considering acceptable the inter-user agreement [10].

5.1 Methodology

We compare our method to recent works on visual interestingness [11] and video summarization [13, 36]. We chose the three methods as our baseline because they share certain similarities to our method – they produce frame-level scores indicating how interesting/important they are, and they do so without making any assumption on the video topic. One difference to our work is that, while our method is purely based on mouse signal, all three baselines are based on visual content of a video. Therefore, our experiments would allow us to measure the effectiveness of mouse signal in comparison to visual signal.

Table 1: Interestingness prediction results, measured in AUC at varying degree of the binarization threshold δ.

	$\delta = 5$	$\delta = 10$	$\delta = 15$	$\delta = 20$
Gygli et al. [13]	0.5141	0.5301	0.5176	0.5153
Grabner et al. [11]	0.5246	0.5377	0.5478	0.5459
Song et al. [36]	0.5741	0.5643	0.5520	0.5421
Our method	**0.6868**	**0.6728**	**0.6577**	**0.6443**

Grabner et al [11] and Gygli et al [13] define a set of visual features for predicting visual interestingness based on attention models and psychological studies. We compute visual interestingness scores by combining visual features as described in [11] and [13]. Song et al. [36] measure the importance of each video frame based on their similarity to the title of that video. We measure the frame-level interestingness by following the description in [36]. We process videos at 6 FPS in all our experiments.

We acknowledge that the two baseline methods [13, 36] are optimized to tackle video summarization, which is slightly different from our problem. Our goal is to measure the level of interestingness in each moment of a video, while the goal of video summarization is to create a concise summary of a video given a time budget (e.g., 15% of the original video length).

Below, we show results on two experiments: (i) performance in predicting the *binarized* interestingness; (ii) correlation between mouse signals and the *real-valued* interestingness scores.

Interestingness Prediction. The performance is computed in terms of Area Under the ROC Curve (AUC), where the *binarized interestingness score* is used as the ground truth for interestingness. The binarized signals is obtained by selecting the $\delta\%$ top interesting moments from the *real-valued interestingness score*. We show results obtained by varying δ between 5 and 30 with a unary step. We report the results in Section 5.2.

Correlation with Interestingness. We assess the correlation between the reference *real-valued interestingness score* and the predicted interestingness scores by computing the Pearson correlation between the two signals. For the sake of comparison, both signals are normalized to zero mean and one standard deviation. We report the results in Section 5.3.

5.2 Interestingness Prediction

Table 1 and Figure 2 (a) show the performances on interestingness prediction obtained with different methods, for the videos with $\alpha > 0.7$. The performances are measured in terms of AUC and computed at varying the binarization threshold δ used for generating the *binarized interestingness score*. We observe that our method outperforms related works where the score is computed based on visual content [11, 13, 36].

Figure 2(b,c) show the performances of our method respectively by varying the value of minimum α_u and N used for selecting the video set on which our analysis is performed. Based on this observation, we can assess that both α and N are good indicators for determining the trustability of the mouse signal. In particular, we experimentally observe that the performance obtained on our dataset with $\alpha_u > 0.7$ can be reached on our dataset in the case of $N > 1,000$.

5.3 Correlation with Interestingness

Table 2 shows the correlation of different mouse features and methods with *real-valued interestingness scores*. In general, we observe that the correlations is low across different methods (below 0.3). We speculate that this is indicative of how challenging

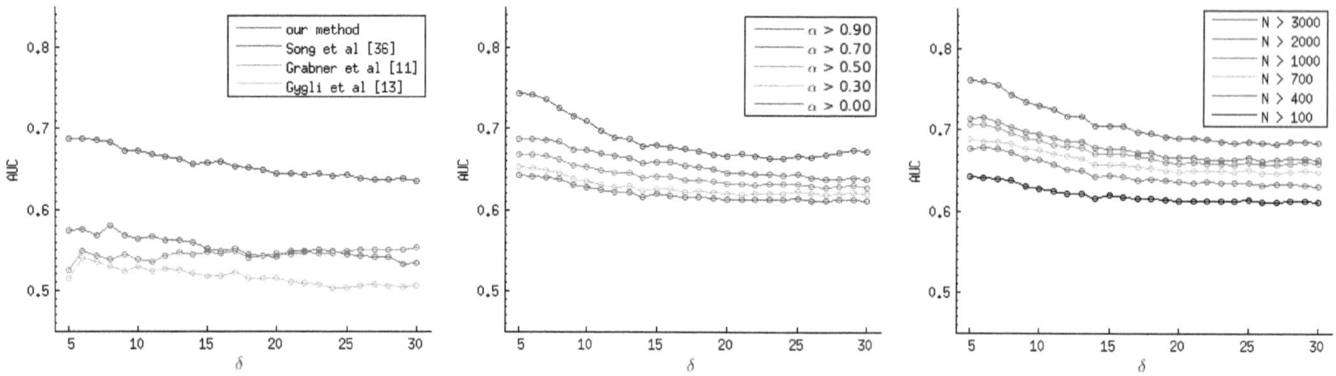

(a) (b) (c)

Figure 2: Overall performance on the prediction of interestingness, measured in AUC at varying δ: (a) our method compared with related works and our method when only videos with a minimum value of (b) N and (c) α are considered. The y-axis limits for (a,b,c) are magnified between 0.45 and 0.85 for sake of clarity.

Table 2: Pearson correlation between *real-valued* interestingness scores and prediction scores obtained using: (top) different mouse features and (bottom) different methods. We report results on two versions of our dataset (all videos and $\alpha_u > 0.7$)

	all videos ($\alpha_u > 0$)	$\alpha_u > 0.7$
mouse	0.250	0.283
local	0.259	0.292
local variation (1st order)	0.136	0.158
local variation (2nd order)	0.007	0.098
spectral	0.259	0.289
global	0.259	0.303
Gygli et al. [13]	0.106	0.133
Grabner et al. [11]	0.057	0.043
Song et al. [36]	0.021	0.038
Our method	**0.268**	**0.301**

the problem is in general. Indeed, videos were retrieved without making any assumption on the video format or content.

Still, just by considering mouse features (Table 2(top)), we obtain a higher correlation with respect to the recent methods based on visual features (Tab. 2(bottom)). From Table 2, we can also observe the benefit of combining mouse features, leading to a higher correlation. Also, if we compare the results obtained by considering all videos from the dataset and only those with $\alpha > 0.7$, reported respectively in the left and right column of Table 2, we observe that the increase in r for the mouse-based signal is more significant with respect to the variation of r obtained for the other methods.

Table 3 reports the two sets of Pearson correlation values computed based on the *real-valued interestingness score* obtained by using (i) the original set of AMT annotations and (ii) the reduced set, which is derived from original AMT annotations by eliminating the outliers. It can be noted that the difference of the results between the two sets is not significant, around 0.01.

5.4 Qualitative Analysis

Figure 4 shows the mouse movement and the interestingness score collected for the video "*Huge Sea Turtle Crashes Wedding*". Figure 3 shows the thumbnail frames uniformly extracted every 2 s from this video. By comparing Figure 3 and Figure 4, it is possible to observe that the *mouse signal* and the *real-valued interestingness*

Table 3: Pearson correlation between *real-valued* interestingness scores and prediction scores. The real-valued interestingness score is obtained using (left) the original set and (right) the reduced set of AMT annotations.

	original AMT set	reduced AMT set
Gygli et al. [13]	0.056	0.057
Grabner et al. [11]	0.103	0.106
Song et al. [36]	0.012	0.021
Our method	0.236	0.250

score exhibit a similar trend, with an increasing interestingness in the transitions from segments where the news anchor is shown, to those depicting the subject of the news (e.g., bride and turtle being shown around the 15th, 25th, 59th and 89th seconds), and vice versa (e.g., news anchor appearing around the 3rd, 21st and 83rd seconds). Interestingly, a value mismatch between the two signal can be observed when a screenshot of the Reddit Post is displayed (i.e., around the 33rd and the 47th second): while a low interesting score has been assigned by the annotators, a peak in the mouse signal can be observed. A similar situation of mismatch was observed in other videos when a screenshot or a map was shown.

Also, it is interesting to notice that the parts of the video for which we observe a drop of interestingness are those where the newcaster is speaking and where the pictures of the celebrities are shown. This may be apparently be in contrast with attention based model theories that indicate the presence of faces or celebrities as a salient cues. Feedback provided by the AMT workers explain this choice, as shown in Table 4. This table reports some of the keywords and keyphrases used by the AMT workers to describe the moments indicated as interesting or uninteresting for one of the videos in the dataset. Some of the negative keyphrases include "*the anchor*", "*host trying to be funny*" or "*lame jokes with the celebrity photos*". This example shows us that, while this kind of subtleties may be difficult to catch with content-based method analysis, directly sensing from the users what is interesting helps disambiguate this kind of situations.

6. CONCLUSION

In this paper, we provide a novel framework for detecting interesting moments in video based on mouse activity signals. Collecting mouse activity signals is computationally efficient, non-

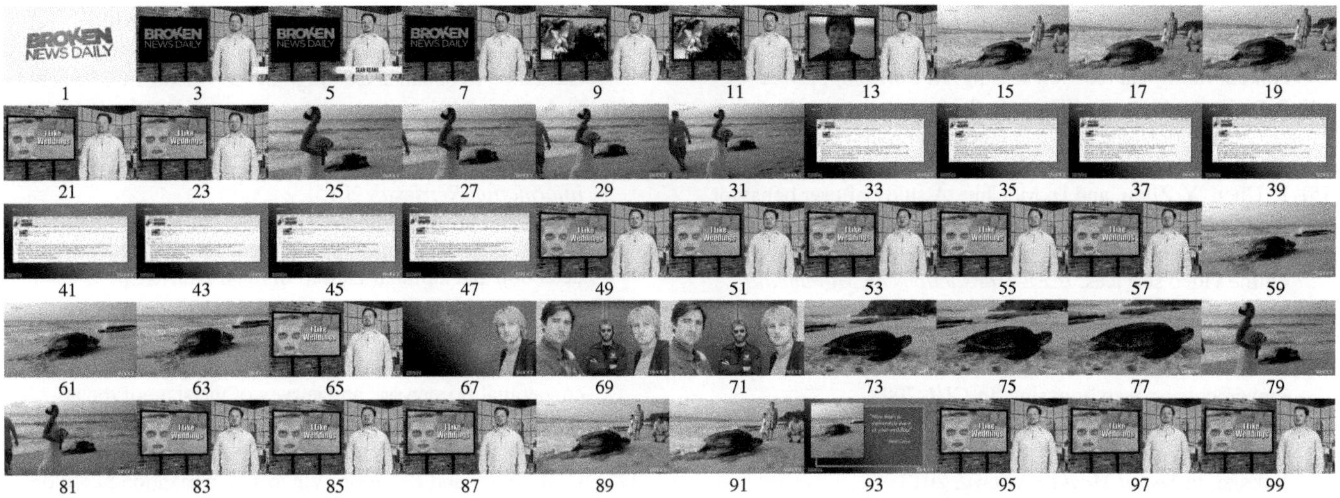

Figure 3: Thumbnail frames uniformly extracted every 2 seconds from the video *"Huge Sea Turtle Crashes Wedding"*. The frames depicting the subjects of the news (e.g. bride and turtle between the 25th and the 31st second and between the 73th and 81th second) are indicated as the most interesting by the AMT workers (see Figure 4, in blue) and also correspond to peaks of the mouse signal (see Figure 4, in black).

Table 4: Sample keywords describing interesting and uninteresting moments for the video *"Huge Sea Turtle Crashes Wedding"*, as indicated by the AMT workers.

	Motivations
Interesting moments	photos of the turtle, wedding, bride, pics of bride and groom, cute animal, unique, surprising, funny, memorable, unexpected, turtle with bride and groom, Jason's comment on Reddit, wedding ceremony on the beach
Not interesting moments	host trying to be funny, Reddit post photograph, references not to turtle and wedding, cheesy, the anchor, repetitive, unnecessary, lame jokes with celebrity photos, the newscater's jokes were terrible, too much text, zombie

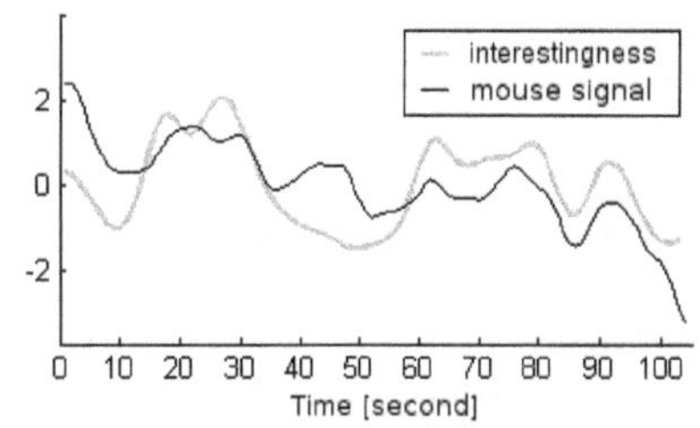

Figure 4: Scores of interestingness based on human judgments (in blue) and mouse signal (in black) for the video *"Huge Sea Turtle Crashes Wedding"*. For sake of comparison, both signals are normalized to zero mean and one standard deviation.

invasive, and scalable to thousand or even millions of users. By analyzing over 100,000 online video watching sessions, we showed that mouse movement can be considered a predictive cue for the interestingness in video, yielding a performance that is significantly higher than the current state-of-the-art computer vision techniques.

As an empirical value, we found that 0.7 is the minimal desirable value of inter-user agreement over the mouse signals collected from users, for which the aggregated mouse signal can be considered significant. We also shown that the number of users watching the video is a good indicator of the mouse signal trustability for predicting interestingness in video. We empirically found that similar performances to the case of $\alpha_u > 0.7$ can be achieved when at least 1,000 users sessions are collected for each video. Considering the growing number of users who watch videos online (so called "cord cutters"), we believe this is a reasonable number for a popular video service provider. This is shown by recent statistics, indicating that the average number of views per video for different categories varies between 2,300 and 9,000.[5]

Over the last few years, the time people spend on watching online video has increased dramatically. Now more than ever, it is important to invest in developing intelligent systems able to predict how users will react to the content. Our work contributes to this line of research, and especially on detecting interesting moments in video. Our method leverages the implicit form of user feedback obtained from the mouse activity, collected from thousands of online users, in order to detect interestingness in video. We showed that our method is computationally efficient and scalable to billions of videos. We also show that our approach can handle a variety of video genres, as we make no assumption on what constitutes interestingness.

Our work has implications on video summarization, which can help improve user experience by generating high quality video previews and efficient video buffering, and also on video recommendation, which would bring more revenue to the service providers.

In the future, we plan to perform a deeper analysis on mouse activities when the user attention is lost (e.g., the user starts interacting with the video player controls, scrolling down to browse related videos, etc.). Also, more analysis is needed to understand what types of features (e.g., visual cues, sound, objects depicted in the video, plot development) drive attention, and in which specific context (e.g., reading text from the screen requires attention, but it probably does not constitute a highlight).

[5] http://www.reelseo.com/average-youtube-views

7. REFERENCES

[1] I. Arapakis, M. Lalmas, and G. Valkanas. Understanding within-content engagement through pattern analysis of mouse gestures. In *CIKM*, 2014.

[2] M. Avlonitis and K. Chorianopoulos. Video pulses: User-based modeling of interesting video segments. *Advances in Multimedia*, 2014.

[3] X. Bao, S. Fan, A. Varshavsky, K. Li, and R. Roy Choudhury. Your reactions suggest you liked the movie: Automatic content rating via reaction sensing. In *UbiComp*, 2013.

[4] P. R. Chakraborty, L. Zhang, D. Tjondronegoro, and V. Chandran. Using viewer's facial expression and heart rate for sports video highlights detection. In *ACM ICMR*, 2015.

[5] L. Chen, Y. Zhou, and D. M. Chiu. A study of user behavior in online vod services. *Computer Communications*, 46, 2014.

[6] L. Chen, Y. Zhou, and D. M. Chiu. Smart streaming for online video services. *IEEE Transactions on Multimedia*, 17(4), 2015.

[7] M. C. Chen, J. R. Anderson, and M. H. Sohn. What can a mouse cursor tell us more?: correlation of eye/mouse movements on web browsing. In *CHI*, 2001.

[8] C. Chênes, G. Chanel, M. Soleymani, and T. Pun. Highlight detection in movie scenes through inter-users, physiological linkage. In *Social Media Retrieval*. 2013.

[9] W.-S. Chu, Y. Song, and A. Jaimes. Video co-summarization: Video summarization by visual co-occurrence. In *CVPR*, 2015.

[10] G. Goldstein and M. Hersen. Handbook of psychological assessment. 2000.

[11] H. Grabner, F. Nater, M. Druey, and L. Van Gool. Visual interestingness in image sequences. In *ACM Multimedia*, 2013.

[12] M. Gygli, H. Grabner, H. Riemenschneider, F. Nater, and L. Van Gool. The interestingness of images. In *ICCV*, 2013.

[13] M. Gygli, H. Grabner, H. Riemenschneider, and L. Van Gool. Creating summaries from user videos. In *ECCV*. 2014.

[14] D. Hauger, A. Paramythis, and S. Weibelzahl. Using browser interaction data to determine page reading behavior. In *UMAP*. 2011.

[15] J. Huang, R. White, and G. Buscher. User see, user point: gaze and cursor alignment in web search. In *CHI*, 2012.

[16] J. Huang, R. W. White, and S. Dumais. No clicks, no problem: using cursor movements to understand and improve search. In *CHI*, 2011.

[17] Y. Ito, K. M. Kitani, J. A. Bagnell, and M. Hebert. Detecting interesting events using unsupervised density ratio estimation. In *ECCV Workshops and Demonstrations*.

[18] Y.-G. Jiang, Y. Wang, R. Feng, X. Xue, Y. Zheng, and H. Yang. Understanding and predicting interestingness of videos. In *AAAI*, 2013.

[19] M. Kamvar, P. Chiu, L. Wilcox, S. Casi, and S. Lertsithichai. Minimedia surfer: browsing video segments on small displays. In *CHI*, 2004.

[20] I. Karydis, M. Avlonitis, K. Chorianopoulos, and S. Sioutas. Identifying important segments in videos: A collective intelligence approach. *International Journal on Artificial Intelligence Tools*, 23(02), 2014.

[21] J. Kim, P. J. Guo, D. T. Seaton, P. Mitros, K. Z. Gajos, and R. C. Miller. Understanding in-video dropouts and interaction peaks in online lecture videos. In *L@S*, 2014.

[22] J. Kim, P. T. Nguyen, S. Weir, P. J. Guo, R. C. Miller, and K. Z. Gajos. Crowdsourcing step-by-step information extraction to enhance existing how-to videos. In *CHI*, 2014.

[23] D. Lagun and E. Agichtein. Inferring searcher attention by jointly modeling user interactions and content salience. In *ACM SIGIR Conference on Research and Development in Information Retrieval*, 2015.

[24] M. Mazloom, A. Habibian, D. Liu, C. G. Snoek, and S.-F. Chang. Encoding concept prototypes for video event detection and summarization. In *ACM ICMR*, 2015.

[25] T. Mei, X.-S. Hua, L. Yang, and S. Li. Videosense: towards effective online video advertising. In *ACM Multimedia*, 2007.

[26] A. G. Money and H. Agius. Video summarisation: A conceptual framework and survey of the state of the art. *Journal of Visual Communication and Image Representation*, 19(2):121–143, 2008.

[27] D. R. Olsen and B. Moon. Video summarization based on user interaction. In *EuroITV*, 2011.

[28] A. V. Oppenheim, R. W. Schafer, J. R. Buck, et al. *Discrete-time signal processing*, volume 2. Prentice-hall Englewood Cliffs, 1989.

[29] W.-T. Peng, W.-T. Chu, C.-H. Chang, C.-N. Chou, W.-J. Huang, W.-Y. Chang, and Y.-P. Hung. Editing by viewing: automatic home video summarization by viewing behavior analysis. *IEEE Transactions on Multimedia*, 13(3), 2011.

[30] D. Potapov, M. Douze, Z. Harchaoui, and C. Schmid. Category-specific video summarization. In *ECCV*, 2014.

[31] K. Rodden, X. Fu, A. Aula, and I. Spiro. Eye-mouse coordination patterns on web search results pages. In *CHI*, 2008.

[32] D. A. Shamma, L. Kennedy, and E. F. Churchill. Tweet the debates: understanding community annotation of uncollected sources. In *ACM SIGMM Workshop on Social media*, 2009.

[33] D. A. Shamma, R. Shaw, P. L. Shafton, and Y. Liu. Watch what I watch: using community activity to understand content. In *ACM Workshop on Multimedia Information Retrieval*, 2007.

[34] A. S. Shirazi, M. Funk, F. Pfleiderer, H. Glück, and A. Schmidt. Mediabrain: Annotating videos based on brain-computer interaction. In *Mensch & Computer*, 2012.

[35] M. Soleymani. The quest for visual interest. In *ACM Multimedia*, 2015.

[36] Y. Song, J. Vallmitjana, A. Stent, and A. Jaimes. TVSum: Summarizing web videos using titles. In *CVPR*, 2015.

[37] M. Sun, A. Farhadi, and S. Seitz. Ranking domain-specific highlights by analyzing edited videos. In *ECCV*, 2014.

[38] A. Tang and S. Boring. #EpicPlay: crowd-sourcing sports video highlights. In *CHI*, 2012.

[39] S.-Y. Wu, R. Thawonmas, and K.-T. Chen. Video summarization via crowdsourcing. In *CHI*, 2011.

[40] B. Yu, W.-Y. Ma, K. Nahrstedt, and H.-J. Zhang. Video summarization based on user log enhanced link analysis. In *ACM Multimedia*, 2003.

Automatic Identification of Sports Video Highlights using Viewer Interest Features

Prithwi Raj Chakraborty
Queensland University of Technology
p1.chakraborty@qut.edu.au

Dian Tjondronegoro
Queensland University of Technology
dian@qut.edu.au

Ligang Zhang
Xi'an University of Technology
lg.zhang@xaut.edu.cn

Vinod Chandran
Queensland University of Technology
v.chandran@qut.edu.au

ABSTRACT

Classification of viewer interest using facial expression and heart rate facilitates automatic identification of interest evoking video segments. Sports video is suitable for testing the effectiveness of such a system as it has structured segments with distinguishable highlight events. Previous work has not investigated the differences in viewer interest characteristics from one sports type to another, which is crucial for appropriate classification methodology. Thus, it is still unclear whether a universal classification model can be used for analyzing viewer interest for all types of sports. This paper addresses this gap by demonstrating a significant difference ($p < 0.05$) in the distributions of viewer interest data in soccer compared to tennis. Based on this finding, this paper proposes an adoption of Gaussian mixture models (GMM) to integrate sports-specific and sports-independent approaches for identifying video segments, which would be of potential interest to individual viewers. The approaches achieve 52% to 64% accuracy, demonstrating that sports-specific approach gets better performance.

Categories and Subject Descriptors

• Human-centered computing • Human-centered computing~Ubiquitous and mobile computing • Human-centered computing~Empirical studies in ubiquitous and mobile computing

Keywords

Viewer interest; sports video; highlight identification

1. INTRODUCTION

Viewer interest is a type of emotion, which involves affect related components, such as attention, facial expression, and physiological responses. It is brief in duration and can be indicative of positive or active experience [1, 2]. The use of multimodal data for viewer interest classification is challenging, as each modality has different sensitivity to video stimuli. Facial expression (FE) and heart rate (HR), have previously been found effective in identifying video events of potential interest to viewers in unseen videos [3, 4]. Similar systems utilizing facial expression, heart rate, respiration, and blood volume pulse have been found effective in affective tagging of music video and movie clips, automatic video editing, personalized video highlight detection, and measuring user engagement to online advertisements [5-9]. However, an effective fusion of multimodal viewer interest signals has not been fully applied for sports video highlights identification, as current approaches (e.g., [10, 11]) have mainly used content-based features to identify highlights. Existing work which has applied a combination of viewer interest signals used either visual or physiological modalities [6, 12, 13]. The applications of these approaches are confined to cognition measurement, fan identification, and topical relevance detection [14-16], but not sports highlights detection.

Automatic classification of viewer interest (into interested vs. not interested categories) is challenging, as the evoked responses to sports video are expected to be subjective and dependent on various factors such as: whether the viewer is a passionate supporter of the sports/team/player; the viewer's personality; the sports type and the characteristics of sports events. The current research gap in identifying *interesting* video segments is to investigate whether the classifier model for viewer interest in sports video can be universal, or it needs to be sports-specific. The distributions of viewer interest can be expected to be different across sports types; however statistical analysis of such distributions has not been investigated in prior work.

This paper aims to study the use of facial expression recognition scores and heart rate data as viewer interest features for identifying sports video highlights. The system provides novel insights into understanding the statistical distributions of viewer interest data across different sports types. It verifies the feasibility of proposed GMM-based generic viewer interest classification model for identifying *interesting* and *non-interesting* segments in different types of sports videos.

2. RELATED WORK

Facial expression and head features have been utilized as visual cues for understanding viewer interest in video content, including face distance, face angle, head roll, and movements of facial points [5, 17]. Optical motion features from the face and upper body images are aggregated into motion history features in [18] which are found to be indicative of viewer attention and positive experience. An attention score has been estimated using a fusion of facial movement, eye movement, and eye blink features in [6]. Time-domain and frequency-domain features from physiological signals can be used for identifying viewer interest. Heart rate variability (HRV) features - including heart rate and its standard deviation, skewness, kurtosis and spectral power in frequency bands - are useful to compute valence-arousal scores [19]. Energy in low frequency band (0.04-0.15 Hz) and high frequency band (0.15-0.40 Hz) is indicative of sympathetic modulation and excitement [20]. Fast and significant changes in these features

ICMR'16, June 6–9, 2016, New York, NY, USA.
© 2016 ACM. ISBN 978-1-4503-4359-6/16/06…$15.00.
DOI: http://dx.doi.org/10.1145/2911996.2912011

indicate emotional trends [13]. Beats-per-minute, heart rate deceleration, and the high-frequency component of HRV can be used to detect emotional patterns evoked by film and sports video stimuli, however, these features are found to vary across film and picture categories [12, 21]. It is not yet determined whether these features are statistically different across sports types.

A reliable system for classifying viewer interest to identify sports video highlights has not been proposed. Thresholding of facial expression and heart rate features can be used to detect potential highlight segments from soccer videos [3]. However, such method is too simplistic and does not capture complex correlations and statistics between features. Machine learning methods such as linear regression can be applied to facial expression and heart rate features for computing valence and arousal scores [7, 18]. Support vector machine (SVM) has been used to classify facial expression features to measure viewer engagement and voter preferences [17, 22]. These methods have been validated against subjective assessments using correlation-based techniques. Correlation is useful to compute the similarity between the extracted features, which subsequently can help to determine the most complementary set of features for classification [12, 19]. A model-based technique such as GMM has been used in estimating interest from music and music video, using content-based features [23, 24].

3. EXPERIMENT PROTOCOL

3.1 Stimuli Dataset

Unlike most of existing studies that use short clips with durations between 2 to 3 minutes (e.g., [4, 13]), this study uses longer clips ranging between 9 to 20 minutes from soccer and tennis videos. Short clips from sports video might lack sufficient information to build-up strong cognitive attention of viewers. Full-length matches are deliberately avoided to maintain the subjects' attention and patience. The sources are heterogeneous as they are selected from popular international leagues including UEFA Euro, English Premier League, Champions League, Australian Open, and ATP World Tour. Descriptions of these clips are provided in Table 1. Soccer clips are trimmed from the beginning of the matches. One tennis clip contains the first three games of the first set of a tennis match while the other tennis clip includes the last three games of the first sets from another tennis match. The frame resolution of the clips is 1280×720 pixels and the frame rate is 25 frames-per-second (fps).

Table 1. Details of the stimuli clips

Clip Id	Type	Duration (min)	No. of Highlights and Rallies			
			Goal	Shot-on-goal	Foul	Rally
1	Soccer	20	1	5	2	-
2	Soccer	15	1	4	2	-
3	Soccer	17	1	5	1	-
4	Tennis	9	-	-	-	15
5	Tennis	11	-	-	-	16

A number of highlight segments from each clip are prepared for obtaining subjects' feedbacks. Highlight segments are expected to be interest-evoking and exciting regardless of a person's sports demographic. For soccer video clips, web-based match reports are used to identify potential highlight segments, which include 3 goals, 14 shots-on-goal, and 5 fouls. The segmentation of these soccer highlight events is manually obtained using play-break frames as described in [25]. A tennis match does not contain conspicuous highlights like soccer. Each game in tennis contains at least 4 points and each point scored is a sequence of shots which is known as a rally as well. All rally events are identified using similar play-break segmentation and used as highlight segments.

3.2 Environment Setup and Participants

A closed and quiet room has been used to record facial expression and heart rate signals of participants concurrently while they are watching stimuli. A video camera is used with natural daylight for recording facial expression. To maintain a non-invasive environment, a strapless heart rate sensor (Mio Alpha) is used for recording heart rate. Video stimuli are presented to each participant through a 21.5-inch monitor. A comfortable revolving chair is used for participants to sit. The distance between the monitor and the viewer is kept approximately 80 - 90 cm. The setup is shown in Figure 1.

Figure 1. Illustration of the environment setup for recording a subject's facial expression and heart rate using a video camera (marked) mounted on the top of a Dell monitor and Mio Alpha (marked) while the subject is watching a tennis clip.

This study involves a total of 15 subjects recruited from university students, who are not familiar with the stimuli video and do not have any visual impairment or heart condition (as confirmed by questionnaire). Subjects are aged between 22 and 30 (mean = 26.2, standard deviation = 3.7) and further characterized by demographic and profile information, including: whether a subject is a fan (or not) of a particular sport, their favorite soccer teams, their favorite soccer and tennis players, and their familiarity with soccer and tennis. After obtaining consents, subjects are invited to participate in data collection study. Out of the 15 subjects, 9 subjects (id: 1, 2, 4, 5, 7 - 11) have participated in the studies using all five clips; while three subjects (id: 3, 6, 12) have participated in clip 1-3 (soccer) and another three (id: 13-15) in clip 4-5 (tennis) studies.

3.3 Data Collection Procedure

Prior to commencing data collection, a short demonstration is presented to the subjects to make them familiar with the setup interface and the sessions. Then a 5-minute resting time (empirically set based on prior studies) is given to stabilize heart rate. Subjects are instructed to avoid rapid body movements, other activities and act naturally during the data collection process. There is a two-week break between two consecutive sessions. Each session has three main parts – recording, feedback, and questionnaire discussed as follows:

1. *Recording:* Each subject is asked to watch a clip and his/her facial video as well as heart rate are recorded during watching. The viewing and recording are continuous for each clip. The sampling frequencies of facial video and heart rate are 25 fps and 1/3 Hz respectively.

2. *Feedback:* Each subject is asked to annotate (i.e., select the starts and ends of) a random number of segments he/she felt *interesting* from the clip viewed in the first session, using a media player tool (*KMPlayer 3.5*). This part is conducted for soccer clips only.

For both soccer and tennis clips, each subject watches the prepared highlight segments (as discussed in Section 3.1) and rates them on a binary scale as **0** (*non-interesting*) or **1** (*interesting*), according to how he/she felt. The binary scale is used to discard any in-between choice of subjects, since segments which do not evoke interest should be rated as *non-interesting.* Both annotations and highlight ratings from soccer clips are obtained to ensure no potentially interesting segment is missed. The use of highlight ratings ensures robustness to the identification of interesting segments.

3. *Post-questionnaire:* Each subject is asked to select his/her favorite players and teams, and rate their performance during the matches in the viewed clips.

3.4 Ground Truth Design

Two types of ground truths are created: subject-independent and subject-dependent. Classification approaches use subject-independent ground truth to verify their generalizability. The subject-dependent ground truth is used in the statistical distribution analysis since the tests are conducted for each subject. The temporal misalignments of the annotated segments are corrected by manually adjusting the starts and ends according to the play-break segmentation. In subject-independent ground truth, each segment from a soccer or tennis clip is marked as *interesting* if more than 50% subjects agree through their feedbacks. Segments that do not fulfill this criterion are labeled as *non-interesting.* By contrast, the subject-dependent ground truth includes segments which are annotated and rated (as *interesting*) by each individual subject. The starting and ending time indices of all these segments are stored along with their respective labels as ground truth.

4. STATISTICAL DISTRIBUTIONS OF EXTRACTED FEATURES

This section explains the proposed methods for feature extraction and statistical validation. A summary of all extracted features from facial expression and heart rate data is provided in Table 2. Features are extracted from the recorded data and statistical hypothesis tests are conducted to validate whether the features are varying across two types of sports. Three separate classification approaches (i.e., sports-specific, cross-sports, sports-independent) are introduced to verify the generalizability of the features. The classification labels are fused using a Naïve Bayes combiner to check whether fusion can perform better than using a single label.

4.1 Facial Expression Recognition

Features from facial expression signals are obtained from the outputs of the facial expression recognition (FER) system described in [30]. The FER system is trained with non-lab-based data from TV, news, and World Wide Web. This system detects the facial region with a Viola-Jones face detector and extracts facial landmark points using a multi-view active shape model tracker. Scale-invariant feature transform (SIFT) features are extracted from detected face regions and dimensionally reduced with the minimum redundancy maximum relevance algorithm. SIFT features are subsequently fused with geometric features. A SVM classifier then predicts the fused features into one of the three emotion categories, namely, positive, negative or neutral, where basic emotions like happiness and surprise constitute positive while fear, sadness, and anger are combined into negative.

Four features acquired from FER ($Feat_1$-$Feat_4$) are intensity scores for positive (POS), negative (NEG), non-neutral (NNEU), and neutral (NEU) categories. Positive, negative, and neutral scores are directly obtained from the output of FER, which is a frame-by-frame probabilistic emotion intensity score for each of the three emotion categories (i.e., $P^{POS,NEG,NEU}$). Each of these scores varies between [0, 1] and their sum equals to 1 (i.e., $P^{POS}+ P^{NEG}+ P^{NEU}=1$). The FER output can be represented as a two-dimensional intensity score signal of time (discrete as frame numbers). A non-neural probabilistic score (i.e., P^{NNEU}) for each frame is computed by taking the maximum of positive or negative scores, where non-neutral means facial expression which is not neutral. It indicates the maximum emotional (regardless of positive or negative) responses of a viewer to the video content. There may be cases of dropped frame when the ASM tracker in FER system cannot track the face due to rapid movement, eye closure etc. The intensity values for the missing frames are obtained using linear interpolation of the intensity scores from two neighboring frames. The mean and standard deviation of the total number of observations are 21144 and 7244 for five clips.

Table 2. Extracted features from facial expression and heart rate data

Modality	Features	Description
Facial expression	$Feat_1$ - $Feat_4$	Intensity scores for positive, negative, non-neutral (i.e., not neutral), and neutral emotion categories
Heart rate	$Feat_5$	Normalized heart rate readings in beats-per-minute
	$Feat_6$ - $Feat_{10}$	Derivative (Rate-of-change), local maxima, variance, gradient, energy in low frequency band

4.2 Heart Rate Feature Extraction

The usefulness of time-domain and frequency-domain features of heart rate signal such as heart rate reading, maximum, derivative, standard deviation, and gradient of heart rate, as well as energy from high and low frequency bands has been proved by previous work [7, 13, 20]. This study computes five heart rate features ($Feat_6$-$Feat_{10}$), including time-derivative, local maxima, variance, gradient, and low-frequency band energy, using a feature extraction algorithm from [3].

Raw heart rate data is normalized by mean subtraction and then smoothed by a 9 seconds moving average low-pass filter. Since the heart rate sampling rate is 1/3 Hz, it is observed that a window smaller than 9 seconds includes less than 4 heart rate observations which would be insufficient to capture the time varying information. This window length is also not large enough where the state of interest can change. Therefore, a 9 seconds sliding window is used for heart rate feature extraction. For estimating the derivative, first order numerical approximation is used as the difference between adjacent time samples, and its absolute value is averaged over the entire window, using equation 1. Here, $\{hr_i, \ldots, hr_{i+3}\}$ are any four consecutive heart rate observations within the sliding window (i.e., $\{t_i, \ldots, t_{i+3}\}$) at a particular point of time. Local maxima and variance are also estimated over each sliding window. The gradient is calculated as the average of a series of directional values for an increasing order of heart rate observations as shown in equation 2. Energy is computed by applying a band-pass filter with passbands between 0.04 and 0.15 Hz over the heart rate samples. Energy only from low-frequency band is computed due to the low sampling rate (1/3 Hz) of heart rate signals. The mean and standard deviation of the number of observations are 284 and 97 for five clips.

$$\text{derivative} = \sum_{i}^{i+3} | hr_{i+3} - hr_i | / (t_{i+3} - t_i) \quad (1)$$

$$\text{gradient} = \mu \mid \delta\{hr_i, .., hr_{i+3}\} / \delta\{i, .., i+3\} \mid \quad (2)$$

4.3 Statistical Hypothesis Tests

The extracted features are expected to have differences across both sports types. To investigate this, statistical hypothesis tests are conducted for each subject over facial expression and heart rate features obtained from the 9 common subjects. Four facial expression and heart rate features are manually selected for hypothesis test including intensity scores of positive, negative, non-neutral emotion categories ($Feat_1$- $Feat_3$) and heart rate reading in beats-per-minute ($Feat_5$). Neutral scores are not used since they are expected to have less correlation with viewer interest. The selected facial expression and heart rate features are smoothed using a moving average low-pass filter respectively of 5 seconds and 9 seconds spans to eliminate rapid fluctuation and over-smoothing.

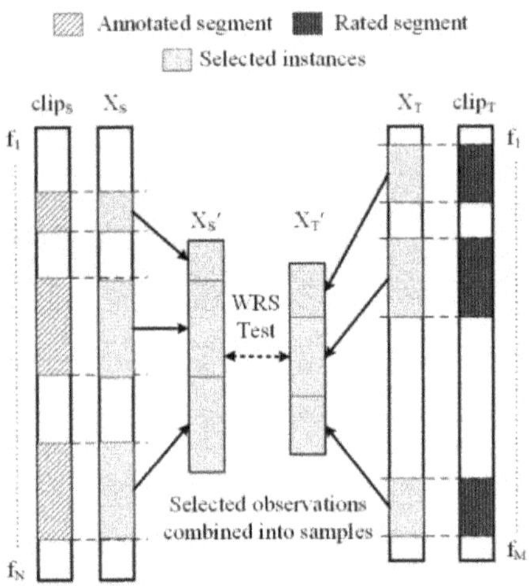

Figure 2. Schematic representation of the data selection procedure for the hypothesis test where X_S and X_T are the response data for soccer clip, clip$_S$ and tennis clip, clip$_T$.

The hypothesis test is conducted over a subset of observations from each of the four selected features, which incorporate interests of individual subjects. The selection of observations is essential since the hypothesis is supposed to be conducted over 'viewer interest' data. The observations are selected based on subject-dependent ground truth (introduced in Section 3.4). This ground truth includes time indices of segments which are annotated (or rated) as *interesting* and thus useful to select the desired observations. Figure 2 illustrates how the observations are selected and combined into samples over which a hypothesis test is conducted. Let X_S and X_T be any feature from {$Feat_1$, $Feat_2$, $Feat_3$, $Feat_5$} of a random subject for a soccer clip (clip$_S$) and tennis clip (clip$_T$). The time stamped observations can be temporally aligned along with the time indices in ground truth. The sampling rate of heart rate signal is different from stimuli frame rate and an additional mapping is obtained to select heart rate observations. Observations which lie between the window of the starting and ending time indices are selected. The selected observations are combined into two samples, say, X_S' and X_T', where $X_S' \subset X_S$ and $X_T' \subset X_T$. A Lilliefors test is done prior to the hypothesis test to confirm that the sample data do not have a normal distribution. A two-sided *Wilcoxon rank sum* (WRS) hypothesis test [26] is then conducted over X_S' and X_T' (i.e., TEST (X_S', X_T')) to validate differences in the distributions of viewer interest data. The WRS test is performed with the null hypothesis that *"two data samples come from the same population"*. The significance level, α is set to 0.05. One outcome of the test is p-value, which indicates the significance of the test result. The other outcome is h = {0, 1}, which indicates the acceptance (0) or rejection (1) of the null hypothesis.

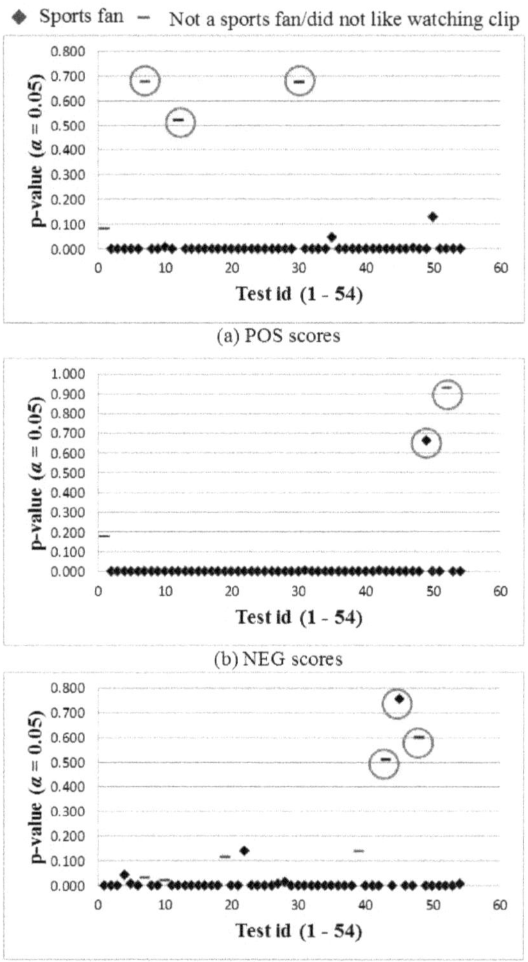

Figure 3. The p-values of 54 hypothesis tests on the distributions of: (a) POS; (b) NEG; and (c) NNEU scores of facial expression samples. Cases where the null hypothesis is accepted with p-values > 0.05 are circled in red.

The hypothesis tests are conducted in 6 combinations between 3 soccer and 2 tennis clips. Therefore, for each of the four features {$Feat_1$, $Feat_2$, $Feat_3$, $Feat_5$}, the total number of trials on 9 subjects' data is 54. The mean sample sizes for five clips are 12.75%, 15.84%, 22.89%, 40%, and 26% of the total number of observations respectively. Besides p-value and h, additional statistics including the mean, standard deviation, skewness, and kurtosis are computed in each test. These statistics are computed to verify the test results.

4.4 Results of Variations in Viewer Interest

According to the WRS test results, the null hypothesis is rejected with significantly low p-values (i.e., $p < \alpha = 0.05$) in most cases (FE: 91%, HR: 100% cases). A *p*-value less than α indicates the rejection of null hypothesis with a significant low value and subsequently suggests significant statistical difference exists between the two data samples. Figure 3 illustrates the scatter plots of all p-values computed from the 54 tests for POS, NEG, and NNEU scores, sorted according to subject id and test id. For example, tests 1-9 contain results for subjects 1-9; tests 10-18 contain results for subjects 1-9 and so on. The figure demonstrates significant statistical variations in the distributions of the features across two sports types. However, in a few cases (circled in red), the distributions of the features are found not to be statistically different, since the p-value is higher than 0.05. In all of these cases, the subject is not a sports fan and/or does not enjoy watching the clip (id: 1, 4, 9, marked as '-'). Data from these subjects do not constitute distinguishable distributions of interest. All other subjects are fans of either/both sports. This suggests subjective preference and profile have influence over viewer interest distributions. To investigate by which property most of the distributions differ, mean, standard deviation, skewness, and kurtosis are computed for each test.

4.4.1 Mean and standard deviation

The means of the distributions have relatively small differences across two sports types. For soccer clips, the means of the POS, NEG, and NNEU scores range between 24% and 46%, while for tennis clips, the means are varying from 23% to 41% of the sample values. The difference is higher for HR (beats-per-minute) samples. The means for HR across soccer and tennis clips vary between 4.7% - 5% and 7% - 7.6% respectively. The standard deviations appear to be about 53% to 75% of the means. The mean varies from subject to subject and the overall mean for tennis clips is higher than for soccer clips. Subjects who are not sports fans tend to have smaller means. Since the means are found to be not statistically significantly different across two sports, higher order statistical moments of the distribution are computed to extract additional information.

4.4.2 Skewness

The distributions are found reversely skewed across soccer and tennis clips in majority (59%) cases, which suggest that the distributions of the samples differ in asymmetry. Figure 4 illustrates the histogram plots of the skewness values of POS, NEG, NNEU, and HR (beats-per-minute) samples. NNEU scores are less different in asymmetry across soccer and tennis (left skewed in 70% cases). The differences are more evident in POS, NEG, and HR samples. POS and NEG scores are right skewed in 81% and 47% cases for soccer and tennis respectively. The majority of the HR samples are found left skewed for soccer (55% cases) while they are right skewed for tennis (60% cases). HR samples are found closer to a normal form, regardless of sports types. Overall, distributions for soccer clips are found right skewed (skewness > 0) in 54% cases, while distributions for tennis clips are found left skewed (skewness < 0) in 51% cases. Average skewness is found higher for soccer than for tennis clips.

4.4.3 Kurtosis

Kurtosis values across two sports types are found statistically different in 61% cases. Figure 5 presents the histogram plots of the kurtosis values for POS, NEG, NNEU, and HR (beats-per-minute) samples for soccer and tennis. The histogram plot of HR samples depicts that most of the kurtosis values are less than three, which indicates flatter distributions for both sports. Overall, the distributions for both sports types are flatter in majority cases (soccer: 72% cases, tennis: 74% cases). Mean kurtosis for soccer is higher than that for tennis. The absolute difference between kurtosis values for both sports types varies between 1.7 and 3.95.

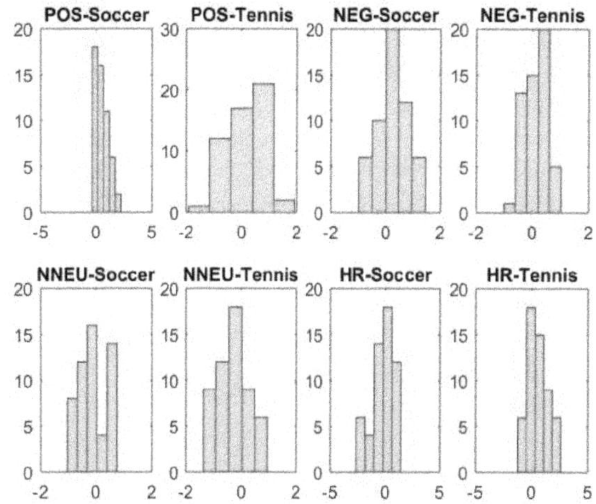

Figure 4. Histogram plots of skewness for the samples of POS, NEG, NNEU scores and HR (bpm).

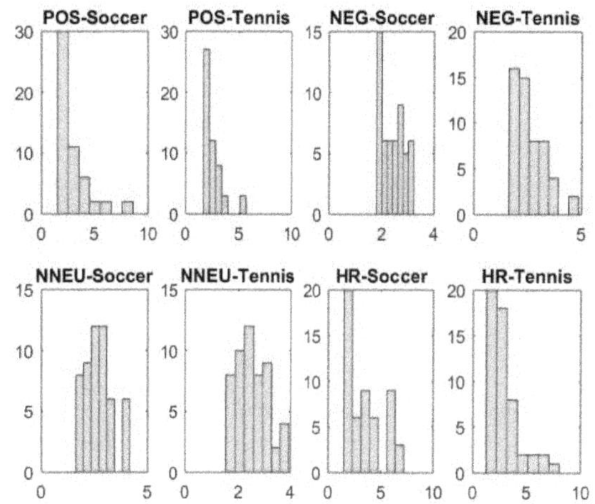

Figure 5. Histogram plots of kurtosis the samples of POS, NEG, NNEU scores and HR (bpm).

In summary, viewer interest data vary across different sports types and it is dependent on the subjective profile. The statistical differences in viewer interest data are apparent through higher order statistics like skewness and kurtosis rather than mean and standard deviation. Therefore, higher order statistics are expected to be useful in classification.

5. VIEWER INTEREST CLASSIFICATION

As statistical differences can be found in the distributions of viewer interest data across different sports types (discussed in Section 4), this section will verify whether a viewer interest classifier needs to be sports-specific. This section focuses on the methods to use GMM models for classifying viewer interest to identify sports video highlights and subsequently verify the generalizability of the models. GMM is well known for its non-parametric modeling capability in supervised learning environment. Two facial expression features and three heart rate features are manually selected and concatenated for classification.

The non-neutral and neutral scores from facial expression $\{Feat_3, Feat_4\}$ are selected, since non-neutral scores combine both positive and negative scores, and thus reduce subjective bias. Three heart rate features including derivative, local maxima, and energy $\{Feat_6, Feat_7, Feat_{10}\}$ are selected for classification, due to the high correlation of variance and gradient with derivative ($r = 0.83, 0.97$). These five features are further normalized using z-score standardization prior to classification. A principle component analysis is applied to reduce data dependency.

For testing generalizability, this study investigates whether a model trained with soccer data (i.e., features) would perform well for tennis data and vice-versa. This is also investigated how well a model trained with both soccer and tennis data would perform against data from each of them. Table 3 shows how data for two sports types are utilized to conduct training and testing as well as the cross-validation methods applied.

Table 3. Strategies to separate features into training-testing sets and to cross-validate

Classification Approach	Training Data	Testing Data	Cross-validation
Sports-specific	Soccer (or Tennis)	Same sports as training	Leave-one-viewer-out
Cross-sports	Soccer	Tennis	Subject-wise
Sports-independent	Soccer + Tennis	Soccer (or Tennis)	Leave-one-viewer-out

5.1 Cross-validation

Training and testing data are split using the sports-specific, cross-sports, and sports-independent approaches (see Table 3). The approaches are identical for facial expression and heart rate features. Totally, 60 sets of facial expression and 60 sets of heart rate features are obtained from the response data of 12 subjects for 5 clips. Let Y_k be an augmented feature vector that contains features from all 12 subjects for the kth clip, $k = \{1, 2, 3, 4, 5\}$. And Y_k is defined as $\{y_1, ..., y_{12}\}$, where y_i designates the ith subject's features. When only 'feature' is denoted, it is generic and applicable to both facial expression and heart rate features.

5.1.1 Sports-specific approach

Both training and testing are done with the same sports type (i.e., soccer vs soccer and tennis vs tennis) in this approach. Clip-wise leave-one-viewer-out cross-validation is applied and iterated for each subject. For example, for each soccer clip, the testing and training data sets are distributed as $y_i : (\bigcup_{k=1}^{3} Y_k) - y_i$, where y_i is a feature from a random subject's data for that clip and k denotes ids $\{1, 2, 3\}$ of three soccer clips. The 'U' symbol indicates the combination of the features from all subjects' data for the soccer clips. For tennis clips, the approach is identical except $k = \{4, 5\}$.

5.1.2 Cross-sports approach

Generalizability of a classification model is tested by training it with soccer data and testing against tennis data, in a subject-wise manner. By subject-wise it is meant that each subject's tennis data was tested against soccer data from all subjects. For example, for each tennis clips, each subject's feature data for that clip is used for testing and feature data from soccer clips from all subjects (i.e., $\bigcup_{k=1}^{3} Y_k$) are used for training.

5.1.3 Sports-independent approach

A model is trained with both soccer and tennis data and tested against each of them individually. A clip-wise leave-one-viewer-out cross-validation is utilized. For each of the five clips, each subject's feature data (i.e., y_i) is used for testing, while the rest feature data (i.e., $(\bigcup_{k=1}^{5} Y_k) - y_i$) are used for training the classification model. This method is iterated for each subject.

5.2 Classification Procedure

Let TR and TS be the dataset splits for training and testing respectively, using the cross-validation approaches described in Section 5.1. The labels of the features are obtained by a temporal mapping with the time indices of ground truth (described in Sections 3.4 and 3.5). The goal here is to examine whether viewer interest can be classified (with the approaches in Table 3) from facial expression and heart rate features. The labels of the time indices are thus utilized to label the features and separate them into *interesting* and *non-interesting* subsets for training $\{TR_I, TR_{NI}\}$ and testing $\{TS_I, TS_{NI}\}$. Two GMMs, γ_I, γ_{NI}, are trained with the *interesting* and *non-interesting* training data (i.e., TR_I, TR_{NI}) respectively using equations 3 and 4. The optimum number of components for each GMM is computed using Akaike Information Criteria (AIC).

$$\gamma_I = \sum_{j=1}^{c} w_j d(TR_I | \mu_j, \Sigma j) \quad (3)$$

$$\gamma_{NI} = \sum_{j=1}^{c} w_j d(TR_{NI} | \mu_j, \Sigma j) \quad (4)$$

where w_j is the weight of the mixture and d is the Gaussian density. In the testing phase, each *interesting* and *non-interesting* feature subset from a subject (i.e., TS_I or TS_{NI}) is then cross-compared against the two GMMs. Each time a posterior probability and a likelihood score are computed as outputs. The label of that particular feature subset is obtained based on the label of the GMM, which produces the higher likelihood score. Testing is done in a clip-wise manner.

5.3 Decision Fusion

A decision-level fusion technique over the classification labels for facial expression and heart rate features is applied, to test the hypothesis that fusion of facial expression and heart rate would perform better than using each individually. A Naïve Bayes combiner is used to fuse the labels as described in [27]. Naïve Bayes combiner is a Bayesian Classifier Combination (BCC) technique which assumes that the classifiers are mutually independent and it utilizes probability scores. Independent BCC is found outperforming the dependent BCC and majority voting approaches [28, 29].

Two c×c (c = 2, for binary classes) confusion matrices for facial expression (CM_{FE}) and heart rate (CM_{HR}) are computed, using the computed labels obtained in the classification phase. The suffixes stand for facial expression and heart rate respectively. Consider, N_1 and N_2 are the numbers of *interesting* and *non-interesting* segments respectively in a particular clip. If $S_{i,j}$ is the number of segments for which the true label is i but assigned as label j in the (facial expression or heart rate) classification phase, each entry of the confusion matrix, $CM_{\{FE,HR\}}(i, j)$ is computed using equation 5.

$$CM_{\{FE,HR\}}(i, j) = (S_{i,j} + (1 / c)) / (N_i + 1) \quad (5)$$

A Naïve Bayes combiner combines labels using the confusion matrices. For each segment (*interesting* or *non-interesting*) and for each class, a posterior probability is computed based on $CM_{\{FE,HR\}}$ and $N_{k=\{1,2\}}$. The label with the maximum posterior probability is used as the final fused label.

Table 4. Clip-wise precision-rates (PR), recall-rates (RR), and accuracy (F1-score in %) of sports-specific, sports-independent, and cross-sports classification models for FE, HR, and their fusion

		Soccer						Tennis					
		Sports-specific			Sports-independent			Sports-specific		Sports-independent		Cross-sports	
		$clip_1$	$clip_2$	$clip_3$	$clip_1$	$clip_2$	$clip_3$	$clip_4$	$clip_5$	$clip_4$	$clip_5$	$clip_4$	$clip_5$
FE	PR	57	48	51	58	49	52	50	51	36	50	52	56
	RR	66	52	50	**64**	**55**	**59**	64	59	**63**	**65**	**67**	**53**
	F1	61	50	50	**61**	**52**	**55**	56	55	**46**	**57**	**59**	**54**
HR	PR	51	41	30	48	41	50	49	48	11	35	46	53
	RR	34	25	11	17	15	19	58	34	9	12	65	21
	F1	41	31	16	25	22	28	53	40	10	18	54	30
FUSION	PR	**64**	**63**	**54**	**72**	**59**	**61**	**61**	**53**	**47**	**53**	**52**	**64**
	RR	**69**	**54**	**51**	52	41	28	**65**	**68**	38	55	36	38
	F1	**66**	**58**	**52**	60	48	38	**63**	**60**	42	54	43	48

5.4 Classification Performance Metrics

Precision, recall, and F1-scores are computed for each subject and further averaged over all subjects for each clip and reported as the precision rate (PR), recall rate (RR), and accuracy in Table 4. Accuracy (i.e., F1-score) has been computed as: 2×(PR×RR)/(PR+RR). The sizes of the comparisons for computing precision-recall are 252 for $clip_1$, $clip_2$, $clip_5$ and 204 for $clip_3$, $clip_4$. These numbers represent the total number of comparisons for all subjects in a clip-wise manner. The performance measures have been done for each clip to inspect any possible stimuli dependence in classification results.

5.5 Results of Classification Performance

The sports-specific approach yields higher performance than cross-sports and sports-independent approaches. The means and standard deviations of the F1-score rates are respectively: 53% and 13% for sports-specific; 44% and 10% for cross-sports; 41% and 17% for sports-independent. The marginal difference between the overall accuracies of sports-independent and cross-sports approaches is small. Fusion achieves higher precision and accuracy than FE and HR in general. The standard deviations of the precision, recall and F1-score rates range between 7% and 31%, which suggests non-uniform variations across subjects and clips. Clip-wise and subject-wise variations are expected due to differences in event characteristics (across clips) and subject demographics.

Table 4 depicts clip-wise F1-socres computed (in %) in three approaches for FE, HR, and their fusion. Sports-specific approach outperforms other two approaches in term of individual modality as well. Overall, FE, HR, and fusion achieve higher accuracy in sports-specific (mean accuracy - FE: 55%, HR: 39%, fusion: 60.4%) approach than sports-independent (mean accuracy - FE: 52.3%, HR: 20.6%, fusion: 48.4%) and cross-sports (mean accuracy - FE: 53.5%, HR: 37%, fusion: 45.5%) approaches. Fusion of FE and HR has higher accuracy than each of them in sports-specific approach. In contrast, FE achieves higher accuracy than HR and fusion in sports-independent and cross-sports approaches, due to low performance of HR. Table 4 also contains clip-wise precision and recall rates for the three classification approaches. FE has higher precision and recall than HR in general. Fusion has higher precision and recall than FE and HR for sports-specific models while for sports-independent and cross-sports models fusion has higher precision only. Results from sports-independent and cross-sports models suggest that FE produces overall higher recall than HR and fusion. In these cases, lower performance of HR features influences the overall performance of fusion.

The results suggest that overall classification performance does not increase in the sports-independent approach and cross-sports model performs poorer compared to the sports-specific approach. This is expected as a statistically significant difference is found in the distributions of the viewers across soccer and tennis clips.

6. DISCUSSION

This study uses long-duration video stimuli to maintain a consistent subjective attention. The distributions of viewer interest data vary significantly between soccer and tennis clips, except for those who are not sports fans and/or did not enjoy watching. This confirms that subjective profile and preference has a strong influence on viewer's experience. The distributions are different in higher order statistics like skewness and kurtosis but not in the mean or the standard deviation. This suggests that the difference is subtle which first order statistics fail to extract.

Classification results demonstrate that a generic classifier is less robust compared to sports-specific models due to the demonstrated statistical differences in distributions. Sports-independent (F1: 41±17%) and cross-sports (F1: 44±10%) models have a similar range of accuracies. This also suggests the influence of statistical differences in viewer interest data. It is also evident that fusion of facial expression and heart rate performs better than each of them individually, which is expected. However, in few cases facial expression is outperforming fusion since the heart rate signal is performing low. Heart rate generally has lower accuracy in generic models compared to sports-specific models, which suggests that heart rate is more sensitive to content than facial expression.

7. CONCLUSION

This paper demonstrates the existence of differences in viewer interest across different sports. The statistical differences in viewer interest distributions are more evident in higher order statistics and found to be sensitive to subjective profile. This paper also validates the feasibility of training a general classifier for highlighting viewer interests in sports videos. However due to the significant statistical differences in the collective viewer interest across different sports, a domain-specific classifier appears to be more effective. The experimental results confirmed that sports-specific models perform better (F1: 53±13%) than sports-independent (F1: 41±17%) and cross-sports (F1: 44±10%) models. Future study will involve more participants, full-length clips, higher accuracy heart rate sensor, and more sophisticated features to improve the performance of the classification models.

8. REFERENCES

[1] Silvia, P. J. 2008. Interest—The curious emotion. *Current Directions in Psychological Science* 17, 1, 57-60.

[2] Silvia, P. J. 2006. *Exploring the psychology of interest.* Oxford University Press, Oxford, UK.

[3] Chakraborty, P. R., Zhang, L., Tjondronegoro, D. and Chandran, V. 2015. Using Viewer's Facial Expression and Heart Rate for Sports Video Highlights Detection. In *Proceedings of the 5th ACM on International Conference on Multimedia Retrieval* (Shanghai, China, June 23 - 26, 2015). ICMR '15. ACM, New York, NY, 371-378.

[4] Soleymani, M., Pantic, M. and Pun, T. 2012. Multimodal emotion recognition in response to videos. *IEEE Transactions on Affective Computing* 3, 2 (Apr. 2012), 211-223.

[5] Joho, H., Staiano, J., Sebe, N. and Jose, J. M. 2011. Looking at the viewer: analysing facial activity to detect personal highlights of multimedia contents. *Multimedia Tools and Applications* 51, 2 (Jan. 2011), 505-523.

[6] Peng, W. T., Chu, W. T., Chang, C. H., Chou, C. N., Huang, W. J., Chang, W. Y. and Hung, Y. P. 2011. Editing by viewing: automatic home video summarization by viewing behavior analysis. *IEEE Transactions on Multimedia* 13, 3 (Jun. 2011), 539-550. DOI: 10.1109/TMM.2011.2131638.

[7] Soleymani, M., Chanel, G., Kierkels, J. J. and Pun, T. 2008. Affective ranking of movie scenes using physiological signals and content analysis. In *Proceedings of the 2nd ACM workshop on Multimedia semantics.* MS '08. ACM, New York, NY, 32-39.

[8] Soleymani, M. and Pantic, M. 2012. *Human-centered implicit tagging: Overview and perspectives.* In *Proceedings of IEEE International Conference on Systems, Man, and Cybernetics.* SMC '12. IEEE. 3304-3309.

[9] Teixeira, T., Wedel, M. and Pieters, R. Emotion-induced engagement in internet video advertisements. *Journal of Marketing Research* 49, 2 (Apr. 2012), 144-159.

[10] Tjondronegoro, D., Chen, Y. P. P. and Pham, B. 20014. Integrating highlights for more complete sports video summarization. *IEEE multimedia* 11, 4 (Oct. 2004), 22-37.

[11] Xu, H. and Chua, T. S. 2004. The fusion of audio-visual features and external knowledge for event detection in team sports video. In *Proceedings of the 6th ACM SIGMM International Workshop on Multimedia Information Retrieval.* MIR '04. ACM, New York, NY, 127-134.

[12] Bos, M. G., Jentgens, P., Beckers, T. and Kindt, M. 2013. Psychophysiological response patterns to affective film stimuli. *PloS one* 8, 4 (Apr. 2013).

[13] Fleureau, J., Guillotel, P. and Huynh-Thu, Q. 2012. Physiological-based affect event detector for entertainment video applications. *IEEE Transactions on Affective Computing* 3, 3 (Jul. 2012), 379-385.

[14] Arapakis, I., Konstas, I. and Jose, J. M. 2009. Using facial expressions and peripheral physiological signals as implicit indicators of topical relevance. In *Proceedings of the 17th ACM International Conference on Multimedia.* MM '09. ACM, New York, NY, 461-470.

[15] Lang, P. J., Greenwald, M. K., Bradley, M. M. and Hamm, A. O. 1993. Looking at pictures: Affective, facial, visceral, and behavioral reactions. *Psychophysiology* 30, 3 (May 1993), 261-273. DOI: 10.1111/j.1469-8986.1993.tb03352.x.

[16] Potter, R. F. and Keene, J. R. 2012. The effect of sports fan identification on the cognitive processing of sports news. *International Journal of Sport Communication* 5, 3 (Sep. 2012), 348-367.

[17] Hernandez, J., Liu, Z., Hulten, G., DeBarr, D., Krum, K. and Zhang, Z. 2013. Measuring the engagement level of TV viewers. In *Proceedings of 10th IEEE International Conference and Workshops on Automatic Face and Gesture Recognition* (April 22 - 26, 2013). FG '13. IEEE, 1-7.

[18] Navarathna, R., Lucey, P., Carr, P., Carter, E., Sridharan, S. and Matthews, I. 2014. Predicting movie ratings from audience behaviors. In *Proceedingds of IEEE Winter Conference on Applications of Computer Vision.* WACV '14. IEEE, 1058-1065. DOI: 10.1109/WACV.2014.6835987.

[19] Soleymani, M., Chanel, G., Kierkels, J. J. and Pun, T. 2008. Affective characterization of movie scenes based on multimedia content analysis and user's physiological emotional responses. In *Proceedings of 10th IEEE International Symposium on Multimedia* (December 15 - 17, 2008). ISM '08. IEEE, 228-235.

[20] Ong, K.-M. and Kameyama, W. 2010. Video summary based on human bio-signals-Evaluation of its applicability to first-time viewers. In *Proceedings of 2nd International Symposium on Aware Computing.* ISAC '10. IEEE, 251-256.

[21] Alpers, G. W., Adolph, D. and Pauli, P. 2011. Emotional scenes and facial expressions elicit different psychophysiological responses. *International Journal of Psychophysiology*, 80, 3 (Jun. 2011), 173-181.

[22] McDuff, D., El Kaliouby, R., Kodra, E. and Picard, R. 2013. Measuring Voter's Candidate Preference Based on Affective Responses to Election Debates. In *Proceedings of Humaine Association Conference on Affective Computing and Intelligent Interaction.* IEEE, 369-374.

[23] Wang, J.-C., Yang, Y.-H., Jhuo, I., Lin, Y.-Y. and Wang, H.-M. 2012. The acousticvisual emotion Guassians model for automatic generation of music video. In *Proceedings of the 20th ACM international conference on Multimedia.* ACM, 1379-1380.

[24] Wang, J. C., Yang, Y. H., Wang, H. M. and Jeng, S. K. 2015. Modeling the affective content of music with a Gaussian mixture model. *IEEE Transaction on Affective Computing* 6, 1 (Jan. 2015), 56-68.

[25] Tjondronegoro, D. W., Chen, Y.-P. P. and Pham, B. 2004. Classification of self-consumable highlights for soccer video summaries. In *Proceedings of IEEE International Conference on Multimedia and Expo.* ICME '04. IEEE, 579-582.

[26] Haynes, W. 2013. Wilcoxon Rank Sum Test. *Encyclopedia of Systems Biology.* Springer, 2354-2355.

[27] Kuncheva, L. I. 20014. *Combining pattern classifiers: methods and algorithms.* John Wiley & Sons., Hoboken, US.

[28] Kim, H. C. and Ghahramani, Z. 2012. Bayesian classifier combination. In *Proceedings of International Conference on Artificial Intelligence and Statistics.* 619-627.

[29] Kuncheva, L. 2003. "Fuzzy" versus" nonfuzzy" in combining classifiers designed by Boosting. *IEEE Transactions on Fuzzy Systems* 11, 6 (Dec. 2003), 729-741.

[30] Zhang, L., Tjondronegoro, D. and Chandran, V. 2014. Facial expression recognition experiments with data from television broadcasts and the World Wide Web. *Image and Vision Computing* 32, 2 (Feb. 2014), 107-119.

Diverse Concept-Level Features for Multi-Object Classification

Youssef Tamaazousti[1,2] Hervé Le Borgne[1] Céline Hudelot[2]
[1]CEA, LIST, Laboratory of Vision and Content Engineering, F-91191 Gif-sur-Yvette, France
[2]University of Paris-Saclay, MICS, 92295 Châtenay-Malabry, France
{youssef.tamaazousti,herve.le-borgne}@cea.fr, celine.hudelot@centralesupelec.fr

ABSTRACT

We consider the problem of image classification with semantic features that are built from a set of base classifier outputs, each reflecting visual concepts. However, existing approaches consider visual concepts independently from each other whereas they are often linked together. When those relations are considered, existing models strongly rely on image low-level features, yielding in irrelevant relations when the low-level representation fails. On the contrary, the approach we propose, uses existing human knowledge, the application context itself and the human categorization mechanism to reflect complex relations between concepts. By nesting this human knowledge and the application context in the concept detection and selection processes, our final semantic feature captures the most useful information for an effective categorization. Thus, it enables to give good representation, even if some important concepts failed to be recognized. Experimental validation is conducted on three publicly available benchmarks of multi-class object classification and leads to results that outperforms comparable approaches.

Keywords

Image-Classification, Semantic-Features, Category-Level

1. INTRODUCTION

The problem of object class recognition in large scale image databases is a topic of high interest in the vision community [1, 3, 14, 24, 26]. In parallel to the mainstream data-driven approach, based on convolutional neural networks (CNNs) [3, 24], several works adopted a concept-driven scheme to design semantically grounded image features, that we name *semantic features* in the following. Given the availability of large-scale image datasets, [14, 26] argued that an image representation based on a bench of object detectors is a promising way to handle natural images according to their category. These object detectors are more generally considered as the outputs of base classifiers. Such

ICMR'16, June 06-09, 2016, New York, NY, USA

DOI: http://dx.doi.org/10.1145/2911996.2912013

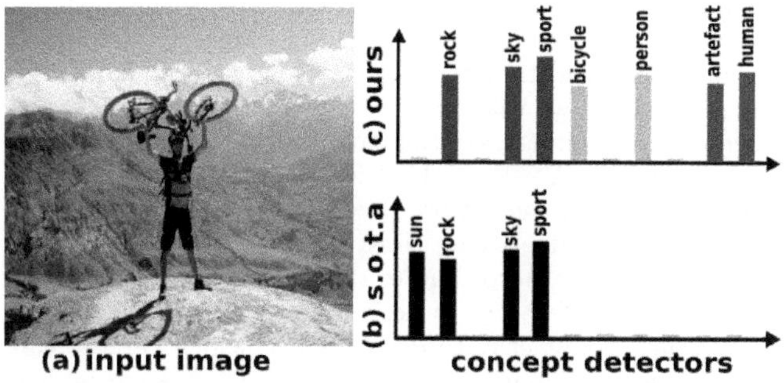

Figure 1: We propose a semantic representation that compute the concepts presence differently according to their categorical level. For an input image (a) with multiple objects, state-of-the-art semantic features (b) would output the concepts illustrated in black and miss useful concepts, such as person and bicycle. In contrast, the proposed scheme (c) capture properties of the image that are useful for categorization, *e.g.* *superordinate* (brown), *basic-level* (gray) and *subordinate* (blue) concepts, making the representation more relevant. Best viewed in color.

approaches offer a rich high-level description of images that is close to the human understanding. Moreover, they can benefit from the advances of the data-driven works that propose better mid-level features in order to improve the base classifiers. Semantic features are also scalable in terms of number of concepts thus being able to cope with a wide variety of content.

Most semantic features in the literature [2, 10, 12, 14, 26] consider visual concepts independently from each other whereas they are often linked together by some semantic relationships (*i.e.*hyponymy, hypernymy, exclusion, etc.). An exception is the work of Bergamo and Torresani [1] that introduces "meta-classes" to address this aspect. Those meta-classes are "abstract" categories (do not really exist in the real-world) that capture common properties among many object classes. They are built using spectral clustering on low-level features of images among a set of categories. The restrictive assumption of this method, is the dependence of the meta-class learning to the visual low-level features. For instance, it leads to irrelevant meta-classes when low-level feature fails to capture the dissimilarity between different categories, making this method a "bottom-up" scheme.

The classical formulation of semantic features exploits all

classifier outputs [1, 2, 14, 26] but it was recently shown that forcing the semantic representation to be sparse (by setting the lowest values to zero) can be beneficial both in terms of scalability and performance [10, 12]. Nevertheless, semantic features with a large set of concept detectors often contains a high number of visually similar concepts to describe the same object. For instance, the right image of Figure 2 would be predicted by a semantic feature as a *palm cockatoo*, but also a *cockatoo*, a *parrot*, a *bird*, a *vertebrate*, and so on, inducing redundant information in the final representation. As far as a human is concerned, he would categorized this image as *a bird*, an *animal* and maybe a *palm cockatoo* if the human is a bird-expert. In fact, psychologists studies such as those of Rosch [20] and Kosslyn [15] showed that a human tends to categorize an object through three categorical-levels (i) basic-level, (ii) superordinate, and (iii) subordinate. They are the most important concept types to categorize objects.

In this paper, we take into account the relations between concepts using human existing knowledge, such as semantic hierarchies (*e.g* WordNet [17]), which makes our approach a "top-down" scheme. More precisely, our main contribution consists in identifying three types of concepts into an existing hierarchy, according to their categorical level, then process them differently to design the semantic feature. It is nevertheless not easy to determine to which categorical-level a concept belongs to. Hence, we propose a method to identify the three groups in practice, for a given supervised classification problem. The proposed semantic representation is named Diverse Concept-Level feature (**D-CL**).

Compared to bottom-up approaches, an advantage of the proposed top-down scheme appears when the concept detectors fails at the subordinate level (*e.g.* the concepts *cockatoo* and *parakeet* are highly activated), which is often the case since the category is finer thus harder to identify. In that case, our descriptor at least capture basic-level and superordinate concepts (*e.g.* bird and animal), making the full representation more robust for classification problems. Moreover, the proposed feature contains only useful concepts (from the three categorical levels), which avoids redundant information that disturbs the image classification.

We validate the proposed Diverse Concept-Level representation, in a multi-object classification task through Pascal VOC 2007, Pascal VOC 2012 and Nus-Wide Object. The experiments show that the proposed approach obtains better results than seven state-of-the-art semantic features.

The remainder of this paper is organized as follows. Section 2 briefly introduces related works. Section 3 details the proposed technical approach. After showing experiments and analytic studies in Section 4, we conclude in Section 5.

2. RELATED WORKS

The current trend in image classification is to exploit mid-level features obtained with deep convolutional neural networks, such as Overfeat [23], Caffe [13] or VGG-Net [24]. Built on top of such mid-level representations, we focus on *semantic features* that: (i) include a rich representation of images, (ii) provide a humanly understandable description of content, and (iii) are more flexible since concepts are learned independently from each other. This semantic-based approach has been introduced by Torresani *et al.* [26] and Li *et al.* [14] with a limited number of concepts. The former used nonlinear LP-β [9] classifiers to learn each concept detector. Recently, Ginsca *et al.* [10] and Jain *et al.* [12] explored linear SVMs in semantic features and shows their effectiveness when the features are constrained to be sparse.

The feature is said *sparse* when, for a given image, only a limited number of dimension is non-zero. For instance, Li *et al.* [14] managed this sparsity aspect at learning time through the regularization of logistic regression by L_1 or L_1/L_2 [27]. Torresani *et al.* [26] did not investigate directly the sparse aspect but showed that classemes was quite robust to a 1-bit quantization. In practice, they forced negative outputs to zero thus they actually performed a sparsification. The difference with further works is that they also unified positive outputs to 1. Recent works such as [10, 12] exhibit very good performances in image retrieval, and action classification on videos, by retaining in the final feature, a small (but fixed) number of the largest classifier outputs (less than 100). In our scheme, the sparsity is a consequence of the proposed concept groups identification . Thus, in terms of sparsity, the key novelty of our work is the selection of concepts regarding their identified categorical-level, yielding to representations containing only useful concepts. Contrary to former works, our sparse representation is adapted to each image, according to its actual content, and relative to the problem of interest.

Regarding the general concepts in semantic features, Bergamo *et al.* [1] proposed "meta-classes", corresponding to "abstract" categories that captures common properties among many object classes. In our work, we also use general concepts, that captures common properties among object classes, but the key difference with their work is the building of these categories. While [1] automatically built the meta-classes using spectral clustering on low-level features of images among a set of categories, our scheme rely on a direct selection of concepts among those of WordNet [17], that have the advantage to match a semantic reality and is thus more relevant on a user point-of-view.

A last line of work deals with cognitive studies in pattern recognition [6, 16, 18, 19]. The main goal of these works is to propose a system that takes as input a set of predicted concepts for an image and outputs the corresponding basic-level concepts. In particular, the work of Deng *et al.* [6] is related to ours since they optimize the trade-off between accuracy and specificity. In other words, if concept detector fails to recognize categories at a specific level, they try to output a more general concept. As in our work, they indirectly reflect in their systems the psychological fact that even if humans tend to categorize an object at a particular level (basic-level), they are still aware of the other levels of categorization. However, the key difference between their work and ours is the method used to integrate this psychological fact as well as its purpose. In fact, our goal is to identify the most important concepts to retain in the semantic feature. In contrast, their goal is to annotate the images, and consequently identify only one concept. More precisely, we opt for an integration of the psychological fact directly in the semantic feature design, while they do it only on the test images, after the prediction of the different concepts.

3. PROPOSED APPROACH

In this section, we detail our proposed approach, a new semantic representation of an image that take into account an available human knowledge. In Section 3.1, we present our main contribution, consisting in identifying three types of concepts into an existing hierarchy (according to their

Superordinate: **vehicle** Superordinate: **animal**
Basic-level: **car** Basic-level: **bird**
Subordinate: **ford_mustang** Subordinate: **palm_cockatoo**

Figure 2: Illustration of concepts that our D-CL feature would predict, for two different images. It select concepts from different categorical levels of a semantic hierarchy, *i.e.*, superordinate, basic-level and subordinate concepts.

categorical level) and then, process their concepts differently. It is nevertheless, not evident to identify these three groups, in practice. Thus, we detail in Section 3.2 how to identify them, for a given supervised classification problem.

3.1 Diverse Concept-Level Feature

A semantic feature is a F-dimensional vector $\mathcal{F}(\mathbf{x}) = [\mathcal{F}_1(\mathbf{x}), \ldots, \mathcal{F}_F(\mathbf{x})]$ extracted from an image I, itself described by a mid-level feature $\mathbf{x}$. The feature $\mathbf{x}$ could be any image descriptor such as Bag-of-Word or Fisher Kernel [11] features, but also mid-level features such as that obtained from a fully-connected layer of a convolutional neural network. Each dimension $\mathcal{F}_i(\mathbf{x})$ of the semantic feature is the output of a classifier for the concept c_i evaluated on $\mathbf{x}$.

While the concepts c_i are potentially linked together by some semantic relationships, most of works consider them independently [2, 10, 12, 14, 26]. A notable exception is the work of Bergamo and Torresani [1] that take into account relations between categories through a "bottom-up" scheme. However, their method can lead to irrelevant identification of relation when the low/mid-level features used fails to capture the dissimilarity between different categories. To cope with such a limitation, we propose to rely on existing human knowledge regarding the relations between concepts. Such a knowledge is, for instance, reflected into existing hierarchies such as WordNet [17] that organize a large set of concepts according to "is-a" relationships, that is to say by defining hyponyms and hypernyms. An advantage of our approach is to remove the dependence to the basic visual descriptor and to introduce human-based information within the process of image representation design.

All the concepts considered in semantic features, are named according existing *categories*. Once again, the *name* of a category is given according to a human judgment, and the exact choice of the word used is far from being neutral, as a large literature has shown it, both in Psychology [15, 20] and Computer Vision[6, 16, 19]. More precisely, they showed the importance to differentiate several levels of categories:

- **Basic-level concepts** are the terms at which most people tend naturally to categorize objects, usually neither the most specific nor the most general available category but the one with the most distinctive attributes of the concept.
- **Superordinate concepts** are categories placed at the top of a semantic hierarchy and thus displays a high degree of class inclusion and a high degree of generality. They include basic-level and subordinate concepts.
- **Subordinate concepts** are found at the bottom of a semantic hierarchy and display a low degree of class inclusion and generality. As hyponyms of basic-level concepts, subordinate categories are highly specific.

At the core of our proposal to design a feature representation, concepts are processed differently according to their categorical level. This asymmetrical process is based on a cognitive study proposed by [15] where they conclude that, concepts are processed differently by humans, *i.e.*, it is purely perceptual for the basic-level and subordinate concepts, while it is inferred using stored semantic information, for superordinate concepts. In our scheme, basic-level and subordinate concepts are computed through a visual process, while superordinate concepts are processed semantically using the hyponym relations between concepts into hierarchies. Figure 2 illustrates for two input images, the three types of concepts that would be retained by our scheme.

More precisely, for an input image, the probability of a basic-level or a subordinate concept is the output of a binary classifier ($\varphi_i^V(\mathbf{x})$) for the concept c_i evaluated on the mid-level feature $\mathbf{x}$, further normalized by a sigmoid function such that $0 < \varphi_i^V(\cdot) < 1$. The binary classifiers, that we name *visual classifiers* in the following, have been learned using images of the concept c_i as positive samples and images of a diversified class as negative samples. Each concept classification model $\varphi_i^V(\cdot)$ is obtained with L_2-regularized linear SVM, but other linear models could be used. Regarding the process of basic-level and subordinate concepts, even if it is similar, a particular difference is that, all basic-level concepts are selected in the final representation, while for subordinate concepts, we select only the most salients. This particular process for subordinate concepts avoid redundancy of information, due to the fact pointed in [20] that there is more concepts at a subordinate level than at the basic-level.

Concepts (c_i) at the highest categorical level (superordinate) are computed, for an input image, through a *semantic classifier*. It is an inference of concepts that have at least one hyponym relation with the superordinate concept (c_i). We thus, define the subsumption function that aims to output the set of concepts having hyponym relations with an input concept. We further, define the semantic classifiers that are used to compute superordinate concepts.

Definition 1. A subsumption function $\varsigma(\cdot)$ takes as input a concept c_i and a semantic hierarchy $\mathcal{H}$ with hyponymy relations and outputs a set $\mathcal{C}_i$ of concepts that are subsumed by the concept c_i, *i.e.*, the concepts that have an hyponymy relation with the concept c_i in a semantic hierarchy.

Definition 2. Considering $x \in \mathbb{R}^N$ a N-dimensional mid-level feature extracted from an image I. A semantic classifier is an operator that predicts the probability of presence of a concept c_i in the image through a semantic inference of purely visual output classifiers: $\varphi_i^S(\mathbf{x}, \mathcal{C}_i) = max(\varphi_{\mathcal{C}_1}^V(\mathbf{x}), \cdots, \varphi_{\mathcal{C}_M}^V(\mathbf{x}))$, where $\mathcal{C}_i$ is the set of concepts subsumed by c_i, $M = card(\mathcal{C}_i)$ and $\varphi^V(\cdot)$ is the output values given by visual classifiers.

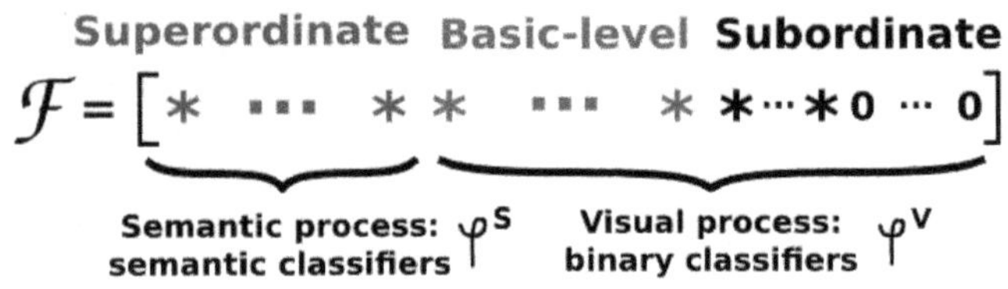

Figure 3: Illustration of the asymmetric process in our D-CL feature. Superordinate concepts are processed semantically through semantic classifiers, while basic-level and subordinate concepts are visually processed through binary classifiers. Stars and zeros represents output values $\mathcal{F}_i(\cdot)$ of each concept of the D-CL feature $\mathcal{F}(\cdot)$. Note that, concepts are grouped by categorical levels, but any order could be obtained in a real scheme.

Finally, the proposed "Diverse Concept-Level" (D-CL) feature computes superordinate concepts through a semantic classifier and all other concepts, *i.e.* basic-levels and subordinates, using visual classifier. It also selects all basic-level and superordinate concepts and retains only the most salients subordinate concepts. Formally, let's $\mathcal{N}$ be the set of all concepts associated to a semantic hierarchy, $\mathcal{BL}$ the set of all basic-level concepts, $\mathcal{P}$ the set of superordinate concepts, $\mathcal{B}$ the set of subordinate concepts and $\mathcal{B}^K$ the set of the K most salient subordinate concepts for each input image. Note that, $\mathcal{N} = \mathcal{P} \cup \mathcal{BL} \cup \mathcal{B}$. Each dimension $\mathcal{F}_i(\mathbf{x})$ of the D-CL feature $\mathcal{F}(\mathbf{x})$ is a concept detector computed through:

$$\mathcal{F}_i(\mathbf{x}) = \begin{cases} \varphi_i^S(\mathbf{x}, \varsigma(i)), & \text{if } c_i \in \mathcal{P} \\ \varphi_i^V(\mathbf{x}), & \text{if } c_i \in \mathcal{BL} \cup \mathcal{B}^K \\ 0 & \text{if } c_i \in \mathcal{B} \setminus \mathcal{B}^K \end{cases} \quad (1)$$

where $\varsigma(\cdot)$ is the subsumption function, $\varphi_i^V(\cdot)$ the visual classifier, $\varphi_i^S(\cdot)$ the semantic classifier and K is a parameter corresponding to the number of subordinate concepts retained in the representation, that can be set by cross-validation. An illustration of the asymmetric process according to the type of concepts is presented in Figure 3.

3.2 Identifying Concept Groups in Practice

In this section, we detail how to identify the three groups of concepts (*i.e.*, basic-level, superordinate and subordinate), in practice, for a given supervised classification problem.

As depicted in Equation 1, the D-CL feature is computed by activating all the basic-level concepts, all the superordinate concepts, the K most salient subordinate concepts and by deactivating all others. Let $\mathcal{F}(\mathbf{x})$ be the D-CL feature of a mid-level feature $\mathbf{x}$ extracted for an image I contained in a targeted dataset. Let $\mathcal{D}^d$ the set of d categories of the targeted dataset.

While basic-level concepts are not available at a large scale, we propose to identify, in an offline phase, the set of basic-level concepts ($\mathcal{BL}$) selected in our D-CL feature by matching it with the set of targeted dataset categories $\mathcal{D}^d$. This latter, is based on the assumption that broader-datasets mostly contain categories at the basic-level. Specifically, all targeted dataset categories d_i are matched with concepts c_i to generate a set of basic-level concepts adapted to the dataset $\mathcal{BL}^d$. In fact, this matching has the advantage to make our D-CL feature adaptable to the application context. Regarding the sets of superordinate $\mathcal{P}$ and most salients subordinate $\mathcal{B}^K$ concepts, they are therefore automatically selected through the subsumption function $\varsigma(\cdot)$ that takes as input concepts from $\mathcal{BL}^d$ and a semantic hierarchy $\mathcal{H}$ with "is-a" relations. Formally, the Equation 1 becomes:

$$\mathcal{F}_i(\mathbf{x}) = \begin{cases} \varphi_i^S(\mathbf{x}, \varsigma(i)), & \text{if } c_i \in \mathcal{P}^d \\ \varphi_i^V(\mathbf{x}), & \text{if } c_i \in \mathcal{BL}^d \cup \mathcal{B}^K \\ 0 & \text{if } c_i \in \mathcal{B} \setminus \mathcal{B}^K \end{cases} \quad (2)$$

where $\mathcal{BL}^d$ and $\mathcal{P}^d$ are, respectively, the set of basic-level and superordinate concepts adapted to the targeted dataset $\mathcal{D}^d$. Selecting a portion of the whole concepts, and setting others to zero is closely related to the sparsification processes that sets to zero the lowest output values and keeps activated only the other concepts. Recent works underlined that such a property of sparsity has the advantage to be effective and computational efficient [10, 12]. The key novelty of our work is the adaptability of the concept selection to the input images. Contrary to former work, the sparsity is adapted to each image, according to its actual content, and relative to the problem of interest.

Our D-CL feature is illustrated in Figure 4. It is able to capture from an image containing multiple objects, all the basic-level concepts (colored in dark green) adapted to the target dataset, all its superordinate concepts (colored in dark red) and the most salient subordinate ones (colored in dark blue). It results in a final representation capturing the most informative concepts for a target collection of images.

4. EXPERIMENT AND ANALYSIS

In this section, we employ the proposed "Diverse Concept-Level" feature (denoted as **D-CL**) on three multi-object classification datasets. We first describe this datasets (Section 4.1) and the implementation details of our model (Section 4.2). Then, we report multi-object classification results on the three datasets (Section 4.3), and we compare it with the best semantic features in the literature. Finally, we evaluate the contribution of the asymmetrical process of concepts in the proposed D-CL descriptor by, first, evaluating the proposed semantic classifier and compare it to traditional binary classifiers (Section 4.4), and then, assessing the contribution of each concept groups selection (Section 4.5).

4.1 Datasets

The effectiveness of the proposed diverse concept-level feature is tested in the context of multi-class object classification. It is evaluated according to a standard experimental protocol as reported in the recent literature on the three following datasets:

- **Nus-Wide Object** [4], is a multi-object classification dataset. As a subset of NUS-WIDE, it consists of 31 object categories and 36,255 images in total. It contains 21,709 images for training and 15,546 images for testing. Each image is labeled by one or several labels from the 31 categories.
- **Pascal VOC 07** [8] is a multi-object classification

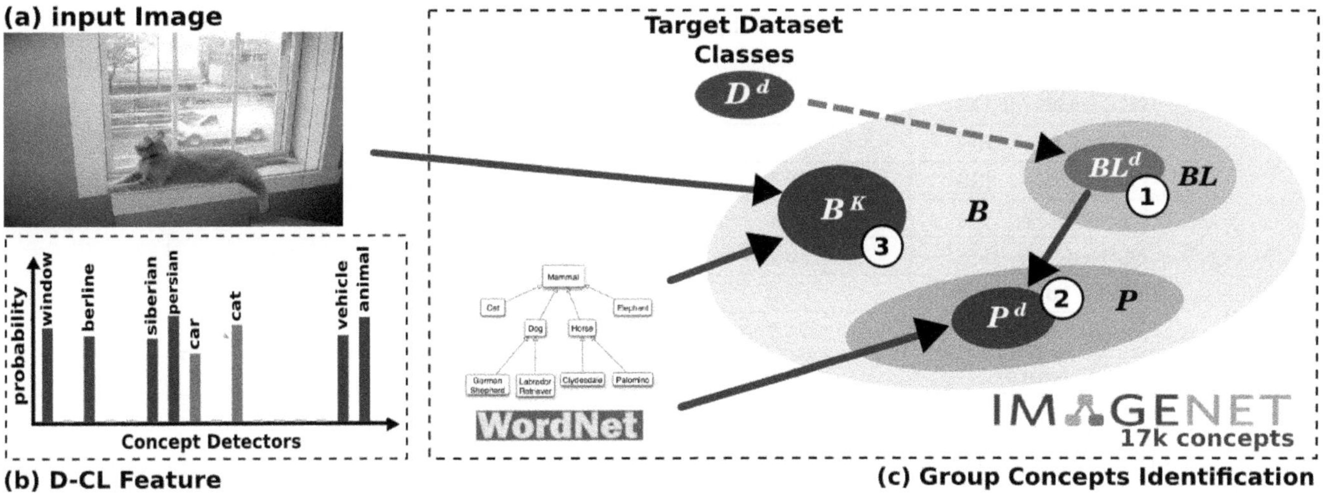

Figure 4: Illustration of the concept groups identification (c) in a practical case, for an input image (a) contained in a dataset collection. The proposed concept groups identification selects (1) in an offline phase (dashed arrow), the concepts of the target dataset categories ($\mathcal{D}^d$) as a portion ($\mathcal{BL}^d$) of all basic-level concepts ($\mathcal{BL}$), (2) the part ($\mathcal{P}^d$) of its superordinate concepts ($\mathcal{P}$) and in a final step (3) the most salient ($\mathcal{B}^K$) subordinate concepts ($\mathcal{B}$). For steps (2) and (3), a semantic hierarchy (WordNet) is used to compute the hyponymy relations. This latter, results in the final D-CL representation (b), to an activation of diverse concept levels (*i.e.*, superordinate, basic-level and subordinate) and a deactivation of all other concepts.

task. It is based on a dataset that contains 9,963 images, each image being labeled by one or several labels from 20 categories. We used the pre-defined split of 5,011 images for training and 4,952 for testing.

- **Pascal VOC 12 [7]** benchmark is similar to VOC 2007 but its number of images is larger: 22,531 images are split into 11,540 images for training and 10,991 images for testing.

4.2 Implementation details

D-CL learning: For all experiments, ImageNet [5] is used to learn our diverse concept-level representation. We especially use a subset of ImageNet with 17,462 concepts, containing more than 100 images each. Thus, we learn each individual concept detector using images representing the concept c_i as positive samples, and images of a diversified class as negative samples. Note that the concepts can be at any categorical-level of a semantic hierarchy, making our method applicable on top of any semantic feature.

Concept Groups Identification: As depicted in Section 3.2, the set of basic-level concepts ($\mathcal{BL}^d$ in Equation 2) is matched with the set of targeted dataset categories, for each dataset. Since all the concepts of ImageNet are organized in accordance to the WordNet [17] hierarchy, we use it as input to the subsumption function $\varphi(\cdot)$ to select the corresponding superordinate concepts ($\mathcal{P}^d$ in Equation 2). Specifically, only the first and the fourth level of the WordNet hierarchy are used. This, avoids redundancy of semantically close superordinate concepts. In fact, those levels contains the most popular superordinate concepts employed in cognitive experiments [15, 20, 25]. For the set of the K most salients subordinate concepts ($\mathcal{B}^K$), the parameter K of Equation 2, is cross-validated on each training dataset using the usual train/val split.

CNN feature: Semantic features (including the proposed D-CL), are built on top of any low-level or mid-level features (CNN). However, the quality of the D-CL feature will directly depend on the low/mid-level feature used. We thus, created semantic features on top of a competitive mid-level feature released in the literature, namely VGG-Net [24]. It is extracted from the last fully-connected layer (layer 16) of a Convolutional Neural Networks (CNN) learned on ILSVRC 2012 dataset [21] (containing 1.2 million images over 1,000 output categories), resulting in 4,096 dimensional vectors. Note that, for a fair comparison, the same mid-level feature is used to build Classemes+ [26] and Semfeat [10], presented in Section 4.3. For our study, fine tuning of the CNN may result into an improvement of the results at the cost of significant computational cost and the possible use of additive data. Such a specific optimization of the CNN has not been considered in our experiment, to insure their reproducibility with the available CNN models.

4.3 Multi-Object Classification Results

In this section, we test the D-CL feature for multi-object classification on the datasets presented in Section 4.1. The evaluation of our method lies in the context of semantic features. Thus we compare its performances to the following four baselines:

- **VGG-16 (fc8) [24]**, is extracted from a fully-connected layer (fc8, 18th layer) of a CNN architecture (D) learned on ILSVRC 2012 dataset [21] that contains 1.2 million images of 1,000 classes. The resulting vector has 1,000 dimensions and can be seen as a semantic feature build on top of the fc7 (16th layer), which the concept detectors are the final outputs of the CNN;
- **Semfeat [10]**, is built on top of a mid-level feature (Overfeat [23]) in their original work. To fairly com-

Method	Nus-Wide Object (20%)	Pascal VOC 2007 (45%)	Pascal VOC 2012 (30%)
ObjectBank [14]	n.a	45.2*	n.a
Classemes [26]	n.a	43.8*	n.a
Classemes+ [26]	70.3	82.4	81.7
Picodes [2]	n.a	43.7*	n.a
Meta-Class [1]	36.5	48.4 (53.2*)	49.3
VGG-16 (fc8) [24]	67.3	77.4	77.2
Semfeat [10]	74.7	82.8	81.7
D-CL (ours)	**76.0**	**85.1**	**83.0**

Table 1: Overall performance (mean Average Precision in %) of the following methods, ObjectBank, Classemes, Classemes+, Picodes, Meta-Class, VGG-16 (fc8), Semfeat and our approach (D-CL) on Nus-Wide Object, Pascal VOC 2007 and Pascal VOC 2012. We mention, for each dataset (in parenthesis), the rate of images labelled with multiple labels. Results marked with * are those reported in the original papers.

pare it to our method, we build it on top of the 16th layer of VGG-16. This layer is used to learn the classifiers of the 17,462 concepts of ImageNet that contains more than 100 images. According to their original work, a fixed sparsification over images is considered;

- **Classemes+** is, for a fair comparison with other methods, our own implementation of **Classemes [26]**. We build it on top of a the 16th layer of VGG-16 with the same concepts as our method and Semfeat, that is to say 17,462 concepts of ImageNet containing more than 100 images. Like in the original work, no sparsification is considered;
- **Meta-Class [1]**, is the output of 15,232 concept detectors. It is based on a concatenation of five low-level features combined with a spatial pyramid histogram with 13 pyramid levels. Since the number of concepts is almost equal to other methods and the code is available, we use it as it is released [1].

To extend the comparison, we also report released scores by other semantic-based approaches in the literature (ObjectBank [14], Picodes [2] and Classemes [26]). Regarding the classification protocol, each class of the datasets is learned by a one-vs-all linear SVM classifier and we use mean Average Precision (mAP) to evaluate the performances. For each dataset, the cost parameter of the SVM classifier and the parameter K of Equation 2 are optimized through cross-validation on the training images, using the usual train/val split. Results are reported in Table 1. Our descriptor significantly outperforms all the other representations. On Pascal VOC 2007, D-CL has better performances than the four baselines Classemes+ (+2.7 points of mAP), Meta-Class (+35), VGG-16-fc8 (+7.7) and Semfeat (+2.3 points of mAP). Our method also outperforms the other semantic-based methods (ObjectBank, Picodes and Classemes) evaluated on Pascal VOC 2007. The same improvements are observed on Pascal VOC 2012 and Nus-Wide Object datasets. However, we note that, compared to all baselines, the improvements of the proposed D-CL feature, is much better on Pascal VOC 2007 than Pascal VOC 2012 and Nus-Wide Object. This result is aligned with the expectation since Pascal VOC 2007 contains a larger part (45%) of images labeled by multiple classes, compared to Pascal VOC 2012 and Nus-Wide Object, that contains only 30% and 20%, respectively. Regarding this, the performances of our method increases with the level of co-occurrence objects in the dataset and even achieves better performances than comparable state-of-the-art methods when the objects in the datasets have a lower level of co-occurrence.

[1]http://vlg.cs.dartmouth.edu/projects/metaclass

4.4 Accuracy of Semantic Classifiers

In this section, we assess the effectiveness of the proposed semantic classifier ($\varphi^S(\cdot)$ of Equation 1), and compare it with purely visual classifiers, *i.e.*, binary classifiers ($\varphi^V(\cdot)$ of Equation 1) on generic concepts (*i.e.* concepts that have at least one hypernym relation with another concept).

This analytic study is an analogy to the experiment conducted by the cognitive works of Stephan Kosslyn [15]. More precisely, they wanted to provide a converging evidence that superordinate concepts are semantically processed by humans, rather than by a visual perception processing. Thus, to respect the analogy with [15], we evaluate the proposed semantic classifier and the visual classifiers on superordinate concepts only.

Regarding our experiment, the selection of superordinate concepts impose, in the Equation 2 of the proposed D-CL representation, to set to zero all the basic-level and subordinate concepts ($\varphi_i^V(\mathbf{x}) = 0, \forall c_i \in \mathcal{BL}^d \cup \mathcal{B}^K$). Thereby, the experiment has been conducted on the context of multi-class object classification through the Pascal VOC 07 dataset. All the images of the dataset have been re-labeled at superordinate level, *e.g.* all images labeled as *bird*, *dog*, *cow*, *horse* or *sheep* are now labeled as *animal*, all images labeled as *chair*, *sofa* or *table* are now labeled as *furniture*, etc (see first and second column of Table 2 for the re-labeling of other classes). Hence, we learn each superordinate class of the dataset by a one-vs-all SVM classifier. The cost parameter of the SVM classifier is optimized through cross-validation on the training dataset, using the usual train/val split. Performance results of both classifiers are reported in Table 2 using average precision (AP in %) for each class and mean Average Precision (mAP in %) over all classes in the last row. The second column of the table corresponds to the basic-level categories of the dataset and the first column

Superordinate	Basic-level	Visual	Semantic (↑)
Animal	bird - cow - dog - horse - sheep	92.9	**97.7** (+4.8)
Electronic equipment	tv monitor	52.1	**72.6** (+20.5)
Furniture	chair - sofa - table	70.0	**74.9** (+4.9)
Person	person	77.2	**85.7** (+8.5)
Plant	potted plant	26.5	**40.5** (+14.0)
Vehicle	airplane - bike - boat - bus - car - mbike - train	93.4	**96.9** (+3.5)
Vessel	bottle	18.7	**31.4** (+12.7)
mAP		61.5	**71.4** (+9.9)

Table 2: Evaluating purely visual binary classifiers (denoted as "Visual") and our proposed semantic classifiers (denoted as "Semantic") for superordinate concepts (first column) of Pascal VOC 07 dataset classes (second column). The improvements of semantic classifiers over visual classifiers are shown in parentheses. Note that, the class *person* of Pascal VOC 2007 is already at the highest level in the WordNet hierarchy.

corresponds to the list of selected superordinate concepts in our D-CL feature. The average precision of each superordinate concept computed through binary classifiers (denoted as **Visual**) and the proposed semantic classifier (denoted as **Semantic**), are presented in the last two columns, respectively. Remarkably, the proposed semantic classifier clearly outperforms binary classifiers (purely visual) for all the superordinate concepts. From this study, we conclude that the superordinate concepts are better recognised by D-CL, due to its ability to compensate low within-category resemblance of generic concepts. The most surprising aspect of this experiment is that it shows, as concluded by the analogical cognitive experiment of Stephan Kosslyn [15], that semantic process is most adapted than purely visual process for superordinate concepts.

Concept Groups Selection	$\mathcal{P}$	$\mathcal{BL}$	$\mathcal{B}$	$\mathcal{B}^K$	mAP
Superordinate	✓				44.4%
Basic-level		✓			76.1%
Subordinate			✓		82.1%
K-Subordinate				✓	78.9%
Fusion 1	✓	✓	✓		82.7%
Fusion 2 (D-CL)	✓	✓		✓	85.1%

Table 3: Evaluation of the contribution of different concept groups selection (check-mark = selected group) in the proposed semantic feature on Pascal VOC 2007 dataset.

4.5 Concept Groups Selection Sensitivity

We evaluate now the contribution of the concepts from different groups (*i.e.* categorical levels) on a multi-object classification task (Pascal VOC 2007). To this end, we need to isolate each group of concepts in the D-CL representation by selecting them individually and setting other groups to zero. It results in four special cases of the D-CL feature (Equation 2), (i) selecting only superordinate concepts ($\forall c_i \in \mathcal{P}^d \cup \mathcal{B}, \varphi(c_i) = 0$) denoted as "Superordinate", (ii) selecting only basic-level concepts ($\forall c_i \in \mathcal{P}^d \cup \mathcal{B}, \varphi(c_i) = 0$) denoted as "Basic-level" (iii) selecting only subordinate concepts ($\forall c_i \in \mathcal{P}^d \cup \mathcal{BL}^d, \varphi(c_i) = 0$), denoted as "Subordinate" and (iv) selecting only the K most salient subordinate concepts ($\forall c_i \in \overline{\mathcal{B}^K}$), denoted as "$K$-Subordinate". We also evaluate the contribution when selecting all the concept groups in the representation ($\forall c_i \in \mathcal{P}^d \cup \mathcal{BL}^d \cup \mathcal{B}, \varphi(c_i) \neq 0$ in Eq. 2), *e.g.*, superordinate, basic-level and subordinate concepts, denoted as "Fusion 1". Finally, we report the results obtained by the proposed D-CL concept groups selection (see Section 3.2), corresponding to the selection of, all the superordinate and basic-level concepts and the K most salient subordinate concepts. It is also a fusion of other groups of concepts that we denote as D-CL. Results are reported in Table 3. For each concept group selection, a check-mark represents the concept groups that had been selected in the final representation. The last column gives the mAP obtained for the different concept selections. Note that, the K parameter of Equation 2 has been cross-validated for the "K-Subordinate" and "D-CL" concept group selections.

Obviously, selecting only superordinate concepts ($\mathcal{P}$) leads to very bad results, compared to basic-level concepts only ($\mathcal{BL}$), which are their-self lower than subordinate concepts only ($\mathcal{B}$). Selecting only the K most salient subordinate concepts ($\mathcal{B}^K$) obtains lower performances than selecting them all. Surprisingly, for the fusion, it is better with the selection of the K most salient concepts (the proposed D-CL) than with the selection of all subordinate concepts (Fusion 2). This experiment shows that the proposed D-CL selection gives a most effective semantic representation.

5. CONCLUSIONS

We propose the Diverse Concept-Level feature (D-CL), a semantic representation based on the exploitation of human knowledge, such as semantic hierarchies, to identify group of concepts, according to their categorical-level. This latter, aims to process the three groups of visual concepts differently from each other. Thus, our scheme outputs only informative concepts in the final representation. In addition, we show that the proposed semantic classifiers are most adapted to recognize superordinate concepts in images, than traditional visual classifiers. We also explored the selection of concepts from the three different categorical-levels, showing that the proposed scheme, consisting in the selection of concepts from all of them, is beneficial to obtain a precise semantic representation.

Experimental validation of the proposed approach has been conducted on three benchmarks (Pascal VOC 2007, Pascal VOC 2012 and Nus-Wide Object) of multi-class object classification. The proposed D-CL feature obtained significantly better performances than the best semantic features in the literature.

The results obtained for image classification are very encouraging and we will pursue the work reported here. We will investigate finer ways to identify basic-level concepts. In particular, large released lists of basic-level concepts [16, 19, 22] will replace the dataset categories that are currently used. This work direction, will aim to handle unsupervised image retrieval problem, where categories of images in the collection are not supposed known.

6. ACKNOWLEDGMENTS

This work is supported by the USEMP FP7 project, partially funded by the European Commission under contract number 611596.

7. REFERENCES

[1] A. Bergamo and L. Torresani. Meta-class features for large-scale object categorization on a budget. In *Computer Vision and Pattern Recognition*, 2012.

[2] A. Bergamo, L. Torresani, and A. W. Fitzgibbon. Picodes: Learning a compact code for novel-category recognition. In *NIPS*, 2011.

[3] K. Chatfield, K. Simonyan, A. Vedaldi, and A. Zisserman. Return of the devil in the details: Delving deep into convolutional nets. *arXiv:1405.3531*, 2014.

[4] T.-S. Chua, J. Tang, R. Hong, H. Li, Z. Luo, and Y.-T. Zheng. Nus-wide: A real-world web image database from national university of singapore. In *Proceedings of ACM Conference on Image and Video Retrieval*, CIVR, 2009.

[5] J. Deng, W. Dong, R. Socher, L.-J. Li, K. Li, and L. Fei-Fei. ImageNet: A Large-Scale Hierarchical Image Database. In *CVPR*, 2009.

[6] J. Deng, J. Krause, A. C. Berg, and L. Fei-Fei. Hedging your bets: Optimizing accuracy-specificity trade-offs in large scale visual recognition. In *Computer Vision and Pattern Recognition*, 2012.

[7] M. Everingham, L. Van Gool, C. K. Williams, J. Winn, and A. Zisserman. The pascal visual object classes challenge 2012.

[8] M. Everingham, L. Van Gool, C. K. Williams, J. Winn, and A. Zisserman. The pascal visual object classes challenge. *International journal of computer vision (IJCV)*, 88(2):303–338, 2010.

[9] P. Gehler and S. Nowozin. On feature combination for multiclass object classification. In *Computer Vision and Pattern Recognition*, CVPR, 2009.

[10] A. L. Ginsca, A. Popescu, H. Le Borgne, N. Ballas, P. Vo, and I. Kanellos. Large-scale image mining with flickr groups. In *Multimedia Modelling*, MM, 2015.

[11] Y. Huang, Z. Wu, L. Wang, and T. Tan. Feature coding in image classification: A comprehensive study. *Transactions on Pattern Analysis and Machine Intelligence (PAMI)*, 36(3):493–506, 2014.

[12] M. Jain, J. C. van Gemert, T. Mensink, and C. G. M. Snoek. Objects2action: Classifying and localizing actions without any video example. In *International Conference on Computer Vision*, ICCV, 2015.

[13] Y. Jia, E. Shelhamer, J. Donahue, S. Karayev, J. Long, R. Girshick, S. Guadarrama, and T. Darrell. Caffe: Convolutional architecture for fast feature embedding. In *International Conference on Multimedia*, ACM, 2014.

[14] L. jia Li, H. Su, L. Fei-fei, and E. P. Xing. Object bank: A high-level image representation for scene classification & semantic feature sparsification. In *Advances in Neural Information Processing Systems*, NIPS, 2010.

[15] P. Jolicoeur, M. A. Gluck, and S. M. Kosslyn. Pictures and names: Making the connection. *Cognitive Psychology*, 16(2):243–275, 1984.

[16] A. Mathews, L. Xie, and X. He. Choosing basic-level concept names using visual and language context. In *Winter Conference on Applications of Computer Vision*, WACV, 2015.

[17] G. A. Miller. Wordnet: a lexical database for english. *Communications of the ACM*, 38(11):39–41, 1995.

[18] V. Ordonez, J. Deng, Y. Choi, A. C. Berg, and T. Berg. From large scale image categorization to entry-level categories. In *International Conference on Computer Vision*, ICCV, 2013.

[19] V. Ordonez, W. Liu, J. Deng, Y. Choi, A. C. Berg, and T. L. Berg. Predicting entry-level categories. *International Journal of Computer Vision (IJCV)*, pages 1–15, 2015.

[20] E. Rosch. Principles of categorization. *Cognition and Categorization*, page 2748, 1978.

[21] O. Russakovsky, J. Deng, H. Su, J. Krause, S. Satheesh, S. Ma, Z. Huang, A. Karpathy, A. Khosla, M. Bernstein, A. C. Berg, and L. Fei-Fei. Imagenet large scale visual recognition challenge. *International Journal of Computer Vision*, 2015.

[22] O. Russakovsky, J. Deng, H. Su, J. Krause, S. Satheesh, S. Ma, Z. Huang, A. Karpathy, A. Khosla, M. Bernstein, A. C. Berg, and L. Fei-Fei. ImageNet Large Scale Visual Recognition Challenge. *International Journal of Computer Vision (IJCV)*, 115(3):211–252, 2015.

[23] P. Sermanet, D. Eigen, X. Zhang, M. Mathieu, R. Fergus, and Y. LeCun. Overfeat: Integrated recognition, localization and detection using convolutional networks. *arXiv:1312.6229*, 2013.

[24] K. Simonyan and A. Zisserman. Very deep convolutional networks for large-scale image recognition. *arXiv:1409.1556*, 2014.

[25] J. W. Tanaka and M. Taylor. Object categories and expertise: Is the basic level in the eye of the beholder? *Cognitive Psychology*, 23(3):457–482, 1991.

[26] L. Torresani, M. Szummer, and A. Fitzgibbon. Efficient object category recognition using classemes. In *European Conference on Computer Vision*, 2010.

[27] M. Yuan and Y. Lin. Model selection and estimation in regression with grouped variables. *Journal of the Royal Statistical Society, series B*, 68:49–67, 2006.

Personalized Privacy-aware Image Classification

Eleftherios Spyromitros-Xioufis[1], Symeon Papadopoulos[1], Adrian Popescu[2], Yiannis Kompatsiaris[1]
[1]CERTH-ITI, 57001 Thessaloniki, Greece, {espyromi,papadop,ikom}@iti.gr
[2]CEA, LIST, 91190 Gif-sur-Yvette, France, adrian.popescu@cea.fr

ABSTRACT

Information sharing in online social networks is a daily practice for billions of users. The sharing process facilitates the maintenance of users' social ties but also entails privacy disclosure in relation to other users and third parties. Depending on the intentions of the latter, this disclosure can become a risk. It is thus important to propose tools that empower the users in their relations to social networks and third parties connected to them. As part of USEMP, a coordinated research effort aimed at user empowerment, we introduce a system that performs privacy-aware classification of images. We show that generic privacy models perform badly with real-life datasets in which images are contributed by individuals because they ignore the subjective nature of privacy. Motivated by this, we develop personalized privacy classification models that, utilizing small amounts of user feedback, provide significantly better performance than generic models. The proposed semi-personalized models lead to performance improvements for the best generic model ranging from 4%, when 5 user-specific examples are provided, to 18% with 35 examples. Furthermore, by using a semantic representation space for these models we manage to provide intuitive explanations of their decisions and to gain novel insights with respect to individuals' privacy concerns stemming from image sharing. We hope that the results reported here will motivate other researchers and practitioners to propose new methods of exploiting user feedback and of explaining privacy classifications to users.

1. INTRODUCTION

Uploading and sharing information in Online Social Networks (OSNs) is nowadays a frequent activity for the majority of Internet users. Such shared pieces of information are aggregated into digital user profiles. These profiles support a business model based on free access to the OSN service and users have little or no control on how their profiles are exploited by the OSN. Typically, OSNs employ sophisticated algorithms to make sense of the data posted by their users in order to create personal profiles that they often use to perform ad targeting. Different research and industrial initiatives point out risks related to different aspects of information sharing. The **Sunlight** project[1] enhances transparency by detecting which textual data are used for personalized advertising. **PleaseRobMe**[2] illustrates a straightforward implication of explicit location disclosure. Note, however, that location disclosure can also be implicit, e.g. through one's posted images. Our own contribution is part of **USEMP**[3], a multidisciplinary European project which develops DataBait[4], a tool that provides feedback about what can be inferred from a user's historical data shared on OSNs.

These above initiatives provide important contributions to understanding the risks related to information sharing. However, most of the challenges related to the proposal of effective privacy preservation tools lie ahead. First, researchers need to operate under the privacy paradox [15] which causes a discrepancy between what users intend to share and what they actually disclose. This discrepancy impedes the wide adoption of privacy preservation methods and tools and an important effort is needed to educate users toward its reduction. Second, privacy breaches might be caused by different types of disclosed data, including multimedia documents and behavioral or social links in OSNs. Research should focus on these data individually, as well as on their interlinking. Third, privacy perception is inherently subjective and dynamic. Consequently, its modeling should include a strong personalization component that caters to each user's needs. Equally important, the models should evolve over time. Fourth, effective privacy preservation tools might be perceived as a threat for current business practices that are built around the exploitation of user profiles. The adoption of such tools by OSNs is conditioned by public demand combined with regulatory requirements. The Privacy Impact Assessment required by the US E-government Act[5] issued in 2002 and the proposed European General Data Protection Regulation[6] are examples of how regulation acts upon business practices. Fifth, the proposed privacy inference methods should work under real-time constraints in order to give immediate feedback to the user, preferably before the information is shared on OSNs. These

ICMR '16, June 6–9, 2016, New York, NY, USA.

ISBN 978-1-4503-4359-6/16/06...$15.00

DOI: http://dx.doi.org/10.1145/2911996.2912018

[1]http://columbia.github.io/sunlight
[2]http://www.pleaserobme.com
[3]http://www.usemp-project.eu
[4]https://databait.hwcomms.com
[5]https://www.gpo.gov/fdsys/pkg/PLAW-107publ347
[6]http://ec.europa.eu/justice/data-protection/reform/index_en.htm

Figure 1: A hardly comprehensible justification (green rectangles highlighting the most discriminative local patches) provided for a private classification by the PicAlert system. Image from [23]

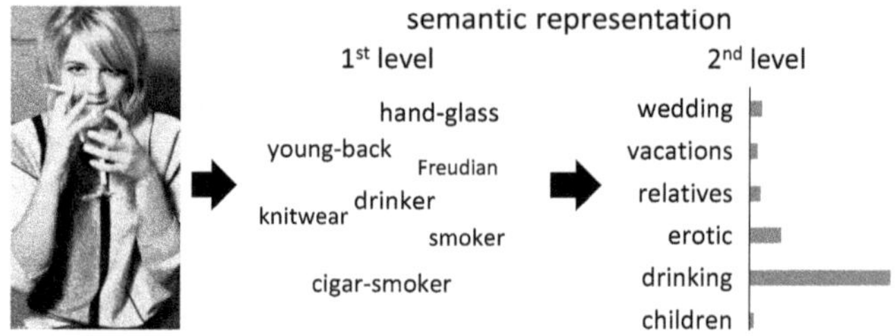

Figure 2: A better justification of the classifier's decision consisting of a tag-cloud of the most prevalent image tags and a projection of those tags into six privacy-related dimensions

methods should also offer high-quality and understandable results in order to be adopted by users. Finally, the creation and sharing of privacy-related evaluation datasets is difficult due to the very nature of the information included. However, such datasets are essential to evaluate the merits of proposed methods in a quantifiable way and facilitate reproducibility.

Here, we tackle the privacy-related risks in the context of image sharing and try to tackle some of the challenges mentioned above. Image sharing is such a widely used and valued service that preventing users from sharing their images cannot be considered as a viable means of protecting their online privacy. Instead, having access to a service that could automatically process one's images before they are shared with the OSN, and being alerted in case their content is found to be sensitive, would be a very practical and transparent way of safeguarding the online privacy of OSN users without affecting their image sharing experience.

A first solution to this problem was presented in [24], where the authors defined the problem of automatically classifying users' images as being of private or public nature, and tested the effectiveness of standard image and text features in a supervised learning setting for solving the problem. In that work, the authors focused on developing models that capture a *generic* ("community") notion of privacy, making the underlying assumption that each user perceives privacy in the same way. However, OSN users often have wildly different perceptions and norms regarding privacy [16]. A further limitation of that solution is that the classification decision was justified by highlighting the most discriminative local patches in the image as shown in Figure 1. Such a justification is hardly comprehensible by non-experts in computer vision. Providing more intuitive, higher-level, explanations would be clearly more desirable. An example is given in Figure 2, where a private classification is accompanied by an automatically generated cloud of the most prevalent image tags and a projection of those tags into a number of privacy-related dimensions.

In this paper, we propose a personalized image privacy scoring and classification system that provides an effective privacy safeguarding mechanism on top of image sharing OSN facilities and alleviates the limitations of previous solutions. In particular, we make the following contributions:

- **Personalized privacy classification:** We demonstrate that by combining feedback from multiple users with a limited amount of user-specific feedback, we can obtain significantly more accurate privacy classifications compared to those obtained from a generic model (Section 4.3).
- **Real-world dataset:** We create a realistic benchmark dataset via a user study where participants annotate their own photos as private or public according to their own notion of privacy. Experiments on this dataset reveal the limitations a generic privacy definition and highlight the necessity of building personalized privacy classification models (Section 4.2).
- **Semantic justification:** We employ a type of semantic features that facilitate the explanation of image privacy classifications and support the discovery of valuable insights with respect to users' privacy concerns (Section 4.4). Importantly, these features are computed based solely on the visual content of the images and, therefore, the approach does not require the existence of manually assigned image tags.
- **State-of-the-art performance:** By using visual features extracted from deep convolutional neural networks (CNNs) we significantly improve the state-of-the-art performance on an existing private image classification benchmark (Section 4.2).

2. RELATED WORK

Most modern OSNs allow users to control the privacy settings of their shared content. Yet, the typical user finds it difficult to understand and correctly configure the offered access control policies [12]. As a result, several studies [11, 12] have identified a serious mismatch between the desired and the actual privacy settings of online shared content. This discrepancy motivated the development of mechanisms that aid users in selecting appropriate privacy settings. In the work of [14], for instance, the authors focused on Facebook posts and evaluated prediction models that make use of users' previous posts and profile preferences in order to suggest appropriate privacy settings for new posts. Despite achieving high performance, the authors noticed differences in user behaviors and concluded that personalized privacy models could further improve the results.

Zerr et al. [24], were among the first to consider the problem of privacy-aware image classification. In their work, a large-scale user study was conducted asking participants to annotate a large number of publicly available Flickr photos as being either "private" or "public". The study was set up as a social annotation game where players were instructed to adopt a common definition of privacy[7] and were rewarded for providing annotations that were similar to those of other players. The resulting dataset, referred to as *PicAlert*, was used to train supervised classification models that capture a generic ("community") notion of privacy.

Extending that work, [21] experimented with combinations of visual and metadata-derived features and achieved better prediction accuracy on PicAlert. [21] also attempted to solve a more complex privacy classification problem where three types of disclosure were defined for each image (view, comment, download) and the task was to assign one of five privacy levels ('Only You', 'Family', 'Friends', 'SocialNetwork', 'Everyone') to each type of disclosure. As in [24], their models captured only a generic perception of privacy.

Differently from the majority of previous works, our paper highlights the limitations of generic image privacy classification models and proposes an effective personalization method. To the best of our knowledge, [4] is the only work that considers privacy classification of personal photos as we do here. However, [4] evaluates only purely personalized models, assuming that each user provides sufficient amount of feedback. In contrast, our method achieves high performance even at the presence of very limited user-specific feedback by leveraging feedback from other users. Moreover, while [4] uses only metadata-based (location, time, etc.) and simple visual features (colors, edges, etc.), we employ state-of-the-art CNN-based semantic visual features that facilitate comprehensible explanations of the classification outputs. Very recently, [22] evaluated the performance of deep features on PicAlert (again in the context of a generic privacy model) and found that they yield remarkable improvements in performance compared to SIFT, GIST and user-assigned tag features. Moreover, the authors evaluated the performance of 'deep tag' features (which are similar to the first level of semantic features that we extract here) but did not exploit them for justifying the classifier's decisions.

3. APPROACH

3.1 Personalized Privacy Models

Privacy classifications based on a generic privacy classification model as the one developed in [24] are undoubtedly useful for preventing users from uploading images that are considered to be private according to a generic notion of privacy. However, as the perception of privacy varies greatly among users depending on factors such as age, social status and culture, it is expected that a generic model would provide inaccurate predictions for certain users, thus decreasing the reliability and usefulness of the alerting mechanism. To overcome this issue, we propose the exploitation of user feedback in order to build personalized privacy models. Such feedback could be acquired either explicitly, by asking OSN users to provide examples of private and public photos, or implicitly, by exploiting logs of the user's interaction with his/her photos (e.g. changes in privacy settings, removal of previously shared images, etc.).

Provided that sufficient amount of feedback is available from each user, one could rely only on user-specific examples for training personalized privacy classification models. This, however, might require considerable effort from the user and cannot be taken for granted. As a result, user-specific privacy classification models might not be able to generalize well. To overcome this problem, we propose the development of semi-personalized models that are learned using a combination of user-specific training examples and examples from other users. The intuition behind such an expansion of the training set is that, although each person has a personal notion of privacy, there are also similarities between different users (since everyone is affected to some degree by general trends and norms) and the expansion of the training set is tailored exactly towards an exploitation of these similarities. Importantly, in order to retain the personalized nature of the models, we assign higher weights to the user-specific examples, effectively increasing their influence on the resulting model.

More formally, given a set of users $U = \{u_1, u_2, \ldots, u_k\}$ and assuming that each user $u_i \in U$ has provided ground truth annotations for a set of personal images $I_{u_i} = \{im^1_{u_i}, im^2_{u_i}, \ldots, im^n_{u_i}\}$, a user-specific dataset $D_{u_i} = \{(\mathbf{x}^1_{u_i}, y^1_{u_i}), (\mathbf{x}^2_{u_i}, y^2_{u_i}), \ldots, (\mathbf{x}^n_{u_i}, y^n_{u_i})\}$ can be constructed where $\mathbf{x}_{u_i} = [x_{1_{u_i}}, x_{2_{u_i}}, \ldots, x_{d_{u_i}}]$ is a vector representation of im_{u_i} and y_{u_i} equals 1 if the image is annotated as private, 0 otherwise. The typical approach is to train a personalized classifier $h_{u_i} : \mathcal{X} \rightarrow \mathcal{Y}$ (where $\mathcal{X} = R^d$ and $\mathcal{Y} = \{0, 1\}$ are the domains of $\mathbf{x}$ and y respectively) using only examples from D_{u_i}. Instead of that, we propose that each classifier h_{u_i} is trained on $\bigcup_{i=1}^{k} D_{u_i}$, i.e. the union of all user-specific datasets, and personalization is achieved by assigning a higher weight w to the examples of D_{u_i}. Example weights are directly handled by some learning algorithms (e.g. decision trees) while other learning algorithms can be "forced" to take weights into account by including duplicates of specific examples in the training set. The effect of weighting is that the classifier is biased towards correct prediction of higher weighted examples and is commonly used in supervised learning techniques, e.g. cost-sensitive learning [6] and boosting [8].

We note that our approach resembles techniques from the domains of *transfer* and *multi-task* learning [17, 5], commonly referred to as *instance sharing* or *instance pooling*. In fact, if we consider the privacy classification of the images of each user as a different learning task, the problem of personalized image privacy classification can be considered as an instance of multi-task learning. These methods are known to work better than methods that treat each learning task independently whenever the tasks are related and there is lack of training data for some of the tasks [1], two conditions that hold in the problem that we tackle here.

3.2 A Realistic Image Privacy Benchmark

The PicAlert dataset is certainly useful for training models that capture a generic notion of privacy. However, there are two limitations that make PicAlert unsuitable as a realistic image privacy classification benchmark: a) it consists of publicly available images with few of them being of really private nature, b) the ground truth collection process makes the unrealistic assumption that all OSN users have common privacy preferences. As a result, a privacy classification model trained on this dataset may practically fail to provide accurate classifications (as shown in Section 4.2). Moreover, the variability of privacy preferences among users is not taken into account when evaluating the accuracy of

[7]"Private are photos which have to do with the private sphere (like self portraits, family, friends, your home) or contain objects that you would not share with the entire world (like a private email). The rest is public." [24]

privacy classifications on PicAlert, resulting to overly optimistic performance estimates.

To overcome these limitations, we created a new privacy-oriented image dataset with two goals: a) the development of personalized image privacy models, and b) the realistic evaluation of both generic and personalized image privacy models. To this end, we conducted a realistic user study where we asked users to provide privacy annotations for photos of their personal collections. A call for contributions that described our research goals and the potential benefits for OSN users was distributed within our workplaces and through our OSN accounts. To reduce the concerns associated with sharing personal images (especially private ones), we provided users with software that automatically extracts the above visual features from the images and helps them share the features and the corresponding annotations (instead of the original images). To provide loose guidance and let users develop their own notion of privacy, we briefly described as public "images that they would share with *all* their OSN friends or even make them publicly visible" and as private "images that they would share only with *close* OSN friends or not share them at all". To ensure a representation of both classes we asked each user to provide (if possible) at least 10 private and 30 public images.

In total, we received feedback from 27 users (22 males and 5 females), with ages ranging from 25 to 39 years. Each user contributed approximately 16.4 private and 39.5 public photos (on average) for a total of 1511 photos. The resulting dataset (features and privacy annotations), named *YourAlert*, is made publicly available[8] for future benchmarks.

3.3 Visual and Semantic Features

In our experiments we focus on privacy classification based on the visual content - a piece of information that is always available in contrast to metadata and manually assigned tags - and extract the following state-of-the-art visual features:

`vlad`: We used the implementation of [20] to extract $d = 24,576$-dimensional VLAD+CSURF vectors from a 128-dimensional visual vocabulary and then performend PCA and whitening to project the vectors to $d' = 512$ dimensions (a projection size that led to near optimal results in preliminary experiments).

`cnn`: standard convolutional neural network features using the VGG-16 model [19] that includes 16 layers and is learned with the training set of the ImageNet ILSVRC 2014 dataset [18]. VGG-16 was chosen because it obtained one of the top results during the ImageNet 2014 challenge but also because it is publicly available and thus facilitates reproducibility. This dataset includes 1,000 specific classes and approximately 1,2 million images. These classes cover a wide range of domains and the obtained model has thus good performance in transfer learning tasks as attested by [9]. We use the output of the last fully connected layer (*fc7*), which consists of 4,096 dimensions.

`semfeat`: semantic image features obtained by exploiting the outputs of a large array of classifiers, learned with low-level features [2]. We use the VGG-16 features described above as basic features for the semantic features. Here, we compute a slightly modified version of the `semfeat` descriptor that was introduced in [9]. Only concepts that have at least 100 associated images are retained and the total size of the descriptor is 17,462. Concept models are learned independently as binary classifiers but with a ratio of 1:100 between positive and negative examples instead of a fixed number of negatives. The negative class includes images that illustrate ImageNet concepts that were not modeled. These images are sorted in order to provide a conceptually diversified sample of negatives for each modeled concept. Following the conclusions of [9] concerning the positive effect of sparsity, only the top $n = 100$ classifier outputs are retained for each image.

[8]https://github.com/MKLab-ITI/image-privacy

Table 1: Privacy-related latent topics along with the top-5 `semfeat` concepts assigned to each topic

Topic	Top-5 `semfeat` concepts assigned to each topic
children	dribbler child godson wimp niece
drinking	drinker drunk tippler thinker drunkard
erotic	slattern erotic cover-girl maillot back
relatives	g-aunt s-cousin grandfather mother g-grandchild
vacations	seaside vacationer surf-casting casting sandbank
wedding	groom bride celebrant wedding costume

Table 2: Dataset statistics

Dataset	# examples (private/public)	Source
PicAlert	26458 (3651/22807)	[24]
YourAlert	1511 (444/1067)	This paper

Compared to `vlad` and `cnn`, `semfeat` have the advantage that they enable result explainability: users can obtain human-understandable feedback about why an image was classified as private or not, in the form of top concepts associated to it. A limitation of this approach is that, having been constructed for general purpose concept detection, the `semfeat` vocabulary contains many concepts that are too specific and unrelated to privacy (e.g. *osteocyte*: 'mature bone cell'). As a result, many of the top n concepts of each image can not be easily linked to privacy.

To address this limitation, we developed a privacy aspect modeling approach that projects the detected `semfeat` concepts into a number of privacy-related latent topics using Latent Dirichlet Allocation (LDA) [3]. More specifically, each image is treated as a document consisting of its top $n = 10$ `semfeat` concepts and a private image corpus is created by combining the private images of the PicAlert and YourAlert datasets. LDA (the Mallet implementation [13]) is then applied on this corpus to create a topic model with 30 topics. Among the detected topics, 6 privacy-related ones are identified: **`children`**, **`drinking`**, **`erotic`**, **`relatives`**, **`vacations`**, **`wedding`** (Table 1). Given such a topic model, the topics of each image are inferred (using Gibbs sampling inference) from its `semfeat` concepts and the assignments to the privacy-related topics are used as a means of justification of the classifier's decision (as shown in Figure 2). We refer to this representation as `semfeat-lda`.

4. EXPERIMENTS

4.1 Experimental Setup

In our experiments we used the PicAlert[9] and YourAlert datasets, of which the statistics are provided in Table 2. To measure the accuracy of a classification model, we use

[9]Since some images of PicAlert are no longer available in Flickr, the version that we use here contains about 18% less images than the original one.

the area under the ROC curve (AUC). This was preferred over other evaluation measures due to the fact that it is unaffected by class imbalance and it is independent of the threshold applied to transform the confidence (or probability) scores of a classification model into hard 1/0 (private/public) decisions. Moreover, AUC has an intuitive interpretation: it is equal to the probability that the classification model will assign a higher score to a randomly chosen private image than a randomly chosen public image. Thus, a random classifier has an expected AUC score of 0.5 while a perfect classifier has an AUC score of 1.

Throughout the experiments, we use an L2-regularized logistic regression classifier (the LibLinear implementation [7]) as it provided a good trade-off between efficiency and accuracy compared to other state-of-the-art classifiers in preliminary experiments. Moreover, the coefficients of a regularized logistic regression model are suitable for identifying features that are strongly correlated with the class variable [10], thus facilitating explanation of the privacy classifications when features with a semantic interpretation such as `semfeat` are used. The regularization parameter was tuned by applying internal 3-fold cross-validation and choosing the value (among $10^r : r \in \{-2, \dots, 2\}$) that leads to the highest AUC. Finally, all feature vectors were normalized to unit length before being fed to the classifier, as suggested in [7].

To facilitate reproducibility of our experimental results we have created a GitHub project[10] where we make available the experimental testbed and the datasets that we used.

4.2 Limitations of Generic Privacy Models

In this section, we evaluate the performance of generic image privacy classification models when applied in a realistic setting where different users have different perceptions of image privacy. To this end, we conduct the following experiment: A generic privacy classification model is trained using a randomly chosen 60% of the PicAlert dataset and then tested on: a) the remaining 40% of PicAlert and b) the YourAlert dataset. In the first case, we have an idealized evaluation setting (similar to the one adopted in [24]), while in the second case we have an evaluation setting that better resembles the test conditions that a privacy classification model will encounter in practice. To ensure reliability of the performance estimates, we repeat the above evaluation procedure five times (using different random splits of PicAlert) and take the average of the individual estimates.

Figure 3 shows the AUC scores obtained on PicAlert (light blue bars) and YourAlert (orange bars) when each of the visual features described in Section 3.3 is used. On PicAlert, we also evaluate the performance with quantized SIFT (`bow`) and edge-direction coherence (`edch`) features, the best performing of the visual features used in [24][11].

The performance on PicAlert indicates that `vlad`, `semfeat` and `cnn` lead to significantly better results than `edch` and `bow`. With `semfeat` and `cnn`, in particular, we obtain a near-perfect 0.95 AUC score which is about 20% better than the AUC score obtained with `bow` (the best visual feature among those used in [24]). `semfeat` have very similar performance with `cnn`, a fact that makes them a very appealing choice, given their sparsity and interpretability properties.

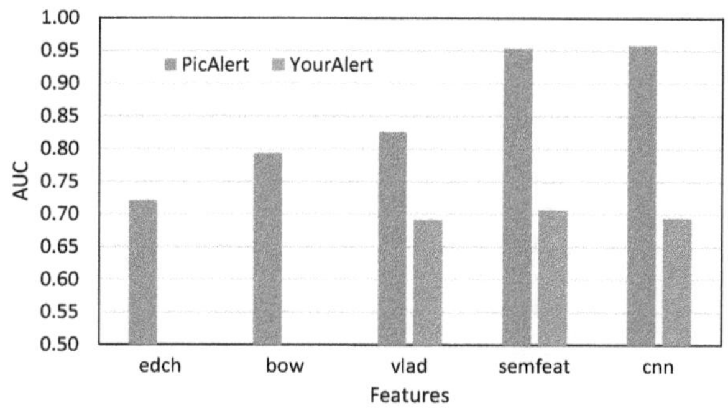

Figure 3: Performance of generic models on PicAlert and YourAlert[13]

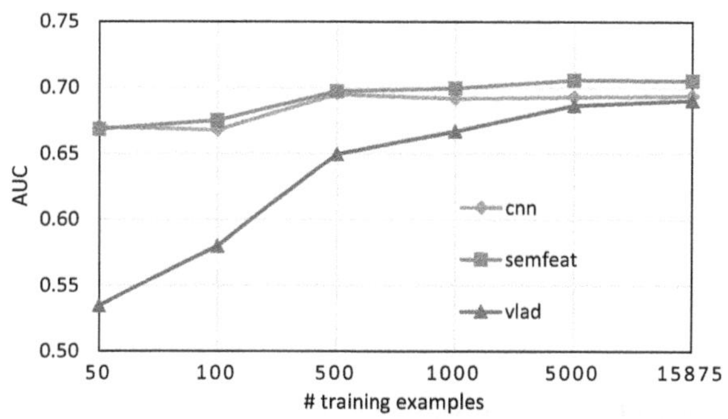

Figure 4: Performance of generic models on YourAlert as a function of the number of training examples

However, the performance of all models drops significantly when they are applied on YourAlert. `cnn` and `semfeat`, for instance, have about 24% lower performance in terms of AUC. As we see, all models perform similarly, which suggests that the accuracy is not expected to improve considerably if better features are used. Moreover, to check whether the performance on YourAlert could improve by using additional training examples from PicAlert, we studied the performance of the generic privacy models as a function of the number of examples. More specifically, for each type of features, we built six generic privacy estimation models using $\{50, 100, 500, 1000, 5000, 15875\}$ training examples from PicAlert and applied them on YourAlert. As above, to ensure reliability of the performance estimates, the evaluation of each model was repeated five times, i.e. five models were built (each trained on a different random subset of PicAlert) for each combination of features and number of training examples, and the averages of the individual performance estimates were taken. The results of this experiment are shown in Figure 4. We observe that for all types of features, the AUC performance reaches a plateau and does not change significantly after 5000 examples. Interestingly, the generic models that use `cnn` and `semfeat` features obtain 96% of their maximum performance with only 50 training examples, while the generic model that uses `vlad` features seems to require about 5000 training examples in order to approach its maximum performance. Clearly, the use of additional generic training examples is not expected to help in attaining better performance on YourAlert.

Figure 5 presents a per-user performance breakdown for generic models based on `vlad`, `semfeat` and `cnn` features (i.e.

[10] https://github.com/MKLab-ITI/image-privacy

[11] `edch` and `bow` were kindly provided by the authors of [24].

[13] `edch` and `bow` could not be tested on YourAlert because we did not have access to their exact implementations.

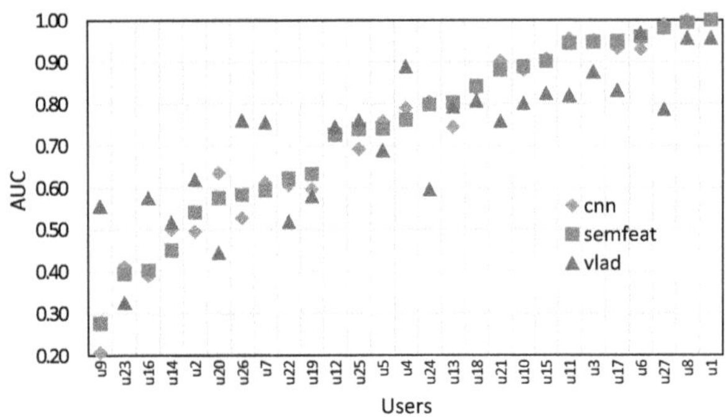

Figure 5: Per-user performance of generic models based on vlad, semfeat and cnn features

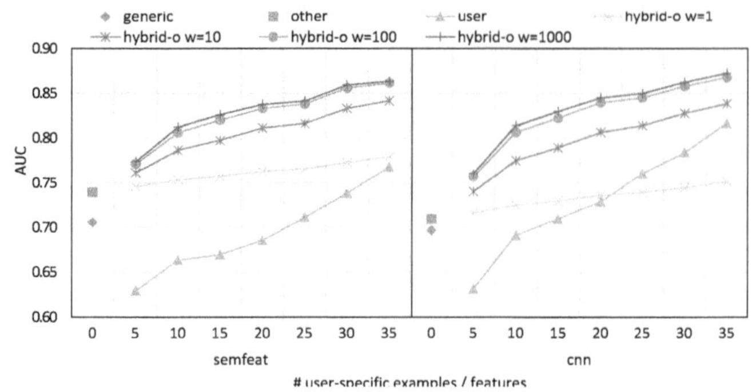

Figure 6: Performance of personalized models as a function of user-specific training examples

a separate AUC score is calculated for each user based on his/her own images). We note that there is a large variability in performance across users. For instance, using **semfeat** features, near-perfect AUC scores are obtained for users $\{u_1, u_8, u_{27}\}$ while the AUC scores are worse than random for users $\{u_9, u_{23}, u_{16}, u_{14}\}$ suggesting that the privacy perceptions of these users deviate strongly from the average notion of privacy. For this type of users, as well as for those for whom the performance of the generic models is close to random (about 40% of users), building personalized privacy classification models is essential to develop a useful alerting mechanism.

4.3 Personalized Privacy Models

This subsection compares the performance of generic privacy classification models to that of models employing user feedback in order to adapt to specific users. Specifically, we evaluate two types of personalized models on YourAlert.

user: Purely personalized models that use only user-specific training examples, i.e. a specific model is built for each YourAlert user from his examples only.

hybrid: Semi-personalized models that use a mixture of user-specific and generic training examples, with user-specific examples being assigned a higher weight to achieve personalization. We experimented with treating as generic examples: a) examples from PicAlert (**hybrid-g** variant) and b) examples from YourAlert that belong to other users (**hybrid-o** variant). Since the two choices lead to similar results, we report results only for **hybrid-o**.

As discussed in Subsection 3.1, *user* models are expected to perform better when a sufficient amount of user-specific examples are available, while *hybrid-o* models are expected to be advantageous with a limited amount of user feedback.

In order to evaluate this type of models ensuring reliable, out-of-sample estimates for all examples of each user, we use a modified k-fold cross-validation procedure ($k = 10$) that works as follows. The examples contributed by each user are randomly partitioned into k folds of approximately equal size, respecting the original class distribution (as in stratified cross-validation). Out of these, a single fold is retained as the test set and used to test the model, and from the remaining $k - 1$ folds we randomly select a specified number of examples (again respecting the original class distribution) and use them as training data either alone (**user** models) or together with generic examples (**hybrid-o** models). This process is repeated k times, with each of the k subsets being used exactly once as the test set. All predictions concerning each user are then aggregated into a single bag to calculate a per-user AUC score, or predictions for all users are combined together to calculate an overall AUC score for the examples of the YourAlert dataset.

Figure 6 plots the AUC scores on YourAlert by **user** and **hybrid-o** models trained on $\{5, 10, 15, 20, 25, 30, 35\}$ user-specific examples using **semfeat** and **cnn** features. We evaluate four variations of **hybrid-o** models, each one using a different weight ($w = \{1, 10, 100, 1000\}$) for the user-specific examples to facilitate a study of the impact of the weight parameter. In addition to the performance of these personalized models, the figure also shows the performance of two types of generic models to allow a direct comparison: a) **generic**: a model trained on a random subset of PicAlert (containing 5000 examples) and b) **other**: a model trained using only examples from other YourAlert users, i.e. a different generic model is build for each user, using the same generic examples as the corresponding **hybrid-o** model.

With respect to the generic models, we see that the performance of **other** is similar to that of **generic** with **cnn** features and better with **semfeat** features. These results suggest that although the examples of YourAlert come from users that adopt a personal, potentially different, notion of privacy, they are equally useful as the PicAlert examples for learning a generic privacy model.

With respect to the personalized models, we see that the performance of **user** models increases sharply as more user-specific training examples become available. When **semfeat** features are used we see that **user** models obtain similar performance with the generic models (**generic** and **other**) with as few as about 30 examples. The situation is even better when **cnn** features are used as we see that the performance of **user** models catches up with the performance of the generic models with as few as 15 examples and improves it by about 15% when 35 user-specific examples are used.

With regard to the semi-personalized, **hybrid-o** models we observe that they outperform significantly the purely personalized **user** models (with both types of features), especially for smaller numbers of user-specific training examples. As expected by the analysis of Subsection 3.1, the gap closes as more user-specific training examples become available. However, we see that for all values of user-specific examples (up to at least 35) **hybrid-o** models provide significantly better performance than both **user** and generic models. Importantly, we see that assigning a higher weight to user-specific examples is crucial for obtaining better per-

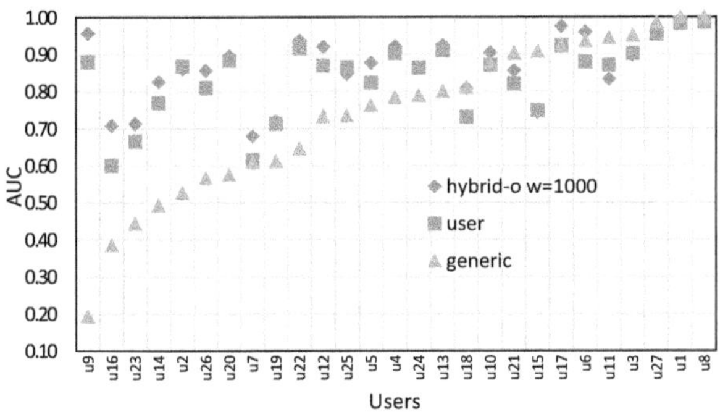

Figure 7: Per-user performance of generic, user and hybrid-o ($w = 1000$) models based on cnn features

formance. Specifically, results improve significantly as we increase w up to 100 but a saturation is observed with higher values.

Overall, the best personalized model (`hybrid-o` with `cnn` features) boosts the performance of the best generic model (`other` with `semfeat` features) by about 4% when the user provides feedback for 5 images to about 18% when the feedback increases to 35 images. Figure 7 presents a per-user performance breakdown for `generic`, `user` and `hybrid-o` ($w = 1000$) models based on `cnn` features (`user` and `hybrid-o` use 35 user-specific examples). `hybrid-o` and `user` provide better performance than `generic` for the majority of users, particularly for those that are poorly predicted by the `generic` model. Moreover, we see that in most cases `hybrid-o` is equally good or better than `user`.

4.4 Image Privacy Insights via SemFeat

Besides facilitating easily comprehensible explanations of privacy classifications (as shown in Figure 2), `semfeat` features can help in identifying users whose privacy concerns deviate strongly from the average perception of privacy. To this end, we build a single generic privacy detection model using the whole YourAlert dataset as well as 27 personalized privacy models trained using only the examples contributed by each user. For each model, we identify the concepts that are assigned the top-50 positive (associated with the private class) and top-50 negative (associated with the public class) coefficients and search for concepts that are strongly correlated to privacy according to the generic model and negatively correlated to privacy according to a personalized model (or vise versa). Despite the fact that less than 1% of the total `semfeat` features are considered in these comparisons, we can still gain valuable insights. For instance, according to the generic model, concepts related to family and relatives, such as `child`, `mate` and `son` are highly correlated to private images, while concepts related to natural scenes, such as `uphill`, `waterside` and `lakefront` are correlated to public images. In addition, we found some interesting deviations from the generic model, e.g. `alcoholic` is strongly correlated with privacy according to the generic model while it is negatively correlated with privacy for users u_{12} and u_{22}. On the other hand, concept `tourist` is private for user u_{11} and public according to the generic model.

Another practical use of `semfeat` is in creating user privacy profiles. To this end we employ the `semfeat-lda` representation that was described in subsection 3.3 and construct a privacy profile for each user by computing the centroid of the `semfeat-lda` vectors of his/her private images. This vector facilitates a summary of the user's concerns with respect to the six privacy-related topics that were identified by the LDA analysis. Given such a representation for each user, cluster analysis can be performed to identify recurring privacy themes among users. To illustrate this, we performed k-means ($k = 5$) clustering on the users of YourAlert and present the clustering results in Figure 8. We see that each cluster captures a different privacy theme. Users clustered at `c0`, for instance, are primarily concerned about preserving the privacy of their `vacations` while users clustered at `c2` are mainly concerned about the privacy of `children` and of photos related to `drinking`.

5. CONCLUSION AND FUTURE WORK

We presented a framework for personalized privacy-aware image classification. Our main immediate contribution is the creation of personalized privacy classification models that, as verified by experiments on a newly introduced image privacy dataset, exhibit significantly better performance than generic ones. Experimenting with different strategies of utilizing user feedback we found that combining user-specific with generic examples during training yields better performance than relying on either the user-specific or the generic examples alone. Furthermore, we exploited a new type of semantic features that, in addition to having an impressive performance, allow the discovery of interesting insights regarding the privacy perceptions of individuals.

There are several interesting directions for future work. First, the current system is limited to binary classification of images. We would like to develop models able to classify a user's photos into finer-grained privacy classes (e.g. close-friends, all-friends, friends-of-friends, public), corresponding to the different OSN audiences photos can be shared with. Second, we intend to design more sophisticated instance sharing strategies (e.g. assigning different weights to the examples of other users based on inter-user similarities) and make a comparison with well-established methods from the multi-task learning domain. Third, a limitation of the current study is that `cnn` features are obtained with the standard 1,000 classes from the ImageNet challenge that are, in a large majority of cases, not linked to privacy. As an alternative, we will explore: 1) the direct training of a neural network with private/public examples, and 2) the training of a network with an increased number of privacy-oriented concepts, based on an analysis similar to the one of subsection 4.4. Such a privacy-oriented set of concepts can also facilitate more meaningful semantic justifications compared to the `semfeat` vocabulary.

In a larger context, we will work toward the structuring of an active research community working on users' privacy preservation. This effort is necessary because the tackling of the challenges presented in the introduction is only possible through the collaboration of a hefty number of research groups with expertise in different areas related to privacy. While important among the data shared in OSNs, images are just a piece of the puzzle. The mining of other types of data (texts, videos, audio content, cookies, etc.) should be combined with social network analysis in order to best serve users. As a first step, we release our implementation under an open source license and also share the features and annotations associated with our dataset to encourage reproducibility. Sharing the dataset itself would be very useful

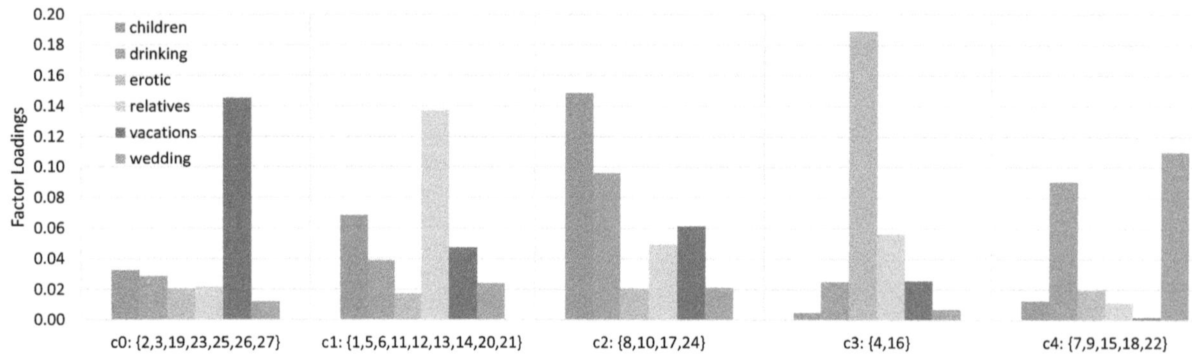

Figure 8: Clustering of YourAlert users based on privacy-related latent topics

but it is challenging due to the highly private nature of its content. The creation of dataset was not straightforward and we are currently investigating ways to enlarge it. One possible way is to provide incentives to users in exchange for the possibility to include their images in the dataset and to share them with the community. Another possibility is to liaise with other research groups from the area in order to gather data in a collaborative manner. The insights gained from this exploration will be shared with the research community in order to facilitate the creation and sharing of datasets for other types of data.

Yet another direction that we will explore is the organization of events to disseminate the topic in the community. Toward this direction, we have already identified the *MediaEval Benchmarking Initiative*[14] as a relevant venue that could host a task on privacy classification for multimedia documents.

Beyond computer science, privacy research should be informed by results from the legal and social sciences domains. A small interdisciplinary European group is already constituted as part of the USEMP project. We will work toward its extension with relevant research groups from other countries in order to include and confront different takes at privacy.

6. ACKNOWLEDGMENT

This work is supported by the USEMP FP7 project, partially funded by the EC under contract number 611596.

7. REFERENCES

[1] M. A. Álvarez, L. Rosasco, and N. D. Lawrence. Kernels for vector-valued functions: A review. *Foundations and Trends in Machine Learning*, 4(3):195–266, 2012.

[2] A. Bergamo and L. Torresani. Meta-class features for large-scale object categorization on a budget. In *CVPR*, 2012.

[3] D. M. Blei, A. Y. Ng, and M. I. Jordan. Latent dirichlet allocation. *JMLR*, 3:993–1022, 2003.

[4] D. Buschek, M. Bader, E. von Zezschwitz, and A. D. Luca. Automatic privacy classification of personal photos. In *Human-Computer Interaction - INTERACT*, 2015.

[5] R. Caruana. Multitask learning. *Machine Learning*, 28(1):41–75, 1997.

[6] C. Elkan. The foundations of cost-sensitive learning. In *IJCAI*, 2001.

[7] R. Fan, K. Chang, C. Hsieh, X. Wang, and C. Lin. LIBLINEAR: A library for large linear classification. *JMLR*, 9:1871–1874, 2008.

[14]http://www.multimediaeval.org

[8] Y. Freund and R. E. Schapire. Experiments with a new boosting algorithm. In *ICML*, 1996.

[9] A. Gînsca, A. Popescu, H. L. Borgne, N. Ballas, P. Vo, and I. Kanellos. Large-scale image mining with flickr groups. In *MultiMedia Modeling Conf.*, 2015.

[10] T. Hastie, R. Tibshirani, J. Friedman, T. Hastie, J. Friedman, and R. Tibshirani. *The elements of statistical learning*. Springer, 2009.

[11] Y. Liu, P. K. Gummadi, B. Krishnamurthy, and A. Mislove. Analyzing facebook privacy settings: user expectations vs. reality. In *Proceedings of the 11th ACM SIGCOMM Internet Measurement Conference*, 2011.

[12] M. Madejski, M. L. Johnson, and S. M. Bellovin. A study of privacy settings errors in an online social network. In *Tenth Annual IEEE International Conference on Pervasive Computing and Communications*, 2012.

[13] A. K. McCallum. Mallet: A machine learning for language toolkit. http://mallet.cs.umass.edu, 2002.

[14] K. D. Naini, I. S. Altingovde, R. Kawase, E. Herder, and C. Niederée. Analyzing and predicting privacy settings in the social web. In *User Modeling, Adaptation and Personalization*, 2015.

[15] P. A. Norberg, D. R. Horne, and D. A. Horne. The Privacy Paradox: Personal Information Disclosure Intentions versus Behaviors. *J. of Consumer Affairs*, 41(1):100–126, 2007.

[16] C. Paine, U. Reips, S. Stieger, A. N. Joinson, and T. Buchanan. Internet users' perceptions of 'privacy concerns' and 'privacy actions'. *Int. J. Hum.-Comput. Stud.*, 65(6):526–536, 2007.

[17] L. Y. Pratt. Discriminability-based transfer between neural networks. In *NIPS*, 1992.

[18] O. Russakovsky, J. Deng, H. Su, J. Krause, S. Satheesh, S. Ma, Z. Huang, A. Karpathy, A. Khosla, M. Bernstein, A. C. Berg, and L. Fei-Fei. Imagenet large scale visual recognition challenge. *IJCV*, 2015.

[19] K. Simonyan and A. Zisserman. Very deep convolutional networks for large-scale image recognition. *CoRR*, 2014.

[20] E. Spyromitros-Xioufis, S. Papadopoulos, I. Kompatsiaris, G. Tsoumakas, and I. Vlahavas. A comprehensive study over vlad and product quantization in large-scale image retrieval. *IEEE Transactions on Multimedia*, 2014.

[21] A. C. Squicciarini, C. Caragea, and R. Balakavi. Analyzing images' privacy for the modern web. In *In ACM Hypertext*, pages 136–147, 2014.

[22] A. Tonge and C. Caragea. Image privacy prediction using deep features. In *AAAI Conference on Artificial Intelligence*, 2016.

[23] S. Zerr, S. Siersdorfer, and J. S. Hare. Picalert!: a system for privacy-aware image classification and retrieval. In *ACM CIKM*, pages 2710–2712, 2012.

[24] S. Zerr, S. Siersdorfer, J. S. Hare, and E. Demidova. Privacy-aware image classification and search. In *ACM SIGIR*, 2012.

The Science and Detection of Tilting

Xingjie Wei*
Psychometrics Centre,
University of Cambridge
xw323@cam.ac.uk

Jussi Palomäki*
Cognitive Science Unit,
University of Helsinki
jussi.palomaki@helsinki.fi

Jeff Yan
School of Computing and
Communications, University of
Lancaster
jeff.yan@lancaster.ac.uk

Peter Robinson
Computer Laboratory,
University of Cambridge
pr10@cl.cam.ac.uk

ABSTRACT

Tilting refers to losing control due to negative emotions, behaving erratically, and thereby suffering adverse consequences. The term *tilt* originated in poker playing communities, where it is often a consequence of so called bad beats, i.e. losing with an unlikely-to-lose poker hand. Often resulting in devastating monetary losses, tilting is ubiquitous and well known in poker, but rarely studied despite its significance. In this paper, we argue that tilting is a fertile topic for interdisciplinary research both for psychologists and computer scientists. Specifically, we propose to study the manifestation of tilting via facial emotion expressions, and motivate the development of an automatic tilt-detection system. The scientific understanding of the psychology of tilting can be increased via a computing approach, which has not been previously attempted. Automatic tilting detection will lead to a practical technology that reduces poker players' monetary losses and improves their well being through reduced tilting. We also argue that while tilting is best known as a poker phenomenon, it also exists in other contexts. Thus, the idea we suggest is a novel application of computer vision, affective computing and multimedia technologies in the real world, across many domains.

Keywords

Tilting; facial expression; poker;affective computing

1. INTRODUCTION

Poker is a popular game played by over a hundred million players worldwide, most notably online. The yearly market value of online poker is estimated in billions of US dollars [20]. Poker is also often featured in various blockbuster movies (James Bond, X-Men, etc.), and dozens of television programs are exclusively dedicated to it, which highlights its cultural significance - nearly everyone is familiar with terms like *bluff* and *poker-face*.

Poker involves constant decision-making and risk analysis with monetary stakes, and it inspired John von Neumann to invent game theory, which is the study of strategic co-operation and conflict between intelligent rational decision-makers. In the recent years, poker has been used by researchers to study human decision-making processes [23], leading to interesting results and our increased scientific understanding of decision-making.

In poker, the term *tilt* refers to losing control and making detrimental, strategically weak decisions due to negative emotions, such as *anger* or *frustration*. Typical poker situations that cause tilt include, but are not limited to 1) losing in a situation where losing is perceivably highly improbable, for example, having a 90% chance of winning a big pot of money, but ending up losing it due to chance (or *bad luck*). This is known as encountering a *bad beat* in the poker community. 2) Prolonged series of losses (losing streaks), and 3) Factors external to the game mechanics, such as fatigue, or *needling* by other players (making provocative or *stingy* comments) [3]. Tilted poker players commonly adopt a sub-optimal and overly aggressive playing style, whereby they almost always end up losing superfluous amounts of money. This can result in losing one's entire life savings in a single 20-minute session [17].

It is well known in poker communities that tilting is a highly prevalent phenomenon. In a recent online study, within their last 6 months of poker playing, 88% of players reported having tilted severely at least once, 43% more than five times, and 24% more than 10 times [18]. This means that most poker players will eventually tilt, if they play long enough. It is thus not a stretch to state that tilting is the *number one destroyer of bankrolls* in poker.

Unfortunately, despite its significance, tilting has been rarely studied. There are only a few scientific studies on tilting in the psychology and gambling communities [17, 16, 18]. These studies have analysed poker players' subjective self-reports and suggested that tilting - in addition to being related to the emotions of anger and frustration - is characterized by strong feelings of *injustice*. In other words, tilting seems to be a state of *moral anger*: losing due to *bad luck* is perceived as *unfair*, which motivates an aggressive retaliation strategy (*in the name of justice*), which, in turn, ends in disappointment in self, and rumination over

*denotes equal contribution.

ICMR'16, June 06 - 09, 2016, New York, NY, USA

ISBN 978-1-4503-4359-6/16/06...$15.00

DOI: http://dx.doi.org/10.1145/2911996.2912019

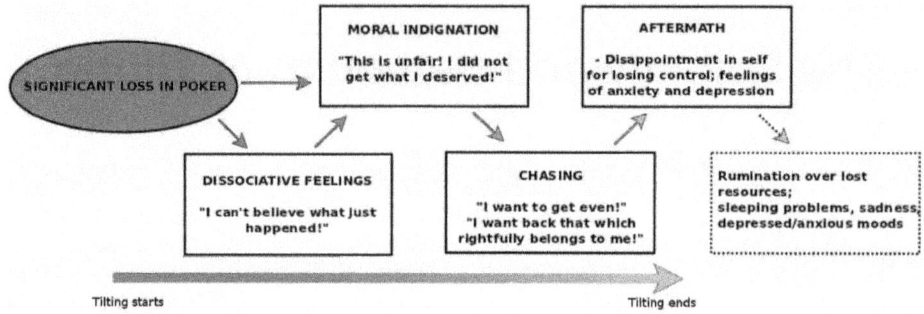

Figure 1: A model illustrating the phenomenology and aetiology of tilting. The small arrows indicate directions of causality. The bottom arrow indicates time.

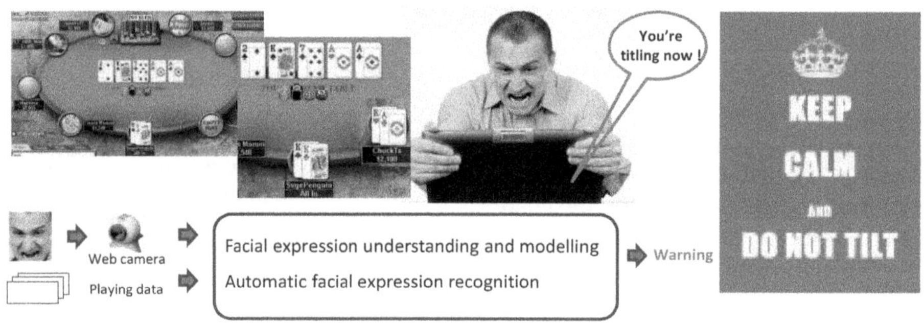

Figure 2: Illustration of poker tilting and automatic detection.

lost resources [16, 17]. This was a particularly common behavioural pattern in inexperienced players. The etiology and phenomenology of tilting is aptly depicted in a model formed by Palomäki, Laakasuo, and Salmela [17], which is based on a qualitative analysis of poker players' self-reported loss-induced emotions (see Figure 1).

It should also be noted that an increasing number of *self-help* books (e.g. [25]) have been published that specifically focus on how to deal with the emotional challenges posed by playing poker - i.e. the mental game of poker. At the heart of the challenges is tilting: each of these books recognises it as a remarkably significant single factor for players to lose excessive amounts of money. In other words, the mental game of poker is almost synonymous with *tilt-control*, and has become an increasingly pellucid subject matter especially during the era of online poker.

Interestingly, an increasing amount of anecdotal and empirical evidence suggests that tilting might in fact be a more universal human behavioural tendency. In a non-poker gambling context, behaviour similar to tilting is often seen in situations where people chase their losses [2]. This refers to people continuing to gamble only to win back what they had previously lost, for example, in slot machines, roulette or blackjack. As can be seen in Figure 1, chasing is also part of the aetiology of the tilting experience, although tilting as a whole is a more complex process.

Since tilting involves a strong moral anger component, it might also be related to *road rage*, which refers to aggressive or even retaliative behaviour in a motor vehicle. Road rage and tilting have a number of similarities, such as the aggressive and dangerous driving in road rage compared to the aggressive and detrimental betting behaviour in tilting, or the tendency to physically chase other motorists compared to the tendency of tilted players to chase their losses. Nonetheless, like tilting, road rage is often discussed colloquially but rarely studied empirically - at least not within a cohesive theoretical framework [5].

Moreover, even in the online communities of the popular *Starcraft* 2 game, the term *tilted* is often used to describe situations where players lose self-control and start playing overly aggressively and erratically. Finally, similar observations have also been made in tennis and golf [22].

Tilting is thus a significant and fascinating psychological phenomenon, and understanding it helps to better understand how emotions influence our behaviour and well-being. However, there seems to be no previous research on tilting in the computer science communities.

In this paper, we motivate the study of the psychology of tilting via a computing approach. Specifically, we propose to examine how tilting is manifested via facial emotion expressions. Methods and algorithms in computer vision, affective computing and multimedia will contribute to increasing the current scientific understanding of the psychology of tilting, a research goal that neither psychologists nor computer scientists would achieve alone. On the other hand, the understanding of how tilting is manifested via facial expressions will enlighten the development of an automatic tilt-detection system, which defines a novel application of computer vision and affective computing and multimedia technologies.

The overall illustration of our idea is shown in Figure 2. Since tilting is originally a poker phenomenon, we will employ poker as a tool to study it. A camera is used to capture videos of the poker players' facial expressions while they are playing. Quantitative data of the players' in-game poker actions (i.e. poker hand data) will be collected, and players will also keep a self-report *diary* to record their own experiences of tilting. Thereafter behaviour analysis and automatic facial expression recognition can be performed on these data. The results will form the basis of the automatic tilt detection system.

There have been no previous attempts to apply automatic facial expression analysis techniques to study the multifaceted and pervasive phenomenon of tilting. Such an interdisciplinary research project needs to draw heavily not only from theories of emotions and decision-making in cognitive psychology, but also from sophisticated techniques of facial expression recognition in computer science.

The rest of this paper is organised as follows. In Section 2 we introduce the theoretical foundations of emotions and facial expressions. In Section 3 we discuss related work. In Section 4 we discuss two important research questions in tilting and outline specific objectives for future research. In Section 5 we present an approach of combining behaviour analysis and facial expression recognition techniques to automatically detect the tilting behaviour. Finally, we conclude in Section 7 with a summary of the significance of our proposed idea, which extends beyond the context of poker.

2. THEORETICAL FOUNDATIONS

2.1 Scientific theories of emotions

It is clear that emotions are at the core of tilting. Emotions are multifaceted phenomena and studied within many different theoretical frameworks. Typically, emotion researchers are interested in the following questions: 1) what is the overall function of emotions (what they are *for*)? 2) what factors determine which emotion is experienced in a given situation; and 3) how do emotions relate to physiological processes in the body [7] ? There is some debate over whether emotions should be conceptualized as *discrete* or *dimensional* phenomena. A discrete model of emotions claims that different emotions correspond to specific physiological reactions and body expressions. According to discrete models, the physiological changes occurring in the body during experiences of *anger* are distinct from those occurring during experiences of *fear*. Dimensional models, in turn, argue that emotions are not so easily distinguished from one another at the physiological level, and that they should instead be defined according to one or more dimensions: for example, arousal (or *activation*; ranging from low to high), *valence* (ranging from unpleasant to pleasant), or *incentive* (ranging from withdrawal to approach) [21].

We focus briefly on two theoretical frameworks in emotion research: cognitive appraisal and evolutionary psychology theories of emotions. These frameworks are not mutually incompatible, but do differ in many key aspects.

According to cognitive appraisal theories [15], emotion elicitation depends on how various situations are *appraised*: two people can experience a very different emotion in an identical situation, if they appraise that situation differently. What is a compliment for some (*nice hair!*) may be a sarcastic insult for others. Appraisal is sometimes viewed as a *cognitive* process that is conceptually separate from *emotional* processes, as emotional reactions are assumed to *follow* cognitive appraisals. However, appraisals can also be unconscious, in which case the distinction between *emotion* and *cognition* becomes less obvious [15]. This framework has previously been adopted in computational modelling of human emotion [13].

However, appraisal theories of emotions are not really *theories* insofar as they mainly aim at describing how situational factors relate to emotion elicitation, but do not answer the deeper questions, such as "*why* do we have emotions?" or "what are emotions *for*"? The evolutionary-psychology theory of emotions is not so much concerned about the distinction between *cognitive* and *emotional* processes, but rather seeks to explain what the overall function or purpose of emotions is. In this paper, we adopt this view of emotions, as will be detailed below, because we believe it has the strongest empirical backing in both psychology and biology [31]. The evolutionary-psychologist theory also draws from both discrete and dimensional conceptualisations of emotions to create a uniform picture of what emotions really are.

2.2 Emotions and facial expressions

According to evolutionary psychologists, emotions are defined as coordinated psycho-physiological changes in the body and mind in response to specific (e.g. threatening or inviting) stimuli, which increased the fitness of our ancestors' genes.

For example, if we accidentally run into a bear while camping, we would freeze, our hearts would start pounding, and we would allocate all our attention towards resolving the threat. In other words, we would feel *fear*, which, in this situation, is a psycho-physiological manifestation of the so-called adaptive flight-or-flight response. We would at this moment also *display* fear on our faces, which is made possible by human facial muscles controlling our facial expressions. It is well known that discrete facial *displays* of emotions are a human universal, and the study of facial emotion expression dates back to Darwin in the 1800s. Putatively, displaying emotions on their faces made communication easier and faster for our ancestors in dangerous environments. The ability to effectively convey or interpret feelings enables quicker reactions in threatening situations. For example, a facial fear expression is a quicker way to signal danger than other more elaborative ways of communication, such as words.

The scientific study of universal facial emotions rose to general popularity in the 1970s, largely because of the cross-cultural studies conducted by psychologist Paul Ekman [6]. However, the early studies were based on human observers and subjective evaluations of facial expressions, which are prone to errors of judgment and thus often unreliable. These limitations have since been overcome by representing facial expressions in terms of a fixed set of facial parameters, which can be calculated based on carefully observed movements in facial muscles. Currently, there is strong evidence for six basic emotions, that people across cultures display on their faces: joy/happiness, sadness, anger, fear, disgust and surprise (for an alternative view of four instead of six basic emotions, see [9]).

The term *macro-expression* is generally used to describe both the six basic facial emotions and other *large-scale* facial muscle movements. Unlike macro-expressions, *micro-expressions* are brief (lasting less than 100ms), involuntary human facial expression associated with experiencing emotions. Micro-expressions typically occur in *high-stakes* situations, in which people have something significant to lose or gain - especially when the person does not consciously know what s/he is feeling, or is consciously trying to hide an emotion [6].

Facial expressions, both macro and micro, can be represented as a fixed set of parameters via the Facial Action Coding System (FACS). FACS defines atomic facial muscle actions as *Action Unit* numbers (AUs), which can describe almost any facial expression. For example, anger can be represented by the combined activation of AUs 4, 5, 7, 23 and 24 (the description of each AU is presented in Table 1).

Also more complex cognitive mental states such as *bothered* or *disbelieving* can be represented as facial expressions, but these are beyond the scope of the current paper.

3. RELATED WORK

As mentioned in Section 1, the only scientific studies on tilting were conducted by Palomäki and colleagues' [17, 16, 18], which are useful in building a preliminary framework for understanding the psychology of tilting. However, these studies relied on poker players' subjective self-reports - observations of actual tilting behaviour were not made. Furthermore, although other facial expressions have been studied in automatic facial expression recognition, there is no previous research on tilting in computer science communities.

Facial expression techniques have been widely employed in human-computer interaction applications. Despite having solid theoretical foundations, automatic micro-expression analysis techniques have not attracted much attention in the field of affective gaming (the study of how human affects and emotions can be recognised, interpreted and processed to enhance the gaming experience).

Compared with other methods used in studies of affective processes, such as measuring body movements or poses, or psycho-physiological emotion-related signals, such as heart beat rates, skin conductance responses, or electroencephalography, the vision based facial macro- and micro-expression analysis system has unique advantages: 1) it requires only a cost-effective camera (even micro-expressions can be detected from videos with a frame-rate of 25 fps and a resolution of 640×480; [4, 19]); 2) it is non-intrusive and easily adopted by poker players [10].

Analysing betting sequences and poker hand records (i.e. monitoring *erratic* betting behaviour by quantitative methods) could be useful for tilt-detection, but very difficult for current artificial intelligence (AI), although tremendous progress in poker AI research has been achieved by leading teams at the University of Alberta and Carnegie Mellon University [1]. Moreover, these teams have not specifically studied tilting at all.

In 2013, the Affective Computing Research Group led by Professor Rosalind Picard at the Massachusetts Institute of Technology were the first to collect naturalistic and spontaneous facial expressions *in-the-wild* via participants' cameras (at 14 fps), but they focused only on the emotion of *joy* [14]. Also in 2013, a leading team in facial expression analysis at the University of Oulu studied micro-expression detection during feelings of joy, sadness, disgust, fear and surprise in a laboratory setting; they were also the first to establish a spontaneous micro-expression database [10].

However, neither of these groups, nor any others, have evaluated the emotion of anger, which is highly relevant to tilting.

4. RESEARCH QUESTIONS

Previous evidence suggests that feelings of anger, frustration and injustice are implicated in tilting, but this knowledge is by no means sufficient to fully and objectively understand the phenomenon. Neither are the six basic emotions necessarily sufficient to fully characterise tilting behaviour. For example, it is not enough to merely look for facial displays of anger (or frustration) during poker play using pre-existing methods of facial expression classification, and, based on these, conclude that tilting had occurred. Various unknown macro- and/or micro-expressions might also be involved, for instance, those related to feelings of injustice (or some other still unascertained emotion). Furthermore, the exact temporal pattern/order of facial expressions during tilting has not been ascertained: do facial macro-expressions of frustration lead to micro-expressions of *injustice*, which, in turn, lead to macro-expressions of *anger*? Or does tilting begin with macro-expressions of anger (e.g. due to a bad beat), followed by micro-expressions of injustice and frustration? Is tilting more about short-lasting moral anger than prolonged feelings of frustration and/or anxiety, or vice versa? These questions are currently unanswered.

In other words, on a general level, we know **how tilting feels** (subjectively), but not **what it actually looks like** (objectively). We do not yet know **what exactly are the objective facial expressions implicated in tilting behaviour**. Thus, we propose to build on the existing anecdotal and empirical evidence on tilting by asking two subsequent simple but deep research questions:

- *How does tilting manifest via facial expressions?*
- *Is this manifestation automatically detectable via computer vision methods?*

People typically play online poker at home, facing a computer monitor, in a secluded environment. Since poker requires active concentration and task immersion, prominent facial expressions unrelated to the game are not likely to occur. Online poker is also played for real money and the stakes are often significant for many players. Arguably, while playing online, poker players do not benefit from attempting to *hide* their emotions (as they would in *live* poker). Micro-expressions are still likely to occur, given the emotional and monetary significance of the game to the players. We thus expect both macro- and micro-expressions to be implicated in online poker, and consequently in tilting.

We outline two specific objectives for future research:

1. Map the facial macro- and micro-expressions detected during actual tilting behaviour by employing facial expression analysis techniques.

2. Pioneer the development of an automatic system that detects expressions of tilting and warns players when tilting is imminent (*Tilt-detector*).

Previous studies of facial expression analysis have shown that detecting anger is more difficult than detecting other basic emotional expressions, such as surprise or joy. The display of anger requires a personal involvement, which is

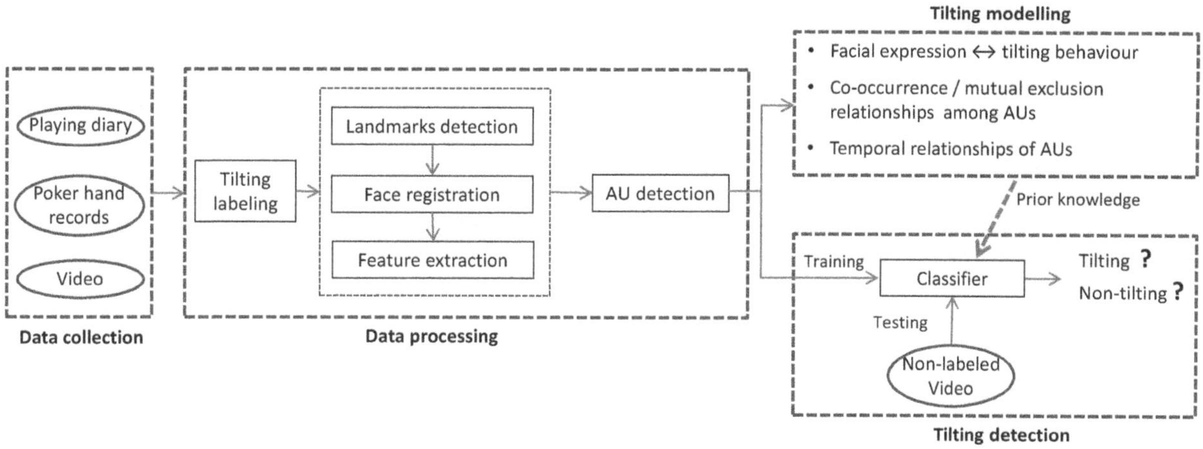

Figure 3: The framework of our research approach.

not easy to evoke using traditional methods of emotion-elicitation. However, this is unlikely to be an issue in the current context, because we rely on the inherent nature of online poker as a naturalistic and emotional environment. This assumption has a strong empirical backing in psychology [18].

5. RESEARCH APPROACH

The framework of our research approach is shown in Figure 3. It contains four main phases: data collection, data processing, tilting modelling and tilting detection. As mentioned in Section 1, the self-report playing diary, quantitative poker hand records and facial expression videos are first collected from the players. During data processing, the video frames are manually labelled for analysis (for the presence of tilting) according to the playing diary and hand record data, and then image processing is performed to extract features and detect AUs in these frames. The detected AUs are used for tilting modelling in three levels, from high level to low level.

In addition, the AUs and the previously extracted features are used to train classifiers for tilting detection, while the information acquired during the modelling process is considered in training. We explain each process in detail in the following sub-sections. Note that in each process, various specific techniques can be used in implementation - our framework is flexible, extendable and not limited to the specific implementation methods introduced hereafter.

5.1 Data collection

For data collection, participants should be active poker players who play for real money and who have had personal experiences of tilting. Special care should be taken in screening for eligible participants. This includes, but is not limited to, assessing their level of poker experience, severity and frequency of self-reported tilting, and personality characteristics. Given that the overwhelming majority (about 95%, see [17, 18]) of poker players are male, female participants will not be included in the experiment due to unknown and possibly confounding gender effects. On the other hand, there is evidence [29] that cultural background affects nonverbal behaviour. To reduce unconstrained variability in the data, the data collection should only focus on western players. This enables performing a more effective analysis with less noisy data. However, we also note that our proposed framework is not necessarily limited to these constraints. Further research and development can be done without such constraints.

For a planned period of time, for example, 2-3 months, participants should be instructed to play as they would normally, with the exception of having their cameras on recording their facial expressions. Standard 25-fps webcams have yielded decent success for detecting micro-expressions, as evidenced in [10, 19]. Furthermore, Moore's law suggests that we will see better webcams widely deployed in the near future, which will further improve facial expression detection.

Participants should keep a playing diary, in which they record and time-stamp their experiences of tilting. These self-reports should include 1) perceived cause (e.g. bad beat), 2) exact time and duration, 3) perceived severity of the tilt, and 4) descriptions of the emotions felt.

Participants should also record their poker hand histories using poker tracking and analysis software such as Poker Tracker (*www.pokertracker.com*) or Hold'Em Manager (*www.holdemmanager.com*). These software import and parse poker hand histories from online poker sites and use this information to build a local database library. They thus allow for monitoring each participant's session-by-session profit or loss, the number of hands played, and the amount of time played. Having detailed quantitative tracking records of the poker hands played will help participants accurately reflect on their playing sessions.

5.2 Data processing

5.2.1 Tilting labelling

After data collection, the video frames can be manually labelled as *tilting*, *non-tilting* and *unknown*, according to participants' self-reports and poker tracking data. For example, if a participant reports in his diary that during one session he started tilting around hand number 85 (the 85th played hand during that session) and stopped tilting around hand number 120, we look at the recorded video frames between the time hands #85 and #120 were played, and label these frames as tilting.

5.2.2 *Face data pre-processing*

For *tilting* and *non-tilting* video frames, a large number of facial landmarks, such as eye and eyebrow corners, nose tip and mouth corners, are automatically detected by the landmarks detector *Face++* [32] in each frame. The face area is normalised according to its geometrical properties such as size and pose using geometrical or morphological transforms and then further normalised with respect to its photometrical properties such as illumination conditions. Thereafter the face area is cropped from the background and re-sized to a constant scale (i.e. 250×250 pixels), and appearance features such as the Local Binary Pattern (LBP) are extracted from a small region (i.e. 20×20 pixels) around each landmark. Finally, dimension reduction is performed using principal component analysis (PCA) to transform high-dimensional features into low-dimensional spaces for efficient classifier learning.

5.2.3 *AU detection*

To evaluate the subtle facial expressions related to tilting, AUs defined by the FACS are used to describe facial muscle actions. Typically, trained experts manually label AUs frame-by-frame from each video, which is time-consuming. In our framework, we adopt the automatic AU detectors BGCS [24] which includes a large number of trained AU models. Detailed information of AUs that can be detected is shown in Table 1.

Table 1: Description of AUs

AU No.	Description	AU No.	Description
1	Inner Brow Raiser	17	Chin Raiser
2	Outer Brow Raiser	18	Lip Pucker
4	Brow Lowerer	20	Lip Stretcher
5	Upper Lid Raiser	22	Lip Funneler
6	Cheek Raiser	23	Lip Tightener
7	Lid Tightener	24	Lip Pressor
9	Nose Wrinkler	25	Lips Part
10	Upper Lip Raiser	26	Jaw Drop
11	Nasolabial Deepener	27	Mouth Stretch
12	Lip Corner Puller	43	Eyes Closed
14	Dimpler	45	Blink
15	Lip Corner Depressor	46	Wink
16	Lower Lip depression		

5.3 Tilting modelling

After the video frames have been labelled for the presence of tilt, automatic AU detection can be applied to these frames for tilting modelling. We create the models in three levels by: 1) building the mapping between tilting behaviour and facial expressions, 2) representing the co-occurrence / mutual exclusion relationships among AUs, and 3) creating models of the temporal relationships of AUs. The outputs of these three levels can tell us *what tilting actually looks like* and they can be used as prior knowledge to aid tilting detection.

Level 1: We first apply sequential regression analysis to assess which AUs are most related to the tilting expressions. Based on a small subset of discriminative AUs (whose frequencies among all the detected AUs exceed a specific threshold) and many iterations of regressions, an additional AU is added to the current subset if it increases the accuracy of predicting tilting expressions. After that, a *tilting AU set* which contains a number of AUs of tilting expressions can be generated. Then we can contrast the *tilting AU set* with AUs detected from the *non-tilt frames.* By examining the differences in these two AU sets, we are able to answer *whether or not tilting actually manifests as specific facial expression patterns.*

In addition, we contrast the AUs of tilting expressions with the AUs of other basic facial expressions. As a hypothetical example, in the tilting frames, activity in AU4 (brow lowerer), AU5 (upper lid raiser), AU7 (lid tightener) and AU23 (lip tightener) might be pronounced. This reflects a facial expression akin to anger and perhaps disgust, which would be reasonable, given that tilting has been characterized in the literature as *moral anger* [17]. However, it should be noted that the expressions we might observe during tilting do not necessarily map directly into previously established emotion-related facial actions.

After these steps, we can see if the tilting expressions are a combination of other basic facial expressions (e.g. *anger+sadness*), or if *new* facial movements are involved. The modelling of Level 1 answers the first research question posed in Section 4.

Level 2: As shown in [24], some AUs usually co-occur to form meaningful expressions. For example, AU6 (cheek raiser) frequently co-occurs with AU12 (lip corner puller) and AU15 (lip corner depressor) when people smile. In contrast, some AUs almost never co-occur. For example, it is very difficult to activate AU24 (lip pressor) and AU25 (lips part) simultaneously.

The work in [27] shows that such co-occurrence and mutual exclusion relationships are important for facial action recognition. The pairwise co-occurrence probability of two AUs is computed as:

$$P(AU_i = 1 | AU_j = 1) = \frac{N_{AU_i + AU_j}}{N_{AU_j}} \tag{1}$$

where $N_{AU_i+AU_j}$ is the number of samples when AU_i and AU_j occur together and N_{AU_j} is the number of samples of AU_j. Similarly, the pairwise mutual exclusion probability of two AUs is computed as:

$$P(AU_i = 0 | AU_j = 0) = \frac{N_{\neg AU_i + \neg AU_j}}{N_{\neg AU_j}} \tag{2}$$

where $N_{\neg AU_i + \neg AU_j}$ is the number of samples when neither AU_i nor AU_j occurs and $N_{\neg AU_j}$ is the number of sample when AU_j does not occur.

We employ the Bayesian Networks (BN) to exploit the relationships among AUs detected in tilt frames. BN is a probabilistic model that represents a set of random variables and their conditional dependencies by a directed acyclic graph (DAG). Each AU is modelled as a node in a BN and the probabilistic dependencies among the AUs are characterised by the links between the nodes. The initial dependencies among the AUs are computed using equation (1) and (2) and a finer BN structure is learned by using structure learning methods [11].

Level 3: Besides the co-occurrence and mutual exclusion relationships, AUs also show strong temporal dependencies [26]. The activation of an AU can activate another AU (i.e. one is the cause and the other is the effect). For example, AU12 (lip corner puller) is usually followed by AU6 (cheek raiser) during smiling.

The static BN in Level 2 captures the spatial dependencies among AUs. In order to represent the temporal relationships of AUs in tilting, we adopt the Dynamic Bayesian Network (DBN) [26], which consist of interconnected time slices of BNs, and where the temporal relationships between two neighbours are modelled by a Hidden Makov Model (HMM). Therefore AUs can be regarded as a sequence of observations over time.

With models built in Level 2 and 3, we are able to better understand the relationships between AUs (i.e., facial micro features) and tilting expressions.

5.4 Tilting detection

After tilting modelling, we adopt facial expression recognition techniques to automatically detect the tilting expression from the videos. We use both the holistic appearance features (e.g., LBP features mentioned in Section 5.2.2) and AU features (See Table 1) for detection.

Baseline: We train a Support Vector Machine (SVM) using the LBP features extracted from tilting and non-tilting video frames as the baseline method, to detect the tilting expression as a whole.

AU based detection: The AU based detection focuses on facial micro features. As mentioned Section 5.3, a number of significant AUs related to tilting expressions are selected and used to train a SVM.

Intuitively, the second approach should generate superior performance to the baseline since it utilises high-level knowledge from the previously established associations between facial expressions and tilting behaviour. However, because the relationship between AUs and tilting expressions is still an open problem, the first approach, which detects tilt expression as a whole, could also prove useful.

6. SIGNIFICANCE

In this section, we summarise the significance of our idea and the proposed framework. Our framework is flexible and extensible, and can be applied to the study of other negative facial expressions.

6.1 Authentic and spontaneous negative emotion data

If data were successfully collected, they will be the first in the world on actual tilting behaviour, and on authentic and spontaneous *negative* emotional expressions, which are more difficult to obtain than positive expressions in naturalistic conditions. Currently, most of the public facial expression databases are limited to posed expressions collected under controlled laboratory conditions [12, 28]. In contrast, the data we propose to collect will contain spontaneous and naturalistic (i.e. uncontrolled) expressions captured in real-application scenarios. These expressions involve challenging elements, such as non-uniform illumination and changes in head poses. These data will be a valuable resource for researchers working in the domains of facial expression recognition, affective computing and psychology - the impact thus reaches far beyond the currently suggested research.

6.2 Tilting prevention solution for poker

An automatic tilt-detector can be developed based on the evaluation results of both the holistic and AU based approaches. The tilt-detector can be used to dissuade tilted players from playing. This can be done by a variety of means, including (but not limited to) force-closing or force-pausing the poker software, displaying *warning*-messages, or setting an upper limit to the number of online poker tables to play on. Moreover, very recently, the idea of studying the AUs and facial expressions simultaneously has attracted attention [30, 11] in the area of automatic facial recognition. We believe our proposed framework, which involves both the low-level (i.e. AUs) and high-level (i.e. tilting expressions) facial activities, will also contribute to the research in this area.

Many poker players strive to increase their skills and profits. This is reflected in the many poker self-help books focusing on the *mental game aspects* of the game, and also in the increased popularity of commercial online poker *training sites* such as *www.deucescracked.com* or *www.pokersavvy.com*, which offer downloadable training videos as well as hands-on coaching from professional poker players. Although tilting is ubiquitous and generally recognised by poker players as the most significant single reason for superfluous losses, there are currently no efficient software-based solutions to reduce tilting. Thus, the suggested research has also tremendous commercial potential. For example, an automatic tilt-detection system can be deployed as a cloud-based software-as-a-service. Poker players need only to switch on their webcam, and let the service do the rest.

Tilting less in poker equals losing much less money, or winning much more. More importantly, for tens of millions of poker players around the world, reduced tilting will undoubtedly result in increased well-being.

6.3 Applications in other contexts

Given that other tilt-like phenomena besides poker tilting exist in various settings - such as other types of gambling or games, road rage, or even sports - the detection of tilt-related facial expressions has wide potential applicability. Casinos will not have a monetary incentive to deter their customers from tilting. However, in terms of responsible gambling, casinos are liable to ensure their customers' general welfare. This means casinos would not have reasonable moral grounds *not* to implement an effective means to reduce their customers' detrimental gambling behaviour (tilting). Likewise, inside a motor vehicle, it would be relatively easy to install computerized devices that automatically detect road rage (i.e. an aggressive behavioural tilt-like expression) and deter drivers from acting out. This application of affective computing could directly impact people's well being by saving lives.

Moreover, since poker is essentially a game of rapid financial investments, it closely resembles active stock trading. Like poker players, online stock traders often need to make multiple financial decisions over short timescales, and such decisions are adversely influenced by emotions. To our knowledge, there is only one pre-existing commercial device designed to reduce emotional arousal during online stock trading: The (Philips) Rationalizer, which measures online stock traders' heartbeat variability via a wristband and warns them if they get too excited or stressed (as indicated by increased heartbeat rates).

The most obvious caveat of the Rationalizer is its inability to differentiate between positive and negative emotions. For example, feeling enthusiastic or angry (positive an negative emotional states with high arousal, respectively) would both be reflected in an increased heartbeat rate and thus flagged by the Rationalizer as potentially "detrimental" for decision-making. Our proposed tilt-detector system does not have this limitation and could thus be easily utilized in an online stock-trading context. Moreover, our system is likely much more cost-effective than the Rationalizer, as the only hardware required is a standard web-camera.

It should also be noted that an early detection of micro-expressions, including those related to tilting, has many potential applications in fields ranging from video security (e.g. surveillance), human-computer-interaction (e.g. robotics) to affective computing (e.g. gaming). Compared with the traditional facial expression recognition, early detection is a relatively unexplored problem [8].

The co-occurrence and mutual exclusion relationships among AUs modelled in Section 5.3 suggest that the presence of one AU can act as a strong prior for the presence or non-presence of others in tilting. In addition, the temporal relationships of tilting AUs enable tilting to be recognised from a sequence of observations over time. This information is helpful for building further models for early detection of tilting. This can be an interesting future research direction.

7. SUMMARY

In this paper, using online poker as a case study, we have motivated the study of the science and detection of tilting and related psychological phenomena. We have proposed a framework for examining how tilting is manifested via facial emotion expressions, and introduced a tilt-detection system based on behaviour analysis and automatic facial expression recognition techniques. On the one hand, the research idea discussed here would definitely produce new knowledge concerning emotion elicitation and facial expressions, e.g. during playing online poker in a very naturalistic setting, thus advancing the scientific understanding of the psychology of emotions and tilting - a significant but under-explored topic. On the other hand, the automatic tilt-detection introduced here defines a new problem for computer vision and affective computing, which is an interesting research area by itself, and can motivate novel applications in the future.

8. REFERENCES

[1] N. Bard, J. Hawkin, J. Rubin, and M. Zinkevich. The annual computer poker competition. *AI Magazine*, 34(2):112, 2013.

[2] R. B. Breen and M. Zuckerman. 'Chasing' in gambling behavior: personality and cognitive determinants. *Pers. Indiv. Differ.*, 27(6):1097–1111, 1999.

[3] B. R. Browne. Going on tilt: Frequent poker players and control. *J. Gambl. Behav.*, 5(1):3–21, 1989.

[4] W.-S. Chu, F. De la Torre, and J. Cohn. Selective transfer machine for personalized facial action unit detection. In *IEEE Conf. Computer Vision and Pattern Recognition (CVPR)*, pages 3515–3522, Jun. 2013.

[5] C. S. Dula and E. Geller. Risky, aggressive, or emotional driving: Addressing the need for consistent communication in research. *J. Safety Res.*, 34(5):559–566, 2003.

[6] P. Ekman. *Emotions Revealed: Recognizing Faces and Feelings to Improve Communication and Emotional Life.* Henry Holt and Co., Apr. 2003.

[7] E. Fox. *Emotion science cognitive and neuroscientific approaches to understanding human emotions.* Palgrave Macmillan, 2008.

[8] M. Hoai and F. De la Torre. Max-margin early event detectors. *Int. J. Comput. Vision*, 107(2):191–202, 2014.

[9] R. E. Jack, O. G. Garrod, and P. G. Schyns. Dynamic facial expressions of emotion transmit an evolving hierarchy of signals over time. *Curr. Biol.*, 24(2):187–192, 2014.

[10] X. Li, T. Pfister, X. Huang, G. Zhao, and M. Pietikainen. A spontaneous micro-expression database: Inducement, collection and baseline. In *IEEE Int. Conf. Automatic Face and Gesture Recognition (FG)*, pages 1–6, Apr. 2013.

[11] Y. Li, S. Wang, Y. Zhao, and Q. Ji. Simultaneous facial feature tracking and facial expression recognition. *IEEE Trans. Image Process.*, 22(7):2559–2573, Jul. 2013.

[12] P. Lucey, J. Cohn, T. Kanade, J. Saragih, Z. Ambadar, and I. Matthews. The extended cohn-kanade dataset (CK+): A complete dataset for action unit and emotion-specified expression. In *IEEE Conf. Computer Vision and Pattern Recognition Workshops (CVPRW)*, pages 94–101, Jun. 2010.

[13] S. Marsella and J. Gratch. Computationally modeling human emotion. *Commun. ACM*, 57(12):56–67, Nov 2014.

[14] D. McDuff, R. El Kaliouby, T. Senechal, M. Amr, J. Cohn, and R. Picard. Affectiva-MIT facial expression dataset (AM-FED): Naturalistic and spontaneous facial expressions collected in-the-wild;. In *IEEE Conf. Computer Vision and Pattern Recognition Workshops (CVPRW)*, pages 881–888, Jun. 2013.

[15] A. Moors, P. C. Ellsworth, K. R. Scherer, and N. H. Frijda. Appraisal theories of emotion: State of the art and future development. *Emotion Review*, 5(2):119–124, 2013.

[16] J. Palomäki, M. Laakasuo, and M. Salmela. "Don't worry, it's just poker!"-experience, self-rumination and self-reflection as determinants of decision-making in on-line poker. *J. Gambl. Stud.*, 29(3):491–505, 2013.

[17] J. Palomäki, M. Laakasuo, and M. Salmela. "This is just so unfair!": A qualitative analysis of loss-induced emotions and tilting in on-line poker. *Int. Gambl. Stud.*, 13(2):255–270, 2013.

[18] J. Palomäki, M. Laakasuo, and M. Salmela. Losing more by losing it: Poker experience, sensitivity to losses and tilting severity. *J. Gambl. Stud.*, 30(1):187–200, 2014.

[19] T. Pfister, X. Li, G. Zhao, and M. Pietikainen. Recognising spontaneous facial micro-expressions. In *IEEE Int. Conf. Computer Vision (ICCV)*, pages 1449–1456, Nov 2011.

[20] K. Philander and I. Fiedler. Online poker in north america: Empirical evidence on its complementary effect on the offline gambling market. *Gaming Law Review and Economics*, 16(7-8):415–423, 2012.

[21] N. A. Remington, L. R. Fabrigar, and P. S. Visser. Reexamining the circumplex model of affect. *J. Pers. Soc. Psychol.*, 79(2):286, 2000.

[22] B. Rotella. *Golf is not a game of perfect.* Simon and Schuster, New York, NY 10020 USA, 1996.

[23] E. J. Schlicht, S. Shimojo, C. F. Camerer, P. Battaglia, and K. Nakayama. Human wagering behavior depends on opponents' faces. *PloS one*, 5(7):e11663, 2010.

[24] Y. Song, D. McDuff, D. Vasisht, and A. Kapoor. Exploiting sparsity and co-occurrence structure for action unit recognition. In *IEEE Int. Conf. Automatic Face and Gesture Recognition (FG)*, May 2015.

[25] J. Tendler and B. Carter. *The mental game of poker: Proven strategies for improving tilt control, confidence, motivation, coping with variance, and more.* Jared Tendler LLC, 2011.

[26] Y. Tong, J. Chen, and Q. Ji. A unified probabilistic framework for spontaneous facial action modeling and understanding. *IEEE Trans. Pattern Anal. Mach. Intell.*, 32(2):258–273, Feb. 2010.

[27] Y. Tong, W. Liao, and Q. Ji. Facial action unit recognition by exploiting their dynamic and semantic relationships. *IEEE Trans. Pattern Anal. Mach. Intell.*, 29(10):1683–1699, Oct. 2007.

[28] M. Valstar and M. Pantic. Induced disgust, happiness and surprise: an addition to the mmi facial expression database. In *Int. Conf. Language Resources and Evaluation, Workshops on EMOTION*, pages 65–70, 2010.

[29] A. Vrij and F. W. Winkel. Cultural patterns in dutch and surinam nonverbal behavior: An analysis of simulated police/citizen encounters. *J. Nonverbal Behav.*, 15(3):169–184, 1991.

[30] J. Wang, S. Wang, M. Huai, C. Wu, Z. Gao, Y. Liu, and Q. Ji. Capture expression-dependent au relations for expression recognition. In *IEEE Int. Conf. Multimedia and Expo Workshops (ICMEW)*, pages 1–6, Jul. 2014.

[31] L. Workman and W. Reader. *Evolutionary psychology.* Cambridge University Press, 2014.

[32] E. Zhou, H. Fan, Z. Cao, Y. Jiang, and Q. Yin. Extensive facial landmark localization with coarse-to-fine convolutional network cascade. In *IEEE Int. Conf. Computer Vision Workshops (ICCVW)*, pages 386–391, Dec. 2013.

Using Photos as Micro-Reports of Events

Siripen Pongpaichet, Mengfan Tang, Laleh Jalali, Ramesh Jain
University of California, Irvine
{spongpai, mengfant, lalehj, jain}@ics.uci.edu

ABSTRACT

Photos serve dual role. Photos are important for capturing, saving, sharing, and reminiscing memories of events and people. Modern photos, however, are becoming more *spontaneous*, *objective*, *compelling*, and *universal* reports of a moment in an event also. In this paper our focus is on millions of photos being captured as informative reports and using them for emerging applications including situation recognition, trend analysis, and cultural dynamics.

EventShop is an open source platform for situation recognition. Utilizing this platform and using a stream of photo reports from various sources as one of the data streams in this platform, we build a visual analytics system to understand the information that could be gleaned from such photo report streams. Our early experiments are based on the Yahoo Flickr Creative Commons 100 Million photos set released recently. We are also using other sources to import and understand the efficacy of these reports for various important applications.

Keywords

Micro-report, Micro-blog, Photo, Situation Recognition, Visual Analytics

1. INTRODUCTION

As of today, phones have already out numbered humans in this world since a person can possess multiple phones at once. 70 percent of world population may own smart phones in 2020. Most people use their phones for reporting and getting useful information from collected and processed reports by other people. Camera is the main reporting instrument, like pen used to be, for reporting. In fact, smartphones are ideal devices to create spontaneous micro-reports. Just a few years ago people used text for reporting; now they hardly use text. The reports using smartphones are increasingly more *spontaneous*, *objective*, *compelling*, and *universal*. Many sensors, particularly the camera, facilitate spontaneous capture of data and information in context and use them, without any text, as reports. This is a rapidly growing trend. There were 1 Trillion digital photos captured in 2014 and more than 75 percent of those were captured and shared using mobile phones! In fact, we are going through a major transformation in the nature of information and knowledge due to rapid progress in technology. In the 20th century, we tolerated photos in our textual documents. In the 21st century, we create visual documents that tolerate text.

Photos play dual role in human experience communication. Photos captured as traditional *kodak moment* were for remembering and keeping records of special events. They were very valuable to us. We wanted to preserve details of content and experiences in each photo. Much of our thinking and research in photo organization, management, analysis, and retrieval in Multimedia Retrieval community is based on that thinking. Our techniques are strongly influenced by photos as *kodak moments.* However, photos have another, possibly even more dominant role. Photos are increasingly used as a compelling and descriptive universal information creation as well as consumption source. Photos communicate independent of language. Photos capture a total moment so the data contains much more than a narrow perspective or interest at the moment. Photos are captured for detailed descriptions as captured in oft use phrase *a picture is worth a thousand words.* This aspect of photos has remained in the domain of special applications such as medical imaging, remote sensing, and plant disease detection. With tremendous changes in the way we now capture photos, information element aspect of photos is likely to become at least as important as the memory aspect.

With smartphones and more importantly with younger generation, we live in the world of SnapChat where photos could be ephemeral. Each photo that one takes is called "a snap", and each snap would get deleted within a couple of seconds. Photos are captured to convey some simple messages, or could be like Instagram where one captures something interesting and wants to share that feeling in visual report with people. Next could be a new kind of photo report mechanism that is more compelling, more universal, more objective, and more spontaneous. None of these characteristics exist in Twitter. This can even go one step further and be used to determine more subtle trends and situations as emerging from such photo-reports posted by people all across the globe.

In these days of Big Data, many emerging applications are related to sensing people and environment in real time to understand evolving situations for taking corrective actions as effectively and as rapidly as possible. All sensors including

ICMR'16, June 06-09, 2016, New York, NY, USA

DOI: http://dx.doi.org/10.1145/2911996.2912020

IoT sensors, environmental sensors, and participatory sensors are to capture micro-reports of the state where an event is taking place. These micro-reports from diverse sensors are used to estimate event state and aggregated to understand situations. In the last decade Twitter emerged as the most popular participatory sensing mechanism to find information about events as well as understand situations and trends. As is well known, Twitter introduced the concept of micro-blogs for sharing short 140 character message to share one's opinion on events or situations. These micro-blogs were suppose to provide reports on events. And tweets have been used to detect situations and trends. However, getting objective information from tweets has been a problem.

Can we look at dense geo-spatial streams of photo-reports in their context and use the fact that each photo is worth a thousand words to understand subtle as well as higher level, possibly obvious, trends and situations? We believe that the time is right to address and explore this now. Using YFCC100M data [23], 100 Million photos, we did several experiments and validated the importance of photos as micro-reports. Encouraged by that, we are building a framework to import photo-reports from diverse sources and explore their efficacy in applications like situation awareness, trend analysis, and cultural dynamics. For the analytics on these reports, we use EventShop platform, and consider photo-reports as an information stream from people to detect situations and trends by combining it with other streams.

Our initial experiments as reported in this paper using 100 Million images set from Yahoo-Flickr clearly demonstrate the potential of these micro-reports for important applications. We discuss limitations of micro-blogs and show why micro-blog based applications, such as those using Tweets, could be dramatically improved using micro-reports. We present information encoded in micro-reports and architecture to harvest micro-reports using EventShop and visual analytics.

2. LIMITATIONS OF MICRO-BLOGS

People use variety of social media applications to broadcast their opinions and capture their moments. Twitter and Facebook Status updates are the most popular examples. At first, people could not see the value in micro-blogging, but soon it became clear that aggregation of information in micro-blogs could be valuable. Though Twitter has proved to provide the first line of information to people during emergency situations, it was not originally designed for detecting real-time situations. Twitter became one of the most successful social and journalistic applications in the last decade. It has become the source of latest alerts, news and popular trends in most areas. In academic world, many research papers have shown how tweets could be used for important social analysis. Despite all the success, there are three most critical problems in using this type of micro-blogs to understand evolving situations: *missing/misleading context*, *noise*, and *subjectivity*.

First, the lack of explicit geo-tagging on a large scale of micro-blogs can undermine the accuracy of situation recognition. This can be considered as insufficient data cause by incomplete gathering of information, however misinterpretation in data can also become an issue. An actual location of a posted micro-blog does not always correspond to the location of the published contents. For example, one of the data set from Web Observatory [24] has more than 6 million tweets related to London Olympic Game in 2012. Only about 1% of tweets are geo-tagged, and only 0.1% are tweeted by users within London.

Second, social media applications usually have very low signal to noise ratio [2, 5, 12, 15]. People tweet more than 100 million times a day, yielding a noisy and informal corpus of 140-character. Extracting accurate and useful information requires significant effort in data pre-processing. The performance of traditional NLP tools and named entity classifications is severely degraded on tweets. Tremendous works have been done in using Latent Dirichlet allocation to detect the topic and sentimental analysis to estimate the feeling of the tweets' content.

Third, the information is usually subjective and limited to textual format. In order to make a right decision, people need to know that the information they receive is a fact or an opinion. In journalism, journalists need to know how reliable statements are before they can report them. Reporting an opinion as a fact is unacceptable. In tweets, the capability to distinguish between facts and opinions is lacking.

In our past study [17], persistent location sensor data, air pollution data and pollen data were combined with citizen contributed Twitter data, to study the situation of asthma risk. The accuracy of situation detection depends on the quality the of data. Micro-blogs from systems like Twitter are very noisy and subjective. Most applications may benefit from objective and factual citizen contributed data.

3. MICRO-REPORTS AND BEYOND

To tackle these problems, we are exploring use of **micro-reports** as compared to **micro-blogs** for radical improvement in the quality of participatory sensing data. Unlike micro-blogs, micro-reports serve like eyewitnesses and field reporters of the events which are more reliable. Among diverse citizen contributed data, photo and video are the biggest data source. Every minute, millions of photos and videos are uploaded by people to social media. More and more photos and videos have timestamp and geo-tag information. With the right tool, photos and videos are more than visual documents. They become the best resources of micro-reports because of their objective and factual nature.

3.1 Basic Characteristics

The following important characteristics are required for micro-reports:

Spontaneous: Micro-reports should be shareable immediately. If creating a report requires thinking and typing a message, fewer people will use it during the event. A report submitted later relies on memory and may not have correct contextual information.

Objective: Micro-reports should emphasize on facts and not subjective opinions of people and their personal attitude toward the facts. Opinions are important, but should appear explicitly as opinions. Objective and subjective components in a report should be clear.

Compelling: Micro-reports should effortlessly capture the moment with rich context along with compelling photo, audio, video and/or other signals. As are well known photos, videos, and audio which make a report of an experience more compelling and more informative.

Universal: Micro-reports need to have a universal language, that is beyond literacy and geographical boundaries. Photos are universal language.

3.2 Emerging Challenges and Opportunities

To make use of all benefits of micro-reports, the existing platforms for social media are unsatisfactory. Because of the unique characteristics of micro-reports that we mentioned, new challenges and opportunities in emerging applications are addressed here.

Situation Recognition: For multiple decades, researchers in multimedia community have been developing approaches like entity resolution, object detection and scene recognition, to make sense of a single media. Now, with trillion of micro-reports, real-world phenomena are being observed by multiple media streams. For example, beyond creating a tree detector and testing it over millions of photos, we can use those millions of photos as micro-reports streams and combine them with other available data to detect plant diseases spreading pattern. In [25], visual report from physical surveillance cameras and social tweets are combined to detect evolving real-world events.

Trend Analysis: Trend analysis in social media has been a significant interest for many researchers. Traditionally trends can be defined as the frequently mentioned topics throughout the stream of social media from temporal point of view. The new challenge is to incorporate both temporal and spatial characteristics along with themes or topics from micro-reports for a better understanding of trends. The result of trend analysis can also be used in creating a situation model to recognize and predict situation in real-time.

Cultural Analytics: A culture in any cities is evolving. With the current mobile and social technologies, an opportunity to learn the culture from the eyes of city crowds has arrived. The term "cultural analytics" was first introduced by Lev Manovich. In his work [9], an informative visualization offers social, cultural and political insights about people's activities from Instagram photos. We need to develop a computational and visualization platform for the analysis of large sets of cultural artifacts beyond text.

3.3 Streaming Micro-Reports in EventShop

The EventShop project was started with the goal of building a platform for situation modeling and recognition from disparate data streams [18]. This framework allows for ingestion of different data streams and converts them to a unifying space, time, and thematic (STT) representation. Using different spatio-temporal operators, disparate data streams with different themes can be combined to generate new spatio-temporal themes of interest in a given application [20]. Pattern recognition operators can detect and recognize different situations allowing for appropriate actions to be taken. The name EventShop was inspired by the popular photo editing software PhotoShop. PhotoShop implements complex image processing algorithms and presents them to the end-user as an intuitive operator. Similarly, EventShop provides a platform that is agnostic to the data source, granularity, and form. The user can use any of the complex operators, and 'plug and play' the desired data to perform complex analyses. This empowers the user to create Complex Event Processing pipelines involving various forms of data, enabling the user to focus on the desired application logic and semantics. The EventShop system is now available as an open-source at http://dabuntu.github.io/es/.

3.4 Visual Analytics

One of the most important steps in micro-report analysis direction is the need to move from confirmatory data analysis to exploratory data analysis, which was first stated in the statistics research community by John W. Tukey in his book "Exploratory data analysis" [8]. At some stage, this community recognized the potential of integrating the user in the knowledge discovery process through effective visualization techniques, interaction capabilities and knowledge transfer leading to visual data exploration or visual data mining. The term Visual Analytics was proposed by Jim Thomas in [4], with a focus on Homeland Security in the United States. Meanwhile, the term is used as a new multidisciplinary field that combines various research areas including data analysis, data management, visualization, human-computer interaction, geo-spatial and temporal data processing and statistics. From a conceptual perspective, how we use EventShop to understand and analyze the underlying situation from a pool of micro-reports is aligned with visual analytics mantra: **"Analyze first, show the important, zoom, filter and analyze further, details on demand"**.

3.5 Numerous Applications

The act of leveraging the human as a 'sensor' and 'actuator' in an environment is referred to as "Participatory Sensing" which offers unprecedented observational capacity at the scale of the individual. EventShop provides an experimental environment in building situation models. Domain experts can browse through the discovered patterns in any space, time and theme dimension to obtain deeper insights that support their assessment, and decision making. By adding different layers of data streams, endless situations can be modeled such as disease incidence and severity, and emergency response and impact. Several applications have used EventShop framework to recognize real world situations [6, 14, 10, 21, 19].

EventShop combines heterogeneous data streams ranging from static information, stationary sensors and human generated contents to get insight evolving situations. Quality of data affects the quality of situation detection. Our systems have been addressing different issues due to sparse availability of data as well as use of micro-blogs. By improving quality and density of data from participatory sensing, we can improve the quality of situation detection and understanding as well as sending right information to right people.

3.5.1 Smart Cities

Some example applications include "Smart Cities", where citizens and local governments alike can report on, and get notifications about air quality, cleanliness, crime, reports and agriculture. One such application is Waze[1], a community-based traffic and navigation app that displays real-time traffic situation. It uses objective crowd sourcing information from GPS sensor of user's smartphone. Drivers become alerted before they approach police, accidents, road hazards or traffic jams, all shared by other drivers in real-time. Another application is *SLN4MOP*, a next generation social networks that have the capability of providing real-time, context-sensitive local information by aggregating data from Sri Lankan farmers through their mobile phones [7].

3.5.2 Public Health

Social media in public health gains increasingly high attentions in the past few years. It is becoming a common

[1]https://www.waze.com

platform for clinicians and public health officials to share information, track diseases, and predict outbreaks. In [11], most of public health mapping tools relying on Tweets, Propeller Health [2] is a distinguished application that uses micro-reports paradigm instead of traditional micro-blogs. Propeller health maps asthma triggers and identifies the severity of asthma attacks from the uses of inhalers equipped with special tracking sensors. Combining these focused and high quality data with other environmental data sources can create the medical knowledge on environmental asthma triggers at both individual and society level.

3.5.3 *Emergency Management*

Emergency reports from social media have proven to be the first line information for people to get the latest status of any emergency situations, for example, hurricane and flood detection, disaster mitigation, flu outbreak, and wildfire detection. In the recent incident, the outbreak of Zika virus disease began in April 2015 in Brazil, and spread to other major countries in South America, Central America and Caribbean. In February 2016, World Health Organization (WHO) declared that cluster of microcephaly cases reported in Brazil was a public health emergency of international concern. They could have contained the outbreak within Brazil if there were a better technology for people to create focused report and for officers to detect the disease outbreak sooner.

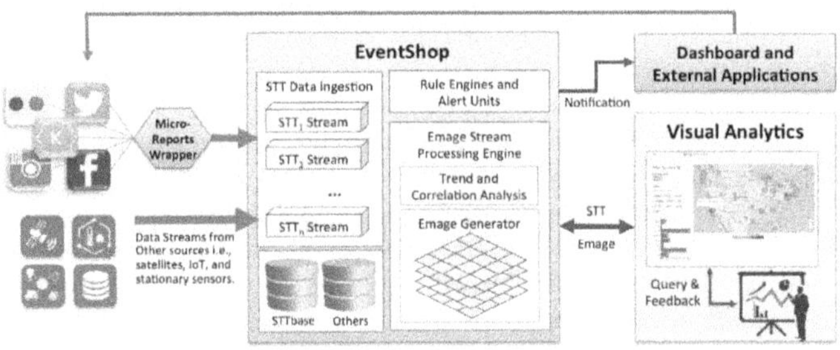

Figure 1: From micro-reports to situation recognition using an open-source EventShop platform

4. SYSTEM ARCHITECTURE

To detect situations from massive volumes of micro-reports, we extend the EventShop framework and implement a new visual analytics tool as shown in Figure 1.

First, micro-reports from variety of social media are transformed into *events* represented in a JSON format. We believe that events are a much better abstraction of human experience and provide a more appropriate means for managing micro-reports. This JSON is designed to capture six facets in E-Model [26]: temporal, spatial, informational, experiential, structural, and causal. An example of micro-report in JSON form is shown in Figure 2.

4.1 Micro-Reports Wrapper

To extract temporal and spatial facets from photo and videos media, we rely on timestamp and geo-location from the GPS of the capture devices. For informational facet, We

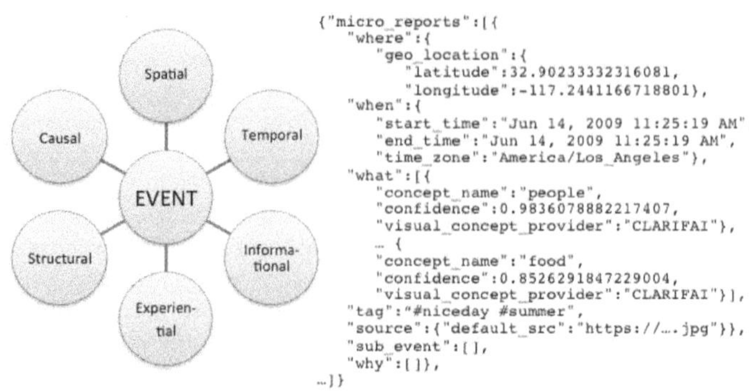

Figure 2: Micro-reports in E-model

not only use user's tag, but also automatically classifying the media contents into a number of predefined concepts [3]. The experiential facet is the media sources themselves. Note that some of the facets may not be inferred at this step. For example, the causal facet which is required more understanding in qualitative causal modeling [13]. As of our knowledge, Krumbs [3] micro-report comes closest to capture the intent of the users with the use of Emjois instead of a single shutter button.

4.2 EventShop

EventShop is an open source platform for situation modeling across heterogeneous data streams. We extend EventShop in several aspects to support situation recognition from micro-reports.

4.2.1 *STT Data Ingestion*

EventShop provides a number of wrappers to ingest data into the system. These wrapper can convert data from Twitter and Flickr APIs, CSV files, and JSON files into the unified STT format. Data from several sources such as PM2.5 measuring stations, satellite Aerosol Optical Depth observations, loop detectors on the freeway an be easily ingested into the system. The limitation is that they only support numerical value as a theme, and only one value is supported. Since our micro-reports can contain more than one concepts, we has to create a new micro-reports wrapper to support our information. The space and time aspect in our wrapper are similar to the existing ones. The list of themes which is the array of key-value pairs can be handled by our new wrapper. As a result, we are now able to ingest our micro-reports into EventShop in real-time.

We also enhance the filter operator in EventShop to query this new version of STT. In the past, user can filter their STTs by geo-coordinate, timestamp, and simple numeric operators on its theme value. Since the theme part is now a list of key-value pairs, We added a new functionality to filter by theme's name and theme's value. For example, we can filter all micro-reports which have theme 'stadium' with the confident value larger than 0.9. The result of the filter operator is the STT stream. Variety of STT streams can be generated from the same pool of micro-reports. This provide a flexibility to explore the data for different type of applications.

[2]http://propellerhealth.com

[3]https://krumbs.net

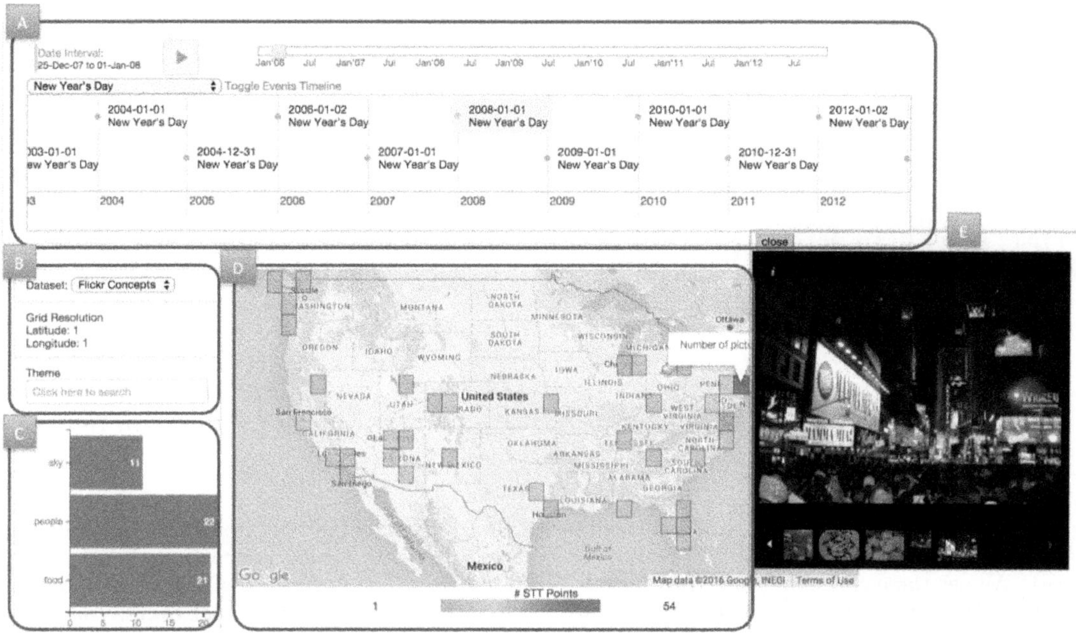

Figure 3: Visual Analytics Tool for Micro-Reports: A) interactive timeline, B) query control, C) theme chart, D) interactive map, and E) media gallery

4.2.2 Data Storage Layer

EventShop only stores JSON and STT data of micro-reports inside its internal database, while the original media sources are still maintained in the cloud of that social media. We can access them when required from the source URL in the JSON file. Currently, we use two data management system: MySQL and AsterixDB [1]. AsterixDB is an open source big data management system that provides scalability like other Big Data platforms, with full functionality of data management. Because of its flexible data model, spatial-temporal query support, and built-in data feed ingestion, AsterixDB well serves our needs.

4.3 Visual Analytics

Our visualization is not only designed for summarizing and retrieving information from large volume of photos, but also facilitate an experimental environment to analyze micro-reports along with other data streams. It is a novel visual analytic tool where the strength of human and machine are combined to shed the light on unexpected and hidden situations. We ease users to explore micro-events streams with zooming, filtering, and aggregating abilities in three dimensions: space, time and theme. Our user interface contains five main components as shown in Figure 3: query control, interactive map, interactive timeline, theme chart, and media gallery.

We developed this UI to work with EventShop. EventShop aggregates the STT stream according to the frame parameters (bounding box, latitude/longitude units, and time-window) to create an Emage stream. Emage is an event-image where each pixel reflects social interest of that specific theme at particular location and time, for more details please refer to [14].

We visualize the information from micro-reports in the center of our UI (D). Users can spatially explore the aggregated micro-report (Emage) over the map. When users detect any interesting incidents, they can zoom-in into particular regions and analyze further. The grid's color represents the total number of photos ranging from green (low) to red (high). By moving mouse over the grid box, the actual number is displayed. While clicking on the box, the media gallery (E) is shown. In this gallery, further detail of each micro-reports can be explored.

On the top, we provide an interactive timeline (A) that allows user to select the Emage over time. Users can also click "play" button to see all Emage in animated fashion like a video. On the left side, we provide a query control (B) where users can select specific micro-report source such as Flickr or instagram, changing latitude and longitude scale of the Emage grid, and filter for some particular themes. The theme chart (C) shows the number of photos with the associated theme. This chart is changing over time, and location. In our example, we can see that number of photo in New York during New Year's day is significantly higher than other areas. When we hover our mouse over the New York grid, the theme chart shows that most of the photos are about sky, people, and food. Then, we can open up the media gallery to see more details about these micro-reports. The demo of the tool can be found at http://slnlab.ics.uci.edu/eventshop.

5. MICRO-REPORTS PROOF OF CONCEPT

An important characteristic of these geo-tagged photo data is its space-time nature. For example, when a public event occurs, people take photos related to the event, which enables detection of event occurrence promptly, simply by observing the photo. In this paper, we investigate the interaction of events, and develop a framework that treats photos as micro-reports to understand evolving situations. Yahoo Flickr Creative Commons 100M (YFCC100M) dataset [22] is used to demonstrate our idea. This dataset contains a list

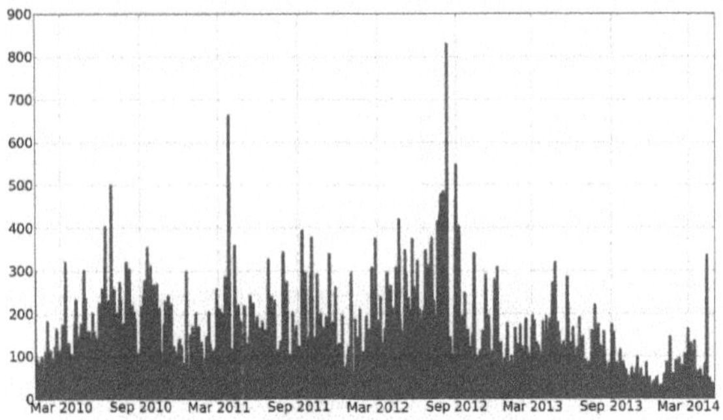

Figure 4: Number of photos taken in London

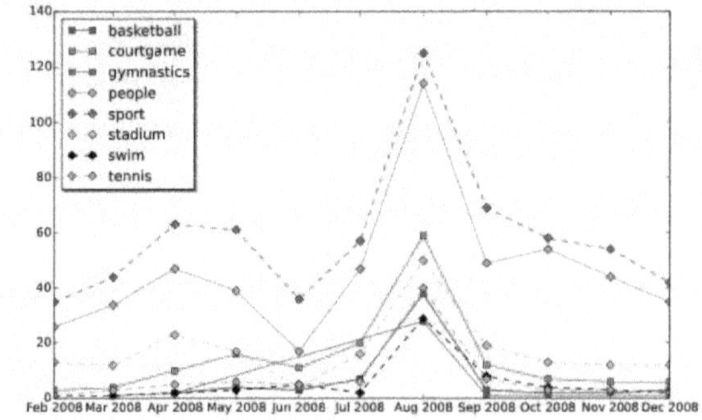

Figure 5: Evolving Concepts in Beijing in the year of 2008

of photos and videos under Creative Commons license. A deep-learning approach was used to detect 1,570 concepts in the photos (such as people, animals, nature, building, sky, and scenery). We use these concepts to create informative and objective micro-reports along with their location and time. Thus, EventShop can convert photo and video to STT data and use them as powerful data streams for situation recognition.

We are interested in detecting meaningful events reported by users through photos. Since time and space are the crucial components in our study, photos with invalid timestamps and unknown geo-location are filtered out, leaving us with about half of the photos (48.5 millions).

5.1 Detecting Evolving Situations from Concepts of Photos

Unlike tweets and user tags which are subjective and noisy, photo visual concepts generated by advanced deep learning technique are objective and standardized. Our experiments provide a proof of concept in detecting real-world situations using these visual concepts.

5.1.1 Detecting Olympic Games

From the year 2010 to 2014, photos in the bounding box of London (-0.489,51.28 0.236,51.686) are selected. Figure 4 shows the total number of photos taken changed over time. There are three big peaks which can be caused by some situations. To understand such situations, we zoom into the concepts of photos. For each day, the probabilities for the same concept is aggregated. Figure 6 gives an example of how four concepts, people, running, sport and swim evolve during the time of interest. Let's first look at the dynamic change in the 'people' concept, we observe that London is less crowded in winter season and attracts more people in summer and autumn. London usually hosts many kinds of sport events, such as swimming, and running, which also can been detected in this figure. However, single data stream ('people' theme) finds itself hard to detect situations.

Social events and trends are usually detected by the concurrences of photo's visual concepts. Figure 5 shows the evolving concepts in Beijing in the year of 2008. As we know, Beijing Olympic Games was held in Beijing in the summer of 2008. This event is clearly reflected in Figure 5 where the number of these ten concepts 'basketball','court game','gymnastics','people','sport','stadium','swim' and 'tennis' reaches peak at the same time of Olympic Games. Thus, the event model of "Olympics Games" can be defined as bag of these photo visual concepts. By computing the similarity between the "Olympics Games" event model with evolving *bag of visual concepts*, similar events can be detected. Figure 9 shows that during the summer of 2012, two events are detected because of similar visual concept evolving patterns. In fact, these two events are 2012 Summer Olympics in July and August and Paralympic Games in September in London.

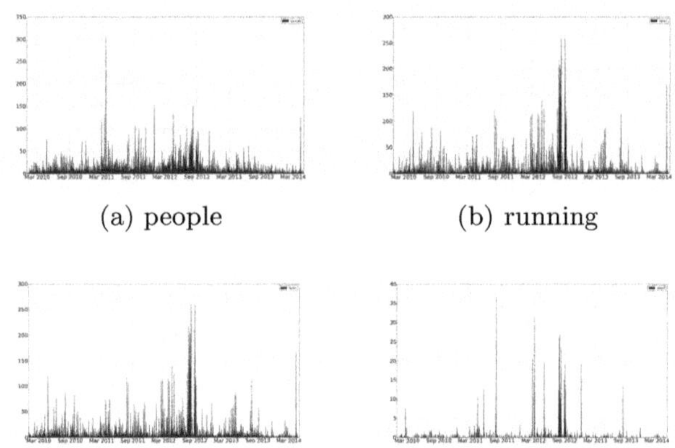

(a) people (b) running

(c) sport (d) swim

Figure 6: Timeline of concepts

5.1.2 Detecting Emergency Situations

We apply the same technique to detect emergency situations such as flood in the city. First, we define the flood event model using the bag of photo concepts. From the historical data and human knowledge, these concepts, 'outdoor', 'water', 'road', and 'car', are highly occurred together during a city flood. In this experiment, we try to detect city flood in Thailand during July 1, 2011 to June 30, 2012. The number of Flickr photos taken during this period are shown in Figure 7. Second, we cluster those photos using WaveCluster algorithm [16] on their spatial and temporal features. Then, we identify which clusters are associated with flood event by monitoring the frequent of its photos and measuring the similarity between photos concepts and flood event model. Figure 8 presents a set of photos in one cluster near Don

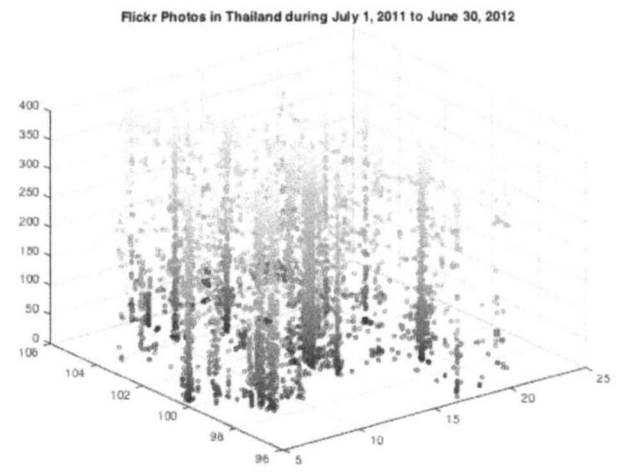

Figure 7: Flick Photos in Thailand during July 1, 2011 to June 30, 2012. X, Y and Z axis represent latitude, longitude and day respectively.

Meuang international airport on November 5, 2011. Each edge represents the similarity value between the photo (circle) and flood event model (rectangle). The shorter length means the higher similarity value. Finally, the cluster is identified as a flood event when a ratio between flood photos and all the photos is higher than user-defined threshold. Our framework successfully detect several city flood events in Bangkok from November 4, 2011 to November 23, 2011.

These two experiments demonstrates that photographs as micro-reports are more informative source of information from citizens. In addition, using advances in deep learning features, we will make them a powerful information stream for detecting evolving situations.

6. CONCLUSIONS AND FUTURE RESEARCH

Photos maybe used as a powerful report for a moment in an event. A stream of photos from different people and posted at different places creates a mosaic of world wide events as they happen. This could be a powerful data source for real time information in many emerging applications. To demonstrate our concept, we developed a prototype for situation recognition from micro-reports using an open source EventShop and a new visual analytics dashboard. We analyzed data from 100M Yahoo photos and global events calendar. Just from these two data sources, we began to realize evolving events around the world from citizens' perspective. We could identify interesting data patterns and relate those to both planed events such as Olympics Games in Beijing and London, and emergency events such as flood in the Bangkok city of Thailand.

We plan to include more data sources ranging from environmental data streams, data from IoT, videos, and focused micro-reports from Krumbs. Using all these data sources, we will explore how could we detect current situations and more importantly predict emerging situations in the context of emergency management and precision health. We plan to work with Krumbs Inc in their effort to create an open standard media-JSON that maybe used by any photo services to convert their photos into a standard report format that could be used by any analytics engine.

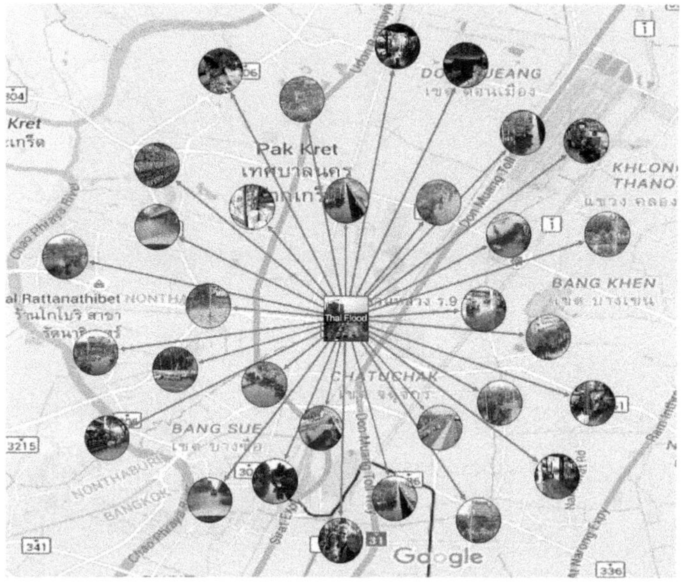

Figure 8: Photos from one of the cluster in Thailand on November 5, 2011. The length of edges in the graph represents a similarity between a flood event model (rectangle) and a photo (circle) considering its visual concepts. The shorter length means the higher similarity. Most of the photos related to flood event can be captured by our framework.

7. REFERENCES

[1] S. Alsubaiee, Y. Altowim, H. Altwaijry, A. Behm, V. Borkar, Y. Bu, M. Carey, I. Cetindil, M. Cheelangi, K. Faraaz, et al. Asterixdb: A scalable, open source bdms. *Proceedings of the VLDB Endowment*, 7(14):1905–1916, 2014.

[2] L. Barbosa and J. Feng. Robust sentiment detection on twitter from biased and noisy data. In *Proceedings of the 23rd International Conference on Computational Linguistics: Posters*, pages 36–44. Association for Computational Linguistics, 2010.

[3] S.-F. Chang, D. Ellis, W. Jiang, K. Lee, A. Yanagawa, A. C. Loui, and J. Luo. Large-scale multimodal semantic concept detection for consumer video. In *Proceedings of the international workshop on Workshop on multimedia information retrieval*, pages 255–264. ACM, 2007.

[4] K. A. Cook and J. J. Thomas. Illuminating the path: The research and development agenda for visual analytics. Technical report, Pacific Northwest National Laboratory (PNNL), Richland, WA (US), 2005.

[5] L. Derczynski, A. Ritter, S. Clark, and K. Bontcheva. Twitter part-of-speech tagging for all: Overcoming sparse and noisy data. In *RANLP*, pages 198–206, 2013.

[6] M. Gao, V. K. Singh, and R. Jain. Eventshop: From Heterogeneous Web Streams to Personalized Situation Detection and Control. In *Proceedings of the 4th Annual ACM Web Science Conference*, WebSci '12, pages 105–108, New York, NY, USA, 2012. ACM.

[7] A. Ginige, L. De Silva, T. Ginige, P. Giovanni, A. I. Walisadeera, M. Mathai, J. Goonetillake,

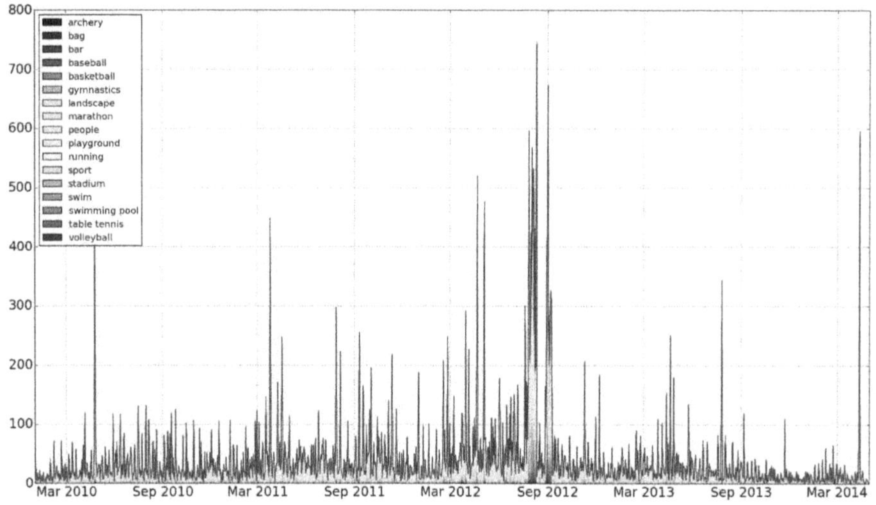

Figure 9: Micro-reports of Flickr Data

G. Wikramanayake, G. Vitiello, M. Sebillo, et al. Towards an agriculture knowledge ecosystem: a social life network for farmers in sri lanka. In *9th Conference of the Asian Federation for Information Technology in Agriculture (AFITA 2014)*, pages 170–179, 2014.

[8] F. Hartwig and B. E. Dearing. *Exploratory data analysis*. Sage, 1979.

[9] N. Hochman and L. Manovich. Zooming into an instagram city: Reading the local through social media. *First Monday*, 18(7), 2013.

[10] L. Jalali and R. Jain. Building Health Persona from Personal Data Streams. In *Proceedings of the 1st ACM International Workshop on Personal Data Meets Distributed Multimedia*, PDM '13, pages 19–26, New York, NY, USA, 2013. ACM.

[11] T. A. Kass-Hout and H. Alhinnawi. Social media in public health. *British Medical Bulletin*, 108(1):5–24, 2013.

[12] E. Kouloumpis, T. Wilson, and J. D. Moore. Twitter sentiment analysis: The good the bad and the omg! *Icwsm*, 11:538–541, 2011.

[13] R. J. L. Jalali. Bringing deep causality to multimedia data streams. In *Proceedings of the 23rd Annual ACM Conference on Multimedia Conference*, pages 221–230. ACM, 2015.

[14] S. Pongpaichet, V. K. Singh, M. Gao, and R. Jain. EventShop: Recognizing Situations in Web Data Streams. In *Proceedings of the 22nd International Conference on World Wide Web Companion*, WWW '13 Companion, pages 1359–1368, 2013.

[15] H. Saif, Y. He, and H. Alani. Alleviating data sparsity for twitter sentiment analysis. CEUR Workshop Proceedings (CEUR-WS. org), 2012.

[16] G. Sheikholeslami, S. Chatterjee, and A. Zhang. Wavecluster: A multi-resolution clustering approach for very large spatial databases. In *VLDB*, volume 98, pages 428–439, 1998.

[17] V. K. Singh, M. Gao, and R. Jain. Situation Recognition: An Evolving Problem for Heterogeneous Dynamic Big Multimedia Data. In *Proceedings of the 20th ACM International Conference on Multimedia*, MM '12, pages 1209–1218. ACM, 2012.

[18] V. K. Singh and R. Jain. *Situation Recognition using EventShop*. Springer; Auflage: 1st ed. 2016, 2016.

[19] M. Tang, P. Agrawal, and R. Jain. Habits vs environment: What really causes asthma? *arXiv preprint arXiv:1601.05141*, 2016.

[20] M. Tang, P. Agrawal, F. Nie, S. Pongpaichet, and R. Jain. A graph based multimodal geospatial interpolation framework. In *Multimedia and Expo (ICME), 2016 IEEE International Conference on.* IEEE, 2016.

[21] M. Tang, P. Agrawal, S. Pongpaichet, and R. Jain. Geospatial interpolation analytics for data streams in eventshop. In *Multimedia and Expo (ICME), 2015 IEEE International Conference on.* IEEE, 2015.

[22] B. Thomee, D. A. Shamma, G. Friedland, B. Elizalde, K. Ni, D. Poland, D. Borth, and L.-J. Li. The new data and new challenges in multimedia research. *arXiv preprint arXiv:1503.01817*, 2015.

[23] B. Thomee, D. A. Shamma, G. Friedland, B. Elizalde, K. Ni, D. Poland, D. Borth, and L.-J. Li. Yfcc100m: The new data in multimedia research. *Commun. ACM*, 59(2):64–73, Jan. 2016.

[24] R. Tinati, X. Wang, T. Tiropanis, and W. Hall. Building a real-time web observatory. *Internet Computing, IEEE*, 19(6):36–45, 2015.

[25] Y. Wang. Socializing multimodal sensors for information fusion. In *Proceedings of the 23rd Annual ACM Conference on Multimedia Conference*, pages 653–656. ACM, 2015.

[26] U. Westermann and R. Jain. Toward a common event model for multimedia applications. *IEEE MultiMedia*, (1):19–29, 2007.

Searching for Audio by Sketching Mental Images of Sound

A Brave New Idea for Audio Retrieval in Creative Music Production

Peter Knees
Dept. of Computational Perception
Johannes Kepler University Linz, Austria
peter.knees@jku.at

Kristina Andersen
Studio for Electro Instrumental Music (STEIM)
Amsterdam, the Netherlands
kristina@steim.nl

ABSTRACT

We propose a new paradigm for searching for sound by allowing users to graphically sketch their mental representation of sound as query. By conducting interviews with professional music producers and creators, we find that existing, text-based indexing and retrieval methods based on file names and tags to search for sound material in large collections (e.g., sample databases) do not reflect their mental concepts, which are often rooted in the visual domain and hence are far from their actual needs, work practices, and intuition. As a consequence, when creating new music on the basis of existing sounds, the process of finding these sounds is cumbersome and breaks their work flow by being forced to resort to browsing the collection. Prior work on organizing sound repositories aiming at bridging this conceptual gap between sound and vision builds upon psychological findings (often alluding to synaesthetic phenomena) or makes use of ad-hoc, technology-driven mappings. These methods foremost aim at *visualizing* the contents of collections or individual sounds and, again, facilitating *browsing* therein. For the purpose of indexing and querying, such methods have not been applied yet. We argue that the development of a search system that allows for visual queries to audio collections is desired by users and should inform and drive future research in audio retrieval. To explore this notion, we test the idea of a sketch interface with music producers in a semi-structured interview process by making use of a physical non-functional prototype. Based on the outcomes of this study, we propose a conceptual software prototype for visually querying sound repositories using image manipulation metaphors.

CCS Concepts

•Information systems → Speech / audio search; *Music retrieval;* **•Human-centered computing →** *Graphical user interfaces;*

Keywords

audio retrieval, retrieval by sketch, cross-domain retrieval, music production

ICMR'16, June 06 - 09, 2016, New York, NY, USA

ISBN 978-1-4503-4359-6/16/06. . . $15.00

DOI: http://dx.doi.org/10.1145/2911996.2912021

1. INTRODUCTION AND CONTEXT

Today's music production is overwhelmingly based on prerecorded or live-generated sound material. The task of composition consequently often consists of combining sound loops and samples with synthesized and processed elements using a so-called digital audio workstation (DAW), an electronic device or computer application for recording, editing and producing audio files [32]. These types of interfaces typically do not require much prior formal knowledge on music theory or composition (such as traditional tonal harmony), in order to be used. In practice, this development has not only changed the way music is produced on a technical level and democratized music composition but also led to new sound aesthetics and the establishment of electronic music as a dedicated art form and music style, cf. [4, 3]. As results of these changes in practice and mainstream music aesthetics, today, the music products industry has become a major economic force and electronically produced music can be found in all areas of the creative industries (see, e.g., [28] for references).

1.1 The Need for Sound Organization

Working in the context of the EU-funded GiantSteps project [27] we engage with musicians and music producers in order to learn about the processes involved in professional music creation and to improve tools used by practitioners, thereby allowing them a strong peer position in the conceptualization and evaluation of new music interfaces. When asked about their wishes and expectations for future technological developments [1], most of these expert users mention very practical requirements for storing and retrieving sound material and the insuffiency of current solutions for sound search due to the sheer amount of available content:

> "Because we usually have to browse really huge libraries [...] that most of the time are not really well organized." (TOK003)
>
> "If you have, like, a sample library with 500,000 different chords it can take a while to actually find one because there are so many possibilities." (TOK015)
>
> "Like, two hundred gigabytes of [samples]. I try to keep some kind of organization." (TOK006)
>
> "You just click randomly and just scrolling, it takes for ever!" (TOK009)
>
> "I easily get lost... I always have to scroll back and forth and it ruins the flow when you're playing" (PA011)

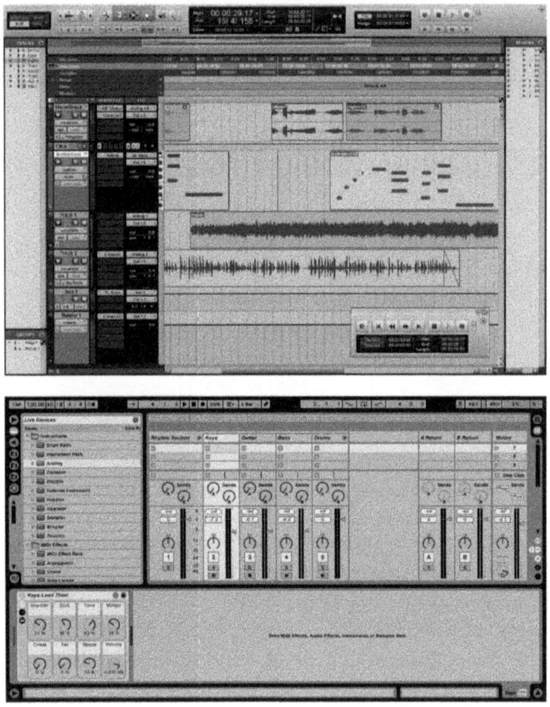

Figure 1: Screenshots of the Avid Pro Tools 9 [53] (top) and the Ableton Live 8 [52] (bottom) DAWs.

Even from this small selection of statements it becomes clear that organization of audio libraries, "semantic" indexing, and efficient retrieval plays a central role in the practice of music creators and producers. However, with the search tools provided by existing DAWs, this aspect is apparently addressed insuffiently.

1.2 Sound Retrieval in DAWs

The user interfaces of different DAWs are typically very similar. Despite the importance of effective retrieval for users, the access to sample libraries and other audio material is literally marginalized in most DAWs. For composition, the most part of the screen is devoted to the arrangement of different tracks which either consist of sequences of sound segments (displayed as blocks and often additionally overlaid with the waveform of the sound [21]) or piano roll segments representing notes that are synthesized using a virtual instrument (see top of fig. 1). In a live setting, i.e., when an artist is performing on stage, this space is instead often devoted to controlling and mixing the pre-composed tracks (see bottom of fig. 1). In the left and/or right margins of the screen, one can typically find repositories of instruments, sound effects, and sound material (samples), organized in alphabetic lists according to filenames or assigned tags. Additionally, thumbnails of the waveforms might be displayed. In addition to a text search field that matches against the displayed identifiers, semantic tagging of the repositories enables the user to narrow down the search by applying filters. However, in reality, collections remain largely untagged, because tagging needs to be done manually for personal material which is a time consuming and tedious task. Ultimately, to find a suited sample, the filtered list needs to be examined entry by entry by listening to the sounds.

1.3 Proposed New Retrieval Paradigm

In order to organize sounds and make sound collections more intuitively accessible, the challenges of "semantic" description and visualization are central (e.g., [30, 22]). In fact, the visual dimension itself already plays a central role in the verbal description of sound. For instance, sound is characterized through terms such as tone color (timbre), chroma (as an attribute of pitch), or texture, which are all visual metaphors. Such visual metaphors for description of sound were also present during interviews we made:

> "Sometimes I don't have all of my kick drums in my head, because there might be 2,000, or I may not remember what it was but I know I am looking for a soft round sound which is short and dry." (TOK002)

Here, our expert user is referring to textural properties (soft, dry), as well as to properties of shape (round) to describe the qualities of the desired drum sample. Since there is evidence that, when thinking of sound, people (and in particular musicians) might hold a mental image of that sound, we infer that allowing users to *retrieve* a sound by visually sketching it, would allow them to find what they are looking for effectively. Hence, in this paper, we propose a *query-by-visual-sketch* paradigm for sound retrieval.

In order to support and contextualize this idea of utilizing sketches of mental images as queries, in sec. 2, we discuss the requirements and perception of our users and connect these with psychological findings on the correspondence of sound and vision. Within music information retrieval (MIR) research, several related techniques for sound retrieval have been proposed — including acoustic sketches (query-by-example) [25, 41], visualization of sound qualities [30, 8, 22], and map-based arrangements of sounds for browsing [38, 22, 19] — which we discuss in sec. 3.

In sec. 4, we propose a non-functional physical prototype to test the idea of visual querying with users and gather practical feedback. Finally, pointing in the direction of future work, we present a concept for a software prototype which incorporates the desired functionality in sec. 5.

2. MENTAL IMAGES OF SOUND

One of our goals is to understand our participants' mental models of sound and music. If we understand the musical perceptions of our users, we may in turn be able to suggest new ways to find sound. To this end, we explore the mental models of sounds of our users by asking them to illustrate the sound they would like to be able to make by drawing it with coal on a small piece of paper.[1] Each participant spends time explaining the illustrations, and this opens up a conversation about their mental model of sound:

> "I don't wanna see the wave, I want to use my ears and as soon as I start being able to see the wave I start getting into this visual world where the whole, my brain totally changes and the way I interact with, what I am doing totally changes." (STE023)

In order to further inspire lateral thinking, some participants are asked to make this drawing on the palm of their

[1] cf. http://ears2.dmu.ac.uk/learning-object/drawing-sounds

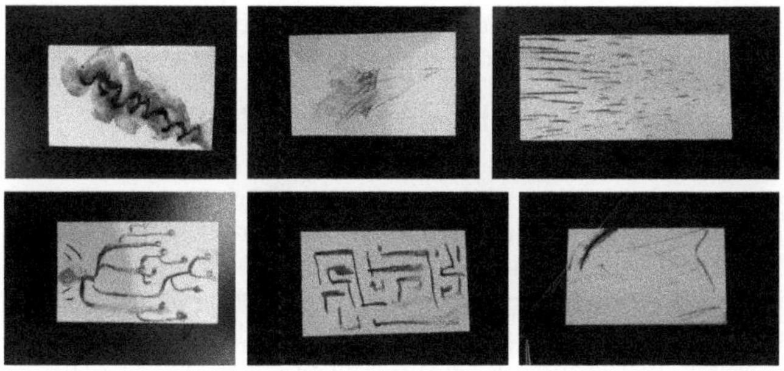

Figure 2: Coal drawings of mental images of sound.

own hand with a black marker. This has the advantage of making the task both much more difficult, but — maybe counter intuitively — also easier, in the same way that an elaborate surrealist art game such as Exquisite Corpse allows easy expression and complex outcomes [5].

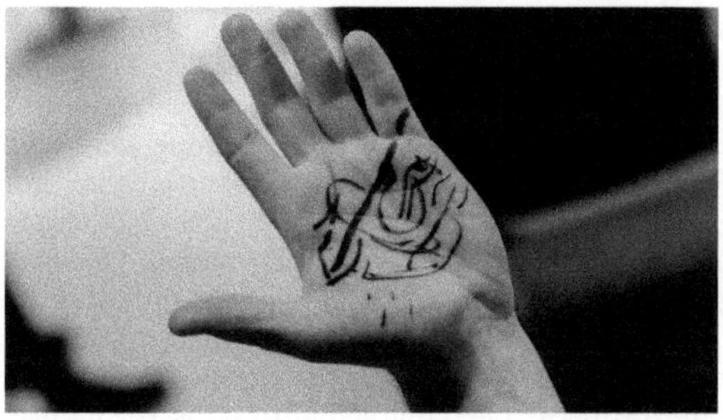

Figure 3: Drawing of "the sound you want to be able to make" on the hand.

> "So it would be really useful to have some kind of sorting system for drums, for example, where I could choose: 'bass drum', and here it is 'bass' and 'bright', and I would like it to have, maybe, bass drum 'round' and 'dry', and you can choose both..." (TOK002)

> "It would be even more useful to be able to search for a particular snare, but I can't really imagine how, I need something short, low in pitch, dark or bright in tone and then it finds it..." (TOK003)

> "There are a lot of adjectives for sound, but for me, if you want a bright sound, for example, it actually means a sound with a lot of treble, if you say you want a warm sound, you put a round bass, well, round is another adjective." (TOK009)

In these quotes, sounds are described by shapes (round), brightness (bright, dark) and textures (soft, dry). While these might be regarded as unusual descriptors of sound, there is some evidence that many humans make, to some degree, use of synaesthetic connections between visual perceptions and sound.

When talking about "synaesthesia" in this artistic context, it needs to be clarified that we use it as "an aesthetic appropriation of the neurological condition in which stimulation of one sensory modality triggers involuntary sensation in another" [11], which is a rare, asymmetric, and individual phenomenon. Thus, we make use of a weak definition of synaestesia as cross-modal associations, cf. [17, 22], and, in the context of computer science, "the more general fact that digital technologies offer, if not a union of the senses, then something akin: the intertranslatability of media, the ability to render sound as image, and vice versa." [11]

Some experiments have found an association of *brightness* with musical scales, modes, and pitch height [10]. Datteri and Howard find an association of the frequency of pure sine tones and color frequency [12], while Rusconi et al. point out that some people associate pitch height with spatial height [42]. As mentioned by Datteri and Howard [12], Marks finds that some participants associate an increase of brightness of grey surfaces with increase in loudness of pure tones, while others associate an increased loudness with a decrease of brightness, and suggests that most participants associate visual brightness with auditory brightness [35]. This diversity is an indication that a universal function to translate visual impressions into sound that generally matches human perception may not exist. In terms of *shape*, there is repeatable evidence of object-sound associations, For example, it was shown that nonsense words such as *baluba*, *maluma*, or *bouba* are associated with rounded, while words such as *takete* or *kiki* are associated with spiky and angular shapes [29, 36].

We find an interesting opportunity in the relation between our users' mental images of sound and the possibilities for using these intuitions for sound retrieval. The emerging goal of this process is to make use of these connections for building a visual-query sound search engine. In the following, we review how this area has been discussed in related work in multimedia retrieval.

3. RELATED WORK: VISUAL — SOUND — RETRIEVAL

Three areas are touched by the idea of using graphical sketches of mental images of sound for audio search: vision, sound, and retrieval. Extensive work — both academically and artistically — has been conducted in all these areas. To discuss the most relevant examples of this related work, in the following, we focus on work at the intersections, precisely, works at the intersection of visual and sound *(VS)*, visual and retrieval *(VR)*, sound and retrieval *(SR)*, and the intersection of all three *(VSR)*, cf. fig. 4.

3.1 Visualization/Sonification

At the intersection of visual and sound, we find work that visualizes sound or sonifies images, or both.

The area of **music visualizations** is a wide field and ranges from software and plug-ins for automatic visualizations of played back music (e.g., the iTunes Visualizer), to stage show effects, to visuals in music performance, to the dedicated VJ culture. The artistic discussion and discourse at the intersection of visual arts and music composition and the motif of synaesthesia, historically, has influenced and been influenced by the works of Kandinsky, Schönberg, Cage, Stockhausen, or Xenakis, cf. [20], to name a few prominent exponents, and is a reoccurring theme of art exhibitions, e.g., [14, 40, 37]. The abstract musical animations by Oskar Fischinger have even reached the mainstream entertainment industry (e.g., through a visualization of Bach's Toccata and Fugue in Walt Disney's Fantasia) [26].

In the field of computer science, various strategies for vi-

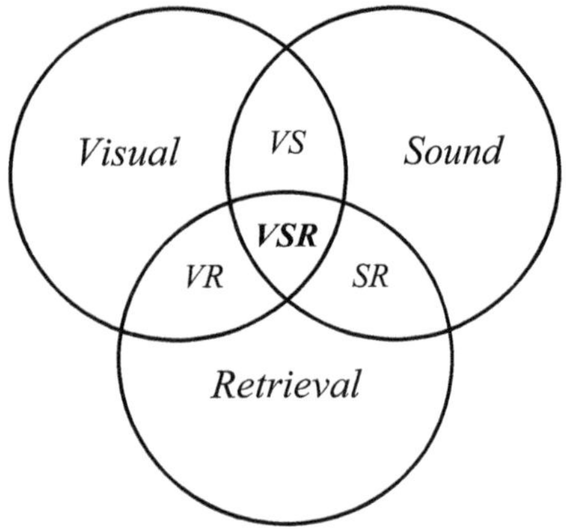

Figure 4: Venn diagram of areas of related work. Our proposed approach to audio retrieval through visual sketches belongs to the central area (*VSR*).

sualizing sounds have been proposed. *ThumbnailDJ* [8] produces visual summaries for audio files using repurposed music notation symbols to display information on aggressiveness, bass, tempo, volume, and genre for DJs. Genre information is also mapped to colors for fast distinction. *Music Icon* [30] generates expressive file system icons for music files using blooms with two rings of petals that reflect music features by color, shape, and number of petals. In order to map musical properties to the eight parameters used to generate a bloom, a neural network is trained using a small set of hand-crafted examples. Grill et al. [22, 23] visually model perceptual qualities of textural sound. In the visualization, they combine two aspects, namely mapping the overall structure of a sound collection and visualizing the qualities of its elements. Since they propose a user interface for visual browsing, we discuss this work in more detail in sec. 3.4.

In the area of **image sonification**, i.e., the generation of non-speech sound or music that conveys information of visual data (cf. [31] for a general definition), the process of visualization is inverted. Existing work is dealing with extraction of visual features, e.g., color, brightness, texture, or shape, and using these to control acoustic properties. Thoret et al. [49], for instance, sonify two-dimensional curves by imitating the sounds of friction of a pencil drawing the shape to sonify. Other approaches often aim at automatically composing music from images, interpreting the two dimensions of images onto two acoustic dimensions, e.g., the position of pixels on the y-axis as pitch and the position along the x-axis as point in time. Lauri Gröhn utilizes a cell-automaton-like concept to filter images by removing pixels in an iterative process.[2] *Bondage* by Atau Tanaka is an interactive installation including the transformation of a displayed picture into sounds.[3] The *Monalisa* project [24] transforms sound into image data and vice versa using software plugins that allow the approach to apply sound effects to image data, and to apply image effects to sounds. *sound/tracks* [39] generates a musical composition from the images of a passing scenery (recorded from trains) by mapping spatial height to octaves and colors to notes using the synaesthetic mapping of composer Alexander Skrjabin's color keyboard.

[2]http://www.synestesia.fi

[3]http://www.ataut.net/site/Bondage

3.2 Image Search and Sketch Retrieval

Content-based retrieval in the visual domain is a well-researched area, e.g., [33]. In the context of this paper we are foremost interested in methods for sketch-based and shape-based retrieval [51]. In sketch-based image retrieval, the goal is to use a schematic (even binary) sketch as query to find similar full color images. Existing methods build upon local gradient histograms, structure tensors [15], bag of features descriptors [16], or keyshapes [43] and can further be applied for 3D-object retrieval [44] and image synthesis and montage applications [7]. In our proposed approach, extracting features and relevant parameters from sketches and matching them to repositories of richer and more complex data is essential in order to achieve our goal.

3.3 Audio Search and Semantic Indexing

Current audio and music search is dominated by the query-by-example paradigm [6]. An early example of a content-based sound retrieval system is *SoundFisher* [54], which lets the user query a database by combining examples with tags and other meta-data. Another early example uses audio features for indexing, classification, and retrieval of audio/video segments in production studios [55]. Query-by-example is also practiced in *mosaicing*, an effect that "reconstructs" a target sound by concatenating similar sounding slices of other recordings [56, 45, 34]. An alternative to direct query-by-example (audio-to-audio) is query-by-semantic-example, which first aims at deriving semantic tags through classification (see also [47]) and then compares sounds on the level of semantic categories [2].

A coarser approach to querying by example is to use an "acoustic sketch," so to say, i.e., articulating (through a microphone) the qualities of the desired sound with voice. So far, this has been applied for retrieving samples or tracks with a similar beat structure for DJs ("query-by-beat-boxing" [25]) and for sound synthesis [41]. In the context of sound synthesis and creation of textures, also sound-to-(haptic)-image, image-to-texture, and haptics-to-texture transformations have been proposed [13]. However, existing methods are either unimodal, i.e., do not take advantage of synaesthetic correspondence with the visual domain, or focus on the translation of parameters for sound synthesis rather than indexing and retrieval. To the best of our knowledge, there is no work that addresses sound search by graphical querying using synaesthetic information.

3.4 Sound Browsing through Collection Visualizations

Finally, we want to discuss existing methods at the intersection of visual, sound, and retrieval, i.e., methods that assist in retrieving sounds from collections by providing a visual browsing tool. Most proposed sound browsing systems are based on maps, i.e., 2D arrangements of sounds. The *Sonic Browser* [18] gives the user the possibility to assign visual properties such as color, shape, size, and location to characteristics of audio files and then navigate through the resulting visualization plane by simultaneously playing sounds within a selected region through stereo spatialization. Pampalk et al. [38] present a hierarchical user interface to drum sample repositories based on self-organizing maps and psychoacoustically motivated descriptors of drum sounds. Coleman [9] extracts event-synchronous audio samples from existing music collections and proposes an interactive scatter plot for browsing. Schwarz and Schnell [46] apply a similarity function developed for mosaicing together with a spring model for layout and multi-dimensional scaling to enable the user to interact with and filter the contents of sound effect and sample databases. Fried et al. [19] present *AudioQuilt*, which optimizes 2D arrangements of audio samples based on user preferences and can be used for navigation in snare drum and synth sound databases.

Grill and Flexer [22] visualize perceptual qualities of sound textures through symbols that are arranged on a map to reflect the structure of the collection (see fig. 5).[4] To this end, they map bipolar qualities of sound that describe spectral and temporal aspects of sound, to visual properties. The spectral qualities of pitch (high vs. low) and tonality (tonal vs. noisy) are mapped to brightness/hue and saturation, respectively. The temporal (or structural) qualities of smoothness vs. coarseness, order vs. chaos, and homogeneity vs. heterogeneity are associated with the jaggedness of an element's outline, the regularity of elements on the grid, and a variation in color parameters, respectively. Evaluation of these correspondences through a survey showed that subjects were able to meaningfully associate sounds with the chosen graphical representations. These parameters could also be used in our proposed search system, i.e., to match user-drawn shapes to sounds.

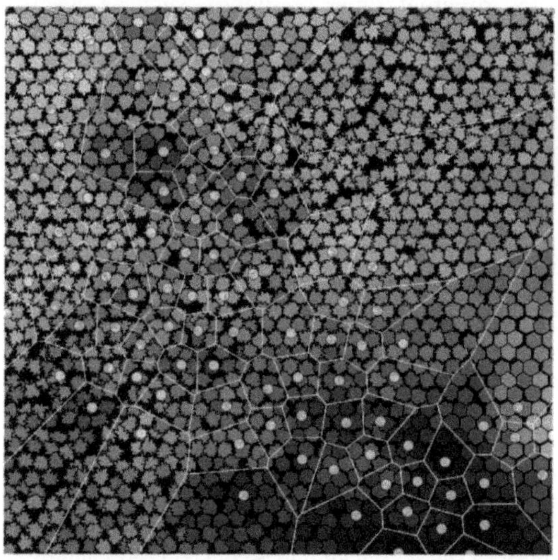

Figure 5: Screenshot of the texture browser by Grill and Flexer [22].

4. A NON-FUNCTIONAL PROTOTYPE TO TEST THE IDEA

In order to explore how our users imagine sound, we decided to build a non-functional prototype. This was the simplest of objects, a cardboard box the size of a hand, a traditional size for a music device or tablet. The purpose of the prototype was to give our idea a physical representation and allow it to function as a conversational prop during interviews. During the interviews, the users were told that this prop would find the sounds they want if they express them visually and asked to do various small exercises: *draw your visualization of a piece of music*, *use small colored pieces of paper to illustrate the piece again*, and *imagine how the box could be used in your particular practice*. This is accompanied by an ongoing conversation about images and sound.

The following quotes are taken from this process, conducted with 21 users at professional music events in Amsterdam and Paris. In the interest of brevity, we will show examples from one user conversation (ST002) here and then summarize the ideas and comments from all the interviews.

Figure 6: Drawing the sound.

User ST002 describing the sound and fig. 6.

> "For me, it's sort of like a chair moving back and forth. You have the note which is the long line and the *(makes high-pitched noise)*. I think they're actually both at the same time. You sort of perceive the note first and then the *(makes noise)*."

Figure 7: Collaging the sound.

Describing the collage in fig. 7

> "This is how you should view it. The base of the track is like the beat, it's not completely rigid to the grid. It doesn't have a lot of swing so it's divided into four but it has a little bit of space. It's also because there's not a lot of variations, there might be some little fills and everything but the basis is still the same. So you have the basis. Over there, there are some sounds and they're not really... they're pretty sort of neutral, so I tried to stay more straight into the neutral colors like grey and blue and a little bit of red, because sometimes it's a bit more calmed down. They're overlapping, but it's not really totally chaotic. You can, when you look at it, it's like fourth,

[4]http://grrrr.org/test/texvis/map.html

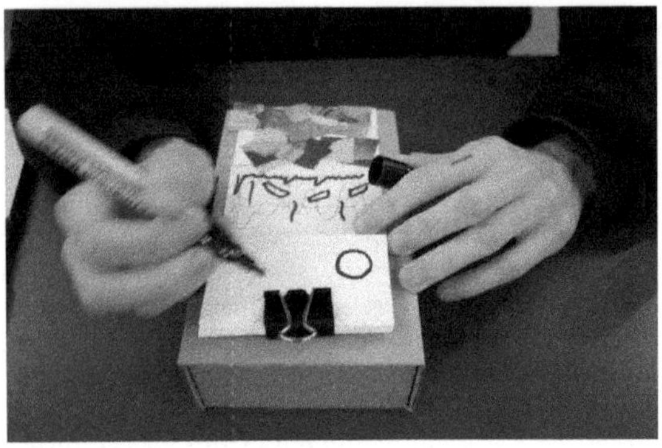

Figure 8: Imagining using the search box.

there's actually a lot going on, but it doesn't actually feel like it. That's what I tried to recreate."

We then start talking about how to use the box, see fig. 8.

> *User ST002*: "Okay, 'I really want a squiggly sound here,' and you get a really round sound and you're like, 'Hey this could also work'. Or you could start modifying your squiggle."
>
> *Interviewer*: "If you could imagine you could constantly change what would come back if it was a live query."
>
> *User ST002*: "Yeah, it could be like, 'I want this sound, okay well this is not what I had in mind, let's try this and this,' then you can really shape your sound to what you want to."

At the end of the interview we talk more generally:

> *Interviewer*: "We had an artist suggest that he was associating particular colors to each of his samples as he made them. He would go 'this is a green sound' but he would have a really detailed opinion about what kind of green."
>
> *User ST002*: "Yeah, no, a lot of artists have that actually. It's really funny. Imagine if their whole song is sort of structures and shapes with colors and everything else."

Over the course of the interviews a number of ideas and notions came up in addition to the importance of brightness, shape, and texture in mental models identified in sec. 2:

- Our expert users have complex mental models of their own sounds and color plays a central role: "I see the music sometimes as more aesthetic and something that I can see more than something that I can hear" (PA013), "When I listen to music I see colors. [...] I remember colors." (PA011), "Different sounds to me have specific colors" (PA009)
- The temporal dimension of sound is important: "a very useful and beautiful way of displaying the track over time, the colors based on timbre and stuff" (ST001)
- For some users, current forms of visualization, especially waveforms, are useful, while others are very dissatisfied: "Listen [...] with the waveform, [is] really useful for me, I can go to the drop directly cause know from the waveform where it is and I can listen to it and then I can jump, like, to the middle section." (TOK011), "The waveform is a beautiful thing to look at, depending on its sound." (TOK014) vs. "You're confronted with these boring waveforms... they bore your eyes... you're already not listening to something because you just see a square wave." (PA008), "If you think about it, most waveforms of songs look like bricks because they've been smashed to shit with brick wall limiters and compression." (TOK007), "Looking at the waveform is not really helpful." (TOK003)
- Users are open to systems that might not work perfectly out of the box but learn their associations over time (personalization): "You could imagine that your computer gets used to you, it learns what you mean by grainy, because it could be different from what that guy means by grainy" (PA008)
- Users would use images as references to find files: "I don't have the actual ability to use images [now], so I just use color." (PA009)

5. PROPOSAL FOR A FUTURE SOUND RETRIEVAL SYSTEM

Based on the findings from our interviews and from surveying the literature, we propose a software interface for sound search based on queries consisting of sketches of mental images. A central requirement for such an interface is that it needs to be able to deal with different sound properties and different types of sounds, such as effects, samples, ambient, tonal, or textured recordings, and therefore needs to comprise *different simultaneous representational models for indexing*. For instance, while tonal aspects might be best represented using symbolic music notation, noise sounds should be modeled primarily via their textural properties. It is expected that modeling and indexing will heavily draw from audio content processing and analysis methods. Methods for source separation will play a particularly important role in order to isolate individual sound objects, cf. [48].

As pointed out before, while some audio-visual associations are more universal (e.g., acoustic representations of shape seem to be more generally agreed on), others, like the correspondence between spatial height and pitch height or the brightness of sound, are more subjective. The association of colors with sound, although appearing to be the most frequent association, seems also to be the most subjective. Thus, another requirement for the sketch search interface is *adaptiveness to the preferences of the user* over time.

A query to the search engine is constructed visually aiming at reflecting the user's mental model of sound (i.e., the information need). To this end, the search interface will resemble more an image manipulation program than a text search engine. Fig. 9 shows a UI mockup of the envisioned system. The central element is the canvas, holding the current query. The user can start with an empty canvas and build the query from scratch or input an existing sound, which is subsequently analyzed, deconstructed, and displayed using the available symbolic representations. While the user is drawing or moving objects on the canvas, the list of search results gets constantly updated, encouraging exploration and modification. The canvas itself features a two-dimensional layout, with the x-axis representing time (or temporal order), and consists of multiple layers, which can be turned on and off selectively, each representing a different type of

Figure 9: UI mockup of the proposed query-by-visual-sketch search engine for sound.

indexing modality. In the different layers, the x- and y-axes are interpreted differently:

1. *symbolic layer*: sequential order vs. spatial area of symbols
2. *waveform layer*: time vs. amplitude
3. *tonal layer* (or spectral or piano roll layer): time vs. pitch (frequency activation)

For indexing and query matching, i.e., similarity calculation, the symbolic layer requires a segmentation of the audio into sound objects which are individually modelled and then can be expressed as a sequence of symbols (i.e., a string). The mappings used by methods discussed in related work (sec. 3) are promising candidates to create such symbols. However, not all of these mappings are isomorphic in the sense that their expressivity can be inverted and not all relevant acoustic dimensions are covered. The waveform and tonal layers basically hold sketches of the expected waveform and the piano roll (or spectrogram) of the sound, repectively, and can be matched by stretch- and (partly) location-invariant image comparison. Alternatively, the tonal layer can be matched using symbolic music retrieval methods such as melody contour matching, e.g., [50].

For sketching the appearance of the individual layers, common image manipulation tools are provided:

- Draw dots, lines, and paths (e.g., waves, zig-zag)
- Draw shapes: circles, ellipses, rectangles, polygons (e.g., stars)
- Fill shapes with texture (from a predefined set)
- Choose color to draw to represent different sound qualities (e.g., tonality, instrument, mood, or any other semantic label)
- Eraser (selectively remove shapes or parts of drawings)

An important addition to the system is that — in contrast to text- or image-based search — in case retrieval delivers no or only unsatisfactory results, sound synthesis can be applied instead, based on the provided parameters, using, e.g., the methods discussed in sec. 3.3. That is, if the desired sound is not present in the database, it can still be built/synthesized given the visual description.

6. CONCLUSIONS

We proposed a new search paradigm for sound retrieval based on visual sketch queries to replace or complement existing text- and tag-based search engines as exemplified in current digital audio workstations. From a substantial amount of interviews with professional music producers, we identified a need for improved organisation of and access to large sound repositories as well as a common conception of sound through visual metaphors and synaesthetic sensations. We argued for making use of the visual mental models of sound for retrieval and presented a mockup UI to allow for visual sketches using image manipulation metaphors.

While an actual implementation of such a search engine is beyond the scope of this paper, we believe that setting such a target points research in content-based audio retrieval into a highly relevant direction (as evidenced not at least by the explicit demand for this type of functionality by users). Existing work that already builds upon audio-visual correspondences for visualization purposes should be tapped for also facilitating the opposite information flow and giving users graphical tools to "build" the sound they want to find. Audio and music information retrieval research has achieved significant improvements in the last years wrt. sound description and indexing. Therefore, although it is without question a very difficult, subjective, and ambiguous task that requires extensive efforts, we believe that visual sound retrieval does not end with browsing interfaces, but should be taken to the level of search engines, to help people find the sounds they already have in mind.

7. ACKNOWLEDGMENTS

This work is supported by the European Union's seventh Framework Programme FP7 / 2007–2013 for research, technological development and demonstration under grant agreement no. 610591 (GiantSteps).

8. REFERENCES

[1] K. Andersen, F. Grote. GiantSteps: Semi-structured conversations with musicians. In *Proc CHI EA*, 2015.
[2] L. Barrington, A. Chan, D. Turnbull, G. Lanckriet. Audio information retrieval using semantic similarity. In *Proc ICASSP*, 2007.
[3] T. Brett. DJ culture in the mix: Power, technology, and social change in electronic dance music. *Popular Music and Society*, 38(3):389–391, 2015.

[4] B. Brewster, F. Broughton. *Last night a DJ saved my life: The history of the disc jockey.* Grove/Atlantic, 2007.
[5] A. Brotchie, M. Gooding, eds. *A book of surrealist games.* Shambhala Redstone Editions, 1995.
[6] M. A. Casey, R. Veltkamp, M. Goto, M. Leman, C. Rhodes, M. Slaney. Content-based music information retrieval: Current directions and future challenges. *Proc IEEE*, 96:668–696, April 2008.
[7] T. Chen, M.-M. Cheng, P. Tan, A. Shamir, S.-M. Hu. Sketch2photo: Internet image montage. *ACM TOG*, 28(5):124, 2009.
[8] Y.-X. Chen, R. Klüber. ThumbnailDJ: Visual thumbnails of music content. In *Proc ISMIR*, 2010.
[9] G. Coleman. Mused: Navigating the personal sample library. In *Proc ICME*, 2007.
[10] W. G. Collier, T. L. Hubbard. Musical scales and brightness evaluations: Effects of pitch, direction, and scale mode. *Musicae Scientiae*, 8:151–173, 2004.
[11] C. Cox. Lost in translation: Sound in the discourse of synaesthesia. *Artforum Int.*, 44(2):236–241, 2005.
[12] D. L. Datteri, J. N. Howard. The sound of color. In *Proc ICMPC*, 2004.
[13] A. Del Piccolo, S. Delle Monache, D. Rocchesso, S. Papetti, D. A. Mauro. To "sketch-a-scratch". In *Proc SMC*, 2015.
[14] S. Duplaix, M. Lista, B. Veret, C. Delineau, eds. *Sons & Lumières – Une histoire du son dans l'art du XXe siècle.* Éditions du Centre Pompidou, 2004.
[15] M. Eitz, K. Hildebrand, T. Boubekeur, M. Alexa. A descriptor for large scale image retrieval based on sketched feature lines. In *Proc SBIM*, 2009.
[16] M. Eitz, K. Hildebrand, T. Boubekeur, M. Alexa. Sketch-based image retrieval: Benchmark and bag-of-features descriptors. *IEEE TVCG*, 17(11):1624–1636, 2011.
[17] K. K. Evans, A. Treisman. Natural cross-modal mappings between visual and auditory features. *JOV*, 10(1):6.1–12, 2010.
[18] M. Fernström, E. Brazil. Sonic browsing: An auditory tool for multimedia asset management. In *Proc ICAD*, 2001.
[19] O. Fried, Z. Jin, R. Oda, A. Finkelstein. AudioQuilt: 2D arrangements of audio samples using metric learning and kernelized sorting. In *Proc NIME*, 2014.
[20] K. Giannakis. A comparative evaluation of auditory-visual mappings for sound visualisation. *OSO*, 11:297–307, Dec. 2006.
[21] K. Gohlke, M. Hlatky, S. Heise, D. Black, J. Loviscach. Track displays in DAW software: Beyond waveform views. In *AES 128*, 2010.
[22] T. Grill, A. Flexer. Visualization of perceptual qualities in textural sounds. In *Proc ICMC*, 2012.
[23] T. Grill, A. Flexer, S. Cunningham. Identification of perceptual qualities in textural sounds using the repertory grid method. In *Proc Audio Mostly*, 2011.
[24] K. Jo, N. Nagano. Monalisa: "See the sound, hear the image". In *Proc NIME*, 2008.
[25] A. Kapur, M. Benning, G. Tzanetakis. Query-by-beat-boxing: Music retrieval for the DJ. In *Proc ISMIR*, 2004.
[26] C. Keefer, J. Guldemond, eds. *Oskar Fischinger 1900-1967: Experiments in cinematic abstraction.* EYE Film Instituut, 2013.
[27] P. Knees, K. Andersen, S. Jordà, M. Hlatky, A Bucci, W. Gaebele, R. Kaurson. The GiantSteps project: A second-year intermediate report. In *Proc ICMC*, 2016.
[28] P. Knees, Á. Faraldo, P. Herrera, R. Vogl, S. Böck, F. Hörschläger, M. Le Goff. Two data sets for tempo estimation and key detection in electronic dance music annotated from user corrections. In *Proc ISMIR*, 2015.
[29] W. Köhler. *Gestalt psychology.* Liveright, 1929.
[30] P. Kolhoff, J. Preuss, J. Loviscach. Music icons: Procedural glyphs for audio files. In *Proc SIBGRAPI*, 2006.
[31] G. Kramer, ed. *Auditory display: Sonification, audification, and auditory interfaces.* Addison-Wesley, 1994.
[32] L. Landy. *Making music with sounds.* Routledge, 2012.
[33] M. S. Lew, N. Sebe, C. Djeraba, R. Jain. Content-based multimedia information retrieval: State of the art and challenges. *ACM TOMCCAP*, 2(1):1–19, Feb. 2006.
[34] E. Maestre, R. Ramírez, S. Kersten, X. Serra. Expressive concatenative synthesis by reusing samples from real performance recordings. *CMJ*, 33(4):23–42, Dec. 2009.
[35] L. E. Marks. On associations of light and sound: The mediation of brightness, pitch, and loudness. *AJP*, 87 (1-2):173–188, 1974.
[36] D. Maurer, T. Pathman, C. J. Mondloch. The shape of boubas: Sound–shape correspondences in toddlers and adults. *Dev. Sci*, 9:3:316-322, 2006.
[37] C. Meyer, ed. *Kandinsky, Kupka, Schönberg – Abstraction and atonality.* Museum Kampa, 2011.
[38] E. Pampalk, P. Hlavac, P. Herrera. Hierarchical organization and visualization of drum sample libraries. In *Proc DAFx*, 2004.
[39] T. Pohle, P. Knees, G. Widmer. sound/tracks: Real-time synaesthetic sonification and visualisation of passing landscapes. In *Proc ACM Multimedia*, 2008.
[40] C. Rainer, S. Rollig, D. Daniels, M. Amme, eds. *See this Sound.* W. König, 2009.
[41] D. Rocchesso, G. Lemaitre, P. Susini, S. Ternström, P. Boussard. Sketching sound with voice and gesture. *IX*, 22(1):38–41, Jan. 2015.
[42] E. Rusconia, B. Kwana, B. L. Giordano, C. Umiltà, B. Butterworth. Spatial representation of pitch height: the SMARC effect. *Cognition*, 99(2):113–129, 2006.
[43] J. M. Saavedra, B. Bustos. Sketch-based image retrieval using keyshapes. *MTAP*, 73(3):2033–2062, 2013.
[44] J. M. Saavedra, B. Bustos, M. Scherer, T. Schreck. Stela: Sketch-based 3D model retrieval using a structure-based local approach. In *Proc ICMR*, 2011.
[45] D. Schwarz. Current research in concatenative sound synthesis. In *Proc ICMC*, 2005.
[46] D. Schwarz, N. Schnell. Sound search by content-based navigation in large databases. In *Proc SMC*, 2009.
[47] M. Slaney. Mixtures of probability experts for audio retrieval and indexing. In *Proc ICME*, 2002.
[48] P. Smaragdis. User guided audio selection from complex sound mixtures. In *Proc UIST*, 2009.
[49] E. Thoret, M. Aramaki, R. Kronland-Martinet, J.-L. Velay, S. Ystad. From shape to sound: Sonification of two dimensional curves by reenaction of biological movements. In *Proc CMMR*, 2012.
[50] R. Typke. *Music retrieval based on melodic similarity.* PhD thesis, Univ Utrecht, 2007.
[51] R. C. Veltkamp. Shape matching: Similarity measures and algorithms. In *Proc SMI*, 2001.
[52] Wikipedia. Ableton, 2016. [Online; acc. 02/11/16].
[53] Wikipedia. Pro Tools, 2016. [Online; acc. 02/11/16].
[54] E. Wold, T. Blum, D. Keislar, J. Wheaten. Content-based classification, search, and retrieval of audio. *IEEE MultiMedia*, 3(3):27–36, 1996.
[55] T. Zhang, C.-C. Kuo. Classification and retrieval of sound effects in audiovisual data management. In *Proc Asilomar SSC*, volume 1, 1999.
[56] A. Zils, F. Pachet. Musical mosaicing. In *Proc DAFX*, 2001.

The LFM-1b Dataset for Music Retrieval and Recommendation

Markus Schedl
Department of Computational Perception
Johannes Kepler University
Linz, Austria
markus.schedl@jku.at

ABSTRACT

We present the LFM-1b dataset of more than one billion music listening events created by more than 120,000 users of Last.fm. Each listening event is characterized by artist, album, and track name, and further includes a timestamp. On the (anonymous) user level, basic demographics and a selection of more elaborate user descriptors are included.

The dataset is foremost intended for benchmarking in music information retrieval and recommendation. To facilitate experimentation in a straightforward manner, it also includes a precomputed user-item-playcount matrix. In addition, sample Python scripts showing how to load the data and perform efficient computations are provided. An implementation of a simple collaborative filtering recommender rounds off the code package.

We discuss in detail the LFM-1b dataset's acquisition, availability, statistics, and content, and place it in the context of existing datasets. We also showcase its usage in a simple artist recommendation task, whose results are intended to serve as baseline against which more elaborate techniques can be assessed. The two unique features of the dataset in comparison to existing ones are (i) its substantial size and (ii) a wide range of additional user descriptors that reflect their music taste and consumption behavior.

Keywords

Dataset, Analysis, Music Information Retrieval, Music Recommendation, Collaborative Filtering, Experimentation

1. MOTIVATION

Research and development in music information retrieval (MIR) and music recommender systems has seen a sharp increase during the past few years, not least due to the proliferation of music streaming services [8, 5]. Having tens of millions of music pieces available at the listeners' fingertips requires novel retrieval, recommendation, and interaction techniques for music.

ICMR'16, June 06 - 09, 2016, New York, NY, USA

ISBN 978-1-4503-4359-6/16/06...$15.00

DOI: http://dx.doi.org/10.1145/2911996.2912004

However, researchers interested in conducting experiments in music retrieval and recommendation on a large scale — in particular those working in academia — are facing the challenge that they frequently have to acquire the data for their experiments themselves, which results in non-standardized collections, hindering reproducibility . While online music platforms such as Spotify,[1] Last.fm,[2] or Soundcloud[3] offer convenient API endpoints that provide access to their databases, it takes a considerable amount of time to build collections of substantial size necessary for large-scale evaluation. The few publicly available datasets for these purposes, the most well-known of which is probably the *Million Song Dataset* (MSD) [2], might represent an alternative, but come with certain restrictions. For instance, while the MSD offers a great variety of pieces of information (among others, genre labels, tags, term weights of lyrics, song similarity information, and aggregated playcount data), user- and listening-specific information is provided rather scarcely, on a high level, or in a summarized form only.

Since we believe that listener-specific information is key to build personalized music retrieval systems, the focus and unique feature of the LFM-1b dataset presented here is detailed information on the level of listeners and of listening events. For instance, the dataset provides user-specific scores about their music taste (among others, measures of mainstreaminess and inclination to listen to novel music). Next to this, the size of the dataset, which includes more than a billion listening events of approximately 120,000 users should be sufficient to perform experimentation on a large scale on real-world data.

The paper is organized as follows. We first review related datasets for music retrieval and recommendation (Section 2). Subsequently, we outline the data acquisition procedure, present the dataset's structure and content, provide basic statistics and analyze them, and point to sample Python scripts that show how to access the components of the dataset (Section 3). We further illustrate how to exploit the dataset for the use case of building a music recommender system that implements various recommendation algorithms (Section 4). We eventually round off the paper with a summary and discussion of possible extensions (Section 5).

2. RELATED WORK

The need for user-aware and multimodal approaches to music retrieval and recommendation has been acknowledged

[1] https://developer.spotify.com/web-api
[2] http://www.last.fm/api
[3] https://developers.soundcloud.com/docs/api/guide

many times and is meanwhile widely accepted [9, 11, 14, 15]. However, respective scientific work is still in its fledgling stage. One of the reasons for this is that involving users, which is an obvious necessity to build user-aware approaches, is time-consuming and hardly feasible on a large scale — at least not in academia. As a consequence, datasets offering user-specific information are scarce.

On the other hand, thanks to evaluation campaigns in the fields of music information retrieval and music recommendation, including the *Music Information Retrieval Evaluation eXchange*[4] (MIREX) and the *KDD Cup 2011*[5] [4], the research community has been given several datasets that can be used for a wide range of MIR tasks, from tempo estimation to melody extraction to emotion classification. Most of these datasets, however, are specific to a particular task, e.g., onset detection or genre classification. What is more, for content-based or audio-based approaches, the actual audio can typically not be shared, because of restrictions imposed by intellectual property rights.

Datasets that can be used to some extent for evaluating personalized approaches to music retrieval and recommendation include the *Yahoo! Music* dataset [4], which currently represents the largest available music recommendation dataset, including more than 262 million ratings of more than 620 thousand music items created by more than one million users. The ratings cover a time range from 1999 to 2010. However, the dataset is completely anonymized, i.e., not only users, but also items are unknown. The absence of any descriptive metadata and ignorance of music domain knowledge therefore restricts the usage of the dataset to rating prediction and collaborative filtering [13].

The *Million Song Dataset*[6] (MSD) [2] is perhaps one of the most widely used datasets in MIR research. It offers a wealth of information, among others, audio content descriptors such as tempo, key, or loudness estimates, editorial item metadata, user-generated tags, term vector representations of lyrics, and playcount information. While the MSD provides a great amount of information about one million songs, it has also been criticized, foremost for its lack of audio material, the obscurity of the approaches used to extract content descriptors, and the improvable integration of the different parts of the dataset. The *MSD Challenge*[7] [10] further increased the popularity of the dataset. Organized in 2012, the goal was to predict parts of a user's listening history, given another part.

Providing more than one million temporally and spatially annotated listening events that have been extracted from microblogs, the *Million Musical Tweets Dataset*[8] (MMTD) [6] particularly supports context-aware recommendation [1]. Each listening event is accompanied by longitude and latitude values, as well as month and weekday. A major shortcoming of this dataset is its uneven geographical distribution of listening events, which is caused by the likewise skewed distribution of microblogging activity around the world.

Another related dataset is constituted of Last.fm data provided by Celma [3]. The dataset comprises two subsets, one containing listening information for about 360 thousand users, only including artists they most frequently listened to. The other subset offers full listening data of nearly a thousand users, where each listening event is annotated with a timestamp, artist, and track name. Both subsets include gender, age, country, and date of registering at Last.fm, as provided by their API.

Other datasets that are related to LFM-1b to a smaller extent include the *AotM-2011* dataset of playlists extracted from Art of the Mix[9] and the *MagnaTagATune*[10] dataset [7] of user-generated tags and relative similarity judgments between triples of tracks.

In comparison to the datasets most similar to the one proposed here — the MSD and Celma's [3] — the LFM-1b dataset offers the following unique features: (i) substantially more listening events, i.e., over one billion, in comparison to roughly 48 and 19 million, respectively, for MSD and Celma's [3]; (ii) exact timestamps of each listening event, unlike MSD; (iii) demographic information about listeners in an anonymous way, unlike MSD; and (iv) additional information describing the listeners' music preferences and consumption behavior, unlike both MSD and Celma's [3]. These additional descriptors include temporal aspects of listening behavior as well as novelty and mainstreaminess scores as proposed in [12], among others.

3. THE LFM-1B DATASET

In the following, we outline the data acquisition procedure from Last.fm, describe in detail the dataset's components, analyze basic statistical properties of the dataset, provide download links, and refer to some sample code in Python, which is also available for download. Please note that the LFM-1b dataset is considered derivative work according to paragraph 4.1 of Last.fm's API Terms of Service.[11]

3.1 Data Acquisition

We first use the overall 250 top tags[12] to gather their top artists[13] using the Last.fm API. For these artists, we fetch the top fans, which results in 465,000 active users. For a randomly chosen subset of 120,322 users, we then obtain their listening histories.[14] For approximately 5,000 users, we cap the fetched listening histories at 20,000 listening events in order to avoid ending up with an extraordinarily uneven user distribution (cf. Section 3.3), in which a few users have an enormous amount of listening events. We define a listening event as a quintuple specified by user, artist, album, track, and timestamp. The period during which we fetched the data ranges from January 2013 to August 2014.

3.2 Dataset Availability and Content

The whole LFM-1b dataset of approximately 8 GB can be downloaded from www.cp.jku.at/datasets/LFM-1b. For ease of access and compatibility, the metadata on artists, albums, tracks, users, and listening events is stored in simple text files, encoded in UTF-8, while the user-artist-playcount matrix is provided as sparse matrix in a Matlab file, which

[4]http://www.music-ir.org/mirex/wiki
[5]http://www.sigkdd.org/kdd2011/kddcup.shtml
[6]http://labrosa.ee.columbia.edu/millionsong
[7]http://www.kaggle.com/c/msdchallenge
[8]http://www.cp.jku.at/datasets/MMTD
[9]http://www.artofthemix.org
[10]http://mi.soi.city.ac.uk/blog/codeapps/the-magnatagatune-dataset
[11]http://www.last.fm/api/tos
[12]http://www.last.fm/api/show/tag.getTopTags
[13]http://www.last.fm/api/show/tag.getTopArtists
[14]http://www.last.fm/api/show/user.getRecentTracks

Table 1: Description of the files constituting the LFM-1b dataset. Attributes of same color are connected to each other.

File	Content
LFM-1b_users.txt	user-id, country, age, gender, playcount, registered_timestamp
LFM-1b_users_additional.txt	user-id, novelty_artist_avg_month, novelty_artist_avg_6months, novelty_artist_avg_year, mainstreaminess_avg_month, mainstreaminess_avg_6months, mainstreaminess_avg_year, mainstreaminess_global, cnt_listeningevents, cnt_distinct_tracks, cnt_distinct_artists, cnt_listeningevents_per_week, relative_le_per_weekday1, ... relative_le_per_weekday7, relative_le_per_hour0, ... relative_le_per_hour23
LFM-1b_artists.txt	artist-id, artist-name
LFM-1b_albums.txt	album-id, album-name, artist-id
LFM-1b_tracks.txt	track-id, track-name, artist-id
LFM-1b_LEs.txt	user-id, artist-id, album-id, track-id, timestamp
LFM-1b_LEs.mat	idx_users (vector), idx_artists (vector), LEs (sparse matrix)

Table 2: Description of the additional user features on preference and consumption behavior.

Attribute	Description
user-id	user identifier
novelty_artist_avg_month	novelty score according to [12], i.e., percentage of new artists listened to, averaged over time windows of 1 month
novelty_artist_avg_6months	novelty score, averaged over time windows of 6 months
novelty_artist_avg_year	novelty score, averaged over time windows of 12 months
mainstreaminess_avg_month	mainstreaminess score according to [12], i.e., overlap between the user's listening history and an aggregate listening history of all users, averaged over time windows of 1 month
mainstreaminess_avg_6months	mainstreaminess score, averaged over time windows of 6 months
mainstreaminess_avg_year	mainstreaminess score, averaged over time windows of 12 months
mainstreaminess_global	mainstreaminess score, computed for the entire period of the user's activity on Last.fm
cnt_listeningevents	total number of the user's listening events (playcounts) included in the dataset
cnt_distinct_tracks	number of unique tracks listened to by the user
cnt_distinct_artists	number of unique artists listened to by the user
cnt_listeningevents_per_week	average number of listening events per week
relative_le_per_weekday[1–7]	fraction of listening events for each weekday (starting on Monday) among all weekly plays, averaged over the user's entire listening history
relative_le_per_hour[0–24]	fraction of listening events for each hour of the day (starting with the time span 0:00-0:59) among all 24 hours, averaged over the user's entire listening history

complies to HDF5 format. This makes the matrix also accessible from a wide range of programming languages. For instance, Python code for data import is provided along with the dataset, cf. Section 3.4.

Table 1 gives an overview of the dataset's content, in particular the included files and respective pieces of information. Keys that are linked to each other are depicted in the same color. Files `LFM-1b_artists.txt`, `LFM-1b_albums.txt`, and `LFM-1b_tracks.txt` contain the metadata for artists, albums, and tracks, respectively. File `LFM-1b_LEs.txt` contains all listening events, described by user, artist, album, and track identifiers. Each event is further attached a timestamp, which is encoded in Unix time, i.e., seconds since January 1, 1970 (UTC). File `LFM-1b_LEs.mat` contains the user-artist-playcount matrix (UAM) as Matlab file in HDF5 format. It comprises 3 items: (i) a 120,175-dimensional vector (idx_users), each element of which links to the user-ids in files `LFM-1b_users.txt`, `LFM-1b_users_additional.txt`, and `LFM-1b_LEs.txt`, (ii) a 585,095-dimensional vector (idx_artists), whose elements link to the artist-ids in `LFM-1b_LEs.txt` and the metadata files, and (iii) a 120,175 $\times$ 585,095 sparse matrix (LEs), whose rows correspond to users and columns to artists. User-specific information is given in `LFM-1b_users.txt` and `LFM-1b_users_additional.txt`. While the former contains basic demographic information as well as overall playcount and date of registration with Last.fm, the latter provides 43 additional user descriptors that represent a unique feature of LFM-1b. Table 2 describes these user features, which are valuable in particular when creating user-aware music recommender systems.

3.3 Dataset Statistics

Table 3 shows basic quantitative statistics of the dataset's composition. The number of unique <user, artist> pairs corresponds to the number of entries in the UAM, which is a 120,175 $\times$ 585,095 sparse matrix. Note that these numbers are smaller than the total numbers of unique users and artists reported in Table 3 since we discarded users who listened to less than 10 unique artists and artists listened to by less than 10 users when creating the UAM. We assume that data about these artists and users is too sparse to be informative, or just noise. In particular, this approach efficiently filters artists that are misspelled, which is evidenced by the substantial reduction of their number by 81.66% (from 3,190,371 to 585,095). The reduction in terms of users is much smaller (by 0.21%, from 120,322 to 120,175), because users with such a narrow music artist taste are almost non-existent on Last.fm. This filtering step yields a UAM that is very well manageable with today's computers (approximately 200 MB).

Table 3: Statistics of items in the dataset.

Item	Number
Users	120,322
Artists	3,190,371
Albums	15,991,038
Tracks	32,291,134
Listening events	1,088,161,692
Unique <user, artist> pairs	61,534,450

In the following, we present a more detailed analysis of the demographic coverage, distribution of listening events, and features related to music preference and consumption behavior.

Demographics

We compute and illustrate the distribution of users among country, age, and gender. Table 4 shows the countries where most users in the dataset originate from. We include all countries with more than 1,000 users. As can be seen, a majority of users do not provide country information (54.13%). The country-specific percentages in the last column of the table are computed only among those users who provide their country. The distribution of users in the dataset reflects that of Last.fm users in general.

A histogram illustrating the age distribution is shown in Figure 1. Among all users, only 38.31% provide this piece of information. It can be seen that the age distribution is quite uneven and skewed towards the right (higher ages), but reflects the composition of Last.fm users. In addition to this, we can spot some seemingly erroneous information provided by some users, i.e., 165 of them indicated an age smaller or equal to 6 years, 149 indicated an age of at least 100 years. However, the share of these users only represents 0.26% of all users in the dataset. The age distribution has its arithmetic mean at 25.4 years, standard deviation of 9.7, a median of 23, and 25- and 75-percentile, respectively, at 20 and 28 years.

Table 5 depicts the gender distribution of users in the dataset. Among those who provide this information, more than two thirds are male, less than one third female. The larger share of male users on Last.fm is a known fact. The number of users who provide information on their gender (64,551 or 53.6%) is very close to the number of users who provide country information (65,132 or 54.1%), and considerably higher than the amount of users who indicate their age (46,095 or 38.3%). Therefore, users seem to be highly reluctant to reveal their age.

Listening events

To gain an understanding of the distribution of listening events in the dataset, Figures 2 and 3 illustrate the sorted amount of listening events for all artists and for all users, respectively, plotted as red lines. The blue plots indicate the number of listeners each artist has (Figure 2) and the number of artists each user listens to (Figure 3). The axes in both figures are logarithmically scaled.

From Figure 2, we observe that especially in the range of artists with extraordinarily high playcounts (left side of the figure), the number of playcounts decreases considerably faster than the number of listeners. For instance, the top-played artist is on average listened to 78.92 times per user,

Table 4: Statistics on country distribution of users. All countries with more than 1,000 users are shown.

Country	No. of users	Pct. in dataset
US	10255	18.581 %
RU	5024	9.103 %
DE	4578	8.295 %
UK	4534	8.215 %
PL	4408	7.987 %
BR	3886	7.041 %
FI	1409	2.553 %
NL	1375	2.491 %
ES	1243	2.252 %
SE	1231	2.230 %
UA	1143	2.071 %
CA	1077	1.951 %
FR	1055	1.912 %
N/A	65132	54.131 %

Table 5: Statistics on gender distribution of users.

Gender	No. of users	Pct. in dataset
Male	39969	71.666 %
Female	15802	28.334 %
N/A	64551	53.649 %

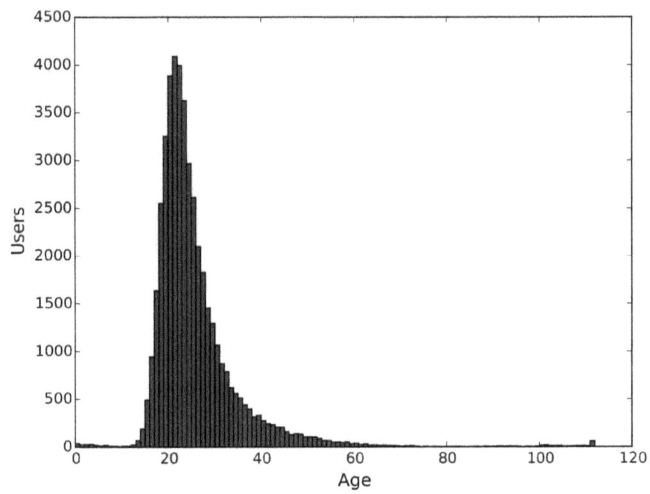

Figure 1: Histogram of age distribution.

while the 1,000th most popular artist is listened to only 22.66 times per user, on average. On the other side, the 100,000 least popular artists are played only 1.99 times on average. This provides strong evidence of the "long tail" of artists [3].

From Figure 3, we see that highly active listeners (in the left half of the figure) tend to have a rather stable relationship between total playcounts and number of artists listened to, whereas the average number of playcounts per artist strongly decreases for less active listeners. Indeed, the 1,000 most active listeners aggregate on average 29.73 listening events per artist, while for the 1,000 least active listeners, this number is only 3.04. Therefore, highly active users tend to listen to tracks by the same artists over and over again, while occasional and seldom listeners tend to play only a few tracks by their preferred artists. Furthermore, we can observe in Figure 3 the considerable number of users for which

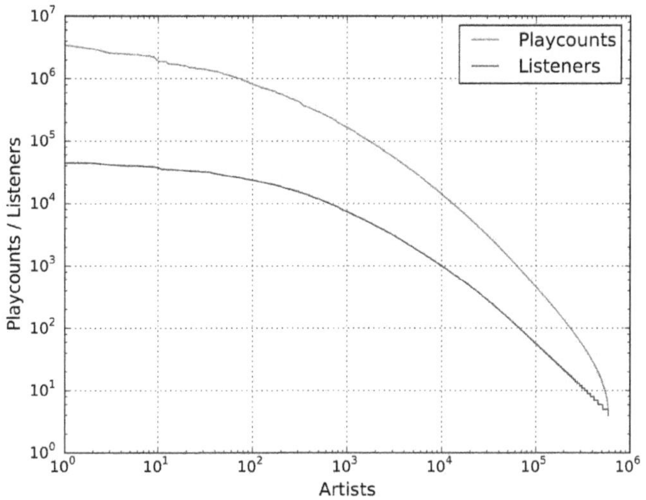

Figure 2: Distribution of listening events by artist, log-log-scaled.

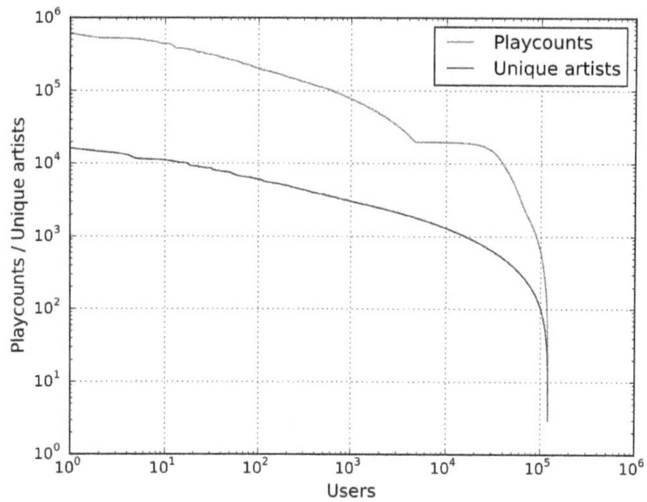

Figure 3: Distribution of listening events by user, log-log-scaled.

we recorded approximately 20,000 listening events, for the reasons given in Section 3.1.

Table 6 shows additional statistics of the listening event distribution, both from a user and an artist perspective (second and third column, respectively). The first row shows the average number and standard deviation of playcounts, per user and per artist, computed from the values of the red plots in Figures 2 and 3. The second row shows the average number of unique artists per user (second column) and the average number of unique users per artist (third column). These numbers are computed from the blue lines in the figures. The third row reveals how often, on average, users play artists they listen to (second column) and how often artists are listened to by users who listen to them at all, on average (third column). The last row is similar to the third one, but uses the median instead of the arithmetic mean to aggregate average playcounts. It shows that there exist strong outliers in the average playcount values, both per user and per artist, because the median values are much smaller than the mean values. For instance, each user listens to each of her artists on average about 21 times, but half of all users listen to each of their artists on average only 5 times or less. Therefore, there are a few users who keep on listening to their artists over and over again, while a large majority do not listen to the same artist more than a few times, on average.

Descriptors of preference and consumption behavior

The LFM-1b dataset provides a number of additional user-specific features (cf. Table 2), in particular information about temporal listening habits and music preference in terms of mainstreaminess and novelty [12]. To characterize temporal aspects, we binned the listening events of each user into weekdays and into hours of the day, and computed the share of each user's listening events over the bins. The distribution of these shares are illustrated in Figure 4 for weekdays and in Figure 5 for hours of the day. These box plots illustrate the median of the data by a horizontal red line. The lower and upper horizontal black lines of the box indicate the 25- and 75-percentiles, respectively. The horizontal black lines further above or below represent the furthest points not considered outliers, i.e., points within 1.5 times the interquartile range. Points beyond this range are depicted as blue plus signs. The red squares illustrate the arithmetic mean.

Table 6: Statistics of the distribution of listening events among users and artists. Values after the $\pm$ sign indicate standard deviations.

	Users	Artists
Playcount (PC)	$8{,}879 \pm 15{,}962$	$1{,}824 \pm 24{,}745$
Unique artists/users	512 ± 622	105 ± 733
Mean PC per artist/user	21.21 ± 46.68	7.89 ± 17.83
Median PC per artist/user	5.16 ± 19.35	2.50 ± 2.98

We can observe in Figure 4 that the share of listening events does not substantially differ between working days. However, during weekend (Saturday and Sunday), there is a much larger spread. A majority of people listens less during weekends than during working days (lower median). At the same time, the top 25% of active listeners consume much more music during weekends (higher 75-percentile for Saturday, and even higher for Sunday). This is obviously the result of working and leisure habits.

In Figure 5, we see that the distribution of listening events over hours of day vary more than over weekdays. It is particularly low during early morning hours (between 4 and 7h) and peaks in the afternoon and early evening (between 17 and 22h) when many people indulge in leisure time activities. While it would be interesting to investigate whether the temporal distribution of listening events varies with demographics, which we presume, such an analysis is unfortunately out of this paper's scope and left for future work.

The main statistics of the novelty and the mainstreaminess scores (both computed on time windows of one year) are given in Table 7. We can see that most users are eager to listen to new music since the average share of new artists listened to every year is approximately 50%. On the other hand, their music taste tends to be quite diverse and far away from the mainstream since the overlap between the user's distribution of listening events and the global distribution (that is how mainstreaminess is defined) is only 5%, on average.

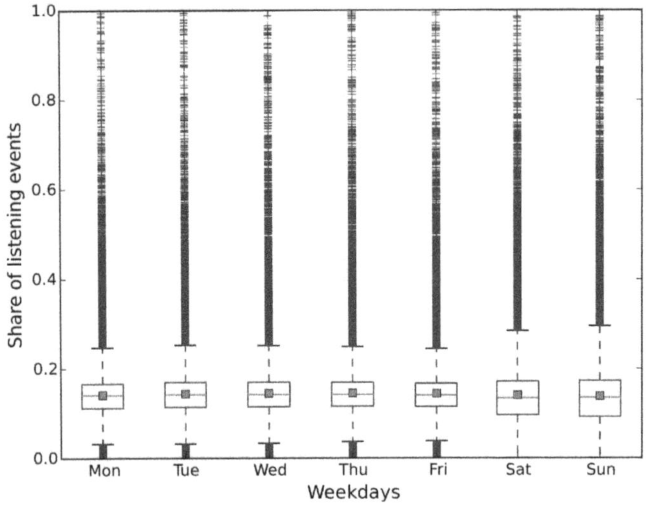

Figure 4: Distribution of listening events over weekdays.

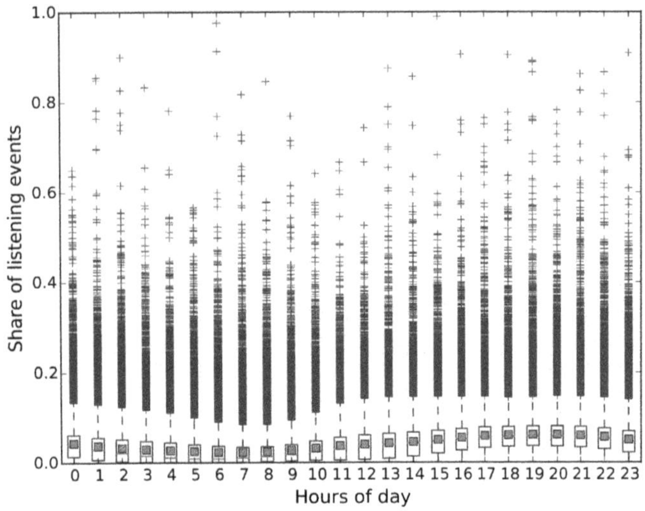

Figure 5: Distribution of listening events over hours of day. Each time range encompasses 0 to 59 minutes after the hour indicated on the x-axis.

Table 7: Statistics of novelty and mainstreaminess scores.

	Novelty	Mainstreaminess
Min.	0.000	0.000
25-perc.	0.354	0.016
Median	0.496	0.045
75-perc.	0.647	0.079
Max.	1.000	0.393
Mean	0.504	0.054
Std.	0.211	0.048

3.4 Sample Source Code

To facilitate access to the dataset, we provide Python scripts that show how to load the data and perform simple computations, e.g., basic statistics, as well as how to implement a basic collaborative filtering music recommender. The code package can be found on www.cp.jku.at/datasets/LFM-1b. File `LFM-1b_stats.py` shows how to load the UAM, compute some of the statistics reported in Section 3.3, and store them in a text file. Based on this text file, `LFM-1b_plot.py` demonstrates how to create plots such as the one shown in Figures 2 and 3. In addition, we implement in `LFM-1b_recommend-CF.py` a simple memory-based collaborative filtering approach, which might serve as reference implementation and starting point for experimentation with various recommendation models.

4. MUSIC RECOMMENDATION EXPERIMENTS USING LFM-1B

Music recommendation has lately become an important task. While the LFM-1b dataset is not restricted to this task, we illustrate its use for building and evaluating a music recommender system that recommends artists. The following results are intended to serve as baseline for further experimentation and investigating more sophisticated approaches.

4.1 Recommendation Algorithms

We implemented several recommendation algorithms, detailed in the following. The results of the experiments are then presented and discussed in Section 4.2.

Collaborative Filtering

A standard memory-based collaborative filtering approach that computes the inner product of the normalized UAM (excluding the artists used for testing) was implemented. After that, the K most similar users to the target user, i.e., the user to whom we want to recommend artists, are determined and the artists these K neighbors, but not the target user, listened to are weighted with respect to their frequency among the neighbors and the similarity of each neighbor to the target. This process yields a score for each artist which is used to rank them. Finally, the top N artists are recommended. For our experiments, we set $K = 25$.

Demographic Filtering

Based on users' gender, age, and country, we define a user-user similarity matrix, from which we identify the K most similar users to the target user and eventually recommend artists using the same weighting as in the CF approach. Demographic similarity is defined binary for gender (1 if same gender, 0 otherwise), and graded for age and country (e.g., 0.8 if the age difference is between 1 and 2 years, 0.2 if the age difference is between 9 and 15 years; 1 if the users reside in the same country, 0.1 if the distance between countries — measured between their midpoint of landmass — is larger than 3,500 kilometers). We then combine these three similarity functions linearly, giving equal weights to all components. Aggregation and recommendation is performed as in the collaborative filtering approach.

Content-based Recommendation

We implemented two content-based approaches, based on different data sources. Exploiting the artist names, we fetch for each artist (i) the mood descriptors from Allmusic[15] and (ii) the links present on the artist's Wikipedia[16] page.[17] We assume that artists that share moods and links are more

[15]http://www.allmusic.com

[16]http://en.wikipedia.org

[17]To determine the correct Allmusic and Wikipedia pages for a given artist, we implemented several heuristics and

similar. Each artist is eventually represented by a set of moods and a set of Wikipedia links, based on which two content-based recommenders are constructed. To estimate similarity between two artists, we calculate the Jaccard index between their sets of moods and between their sets of links, i.e., we compute the share of overlapping elements in both artists' item sets, separately for mood and for links. Artists similar to the ones listened to by the target user are then determined, weighted, aggregated, and ranked in a similar way than in the CF approach. Eventually, the N artists with highest scores, not known by the target user, are recommended. In our experiments, we considered up to $K = 25$ most similar artists for each artist in the target listener's training set.

Hybrid Recommender

In order to create a hybrid recommender, we follow a late fusion strategy by integrating the results of the content-based and the collaborative filtering recommenders. To this end, we first median-normalize the ranking scores given by the two recommenders to fuse. For artists suggested by both recommenders, we compute the new score as the arithmetic mean of both original scores; for all others, we take the original normalized scores. Based on the ranking obtained by sorting with respect to the new scores, we eventually recommend the top N artists.

Popularity-based Recommendation

This recommender simply sorts all artists according to their overall playcounts and recommends the top N, excluding those which the target user already knows.

Random Baselines

To contextualize the results of the recommender systems algorithms, we implemented two baselines: one that randomly selects N artists out of all artists the target user has not listened to, and one that randomly selects users and recommends N artists they listened to and are unknown to the target user.

4.2 Experiments and Results

For computational reasons, we ran the evaluation experiments on a subset of 1,100 users randomly sampled from LFM-1b. We performed 10-fold cross-validation on the listener level, i.e., we used 90% of each target user's listening history for training the system and the remaining 10% as ground truth to evaluate the recommendations made by the system. We repeated this procedure 10 times in a way that each listening event of the user occurs exactly once in the 10% test data. Varying the number of recommended artists N allows us to investigate precision at different levels of recall. The results are shown in Figure 6. As expected, CF and hybrid recommendations outperform all others. While CF has a slightly better performance when recommending a small number of artists N (higher precision at same recall), the hybrid approach outperforms CF for a large number of recommendations (higher precision and higher recall). The content-based recommender based on Wikipedia links also performs considerably well, in contrast to the mood-based one, for which data seems too sparse. All others perform substantially worse. Among the baselines, the random user selection performs slightly better than the random artist selection, which is due to the fact that the former tends to recommend artists that are more frequently listened to, while the latter performs a completely random selection.

filtering pipelines, a discussion of which is unfortunately not possible due to space limitations.

5. CONCLUSIONS AND FUTURE WORK

We presented the LFM-1b dataset that enables large-scale experimentation in music retrieval and recommendation. It can be downloaded from www.cp.jku.at/datasets/LFM-1b and provides information on the level of artists, albums, tracks, and users, as well as individual listening events. In addition to this standard content seen in other datasets as well, a unique feature of the LFM-1b dataset — next to its size — is the inclusion of detailed additional user-specific descriptors that model music preferences and consumption behavior. We strongly believe that this dataset, if not becoming a standard in benchmarking user-aware music recommendation approaches that go beyond rating prediction, will at least nicely complement existing datasets.

While the LFM-1b dataset can be used for experimentation in music retrieval and recommendation, particularly for collaborative filtering, demographic filtering, and personalized approaches, we contemplate several extensions. In particular, we would like to add audio-based features that allow to build content-based recommenders and retrieval systems. While audio is generally not available for the tracks in the dataset, preview snippets provided by several online music stores could be acquired and audio features computed thereon. Next to audio descriptors, features modeling the music context or background, such as TF·IDF weights computed on web pages related to artists or on lyrics, could be included too. Finally, we are investigating additional user-specific features relating to music consumption behavior, which we plan to include in a possible extension of the current dataset.

6. ACKNOWLEDGMENTS

This research is supported by the Austrian Science Fund (FWF): P25655. It would not have been possible without the help of numerous students, in particular, David Hauger, Andreas Frank, Matthias Freßdorf, Fabian Schneider, Georg Eschbacher, Hubert Scharfetter, and Nino Kratzer. Finally, we would like to thank Last.fm for providing an extensive API and for their liberal way of allowing to share data provided by their API, for non-commercial purposes. This strongly supports research in music recommendation, as evidenced by many publications that exploit Last.fm data.

7. REFERENCES

[1] G. Adomavicius, B. Mobasher, F. Ricci, and A. Tuzhilin. Context-aware Recommender Systems. *AI Magazine*, 32:67–80, 2011.

[2] T. Bertin-Mahieux, D. P. Ellis, B. Whitman, and P. Lamere. The Million Song Dataset. In *Proceedings of the 12th International Society for Music Information Retrieval Conference (ISMIR)*, Miami, FL, USA, October 2011.

[3] O. Celma. *Music Recommendation and Discovery – The Long Tail, Long Fail, and Long Play in the Digital Music Space.* Springer, Berlin, Heidelberg, Germany, 2010.

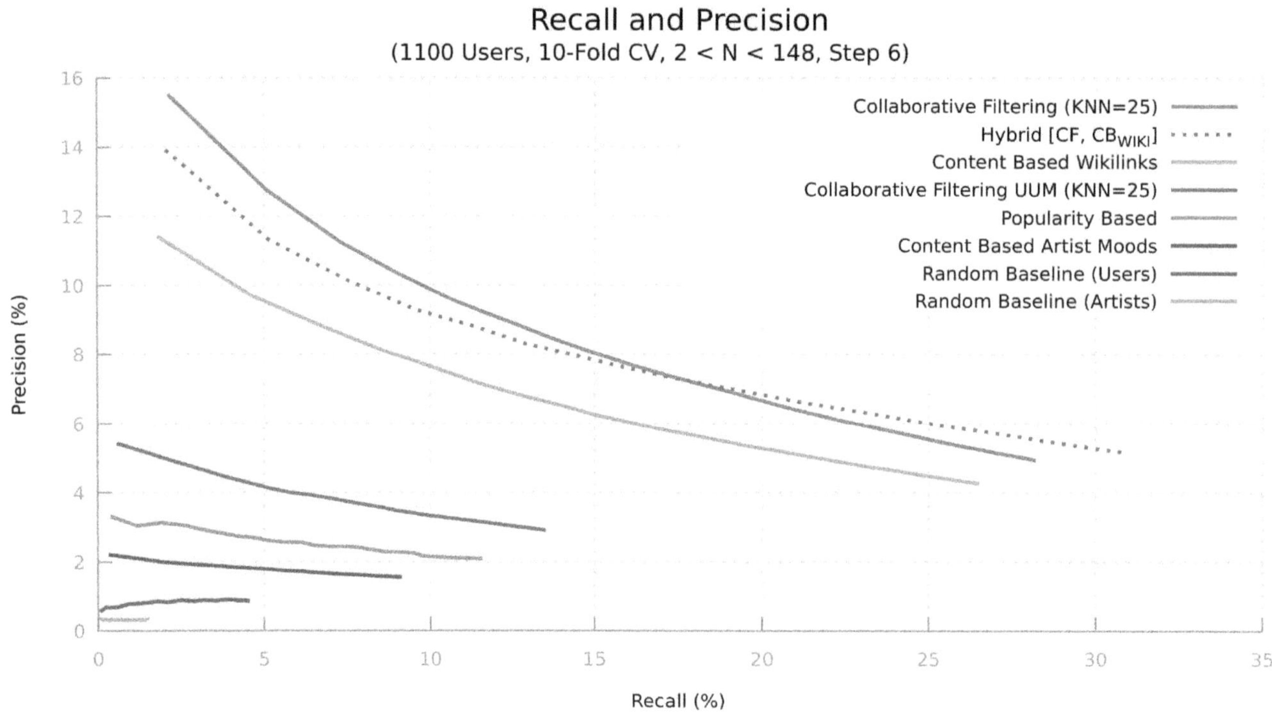

Figure 6: Precision/Recall plot of various recommendation algorithms, applied to a random subset of 1,100 users from the LFM-1b dataset. Ten-fold cross-validation was used. Precision and recall are plotted for various numbers of recommended artists N, ranging from 2 to 148 using a step size of 6.

[4] G. Dror, N. Koenigstein, Y. Koren, and M. Weimer. The Yahoo! Music Dataset and KDD-Cup'11. *JMLR: Proceedings of KDD-Cup 2011 Competition*, 18:3–18, October 2012.

[5] M. Grachten, M. Schedl, T. Pohle, and G. Widmer. The ISMIR Cloud: A Decade of ISMIR Conferences at Your Fingertips. In *Proceedings of the 10th International Society for Music Information Retrieval Conference (ISMIR)*, Kobe, Japan, October 2009.

[6] D. Hauger, M. Schedl, A. Košir, and M. Tkalčič. The Million Musical Tweets Dataset: What Can We Learn From Microblogs. In *Proceedings of the 14th International Society for Music Information Retrieval Conference (ISMIR)*, Curitiba, Brazil, November 2013.

[7] E. Law, K. West, M. Mandel, M. Bay, and J. S. Downie. Evaluation of Algorithms Using Games: The Case of Music Annotation. In *Proceedings of the 11th International Society for Music Information Retrieval Conference (ISMIR)*, Utrecht, the Netherlands, August 2010.

[8] J. H. Lee, M. C. Jones, and J. S. Downie. An Analysis of ISMIR Proceedings: Patterns of Authorship, Topic, and Citation. In *Proceedings of the 10th International Society for Music Information Retrieval Conference (ISMIR)*, Kobe, Japan, October 2009.

[9] C. Liem, M. Müller, D. Eck, G. Tzanetakis, and A. Hanjalic. The Need for Music Information Retrieval with User-centered and Multimodal Strategies. In *Proceedings of the 1st International ACM Workshop on Music Information Retrieval with User-centered and Multimodal Strategies (MIRUM)*, Scottsdale, AZ, USA, November 2011.

[10] B. McFee, T. Bertin-Mahieux, D. Ellis, and G. Lanckriet. The Million Song Dataset Challenge. In *Proceedings of the 4th International Workshop on Advances in Music Information Research (AdMIRe)*, Lyon, France, April 2012.

[11] M. Müller, M. Goto, and M. Schedl, editors. *Multimodal Music Processing*, volume 3 of *Dagstuhl Follow-Ups*. Schloss Dagstuhl–Leibniz-Zentrum für Informatik, Dagstuhl, Germany, 2012.

[12] M. Schedl and D. Hauger. Tailoring Music Recommendations to Users by Considering Diversity, Mainstreaminess, and Novelty. In *Proceedings of the 38th Annual International ACM SIGIR Conference on Research and Development in Information Retrieval*, Santiago, Chile, August 2015.

[13] M. Schedl, P. Knees, B. McFee, D. Bogdanov, and M. Kaminskas. *Recommender Systems Handbook*, chapter Music Recommender Systems. Springer, 2nd edition, 2015.

[14] B. L. Sturm. The State of the Art Ten Years After a State of the Art: Future Research in Music Information Retrieval. *Journal of New Music Research*, 43(2):147–172, 2014.

[15] Yuan Cao Zhang, Diarmuid O Seaghdha, Daniele Quercia, Tamas Jambor. Auralist: Introducing Serendipity into Music Recommendation. In *Proceedings of the 5th ACM International Conference on Web Search and Data Mining (WSDM)*, Seattle, WA, USA, February 2012.

Foreground Object Sensing for Saliency Detection

Hengliang Zhu[1], Bin Sheng[1], Xiao Lin[2], Yangyang Hao[1], Lizhuang Ma[1]
[1]Dept. of Computer Science and Engineering, Shanghai Jiao Tong University, China
[2]School of Optical-electrical and Computer Engineering, University of Shanghai for science and technology, China
{hengliang_zhu, haoyangyang2014}@sjtu.edu.cn, lin6008@126.com, {shengbin, ma-lz}@cs.sjtu.edu.cn

ABSTRACT

Many state-of-the-art saliency detection algorithms rely on the boundary prior, but these algorithms simply suppose the boundaries around an image as background regions. Here we propose a fast and effective algorithm for salient object detection. First, a novel method is proposed to approximately locate the foreground object by using the convex hull from Harris corner. On this basis, we divide the saliency values of different regions into two parts and generate the corresponding cue maps (foreground and background), which are combined into a convex hull prior map. Then a new prior based on distance to the convex hull center is proposed to replace the center prior. Finally, the convex hull prior map and the convex hull center-biased map are combined to be the saliency map, which is then optimized to get the final result. Compared with eighteen existing algorithms and tested on several datasets, the present algorithm performs well in terms of precision and recall.

CCS Concepts

•**Computing methodologies** → **Interest point and salient region detections;**

Keywords

Foreground object; Harris corner; Convex hull; Saliency map

1. INTRODUCTION

Following the study on the information processing mechanism of the biological (human) vision system, the task of visual saliency detection has rapidly progressed in recent years and is successfully used in numerous computer vision applications, such as object segmentation [34], image compression [13, 23], image resizing [29], image retrieval [8,35], and image quality assessment [46]. The aim of "visual saliency" is to find the abundant information regions of an image, where the salient regions are perceptually distinguishable from non-salient regions.

From the psychophysical perspective [22], saliency detection can be classified into bottom-up (data-driven) methods [7,12,15,32,39, 45,48] and top-down (goal-driven) methods [20,27,47]. In contrast to the latter taking advantage of high-level prior knowledge of an image, the former makes use of low-level features of the image (e.g. color, location, and texture) to detect saliency regions. With these primitive features, in the previous works [1, 18, 28, 37, 48], prior assumptions, such as the center prior, contrast prior, and boundary prior, were raised to improve the accuracy of salient object detection. In this paper, we mainly focus on the bottom-up saliency detection.

In recent years, the image boundary prior is adopted for saliency detection, assuming that a narrow border of the image is the non-salient regions. In other words, the image boundary tends to be background. There are many state-of-the-art algorithms rely on the boundary prior [19,41,45,48], which achieves better performance. However, one limitation of these works is that the salient object may slightly touch the image edge. In other words, the detected salient object is incomplete at the image boundary regions.

To address this problem, we propose a simple and effective algorithm for saliency region detection (see the workflow inFigure 1). First, based on the corner detection algorithm (Harris corner [40]), a new foreground object location algorithm is proposed, which uses two convex hull intersections to approximately locate the foreground object. The intersecting region excludes more scattered background and concentrates on the surrounding of a salient object. Second, by incorporating global contrast cues, we introduce a new region (image patch) saliency computation step (elaborated in Section 3). We divide the saliency value of a region into two parts: one part inside of convex hull (salient regions, which may contain some background) and the other part outside of convex hull (background regions). They are used to generate two cue maps (foreground and background) that are combined into a convex hull prior map. Finally, the saliency map is optimized.

The remainder of the article is organized as follows. Section 2 reviews the related work. The details of the proposed saliency computation method is presented in Section 3 and Section 4. Section 5 presents the experimental results and discussions. The conclusions are given in Section 6.

2. RELATED WORKS

A detailed summary of saliency detection is provided in [4, 5]. The fixation prediction models [3, 11, 14, 16], which track the eye movements, are based on the exploitation of physical devices. Instead, this work is based on the study of image processing. In this section, we briefly review the major salient detection algorithms and their differences.

The pioneering research about saliency detection was conducted by Itti et al. [17], who defined the saliency value of a pixel as the local center-surround difference. The detection is based on a multiscale of image features, including color, intensity, and orientation.

ICMR'16, June 06-09, 2016, New York, NY, USA
© 2016 ACM. ISBN 978-1-4503-4359-6/16/06...$15.00
DOI: http://dx.doi.org/10.1145/2911996.2912008

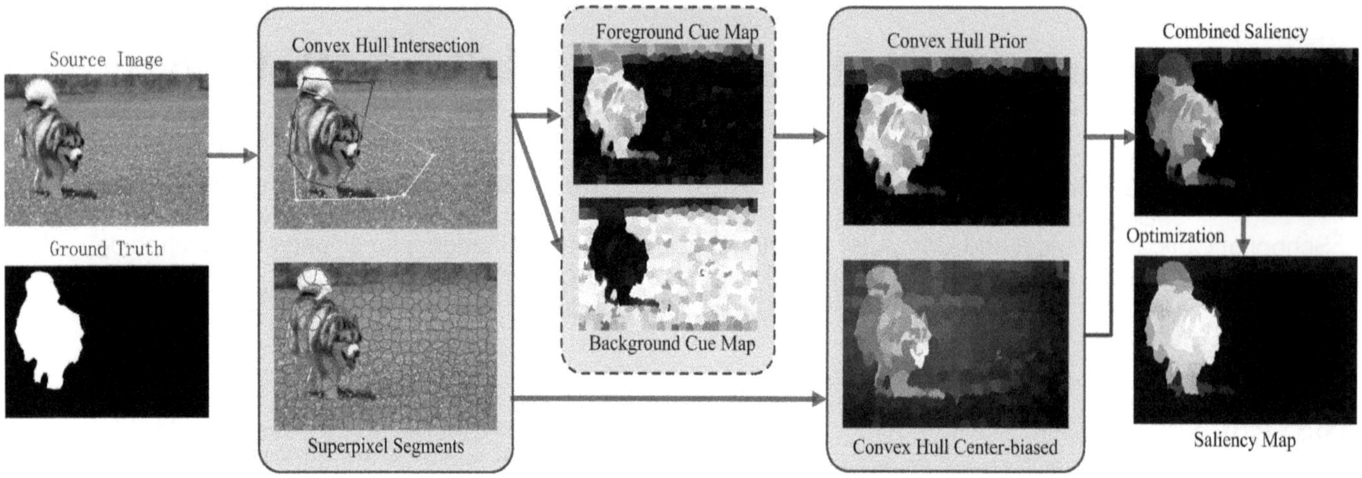

Figure 1: Workflow of the new saliency detection algorithm. The intersection of two convex hulls is approximately estimated by using the Harris corner points, and used to construct two cue maps (foreground and background). Then these two cue maps are combined into a convex hull prior map, which is integrated with a convex hull center-biased map to form the final saliency map.

Later, the contrast prior, including the local or global contrast, has been extensively exploited to detect salient objects and regions. For example, Ma et al. [28] proposed a local contrast-based method for salient region detection, which operates at a single scale. Cheng et al. [7] considered a global contrast prior for saliency computation. Perazzi et al. [32] used the uniqueness and spatial distribution for computing a saliency map. Goferman et al. [12] proposed a context-aware saliency detection model. Achanta et al. [1] proposed a multi-scale method to generate saliency maps. All these methods make use of the low-level features of an image to characterize the visual saliency. Also, some works [19, 20, 27] used the primitive features in machine learning ways, and more favorable results are generated.

Recently, the boundary prior is applied to detect salient regions, where the image boundary areas are simply treated as background. Intuitively, salient regions are much less connected to the image border than the ones in the background. Wei et al. [41] proposed a geodesic saliency approach, which considers the background as cues instead of salient object. Chuan Yang et al. [45] proposed a graph-based manifold ranking method, which uses the image background regions as queries. W. Zhu et al. [48] proposed a saliency measure called boundary connectivity, which exploits the spatial relationship between an image patch with the image boundary. X. Li et al. [24] measured the saliency from dense and sparse reconstruction errors by using the background templates. In order to exploit the intrinsic relationship of regions with it's neighbors, Q. Yao et al. [33] treated the salient object detection as a Cellular Automata evolution process. But from a different viewpoint, another important cue for saliency detection is foreground object location. The convex hull of Harris points has been extensively used to approximately estimate the foreground regions. For instance, the low-level cues based on the convex hull can be used to estimate saliency [42, 43]. R.Liu et al. [26] used the Harris operator to obtain the candidate foreground and background. Pan et al. [31] proposed an edge preserving filter method by using the image matting model.

However, the boundary prior algorithms simply consider the image boundary as background, and convex-hull-based algorithms may include more non-salient regions. To overcome these difficulties, we propose the foreground object sensing measure for saliency detection.

3. FOREGROUND OBJECT SENSING

The steps of our algorithm are as follows. First, we present a new method to approximately localize a foreground object. After that, two saliency cue maps (foreground and background) are generated and finally integrated into a convex hull prior map in a simple way. Then we propose a weighted global contrast algorithm based on convex hull center-biased. These details are talked about in Section 3.1-3.3, respectively.

3.1 Object location estimation

According to the vision attention mechanism, many studies indicate that a salient region has an obviously different appearance and can be distinguished from its surroundings. Inspired by this principles, we use the feature points of an image to acquire the convex hull and then approximately locate the foreground object.

There are many feature point detectors, such as scale-invariant feature transform (SIFT), speeded-up robust features (SURF) and Harris. Considering the low complexity in computation, we utilize Harris corner points to roughly detect the feature points of a salient object. In the experiment, we find that the only use of Harris corner points to calculate the convex hull of salient regions is not appropriate, because the convex hull region may contain too much background. In order to more accurately locate the foreground object, we need to further eliminate the background influence in the convex hull region.

Generally, the salient object is the most informative region in an image, and its edges or contours are discontinuous on the intensity or color at a pixel. In the frequency domain, however, brightness variations are likely to correspond to the high-frequency component. Thus, in order to suppress some high-frequency components belonging to the background, we can use low-pass filters to smooth the original image, such as averaging filter, and Gaussian low-pass filter. Then we use the Harris operator again to detect the corner points in the filtered image and get the corresponding convex hull. The two convex hull regions are represented as R_1 and R_2, respectively (Figure 2(b) and 2(c)), and their intersection is then determined. We define this intersection region as

$$R_F = R_1 \cap R_2, \tag{1}$$

Figure 2 shows the localization of the foreground object region

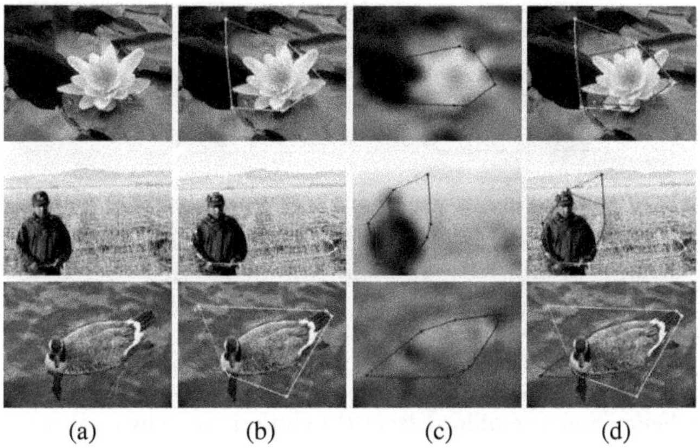

Figure 2: Foreground object region detection by using convex hull. (a) Original image. (b) The convex hull of the original image. (c) The convex hull of the filtered image. (d) Intersection of the two convex hull regions (red polygon).

using convex hull. The intersection region (red polygon) excludes more scattered background (Figure 2(d)) and can be approximately regarded as a foreground object region. Also the background (outside of R_F) region of an image is expressed as R_B. In our experiments, we use an averaging filter and set its size as 35.

3.2 Saliency computation

Before computing the saliency map, we segment the original image into superpixel regions using the simple linear iterative clustering algorithm (SLIC) [2], which can efficiently generate compact and uniform superpixels. We set the number of superpixels to be 300 for an image in our experiments. The superpixel region set is denoted as $X = \{r_1, r_2, \cdots, r_N\}$, and its corresponding saliency values are $V = \{v_1, v_2, \cdots, v_N\}$, where v_i is saliency value of a superpixel region r_i, and N is the number of superpixels.

Based on the location of the foreground object, we divide the saliency value of each superpixel into two parts: one inside of convex hull and one outside of convex hull, denoted as SF_i and SB_i, respectively. Then we construct an undirected graph by connecting all adjacent superpixels r_i and r_j, and the weight of its edges is the Euclidean distance between the average colors of superpixels in the CIELab color space. Thus, based on this graph, we compute the difference between two superpixel regions using the geodesic distance, which is easily computed with the shortest path algorithm.

Therefore, we define SF_i for a superpixel region as a sum of geodesic distances compared with all the regions in R_F. Thus, SF_i is written as

$$SF_i = \sum_{j=1}^{N_1} shtDist(c_i, c_j), r_j \in R_F \tag{2}$$

where $shtDist(c_i, c_j)$ is the shortest path between two regions r_i and r_j; c_i and c_j are the mean colors of superpixels r_i and r_j, respectively, in the CIELab color space, and region r_j belongs to R_F; N_1 is the total number of superpixels inside of convex hull. Examples are showed in Figure 3(b).

Like SF_i, we define the SB_i of a superpixel region as a sum of geodesic distances compared to all the regions in R_B. Thus, SB_i

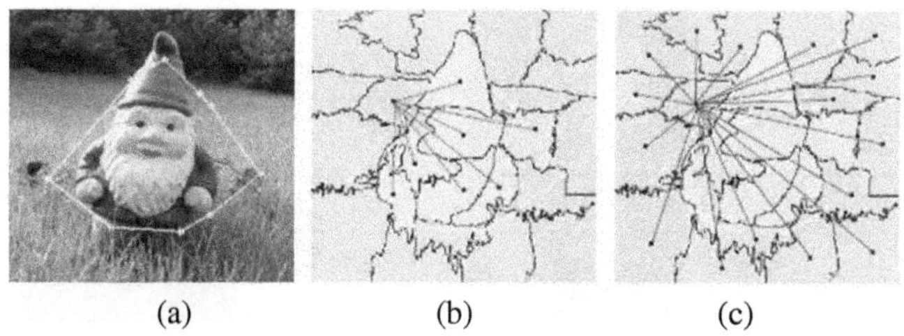

Figure 3: A region's saliency value is divided into two parts. (a) Convex hull region (yellow polygon R_F). (b) A region's value SF_i indicates that this region compares with all the regions in R_F (pink regions). (c) A region's value SB_i indicates that this region compares with all the regions in R_B (blue regions).

is computed as follows:

$$SB_i = \sum_{j=1}^{N_2} shtDist(c_i, c_j), r_j \in R_B \tag{3}$$

where r_j belongs to R_B; N_2 is the total number of superpixels outside of convex hull, as illustrated in Figure 3(c). Note that $N = N_1 + N_2$.

Foreground Cue Map Salient regions are generally the important and attractive place [5] and usually stand out from their surroundings. Thus, the saliency value of a superpixel region in R_F is higher than in R_B. For a given region r_i, if it is inside of convex hull, SF_i is smaller than SB_i, so SB_i/SF_i is high; if it is outside of convex hull, SF_i is larger than SB_i, so SB_i/SF_i is low.

Given this fact, we construct the foreground cue map using the convex hull region. The saliency value of each superpixel region in an image is defined as

$$FC_i = SB_i/SF_i, \tag{4}$$

Equation 4 guarantees that the saliency value of a region in the foreground R_F is higher than in the background R_B. Figure 4(b) shows some results of foreground cue maps. Clearly, the entire foreground object regions are prominently highlighted, and have larger values than the regions outside of the convex hull (background).

Background Cue Map Contrary to the foreground cue map, we can construct the corresponding background cue map. A superpixel region in the background R_B has a larger saliency value than in the foreground region. Like Eqs. 4, the background cue map is defined as

$$BC_i = SF_i/SB_i, \tag{5}$$

where BC_i is the saliency value of a region in an image. As shown in Figure 4(c), we can see that the background regions are almost highlighted.

Convex Hull Prior Map The foreground cue map is not homogeneous enough, since some background regions have high saliency values (Figure 4(b)), but the background cue map highlights the non-salient regions more significantly (Figure 4(c)). Therefore, we propose an algorithm to combine these two cue maps into a convex hull prior map as follows:

$$CH_i = \begin{cases} FC_i * \exp(-\sigma_1 BC_i), r_i \in R_F \\ FC_i * \exp(-\sigma_2 BC_i), r_i \in R_B \end{cases} \tag{6}$$

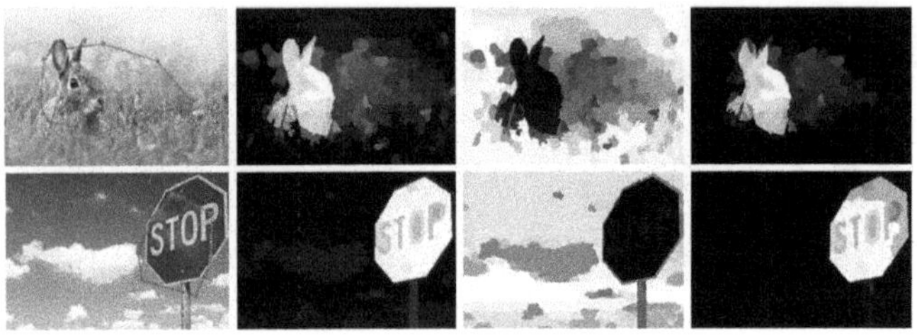

(a) (b) (c) (d)

Figure 4: Saliency cue maps based on convex hull regions. (a) Source image and convex hull region in red polygon. (b) Foreground cue maps. (c) Background cue maps. (d) Convex hull prior maps generated by (b) and (c).

where r_i is a superpixel region. In fact, the background cue map has a great effect on background, so its effect is balanced by the parameters σ_1 and σ_2. When $r_i \in R_F$, we assign σ_1's with a smaller value; when $r_i \in R_B$, we set σ_2's with a larger value. Note that we set σ_1 and σ_2 with constant values in our experiments. Empirically, we set $\sigma_1 = 2.5$ and $\sigma_2 = 6$.

Also, the convex hull prior map is normalized to the range [0, 1]. According to some visual comparisons (Figure 4(d)), the background regions are obviously weakened.

3.3 Convex hull center-biased algorithm

Vision attention study shows that humans tend to focus on the central area in an image [38]. There are some saliency models using the center prior [18,44], which consider the region close to the center of an image could be a salient object. In other words, the background regions tends to be far away from the image center. In many situations, however, the center prior model may be ineffective and miss some salient regions. Thus, we sufficiently utilize a convex hull center-biased as a weighted factor for global region contrast [7]. Let the center of convex hull be $\mu(x_c, y_c)$, then a region's global contrast in our algorithm is written as

$$G(r_i) = \sum_{j=1}^{N} \phi(r_i, r_j)||c_i - c_j||_2 \psi(r_i, \mu), \quad (7)$$

where $\phi(r_i, r_j)$ is a Gaussian weighting function and set to be $\exp(-d(r_i, r_j)/(2\delta_1^2))$, representing the spatial distance between two region centers of r_i and r_j; $\psi(r_i, \mu)$ is a weighted factor and set to be $\exp(-d(r_i, \mu)/(2\delta_2^2))$; $d(r_i, \mu)$ denotes the Euclidean distance between the centers of region r_i and convex hull. Empirically, δ_1 and δ_2 are set to be 0.4 and 0.2 in our experiments, respectively. As shown in Figure 5, the second and third rows present some cases when the foreground object is not in the center of an image and Figure 5(c) shows the results of our algorithm.

3.4 Integration and optimization

The convex hull prior map and convex hull center-biased map are complementary to each other. As shown in Figure 5(b), we can see that the foreground objects are obviously highlighted, but there are still some background regions not clearly separated from the salient objects.

Compared with the foreground object, the background regions in the saliency maps are weakened (Figure 5(c)). Thus, we can take the advantage of these two saliency maps and combine them into the final saliency map in a simple way. We define our combined saliency map as

$$S_i = CH_i * G_i, \quad (8)$$

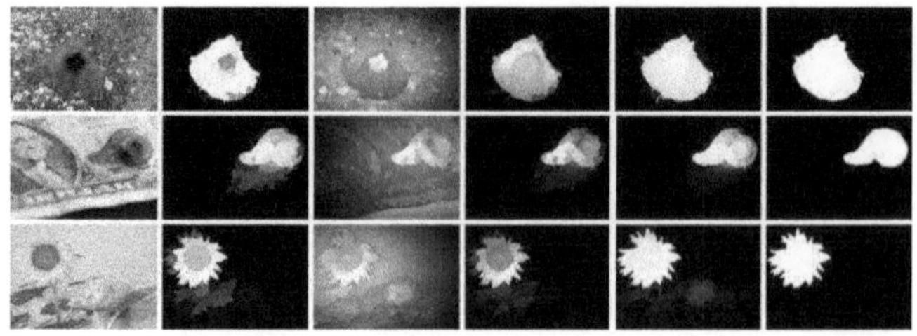

(a) (b) (c) (d) (e) (f)

Figure 5: Saliency maps of each step. (a) Source images and (f) ground truth. (b) The convex hull prior maps. (c) Saliency maps based on the convex hull center-biased algorithm. (d) Saliency maps combined from (b) and (c). (e) The final optimized saliency map.

As shown in the combined saliency map (Figure 5(d)), we can see that the background regions are greatly eliminated by Eq. 8. In order to further generate a uniformly-highlighted saliency map, we refine our results using the optimization function reported in [48]. With different coefficients, the optimization function is rewritten as

$$\sum_{i=1}^{N} B_i v_i^2 + \sum_{i=1}^{N} S_i(1 - v_i)^2 + \sum_{i,j} \phi(r_i, r_j)(v_i - v_j)^2, \quad (9)$$

where v_i is a superpixel's saliency value, and B_i can be determined from Eqs. 5 and 8 as $B_i = (1 - S_i)BC_i$. The coefficients B_i and S_i control the background and foreground saliency values, respectively. The third term is a smooth constraint, which controls the smooth transition from foreground to background. Some examples are shown in Figure 5(e), and clearly, the salient objects are well highlighted after optimization.

4. EXPERIMENTS

To test the performance of our algorithm, we conducted two types of experiments: (1) performance evaluation, including precision and recall (PR) curves, F-measure and mean absolute error (MAE), which are computed as described previously [15,32]; (2) some evaluations of each component in the proposed algorithm that contribute to the final saliency map.

We compare our algorithm (denoted as FOS) with the existing eighteen state-of-the-art saliency detection algorithms, including IT [17], FT [15], SR [16], CA [12], SF [32], GS [41], GC [10], HS [44], PCA [30], RC [7], SVO [6], LMLC [43], GMR [45], D-SR [24], HDCT [21], wCO [48], BL [33], and BSCA [39]. Results of these algorithms are determined using the corresponding authors' publicly available source code or demo. The experiments are tested on six benchmark datasets (ASD [15], MSRA5000 [27], THUS10000 [9], ECSSD [44], Pascal-S [25] and SED2 [36]).

4.1 Quantitative evaluation

We choose two objective evaluation methods (fixed threshold and adaptive threshold) to evaluate all saliency detection algorithms. First, for each saliency map, a binary map is generated using a fixed threshold lying in the range [0, 255] with an increment of 1. Then we use the results of precision and recall to compare with the ground truth maps. The results of precision-recall (PR) curves are shown in Figure 6(a) and 6(b), where the results from top row to bottom row are MSRA5000, THUS10000, ECSSD and Pascal-S, respectively. Our algorithm outperforms other algorithms in terms of precision and recall.

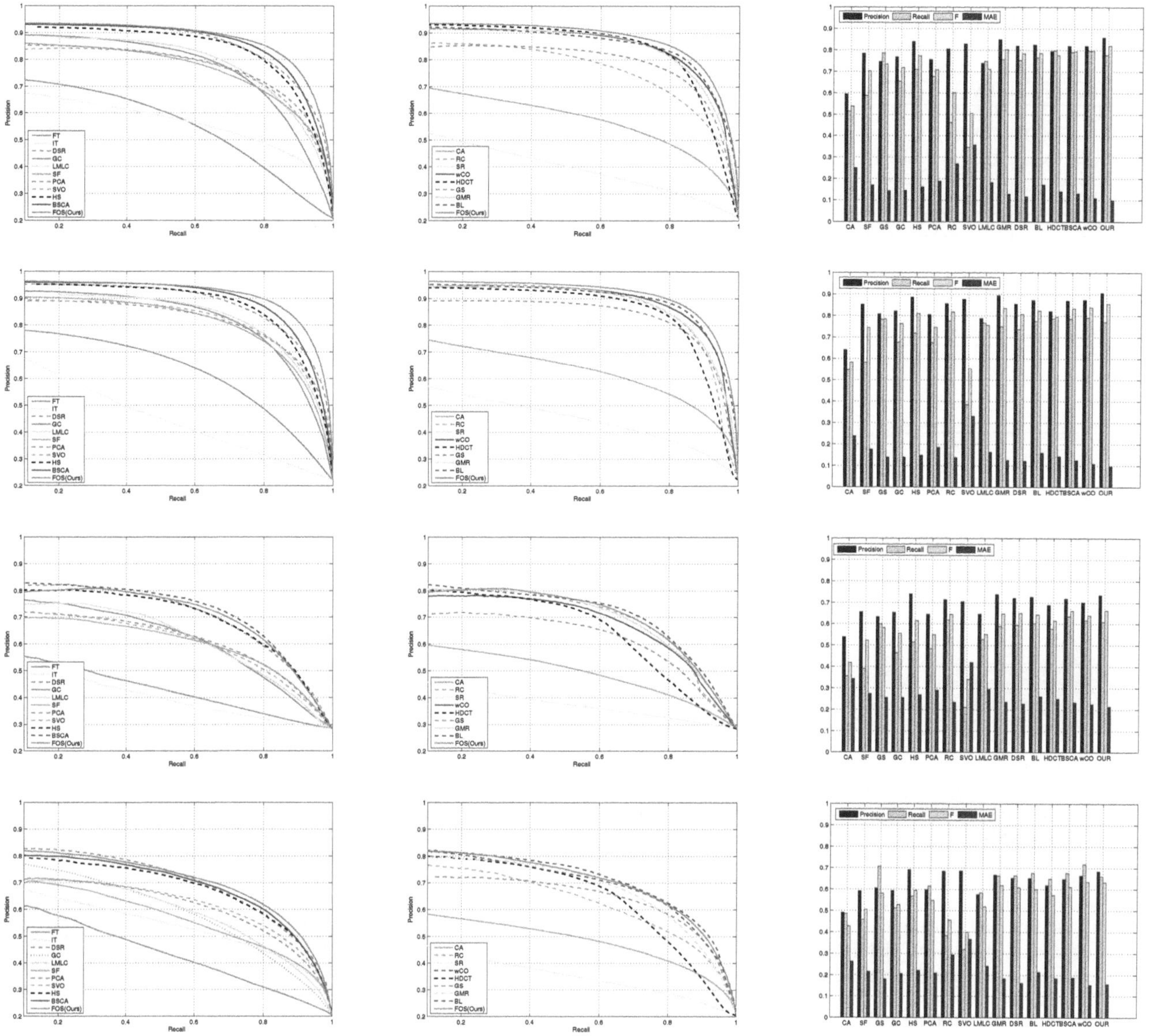

(a) (b) (c)

Figure 6: Comparison of our results with the state-of-the-art methods on four data sets. From top to bottom, the results are M-SRA5000, THUS10000, ECSSD and Pascal-S, respectively. (a)-(b) Precision and recall curves of saliency methods. (c) The bar charts of average precision, recall, F-measure and MAE values.

Second, we also estimate the average precision, recall, F-measure and MAE values for each algorithm. According to the setting in [15], we set adaptive threshold $T = 2{*}Mean(S)$ (S is the saliency map) and the expression of F-measure as

$$F_{\omega} = \frac{(1+\omega^2) * precision * recall}{\omega^2 * precision + recall}, \quad (10)$$

where we set $\omega^2 = 0.3$. The results of these values are shown in Figure 6(c) bar charts. On the whole, our algorithm achieves favorable results compared with other eighteen algorithms, especially in terms of F-measure and MAE.

To clearly evaluate the performances of these saliency algorithms, we provide some quantitative results of F-measure and MAE with twelve representative algorithms on five datasets (Table 1). We can see that our algorithm significantly outperforms other state-of-the-art algorithms.

4.2 Qualitative evaluation

We provide some saliency maps of the proposed algorithm and other ten state-of-the-art algorithms in Figure 9. From the results we can see that the saliency maps generated by our algorithm can clearly separate the salient objects from the background. When an image has complex background structures, our algorithm still produces favorable results with fewer noisy background. For example, in the fourth and fifth rows, our saliency maps can uniformly highlight the foreground object of the images, but other algorithms fail to extract the salient object from the scattered background. In addition, when a salient object has similar appearance as the back-

Table 1: Some quantitative results of F-measure scores and MAE. We compare our method with twelve representative saliency methods on five datasets. The upper part is F-measure scores, and the bottom part is MAE values. Our results are shown in red color.

F-measure	SVO	RC	PCA	SF	GS	HS	GMR	DSR	HDCT	wCO	BL	BSCA	FOS
ASD	0.579	0.719	0.797	0.835	0.830	0.865	0.901	0.860	0.832	0.888	0.874	0.879	**0.908**
MSRA5000	0.506	0.601	0.709	0.703	0.736	0.774	0.803	0.785	0.776	0.797	0.785	0.795	**0.820**
THUS10k	0.553	0.818	0.745	0.743	0.785	0.810	0.835	0.807	0.795	0.838	0.823	0.834	**0.855**
ECSSD	0.342	0.646	0.548	0.521	0.583	0.614	0.649	0.651	0.614	0.641	0.644	0.661	**0.664**
PASCAL-S	0.400	0.456	0.548	0.506	0.581	0.595	0.619	0.608	0.573	**0.635**	0.600	0.610	**0.632**
MAE													
ASD	0.336	0.237	0.155	0.130	0.106	0.114	0.074	0.076	0.118	0.064	0.128	0.085	**0.059**
MSRA5000	0.358	0.269	0.189	0.171	0.144	0.161	0.129	0.117	0.142	0.110	0.172	0.131	**0.100**
THUS10k	0.331	0.137	0.185	0.175	0.139	0.149	0.126	0.121	0.143	0.109	0.159	0.125	**0.099**
ECSSD	0.420	0.235	0.291	0.274	0.255	0.269	0.237	0.226	0.249	0.225	0.262	0.233	**0.215**
PASCAL-S	0.368	0.295	0.209	0.216	0.181	0.223	0.184	0.163	0.185	**0.154**	0.214	0.188	**0.158**

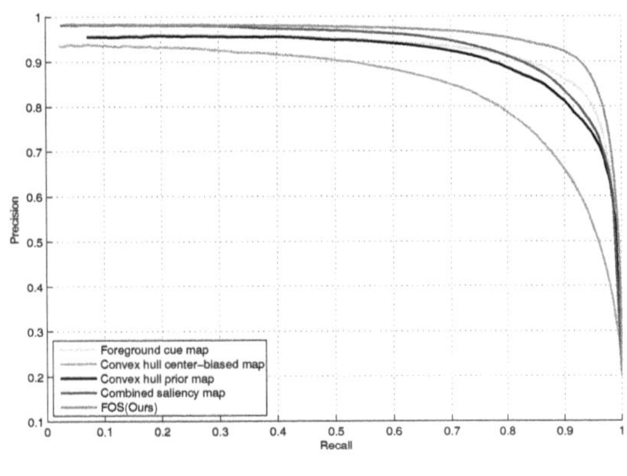

Figure 7: Evaluation of each component in the proposed algorithm on dataset ASD.

ground, our algorithm is able to detect salient regions accurately as shown in the first and third rows. Generally, our algorithm can generate the saliency maps with highlighted salient objects and effectively restrain the background regions (Figure 9).

4.3 Analysis of our algorithm

To demonstrate the effectiveness of our proposed algorithm, we also evaluate the performance of each component in our algorithm. Each component contributes to the final results, such as the foreground cue map, convex hull prior map, convex hull center-biased map, combined saliency map and the final saliency map. Figure 7 shows the precision and recall for each individual component of our algorithm on ASD (MSRA1000) dataset. It is clear that the foreground cue map, convex hull prior map and combined saliency map can also generate high accuracy results.

4.4 Limitations

We also present the experimental results of our algorithm with other saliency detectors on the dataset SED2 (100 images). SED2 contains more than one salient object, which is a big challenge for saliency detection. The results are illustrated in Figure 8. We can see that the performance of our algorithm is not the best on dataset SED2. As shown in PR curves (Figure 8), the precision constantly drops quickly with the increase of recall rate. Intuitively, when an image contains multiple salient objects with very large spatial distance, our algorithm has some limitations at detecting these salient objects, especially in terms of accuracy. Since the sizes and positions of multi-objects in an image are both very different and diverse, and can be hardly covered in only one convex hull, which is used in our algorithm, as shown in the failure case in Figure 8. Perhaps we could use more than one convex hull to improve the algorithmic ability in multi-object detection.

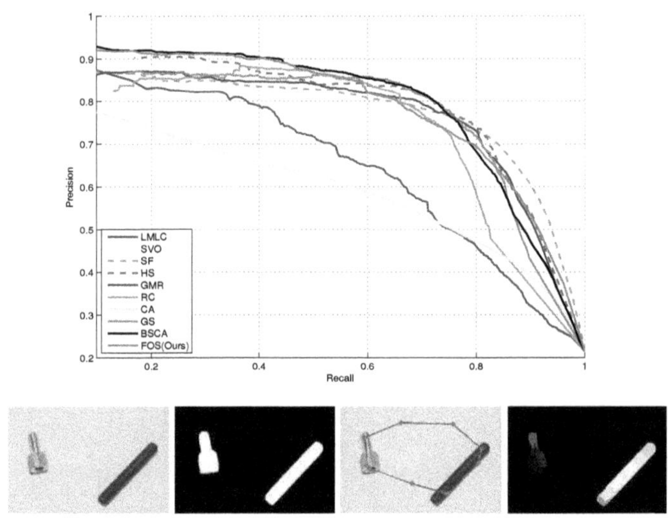

Figure 8: The top part is PR curves on dataset SED2. The bottom part is the failure case of the proposed algorithm. From left to right: source image, ground truth, convex hull and saliency map.

4.5 Time Complexity

We compare the speed of FOS (ours) with the most representative or the newest algorithms on ASD dataset. The average running time for each algorithm is listed in Table 2. We use the corresponding authors' public source code for their algorithms, and our algorithm is based on implementation in Matlab R2013a. All experiments are conducted on a PC with Intel Core i5-3470 CPU@ 3.2GHz with 4G RAM, Windows 8. It is clear that our algorithm has a low complexity in computation.

Table 2: Running time on ASD dataset. (All the algorithms are Matlab code).

Method	PCA	GMR	BL	HDCT	wCO	FOS
Time (s)	3.821	0.873	1.741	3.635	0.212	0.441

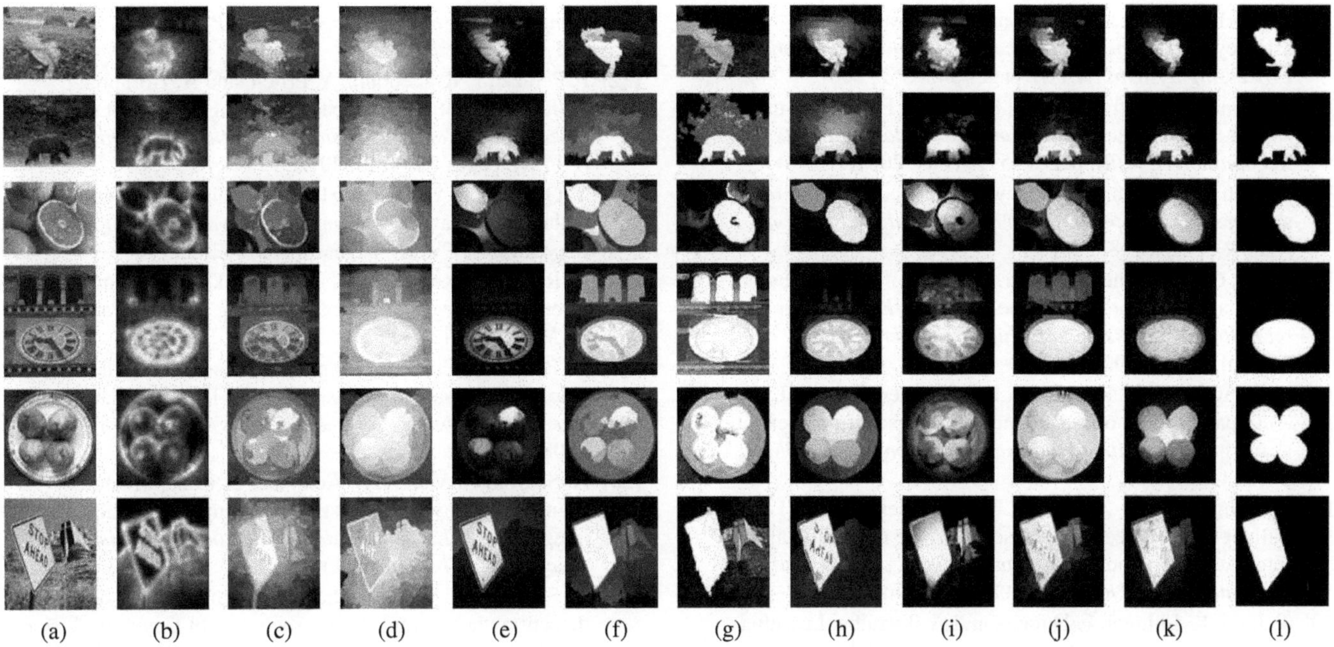

Figure 9: Comparison of our saliency maps with other ten state-of-the-art algorithms. (a) Source image (b) CA [12] (c) RC [7] (d) SVO [6] (e) SF [32] (f) HS [44] (g) LMLC [43] (h) GMR [45] (i) DSR [24] (j) wCO [48] (k) FOS (Ours) (l) Ground truth.

5. CONCLUSIONS

In this paper, we present an efficient saliency region detection algorithm via foreground object sensing. In order to accurately locate the foreground object, we first introduce a new approach to approximately estimate the location of the salient object, which can eliminate most background information. We also propose a convex hull center-biased algorithm to enhance the contrast of the foreground regions and weaken the background influence. Extensive experimental results show that the new algorithm can generate high-quality homogeneous saliency map and uniformly highlight the salient regions. In the future, we will improve our algorithm for detection of multiple salient objects.

6. ACKNOWLEDGMENTS

The work is supported by the Natural Science Foundation of China (No. 61133009, 61472245, 61202154, 61572316, 61133009, 61502220 and U1304616), National High-tech R&D Program of China (863 Program) (No. 2015AA015904), the Interdisciplinary Program of Shanghai Jiao Tong University (No. 14JCY10), the Science and Technology Commission of Shanghai Municipality Program (No. 13511505000).

7. REFERENCES

[1] R. Achanta, F. Estrada, P. Wils, and S. Süsstrunk. Salient region detection and segmentation. *Computer Vision Systems*, pages 66–75, 2008.

[2] R. Achanta, A. Shaji, K. Smith, A. Lucchi, P. Fua, and S. Süsstrunk. Slic superpixels compared to state-of-the-art superpixel methods. *IEEE Transactions on Pattern Analysis and Machine Intelligence*, 34(11):2274–2282, Nov 2012.

[3] B. Ali, D. N. Sihite, and I. Laurent. Quantitative analysis of human-model agreement in visual saliency modeling: a comparative study. *IEEE Transactions on Image Processing*, 22(1):55–69, 2013.

[4] A. Borji, M.-M. Cheng, H. Jiang, and J. Li. Salient object detection: A survey. *Eprint Arxiv*, 16(7):3118, 2014.

[5] A. Borji, D. N. Sihite, and L. Itti. Salient object detection: A benchmark. In *European Conference on Computer Vision (ECCV)*, 2012.

[6] K.-Y. Chang, T.-L. Liu, H.-T. Chen, and S.-H. Lai. Fusing generic objectness and visual saliency for salient object detection. In *International Conference on Computer Vision (ICCV)*, pages 914–921, 2011.

[7] M. Cheng, N. J. Mitra, X. Huang, P. H. S. Torr, and S. Hu. Global contrast based salient region detection. In *Computer Vision and Pattern Recognition (CVPR)*, pages 409–416, 2011.

[8] M.-M. Cheng, N. J. Mitra, X. Huang, and S.-M. Hu. Salientshape: Group saliency in image collections. *The Visual Computer*, pages 1–10, 2013.

[9] M. M. Cheng, N. J. Mitra, X. Huang, P. H. S. Torr, and S. M. Hu. Salient object detection and segmentation. *IEEE Transactions on Pattern Analysis and Machine Intelligence*, 37(3):1, 2011.

[10] M.-M. Cheng, J. Warrell, W.-Y. Lin, S. Zheng, V. Vineet, and N. Crook. Efficient salient region detection with soft image abstraction. In *International Conference on Computer Vision (ICCV)*, pages 1529–1536, 2013.

[11] D. Gao, V. Mahadevan, and N. Vasconcelos. The discriminant center-surround hypothesis for bottom-up saliency. *Advances in Neural Information Processing Systems (NIPS)*, 20:497–504, 2007.

[12] S. Goferman, L. Zelnik-Manor, and A. Tal. Context-aware saliency detection. In *Computer Vision and Pattern Recognition (CVPR)*, pages 2376–2383, 2010.

[13] C. Guo and L. Zhang. A novel multiresolution spatiotemporal saliency detection model and its applications in image and video compression. *IEEE Transactions on Image Processing*, 19(1):185–198, 2010.

[14] J. Harel, C. Koch, and P. Perona. Graph-based visual saliency. In *Annual Conference on Neural Information Processing Systems (NIPS)*, pages 545–552, 2007.

[15] S. Hemami, F. Estrada, and S. Susstrunk. Frequency-tuned salient region detection. In *Computer Vision and Pattern Recognition (CVPR)*, pages 1597–1604, 2009.

[16] X. Hou and L. Zhang. Saliency detection: A spectral residual approach. In *Computer Vision and Pattern Recognition (CVPR)*, pages 1–8, 2007.

[17] L. Itti, C. Koch, and E. Niebur. A model of saliency-based visual attention for rapid scene analysis. *IEEE Transactions on Pattern Analysis and Machine Intelligence*, 20(11):1254–1259, 1998.

[18] H. Jiang, J. Wang, Z. Yuan, T. Liu, N. Zheng, and S. Li. Automatic salient object segmentation based on context and shape prior. In *British Machine Vision Conference (BMVC)*, pages 1–12, 2011.

[19] H. Jiang, J. Wang, Z. Yuan, Y. Wu, N. Zheng, and S. Li. Salient object detection: A discriminative regional feature integration approach. In *Computer Vision and Pattern Recognition (CVPR)*, pages 2083–2090, June 2013.

[20] T. Judd, K. Ehinger, F. Durand, and A. Torralba. Learning to predict where humans look. In *International Conference on Computer Vision*, 2009.

[21] J. Kim, D. Han, Y.-W. Tai, and J. Kim. Salient region detection via high-dimensional color transform. In *Computer Vision and Pattern Recognition (CVPR)*, pages 883–890, June 2014.

[22] C. Koch and S. Ullman. Shifts in selective visual attention: Towards the underlying neural circuitry. In *Matters of Intelligence*, volume 188, pages 115–141. 1987.

[23] I. Laurent. Automatic foveation for video compression using a neurobiological model of visual attention. *IEEE Transactions on Image Processing*, 13(10):1304–18, 2004.

[24] X. Li, H. Lu, L. Zhang, X. Ruan, and M.-H. Yang. Saliency detection via dense and sparse reconstruction. In *International Conference on Computer Vision (ICCV)*, pages 2976–2983, Dec 2013.

[25] Y. Li, X. Hou, C. Koch, J. M. Rehg, and A. L. Yuille. The secrets of salient object segmentation. In *Computer Vision and Pattern Recognition (CVPR)*, pages 280–287, 2014.

[26] R. Liu, J. Cao, Z. Lin, and S. Shan. Adaptive partial differential equation learning for visual saliency detection. In *Computer Vision and Pattern Recognition (CVPR)*, pages 3866–3873, June 2014.

[27] T. Liu, Z. Yuan, J. Sun, J. Wang, N. Zheng, T. X., and S. H.Y. Learning to detect a salient object. *IEEE Transactions on Pattern Analysis and Machine Intelligence*, 33, 2011.

[28] Y. F. Ma and H. J. Zhang. Contrast-based image attention analysis by using fuzzy growing. In *Eleventh ACM International Conference on Multimedia*, pages 374–381, 2003.

[29] L. Marchesotti, C. Cifarelli, and G. Csurka. A framework for visual saliency detection with applications to image thumbnailing. In *International Conference on Computer Vision (ICCV)*, pages 2232–2239, 2009.

[30] R. Margolin, A. Tal, and L. Zelnik-Manor. What makes a patch distinct? In *Computer Vision and Pattern Recognition (CVPR)*, pages 1139–1146, June 2013.

[31] J. Pan, Z. Su, M. Bian, and R. Liu. Saliency detection based on an edge-preserving filter. In *2013 20th IEEE International Conference on Image Processing (ICIP)*, pages 1757–1761, 2013.

[32] F. Perazzi, P. Krähenbühl, Y. Pritch, and A. Hornung. Saliency filters: Contrast based filtering for salient region detection. In *Computer Vision and Pattern Recognition (CVPR)*, pages 733–740, 2012.

[33] Y. Qin, H. Lu, Y. Xu, and H. Wang. Saliency detection via cellular automata. In *Computer Vision and Pattern Recognition (CVPR)*, pages 110–119, 2015.

[34] C. Rother, V. Kolmogorov, and A. Blake. "GrabCut"– Interactive foreground extraction using iterated graph cuts. *ACM TOG*, 23(3):309–314, 2004.

[35] H. P. S and J. Pujari. Content based image retrieval using color boosted salient points and shape features of an image. *International Journal of Image Processing*, pages 10–17, 2008.

[36] A. Sharon, G. Meirav, B. Achi, and B. Ronen. Image segmentation by probabilistic bottom-up aggregation and cue integration. *IEEE Transactions on Pattern Analysis and Machine Intelligence*, 34(2):1–8, 2007.

[37] X. Shen and Y. Wu. A unified approach to salient object detection via low rank matrix recovery. In *Computer Vision and Pattern Recognition (CVPR)*, pages 853–860, June 2012.

[38] B. W. Tatler. The central fixation bias in scene viewing: selecting an optimal viewing position independently of motor biases and image feature distributions. *Journal of Vision*, 7(14):4.1–17, 2007.

[39] N. Tong, H. Lu, X. Ruan, and M.-H. Yang. Salient object detection via bootstrap learning. In *Computer Vision and Pattern Recognition (CVPR)*, pages 1884–1892, 2015.

[40] J. Van, de Weijer, T. Gevers, and A. D. Bagdanov. Boosting color saliency in image feature detection. *IEEE Transactions on Pattern Analysis and Machine Intelligence*, 28(1):150–156, 2006.

[41] Y. Wei, F. Wen, W. Zhu, and J. Sun. Geodesic saliency using background priors. In *European Conference on Computer Vision (ECCV)*, volume 7574 of *Lecture Notes in Computer Science*, pages 29–42. Springer Berlin Heidelberg, 2012.

[42] Y. Xie and H. Lu. Visual saliency detection based on bayesian model. In *IEEE International Conference on Image Processing (ICIP)*, pages 645–648, Sept 2011.

[43] Y. Xie, H. Lu, and M.-H. Yang. Bayesian saliency via low and mid level cues. *IEEE Transactions on Image Processing*, 22(5):1689–1698, May 2013.

[44] Q. Yan, L. Xu, J. Shi, and J. Jia. Hierarchical saliency detection. In *Computer Vision and Pattern Recognition (CVPR)*, pages 1155–1162, June 2013.

[45] C. Yang, L. Zhang, H. Lu, R. Xiang, and M. H. Yang. Saliency detection via graph-based manifold ranking. In *Computer Vision and Pattern Recognition (CVPR)*, pages 3166–3173, 2013.

[46] L. Zhang, Y. Shen, and H. Li. Vsi: A visual saliency-induced index for perceptual image quality assessment. *IEEE Transactions on Image Processing*, 23(10):4270–4281, Oct 2014.

[47] L. Zhang, M. Tong, T. Marks, H. Shan, and G. Cottrell. SUN: A bayesian framework for saliency using natural statistics. *Journal of Vision*, 8(7):32:1–20, 2008.

[48] W. Zhu, S. Liang, Y. Wei, and J. Sun. Saliency optimization from robust background detection. In *Computer Vision and Pattern Recognition (CVPR)*, pages 2814–2821, June 2014.

Constrained Local Enhancement of Semantic Features by Content-Based Sparsity

Youssef Tamaazousti[1,2] Hervé Le Borgne[1] Adrian Popescu[1]
[1]CEA, LIST, Laboratory of Vision and Content Engineering, F-91191 Gif-sur-Yvette, France
[2]University of Paris-Saclay, MICS, 92295 Châtenay-Malabry, France
{youssef.tamaazousti,herve.le-borgne,adrian.popescu}@cea.fr

ABSTRACT

Semantic features represent images by the outputs of a set of visual concept classifiers and have shown interesting performances in image classification and retrieval. All classifier outputs are usually exploited but it was recently shown that feature sparsification improves both performance and scalability. However, existing approaches consider a fixed sparsity level which disregards the actual content of individual images. In this paper, we propose a method to determine automatically a level of sparsity for the semantic features that is adapted to each image content. This method takes into account the amount of information contained by the image through a modeling of the semantic feature entropy and the confidence of individual dimensions of the feature. We also investigate the use of local regions of the image to further improve the quality of semantic features. Experimental validation is conducted on three benchmarks (Pascal VOC 2007, VOC 2012 and MIT Indoor) for image classification and two of them for image retrieval. Our method obtains competitive results on image classification and achieves state-of-the-art performances on image retrieval.

Keywords

Image-Retrieval, Image-Classification, Semantic-Features, Concept-Sparsification

1. INTRODUCTION

The problem of image recognition and retrieval in image databases is a topic of high interest in the vision community [1, 2, 14, 23, 25]. In parallel to the mainstream "bottom-up" approach based on convolutional neural networks (CNN) [2], several works adopted a "top-down" scheme to design semantically grounded image features, that we name *semantic features* in the following. Given the availability of large-scale image datasets, [14, 25] argued that an image representation based on a bench of object detectors is a promising way to handle natural images. These object detectors are more generally considered as the outputs of base classifiers. Such approaches offer a rich, high level description of images that is close to the human understanding. Moreover, they can easily integrate the advances of the "bottom-up" works that propose better mid-level features in order to improve the base classifiers. Even more importantly, semantic features are scalable in terms of number of classes recognisable in order to cope with a wide variety of content. In image retrieval, they can be represented with inverted index implementation that is particularly efficient for large-scale databases. In classification, the compactness of the features insures computational efficiency, in particular at testing time. The classical formulation of semantic features exploits all classifier outputs [25] but it was recently shown that feature sparsification can be beneficial both in terms of scalability and performance [9].

The contribution of this paper is two-fold. First, we propose a method to determine automatically an appropriate level of semantic feature sparsity that accounts for the amount of information contained by the image that is modelled with the Shannon entropy and the confidence of the individual prediction of semantic feature dimensions. We study the importance of both components for an appropriate modelling of image content. Above the particular method proposed, such an adaptation of the level of sparsity has never been proposed to date in the domain of semantic features.

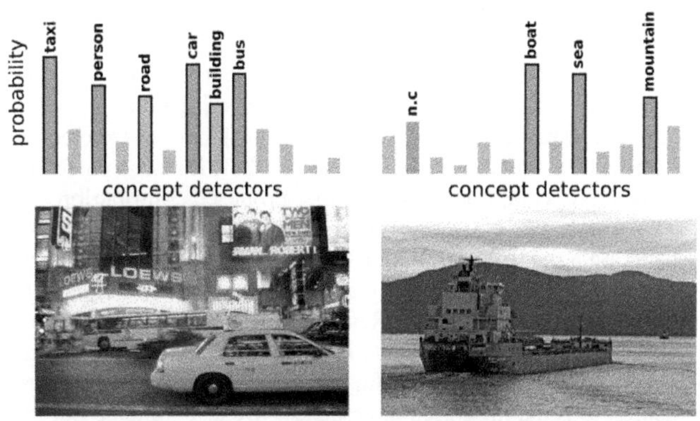

Figure 1: Illustration of the "Content-Based Sparsity" (CBS) method that adapts the sparsification of semantic features to the actual content of the image. Two images with different semantic profiles are presented, i.e. large and low number of detected concepts to the left and right, respectively. A fixed sparsity scheme would select the concepts illustrated in red and it would miss some useful concepts in the left image and would select noisy concepts (n.c.) in the right image. In contrast, CBS adapts the number of selected concepts (surrounded in black) and keeps a larger number in the left image and a lower one in the right image. Best viewed in color.

ICMR'16, June 06-09, 2016, New York, NY, USA
© 2016 ACM. ISBN 978-1-4503-4359-6/16/06...$15.00
DOI: http://dx.doi.org/10.1145/2911996.2912009

Second, inspired by Object Bank scheme [14], we also deal with the problem of the content-locality aspect in images. In Object Bank, the spatial location of the objects is encoded with a three level pyramid computed at multiple scales of the image. However, the final feature in [14] results from the concatenation of the features in all grids. While concatenation is not problematic in Object Bank since it only includes approximately 200 detectors, it has significant negative effect on scalability when exploiting tens of thousand detectors [1, 9]. As an alternative for locality modelling, we apply a pooling of local regions that does not change the total size of the feature and its sparsity level. The amount of useful information varies from one region to another and this variability is accounted through a max-pooling scheme that selects the top score of each individual concept and merges these individual scores into a single vector before sparsification. The proposed locality modelling scheme is named "Constrained Local Enhancement" (CLE) and built on top of the first contribution. The use of max-pooling and spatial pyramid is not novel in itself since it has been used in the domain of bag-features [2] and CNNs [12], but nevertheless its use is novel for semantic features, and we show it makes particular sense when it is combined with the first proposed contribution.

We validate our work on three publicly available benchmarks, focusing on a scene classification task with the MIT Indoor benchmark and on multi-class object classification task with PascalVOC 2007 and Pascal VOC 2012. Result shows that the proposed approach CLE obtains competitive results compared to the best approaches in the literature and achieves state-of-the-art performances compared to semantic-based approaches. We also validate our approach on image retrieval over two datasets, Pascal VOC 2007 and MIT Indoor 67, when CLE achieves state-of-the-art performances.

2. RELATED WORK

The current trend in image classification and retrieval is to exploit mid-level features obtained with deep convolutional neural networks, such as Overfeat [21], Caffe [13] and VGG-Net [24]. Building on such features, we focus on "semantic features" that: (i) include a rich representation of images, (ii) provide a humanly understandable description of content, and (iii) are more flexible since concepts are learned independently from one another. The *semantic feature* approach has been introduced in [14, 25] with a limited number of concepts, with several proposals to determine the level of sparsity for these features. For instance, [14] managed this sparsity aspect at learning time through the regularisation of logistic regression.[25] adopted a more direct scheme by retaining only a portion of the most probable base classifier outputs. In practice they selected $1,500$ non-zero dimensions among $2,659$ possible visual concepts. However, recent works such as [9] exhibits very good performances in image retrieval by retaining a small and fixed number of classifier outputs (*i.e.* less than 100 dimensions) for all images. To the best of our knowledge, our work is the first that proposes to adapt the level of sparsity to the content of each image.

The number of base classifiers used was limited and hand-picked in the first works [14, 25] but [1] learned a larger number of visual concepts to provide better coverage of semantic features. However, their approach is based on 13 different features and then "lifting-up" each one to approximate a non-linear kernel, resulting in a significant computational cost. In order to gain in efficiency, they showed that a binarization of their $15,458$-dimensional vector resulting from a hierarchy of $8,000$ synsets still leads to good results, though inferior to those obtained with the full feature. Recently, [9] exploited $17,000$ concepts from ImageNet or $30,000$ concepts from Flickr Groups and obtained interesting results in image retrieval using simpler linear classifiers learned over mid-level CNN features. Relating to the choice of the visual concepts of reference, we adopted a scheme similar to [9], that has the advantage to be efficient and easy to reproduce.

Regarding semantic feature locality, Object Bank [14] accounts for the spatial location of the objects using a three level pyramid computed at multiple scales of the image to reduce scale variance. As we mentioned, this concatenation based approach scales poorly when using a large number of base classifiers. However, the contribution of our paper does not relate to obtain the exact localisation of an object but to include such a possible locally present object into a global signature. Regarding the modelling of the local information, our contribution is inspired by the spatial pyramid pooling (SPP) [12]. However, in this last paper, SPP is applied at a lower level (that of the mid-level features) and requires a much larger number of regions than in our case. In our case, we show that when it is applied at a higher level (semantic feature) and it is combined with the CBS that adapt the number of active concept to the actual content of each region, SPP makes sense with a small number of regions. This latter is specifically due to the ability of our approach to consider informative regions and neglect confusing ones.

3. IMPROVED SEMANTIC FEATURES

We first present the formalism of existing semantic features [1, 9, 25]. Then, we detail the "Content-Based Sparsity" (CBS) scheme that automatically adapts the level of sparsity to the content of the image. Finally, we introduce "Constrained Local Enhancement" (CLE), the main contribution of this paper which applies CBS to image regions to integrate only informative local regions.

An image I is first described by a global feature $\mathbf{x}$. Then, a *raw* semantic feature is defined as a C-dimensional vector $\zeta^{raw}(\mathbf{x}) = [\phi_1^{raw}(\mathbf{x}), \ldots, \phi_C^{raw}(\mathbf{x})]$ where each dimension $\phi_c(\mathbf{x})$ is the output of a binary classifier evaluated on $\mathbf{x}$, further normalized by a sigmoid function, such that $0 < \phi_c(\mathbf{x}) < 1$. First works in the domain [1, 25] used the LP-β kernel combiner of [8] on 13 features. These approaches had an important computational complexity, but [9] showed that linear classifiers could be used under the constraint of (i) using a significantly larger C (ii) using more powerful mid-level features $\mathbf{x}$. Following [9], the semantic feature is learned on top of ImageNet [3] concepts that have at least 100 associated images, results in $17,462$ dimensions. To study its robustness for different mid-level features that are used to learn object classifiers, it is implemented on top of Overfeat, Caffe and VGG-Net architectures and results are discussed in Section 4.4. A diversified negative class is used when learning classifiers. This class is composed of images that are pooled from ImageNet concepts that are not included in the semantic feature. Its content is sorted in such a way a maximum of concepts are used when learning base classifiers. We empirically determined that best results are obtained for a ratio of $1/100$ between positive and negative samples and this ratio is used in experiments. Finally, we chose to learn each classification model $\phi_c(.)$ with L_2-regularized linear SVM.

Given a *raw* semantic feature, it has been shown that the performances in retrieval and classification could be almost the same when the descriptor is quantized on a limited number of bits [25, 1], or even improved when one sparsifies the feature by retaining only the d largest values and set the other to zero [9]. Formally, the signature with a "fixed" level d of sparsification is expressed as:

$$\phi_c^d(\mathbf{x}) = \begin{cases} \phi_c^{raw}(\mathbf{x}) & \text{if } \phi_c^{raw}(\mathbf{x}) \in \mathcal{H}_d(\zeta^{raw}(\mathbf{x})) \\ 0 & \text{otherwise,} \end{cases} \quad (1)$$

where $\mathcal{H}_d(A)$ is the subset of the d largest values of the set $A \subset \mathbb{R}$. The semantic feature with a fixed level of sparsification d is then

$\zeta^d(\mathbf{x}) = [\phi_1^d(\mathbf{x}), \ldots, \phi_C^d(\mathbf{x})]$. Equation (1) correspond to the "fast encoding" of locality-constrained coding [26], an efficient method of sparse coding used in the bag-of-visual-word framework. It introduces a locality constraint to the feature representation that leverages the manifold geometry induced by the set of visual concepts, locally homeomorphic to an Euclidean space [26], and improves the recognition performances in practice [9]. In addition, such a sparsification leads to a much smaller memory footprint since, if a float and an index are both coded on 4 bytes, then ϕ_c^{raw} occupies $4 \times C$ bytes while ϕ_c^d only $8 \times d$ bytes (with $d \ll C$).

3.1 Content-based Sparsity for Semantic Features

We make two hypotheses that motivates our proposal.First, the level of sparsity of a semantic feature should be adapted to the number of objects/concepts contained in the image. As illustrated in Figure 1, it seems desirable that an image containing lots of object (Fig. 1, left image) has a semantic feature with more non-zero dimensions than that of an image with few objects (Fig. 1, right image). Retaining a fixed number of concepts as it has been proposed to date leads to an incomplete description for the first image and to an over-complete one for the second one.

Second, it is equally important that the number of non-zero dimensions to retain also depends on the confidence that can be placed into the quality of visual concept detections. For instance, if the confidence of concept detections is low (bottom of Figure 2), only a small number of concepts should be retained. On the contrary, if confidence is high (top-right of Figure 2), a larger number of concepts would probably be useful in the image representation. In [25] such a selection is proposed but is based on a cross-validation error of the ϕ_c and is thus the same of all images. As well, [1] proposed a simple thresholding on the values of $\phi_c(\mathbf{x})$ that is not adapted to each image. To our kowledge, our proposal is the first to propose an adaptation to *each* image.

The combination of the two hypotheses leads to four prototypical semantic feature profiles that are depicted in Figure 2. When few visual concepts are present in the image (see left of Figure 2), the profiles include a small number of dominating values (values with high confidence) and profiles are naturally sparse. On the contrary, the presence of a large number of visual concepts (see Figure 2, right schemes) leads to a flatter profile, typical of a distributed activity. In addition, the value of the largest concept (thus on the left of the profiles in Figure 2) indicates the confidence one can place into the quality of the visual concepts detected. If the two hypotheses above are combined, we should retain a large number of concepts when the profile indicates both a confident detection and many dominant concepts (top-right of Figure 2), while we should keep few concepts for the other three cases.

Let $\zeta^{raw}(\mathbf{x}) = [\phi_1^{raw}(\mathbf{x}), \ldots, \phi_C^{raw}(\mathbf{x})]$ be the raw semantic feature. Equation (1) proposes a fixed sparsity level that does account for the two hypotheses that support an appropriate modeling of individual images. We propose to incorporate these hypotheses and thus adapt sparsity to image content using:

$$\phi_c^{CBS}(\mathbf{x}) = \begin{cases} \phi_c^{raw}(\mathbf{x}) & \text{if } \phi_c^{raw}(\mathbf{x}) \geq \Gamma(I) \\ 0 & \text{otherwise,} \end{cases} \quad (2)$$

where $\Gamma(.)$ is a threshold that reflects "semantic feature profile" of each image, that is to say, the way its values decrease, when they are sorted in decreasing order.

Each dimension of the raw semantic signature $\phi_i^{raw}(\mathbf{x})$ can be seen as a piece of information related to the content of the image. We propose to consider the raw semantic signature of an image as a source of information on its semantic content and to model the

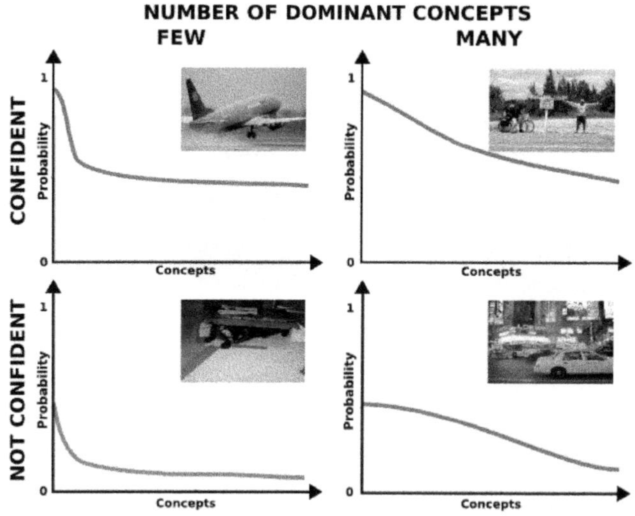

Figure 2: Four configurations of semantic feature profiles. Each configuration illustrates the raw semantic signature with $\phi_i^{raw}(\mathbf{x})$ sorted by decreasing values. The top graphics illustrate high confidence detections (well recognizable objects in the images) and the bottom ones low confidence detections (incomplete objects in the image). The left graphics correspond to the schemes containing few dominant visual concepts (few object in the image), while the right ones, depict schemes with a lot of dominant visual concepts (several objects in the image).

quantity of information it conveys using the Shannon entropy. This choice is formally supported by the fact that the entropy is defined as the average amount of information generated by a source. If appropriately normalised to be considered a random variable, ζ^{raw} can be considered as such a source of information. Formally, for an image I from which a mid-level feature $\mathbf{x}$ was extracted:

$$H(I, \mathbf{x}) = \sum_{i=1}^{C} \frac{\phi_i^{raw}(\mathbf{x})}{\sum_{j=1}^{C} \phi_j^{raw}(\mathbf{x})} \log_2 \left(\frac{\sum_{j=1}^{C} \phi_j^{raw}(\mathbf{x})}{\phi_i^{raw}(\mathbf{x})} \right) \quad (3)$$

The value $\frac{\phi_i^{raw}(\mathbf{x})}{\sum_{j=1}^{C} \phi_j^{raw}(\mathbf{x})}$ is the probability to get concept i into the image. With such a normalization, the semantic feature is the probability mass function of a discrete random variable whose value is subject to variations due to the presence of object/concepts into the image. Hence, equation 3 computes Shannon entropy of this source of information. It results into a lower entropy when profiles are distributed and higher for the profiles having a small number of dominant concepts. The threshold $\Gamma(.)$ should therefore be a decreasing function with respect to $H(I, \mathbf{x})$.

Equation 3 reflects the number of dominant concepts but does not take into account the absolute confidence of their detection. For this, we propose to consider the value of the largest semantic dimension of the profile, noted $\phi_{max}(\mathbf{x})$ that is normalized in $[0, 1]$, as the proportion of concepts to retain among the C available. For instance, for an almost flat profile, our proposal means that if the output classifiers have a confidence around 0.5 we decide to retain half of them, while for a confidence around 0.75 we retain the three quarters of them. In accordance to our hypothesis, the more confident detections are, the more dimensions will be retained. Hence, the threshold $\Gamma(.)$ should therefore be an increasing function with respect to $\phi_{max}(\mathbf{x}) \times C$.

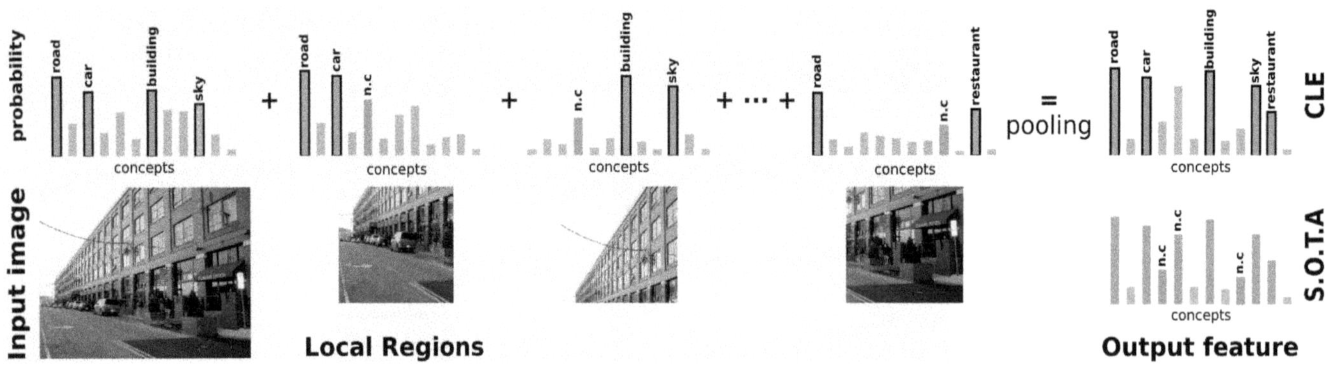

Figure 3: Illustration of our "Constrained Local Enhancement" (CLE) method over semantic features. Concepts illustrated in red are selected by the fixed sparsity, while concepts surrounded in black are selected by our "Content-Based Sparsity" (CBS). The use of fixed sparsity on local regions results in a final representation (bottom) that contains a lot of noisy concepts (n.c.). On the contrary, CBS selects only relevant concepts per region and results in a relevant output feature (top). Using max-pooling, selected concepts from the global image representation are updated with higher scores from image regions. Equally important, new relevant concepts with strong activations in image regions appear in the final representation. Best view in color.

Combining the two modeling of our hypotheses, we finally propose to estimate the threshold as:

$$\Gamma(I) = \alpha \times \frac{\phi_{max}(\mathbf{x}) \times C}{H(I, \mathbf{x})} \quad (4)$$

where the denominator $H(I, \mathbf{x})$ is the entropy computed according to equation (3), $\alpha \in [0, 1]$ is a normalizing parameter that can be set by cross-validation, C is the total number of visual concepts that are considered in the semantic signature and $\phi_{max}(\mathbf{x})$ the largest value of the semantic feature, named "confidence parameter".

3.2 Constrained Local Enhancement

The mid-level CNN features used to produce the semantic features are not scale-independent [19] and small objects have smaller detection scores if only the full image is exploited. In Figure 3, we illustrate the importance of using local regions with the examples of *car*, whose score is taken from a local region and *restaurant*, which does not appear at all in the representation of the full image. We enhance image semantic features by adding local image information. Let's consider an image I from which we identify a set of regions $\{\mathcal{R}_i, i \in [1, N]\}$. A mid-level feature $\mathbf{x}_i$ is extracted from each region and the corresponding semantic feature $\zeta_i^{d_i}(\mathbf{x}_i)$ is computed with a level of sparsity d_i. Then, the final feature of the image results from the pooling of all these local semantic features:

$$\zeta_{loc}(I) = \underset{i=1...N}{\mathcal{P}}(\zeta_i^{d_i}(\mathbf{x}_i)), \quad (5)$$

where $\mathcal{P}$ is a pooling operator such as sum, $average$ or max that operates on individual components of semantic features of image regions. The pooling procedure is well established by biophysical evidence in visual cortex [22] and is empirically justified by many algorithms applied to image categorisation.

One advantage of the method is that, unlike concatenation-based region modeling schemes such as spatial pyramid matching (SPM) [10, 16], the resulting feature has the same size as the original semantic feature computed on the full image. Moreover, it contains information extracted at a local level that represents more faithfully the content of the image.

Naturally, the performance of the local enhancement of the feature depends on the choice of initial regions $\mathcal{R}_i$. Here we propose a simple strategy in order to demonstrate the efficiency of the principle and adopt a scheme inspired by SPP [12]. The region $\mathcal{R}_0$ is the full image and the following $\mathcal{R}_{i>0}$ are extracted according to regular grid at smaller scale. Unlike SPM, we use overlapping rectangular regions to reduce the risk of cutting the objects represented in the image.

A semantic feature can be enhanced locally with a fixed-sized sparsity (d_i fixed $\forall i \in [1, N]$), but it results into the assignment of the same number of visual concepts to all local regions. Such an approach is suboptimal since some regions could contain a lot of information while others may contain much less. Hence, we hypothesize that we should assign automatically a weight to each region, in order to determine which ones should be most considered. As illustrated in Figure 3, our first contribution, "Content-Based Sparsity" (CBS) method, has the ability to assign a sparsity level to regions based on their amount of information. Finally, when the level of sparsity d_i used in equation 5 is determined by the CBS method (equation 4) on all regions before the pooling, we obtain our main contribution, namely "Constrained Local Enhancement" (CLE). Formally, the final feature is computed through

$$\zeta_{loc}(I) = \underset{i=1...N}{\mathcal{P}}(\zeta_i^{CBS}(\mathbf{x}_i)), \quad (6)$$

where $\mathcal{P}$ is a pooling operator such as sum, $average$ or max that operates on individual components of semantic features of image regions. The sparsification of each region is computed by our "Content-Based Sparsity" (CBS) defined by Eq. (2) and (4).

4. EXPERIMENTS

The effectiveness of our approach is tested in image classification (Section 4.2) and image retrieval (Section 4.3) tasks. To facilitate reproducibility and comparability, evaluation is done with publicly available datasets and using standard experimental protocols. Image classification evaluation is conducted on Pascal VOC 2007 [7], Pascal VOC 2012 [6] (object recognition) and MIT Indoor 67 [18] (scene recognition). For image retrieval, we evaluate our approach on Pascal VOC 2007 and MIT Indoor 67. [1]

The proposed "Constrained Local Enhancement" method can be applied to a semantic feature built on top of any mid-level feature.

[1]Pascal VOC 2012 is excluded due to the unavailability of an evaluation protocol and ground truth for image retrieval.

However, based on the experiments reported in Section 4.4, the quality of the semantic feature will directly depend on that of the mid-level feature used. We thus created semantic features on top of a competitive mid-level CNN feature released in the literature, namely VGG-Net [24]. For our study, fine tuning of the CNN may result into an improvement of the results at the cost of significant computational cost and the possible use of additive data. Such a specific optimization of the CNN has not been considered in our experiment, to insure their reproducibility with original and available CNN models.

4.1 Baseline Methods

Our work is focused on semantic features and it is important to compare the performance of the proposed CLE method to several state-of-the-art semantic-based approaches. We also compare it to a very competitive CNN feature.

- **VGG-Net** [24], is extracted from a fully-connected layer (fc7, 16th layer) of a CNN architecture (D) learned on ILSVRC 2012 dataset [20] that contains 1.2 million images of 1,000 classes. The resulting vector has $4,096$ dimensions. The 18th and last layer (fc8), of size $1,000$, can be seen as a semantic feature build on top of the fc7, which the base classifiers are the final outputs of the CNN.

- **Semfeat** [9] is built on top of a mid-level CNN feature using the Caffe reference model [13]. To ensure a fair comparison with our method, we rebuild Semfeat using VGG-Net as basic feature. The same 17,462 ImageNet concepts from [9], represented by at least 100 images, are modeled here. A fixed sparsification is used to replicate their methodology.

- **Classemes+**, is our own implementation of **Classemes** [25]. Again, for a fair comparison with other methods, it is built on top of a VGG-Net feature with exactly the same concepts as Semfeat. Following [25], no sparsification is considered and **Classemes+** thus corresponds to ζ^{raw}.

- **Meta-Class** [1] is the output of 15,232 classifiers. It is based on a concatenation of five low-level features combined with a spatial pyramid histogram with 13 pyramid levels. Since the number of concepts is rather similar to other methods and the code is available, we use it as it is released. [2]

4.2 Image Classification Experiments

We report and analyse the experimental results on image classification task using the Pascal VOC 2007, Pascal VOC 2012 and MIT Indoor 67 datasets.

4.2.1 Object Classification

The Pascal VOC 2007 object classification task [7] is run on a dataset that contains $9,963$ images. Each image is labelled with one or more categories from a total of 20. We used the pre-defined split of $5,011$ images for training and $4,952$ for testing, with the publicly available evaluation tools and ground truth. The Pascal VOC 2012 benchmark [6] is similar to VOC 2007 but its number of images is larger: $22,531$ images are split into training ($5,717$ images), validation ($5,823$ images) and test data ($10,991$ images). A server is available to estimate the performances of an algorithm on the test dataset, with a limited number of submission allowed. Hence, we measured the performance on the official testing dataset.

[2]http://vlg.cs.dartmouth.edu/projects/metaclass/metaclass/Home.html

For both datasets, we learn each class by a one-vs-all SVM classifier and we use mean Average Precision (mAP) to evaluate performance. The cost parameter of the SVM classifier and the α parameter from equation (4) are optimised through cross-validation on the training dataset, using the usual train/val split. In addition to the baselines presented in Subsection 4.1, we also report the best existing state-of-the-art results in the literature.

Classification results for Pascal VOC 2007 and 2012 are presented in Table 1. Our method leads to significant better results than previous approaches based on semantic features [25, 1, 9], as well as those obtained from the mid-level feature it is based on (VGG-Net [24]). Note that we get better results than VGG-16 (our method is built on top of this mid-level features) but [24] report results above ours with VGG-19, a multi-scale VGG-Net feature of 19 layers. However, this is obtained when descriptors are aggregated over five scales and they note that their performances is much below when only three scales are used (although they do not give the corresponding score). On our side, we obtain 88.2 with only two scales and a VGG-Net features of 16 layers only. The improvement due to our method with regards to the mid-level feature used is discussed in Section 4.4. In the same vein, Wei *et al.* [27] achieves 2% better mAP on VOC12 when their method is trained on an extended 2000-classes ILSVRC dataset but is 5% of mAP below our method when they use a comparable dataset as ours to train their CNN. Note that our proposal is always better on VOC07 (from 3% to 7% mAP), even in comparison to the method trained with the extended dataset.

Method		**VOC 2007** mAP (in%)	**VOC 2012** mAP (in%)
CNN	Oquab *et al.* [19]	77.7	n.a.
	Chatfield *et al.* [2]	82.42	83.2
	Wei *et al.* [27]	81.5(85.2**)	81.7(**90.3****)
	VGG-Net (fc7) [24]	86.1(**89.7***)	84.5 (89.3*)
Semantic	VGG-Net (fc8) [24]	77.4	77.2
	Meta-Class [1]	48.4 (53.2†)	49.3
	Classemes+ [25]	82.4	81.7
	Semfeat [9]	82.8	81.7
	CLE (ours)	**88.2**	**86.6**

Table 1: Comparison with the state of the art on Pascal VOC 2007, Pascal VOC 2012. Our model is denoted as "CLE". Results marked with * where achieved using multi-scale scheme with a CNN architecture (E) of 19 layers. Results marked with ** were achieved using a CNN pre-trained on the extended ILSVRC dataset (2000 classes). Results marked with † are reported scores in the original paper.

4.2.2 Scene Classification

The MIT Indoor database [18] is a scene recognition benchmark that consists of 67 categories of indoor places. All experiments in this database where performed using the usual training-test split, taking 80 images per class for training and 20 for testing. It results in $5,360$ images in training and $1,360$ in testing.

We learn a SVM classifier on each class (one-versus-all strategy) and cross-validate the cost parameter and the α parameter of the equation (4) by splitting the training dataset into 60 images per class for training and 20 images per class for validation. Similar to Pascal VOC experiments, the proposed CLE method is compared to related baselines but also with other state-of-the-art approaches that were evaluated MIT Indoor 67. All results are reported in the

Table 2. We report classification accuracy to evaluate the performances. Zhou *et al.* [30] report an accuracy of 56.79 on MIT Indoor 67, using a generic CNN architecture similar to Caffe. With this mid-level feature, our method gets 57.3. They also report a score of 68.24 when they fine-tune the network with 2.5 million additional images representing places. When they combine with the original ImageNet images and remove the overlapping scene categories, they obtain an Hybrid-CNN trained on 3.5 million images from 1,183 categories that report 70.8 classification accuracy. Our CLE method based on VGG-Net obtain better results (71.6) while we use a CNN pre-trained on object images only while their deep network is adapted to recognize places. Our proposed approach also outperforms over all semantic-based approaches and even other state-of-the-arts works such as ONE+SVM [28].

	Method	MIT Indoor 67 Classification Accuracy (in%)
	Doersch *et al.* [4]	66.9
	Oquab *et al.* [19]	69.0
	VGG-Net (fc7) [24]	65.8
	Zhou *et al.* [30]	68.2* (70.8**)
	ONE+SVM [28]	70.1
Semantic	VGG-Net (fc8) [24]	48.7
Semantic	Meta-Class [1]	35.7 (44.6†)
Semantic	Classemes+ [25]	58.9
Semantic	Semfeat [9]	61.5
Semantic	CLE (ours)	**71.6**

Table 2: Comparison with the state of the art on MIT Indoor 67. Our model is denoted as "CLE". Results marked with * where achieved using a CNN pre-trained on 2.5 million scene images. Results marked with ** where achieved using the previous pre-trained CNN with fine-tuning. Results marked with † are reported scores in the original paper.

4.3 Image Retrieval Experiments

We report and analyse the experimental results on visual retrieval over Pascal VOC 2007 and MIT Indoor 67 datasets. Pascal VOC 2012 has not been evaluated because of the absence of ground-truth on test images. For both evaluated datasets, we adopt Average Precision at top K retrieved results (AP@K) defined as in [29]:

$$AP@K = \frac{1}{min(R,K)} \sum_{j=1}^{K} \frac{R_j}{j} \times I_j, \qquad (7)$$

where R is the number of relevant images within the collection and R_j is the number of relevant images among top j search results. I_j is set to 1 if the j-th image is relevant, and 0 otherwise. We averaged AP@K over all queries to obtain mAP@K as overall evaluation metric. $K \in \{1, 2, \cdots, 100\}$ for Pascal VOC 2007 and $K \in \{1, 2, \cdots, 80\}$ for MIT Indoor 67, because the number of relevant images within the dataset is set to 80 per query. Similarity between images are computed using cosine measure.

Object retrieval evaluation is run with the Pascal VOC 2007 dataset, using the train images as collection and the test images as queries. In Figure 4, we present mAP@100 curves for CLE, Classemes+ and Semfeat, the best semantic feature baselines, and also for VGG-Net. Figure 5 reports detailed performance (AP) of individual concepts for the CLE, Semfeat VGG-Net.

Scene retrieval is evaluated with the MIT Indoor 67 dataset, using the same split as for classification, with training images considered

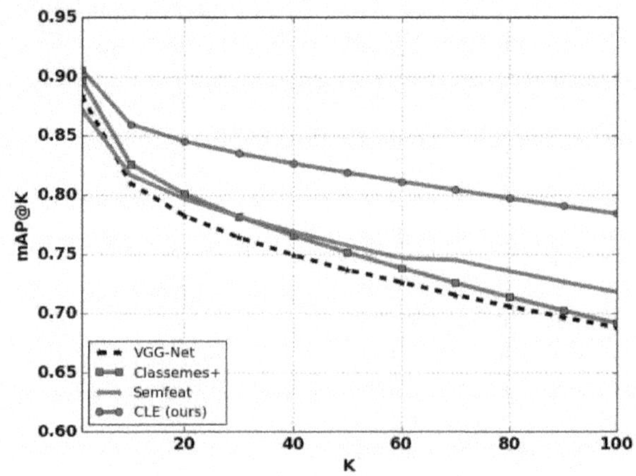

Figure 4: Overall performance (mAP@K) of visual retrieval using all images of the released test split as queries on Pascal VOC 07. We compare our CLE method, with the best semantic-based state-of-the-art approaches (Classemes+ [25] and Semfeat [9]) and the best CNN-based method (VGG-Net [24]) represented in dashed line.

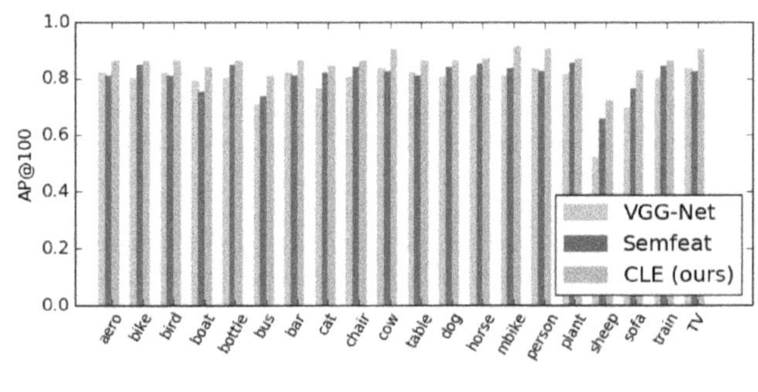

Figure 5: Detailed performance (AP@100) of individual categories for the best semantic-based (Semfeat [9]) and CNN-based (VGG-Net [24]) approaches reported in the Figure 4 for image retrieval on Pascal VOC 2007 dataset.

to be the collection and test images considered as queries. Figure 6 gives mAP@K curves for CLE, Classemes+, Semfeat and VGG-Net. For each query, there are at most 80 true positives in the ground-truth and we set K=80. Figure 7 reports detailed performance (AP) of individual concepts for the best semantic-based (Semfeat) and CNN-based (VGG-Net) approaches.

The obtained results show that the proposed CLE method outperforms all other tested methods on both of the evaluated datasets. For instance, on Pascal VOC 07, CLE improves the performance of VGG-Net, Classemes+ and Semfeat by around 10%, 8% and 7% in terms of mAP@100, respectively. CLE achieves best results over all methods (CNN and semantic-based) on all categories. On MIT Indoor 67, CLE improves the performances of VGG-Net, Classemes+ and Semfeat by around 6%, 7% and 5% in terms of mAP@20, respectively. Nevertheless, we observe on the detailed performances (AP@20) of individual categories that, for a few categories, VGG-Net performs better, this can be due to the fact that some scene categories like *pool inside*, do not contain any object but only basic shapes, while CLE has the ability to recognize ob-

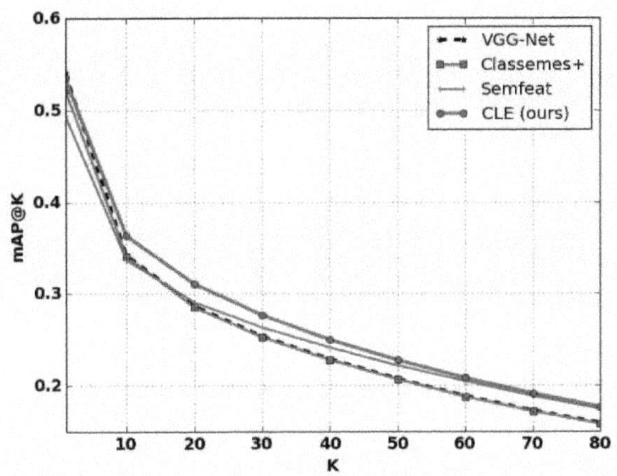

Figure 6: Overall performance (mAP@K) of visual retrieval using all images of the released test split as queries on MIT Indoor 67. We compare our CLE method, with the best semantic-based state-of-the-arts approaches (Classemes+ [25] and Semfeat [9]) and the best CNN-based method (VGG-Net [24]) represented in dashed line.

jects only. Based on that, our proposed CLE outperforms all the methods when scene categories contain objects. The above phenomenons of performance comes from an effective cooperation of local representations and a Content-Based Sparsity that keeps in the final representation only relevant concepts. On the contrary, Semfeat forces a level of sparsification and Classemes+ keeps all the concepts in the final representation, yielding in a consideration noisy concepts in the final feature.

4.4 Mid-level Feature Sensitivity

The low-level or mid-level features used to build concept detectors are a core component of semantic features. We evaluate their influence on performance by using three publicly available CNN models using the Pascal VOC 2007 dataset. Overfeat [21], Caffe [13] and VGG-Net [24] are used as basic features. Overfeat and Caffe architectures are similar since both of them are based on the original AlexNet model [15]. VGG-Net [24] uses a deeper CNN architecture, with smaller kernels and exhibits significantly better results than Overfeat and Caffe on the ImageNet challenge. In all cases, we extracted features from the last fully-connected layer, resulting in $4,096$ dimensional vectors. Regarding the resulting semantic features, note that, Classemes was initially designed with low-level features only, as well as Semfeat, was initially designed with Overfeat features only. Thus, we implemented Classemes [25], Semfeat [9] and our CLE method on top of the three mid-level features (Overfeat, Caffe and VGG-Net). For Semfeat, the sparsity parameter is fixed as formalised by equation (1). It has been cross-validated on several levels of sparsity, and we report the best results, corrseponding to $d = 50$. For our "Constrained Local Enhancement" (CLE), the parameter α of equation 4 has been cross validated on the validation data and we report the best results, corresponding to $\alpha = 0.1$.

Results are reported in Table 3 and, as expected, they are correlated to the quality of the mid-level feature used. For all the semantic methods, best performance is obtained with VGG-Net followed by Caffe and Overfeat. This suggests that, the more the mid-level features are deeper, the more the obtained results by semantic features will be better. Equally important, regardless the mid-level feature used, our CLE approach is better than other semantic-based ones. This validates the robustness of our approach and, since other mid-level features are easy to plug into the CLE pipeline, it will be easy to make it evolve in order to take advantage of progress in deep learning architecture design.

Method	Pascal VOC 2007 mAP (in %)		
	Overfeat [21]	Caffe [13]	VGG-Net [24]
CNN only	72.0	76.3	86.1
Classemes+ [25]	72.2	72.4	82.4
Semfeat [9]	73.6	76.0	82.8
CLE (ours)	78.4	80.5	88.2

Table 3: Evaluation of effects of CNN architecture (Overfeat, Caffe and VGG-Net) used to compute semantic features (Classemes, Semfeat and Ours) on object classification over Pascal VOC 2007 dataset.

5. CONCLUSIONS

We introduce a novel method to design semantic features that integrates adaptive sparsification and information from informative local regions only. In contrast to existing works, which perform sparsification regardless of image content, we propose a scheme that considers individual image profile to do so. The informational content of images is modelled using the Shannon entropy, a theoretically grounded method, and also accounts for the confidence that can be placed in visual concept detections. Finally, modelling local regions of the image further improves the semantic features through an improved integration of localized objects.

Evaluation is carried out for classification and retrieval tasks and results show that the proposed method outperforms existing semantic features and also the mid-level CNN feature it is based upon. Interestingly, our CLE scheme is the only semantic feature whose classification performance is above that of the mid-level features, with existing semantic features all having lower performance. Equally important, the proposed approach is also competitive with optimizations of CNN features reported in the literature and even state-of-the-art on the MIT Indoor 67 benchmark. Content-based image retrieval results place CLE favourably when compared to all other tested approaches. In addition to performance, it is also important to note that CLE representations are sparse and thus more scalable than CNN features. Sparsity is particularly important for retrieval since images can be efficiently represented using inverted index structures which accelerate the search process.

The results obtained for still images are very encouraging and we will pursue the work reported here. We will investigate finer ways to model local information. In particular, interesting region detection [5] will replace the fixed regions that are currently used. A second work direction concerns video classification and retrieval that can be dealt with the CLE pipeline. Replacing local regions by frames in CLE, will bring to our proposed approach, the ability to assess the amount of information of each frame. This information can be used in future work to stop-frame removal [11] (removing less informative frames) or even concept-prototyping [17] (selecting a set of relevant frames) for web-videos.

Acknowledgments
This work is supported by the USEMP FP7 project, partially funded by the European Commission under contract number 611596.

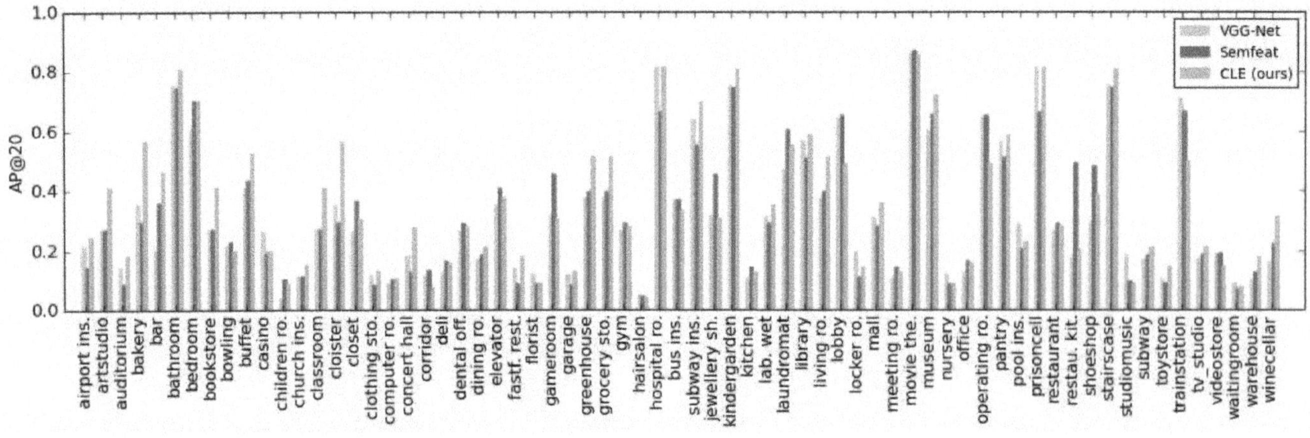

Figure 7: Detailed performance (AP@20) of individual categories for the best semantic-based (Semfeat [9]) and CNN-based (VGG-Net [24]) approaches reported in the Figure 6 for image retrieval on MIT Indoor 67 dataset. Our model is denoted as CLE.

6. REFERENCES

[1] A. Bergamo and L. Torresani. Meta-class features for large-scale object categorization on a budget. In *CVPR*, 2012.

[2] K. Chatfield, K. Simonyan, A. Vedaldi, and A. Zisserman. Return of the devil in the details: Delving deep into convolutional nets. *arXiv:1405.3531*, 2014.

[3] J. Deng, W. Dong, R. Socher, L.-J. Li, K. Li, and L. Fei-Fei. ImageNet: A Large-Scale Hierarchical Image Database. In *Computer Vision and Pattern Recognition*, CVPR, 2009.

[4] C. Doersch, A. Gupta, and A. A. Efros. Mid-level visual element discovery as discriminative mode seeking. In *Advances in Neural Information Processing Systems*, NIPS. 2013.

[5] P. Dollár and C. L. Zitnick. Fast edge detection using structured forests. *PAMI*, 2015.

[6] M. Everingham, L. Van Gool, C. K. Williams, J. Winn, and A. Zisserman. The pascal visual object classes challenge 2012.

[7] M. Everingham, L. Van Gool, C. K. Williams, J. Winn, and A. Zisserman. The pascal visual object classes challenge. *International journal of computer vision*, 88(2):303–338, 2010.

[8] P. Gehler and S. Nowozin. On feature combination for multiclass object classification. In *Computer Vision, 2009 IEEE 12th International Conference on*, pages 221–228, Sept 2009.

[9] A. L. Ginsca, A. Popescu, H. Le Borgne, N. Ballas, P. Vo, and I. Kanellos. Large-scale image mining with flickr groups. In *Multimedia Modelling*, MM, 2015.

[10] K. Grauman and T. Darrell. The pyramid match kernel: Discriminative classification with sets of image features. In *International Conference on Computer Vision*, ICCV, 2005.

[11] A. Habibian and C. G. Snoek. Stop-frame removal improves web video classification. In *Proceedings of International Conference on Multimedia Retrieval*, ICMR, 2014.

[12] K. He, X. Zhang, S. Ren, and J. Sun. Spatial Pyramid Pooling in Deep Convolutional Networks for Visual Recognition. *arXiv 1406.4729*, 2014.

[13] Y. Jia, E. Shelhamer, J. Donahue, S. Karayev, J. Long, R. Girshick, S. Guadarrama, and T. Darrell. Caffe: Convolutional architecture for fast feature embedding. In *International Conference on Multimedia*. ACM, 2014.

[14] L. jia Li, H. Su, L. Fei-fei, and E. P. Xing. Object bank: A high-level image representation for scene classification & semantic feature sparsification. In *NIPS*. 2010.

[15] A. Krizhevsky, I. Sutskever, and G. E. Hinton. Imagenet classification with deep convolutional neural networks. In *Advances in Neural Information Processing Systems*, NIPS, pages 1097–1105. 2012.

[16] S. Lazebnik, C. Schmid, and J. Ponce. Beyond bags of features: Spatial pyramid matching for recognizing natural scene categories. In *Computer Vision and Pattern Recognition*, CVPR, 2006.

[17] M. Mazloom, A. Habibian, D. Liu, C. G. Snoek, and S.-F. Chang. Encoding concept prototypes for video event detection and summarization. In *International Conference on Multimedia Retrieval*, ICMR, 2015.

[18] A. Quattoni and A. Torralba. Recognizing indoor scenes. In *Computer Vision and Pattern Recognition*, CVPR, 2009.

[19] A. S. Razavian, H. Azizpour, J. Sullivan, and S. Carlsson. Cnn features off-the-shelf: an astounding baseline for recognition. *CoRR*, abs/1403.6382, 2014.

[20] O. Russakovsky, J. Deng, H. Su, J. Krause, S. Satheesh, S. Ma, Z. Huang, A. Karpathy, A. Khosla, M. Bernstein, A. C. Berg, and L. Fei-Fei. Imagenet large scale visual recognition challenge. *International Journal of Computer Vision*, 2015.

[21] P. Sermanet, D. Eigen, X. Zhang, M. Mathieu, R. Fergus, and Y. LeCun. Overfeat: Integrated recognition, localization and detection using convolutional networks. *arXiv:1312.6229*, 2013.

[22] T. Serre, L. Wolf, and T. Poggio. Object recognition with features inspired by visual cortex. In *Computer Vision and Pattern Recognition*, CVPR, 2005.

[23] M. Shi, Y. Avrithis, and H. Jégou. Early burst detection for memory-efficient image retrieval. In *Computer Vision and Pattern Recognition*, CVPR, 2015.

[24] K. Simonyan and A. Zisserman. Very deep convolutional networks for large-scale image recognition. *arXiv:1409.1556*, 2014.

[25] L. Torresani, M. Szummer, and A. Fitzgibbon. Efficient object category recognition using classemes. In *European Conference on Computer Vision*, ECCV, 2010.

[26] J. Wang, J. Yang, K. Yu, F. Lv, T. Huang, and Y. Gong. Locality-constrained linear coding for image classification. In *Conference on Computer Vision and Pattern Recognition*, 2010.

[27] Y. Wei, W. Xia, J. Huang, B. Ni, J. Dong, Y. Zhao, and S. Yan. Cnn: Single-label to multi-label. *arXiv:1406.5726*, 2014.

[28] L. Xie, Q. Tian, R. Hong, and B. Zhang. Image classification and retrieval are one. In *International Conference on Multimedia Retrieval*, ICMR, 2015.

[29] Y. Yang, H. Zhang, M. Zhang, F. Shen, and X. Li. Visual coding in a semantic hierarchy. In *Proceedings of the 23rd Annual ACM Conference on Multimedia Conference*, pages 59–68. ACM, 2015.

[30] B. Zhou, A. Lapedriza, J. Xiao, A. Torralba, and A. Oliva. Learning deep features for scene recognition using places database. In *Advances in Neural Information Processing Systems*, NIPS, 2014.

Event Detection with Zero Example: Select the Right and Suppress the Wrong Concepts

Yi-Jie Lu†, Hao Zhang†, Maaike de Boer*‡, Chong-Wah Ngo†
†City University of Hong Kong, ‡Radboud University
*Netherlands Organization for Applied Scientific Research (TNO)
{yijie.lu, hzhang57-c}@my.cityu.edu.hk, maaike.deboer@tno.nl, cscwngo@cityu.edu.hk

ABSTRACT

Complex video event detection without visual examples is a very challenging issue in multimedia retrieval. We present a state-of-the-art framework for event search without any need of exemplar videos and textual metadata in search corpus. To perform event search given only query words, the core of our framework is a large, pre-built bank of concept detectors which can understand the content of a video in the perspective of object, scene, action and activity concepts. Leveraging such knowledge can effectively narrow the semantic gap between textual query and the visual content of videos. Besides the large concept bank, this paper focuses on two challenges that largely affect the retrieval performance when the size of the concept bank increases: (1) How to choose the right concepts in the concept bank to accurately represent the query; (2) if noisy concepts are inevitably chosen, how to minimize their influence. We share our novel insights on these particular problems, which paves the way for a practical system that achieves the best performance in NIST TRECVID 2015.

General Terms

Algorithms, Experimentation, Performance

Keywords

Multimedia Event Detection; Video Search; 0Ex; Concept Selection; Semantic Pooling; Concept Bank

1. INTRODUCTION

Today, almost all real-world solutions of video retrieval, such as YouTube, are mainly based on text matching. This matching requires the availability of textual metadata such as titles and tags provided by video uploader [6]. In contrast to text matching, multimedia research communities have kept promoting video content understanding for years, expecting that machines can search by visual cues as well as high-level semantics, rather than requiring humans to annotate the videos beforehand [31]. Among those practices,

ICMR'16 June 6–9, 2016, New York, NY, USA
© 2016 ACM ISBN 978-1-4503-4359-6/16/06 ...$15.00
DOI: http://dx.doi.org/10.1145/2911996.2912015

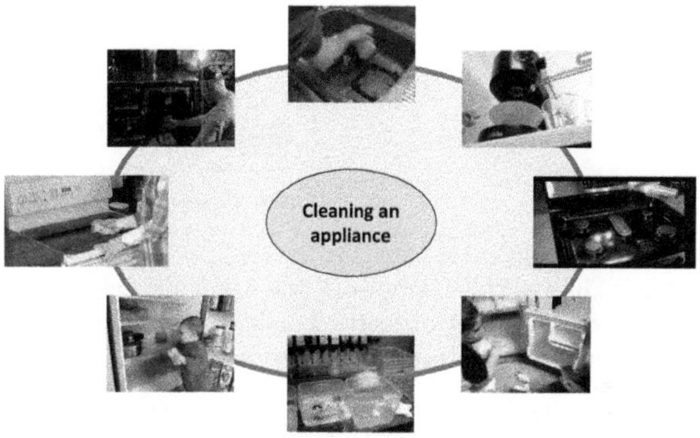

Figure 1: Visual diversity of the event "cleaning an appliance".

in recent years, TRECVID has brought up the problem of multimedia event detection (MED), which is specialized in searching complex multimedia events in a very large video corpus [26]. MED has the following distinctions that cause great difficulty for video retrieval: (1) The query is a description of an everyday event, which is complex and diverse by nature in both of its visual and semantic cues. The diversity is caused by the varieties of appliance types, change of surroundings, illumination, and viewpoints. Figure 1 takes the event "cleaning an appliance" as an example: the definition of an appliance includes large household machines such as air conditioner, dishwasher, refrigerator, kitchen stove, etc. It can also include small devices like coffee makers. The camera position may vary dramatically between videos, causing great difficulty for object recognition. The cleaning operation usually happens in a kitchen or shop, but is not limited to such indoor scenes. For example, people may clean their grill in the backyard, which substantially increases visual diversity. Moreover, although the appearance of a refrigerator in a kitchen is helpful for video screening, key evidence such as spraying cleaning fluid is critical to make a judgement. (2) The task concerned by this paper, namely zero-example event detection (0Ex), focuses on the case that no visual examples are given to train an event classifier. Instead, only textual definition of the event is provided as a information need. Therefore, a search system has to leverage external knowledge to bridge the gap between textual information in the query and visual content in the video corpus. (3) The large video corpus for event search contains 200,000 unconstrained Internet videos with variable length and quality [29], which sets a high demand on both performance and efficiency for a search system.

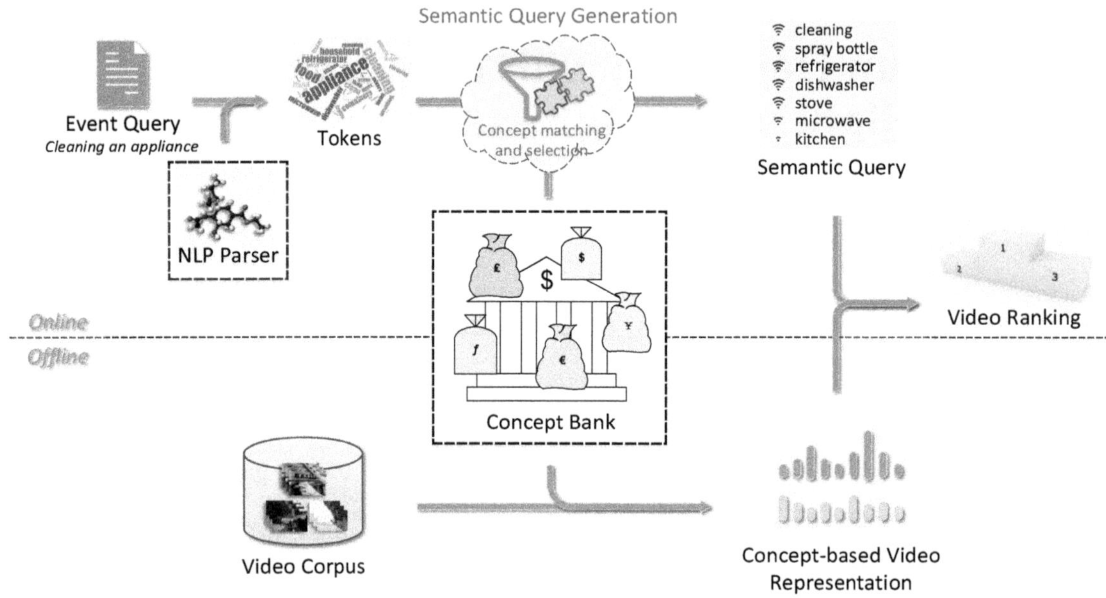

Figure 2: The overall framework for event detection with zero example. The core of the framework is a large concept bank containing detectors of objects, scenes, actions, and activities. Semantic query generation which maps the tokens (noun and verb phrases) to an internal query representation, namely *semantic query*, is essential to system performance.

The state-of-the-art systems for 0Ex are mostly based on the selection of a handful of relevant concepts that can integrally describe an event query, assuming that there is a classifier for each of the selected concepts [15]. We develop our automatic system likewise, which is shown in Figure 2. In the offline phase, all videos are represented by a concept-based representation in which each dimension represents the likelihood of presence of a particular concept. In the online phase, given an event query, e.g. "cleaning an appliance" with detailed description, the noun and verb phrases are first extracted as tokens. Then these tokens are mapped to an internal query representation called *semantic query* by concept matching. In this way, the query is converted to concept-based representation as well. Finally, event search is performed having all the concept-based representations of both queries and videos.

This framework directly raises an important concern: *How to build a large concept bank generalizable for everyday events?* In order to provide good coverage in the first place, we basically mix thousands of concepts in different granularity, i.e. from common objects to activities. Then comes the fundamental problem this paper aims to focus: *How to pick up the right concepts in the concept bank to represent an event query?* Intuitively, one may expect of using more and more relevant concepts for describing an event from different aspects, given that these concepts may help reinforce with each other. This idea, however, turns out to be impractical: Through experiments, we surprisingly find that only selecting a few relevant concepts could already provide a good performance for most events, as long as the selected concepts are accurate. Adding more concepts that are less relevant to the query almost always risks a performance plunge. Hence, a conservative strategy is to simply cap the number of concepts in semantic query by keeping the best matches. Although this strategy generally shows good performance, the optimal number of concepts is hard to determine because it varies among events. In addition, due to imperfection of concept matching, false positives are inevitable even for the top ten relevant concepts. As a result, capping the number of concepts turns to be risky when concept matching becomes unreliable, because a single noisy concept would count in a representation with a small number of concepts. We hereby propose to improve the video representation by pooling the key evidence, rather than pooling all the keyframes. In this new representation, noisy concepts are less likely to have an impact.

The novelty of this paper can be summarized as follows:

- We focus on the problem of choosing the right concepts from a large concept bank for event detection without training examples. We show that, with a large concept bank, concept selection is crucial to the performance. To the best of our knowledge, concept selection in the scope of 0Ex has not been systematically investigated.
- We propose to represent the videos only by their evidential shots to create a system robust to wrong concepts in the semantic query. The detection of the evidential shots is unsupervised, which well fits to the 0Ex pipeline. The representation can lead to more than 50% of improvement without capping the number of concepts in semantic query generation.

The efficiency of the proposed methods was backed by experimental results on a large corpus: According to TRECVID 2015's evaluation on 200,000 videos, addressing the aforementioned problems paved our way to a practical system that achieved the best performance in the 0Ex task of MED.

2. RELATED WORK

Multimedia event detection typically makes use of training examples. Event classifiers are trained by low-level features [9, 25, 33] or semantic features [11, 12, 27] that are directly extracted from exemplar videos. *Zero-example* multimedia event detection (0Ex) is an emerging topic yet to be explored. In contrast to zero-shot learning which focuses on the recognition of images with unseen labels, 0Ex emphasizes the use of general and external knowledge for textual-to-visual relation. A few pilot studies were proposed very recently [5, 34, 2]. These works built a small concept library, typically hundreds of concepts, for textual-to-visual relation. Mazloom et al. [20] proposed to use tag propagation which propagates tags from a labeled video source to unlabelled videos. For 0Ex retrieval, they found that using tags propagated by concept vector similarity overwhelms bag of visual words similarity, which renders the importance of concepts. More recent work starts to resort to a larger concept library. Ye et al. [35] collected a dataset with 500 events in which more than 4,000 concepts were hierarchically organized. Singh et al. [28] automatically discovered salient visual concepts by web search according to the text query. In event search phase, Habibian et al. [10] indexed concepts by AND/OR composition. Chang et al. [3] proposed a rank aggregation framework that addressed the incomparable scales of scores when merging concepts from different feature spaces. Jiang et al. studied pseudo relevance feedback [14] and self-paced reranking [13] that further improved the performance by reranking. Jiang et al. [15] also systematically investigated 0Ex problem. This work explored the contribution of multiple features including thousands of concepts, as well as the performance of several search models. Our work relies on a large number of concepts as well. But different from previous studies which analyze many components like feature types and search models, we especially focus on the crucial problems raised when the size of the concept library is increased.

Regarding the retrieval performance of an 0Ex system, semantic query generation, which translates event query to an internal query representation, is the crux. With a large concept bank, while trying to avoid relating queries to wrong concepts on the one hand, an alternative to improve performance is to somehow tolerate the wrong concepts in event search. We draw inspiration from semantic pooling [36]. Rather than simply averaging the frame-level concept responses for the whole video [19, 21], recent studies suggest to only pool the evidential parts that are semantically important to an event query [22, 36]. The idea is based on the underlying assumption that important evidence is sparsely scattered in a video's timeline, thus aggregating all keyframes like average pooling would collect a bunch of junk information. Yu et al. [36] learned the concept importance of a small concept set and pooled the low-level features according to the importance of their related concepts. Mettes et al. [22] clustered the keyframes into fragment proposals and learned the importance of each proposal. Lately, more complex work tends to optimize the event detection by jointly discovering the evidence, given that a good recounting should assist detection in the first place [4, 30], rather than only interpret detection [8]. All the above works need training examples to discover discriminative segments for pooling. Furthermore, Bhattacharya et al. [1] conducted intensive user study and found that a human can recognize most events by merely looking into very few sample segments of a video. Inspired by this finding, we take query words to locate key evidence in a video for pooling. Unlike previous works, the key evidence is proposed without any need of training videos. We show that event search is robust to noisy concepts even by exploiting as few as three pieces of key evidence for video representation.

3. SEMANTIC QUERY GENERATION

Semantic query generation, as shown in Figure 2, maps the user generated *event query* to an internal, concept-based representation, a.k.a. *semantic query*. This query translation has two goals in general: First, the semantic query can be directly used for event search by the system. Second, the semantic query is able to reflect the essentials of event query for event detection purpose. In addition, the readability, i.e. how concise the semantic query is, is an optional goal if humans are considered to interactively refine the semantic query. We investigate two major steps that have significant impact on retrieval performance in semantic query generation.

3.1 Concept matching

Matching concepts in concept bank requires to measure how close each concept is to the query. We design a flexible phrase matching method that can easily combine with word similarities of WordNet [23], and weighting policies, such as TF-IDF and word specificity.

The concept matching process can be formalized as a mapping from query tokens $\boldsymbol{q}$ to the concepts $\boldsymbol{c}$, denoted as $map(\boldsymbol{q}, \boldsymbol{c})$. Then, we denote the name of one of the concepts as $\boldsymbol{c}_i$, a noun or verb phrase from the query tokens as $\boldsymbol{q}_j$, and the set of common words[1] between them as $\boldsymbol{U}$. Obviously, $\boldsymbol{U} = \boldsymbol{T}(\boldsymbol{c}_i) \cap \boldsymbol{T}(\boldsymbol{q}_j)$, where $\boldsymbol{T}(\boldsymbol{c}_i)$ stands for the set of words in the concept name $\boldsymbol{c}_i$, and $\boldsymbol{T}(\boldsymbol{q}_j)$ likewise. The concept matching is solved by first calculating the similarities for each $(\boldsymbol{c}_i, \boldsymbol{q}_j)$ pair, then selecting the concept with the maximum similarity for each phrase $\boldsymbol{q}_j$, thus forming a set of event-related concepts.

Specifically, a similarity matrix $\boldsymbol{S}$ is first obtained by calculating the similarity for each $(\boldsymbol{c}_i, \boldsymbol{q}_j)$ pair via word-to-word matching, given

$$sim(\boldsymbol{c}_i, \boldsymbol{q}_j) = \frac{|\boldsymbol{U}|}{|\boldsymbol{c}_i|} \cdot \max(\boldsymbol{t_U} \odot \log \boldsymbol{s_U}) \quad (1)$$

where $\boldsymbol{t_U}$ is the TF-IDF weights, in which TF (term frequency) represents the frequency of appearance in event query for the words in $\boldsymbol{U}$, and IDF (inverse document frequency) is estimated based on a collection of Wikipedia pages downloaded from the Web. $\boldsymbol{s_U}$ is the word specificity vector defined by the minimum depths of word for the words in $\boldsymbol{U}$ based on WordNet hierarchy. $\odot$ stands for element-wise product. $\max(\cdot)$ operation only picks up the maximum value. $|\boldsymbol{U}|$ means the number of common words, and $|\boldsymbol{c}_i|$ likewise. $\frac{|\boldsymbol{U}|}{|\boldsymbol{c}_i|}$ gives credits to an exact match of the concept name compared to a partial match. Note that for the concepts which do not have any overlapped words with token phrases, the corresponding similarities are set to 0. Then, we define the max-filtered similarity matrix $\boldsymbol{S^F}$ as

$$[\boldsymbol{S}^{\boldsymbol{F}}_{ij}] = \begin{cases} sim(\boldsymbol{c}_i, \boldsymbol{q}_j) & \text{if } sim(\boldsymbol{c}_i, \boldsymbol{q}_j) = \max\limits_{k} sim(\boldsymbol{c}_k, \boldsymbol{q}_j); \\ 0 & \text{otherwise} \end{cases} \quad (2)$$

[1]We find it helpful to consider synonyms as common words as a supplement to the overlapped words. For example, "baby" and "infant" can be regarded as common words.

Type	*Concepts*
Relevant	Rock climbing, bouldering, sport climbing, artificial rock wall
Non-discriminative	Rope climbing, climbing, rock
False positive	Rock fishing, rock band performance
Different context	Stone wall, grabbing rock

Table 1: Concept examples for manual concept selection regarding the event *rock climbing*.

in which we only retain the concept with the maximum similarity given a phrase $\boldsymbol{q}_j$. Finally, we map the text queries $\boldsymbol{q}$ to concepts $\boldsymbol{c}$ by

$$\boldsymbol{w} = map(\boldsymbol{q}, \boldsymbol{c}) = \boldsymbol{S^F} \cdot \mathbb{1} \tag{3}$$

which results in a sparse weight vector $\boldsymbol{w}$, with each dimension representing the importance of a concept.

Given the concept detector responses of all the videos $\boldsymbol{R}$, the event search now can simply be performed by calculating the product of the videos and query:

$$\boldsymbol{h} = \boldsymbol{R}\boldsymbol{w} \tag{4}$$

3.2 Concept selection

Given an event query, concept matching can basically match to dozens of concepts with a concept bank sized about 3,000. Using all of the matches for event search would eventually result in poor performance. On the one hand, this is because concepts with lower importance are less discriminative to the event. For instance, although the concept *water* frequently appears in the event *distinguishing a fire*, water is too common to be seen in many other events such as *competitive swimming*, *bungee jumping*, and *cleaning an appliance*. On the other hand, a concept with low importance is more likely to be a false positive example. Therefore, it makes sense to deploy a concept selection module aiming to filter out irrelevant concepts.

Automatic concept selection simply rank the concepts by importance given the weight vector $\boldsymbol{w}$, then select the top k concepts for semantic query generation.

Manual concept selection employs human subjects to perform concept screening. Along this process, all noisy concepts are expected to be removed, leaving only relevant and discriminative concepts. We basically follow the criteria below for manual concept screening:

- *Relevancy*: Remove false positives by looking at the names of concepts;
- *Context relatedness*: Remove concepts for which training videos appear in different context based on human's common sense;
- *Discrimination*: Only include concepts that are discriminative to this event if a higher-level activity/event detector that matches the event is found.

These criteria are exploited based on the results of automatic concept selection. Take the event *rock climbing* as an example, semantic query generation can pick up roughly 50 concepts by automatic concept matching. A human judge then needs to quickly screen these concepts and remove irrelevant ones. Table 1 shows different types of irrelevant concepts, which considers relevancy, discrimination, and context relatedness. For example, *Rope climbing* is not discriminative because it can also appear in the event *climbing a tree*; *grabbing rock* is removed as it may present in different context, e.g. alongside a river. It's worth to mention that *artificial rock wall* can be regarded as a relevant concept because, based on common sense, artificial rock wall is only used for practicing rock climbing. As a rule of thumb, it's practically effective to only represent an event by relevant concepts. The non-discriminative concepts and concepts that come out in different context are still helpful if no relevant concepts can be found.

Algorithm 1 Evidential pooling for one video

input: weight vector $\boldsymbol{w}$, keyframe-level concept detector responses $\boldsymbol{J}$, number of concepts restricted for evidence proposal k_e, number of evidential shots m
output: video-level concept detector responses $\boldsymbol{r}$

For concepts not ranking in the top k_e of $\boldsymbol{w}$, set their weights in $\boldsymbol{w}$ to 0, getting $\boldsymbol{w_e}$;
Calculate $\boldsymbol{J}\boldsymbol{w_e}$, the importance scores for all the keyframes;
Rank all the keyframes by their importance scores;
$n \leftarrow 0$, $G \leftarrow \varnothing$;
while $n < m$ **and** not all the keyframes are processed **do**
    get the next important keyframe y in the rank list;
    if $G = \varnothing$ **or** y is not adjacent to any of the keyframes in G **then**
        add y to a new set P;
        add set P to G;
        $n \leftarrow n + 1$;
    else
        add y to the existing set P in G where P has a keyframe adjacent to y;
    end if
    if $n > 1$ **then**
        for each $(P_i, P_j) \in G$ **do**
            if P_i has a keyframe adjacent to P_j **then**
                merge P_i and P_j into one set;
                $n \leftarrow n - 1$;
            end if
        end for
    end if
end while
$\boldsymbol{r} \leftarrow$ Average pooling J for the selected keyframes in G only;
return $\boldsymbol{r}$;

4. EVIDENTIAL POOLING

Automatic concept selection simply caps the number of concepts used in semantic query in order to avoid the involvement of irrelevant concepts. Although this method is generally simple and efficient, it has two major drawbacks. First, it is difficult to determine a threshold k because the number of concepts that achieves the best performance varies between events; second, using fewer number of concepts for event representation is more sensitive to noisy concepts, given that each concept would count much. We would like to have a best of both worlds approach that, it can both benefit from a representation with larger number of concepts and resist the negative impact from less relevant or even irrelevant concepts.

Our idea is majorly enlightened by Bhattacharya et al.[1] that, for event recognition, humans can make a quick decision in most cases by just looking into several shots of a video. This fact indicates that merely a few shots can provide sufficient information to reach a decision. We further hypothesis that using few sample shots of a video is more discriminative than using all of its content. Specifically, consider the case of a video only represented by the most evidential shot: a large portion of the video is thus stripped

Figure 3: Concept bank overview. 2,774 concept
off-the-shelf datasets are collected. *ImageNet 1(*
cialized in objects, *Places 205* in scenes. *Sport*
FCVID 239 mainly contain higher-level semanti
activities and events. *Research Collection (RC*
SIN 346 are mixed with concepts of different gra

off, making the representation sparse and "clean'
a neat outcome of this clean representation – *it is relatively robust against the noisy concepts in the semantic query.* For instance, a typical video clip of *bike trick* might happen on a street. A prolonged clip would capture many objects on the street, such as cars, buses and traffic lights. If a given event query *parking a car* also expects the presence of such street objects, the clip of *bike trick* is likely to be detected as a false positive, simply because it happily responds to the semantic query that expects these non-discriminative street objects. But the clean representation which takes only the most evidential shot is less likely to suffer from this problem, as the representation is more concentrated. Rare concepts such as buses and traffic lights are naturally filtered out.

Algorithm 1 details the evidential pooling. The pivot is finding m evidential shots. The algorithm takes the semantic query as information need to rank keyframes in a video (steps 1–3). Evidential keyframes are sequentially selected based on the rank (steps 5–22) while aggregating them into evidential shots (steps 15–20). Video representation is formed by pooling through m evidential shots only, rather than all the keyframes of the video clip (step 23). It is important to note that the ranking of keyframes is based on $\boldsymbol{w}_e$, where the number of concepts is restricted to k_e (step 1). Basically, k_e is set to a small number concerning that the evidential shots should be proposed by the most relevant concepts selected by k_e. We actually find that k_e can be chosen from a wide range that does not affect the performance. It is also worth noting that k_e is different from k which is used for automatic concept selection. With evidential pooling, the event search should be tolerant to noise, i.e., less sensitive to the value of k in the automatic concept selection phase.

5. EXPERIMENTS

5.1 Setups

The experiments are conducted on the TRECVID Multimedia Event Detection (MED) datasets. We use the event kits that contain 20 event queries from E021 to E040. The test set, named MED14Test, includes around 25,000 testing videos with no textual metadata. The performance is evaluated by the standard metric Mean Average Precision (MAP). The ground truth of MED14Test set is officially provided for self-evaluation [26]. As for 0Ex, no training videos are used throughout the experiments. Besides, we

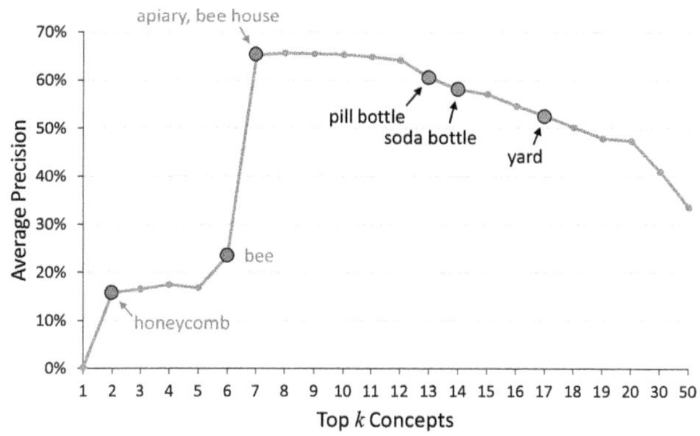

Figure 4: For the exemplar event query *beekeeping*, the performance drops significantly when adding more concepts to the semantic query. Concepts having a large impact are marked in the figure.

also show the official results on MED15Eval released by NIST. MED15Eval set has two divisions: MED15EvalFull contains 200,000 videos without textual metadata; MED15-EvalSub is a random subset of MED15EvalFull, which contains around 32,000 videos. No ground truth is provided for MED15Eval.

5.2 Concept bank

We build a large concept bank containing a total of 2,774 semantic concepts with varied granularity. They are sourced from off-the-shelf datasets with concept types covering objects, scenes, actions and activities. The six datasets and their settings are listed below:

- ***ImageNet 1000:*** We use the same DCNN architecture proposed in [18]. Specifically, the DCNN architecture can be denoted as $Image - C48 - P - N - C128 - P - N - C192 - C192 - C128 - P - F4096 - F4096 - F1000$, in which C are the convolutional layers followed by the number of filters, F are the fully-connected layers, P are the max-pooling layers and N are the local contrast normalization layers. The parameters of DCNN are learnt on ILSVRC 2012 [7]. The neural responses of the eight layer (F1000) are extracted for each keyframe of a test video.
- ***SIN 346:*** A set of 346 concept detectors fine-tuned with AlexNet DCNN structure on the TRECVID SIN 2014 dataset [37]. The concept responses are extracted for each keyframe of a test video.
- ***Research Collection 497:*** Similar to [24], we select 497 frequent concepts from the MED'14 Research Collection dataset [29]. At most 200 positive keyframes are manually annotated for each concept. We fine-tune 497 concept detectors using the AlexNet DCNN architecture. As with previous methods, we extract the responses of the concept detectors for each keyframe of a test video.
- ***Places 205:*** Multimedia events usually take place in notable scenes, e.g., *bike trick* is played in a park or on a street, whereas *cleaning an appliance* happens in a kitchen or shop. To capture the scene information, we fine-tune 205 scene categories on the MIT Places dataset [38] using the AlexNet DCNN architecture. The concept responses are extracted for each keyframe of a test video.

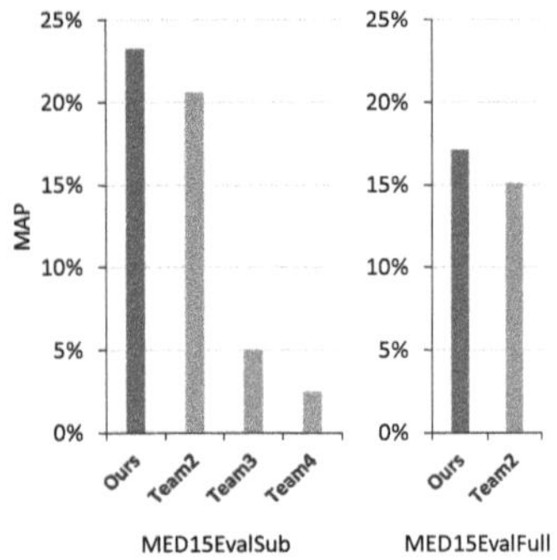

Figure 5: The official results of 0Ex MAP performance on MED15Eval released by NIST.

Dataset	*#Concepts*	*Optimum k*	*MAP*
Sports	487	10	0.103
FCVID	239	1	0.071
Research Collection	497	2	0.053
ImageNet	1,000	3	0.049
Places	205	2	0.020
SIN	346	5	0.014
Concept Bank	2,774	9	0.129
AutoSQGSys [15]	4,043	-	0.115

Table 2: The optimum of concepts k per dataset using automatic concept selection. The MAP is reported on MED14Test.

- ***FCVID 239:*** To capture the high level activities of multimedia events, 239 concept detectors are trained with SVMs on FCVID [16] dataset. Specifically, as concepts in this dataset are mainly annotated at video level, we first extract the AlexNet Layer-7 [18] responses for each keyframe in a training video. Then, the training features for a video are generated by average pooling the responses of all the keyframes. The concept detectors are trained by these video-level training features. A similar pipeline can be applied to test videos to extract video-level testing features. Finally, the responses of 205 concept detectors can be directly extracted for test videos.
- ***Sports 487:*** The 487 concepts of general sports are trained with the 3D-CNN architecture [32] on the Sport-1M dataset [17] that contains one million videos. The concept responses are extracted for each of 15-frame segments of a test video.

Figure 3 summarizes the granularity of concepts for the six datasets.

5.3 Concept selection

Automatic concept selection To demonstrate the importance of concept selection, we illustrate an event *beekeeping* in Figure 4. By concept matching, 34 concepts are chosen as candidates for this event. We then employ automatic concept selection to only retain the top k concepts. As the number k increases, the performance increases at first, but decreases dramatically when $k > 12$, dropping almost a half at the end. From the figure, we see three concepts that largely contribute to the performance increase: *honeycomb*, *bee* and *apiary (bee house)*. These concepts are relevant and discriminative. In contrast, as k further increases, more

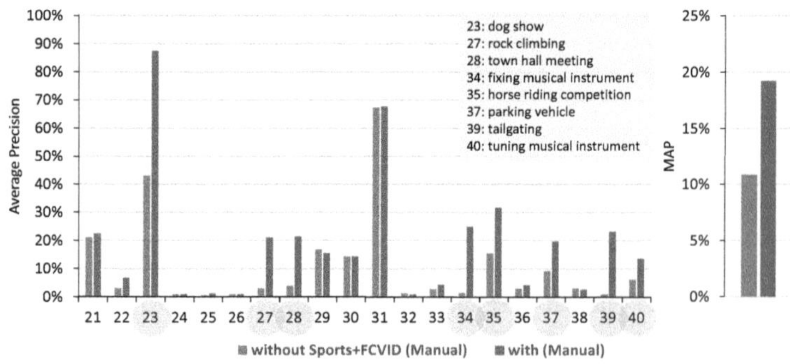

Figure 6: The contribution of concepts from Sports 487 and FCVID 239 on MED14Test. Both the Average Precision (AP) per event and MAP are shown. Concepts from these two datasets have a large contribution on 8 of the 20 events, leading to a boost of MAP.

k_e	2	4	8	16
MAP	0.0725	0.0771	0.0775	0.0770

Table 3: Evidential pooling is not sensitive to the number of concepts k_e used for evidence proposal. For this test, all the matched concepts are used for event search. The MAP is based on MED14Test.

concepts that are less relevant are involved. For example, a *bottle* as beekeeping container is different from a *pill bottle*. Although there is a partial match in their names, the context of these two concepts is different. *Yard* is another example which turns down the performance. One might intuitively think that *yard* can be helpful in recognizing beekeeping, given that beekeeping usually takes place in a yard. However, due to the presence of more accurate and discriminative concepts like *honeycomb* and *apiary*, high performance has already been achieved. Adding a less discriminative concept *yard* would decrease the performance in this case, since *yard* is commonly seen in many other activities, which tends to introduce noise.

As the performance is sensitive to the number of concepts, a good practice for automatic concept selection is to stop at a small k. For the beekeeping example shown above, the optimal number k is 8. We find that the optimum k is bound to both event query and concept bank. Table 2 lists the optimum k for each individual dataset as well as the merged concept bank tested on MED14Test. As you can see, many datasets have their best performance by less than 4 concepts. Note that the performance of our concept bank with automatic concept selection has already exceeded the state-of-the-art full system AutoSQGSys as described by Jiang et al. [15] even without combining the ASR and OCR features.

Manual concept selection By concept screening according to the rules in Section 3.2, we refine the automatically matched concepts for all the 20 events. Note that manual concept screening is allowed in TRECVID and used by many teams [15, 26]. The manually refined semantic queries, combined with ASR and OCR features, provide us clear advantage against other teams (Figure 5), based on the 0Ex evaluation in TRECVID 2015.

We further investigate the contribution of concepts according to their source datasets. Figure 6 shows a large

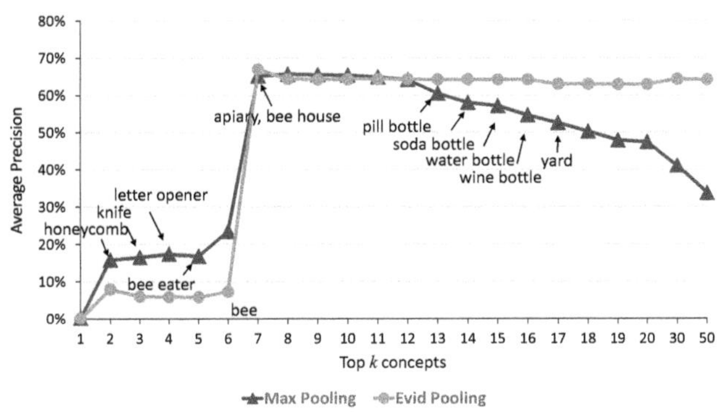

Figure 7: Evidential pooling vs. max pooling regarding the event query *beekeeping*.

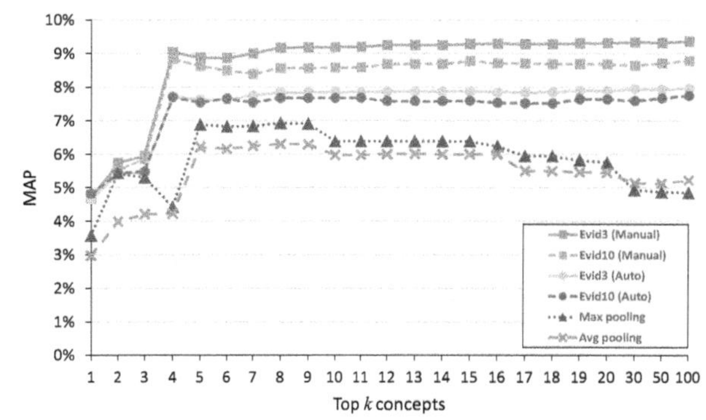

Figure 8: Evidential pooling with various settings for the 20 events in MED14Test. The MAP with regard to the top k concepts is shown for each pooling method.

Pooling Method	*MAP*
3 shots proposed by manually refined SQ	0.0936
10 shots proposed by manually refined SQ	0.0879
3 shots proposed by automatic SQ	0.0797
10 shots proposed by automatic SQ	0.0775
Max pooling	0.0485
Average pooling	0.0522

Table 4: The performance summarization of Figure 8 when all the matched concepts are used for event search. The settings are exactly the same as in Figure 8. SQ stands for Semantic Query. The k_e in automatic SQ is set to 8.

gap of MAP between systems with and without the higher-level concepts from Sports-1M and FCVID. Semantic queries for both systems are manually refined. As seen in the figure, the MAP drops more than 40% by removing these two datasets. We therefore conclude that both lower and higher level concepts devote to a good overall performance. Higher-level concept detectors, such as the activity detectors from FCVID, are accurate and discriminative. However, they require exact matches to the information need, otherwise they are not applicable. For instance, the activity *"professional American football"* would only satisfy queries of American football game. In contrast, lower-level concepts such as objects are componential and complementary. Although they are less discriminative, they offer help in case no exact match can be found among the higher-level concepts. Figure 6 also gives such insights when looking into the comparison of each individual event: Almost half of the events are the events with exact matches in Sports-1M or FCVID, hence their performance boosts. On the opposite side, for the events in which exact matches are not found, the contributions of Sports-1M and FCVID are relatively low.

5.4 Evidential pooling

Algorithm 1 tries to localize key evidence in a video according to a given semantic query. To generate a semantic query suitable for evidence proposal, we first cap the number of concepts k_e to a small value. This makes sense because, for localizing key evidence, we only need to focus on precision regardless of recall. We hence expect the semantic query to be as precise as possible. Table 3 indeed proves that it is acceptable to choose from a wide range of k_e. Even a very risky setting, e.g. $k_e = 2$, can have a satisfactory retrieval performance. We simply choose $k_e = 8$ and keep it fixed for all the automatic runs. Then, for each video clip, we locate the evidential shots regarding the semantic query. It is worth mentioning that the evidential shots can be generated for arbitrary videos, but in this case the content of these shots is likely to be arbitrary too.

We compare the evidential pooling to the conventional max/average pooling[2]. First, we review the *beekeeping* event in Figure 7. The evidential pooling shows clear advantage over max pooling: As the number of concepts k increases, max pooling tends to suffer much from less relevant and noisy concepts. In contrast, evidential pooling is considerably robust. By using all of the 34 matched concepts, max pooling drops to an AP of 0.336, while evidential pooling stays above 0.64, which is almost twice the AP of max pooling. To investigate whether this observation is generalizable, we further conduct experiments on all the 20 events in MED14Test. Figure 8 shows the performance of evidential pooling with various settings. The corresponding MAP scores are summarized in Table 4. The benefit of evidential pooling is clearly seen over the 20 events. First, both max and average pooling are sensitive to k, whereas evidential pooling is robust to a wide range of k. Second, using all the matched concepts without concept selection, evidential pooling clearly overwhelms max and average pooling by more than 50% of MAP. Third, merely exploiting three evidential shots for pooling can achieve a great performance. Fourth, although proposing evidence by manually refined semantic query performs better, automatic semantic query is not far behind. Most importantly, the event detection using evidential pooling with automatic semantic query is not sensitive to the parameter k_e. Finally, we see that evidential pooling is not only robust, the MAP it reaches by using all the concepts is but also higher than the peak MAP of max pooling by picking the top 8 concepts.

[2]These experiments use a smaller concept bank that does not include FCVID and Sports-1M datasets as lacking of keyframe-based concept responses.

6. CONCLUSION

We presented a framework that practically achieved good performance in 0Ex. Because query representation relying on a large concept bank is sensitive to noisy concepts, restricting the number of concepts and manually removing the weakly relevant concepts are crucial to the performance. Evidential pooling, nevertheless, can involve more concepts including that of weakly relevant without sacrificing performance. From the experimental results we arrive at the following conclusions:

- An effective practice for generating the semantic query is to keep the concepts precise and discriminative. Using fewer but precise concepts performs better than more but less precise concepts.
- For manual concept screening, we recommend to remove concepts based on their relevancy, context relatedness and discrimination.
- Pooling from the evidential shots rather than all the keyframes can be robust to the noise in the semantic query as potentially non-evidential information is excluded from the search process.

Acknowledgements

The work described in this paper was fully supported by a grant from the Research Grants Council of the Hong Kong Special Administrative Region, China (CityU 120213).

7. REFERENCES

[1] S. Bhattacharya, F. X. Yu, and S.-F. Chang. Minimally needed evidence for complex event recognition in unconstrained videos. In *ICMR*, pages 105–112, New York, NY, USA, 2014.

[2] M. Boer, K. Schutte, and W. Kraaij. Knowledge based query expansion in complex multimedia event detection. *Multimedia Tools and Applications*, pages 1–19, 2015.

[3] X. Chang, Y. Yang, A. G. Hauptmann, E. P. Xing, and Y.-L. Yu. Semantic concept discovery for large-scale zero-shot event detection. In *IJCAI*, 2015.

[4] X. Chang, Y.-L. Yu, Y. Yang, and A. G. Hauptmann. Searching persuasively: Joint event detection and evidence recounting with limited supervision. In *23rd ACM MM*, pages 581–590, New York, NY, USA, 2015. ACM.

[5] J. Dalton, J. Allan, and P. Mirajkar. Zero-shot video retrieval using content and concepts. In *22Nd CIKM*, pages 1857–1860, New York, NY, USA, 2013. ACM.

[6] J. Davidson, B. Liebald, J. Liu, P. Nandy, T. Van Vleet, U. Gargi, S. Gupta, Y. He, M. Lambert, B. Livingston, and D. Sampath. The youtube video recommendation system. In *4th ACM RecSys*, pages 293–296, New York, NY, USA, 2010.

[7] J. Deng, W. Dong, R. Socher, L.-J. Li, K. Li, and L. Fei-Fei. ImageNet: A Large-Scale Hierarchical Image Database. In *CVPR*, 2009.

[8] N. Gkalelis, V. Mezaris, I. Kompatsiaris, and T. Stathaki. Video event recounting using mixture subclass discriminant analysis. In *ICIP*, pages 4372–4376, Sept 2013.

[9] A. Habibian, T. Mensink, and C. G. Snoek. Videostory: A new multimedia embedding for few-example recognition and translation of events. In *22Nd ACM MM*, pages 17–26, New York, NY, USA, 2014.

[10] A. Habibian, T. Mensink, and C. G. M. Snoek. Composite concept discovery for zero-shot video event detection. In *ICMR*, pages 17–24, New York, NY, USA, 2014.

[11] A. Habibian, K. E. van de Sande, and C. G. Snoek. Recommendations for video event recognition using concept vocabularies. In *ICMR*, pages 89–96, New York, 2013.

[12] L. Jiang, A. G. Hauptmann, and G. Xiang. Leveraging high-level and low-level features for multimedia event detection. In *20th ACM MM*, pages 449–458, New York, NY, USA, 2012.

[13] L. Jiang, D. Meng, T. Mitamura, and A. G. Hauptmann. Easy samples first: Self-paced reranking for zero-example multimedia search. In *22Nd ACM MM*, pages 547–556, New York, 2014.

[14] L. Jiang, T. Mitamura, S.-I. Yu, and A. G. Hauptmann. Zero-example event search using multimodal pseudo relevance feedback. In *ICMR*, pages 297–304, New York, NY, USA, 2014.

[15] L. Jiang, S.-I. Yu, D. Meng, T. Mitamura, and A. G. Hauptmann. Bridging the ultimate semantic gap: A semantic search engine for internet videos. In *5th ICMR*, pages 27–34, New York, NY, USA, 2015.

[16] Y.-G. Jiang, Z. Wu, J. Wang, X. Xue, and S.-F. Chang. Exploiting feature and class relationships in video categorization with regularized deep neural networks. *arXiv:1502.07209*, 2015.

[17] A. Karpathy, G. Toderici, S. Shetty, T. Leung, R. Sukthankar, and L. Fei-Fei. Large-scale video classification with convolutional neural networks. In *CVPR*, pages 1725–1732. IEEE, 2014.

[18] A. Krizhevsky, I. Sutskever, and G. E. Hinton. Imagenet classification with deep convolutional neural networks. In F. Pereira, C. Burges, L. Bottou, and K. Weinberger, editors, *Advances in Neural Information Processing Systems 25*, pages 1097–1105. Curran Associates, Inc., 2012.

[19] M. Mazloom, A. Habibian, and C. G. Snoek. Querying for video events by semantic signatures from few examples. In *21st ACM MM*, pages 609–612, New York, NY, USA, 2013.

[20] M. Mazloom, X. Li, and C. G. M. Snoek. Few-example video event retrieval using tag propagation. In *ICMR*, pages 459–462, New York, NY, USA, 2014.

[21] M. Merler, B. Huang, L. Xie, G. Hua, and A. Natsev. Semantic model vectors for complex video event recognition. *IEEE Transactions on Multimedia*, 14(1):88–101, Feb 2012.

[22] P. Mettes, J. C. van Gemert, S. Cappallo, T. Mensink, and C. G. Snoek. Bag-of-fragments: Selecting and encoding video fragments for event detection and recounting. In *5th ICMR*, pages 427–434, New York, NY, USA, 2015.

[23] G. A. Miller. Wordnet: A lexical database for english. *Commun. ACM*, 38(11):39–41, Nov. 1995.

[24] P. Natarajan, S. Wu, F. Luisier, X. Zhuang, and M. Tickoo. BBN VISER TRECVID 2013 multimedia event detection and multimedia event recounting systems. In *NIST TRECVID Workshop*, 2013.

[25] S. Oh, S. Mccloskey, I. Kim, A. Vahdat, K. J. Cannons, H. Hajimirsadeghi, G. Mori, A. G. Perera, M. Pandey, and J. J. Corso. Multimedia event detection with multimodal feature fusion and temporal concept localization. *Mach. Vision Appl.*, 25(1):49–69, Jan. 2014.

[26] P. Over, G. Awad, M. Michel, J. Fiscus, W. Kraaij, A. F. Smeaton, G. Queenot, and R. Ordelman. TRECVID 2015 – an overview of the goals, tasks, data, evaluation mechanisms and metrics. In *Proceedings of TRECVID 2015*. NIST, USA, 2015.

[27] B. Safadi, M. Sahuguet, and B. Huet. When textual and visual information join forces for multimedia retrieval. In *ICMR*, pages 265–272, New York, NY, USA, 2014.

[28] B. Singh, X. Han, Z. Wu, V. I. Morariu, and L. S. Davis. Selecting relevant web trained concepts for automated event retrieval. In *ICCV*, pages 4561–4569, Dec 2015.

[29] S. Strassel, A. Morris, J. Fiscus, C. Caruso, H. Lee, P. Over, J. Fiumara, B. Shaw, B. Antonishek, and M. Michel. Creating HAVIC: Heterogeneous audio visual internet collection. In N. C. C. Chair), K. Choukri, T. Declerck, M. U. Dogan, B. Maegaard, J. Mariani, J. Odijk, and S. Piperidis, editors, *LREC*, Istanbul, Turkey, may 2012. ELRA.

[30] C. Sun and R. Nevatia. Discover: Discovering important segments for classification of video events and recounting. In *CVPR*, pages 2569–2576, June 2014.

[31] C. V. Thornley, A. C. Johnson, A. F. Smeaton, and H. Lee. The scholarly impact of TRECVid (2003-2009). *J. Am. Soc. Inf. Sci. Technol.*, 62(4):613–627, Apr. 2011.

[32] D. Tran, L. Bourdev, R. Fergus, L. Torresani, and M. Paluri. Learning spatiotemporal features with 3d convolutional networks. In *ICCV*, pages 4489–4497, 2015.

[33] F. Wang, Z. Sun, Y.-G. Jiang, and C.-W. Ngo. Video event detection using motion relativity and feature selection. *IEEE Transactions on Multimedia*, 16(5):1303–1315, Aug 2014.

[34] S. Wu, S. Bondugula, F. Luisier, X. Zhuang, and P. Natarajan. Zero-shot event detection using multi-modal fusion of weakly supervised concepts. In *CVPR*, pages 2665–2672, June 2014.

[35] G. Ye, Y. Li, H. Xu, D. Liu, and S.-F. Chang. Eventnet: A large scale structured concept library for complex event detection in video. In *23rd ACM MM*, pages 471–480, New York, NY, USA, 2015. ACM.

[36] Q. Yu, J. Liu, H. Cheng, A. Divakaran, and H. Sawhney. Semantic pooling for complex event detection. In *21st ACM MM*, pages 733–736, New York, NY, USA, 2013.

[37] W. Zhang, H. Zhang, T. Yao, Y. Lu, J. Chen, and C.-W. Ngo. VIREO @ TRECVID 2014: instance search and semantic indexing. In *NIST TRECVID Workshop*, 2014.

[38] B. Zhou, A. Lapedriza, J. Xiao, A. Torralba, and A. Oliva. Learning deep features for scene recognition using places database. In *Advances in Neural Information Processing Systems*, pages 487–495, 2014.

Homemade TS-Net for Automatic Face Recognition

Shilun Lin
Beijing University of Posts and Telecommunications
linshilun@bupt.edu.cn

Zhicheng Zhao
Beijing University of Posts and Telecommunications
zhaozc@bupt.edu.cn

Fei Su
Beijing University of Posts and Telecommunications
sufei@bupt.edu.cn

ABSTRACT

Inspired by how human being accomplishes face recognition task, a new architecture, called transfer and specialized net (TS-Net) is proposed in this paper, which fuses the general and specialized knowledge by combining a Transfer FaceNet and a Specialized FaceNet. The former is obtained by fine-tuning the pre-trained GoogleNet to transfer object-recognition knowledge to face recognition, and the latter is trained on global and local face patches to provide the discriminative specialized knowledge for face recognition. The final face representation is formed by fusing the features from both FaceNets. The advantages of our proposed architecture come from that: (i) By explicitly assigning different learning rates to different layers we successfully transfer the well-trained GoogleNet from object recognition task to a distinctly different task - face recognition; (ii) We construct the Specialized FaceNet with 6 simple networks to imitate the capture of featured-based and configural information in human vision process; (iii) Both Transfer FaceNet and Specialized FaceNets can be trained with a relatively small amount of training data (about 0.4 million samples) and a low configuration hardware (for example, a Titan-Z GPU). Experimental results show that TS-Net achieves competitive performance on both LFW and CASIA-Webface datasets. Also, it is promising that only slight dropping is found on verification and identification accuracy when 300 dimensional binary face representations are applied with Cosine distance as measure, which is implemental to develop practical human face retrieval and recognition system.

Keywords

Face Recognition, Convolutional Neural Network, Deep Learning, Transfer Learning, Specialized Learning

1. INTRODUCTION

In the past few years, face recognition under uncontrolled environments becomes one of the most extensively researched fields in computer vision [4, 26, 6, 24, 21, 19, 3, 2], due to the publication of LFW [9], an extensively reported dataset for evaluation of face recognition algorithms.

Figure 1: The basic idea of our proposed TS-Net. Simulating the transfer learning mechanism and the visual attention mechanism of human, we combine the transfer knowledge with the specialized knowledge to solve the face recognition problem by the machine.

In this paper, we try to use some hints given by experiments on human cognitive process to guide the construction of our system. Most of the existing works directly train specific networks from scratch for face recognition, therefore they require plenty of training data and computational effort. However, behavioral experiments reveal that human being can leverage experience in previous tasks into improved performance on different tasks [5]. Thus we can reasonably conjecture that common knowledge learned from general object recognition could be transferred to boost the performance of face recognition, especially when considering face recognition as a special case of object recognition. Even so, learning specialized knowledge about face, without doubt, is still necessary because face recognition involves small inter-personal variations and large intra-personal variations. Cognitive experiments on human memory suggest that humans use both feature-based and configural information to recognize faces [1]. Distortions of the relative positions of the mouth, eyes, and nose [1], as well as inverting a face [27] can strongly affect human recognition accuracy. In the perspective of top-down visual attention mechanism [8], driven by a specific goal, human usually uses feature-based attention to highlight specific features throughout a scene, and applies spatial attention to capture more information including configural information at the surrounding areas of the feature regions. Inspired by this fact, we will let our model to learn specialized knowledge from different face

ICMR'16, June 06-09, 2016, New York, NY, USA
© 2016 ACM. ISBN 978-1-4503-4359-6/16/06...$15.00
DOI: http://dx.doi.org/10.1145/2911996.2911999

regions to imitate human top-down visual attention. Therefore, to simulate the biological transfer learning mechanism and the visual attention mechanism mentioned above, we propose an approach, as shown in Fig. 1, which combines deep transfer learning and deep specialized learning based on various face patches to accomplish the recognition task.

We adopt the well-trained off-the-shelf deep model of object recognition, GoogleNet [23], and transfer it to face recognition task by transfer learning. To determine what kind of knowledge contained in the source model can be transferred to target domain, we analyze the filters and feature maps of different layers in original GoogleNet by visualization. The results of visualization indicate that knowledge learned by lower layers, including Gabor-like filters and color blobs, is so general that can be transferred directly. However, as the layer goes up, the semantics contained in the response of the higher layers are increasingly inclined to tell us whether the object in the image is a person instead of whom the person is, since GoogleNet is originally designed for object recognition. Thus, these higher layers should be retrained with the target domain data. By performing transfer learning on GoogleNet based on the transferability of different layers discussed above, we obtain a model, named Transfer FaceNet, which reuses the source domain knowledge selectively. Interestingly, we find that with a relatively small amount of training data, much less than training from scratch, transfer learning can make the response of higher layers of the original GoogleNet gradually focused on parts of the face (e.g., eyes and mouth), like the result of feature-based attention. The details will be given in section 3.

To further obtain both feature-based and configural knowledge about a face, we propose Specialized FaceNet which consists of 6 CNNs, each operating on one of 3 kinds of global and 3 kinds of local face patches. Identification and verification supervision signals are applied to 3 global patch based networks to imitate featured-based attention and find specific features throughout the face. To obtain configual information, we design three relatively simple networks with only identification supervision signals for local patches which cover upper, middle and lower regions of a face respectively. The response of these three simple networks is supposed to simulate human's quick eye movements from one fixation to another to capture spatial dependency on facial configurations. Batch normalization [10] is applied to the local patch based networks with the purpose of fixing the internal covariate shift problem, which allows us to use a big learning rate to accelerate convergence steadily. In addition, we use Leaky ReLU [15] to "close the distance" between supervision signals and lower layers in both the global and local patch based networks. This trick makes our approach more efficient in computation and memory than previous methods, where supervision signals were applied to lower layers through full-connected layers [22].

We combine the Transfer FaceNet with Specialized FaceNet to build a multi-model face recognition system, namely TS-Net. Proper reuse of the high performance GoogleNet and careful design of Specialized FaceNet make TS-Net outstanding and economical. Extensive experiments on both LFW and CASIA-Webface datasets indicate that superior performance is achieved with TS-Net. Using CASIA-Webface dataset as training data, we achieve 99.03% verification accuracy on LFW with the unsupervised protocol. From Scratch [26] achieves 97.30% using the same protocol and MM-DFR-JB [6] achieves 99.02% under the supervised paradigm. Face identification experiment is conducted on CASIA-Webface dataset. We try to identify 2,003 subjects (8,012 probe and 76,575 gallery images) and achieve 88.70% Rank-1 identification rate. Furthermore, we also verify the performance of using binarized face representations produced by TS-Net for both face verification and identification tasks. It's encouraging that the verification accuracy on LFW and Rank-1 identification rate on CASIA-Webface just drop slightly (from 98.52% to 98.41% and 88.70% to 87.51% respectively using Cosine distance as similarity measure). So TS-Net can offer a flexible and reasonable tradeoff between performance and storage and computational costs in real world applications.

2. RELATED WORK

2.1 Deep Transfer Learning

Traditional machine learning algorithms make prediction on the test data using statistical models which are trained on previously collected labeled or unlabeled training data [17]. Most of them assumed that the distributions of the training data and the test data are the same. Transfer learning aims to address the problem when the distribution of the training data from the source domain is different from that of the future data from the target domain. Transfer learning across tasks using deep representations has been extensively studied. Donahue *et al.* [7] empirically validated that a generic visual feature based on a convolutional network trained on ImageNet (Berg *et al.*, 2012 dataset) outperformed a host of conventional representations on standard object recognition tasks. Oquab *et al.* [16] transferred the CNN representations learned on ImageNet to recognize general object in Pascal VOC dataset without an explicit consideration of the transferability in different layers. However, face recognition has a distinct difference from general object recognition because of its small inter-class differences but big intra-class variations. This leaves a question: can deep transfer learning play a role in such distant tasks? We explore this question by transferring the source model for object recognition to face recognition task, and find that transferring according to the transferability of different layers in source model leads to a fairly good face model with an acceptable computation overhead.

2.2 Deep Face Representation Learning

Data and algorithm are two essential components for face recognition, especially for deep face representation learning. The publication of a milestone dataset, LFW, including 13,233 images of 5,749 identities, promotes the studies of unconstrained face recognition. Several excellent face features were learned by different deep networks, and achieved high performance on LFW face verification task. Taigman *et al.* [24] proposed the DeepFace, which was a multi-class network trained to perform the face identification task on 4.4 million faces of over 4,000 identities. Through an ensemble of three networks using different alignments and color channels they obtained high accuracy approaching the human-level. Sun *et al.* [21] proposed to combine the identification and verification losses for reducing intra-personal variations while enlarging inter-personal differences during the training of DeepID2. They concatenated the features from 25 of such networks, each operating on a different face patch, and then PCA was applied to get the compact face representation. Schroff *et al.* [19] presented a system, called FaceNet, which directly learned a mapping from face images to a compact Euclidean space with 100-200 million training face thumbnails consisting of about 8 million different identities. In common, the above works employed private face databases for training. Thus, the performance of the above works could not be compared directly because of the distinct size and unknown distribution of the unavailable data. Recently, Yi *et al.* [26] released the CASIA-Webface database which contained 494,414 labeled images of 10,575 subjects to fill this gap. All the models in this paper are trained on CASIA-WebFace dataset, which makes the results of this work directly comparable. In addition, most of the multi-model based methods treat face patches equally which may involve redundant operations. Our proposed TS-Net uses complex networks (e.g., Transfer FaceNet) based on global patches to imitate the process of feature-based visual attention, and relatively simple networks based on U-M-L (upper, middle and lower) face patches to simulate spatial saccades on different local fixation areas.

3. TRANSFER FACENET

The source model we choose is GoogleNet, a 22-layer network which is consisting of local inception modules stacked upon each other and achieves the best result at the ILSVRC14 visual recognition challenge [18]. However, on the one hand, due to the distance between general object recognition and face recognition task, directly using pre-trained GoogleNet for face recognition may not be suitable. On the other hand, based on GoogleNet structure retraining a brand new deep model for face recognition is not easy. In general, it requires a lot of time and a dataset of sufficient size (e.g., ImageNet, which contains 1.2 million images with 1,000 categories) that we may not have in practice. In such cases, knowledge transfer, if done successfully, would produce a nice model for the target task through reusing the source model, which can alleviate some expensive data-labeling efforts and save a lot of time.

In this session, we present the Transfer FaceNet which transfers the knowledge learned for object recognition to face recognition by fine-tuning the pre-train GoogleNet to recognize 10,370 face identities in CASIA-Webface. In test phase, face representations are extracted from the bottleneck layer (the layer before the last fully-connected layer). Transfer FaceNet achieves a good performance and reduces the training time and the amount of training data through reuse the powerful but hard-to-train source model. The flowchart of Transfer FaceNet is shown in Fig. 2.

3.1 Transferability

We believe that knowledge especially the common knowledge learned for object recognition can be transferred to face recognition. As can be seen in Fig. 3 (left), the first convolutional layer of original GoogleNet learns Gabor-like filters and color blobs. Such first-layer features appear not to be specific to a particular dataset or task, but are general for a wide range of applications. For instance, Gabor-based features, as a local and nonlinear handcrafted feature, have been widely used in the fields of face recognition and some significant results have been obtained [14]. Thus, we can transfer this basic knowledge to face identification directly.

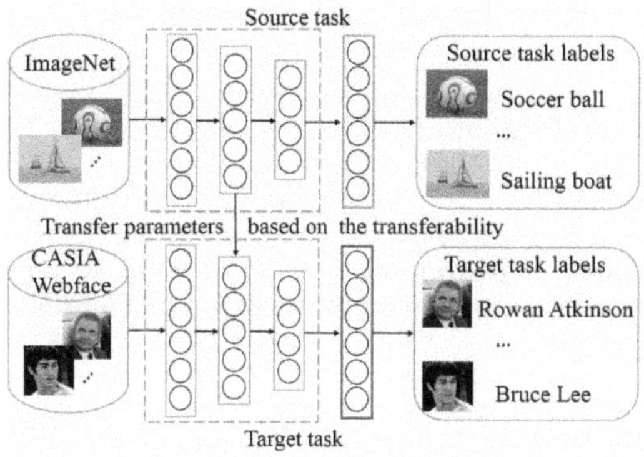

Figure 2: The flowchart of Transfer FaceNet.

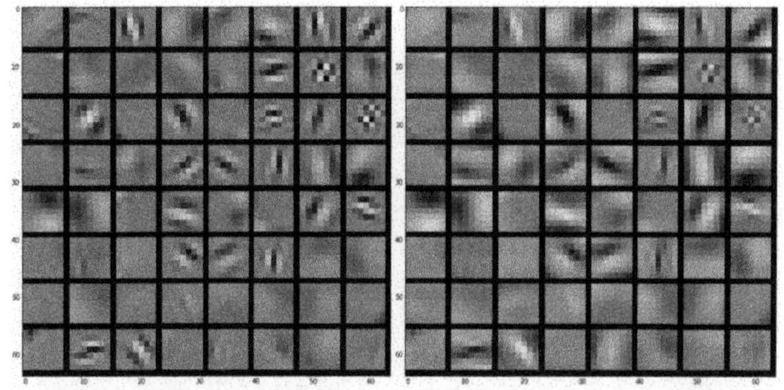

Figure 3: Visualization of the first convolution layer filters of both original GoogleNet (left) and Transfer FaceNet (right). Best viewed in color.

Through the output of an intermediate layer of original GoogleNet, as shown in Fig. 4 (left), we can find that on this layer the network learns face concepts like mouth to some degree (see third column of second row, for an example). But these concepts are not clear enough, so the knowledge learned by intermediate layers should be slightly modified to enhance the face concepts.

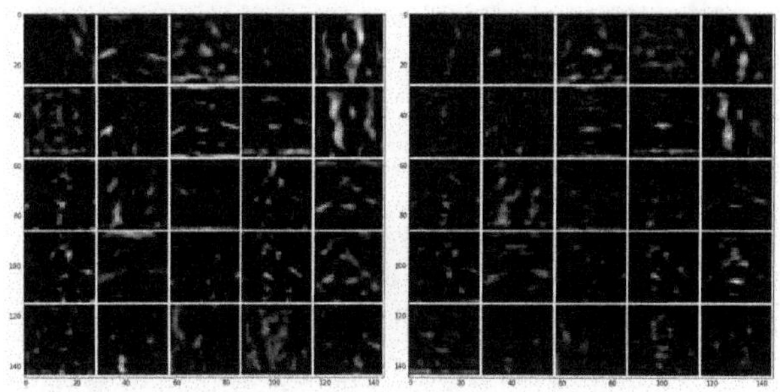

Figure 4: Visualization of first 25 feature maps output from the inception_3a/5×5 layer of original GoogleNet (left) and Transfer FaceNet (right) on image of Aaron Eckhart.

The specialization of higher layer neurons to their source task weakens the transferability of these layers. Particularly, the last output layer with an N-dimensional (1,000 of GoogleNet) softmax has been successfully trained toward a specific supervised classification objective, and each output unit will be specific to a particular class. Doubtlessly, the knowledge obtained by the top layers of the source model should be forgotten and learnt from target data renewedly.

3.2 Transfer based on Transferability

From what has been discussed above, we may reasonably arrive at the conclusion that transferring the knowledge from object recognition (source domain) to face identification (target domain) according to transferability of different layers is feasible.

We use the pre-trained GoogleNet available in the Caffe deep learning framework (Jia *et al.* [11]) as the source model. This model was trained by using 1.2 million images of the ImageNet to discriminate among 1,000 leaf-node categories of the ImageNet hierarchy. Around 380,000 images from 10,370 identities are used as target domain labeled data in transfer learning. All face images are normalized to 256×256 according to five facial landmarks before input to the network.

To explicitly take the transferbility of different layers into account in the transfer learning process, we assign different learning rates to different levels of the network to capture the desired information and forget the specialized source domain knowledge contained in the pre-train model. We freeze the weights of the first three layers to maintain the general knowledge learned in the source domain. For intermediate layers, the initial learning rate is set to 0.001 which is helpful to add some fresh knowledge into these layers. With the purpose of forgetting the concepts learned for the specific mission in the source domain, the initial learning rates of the last three inception modules and the full-connected layer are all set to tenfold bigger than the intermediate layers. So these layers can learn more from the target domain data. All the learning rates are divided by 10 after 150,000 iterations.

3.3 Performance of Transfer FaceNet

After about 200,000 iterations, the learning of Transfer FaceNet slows down and the loss function reaches convergence. 81.2% top-1 accuracy is achieved on CASIA-Webface test set to identify 10,370 persons. Next, we will investigate whether the knowledge is transferred from source domain to target domain.

Fig. 3 (right) gives the visualization of the convolutional filters on the first layer of Transfer FaceNet. They are almost the same as those in original GoogleNet (Fig. 3, left), which indicates that most of the knowledge learned by early layers in the source network has been transferred to the one in the target domain.

Fig. 4 shows feature maps from the inception_3a/5×5 layer of original GoogleNet (left) and Transfer FaceNet (right). We can see that the response of face concepts like mouth and eyes is more visible in Transfer FaceNet than in GoogleNet (see last column of fourth row, for an example), which is instrumental in boosting the face recognition performance. Because of the intense learning on the top layers of Transfer FacceNet, these layers obtain sufficient specialized knowledge for face recognition. Fig. 5 gives the comparison between higher layers of original GoogleNet (left) and Transfer FaceNet (right). We can see that the response of the source model is focused on the entire face (for example, third column of second row), because the source task is object recognition with the purpose of distinguishing categories of the objects in images. It might tell you there is a person face in the image but not whom this person is. In contrast to the source model, concepts for identifying a particular person, like eyes, nose and mouth, are more clearly shown in the feature maps of Transfer FaceNet. Comparing feature maps of different persons (top *vs.* bottom) in Fig. 5, we can find that the inter-personal variations of feature maps produced by higher layer in source model is small, since in object recognition task, people are regarded as in the same class. However, the feature maps produced by higher layer of Transfer FaceNet for two persons have a significant difference and are focused on specific feature regions (e.g., eyes) in the face, as like feature-based visual attention does.

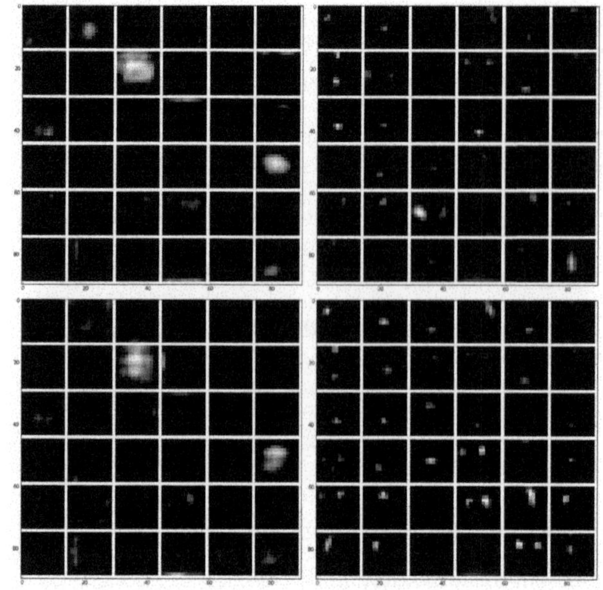

Figure 5: Visualization of the first 36 feature maps produced by the inception_4e/5×5 layer of original GoogleNet (left) and Transfer FaceNet (right) on images of Aaron Peirsol(top) and Abdel Nasser Assidi(bottom).

We test the Transfer FaceNet on LFW face verification task. 1024-dimensional representations in pool5_7×7/s1 layer of both the original GoogleNet and the Transfer FaceNet are extracted and then reduced to 300-D by PCA that is learned on CASIA-Webface dataset. Cosine distance is employed to measure the similarity between face representations. Finally, we achieve 97.24% single model face verification accuracy on LFW based on transfer learning, while only 63.40% verification accuracy is achieved by using features extracted from original GoogleNet. The training of our Transfer FaceNet only demands about 0.4 million training images and 96 hours using a Titan Black GPU. Such an amount of samples even can not make a brand new GoogleNet convergent in our experiments. A lot of more samples, such as 200 million images [19], is often required to train a GoogleNet from scratch.

4. SPECIALIZED FACENET

Whenever talking about face recognition, how to learn effective face representations closing the intra-personal distance and enlarging the inter-personal gap is always a key topic. To tackle such a challenging task, we follow the hints given by human vision process to capture feature-based and configural information from various global and local face regions, and then come up with an architecture consisting of 6 deep CNNs trained from scratch, namely, Specialized

FaceNet. Several tricks, such as Leaky ReLU and Batch Normalization, are applied to the training of Specialized FaceNet to make the training process efficient.

4.1 Global and local face patches

The top-down attention mechanism pays feature-based attention to the whole scene to highlight specific features and spatial attention to the surrounding area of feature regions for additional configural information. We train the multi-model system on various global and local face patches extracted from CASIA-Webface dataset (all face patches are converted to gray scale and aligned by five facial landmarks before feeding to the network) to simulate the mechanism. Afterwards we fuse multiple features extracted from these models for the face recognition task.

For global face patches, inspired by random crop (one form of data augmentation) [12], we randomly extract 88×88 and 74×74 patches from each 100×100 image which is a scale-down version of the 250×250 original face image and then double the number of patches by mirror operation. This not only increases the size of our training set which can avoid over fitting efficiently, but also improves the feature robustness for pose variations and face position offset. In feature extraction, only the central patch is used. We notice that to recognize a face, people often scan the face from one fixation location to another quickly, which can helps them to dig the spatial dependency information of facial configurations. Thus to simulate such a scan, we design 74×74 U-M-L (upper, middle and lower) local patches from top to bottom in 160×160 resized face images with a stride of 23 pixels. Fig. 6 depicts an example.

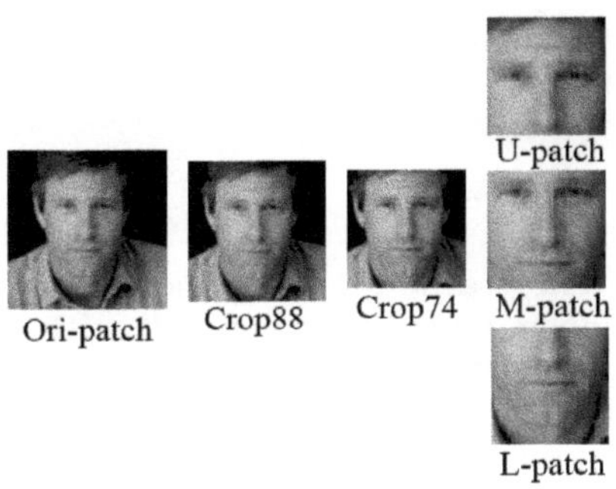

Figure 6: Global and local face patches. Original 250×250 images in CASIA-Webface (for training) and LFW (for testing) dataset are normalized by five facial landmarks and converted to gray scale.

4.2 Architecture of Specialized FaceNet

Specialized FaceNet consists of a set of 6 sub-networks. The basic element of Specialized FaceNet is borrowed from VGG net [20] that reduces the number of learnable parameters, maintains more spatial information, and enhances the nonlinearity of the network by using small convolutional size (3×3), small convolutional stride (1×1), small pooling window (2×2), and deep architecture.

To simulate feature-based attention to the whole scene to highlight specific features, a Siamese network, as shown in Fig. 7, is served as the subnet for each kind of global patches (Ori-patch, Crop88, and Crop74). Both face identification and verification supervision signals are applied to the Siamese network, because we think that to find specific features throughout a scene, a strong goal guidance is needed. The softmax layer is trained to identify 9,976 subjects in CASIA-Webface, while the contrastive layer learns to judge whether the persons in a pair of input images are the same. We get the same conclusion that dense and compact face feature is better than the sparse one, which is intuitively advocated in [26] and experimentally justified in [6]. So Leaky ReLU instead of ReLU is utilized after all convolutional layers but the Conv52.

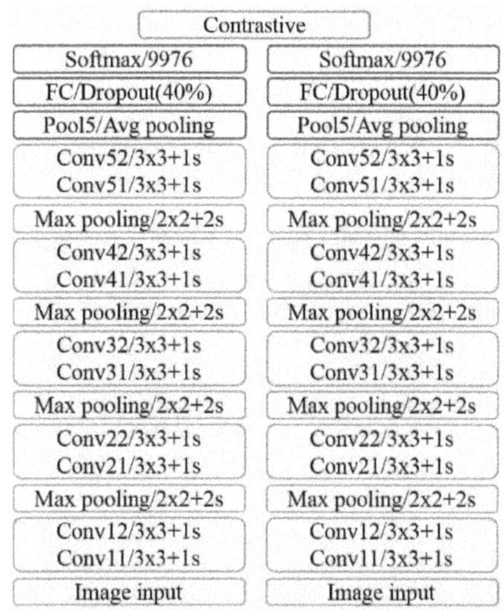

Figure 7: Siamese network with identification (softmax) and verification (contrastive) supervisory signals. Nets in the left and right have the same architecture but with different input face images (positive pair for the same identity, and negative one for different people).

ReLU can "die" if a large enough gradient changes the weights such that the neuron never activates on new data. Further, like the vanishing gradients problem, the learning of lower layers might be insufficient when training a deep ReLU network with constant 0 gradients. Leaky ReLU is first introduced in acoustic model [15] as an attempt to fix the "dying ReLU" problem which is defined as:

$$y = \max(0, Wx + b) + \alpha \min(0, Wx + b) \quad (1)$$

where α is a fixed parameter in the range $(0, +\infty)$. We set α to 0.01, which can avoid zero gradients and is potentially to "close the distance" between the top supervisory signals and the earlier convolutional layers.

The key aim of modeling on U-M-L local patches is to extract spatial dependency on facial configurations. Intuitively, human accomplishes this task by spatial saccades which move from one local face region to another quickly. This quick scan does not allow one to make much effort at each fixation location. To simulate this rough scanning process, we use three small networks (one branch of the structure shown in Fig. 7) respectively operating on U-M-L local patches to gather configural information of a face. Only identification supervision signal is used to train the small but efficient network with Leaky ReLU and Batch Normalization. The distribution of each layer's input may change during the training of deep neural networks. This phenomenon is called internal covariate shift (ICS). In the process of training deep CNNs based on U-M-L patches, ICS slows down the learning by requiring lower learning rates to ensure that loss drops smoothly. To address this problem, Batch Normalization (BN), which was first brought into use by [10], is applied to train the subnets on U-M-L patches.

4.3 Performance of Specialized FaceNet

The training set for the Siamese network includes 217,856 positive pairs (same person) and 217,856 negative pairs (different person), which are from face images of 9,976 subjects contained in CASIA-Webface. As for the models trained by the U-M-L patches, 386,468 images from 10,370 identities are used as training data. A 320-dimensional feature in pool5 layer is extracted and then reduced to 160-D by PCA. The similarity between two 160-dimensional face representations is measured by the Cosine distance.

The performance achieved by Siamese CNNs trained on global patches (Ori-patch and random crop patches) with Leaky ReLU or ReLU as activation function are presented in Table 1. Experiment results have indicated that Leaky ReLU typically boosts the result of the face verification task on LFW by 0.5%.

Table 1: Performance of Leaky ReLU and ReLU on LFW.

patch	Leaky ReLU(%)	ReLU(%)
Ori-patch	97.08	96.55
Crop88	97.31	96.74
Crop74	97.07	96.48

Table 2: Performance of U-M-L based CNNs.

patch	Cosine Distance(%)
U-patch	95.92
M-patch	96.02
L-patch	94.41

Table. 2 presents the performance of the CNNs trained on U-M-L patches. The accuracy of a single model is not satisfactory because these models are designed to capture spatial information with a relatively simple structure. However as shown in Fig. 8, the feature maps of these models present configural information that global patch based models cannot capture and boost the final result of the face verification task on LFW by 0.24%. Through the comparison between Fig. 5 (right) and Fig. 9, we can find that the response on a higher layer of Transfer FaceNet highlights specific features (e.g., eyes and mouth) on a face (similar effects can be observed from feature maps of heigher layers in global patch based Siamese networks), while feature maps on higher layer of a local patch based network are dense and reflect more information including the spatial correlation of facial components, such as the T-structure (e.g., Fig. 9, left), as like spatial attention does. During training process of the local patch based model, BN layer allows one to use a big learning rate to speed up convergence along with a steady loss decline, as shown in Fig. 10 for U-patch based model for instance. Although earlier drop of the learning rate can keep the loss to decrease without Batch Normalization, this will lead to performance degradation of the model.

The ROC curves of the Transfer and Specialized FaceNet are illustrated in Fig. 11. To further improve our system, we will propose the TS-Net in the next section, which combines the Transfer FaceNet and Specialized FaceNet.

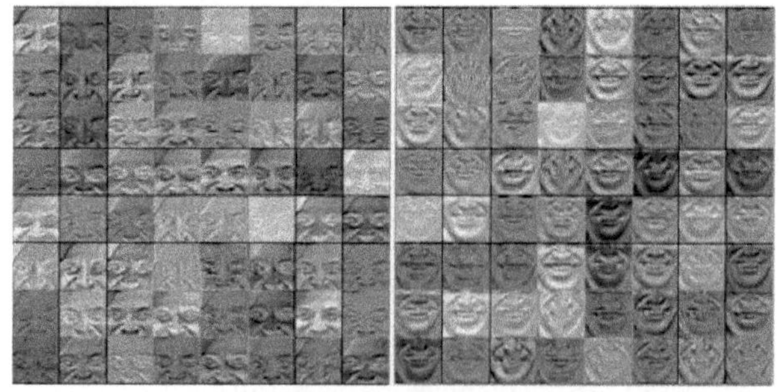

Figure 8: Visualization of feature maps output from Conv12 layer of the subnets of Specialized FaceNet trained by U-patch (left) and L-patch (right).

Figure 9: Visualization of feature maps output from Conv41 layer of the subnets of Specialized FaceNet trained by U-patch (left) and L-patch (right).

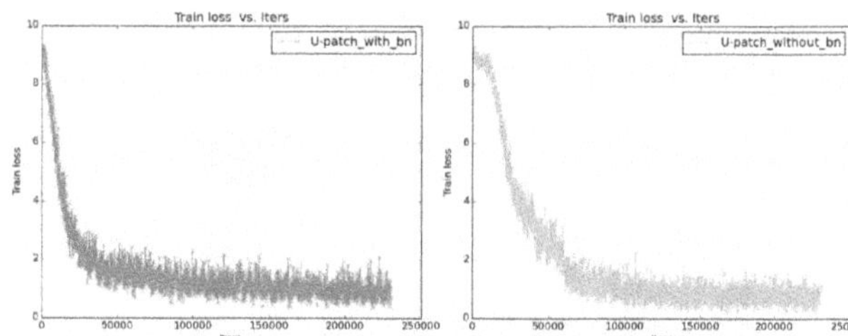

Figure 10: The training loss of the subnets of Specialized FaceNet trained on U-patch with (left) and without (right) Batch Normalization, *vs.* the number of iterations.

5. TS-NET

In this section, we propose a multi-model system, called TS-Net, by combining Transfer FaceNet with Specialized FaceNet, which achieves a high performance with reasonable memory and computation overhead. Joint Bayesian that has been highly successful in face verification [3] is applied to TS-Net.

A 1024-dimensional feature extracted from Transfer FaceNet and six 320-dimensional features produced by Specialized FaceNet are concatenated to form a 2,944 long vector, and then this vector is reduced to 300 dimensions by PCA as the final face representation. Joint Bayesian learned on the CASIA-Webface identities (exclusive from people in LFW) achieves 99.03% accuracy on LFW face verification task. The actual performance of TS-Net reaches 99.11% when excluding a few wrongly labeled test face pairs in LFW. The ROC curve of human performance [13] (using the cropped LFW images) and TS-Net are illustrated in Fig. 11. Predictably, performances of sub-models considering only one aspect of the knowledge are not as good as human. Merging transfer and specialized knowledge makes TS-Net outperform human, demonstrating the complementarity of those two kinds of knowledge.

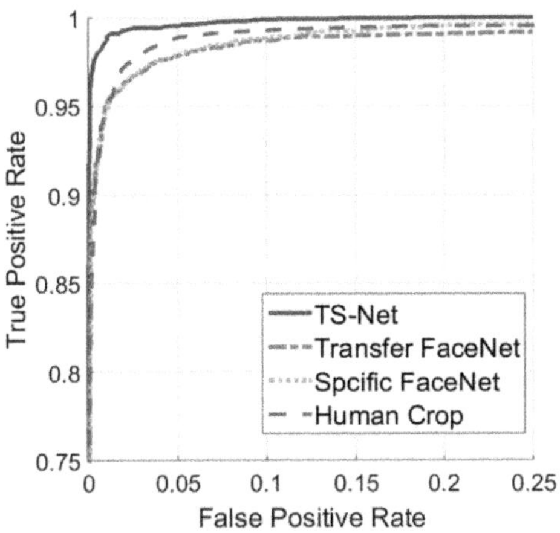

Figure 11: Performance comparisons between sub-models, human performance and TS-Net on LFW face verification task. Best viewed in color.

Using private face datasets for training, several existing systems achieved high performances on LFW (results and ROC curves are illustrated in Table. 3 and Fig. 12). DeepFace [24] trained on 4 million facial images with 3D alignment achieves 97.35% accuracy. DeepID2 [21] trained a total of 200 deep ConvNets and then selected 25 effective and complementary ConvNets form them to extract representations. With all the 25 selected ConvNets, DeepID2 achieves 98.97% accuracy. The result is increased from 98.97% to 99.15% through learning the Joint Bayesian model on each of the seven groups of features extract by selected models respectively (repeat the model selection algorithm for another six times) and fusing seven Joint Bayesian scores on each pair of compared faces by further learning a SVM. Based on DeepID2, DeepID2+ [22] increases final feature representation from 160 to 512 dimensions and enhances the supervision by connecting a 512-dimensional fully-connected layer to each of the four convolutional layers, and the accuracy is improved by 0.32%. TS-Net could achieve a promising result with only 300 dimensional features produced by 7 networks. FaceNet [19] achieves the highest accuracy of 99.63% by a model trained on a CPU cluster with 200 million images for about 2,000 hours. However, our TS-Net can be trained on a Titan-Z GPU with about 0.4 million images in a week, but achieves a comparable performance. TS-Net provides a reasonable compromise between performance and overhead.

To make a fair comparison, Table. 4 presents the results of approaches using the publicly available CASIA-Webface dataset as training data (the term "unsupervised" means that the model is not trained on LFW in a supervised way). Although the verification performance of MM-DFR-JB [6] is comparable to ours, their system is developed by a supervised way. For the more challenging task [25], face identification, experiment is made on 84,587 images of 2,003 identities in CASIA-Webface dataset. Four images of each identity outside the training set are selected to make up the probe set (8,012 images), and the other images compose the gallery set (76,575 images). TS-Net achieves 88.70% Rank-1 identification rate.

With the purpose of building a storage economic and fast face recognition system, we convert the face representation extracted from TS-Net to binary code by direct zero-thresholding and compare its face recognition ability with the original one. As shown in Table. 5, using the 300 dimensional binary features achieves 98.41% face verification accuracy on LFW (drops from 98.52%) and 87.51% Rank-1 identification rate on CASIA-Webface (drops from 88.70%) even by calculating the Cosine distance directly. A similar fact (97.47%) was reported in DeepID2+ with 512-D binary features and Hamming distance measure [22]. This is advantageous for practical retrieval system development.

Table 3: Performance comparison on LFW.

method	#Nets	accuracy(%)$\pm S_E$
High-dim LBP[4]	1	95.17±1.13
TL Joint Bayesian[2]	1	96.33±1.08
DeepFace[24]	7	97.35±0.25
DeepID2[21]	25	99.15±0.13
DeepID2+[22]	25	99.47±0.12
FaceNet[19]	1	99.63±0.09
TS-Nets	**7**	**99.03±0.27**

Table 4: Performance of CASIA-Webface based method on LFW.

method	accuracy(%)$\pm S_E$	protocol
From Scratch[26]	97.30±0.31	unsupervised
MM-DFR-JB[6]	99.02±0.19	supervised
TS-Nets	**99.03±0.27**	**unsupervised**

Table 5: Performance comparison of the original and binarized TS-Net features on LFW (verification) and CASIA-Webface (identification).

	Verification (%)	Identification (%)
binary	98.41	87.51
real	98.52	88.70

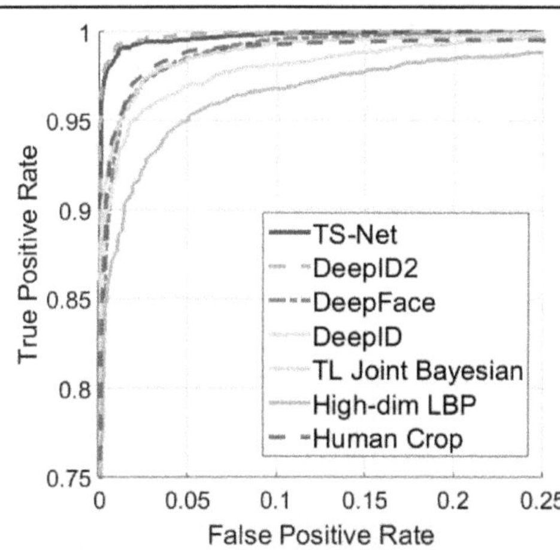

Figure 12: The ROC curves of various methods on LFW face verification task. Best viewed in color.

6. CONCLUSION

This paper proposes a high-performance TS-Net by simulating the transfer learning mechanism and the visual attention mechanism of human being. We offer an insight to transferability of different layers in GoogleNet, and selectively transfer its object-recognition capacity to face recognition, which reduces the dependence on big data as well as the computation consumption load in training. For specialized learning, we apply tricks including Leaky ReLU, Batch Normalization and Siamese network to train a set of CNNs on global and local face patches from scratch, which is economical to obtain robust, compact and discriminative face representations. In addition, visualization of TS-Net provides intuitive insights to help people to understand what this black box has learned. Further, the validity of the binary features is experimentally justified, which is implemental to develop practical face retrieval and recognition system.

7. ACKNOWLEDGMENT

This work is supported by Chinese National Natural Science Foundation (61532018, 61372169, 61471049), Special Funds of Beijing Municipal Co-construction Project, and Beijing Key Lab of Network System and Network Culture.

8. REFERENCES

[1] J. C. Bartlett and J. Searcy. Inversion and configuration of faces. *Cognitive psychology*, 25(3):281–316, 1993.

[2] X. Cao, D. Wipf, F. Wen, G. Duan, and J. Sun. A practical transfer learning algorithm for face verification. In *Computer Vision (ICCV), 2013 IEEE International Conference on*, pages 3208–3215. IEEE, 2013.

[3] D. Chen, X. Cao, L. Wang, F. Wen, and J. Sun. Bayesian face revisited: A joint formulation. In *Computer Vision–ECCV 2012*, pages 566–579. Springer, 2012.

[4] D. Chen, X. Cao, F. Wen, and J. Sun. Blessing of dimensionality: High-dimensional feature and its efficient compression for face verification. In *Computer Vision and Pattern Recognition (CVPR), 2013 IEEE Conference on*, pages 3025–3032. IEEE, 2013.

[5] D. J. Cook, L. B. Holder, and G. M. Youngblood. Graph-based analysis of human transfer learning using a game testbed. *Knowledge and Data Engineering, IEEE Transactions on*, 19(11):1465–1478, 2007.

[6] C. Ding and D. Tao. Robust face recognition via multimodal deep face representation. *arXiv preprint arXiv:1509.00244*, 2015.

[7] J. Donahue, Y. Jia, O. Vinyals, J. Hoffman, N. Zhang, E. Tzeng, and T. Darrell. Decaf: A deep convolutional activation feature for generic visual recognition. *arXiv preprint arXiv:1310.1531*, 2013.

[8] E. Goldstein. *Sensation and perception*. Cengage Learning, 2013.

[9] G. B. Huang, M. Ramesh, T. Berg, and E. Learned-Miller. Labeled faces in the wild: A database for studying face recognition in unconstrained environments. Technical report, Technical Report 07-49, University of Massachusetts, Amherst, 2007.

[10] S. Ioffe and C. Szegedy. Batch normalization: Accelerating deep network training by reducing internal covariate shift. *arXiv preprint arXiv:1502.03167*, 2015.

[11] Y. Jia. Caffe: An open source convolutional architecture for fast feature embedding, 2013.

[12] A. Krizhevsky, I. Sutskever, and G. E. Hinton. Imagenet classification with deep convolutional neural networks. In *Advances in neural information processing systems*, pages 1097–1105, 2012.

[13] N. Kumar, A. C. Berg, P. N. Belhumeur, and S. K. Nayar. Describable visual attributes for face verification and image search. *Pattern Analysis and Machine Intelligence, IEEE Transactions on*, 33(10):1962–1977, 2011.

[14] Z. Lei, S. Liao, M. Pietikäinen, and S. Z. Li. Face recognition by exploring information jointly in space, scale and orientation. *Image Processing, IEEE Transactions on*, 20(1):247–256, 2011.

[15] A. L. Maas, A. Y. Hannun, and A. Y. Ng. Rectifier nonlinearities improve neural network acoustic models. In *Proc. ICML*, volume 30, 2013.

[16] M. Oquab, L. Bottou, I. Laptev, and J. Sivic. Learning and transferring mid-level image representations using convolutional neural networks. In *Computer Vision and Pattern Recognition (CVPR), 2014 IEEE Conference on*, pages 1717–1724. IEEE, 2014.

[17] S. J. Pan and Q. Yang. A survey on transfer learning. *Knowledge and Data Engineering, IEEE Transactions on*, 22(10):1345–1359, 2010.

[18] O. Russakovsky, J. Deng, H. Su, J. Krause, S. Satheesh, S. Ma, Z. Huang, A. Karpathy, A. Khosla, M. Bernstein, et al. Imagenet large scale visual recognition challenge. *International Journal of Computer Vision*, pages 1–42, 2014.

[19] F. Schroff, D. Kalenichenko, and J. Philbin. Facenet: A unified embedding for face recognition and clustering. *arXiv preprint arXiv:1503.03832*, 2015.

[20] K. Simonyan and A. Zisserman. Very deep convolutional networks for large-scale image recognition. *arXiv preprint arXiv:1409.1556*, 2014.

[21] Y. Sun, Y. Chen, X. Wang, and X. Tang. Deep learning face representation by joint identification-verification. In *Advances in Neural Information Processing Systems*, pages 1988–1996, 2014.

[22] Y. Sun, X. Wang, and X. Tang. Deeply learned face representations are sparse, selective, and robust. *arXiv preprint arXiv:1412.1265*, 2014.

[23] C. Szegedy, W. Liu, Y. Jia, P. Sermanet, S. Reed, D. Anguelov, D. Erhan, V. Vanhoucke, and A. Rabinovich. Going deeper with convolutions. *arXiv preprint arXiv:1409.4842*, 2014.

[24] Y. Taigman, M. Yang, M. Ranzato, and L. Wolf. Deepface: Closing the gap to human-level performance in face verification. In *Computer Vision and Pattern Recognition (CVPR), 2014 IEEE Conference on*, pages 1701–1708. IEEE, 2014.

[25] Y. Taigman, M. Yang, M. Ranzato, and L. Wolf. Web-scale training for face identification. *arXiv preprint arXiv:1406.5266*, 2014.

[26] D. Yi, Z. Lei, S. Liao, and S. Z. Li. Learning face representation from scratch. *arXiv preprint arXiv:1411.7923*, 2014.

[27] R. K. Yin. Looking at upside-down faces. *Journal of experimental psychology*, 81(1):141, 1969.

Pooling Objects for Recognizing Scenes without Examples

Svetlana Kordumova, Thomas Mensink, Cees G.M.Snoek
University of Amsterdam, The Netherlands
{s.kordumova, tmensink, cgmsnoek}@uva.nl

ABSTRACT

In this paper we aim to recognize scenes in images without using any scene images as training data. Different from attribute based approaches, we do not carefully select the training classes to match the unseen scene classes. Instead, we propose a pooling over ten thousand of off-the-shelf object classifiers. To steer the knowledge transfer between objects and scenes we learn a semantic embedding with the aid of a large social multimedia corpus. Our key contributions are: we are the first to investigate pooling over ten thousand object classifiers to recognize scenes without examples; we explore the ontological hierarchy of objects and analyze the influence of object classifiers from different hierarchy levels; we exploit object positions in scene images and we demonstrate new scene retrieval scenarios with complex queries. Finally, we outperform attribute representations on two challenging scene datasets, SUNAttributes and Places2.

1. INTRODUCTION

This paper strives to recognize the scene of an image, such as *beach*, *supermarket* or *youth hostel*, without using any labeled scene example. Evidence from *supervised* scene recognition suggests that objects emerge in the representations learned from millions of labeled scene images [29], inspiring us to explore whether object classifiers can be leveraged to recognize scenes without examples.

The common approach to address classification without examples is to define scene-specific attributes, train attribute detectors and rely on an attribute-to-scene mapping for classification [12, 20, 10, 13]. In [12] for example, Lampert *et al.* use attribute annotations on images from the SUNAttributes [19] dataset, to learn attribute models and create attribute-to-scene mappings. Rather than relying on attributes and attribute-to-class mappings, recent works [9, 4] showed that events, actions and emoji's can be recognized without examples using a representation based on object classifier scores and object-class affinities estimated from a social media corpus [24]. Inspired by these efforts, we explore in this paper whether object classifier scores, together with a semantic embedding learned from social media, are as well a suitable representation for scene recognition without examples.

ICMR'16, June 06-09, 2016, New York, NY, USA
© 2016 ACM. ISBN 978-1-4503-4359-6/16/06...$15.00
DOI: http://dx.doi.org/10.1145/2911996.2912007

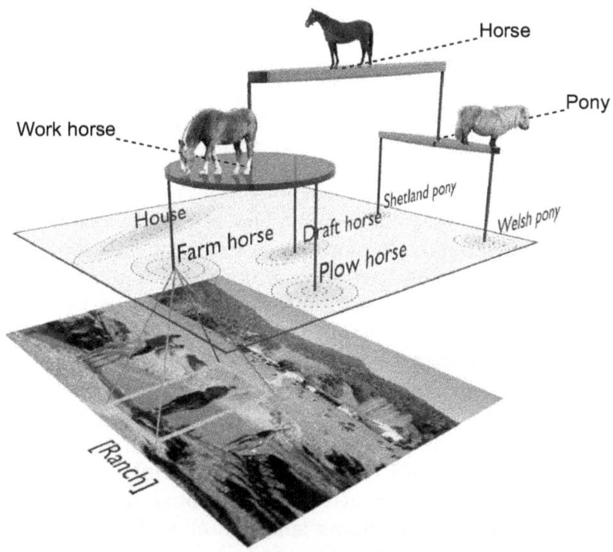

Figure 1: We investigate four approaches of object pooling for scene recognition without examples and rely on a freely available large-scale object corpus, social media text and an ontology.

Supervised image recognition is currently dominated by deep learning. Convolutional neural networks, the deeper the better [23, 8], learn the optimal image representation by tuning its millions of network parameters from huge amounts of labeled data, such as ImageNet [6] (for objects) or Places2 [30] (for scenes). In [29], Zhou *et al.* show evidence that objects emerge in deep nets learned from scene images. Motivating us to rely on a representation of objects to recognize scenes. By doing so we don't need any scene example. Our object classifiers correspond to the output of the last softmax layer of a very deep convolutional neural network trained on ImageNet [23]. These object classifiers have a lingual correspondence derived from nouns in WordNet [16], making them well suited for recognition without examples using a semantic word embedding, *e.g.* [15, 18, 22], as prior knowledge. Rather than simply using the response of all available object classifiers, we pose the question: *What objects to pool when representing scenes?*.

In [9] Jain *et al.* evaluate two methods for pooling object classifiers to recognize unseen actions in video; one based on the semantics of the class and the other based on the appearance of the test imagery. We adopt and adapt their methods for scene recognition in images. In addition, we introduce a hierarchical pooling taking into account the ontological relations of objects as defined in WordNet, see Figure 1. Finally, we also introduce a pooling that considers the spatial extent of object classifiers by exploiting a recent box proposal [32]. This spatial pooling allows to answer complex search queries like "finding beach scenes with a human on the right of the image". We evaluate our proposals on two scene datasets SUNAttributes [19] and Places2 [30].

2. RELATED WORK

The goal of recognition without examples, as introduced by Lampert *et al.* [12], is to recognize a set of unseen classes Z using some set of training classes Y, which do not overlap with the test classes ($Z \cap Y = \emptyset$). To allow for knowledge transfer in between, usually a set of attributes A is defined, which semantically relates to both the training classes Y and the unseen test classes Z. The attributes come with annotated examples X, forming a training dataset $D = \{X, Y, A\}$, from which attribute models are learned, and a human defined class-to-attribute mapping is used to transfer knowledge. In this paper, instead of manually and carefully choosing training classes Y and attributes A to well fit the characteristics of the unseen scene classes, like scene attributes [19], we investigate pooling off-the-shelf object classifiers derived from ImageNet [21], with 15K diverse object categories, to recognize scenes without examples.

Instead of relying on attributes, Norouzi [18] proposed to use a semantic embedding space to allow for knowledge transfer between the training classes Y and unseen classes Z. The semantic embedding space is trained to minimize the distance between words with similar semantics. We use the word2vec semantic embedding [15]. This is a single hidden layer neural network, trained to predict the surrounding words given an input word. The semantic embedding representation is a d-dimensional vector derived from the activation values of the hidden layer. This ensures that, the similarity between two words in the word2vec space will be close only if the words are found in similar semantic context. Cappallo *et al.* [4], show that a word2vec model trained using the textual data accompanied with images, works better than a model trained on Wikipedia, probably because of the more visual nature of these descriptions. We follow their approach and train on a large social media dataset [24], containing the surrounding text (tags, captions, *etc.*) of 100 million Flickr images. Although semantic embeddings have been used before for zero-shot learning [9, 18, 4] it has not yet been explored for objects and scenes.

To represent scene and object class names composed of multiple words, we aggregate them using Fisher vectors [5]. The Fisher vector characterizes each word by its deviation in the semantic embedding space *w.r.t.* a Gaussian mixture model. This has shown to perform better than simple word averaging [5], also in the context of recognizing actions and events in a zero-shot setting [9]. We use the Fisher vector for computing similarities between objects and scenes names.

The semantic structure defined by an ontology has been explored for many retrieval and classification problems. Fergus *et al.* [7] leverage the WordNet hierarchy to define semantic distance between any two categories, and use it to share labels for training classifiers. Zhu *et al.* [31] use the WordNet hierarchy to complete imprecise and incomplete social media tags by, transferring tag examples from child to parent nodes. When a tag occurs rarely in social media, Kordumova *et al.* use semantics from the WordNet ontology to enrich training data [11]. In [26] Vreeswijk *et al.*, compare training a classifier of a parent node with an union of their constituting child nodes. Different from these approaches, we investigate the WordNet hierarchy to steer the object representation in a semantic embedding for recognizing scenes without examples.

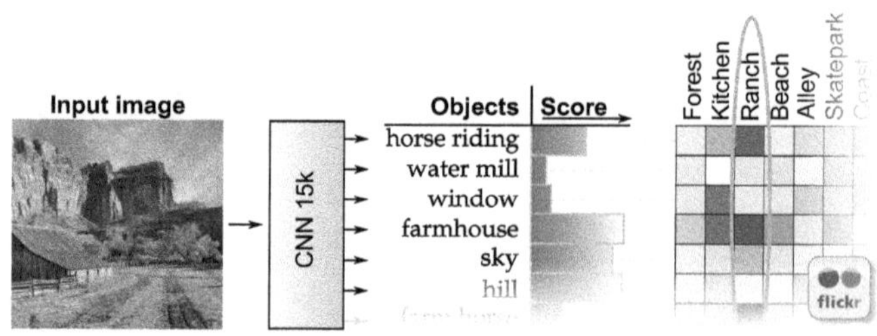

Figure 2: Flow of data when recognizing scenes without examples using object pooling. For an input test image we calculate its object prediction scores from a very deep convolutional neural network, learned to classify 15K objects from ImageNet. We calculate a knowledge transfer matrix between objects and scenes from a semantic similarity embedding learned using text of Flickr images. The scene with the highest score is assigned to the input test image.

Object proposals [2, 25, 32] suggest the most likely positions in an image to contain an object. Besides being successful in object detection, they have also proven to obtain better results for image retrieval and classification [27]. Inspired by [27], we use (unsupervised) object proposals with object classifiers trained on the whole image, for the task of recognizing scenes. We prefer object proposals over object detectors, for two reasons: detection increases the complexity of our approach, and limits the number of object categories to at most 1K, for which bounding box annotations are available. Encoding the spatial layout of objects allows us to answer complex queries, where instead of just querying with the scene name, we include object names and rough estimates of their position, like "finding castle scenes with grass on the bottom of the image". Different from other complex query approaches [28, 17, 14, 3], which all emphasize on word combinations, we propose a complex query with a scene, an object *and* its position. Next we describe our approach.

3. POOLING OBJECTS FOR SCENES

Our goal is to recognize unseen scenes Z, using a set of off-the-shelf object classifiers Y, which do not overlap with the scene classes, *i.e.* ($Z \cap Y = \emptyset$), and a semantic embedding space S. Similar to [18] we use a convex combination of object scores and semantic similarities to assign a class z to a test image v:

$$C(v) = \operatorname*{argmax}_{z \in Z} \sum_{y \in Y} s(z, y)\; p(y|v), \tag{1}$$

where $p(y|v)$ is the object prediction score for class y given test example v and $s(z, y)$ denotes the semantic similarity between unseen class z and object class y.

The object prediction $p(y|v)$ is the last network layer (after softmax normalization) of a very deep convolutional neural network [23]. We use 15K object categories from the ImageNet dataset, for which at least 200 images are available for training, similar to [9, 4].

The semantic similarity $s(z, y)$, is the cosine similarity between a scene z and an object y:

$$s(z, y) = cos(s(y), s(z)) = s(y)^\top s(z), \tag{2}$$

where $s(\cdot)$ denotes the d-dimensional Fisher vector encoding of a word2vec vector. We visualize the flow of data for recognizing a scene in an input image in Figure 2.

When considering off-the-shelf object classifiers, we expect that not all objects will contribute equally in describing scenes. ImageNet follows a hierarchical structure, derived from WordNet nouns, where objects like *animal, vehicle, plant, food* appear high in the hierarchy, followed by object categories like types of animals *cat, dog, bird, horse*, and fine-grained objects in the lowest level of the hierarchy, for example types of horses *tarpan, hackney, clydesdale*. However, it is not clear how specific the objects need to be in order to better retrieve scenes. We also expect that for different scenes, different objects should matter. To recognize a *beach* scene objects like *sand, ocean, sky* would be beneficial, whereas *bed, apple, church* would have a negligible or no influence. We describe and investigate four ways of pooling objects for scene recognition.

Semantic Pooling. This method considers the semantically closest objects for each scene class. Similarly as in [9], it does so by first ranking the objects based on their semantic similarity scores to a scene, calculated with Equation 2. For each scene $z \in Z$, we then select the closest objects, forming a subset of Y_z from the complete objects set Y:

$$Y_z = \{y \in Y \mid s_{yz} > t_s\}, \tag{3}$$

where t_s is a hyper parameter of selecting the objects with larger scene similarity, or the similarity value of the m-th closest object, so that we select the top m objects. In this case, for a test image, scene scores will be computed as in Equation 1, and only changing the summation over the set Y to the subset Y_z.

Appearance Pooling. A test image v is represented with probability values for each object category $p_{vy}, \forall y \in Y$. Each probability p_{vy} approximates the presence of an object of class y in the image. We follow [9, 18] and we sample only the prominent objects present in an image, resulting in a subset of objects:

$$Y_v = \{y \in Y \mid p_{vy} > t_p\}, \tag{4}$$

where t_p is a hyper parameter which regulates selecting objects with minimum presence probability in the image. To select the top m present objects, t_p takes the value of the $m - th$ ranked object. In this case, the scene scores of a test image will be computed as in Equation 1, with the only difference in the summation over the objects set, from Y to a subset Y_v. Doing so, we avoid summing over many unrelated object classes for an image with low probability scores, which do not appear in the image and will not contribute to the scene recognition.

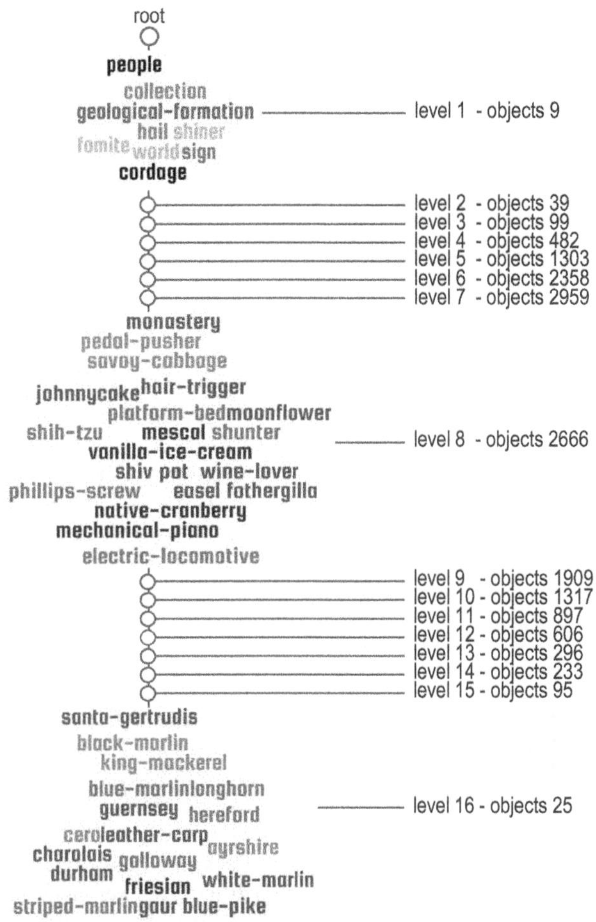

Figure 3: Flattened hierarchy tree of the ImageNet objects, indicating the number of objects per level. The first level contains very general objects, becoming more specific as the levels grow, narrowing down to fine-grained objects. We show word clouds of typical object names in the first, middle and last level.

Hierarchy Pooling. The hierarchical structure of objects portrays parent-child relationship of object categories, where the children objects are a subcategory of their parent class. The leaf nodes represent the most fine-grained object classes of their tree branch. We question how important are objects from different hierarchy levels for recognizing a scene. One would most naturally expect to find a *tree* in a *forest*, and a *sofa* in a *living room*, and to discriminate these two scenes the specificity of objects like *tree, sky, sofa, tv* would be sufficient, without going further into knowing the type of a tree. To discriminate a *bamboo forest* from a *broadleaf forests*, specific types of tree objects might matter.

The hierarchical structure of objects, as defined in the WordNet ontology, forms a tree. In Figure 3 we show a flattened tree version of a WordNet subspace, using only the nouns from ImageNet object categories. We denote as $L = \{L_1, ...L_k\}$ the set of all $k = 16$ tree levels from the flattened tree. Each level $L_i, i \in \{1, ..., k\}$ is a subset from all objects Y with depth i:

$$L_i = \{y \in Y \mid depth(y) = i\}. \tag{5}$$

For a new test example, we investigate how accurate will the objects from different levels predict its scene class. We use objects from each level separately by changing the summation over the set Y in Equation 1, to objects from only one level set L_i at a time.

Position Pooling. We employ [32] to generate bounding box coordinates over the image $[x_{min}, y_{min}, x_{max}, y_{max}]$, most likely to contain an object. For a test image, we exploit whether being more precise by object scoring the bounding box regions in an image, helps in recognizing the scene. Same as for the whole image, we use the last network layer with softmax normalization of [23], to compute object prediction scores on image regions. For m bounding boxes $\{b_i\}_{i=1}^{m}$, generated with an object proposal method, the object scores are $p(y|b_i), y \in Y$. There are multiple ways to pool object classifiers when objects scores of image regions are known. We employ two simple approaches, max pooling and average pooling. For max pooling, we consider object classifiers with the largest prediction scores from all generated positions in an image:

$$Y_b = \{y \in Y \mid max(p(y|b_1), ..., p(y|b_m)) > t_b\}, \quad (6)$$

where t_b is a hyper parameter, selecting the top scored objects among all image regions. For average pooling we consider object classifiers with average prediction scores of all bounding box positions in an image, larger then a value parameter t_a:

$$Y_a = \{y \in Y \mid avg(p(y|b_1), ..., p(y|b_k)) > t_a\}. \quad (7)$$

The position of objects in scene images allows for new scene retrieval scenarios. With a (textual) scene query, one can also specify what object(s) to be present, as well as where in the scene the object(s) should be. We choose three adjectives to approximate the *where* for horizontal position, *(left, center, right)*, and three for vertical position *(bottom, middle, top)*. Thus, an example query would be: *beach* with *human* on the *right*. We first find all images where the query scene was recognized, and then we rerank them based on the maximum prediction response for that object. If the query has specified also the object position, we consider object responses only from bounding boxes which center falls in that scene area. We compute the horizontal and vertical center of bounding boxes as $b_h = (x_{max} - x_{min})/2 + x_{min}$, and $b_v = (y_{max} - y_{min})/2 + y_{min}$. If I_h, I_w are the image width, height, and $t_w = I_w/3$, $t_h = I_h/3$, is one third of the image horizontal and vertical area, for (*left, center, right*) we consider the boxes which center falls in the intervals $(0, t_w), (t_w, 2t_w), (2t_w, I_h)$, and for (*bottom, middle, top*) we consider bounding boxes with center in the intervals $(0, t_h), (t_h, 2t_h), (2t_h, I_h)$ respectively.

We are now ready to evaluate our proposal quantitatively and qualitatively.

4. EXPERIMENTS

4.1 Datasets

SUNAttributes. The SUNAttributes dataset has 14,340 images hierarchically grouped in 3 levels [19]. Level 3 has 717 fine-grained scenes like *airplane cabin, athletic field outdoor, cybercafe.* Level 2 groups the fine-grained scenes in 16 categories like *shopping and dining* or *water, ice, snow,* and level 1 has three general categories of scenes *indoor, outdoor natural* and *outdoor man made.* Each of the 717 scenes in level 3 has 20 images per scene, which we use as test data. We scale all images to same dimension of 256x256 pixels.

The dataset also comes with 102 attribute annotations. When using attributes [12], the dataset is split into two parts of 10 random splits, where 90% of the images are used for attribute learning, and the rest for testing. We follow the same approach, and create 10 random splits. Because the data is split into disjoint train (90%), and test classes (10%), 71 classes of the dataset are present at test time for each random split. For our approach we only use the images from the test splits, since we do not need any scene images for learning. Same as in [12], we report results in accuracy. For scene level one and two, a prediction is considered correct if the ground truth class and the predicted class paths run through a common node in that level.

Places2. The Places2 dataset [30] contains more than 10 million images comprising 401 unique scene categories. The scene categories vary from indoor scenes like *bazaar indoor, cafeteria, toyshop,* and outdoor scenes like *bazaar outdoor, creek, desert sand.* The dataset features up to 30,000 training images and 50 validation images per class, scaled to 256x256 pixels. Since our goal is to retrieve scenes without any training example, we do not use the training set, and evaluate our approach on the validation set. This dataset was first released in the scene recognition subtask of the ImageNet 2015 challenge [21], and to the best of our knowledge, we are the first to report scene recognition results without examples on this dataset. As evaluation metric we report top-5 accuracy, as set by the challenge.

4.2 Implementation details

Object classifiers. We train an off-the-shelf deep convolutional network [23], with 22 layers, on all ImageNet categories having more than 200 images available for training. As object classifier scores we use the last network layer with softmax normalization. After removing 304 objects having an exact overlap in name with the scene classes, we end up with 14,989 object classifiers.

Object hierarchy. We use the parent-child noun relationships provided by WordNet [16] to construct a hierarchical tree[1]. The WordNet tree has 20 depth levels, from which we create a flattened subset version, where we take only the nouns that appear as object classes in ImageNet, and keep their depth position as in WordNet. Besides the *sun* object which appears in the second level, the first four levels do not contain objects from ImageNet. Therefore, we ignore them, and start counting from the fifth as a first level, resulting in a 16-level flattened tree, see again Figure 3, with ImageNet objects only.

Objects positions. We generate object positions with EdgeBoxes [32]. As we observe a stable recall, we use the top 25% of bounding boxes after ranking by their objectness score. The number of bounding boxes varies per image, between 2 and 1025 for SUNAttributes, and between 1 and 1077 for Places2. We also employ the common non-maximal suppression on the sorted boxes with an overlap threshold of 0.5 [32, 2, 25].

Semantic embedding. We train a 500-dimensional skipgram word2vec model using the metadata of the YFCC100M dataset [24]. This dataset has 100 million Flickr images accompanied with titles, descriptions and tags. We encode the word2vec vectors with Fisher vectors, following the setting

[1]Visualisation: *isis-data.science.uva.nl/svetlana/WordNetTree*

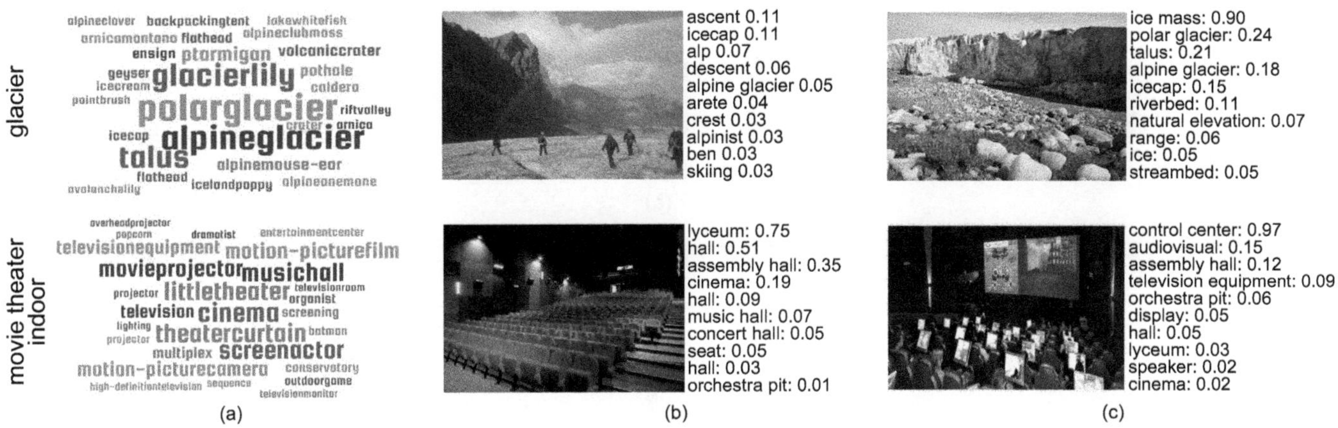

Figure 4: Pooled objects for two scenes, (a) word clouds of semantically pooled closest objects, (b) and (c) image examples with their top-scoring object predictions. With appearance pooling, the correct scene was assigned to the images in (b), whereas in (c) the *glacier* image was misclassified as *ice shelf* scene, and the *movie theater indoor* image as a *steel mill* scene. This happens when the top predicted objects in an image are closer in the semantic embedding space to the misclassified scenes. Overall, all pooled objects look reasonable.

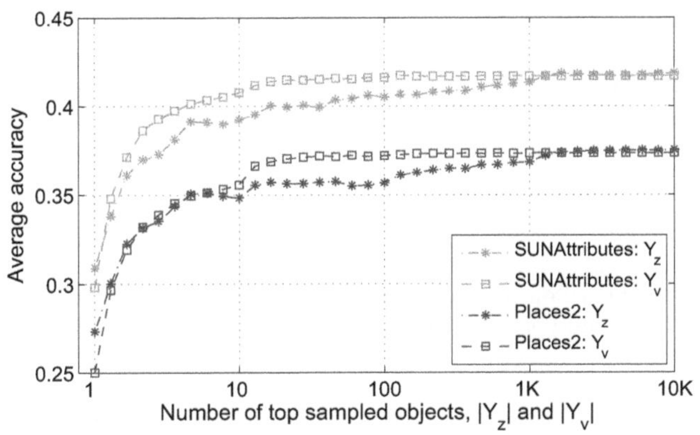

Figure 5: Impact of the number of semantically closest objects per scene $|Y_z|$, and most prominent objects per image $|Y_v|$, for scene recognition with no examples on the SUNAttributes and Places2 datasets.

of [9]. We learn k=2 Gaussian Mixture components, apply PCA to reduce the dimensionality by a factor of 2, and use only the partial derivatives *w.r.t* the mean. In this way, the encoded word2vec Fisher vector keeps the dimensionality, $d = 500$, as the original word2vec.

4.3 Semantic pooling and appearance pooling

We first investigate semantic pooling and appearance pooling, where the first selects the semantically closest objects to scenes Y_z, and the second the most prominent objects per image Y_v. We show pooled object examples for two scenes in Figure 4. We vary the threshold parameters, t_z and t_v, in a way that we select the top m ranked objects, where $m = |Y_z|$ or $m = |Y_v|$. In both cases, we see similar pattern in the results, see Figure 5.

When only selecting the single most semantically similar object per scene, $|Y_z| = 1$, the average accuracy for SUNAttributes is 30.91%, and for Places2 is 27.32%. When compared to random accuracy, 1.41% and 0.25% respectively, the results indicate that even one object per scene can help in discriminating scenes. As we sample more objects the accuracy improves. Up to 10 objects it grows rapidly, followed by a slow progress, which saturates after about 1K sampled objects. If we select the single most prominent object in an image, $|Y_v| = 1$, the accuracy for SUNAttributes is 29.82%, and for Places2 is 25.02%. Thus, when one object is selected, the most semantically similar one is more informative than the most prominent one. However, as we sample more prominent objects, the accuracy comes close to the maximum after only 100 objects are selected.

Object classifiers recognize scenes without examples reasonably. We expect that as object classifiers improve further [8], the more accurate the scene recognition without examples will become. From now on we use the 100 most prominent objects in an image to recognize its scene.

4.4 Hierarchy pooling

Here we investigate what is the discriminative power of objects from different hierarchy levels when recognizing scenes without examples. In Figure 6 (a), we show results when we pool objects from each level individually. Interestingly, the top- and low-level objects show lowest accuracy. The top-levels contain mostly general object categories, and the low-levels have fine-grained object categories, see Figure 3. From the results we conclude that general and fine-grained object categories from the top- and low-levels of the ImageNet hierarchy, are not discriminative for recognizing scenes. The objects from level 6 and 7 show best performance. If we use objects from only these two levels, in total 5317, or one third of all objects, we already achieve an accuracy of 32.5% for Places2, and 34.5% for SUNAttributes.

The number of objects in each level varies. In our experiments we use the top 100 most prominent objects in an image. Level 1,2,3,15,16 contain less than 100 objects, thus, we believe that the number of objects present might also influence the scene recognition. Therefore, we perform two additional experiments where we investigate what happens

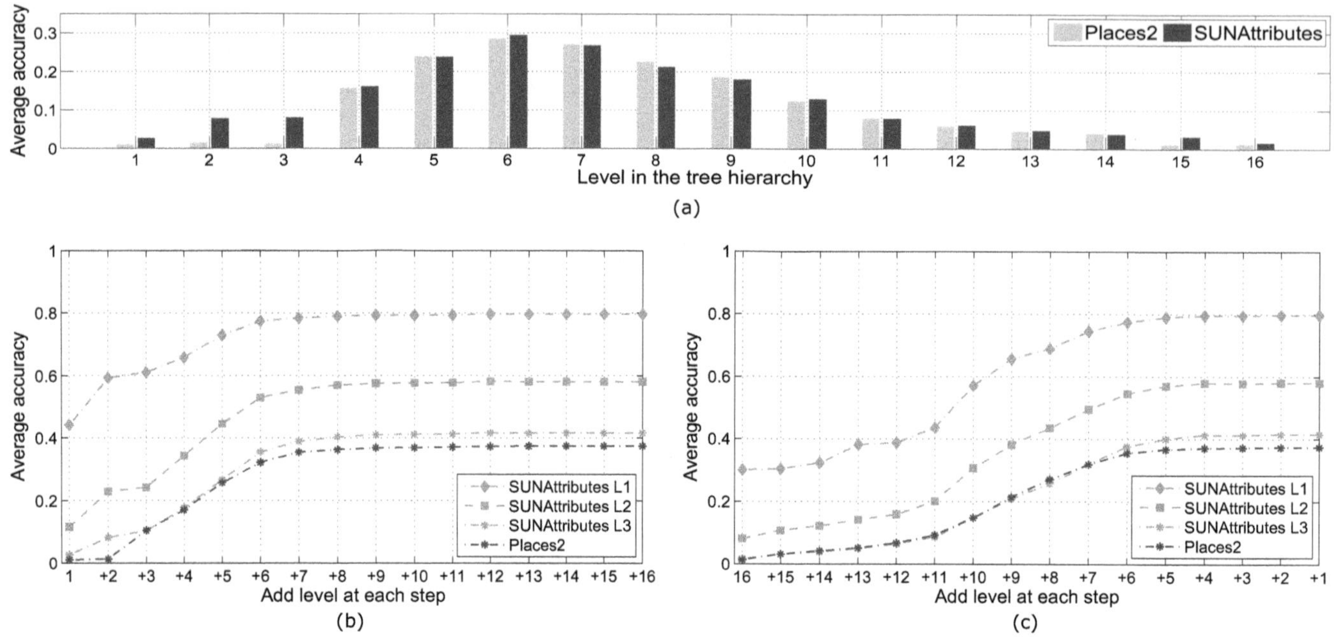

Figure 6: Scene recognition without examples using a representation containing classification scores from ImageNet objects, where we vary the objects in the representation using hierarchy levels. In (a), each hierarchy level forms one object representation, and we show results on Places2, and Level3 SUNAttribute scenes. Object classifiers from the middle levels are most discriminative, whereas the first levels (general objects), and the last levels (fine-grained objects), are not discriminative for recognizing scenes. In (b), in each step objects from the next level of the hierarchy are added, and in (c) in each step objects from the previous level of the hierarchy are added. Again we conclude that the objects from the middle level contribute the most for discriminating scenes.

if in each step we add objects from the next level, and see how much each level contributes. We first start from level one, and continue adding up objects from the next levels until all objects are used. We show the results in Figure 6 (b), for Places2 scene categories, as well as for all three scene levels of SUNAttributes. We see a similar pattern for all scene categories. The average recognition accuracy grows substantially up to level eight. From the ninth level on, there is minor growth in the accuracy. This again confirms that the lower levels do not add extra information which contributes for the recognition of scenes. As we go the other way around, we start from the lowest level and add up objects from the previous levels, see Figure 6 (c), the results confirm the previous findings. The fine-grained object classifiers have a small contribution for discriminating scenes, middle level objects help the most, and the general objects from the top levels do not contribute in recognizing scenes.

4.5 Position pooling

When we sample the top 100 objects by average pooling over image positions, as generated with EdgeBoxes, we get slightly better results than max pooling, 32.57% vs 32.31% for SUNAttributes, and 31.87% vs 31.35% for Places2. When we merge pooled objects from image positions, for $t_a = 0.3$, with objects pooled from the whole image, the scores do not change much. For SUNAttributes it changes from 41.62% to 41.46%, and for Places2 from 37.23% to 37.63%, for appearance and apperance+position pooling respectively. When we look into individual scene accuracy, in some cases position pooling helps, whereas in others, appearance pooling from the whole image is enough. For example the objects *milldam* and *waterspout* pooled from positions, helped to correctly classify a *dam* scene which was misclassified as *river*. In another example, a *field cultivated* image was misclassified into a *pasture* scene, when the objects *geyser, waterspout, parhelion, cloud, azure,...* were pooled from image positions. We did not find a general rule on when position pooling helps over the whole image, and since it requires more processing, we recommend to use appearance pooling from the whole image only.

A more interesting benefit of knowing the object positions is that they allow retrieval with complex queries. In Figure 7 we show qualitative results for four different queries, two with scene+object and two with scene+object+position. We show the top and bottom retrieved images for each query. For the top retrieved images we also draw the bounding box which contributes the most for the object. We do not show bounding boxes on the lowest ranked images, since the object is not present, the object scores are low and do not make sense. Interestingly, the top retrieved scenes contain the object we query with. When an object position is specified, like *right* or *bottom* as in the last two queries in Figure 7, the most contributing bounding box of the object in the top retrieved images, comes from the *right* or *bottom* area in the scene. The bottom ranked images, in all cases are missing the object we query with from the scene. Thus, we observe that knowing the object positions in scene images can indeed be used for retrieving images with complex queries of scenes, objects and their spatial extent.

Figure 7: Top and bottom ranked images when as query we use scenes+object (first two rows), and scenes+object+position (last two rows). Over the top retrieved images we draw the bounding box which contributes the most for finding the object. We do not show bounding boxes on the lowest ranked images, since the objects are not present and the object scores are low, so it does not make sense. Interestingly, the top ranked images are quite relevant to the query, and when the object position is specified, the filtered bounding boxes from only that area in the image indeed help. The bottom ranked images, in all cases are missing the object we query with from the scene.

4.6 Comparison with attributes

Finally we compare pooling off-the-shelf objects with attribute representations for recognizing scenes without examples. We report all results in Table 1.

Our object pooling performs better than the direct attribute prediction (DAP) reported by Lampert *et al.* [12], 41.63% vs 22.20%, on the SUNAttributes dataset. Since their results were calculated using GIST and HOG features, we repeat their experiment with our convolutional neural network features, for fair comparison. We take features from the layer before the last one, of the same network we use throughout all our experiments. We L_2 normalize the features, and for each attribute we learn a linear binary classifier with libsvm and probability outputs. In this setting, the DAP approach improves from 22.20% to 34.78% on SUNAttributes. Still the result does not go over our accuracy with object pooling.

We can not report results with DAP on Places2, since this approach requires attribute-to-scene mapping, which is not available on this dataset. Instead, we investigate how attributes work with a semantic embedding [18], when attribute annotations are missing. For all 102 attribute names of SUNAttributes we find their match among the 15K objects. 22 attributes have an exact name match, and for 80 we use the closest object, like *sailing/boating* with *sailboat*, or *sunbathing* with *sunbather*. As expected, the attributes with semantic embedding perform lower then a DAP setting, with an accuracy of 10.07% on SUNAttributes (71 classes), and 1.27% on the more challenging Places2 dataset (401 classes). The results are comprehensible, since there are only 102 attributes, and in our setting we use 100 objects pooled from a set of 15K object classifiers.

We also consider an upper limit comparison with a supervised alternative. The best reported number on the 2015 Places2 challenge [1] with supervised deep learning is 83.12%, and with our method, where no scene examples are used, we achieve an accuracy of 42.72%. While encouraging, there is a lot of space left for further improvement.

We conclude, rather than using attributes scenes are better recognized without examples by pooling relevant objects from the image representation, when a large corpus of object classifiers is available, and with a semantic embedding learned from a large social media corpus to guide the knowledge transfer between objects and scenes.

5. CONCLUSIONS

In this paper we recognize scenes without examples by using off-the-shelf object classifiers from a large collection of 15K object classes. We pose the question *what objects to pool when representing scenes?*. Throughout extensive analysis by experiments on two large-scale scene datasets we conclude that object classifiers from a large objects collection are suited for scene recognition without examples. From the four pooling methods considered we recommend object pooling by appearance, as it requires only 100 objects per image. General and fine-grained object categories, from the top and bottom level of the WordNet hierarchy, do not contribute much for scene recognition and can be avoided in the image representation. When the object classifiers are run on object proposals instead of the full image, our proposal allows for complex queries including position

	SUN Attributes	Places2
Random	1.41	0.25
Attributes DAP [12]	22.20 ± 1.60	n.a.
Using deep learning:*		
Attributes DAP [12]	34.78 ± 2.54	n.a.
Attributes-Embedding [18]	10.07 ± 2.22	1.27
Object pooling	$\mathbf{41.63 \pm 3.16}$	**37.46**

Table 1: Comparison of object pooling by appearance vs attributes for recognizing scenes without examples. Between the lines marked with deep learning*, we show results which are not available in the cited papers, but computed using their approach with our deep learning setting. Object pooling recognizes scenes better then attribute representations on both datasets.

quantifiers, like "finding beach scenes with a human on the right of the image". Finally, object pooling outperform attribute representation for scene recognition without examples, with the additional benefit of learning the knowledge transfer from social multimedia, rather than manually specifying the scene-to-attribute mappings.

Acknowledgments. This research is supported by the STW STORY project, the NWO VENI What&Where project and the Dutch national program COMMIT. Thanks to Morris Franken for helping with the visualisations.

6. REFERENCES

[1] http://places2.csail.mit.edu/results2015.html.

[2] B. Alexe, T. Deselaers, and V. Ferrari. Measuring the objectness of image windows. *PAMI*, 34(11):2189–2202, 2012.

[3] D. Borth, R. Ji, T. Chen, T. Breuel, and S.-F. Chang. Large-scale visual sentiment ontology and detectors using adjective noun pairs. In *MM*, 2013.

[4] S. Cappallo, T. Mensink, and C. Snoek. Image2emoji: Zero-shot emoji prediction for visual media. In *MM*, 2015.

[5] S. Clinchant and F. Perronnin. Textual similarity with a bag-of-embedded-words model. In *ICTIR*, 2013.

[6] J. Deng, W. Dong, R. Socher, L.-J. Li, K. Li, and L. Fei-Fei. ImageNet: A Large-Scale Hierarchical Image Database. In *CVPR*, 2009.

[7] R. Fergus, H. Bernal, Y. Weiss, and A. Torralba. Semantic label sharing for learning with many categories. In *ECCV*, 2010.

[8] K. He, X. Zhang, S. Ren, and J. Sun. Deep residual learning for image recognition. 2016.

[9] M. Jain, J. van Gemert, T. Mensink, and C. Snoek. Objects2action: Classifying and localizing actions without any video example. In *ICCV*, 2015.

[10] D. Jayaraman and K. Grauman. Zero-shot recognition with unreliable attributes. In *NIPS*, 2014.

[11] S. Kordumova, J. van Gemert, and C. Snoek. Exploring the long tail of social media tags. In *MMM*, 2016.

[12] C. Lampert, H. Nickisch, and S. Harmeling. Attribute-based classification for zero-shot visual object categorization. *PAMI*, 36(3):453–465, 2013.

[13] H. Li, D. Li, and X. Luo. Bap: Bimodal attribute prediction for zero-shot image categorization. In *MM*, 2014.

[14] X. Li, C. Snoek, M. Worring, and A. Smeulders. Harvesting social images for bi-concept search. *TMM*, 14(4):1091–1104, 2012.

[15] T. Mikolov, I. Sutskever, K. Chen, G. Corrado, and J. Dean. Distributed representations of words and phrases and their compositionality. In *NIPS*, 2013.

[16] G. A. Miller. Wordnet: A lexical database for english. In *CACM*, 1995.

[17] L. Nie, S. Yan, M. Wang, R. Hong, and T.-S. Chua. Harvesting visual concepts for image search with complex queries. In *MM*, 2012.

[18] M. Norouzi, T. Mikolov, S. Bengio, Y. Singer, J. Shlens, A. Frome, G. Corrado, and J. Dean. Zero-shot learning by convex combination of semantic embeddings. In *ICLR*, 2014.

[19] G. Patterson, C. Xu, H. Su, and J. Hays. The SUN attribute database: Beyond categories for deeper scene understanding. *IJCV*, 108(1-2):59–81, 2014.

[20] B. Romera-Paredes and P. Torr. An embarrassingly simple approach to zero-shot learning. In *ICML*, 2015.

[21] O. Russakovsky, J. Deng, H. Su, J. Krause, S. Satheesh, S. Ma, Z. Huang, A. Karpathy, A. Khosla, M. Bernstein, A. C. Berg, and L. Fei-Fei. ImageNet Large Scale Visual Recognition Challenge. *IJCV*, 115(3):211–252, 2015.

[22] T. Schnabel, I. Labutov, D. Mimno, and T. Joachims. Evaluation methods for unsupervised word embeddings. In *EMNLP*, 2015.

[23] C. Szegedy, W. Liu, Y. Jia, P. Sermanet, S. Reed, D. Anguelov, D. Erhan, V. Vanhoucke, and A. Rabinovich. Going deeper with convolutions. In *CVPR*, 2015.

[24] B. Thomee, B. Elizalde, D. Shamma, K. Ni, G. Friedland, D. Poland, D. Borth, and L.-J. Li. YFCC100M: The new data in multimedia research. *CACM*, 59(2):64–73, 2016.

[25] J. Uijlings, K. van de Sande, T. Gevers, and A. Smeulders. Selective search for object recognition. *IJCV*, 104(2):154–171, 2013.

[26] D. Vreeswijk, K. van de Sande, C. Snoek, and A. Smeulders. All vehicles are cars: Subclass preferences in container concepts. In *ICMR*, 2012.

[27] L. Xie, Q. Tian, R. Hong, and B. Zhang. Image classification and retrieval are one. In *ICMR*, 2015.

[28] J. Yuan, Z.-J. Zha, Y.-T. Zheng, M. Wang, X. Zhou, and T.-S. Chua. Learning concept bundles for video search with complex queries. In *MM*, 2011.

[29] B. Zhou, A. Khosla, A. Lapedriza, A. Oliva, and A. Torralba. Object detectors emerge in deep scene cnns. In *ICLR*, 2015.

[30] B. Zhou, A. Khosla, A. Lapedriza, A. Torralba, and A. Oliva. Places2: A large-scale database for scene understanding. In *arXiv*, 2015.

[31] S. Zhu, C.-W. Ngo, and Y.-G. Jiang. Sampling and ontologically pooling web images for visual concept learning. *TMM*, 14(4):1068–1078, 2012.

[32] C. L. Zitnick and P. Dollár. Edge Boxes: Locating Object Proposals from Edges. In *ECCV*, 2014.

Multilingual Visual Sentiment Concept Matching

Nikolaos Pappas
Idiap Research Institute
Martigny, Switzerland
npappas@idiap.ch

Miriam Redi
Yahoo Inc.
London, United Kingdom
redi@yahoo-inc.com

Mercan Topkara
JW Player
New York, NY, USA
mercan@jwplayer.com

Brendan Jou
Columbia University
New York, NY, USA
bjou@ee.columbia.edu

Hongyi Liu
Columbia University
New York, NY, USA
hongyi.liu@columbia.edu

Tao Chen
Columbia University
New York, NY, USA
taochen@ee.columbia.edu

Shih-Fu Chang
Columbia University
New York, NY, USA
sfchang@ee.columbia.edu

ABSTRACT

The impact of culture in visual emotion perception has recently captured the attention of multimedia research. In this study, we provide powerful computational linguistics tools to explore, retrieve and browse a dataset of 16K multilingual affective visual concepts and 7.3M Flickr images. First, we design an effective crowdsourcing experiment to collect human judgements of sentiment connected to the visual concepts. We then use word embeddings to represent these concepts in a low dimensional vector space, allowing us to expand the meaning around concepts, and thus enabling insight about commonalities and differences among different languages. We compare a variety of concept representations through a novel evaluation task based on the notion of *visual semantic relatedness*. Based on these representations, we design clustering schemes to group multilingual visual concepts, and evaluate them with novel metrics based on the crowdsourced sentiment annotations as well as visual semantic relatedness. The proposed clustering framework enables us to analyze the full multilingual dataset in-depth and also show an application on a facial data subset, exploring cultural insights of portrait-related affective visual concepts.

Keywords

Multilingual; Language; Cultures; Cross-cultural; Emotion; Sentiment; Ontology; Concept Detection; Social Multimedia

1. INTRODUCTION

Everyday, billions of users from all around the world share their visual memories in online photo sharing platforms. Web users speak hundreds of different languages, come from different countries and backgrounds. Such multicultural diversity also results in users representing the visual world in very different ways. For instance, [1] showed that Flickr users with different cultural backgrounds use different concepts to describe visual emotions. But how can we build tools to analyze and retrieve the multimedia data generated by such a diverse population?

ICMR'16, June 06-09, 2016, New York, NY, USA
© 2016 ACM. ISBN 978-1-4503-4359-6/16/06...$15.00
DOI: http://dx.doi.org/10.1145/2911996.2912016

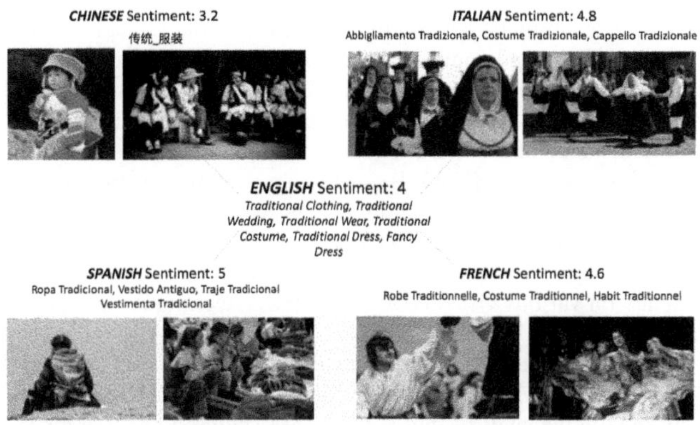

Figure 1: Example images from four languages from the same "traditional clothing" cluster. Even though all images are tagged with semantically similar concepts, each culture interprets such concepts with different visual patterns and sentimental values.

Multimedia retrieval in a multilingual and multicultural environment cannot be independent of the spoken language used by users to describe their visual content. For example, among the vast content of photo sharing platforms such as in Flickr, it is easy to find pictures of traditional costumes from all around the world. However, a basic keyword search, e.g. *traditional costumes*, would not return multiculturally rich results: the returned content would very likely come from Western countries, especially from countries where English is the primary language. The problem we tackle is to analyze, index and develop a deeper understanding of multicultural content in the context of a large social photo sharing platform. A purely image-based analysis would not provide a complete understanding as it clusters visually-similar images together, missing the differences between cultures, e.g. how an *old house* or *good food* look in each culture. We mitigate the problems of pure image-based analysis with the aid of analytical language tools.

In this paper, we focus on one dimension which characterizes users' cultural background, namely their spoken language, and we build the first complete framework for analyzing, exploring, and retrieving multilingual emotion-biased visual concepts. This allows to retrieve examples of concepts such as *traditional costumes* from visual collections of different languages (see Fig. 1). Our goal is to study the lexical differences of sentiment-biased visual concepts across multiple languages from the MVSO dataset [1]. Complementarily, we also seek to investigate the visual differences for images related to similar visual concepts across languages. To achieve this, it is essential to match lexical expressions of concepts from one language to another. One way to achieve this is through *exact matching*, arising from the translation of all languages to a single one, e.g. English. However, given that lexical choices for the same concepts vary across languages, the exact matching of multilingual concepts has a small coverage across languages. To overcome this sparsity issue, we propose an *approximate matching* approach. We represent multilingual concepts in a common semantic embedding based on pre-trained word embeddings. This allows us to compute the semantic proximity or distance between visual concepts and cluster concepts from multiple languages. Furthermore, the approximate matching enables a better connectivity between visual concepts of different languages. This allows discovery of multilingual clusters of visual concepts, whereas exact matching clusters are mostly dominated by a single language.

The contributions of our work can be summarized as follows:
(1) We design a crowdsourcing experiment to annotate the sentiment score of visual concepts from 11 languages in MVSO, and make the resulting data publicly available.
(2) We evaluate and compare a variety of unsupervised distributed word and concept representations. To do so, we define a novel evaluation metric called *visual semantic relatedness*, defined as the cosine distance of the multilingual concept co-occurrence on real-world images from MVSO. By analyzing sentiment values across languages and their translations, we prove the need of effective multilingual sentiment analysis tools.
(3) We design new tools to evaluate sentiment and semantic consistency on various visual concept clustering techniques that allow us to organize MVSO in an hierarchical manner by obtaining rich multilingual clusters of affective concepts.
(4) We demonstrate the applicability of the proposed approaches with qualitative analysis and a novel case study on analyzing portrait images in MVSO. We find that Eastern and Western languages tend to attach different visual concepts to portrait images, but that many languages similarly attach positive concepts to face pictures.

2. RELATED WORK

Research on distributed word representations [3, 4, 5, 6] have recently extended to multiple languages either by using bilingual word alignments or parallel corpora to transfer linguistic information from multiple languages. For instance, [7] proposed to learn distributed representations of words across languages by using a multilingual corpus from Wikipedia. [8, 9] proposed to learn bilingual embeddings in the context of neural language models utilizing multilingual word alignments. [10] proposed to learn joint-space embeddings across multiple languages without relying on word alignments. Similarly, [11] proposed auto-encoder-based methods to learn multilingual word embeddings. A limitation when dealing with many languages is the scarcity of data for all pairs. In this study, we use a pivot language to align the multiple languages using machine translation.

To our knowledge, the visual context of sentiment concepts for evaluating multilingual embeddings have not been considered before. However, studies on multimodal distributional semantics have combined visual and textual features to learn more informed word embeddings and have used the notion of semantics [12, 13] and visual similarity to evaluate word embeddings [14, 15]. Furthermore, there are studies which have combined language and vision for image caption generation and retrieval [16, 17, 18, 19] based on multimodal neural language models. We argue that our evaluation metric is a rich resource for learning more informed multimodal embeddings which can benefit these systems. Perhaps the most related study to ours is in [20] which aimed to learn visually grounded word embeddings to capture visual notions of semantic relatedness using abstract visual scenes. Our differences are that we focus on

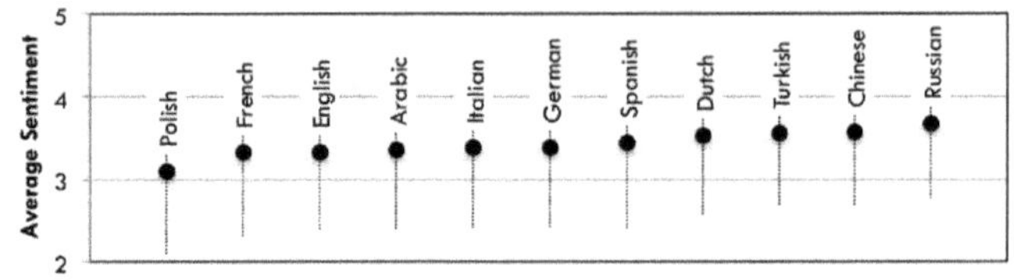

Figure 2: Crowdsourced visual sentiment per language in MVSO.

sentiment concepts and we define visual semantic relatedness based on real-world images which are annotated by community users of Flickr instead of abstract scenes.

3. VISUAL SENTIMENT OF CONCEPTS

In this work, we make use of the MVSO dataset [1]. One drawback of MVSO is that the sentiment scores assigned to affective visual concepts were automatically inferred through sentiment analysis tools. Although such tools have achieved impressive performances in the recent years, they are typically based on text modalities alone. To counter this, we designed a crowdsourcing experiment with CrowdFlower[1] to annotate the sentiment of the multilingual adjective-noun pairs (ANPs) in MVSO. We considered 11 out of 12 languages in MVSO, leaving out Persian due to the limited number of ANPs. We constructed separate tasks for each language, using all ANPs in MVSO for that language.

Task Interface. We asked crowdsourcing workers to evaluate the sentiment value of ANPs on a scale from 1 to 5. We provided annotators with intuitive instructions, along with examples ANPs with different sentiment values. Each task showed five ANPs from a given language along with Flickr images associated to those ANPs. Annotators rated the sentiment expressed by each ANP, choosing between "very negative," "slightly negative," "neutral," "slightly positive" or "very positive".

Task Setup. The sentiment of each ANP was judged by five or more independent workers. Similar to the MVSO setup, we required that workers were both native speakers of the task's language and highly ranked on the platform. We also developed a subset of test questions with an expert-labeled gold standard: to access a crowdsourcing task, workers needed to correctly answer 7 of 10 test questions. Their performance was also monitored throughout the task by randomly inserting a test question in each task.

Crowdsourcing Results. To assess the quality of the collected annotations, we computed the level of agreement between contributors. And although sentiment assessment is intrinsically a subjective task, we found an average agreement of $\sim$68%. We found an average correlation of 0.54 between crowdsourced sentiment scores and the automatically assigned sentiment scores in [1]. Although this value is reasonably high, it still shows that the two sets of scores do not completely overlap. A high-level summary of the average sentiment collected per language is shown in Figure 2. Unlike the findings of previous work using automatic sentiment scores [1], we find that visual concepts from Chinese and Russian users carry more positive sentiment on the average when compared to concepts shared by speakers of other languages.

4. EXACT CONCEPT MATCHING

To match visual sentiment concepts (ANPs) across languages we translated them from each language $L = \{l_ij \mid i = 1 \dots m, j = 1 \dots n_i\}$ to the concepts of a pivot language $C = \{c_i \mid i = 1 \dots N\}$ using the Google Translate API[2]. We selected English as the pivot

[1] http://www.crowdflower.com
[2] https://cloud.google.com/translate

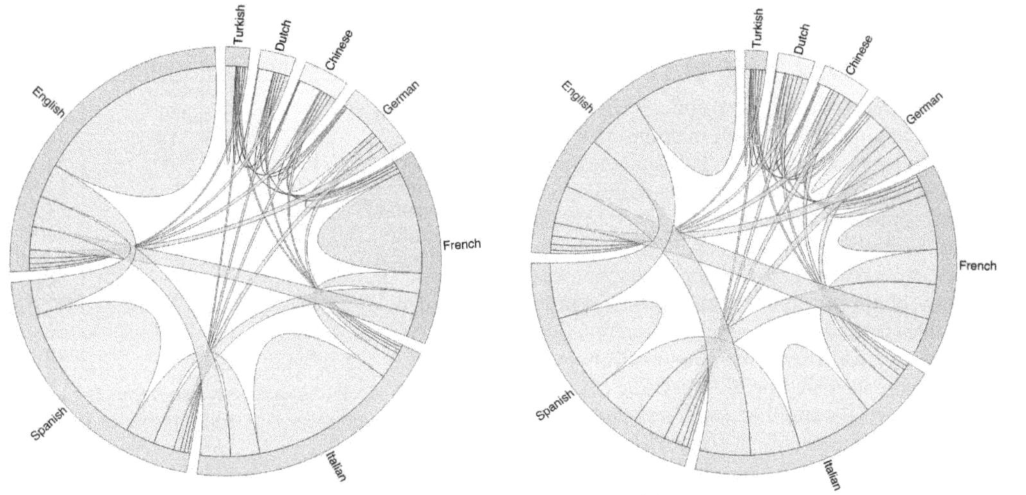

(a) Exact matching (b) Approximate matching

Figure 3: Clustering connectivity across top-8 most popular languages in MVSO measured by the number of concepts in the same cluster of a given language with other languages represented in a chord diagram. On the left (a), the clusters based on exact matching are mostly dominated by a single language, while on the right (b), based on approximate matching, the clusters are enriched with multiple languages.

language because it has the most complete translation resources (parallel corpora) for each of the other languages due to its popularity in relevant studies. For instance, the concepts *chien heureux* (French), *perro feliz* (Spanish) and *glücklicher hund* (German) are translated to the English concept *happy dog*. Rightly so, one would expect that the visual sentiment concepts in the pivot language might have shifted in terms of sentiment and meaning as a result of the translation process. And so, we examine and analyze the effects of translation to the sentiment and meaning of the multilingual concepts as well as the matching coverage across languages.

4.1 Sentiment and Meaning Shift

To quantitatively examine the effect of translation to the sentiment of concepts, we used the crowdsourced sentiment values and count the number of concepts for which the sentiment is shifted after translation in English. The higher this number for a given language, the higher the specificitiy of the visual sentiment for that language. To avoid counting sentiment shifts caused by small sentiment values we define a sentiment threshold t below which we do not consider sign changes, as follows: $|\text{sent}(c_i)| > t$. Table 1 displays the percentage of concepts with shifted sign due to translation. The percentages are on average about 33% for $t = 0$. The highest percentage of sign shift is 60% from Arabic and the lowest percentage is 18.6% for Dutch. Moreover, the percentage of concepts with shifted sign decreases for most languages as we increase the absolute sentiment value threshold t from 0 to 0.3. This result is particularly interesting since it suggests that visual sentiment understanding can be enriched by considering the language dimension.

The translation can affect also the meaning of the original concept in the pivot language. For instance, a concept in the original language which has intricate compound words (adjective and noun) could be translated to simpler compound words. This might be due to the lack of expressivity of the pivot language, or to compound words with shifted meaning, because of translation mistake, language idioms, or lack of large enough context. For example, 民主法治 (Chinese) is translated to *democracy and the rule of law* in English, while *passo grande* (Italian) is translated to *plunge* and *marode schönheit* (German) is translated in to *ramshackle beauty*. Examining the extent of this effect quantitatively is very costly because it requires language experts from all languages at hand. Sentiment and meaning shift effects are very interesting open problems, however, in this study, we focus specifically on how to increase the matching coverage among languages rather than what is the optimal modeling of sentiment and meaning, hence we leave them as future work.

Language	$t = 0.0$	$t = 0.1$	$t = 0.2$	$t = 0.3$
Italian	28.9 (6.0)	16.7 (3.3)	11.4 (2.4)	7.3 (2.2)
French	36.2 (8.1)	23.6 (5.3)	16.8 (3.8)	9.7 (3.3)
Chinese	24.4 (6.3)	11.8 (5.5)	5.5 (1.4)	3.1 (0.8)
German	27.1 (6.2)	15.5 (3.5)	8.3 (1.9)	7.7 (1.8)
Dutch	18.6 (5.4)	8.2 (2.4)	6.2 (1.8)	3.1 (0.9)
Russian	25.6 (8.3)	20.5 (6.6)	5.1 (1.7)	2.6 (0.8)
Turkish	33.3 (8.2)	22.2 (5.5)	7.4 (1.8)	3.7 (0.9)
Arabic	60.0 (21.4)	40.0 (14.3)	10.0 (3.6)	10.0 (3.6)

Table 1: Percentage of concepts with sentiment sign shift after exact match and over all ANPs in a given language (in parenthesis).

4.2 Matching Coverage

The matching coverage is an essential property for multilingual concept matching and clustering. We examine this property by performing k-Means clustering of multilingual concepts, and counting the number of concepts between two languages that belong to the same cluster. This reveals the connectivity of language clusters based on exact matching, as shown in Figure 3 (a) for the top-8 most popular languages in MVSO. From the connection stripes which represent the number of concepts between two languages, we can observe that, when using exact matching, concept clusters are dominated by single languages. For instance, in all the languages there is a connection stripe which connects back to the same language: this means that many clusters contain monolingual concepts. Another example which highlights the disadvantage of exact matching is that out of all the German translations (781), the ones matched with Dutch concepts (39) were more numerous than the ones matched with Chinese concepts (23). This was striking given that there were less (340) translations from Dutch than from Chinese (472). This demonstrates that the matching of concepts among languages is generally very sparse and does not depend necessarily on the number of translated concepts; this hinders our ability to compare concepts across languages in a unified manner.

Moreover, we want be able to know the relation among concepts from original languages where we cannot have a direct translation. To address the limitations of exact matching coverage of concepts, we propose below to expand the exact match translation and approximate translations based on compound word semantics.

5. APPROXIMATE CONCEPT MATCHING

We saw that matching sentiment-biased visual concepts in different languages with exact matching has several limitations, in terms of translation correctness and concept coverage. To overcome these limitations, we relax the exact condition for matching multilingual concepts, and instead we *approximately* match concepts based on their semantic meaning. Intuitively, in order to match concepts from different languages, we need a proximity (or distance) measure reflecting how 'close' or similar concepts are in the semantic distance space. This enables to achieve our main goal: comparing visual concepts cross-lingually, and cluster them in to multilingual groups. When using, approximate matching the clustering connectivity between languages is greatly enriched, as shown in Figure 3 (b): connection stripes are more evenly distributed for all languages. To learn such representations of meaning we make use of the recent advances in distributional lexical semantics [5, 6, 21, 22] utilizing the skip-gram model provided by word2vec toolkit[3] trained on large text corpora.

5.1 Distributed Word Representations

To represent words in a semantic space we use unsupervised word embeddings based on the skip-gram model via word2vec. Essentially, the skip-gram model aims to learn vector representations for words by predicting the context of a word in a large corpus. The context is defined as a window of w words before and w after the current word. We consider the following corpora in English on which the skip-gram model is trained:

1. **Google News**: A corpus of news which contains 100 billion tokens and 3,000,000 unique words which have at least 5 occurrences from [23]. News are typically used to describe real-world events which contains accurate word meanings, however it has indirect relevance to visual content.

2. **Wikipedia**: A corpus of Wikipedia articles which contains 1.74 billion tokens and 693,056 unique words which have at least 10 occurrences. The pre-processed text of this corpus was obtained from [24]. Wikipedia articles are more thorough descriptions of real-world events, entities, objects, and concepts. Similar to Google news, the visual content is indirectly connected to the word usage.

3. **Wikipedia + Reuters + Wall Street Journal**: A mixture corpus of Wikipedia articles, Wall Street Journal (WSJ) and Reuters news which contains 1.96 billion tokens and 960,494 unique words which have at least 10 occurrences. The pre-processed text of this corpus was obtained from [24]. This combination of news articles and Wikipedia articles captures a balance between these two different types of word usage.

4. **Flickr 100M**: A corpus of image metadata which contains 0.75 billion tokens and 693,056 unique words (with frequency higher than 10) available from Yahoo! [4]. For the first time in this paper, this corpus is used to train skip-gram models. In contrast to the previous corpora, the description of real-world images contains spontaneous word usage which is directly related to visual content. Hence, we expect it to provide embeddings able to capture visual properties.

For the Google News corpus, we used pre-trained embeddings of 300 dimensions with a context window of 5 words provided by [23]. For the other corpora, we trained the skip-gram model with a context window w of 5 and 10 words, fixing the dimensionality of the word embeddings to 300 dimensions. In addition to training the vanilla skip-gram model on word tokens we propose to train each of the corpora (except Google news due to lack of access to original documents used for training) by treating ANPs (concepts) as unique tokens. This pre-processing step allows the skip-gram model to directly learn concepts embeddings while taking advantage from the word contextual information over the above corpora.

[3]https://code.google.com/p/word2vec

[4]http://webscope.sandbox.yahoo.com

Language	Abbrev.	# Concepts	# Pairs	# Images
English	EN	4,421	1,109,467	447,997
Spanish	ES	3,381	97,862	37,528
Italian	IT	3,349	44,794	25,664
French	FR	2,349	34,747	16,807
Chinese	ZH	504	21,049	5,562
German	DE	804	14,635	7,335
Dutch	NL	348	3,491	2,226
Russian	RU	129	1,536	800
Turkish	TR	231	941	638
Polish	PL	63	727	477
Persian	FA	15	56	34
Arabic	AR	29	46	23

Table 2: ANP co-occurrence statistics for 12 languages, namely the number of concept tags and number of images with concept tags.

5.2 Distributed Concept Representations

To represent concepts in a semantic space we use the word embeddings in the pivot language (English), and compose the representation of a concept based on its compound words. Each sentiment-biased visual concept c_i comprises zero or more adjective and one or more noun words (as translation does not necessarily preserve the adjective-noun pair structure of the original phrase). Given the word vector embeddings, $\vec{x}_{\text{adj}}$ and $\vec{x}_{\text{noun}}$, we compute the concept embedding $\vec{c}_i$ using the sum operation for composition: $\vec{c}_i = \vec{x}_{\text{adj}} + \vec{x}_{\text{noun}}$ or the concept embedding $\vec{c}_i$ which is directly learned from the skip-gram model. This enables the comparison of multilingual concepts using the pivot language (English). At this stage, we note that there are several other ways to define composition of short phrases, e.g. [25, 26, 23]; however, here, we focus on the type of corpora used for obtaining the word embeddings rather than on the composition function.

6. EVALUATION

6.1 Visual Semantic Relatedness

Evaluating word embeddings learned from text is typically performed on tasks such as semantic relatedness, syntactic relations and analogy relations [5]. These tasks are not able to capture concept properties related to visual content. For instance, while *deserted beach* and *lonely person* seem unrelated according to text, in the context of an image they share visual semantics. An individual person in a deserted beach gives to a remote observer the impression of loneliness. To obtain groundtruth for visual semantic distance we collected co-occurrence statistics of ANPs (concepts) translated in English from 12 languages by analyzing the MVSO image tags (1,000 samples per concept), as displayed in Table 2. We compute the visually anchored semantic distance using cosine distance between two co-occurrence vectors: $d(\vec{h}_i, \vec{h}_j) = 1 - \text{cosine}(\vec{h}_i, \vec{h}_j)$. We now compare the performance of the various concept embeddings of Section 5.1 on the visual semantic relatedness task. Figure 4 displays their performance over all languages in terms of Mean Squared Error (MSE), and Table 3 displays their performance per language accoring to the MSE score for all the pairs of concept embeddings $\vec{c}_i$ and $\vec{c}_j$, as:

Method \ Language	EN	ES	IT	FR	ZH	DE	NL	RU	TR	PL	FA	AR
wiki (w=10)	3.81	5.62	6.47	7.18	5.30	8.33	11.65	14.67	19.59	16.62	17.25	31.17
wiki-anp (w=10)	3.46	5.38	6.33	7.20	4.98	8.56	11.99	15.26	20.97	17.14	19.31	35.15
wiki-anp-l (w=10)	3.27	4.78	6.49	7.29	4.57	8.57	13.54	16.05	24.30	22.05	21.47	38.40
wiki_rw (w=10)	10.17	12.01	12.08	12.11	13.62	12.98	11.02	13.74	**12.71**	**12.28**	**6.51**	**16.16**
wiki_rw-anp (w=10)	3.79	5.54	6.38	7.23	5.16	8.53	11.67	14.94	19.79	16.48	17.91	32.34
wiki_rw-anp-l (w=10)	3.57	4.90	6.43	7.21	4.90	7.91	13.28	15.27	23.29	21.15	20.15	34.59
flickr (w=10)	6.27	6.75	7.23	7.84	6.91	9.03	**10.31**	**13.59**	15.83	13.41	10.36	24.98
flickr-anp (w=10)	3.38	4.81	6.89	6.59	4.69	**7.85**	11.33	14.05	18.66	16.26	15.61	31.43
flickr-anp-l (w=10)	2.72	4.12	5.95	6.73	4.04	8.55	14.09	14.59	25.00	22.23	21.12	34.92
gnews (w=5)	4.59	5.81	6.85	7.51	5.63	8.76	11.08	14.02	18.29	14.88	14.08	28.61
wiki (w=5)	3.01	5.08	6.16	7.04	4.83	8.30	12.34	15.07	21.16	17.57	19.30	35.43
wiki-anp (w=5)	2.91	5.01	6.09	7.10	4.71	8.36	12.39	15.53	21.91	17.79	20.86	37.42
wiki-anp-l (w=5)	2.73	4.56	6.36	7.23	4.30	8.42	13.71	16.33	25.06	22.66	22.40	40.53
wiki_rw (w=5)	5.70	7.36	8.12	8.47	8.51	9.48	10.52	13.60	15.34	13.43	10.12	22.40
wiki_rw-anp (w=5)	3.20	4.99	6.08	7.04	4.65	8.32	12.22	15.21	21.37	17.49	19.26	36.30
wiki_rw-anp-l (w=5)	3.03	4.58	6.35	7.21	4.55	8.47	13.74	15.78	24.50	22.18	21.24	37.86
flickr (w=5)	5.48	6.19	6.79	7.53	6.19	8.79	10.64	13.71	16.60	14.03	11.87	28.04
flickr-anp (w=5)	2.87	4.52	**5.85**	**6.56**	4.41	7.91	11.85	14.34	20.18	17.14	16.67	34.31
flickr-anp-l (w=5)	**2.21**	**4.12**	6.04	6.84	**3.94**	8.28	14.66	15.54	26.10	23.16	21.82	36.85

Table 3: Comparison of the various concept embeddings on visual semantic relatedness in terms of MSE (%) per language (lower is better). The embeddings are from Flickr ('flickr'), Wikipedia ('wiki') and Wikipedia + Reuters + Wall Street Journal ('wiki-rw') trained on a context window of $w \in \{10, 5\}$ words using words as tokens or words and ANPs as tokens ('-anp'). All embeddings use the sum operation of noun and adjective vectors to compose ANP embedding for a given ANP except from the ones abbreviated with '-l' which use instead learned ANP embeddings when available. The best score per language is marked in bold.

$$\text{MSE} = \frac{1}{T}\sum_{i}^{N}\sum_{j:j\neq i\ \&\ Uij\neq 0}^{|\{i,\ldots,N\}|}(d(\vec{c}_i,\vec{c}_j) - d(\vec{h}_i,\vec{h}_j))^2, \quad (1)$$

where U_{ij} is the co-occurrence between concepts i and j, and T is the total number of comparisons, that is $T = \frac{(N^2 - N - |\{Uij=0\}|)}{2}$. Note that to avoid redundancy, we have excluded from the comparisons the diagonal and the lower triangular matrix of the concept co-occurrence matrix ($N \times N$). This does not affect the average mean squared error calculation because the cosine distance is symmetric. From the comparisons T we further exclude ANP pairs with zero co-occurrence to penalize embeddings which tend to separate most of the concepts apart.

The best performance over all languages (Figure 4) is achieved by the flickr-anp-l (w=5) embeddings, followed by the wiki-anp-l (w=5) embeddings. The superior performance of flickr-anp-l (w=5) is attributed to its ability to learn directly the embedding of a given concept (ANP). The lowest performance is observed by wiki-reu-wsj (w=10) and flickr (w=10). The larger context (w=10) performed worse than the smaller context (w=5); it appears that the semantic relatedness prediction over all languages does not benefit from large contexts. When the concept embeddings are evaluated per language in Table 3 we obtain slightly different ranking of the methods. In the languages with the most data, namely English (EN), Spanish (ES), Italian (IT), French (FR) and Chinese (ZH), the ranking is similar as before, with flickr-anp-l (w=5), flickr-anp (w=5) and wiki-anp (w=5), wiki-anp-l (w=5) embeddings having the lowest error in predicting semantic relatedness.

Generally, we observed that for well-resourced languages the quality of concept embeddings learned by a skip-gram model improves when the model is trained using ANPs as tokens (both when using directly learned concept embeddings or composition of word embeddings with sum operation). Furthermore, the usage of learned embeddings abbreviated with $-l$ on the top-5 languages outperforms on average all other embeddings in English, Spanish and Chinese languages and performs similar to the best embeddings on Italian and French. In the low resourced languages the results are the following: in German (DE) language the lowest error is from flickr-anp (w=10), in the Dutch (NL) and Russian (RU) is the flickr (w=10). Lastly, the lowest error in the Turkish (TR), Persian (FA)

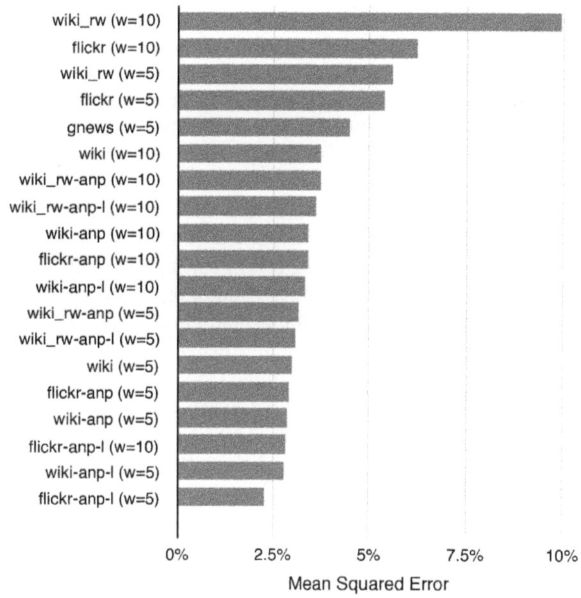

Figure 4: Comparison of the various concept embeddings over all languages on visual semantic relatedness in terms of descending MSE (%). For the naming conventions please refer to Table 3.

and Arabic (AR) languages is from wiki-reu-wsj (w=10). It appears that for the languages with small data the large context benefits the visual semantic relatedness task.

Moreover, the performance of embeddings with a small context window (w = 5), are outperformed by the ones that use a larger one (w = 10) as the pool of examples of the languages narrows. This is likely due to the different properties which are captured by different context windows, namely more abstract semantic and syntactic relations with a larger context window and more specific relations with a smaller one. Note that the co-occurrence of concepts in MVSO images is computed on the English translations and hence some of the syntactic properties and specific meaning of words of low-resourced languages might have vanished due to errors in the translation process. Lastly, the superior performance of the embeddings learned from the Flickr 100M corpus in the top-5 most resourced languages, validates our hypothesis that word usage directly related to the visual content helps to learn concept embeddings with superior visual semantic properties.

6.2 Multilingual Concept Clustering

Given a common way to represent multilingual concepts, we are now able to cluster them. We normalize the concept vectors to perform k-means clustering over Euclidean distances. We perform part-of-speech tagging on the translation to extract the representative noun or adjective with TreeTagger [27]. We then experimented with two types of clustering approaches: a one-stage and a two-stage approach. The **one-stage** approach directly clusters all the concept vectors using k-means. The **two-stage** clustering operates first on the noun or adjective word vectors and then second on concept vectors. Here, we first split the translated concepts into different groups based on the clusters their nouns belong to, and then run another round of k-means clustering within the groups formed in the first stage. In the case when a translation phrase has more than one noun, we select the last noun as the representative and use it in the first stage of clustering. The second stage uses the sum of vectors for all the concepts that comprise that translation for clustering. We also experimented with first clustering by adjectives and then by nouns using the same process.

We experimented with different number of clusters k. For the two-stage clustering, we adjust the number of clusters k in the last stage based on the number of concepts in each first-stage cluster, e.g. concepts in each noun-cluster ranged from 3 to 253 in one setup, to bring the final number of clusters in two-stage clustering to our desired number for fair comparison of clustering with different setups. We ended up with clusters such as *beautiful music, beautiful concert, beautiful singer* that clusters concepts like *musique magnifique* (French), *bella musica* (Italian), *bellissimo concerto*. While noun-first clustering brings concepts that talk about similar objects, e.g. estate/unit/property/building, adjective-based clustering yields concepts about similar and closely related emotions, e.g. grateful/festive/joyous/floral/glowing/delightful (examples are from two-stage clustering with the Google News corpus).

To evaluate the clustering of affective visual concepts, we consider two dimensions: (1) *Semantics*: ANPs are concepts, so we seek a clustering method to group ANPs with similar semantic meaning, such as for example *beautiful woman* and *beautiful lady*, (2) *Sentiment*: Given that ANPs have an *affective* bias, we need a clustering method that groups ANPs with similar sentiment values, thus ensuring the integrity of ANPs sentiment information after clustering. To evaluate clustering over both dimensions, we score clustering methods using two evaluation metrics specifically designed for this task, one for semantics and one for sentiment, and then combine the resulting ratings into a single score.

Semantic Consistency. Each clustering method produces k ANPs clusters, out of which C contains two or more ANPs. For each of these multi-ANP clusters, each with N_c ANPs, we compute the average visually grounded semantic distance (Eq. 1) between all pairs of ANPs, and then average it over all C clusters, thus obtaining a Semantic Consistency sem_C metric for a given clustering method:

$$\text{sem}_C = \frac{1}{C}\sum_{c=1}^{C}\frac{\sum_{j:j\neq i\ \&\ Uij\neq 0}^{|\{i,\ldots,N_c\}|} d(\text{ANP}_{c,i},\text{ANP}_{c,j})}{N_c} \quad (2)$$

Sentiment Consistency. For each multi-ANP cluster c, we compute a *sentiment quantization error*, namely the average difference between the sentiment of each ANP in the cluster, and the average sentiment of the cluster. So, given $\text{sen}_c = \sum_{i=1}^{N_c}\text{sen}(\text{ANP}_i)/N_c$ as the average sentiment for a clusterc, we obtain a Sentiment Consistency sen_C metric for a given clustering method as follows:

$$\text{sen}_C = \frac{1}{C}\sum_{c=1}^{C}\frac{\sum_{i=1}^{N_c}(\text{sen}(\text{ANP}_{c,i}) - \text{sen}_c)^2}{N_c} \quad (3)$$

Method	Embeddings	sen_C	sem_C	μ
2-stage_noun	wiki (w=10)	0.511	0.588	0.549
2-stage_noun	wiki_rw (w=10)	0.529	0.604	0.566
2-stage_noun	flickr (w=10)	0.538	0.528	0.533
2-stage_noun	wiki (w=5)	0.534	0.586	0.560
2-stage_noun	wiki_rw (w=5)	0.510	0.614	0.562
2-stage_noun	flickr (w=5)	0.526	0.513	0.519
2-stage_noun	gnews (w=5)	0.309	0.569	0.439
2-stage_adj	wiki (w=10)	0.483	0.567	0.524
2-stage_adj	wiki_rw (w=10)	0.476	0.536	0.506
2-stage_adj	flickr (w=10)	0.459	0.536	0.497
2-stage_adj	wiki (w=5)	0.581	0.930	0.755
2-stage_adj	wiki_rw (w=5)	0.472	0.560	0.516
2-stage_adj	flickr (w=5)	0.455	0.519	0.487
2-stage_adj	gnews (w=5)	0.178	0.522	0.350
1-stage	wiki-anp (w=10)	0.240	0.576	0.408
1-stage	wiki_rw-anp (w=10)	0.257	0.508	0.382
1-stage	flickr-anp (w=10)	**0.262**	**0.489**	0.375
1-stage	wiki-anp (w=5)	0.250	0.583	0.416
1-stage	wiki_rw-anp (w=5)	0.281	0.522	0.402
1-stage	flickr-anp (w=5)	0.280	0.502	**0.391**

Table 4: Sentiment and semantic consistency of the clusters from the two-stage and one-stage k-Means clustering methods with $k =$ 1000, trained with the various concept embeddings.

Clustering Evaluation Results. We evaluate all the clustering methods using these two scoring methods and an overall *consistency* metric (average of semantic and sentiment consistencies). The lower the value of the metrics, the higher the quality of the clustering method. We observe that semantic consistency and sentiment consistency are actually highly related. When we correlate the vector containing semantic consistency scores for all clustering methods with the vector containing sentiment consistency scores, we find that the Pearson's coefficient is around 0.7, thus suggesting that the higher the semantic relatedness of the clusters resulting from one method, the higher their respective sentiment coherence.

We observed that as the total cluster size k increases, the consistency within a cluster also increases, even though the images and ANPs come from different languages and though the source of training corpus for word vectors did not always come from social content. Word vectors trained on Flickr data provided clustering with top consistency in all evaluation measures. Based on the analysis of sentiment consistency, we observed that 9 out of top 10 two-stage clustering setups were based on adjective-first clustering. This confirms our intuition that similar sentiments are clustered together when we first cluster ANPs with similar adjectives. Lastly, the vectors trained on full ANP tokens lead to increased semantic consistency, similar to on the full corpus (Section 6.1).

7. PORTRAIT CONCEPT CLUSTERING

The proposed multilingual concept clustering framework can be a useful tool for exploring and analyzing any large, multilingual collections of visual concepts. As an example application, we applied this concept matching framework to study how affective concepts attach to human *portraits*, i.e. photos with faces, through the viewing lens of different languages.

7.1 Portrait-based Sentiment Ontology

Portrait and face-centric photography has been a subject of research in multiple disciplines for years. Facial perception is among the most developed human capabilities, where our brains even contain a dedicated sub-network of neurons for face processing [28]. Recently, computational understanding portrait modeling has attracted much attention from the multimedia community, e.g. in computational aesthetics [29], animated GIFs [30], and social dynamics [31]. Here, we seek to unpack what sentiment-biased visual concepts, specifically ANPs, languages attach to faces.

Face Detection and ANP Filtering. To obtain a corpus of visual concepts relating to faces, we ran a frontal face detector [32] which projects images onto a normalized pixel difference feature space and performs quadtree-based face detection. A total of 3,858,869 faces were detected across the 7,368,364 images in the MVSO image dataset [1]. Over 53.67% of these detections came from the English image subset (2,071,078 detections), where the next leading language subset was Spanish at 23.68% (913,596 detections). We then computed a *portrait score* for each ANP which we define as the ratio of detected faces to all images in each ANP. We then selected the subset of ANPs whose portrait score was greater than 0.6. To ensure statistical significance, we only considered languages with 20 or more face-dominated ANPs: Turkish, Russian, German, Chinese, French, Spanish, Italian and English. Of the 11,832 concepts from the full MVSO dataset, we retained 2,345 face ANPs. We found that in general, detected faces from the French and German datasets we larger in size on average than other languages. In addition, images originating from the Italian subset typically contained more than one person while images in the Chinese and Turkish subset tended to contain mostly single-subject portraits.

Concept Sentiment and Face Portraits. To explore the sentiment correlations of different languages to the presence of faces, we computed the Pearson's correlation coefficient ρ for each language between ANP portrait scores and the ANP sentiment values, as shown in Table 5. The higher the correlation, the higher the tendency of a given language to associate positive sentiment with a face image. Here, for all languages except Turkish, the presence of portraits in an ANP image pool tended to be positively correlated with the ANP sentiment. In particular, the languages having the strongest tendency to attach positive sentiments to portraits are Russian and Chinese.

7.2 Multilingual Portraits

We sought to investigate how similar/different languages are with regard to affective visual concepts (ANPs) and their face images. We clustered face ANPs from the subset of eight languages using our approximate match-based clustering techniques, and evaluated different clustering approaches to find that the *single-step* clustering over Flickr-trained word2vec vector with $w = 5$ and $k = 1000$ gave us the best results when combining semantic and sentiment consistency metrics. This method output 1,000 multilingual clusters of affective visual concepts related to portraits. This provides a powerful tool to analyze the visual concept preferences for different languages, i.e. if the ANPs of two languages fall often in similar clusters, such languages tend to attach similar concepts to face images.

	ρ**(face,sent)**	**sent(faces)**	**sent(all)**	**diff(%)**	**face size(%)**	**#faces(%)**
Turkish	0.00	3.54	3.55	-0.26	63.46	0.95
Russian	**0.23**	**4.13**	3.67	**12.48**	58.25	1.23
German	0.18	3.75	3.39	10.70	65.49	0.99
Chinese	**0.23**	**4.30**	3.57	**20.33**	64.12	0.93
French	0.14	3.48	3.32	4.79	**65.88**	1.01
Spanish	0.16	3.72	3.44	7.93	65.08	1.23
Italian	0.15	3.75	3.38	10.97	61.72	**1.37**
English	0.15	3.51	3.32	5.49	56.78	1.04

Table 5: Sentiment statistics per language (face and all ANPs).

Languages, Sentiments, Face Sizes. Among the clusters found by this method, around 60% are monolingual clusters: English and Spanish are the languages with the highest percentage of monolingual clusters ($\sim$32% and 31% respectively), probably due to the large number of ANPs, implying a wider vocabulary compared to other languages. Around 22% of the face ANP clusters are bilingual, out of which 40% contains 2 of the 4 Western-most languages in the corpus (French, Italian, English and Spanish), while the others contain a mixture of other languages. The remaining 18% of clusters show three languages or more. But what is the relation between multilingual clusters and portrait sentiment? Do languages agree more on positive or negative sentiment for similar visual concepts? To answer these, we computed the correlation between the number of languages falling into each cluster and the average sentiment of the ANPs in that cluster. These two dimensions statistically significantly correlate with a coefficient of 0.13, showing that different languages tend to associate similar visual concepts to portraits when concepts carry positive sentiment.

We also analyze the relation between cluster multilingual-ness and face sizes. Do visual concepts shared by different languages refer to portraits with bigger or smaller faces? We compute here the correlation between the number of languages falling into each cluster and the average face sizes for the ANPs in that cluster. The correlation coefficient stands at 0.17, showing that, the bigger the average face sizes of portraits related to a visual concept, the higher the possibility that different languages share such concept.

Clustering Analysis. Which languages are more similar when tagging portraits? To further understand language-specific concepts used when tagging face images, we perform a multivariate analysis of language distribution across visual concepts. To better understand which groups of languages tend to attach similar affective concepts to face images, we proceed as follows. We create eight k-dimensional vectors, one for each language. Each element of such vectors corresponds to the number of ANPs falling into each cluster, normalized by the total number of ANPs for a given language. Finally, we cluster these vectors using k-means with cosine distance, progressively raising k from 2 to 6, thus separating languages into different groups, as shown in Figure 5. The binary subdivision of the languages in two clusters ($k = 2$) shows immediately a clear separation between more Eastern (Turkish, Chinese, Russian) versus Western (Italian, Spanish, French, English, German) languages. When we raise the number of clusters to 3, Turkish is the first one to detach from the Eastern clusters, suggesting that Turkish images tend to have more unique ways to assign concepts to portraits. Within the Western languages, when $k = 4$ we see a separation: Italian gets clustered with Spanish and English, while French gets clustered with German. Chinese and Russian become independent clusters for $k = 5$. Finally, when raising k to 6, Western languages split again: English becomes an independent cluster, leaving two bilingual clusters: Italian/Spanish and French/German.

What Do Different Languages Say About Portraits? According to our clustering method, $\sim$3% of the clusters contain five or more languages. The limited size of this data allows us to proceed with manual inspection, to understand the topics of the ANPs falling in highly multilingual clusters. The most highly multilingual cluster contains 8 languages and 20 ANPs: its main topic is about *little guy* or *little girl* (e.g. *piccola bimba* in Italian, or *petit fille* in French). One interesting observation is that not all languages agree on the sentiment value for this concept: while Chinese and Turkish give a score slightly below 3, Italian, Spanish and Russian languages consider it a very positive concept, having respectively an average sentiment value of 4.0, 4.0 and 4.6, respectively, for this cluster. The

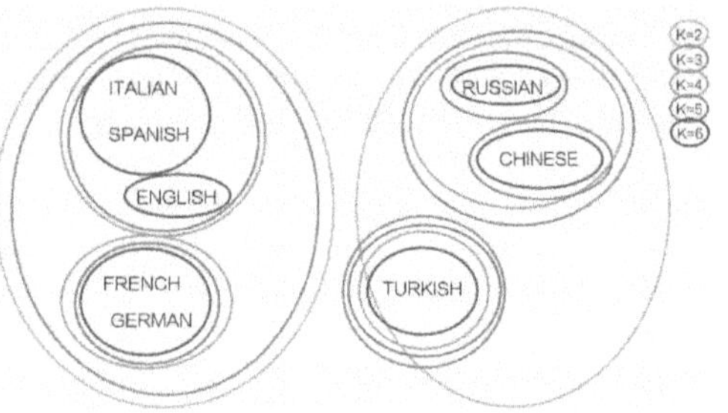

Figure 5: Groups of languages according to their similarity when associating affective concepts to faces. Each color corresponds to the output of a different clustering granularity k.

second biggest cluster, spanning seven languages (all apart from Chinese) with 24 ANPs, contained concepts like *gorgeous girl* in English or *belle fille* in French. Here, all languages agree on the highly positive value of this concept sentiment. Other highly multilingual noun clusters contain concepts related to *happy children*, *young women*, *healthy food*, *beautiful women*, etc, and also negative concepts such as *sexual violence*.

8. CONCLUSIONS & FUTURE WORK

In this study, we showed that visual sentiment concepts from multiple languages can be effectively represented in a common semantic space using a pivot language (English) and existing advances in distributional semantics of words. The best results on the prediction of visually grounded semantic distance was achieved by a skip-gram model trained on real-world image metadata, namely titles and descriptions from the Flickr 100M corpus, with a summed combination of concept word embeddings or also by direct learning. This enabled multilingual clustering of visual sentiment concepts in 11 languages, and allowed us to better hierarchically organize an ontology in [1] as well as provide deep analysis into portrait imagery from a multilingual perspective.

In the future, we plan to learn visually grounded concept embeddings in multiple languages directly from the groundtruth cooccurrence data (Section 5.2), e.g. by modeling the proposed visual semantic distance. An essential element for achieving this goal is to semantically align multiple languages using parallel corpora, as it has been effectively done in previous studies in multilingual representation learning. Finally, we plan to evaluate such word and concept embeddings on visual sentiment concept prediction, concept recommendation and caption generation.

9. REFERENCES

[1] B. Jou, T. Chen, N. Pappas, M. Redi, M. Topkara*, and S.-F. Chang, "Visual affect around the world: A large-scale multilingual visual sentiment ontology," in *ACM International Conference on Multimedia*, (Brisbane, Australia), pp. 159–168, 2015.

[2] H. Liu, B. Jou, T. Chen, M. Topkara, N. Pappas, M. Redi, and S.-F. Chang, "Complura: Exploring and leveraging a large-scale multilingual visual sentiment ontology," in *ACM Interational Conference on Multimedia Retrieval*, (New York, NY, USA), 2016.

[3] J. Turian, L. Ratinov, and Y. Bengio, "Word representations: A simple and general method for semi-supervised learning," in *48th Annual Meeting of the Association for Computational Linguistics*, ACL '10, (Uppsala, Sweden), pp. 384–394, 2010.

[4] R. Collobert, J. Weston, L. Bottou, M. Karlen, K. Kavukcuoglu, and P. Kuksa, "Natural language processing (almost) from scratch," *Journal of Machine Learning Research*, vol. 12, pp. 2493–2537, 2011.

[5] T. Mikolov, K. Chen, G. Corrado, and J. Dean, "Efficient estimation of word representations in vector space," *CoRR*, vol. abs/1301.3781, 2013.

[6] J. Pennington, R. Socher, and C. D. Manning, "GloVe: Global vectors for word representation," in *Empirical Methods in Natural Language Processing*, pp. 1532–1543, 2014.

[7] R. Al-Rfou, B. Perozzi, and S. Skiena, "Polyglot: Distributed word representations for multilingual NLP," *CoRR*, vol. abs/1307.1662, 2013.

[8] A. Klementiev, I. Titov, and B. Bhattarai, "Inducing crosslingual distributed representations of words," in *Proceedings of COLING 2012*, (Mumbai, India), pp. 1459–1474, 2012.

[9] W. Y. Zou, R. Socher, D. Cer, and C. D. Manning, "Bilingual word embeddings for phrase-based machine translation," in *Proceedings of the 2013 Conference on Empirical Methods in Natural Language Processing*, (Seattle, WA, USA), pp. 1393–1398, 2013.

[10] K. M. Hermann and P. Blunsom, "Multilingual models for compositional distributed semantics," in *Annual Meeting of the Association for Computational Linguistics*, (Baltimore, Maryland), pp. 58–68, 2014.

[11] A. P. S. Chandar, S. Lauly, H. Larochelle, M. M. Khapra, B. Ravindran, V. C. Raykar, and A. Saha, "An autoencoder approach to learning bilingual word representations," *CoRR*, vol. abs/1402.1454, 2014.

[12] F. Hill, R. Reichart, and A. Korhonen, "Simlex-999: Evaluating semantic models with (genuine) similarity estimation," *CoRR*, vol. abs/1408.3456, 2014.

[13] E. Bruni, N. K. Tran, and M. Baroni, "Multimodal distributional semantics," *Journal of Artificial Intelligence Research*, vol. 49, pp. 1–47, Jan. 2014.

[14] C. Silberer and M. Lapata, "Learning grounded meaning representations with autoencoders," in *52nd Annual Meeting of the Association for Computational Linguistics*, (Baltimore, Maryland), pp. 721–732, June 2014.

[15] A. Lazaridou, N. T. Pham, and M. Baroni, "Combining language and vision with a multimodal skip-gram model," in *Conference of the North American Chapter of the Association for Computational Linguistics: Human Language Technologies*, (Denver, Colorado), pp. 153–163, 2015.

[16] A. Karpathy, A. Joulin, and F. Li, "Deep fragment embeddings for bidirectional image sentence mapping," in *Advances in Neural Information Processing Systems 27*, pp. 1889–1897, Curran Associates, Inc., 2014.

[17] R. Kiros, R. Salakhutdinov, and R. S. Zemel, "Unifying visual-semantic embeddings with multimodal neural language models," *CoRR*, vol. abs/1411.2539, 2014.

[18] R. Socher, A. Karpathy, Q. V. Le, C. D. Manning, and A. Y. Ng, "Grounded compositional semantics for finding and describing images with sentences," *TACL*, vol. 2, pp. 207–218, 2014.

[19] J. Mao, W. Xu, Y. Yang, J. Wang, and A. L. Yuille, "Explain images with multimodal recurrent neural networks," *CoRR*, vol. abs/1410.1090, 2014.

[20] S. Kottur, R. Vedantam, J. M. F. Moura, and D. Parikh, "Visual word2vec (vis-w2v): Learning visually grounded word embeddings using abstract scenes," *CoRR*, vol. abs/1511.07067, 2015.

[21] T. Schnabel, I. Labutov, D. Mimno, and T. Joachims, "Evaluation methods for unsupervised word embeddings," in *Conference on Empirical Methods in Natural Language Processing*, (Lisbon, Portugal), pp. 298–307, 2015.

[22] O. Levy, Y. Goldberg, and I. Dagan, "Improving distributional similarity with lessons learned from word embeddings," *Transactions of Association for Computational Linguistics*, vol. 3, pp. 211–225, 2015.

[23] T. Mikolov, I. Sutskever, K. Chen, G. S. Corrado, and J. Dean, "Distributed representations of words and phrases and their compositionality," in *Advances in Neural Information Processing Systems 26*, pp. 3111–3119, 2013.

[24] R. Lebret and R. Collobert, "Word embeddings through hellinger pca," in *Conference of the European Chapter of the Association for Computational Linguistics*, (Gothenburg, Sweden), pp. 482–490, 2014.

[25] M. Baroni and R. Zamparelli, "Nouns are vectors, adjectives are matrices: Representing adjective-noun constructions in semantic space," in *Conference on Empirical Methods in Natural Language Processing*, (Cambridge, MA, USA), pp. 1183–1193, 2010.

[26] R. Socher, B. Huval, C. D. Manning, and A. Y. Ng, "Semantic compositionality through recursive matrix-vector spaces," in *Joint Conference on Empirical Methods in Natural Language Processing and Computational Natural Language Learning*, (Jeju Island, Korea), pp. 1201–1211, 2012.

[27] H. Schmid, "Probabilistic part-of-speech tagging using decision trees," in *International Conference on New Methods in Language Processing*, (Manchester, UK), 1994.

[28] W. A. Freiwald and D. Y. Tsao, "Neurons that keep a straight face," *National Academy of Sciences*, vol. 111, no. 22, pp. 7894–7895, 2014.

[29] M. Redi, N. Rasiwasia, G. Aggarwal, and A. Jaimes, "The beauty of capturing faces: Rating the quality of digital portraits," in *IEEE International Conference and Workshops on Automatic Face and Gesture Recognition*, (Ljubljana, Slovenia), pp. 1–8, 2015.

[30] B. Jou, S. Bhattacharya, and S.-F. Chang, "Predicting viewer perceived emotions in animated GIFs," in *ACM International Conference on Multimedia*, (Orlando, Florida, USA), pp. 213–216, 2014.

[31] S. Bakhshi, D. A. Shamma, and E. Gilbert, "Faces engage us: Photos with faces attract more likes and comments on instagram," in *ACM Conference on Human Factors in Computing Systems*, (Toronto, ON, Canada), pp. 965–974, 2014.

[32] S. Liao, A. K. Jain, and S. Z. Li, "A fast and accurate unconstrained face detector," *IEEE Transactions on Pattern Analysis and Machine Intelligence*, vol. 38, pp. 211–223, Feb 2016.

Action Recognition by Learning Deep Multi-Granular Spatio-Temporal Video Representation*

Qing Li [1], Zhaofan Qiu [1], Ting Yao [2], Tao Mei [2], Yong Rui [2], Jiebo Luo [3]
[1] University of Science and Technology of China, Hefei 230026, P. R. China
[2] Microsoft Research, Beijing 100080, P. R. China
[3] University of Rochester, NY 14627, USA
{sealq, qiudavy}@mail.ustc.edu.cn; {tiyao, tmei, yongrui}@microsoft.com;
jluo@cs.rochester.edu

ABSTRACT

Recognizing actions in videos is a challenging task as video is an information-intensive media with complex variations. Most existing methods have treated video as a flat data sequence while ignoring the intrinsic hierarchical structure of the video content. In particular, an action may span different granularities in this hierarchy including, from small to large, a single *frame*, consecutive frames (*motion*), a short *clip*, and the entire *video*. In this paper, we present a novel framework to boost action recognition by learning a deep spatio-temporal video representation at hierarchical multi-granularity. Specifically, we model each granularity as a single stream by 2D (for *frame* and *motion* streams) or 3D (for *clip* and *video* streams) convolutional neural networks (CNNs). The framework therefore consists of multi-stream 2D or 3D CNNs to learn both the spatial and temporal representations. Furthermore, we employ the Long Short-Term Memory (LSTM) networks on the *frame*, *motion*, and *clip* streams to exploit long-term temporal dynamics. With a *softmax* layer on the top of each stream, the classification scores can be predicted from all the streams, followed by a novel fusion scheme based on the multi-granular score distribution. Our networks are learned in an end-to-end fashion. On two video action benchmarks of UCF101 and HMDB51, our framework achieves promising performance compared with the state-of-the-art.

Keywords

Action Recognition; Video Analysis; Deep Learning.

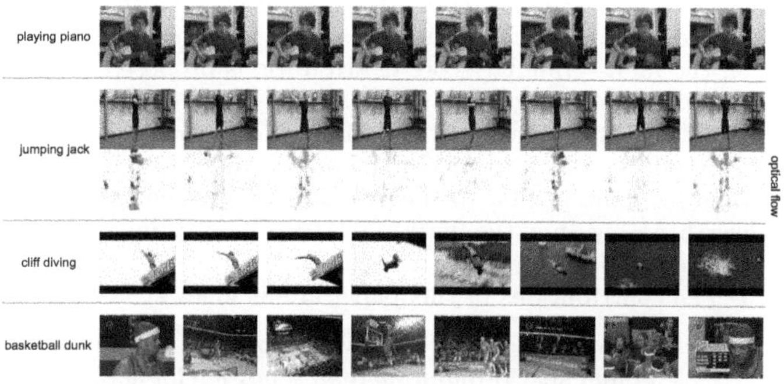

Figure 1: An action may span different granularities. For example, the action of "playing piano" can be recognized from individual *frames*, "jumping jack" may have high correlation with the optical flow images (*motion* computed from consecutive frames), "cliff diving" should be recognized from a short *clip* since this action usually lasts for few seconds, while "basketball dunk" can be reliably identified at the video granularity due the complex nature of this action. Recognizing actions therefore should take the hierarchical multi-granularity and spatio-temporal properties into consideration.

1. INTRODUCTION

Recognizing actions in videos is one of the fundamental problems of computer vision for a wide variety of applications, ranging from video surveillance, indexing and retrieval, to human computer interaction [9, 23, 29, 32]. However, video is an information-intensive media with large variations and complexities, e.g., intra-class variations caused by camera motion, cluttered background, illumination conditions, and so on. These have made action recognition a very challenging task. Moreover, as shown in Figure 1, an action may span different granularities in a video including, from small to large, a single *frame*, consecutive frames (*motion*), a short *clip*, and the entire *video*. Therefore, recognizing actions in videos therefore should take the hierarchical multi-granularity and spatio-temporal properties into consideration.

There has been extensive research on video action recognition, including hand-crafted feature-based methods [14, 15, 22, 28, 29, 33, 34, 36] or deep learning of video representations [9, 20, 16, 26, 27, 32]. The first category of research predominantly focuses on the detection of spatio-temporal interest points followed by the description of these points with local representations, while the deep learning methods heavily rely on using the Convolutional Neural Networks (CNNs) to learn visual appearance or the Recurrent Neural Networks (RNNs) to model the temporal dynamics in the video. However, most these methods treat video as a flat

* This work was performed at Microsoft Research Asia. The first two authors made equal contributions to this work.

ICMR'16, June 06-09, 2016, New York, NY, USA

DOI: http://dx.doi.org/10.1145/2911996.2912001

data sequence while ignoring the aforementioned intrinsic hierarchical structure of the video content deeply.

In this work, we aim at investigating a multi-granular architecture to learn the deep spatio-temporal video representation for action recognition. A video is represented by a hierarchical structure with multiple granularities, including from small to large, a single *frame*, consecutive frames (*motion*), a short *clip*, and the entire *video*. We model each video granularity as a single stream by 2D CNN (for *frame* and *motion* streams) or 3D CNN (for *clip* and *video* streams). The framework therefore learns both the spatial and temporal representations via the multi-stream 2D or 3D CNNs. Furthermore, we employ the Long Short-Term Memory (LSTM) networks on the *frame*, *motion*, and *clip* streams to exploit long-term temporal dynamics. With a *softmax* layer on the top of each stream, the classification scores can be predicted from each stream. A novel fusion scheme based on the multi-granular score distribution is proposed to predict the final recognition results, where the weights of each individual stream are learnt on the score distribution. This is an effective way to reflect the importance of each stream (and its components) to the overall action recognition. It is worth noting that the entire architecture is trainable in an end-to-end fashion.

The contributions of this paper are as follows.

- We propose a novel framework to learn a deep multi-granular spatio-temporal representation for action recognition. The learned representation can capture not only the spatio-temporal nature of video sequence but also the contributions from different granularities for action recognition.
- We adopt the LSTM to model long-term temporal dynamics on the top of frame, motion and clip streams, and optimize the recognition results from all the streams through a novel fusion scheme based on the multi-granular score distribution.
- We conduct extensive experiments and show that our framework outperforms several state-of-the-art methods by clear margins on two well-known benchmarks.

The remaining sections are organized as follows. Section 2 describes related work on action recognition. Section 3 presents our multi-granular architecture for action recognition, while Section 4 formulates the importance of each component over the predicted score distribution. Implementation details are given in Section 5. Section 6 provides empirical evaluations on two popular datasets, i.e., UCF101 and HMDB51, followed by the conclusions in Section 7.

2. RELATED WORK

Video action recognition has attracted intensive research attention. We briefly group the methods for action recognition into two categories: hand-crafted feature-based and deep learning-based methods.

Hand-crafted feature-based methods usually start by detecting spatio-temporal interest points and then describe these points with local representations. Many video representations are derived from image domain and extended to measure the temporal dimension of 3D volumes. For example, Laptev and Lindeberg propose space-time interest points (STIP) by extending the 2D Harris corner detector into 3D space [14]. The global color moment feature [34], Histogram of Gradient (HOG) and Histogram of Optical Flow (HOF) [15], 3D Histogram of Gradient (HOG3D) [10], SIFT-3D [21], Extended SURF [31], and Cuboids [2] are good descriptors as the local spatio-temporal features. Recently, Wang *et al.* propose dense trajectory features, which densely sample local patches from each frame at different scales and then track them in a dense optical flow field [28, 29]. The further improvements are achieved by the compensation of camera motion [6], and the use of advanced feature encoding methods such as Bag-of-Words (BoW) [15] and Fisher Vectors [19, 22].

The most recent approaches to action recognition are to devise deep architectures for learning video representations. Qiu *et al.* perform action recognition using the Support Vector Machine with mean pooling of the CNN-based representations over frames [20]. Karparthy *et al.* extend the CNN-based architecture by stacking visual features in a fixed size of windows and using spatio-temporal convolutions for video classification [9]. Later in [27], Tran *et al.* employ 3D ConvNets trained on the Sports-1M dataset to learn video descriptors. Zha *et al.* leverage both spatial and temporal pooling on the CNN features computed on patches of video frames [35]. The late fusion is then exploited to combine spatio-temporal representations. In the work by Wang *et al.* [30], the local ConvNet responses over the spatio-temporal tubes centered at the trajectories are pooled as the video descriptors. Fisher vector is then used to encode these local descriptors to a global video representation. Most recently, the LSTM-RNN networks have been successfully employed for modeling temporal dynamics in videos. In [16], temporal pooling and LSTM are used to combine frame-level (optical flow images) representation and discover long-term temporal relationships. Srivastava *et al.* further formulate the video representation learning as an autoencoder model, which consists of the encoder and decoder LSTMs [26]. Wu *et al.* present an approach using regularization in neural networks to exploit feature and class relationships [32].

It can be observed that most existing methods treat video as a flat data sequence while ignoring the aforementioned intrinsic hierarchical structure of video content deeply. The most closely related work is the two-stream CNN approach [23]. The work applies the CNN separately on visual frames and stacked optical flows. Our method is different from [23] in that we extend two-stream to hierarchical multi-granular streams, employ 3D CNN to learn the spatio-temporal representation of video, and further utilize LSTM networks to model long-term temporal cues. In addition, our work is able to derive the fusion weights of each component from all the streams in a principled way.

3. MULTI-GRANULAR ARCHITECTURE FOR ACTION RECOGNITION

Video is essentially an information-intensive media with multiple granularities. For example, a video can be represented by a hierarchical structure including, from large to small, the entire *video*, short *clips*, consecutive frames (called *motion*, or optical flow), and individual *frames*. Different granularity depicts distinct capability to describe different actions. Recognizing actions from videos should take this intrinsic structure into account. Motivated by the above observations, we exploit such hierarchical nature of video structure and decompose video representation into multi-

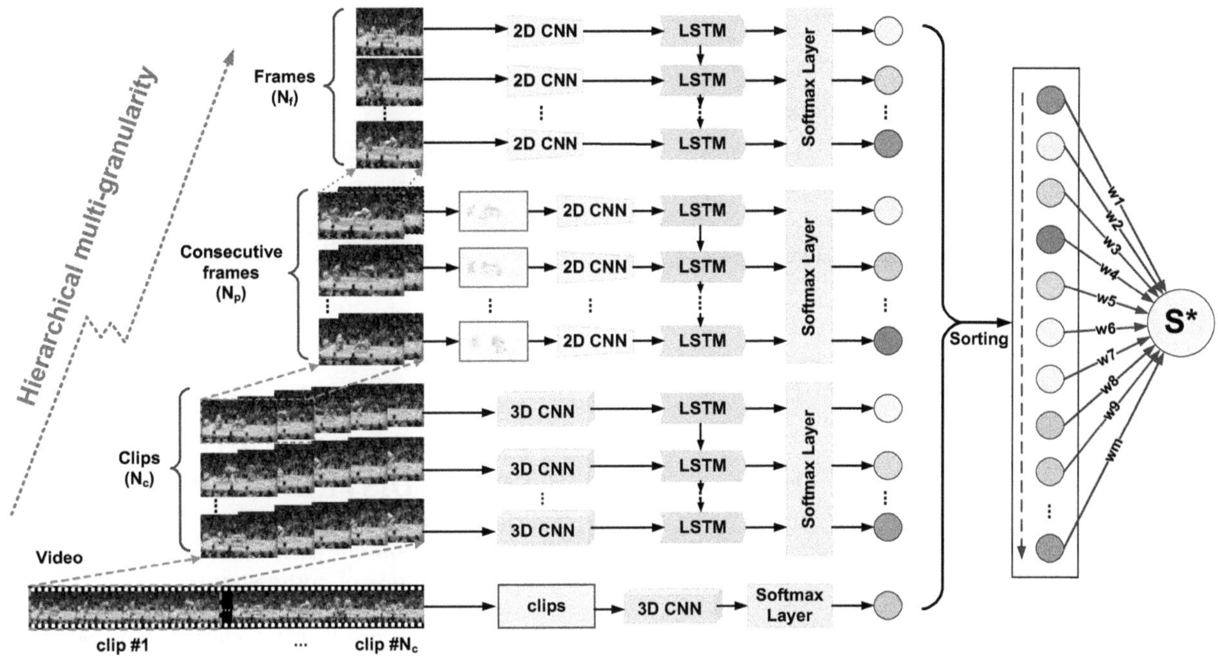

Figure 2: Multi-granular spatio-temporal architecture for video action recognition. A video is represented by the hierarchical structure with multiple granularities including, from small to large, *frame*, consecutive frames (*motion*), *clip*, and *video*. Each granularity is modeled as a single stream. 2D CNNs are used to model the *frame* and *motion* (optical flow images) streams, while 3D CNNs are used to model the *clip* and *video* streams. LSTMs are used to further model the temporal information in the *frame*, *motion*, and *clip* streams. A *softmax* layer is built on the top of each stream to obtain the prediction from each component. Suppose we have N_c clips, N_p motions (consecutive frame pairs), and N_f frames, then we have $N_c + N_p + N_f + 1$ components. The final action recognition result of the input video is obtained by linearly fusing the prediction scores from all the components with the weights learned on the score distribution. Note that this deep architecture is trainable in an end-to-end fashion.

granular streams. We design a deep architecture consisting of modeling of individual streams, 2D/3D CNNs with LSTM networks for learning spatio-temporal representations, and a novel multi-granularity score distribution scheme for fusion. Figure 2 shows the overall framework of our proposed multi-granular architecture for action recognition.

3.1 Modeling Frame Stream

For action recognition, individual video frames can provide useful characteristics as some actions are strongly associated with particular scenes and objects. To make full use of static frame appearance, VGG_19 [24], the recent superior CNN architecture for image classification, is adopted to extract high level visual features for each sampled video frame. VGG_19 is a very deep convolutional network with up to 19 weight layers (16 convolutional layers and 3 fully-connected layers). Thanks to the pre-train process using large dataset from ImageNet challenge, the VGG_19 model can be used to extract plentiful visual concepts like scenes and objects. Thus, we choose the outputs of the fully-connected layer in VGG_19 as the deep representation of a single frame.

3.2 Modeling Motion Stream

To model the displacement of consecutive frames, optical flow is extracted to describe the motion between consecutive frames. As the input to 2D CNN, the optical flow is firstly computed between a temporal window of consecutive frames with [1], and then converted to flow "image" by centering horizontal (x) and vertical (y) flow values around 128 and multiplying by a scalar such that flow values fall between 0 and 255. By this transformation, we can obtain two channels of optical flow "image," while the third channel is created by calculating the flow magnitude. Furthermore, to suppress the displacement caused by camera motion, which may introduce additional noise into CNN, a global motion component is estimated by the mean vector of each flow and then subtracted from the flow [23]. Although the input image is generated from optical flow, we also choose the pre-trained VGG_19 architecture as used for frame stream, and then fine-tune on the extracted optical flow "images."

3.3 Modeling Clip and Video Streams

Besides static frame and motion information between consecutive frames, 3D CNN is used to construct video clip features from both spatial and temporal dimensions by utilizing 3D convolutions. Unlike traditional 2D CNN, 3D CNN architecture takes video clip (multiple continuous frames) as the inputs and consists of alternating 3D convolutional and 3D pooling layers, which are further topped by a few fully-connected layers as described in [7]. For describing video clip by more powerful feature using 3D CNN, we choose the superior architecture in [27], named C3D, which aims to learn spatio-temporal features for videos using 3D CNN trained on Sports-1M video dataset [9]. As the deep network architecture is pre-trained on a large-scale video dataset, C3D can model general appearance and motion information simultaneously, which is important for action recognition. Similar to 2D CNN used for single frame and optical flow "image," we regard fully-connected layer outputs of C3D as the ex-

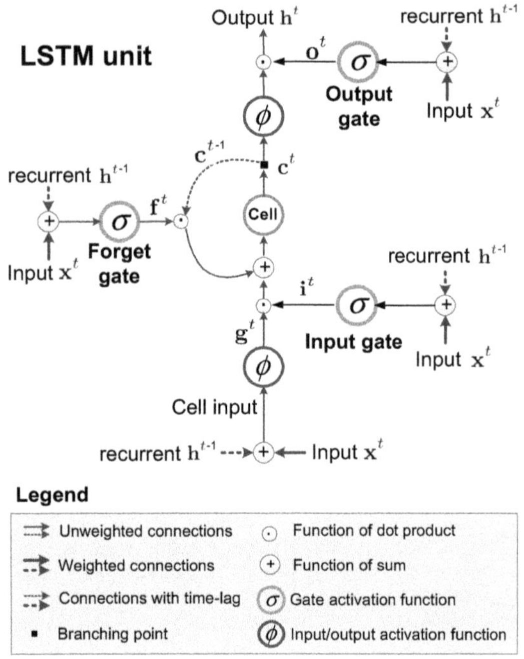

Figure 3: A diagram of a LSTM memory cell.

tracted features for sampled video clips. With the extracted features of each sampled video clip from a video by C3D, we simply perform mean pooling over all the video clips to generate video-level representations.

3.4 Modeling Temporal Dynamics with LSTM

To model the long-term temporal information in videos, we apply the Long Short-Term Memory (LSTM) on the frame, optical flow and video clip streams. The standard LSTM is a variant of RNN, which can capture long-term temporal information in the sequential data. To address the *vanishing/exploding gradients* issues when training traditional RNN, LSTM introduces a new structure called a *memory cell*. As illustrated in Figure 3, a memory cell is composed of four main elements: an input gate, a neuron with a self-recurrent connection, a forget gate and an output gate. The self-recurrent connection has a weight of 1.0 and ensures that, barring any outside interference, the state of a memory cell can remain constant from one timestep to another. The gates serve to modulate the interactions between the memory cell itself and its environment. The input gate can allow incoming signal to alter the state of the memory cell or block it. On the other hand, the output gate can allow the state of the memory cell to have an effect on other neurons or prevent it. Finally, the forget gate can modulate the memory cell's self-recurrent connection, allowing the cell to remember or forget its previous state, as needed. Many improvements have been made to the LSTM architecture since its original formulation [5] and we adopt the LSTM architecture as described in [17].

For timestep t, $\mathbf{x}^t$ and $\mathbf{h}^t$ are the input and output vector respectively, $\mathbf{T}$ are input weights matrices, $\mathbf{R}$ are recurrent weight matrices and $\mathbf{b}$ are bias vectors. *Logic sigmoid* $\sigma(x) = \frac{1}{1+e^{-x}}$ and *hyperbolic tangent* $\phi(x) = \frac{e^x - e^{-x}}{e^x + e^{-x}}$ are element-wise non-linear activation functions, mapping real values to $(0, 1)$ and $(-1, 1)$ separately. The dot product and sum of two vectors are denoted with $\odot$ and $\oplus$ respectively. Given inputs $\mathbf{x}^t$, $\mathbf{h}^{t-1}$ and $\mathbf{c}^{t-1}$, the LSTM unit updates for timestep t are:

$$\begin{aligned}
\mathbf{g}^t &= \phi(\mathbf{T}_g\mathbf{x}^t + \mathbf{R}_g\mathbf{h}^{t-1} + \mathbf{b}_g) && \textit{cell input}\\
\mathbf{i}^t &= \sigma(\mathbf{T}_i\mathbf{x}^t + \mathbf{R}_i\mathbf{h}^{t-1} + \mathbf{b}_i) && \textit{input gate}\\
\mathbf{f}^t &= \sigma(\mathbf{T}_f\mathbf{x}^t + \mathbf{R}_f\mathbf{h}^{t-1} + \mathbf{b}_f) && \textit{forgetgate}\\
\mathbf{c}^t &= \mathbf{g}^t \odot \mathbf{i}^t + \mathbf{c}^{t-1} \odot \mathbf{f}^t && \textit{cell state}\\
\mathbf{o}^t &= \sigma(\mathbf{T}_o\mathbf{x}^t + \mathbf{R}_o\mathbf{h}^{t-1} + \mathbf{b}_o) && \textit{output gate}\\
\mathbf{h}^t &= \phi(\mathbf{c}^t) \odot \mathbf{o}^t && \textit{cell output}
\end{aligned}$$

4. FUSION WITH MULTI-GRANULAR SCORE DISTRIBUTION (MSD)

Given the multi-granular streams in a video, we can predict the action score for each component from each stream. Inspired by the idea of addressing the temporal ambiguity of actions by learning score distribution in [4], we develop a multi-granular score fusion architecture in our deep networks rather than only using *max* or *mean*. Consequently, an improved action recognition score will be obtained by automatically aligning the relative importance to each component from all the streams based on the score distribution.

4.1 Formulation

Given a video, we combine the scores of all the components from multi-granular streams in a distribution matrix as

$$\mathbf{S} = (\mathbf{s}_1, ..., \mathbf{s}_c, ..., \mathbf{s}_C) \in \Re^{L\times C}, \quad (1)$$

where $\mathbf{s}_c \in \Re^L$ denotes the score column vector of L components from all the streams on the cth action class. Next, we will define a *sort* function on the score distribution matrix as

$$sort(\mathbf{S}) = \big(sort(\mathbf{s}_1), ..., sort(\mathbf{s}_c), ..., sort(\mathbf{s}_C)\big) \in \Re^{L\times C}, \quad (2)$$

where $sort(\mathbf{s}_c) \in \Re^L$ is a function to reorder all elements of the vector $\mathbf{s}_c$ in descending order. With large L, $sort(\mathbf{s}_c)$ can represent the score distribution of all the components on the cth action class.

Given N videos, each represented by the score distribution matrix $sort(\mathbf{S})$, we can learn a MSD classifier by formulating the optimization problem as

$$\min_{\mathbf{w}_c, b_c} \quad \sum_{i=1}^{N}\sum_{c=1}^{C} \max\{1 - y_i^c(\mathbf{w}_c \cdot sort(\mathbf{s}_c) + b_c), 0\} \quad (3)$$

$$s.t. \quad \sum_{l=1}^{L} w_c^l = 1, \quad c = 1, ..., C \ , \quad (4)$$

$$w_c^1 \geq w_c^2 \geq ... \geq w_c^L \geq 0, \quad c = 1, ..., C. \quad (5)$$

For the cth action class, the weight vector $\mathbf{w}_c$ and the bias item b_c can separate score distributions of positive and negative data. The loss function (3) is the sum of Hinge Losses. The constraint (4) requires the weights to have unit sum because we are learning weights for each component. The constraint (5) requires the weights to be monotonic and non-negative, because $sort(\mathbf{s}_c)$ are classification scores in descending order and we want to emphasize the relative importance of the components with high classification scores.

From the constraints, we can see that the feasible set of $\mathbf{w}_c$ includes two special cases: 1) $w_c^1 = 1, w_c^2 = ... = w_c^L = 0$, 2) $w_c^1 = w_c^2 = ... = w_c^L = \frac{1}{L}$. The former corresponds to *max* pooling, while the later refers to *mean* pooling.

4.2 Solution

As our architecture is an "end-to-end" neural network which is learnt by using standard backpropagation, we solve the optimization problem (3) by using stochastic gradient descent in a deep learning framework *Caffe* [8]. However, the two constraints (4) and (5) make the optimization difficult to be solved. To address this problem, we relax the two constraints by appending two penalty terms to the cost function J as

$$J = \mathcal{L} + \alpha \sum_{c=1}^{C} \|\mathbf{w}_c\|^2 + \beta \sum_{c=1}^{C} \Big(1 - \sum_{l=1}^{L} w_c^l\Big)^2 + \gamma \sum_{c=1}^{C} \sum_{l=1}^{L} m_c^l, \quad (6)$$

$$m_c^l = \begin{cases} w_c^{l+1} - w_c^l, & if\ w_c^{l+1} > w_c^l \\ 0, & if\ w_c^{l+1} \le w_c^l \end{cases} \quad l = 1, ..., L \text{ and } w_c^{L+1} = 0, \quad (7)$$

where the first part $\mathcal{L}$ is the loss function in Eq. (3), the second is a regularization term preventing over-fitting, the rest are two penalty terms and α, β, γ are the tradeoff parameters.

Finally, the above cost function J is minimized with respect to $\{\mathbf{w}_c\}_{c=1}^{C}$ and the gradients are calculated by

$$\frac{\partial J}{\partial w_c^l} = \frac{\partial \mathcal{L}}{\partial w_c^l} + 2\alpha w_c^l - 2\beta(1 - w_c^l) + \gamma\Big(\frac{\partial m_c^l}{\partial w_c^l} + \frac{\partial m_c^{l-1}}{\partial w_c^l}\Big), \quad (8)$$

$$\frac{\partial m_c^l}{\partial w_c^l} = \begin{cases} -1, & if\ w_c^{l+1} > w_c^l \\ 0, & if\ w_c^{l+1} \le w_c^l \end{cases} \quad l = 1, ..., L, \quad (9)$$

$$\frac{\partial m_c^{l-1}}{\partial w_c^l} = \begin{cases} 1, & if\ w_c^l > w_c^{l-1} \\ 0, & if\ w_c^l \le w_c^{l-1} \end{cases} \quad l = 2, 3, ..., L \text{ and } \frac{\partial m_c^0}{\partial w_c^1} = 0. \quad (10)$$

Each gradient is calculated upon a sorted score distribution. As the score order changes in each SGD iteration, backpropagation of the sorting operator is similar to that of max pooling layer. We store the index of sorted score in original vector and propagate the gradients to the corresponding element in the original vector when backpropagation. After the optimization of J in Eq. (6), we can obtain the optimal $\{\mathbf{w}_c\}_{c=1}^{C}$. With this, we compute the final improved action score for the video as

$$p_c = \mathbf{w}_c \cdot sort(\mathbf{s}_c) + b_c. \quad (11)$$

5. IMPLEMENTATIONS

Frame stream. We uniformly select 25 frames per video and adopt the VGG_19 [24] to extract frame features. The VGG_19 is first pre-trained with the ILSVRC-2012 training set of 1.2 million images and then fine-tuned by using the video frames, which is observed to be better than training from scratch. Following [23], we also use data augmentation like cropping and flipping. The learning rate starts from 10^{-3} and decreases to 10^{-4} after 14,000 iterations, then to 10^{-5} after 20,000 iterations. For temporal modeling, we extract the outputs of 4096-way fc6 layer from VGG_19 as inputs and adopt one-layer LSTM. We conduct experiments with different number of hidden states in LSTM. The LSTM weights are learnt by using the BPTT algorithm with a mini-batch size of 10. The learning rate starts from 10^{-2} and decreases to 10^{-3} after 100K iterations. The training is stopped after 150,000 iterations.

Table 1: The accuracy of *frame* and *motion* streams on UCF101 (split 1).

(a) The accuracy of different 2D CNN and LSTM used on *frame* and *motion* streams. The results are reported for late fusion.

Training setting	Frame	Motion
AlexNet	67.1%	68.4%
AlexNet + LSTM	69.3%	70.3%
VGG_19	77.9%	70.6%
VGG_19 + LSTM	79.3%	73.8%
VGG_19 + LSTM + Augmentation	**80.2%**	**74.6%**

(b) The effect of hidden layer size in the LSTM (VGG_19).

Hidden layer size	Frame	Motion
128	78.2%	71.2%
256	78.8%	72.6%
512	79.1%	73.5%
1024	**79.3%**	**73.8%**
2048	78.5%	73.1%

Motion stream. We compute the optical flow between consecutive frames using the GPU implementation of [1] in OpenCV toolbox. The optical flow is converted to a flow "image" by linearly rescaling horizontal (x) and vertical (y) flow values to [0, 255] range. The transformed x and y flows are the first two channels for the flow image and the third channel is created by calculating the flow magnitude. Moreover, the settings of VGG_19 and LSTM are the same with frame stream.

Clip stream. We define a *clip* as consecutive 16 frames, which is the same setting as [27]. The C3D is exploited to model video clip, which is pre-trained on Sports-1M [9] dataset with 1.1 million sports videos and then fine-tuned on UCF101 and HMDB51, respectively. As designed in C3D architecture, the input of C3D model is 16-frame clip and we uniformly sample 20 clips in each video. The learning rate starts from 10^{-4} and decreases to 10^{-5} after 10,000 iterations, then the training is stopped after 20,000 iterations. Again, the LSTM setting is the same with frame stream.

Video stream. The settings of video stream are similar to the clip stream. The only difference is that we do not involve LSTM after C3D and simply fuse the features of all video clips by *mean* pooling to generate the video-level representations.

6. EXPERIMENTS

6.1 Datasets

We empirically evaluate our multi-granular framework on the UCF101 [25] and HMDB51 [12] datasets. The UCF101 dataset is one of the most popular action recognition benchmarks. It consists of 13,320 videos from 101 action categories. The action categories are divided into five groups: Human-Object Interaction, Body-Motion Only, Human-Human Interaction, Playing Musical Instruments, and Sports. The HMDB51 dataset contains 6,849 video clips divided into 51 action categories, each containing a minimum of 101 clips. The experimental setup is the same for both datasets and three training/test splits are provided by the dataset organisers. Each split in UCF101 includes about 9.5K training and 3.7K test video, while a HMDB51 split

Table 2: The accuracy of *clip* and *video* streams on UCF101 (split 1) and HMDB51 (split 1).

(a) The comparisons of using features from different layers of C3D on *clip* stream.

Dataset	fc6	fc7	prob	fc6+LSTM
HMDB51	50.36%	48.65%	38.97%	**51.3%**
UCF101	83.11%	81.23%	69.81%	**83.9%**

(b) The comparisons of using the features from different layers of C3D on *video* stream.

Dataset	fc6	fc7	prob
HMDB51	**51.09%**	48.52%	39.10%
UCF101	**83.77%**	80.76%	67.01%

contains 3.5K training and 1.5K test videos. Following [23], we conduct our analyses of different streams on the first split of the UCF101 and HMDB51 datasets. The average accuracy over three splits on both datasets are reported when compared with the state-of-the-art techniques.

6.2 Evaluation of Frame and Motion Streams

We first examine the recognition performances of frame and optical flow streams from three aspects: 1) when different 2D CNN are used, 2) when LSTM is utilized to explore longer-term temporal information, and 3) how performance is affected by the size of hidden layer in LSTM learning.

The results and comparisons on UCF101 (split 1) are summarized in Table 1. Table 1a compares the accuracy of different CNN and LSTM on frame and optical flow stream, respectively, while Table 1b compares the performances with the hidden layer size of LSTM in the range of 128, 256, 512, 1024, and 2048. Compared to AlexNet [11], VGG_19 [24] with a deeper CNN exhibits significantly better performance on frame stream. Interestingly, using VGG_19 on optical flow stream gives only marginal performance gain. By additionally utilizing LSTM to explore longer-term temporal information, the improvements can be expected on both frame and optical flow streams. Furthermore, when augmenting the test frame (flow image) by cropping and flipping four corners and the center of the frame and averaging the scores across the frame and its crops, the performance can achieve 80.2% and 74.6% on frame and optical flow, respectively.

In general, increasing the hidden layer size of LSTM can lead to the improvement of the accuracy. When the hidden layer size reaches 1024 in our case, no further improvement can be obtained on both frame and optical flow streams. Note that the performances are reported based on the original frame or optical flow image with only cropping center and no flipping operation in this comparison.

6.3 Evaluation of Clip and Video Streams

Next, we turn to measure the performance of the clip and video streams in terms of features extracted from different layers of 3D CNN (C3D) on both datasets. We extract C3D features: fc6, fc7, and prob for each video clip. The recognition score is computed by late fusing the predicted score on each video clip and the accuracy comparison by using the outputs from these three different layers is shown in Table 2a. As indicated by our results, the recognition using the C3D feature of fc6 layer leads to a larger performance boost against the C3D features of fc7 and prob layers. Furthermore, the accuracy by using the feature of fc6 can achieve 51.3% and 83.9% on HMDB51 and UCF101 after longer-term temporal modeling with LSTM networks, respectively. The features for video stream are computed by averaging the video clip features separately for each type of feature and Table 2b reports the comparison of different C3D features on video stream. Similar to the observations on video clip stream, the features of fc6 layer achieves the best performance among all the three layers with a large margin.

Table 4: The performance in terms of mean accuracy (over three splits) on UCF101 and HMDB51. Please note that the methods in [29, 18, 13] are based on traditional dense trajectory which is computationally expensive, while the methods in [35, 30] combine dense trajectory and deep learning based algorithms. Our approach outperforms the deep learning-based methods without combination of dense trajectory [3, 23, 16] with a large margin. "–" means that the authors did not report their performance on this dataset. IDT: improved dense trajectory [29]; MIFS: Multi-skip Feature Stacking [13]; LRCN: Long-term Recurrent Convolutional Networks [3]; C3D: Convolutional 3D [27]; TDD: Trajectory-pooled Deep-convolutional Descriptor [30].

Method	UCF101	HMDB51
IDT [29]	85.9%	57.2%
IDT w/ Encodings [18]	87.9%	61.1%
MIFS [13]	89.1%	**65.1%**
"Slow Fusion" ConvNet [9]	65.4%	–
LRCN [3]	82.9%	–
C3D [27]	85.2%	–
Two-stream model [23]	88.0%	59.4%
Composite LSTM [26]	84.3%	–
CNN + IDT [35]	89.6%	–
Temporal Pooling + LSTM [16]	88.6%	–
TDD [30]	90.3%	63.2%
Ours	**90.8%**	**63.6%**

6.4 Evaluation of MSD

Here we evaluate the complete multi-granular architecture, which combines the four streams with the MSD fusion method. Table 3 details the accuracy across different fusion strategies on three splits of HMDB51 and UCF101, respectively. MSD consistently outperforms Max and Mean in every split of both two datasets. The improvement is observed in different types of actions. For instance, the actions "playing piano" and "biking" are better fused with Mean as the videos relevant to the two actions are consistent in content. On the other hand, the recognition of actions "cliff diving" and "basketball dunk" show much better results with Max fusion. In the experiment, MSD boosts the accuracy of these actions. Figure 4 shows the top eight weights learnt by MSD and their corresponding components of three exemplary videos from category "baseball pitch," "front crawl," and "hammering." We can easily see that all the eight components are highly related to each action. More importantly, the top eight components come from four different streams, which validates the effectiveness of MSD on fusing multi-granular information.

6.5 Comparisons with State-of-the-Art

We compare with several state-of-the-art techniques on three splits of UCF101 and HMDB51. As shown in Table 4, our multi-granular spatio-temporal architecture shows the

Table 3: The comparisons of the proposed MSD with Mean and Max fusion schemes in terms of accuracy on three splits of HMDB51 and UCF101.

Dataset	split 1			split 2			split 3		
	Mean	Max	MSD	Mean	Max	MSD	Mean	Max	MSD
HMDB51	61.5%	59.6%	**63.1%**	61.8%	59.5%	**63.5%**	62.1%	60.1%	**64.1%**
UCF101	89.6%	87.6%	**90.2%**	89.6%	87.4%	**90.3%**	91.2%	88.1%	**91.9%**

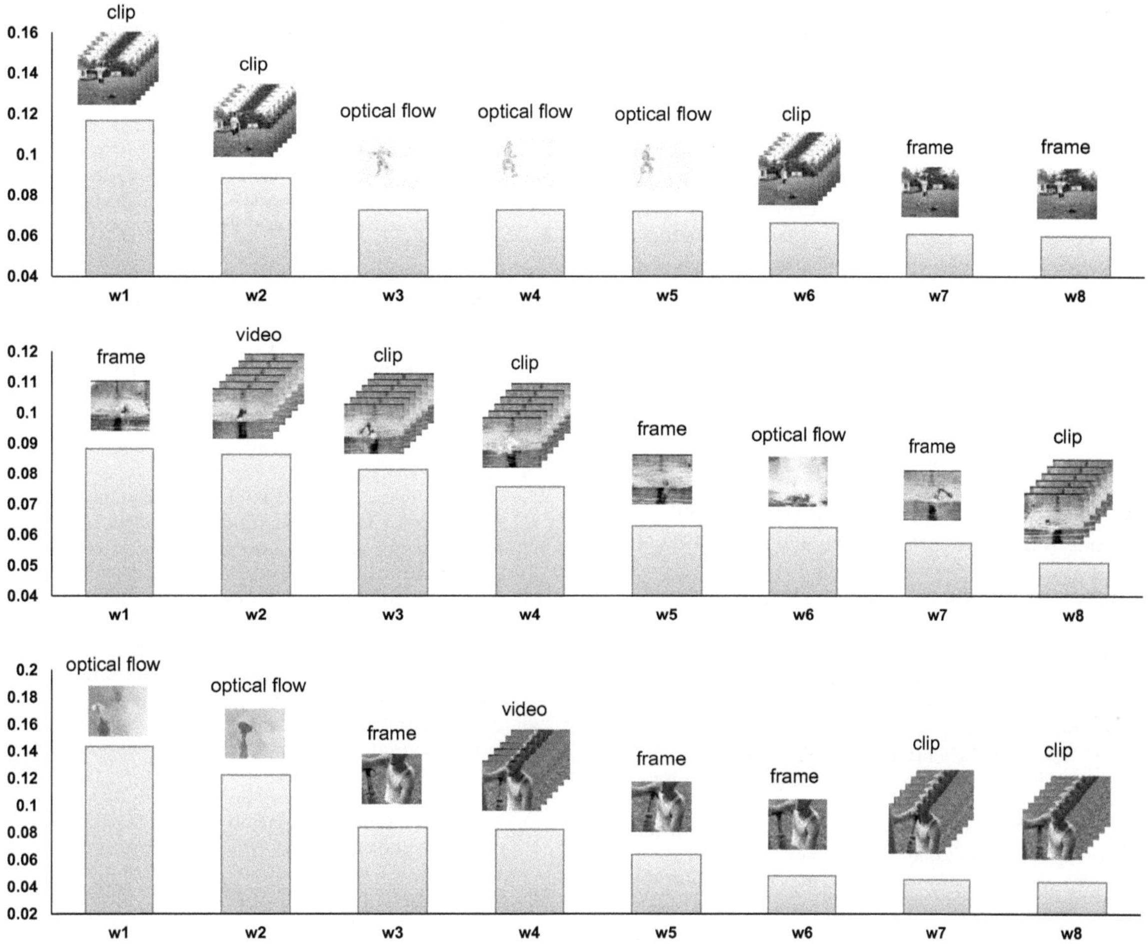

Figure 4: Examples showing the top eight weights learned by the MSD and their corresponding components in a video (top: baseball pitch, middle: front crawl, bottom: hammering). We can see that MSD is able to learn the contributions from different components for particular actions. For example, two *clip* components play important roles for recognizing "baseball pitch," while two *motion* (optical flow) components contribute more to the recognition of "hammering."

best performance on UCF101 dataset. It makes the improvement over [30] by 0.5%, which is generally considered as a significant progress on this dataset. On the HMDB51, the works [13, 30] with competitive results are based on the motion trajectory, while our approach fully relies on the deep learning architecture and is trained end-to-end. Compared with the two-stream model [23], our architecture by additionally incorporating more temporal modeling and utilizing a sophisticated fusion strategy leads to a performance boost on both datasets. It is also worth noting that in the training of the HMDB51 dataset, the work in [23] exploits UCF101 as additional training data through multi-task learning, while our approach is purely trained on HMDB51 only. In addition, the recent works in [3, 16, 26] also use the LSTM to exploit temporal information. Our approach achieves more promising results as more dimensions of cues are included.

Table 5: Run time of different streams averaged over all test videos in UCF101 dataset (milliseconds).

Stream	2D/3D CNN	LSTM	SUM
frame	750	12	762
motion	750	12	762
clip	490	10	500
video	490	–	490

6.6 Run Time

Table 5 listed the detailed run time of each stream averaged over all test videos in UCF101 dataset. The experiments are conducted on a regular server (Intel Xeon 2.40GHz CPU and 256 GB RAM) with a single NVidia K80 GPU. As each stream could be executed in parallel and the fusion with MSD provides instant responses, the average prediction time of our architecture on each video in UCF101 is about 762 milliseconds, which is very efficient. This is much faster than trajectory-based approaches, e.g. IDT, which requires about seven minutes on each video in UCF101.

7. CONCLUSIONS

We have presented a multi-granular deep architecture for action recognition in videos, which is able to incorporate information at a multitude of granularity including frame, consecutive frames (motion), clip and the entire video. Specifically, we model each granularity with two types of CNNs (2D CNN trained on frame and motion streams, and 3D C-NN on clip and video streams). We employ LSTM networks to incorporate long-term temporal modeling based on the granularity features. To fuse the recognition scores of individual components in multiple streams, the distribution of scores is exploited to find the optimal weight for each component. We show that our approach outperforms several state-of-the-art methods on two benchmark datasets.

Our future works are as follows. First, video action recognition can be enhanced by further considering audio information. The audio features can be exploited together with current four streams to more comprehensively characterize the actions. Second, the method of learning the representations of the entire video could be explored by using RNNs in an encoder-decoder framework. In addition, we will continue to conduct more in-depth investigations on how fusion weights of individual streams can be dynamically determined to boost the action recognition performance.

8. REFERENCES

[1] T. Brox, A. Bruhn, N. Papenberg, and J. Weickert. High accuracy optical flow estimation based on a theory for warping. In *ECCV*. 2004.

[2] P. Dollár, V. Rabaud, G. Cottrell, and S. Belongie. Behavior recognition via sparse spatio-temporal features. In *VS-PETS*, 2005.

[3] J. Donahue, L. A. Hendricks, S. Guadarrama, M. Rohrbach, S. Venugopalan, K. Saenko, and T. Darrell. Long-term recurrent convolutional networks for visual recognition and description. *arXiv preprint arXiv:1411.4389*, 2014.

[4] M. Hoai and A. Zisserman. Improving human action recognition using score distribution and ranking. In *ACCV*, 2014.

[5] S. Hochreiter and J. Schmidhuber. Long short-term memory. *Neural computation*, 9(8):1735–1780, 1997.

[6] M. Jain, H. Jégou, and P. Bouthemy. Better exploiting motion for better action recognition. In *CVPR*, 2013.

[7] S. Ji, W. Xu, M. Yang, and K. Yu. 3d convolutional neural networks for human action recognition. *IEEE Trans. on PAMI*, 35(1):221–231, 2013.

[8] Y. Jia, E. Shelhamer, J. Donahue, S. Karayev, J. Long, R. Girshick, S. Guadarrama, and T. Darrell. Caffe: Convolutional architecture for fast feature embedding. *arXiv preprint arXiv:1408.5093*, 2014.

[9] A. Karpathy, G. Toderici, S. Shetty, T. Leung, R. Sukthankar, and L. Fei-Fei. Large-scale video classification with convolutional neural networks. In *CVPR*, 2014.

[10] A. Kläser, M. Marszalek, and C. Schmid. A spatio-temporal descriptor based on 3d-gradients. In *BMVC*, 2008.

[11] A. Krizhevsky, I. Sutskever, and G. E. Hinton. Imagenet classification with deep convolutional neural networks. In *NIPS*, 2012.

[12] H. Kuehne, H. Jhuang, E. Garrote, T. Poggio, and T. Serre. HMDB: a large video database for human motion recognition. In *ICCV*, 2011.

[13] Z. Lan, M. Lin, X. Li, A. G. Hauptmann, and B. Raj. Beyond gaussian pyramid: Multi-skip feature stacking for action recognition. In *CVPR*, 2015.

[14] I. Laptev and T. Lindeberg. Space-time interest points. In *ICCV*, 2003.

[15] I. Laptev, M. Marszalek, C. Schmid, and B. Rozenfeld. Learning realistic human actions from movies. In *CVPR*, 2008.

[16] J. Y.-H. Ng, M. Hausknecht, S. Vijayanarasimhan, O. Vinyals, R. Monga, and G. Toderici. Beyond short snippets deep networks for video classification. In *CVPR*, 2015.

[17] Y. Pan, T. Mei, T. Yao, H. Li, and Y. Rui. Jointly modeling embedding and translation to bridge video and language. *arXiv preprint arXiv:1505.01861v3*, 2015.

[18] X. Peng, L. Wang, X. Wang, and Y. Qiao. Bag of visual words and fusion methods for action recognition: Comprehensive study and good practice. *arXiv preprint arXiv:1405.4506*, 2014.

[19] F. Perronnin, J. Sánchez, and T. Mensink. Improving the fisher kernel for large-scale image classification. In *ECCV*, 2010.

[20] Z. Qiu, Q. Li, T. Yao, T. Mei, and Y. Rui. Msr asia msm at thumos challenge 2015. In *CVPR THUMOS Challenge Workshop*, 2015.

[21] P. Scovanner, S. Ali, and M. Shah. A 3-dimensional sift descriptor and its application to action recognition. In *ACM MM*, 2007.

[22] K. Simonyan, A. Vedaldi, and A. Zisserman. Deep fisher networks for large-scale image classification. In *NIPS*, 2013.

[23] K. Simonyan and A. Zisserman. Two-stream convolutional networks for action recognition in videos. In *NIPS*, 2014.

[24] K. Simonyan and A. Zisserman. Very deep convolutional networks for large-scale image recognition. In *ICLR*, 2015.

[25] K. Soomro, A. R. Zamir, and M. Shah. UCF101: A dataset of 101 human action classes from videos in the wild. *CRCV-TR-12-01*, 2012.

[26] N. Srivastava, E. Mansimov, and R. Salakhutdinov. Unsupervised learning of video representations using lstms. In *ICML*, 2015.

[27] D. Tran, L. D. Bourdev, R. Fergus, L. Torresani, and M. Paluri. Learning spatiotemporal features with 3d convolutional networks. *arXiv preprint arXiv:1412.0767*, 2014.

[28] H. Wang, A. Kläser, C. Schmid, and C.-L. Liu. Action recognition by dense trajectories. In *CVPR*, 2011.

[29] H. Wang and C. Schmid. Action recognition with improved trajectories. In *ICCV*, 2013.

[30] L. Wang, Y. Qiao, and X. Tang. Action recognition with trajectory-pooled deep-convolutional descriptors. In *CVPR*, 2015.

[31] G. Willems, T. Tuytelaars, and L. J. V. Gool. An efficient dense and scale-invariant spatio-temporal interest point detector. In *ECCV*, 2008.

[32] Z. Wu, Y.-G. Jiang, J. Wang, J. Pu, and X. Xue. Exploring inter-feature and inter-class relationships with deep neural networks for video classification. In *ACM MM*, 2014.

[33] T. Yao, T. Mei, C.-W. Ngo, and S. Li. Annotation for free: Video tagging by mining user search behavior. In *ACM MM*, 2013.

[34] X. Yuan, W. Lai, T. Mei, X.-S. Hua, and X.-Q. Wu. Automatic video genre categorization using hierarchical svm. In *ICIP*, 2006.

[35] S. Zha, F. Luisier, W. Andrews, N. Srivastava, and R. Salakhutdinov. Exploiting image-trained CNN architectures for unconstrained video classification. *arXiv preprint arXiv:1503.04144*, 2015.

[36] Z.-J. Zha, T. Mei, Z. Wang, and X.-S. Hua. Building a comprehensive ontology to refine video concept detection. In *ACM SIGMM Workshop on MIR*, 2007.

A Short Survey of Recent Advances in Graph Matching

Junchi Yan*
East China Normal University
IBM Research – China
jcyan@sei.ecnu.edu.cn

Xu-Cheng Yin
University of Science and Technology Beijing
xuchengyin@ustb.edu.cn

Weiyao Lin
Shanghai Jiao Tong University
wylin@sjtu.edu.cn

Cheng Deng
Xidian University
chdeng@mail.xidian.edu.cn

Hongyuan Zha
Georgia Institute of Technology
zha@cc.gatech.edu

Xiaokang Yang
Shanghai Jiao Tong University
xkyang@sjtu.edu.cn

ABSTRACT
Graph matching, which refers to a class of computational problems of finding an optimal correspondence between the vertices of graphs to minimize (maximize) their node and edge disagreements (affinities), is a fundamental problem in computer science and relates to many areas such as combinatorics, pattern recognition, multimedia and computer vision. Compared with the exact graph (sub)isomorphism often considered in a theoretical setting, inexact weighted graph matching receives more attentions due to its flexibility and practical utility. A short review of the recent research activity concerning (inexact) weighted graph matching is presented, detailing the methodologies, formulations, and algorithms. It highlights the methods under several key bullets, e.g. how many graphs are involved, how the affinity is modeled, how the problem order is explored, and how the matching procedure is conducted etc. Moreover, the research activity at the forefront of graph matching applications especially in computer vision, multimedia and machine learning is reported. The aim is to provide a systematic and compact framework regarding the recent development and the current state-of-the-arts in graph matching.

Keywords
Survey; graph matching; correspondence; similarity

1. INTRODUCTION
Graph matching, which refers to a class of computational problems of finding an optimal correspondence between the vertices of graphs to minimize (maximize) their node and edge disagreements (affinities), has been a fundamental problem in computer science and relates to many areas such as pattern recognition, computer vision, graphics, bioinformatics, whereby correspondence and similarity between graphs are required. One main advantage for describing the relational information by attributed graphs instead of vectors is that graphs allow for a more powerful representation of structural relations. In the general case, nodes and edges are assigned with arbitrary attributes [124, 4]. This modeling is rather flexible from the application-oriented point of view, as most real-world graphs fall into this category.

The GM problem can be divided into two general categories: exact matching and inexact matching. In the former task, a strict correspondence is required to be found, or at least among their substructures. In the latter, this requirement is substantially relaxed to find the bijection between the vertex that optimizes a certain affinity or distortion criterion – thus is also called error-tolerant/correcting GM in literature [14, 13], since matchings between non-identical graphs need to be addressed for real-world problems.

Different from the point based registration methods, such as RANSAC [45] and Iterative Closet Point (ICP) [151], GM methods incorporate both the unary *node-to-node*, and the second-order, or even higher-order, *(hyper)edge-to-(hyper)edge* structural similarities. By encoding such geometrical cues in the graph representation and matching process, GM methods can in general find better correspondence. Although extensive research has been done, deriving optimal GM is still a challenging problem in both theory and practice: in deed the GM problem can be formulated as a quadratic assignment problem (QAP) [77], being well-known NP-complete [49].

To our surprise, there is scarcely any focused whole-picture of up-to-date development on inexact weighted graph matching though it has already attracted considerable attentions due to its flexibility in modeling real-world problems.

Several surveys e.g. [15, 30, 46, 125] involve the broad literature on graph-based techniques, especially in the context of pattern recognition. They cover various areas beyond weighted graph matching, e.g. graph kernel, graph embedding, graph clustering, while devote only a minor portion of the space to the recent development of GM especially in computer vision and machine learning. For instance, despite the title of the survey [76], it is mostly dedicated to graph embedding and graph kernels. These concepts are related to GM as they help evaluate the similarity among graphs, but they are out of the scope of this survey. There are also

*Corresponding author. This work is partially supported by the Shanghai Science and Technology Committee (15JC1401700, 14XD1402100) NSFC 61471235 and Microsoft Research Asia Collaborative Research Award.

ICMR'16, June 06-09, 2016, New York, NY, USA
© 2016 ACM. ISBN 978-1-4503-4359-6/16/06...$15.00
DOI: http://dx.doi.org/10.1145/2911996.2912035

a few specific reports on one or a few small areas related to GM. [106] presents a comparative evaluation of four exact algorithms for graph isomorphism and graph-subgraph isomorphism. [48] focuses on the graph edit distance based methods for both attributed and non-attributed graphs. On the other hand, are reviews on the applications of GM to computer vision and pattern recognition [31, 126]. However, many recent work studied in this paper are not covered in these surveys. One focused review on inexact weighted graph matching [131], which is the emphasis of this survey, is dated back one decade ago [18].

This paper is aimed to address the above gap between a too broad (but often rather general) survey and a too narrow one, especially for those emerging topics in GM, and the vitality of this survey involves two main regards:

i) It provides a systematic view of looking at the recent development on (inexact) weighted graph matching, concerning how the problem is formulated, two or multiple graphs are involved, how the affinity is modeled etc. Most of these perspectives are fresh compared with existing surveys, which we believe relates to the recent emerging research advances.

ii) This paper involves more recent GM works, especially from the computer vision and machine learning community. A majority of these works have not been covered in [125, 46, 76, 126], perhaps due to these existing surveys often focus on the area of pattern recognition. This survey aims to strengthen the tie between different communities.

The survey is organized as follows. We first give a brief on exact graph matching, which is commonly regarded too idealistic for practical problems. Then we are devoted to the recent advance in inexact weighted graph matching – a more realistic setting. It is followed by a study on the applications especially in multimedia and a conclusive remark.

2. BRIEF ON EXACT GRAPH MATCHING

Classical exact graph matching algorithms employ the concepts of graph and subgraph isomorphisms, such that requires a bijective node mapping between two (sub)graphs, and preserves the edges of both graphs with zero-distortion, which is termed isomorphism. Graph isomorphism, which involves to verify whether a zero-distortion node mapping exists, is known to be in NP, neither known to be in P nor NP-complete [49]. There are special structure where graph isomorphism can be solved in polynomial time. For instance, checking the isomorphism between planar graphs [42], or graphs with bounded vertex degree [78], is known to be solvable in a linear time .

One weaker form of exact GM is subgraph isomorphism, which requires the existence of an isomorphism between one graph and the subgraph of the other. Subgraph isomorphism is known to be NP-complete [32]. One more practical, while still NP-hard problem is the maximum common subgraph (MCS) [68]. It is aimed to find the largest subgraph in one graph that is isomorphic to a subgraph in the other.

3. INEXACT GRAPH MATCHING

GM is often integrated with an 'inexact' flavor to account for ubiquitous noises, involving finding a correspondence concerning minimum rather than zero-distortion, or equivalently a maximum affinity, when exact matching is impossible. In such cases, the concept of inexact [7], also termed as error-correcting [14] or error-tolerant [13] matching, is called for. Specifically, this survey pays more attention on the general quadratic assignment programming based formulations and the variants for weighted graphs [131], though there are similar forms under different residual norms [124, 4].

3.1 Some basic formulations

3.1.1 Second-order affinity matrix based model

Most GM methods try to find correspondences between two graphs e.g. [66, 50, 25, 17, 41]. In general, the two-graph matching problem can be formulated as a quadratic assignment problem (QAP). As a most general form, the Lawler's QAP [60] to maximize the affinity score is:

$$J(\mathbf{X}) = \text{vec}(\mathbf{X})^\top \mathbf{K} \text{vec}(\mathbf{X}) \tag{1}$$
$$\mathbf{X}\mathbf{1}_{n_2} = \mathbf{1}_{n_1}, \mathbf{X}^T\mathbf{1}_{n_1} \leq \mathbf{1}_{n_2}$$

where $\mathbf{X}$ refers to the assignment matrix between two graphs. The assignment constraint is one typical setting in GM. Here it refers to the two-way one-to-one node mapping: a node from graph $\mathcal{G}_1$ of node size n_1 can match at most one node in $\mathcal{G}_2$ of size n_2 and every node in $\mathcal{G}_2$ is corresponding to one node in $\mathcal{G}_1$. There is no (one/many)-to-many matchings between two graphs, though there is a line of studies on these more general cases [3, 145, 115, 37, 159] beyond the one-to-one mapping constraint. $\mathbf{K}$ is the second-order affinity matrix. A large portion of recent GM works including both two-graph matching e.g. [50, 25, 154] and multi-graph matching e.g. [135, 136] adopt the Lawler's formula.

The Koopmans-Beckmann's QAP [77] is another QAP form for two-graph matching, which can be written by

$$J(\mathbf{X}) = \text{tr}(\mathbf{X}^\top \mathbf{F}_i \mathbf{X} \mathbf{F}_j) + \text{tr}(\mathbf{K}_p^\top \mathbf{X}) \tag{2}$$

The vector $\mathbf{F}_i$, $\mathbf{F}_j$ are the weighted adjacency matrices and $\mathbf{K}_p$ is the node-to-node similarity matrix. Note the Koopmans-Beckmann's QAP can always be represented as a special case of the Lawler's by setting $\mathbf{K} = \mathbf{F}_j \otimes \mathbf{F}_i$.

3.1.2 Factorized affinity matrix

There are recent advances in the interpretation of the affinity matrix. [154] show how to factorize the affinity matrix as a Kronecker product of smaller matrices. One formulation for the undirected graphs is written by:

$$\mathbf{K} = (\mathbf{H}_2 \otimes \mathbf{H}_1)\text{diag}(\text{vec}(\mathbf{L}))(\mathbf{H}_2 \otimes \mathbf{H}_1)^T \tag{3}$$
$$\text{where} \quad \mathbf{H}_i = [\mathbf{G}_i, \mathbf{I}_{n_i}] \in \{0,1\}^{n_i \times (m_i+n_i)}, \quad i = 1,2$$
$$\mathbf{L} = \begin{bmatrix} \mathbf{K}^q & -\mathbf{K}^q\mathbf{G}_2^T \\ -\mathbf{G}_1\mathbf{K}^q & \mathbf{G}_1\mathbf{K}^q\mathbf{G}_2^T + \mathbf{K}^p \end{bmatrix}$$

where n_i and m_i is the number of nodes and edges in graph i respectively and $\otimes$ is the Kronecker product operation between matrices. $\mathbf{K}^p \in \mathbb{R}^{n_1 \times n_2}$ denotes the node affinity matrix, and $\mathbf{K}^q \in \mathbb{R}^{m_1 \times m_2}$ for the edge affinity matrix. The graph structure is specified by the node-edge incidence matrix $\mathbf{G} \in \mathbb{R}^{n \times m}$ such that the non-zero elements in each column of $\mathbf{G}$ indicate the starting and ending nodes in the corresponding edge. The factorization provides a taxonomy for GM and reveals the connection among several methods. Readers are referred to [154] for greater details.

3.1.3 *Higher-order affinity tensor based model*

Based on tensor marginalization as adopted by several hypergraph matching works [148, 21, 39, 139]:

$$\mathbf{x}^* = \arg\max(\mathbf{H} \otimes_1 \mathbf{x} \otimes_2 \mathbf{x} \ldots \otimes_m \mathbf{x}) \quad s.t. \qquad (4)$$
$$\mathbf{X}\mathbf{1}_{n_2} = \mathbf{1}_{n_1}, \mathbf{X}^T\mathbf{1}_{n_1} \leq \mathbf{1}_{n_2}, \mathbf{x} = \text{vec}(\mathbf{X}) \in \{0,1\}^{n_1 n_2 \times 1}$$

where m is the affinity order and $\mathbf{H}$ is the m-order affinity tensor whose element encodes the affinity between two hyperedges from the graphs. $\otimes_k$ is the tensor product [63]. Readers are referred to Sec. 3.1 in [39] for details on tensor multiplication. The above works all assume the affinity tensor is invariant w.r.t. the index of the hyperedge pairs.

3.1.4 *Graph edit distance based graph matching*

[102] firstly introduces the graph edit distance (GED), as an important way to measure the similarity between pairwise graphs. GED is defined from the notion of edit path which corresponds to a sequence of elementary transformations of a graph into another. An standard edit operation, associated with non-negative value, is a transformation performed on the structure of a graph, restricted to be elementary: node or edge insertion, removal and substitution. The cost of the edit path is defined as the sum of all its elementary operation's costs [14] and the GED distance between two graphs can then be defined as the minimum cost required to transform one of the given graphs into the other. Computing the GED is known NP-complete and a classic method is by means of a tree search procedure that basically evaluates all possible node-to-node correspondences [102].

A number of approximate methods have been proposed to render the computation of graph edit distance feasible [48]. Among these, we examine two approximate formulations. One is called bipartite GED [98, 99] solved by linear assignment; the other is based on the quadratic assignment formulation [88, 10], which transforms the GED problem to a graph matching one, though computing the GED is generally not equivalent to solving a graph matching problem.
Bipartite GED [98] and its variants e.g. [109, 110] approximate the GED problem by a linear assignment problem, which can be solved efficiently via e.g. the Hungarian method [85]. These methods approximate graph structure by a node-to-node cost matrix that encodes local clique structure. However, edit operations on nodes and edges are not handled simultaneously, which limits the efficacy of such a first-order approximation strategy.
QAP based GED To improve the above Bipartite GED models, [88] firstly shows that the GED problem can be formalized as a Quadratic Assignment Programming problem, through the definition of fuzzy paths. In the more recent work, [10] then gives a further formal and more general analysis on how and in what conditions the GED can be transformed to a QAP form, which is directly related to weighted GM solvers e.g. [65] as used in [10].

3.2 Affinity/cost modeling

3.2.1 *Attribute/affinity learning*

A large number of GM methods are fed with a manually-predefined affinity matrix/tensor and keep it unchanged during the entire matching process. This would be too restricted to cope with noisy real-world data. Recent work leverage various leaning algorithms for computing the optimal affinity matrix [66, 17, 67, 23, 54], and these methods in general fall into either supervised [17], unsupervised [66], or semi-supervised [67] learning paradigm, based on to what extent the supervision information is used.

The authors in [23] present a unified parameterized graph structure learning model, and solve it in a max-margin framework. They define a joint feature map by the vector form:

$$\Phi(\mathcal{G}, \mathcal{G}', \pi) = [\cdots, s_v(a_i, a_{\pi(i)}), \cdots, s_e(a_{ij}, a_{\pi(i)\pi(j)}) \cdots]^T$$

By introducing weights on all elements of this feature map, one obtains a score function: $S(\mathcal{G}, \mathcal{G}', \pi, \beta) = \beta\Phi(\mathcal{G}, \mathcal{G}', \pi)$ where β is a weight vector of the node and edge similarity.

As observed by [23], many previous learning based GM methods can be viewed as a special case for the above formulation. Specifically, [17] uses a 60-dimensional similarity function s_v for appearance similarity and a simple binary similarity s_e for edges. [123] adopts 2-dimensional s_v and s_e functions to measure appearance similarity, geometric compatibility and occlusion. [66] employs a multi-dimensional s_e to model similarity without considering s_v.

3.2.2 *Graph edit cost learning*

In [14], the authors theoretically prove that the graph edit costs is critical to the performance of the GED based methods. In complex tasks a manual procedure for cost setting is difficult, or even impossible to apply. To address this issue, [87] aims to learn the edit cost by a probabilistic framework, to reduce the intra-class edit distance and increase the inter-class one. Alternatively, [86] proposes to use self-organizing maps to learn the edit cost.

3.3 Joint matching multiple graphs

Dating back to the simpler setting of matching a set of point sets based on their node-wise attributes[95, 36], here is an emerging line of work for devising advanced multi-graph matching methods [117, 55, 93, 135, 118, 134, 20, 114], because directly using on-the-shelf two-graph solvers is incapable of fully utilizing the cross-graph information of affinity and matching consistency. Most multi-graph matching methods involve the following aspects:

i) One limitation of employing a two-graph matching method for multi-graph is that the so-called cycle-consistency need additional care. Consider one toy example, for graphs $\mathcal{G}_i$, $\mathcal{G}_j$, $\mathcal{G}_a$, $\mathcal{G}_b$ of equal size with no outliers, the four matching solutions between two graphs $\mathbf{X}_{ij}$, $\mathbf{X}_{ia}$, $\mathbf{X}_{aj}$, $\mathbf{X}_{ib}$, which are computed by two-graph matching independently, can lead to cycle-inconsistency: $\mathbf{X}_{ia}\mathbf{X}_{aj} \neq \mathbf{X}_{ib}\mathbf{X}_{bj}$ [135].

Many multi-graph matching models capture the above consistency often in an iterative or a one-shot setting:

Iterative methods aim to maximize the affinity and meanwhile account for consistency. [135, 136] enforce the cycle-consistency by obeying the strict equality constraints $\mathbf{X}_{ij} = \mathbf{X}_{ib}\mathbf{X}_{bj}$ over the whole iterative variable updating procedure. The performance is often sensitive to the starting solution and variable rotating order – inherently vulnerable to error accumulation. Similar hard constraint is devised by [118] which extends the Graduated Assignment algorithm for two-graph matching [50] to multi-graph one. [134, 133] propose a more flexible and robust mechanism, where they gradually infuse consistency over iterations.

One-shot methods try to enforce overall consistency immediately. [93, 20, 158] achieve consistency as a post-step whose inputs are the putative two-graph matchings $\{\mathbf{X}\}_{i,j=1}^N$ obtained by a two-graph matching solver. Since no reinforcement is performed to boost the affinity, these methods are found often sensitive to the quality of initial inputs.

ii) In a line of recent work [118, 135, 136, 134, 133], the authors write out the objective for multi-graph matching by adding up pairwise affinity terms $\{\text{vec}(\mathbf{X})^\top \mathbf{K}\text{vec}(\mathbf{X})\}_{i,j=1}^N$, and the two-graph matchings $\{\mathbf{X}\}_{i,j=1}^N$ are iteratively updated such that strictly, or gradually satisfy the cycle-consistency constraints. While for the two non-iterative methods [93, 20], affinity information is only considered locally for a pair of graphs at hand. The affinity information is ignored in their post-step where consistency is enforced.

Based on the above two groups of methods, the authors in [138] make two observations: first, cycle-inconsistency is caused by the use of two-graph matchings – a distributed and redundant representation for multi-graph matching; second, for affinity modeling, existing multi-graph matching methods are mostly based on the two-graph affinity representation. Motivated by this, they present a novel formulation where the affinity among graphs is encoded by a matrix stacked by the vectorized attributes of graphs, and the variables are reduced to a set of non-redundant bases inherent free from the consistency constraint.

3.4 Higher-order graph matching

Higher-order attributes for matching hypergraphs have recently drawn considerable attentions, with the aim of improving the matching robustness by incorporating higher-order cues. Third-order models, for instance using the angles of sampled triplets [39, 63, 139], are often explored in for their tradeoff between efficiency and modeling capability.

The approximate linear assignment framework is often inherited for extending the second-order methods [50, 64, 65, 25, 121] to their hypergraph variants [19, 39, 63, 139]. In the seminal work, [39] resorts to a tensor to encode the higher-order affinity to generalize second-order to higher-order. They also extend the spectral matching method [64] via a multi-dimensional power method [51]. Re-weighted Random Walks is devised for second-order [25], and subsequently for higher-order [63]. Chang and Kimia [19] generalize GAGM [50] to the higher-order. The probabilistic method [148] assumes the higher-order correspondences are conditional independence. This hurts its applicability and performance [63]. [139] generalize the convergence analysis and algorithm from the second-order [121] to higher-order. The local property of graph structure is taken special care in [156] such that the matching accuracy is improved.

There are also specialized hypergraph matching solvers [8, 94]. The former is tailored to finding 3-D and 2-D projection correspondence. The latter assumes the affinity tensor is redundant as it requires there are many tuples of feature points whose corresponding angles are close to each other.

Another interesting work [89] proposes a novel flexible tensor block coordinate ascent method for hypergraph matching, with the guarantee of monotonic ascent in the matching score on the set of discrete assignment matrices.

3.5 Recent representative solvers

We refer the readers to a partial review of recent GM methods, of which most are after year 2000, under several bullets to highlight the main characters. Note that due to the complexity and non-triviality of GM algorithms, they are often mixed by multiple features, and the bullets below are not strictly orthogonal to each other in algorithm design.

3.5.1 (Quasi-)discrete methods

Several methods tend to directly compute the solution in discrete assignment space. Integer Projected Fixed Point (IPFP) [65] is one of the most popular (quasi) discrete graph matching solvers in this spirit. By a similar first-order linearization idea, [139] proposes a full discrete method for hyper-graph matching. [1] devises a tailored Tabu search for graph matching. Another line of work are sampling based methods which directly generate discrete solutions: the Markov chain Monte Carlo model [62] and its efficient extension based on Sequential Monte Carlo Sampling [119].

3.5.2 Spectral, SDP and double-stochastic relaxation

There are different relaxation strategies used in graph matching to mitigate the hard combinatorial problem in nature, and enable practitioners to bring gradient-descent-type algorithms to bear [80]. Here we briefly mention three popular relaxation methodologies.

Spectral matching methods e.g. [57] are based on the fact that the eigenvalues of a matrix keep unchanged whatever the rows and columns are permuted, which are often efficient but more sensitive to noises. [64] proposes to relax the assignment matrix into a unit vector, and the relaxed solution can be obtained by computing the maximum eigen vector of the affinity matrix. [35] uses the affine constrain to better approximate the raw problem.

Semidefinite-programming (SDP) is a general tool for combinatorial problems, and SDP methods [122, 107] approximate GM by relaxing the non-convex constraint to a new one: $\mathbf{Y} = \text{vec}(\mathbf{X})\text{vec}(\mathbf{X})^T$ where $\mathbf{Y}$ is an introduced variable, to a convex semi-definite one: $\mathbf{Y} - \text{vec}(\mathbf{X})\text{vec}(\mathbf{X})^T \succeq 0$. Given $\mathbf{Y}$, $\mathbf{X}$ can be obtained by a winner-take-all strategy [107], or a randomized algorithm [122]. Though there is some theoretical bound on its approximation capability, while in practice it is often computationally expensive.

Most GM methods adopt the doubly-stochastic relaxation on $\mathbf{X}$ – the convex hull on the assignment matrix. GM is transformed to convex quadratic programming that enable different solvers e.g. [50, 64, 65]. However, the applicability of such a relaxation is poorly understood until the recent theoretical findings [80, 2]. Among them, a line of methods adopt a probabilistic paradigm. [41] presents a method for maximum-likelihood estimation of the assignment matrix, as an probabilistic interpretation of the spectral matching algorithm. [52, 25] adopts random walk based methods which are inspired from PageRank. The work [148] proposes a convex relative-entropy error from a probabilistic interpretation to the hypergraph matching problem.

3.5.3 Continuation and path-following methods

One thread of these work adopt a path-following strategy [147, 74, 73, 154, 155]. The authors in [154, 155] propose an affinity matrix factorization technique, based on which a convex-concave relaxation procedure controlled by a continuation parameter is devised, and it is iteratively solved by an modified Frank-Wolfe algorithm [47]. [147, 74] devise similar path-following methods independent of the factorization form of affinity matrix. [73, 75] further propose several implicit convex-concave path-following algorithms, which are more flexible because it does not require the two graphs are of equal size and can handle partial permutation matrix.

Graduated assignment [50] and its variants [19, 118] are another line of continuation methods where a deterministic annealing procedure is performed in the continuous space. Though in general its convergence cannot be guaranteed [121], while adding an appropriate identity matrix to the affinity matrix can ensure it converges to a fixed point in the assignment space as proved in [97] by constructing discrete time Lyapunov functions. [139] generalizes this to tensor.

3.6 Other techniques

3.6.1 Progressive methods

Recently, progressive methods which iteratively enrich the candidate matches and reject the wrong ones have attracted a lot of attentions due to its high precision/recall and efficiency. [26] propagates the matches to neighbor points and refine the candidates by graph matching, where the former part promotes recall and the latter boosts the precision. In [143], a geometric consistency based on a high-order affine invariant constraint is established and a Markov Random Field optimization encoding both appearance and geometric cues is used to reject mismatches. [127] addresses the challenges of outliers and many-to-many node correspondence by a density maximization framework which maximizes the values of a proposed graph density estimator both locally and globally. [84] also proposes a progressive framework by hierarchically matching the sub-structures of the graphs.

3.6.2 Integrated matching pipeline

There are several integrated systems where GM is adopted. [123] allows nodes to be assigned in an unmatchable status in an energy function induced on the Markov Random Field. However, its complex objective function is designed that account for various similarity measurements *e.g.* appearance descriptors, occlusions, spatial proximity. [29] integrates the point detection and matching synergically, which shows robustness to visual problems by fusing various information.

3.6.3 Miscellaneous methods

In the recent work, [90] proposes the clique-graph, and a clique-graph matching method by preserving global and local structures. To address the problem of outliers, [27] presents a max-pooling based approach which is effective in handling massive outliers in one graph. In [79], the authors devise a seeded graph matching model embedding the graphs into a common Euclidean space and matching across embedded graphs, derived from the Joint Optimization of Fidelity and Commensurability [96] algorithm. In particular, [3] offers a game-theoretic perspective that formulates the matching problem as a non-cooperative game. This mechanism enable its capability of dealing with the general many-to-many matching problem. Their method is further improved in [12] by a fast evolutionary approach.

3.6.4 Relation to point registration

For point set registration, the goal is usually finding the correspondence and the geometric transformation between points such that the sum of distances between aligned point sets is minimized. One fundamental difference between GM and point set registration [151, 137] is that the former is a non-parametric model in terms of the transformation between two point sets while the latter assumes a parametric transformation function. The parameterization can vary dependent on the specific problem, such as similarity, affine and RBF non-rigid transformation as used in 2-D space.

Recently, by the factorization formulation, [154] shows that the point registration problem is a special case for the GM problem that only involve the linear term, when the transformation regularization term is given.

There is also a trend for the mixture of graph matching models and registration methods, as evidenced from the recent studies [103, 104, 137, 154].

4. APPLICATION AND DATASET

This section provides a study on several representative areas, and in particular for multimedia retrieval and analysis.

4.1 Applications

Multimedia and computer vision Graph representation of the objects that flexibly captures the geometrical characteristics, calls for GM techniques: image registration [112], understanding [43], extrapolation [128] and recognition [7], object recognition [40] and tracking [91], scene understanding [129] and parsing [144], weak-perspective 3-D reconstruction [158], action recognition [142], robotics [105], video surveillance [72] and person re-identification [113].

In particular, there are various multimedia retrieval applications where graph matching is intensively used, such as motion retrieval [132], object retrieval in video [22] and image [61], content-based image retrieval [9, 53], near-duplicate image detection [149, 152], shape retrieval [56], satellite imagery retrieval [59], CAD component detection [33] etc.

Other scenarios [120] releases a subgraph matching tool for biological graphs. [71] applies the spectral method to the problem of aligning multiple protein networks, and metabolic networks for [141]. [146] formulates to a GM problem and solves it by a path-following algorithm. [44] uses GM and sparse coding to infer the brain connectivity from alignment-free functional magnetic resonance imaging (fMRI) data.

We collect a partial list of other applications: grid anomaly detection [5], business process management [38], schema [81] and RDF [11] matching, network monitoring [116], case based reasoning [101], task assignment [111], information fusion [130], document classification [108], semantic search [153], assembling [6], product design [100], among others.

4.2 Public datasets

There are several benchmark datasets available online like: i) CMU motion sequences [154, 135]; ii) Willow-ObjectClass dataset collected and annotated by [23]; iii) QAPLib benchmark dataset [16]; iv) Tarragona Databases [34, 83]; v) human connectomics by DT-MRI scans as used in [80]; vi) Fish and character shape dataset from UCF shape dataset [28] which has been historically widely used for ICP registration algorithms, but recently also used in GM [137, 154].

5. CONCLUSION AND OUTLOOK

We have presented a focused survey on various graph matching methods, whereby methods are categorized by different topics. In particular, it covers many recent papers in the computer vision and machine learning communities.

Looking forward, we think the scalability of GM methods is the key issue for its real-world impact. This is because not only in multimedia applications, but also a wide spectrum of miscellaneous problems e.g. heterogenous social network [150], protein networks [146], smart grids [5], CAD [92], head [140] and face [70, 69] where graph representation is natural, call for scalable GM algorithms. The matching procedure is also expected to handle the dynamic change of the graph, where dynamic assignment algorithms e.g. [82] are suited.

Back to multimedia and computer vision, one specific direction is developing principled methods for weakly-supervised object discovery and localization in images [24]. Another potential is developing tailored GM method integrated in the system for addressing the object (weak) reconstruction from multiple images where several recent advancements have been made [158, 58]. For social media, we are witnessing the emerging problems for aligning multiple heterogenous social network [150] for cross-network data mining, and the behavior data-generated diffusion network structure [157].

6. REFERENCES

[1] K. Adamczewski, Y. Suh, and K. Lee. Discrete tabu search for graph matching. In *ICCV*, 2015.

[2] Y. Aflalo, A. Bronstein, and R. Kimmel. On convex relaxation of graph isomorphism. *Proceedings of the National Academy of Sciences*, 112(10):2942–2947, 2015.

[3] A. Albarelli, S. Bulo, A. Torsello, and M. Pelillo. Matching as a non-cooperative game. In *ICCV*, pages 1319–1326, 2009.

[4] H. A. Almohamad and S. O. Duffuaa. A linear programming approach for the weighted graph matching problem. *PAMI*, 1993.

[5] A. Anwar and A. N. Mahmood. Anomaly detection in electric network database of smart grid: Graph matching approach. *Electric Power Systems Research*, 133:51–62, 2016.

[6] A.S.Deshmukh, A. G. Banerjee, S. GuPta, and R. Sriram. Content-based assembly search: A step towards assembly reuse. *ComPuter-Aided Design*, pages 244–261, 2008.

[7] S. Auwatanamongkol. Inexact graph matching using a genetic algorithm for image recognition. *Pattern Recognition Letters*, 28(12):1428–1437, 2007.

[8] M. Bansal and K. Daniilidis. Geometric polynomial constraints in higher-order graph matching. *arXiv preprint arXiv:1405.6261*, 2014.

[9] S. Berretti, A. D. Bimbo, and E. Vicario. Efficient matching and indexing of graph models in content-based retrieval. *IEEE Transactions on Pattern Analysis and Machine Intelligence*, 23(10):1089–1105, 2001.

[10] S. Bougleux, L. Brun, V. Carletti, P. Foggia, B. Gaüzère, and M. Vento. A quadratic assignment formulation of the graph edit distance. *arXiv preprint arXiv:1512.07494*, 2015.

[11] M. Brocheler, A. Pugliese, and V. Subrahmanian. Dogma: A disk-oriented graph matching algorithm for rdf database. In *ISWC*, 2009.

[12] S. R. Bulò, M. Pelillo, and I. M. Bomze. Graph-based quadratic optimization: A fast evolutionary approach. *Computer Vision and Image Understanding*, 115(7):984–995, 2011.

[13] H. Bunke. Error-tolerant graph matching: a formal framework and algorithms. In *Advances in Pattern Recognition*, pages 1–14. 1998.

[14] H. Bunke. Error correcting graph matching: on the influence of the underlying cost function. *PAMI*, 21(9), 1999.

[15] H. Bunke. Graph matching: theoretical foundations, algorithms, and applications. In *Vision Interface*, 2000.

[16] R. Burkard, S. Karisch, and F. Rendl. Qaplib–a quadratic assignment problem library. *Journal of Global optimization*, 10(4):391–403, 1997.

[17] T. Caetano, J. McAuley, L. Cheng, Q. Le, and A. J. Smola. Learning graph matching. *TPAMI*, 31(6):1048–1058, 2009.

[18] R. M. Cesar, E. Bengoetxea, I. Bloch, and P. Larrañaga. Inexact graph matching for model-based recognition: Evaluation and comparison of optimization algorithms. *Pattern Recognition*, 38(11):2099–2113, 2005.

[19] M. C. Chang and B. B. Kimia. Measuring 3d shape similarity by graph-based matching of the medial scaffolds. *Computer Vision and Image Understanding*, pages 707–720, 2011.

[20] Y. Chen, G. Leonidas, and Q. Huang. Matching partially similar objects via matrix completion. In *ICML*, 2014.

[21] M. Chertok and Y. Keller. Efficient high order matching. *TPAMI*, 2010.

[22] F. Chevalier, J. Domenger, J. Benois-Pineau, and M. Delest. Retrieval of objects in video by similarity based on graph matching. *Pattern Recognition Letters*, 28(8):939–949, 2007.

[23] M. Cho, K. Alahari, and J. Ponce. Learning graphs to match. In *ICCV*, 2013.

[24] M. Cho, S. Kwak, C. Schmid, and J. Ponce. Unsupervised object discovery and localization in the wild: Part-based matching with bottom-up region proposals. In *CVPR*.

[25] M. Cho, J. Lee, and K. M. Lee. Reweighted random walks for graph matching. In *ECCV*, 2010.

[26] M. Cho and K. M. Lee. Progressive graph matching: Making a move of graphs via probabilistic voting. In *CVPR*, 2012.

[27] M. Cho, J. Sun, O. Duchenne, and J. Ponce. Finding matches in a haystack: a max-pooling strategy for graph matching in the presence of outliers. In *CVPR*, 2014.

[28] H. Chui and A. Rangarajan. A new point matching algorithm for non-rigid registration. *CVIU*, 2003.

[29] T. Collins, P. Mesejo, and A. Bartoli. An analysis of errors in graph-based keypoint matching and proposed solutions. In *ECCV*, 2014.

[30] D. Conte, P. Foggia, C. Sansone, and M. Vento. Thirty years of graph matching in pattern recognition. *IJPRAI*, 2004.

[31] D. Conte, P. Foggia, C. Sansone, and M. Vento. How and why pattern recognition and computer vision applications use graphs. In *Applied Graph Theory in Computer Vision and Pattern Recognition*, pages 85–135. Springer, 2007.

[32] D. J. Cook and L. B. Holder. *Mining graph data*. John Wiley & Sons, 2006.

[33] L. Cordella, P. Foggia, C. Sansone, and M. Vento. Fast graph matching for detecting cad image components. In *ICPR*, 2000.

[34] X. Cortés and F. Serratosa. Learning graph-matching edit-costs based on the optimality of the oracle's node correspondences. *Pattern Recognition Letters*, 56:22–29, 2015.

[35] T. Cour, P. Srinivasan, and J. Shi. Balanced graph matching. In *NIPS*, 2006.

[36] S. Deb, M. Yeddanapudi, K. Pattipati, and Y. Bar-Shalom. A generalized sd assignment algorithm for multisensor-multitarget state estimation. *IEEE Transactions on Aerospace and Electronic Systems*, 33(2):523–538, 1997.

[37] M. F. Demirci, B. Platel, A. Shokoufandeh, L. L. Florack, and S. J. Dickinson. The representation and matching of images using top points. *Journal of Mathematical Imaging and Vision*, 35(2):103–116, 2009.

[38] R. Dijkman, M. Dumas, Z. Gao, and L. Garcia-Banuelos. Graph matching algorithms for business process model similarity search. In *Business Process Management*, pages 48–63. Springer, 2009.

[39] O. Duchenne, F. Bach, I. Kweon, and J. Ponce. A tensor-based algor ithm for high-order graph matching. *PAMI*, 2011.

[40] O. Duchenne, A. Joulin, and J. Ponce. A graph-matching kernel for object categorization. In *ICCV*, 2011.

[41] A. Egozi, Y. Keller, and H. Guterman. A probabilistic approach to spectral graph matching. *TPAMI*, 2013.

[42] D. Eppstein. Subgraph isomorphism in planar graphs and related problems. In *SODA*, 1995.

[43] M. Eshera and K.-S. Fu. An image understanding system using attributed symbolic representation and inexact graph-matching. *IEEE Transactions on Pattern Analysis and Machine Intelligence*, (5):604–618, 1986.

[44] M. Fiori, P. Sprechmann, J. Vogelstein, P. Muse, and G. Sapiro. Robust multimodal graph matching: Sparse coding meets graph matching. In *NIPS*, 2013.

[45] M. A. Fischler and R. C. Bolles. Random sample consensus: A paradigm for model fitting with applications to image analysis and automated cartography. *Commun. ACM*, 1981.

[46] P. Foggia, G. Percannella, and M. Vento. Graph matching and learning in pattern recognition in the last 10 years. *IJPRAI*, 33(1), 2014.

[47] M. Frank and P. Wolfe. An algorithm for quadratic programming. *Naval Research Logistics Quarterly*, 1956.

[48] X. Gao, B. Xiao, D. Tao, and X. Li. A survey of graph edit distance. *Pattern Analysis and Applications*, 2010.

[49] M. R. Garey and D. S. Johnson. *Computers and Intractability; A Guide to the Theory of NP-Completeness*. Freeman and Co., NY, USA, 1990.

[50] S. Gold and A. Rangarajan. A graduated assignment algorithm for graph matching. *TPAMI*, 1996.

[51] G. Golub and C. Loan. Matrix computations. *Johns Hopkins University Press*, 1996.

[52] M. Gori, M. Maggini, and L. Sarti. Exact and approximate graph matching using random walks. *PAMI*, 2005.

[53] A. Hlaoui and S. Wang. A new algorithm for graph matching with application to content-based image retrieval. In *Structural, Syntactic, and Statistical Pattern Recognition*, pages 291–300. 2002.

[54] N. Hu, R. M. Rustamov, and L. Guibas. Graph mmatching with anchor nodes: a learning approach. In *CVPR*, 2013.

[55] Q. Huang, G. Zhang, L. Gao, S. Hu, A. Butscher, and L. Guibas. An optimization approach for extracting and encoding consistent maps in a shape collection. *ACM Transactions on Graphics (TOG)*, 2012.

[56] B. Huet and E. Hancock. Shape retrieval by inexact graph matching. In *IEEE International Conference on Multimedia Computing and Systems*, volume 1, pages 772–776, 1999.

[57] U. Kang, M. Hebert, and S. Park. Fast and scalable approximate spectral graph matching for correspondence problems. *Information Sciences*, 220:306–318, 2013.

[58] A. Kar, S. Tulsiani, J. Carreira, and J. Malik. Category-specific object reconstruction from a single image. In *CVPR*, pages 1966–1974, 2015.

[59] A. Kitamoto, C. Zhou, and M. Takagi. Similarity retrieval of noaa satellite imagery by graph matching. In *IS&T/SPIE's Symposium on Electronic Imaging: Science and Technology*, pages 60–73, 1993.

[60] E. L. Lawler. The quadratic assignment problem. *Management Science*, pages 586–599, 1963.

[61] J. Lebrun, P. Gosselin, and S. Philipp-Foliguet. Inexact graph matching based on kernels for object retrieval in image databases. *Image and Vision Computing*, 29(11):716–729, 2011.

[62] J. Lee, M. Cho, and K. Lee. A graph matching algorithm using data-driven markov chain monte carlo sampling. In *ICPR*, 2010.

[63] J. Lee, M. Cho, and K. M. Lee. Hyper-graph matching via reweighted randomwalks. In *CVPR*, 2011.

[64] M. Leordeanu and M. Hebert. A spectral technique for correspondence problems using pairwise constraints. In *ICCV*, 2005.

[65] M. Leordeanu, M. Hebert, and R. Sukthankar. An integer projected fixed point method for graph matching and map inference. In *NIPS*, 2009.

[66] M. Leordeanu, R. Sukthankar, and M. Hebert. Unsupervised learning for graph matching. *Int. J. Comput. Vis.*, pages 28–45, 2012.

[67] M. Leordeanu, A. Zanfir, and C. Sminchisescu. Semi-supervised learning and optimization for hypergraph matching. In *ICCV*, 2011.

[68] G. Levi. A note on the derivation of maximal common subgraphs of two directed or undirected graphs. *Calcolo*, 9(4):341–352, 1973.

[69] C. Li, Q. Liu, W. Dong, X. Zhu, J. Liu, and H. Lu. Human age estimation based on locality and ordinal information. *IEEE Transaction on Cybernetics*, 2015.

[70] C. Li, Q. Liu, J. Liu, and H. Lu. Learning ordinal discriminative features for age estimation. In *CVPR*, 2012.

[71] C. S. Liao, K. Lu, M. Baym, R. Singh, and B. Berger. Isorankn: spectral methods for global alignment of multiple protein networks. *Bioinformatics*, 2009.

[72] L. Lin, Y. Lu, Y. Pan, and X. Chen. Integrating graph partitioning and matching for trajectory analysis in video surveillance. *IEEE Transactions on Image Processing*, 21(12):4844–4857, 2012.

[73] Z. Liu and H. Qiao. Gncgcp - graduated nonconvexity and graduated concavity procedure. *IEEE PAMI*, 2014.

[74] Z. Liu, H. Qiao, and L. Xu. An extended path following algorithm for graph-matching problem. *TPAMI*, pages 1451–1456, 2012.

[75] Z. Liu, H. Qiao, X. Yang, and S. Hoi. Graph matching by simplified convex-concave relaxation procedure. *IJCV*, 2014.

[76] L. Livi and A. Rizzi. The graph matching problem. *Pattern Analysis and Applications*, 16(3):253–283, 2013.

[77] E. M. Loiola, N. M. de Abreu, P. O. Boaventura-Netto, P. Hahn, and T. Querido. A survey for the quadratic assignment problem. *EJOR*, pages 657–90, 2007.

[78] E. M. Luks. Isomorphism of graphs of bounded valence can be tested in polynomial time. *Journal of Computer and System Sciences*, 1982.

[79] V. Lyzinski, S. Adali, J. T. Vogelstein, Y. Park, and C. E. Priebe. Seeded graph matching via joint optimization of fidelity and commensurability. *stat*, 1050:16, 2014.

[80] V. Lyzinski, D. E. Fishkind, M. Fiori, J. T. Vogelstein, C. E. Priebe, and G. Sapiro. Graph matching: Relax at your own risk. *IEEE Transactions on Pattern Analysis and Machine Intelligence*, 38(1):60–73, 2016.

[81] S. Melnik, H. Garcia-Molina, and E. Rahm. A versatile graph matching algorithm and its application to schema matching. *Data Engineering*, 2002.

[82] G. A. Mills-Tettey, A. Stentz, and M. B. Dias. The dynamic hungarian algorithm for the assignment problem with changing costs. 2007.

[83] C. F. Moreno-García and F. Serratosa. Correspondence consensus of two sets of correspondences through optimisation functions. *Pattern Analysis and Applications*, pages 1–13, 2015.

[84] P. Morrison and J. J. Zou. Inexact graph matching using a hierarchy of matching processes. *Computational Visual Media*, 1(4):291–307, 2015.

[85] J. Munkres. Algorithms for the assignment and transportation problems. *Journal of the Society for Industrial & Applied Mathematics*, 5(1):32–38, 1957.

[86] M. Neuhaus and H. Bunke. Self-organizing maps for learning the edit costs in graph matching. *IEEE Transactions on Systems, Man, and Cybernetics, Part B: Cybernetics*, 35(3):503–514, 2005.

[87] M. Neuhaus and H. Bunke. Automatic learning of cost functions for graph edit distance. *Information Sciences*, 177(1):239–247, 2007.

[88] M. Neuhaus and H. Bunke. A quadratic programming approach to the graph edit distance problem. In *Graph-Based Representations in Pattern Recognition*, pages 92–102. 2007.

[89] Q. Ngoc, A. Gautier, and M. Hein. A flexible tensor block coo rd inate ascent scheme for hypergraph matching. In *CVPR*, 2015.

[90] W. Nie, A. Liu, Z. Gao, and Y. Su. Clique-graph matching by preserving global & local structure. In *CVPR*, 2015.

[91] W. Nie, A. Liu, Y. Su, H. Luan, Z. Yang, L. Cao, and R. Ji. Single/cross-camera multiple-person tracking by graph matching. *Neurocomputing*, 2014.

[92] Z. Niu, R. Martin, F. Langbein, and M. Sabin. Rapidly finding cad features using database optimization. *Computer-Aided Design*, 69:35–50, 2015.

[93] D. Pachauri, R. Kondor, and S. Vikas. Solving the multi-way matching problem by permutation synchronization. In *NIPS*, 2013.

[94] S. Park, S. Park, and M. Heber. Fast and scalable approximate spectral matching for higher-order graph matching. *PAMI*, 2013.

[95] A. Poore. Multidimensional assignment formulation of data association problems arising from multitarget and multisensor tracking. *Computational Optimization and Applications*, 3(1):27–57, 1994.

[96] C. E. Priebe, D. J. Marchette, Z. Ma, S. Adali, et al. Manifold matching: Joint optimization of fidelity and commensurability. *Brazilian Journal of Probability and Statistics*, 27(3):377–400, 2013.

[97] A. Rangarajan, A. Yuille, and E. Mjolsness. Convergence properties of the softassign quadratic assignment algorithm. *Neural Computation*, 1999.

[98] K. Riesen and H. Bunke. Approximate graph edit distance computation by means of bipartite graph matching. *Image and Vision Computing*, 27(7):950–959, 2009.

[99] K. Riesen, M. Ferrer, and H. Bunke. Approximate graph edit distance in quadratic time. *IEEE/ACM Transactions on Computational Biology and Bioinformatics*, 2015.

[100] C. Romanowski, R. Nagi, and M. Sudit. Data mining in an engineering design environment: Or applications from graph matching. *Computers & operations research*, 33(11):3150–3160, 2006.

[101] K. Sanders, B. Kettler, and J. Hendler. The case for graph-structured representations. In *Case-Based Reasoning Research and Development*, pages 245–254. 1997.

[102] A. Sanfeliu and K.-S. Fu. A distance measure between attributed relational graphs for pattern recognition. pages 353–362, 1983.

[103] G. Sanromà, R. Alquézar, and F. Serratosa. Attributed graph matching for image-features association using sift descriptors. In *Structural, Syntactic, and Statistical Pattern Recognition*, pages 254–263. 2010.

[104] G. Sanromà, R. Alquézar, and F. Serratosa. Smooth simultaneous structural graph matching and point-set registration. In *Graph-Based Representations in Pattern Recognition*, pages 142–151. Springer, 2011.

[105] G. Sanromà Güell, R. Alquézar Mancho, and F. Serratosa Casanelles. Graph matching using sift descriptors: an application to pose recovery of a mobile robot. In *5th International Conference on Computer Vision Theory and Applications*, pages 249–254, 2010.

[106] M. D. Santo, P. Foggia, C. Sansone, and M. Vento. A large database of graphs and its use for benchmarking graph isomorphism algorithms. *Pattern Recognition Letters*, 24(8):1067–1079, 2003.

[107] C. Schellewald and C. Schnörr. Probabilistic subgraph matching based on convex relaxation. In *EMMCVPR*, 2005.

[108] A. Schenker, M. Last, H. Bunke, and A. Kandel. Classification of web documents using graph matching. *International Journal of Pattern Recognition and Artificial Intelligence*, 18(03):475–496, 2004.

[109] F. Serratosa. Fast computation of bipartite graph matching. *Pattern Recognition Letters*, 45:244–250, 2014.

[110] F. Serratosa. Speeding up fast bipartite graph matching through a new cost matrix. *International Journal of Pattern Recognition and Artificial Intelligence*, 29(02):1550010, 2015.

[111] C. Shen and W. Tsai. A graph matching approach to optimal task assignment in distributed computing systems using a minimax criterion. *IEEE Transactions on Computers*, 100(3):197–203, 1985.

[112] D. Shen and C. D. Hammer. Hierarchical attribute matching mechanism for elastic registration. *TMI*, 2002.

[113] Y. Shen, W. Lin, J. Yan, M. Xu, J. Wu, and J. Wang. Person re-identification with correspondence structure learning. In *ICCV*, 2015.

[114] X. Shi, H. Ling, W. Hu, J. Xing, and Y. Zhang. Tensor power iteration for multi-graph matching. In *CVPR*, 2016.

[115] A. Shokoufandeh, Y. Keselman, M. F. Demirci, D. Macrini, and S. Dickinson. Many-to-many feature matching in object recognition: a review of three approaches. *Computer Vision, IET*, 6(6):500–513, 2012.

[116] P. Showbridge, M. Kraetzl, and D. Ray. Detection of abnormal change in dynamic networks. In *Information, Decision and Control*, pages 557–562, 1999.

[117] A. Solé-Ribalta and F. Serratosa. Models and algorithms for computing the common labelling of a set of attributed graphs. *CVIU*, 2011.

[118] A. Sole-Ribalta and F. Serratosa. Graduated assignment algorithm for multiple graph matching based on a common labeling. *IJPRAI*, 2013.

[119] Y. Suh, M. Cho, and K. M. Lee. Graph matching via sequential monte carlo. In *ECCV*, 2012.

[120] Y. Tian, R. Mceachin, C. Santos, and J. Patel. Saga: a subgraph matching tool for biological graphs. *Bioinformatics*, 2007.

[121] Y. Tian, J. Yan, H. Zhang, Y. Zhang, X. Yang, and H. Zha. On the convergence of graph matching: Graduated assignment revisited. In *ECCV*, 2012.

[122] P. H. S. Torr. Solving markov random fields using semidefinite programmin. In *AISTATS*, 2003.

[123] L. Torresani, V. Kolmogorov, and C. Rother. Feature correspondence via graph matching: Models and global optimization. In *ECCV*, 2008.

[124] S. Umeyama. An eigendecomposition approach to weighted graph matching problems. *TPAMI*, 1988.

[125] M. Vento. A long trip in the charming world of graphs for pattern recognition. *Pattern Recognition*, 48(2):291–301, 2015.

[126] M. Vento and P. Foggia. Graph matching techniques for computer vision. *Graph-Based Methods in Computer Vision: Developments and Applications: Developments and Applications*, page 1, 2012.

[127] C. Wang, L. Wang, and L. Liu. Density maximization for improving graph matching with its applications. *IEEE Transactions on Image Processing*, 2015.

[128] M. Wang, Y. Lai, Y. Liang, R. R. Martin, and S.-M. Hu. Biggerpicture: data-driven image extrapolation using graph matching. *ACM Transactions on Graphics*, 33(6), 2014.

[129] W. Wang, W. Lin, Y. Chen, J. Wu, J. Wang, and B. Sheng. Finding coherent motions and semantic regions in crowd scenes: a diffusion and clustering approach. In *ECCV*, 2014.

[130] M. L. Williams, R. C. Wilson, and E. Hancock. Multiple graph matching with bayesian inference. *Pattern Recognition Letters*, pages 1275–1281, 1997.

[131] R. C. Wilson and E. R. Hancock. A bayesian compatibility model for graph matching. *Pattern Recognition Letters*, 17(3):263–276, 1996.

[132] Q. Xiao, Y. Wang, and H. Wang. Motion retrieval using weighted graph matching. *Soft Computing*, 19(1), 2015.

[133] J. Yan, M. Cho, H. Zha, X. Yang, and S. Chu. Multi-graph matching via affinity optimization with graduated consistency regularization. *TPAMI*, 2016.

[134] J. Yan, Y. Li, W. Liu, H. Zha, X. Yang, and S. Chu. Graduated consistency-regularized optimization for multi-graph matching. In *ECCV*, 2014.

[135] J. Yan, Y. Tian, H. Zha, X. Yang, Y. Zhang, and S. Chu. Joint optimization for consistent multiple graph matching. In *ICCV*, 2013.

[136] J. Yan, J. Wang, H. Zha, and X. Yang. Consistency-driven alternating optimization for multigraph matching: A unified approach. *IEEE Transactions on Image Processing*, 2015.

[137] J. Yan, J. Wang, H. Zha, X. Yang, and S. Chu. Multi-view point registration via alternating optimization. In *AAAI*, 2015.

[138] J. Yan, H. Xu, H. Zha, X. Yang, H. Liu, and S. Chu. A matrix decomposition perspective to multiple graph matching. In *ICCV*, 2015.

[139] J. Yan, C. Zhang, H. Zha, W. Liu, X. Yang, and S. Chu. Discrete hyper-graph matching. In *CVPR*, 2015.

[140] Y. Yan, E. Ricci, R. Subramanian, G. Liu, O. Lanz, and N. Sebe. A multi-task learning framework for head pose estimation under target motion. 2016.

[141] Q. Yang and S. Sze. Path matching and graph matching in biological networks. *Journal Of Computational Biology*, 2007.

[142] B. Yao and F. Li. Action recognition with exemplar based 2.5 d graph matching. In *ECCV*, 2012.

[143] C. Yu, L. Tian, H. Hu, Y. Duan, and J. Zhou. Progressive feature matching via triplet graph. In *ICIP*, 2015.

[144] T. Yu and R. Wang. Scene parsing using graph matching on street-view data. *CVIU*, 2016.

[145] M. Zaslavskiy, F. Bach, and J.-P. Vert. Many-to-many graph matching: a continuous relaxation approach. In *Machine Learning and Knowledge Discovery in Databases*, pages 515–530. Springer, 2010.

[146] M. Zaslavskiy, F. R. Bach, and J.-P. Vert. Global alignment of proteinÍcprotein interaction networks by graph matching methods. *Bioinformatics*, 2009.

[147] M. Zaslavskiy, F. R. Bach, and J.-P. Vert. A path following algorithm for the graph matching problem. *TPAMI*, 2009.

[148] R. Zass and A. Shashua. Probabilistic graph and hypergraph matching. In *CVPR*, 2008.

[149] D. Zhang and S. Chang. Detecting image near-duplicate by stochastic attributed relational graph matching with learning. In *ACM MM*, pages 877–884, 2004.

[150] J. Zhang and P. Yu. Multiple anonymized social networks alignment. In *ICDM*, 2015.

[151] Z. Zhang. Iterative point matching for registration of free-form curves and surfaces. *IJCV*, 1994.

[152] W.-L. Zhao, C.-W. Ngo, H.-K. Tan, and X. Wu. Near-duplicate keyframe identification with interest point matching and pattern learning. *IEEE Transactions on Multimedia*, 9(5):1037–1048, 2007.

[153] J. Zhong, H. Zhu, J. Li, and Y. Yu. Conceptual graph matching for semantic search. In *Conceptual structures: Integration and interfaces*, pages 92–106. 2002.

[154] F. Zhou and F. Torre. Factorized graph matching. *IEEE PAMI*, 2016.

[155] F. Zhou and F. D. Torre. Deformable graph matching. In *CVPR*, 2013.

[156] J. Zhou, H. Yan, and Y. Zhu. Local topology preserved tensor models for graph matching. In *IEEE International Conference on Systems, Man, and Cybernetics*, pages 2153–2157, 2015.

[157] K. Zhou, H. Zha, and L. Song. Learning triggering kernels for multi-dimensional hawkes processes. In *ICML*, pages 1301–1309, 2013.

[158] X. Zhou, M. Zhu, and K. Daniilidis. Multi-image matching via fast alternating minimization. In *ICCV*, 2015.

[159] H. Zhu, D. Liu, S. Zhang, Y. Zhu, L. Teng, and S. Teng. Solving the many to many assignment problem by improving the kuhn–munkres algorithm with backtracking. *Theoretical Computer Science*, 2016.

The ImageNet Shuffle: Reorganized Pre-training for Video Event Detection

Pascal Mettes, Dennis C. Koelma, Cees G. M. Snoek

University of Amsterdam

ABSTRACT

This paper strives for video event detection using a representation learned from deep convolutional neural networks. Different from the leading approaches, who all learn from the 1,000 classes defined in the ImageNet Large Scale Visual Recognition Challenge, we investigate how to leverage the complete ImageNet hierarchy for pre-training deep networks. To deal with the problems of over-specific classes and classes with few images, we introduce a bottom-up and top-down approach for reorganization of the ImageNet hierarchy based on all its 21,814 classes and more than 14 million images. Experiments on the TRECVID Multimedia Event Detection 2013 and 2015 datasets show that video representations derived from the layers of a deep neural network pre-trained with our reorganized hierarchy *i)* improves over standard pre-training, *ii)* is complementary among different reorganizations, *iii)* maintains the benefits of fusion with other modalities, and *iv)* leads to state-of-the-art event detection results. The reorganized hierarchies and their derived Caffe models are publicly available at http://tinyurl.com/imagenetshuffle.

Keywords

Event Detection; Video Representation Learning

1. INTRODUCTION

The goal of this work is to detect events such as *Renovating a home*, *Birthday party*, and *Attempting a bike trick* in web videos. The leading approaches [8, 13, 16, 26] attack this challenging problem by learning video representations through a deep convolutional neural network [10, 23]. The deep network is pre-trained on a collection of 1,000 ImageNet classes [2, 19], used to extract features for video frames, and then followed by a pooling operation over the frames to arrive at a video representation. We also learn representations for event detection with a deep convolutional neural network, but rather than relying on the default 1,000 class subset, we investigate how to leverage the complete ImageNet hierarchy for pre-training the representation.

ICMR'16, June 06-09, 2016, New York, NY, USA

© 2016 ACM. ISBN 978-1-4503-4359-6/16/06...$15.00

DOI: http://dx.doi.org/10.1145/2911996.2912036

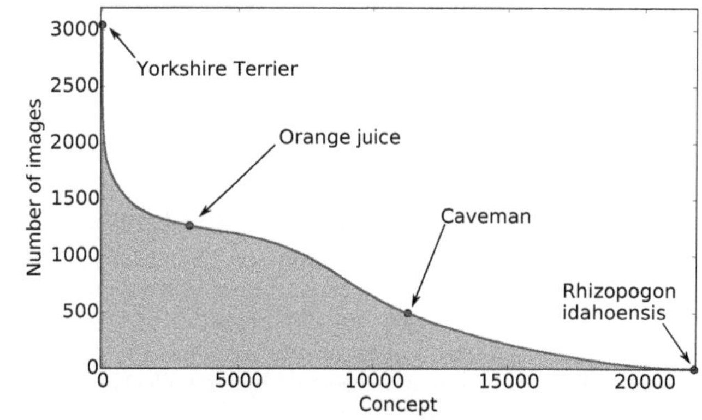

(a) Distribution of the number of images for the 21,814 ImageNet classes. Note the class imbalance.

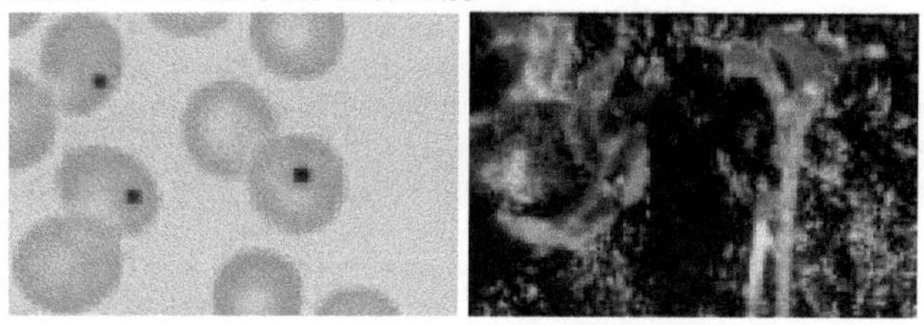

(b) An image of *Siderocyte* (left) and *Gametophyte* (right), two classes which seem over-specific for event detection.

Figure 1: Two problems when using the full ImageNet hierarchy for network pre-training: (a) image imbalance and (b) over-specific classes. In this work, we aim to reorganize the hierarchy into a balanced set of classes for more effective pre-training of video representations for event detection.

The complete ImageNet dataset consists of over 14 million images and 21,814 classes which are connected in a hierarchy as a subset of WordNet [14]. State-of-the-art event detectors are pre-trained on a 1,000 class (1.2 million images) subset of ImageNet, as prescribed by the Large Scale Visual Recognition Challenge [19]. Hence, more than 90% of the images in the hierarchy remain untouched during pre-training. We present an empirical investigation of the effect of using the full ImageNet dataset for event detection in web videos.

We identify two problems when trying to pre-train a deep network on the complete ImageNet hierarchy. First, there is an imbalance in the number of examples for each class, as is shown in Figure 1a. For example, the class *Yorkshire Terrier* contains 3,072 images, whereas 296 other classes contain just a single image. Second, some classes seem over-specific for event detection in web videos. Consider for example the ImageNet categories *Siderocyte* and *Gametophyte* in Figure 1b. As a result, it seems suboptimal to directly pre-train a deep network on all 21,814 classes.

In this work, we introduce pre-training protocols that reorganize the full ImageNet hierarchy for more effective pre-training. The reorganization tackles the image imbalance and over-specific class problems. We propose two contrasting approaches that utilize the graph structure of ImageNet to combine and merge classes into balanced and reorganized hierarchies. We empirically evaluate our event detection using reorganized pre-training on the 2013 and 2015 NIST TRECVID Multimedia Event Detection datasets, for both datasets leading to state-of-the-art results. The Caffe models and detailed video feature extraction instructions are available at http://tinyurl.com/imagenetshuffle.

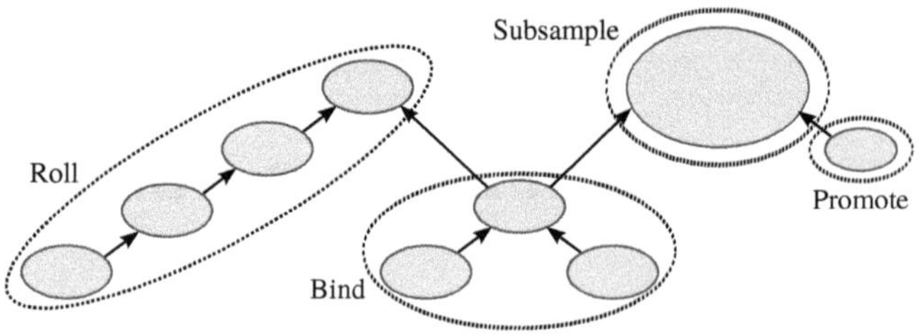

Figure 2: Overview of where in the hierarchy the four operations are applied in the bottom-up approach. **Roll:** Roll up classes with a single chld-parent connection. **Bind:** Bind sub-trees for which the individual classes do not have enough images. **Promote:** Promote individual classes to their parent class if they do not have enough images. **Subsample:** Randomly subsample images from classes with too many images.

2. RELATED WORK

2.1 Event detection with pre-trained networks

The state-of-the-art for event detection in videos focuses on representations learned with the aid of deep convolutional neural networks [3, 8, 13, 16, 26]. The pipeline of these approaches consists roughly of three components. (1) A deep network is pre-trained on a large-scale image collection. Different deep networks have been employed for event detection, such as AlexNet [10] in [8, 13, 16] and VGGnet [21] in [26]. (2) Sampled video frames are fed to the network and features at fully-connected and/or soft-max layers are used as frame representations. (3) The frame representations are pooled into a fixed-sized video representation. A simple and effective pooling method is average pooling, where the frame representations are averaged over the video [9, 13]. Recently, several works have shown that clustering deep frame representations into a codebook, followed by a VLAD [6] in [26] or Fisher Vector encoding [20] in [16], leads to strong video representations. In this work, we aim for a similar pipeline of pre-training, frame representation, and video pooling. However, rather than relying on the standard pre-training protocol using 1,000 ImageNet classes, we leverage the complete ImageNet hierarchy for more effective pre-training.

Web videos provide a wide range of information about events, such as visual, motion, audio, and optical character information [18]. Naturally, multiple works have investigated the fusion of information from different modalities [11, 15, 17]. In this work, we also investigate the effect of fusing our deep representations with Motion Boundary Histogram (motion) features [25] and MFCC (audio) features [15], both of which are encoded into a video representation using Fisher Vectors [20]. This fusion allows us to compare the effectiveness of our deep representations to heterogeneous representations and to investigate how well our deep representations fare when combined with other sources of information.

2.2 (Re)organizing hierarchies for events

Various works have investigated the use of semantic hierarchies and ontologies for event detection. The work of Ye *et al.* [27] focuses on hierarchical relations between events, to find a large collection of videos and event-specific concept classes. Their proposed EventNet has shown to yield an effective event detection [27]. In our work, we focus on different hierarchical relations, namely between concept classes instead of events, to discover a general set of concepts for deep network pre-training. Other recent work on event detection has investigated relations among concept classes to rerank concept scores in the video representation [8]. We similarly focus on hierarchical relations among concept classes, but for the purpose of merging classes into a reorganized hierarchy for pre-training. For the hierarchy of ImageNet specifically, the work of Vreeswijk *et al.* [24] has shown that images from different layers of the hierarchy are visually different and that general concepts benefit from including linked concepts deeper in the hierarchy. We build upon these observations in our operations to reorganize the ImageNet hierarchy.

An alternative approach is to adjust concept hierarchies after feature extraction. For example, the selection of event-specific concepts based on the similarity to a textual event description has shown to yield effective event detection results without positive examples [8]. Mazloom *et al.* [12] show that concept selection is also beneficial for few-example event detection. Habibian *et al.* [4] in turn, jointly learn a classifier for event detection and combine correlated concepts. Rather than changing the representations *a posteriori* using text or video examples, we focus in this paper on reorganizing the hierarchical structure of visual ontologies *before* event training,

3. REORGANIZED PRE-TRAINING

The classes in the ImageNet dataset are a subset of the WordNet collection [14] and the classes are therefore connected in a hierarchy. The connectivity between classes provides information about their semantic relationship. We utilize the hierarchical relationship of WordNet for combining classes to generate reorganized ImageNet hierarchies for pre-training. We focus on two opposing approaches for reorganization, namely a bottom-up and top-down approach.

3.1 Bottom-up reorganization

For the bottom-up reorganization, we start from the original ImageNet hierarchy and introduce four reorganization operations. An overview of where in the hierarchy the four operations are performed is shown in Figure 2 and visual examples for each operation are shown in Figure 3. We outline each operation separately.

(a) Roll.

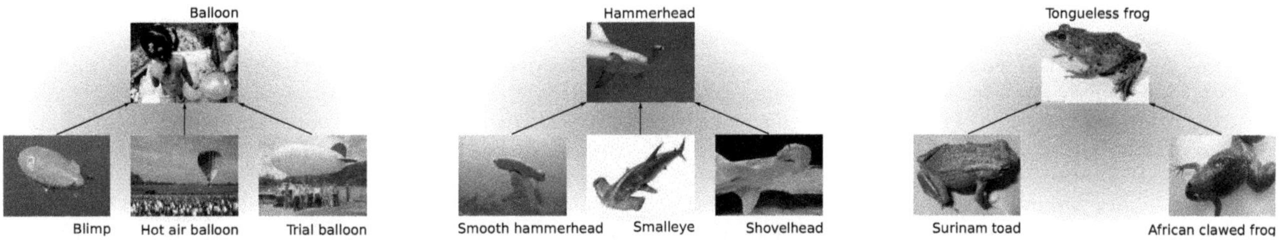

(b) Bind.

(c) Promote.

(d) Subsample.

Figure 3: Visual examples for each of the four operations for the bottom-up reorganization.

Roll. The roll operation is performed on single-link subtrees of classes. In other words, the roll operation merges classes with a single child-parent connection, as shown in Figure 2 on the left. The motivation behind this operation is two-fold: *i)* there is little semantic difference between a child and a parent if the parent has no other children. Treating the child and parent as separate classes during pre-training will dominate the backpropagation gradients to keep these classes separated. *ii)* A single child of a parent is more likely to be over-specific for event detection. Single child-parent connections typically occur deep in the hierarchy, where details between classes become more fine-grained. In our evaluation, we indeed observe that the single child-parent connections occur predominantly in the deeper layers of the ImageNet hierarchy. Three chains of single child-parent connections are shown in Figure 3a. For example, the class *Mamba* is a type of snake and has a single child, namely *Black mamba*. In turn, the *Black mamba* has a single child: *Green mamba* (the green phase of the black mamba). In this example, we move all the images from the *Black mamba* and *Green mamba* classes to the *Mamba* class.

Bind. The bind operation is performed on sub-trees where the individual classes are sparse in the number of images. Let S denote a sub-tree and let c^i denote the number of images in class c. Then the bind operation is performed on subtree S if $\sum_{c \in S} c^i < t_b$, where t_b denotes the threshold on the number of images. The notion behind the bind operation is to deal with small and semantically coherent classes consisting of a parent and multiple children. The children individually do not contain enough images to treat them as separate classes. However, the combined set of parent and children forms a semantically consistent set with a desirable number of images. Three merged sub-trees that are combined with the bind operation are shown in Figure 3b. For example, the *Hammerhead shark* has three children with a small number of images, namely *Smooth hammerhead*, *Smalleye hammerhead*, and *Shovelhead*. Therefore, we opt to combine all these shark images into a single class.

Promote. The promote operation is a unary operation. It is performed after the roll and bind have been performed. The promote operation simply promotes a class to its parent if its number of images is below a threshold t_p. This operation directly targets the imbalance problem, by adding images of classes with few examples to parent classes with more images. Figure 3c shows three cases of the promote operation. For example, the class *Triclinium* (a dining table with couches at three sides) only contains 5 images. Therefore, the images are added to the *Dining table* class, such that the *Triclinium* images are still being used for pre-training without creating an imbalance in the hierarchy.

Subsample. The subsample operation is also a unary operation and deals with the reverse problem of the other three operations. The subsample operation subsamples images from classes for which the number of images is above a threshold t_s. The operation selects a subset of images from classes with a lot of examples. The reason for this operation is again for balancing purposes. If all images of overpopulated classes are used in the optimization of the deep network, the network will overfit to these classes, resulting in suboptimal frame representations for event detection. Four examples of the subsample operation are shown in Figure 3d, such as *Keyboard*, *Coffee mug*, and *Herb*.

We employ the defined operations in the described order. First, all single child-parent connections are rolled up. Second, all sub-trees in the hierarchy are binded based on threshold t_b for their combined number of images. Third, all remaining classes with less than t_p images are promoted to their parent. Fourth, during network pre-training, examples for all classes with more than t_s images are randomly subsampled before the stochastic gradient descent optimization.

3.2 Top-down reorganization

An alternative complementary reorganization strategy is not to start from the deepest classes in the hierarchy, but from the head node. Here, we investigate a breath-first search approach. Let t_t denotes the threshold stating the minimum amount of images required for class in order to be used in the top-down reorganization. Then, starting from layer 0 in the hierarchy, i.e. the head node, we iteratively move down in the hierarchy and keep adding classes with at least t_t images until we reach a desired amount of classes.

The breath-first search approach is outlined as follows. Let l denote the previous layer of the hierarchy. We list all ImageNet classes in layer $l+1$ based on connections from classes in layer l and order the classes in $l+1$ by their number of images. The sorting ensures that we select the classes with the highest number of images first, in case we reach the desired amount of classes before the end of the list. Then, we move through the ordered list and select all classes with at least t_t images as long as the desired amount of selected classes is not reached. Afterwards, we move to the next layer and repeat the ordering and selection procedure.

By using a top-down approach, we ensure that only the most general classes are maintained for pre-training, while simultaneously keeping a balance in the image distribution through the threshold t_t.

4. EXPERIMENTAL SETUP

4.1 Dataset

TRECVID Multimedia Event Detection 2013. The TRECVID Multimedia Event Detection 2013 dataset consists of roughly 27,000 test videos [18]. The dataset contains annotations for 20 everyday events, including *Birthday Party*, *Making a sandwich*, *Attempting a bike trick*, and *Dog show*. The dataset has two different tasks, one where 10 positive videos are given for each event (10 Ex.), and one where 100 positive videos are given for each event (100 Ex.). For an event, a classifier is trained on the 10 or 100 positive videos and a background set of roughly 5,000 negative videos. The classifier is in turn used to rank the 27,000 test videos and its performance is evaluated using the (mean) Average Precision score on the ranked test videos.

4.2 Implementation details

Deep convolutional networks. We focus our evaluation on the recent GoogLeNet of Szegedy *et al.* [23]. The GoogLeNet is a deep convolutional neural network consisting of 22 layers. We also compare against the AlexNet of Krizhevsky *et al.* [10]. The AlexNet consists of 5 convolutional layers and 3 fully-connected layers. To pre-train the deep networks, we utilize the open-source Caffe library [7] and the provided layer definitions and hyper-parameters for both networks.

Feature extraction. After pre-training, we extract features both at the fully connected layer and the soft-max layer. In AlexNet, we use the features from the second fully-connected layer, with a 4,096-dimensional frame representation. In GoogLeNet, we use the features at the pool5 layer, with a 1,024-dimensional frame representation. The dimensionality at the soft-max layer, which provides a probability score of each concept, for both networks is equal to the number of classes in the corresponding hierarchy.

Pooling and Event Classification. For event detection, we average the representations of the frames over each video unless stated otherwise, followed by ℓ_1-normalization. We train an SVM classifier for each event separately with a χ_2 kernel. We set the C parameter to 100 in all our experiments.

5. EXPERIMENTS

We consider four experiments. First, we evaluate the effect of different settings of the operations in our bottom-up reorganized pre-training. Second, we compare standard pre-training versus both the bottom-up and top-down reorganized pre-training. Third, we perform various fusions between deep representations and representation from other modalities. Fourth, we compare our results to the state-of-the-art on multimedia event detection.

5.1 Bottom-up operation parameters

Experiment 1. For the first experiment, we investigate the parameters for the bind and promote operations in our bottom-up reorganization, which have a significant influence on the amount of remaining classes. In total, we have trained three separate GoogLeNets [23] based on different parameters for the bind and promote operations:

- **Bottom-up [4k]:** Deep network pre-trained on 4,437 classes with $t_b = 7,000$ and $t_p = 1,250$.
- **Bottom-up [8k]:** Deep network pre-trained on 8,201 classes with $t_b = 7,000$ and $t_p = 500$.
- **Bottom-up [13k]:** Deep network pre-trained on 12,988 classes with $t_b = 3,000$ and $t_p = 200$.

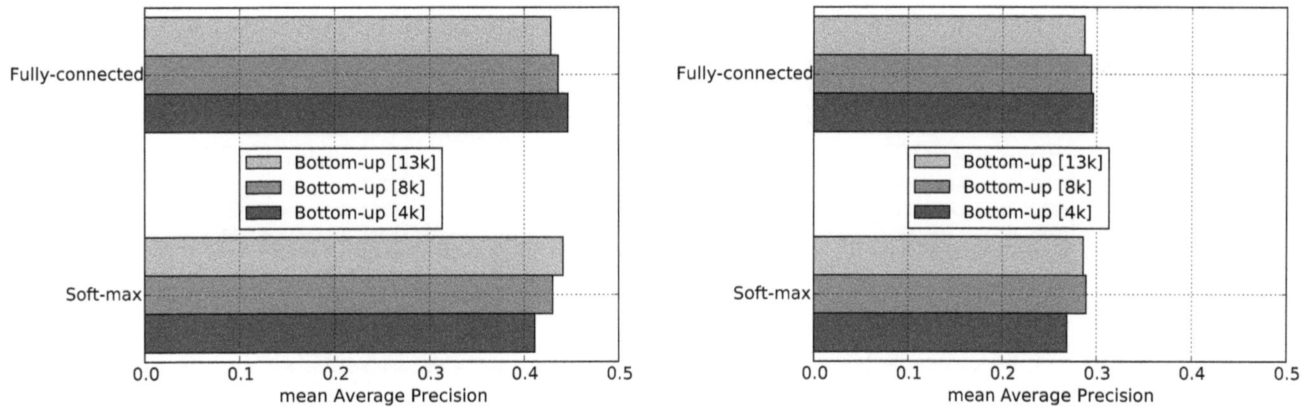

(a) TRECVID MED 2013 with 100 positives.

(b) TRECVID MED 2013 with 10 positives.

Figure 4: Mean Average Precision scores for the three bottom-up variants on TRECVID Multimedia Event Detection 2013. We observe that the more classes are maintained in the bottom-up reorganization, the better the performance using the soft-max (i.e. semantic) layer. The reserve happens for the fully-connected layer.

For all the variants, we set the subsample threshold to $t_s = 2,000$. An overview of mean Average Precision scores using the fully-connected and soft-max layers on TRECVID Multimedia Event Detection 2013 is shown in Figure 4. We report the mean Average Precision scores both for the task with 10 positive videos and with 100 positive videos per event.

Results. From Figure 4, we observe that the best scores using the fully-connected layer are achieved with the bottom-up [4k] variant. This result shows that the fully-connected layer translates best to events when merging more classes into a generic hierarchy. Interestingly, we observe the reverse pattern for the soft-max layer; the more classes are maintained the better the event detection performance. This result follows the work of Habibian et al. [5], which states that using more semantic classifiers is preferred over using better semantic classifiers. Here, we show that this observation translates to deep networks for event detection.

From this experiment, we conclude that the choice of the bottom-up reorganized variant depends on the desired deep network representation. The highest overall results are achieved by the features from the non-semantic fully-connected layer of the variant from 4,437 classes (0.446 mean Average Precision using 100 positives per event, 0.296 using 10 positives). However, the variant from 12,988 classes performs best using the semantic features from the soft-max layer (0.441 using 100 positives, 0.286 using 10 positives).

5.2 Standard versus reorganized pre-training

Experiment 2. For the second experiment, we compare our bottom-up and top-down reorganized pre-training against the conventional pre-training setup using the ImageNet 1,000 class subset [19]. For all networks, we report the Average Precision scores using both the fully-connected layer and the soft-max layer. For the bottom-up approach, we use the deep network pre-trained on 4,437 classes. For the top-down approach, we select the top 4,000 classes, with $t_t = 1,200$ for the threshold on the number of images required for each class. We compare our two approaches to two standard pre-trained deep networks:

- **AlexNet [std]:** AlexNet pre-trained on 1,000 ImageNet classes [10].
- **GoogLeNet [std]:** GoogLeNet pre-trained on 1,000 ImageNet classes [23].

Results. An overview of the comparison between standard and reorganized pre-training is shown in Figure 5. We observe that the top-down and bottom-up reorganization approaches achieve comparable performance. While bottom-up performs slightly better using the fully-connected layer, top-down performs slightly better using the soft-max layer. We also note our reorganized pre-training approaches on GoogLeNet significantly outperform the standard pre-trained GoogLeNet. This holds especially for the soft-max layer, where the difference between standard pre-training and our top-down pre-training is 8.6% and 9.2% in absolute mean Average Precision for respectively the 100 and 10 positive video tasks. Lastly, we note that the difference in performance to the pre-trained AlexNet is even bigger. This result shows that GoogLeNet provides overall better visual representations, leading to improved event detection.

From this experiment, we conclude that our two approaches to reorganized ImageNet pre-training yield strong event detection results and significantly improve over standard pre-trained deep networks.

5.3 Fusing representations and modalities

Experiment 3. For the third experiment, we investigate the effect of feature fusion. Here, fusion is performed in a late fashion, by averaging the classifier scores of different classifiers. We investigate feature fusion in two aspects: *i)* we investigate the effect of fusing different layers and video encodings from different pre-trained deep networks for event detection, *ii)* we investigate the effect of fusing our deep visual representations with two other representations:

- **Audio modality:** MFCC features with first and second order derivatives, 30 dimensions for each of the three features, aggregated into a 46,080-dimensional video representation using Fisher Vectors with 256 clusters.

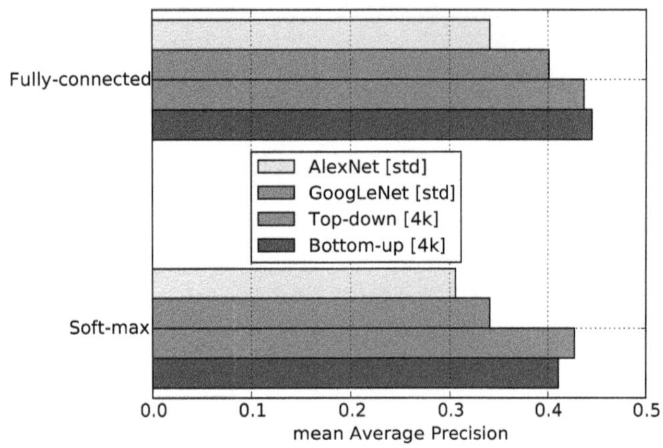

(a) TRECVID MED 2013 with 100 positives.

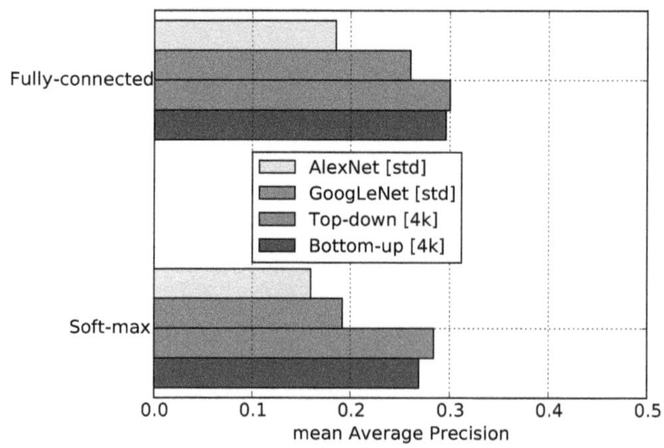

(b) TRECVID MED 2013 with 10 positives.

Figure 5: Mean Average Precision scores for our bottom-up and top-down reorganized pre-training (blue), compared to standard pre-training (green) on TRECVID MED 2013. Our approaches both clearly outperform standard pre-training, while being competitive and potentially complementary to each other.

- **Motion modality:** MBHx, MBHy, and HOG features computed along dense trajectories [25], reduced to 128 dimensions using PCA, aggregated into a 65,536-dimensional video representation using Fisher Vectors with 256 clusters.

Results for Fusing Networks. In Table 1, we show an overview of fusion results using deep networks. Comparing index (1) to (3) and comparing index (2) to (4), we see that for both the bottom-up and top-down approach, it is beneficial to fuse the scores from the fully-connected and soft-max layers. This result is surprising, given that the layers come from the same network and it indicates that the layers contain different information useful for event detection. This result is furthermore interesting from a computational perspective, as the features from both layers can be extracted from a single pass through the same network. Hence, the improvement is obtained for free.

The fusion of (3) and (4), i.e. the fusion of the bottom-up and top-down reorganizations, also yields complementary results, with a mean Average Precision of 0.475 and 0.324 for respectively the 100 and 10 positive video tasks of the TRECVID Multimedia Event Detection 2013 dataset. This result clearly shows that pre-training deep networks on different hierarchies results in different and complementary representations. Figure 6 shows that, although the mean Average Precision of the individual approaches is similar, the scores per event vary notably (on average 2.7% per event), resulting in improved performance upon fusion.

Multiple recent works have investigated complex and high-dimensional video representations from deep frame representations beyond frame averaging [16, 26]. Here, we similarly investigate such representations using the frame features with reorganized pre-training. We have employed both VLAD and Fisher Vector encoding and report the results for VLAD in Table 1, as that yielded the highest scores. For the VLAD encoding, we create a codebook from 10 clusters per event, resulting in a 10,240-dimensional feature vector using the fully-connected layer and a 44,370-dimensional feature vector using the soft-max layer. The results using the bottom-up reorganization show that a VLAD encoding improves over averaging, especially for the 10 positive videos per event task (0.339 mAP versus 0.305 for averaging).

TRECVID MED 2013		
Method	100 Ex.	10 Ex.
Averaging		
(1) Bottom-up (fc)	0.446	0.296
(2) Top-down (fc)	0.438	0.300
(3) Bottom-up (fc + soft-max)	0.452	0.305
(4) Top-down (fc + soft-max)	0.454	0.317
(3) + (4)	0.475	0.324
VLAD		
Bottom-up (fc + soft-max)	0.465	0.339

Table 1: Mean Average Precision scores for fusions of different layers, networks, and encodings within deep representations, which all yield complementary results.

We conclude from this fusion experiment that combining information from different pre-trained deep networks and even different layers from the same deep network improves the Average Precision scores. Furthermore, performing a VLAD encoding instead of averaging frames results in a boost for individual networks, especially for the 10 positive videos task.

Results for Fusing Modalities. In Table 2, we show the results of the deep networks with the audio and motion modalities. The Table clearly states that individually, the event detection scores using our deep networks improve over the motion and audio scores. Upon combining the modalities, we observe a jump in performance. This result shows the complementary natures of the different modalities: individually the motion and audio features are clearly outperformed, but they contain information not captured in deep networks which result in improved fusion results. This is naturally due to the nature of deep convolutional neural networks, which focus on spatially visual information and exclude temporal and audio information.

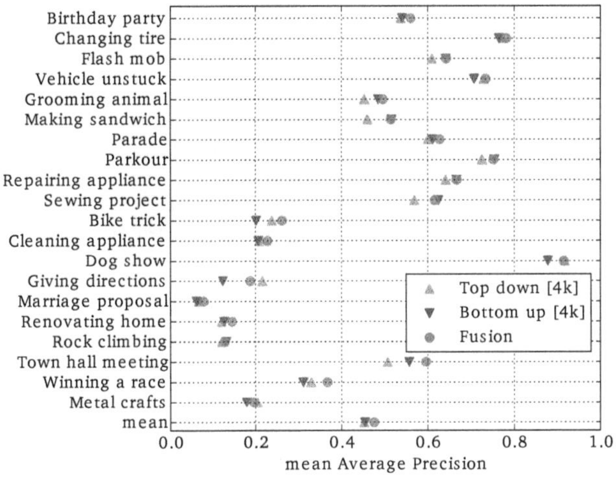

Figure 6: The Average Precision scores per event for bottom-up, top-down, and their fusion. Note that the scores per event are different for the two approaches, resulting in complementary fusion results.

TRECVID MED 2013		
Method	100 Ex.	10 Ex.
Individual		
(1) Audio (MFCC)	0.114	0.053
(2) Motion (MBH)	0.341	0.192
(3) Visual (ours, avg)	0.475	0.324
Fusion		
(2) + (3)	0.504	0.345
(1) + (2) + (3)	0.526	0.348

Table 2: Mean Average Precision scores for fusing our deep representations with other modalities. We outperform motion and audio features, while the fusion leads to further improvement.

We have furthermore attempted to fuse the VLAD encoding of Table 1 with the motion and audio features, but this did not result in improved performance. Since the VLAD encoding requires more computational effort and has a higher storage requirement, we have opted to focus on averaging.

5.4 Comparison to the state-of-the-art

Experiment 4. For the fourth experiment, we compare our results to the current state-of-the-art on multimedia event detection. We perform a comparison on both the TRECVID MED 2013 test set and the TRECVID MED 2015 benchmark.

Results on the TRECVID MED 2013 Test set. The comparison to the state-of-the-art on the TRECVID Multimedia Event Detection 2013 dataset is shown in Table 3. As the Table shows, we outperform the current state-of-the-art on both the 100 and 10 positive videos per event task using deep networks only. Upon a fusion with motion and audio features, we improve further over related work.

Results on the TRECVID MED 2015 Benchmark. We furthermore compare our results achieved on the latest TRECVID 2015 benchmark for Multimedia Event Detection. This benchmark is similar in nature to the 2013 dataset in training and evaluation. However, the 2015 dataset contains 20 new events. Furthermore, the benchmark comparison is performed in a large-scale setup, with a test set of about 200,000 videos. In Figure 7, we show the inferred mean Average Precision scores for our entries and the entries of the other participants. We report results both for the pre-specified (where the events and video labels are given well before the benchmark deadline) and ad-hoc (where the events and video labels are given shortly before the benchmark deadline) tasks. The Figure paints a similar picture to the results on the 2013 dataset; we outperform the current state-of-the-art by fusing deep representations with motion and audio modalities, while our deep representations only are already among the top contenders.

TRECVID MED 2013		
Method	100 Ex	10 Ex
Habibian et al. [4]	-	0.196
Sun et al. (visual) [22]	0.350	-
Nagel et al. [16]	0.386	0.218
Sun et al. (fusion) [22]	0.425	-
Xu et al. [26]	0.446	0.298
Chang et al. [1]	-	0.310
Ours, deep network	0.475	0.324
Ours, multimodal fusion	0.526	0.348

Table 3: Comparison to other works on TRECVID MED 2013 test set for both our best deep network results and our fusion results. We yield better results for both the 100 and 10 positive videos per event task.

6. CONCLUSIONS

In this work, we leverage the complete ImageNet dataset for pre-training deep convolutional neural networks for video event detection, rather than the prescribed 1,000 ImageNet subset. We propose two contrasting and complementary approaches to reorganize the ImageNet hierarchy. The bottom-up approach aims to merge classes from the deepest parts of hierarchy upwards, while the top-down approach aims to select rich generic classes starting from the top of the hierarchy. The new hierarchies are in turn used as input to pre-train deep networks and are employed for frame representation in video event detection. Experimental evaluation performed on the challenging TRECVID MED 2013 dataset shows that deep networks trained on our hierarchies *i)* outperform standard pre-trained networks, *ii)* are complementary, *iii)* maintain the benefits of fusion with other modalities, and *iv)* reach state-of-the-art result. The pre-trained models are available online at http://tinyurl.com/imagenetshuffle and can be used directly to extract state-of-the-art video representations using the Caffe library.

Acknowledgements

This research is supported by the STW STORY project.

7. REFERENCES

[1] X. Chang, Y.-L. Yu, Y. Yang, and A. G. Hauptmann. Searching persuasively: Joint event detection and evidence recounting with limited supervision. In *MM*, 2015.

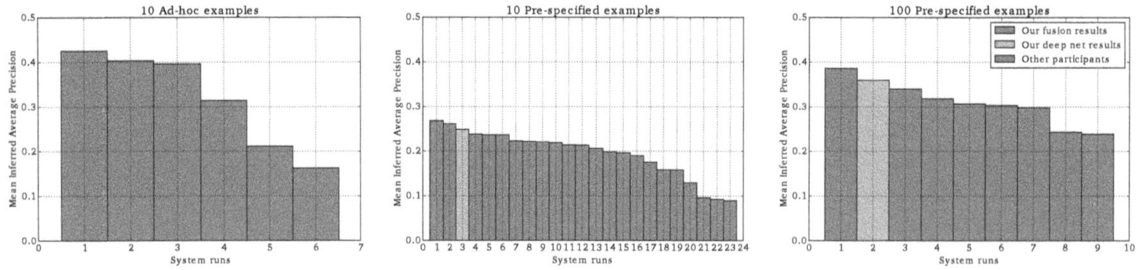

Figure 7: Comparison between our results (blue) and the results of all other participants in the TRECVID Multimedia Event Detection benchmark 2015. Our deep networks and their fusion with motion and audio information are the top contenders for all tasks.

[2] J. Deng, W. Dong, R. Socher, L.-J. Li, K. Li, and L. Fei-Fei. ImageNet: A large-scale hierarchical image database. In *CVPR*, 2009.

[3] C. Gan, N. Wang, Y. Yang, D.-Y. Yeung, and A. G. Hauptmann. Devnet: A deep event network for multimedia event detection and evidence recounting. In *CVPR*, 2015.

[4] A. Habibian, T. Mensink, and C. G. M. Snoek. Videostory: A new multimedia embedding for few-example recognition and translation of events. In *MM*, 2014.

[5] A. Habibian, K. E. A. van de Sande, and C. G. M. Snoek. Recommendations for video event recognition using concept vocabularies. In *ICMR*, 2013.

[6] H. Jégou, F. Perronnin, M. Douze, J. Sanchez, P. Perez, and C. Schmid. Aggregating local image descriptors into compact codes. *TPAMI*, 34(9):1704–1716, 2012.

[7] Y. Jia, E. Shelhamer, J. Donahue, S. Karayev, J. Long, R. Girshick, S. Guadarrama, and T. Darrell. Caffe: Convolutional architecture for fast feature embedding. In *MM*, 2014.

[8] L. Jiang, S.-I. Yu, D. Meng, Y. Yang, T. Mitamura, and A. G. Hauptmann. Fast and accurate content-based semantic search in 100m internet videos. pages 49–58, 2015.

[9] A. Karpathy, G. Toderici, S. Shetty, T. Leung, R. Sukthankar, and L. Fei-Fei. Large-scale video classification with convolutional neural networks. In *CVPR*, 2014.

[10] A. Krizhevsky, I. Sutskever, and G. E. Hinton. Imagenet classification with deep convolutional neural networks. In *NIPS*, 2012.

[11] Z.-Z. Lan, L. Bao, S.-I. Yu, W. Liu, and A. G. Hauptmann. Multimedia classification and event detection using double fusion. *MTA*, 71(1):333–347, 2014.

[12] M. Mazloom, E. Gavves, and C. G. M. Snoek. Conceptlets: Selective semantics for classifying video events. *TMM*, 16(8):2214–2228, 2014.

[13] P. Mettes, J. C. van Gemert, S. Cappallo, T. Mensink, and C. G. M. Snoek. Bag-of-fragments: Selecting and encoding video fragments for event detection and recounting. In *ICMR*, 2015.

[14] G. A. Miller. Wordnet: a lexical database for english. *Comm. ACM*, 38(11):39–41, 1995.

[15] G. K. Myers, R. Nallapati, J. van Hout, S. Pancoast, R. Nevatia, C. Sun, A. Habibian, D. C. Koelma, K. E. A. van de Sande, A. W. M. Smeulders, and C. G. M. Snoek. Evaluating multimedia features and fusion for example-based event detection. *MVA*, 25(1):17–32, 2014.

[16] M. Nagel, T. Mensink, and C. G. M. Snoek. Event fisher vectors: Robust encoding visual diversity of visual streams. In *BMVC*, 2015.

[17] P. Natarajan, S. Wu, S. Vitaladevuni, X. Zhuang, S. Tsakalidis, U. Park, R. Prasad, and P. Natarajan. Multimodal feature fusion for robust event detection in web videos. In *CVPR*, 2012.

[18] P. Over et al. Trecvid 2014 – an overview of the goals, tasks, data, evaluation mechanisms and metrics. In *TRECVID Workshop*, 2014.

[19] O. Russakovsky, J. Deng, H. Su, J. Krause, S. Satheesh, S. Ma, Z. Huang, A. Karpathy, A. Khosla, M. Bernstein, et al. Imagenet large scale visual recognition challenge. *IJCV*, 115(3):211–252, 2015.

[20] J. Sánchez, F. Perronnin, T. Mensink, and J. Verbeek. Image classification with the fisher vector: Theory and practice. *IJCV*, 105(3):222–245, 2013.

[21] K. Simonyan and A. Zisserman. Very deep convolutional networks for large-scale image recognition. *ICLR*, 2015.

[22] C. Sun, B. Burns, R. Nevatia, C. G. M. Snoek, B. Bolles, G. Myers, W. Wang, and E. Yeh. Isomer: Informative segment observations for multimedia event recounting. In *ICMR*, 2014.

[23] C. Szegedy, W. Liu, Y. Jia, P. Sermanet, S. Reed, D. Anguelov, D. Erhan, V. Vanhoucke, and A. Rabinovich. Going deeper with convolutions. *CVPR*, 2015.

[24] D. T. J. Vreeswijk, C. G. M. Snoek, K. E. A. van de Sande, and A. W. M. Smeulders. All vehicles are cars: subclass preferences in container concepts. In *ICMR*, 2012.

[25] H. Wang and C. Schmid. Action recognition with improved trajectories. In *ICCV*, 2013.

[26] Z. Xu, Y. Yang, and A. G. Hauptmann. A discriminative cnn video representation for event detection. *CVPR*, 2015.

[27] G. Ye, Y. Li, H. Xu, D. Liu, and S.-F. Chang. Eventnet: A large scale structured concept library for complex event detection in video. In *MM*, 2015.

Learning for Traffic State Estimation on Large Scale of Incomplete Data

Yiyang Yao
Information & Communication Branch, State Grid Zhejiang Company
Hangzhou, China
yao_yiyang@zj.sgcc.com.cn

Yingjie Xia*
College of Computer Sciences, Zhejiang University
Hangzhou, China
xiayingjie@zju.edu.cn

Zhenyu Shan
Institute of Service Engineering, Hangzhou Normal University
Hangzhou, China
shanzhenyu@zju.edu.cn

Zhengguang Liu
National University of Singapore
Singapore
lzg@nus.edu.sg

ABSTRACT

Traffic state estimation is one of the very basic and most important tasks in intelligent transportation systems. Data collected from multiple types of traffic sensors are valuable sources to estimate traffic state. However, those data are always incomplete for the cases such as sensors broken, data missing, etc. The incomplete data can also be used to accurately estimate taffic state by data prediction and data fusion. Firstly, the missing data are predicted based on the data correlations extracted on large amount of historical taxi GPS data. Then, data collected from multiple sensors are fused to get more accurate results. Finally, computing of data fusion is parallelized. The main research focus is placed on learning for extracting the inherent spatio-temporal correlations of traffic data and fusing multimedia traffic data. Accuracy and efficiency experiments are conducted and the experimental results demonstrate that our method can process incomplete data and achieve accurate and real-time traffic state estimation.

CCS Concepts

•**Computer systems organization** → **Embedded systems;** *Redundancy;* Robotics; •**Networks** → Network reliability;

Keywords

traffic state estimation; random forest; perceptual feature; incomplete data

---

*Yingjie Xia is the corresponding author.

ICMR'16, June 06-09, 2016, New York, NY, USA
© 2016 ACM. ISBN 978-1-4503-4359-6/16/06...$15.00
DOI: http://dx.doi.org/10.1145/2911996.2912037

1. INTRODUCTION

Nowadays, urban traffic jam problem becomes more and more serious. Traffic state estimation is implemented to estimate the traffic states of road segments for congestion controlling, routine planning, traffic management, and road infrastructure planning. Traditionally, traffic data collected from different types of sensors are used to estimate traffic state, such as from traffic surveillance videos, Global Positioning System (GPS) installed in probe vehicles, Sydney Coordinated Adaptive Traffic System (SCATS) loop detectors [2] and remote traffic microwave sensors (RTMS) [5]. SCATS [2] detector is buried within road pavement, and video and RTMS [5] sensors are deployed at roadside. These sensors can detect traffic flow volume or velocity, as essential elements for traffic state estimation. However, for high cost of devices and maintenance, these sensors are always deployed on some important road segments, which indicates incomplete traffic data collection. GPS devices are widely installed in probe vehicles, such as taxi [4]. Although the amount of probe vehicles is limited, their historically aggregated data can demonstrate the overall traffic status of the city and can be used to mine the correlations among road segments.

Therefore, aiming to estimate traffic state more accurately and in real-time, there are the following three challenges we must solve. (1) SCATS, RTMS, GPS, and video data need to be preprocessed respectively. (2) incomplete data need to be dealt with to get more accurate results. (3) large amount of data collected from the whole city should be computed efficiently to achieve real time.

In this paper, towards challenge (1) we propose the respective traffic flow speed and flux calculation methods for preprocessing multimedia traffic data. Towards challenge (2), we use the multiple linear regression model to extract the GPS data spatio-temporal correlations and fill the data gap in the incomplete data. Then, a robust data fusion method is designed to fuse the multi-sensor to improve the accuracy of traffic state estimation. Towards challenge (3), parallel computing techniques applying to the data-intensive computation by quadtree-based data decomposition and parallelized fusion are adopted to implement the real-time traffic state estimation [13].

The technical contributions of this paper are summarized as: (1) by understanding the data characteristics from different types of sensors, we propose the repsective methods to process them. (2) By using the multiple linear regression model to mine the large amount of GPS data uploaded by taxies, we extract the inherent spatio-temporal correlations of traffic states of road segments. (3) We applying the data-intensive parallel computing techniques to accelerate the data fusion.

The rest of the paper is organized as follows. Some related work about traffic state estimation with complete and incomplete multi-sensor data is reviewed in Section 2. Section 3 proposes mutli-sensor data calculation methods. Section 4 presents incomplete data fusion and its quadtree-based parallel computing techniques. Experimental results on the accuracy and efficiency are given in Section 5. Finally, a conclusion with remarks on future work is drawn in Section 6.

2. RELATED WORK

Data-driven intelligent transportation systems (ITS) are the systems which interactively utilize data resources pertaining to transportation systems. Data-driven ITS mainly focus on processing data collected from multiple sources [14], such as video sensor, SCATS loop detector, GPS, and RTMS, to play complementary roles for each other [11]. Traffic Video data are mainly analyzed to detect [18] and recognize [17] objects; SCATS data are collected from loop detectors for vehicle volume [2]; and GPS data are used to locate and trace the probe vehicles [5]. These However, each kind of sensor has its inherent disadvantage. Video sensor is easily subject to environmental constraints, e.g., lighting, weather, and shadow [9]. SCATS loop detector suffers from high installation and maintenance costs for its high failure ratio [12]. GPS suffers from the poor statistical representation and errors in the map-matching process [8].

Multi-sensor traffic data fusion is a popular and useful tool for traffic state estimation, even in some cases that data are incomplete. For example, a large amount of probe vehicle data and RTMS data are used to train the traffic state estimation model by the neural network model [1]. The work can provide good speed estimation in the arterial roads. Some other methods are designed to fuse the multi-sensor traffic data, such as the weighted least-square method [3], D-S evidential theory [12], rough set theory [16]. All these methods are aiming to optimize traffic state estimation. However, their results are always affected by the issue of data incompleteness. This problem also exists in Xia et al.âĂŹs work [10], which uses Cyber-Infrastructure to design a cyber-ITS framework for massive traffic data analysis. The framework is based on the assumption that more than two kinds of traffic sensors are deployed on a single road segment.

Some work has already considered the issue of data incompleteness, and uses different methods to deal with the result inaccuracy. The aforementioned D-S evidential theory is a typical fusion method to construct classifiers for incomplete data [4]. However, the basic condition is the existence of at least one kind of sensor deployed on the road segment. In the condition of data missing, the spatio-temporal related data are used to classify the road segments and estimate the traffic state of the road segment without sensors [7]. The spatio-temporal relation is mined from the historical data, and the diurnal speed/time pattern is determined by Gaussian Mixture Model without pre-classification [8]. This work considers both temporal correlation and spatio correlation in historical data, and therefore can use the traffic flow evolvement and relevance between neighboring road segments to fill the gap of data incompleteness. GPS data collected from taxies are a good type of traffic data resources. Some work [8] [6] uses different number of taxies and different timeslots to analyze the traffic data. All these work finds a lot of spatio-temporal vacancies in the dataset. Therefore, the method to deal with traffic data incompleteness is necessary in data-driven intelligent transportation systems.

Although there has been some work using incomplete data to estimate traffic state, in most cases the results always show the accuracy restriction caused by the data incompleteness. As a common solution, the inherent correlation between the existed data and vacant data is extracted according to their temporal and spatial relations. Then, the correlation is used to estimate the vacant data. In this paper, we implement a traffic state estimation method by extracting the data spatio-temporal correlation and fusing incomplete data fusion.

3. MUTLI-SENSOR TRAFFIC DATA CALCULATION METHODS

3.1 SCATS data calculation for traffic state estimation

In urban traffic network, the SCATS data can be calculated into speed on a specified road segment at specified time by the combination of traffic wave theory and Greenshields linear model. The velocity calculation by the traffic wave theory is expressed as

$$V_{SCATS} = (q_2 - q_1)/(k_2 - k_1) \tag{1}$$

where q_1 and q_2 denote the fluxes of upstream and downstream of a road segment during one phase, and k_1 and k_2 denote the densities of the upstream and downstream. q and k can be collected from the SCATS sensor. The Greenshields linear model reinforces the traffic wave theory for the jam feature of the urban traffic.

3.2 GPS data calculation for traffic state estimation

GPS data can be used to calculate the speeds of road segments. The data preprocessing consists of three steps: coordinates transforming, map matching, and curve approximating. Afterwards, the speed v_0 at time t_0 along the road segment can be calculated as

$$v_0(t_0) = (\int_0^L v(l,t)|_{t=t_0} dl)/L \tag{2}$$

where $v(l, t)$ represents the speed at space l and time t from GPS data attributes, and L is the length of the road segment. Therefore, the mean speed along the whole road segment in the time interval from $(k-1)T$ to kT can be estimated as

$$v_G = (\int_{(k-1)T}^{kT} v_0(t)dt)/T \tag{3}$$

3.3 RTMS data calculation for traffic state estimation

RTMS data contain the attributes of vehicle velocity and flux. We can calculate the average velocity V_{RTMS} and flux F_{RTMS} of road segments by

$$V_{RTMS} = \sum_{i=1}^{n} v_i/n \tag{4}$$

$$F_{RTMS} = n \tag{5}$$

3.4 Video data calculation for traffic state estimation

In tafffic video data, the quantity of corners detected is the global character of the ROI region. It is not qualified to be utilized as a distinctive feature for traffic state estimation. For understanding the traffic scene accurately, the spatial distribution of corners should reveal the local changes of the scenario.

In our model, we divide the ROI region into 16 blocks with the same width and height. The corners in each block are summed up as a value of the feature vector, and these feature values can represent the distribution status of each block, and can significantly indicates the variations caused by vehicles movements.

As shown in Figure 1, we specify the region of one-way lanes for traffic state estimation, and the region is divided into 16 regions for the spatial corner distribution evaluation. Accordingly, 16 values, each of which refers to the number of corners in corresponding blocks, can be obtained and constitute the 16 features of the feature vector.

Figure 1: The spatial distribution of corners

As a result, the feature vector consists of two perceptual features: a global feature which refers to the total quantity of vehicle corners, and the spatial corner distribution feature constituted with 16 feature values. This feature vector will be sent to the classifier of the random forest model for traffic state training and classification.

4. INCOMPLETE TRAFFIC DATA ESTIMATION AND FUSION

We first determine the scale of candidate road segments which can restrict the number of input for the incomplete traffic data estimation. Then, the data of candidate road segments are input to the Bayesian recursive filtering method to estimate traffic state of the target road segment without specified data. Finally, the estimated traffic state is fused with data from other sensors to get more accurate traffic state estimation.

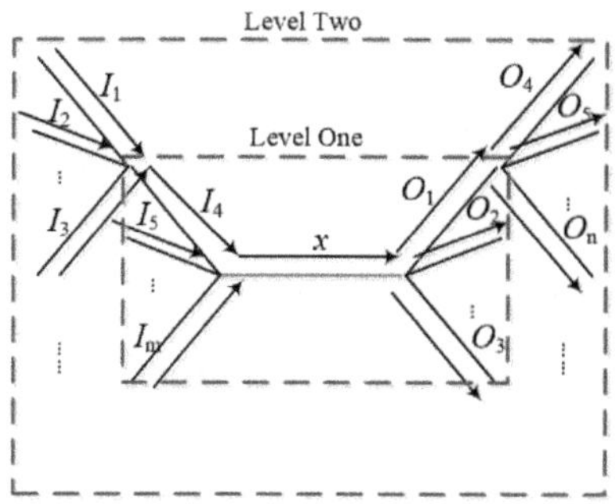

Figure 2: Candidate region scales

4.1 Candidate Road Segments Scale Determination

Firstly, by taking the road segment x as the target road segment, we determine the candidate road segments which are near the target. Iteratively, we check the conditions of road segments connected the target road segment from the first level (directly connected) to bigger levels (indirectly), as Figure 2. The checking conditions focus on the number and type of candidate road segments. For example, we first check the road segments in level one and find more than 30% road segments are missing data, and then we need to check level two. In another case, if all the qualified candidate road segments are input road segments or output road segment, we also need to extend the checking level. The threshold of the checking level can be customized.

4.2 Incomplete Data Estimation

After determining the candidate road segments scale, we use the data of candidate road segments to estimate the incomplete data of our target road segment by adopting the Bayesian recursive filtering method. The basic formula of the method is as following.

$$P(s_{x,k}|Z^k) = P(Z_k|s_{x,k}) * P(s_{x,k}|Z^{k-1})/P(Z_k|Z^{k-1}) \tag{6}$$

where

$$\begin{aligned} Z_k = \{&Z_{I_1,k-t_{I_1}}, Z_{I_2,k-t_{I_2}}, ..., Z_{I_m,k-t_{I_m}}, \\ &Z_{O_1,k+t_{O_1}}, Z_{O_2,k+t_{O_2}}, ..., Z_{O_n,k+t_{O_n}}\} \end{aligned} \tag{7}$$

$$t_i = \sum_{j\epsilon(i \to x)} \left\lceil (\frac{l_j}{2\bar{v}_j} + \frac{l_x}{2\bar{v}_x})/T \right\rceil \tag{8}$$

$$\begin{aligned} \bar{v} &= (\int_{(k-p)T}^{kT} \bar{v}_0\,(t)\,dt)/(p \cdot T), \bar{v}_0(t) \\ &= (\int_0^l v(l,t)dl)/l, v(l,t) = \sum_{a=0}^{3}\sum_{b=0}^{3} c_{ab} l^a t^b \end{aligned} \tag{9}$$

$$Z^{k-1} = \underbrace{\{Z_{k-1}, Z_{k-2}, ..., Z_{k-p}\}}_{p} \tag{10}$$

In the above formulas, t_i is the time slot of traffic flow between the candidate road segment i and the target road segment x. Road segment j is the correlated road segment between i and x. l_j and l_x are the respective length of road segments j and x. T is the time slot between two neighboring road segments. $overlinev_i$ and $overlinev_x$ denote the average speed in the previous p time slots. The number p is the scale of candidate data in temporal dimension, and the number of elements in Z_k is the scale of candidate road segments in spatial dimension. $Z_{i,k-t_i}$ denotes the multi-sensor data set on the road segment i at the time slot $k - t_i$.

4.3 Mutli-Sensor Data Fusion

The estimated traffic state from SCATS, GPS, RTMS, and video sensors are fused by D-S evidential method to implement more accurate traffic state estimation. The basic principle of the D-S evidential fusion method is calculating the basic probability assignment of different sensors by learning from historical data, and achieve a final estimation by using the probability to compensate each other. The basic formular of D-S evidential fusion method is as following [15].

$$\begin{aligned} m(s_{x,t})|_{s_{x,t}=s'} =& m_1(s_{1,x,t})|_{s_{1,x,t}=s'} \oplus m_2(s_{2,x,t})|_{s_{2,x,t}=s'} \\ & \cdots \oplus m_n(s_{n,x,t})|_{s_{n,x,t}=s'} \\ =& \frac{\prod_{i=1}^{n}(m_i(s_{i,x,t})|_{s_{i,x,t}=s'})}{1 - \sum_{(\forall s_{i,x,t \in ss, i=1 \ldots n}) \wedge \bigcap_{i=1}^{n} s_{i,x,t}=\emptyset}^{\prod_1^n m_i(s_{i,x,t})}} \end{aligned} \tag{11}$$

where $m_i(s_{i,x,t})$ denotes probability of the traffic state of the road segment x from the ith sensor at time t. Different state condition is specified by $s_{x,t} = s'$. Since the data fusion method is applied to each road segment with different sensor data or estimated incomplete data, massive road segments in a big city with a large scale of data can be parallelized by region-based data decomposition. The data decomposition is implemented by using quadtree to divide the data set until each sub-data set reaching the threshold. These decomposed sub-data sets are scheduled to different computing nodes to achieve the load balance.

5. EXPERIMENTAL RESULTS AND ANALYSIS

5.1 Experiment Setup

We use RTMS and GPS data collected from some main road segments in the downtown of Hangzhou to test our method. Two metrics, accuracy of missing data estimation and accuracy of multi-sensor data fusion are evaluated. In the accuracy test of missing data estimation, our method is compared with historical average method, temporal correlation method, and spatial correlation method. In the accuracy test of multi-sensor data fusion, our method is compared with the method only using RTMS and the method only using GPS. The experimental results and their analysis are delivered below.

5.2 Results and Analysis

5.2.1 Accuracy test of missing data estimation

We choose 12 road segments which do not deploy RTMS sensors. The spatio-temporal correlations of these road segments are extracted by using historical GPS data collected from taxies. We use the extracted correlations to estimate the missing data on these 12 road segments from

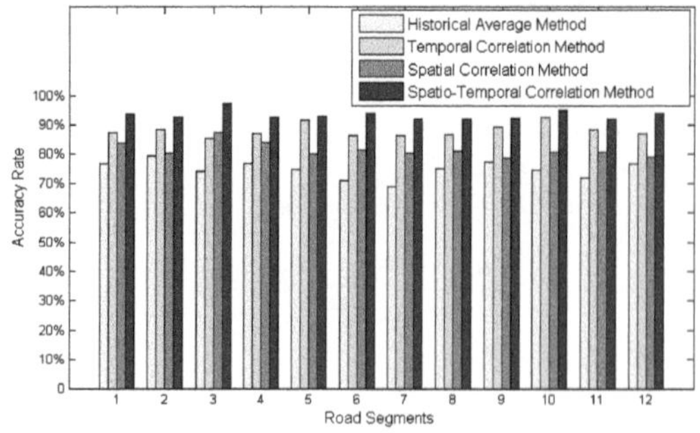

Figure 3: Average accuracy rate of missing data estimation

their neighboring road segments which deploy RTMS sensors. The ground truth of the accuracy test is manually evaluated. The average accuracy results of the four methods are shown in Figure 3. In comparison with the other three methods, our method using spatio-temporal correlation performs better, the accuracy rate always more than 90%. The accuracy rate of the historical average method is the smallest, because this method only uses the ideal data regulation, but neglecting either the temporal correlation or the spatial correlation. In the figure, we also find that the accuracy rates of the temporal correlation method are mostly higher than those of the spatial correlation method. This is because the spatial correlation is affected by many other factors which have impact on the accuracy of missing data estimation.

5.2.2 Accuracy test of data fusion

After estimating the missing RTMS data, we fuse RTMS data and GPS data to get the final traffic state. The accuracy of traffic state estimation is evaluated for each road segment through dividing the number of correctly estimated traffic states by the total number of estimated traffic states. The accuracy test is conducted on the data collected from 8:00 to 17:00 during one day. The accuracy metric is defined as the following formula.

$$Acc = N_c/N_{all} \tag{12}$$

where Acc denotes the accuracy of data fusion, Nc is the number of correct records, and $Nall$ is the total number of records. Accuracy tests on three test cases, multi-sensor data fusion, using only GPS data, and using only RTMS data, are conducted and the experimental results are shown in Figure 4. We find that traffic state estimation by using only GPS data is less accurate than that by using RTMS data, because GPS data collected by taxies are uneven and unstable. RTMS is a kind of stationed sensor, and its data condition is more stable and complete. The accuracy of the fusion method is the highest, and therefore show that our method can improve the accuracy of traffic state estimation.

6. CONCLUSIONS AND FUTURE WORK

This paper designs a method for dealing with incomplete traffic data and fusing data to accurately estimate traffic state. The steps of the method include: (1) SCATS, G-

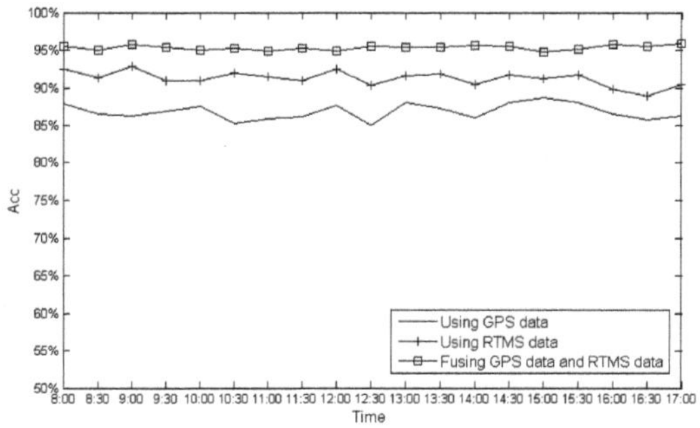

Figure 4: Average accuracy rate of traffic state estimation by using three types of data

PS, RTMS, and video source data are respectively transformed to speed and traffic state; (2) we determine the scale of candidate road segments for the target road segment with incomplete data; (3) we use Bayesian recursive filtering algorithm to estimate traffic state of the target road segment; and (4) the estimated data and existed data are fused to get more accurate traffic state. Some experiments on real urban road networks and real sensor data are conducted. The results of accuracy experiments show that our method can improve the accuracy of traffic state estimation under incomplete data conditions. Moreover, the results of efficiency experiments show that our method is also in real time.

In the future, we want to improve the method to determine the scale of candidate road segments. We also place some interests in new methods for incomplete data estimation, especially those methods based on traffic-related theories.

7. ACKNOWLEDGEMENTS

This research is supported in part by the following funds: National Natural Science Foundation of China under grant number 61472113 and 61304188, and Zhejiang Provincial Natural Science Foundation of China under grant number LZ13F020004 and LR14F020003.

8. REFERENCES

[1] R. L. Cheu, D.-H. Lee, and C. Xie. An arterial speed estimation model fusing data from stationary and mobile sensors. In *Intelligent Transportation Systems, 2001*, pages 573–578. IEEE, 2001.

[2] B. Coifman. Improved velocity estimation using single loop detectors. *Transportation Research Part A: Policy and Practice*, 35(10):863–880, 2001.

[3] N.-E. El Faouzi. Data-driven aggregative schemes for multisource estimation fusion: A road travel time application. In *Defense and Security*, pages 351–359. International Society for Optics and Photonics, 2004.

[4] N.-E. El Faouzi and E. Lefevre. Classifiers and distance-based evidential fusion for road travel time estimation. In *Defense and Security Symposium*, pages 62420A–62420A. International Society for Optics and Photonics, 2006.

[5] S. Gidel, P. Checchin, C. Blanc, T. Chateau, and L. Trassoudaine. Pedestrian detection and tracking in an urban environment using a multilayer laser scanner. *IEEE Transactions on Intelligent Transportation Systems*, 11(3):579–588, 2010.

[6] Z. Li, Y. Zhu, H. Zhu, and M. Li. Compressive sensing approach to urban traffic sensing. In *Distributed Computing Systems (ICDCS), 2011 31st International Conference on*, pages 889–898. IEEE, 2011.

[7] W. Toplak, H. Koller, M. Dragaschnig, D. Bauer, and J. Asamer. Novel road classifications for large scale traffic networks. In *13th International IEEE Conference on Intelligent Transportation Systems (ITSC)*, pages 1264–1270. IEEE, 2010.

[8] P. Widhalm, M. Piff, N. Brandle, H. Koller, and M. Reinthaler. Robust road link speed estimates for sparse or missing probe vehicle data. In *15th International IEEE Conference on Intelligent Transportation Systems (ITSC)*, pages 1693–1697. IEEE, 2012.

[9] Y. Xia, J. Chen, X. Lu, C. Wang, and C. Xu. Big traffic data processing framework for intelligent monitoring and recording systems. *Neurocomputing*, 2016(181):139–146, 2016.

[10] Y. Xia, J. Hu, and M. Fontaine. A cyber-its framework for massive traffic data analysis using cyber-infrastructure. *The Scientific World Journal*, 2013(462846):1–9, 2013.

[11] Y. Xia and X. Li. Multi-sensor heterogeneous data representation for data-driven its. In *16th International IEEE Conference on Intelligent Transportation Systems (ITSC)*, pages 1750–1755. IEEE, 2013.

[12] Y. Xia, X. Li, and Z. Shan. Parallelized fusion on multisensor transportation data: A case study in cyberits. *International Journal of Intelligent Systems*, 28(6):540–564, 2013.

[13] Y. Xia, C. Wu, Q. Kong, Z. Shan, and L. Kuang. A parallel fusion method for heterogeneous multi-sensor transportation data. In *Modeling Decision for Artificial Intelligence*, pages 31–42. Springer, 2011.

[14] Y. Xia, L. Zhang, and Y. Liu. Special issue on big data driven intelligent transportation systems. *Neurocomputing*, 2016(181):1–3, 2016.

[15] Y. Xia, T. Zhang, and S. Wang. A generic methodological framework for cyber-its: Using cyber-infrastructure in its data analysis cases. *Fundamenta Informaticae*, 133(1):35–53, 2014.

[16] H. Zhang, Y. Zhang, D. Yao, and D. Hu. An architecture of traffic state analysis based on multi-sensor fusion. In *Intelligent Vehicles Symposium*, pages 855–860. IEEE, 2005.

[17] L. Zhang, Y. Gao, Y. Xia, and k. Lu. Representative discovery of structure cues for weakly-supervised image segmentation. *IEEE Transactions on Multimedia*, 16(2):470–479, 2014.

[18] L. Zhang, M. Song, Y. Yang, Q. Zhao, C. Zhao, and N. Sebe. Weakly supervised photo cropping. *IEEE Transactions on Multimedia*, pages 94–107, 2014.

Diverse Yet Efficient Retrieval using Locality Sensitive Hashing

Vidyadhar Rao
IIIT Hyderabad, India
vidyadhar.rao@research.iiit.ac.in

Prateek Jain
Microsoft Research India
prajain@microsoft.com

C.V Jawahar
IIIT Hyderabad, India
jawahar@iiit.ac.in

ABSTRACT

Typical retrieval systems have three requirements: a) Accurate retrieval, i.e., the method should have high precision, b) Diverse retrieval, i.e., the obtained set of samples should be diverse, and c) Retrieval time should be small. However, most of the existing methods address only one or two of the above mentioned requirements. In this work, we present a method based on *randomized* locality sensitive hashing which tries to address all of the above requirements simultaneously. While earlier hashing-based approaches considered approximate retrieval to be acceptable only for the sake of efficiency, we argue that one can further exploit approximate retrieval to provide impressive trade-offs between accuracy and diversity. We also extend our method to the problem of multi-label prediction, where the goal is to output a diverse and accurate set of labels for a given document in real-time. Finally, we present empirical results on image and text retrieval tasks and show that our method retrieves diverse and accurate images/labels while ensuring $100\times$-speed-up over the existing diverse retrieval approaches.

1. INTRODUCTION

Nearest neighbor (NN) retrieval [15, 17] is a critical sub-routine for machine learning, databases, and a variety of other disciplines. Basically, we have a database of points, and given an input query, the goal is to return the nearest point(s) to the query using some similarity metric. As a naïve linear scan of large databases is infeasible in practice, most of the research for NN retrieval has focused on making the retrieval efficient with either novel index structures [7, 39] or by approximating the distance computations [4, 19]. That is, the goal of these methods is: a) accurate retrieval, b) fast retrieval.

However in practice, NN retrieval methods [12, 21] are expected to meet one more criteria: diversity of retrieved data points. That is, it is typically desirable to find data-points that are diverse and cover a larger area of the space while maintaining high accuracy levels. For instance, when a user is looking for *flowers*, a typical NN retrieval system would tend to return all the images of the same flower (say *"lilly"*). But, it would be more useful to show a diverse range of images consisting of *sunflowers*, *lillies*, *roses*, etc. In this work, we propose a simple retrieval scheme that addresses all of the above mentioned requirements, i.e., a) good accuracy, b) fast retrieval time, and c) high diversity.

Our algorithm is based on the following simple observation: in most of the cases, one needs to trade-off accuracy for diversity. That is, rather than finding the nearest neighbor, we would need to select a point which is a bit farther from the given query but is *dissimilar* to the other retrieved points. Hence, we hypothesize that *approximate nearest neighbors can be used as a proxy to ensure that the retrieved points are diverse*. Figure 1 contrasts our approach with the different retrieval methods.

We propose a Locality Sensitive Hashing (LSH) [2, 8] based algorithm that guarantees approximate nearest neighbor retrieval in sub-linear time retrieval and superior diversity. We show that the effectiveness of our method depends on *randomization* in the design of the hash functions. Further, we modify the standard hash functions to take into account the distribution of the data for better performance. Our method retrieves points that are sampled uniformly at *random* to ensure diversity in the retrieval while maintaining reasonable number of relevant ones.

In our approach, it is easy to see that we can obtain higher accuracy with poor diversity and higher diversity with poor accuracy. Therefore, similar to precision and recall, there is a need to balance between accuracy and diversity in the retrieval. The later is important as there is a wide variety of diversity in what diversity means [14]. Evaluating the algorithms requires a measure that appropriately rewards diversity in the result list [29]. In this work, we keep a balance between accuracy and diversity and try to maximize these two criteria, simultaneously. We use harmonic mean between accuracy and diversity as the main performance measure. We believe that this performance measure is suitable for several applications i.e., the results would not change in essence with different notions of diversity and helps us empirically compare different methods. The major contributions of this paper are:

1. While approximate retrieval is acceptable only for the sake of efficiency, we argue that one can further exploit approximate retrieval to provide impressive trade-offs between accuracy and diversity. (*see Lemma 4.1 and Section 6*)

2. We propose hash functions that characterize the locality sensitive hashing to retrieve approximate nearest neighbors in sub-linear time with superior diversity. (*see Section 4*)

3. We extend the proposed method to diverse multi-label prediction problem and show that our method is not only orders of magnitude faster than the existing methods but also produces more accurate and diverse set of labels. (*see Section 5 and Section 8*)

ICMR'16, June 06-09, 2016, New York, NY, USA

 ISBN 978-1-4503-4359-6/16/06...$15.00
DOI: http://dx.doi.org/10.1145/2911996.2911998

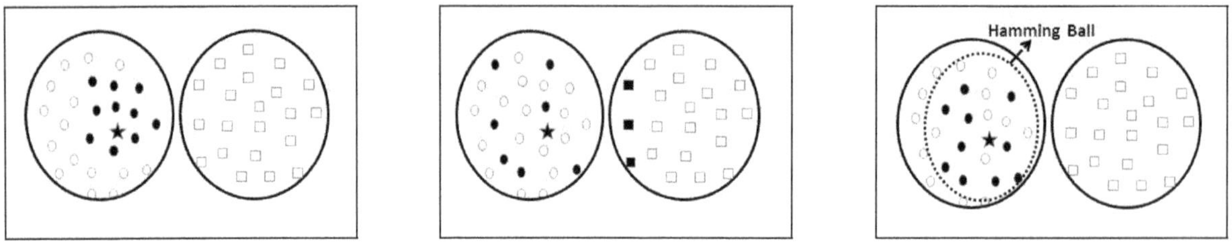

(a) Accurate, Not diverse (b) Not Accurate, diverse (c) Accurate, diverse

Figure 1: Consider a toy dataset with two classes: class A (○) and class B (□). We show the query point (⋆) along with ten points (●, ■) retrieved by various methods. Herein, we measure diversity to be the average pairwise distance between the retrieved set of points. a) A conventional similarity search method (e.g: k-NN) chooses points very close to the query and therefore, shows poor diversity. b) Greedy methods offer diversity but might make poor choices by retrieving points from the class B. c) Our method finds approximate nearest neighbors within a hamming ball of a certain radius around the query point and also ensures diversity among the points.

2. RELATED WORK

2.1 Optimizing Relevance and Diversity

Many of the diversification approaches [3, 5, 10, 32] are centered around an optimization problem that is derived from both relevance and diversity criteria. These methods can be broadly categorized into the following two approaches: (a) *Backward selection*: retrieve all the relevant samples and then rerank them using a clustering step to find a subset with high diversity [3, 10], (b) *Forward selection*: retrieve points sequentially by combining the relevance and diversity scores with a greedy algorithm [5, 16]. Most popular among these methods is MMR optimization [5] which recursively builds the result set by choosing the next optimal selection given the previous optimal selections. However, these methods result in high running times for massive databases.

Some studies attack the diversification problem in different ways. It was shown [31, 33] that natural forms of diversification arise via optimization of rank-based relevance criteria such as average precision and reciprocal rank. It is conjectured that optimizing n-*call@k* metric correlates more strongly with diverse retrieval. More specifically, it is theoretically shown [31] that greedily optimizing expected 1-*call@k* w.r.t a latent subtopic model of binary relevance leads to a diverse retrieval algorithm that shares many features to the MMR optimization. Again, as it turns out, these methods render the task of obtaining diverse solutions extremely time-consuming and thus, are not scalable for several real-time tasks.

Complementary to all the above methods, our work ensures diversity in retrieval using randomization rather than optimization. In our work, instead of finding exact nearest neighbors to a query, we retrieve approximate nearest neighbors that are diverse. In our finding, we theoretically show that approximate NN retrieval via LSH naturally retrieves points that are diverse. Furthermore, our approach is quickly manageable for arbitrary databases of large sizes.

2.2 Application to Multi-label Prediction

A typical application of multi-label learning is automatic image/video tagging [6, 36], where the goal is to tag a given sample with all the relevant concepts/labels. The query is typically an instance (*e.g.*, image, text article) and the goal is to find the most relevant labels (*e.g.*, objects, topics). Moreover, one would like the labels to be diverse. For instance, for a given image, we would like to tag it with a small set of diverse labels rather than several very similar labels. However, the given labels are just some names and we typically do not have any features for the labels. E.g., for a given image of a lab, the appropriate tags might be chair, table, carpet, fan etc. In addition to the above requirement of accurate prediction of the positive labels (tags), we also require the obtained set of positive labels (tags) to be *diverse*. That is, for an image of a lab, we would prefer tags like {table, fan, carpet}, rather than tags like {long table, short table, chair}. Existing multi-label algorithms run in time linear in the number of labels which renders them infeasible for several real-time tasks [37, 40]; exceptions include random forest based methods [1, 28], however, it is not clear how to extend these methods to retrieve diverse set of labels.

To address this, we propose a method that extends our diverse NN retrieval based method to obtain diverse and sub-linear (in the number of labels) time multi-label prediction. Our method is based on the LEML method [40] which is an embedding based method. The key idea behind embedding based methods for multi-label learning is to embed both the given set of labels as well as the data points into a common low-dimensional space. The relevant labels are then recovered by NN retrieval for the given query point (in the embedded space). That is, we embed each label i into a d-dimensional space (say $y_i \in \mathbb{R}^d$) and the given test point is also embedded in the same space (say $x_q \in \mathbb{R}^d$). The relevant labels are obtained by finding y_i's that are closest to x_q. As the final prediction reduces to just NN retrieval, we can apply our method to obtain diverse set of labels in sub-linear time.(*see Section 5*)

3. OPTIMIZATION PROBLEM

Given a set of data points $\mathcal{X} = \{(x_1, y_1), \ldots, (x_n, y_n)\}$ where $x_i \in \mathbb{R}^d$, y_i is a label and a query point $q \in \mathbb{R}^d$, the goal is two-fold: a) retrieve a set of points $\mathcal{R}_q = \{x_{i_1}, \ldots, x_{i_k}\}$ such that a majority of their labels correctly predicts the label of q. b) The set of retrieved points $\mathcal{R}_q$ is "diverse". Note that in this work we are only interested in finding k points that are relevant to the query.

Although it is not quite clear on how relevance and diversity should be combined, we adopt a reminiscent [23] of the general paradigm in machine learning of combining loss functions that measures quality (e.g., training error, prior, or "relevance") and a regularization term that encourages desirable properties (e.g. smoothness, sparsity, or "diversity"). To this end, we define the following optimization problem:

$$\begin{aligned} \min\ & \lambda \Sigma_{i=1}^n \alpha_i \|q - x_i\|^2 - (1-\lambda)\Sigma_{ij}\alpha_i\alpha_j\|x_i - x_j\|^2 \\ \text{s.t. } & \Sigma_{i=1}^n \alpha_i = k; \forall i \in \{1, \ldots n\}\ \alpha_i \in \{0, 1\} \end{aligned} \quad (1)$$

where $\lambda \in [0, 1]$ is a parameter that defines the trade-off between the two terms, and α_i takes the value 1 if x_i is present in the result and 0 if it is not included in the retrieved result. Here, the first term measures the overall relevance of the retrieved set with respect to the query. The second term measures the similarity among the retrieved points. That is, it penalizes the selection of multiple relevant points that are very similar to each other. By including this term in the objective function, we seek to find a set of points that are relevant to the query, but also dissimilar/diverse to each other.

Without loss of generality, we assume that x_i, q are normalized to unit norm, and with some simple substitutions like $\alpha = [\alpha_1, \dots \alpha_n]$, $c = -[q^T x_1, \dots, q^T x_n]$, G be gram matrix with $G_{ij} = x_i^T x_j$, the above objective is equivalent to

$$\begin{aligned} &\min\ \lambda c^T \alpha + (1-\lambda)\alpha^T G \alpha \\ &\text{s.t. } \alpha^T 1 = k; \alpha \in \{0,1\}^n \end{aligned} \tag{2}$$

From now on, we refer to the diverse retrieval problem in the form of the optimization problem in Eq.(2). Finding optimal solutions for the quadratic integer program in Eq.(2) is NP-hard [38]. Usually QP relaxations [30] (which are often called linear relaxations), where integer constraints are relaxed to interval constraints, are efficiently solvable. In this work, we consider the following simple approach[1] to solve Eq.(2): We first remove the integrality constraints on the variables i.e., allow variables to take on non-integral values and solve the relaxed optimization problem. Although, this method yields a good solution to Eq.(2) i.e., obtains accurate and diverse retrieval, solving the QP Relaxation is much more time consuming than the existing solutions (*see Table 1*).

To this end, the existing approaches i.e., greedy MMR optimization methods for Eq.(1) and the QP relaxation method for Eq.(2) suffer from three drawbacks: a) Running time of the algorithms is very high as it is required to recover several exact nearest neighbors. b) The obtained points might all be from a very small region of the space and hence the diversity of the selected set might not be large. c) Computation of the gram matrix may require an unreasonably large amount of memory overhead for large datasets. Therefore, it is of greatest interest to look for computationally efficient solutions for the diverse retrieval problem.

In this work, we propose an approach to overcome the above three issues based on the following high-level idea: instead of finding exact nearest neighbors, we perform *randomized approximate* nearest neighbor search using LSH which guarantees sub-linear time retrieval. We show that randomized hash functions selects points randomly around the query and hence are diverse, while still being relevant to the query.

4. METHODOLOGY

To find nearest neighbors, the basic LSH algorithm [8] concatenates a number of functions $h \in \mathcal{H}$ into one hash function $g \in \mathcal{G}$. Informally, we say that $\mathcal{H}$ is *locality-sensitive* if for any two points a and b, the probability that a and b collide under a random choice of hash function depends only on the distance between a and b. Several such families are known in the literature, see [2] for an overview.

DEFINITION 1. *(Locality Sensitive Hashing [2]): A family of hash functions $\mathcal{H} : R^d \rightarrow \{0,1\}$ is called (r, ϵ, P_1, P_2)-sensitive if for any $a, b \in R^d$*

$$\begin{cases} Pr_{h\in\mathcal{H}}[h(a) = h(b)] \geq P_1, & \text{if } d(a,b) \leq r \\ Pr_{h\in\mathcal{H}}[h(a) = h(b)] \leq P_2, & \text{if } d(a,b) \geq (1+\epsilon)r \end{cases}$$

Here, $\epsilon > 0$ is an arbitrary constant, $P_1 > P_2$ and $d(.,.)$ is some distance function.

[1]We refer to this method with QP-Rel in our experimental evaluations as one of our baselines.

In this work, we use ℓ_2 norm as the distance function and adopt the following hash function:

$$h(a) = sign(\rho \cdot a) \tag{3}$$

where $\rho \sim \mathcal{N}(0, I)$. It is well known that $h(a)$ is a LSH function w.r.t ℓ_2 norm and it is shown to satisfy the following [8]:

$$Pr(h(a) \neq h(b)) = \frac{1}{\pi}\cos^{-1}\left(\frac{a \cdot b}{\|a\|_2\|b\|_2}\right). \tag{4}$$

Algorithm 1: LSH with random hash functions (LSH-Div)

Input: $\mathcal{X} = \{x_1 \dots, x_n\}$, where $x_i \in R^d$, a query $q \in \mathbb{R}^d$ and k an integer.

1 **Preprocessing**: For each $i \in [1 \dots L]$, construct a hash function, $g_i = [h_{1,i}, \dots, h_{l,i}]$, where $h_{1,i}, \dots, h_{l,i}$ are chosen at random from $\mathcal{H}$. Hash all points in $\mathcal{X}$ to the ith hash table using the function g_i
2 $R \leftarrow \phi$
3 **for** $i \leftarrow 1$ ***to*** L **do**
4   Perform a hash of the query $g_i(q)$
5   Retrieve points from i^{th} hash table & append to $\mathcal{R}_q$
6 $\mathcal{S}_q \leftarrow \phi$
7 **for** $i \leftarrow 1$ ***to*** k **do**
8     $x^* \leftarrow \text{argmin}_{(x\in\mathcal{R}_q)}(\lambda\|q-x\|^2 - (1-\lambda)\Sigma_{s\in\mathcal{S}_q}\|x-s\|^2)$
9     $\mathcal{R}_q \leftarrow \mathcal{R}_q \setminus x^*$
10     $\mathcal{S}_q \leftarrow \mathcal{S}_q \cup x^*$

Output: $\mathcal{S}_q$, k diverse set of retrieved points for query q

We provide the details of our approach in the Algorithm 1: Given a query q, the algorithm executes in two phases: i) perform search through the hash tables, line(2-5), to report the approximate nearest neighbors, $R_q \subset \mathcal{X}$, and ii) perform k iterations, line(6-9), to report a diverse set of points, $S_q \subset R_q$. The essential control variables that maintain the trade-off between the accuracy and diversity of the retrieved points are: i) the number of points retrieved from hash table, $|R_q|$, and ii) the number of diverse set of points to be reported, k. Here, R_q can be controlled at the design of hash function, i.e., the number of matches to the query is proportional to $n^{\frac{1}{1+\epsilon}}$ (see Section 6). Therefore, line 7 is critical for the efficiency of the algorithm, since it is an expensive computation, especially when $|R_q|$ is very big, or k is large.

4.1 Diversity in Randomized Hashing

An interesting aspect of the above mentioned LSH function in Eq.(4) is that it is unbiased towards any particular direction, i.e., $Pr(h(q) \neq h(a))$ is dependent only on $\|q-a\|_2$ (assuming q, a are both normalized to unit norm vectors). But, depending on a sample hyper-plane $\rho \in \mathbb{R}^d$, a hash function can be biased towards one or the other direction, hence preferring points from a particular region. If the number of hash bits is large, then all the directions are sampled uniformly and hence the retrieved points are sampled uniformly from all the directions. *That is, the retrieval is not biased towards any particular region of the space.* We formalize the above observation in the following lemma.

DEFINITION 2. **(Hoeffding Inequality** *[25]) Let $Z_1, \dots, Z_n$ be n i.i.d. random variables with $f(Z) \in [a, b]$. Then, with probability at least $1 - \delta$ we have*

$$P[\|\frac{1}{n}\sum_{i=1}^{n} f(Z_i) - E(f(Z))\|] \leq (b-a)\sqrt{\frac{\log(\frac{2}{\delta})}{2n}}$$

LEMMA 4.1. *Let $q \in \mathbb{R}^d$ and let $\mathcal{X}_q = \{x_1, \ldots, x_m\}$ be unit vectors such that $\|q - x_i\|_2 = \|q - x_j\|_2 = r, \forall i, j$. Let $p = \frac{1}{\pi}\cos^{-1}(1 - r^2/2)$. Also, let $r_1, \ldots, r_\ell \sim \mathcal{N}(0, I)$ be ℓ random vectors. Define hash bits $g(x) = [h_1(x) \ldots h_\ell(x)] \in \{0,1\}^{1\times\ell}$, where hash functions $h_b(x) = sign(r_b \cdot x), 1 \le b \le \ell$. Then, the following holds $\forall i$:*

$$p - \sqrt{\frac{\log(\frac{2}{\delta})}{2l}} \le \frac{1}{l}\|g(q) - g(x_i)\|_1 \le p + \sqrt{\frac{\log(\frac{2}{\delta})}{2l}}$$

That is, if $\sqrt{l} \gg 1/p$, then hash-bits of the query q are almost equi-distant to the hash-bits of each x_i.

PROOF. Consider random variable Z_{ib}, $1 \le i \le m$, $1 \le b \le \ell$ where $Z_{ib} = 1$ if $h_b(q) \ne h_b(x_i)$ and 0 otherwise. Note that Z_{ib} is a Bernoulli random variable with probability p. Also, Z_{ib}, $\forall 1 \le b \le \ell$ are all independent for a fixed i. Hence, applying Hoeffding's inequality, we obtain the required result. □

The above lemma shows that if $x_1, \ldots, x_m$ are all at distance r from a given query q then their respective hash bits are also at a similar distance to the hash bits of q. *That is, assuming randomized selection of the candidates from a hash bucket, probability of selecting any x_i is almost the same. That is, the points selected by LSH are nearly uniformly at random and are diverse.*

4.2 Randomized Compact Hashing

The conventional LSH approach [8] considers only random projections. Naturally, by doing random projection, we will lose some accuracy. But we can easily fix this problem by doing multiple rounds of random projections. However, we need to perform a large number of projections to increase the probability that similar points are mapped to similar hash codes. A fundamental result of the Johnson and Lindenstrauss Theorem [20] says that $O(\frac{\ln n}{\epsilon^2})$ random projections are needed to preserve the distance between any two pair of points, where ϵ is the relative error.

Using many random vectors to generate the hash tables (a long codeword), leads to a large storage space and a high computational cost, which would slow down the retrieval procedure. In practice, however, the data lies in a very small dimensional subspace of the ambient dimension and hence a random hyper-plane may not be very informative. Instead, we wish to use more data-driven hyper-planes that are more discriminative and separate out neighbors from far-away points. To this end, we obtain the hyper-planes ρ using principal components of the given data matrix. Principal components are the directions of highest variance of the data and capture the geometry of the dataset accurately. Hence, by using principal components, we aim to reduce the required number of hash bits and hash tables required to obtain the same accuracy in retrieval.

Precisely, given a data matrix $X \in \mathbb{R}^{d\times n}$ where i-th column of X is given by x_i, we obtain top-α principal components of X using SVD. That is, let $U \in \mathbb{R}^{d\times\alpha}$ be the singular vectors corresponding to the top-α singular values of X. Then, a hash function is given by: $h(x) = sign(\rho^T U^T x)$ where $\rho \sim \mathcal{N}(0, I)$ is a random α-dimensional hyper-plane. In the subsequent sections, we denote this algorithm using LSH-SDiv.

Many learning based hashing methods [22, 35] are proposed in literature. The simplest of all such approaches is PCA Hashing [34] which chooses the random projections to be the principal directions of the data directly. Our algorithm LSH-SDiv method is different from PCA Hashing in the sense that we still select random directions in the top components. Note that the above hash function has reduced randomness but still preserves the discriminative power by projecting the randomness onto top principal components of X. As shown in Section 8, the above hash function provides better nearest neighbor retrieval while recovering more diverse set of neighbors.

Algorithm 2: LSH based Multi-label Classification

Input: Train data: $\mathcal{X} = \{x_1, \ldots, x_n\}, \mathcal{Y} = \{y_1, \ldots, y_n\}$. Test data: $\mathcal{Q} = \{q_1, \ldots, q_m\}$. Parameters: α, k.
[W, H]=LEML($\mathcal{X}$, $\mathcal{Y}$, k);
$\mathcal{S}_q$ = LSH-SDiv($W, H^T q, \alpha$), $\forall q \in \mathcal{Q}$;
$\widehat{y}_q$ = Majority($\{y_i$ s.t. $x_i \in \mathcal{S}_q\}$), $\forall q \in \mathcal{Q}$;
Output: $\widehat{\mathcal{Y}}_Q = \{\widehat{y}_{q_1}, \ldots, \widehat{y}_{q_m}\}$

5. DIVERSE MULTI-LABEL PREDICTION

We now present an extension of our method to the problem of multi-label classification. Let $\mathcal{X} = \{x_1, \ldots, x_n\}$, $x_i \in \mathbb{R}^d$ and $\mathcal{Y} = \{y_1, \ldots, y_n\}$, where $y_i \in \{-1, 1\}^L$ be L labels associated with the i-th data point. Then, the goal in the standard multi-label learning problem is to predict the label vector y_q accurately for a given query point q. In practice, the number of labels L is very large, so we require the diverse multi-label predictions to scale sub-linearly with L.

In this work, we build upon the LEML method proposed in [40] that can solve multi-label problems with a large number of labels and data points. In particular, LEML learns matrices W, H s.t. given a point q, its predicted labels is given by $y_q = sign(WH^T x)$ where $W \in \mathbb{R}^{L\times k}$ and $H \in R^{d\times k}$ and k is the rank of the parameter matrix WH^T. Typically, $k \ll \min(d, L)$ and hence the method scales linearly in both d and L with its prediction time being given by $O((d + L) \cdot k)$.

However, for several widespread problems, the $O(L)$ prediction time is quite large and makes the method infeasible in practice. Moreover, the obtained labels from this algorithm can all be very highly correlated and might not provide a diverse set of labels which we desire. We overcome both of the above limitations of the algorithm using the LSH based algorithm introduced in the previous section. We now describe our method in detail. Let $W_1, W_2, \ldots, W_L$ be L data points where $W_i \in \mathbb{R}^{1\times k}$ is the i-th row of W. Also, let $H^T x$ be a query point for a given x. Note that the task of obtaining α positive labels for given x is equivalent to finding α largest $W_i \cdot (H^T x)$. Hence, the problem is the same as nearest neighbor search with diversity where the data points are given by $\mathcal{W} = \{W_1, W_2, \ldots, W_L\}$ and the query point is given by $q = H^T x$.

We now apply our LSH based methods to the above setting to obtain a "diverse" set of labels for the given data point x. Moreover, the LSH Theorem in [13] shows that the time of retrieval is sub-linear in L which is necessary for the approach to scale to a large number of examples. See Algorithm 2 for the pseudo-code of our approach.

6. ALGORITHMIC ANALYSIS

Like most indexing strategies, LSH consists of two phases: *hash generation*, where the hash tables are constructed and *querying*, where the hash tables are used to look up for points similar to the query. Here, we discuss these two steps in more detail with respect to the suggested algorithms in the previous sections.

Accuracy: The data structure used by LSH scheme is randomized: the algorithm must output all points within the distance r from q, and can also output some points within the distance $(1+\epsilon)r$ from q. The algorithm guarantees that each point within the distance r from q is reported with a constant (tunable) probability. The parameters l and L are chosen [18] to satisfy the requirement that neighbors are reported with a probability at least $(1-\delta)$. Note that the correctness probability is defined over the random bits selected by the algorithm, and we do not make any probabilistic assumptions about the data.

Diversity: In lemma 4.1, if the number of hash bits is large, i.e., if $\sqrt{l} \gg 1/p$, then hash-bits of the query q are almost equidistant to the hash-bits of each point in x_i. Then all the directions are sampled uniformly and hence the retrieved points are uniformly spread in all the directions. Therefore, for reasonable choice of the parameter l, the proposed algorithm obtains diverse set of points, $\mathcal{S}_q$ and has strong probabilistic guarantees for large databases of arbitrary dimensions.

Scalability: The time for evaluating the g_i functions for a query point q is $O(dlL)$ in general. For the angular hash functions chosen in our algorithm, each of the l bits output by a hash function g_i involves computing a dot product of the input vector with a random vector defining a hyperplane. Each dot product can be computed in time proportional to the number of non-zeros ζ rather than d. Thus, the total time is $O(\zeta lL)$. For an interested reader, see that the Theorem 2 of [8] which guarantees that L is at most $O(n^{\frac{1}{(1+\epsilon)}})$, where n denotes the total number of points in the database. Note that, in practice, the queries tend to follow the distribution of the data, and therefore, provide skewed accesses conforming to that of a data set.

7. EXPERIMENTAL SETUP

We demonstrate our approach applied to the following two tasks: (a) Image Category Retrieval and (b) Multi-label Prediction.

7.1 Evaluation Criteria

In both these experiments, our goal is two-fold: 1) improve diversity in the retrieval and 2) demonstrate speed-ups of our proposed algorithms. We measure the performance of our methods on three key aspects and characterize them in terms of the following metrics:

- **Accuracy:** We denote precision at k ($P@k$) as the measure of accuracy of the retrieval. This is the proportion of the relevant instances in the top k retrieved results.
- **Diversity:** For image retrieval, the diversity in the retrieved images is measured using entropy as $D = \frac{\Sigma_{i=1}^{m} s_i \log s_i}{\log m}$, where s_i is the fraction of images of ith subcategory, and m is the number of subcategories for the category of interest. Sub-topic recall(SR) is measured as the fraction of subcategories retrieved for a given categorical query. For multilabel classification, the relationships between the labels is not a simple tree. It is better captured using a graph and the diversity is then computed using drank [26].
- **Efficiency:** Given a query, we consider retrieval time to be the time between posing a query and retrieving images/labels from the database. For LSH based methods, the hash tables are processed off-line, and so we do not consider the time spent to load the hash tables into the retrieval time. All the retrieval times are based on a Linux machine with Intel E5-2640 processor(s) and 96GB RAM.

7.2 Combining Accuracy and Diversity

Trade-offs between accuracy and efficiency in NN retrieval have been studied well in the past [4, 19, 39]. Many methods compromise on the accuracy for better efficiency. Similarly, emphasizing higher diversity may also lead to poor accuracy and hence, we want to formalize a metric that captures the trade-off between diversity and accuracy. To this end, we use (per data point) harmonic mean of accuracy and diversity as overall score for a given method (similar to f_{score} providing a trade off between precision and recall). That is, $h_{score}(\mathcal{A}) = \sum_i \frac{2 \cdot Acc(x_i) \cdot Diversity(x_i)}{Acc(x_i) + Diversity(x_i)}$, where $\mathcal{A}$ is a given algorithm and x_i's are given test points. In all of our experiments, parameters are chosen by cross validation such that the overall h_{score} is maximized.

8. EMPIRICAL RESULTS

8.1 Image Category Retrieval

For the image category retrieval, we consider a set of $42K$ images from ImageNet database [9] with 7 categories (*animal, bottle, flower, furniture, geography, music, vehicle*) with five subtopics for each. Images are represented as a bag of visual words histogram with a vocabulary size of $48K$ over the densely extracted SIFT [24] vectors. For each categorical query, we train an SVM hyperplane using LIBLINEAR [11]. Since, there are only seven categories in our dataset, for each category we created 50 queries by randomly sampling 16.67% of the images for training. After creating the queries (classifiers), we use the left over $35K$ images for the retrieval task.

We conducted two sets of experiments, 1) Retrieval without using hash functions and 2) Retrieval using hash functions, to evaluate the effectiveness of our proposed method. In the first set of experiments, we directly apply the existing diverse retrieval methods on the complete dataset. In the second set of experiments, we first select a candidate set of points by using the hash functions and then apply one of these methods to retrieve the images.

We hypothesize that using hash functions in combination with any of the retrieval methods will improve the diversity and the overall performance (h_{score}) with significant speed-ups. To validate our hypothesis, we evaluate various diverse retrieval methods in combination with our hash functions as described in Algorithm 1. It can be noted that lines 6-10 in Algorithm 1 can be replaced with various retrieval methods and can be compared against the methods without hash functions. In particular, we show the comparison with the following retrieval methods: the k-nearest neighbor (NN), the QP-Rel method and the diverse retrieval methods like Backward selection (Rerank), MMR [5].

In Table 1, we denote NH as Null Hash i.e., without using any hash function, LSH-Div with the random hash function and LSH-SDiv with the (randomized) PCA hash function. We report the quantitative results in Table 1 by the mean performance of all 350 queries. We can see in Table 1 that our hash functions in combination with various methods are superior to the methods with NH. Our extensions based on LSH-Div and LSH-SDiv hash functions outperform in all cases with respect to sub-topic recall (SR), diversity (D) and the h_{score}. Interestingly, LSH-Div and LSH-SDiv with NN report maximum h_{score} than any other methods. This observation implies that the approximate nearest neighbor search using standard LSH naturally favours diversity in the retrieval. This is in persistence to our result from Lemma 4.1. We also report a significant speed-up even for a moderate database of $35K$ images.

Readers familiar with LSH will also agree that our methods will enjoy better speed-up even in presence of larger databases and higher dimensional representations. In Table 3, we show a few qualitative results on this dataset with the top-10 images retrieved by different retrieval methods. Notice that the LSH-Div and LSH-SDiv methods consistently retrieve accurate and diverse set of images.

Table 1: We show the performance of various diverse retrieval methods on the ImageNet dataset. We evaluate the methods in terms of precision(P), sub-topic recall(SR) and Diversity(D) measures at top-10, top-20 and top-30 retrieved images. Numbers in **bold** indicate the top performers in SR, D, h_{score} and retrieval time. **NH** corresponds to the method without using any hash function. Notice that LSH-Div and LSH-SDiv hash functions consistently outperform the methods using NH in terms of h_{score}. In some cases, methods with NH show high h_{score} but our methods using hashing are fast in terms of retrieval time.

		precision at 10					precision at 20					precision at 30				
Method	**Hash Function**	P	SR	D	h_{score}	time (sec)	P	SR	D	h_{score}	time (sec)	P	SR	D	h_{score}	time (sec)
NN	NH	1.00	0.60	0.53	0.66	0.621	0.99	0.72	0.60	0.73	0.721	0.99	0.79	0.65	0.77	0.845
	LSH-Div	0.97	**0.79**	**0.76**	**0.84**	**0.112**	0.93	**0.93**	**0.86**	**0.89**	**0.137**	0.89	**0.98**	**0.91**	**0.90**	**0.179**
	LSH-SDiv	0.98	**0.76**	**0.73**	**0.83**	**0.181**	0.95	**0.89**	**0.85**	**0.89**	**0.183**	0.92	**0.95**	**0.89**	**0.90**	**0.106**
Rerank	NH	1.00	0.73	0.69	0.81	0.804	0.99	0.79	0.70	0.81	0.793	0.99	0.88	0.77	0.86	0.901
	LSH-Div	0.93	**0.80**	**0.76**	**0.83**	**0.142**	0.92	**0.93**	**0.86**	**0.88**	**0.146**	0.87	**0.98**	**0.90**	**0.88**	**0.214**
	LSH-SDiv	0.95	**0.79**	**0.76**	**0.84**	**0.154**	0.94	**0.91**	**0.85**	**0.89**	**0.179**	0.90	**0.95**	**0.88**	**0.89**	**0.203**
MMR	NH	0.95	0.75	0.71	0.80	5.686	0.98	0.86	0.77	0.85	11.193	0.97	0.90	0.80	0.87	17.162
	LSH-Div	0.91	**0.77**	**0.73**	**0.80**	**1.135**	0.91	**0.92**	**0.85**	**0.87**	**2.378**	0.87	**0.97**	**0.89**	**0.88**	**3.828**
	LSH-SDiv	0.92	**0.78**	**0.75**	**0.81**	**1.102**	0.93	**0.91**	**0.84**	**0.88**	**2.085**	0.89	**0.96**	**0.88**	**0.88**	**4.106**
QP-Rel	NH	1.00	0.74	0.69	0.81	704.9	1.00	0.82	0.73	0.84	947.09	1.00	0.87	0.76	0.86	1137.19
	LSH-Div	0.93	**0.80**	**0.77**	**0.83**	**0.487**	0.92	**0.94**	**0.86**	**0.88**	**0.499**	0.86	**0.98**	**0.90**	**0.88**	**0.502**
	LSH-SDiv	0.97	**0.78**	**0.74**	**0.83**	**0.447**	0.96	**0.89**	**0.82**	**0.88**	**0.464**	0.93	**0.95**	**0.86**	**0.89**	**0.473**

8.2 Multi-label Prediction

We use one of the largest multi-label datasets, LSHTC [27], to show the effectiveness of our proposed method. This dataset contains the Wikipedia documents with more than $300K$ labels. Since, the dataset is highly skewed, we selected only the documents which have at least 4 or more labels. Thus, we have a dataset of $754K$ documents with $259K$ unique labels. For our experiment, we randomly divide the data in 4:1 ratio for training and testing respectively. We use the large scale multi-label learning (LEML) [40] algorithm to train a linear multi-class classifier. This method is shown to provide state of the art results on many large multi-label prediction tasks.

In LSHTC3 dataset, the labels are associated with a category hierarchy which is cyclic and unbalanced, i.e., both the documents and subcategories are allowed to belong to more than one other category. In such cases, the notion of diversity, i.e., the extent to which the predicted labels belong to multiple categories can be estimated using drank [26]. If the labels belong to the same/few categories, it is considered to have low diversity. Relatively, if the labels belong to different categories, it is considered to have more diversity. Since, the category hierarchy graph is cyclic, we prune the hierarchy graph to obtain a balanced tree by using the Breadth First Search (BFS) traversal. Diversity of the predicted labels is computed as the drank score on this balanced tree. Accuracy for the predictions is computed as Precision, Recall and f_{score}.

Since, the number of labels for each document varies, we used a threshold parameter to limit the number of predicted labels to the documents. We select this threshold by cross validating such that it maximizes the f_{score}. It turns out that all methods produce a small number of diverse label predictions, which results in low recall. These low recall scores affect the f_{score}, which are consequently low as well. This is mainly due to the restrictive nature of these algorithms, as evidenced by the number of predicted labels, being very low for all methods. To quantify the over all performance of these methods, we compute the h_{score} as a harmonic mean of precision and drank score. We demonstrate that the proposed algorithm is effective and robust, since, it improves diversity even when retrieving relevant labels is difficult.

Table 2: Results on LSHTC3 challenge dataset with LEML, MMR, PCA-Hash, LSH-Div and LSH-SDiv methods. LSH-SDiv method significantly outperforms all other methods in terms of overall performance, h_{score} as well as the retrieval time.

Method	P	R	f_{score}	D	h_{score}	time (msec)
LEML [40]	0.304	0.196	0.192	0.827	0.534	137.1
MMR [5]	0.275	0.134	0.175	0.865	0.418	458.8
LSH-Div	0.144	0.088	0.083	0.825	0.437	7.2
PCA-Hash	0.265	0.096	0.121	0.872	0.669	5.9
LSH-SDiv	0.318	0.102	0.133	**0.919**	**0.734**	**5.7**

In Table 2, we report the performance of label prediction with LEML and MMR [5], and the proposed methods that predict diverse labels efficiently. As can be seen, the LSH-Div method shows a reasonable speed-up but fails to report many of the accurate labels, i.e., has low precision. The LSHTC3 dataset is highly sparse in a large dimension (20L), random projections generated by LSH-Div method are a bit inaccurate and have resulted in poor accuracy. In contrast, the LSH-SDiv method can successfully preserve the distances, i.e., reports accurate labels by projecting onto a set of principal components of the data while still producing diverse labels. Clearly, LSH-SDiv based hash function improves the diversity within the labels and outperforms LEML, MMR, PCA-Hash and LSH-Div methods in terms of h_{score}.

Figure 2 illustrates the performance of proposed method with respect to the parameter ϵ. In the figure, we show the performance obtained when 100 random projections are selected for the LSH-Div method. Notice that the conventional LSH fails to retrieve accurate labels and it requires a large number of random projections to retrieve accurate labels, which would slow down the retrieval procedure. For the LSH-SDiv method we project the 100 random projections onto the top-200 singular vectors obtained from the data. Moreover, LSH-SDiv typically requires much smaller number of hash functions than the standard LSH method and hence, is much faster as well. In summary, LSH-SDiv methods produces accurate as well as diverse labels, and we obtain a speed-up greater than 20 over LEML method and greater than 80 over MMR method.

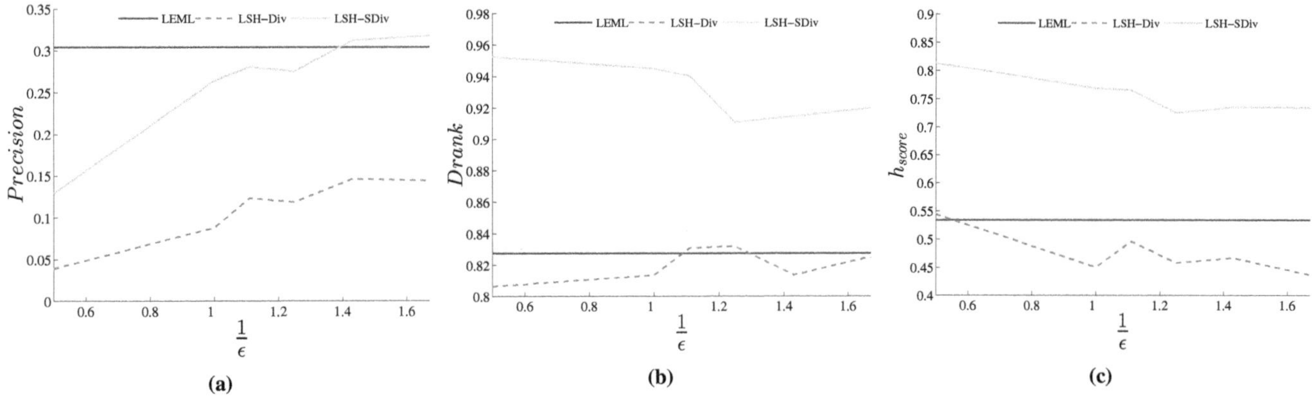

Figure 2: Sensitivity analysis of LSH based methods with respect to the parameter ϵ. We use LSHTC3 dataset for our study. (a) LSH-SDiv method gives better precision than LSH-Div method. (b) LSH-SDiv method shows better diversity than LEML and LSH-Div methods. (c) LSH-SDiv method performs significantly better than the LEML and LSH-Div methods in terms of h_{score}. *(Figure best viewed in color)*

9. CONCLUSIONS

In this paper, we present an approach to efficiently retrieve diverse results based on *randomized* locality sensitive hashing. We argue that standard hash functions retrieve points that are sampled uniformly at random in all directions and hence ensure diversity by default. We show that, for two applications (image and text retrieval), our methods retrieve significantly more diverse and accurate data points, when compared to the existing methods. Our results are appealing: a good balance between accuracy and diversity is obtained by using only a small number of hash functions. We obtained $100\times$-speed-up over existing diverse retrieval methods while ensuring high diversity in retrieval. The proposed solution is highly efficient with theoretical guarantees for sub-linear retrieval time and therefore, the algorithms are interesting and should be very useful and attractive for all practical purposes.

10. REFERENCES

[1] R. Agrawal, A. Gupta, Y. Prabhu, and M. Varma. Multi-label learning with millions of labels: Recommending advertiser bid phrases for web pages. In *WWW*, 2013.

[2] A. Andoni and P. Indyk. Near-optimal hashing algorithms for approximate nearest neighbor in high dimensions. In *FOCS*, 2006.

[3] T. Aytekin and M. Ö. Karakaya. Clustering-based diversity improvement in top-n recommendation. *IIS*, 2014.

[4] R. Basri, T. Hassner, and L. Zelnik-Manor. Approximate nearest subspace search. *TPAMI*, 2011.

[5] J. Carbonell and J. Goldstein. The use of MMR, diversity-based reranking for reordering documents and producing summaries. In *SIGIR*, 1998.

[6] G. Carneiro, A. B. Chan, P. J. Moreno, and N. Vasconcelos. Supervised learning of semantic classes for image annotation and retrieval. *TPAMI*, 2007.

[7] L. Cayton and S. Dasgupta. A learning framework for nearest neighbor search. In *NIPS*, 2008.

[8] M. S. Charikar. Similarity estimation techniques from rounding algorithms. In *STOC*, 2002.

[9] J. Deng, W. Dong, R. Socher, L.-J. Li, K. Li, and L. Fei-Fei. Imagenet: A large-scale hierarchical image database. In *CVPR*, 2009.

[10] T. Deselaers, T. Gass, P. Dreuw, and H. Ney. Jointly optimising relevance and diversity in image retrieval. In *CIVR*, 2009.

[11] R.-E. Fan, K.-W. Chang, C.-J. Hsieh, X.-R. Wang, and C.-J. Lin. Liblinear: A library for large linear classification. *JMLR*, 2008.

[12] G. Ference, W.-C. Lee, H.-J. Jung, and D.-N. Yang. Spatial search for k diverse-near neighbors. In *CIKM*, 2013.

[13] A. Gionis, P. Indyk, and R. Motwani. Similarity Search in High Dimensions via Hashing. In *VLDB*, 1999.

[14] P. B. Golbus, J. A. Aslam, and C. L. Clarke. Increasing evaluation sensitivity to diversity. *Information Retrieval*, 2013.

[15] X. Han, S. Li, and Z. Shen. A k-nn method for large scale hierarchical text classification at lshtc3. *ECML PKDD*, 2015.

[16] J. He, H. Tong, Q. Mei, and B. Szymanski. Gender: A generic diversified ranking algorithm. In *NIPS*, 2012.

[17] M. E. Houle, X. Ma, V. Oria, and J. Sun. Improving the quality of k-nn graphs for image databases through vector sparsification. In *ACM ICMR*, 2014.

[18] P. Indyk and R. Motwani. Approximate nearest neighbors: towards removing the curse of dimensionality. In *STOC*, 1998.

[19] P. Jain, S. Vijayanarasimhan, and K. Grauman. Hashing hyperplane queries to near points with applications to large-scale active learning. In *NIPS*, 2010.

[20] W. B. Johnson and J. Lindenstrauss. Extensions of lipschitz mappings into a hilbert space. 1984.

[21] O. Kucuktunc and H. Ferhatosmanoglu. λ-diverse nearest neighbors browsing for multidimensional data. *TKDE*, 2013.

[22] B. Kulis and T. Darrell. Learning to hash with binary reconstructive embeddings. In *NIPS*, 2009.

[23] H. Lin and J. Bilmes. A class of submodular functions for document summarization. In *HLT*. ACL, 2011.

[24] D. G. Lowe. Distinctive image features from scale-invariant keypoints. *IJCV*, 2004.

[25] G. Lugosi. Concentration-of-measure inequalities. 2004.

[26] P. K. R. Mittapally Kumara Swamy and S. Srivastava. Extracting diverse patterns with unbalanced concept hierarchy. In *PAKDD*, 2014.

[27] I. Partalas, A. Kosmopoulos, N. Baskiotis, T. Artieres, G. Paliouras, E. Gaussier, I. Androutsopoulos, M.-R. Amini, and P. Galinari. Lshtc: A benchmark for large-scale text classification. *arXiv preprint arXiv:1503.08581*, 2015.

[28] Y. Prabhu and M. Varma. Fastxml: a fast, accurate and stable tree-classifier for extreme multi-label learning. In *KDD*, 2014.

Table 3: Top-10 images retrieved for sample queries from the ImageNet database are shown: the first coloumn with the simple NN method, the second coloum with method based on MMR optimization, and the third coloumn with the proposed LSH-SDiv method. Notice that the greedy method fails to retrieve accurate images for some of the queries. Images marked with red box are incorrectly retrieved ones. Our method, consistently retrieves relevant images and simultaneouly shows better diversity. (*Image best viewed in color*)

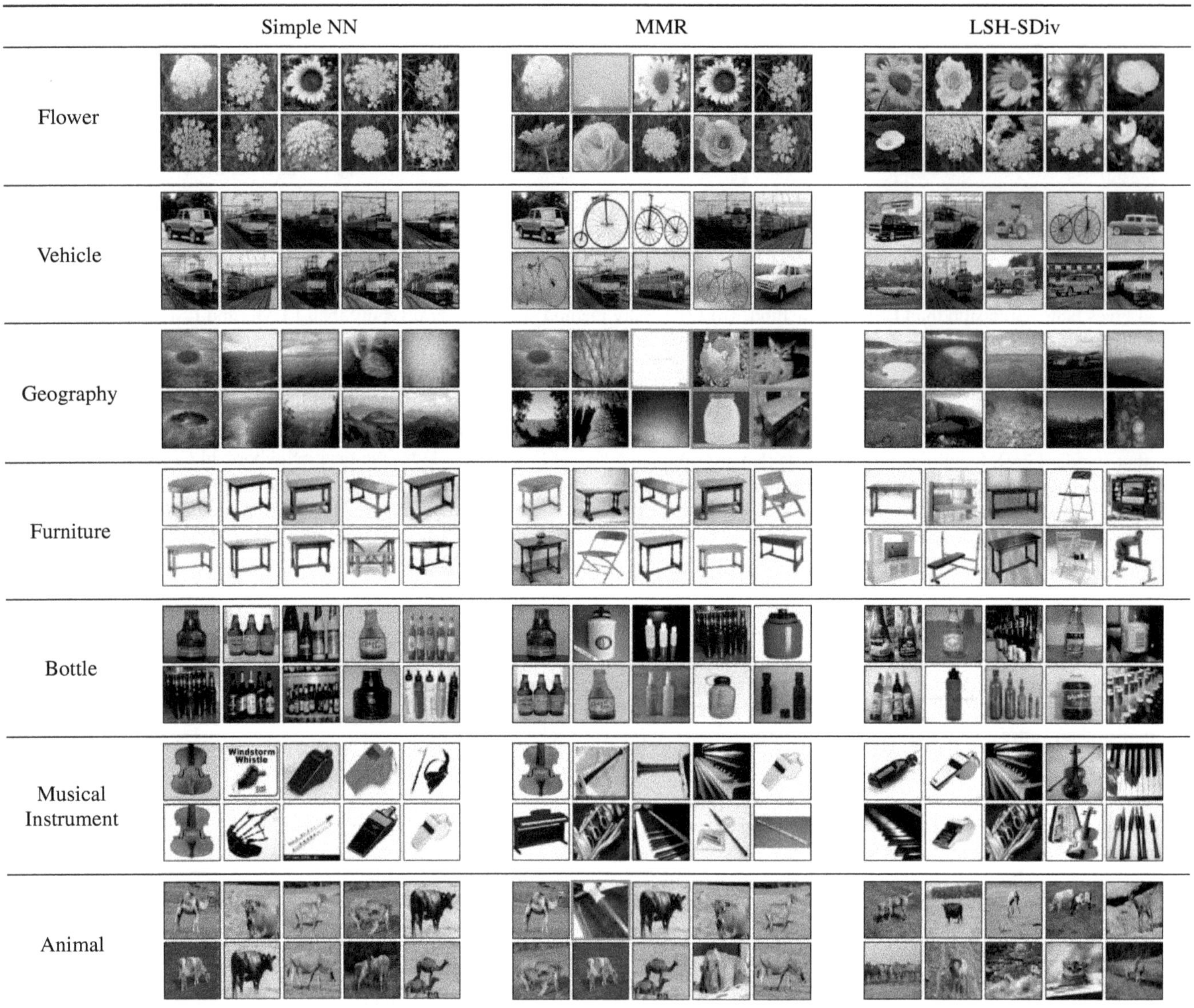

[29] F. Radlinski, P. N. Bennett, B. Carterette, and T. Joachims. Redundancy, diversity and interdependent document relevance. In *ACM SIGIR*, 2009.

[30] P. Ravikumar and J. Lafferty. Quadratic programming relaxations for metric labeling and markov random field map estimation. In *ICML*, 2006.

[31] S. Sanner, S. Guo, T. Graepel, S. Kharazmi, and S. Karimi. Diverse retrieval via greedy optimization of expected 1-call@k in a latent subtopic relevance model. In *CIKM*, 2011.

[32] E. Spyromitros-Xioufis, S. Papadopoulos, A. L. Ginsca, A. Popescu, Y. Kompatsiaris, and I. Vlahavas. Improving diversity in image search via supervised relevance scoring. In *ACM ICMR*, 2015.

[33] J. Wang and J. Zhu. On statistical analysis and optimization of information retrieval effectiveness metrics. In *Proceedings of ACM SIGIR conference on Research and development in information retrieval*, 2010.

[34] X.-J. Wang, L. Zhang, F. Jing, and W.-Y. Ma. Annosearch: Image auto-annotation by search. In *CVPR*, 2006.

[35] Y. Weiss, A. Torralba, and R. Fergus. Spectral hashing. In *NIPS*, 2009.

[36] J. Weston, S. Bengio, and N. Usunier. Large scale image annotation: learning to rank with joint word-image embeddings. *JMLR*, 2010.

[37] J. Weston, S. Bengio, and N. Usunier. WSABIE: scaling up to large vocabulary image annotation. In *IJCAI*, 2011.

[38] L. A. Wolsey. *Integer programming*. 1998.

[39] H. Yu, I. Ko, Y. Kim, S. Hwang, and W.-S. Han. Exact indexing for support vector machines. In *SIGMOD*, 2011.

[40] H.-F. Yu, P. Jain, P. Kar, and I. Dhillon. Large-scale multi-label learning with missing labels. In *ICML*, 2014.

Correlation Autoencoder Hashing for Supervised Cross-Modal Search*

Yue Cao, Mingsheng Long, Jianmin Wang, and Han Zhu
School of Software, Tsinghua University, Beijing, China
Tsinghua National Laboratory for Information Science and Technology
{caoyue10, zhuhan10}@gmail.com {mingsheng, jimwang}@tsinghua.edu.cn

ABSTRACT

Due to its storage and query efficiency, hashing has been widely applied to approximate nearest neighbor search from large-scale datasets. While there is increasing interest in cross-modal hashing which facilitates cross-media retrieval by embedding data from different modalities into a common Hamming space, how to distill the cross-modal correlation structure effectively remains a challenging problem. In this paper, we propose a novel supervised cross-modal hashing method, Correlation Autoencoder Hashing (CAH), to learn discriminative and compact binary codes based on deep autoencoders. Specifically, CAH jointly maximizes the feature correlation revealed by bimodal data and the semantic correlation conveyed in similarity labels, while embeds them into hash codes by nonlinear deep autoencoders. Extensive experiments clearly show the superior effectiveness and efficiency of CAH against the state-of-the-art hashing methods on standard cross-modal retrieval benchmarks.

1. INTRODUCTION

While big data with large volume, high dimensions, and multiple modalities are pervasive in search engines and social networks, it has attracted increasing attention to distill the correlation across heterogenous data modalities. For instance, an uploaded image on Flickr may be annotated with some relevant descriptions or tags, while a featured article on Wikipedia may consist of some correlative images. As relevant data from different modalities may endow semantic correlations, it is desirable to support *cross-modal search* that retrieves semantically-relevant results of one modality in response to a query of different modality. Taking Flickr as example, when a query image is given, the system should return not only relevant images but also relevant tags. Due to large volume and the well-known semantic gap [19], effective and efficient cross-modal retrieval remains a challenge.

When the reference database is large-scale or that the distance calculation between query item and database item is costly, an efficient solution to enabling similarity search is hashing methods [27], which perform approximate nearest neighbor (ANN) search with computation efficiency and search quality. The principle of hashing is to transform high-dimensional data into binary codes and generate similar binary codes for similar data items. The seminal work includes Locality Sensitive Hashing (LSH) [1], Spectral Hashing (SH) [29] and Product Quantization (PQ) [9]. However, the *unimodal* hashing methods cannot enable cross-modal search because ANN cannot be computed across modalities.

Recently, several *cross-modal hashing* methods have been proposed in the literature, which constructs correlation structures across modalities in the process of hash function learning and indexes cross-modal data into an isomorphic Hamming space [3, 12, 33, 34, 20, 28, 30, 14, 31, 6, 15]. These methods can be categorized into unsupervised methods [12, 33, 20] and supervised methods [3, 14, 31]. While unsupervised methods are more general and can be trained without semantic labels, they are also limited by the scarcity of correlation information and the semantic gap issue [19]. Supervised methods, on the contrary, can well explore the semantic labels for enhancing the cross-modal correlations and reducing the semantic gap [19], hence they generally outperform unsupervised methods for cross-modal search. The latest cross-modal retrieval models via deep learning [21, 28, 6, 24, 4] have shown that deep models can distill complex cross-modal correlations more effectively. Despite of the success of deep models for cross-modal search, existing cross-modal retrieval methods are mainly unsupervised and not tailored to hash function learning. Hence it remains an open problem how to explore both feature correlation revealed by bimodal data, and semantic correlation conveyed in similarity labels, using a unified deep model for cross-modal hashing.

In this paper we propose Correlation Autoencoder Hashing (CAH), a novel model towards supervised cross-modal hashing via deep learning. CAH embeds data from different modalities into a common Hamming space by jointly maximizing the feature correlation revealed by bimodal data and the semantic correlation conveyed in similarity labels. More specifically: (1) We explore the *feature correlation* by reconstructing the feature vectors of one modality from the corresponding hash codes of another modality, and capture the cross-modal correlations revealed by the feature vectors; (2) We explore the *semantic correlation* by maximizing the inter-category separation margin and minimizing the intra-category variance, which will produce more discriminative and semantically consistent hash codes; (3) Since cross-modal data (e.g. image and text) are heterogeneous and are difficult to correlate by linear or shallow models [28, 6, 4], we enhance both cross-modal correlations in a deep architecture, which will make the embedded hash codes generalize better across different modalities. Comprehensive results on large-scale benchmarks show that CAH significantly outperforms state-of-the-art cross-modal hashing methods.

The rest of this paper is organized as follows. We review the

*Corresponding author: Mingsheng Long.

ICMR'16, June 06-09, 2016, New York, NY, USA

DOI: http://dx.doi.org/10.1145/2911996.2912000

related work in Section 2. We formally present our correlation autoencoder hashing method in Section 3. Empirical evaluation is reported in Section 4, while the conclusion is enclosed in Section 5.

2. RELATED WORK

Recently, hashing-based cross-modal search has been a prevalent research focus in machine learning, computer vision, and multimedia search communities [3, 6, 7, 12, 14, 20, 25, 28, 30, 31, 33, 34, 15], which performs approximate similarity search on multimedia database with significant speedup and acceptable accuracy. See [27] for a comprehensive survey.

Prior cross-modal hashing methods can be categorized into unsupervised methods and supervised methods. IMH [20] and CVH [12] are unsupervised methods, which extend spectral hashing [29] to multimodal scenarios and learn the hash functions using eigenvalue decomposition. CMSSH [3] and SCM [31] are supervised methods, which extend supervised learning methods to fit pairwise labels indicating whether two points are known to be similar or dissimilar (in sense of semantic similarity), and if two points are similar then their corresponding hash codes should also be similar. Since supervised methods can explore the semantic labels for enhancing the cross-modal correlations and reducing the semantic gap [19], they can achieve superior accuracy than unsupervised methods for cross-modal similarity search.

A limitation of previous supervised cross-modal hashing methods is that they cannot exploit *nonlinear* correlation across different modalities. As cross-modal data (e.g. image and text) are heterogeneous in nature, it is unlikely that the correlation across modalities can be captured by shallow models. Furthermore, the latest cross-modal retrieval models via deep learning [21, 28, 6, 25] have shown that deep models can distill nonlinear cross-modal correlations more effectively. Despite the success of deep models in cross-modal search, it remains unclear how to explore both feature correlation and semantic correlation in a deep model for cross-modal hash learning. This work will formally study this problem. While deep convolutional neural networks (CNNs) are powerful for content-based image retrieval [24], how to jointly handle cross-modal retrieval for image and text in CNNs is still an open problem. Hence we will focus on deep autoencoders [23] in this work.

3. CORRELATION AUTOENCODER HASHING

3.1 Problem Definition

For ease of presentation, we describe the CAH approach with only two modalities (e.g. image and text), which can be readily extended to multiple modalities. In cross-modal search system, the database consists of objects from one modality while the query consists of objects from a different modality. To distill the correlation structure across different modalities, we are given a training set of n bimodal objects $\{(\boldsymbol{x}_i, \boldsymbol{y}_i)\}_{i=1}^n$, where $\boldsymbol{x} \in \mathbb{R}^{d_x}$ and $\boldsymbol{y} \in \mathbb{R}^{d_y}$ denote the two modalities of feature dimensions d_x and d_y, respectively. In supervised cross-modal search, we are further given semantic labels of training objects, that is, $\{(\boldsymbol{x}_i, \boldsymbol{y}_i), \boldsymbol{l}_i\}_{i=1}^n$, where $\boldsymbol{l} \in \mathbb{R}^c$ denotes the label vector of a bimodal object, and c is the number of categories. Assume each object is associated with at least one of the c categories, hence $l_{ik} = 1$ if object i is associated with category k, and $l_{ik} = 0$ otherwise.

The problem of CAH can be formally defined as jointly learning two hashing functions for the two modalities, i.e. $h_x(\boldsymbol{x}) : \mathbb{R}^{d_x} \mapsto \{-1, 1\}^b$ and $h_y(\boldsymbol{y}) : \mathbb{R}^{d_y} \mapsto \{-1, 1\}^b$, where b is the length of the binary hash code. These hashing functions map feature vectors

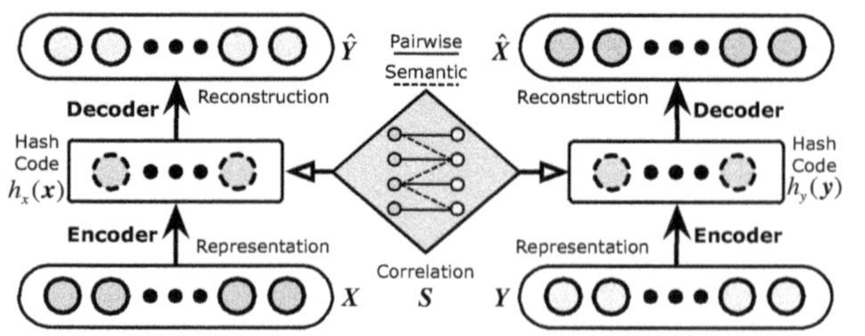

Figure 1: Correlation Autoencoder Hashing (CAH). Both feature correlation (solid lines) and semantic correlation (dashed lines) are maximized. Note that the features are reconstructed across modalities for feature correlation maximization.

in the corresponding modality into the common Hamming space, where the similarity between different modalities can be efficiently computed. We adopt the widely-used linear-sign hashing functions defined as $h_x(\boldsymbol{x}) = \operatorname{sgn}(\boldsymbol{W}_x^{\mathsf{T}}\boldsymbol{x})$ and $h_y(\boldsymbol{y}) = \operatorname{sgn}(\boldsymbol{W}_y^{\mathsf{T}}\boldsymbol{y})$, where $\operatorname{sgn}(\cdot)$ denotes the element-wise sign function, while $\boldsymbol{W}_x \in \mathbb{R}^{d_x \times b}$ and $\boldsymbol{W}_y \in \mathbb{R}^{d_y \times b}$ are the projection matrices. In this paper, we propose to learn these modality-specific hashing functions by maximizing cross-modal *deep* correlations conveyed in *both* feature vectors and semantic labels. An intuitive illustration of the proposed CAH model can be found in Figure 1, which constitutes cross-modal reconstructive embedding and cross-modal semantic correlation.

3.2 Cross-modal Reconstructive Embedding

In the context of similarity search, our goal is to rank the most relevant database objects that are similar to the query objects in terms of a pre-defined similarity measure, e.g. Hamming distance. Hence, preserving the similarity information conveyed in original feature vectors serves as an important learning criterion for hashing quality. This criterion can be achieved by minimizing the quantization error of transforming original feature vectors to binary hash codes, or equivalently, minimizing the reconstruction error of transforming binary hash codes to original feature vectors [17, 6]. A common practice is to learn a pair of modality-specific transformation matrices $\boldsymbol{V}_x \in \mathbb{R}^{d_x \times b}$ and $\boldsymbol{V}_y \in \mathbb{R}^{d_y \times b}$ such that the reconstruction errors within each modality are minimized,

$$\min_{\boldsymbol{V}_x, \boldsymbol{V}_y} \sum_{i=1}^{n} \left(\|\boldsymbol{x}_i - \boldsymbol{V}_x h_x(\boldsymbol{x}_i)\|_2^2 + \|\boldsymbol{y}_i - \boldsymbol{V}_y h_y(\boldsymbol{y}_i)\|_2^2 \right), \quad (1)$$

in which $h_x(\boldsymbol{x}) = \operatorname{sgn}(\boldsymbol{W}_x^{\mathsf{T}}\boldsymbol{x})$ and $h_y(\boldsymbol{y}) = \operatorname{sgn}(\boldsymbol{W}_y^{\mathsf{T}}\boldsymbol{y})$ are the hashing functions. We can observe that Equation (1) takes a similar form as autoencoders [2], but with a different sgn activation function that can learn binary hash codes.

While the reconstructive embedding in Equation (1) can preserve the similarity information within each modality, it may fail to distill the correlation structure across different modalities and restrict the cross-modal search performance. To this end, we propose to reconstruct the original feature vectors from its pairwise hash codes in a different modality. The *cross-modal* reconstructive embedding is formulated as

$$\min_{\boldsymbol{V}_x, \boldsymbol{V}_y} L = \sum_{i=1}^{n} \left(\|\boldsymbol{x}_i - \boldsymbol{V}_x h_y(\boldsymbol{y}_i)\|_2^2 + \|\boldsymbol{y}_i - \boldsymbol{V}_y h_x(\boldsymbol{x}_i)\|_2^2 \right), \quad (2)$$

where L is the aggregate error function. The demonstration of the cross-modal reconstructive embedding can be found in Figure 1. The hash function learning of one modality explores the similarity information from another modality and vice-versa. In this way, we can capture the cross-modal correlations conveyed in the feature vectors using bimodal data. Note that our work learns binary hashing functions whereas the similar previous work [6] learns continuous feature representations.

3.3 Cross-modal Semantic Correlation

The aforementioned unsupervised cross-modal reconstructive embedding may still suffer from two limitations: (1) Without exploring semantic information, we only know the *pairwise correlation* conveyed in bimodal data, i.e. the hash codes of the two modalities within each training object should be similar. Such pairwise correlation in feature vectors is insufficient to distill the cross-modal correlations, since we cannot successfully infer whether unpaired modalities may convey correlations, i.e. whether $\boldsymbol{x}_i$ and $\boldsymbol{y}_j$ $(i \neq j)$ are correlated and should have similar embeddings. (2) Due to the well-known *semantic gap* [19] issue, high-level semantic description of an object often deviates from low-level feature descriptors, hence returning nearest neighbors according to similarity measures between original feature vectors cannot always guarantee satisfactory search quality. To address the above two limitations, we need to enhance the cross-modal correlation by exploring semantic information. Previous works usually require objects of the same category to have similar embeddings [26, 13, 31, 30, 32]. However, this requirement is indeed too strict for real-world problems as there is large intra-class variance (e.g. with subclasses) such that objects of the same category may have different embeddings, especially for the objects across different modalities.

In this paper, we propose a novel cross-modal semantic correlation approach by taking the following justifications into consideration: (1) object pairs from different categories should be separated and have discriminative embeddings (this is to maximize the inter-category separation margin); (2) object pairs from the same category should have similar embeddings only if they are similar in the original feature spaces (this is to circumvent the large intra-class variance). Denote by $\boldsymbol{S}^b$ and $\boldsymbol{S}^w$ the between-class and within-class similarity matrices respectively, then the two learning criteria for maximizing the cross-modal semantic correlations are

$$\begin{aligned} &\max_{\boldsymbol{W}_x,\boldsymbol{W}_y} \sum_{i=1}^{n}\sum_{j=1}^{n} S_{ij}^b \left\| h_x(\boldsymbol{x}_i) - h_y(\boldsymbol{y}_j) \right\|_2^2, \\ &\min_{\boldsymbol{W}_x,\boldsymbol{W}_y} \sum_{i=1}^{n}\sum_{j=1}^{n} S_{ij}^w \left\| h_x(\boldsymbol{x}_i) - h_y(\boldsymbol{y}_j) \right\|_2^2. \end{aligned} \tag{3}$$

The above criterion is similar to Linear Discriminant Analysis (LDA) [22], but with two notable distinctions: (1) the pairwise similarity of embedding is defined on cross-modal binary hash codes $h_x(\boldsymbol{x}_i)$ and $h_y(\boldsymbol{y}_j)$, while LDA defines it on intra-modal continuous embeddings; (2) we also require the locality constraint for intra-class object pairs, which can extract more discriminative and fine-grained hash codes by exploring subclass structures that potentially hide underlying the large intra-class variance.

To formally define the locality-aware similarity matrices, we need to first construct a nearest neighbor affinity matrix $\boldsymbol{A}$ to capture cross-modal locality information as follows,

$$A_{ij} = \begin{cases} d(\boldsymbol{x}_i, \boldsymbol{y}_j), & \text{if } \boldsymbol{l}_i = \boldsymbol{l}_j \wedge \begin{cases} \boldsymbol{x}_i \in \mathcal{N}_k(\boldsymbol{x}_j) \vee \boldsymbol{x}_j \in \mathcal{N}_k(\boldsymbol{x}_i) \\ \boldsymbol{y}_i \in \mathcal{N}_k(\boldsymbol{y}_j) \vee \boldsymbol{y}_j \in \mathcal{N}_k(\boldsymbol{y}_i) \end{cases} \\ 0, & \text{otherwise,} \end{cases} \tag{4}$$

where $\mathcal{N}_k(\boldsymbol{x})$ represents the k-nearest neighbors of $\boldsymbol{x}$ and $d(\boldsymbol{x}_i, \boldsymbol{y}_j) = e^{-\|\boldsymbol{x}_i - \boldsymbol{x}_j\|_2^2/2\sigma_x^2} + e^{-\|\boldsymbol{y}_i - \boldsymbol{y}_j\|_2^2/2\sigma_y^2}$ is the cross-modal similarity between $\boldsymbol{x}_i$ and $\boldsymbol{y}_j$. Heat kernel parameter $\sigma_x^2 = \frac{1}{n}\sum_{ij}\|\boldsymbol{x}_i - \boldsymbol{x}_j\|_2^2$ is the expectation of all pairwise distances in $\{\boldsymbol{x}_i\}_{i=1}^n$, while similar definition applies to σ_y^2. With the locality affinity matrix $\boldsymbol{A}$, which may be sparse using a practical choice of $k = 10$, we can formulate the similarity matrices involving the semantic information as

$$\begin{aligned} S_{ij}^b &= \begin{cases} A_{ij}\left(1/n - 1/n_c\right), & \text{if } \boldsymbol{l}_i = \boldsymbol{l}_j = c \\ A_{ij}/n, & \text{if } \boldsymbol{l}_i \neq \boldsymbol{l}_j, \end{cases} \\ S_{ij}^w &= \begin{cases} A_{ij}/n_c, & \text{if } \boldsymbol{l}_i = \boldsymbol{l}_j = c \\ 0, & \text{if } \boldsymbol{l}_i \neq \boldsymbol{l}_j, \end{cases} \end{aligned} \tag{5}$$

where n_c is the number of objects within the c-th category. The above semantic similarity matrices are consistent with LDA, except for introducing the locality affinity matrix $\boldsymbol{A}$. As can be examined, far apart object pairs in the same category have less influence on $\boldsymbol{S}^b$ and $\boldsymbol{S}^w$ with smaller weight A_{ij}. Note that we reweight the values for the object pairs in different categories since we want to separate them more from each other if they are similar in original feature space.

For expression conciseness, we rewrite the cross-modal *semantic correlation* criterion into a unified formulation as

$$\min_{\boldsymbol{W}_x,\boldsymbol{W}_y} R = \sum_{i=1}^{n}\sum_{j=1}^{n} S_{ij} \left\| h_x(\boldsymbol{x}_i) - h_y(\boldsymbol{y}_j) \right\|_2^2, \tag{6}$$

where R is the penalty of cross-modal semantic correlation, and the unified semantic similarity matrix $\boldsymbol{S} = \boldsymbol{S}^w - \boldsymbol{S}^b$ is

$$S_{ij} = \begin{cases} A_{ij}\left(2/n_c - 1/n\right), & \text{if } \boldsymbol{l}_i = \boldsymbol{l}_j = c \\ -A_{ij}/n, & \text{if } \boldsymbol{l}_i \neq \boldsymbol{l}_j. \end{cases} \tag{7}$$

It is worth noting that, in the proposed CAH approach, the semantic information is not necessary to be semantic labels. The approach also supports other forms of pairwise labels indicating whether two data points are known to be similar or dissimilar, e.g. the relevance feedback in real-world search engines.

3.4 Unified Optimization Problem

An original motivation of this work is to jointly explore both *feature correlation* (2) and *semantic correlation* (6) in a unified learning framework for cross-modal hashing. This motivation leads to the Correlation Autoencoder Hashing (CAH) model, with the joint optimization problem formulated as

$$\begin{aligned} &\min_{\boldsymbol{V}_x,\boldsymbol{V}_y,\boldsymbol{W}_x,\boldsymbol{W}_y} O = L + \lambda R \\ &h_x(\boldsymbol{x}) = \operatorname{sgn}\left(\boldsymbol{W}_x^{\mathsf{T}}\boldsymbol{x}\right), h_y(\boldsymbol{y}) = \operatorname{sgn}\left(\boldsymbol{W}_y^{\mathsf{T}}\boldsymbol{y}\right), \end{aligned} \tag{8}$$

where λ is a penalty parameter for trading off the relative importance of feature correlation and semantic correlation. In summary, CAH is the first cross-modal hashing method that simultaneously distills feature correlation and semantic correlation in a unified optimization framework: (1) CAH enhances feature correlation by cross-modal reconstructive embedding, which reconstructs the original feature vectors from its pairwise hash codes in another different modality; (2) CAH maximizes the inter-category separation margin for learning more discriminative hash codes; and (3) CAH minimizes the intra-category variance by further exploring the cross-modal locality information, which produces more fine-grained hash codes that characterize the subclass structures of each category to facilitate more accurate similarity ranking. Because different modalities are mapped into the common Hamming space by CAH, it is ready to use the model for cross-modal retrieval, e.g. using a text query to search relevant images from the database.

One of the most difficult issues in hash function learning is that hash codes are binary, making the objective neither continuous nor differentiable, and it is NP-hard to directly compute the best binary

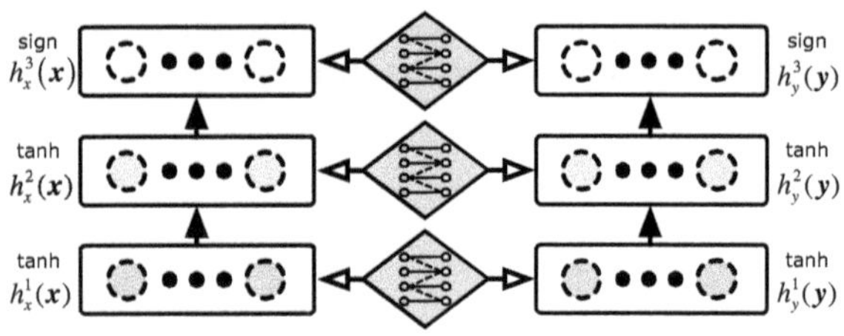

Figure 2: Deep architecture of the CAH model (only hash code layers are shown). At each layer, CAH maximizes both feature and semantic correlation.

hash functions of the problem (8). Most of the existing methods hence resort to the continuous relaxation of hash codes for numerical optimization [27]. A widely adopted option is spectral relaxation $h(\boldsymbol{x}) = \boldsymbol{W}^{\mathsf{T}}\boldsymbol{x}$ [29, 26, 31]. Yet, such relaxation incurs large binarization error as $\boldsymbol{W}^{\mathsf{T}}\boldsymbol{x} \in (-\infty, +\infty)$ while $\mathrm{sgn}(\boldsymbol{W}^{\mathsf{T}}\boldsymbol{x}) \in \{-1, 1\}$. In this paper, we are motivated by the success of logistic regression in squashing continues predictions to binary categories of $[-1, 1]$, and adopt the hyperbolic tangent function $\tanh(x) = \frac{e^x - e^{-x}}{e^x + e^{-x}}$ as the reasonable surrogate for $\mathrm{sgn}(x)$. Besides that tanh and sgn have consistent value ranges of $[-1, 1]$ and guarantee minimized binarization error, another benefit of tanh is that it injects nonlinearity to the CAH problem (8), making it viable for learning deep hash codes by layerwise abstraction. Detailed learning algorithms are presented in Section 3.6.

3.5 Deep Architecture

Cross-modal data have significantly different statistical properties, which makes it very challenging to capture the correlation structures across modalities directly. Recently, it has been witnessed that deep learning methods [2], such as deep autoencoders and convolutional networks, have made performance breakthroughs on many real-world recognition problems. Deep architectures are particularly powerful for distilling the cross-modal correlation since they can extract multilayer feature representations with different abstraction levels [21, 6]. Hence we propose a deep architecture with CAH as building block to enhance cross-modal correlation.

We adopt the stacked autoencoders architecture [28]. After the first layer CAH is trained, we can construct the deep architecture by stacking multiple CAH's on top of it in a layerwise manner, where the *hidden* output of the lower layer is used as the input of the upper layer. We train the Stacked CAH in a greedy layerwise manner by using the Stochastic Gradient Descent (SGD) [23] algorithm, detailed in Section 3.6. An illustration of Stacked CAH is shown in Figure 2. To guarantee accurate hidden representation, we only perform binarization on the top layer to obtain the hash codes. An important advantage of our deep architecture over[6] is that the feature correlation and semantic correlation are distilled in each layer, and can be strengthened layer by layer.

3.6 Learning Algorithm

When training each CAH by back-propagation (BP) using mini-batch SGD, we only need to consider the gradient of objective (8) w.r.t. each data point $\boldsymbol{x}_i$ and its correlated points $\boldsymbol{y}_j$'s such that $S_{ij} \neq 0$. CAH can be seen as a neural network with one hidden layer for hash codes. The output layer is similar to standard autoencoders [23] and can be computed in a similar procedure, while the hidden layer is different from standard autoencoders due to the cross-modal semantic correlation regularizer in Equation (6). Hence for each data point $\boldsymbol{x}_i$, we need to compute the gradient of (6) involving $\boldsymbol{x}_i$, i.e. $R(\boldsymbol{x}_i)$ w.r.t. parameters $\boldsymbol{W}_x$. For instance,

$$\begin{aligned}\frac{\partial R(\boldsymbol{x}_i)}{\partial \boldsymbol{W}_{pq}^x} &= \frac{\partial}{\partial \boldsymbol{W}_{pq}^x}\sum_{j=1}^n S_{ij}\left\|h(\boldsymbol{W}_x^{\mathsf{T}}\boldsymbol{x}_i) - h(\boldsymbol{W}_y^{\mathsf{T}}\boldsymbol{y}_j)\right\|_2^2 \\ &= \sum_{j=1}^n 2S_{ij}\left[h(\boldsymbol{W}_{*q}^{x\mathsf{T}}\boldsymbol{x}_i) - h(\boldsymbol{W}_{*q}^{y\mathsf{T}}\boldsymbol{y}_j)\right]h'(\boldsymbol{W}_{*q}^{x\mathsf{T}}\boldsymbol{x}_i)\boldsymbol{x}_{pi},\end{aligned} \tag{9}$$

where $\boldsymbol{W}_{*q}^x$ is the q-th column of $\boldsymbol{W}_x$ and $\boldsymbol{x}_{pi}$ is the p-th element of $\boldsymbol{x}_i$, and h' is the gradient of the tanh function, which is $h'(x) = 1 - (h(x))^2$. Similarly, for each data point $\boldsymbol{y}_i$, the gradient $\frac{\partial R(\boldsymbol{y}_i)}{\partial \boldsymbol{W}_{pq}^y}$ can be computed in the above way.

After getting the gradient of the cross-modal correlation regularizer (6), we can compute the gradient of the overall objective function (8) w.r.t. each point $(\boldsymbol{x}_i, \boldsymbol{y}_i)$ as follows,

$$\frac{\partial O(\boldsymbol{x}_i, \boldsymbol{y}_i)}{\partial \boldsymbol{W}_{pq}^x} = \frac{\partial L(\boldsymbol{y}_i)}{\partial \boldsymbol{W}_{pq}^x} + \lambda\frac{\partial R(\boldsymbol{x}_i)}{\partial \boldsymbol{W}_{pq}^x}, \tag{10}$$

where $\frac{\partial L(\boldsymbol{y}_i)}{\partial \boldsymbol{W}_{pq}^x}$ is computed by BP for standard autoencoders.

Computational Complexity: The standard autoencoder requires $O(tbdn)$ cost, where t is the number of epochs, b is the number of hidden units, d is the feature dimension, and n is the number of samples. We denote by z the average number of nonzero elements in each row of the semantic similarity matrix $\boldsymbol{S}$, then computing Equation (9) for all $\{\boldsymbol{x}_i\}_{i=1}^n$ requires $O(tb^2dzn)$. The overall computational complexity is $O(tb^2dzn)$, which scales linearly w.r.t. n. Though naively building affinity matrix $\boldsymbol{A}$ requires $O(zn^2)$, the cost can be reduced to $O(n\log n)$ by heap structure [10].

Table 1: The Statistics of the Three Benchmark Datasets

Dataset	NUS-WIDE	Wiki	Flickr
Complete Set	195,834	2,866	1,000,000
Database	191,834	2,173	997,000
Query Set	2,000	393	2,000
Training Set	10,000	2,173	22,000
Validation Set	2,000	300	1,000

4. EXPERIMENTS

In this section, we conduct comprehensive experiments to evaluate the effectiveness of the proposed CAH model in comparison with several state-of-the-art hashing methods on three public cross-modal datasets. We investigate the widely adopted evaluation criteria including mean average precision (MAP) and precision-recall curve. The code and experimental configurations will be made available online.

4.1 Datasets

We conduct our experimental evaluation on three public benchmark datasets, i.e. **NUS-WIDE** [5], **Wiki** [18], and **Flickr** [8]. Detailed statistics are summarized in Table 1.

NUS-WIDE[1] is a public Web image dataset containing 269, 648 images downloaded from Flickr, together with the associated raw tags of these images. There are 81 ground truth concepts (categories) manually annotated for search evaluation. Following previous works [35, 28], we prune the original NUS-WIDE dataset to form a new dataset consisting of 195,834 image-text pairs that belong to one of the 21 most frequent concepts. The images are represented by 500-dimensional bag-of-visual words and the texts are represented by 1000-dimensional tag occurrence vectors.

[1] http://lms.comp.nus.edu.sg/research/NUS-WIDE.htm

Wiki[2] is crawled from the Wikipedia's featured articles, with 2,866 image-text pairs. A Wikipedia article contains multiple sections, and the text information and its associated image in one section is considered as an image-text pair, which is annotated by semantic labels of 10 categories. Each image is represented by a 128-dimensional bag-of-words feature vector extracted from SIFT features, and each text is represented by the probability distribution over 10 topics learned by Latent Dirichlet Allocation (LDA).

Flickr includes 1 million images associated with tags from Flickr, in which 25,000 are labeled with 38 concepts while the remaining 975,000 are unlabeled. Each image of the public available preprocessed dataset[3] is represented by a 3,857-dimensional vector concatenated by local SIFT feature, color histogram, global GIST feature, and etc [21]. Each text is represented by a 2,000-dimensional feature vector extracted from tag occurrences like NUS-WIDE.

To make results comparable, we adopt the data preprocessing strategy, ZCA whitening [11, 28], to normalize each dimension of the feature to be zero mean and unit variance.

4.2 Comparison Methods

We compare CAH with five state-of-the-art cross-modal hashing methods: **IMH**[4] [20], **CVH**[5] [12], **CMSSH**[5] [3], **SCM** [31] and **CorrAE**[6] [6], which can be organized into three categories:

- **Unsupervised shallow hashing: IMH** embeds intra-media and inter-media similarities into a common Hamming space, and integrates a linear regression to learn hash functions such that hash codes for new data can be efficiently generated. **CVH** extends spectral hashing [29] to cross-modal scenario by mapping similar objects across different modalities to similar binary codes.
- **Supervised shallow hashing: CMSSH** is a among the first works which embeds cross-modal data into a common Hamming space via supervised similarity learning. **SCM** is the most recent work which seamlessly integrates semantic labels into the hash function learning procedure for the large-scale data modeling.
- **Unsupervised deep hashing: CorrAE** learns a cross-modal deep autoencoder by integrating unsupervised representation learning and correlation modeling together. It is worth noting that CorrAE is an embedding approach (instead of hashing approach) to cross-modal retrieval, so we directly apply the *sign* function to the CorrAE embedding for generating binary hash codes.

In order to study the effectiveness of our approach with respect to either feature correlation, semantic correlation or data locality, we further evaluate two variants of **CAH** : 1) CAH with only feature correlation, that is $\boldsymbol{S} = \boldsymbol{I}$ in (8), termed **CAH-F**; 2) CAH without using data locality, that is $\boldsymbol{A} = \mathbf{1}\mathbf{1}^{\mathsf{T}}$ in (8), termed **CAH-L**. All variants use a 3-layer deep architecture.

4.3 Evaluation Protocols

We adopt *Mean Average Precision* (MAP) to measure cross-modal search quality, as it is widely adopted in the literature [20, 35, 28, 30, 6]. Given a query and a set of R retrieved documents,

[2] http://www.svcl.ucsd.edu/projects/crossmodal
[3] http://www.cs.toronto.edu/~nitish/multimodal
[4] http://staff.itee.uq.edu.au/shenht/UQ_IMH
[5] http://www.cse.ust.hk/~dyyeung/code/mlbe.zip
[6] https://github.com/fangxiangfeng/deepnet

Table 2: MAP Results on the NUS-WIDE Dataset

Task	Method	NUS-WIDE			
		8 bits	16 bits	32 bits	64 bits
$I \to T$	IMH	0.4345	0.4399	0.4203	0.4115
	CVH	0.4227	0.4287	0.4074	0.3999
	CMSSH	0.3950	0.4052	0.4076	0.3516
	SCM	0.4693	0.4648	0.4619	0.4851
	CorrAE	0.4398	0.4522	0.4699	0.4944
	CAH-F	0.4439	0.4711	0.4922	0.5234
	CAH-L	0.4880	0.5050	0.5219	0.5581
	CAH	**0.4920**	**0.5084**	**0.5407**	**0.5628**
$T \to I$	IMH	0.4380	0.4582	0.4186	0.4051
	CVH	0.4787	0.4689	0.4522	0.4453
	CMSSH	0.3783	0.3499	0.3944	0.4015
	SCM	0.4449	0.4859	0.5105	0.5259
	CorrAE	0.4303	0.4501	0.4634	0.4880
	CAH-F	0.4433	0.4666	0.4885	0.5157
	CAH-L	0.4933	0.5053	0.5205	0.5250
	CAH	**0.5019**	**0.5135**	**0.5451**	**0.5800**

Average Precision (AP) is defined as

$$\mathrm{AP}@R = \frac{\sum_{r=1}^{R} P(r)\,\delta(r)}{\sum_{r'=1}^{R} \delta(r')}, \tag{11}$$

where $P(r)$ denotes the precision of the top r retrieved results, and $\delta(r) = 1$ if the r-th retrieved result is a true neighbor of the query, otherwise $\delta(r) = 0$, and here we follow literatures [16, 30, 28] to adopt AP@$R = 50$. Then MAP is computed as the mean of all the queries' average precision.

Furthermore, we also report a widely adopted metric, *precision-recall* curve [35, 28] that shows the variation of precision in different recall levels for fine-grained analysis.

The CAH approach only involves one model parameter, penalty coefficient λ, for trading off the relative importance of feature correlation and semantic correlation. Here we can automatically select λ using cross-validation via annotation ground truths in the validation sets (see Table 1). In Section 4.6, we further study parameter sensitivity for λ to validate that CAH can consistently outperform the state-of-the-arts with a wide range of parameter configurations. We follow literature convention [6, 28] to set the number of units u_ℓ in each layer of the deep autoencoders: $u_{\ell-1} = 2u_\ell$ and the number of units in the last layer is set to hash code length b.

For comparison methods, we also use cross-validation to carefully tune their parameters using the validation sets. Subject to computation burden, it is too costly to train IMH and CMSSH on the complete datasets, hence for fair comparison, we adopt a literature convention [31, 6] and randomly sample 10,000 image-text pairs to train all models. Average results with ten repeated experiments are reported.

4.4 Experimental Results

We compare CAH against state-of-the-art methods on cross-modal retrieval tasks (image query on text database $I \to T$ and text query on image database $T \to I$) in terms of MAP and precision-recall.

4.4.1 *Results on NUS-WIDE*

The MAP results of CAH and the comparison methods are demonstrated in Table 2. One can see that CAH achieves significantly better performance on all cross-modal tasks. To zoom-in the CAH model for a deeper understanding on where the performance improvements have come, we further show the MAP results of two

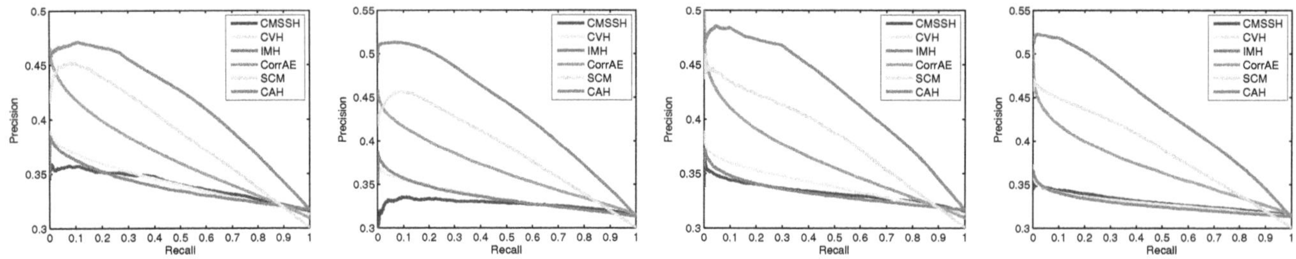

(a) $I \to T$ @ 16 bits (b) $I \to T$ @ 32 bits (c) $T \to I$ @ 16 bits (d) $T \to I$ @ 32 bits

Figure 3: Precision-recall curves on the NUS-WIDE cross-modal search tasks $I \to T$ and $T \to I$ with hash codes @ 16 and 32 bits.

Table 3: MAP Results on the Wiki Dataset

Task	Method	Wiki			
		8 bits	16 bits	32 bits	64 bits
$I \to T$	IMH	0.1734	0.1896	0.1714	0.1601
	CVH	0.1673	0.1877	0.1716	0.1696
	CMSSH	0.1672	0.1727	0.1750	0.1759
	SCM	0.2258	0.2372	0.2381	0.2378
	CorrAE	0.1990	0.2078	0.2105	0.2177
	CAH-F	0.2276	0.2323	0.2233	0.2339
	CAH-L	0.2208	0.2342	0.2420	0.2456
	CAH	**0.2308**	**0.2415**	**0.2465**	**0.2530**
$T \to I$	IMH	0.2394	0.2227	0.2333	0.1896
	CVH	0.2309	0.2219	0.2214	0.2350
	CMSSH	0.2926	0.2991	0.2537	0.2582
	SCM	0.3157	0.3698	0.4239	0.4369
	CorrAE	0.2712	0.2948	0.3111	0.3220
	CAH-F	0.2608	0.3311	0.3418	0.3693
	CAH-L	0.3302	0.3744	0.4156	0.4325
	CAH	**0.3424**	**0.3956**	**0.4284**	**0.4569**

Table 4: MAP Results on the Flickr Dataset

Task	Method	Flickr			
		8 bits	16 bits	32 bits	64 bits
$I \to T$	IMH	0.5449	0.5646	0.5936	0.5539
	CVH	0.6091	0.6225	0.6364	0.6199
	CMSSH	0.5076	0.5272	0.5357	0.5219
	SCM	0.6361	0.6493	0.6495	0.6440
	CorrAE	0.6301	0.6329	0.6357	0.6401
	CAH-F	0.6493	0.6470	0.6544	0.6786
	CAH-L	0.6520	0.6584	0.6710	0.6920
	CAH	**0.6608**	**0.6875**	**0.7035**	**0.7072**
$T \to I$	IMH	0.5374	0.5536	0.5513	0.5583
	CVH	0.5972	0.6032	0.5738	0.5794
	CMSSH	0.5868	0.5732	0.6176	0.6323
	SCM	0.6037	0.5998	0.5805	0.6078
	CorrAE	0.6142	0.6198	0.6247	0.6431
	CAH-F	0.6324	0.6406	0.6508	0.6765
	CAH-L	0.6328	**0.6734**	**0.6978**	0.7201
	CAH	**0.6496**	0.6612	0.6908	**0.7263**

invariants of CAH: (1) CAH-F achieves worse performance than CAH-L and CAH, which highlights that it is crucial to simultaneously distill feature correlation and semantic correlation for cross-modal search; (2) CAH-L achieves worse performance than CAH, this confirms that it makes no sense to make the far-apart objects in the same category have similar hash codes. By exploring locality-aware semantic similarity, CAH can successfully address the large intra-class issue, which may severely deteriorate search performance but remains a rarely touched issue by previous methods.

An interesting observation is that the unsupervised deep model CorrAE generally performs much better than unsupervised shallow models IMH and CVH. This confirms that cross-modal hashing based on deep models can extract the complex cross-modal correlation more effectively than shallow models. Furthermore, CorrAE even significantly outperforms the conventional supervised method CMSSH and approaches the latest state-of-the-art supervised method SCM. This strongly convinces us the powerfulness of deep models and explains why CAH further outperforms SCM.

The precision-recall curves [35, 28] of all methods are illustrated in Figure 3. CAH establishes the best cross-modal retrieval performance at all recall levels. This validates that CAH is capable for diverse retrieval scenarios, for example, to target a higher recall by tolerating fairly lower precision.

4.4.2 *Results on Wiki*

Table 3 shows the MAP scores of CAH and the state-of-arts on the Wiki dataset, which demonstrates that CAH achieves significantly better cross-modal search performance. We also observe that the MAP on $I \to T$ is substantially lower than the MAP on $T \to I$. This is an excellent example of the semantic gap issue [19]: the images of Wiki dataset are low-quality and are poorly related to the semantic labels; on the contrary, the texts of Wiki dataset are well-edited featured articles and are more relevant to the semantic labels. We can observe that CAH still performs more effective cross-modal search in the presence of very large semantic gap. The precision-recall curves in Figure 4 show that CAH gives the best cross-modal search quality at all recall levels.

4.4.3 *Results on Flickr*

We report the MAP results on the Flickr dataset in Table 4 and show the detailed precision-recall curves in Figure 5. We may observe that CAH can significantly outperform the comparison methods on the two cross-modal search tasks.

4.5 Quantization Error Analysis

The search quality with binary codes in Hamming distance is evidently inferior to searching with continuous features in Euclidean distance, due to substantial information loss by quantizing continuous features to binary codes [28]. Hence, how to minimize the quantization error has been the main effort in the hashing research community. In this regard, we further evaluate IMH, CorrAE and CAH using MAP @ 64 bits with continuous features and binary codes, respectively, with results shown in Figure 6. We can see that CorrAE incurs significantly less loss on search quality than

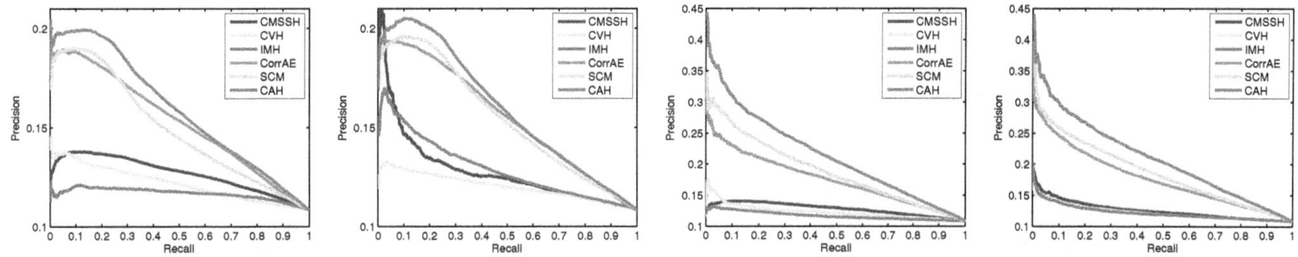

(a) $I \to T$ @ 16 bits (b) $I \to T$ @ 32 bits (c) $T \to I$ @ 16 bits (d) $T \to I$ @ 32 bits

Figure 4: Precision-recall curves on the Wiki cross-modal search tasks $I \to T$ and $T \to I$ with hash codes @ 16 and 32 bits.

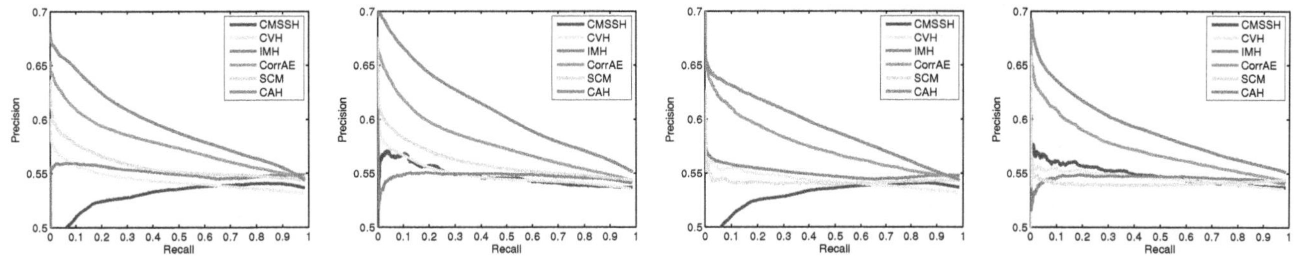

(a) $I \to T$ @ 16 bits (b) $I \to T$ @ 32 bits (c) $T \to I$ @ 16 bits (d) $T \to I$ @ 32 bits

Figure 5: Precision-recall curves on the Flickr cross-modal search tasks $I \to T$ and $T \to I$ with hash codes @ 16 and 32 bits.

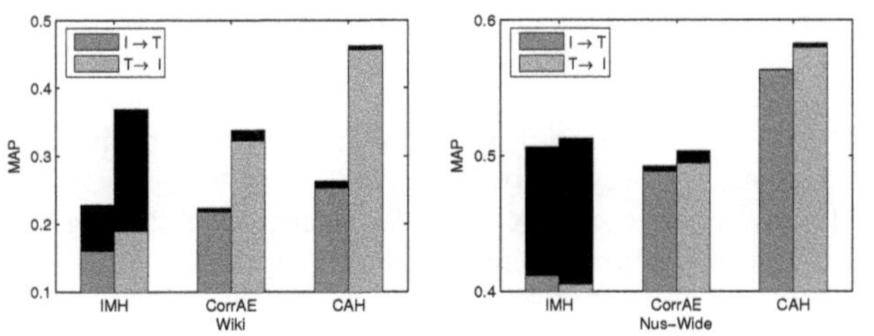

(a) Quantization Error on Wiki (b) Quantization Error on NUS-WIDE

Figure 6: Quantization error: search quality loss due to binarization from continuous features to binary codes (black bars).

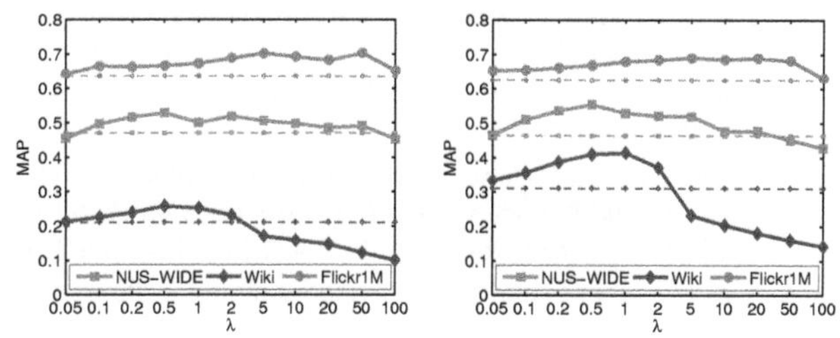

(a) $I \to T$ @ 32 bits (b) $T \to I$ @ 32 bits

Figure 7: The MAP @ 32 bits v.s. different values of λ for both cross-modal retrieval tasks on NUS-WIDE, Wiki, and Flickr.

IMH by using binary codes instead of continuous features, while CAH performs even better than CorrAE. This reveals the vital importance of designing good continuous relaxation method for optimization. Our results suggest that the widely-adopted spectral relaxation $\mathrm{sgn}(x) \approx x$ may be too lossy while $\mathrm{sgn}(x) \approx \tanh(x)$ is a very accurate surrogate.

4.6 Parameter Sensitivity

The stability of performance against parameter variation is crucial as model selection is time-consuming for large-scale problems. We show in Figure 7 the performance of CAH using MAP @ 32 bits on both cross-modal retrieval tasks by varying $\lambda \in [0.05, 100]$. We see that CAH consistently outperforms the strongest baseline CorrAE on all datasets when λ is varied in a large range $[0.1, 2]$.

5. CONCLUSION AND FUTURE WORK

In this paper, we have formally approached the problem of supervised cross-modal hashing. The proposed Correlation Autoencoder Hashing (CAH) model simultaneously maximizes the feature correlation revealed by bimodal data and the semantic correlation conveyed in similarity labels, while embeds these correlations into binary hash codes by deep autoencoders. CAH can successfully consolidate the correlation structure across modalities and enhance the generalizability of the embedded hash codes for cross-modal retrieval. Extensive results show that CAH significantly outperforms state-of-the-art cross-modal hashing methods.

In the future, we plan to extend our approach to a hybrid deep learning architecture, which will model text by autoencoders but model image by convolutional neural networks, since each has successful witness in its respective domains. How to seamlessly integrate the heterogeneous deep models for cross-modal hashing remains a very interesting problem.

Acknowledgments

This work was supported by National Natural Science Foundation of China (61325008, 61502265), China Postdoctoral Science Foundation (2015T80088), National Science and Technology Supporting Program (2015BAH14F02), and Tsinghua National Laboratory (TNList) Special Fund for Big Data Science and Technology.

6. REFERENCES

[1] A. Andoni and P. Indyk. Near-optimal hashing algorithms for approximate nearest neighbor in high dimensions. In *IEEE Symposium on Foundations of Computer Science*, 2006.

[2] Y. Bengio, A. Courville, and P. Vincent. Representation learning: A review and new perspectives. *Pattern Analysis and Machine Intelligence, IEEE Transactions on*, 35(8):1798–1828, Aug 2013.

[3] M. Bronstein, A. Bronstein, F. Michel, and N. Paragios. Data fusion through cross-modality metric learning using similarity-sensitive hashing. In *Computer Vision and Pattern Recognition, 2010 IEEE Conference on*, CVPR'10, pages 3594–3601. IEEE, June 2010.

[4] Y. Cao, M. Long, J. Wang, H. Zhu, and Q. Wen. Deep quantization network for efficient image retrieval. In *AAAI Conference on Artificial Intelligence*, 2016.

[5] T.-S. Chua, J. Tang, R. Hong, H. Li, Z. Luo, and Y.-T. Zheng. Nus-wide: A real-world web image database from national university of singapore. In *Proc. of ACM Conf. on Image and Video Retrieval*, Santorini, Greece, July 8-10, 2009.

[6] F. Feng, X. Wang, and R. Li. Cross-modal retrieval with correspondence autoencoder. In *Proceedings of the ACM International Conference on Multimedia*. ACM, 2014.

[7] Y. Hu, Z. Jin, H. Ren, D. Cai, and X. He. Iterative multi-view hashing for cross media indexing. In *Proceedings of the ACM International Conference on Multimedia*, MM '14, pages 527–536. ACM, 2014.

[8] M. J. Huiskes and M. S. Lew. The mir flickr retrieval evaluation. In *MIR '08: Proceedings of the 2008 ACM International Conference on Multimedia Information Retrieval*. ACM, 2008.

[9] H. Jegou, M. Douze, and C. Schmid. Product quantization for nearest neighbor search. *IEEE Transactions on Pattern Analysis and Machine Intelligence*, 33(1):117–128, Jan 2011.

[10] Z. Jiang, G. Zhang, and L. S. Davis. Submodular dictionary learning for sparse coding. In *CVPR*. IEEE, 2012.

[11] A. Krizhevsky. Learning multiple layers of features from tiny images. Technical report, University of Toronto, 2009.

[12] S. Kumar and R. Udupa. Learning hash functions for cross-view similarity search. In *Proceedings of the Twenty-Second International Joint Conference on Artificial Intelligence*, IJCAI '11, pages 1360–1365, 2011.

[13] W. Liu, J. Wang, R. Ji, Y.-G. Jiang, and S.-F. Chang. Supervised hashing with kernels. In *CVPR*. IEEE, 2012.

[14] X. Liu, J. He, C. Deng, and B. Lang. Collaborative hashing. In *CVPR*. IEEE, 2014.

[15] M. Long, Y. Cao, J. Wang, and P. S. Yu. Composite correlation quantization for efficient multimodal retrieval. In *Proceedings of the 39th International ACM SIGIR Conference on Research and Development in Information Retrieval*, SIGIR '16. ACM, 2016.

[16] X. Lu, F. Wu, S. Tang, Z. Zhang, X. He, and Y. Zhuang. A low rank structural large margin method for cross-modal ranking. In *Proceedings of the 36th International ACM SIGIR Conference on Research and Development in Information Retrieval*, SIGIR '13. ACM, 2013.

[17] M. Norouzi and D. J. Fleet. Cartesian k-means. In *Proceedings of the 2013 IEEE Conference on Computer Vision and Pattern Recognition*, CVPR '13. IEEE, 2013.

[18] J. C. Pereira, E. Coviello, G. Doyle, N. Rasiwasia, G. R. G. Lanckriet, R. Levy, and N. Vasconcelos. On the role of correlation and abstraction in cross-modal multimedia retrieval. *IEEE Transactions on Pattern Analysis and Machine Intelligence*, 36(3):521–535, 2014.

[19] A. W. Smeulders, M. Worring, S. Santini, A. Gupta, and R. Jain. Content-based image retrieval at the end of the early years. *TPAMI*, 22(12):1349–1380, 2000.

[20] J. Song, Y. Yang, Y. Yang, Z. Huang, and H. T. Shen. Inter-media hashing for large-scale retrieval from heterogeneous data sources. In *Proceedings of the 2013 ACM SIGMOD International Conference on Management of Data*, SIGMOD '13, pages 785–796. ACM, 2013.

[21] N. Srivastava and R. Salakhutdinov. Multimodal learning with deep boltzmann machines. *Journal of Machine Learning Research*, 15:2949–2980, 2014.

[22] M. Sugiyama. Dimensionality reduction of multimodal labeled data by local fisher discriminant analysis. *JMLR*, 8:1027–1061, 2007.

[23] P. Vincent, H. Larochelle, I. Lajoie, Y. Bengio, and P.-A. Manzagol. Stacked denoising autoencoders: Learning useful representations in a deep network with a local denoising criterion. *JMLR*, 11:3371–3408, 2010.

[24] J. Wan, D. Wang, S. C. H. Hoi, P. Wu, J. Zhu, Y. Zhang, and J. Li. Deep learning for content-based image retrieval: A comprehensive study. In *MM*. ACM, 2014.

[25] D. Wang, P. Cui, M. Ou, and W. Zhu. Deep multimodal hashing with orthogonal regularization. In *Proceedings of the Twenty-Second International Joint Conference on Artificial Intelligence*, 2015.

[26] J. Wang, S. Kumar, and S.-F. Chang. Semi-supervised hashing for large-scale search. *TPAMI*, 34(12):2393–2406, 2012.

[27] J. Wang, H. T. Shen, J. Song, and J. Ji. Hashing for similarity search: A survey. Arxiv, 2014.

[28] W. Wang, B. C. Ooi, X. Yang, D. Zhang, and Y. Zhuang. Effective multi-modal retrieval based on stacked auto-encoders. In *Proceedings of the VLDB Endowment*, VLDB '14, pages 649–660. ACM, 2014.

[29] Y. Weiss, A. Torralba, and R. Fergus. Spectral hashing. In *Advances in Neural Information Processing Systems 21*, pages 1753–1760. Curran Associates, Inc., 2009.

[30] Z. Yu, F. Wu, Y. Yang, Q. Tian, J. Luo, and Y. Zhuang. Discriminative coupled dictionary hashing for fast cross-media retrieval. In *Proceedings of the 37th International ACM SIGIR Conference on Research and Development in Information Retrieval*. ACM, 2014.

[31] D. Zhang and W.-J. Li. Large-scale supervised multimodal hashing with semantic correlation maximization. In *Proceedings of the Twenty-Eighth AAAI Conference on Artificial Intelligence*, 2014.

[32] P. Zhang, W. Zhang, W.-J. Li, and M. Guo. Supervised hashing with latent factor models. In *SIGIR*, 2014.

[33] Y. Zhen and D.-Y. Yeung. Co-regularized hashing for multimodal data. In *Advances in Neural Information Processing Systems 24*, 2012.

[34] Y. Zhen and D.-Y. Yeung. A probabilistic model for multimodal hash function learning. In *Proceedings of the 18th ACM SIGKDD International Conference on Knowledge Discovery and Data Mining*, KDD '12. ACM, 2012.

[35] X. Zhu, Z. Huang, H. T. Shen, and X. Zhao. Linear cross-modal hashing for efficient multimedia search. In *Proceedings of the 21st ACM International Conference on Multimedia*, MM '13, pages 143–152. ACM, 2013.

Regional Subspace Projection Coding for Image Retrieval

Mingmin Zhen Wenmin Wang* Ronggang Wang

School of Electronic and Computer Engineering, Shenzhen Graduate School, Peking University
Lishui Road 2199, Nanshan District, Shenzhen, China 518055

mingminzhen@pku.edu.cn wangwm@ece.pku.edu.cn rgwang@ece.pku.edu.cn

ABSTRACT

For image retrieval task, hamming embedding, being proved to be one of the state-of-the-art methods, has been prevalently utilised. The basic idea is to project local features into orthogonal space randomly, in which the binary signature is generated based on a single partition of feature space. However, the binary signature generation process is coarse and heuristic. On the one hand, the same projection is carried out for all visual word space without consideration of difference among subspaces. On the other hand, the projection matrix is generated randomly regardless of the distribution of feature data. Therefore, the performance of hamming embedding is limited and far from the optimal. In this paper, we firstly analyse the limitation of hamming embedding and compare different orthogonal projection methods. Then we propose a regional subspace projection coding method that is based on the distribution of local features assigned to each visual word. Finally, our experiments on two benchmark datasets demonstrate that our proposed method outperforms current state-of-the-art methods.

Keywords

Image Retrieval, Bag of Features, Inverted files, Hamming embedding

1. INTRODUCTION

Image retrieval is one of the most popular and significant tasks in multimedia community [28]. Its goal is to retrieve all the images containing the same object or scene with the query in real time for an given image. In order to perform such a research task, many models have been proposed in last few years [31, 11, 25]. In all these methods, local feature based methods have been widely used in many state-of-the-art image systems. Among them the Bag of Visual Words (BoVW) method is the representative one due to its effectiveness and efficiency. For BoVW method, an image is described by local features, which are firstly detected from images with effective detectors such as the Hessian-Affine [24] detector and described by using features descriptors, e.g., the Scale Invariant Feature Transform (SIFT) [22] descriptor. The descriptors from one image are then quantized into discrete visual words, which are generated by cluster algorithm such as K-means algorithm. Finally, all the information is integrated into an inverted index [29] to reduce memory requirements and accelerate online retrieval.

To improve the performance of image retrieval, a series of methods have been proposed [14, 16, 10, 11]. Hamming Embedding (HE) is a powerful method which is proposed to refine the matching process. For HE, local feature is transformed into binary signature and similarity is computed by comparing the hamming distance other than Euclidean distance between these binary signatures. Moreover, in order to reduce quantization errors when assigning and matching feature descriptors, multiple descriptor assignment [13, 12] and soft quantization [7] which assign the feature descriptors to more than one visual word are proposed. Burstiness, as an another problem pointed out in [16, 30], is addressed by power normalization [16, 15] and burstiness weight [16]. A novel method for burst detection is proposed in [30].

There are also other methods which are very effective and competitive for image retrieval, such as Vector of Locally Aggregated Descriptors (VLAD) [14, 15, 2] and Fisher Vector [26, 27]. By aggregating all the features assigned to the same visual word, the main difference for VLAD and Fisher Vector is that different cluster algorithms are used in fact. By this aggregation method, images can be represented by a few dozens bytes after the dimensionality reduction and compression. Both the retrieval accuracy and efficiency can still preserve high while searching even in hundred millions images. Furthermore, by taking the non-aggregation kernel and aggregation kernel, Tolias et al. [32] introduce a framework to bridge the gap between the "matching-based" approaches, such as HE and VLAD. Non-aggregated kernels individually match all the elements belonging to the same visual word while aggregated kernels pre-combine all the elements on one visual word and match them as an entirety. Then, the selectivity of both of the non-aggregated and aggregated kernels are studied. Moreover, the Selective Match Kernel (SMK) and Aggregated Selective Match Kernel (ASMK) are proposed in [32], which combine the matching-based approaches to achieve better image retrieval performances. In essence, both SMK and ASMK compare the similarity between images by matching the features assigned to the same visual word. Thus, binary signatures

*W. Wang is the corresponding author.

ICMR'16, June 06-09, 2016, New York, NY, USA

© 2016 ACM. ISBN 978-1-4503-4359-6/16/06...$15.00

DOI: http://dx.doi.org/10.1145/2911996.2912003

which are generated firstly for both SMK and ASMK are used to compare the similarity. This is similar to HE.

Based on previous works, we can see that the core point of both the aggregated methods and non-aggregated methods is the right match for features assigned to the same visual word. This means that a good binary signature generation process can boost the performance of image retrieval system. But the binary signature generation process for either HE or ASMK is very simple and coarse obviously. Firstly the same projection for all visual word space is performed. Obviously the difference for different visual word space is not taken into consideration. Then the projection matrix is generated randomly, which will result in unpredictable even ambiguous match result. In order to make an in-depth investigation of the binary signature generation for these features assigned to the same visual word, we analyse the difference for different visual word space firstly and compare the different binary signature generation methods. What's more, we further propose a regional subspace projection coding method which make use of the data distribution of each visual word space. We will introduce it in detail in Section 4.

However, in order to further enhance the performance of image retrieval system, we try to find a better binary signature generation method that can boost the matching performance. In our work, we choose HE [11] as our baseline and do not employ SMK or ASMK since HE framework exhibits quite excellent and remarkable retrieval quality [19, 20, 18, 21, 17]. The experiments on two benchmark datasets demonstrate that our proposed method can significantly boost and enhance the retrieval result.

The remainder for this paper is organized as follows. Section 2 introduces related works. The HE framework is illustrated in Section 3 briefly. Section 4 gives the details of our algorithm. After exhibiting experiments in Section 5, we conclude in Section 6.

2. RELATED WORK

There are so many literatures proposed to improve the performance based on the BoVW model. Quantization error is a problem where many works pay attention to. To address this problem, soft matching [9, 7] assigns each descriptor to multiple visual words, but instead the query time and memory overload are added. [4] designs quantization method by kernel density estimation, while [3] utilize binary features to improve efficiency and reduce quantization error.

Encoding spatial constraints into the search framework, such as the weak geometric consistency [11] and RANSAC verification [28], is another popular issue. The geometric context among local features can be also encoded into visual word assemblies [41, 42, 40]. By analysing the spatial contexts [43, 35] of SIFT features, inconsistent matches are filtered out. In order to address burstiness problem, burstiness weight is used in [16] and an early burst detection method is proposed in [30]. Merging multiple vocabularies such as [20, 2] can also enhance the performance, which mainly address the vocabulary correlation problem.

In [8], the distance to hyperplane is embedded to improve the vector-to-binary comparison. However, the key issue of feature-to-feature matching which is comparing the similarity of binary signature is ignorable all the time. Thus it is necessary to find a better binary signature generation method for HE-like framework.

3. HE FRAMEWORK

HE framework exhibits extraordinary retrieval quality and is enhanced and modified constantly since it was proposed by Jégou Hervé [11]. To facilitate the description of our proposed method, the HE framework is described in brief in this section.

Local descriptors and vocabulary. Generally, affine invariant interest regions are detected firstly in order to extract local invariant descriptors. There are many excellent algorithms for this, such as MSER [6, 25] or Hessian interest points [24, 28, 23]. Then an affine invariant descriptor is extracted from the located regions. The SIFT is often used for image retrieval task. As suggested in [1], the RootSIFT variant is also implemented due to its excellent effectiveness. Vocabulary is often trained on a large number of descriptor vectors by cluster algorithm. Typically, either flat K-means or hierachical K-means is employed as suggested in [28].

Thus we can describe an image as a set $\chi = \{\mathbf{x_1}, \mathbf{x_2}, ..., \mathbf{x_n}\}$ of n d-dimensional local features (for SIFT descriptor, $d = 128$). The vocabulary learned offline can be represented as $C = \{\mathbf{c_1}, \mathbf{c_2}, ..., \mathbf{c_K}\}$ with K words. The descriptors can be quantized by a K-means quantizer

$$q : \mathbb{R}^d \rightarrow C \subset \mathbb{R}^d \quad (1)$$

$$\mathbf{x} \rightarrow q(\mathbf{x}) \quad (2)$$

where $q(\mathbf{x})$ denotes that descriptor is quantized based on approximate nearest neighbor algorithm.

HE. HE mainly subdivides each cell associated with a given visual word into regions and then transforms a given descriptor assigned to the visual word into binary signature. This refines the matching, as two descriptors $\mathbf{x}$ and $\mathbf{y}$ match if they are assigned to the same visual word, i.e., if $q(\mathbf{x}) = q(\mathbf{y})$, and if the Hamming distance $h(s(\mathbf{x}), s(\mathbf{y}))$ between their binary signatures is lower or equal than a threshold h_t. The detail of binary signature generation process is presented in Section 4 clearly.

Weighting for HE. The hamming distance between two descriptors can reflect the closeness of descriptors and then be weighted. Since smaller distances reflect higher confidence, higher score should be weighted for them. The weight $w(h_d)$ associated with a Hamming distance $h_d = h(s(\mathbf{x}), s(\mathbf{y}))$ between binary signatures $s(\mathbf{x})$ and $s(\mathbf{y})$ is obtained with a Gaussian function:

$$w(h_d) = \begin{cases} e^{-h_d^2/\sigma^2}, & h_d \leq h_t \\ 0, & otherwise \end{cases} \quad (3)$$

The matching score is obtained by

$$sim(\mathbf{x}, \mathbf{y}) = w(h(s(\mathbf{x}), s(\mathbf{y}))) \times IDF(q(\mathbf{x}))^2 \quad (4)$$

where $IDF(q(\mathbf{x}))$ denotes the Inverse Document Frequency (IDF) weight of the visual word $q(\mathbf{x})$. In [19], an effective $L_p{-}norm$ IDF method is proposed which achieves the state-of-the-art.

4. OUR METHOD

4.1 Baselines

HE framework provides a complete pipeline for image retrieval task. It is noteworthy that the score which will be used for measuring the similarity between images is based on

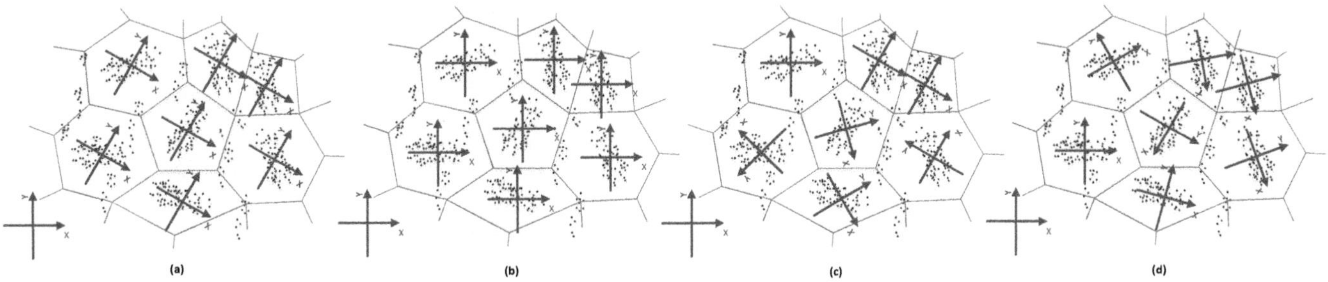

Figure 1: An illustration of the baselines $\mathbf{B_0}$, $\mathbf{B_1}$, $\mathbf{B_2}$ and our proposed method. (a) The same projection matrix is used for all the descriptors in the baseline $\mathbf{B_0}$; (b) The descriptors are transformed in original space in baseline $\mathbf{B_1}$; (c) The different projection matrices are used for the descriptors assigned to different visual words in the baseline $\mathbf{B_2}$; (d) Our proposed method.

the hamming distance between binary signatures. In other words, good binary signature can boost the performance of image retrieval system.

In the original HE framework, the binary signature generation process is divided into two steps, i.e., **offline step** and **online step**.

- **offline step** In the offline step, a $d_b \times d$ orthogonal projection matrix P is generated randomly and median vector $\tau_\mathbf{k}$ for $k-$th cluster is learned by

$$\tau_\mathbf{k} = median(P \times \mathbf{x_{k,1}}, P \times \mathbf{x_{k,2}}, ..., P \times \mathbf{x_{k,m}}) \quad (5)$$

  where $\mathbf{x_{k,j}}$ denotes the descriptor from training data which is assigned to $k-$th cluster. Obviously, the $\tau_\mathbf{k}$ is a d_b-dimensional vector.

- **online step** For a given descriptor $\mathbf{x_i}$ assigned to $k-$th cluster, it is firstly projected. A vector $\mathbf{s}$ is computed by

$$\mathbf{s} = P \times \mathbf{x_i} \quad (6)$$

  where $\mathbf{s} = [s_1(\mathbf{x_i}), s_2(\mathbf{x_i}), ..., s_{d_b}(\mathbf{x_i})]^T$. The final binary signature $\mathbf{b}(\mathbf{x_i}) = [b_1, b_2, ..., b_{d_b}]^T$ can be obtained by

$$b_i = \begin{cases} 1, & if \quad s_i - \tau_{k,i} > 0 \\ 0, & otherwise. \end{cases} \quad (7)$$

Based on the binary signature generation process, we can conclude that the key issue of the binary signature is the projection matrix. In order to distinguish from other methods, we refer to the original method as $\mathbf{B_0}$.

Motivated by original process, another two coding methods are deduced easily.

- $\mathbf{B_1}$ For all descriptors, we transform them into the binary signatures in the original space. In other words, the projection matrix P is set to I_{d_b} where I_{d_b} is a identity matrix with d_b dimension.

- $\mathbf{B_2}$ The descriptors associated with different visual word should be transformed into binary signatures by using different projection matrix. Thus a orthogonal projection matrix P_k for $k-$th visual word is generated and all the obtained matrices are different.

As shown in Fig. 1, different coding methods can lead to different partition of the subspace for each visual word. As a result, a descriptor associated with some visual word can be transformed into different binary signatures as different methods are used. This will have significant impact on the performance.

4.2 Regional subspace projection coding

Based on previous analysis, a better projection method is expected. For the objective $\mathbf{b_k}(\mathbf{x_i})$ for descriptor $\mathbf{x_i}$ associated with $k-$th visual word, the information loss in the transformation process should be reduced and we try to find a optimal projection matrix for each visual word space. Therefore, we try to minimize the objective function

$$\min_{\mathbf{P_k}, \mathbf{b_k}(\mathbf{x_i})} \sum_{\mathbf{x_i} \in \chi_\mathbf{k}} \|\mathbf{b_k}(\mathbf{x_i}) - \mathbf{P_k}(\mathbf{x_i} - \mathbf{c_k})\|_F^2 \quad (8)$$

where $\|.\|_F$ denotes the Frobenius norm, $\chi_\mathbf{k}$ is a set of descriptors assigned to $k-$th visual word. For the solution of this function, an optimal projection matrix $\mathbf{P_k}$ can be obtained. It's noteworthy that the SIFT descriptor is shifted firstly as suggested in [33]. Thus it is not necessary to minus the $\tau_\mathbf{k}$ since the median vector τ_k for shifted descriptors is very close to $\mathbf{0}$. To solve this objective function, a initial projection matrix $\mathbf{P_k}$ is necessary. We do not use a random matrix here in order to adapt to the training data for the visual word.

4.3 Initial projection matrix

Motivated by LLC-like methods [34, 37, 38, 39], the descriptors assigned to the same visual word are encoded by following objective function

$$\min_{\mathbf{y_i}} \sum_{\mathbf{x_i} \in \chi_\mathbf{k}} \{\|\mathbf{x_i} - \mathbf{M_k}\mathbf{y_i}\|_F^2 + \lambda d(\mathbf{x_i}, \mathbf{M_k})\|\mathbf{y_i}\|_2^2\} \quad (9)$$

where $d(\mathbf{x_i}, \mathbf{M_k})$ indicates the value of proximity measure of $\mathbf{x_i}$ to projection subspace and $\lambda > 0$ is a regularization parameter. Clearly the solution for this function can be decoupled into Ridge regression problems for the coding result $\mathbf{y_i}$. The solution is

$$\mathbf{y_i} = (\mathbf{M_k}^T\mathbf{M_k} + \lambda d(\mathbf{x_i}, \mathbf{M_k})\mathbf{I})^{-1}\mathbf{M_k}^T\mathbf{x_i} \quad (10)$$

where $\mathbf{I}$ is an identity matrix. Thus the initial projection matrix can be set to

$$\mathbf{P_k} = (\mathbf{M_k}^T\mathbf{M_k} + \lambda d(\mathbf{x_i}, \mathbf{M_k})\mathbf{I})^{-1}\mathbf{M_k}^T. \quad (11)$$

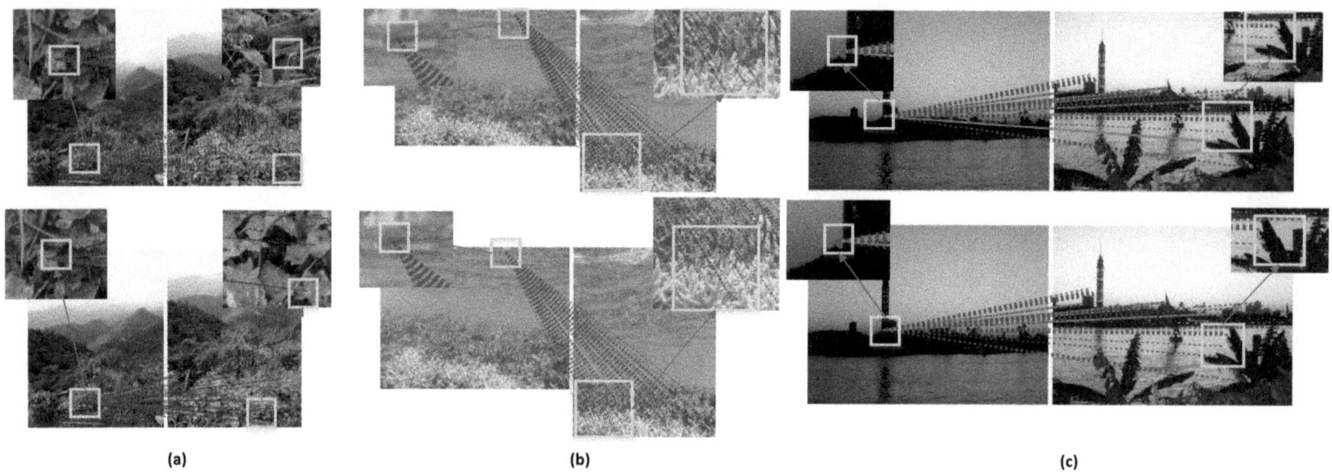

Figure 2: Three examples about the advantage of our method compared with baseline B_0. The top is the result for B_0 and the bottom is the result for our method. In addition, left image is the query image and the right is the annotated good result in dataset. Red line represents the right matching and blue line indicates the hamming distance is too large, thus the matching is filtered out. (a) For the baseline B_0, the rank is 11; the rank of our method is 1. (b) For the baseline B_0, the rank is 8; the rank of our method is 1. (c) For the baseline B_0, the rank is 12; the rank of our method is 1.

We use PCA matrix as the matrix which can represent the distribution of that data associated to visual word. On the one hand, PCA matrix is an orthogonal matrix. On the other hand, each vector of the matrix represents the principal direction of the data space. As shown in Fig. 1 (d), the PCA projection can partition the visual word space based on the distribution of data.

For the matrix $\mathbf{M_k}$, we firstly compute the covariance matrix Σ_k as follows

$$\Sigma_k = \frac{1}{d} \sum_{j=1,i=1} (\mathbf{x_j} - \mathbf{c_k})(\mathbf{x_i} - \mathbf{c_k})^T \quad (12)$$

where $\mathbf{x_j}$ and $\mathbf{x_i}$ are the descriptors assigned to the cluster center $\mathbf{c_k}$. In fact, $\mathbf{c_k}$ is also the mean of descriptors assigned to the $k-$th cluster. Then, we compute the eigenvalues and eigenvectors of Σ_k:

$$(\lambda_1^k, \lambda_2^k, ..., \lambda_d^k) = eigval(\Sigma_k) \quad (13)$$

$$(u_1^k, u_2^k, ..., u_d^k) = eigvect(\Sigma_k) \quad (14)$$

with $\lambda_1^k \geq \lambda_2^k \geq ... \geq \lambda_d^k$ and u_t^k associated with λ_t^k. In fact, u_t^k describes the principal direction of features distribution in the visual word subspace. Finally, we can form the matrix

$$\mathbf{M_k} = [u_1^k, u_2^k, ..., u_d^k] \quad (15)$$

where the obtained matrix $\mathbf{M_k}$ is of the size $d \times d$.

As the eigenvectors are orthogonal, we can simplify the Eq. 11 like this

$$\mathbf{P_k} = (1 + \lambda d(\mathbf{x_i}, \mathbf{M_k}))^{-1} \mathbf{M_k}^T. \quad (16)$$

In this case, we compute the proximity measure term

$$d(\mathbf{x_i}, \mathbf{M_k}) = \Sigma_{j=1}^{d} \|\mathbf{x_i} - \mathbf{M_k(j)}\|_2^2 \quad (17)$$

In order to simplify the computation, we set the parameter λ to 1 in all our experiments. The rows of matrix $\mathbf{P_k}$ are orthogonal since the rows of matrix $\mathbf{M_k}^T$ are orthogonal.

4.4 Solution for the objective function

For the initial projection matrix, the binary signature can be easily obtained through Eq. 7 where $\tau_\mathbf{k}$ is set to $\mathbf{0}$. It is clear and obvious that the original objective function can be solved by Coordinate Descent method to iteratively optimize projection matrix $\mathbf{P_k}$ based on existing $\mathbf{b_k}(\mathbf{x_i})$. But in practice, it is slow and can consume too much memory. In fact, the rows of initial matrix $\mathbf{P_k}$ are orthogonal. Thus we can further restrict the projection matrix which is always kept orthogonal. Therefore, we get the final objective function

$$\min_{\mathbf{P_k}} \|\mathbf{Z_k} - \mathbf{P_k}\mathbf{X_k}\|_F^2 \quad \text{s.t.} \quad \mathbf{P_k}\mathbf{P_k}^T = \mathbf{P_k}^T\mathbf{P_k} = I \quad (18)$$

where $\mathbf{Z_k} = [\mathbf{b_k}(\mathbf{x_1}), \mathbf{b_k}(\mathbf{x_2}), ...]$ and $\mathbf{X_k} = [\mathbf{x_1} - \mathbf{c_k}, \mathbf{x_2} - \mathbf{c_k}, ...]$. The solution for this objective function corresponds to the Orthogonal Procrustes problem [5]. Thus we firstly perform the singular value decomposition (SVD) of the $d \times d$ matrix $\mathbf{Z_k}\mathbf{X_k}^T$, i.e., $svd(\mathbf{Z_k}\mathbf{X_k}^T) = \mathbf{U_k}\Sigma_k\mathbf{V_k}^T$. Then the solution for Eq. 18 is $\mathbf{P_k} = \mathbf{U_k}\mathbf{V_k}^T$. For the final obtained matrix $\mathbf{P_k}$, we can select first d_b rows to form the optimal projection matrix which can be used for the **online step**.

In conclusion, when projection matrix is obtained, the binary signature is easily computed. Conversely, the projection matrix can be generated by solving the Orthogonal Procrustes problem. By this way, an optimal projection matrix can be generated after several iterations. Because each projection matrix corresponds to a visual word, we set iteration times to 10 in order to speed up the computation in our experiments. In fact, the projection matrix is optimized in **offline step**. This will not impact the computation speed for **online step** compared with original method. Thus our method is effective and efficient.

4.5 Discussion

We take the information loss into consideration and then propose a novel coding method which apply the different

Table 1: **Details of datasets in the experiments.**

Datasets	#images	#queries	#descriptors
Holidays	1491	500	4,454,440($thres$=500)
			12,926,355($thres$=100)
Oxford5k	5062	55	15,884,280($thres$=500)
			40,016,075($thres$=100)

projection to different visual word space. Our method concentrates on the data distribution of regional subspace, i.e., visual word space. Compared with the baseline $\mathbf{B_0}$, our proposed method not only try to find a optimal projection matrix for corresponding visual word space but also make the binary signature being generated closely based on the distribution of the data.

As shown in Fig. 2, the three examples are illustrated. For the left query image, an interest feature point is selected randomly. The weights of hamming distance between the descriptor of this point and all the descriptors assigned to the same visual word are computed. Then we can find that

- (a) The wrong matching for the interest point from a "leaf" and an interest point from "tree trunk" can be rectified by our proposed method.
- (b) In the result image, the descriptors associated with the descriptors assigned to the same visual word are wrong intuitively. Thus our method can help filter out these wrong matching.
- (c) In this example the wrong matching points are filtered out partly. This is beneficial to the retrieval result.

All in all, our proposed method is effective and powerful to image retrieval system. The experiments can further demonstrate that our method yields competitive results with the state-of-the-art methods.

5. EXPERIMENTS

5.1 Experimental setup

In order to evaluate our proposed method, we perform experiments on two benchmark datasets, i.e., Holidays [11] and Oxford5k [28]. These two benchmark datasets are used in many previous works.

- **Holidays** This dataset contains 1491 high resolution personal holiday photos with a variety of scene types. The retrieval accuracy is measured by mean average precision (mAP) after removing the query image from the ranked list. For each query, a few (mostly 1 or 2) ground truth images are annotated.
- **Oxford5k** Oxford 5K dataset was collected from Flickr and a total number of 5062 images have been obtained. This dataset has been generated as a comprehensive ground truth for 11 distinct landmarks, each containing 5 queries. In total there are 55 query images. Similar to Holidays dataset, mAP is also used to evaluate the performance.

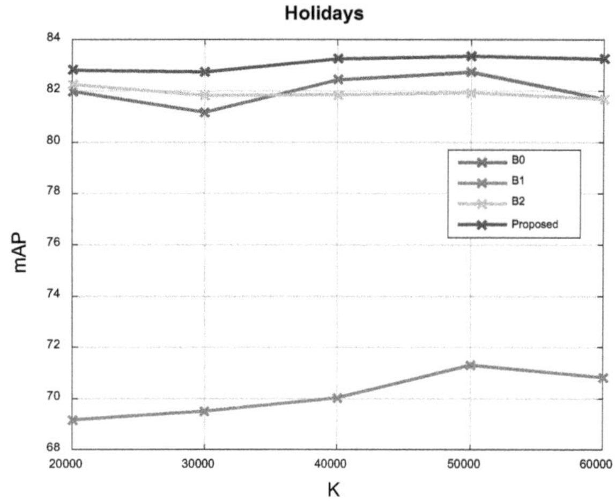

Figure 3: The comparison between proposed method and baselines on large vocabularies for dataset Holidays.

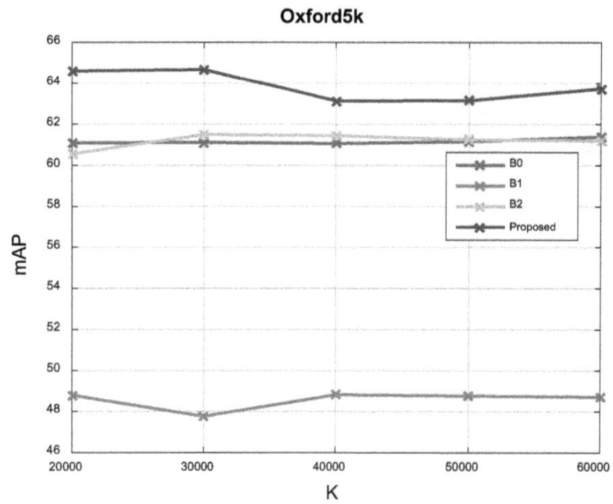

Figure 4: The comparison between proposed method and baselines on large vocabularies for dataset Oxford5k.

The details of datasets are reported in Table 1. Moreover, in order to make a fair comparison with state-of-the-art techniques, we follow the experimental implementations of [11, 20]. In particular, the implementation details are listed as follows.

- The Hessian-Affine detector and the SIFT descriptor are employed for local feature detection and description as suggested in [11]. It should be noted that most of the following evaluations are based on the default detector threshold value (as shown in Table 1,$thres$ = 500). The large sets of features are also used by lowering the detector threshold ($thres$ = 100). Additionally, we follow [1] to post-process the SIFT descriptors and average IDF [19] is used in our experiments.
- The vocabulary is trained by Approximate K-means (AKM) method as suggested in [28, 20]. Quantifica-

Table 2: **Retrieval results on large and small set of descriptors.**

Dataset	methods	Small		Large	
		SA	MA	SA	MA
Holidays	B0	78.36	81.57	86.41	87.49
	Ours	80.23	84.22	87.77	**89.29**
Oxford5k	B0	56.65	62.77	66.37	72.00
	Ours	57.93	64.73	67.77	**73.90**

tion applies the approximate nearest neighbors (ANN) indexing structure. The train data is an independent dataset Flickr6k.

- For the parameters σ and h_t in Eq. (3), we set $\sigma = 20$ and $h_t = 50$ in all the experiments.
- In order to make a fair comparison, both of the spatial re-ranking and query expansion techniques are not implemented by all the comparative approaches for performing experiments.

5.2 Comparison with baselines

We first compare our method with baselines $\mathbf{B_0}$, $\mathbf{B_1}$ and $\mathbf{B_2}$ as shown in Fig. 3, Fig. 4, Fig. 5 and Fig. 6. we report the results on both large vocabularies and small vocabularies. From the results we can find that

- For the original space (Baseline $\mathbf{B_1}$), the projection process is necessary since the performance of $\mathbf{B_1}$ is far inferior to other methods.
- **$\mathbf{B_2}$ versus $\mathbf{B_0}$** These two methods exhibit similar results on both large vocabularies and small vocabularies.
- **Our method** It is clear that our method has better performance than other methods, especially on small vocabularies. In particular, take vocabulary size=64 as example, the improvements for $\mathbf{B_0}$ and $\mathbf{B_1}$ are nearly the same 15% for Holidays dataset, and 19.39%, 14.29 for Oxford5k dataset. We speculate that there are more data associated with a visual word for small vocabulary so that a better projection matrix is learned for this visual word space.
- **Vocabulary size** Obviously, the vocabulary size have significant impact on the effectiveness of methods. As the vocabulary size increases, the retrieval mAP is also enhanced and is basically constant for very large vocabulary. In addition, our method exceeds other baseline methods consistent for all vocabulary sizes.

5.3 Impact of multiple assignment and number of bits

Multiple assignment [11] can further reduce the quantization error for improving the performance. In addition, the parameter d_b in Eq. 5 determines the length of obtained binary signature at last. For a short binary signature, the speed of computation for hamming distance can be boosted significantly. This will also speed up the computation for whole image retrieval process.

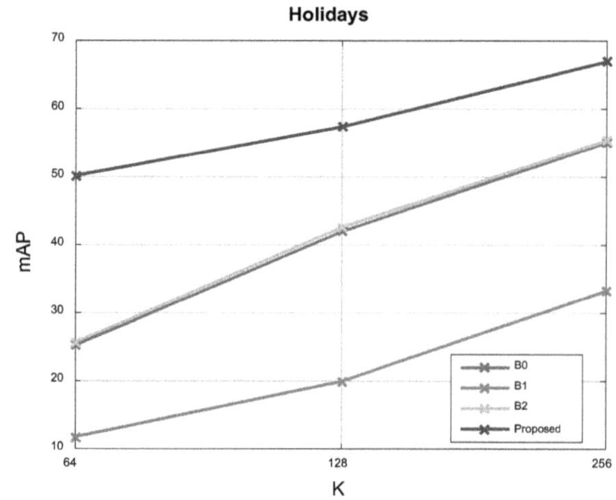

Figure 5: The comparison between proposed method and baselines on small vocabularies for dataset Holidays.

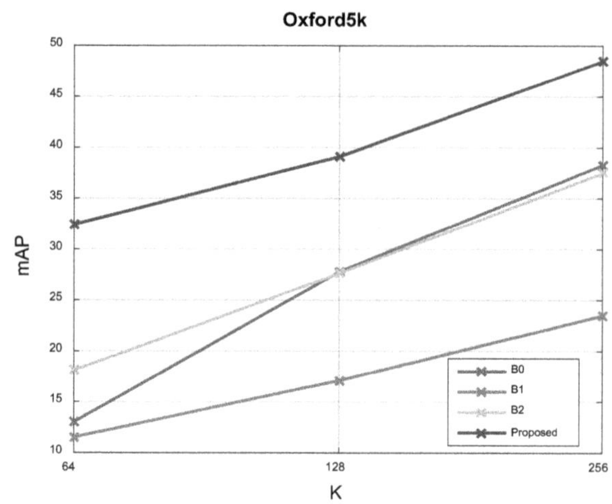

Figure 6: The comparison between proposed method and baselines on small vocabularies for dataset Oxford5k.

We present the results for the impact of multiple assignment and number of bits in Fig. 7 and Fig. 8. Meanwhile, the impact of single assignment is also shown. Firstly, it is clear that the longer binary signature is of better performance for retrieval since less information is lost in the binary generation process. Then we find that multiple assignment has positive effect on binary signature with 128 bits but negative influence on other number of bits.

5.4 Large size of descriptors

The large size of descriptors can represent and describe the image better. By lowering the extracting threshold, we can get a large set of local descriptors, which is presented in Table 1. The results on single assignment (SA) and multiple assignment (MA) are illustrated in Table 2 on both large and small set of descriptors. Here we set the MA to 5 in

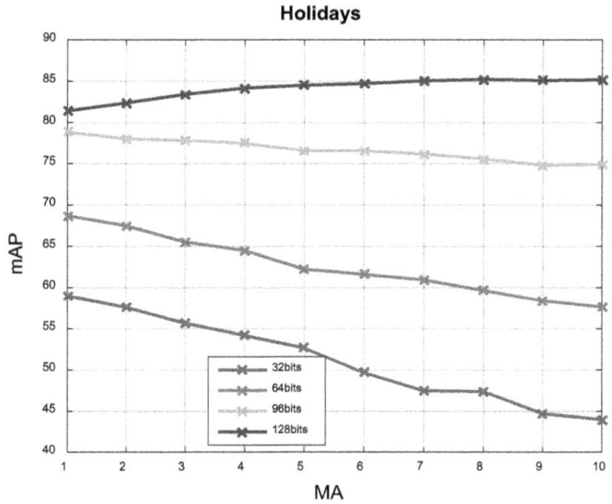

Figure 7: The impact of multiple assignment and number of bits for the performance on Holidays dataset.

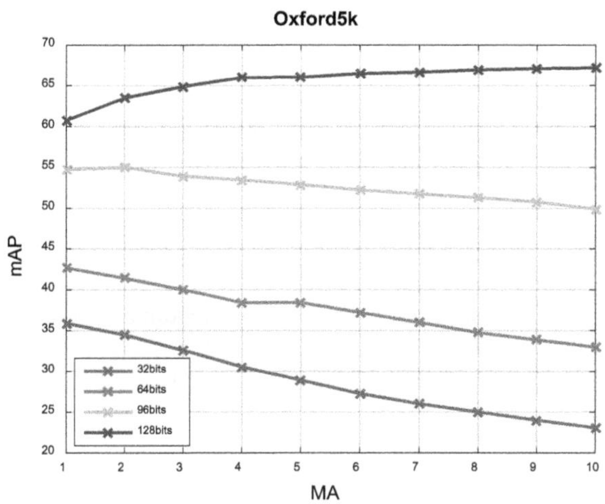

Figure 8: The impact of multiple assignment and number of bits for the performance on Oxford5k dataset.

our experiments and vocabulary size is set to 50000. And we use 128 bits as length of binary signature.

It can be observed that the mAP performances achieved on large set of descriptors are higher than that on small set of descriptors. Multiple assignment also has good effect on the result. In addition, our proposed method have better performance than original method.

5.5 Comparison to the state of the art

As shown in Table 3, we compare out method with a series of state-of-the-art methods. It's noteworthy that some post-processing techniques such as spatial re-ranking and query expansion are not taken into consideration. In addition, we mainly compare our methods with HE-like methods. It is obvious that our method outperforms other methods. This will prove the strength of our work again.

In fact, our method can be easily embedded into the pipeline with some post-processing methods. In this work we just focus on the improvement of HE framework. We will further combine our work with some good post-processing methods.

Table 3: Performance comparison with state-of-the-art methods without post-processing techniques.

Methods	MA	K	Holidays	Oxford5k
HE [12]		200k	74.5	51.7
HE [12]	×	200k	77.5	56.1
HE+BURST [16]		20k	80.7	59.6
HE+BURST [16]	×	20k	83.9	64.7
Nested SIFT [36]		1M	-	72.0
AHE+BURST [8]		20k	79.4	66.0
AHE+BURST [8]	×	20k	81.9	70.4
HE+Bayes[20]	×	20k	81.9	65.0
HE+coupled MI[21]	×	20k	84.0	-
Ours (Small)	×	50k	84.2	63.2
Ours (Large)	×	50k	**89.3**	**73.9**

6. CONCLUSION

In this paper, we present a novel projection method which takes the data distribution of each visual word into consideration. Compared with original method, the projection matrix is not generated randomly firstly. In addition, an optimal projection matrix is computed for each visual word space by optimizing the objective function. We also demonstrate that the projection is necessary for binary signature generation process since the direct signature generation in original space exhibits very inferior result. The experiments on two benchmark datasets show that our method yields very competitive and effective result.

In future, we will make effort to combine our method with some post-processing techniques which are helpful to image retrieval. More attempts will be made to apply our method to other HE-like methods such as ASMK and SMK.

7. ACKNOWLEDGMENTS

This project was supported by Shenzhen Peacock Plan (20130408-183003656).

8. REFERENCES

[1] R. Arandjelović and A. Zisserman. Three things everyone should know to improve object retrieval. In *CVPR*, 2012.

[2] R. Arandjelovic and A. Zisserman. All about vlad. In *CVPR*, 2013.

[3] X. Boix, G. Roig, C. Leistner, and L. V. Gool. Nested sparse quantization for efficient feature coding. *ECCV*, 2012.

[4] Y. Cai, W. Tong, L. Yang, and A. G. Hauptmann. Constrained keypoint quantization: towards better bag-of-words model for large-scale multimedia retrieval. In *ICMR*, 2012.

[5] R. Everson. Orthogonal, but not orthonormal, procrustes problems. *Advances in Computational Mathematics*, 1997.

[6] M. S. Extremal, J. Matas, O. Chum, M. Urban, and T. Pajdla. Robust wide baseline stereo from. In *BMVC*, 2002.

[7] V. Gemert, J. C., Veenman, C. J., Smeulders, A. W. M., and J. M. Geusebroek. Visual word ambiguity. *IEEE Transactions on Pattern Analysis and Machine Intelligence*, 32(7):1271–1283, 2010.

[8] M. Jain, H. Jégou, and P. Gros. Asymmetric hamming embedding: taking the best of our bits for large scale image search. In *ACM MM*, 2011.

[9] P. James, C. Ondrej, I. Michael, S. Josef, and Z. Andrew. Lost in quantization: Improving particular object retrieval in large scale image databases. In *CVPR*, 2008.

[10] H. Jégou and O. Chum. Negative evidences and co-occurences in image retrieval: The benefit of pca and whitening. In *ECCV*, 2012.

[11] H. Jégou, M. Douze, and C. Schmid. Hamming embedding and weak geometric consistency for large scale image search. In *ECCV*, 2008.

[12] H. Jégou, M. Douze, and C. Schmid. Improving bag-of-features for large scale image search. *International Journal of Computer Vision*, 87(3):316–336, 2010.

[13] H. Jégou, H. Harzallah, and C. Schmid. A contextual dissimilarity measure for accurate and efficient image search. In *CVPR*, 2007.

[14] H. Jégou, D. M, and S. C. Aggregating local descriptors into a compact image representation. In *CVPR*, 2010.

[15] H. Jégou, F. Perronnin, M. Douze, J. Sanchez, P. Perez, and C. Schmid. Aggregating local image descriptors into compact codes. *Pattern Analysis and Machine Intelligence*, 2012.

[16] M. Jégou, Hervéand Douze and C. Schmid. On the burstiness of visual elements. In *CVPR*, 2009.

[17] Z. Liang, W. Shengjin, and T. Qi. Coupled binary embedding for large-scale image retrieval. *Image Processing, IEEE Transactions on*, 23(8):3368–3380, 2014.

[18] Z. Liang, W. Shengjin, and T. Qi. Lp-norm idf for scalable image retrieval. *Image Processing, IEEE Transactions on*, 23(8):3604–3617, 2014.

[19] Z. Liang, W. Shengjin, L. Ziqiong, and T. Qi. Lp-norm idf for large scale image search. In *CVPR*, 2013.

[20] Z. Liang, W. Shengjin, L. Ziqiong, and T. Qi. Bayes merging of multiple vocabularies for scalable image retrieval. In *CVPR*, 2014.

[21] Z. Liang, W. Shengjin, L. Ziqiong, and T. Qi. Packing and padding: Coupled multi-index for accurate image retrieval. In *CVPR*, 2014.

[22] D. Lowe. Distinctive image features from scale-invariant keypoints. *International Journal of Computer Vision*, 2004.

[23] O. C. Michal Perdóch and J. Matas. Efficient representation of local geometry for large scale object retrieval. In *CVPR*, 2009.

[24] K. Mikolajczyk and C. Schmid. Scale & affine invariant interest point detectors. *International Journal of Computer Vision*, 2004.

[25] D. Nistér and H. Stewénius. Scalable recognition with a vocabulary tree. In *CVPR*, 2006.

[26] F. Perronnin and C. R. Dance. Fisher kernels on visual vocabularies for image categorization. In *CVPR*, 2007.

[27] F. Perronnin, J. SÃąnchez, and T. Mensink. Improving the fisher kernel for large-scale image classification. In *ECCV*, 2010.

[28] J. Philbin, O. Chum, M. Isard, J. Sivic, and A. Zisserman. Object retrieval with large vocabularies and fast spatial matching. In *CVPR*, 2007.

[29] G. Salton and C. Buckley. Term-weighting approaches in automatic text retrieval. *Information Processing and Management*, 24(5):513–523, 1988.

[30] M. Shi, Y. Avrithis, and H. Jégou. Early burst detection for memory-efficient image retrieval. In *CVPR*, 2015.

[31] J. Sivic and A. Zisserman. Video google: A text retrieval approach to object matching in videos. In *ICCV*, 2003.

[32] G. Tolias, Y. Avrithis, and H. Jégou. To aggregate or not to aggregate: Selective match kernels for image search. In *ICCV*, 2013.

[33] G. Tolias and H. Jégou. Visual query expansion with or without geometry: Refining local descriptors by feature aggregation. *Pattern Recognition*, 2014.

[34] J. Wang, J. Yang, K. Yu, F. Lv, T. Huang, and Y. Gong. Locality-constrained linear coding for image classification. In *CVPR*, 2010.

[35] X. Wang, M. Yang, T. Cour, S. Zhu, K. Yu, and T. Han. Contextual weighting for vocabulary tree based image retrieval. In *ICCV*, 2011.

[36] P. Xu, L. Zhang, K. Yang, and H. Yao. Nested-sift for efficient image matching and retrieval. *IEEE MultiMedia*, 20(3):34–46, 2013.

[37] J. Yang, K. Yu, and T. Huang. Efficient highly over-complete sparse coding using a mixture model. *ECCV*, 2010.

[38] K. Yu and T. Zhang. Improved local coordinate coding using local tangents. In *ICML*, 2010.

[39] K. Yu, T. Zhang, and Y. Gong. Nonlinear learning using local coordinate coding. In *NIPS*, 2009.

[40] S. Zhang, Q. Huang, G. Hua, S. Jiang, W. Gao, and Q. Tian. Building contextual visual vocabulary for large-scale image applications. In *ACM MM*, 2010.

[41] S. Zhang, Q. Tian, G. Hua, Q. Huang, and S. Li. Descriptive visual words and visual phrases for image applications. In *ACM MM*, 2009.

[42] L. Zheng and S. Wang. Visual phraselet: Refining spatial constraints for large scale image search. *Signal Processing Letters, IEEE*, 20(4):391–394, 2013.

[43] W. Zhou, Y. Lu, H. Li, Y. Song, and Q. Tian. Spatial coding for large scale partial-duplicate web image search. In *ACM MM*, 2010.

Scaling Group Testing Similarity Search

Ahmet Iscen
Inria
Rennes, France
ahmet.iscen@inria.fr

Laurent Amsaleg
CNRS-IRISA
Rennes, France
laurent.amsaleg@irisa.fr

Teddy Furon
Inria
Rennes, France
teddy.furon@inria.fr

ABSTRACT

The large dimensionality of modern image feature vectors, up to thousands of dimensions, is challenging the high dimensional indexing techniques. Traditional approaches fail at returning good quality results within a response time that is usable in practice. However, similarity search techniques inspired by the group testing framework have recently been proposed in an attempt to specifically defeat the curse of dimensionality. Yet, group testing does not scale and fails at indexing very large collections of images because its internal procedures analyze an excessively large fraction of the indexed data collection. This paper identifies these difficulties and proposes extensions to the group testing framework for similarity searches that allow to handle larger collections of feature vectors. We demonstrate that it can return high quality results much faster compared to state-of-the-art group testing strategies when indexing truly high-dimensional features that are indeed hardly indexable with traditional indexing approaches.

1. INTRODUCTION

Despite several decades of intensive activity, the field of image retrieval and similarity search is still very active, with recent and strong contributions to the domains of image description as well as high-dimensional indexing. The state-of-the-art for extracting low-level features from images made significant progresses during the last few years. On one hand, researchers designed sophisticated aggregation techniques for local features [2, 3, 12, 15]. Such features were limiting the ability to scale to indexing very large collections, as managing millions or billions of local descriptors is very resource consuming. Aggregation turns the many local descriptors of one image into a unique higher-dimensional vector by taking advantage of the locality and co-variant properties of the local features, preserving most of the discriminative power of the original features. On the other hand, another recent and even more promising progress uses the response of a deep learning architecture as a global descriptor [3], or aggregates the activation of intermediate layers into a descriptor [8].

Overall, such techniques facilitate scaling to larger collections as there are much fewer descriptors to manage. Yet, indexing these descriptors is required for efficiently answering queries, but this turns out to be very challenging. Those (modern) descriptors typically lie within extremely high-dimensional spaces; not only their representational dimension is high as they have thousands of components, but their intrinsic dimensionality is also high as most of these components are needed for discriminability.

In turn, most of the traditional high-dimensional indexing techniques fail due to the curse of dimensionality [19]. The partitioning strategies they all use eventually fail at preserving neighbors in the same partitions, forcing the search procedure to scan many partitions in order to determine good candidates for a query [13]. This extensive scanning is very inefficient and dramatically increases resource consumption and response time.

Similarity search techniques inspired by the group testing framework have recently been proposed in an attempt to specifically defeat the curse of dimensionality. Group testing has found applications in pharmacology, genome screening and has first been adapted to image retrieval by Shi et al. [18] and then extended by Iscen et al. [10]. In this context, group testing specifically exploits the properties underpinning truly high-dimensional spaces: the correlation between two random unit vectors concentrates around zero as their dimension increases, facilitating by contrast the identification of correlated (hence similar) vectors.

Like some traditional high-dimensional indexing schemes, group testing first forms overlapping groups of features and computes a representative vector for each group. Then, at query time, a test is performed on each group by checking the query against the representative vector. The output of the test reveals how likely the query matches one of the features *in* that group. The decoding step identifies some candidate features by analyzing all the test outputs. A final verification step computes the true similarities of the candidate features with the query, and gives back a ranking from which it is easy to return the final result to the user.

Compared to more traditional high-dimensional indexing methods, the key differences with group testing are in the group formation strategies, the procedure to compute representatives and the decoding process that identifies candidates features from the test outputs. Works [18] and [10] prove group testing is particularly robust at higher dimensionalities and allows to return high-quality results faster

ICMR'16, June 06 - 09, 2016, New York, NY, USA

ACM ISBN 978-1-4503-4359-6/16/06. . . $15.00

DOI: http://dx.doi.org/10.1145/2911996.2912010

than the sequential scan, which is often the de facto preferred method to run at high-dimension.

The group testing paradigm as it is applied in [18] and [10] can hardly be scaled to searching very large image collections. First, too many tests are performed at query time when checking the query against the group representatives — the larger the collection, the more such representatives, which limits scalability. Second, unnecessary computations are done at decoding time because most of the tests indeed yield negative output.

This paper tackles these difficulties and proposes extensions to the group testing in order to handle larger collections of feature vectors. Specifically, it shows that it is surprisingly worth indexing the representatives, allowing to very quickly identify the few positive tests. It also shows that these few positive tests not only deliver enough information to identify the good candidates, but also accelerate the decoding step. In terms of quality, it shows that the group testing technique proposed here performs almost as well as other traditional indexing strategies (FLANN [14], LSH [5, 7, 9]) at a much lower cost, however.

The paper is organized as follows. Section 2 briefly reviews prior works on group testing and sketches traditional high-dimensional indexing methods such as the ones implemented in the FLANN library. Section 3 presents sGT, which stands for *scalable Group Testing*. We detail its grouping and searching strategies designed to better cope with large scale image collections. The evaluation in Section 4 shows the interest of sGT in a large-scale scenario. Section 5 concludes the paper.

2. RELATED WORK

Similarity search for image retrieval often boils down to running a k-nearest neighbor process. Assume that the dataset $\mathbf{X}$ is composed of N d-dimensional vectors $\{\mathbf{x}_i\}_{i=1}^N$ such that $\|\mathbf{x}_i\| = 1, \forall 1 \le i \le N$. The similarity between two vectors $\mathbf{x}_i$ and $\mathbf{x}_j$ can be measured with the scalar product $\mathbf{x}_i^\top \mathbf{x}_j$ when all vectors are unit normalized.

2.1 Group testing

Group testing has been used in other computer science fields in the past to solve typical 'needles in a haystack' problems. It did not receive attention in the image retrieval community until the pioneering work of Shi et al. [18].

Their algorithm randomly assigns each feature to m multiple groups, and each group consists of n features. This gives M groups in total, such that

$$M = \frac{mN}{n}. \tag{1}$$

The representative vector for each group is simply the sum of features belonging to that group. More precisely, let $[\mathbf{x}_i]_{\mathcal{M}_j}$ be the $d \times n$ matrix storing the features of jth group, then the representative vector $\{\mathbf{y}_j\}_{j=1}^M$ is computed as:

$$\mathbf{y}_j = \sum_{\mathbf{x}_i \in \mathcal{M}_j} \mathbf{x}_i. \tag{2}$$

At search time, the query is compared to all the representative vectors. Assume that $\mathbf{Y} \in \mathbb{R}^{d \times M}$ is the matrix containing the representative vectors in each column. Then, M group similarities for a given query $\mathbf{q}$ are calculated as:

$$\mathbf{v} = [v_1, ..., v_M]^\top = \mathbf{Y}^\top \mathbf{q}. \tag{3}$$

The group similarity v_j is seen as a test output measure roughly indicating whether or not the query is matching one of the features of the j-th group. This step has a complexity in $O(Md)$.

The score u_i reveals how likely feature i matches the query. It is simply the sum of the group similarities it belongs to:

$$u_i = \sum_{j \in \mathcal{L}_i} v_j, \tag{4}$$

where $\mathcal{L}_i$ is the set of groups where the i-th feature is stored. This step has a complexity in $O(NM)$.

Finally, a shortlist of size $R << N$ is created based on the top scores of $\mathbf{u}$, and a verification step reranks these candidate features based on their true similarities with the query. This final step has a complexity in $O(Rd)$.

Another more recent work [10] optimizes the offline construction of the representative vectors by assuming that the query is a quasi-copy of a feature stored in some groups. It uses the Moore-Penrose pseudo-inverse [17]:

$$\mathbf{y}_j = [\mathbf{x}_i]_{\mathcal{M}_j} ([\mathbf{x}_i]_{\mathcal{M}_j}^\top [\mathbf{x}_i]_{\mathcal{M}_j})^{-1} \mathbf{1}_n. \tag{5}$$

The authors show this is superior to the simple *sum* construction that is used in equation (2), theoretically and empirically, especially as the dimensionality d of the features grows. The decoding step is also optimized by applying the Neyman-Pearson hypothesis test in the form of $u_i = \sum_{j \in \mathcal{L}_i} f_j(v_j)$. The total complexity is unchanged.

2.2 FLANN

FLANN is a well-known approximate similarity search library which implements various high-dimensional indexing strategies [14]. Two of these strategies are the randomized k-d tree and the priority search k-means tree algorithms.

The classic k-d tree algorithm [6] splits the space according to the dimension with the highest variance. In contrast, FLANN's k-d tree splits the space along a dimension chosen randomly from the top D dimensions that have the highest variance. In addition, FLANN creates a forest of random k-d trees that are all probed at query time. The relevant leaves identified in the trees are scanned for nearest neighbors, and that form of multiprobing helps the performance.

The priority search k-means tree algorithm recursively clusters the data points in K clusters at each level of the hierarchy of centroids, until the number of points in a cluster is less than K. At query time, the branches of the hierarchy are explored according to a distance-based priority.

2.3 Discussion

We have briefly described some background work. We now discuss the cons (first) and then the pros of using group testing versus using traditional similarity search techniques when indexing large collections of high-dimensional features like Fisher vectors [15], VLAD [2], T-embedding [12] or other CNN-based [3, 8] descriptors. This discussion ends with a list of requirements that group testing approaches must meet in order to cope with scale, i.e., indexing very large collections of high-dimensional vectors.

Even though it is a state-of-art library, FLANN does not perform well for *truly* high-dimensional data, as acknowledged by its authors [14]. The experiments described later confirm that the effectiveness of FLANN decreases when indexing such high-dimensional descriptors. It is only possible to return high-quality results, however, at the expense of a dramatic increase in the response time. This is caused by FLANN performing a very large number of checks to eventually gather enough good neighbors. This problem is not specific to FLANN but caused by the curse of dimensionality whose effects are mitigated with extensive multiprobing.

In contrast, group testing is less sensitive to the curse of dimensionality and better handles high-dimensional features. Yet, its recent application to image search [10, 18] experiences scalability problems. First, group testing has to compare the query to all the representatives group vectors and that comparison is currently done using a linear scan. This is clearly not scalable when the number of representative group vectors grows, which is the case when indexing larger collections of images. Indexing larger collections (N grows) means for [10, 18] that M as to grow too. At scale, this comparison step becomes excessively costly.

By construction, only a handful of group representative vectors are meaningful for a given query, hence most comparisons between the query and the group representative vectors are done in a pure waste. Quickly identifying the best representatives is therefore a key requirement for designing scalable group testing approaches.

More importantly, the effectiveness of the group testing proposed in [10, 18] vanishes as N grows. Compared to a linear scan of the features in $O(Nd)$, the gain in complexity (as detailed in Sect. 2.1) is:

$$\gamma = \frac{M}{N} + \frac{M}{d} + \frac{R}{N}. \tag{6}$$

The second term shows that having $M << N$ is not sufficient: At scale, M will become larger than d, spoiling the gain in complexity. This is solely due to the decoding procedure of [18] and [10].

Furthermore, equation (4) is likely to sum extremely small values for the v_j associated to the representatives that turn out not to be relevant for a query. Therefore, identifying the best representatives and ignoring the others, i.e., setting their v_j to zero, diminishes the cost of decoding as many factors can now be excluded from the sum in equation (4). It is not needed to take into account similarities to *all* representatives as [18] and [10] do.

Finally, the contributions in [18] and [10] compute the true similarities between the query and $R << N$ features. According to [18] and [10], R is typically equal to $N/10$, which, at scale, becomes prohibitively expensive as well. Therefore, the value of R has to be significantly reduced to allow scaling. Works [18] and [10] can not easily diminish R without severely endangering quality. They essentially keep M small to control the cost of evaluating equation (4) (which corresponds also to the second term of (6)). This is done by choosing m small(see eq. (1)). This implies that [18] and [10] have a rather small number m of evidences (i.e., test outputs v_j) to evaluate the likelihood u_i of being a match. Very efficiently identifying the best representatives allows to use a larger value for m which strengthens the redundancy between the groups.

Consequently, the likelihood scores of the database features identified become more reliable because these scores are computed from more test outputs. For the non matching features, their likelihoods become less noisy, i.e., shrink to zero, because $v_j = 0$ for irrelevant representative group vectors. This improves the reliability of the decoding and makes possible the use of a lighter verification step, i.e., using a small value for R.

On the pro side, the lessons learnt from the two group testing papers are the following ones. The most salient property of the group testing framework is its capacity to cope with truly high-dimensional datasets. This has been demonstrated in [18] where the performance improves as the dimensionality of the features increases. Iscen et al. [10] show that the Moore-Penrose pseudo-inverse construction (see eq. (5)) produces more informative representatives compared to the simple sum that is used in [18]. [10] also demonstrates that representatives are more informative when some form of similarity between features is used to weakly guide the creation of the groups instead of relying on a pure random strategy. They derived groups from running a k-means which clusters similar features in groups of very different cardinalities. However, reducing the unbalanced cardinalities between these groups is key to avoid similarities being dominated by overcrowded groups.

Taking the lessons learnt from [10, 18] for granted, the above discussion allows to isolate two main requirements that must be addressed in order to design scalable group testing techniques:

- **Requirement R1**: Quick identification of the best representatives for a query and removal of the bottleneck from eq. (4) by ignoring irrelevant v_j values.
- **Requirement R2**: Increasing the groups redundancy to improve quality (m) allowing to decrease the number of true similarities calculations (R).

3. SCALING GROUP TESTING

This section describes the extensions to the group testing framework in order to facilitate scaling. The resulting extended group testing algorithm is called sGT which stands for scalable group testing. We detail how the learnt lessons and the requirements detailed above can be addressed.

3.1 Even-Size Groups of Similar Vectors

We first address the lessons learnt from [10, 18]. In order to create even-size groups of similar features, we propose to use the random k-d tree algorithm from FLANN. That algorithm gradually cuts in two equal subsets the collection of vectors to be indexed, until the bottom leaf of the k-d tree contains one unique feature. It is easy to navigate down a fully constructed k-d tree and identify the node where the two child sub-trees each consist of a total of n vectors. This is where we take control of the algorithm in the FLANN library: All the vectors below that particular node now go into two distinct groups. In order to have each feature assigned to m groups, we simply launch the creation of m random k-d trees.

Once the groups have been formed this way, we compute the pseudo-inverse for each group in order to determine its representative (see eq. (5)). It is important to note that we take control of the *construction process* of the k-d trees in FLANN. Once the representatives are stored, the k-d trees are no longer needed and they are deallocated.

Please note that we have taken control of the k-d tree construction *per se* and there is nothing really specific to FLANN here. Using FLANN is handy because it is a state-of-the-art library anyone can download, facilitating the reproduction of our methodology, and because it better copes with high-dimensionality (compared to the regular k-d tree) thanks to his enhanced dimension splitting criterion.

3.2 Indexing Representative Vectors

We then address requirements **R1** and **R2**. It is rather straightforward to insert the group representative vectors into an index in order to circumvent the linear scanning (see eq. (3)) limiting the scalability of [18] and [10]. Instead of determining the similarities to all M representatives, it is worth probing the index and get back the k representatives with the highest similarities to the query.

First, this is faster especially because most modern high-dimensional techniques are approximate and trade response-time for efficiency. Second, it is safe to force to zero the similarities v_j between the query and the $(M-k)$ representatives that remain. Since k is typically orders of magnitude smaller than M, $(M-k)$ is a large value which saves a lot of resource consumption when running the decoding step: many $v_j = 0$, making the computation of equation (4) very sparse. Requirement **R1** is hereby addressed.

Two comments are in order, however. First, most high-dimensional indexing schemes work for Euclidean distances. This is the case for some of the algorithms implemented within the FLANN library. It is not very complicated to translate a L_2 distance into a dot product as it is needed to evaluate equation (3). We L_2−normalize the representative vectors to be compatible with the query whose norm equals one. We ask FLANN to index the database of these normalized representative vectors $\bar{\mathbf{y}}_j = \mathbf{y}_j/\|\mathbf{y}_j\|$. For the k nearest neighbors output by FLANN, we compute the similarities:

$$v_j = \frac{2 - \|\bar{\mathbf{y}}_j - \mathbf{q}\|^2}{2}\|\mathbf{y}_j\| = (\bar{\mathbf{y}}_j^\top \mathbf{q})\|\mathbf{y}_j\| = \mathbf{y}_j^\top \mathbf{q}. \quad (7)$$

This conversion needs the extra storage of one scalar, $\|\mathbf{y}_j\|$, per representative vector. After obtaining these similarities, we compute (4) and re-rank R top scoring features based on their true similarities with the query.

Second, indexing the M representatives facilitates increasing m, which is the number of groups each feature is assigned to. This addresses the requirement **R2** and also positively impacts the quality of the results returned by group testing indexing algorithms. The time it takes to retrieve k representatives indeed does not change that much when M increases. It is anyway much faster than the linear scan. Works [18] and [10] had to set m to a small value in order to reduce the complexity of their implementations when analyzing the M representatives. They had a *complexity* objective. In contrast, indexing these representatives to quickly retrieve k of them allows us to set m such that it is possible to meet a *quality* objective. At last, this better quality yields a more reliable ranking of the candidates. The true matching features are ranked higher. This allows us to reduce the size R of the shortlist and to decrease the complexity of the final verification step.

3.3 Summary

We argue that it is possible to scale group testing high-dimensional approaches provided that these lessons learnt from [10, 18] are enforced and the two requirements presented above are addressed. We therefore implemented within the sGT algorithm a group construction strategy based on k-d tree to marry fixed size groups and some similarity between the vectors of each group. sGT also includes the implementation of the indexing of the representative vectors to quickly identify the k best representatives. This, in turn, allows to increment the redundancy of vectors in groups (m), improving quality. The candidate vectors being more accurate, it allows to decrease the length of the candidate list R, which saves response time.

The next section demonstrates that these extensions indeed make group testing approaches easier to scale to larger collections of very high-dimensional vectors.

4. EXPERIMENTS

This section basically compares the behavior of three high-dimensional indexing schemes. Two of them are state-of-the-art: the first technique is the traditional k-d tree based index from the FLANN library [14]. The second technique is our own implementation of the original group testing scheme proposed by Shi et al. [18]. The third technique is sGT which includes the various extensions discussed in the previous section aiming at better handling large scale collections.

We first describe our experimental setup before moving to the experiments themselves where the comparison of the behavior of the three techniques is made using the mean average precision and running time indicators.

4.1 Experimental Setup

We use a public large-scale image retrieval benchmark dataset known as Holidays+Flickr1M for our experiments. This dataset is the combination of the original Holidays image dataset [11] with 1 million distractor images from Flickr1M [10]. The dataset contains N=1,001,491 images in total. The image retrieval quality is evaluated with the provided ground-truth for 500 queries and measured by mean average precision (mAP).

To facilitate the direct comparison with existing methods [10, 18], we use the same T-embedding features [12] with d = 1,920 which corresponds to a codebook vocabulary of size 16. These features are made available online.[1] Following the pipeline presented in the original paper [12], we post-process these features with power-law normalization, setting $\alpha = 0.5$.

4.2 Image Features are Hardly Indexable

We first show that the T-embedding features extracted from the images can hardly be indexed due to their dimensionality. This motivates the need for alternative high-dimensional indexing schemes such as group testing based approaches better coping with the curse of dimensionality.

We started by using the linear search option of FLANN in order to determine the quality and the time it takes when using the 500 queries. It takes 901 seconds to run the entire query set, and the resulting mAP is equal to 51.9. These values form the baseline we will refer to in the remainder of this paper.

We then ask FLANN to determine what would be the best high-dimensional strategy in order to index the image features. We therefore set the `FLANNParameters` internal data structure to `AUTOTUNED` with a target precision set to 0.95. The resulting index determined by FLANN is a k-d tree. It takes 677 seconds to probe the index with the 500 queries. Using the index instead of relying on the linear scan is only

[1] http://people.rennes.inria.fr/Ahmet.Iscen/memoryvectors.html

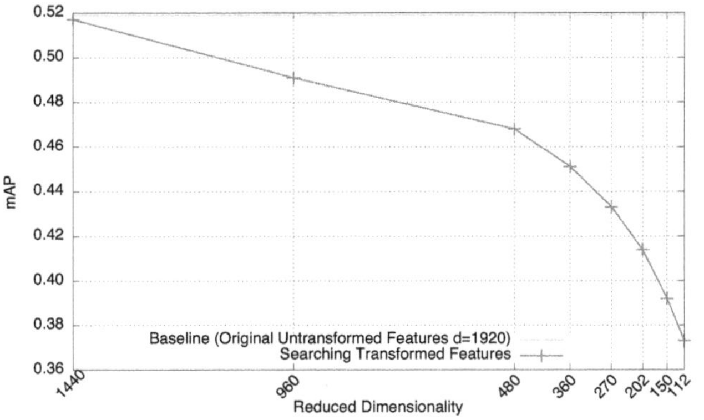

Figure 1: Observed mAP after PCA applied to the T-embeddings image features. Varying number of retained dimensions.

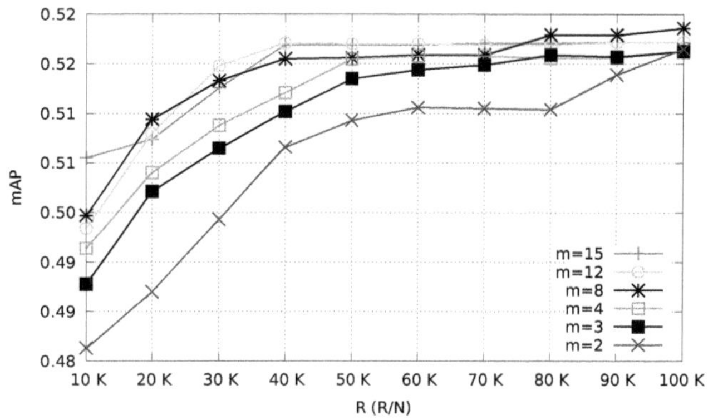

Figure 2: Search quality with different m and R. Percentages in parenthesis give R/N.

1.29 times faster. This little speedup is explained by the very large number of checks FLANN has to perform in order to meet the required precision. Observing the logs produced by FLANN shows that close to 450,000 checks are done for each query – so half of the features are indeed scanned, making the indexing useless as it can not confine the search to a small portion of the database. This is a direct consequence of the high-dimensionality of the indexed features.

The T-embedding features are indeed of a very large dimensionality. Their *representational* dimension is 1,920 while their local intrinsic dimensionality (see [1]) is estimated to be 150.3±41.3. This is a very high value, which emphasizes the negative consequences of the curse of dimensionality. Please note that FLANN proved to work with descriptors having a much smaller intrinsic dimensionality. For example, SIFT has a *representational* dimension equal to 128 while its estimated local intrinsic dimensionality is 12.3 ± 3.0 (again, see [1], Section 6.3). Their indexing is thus much easier.

One obvious approach to circumvent this dimensionality problem is to apply a dimension reduction technique to the features with the hope not to degrade too severely the resulting mAP. We therefore took our collection of image features, applied a PCA and kept a varying number of the most significant resulting dimensions. We then ran the (PCA-ed) queries against that transformed collection and computed the resulting mAP when using a linear scan. Figure 1 plots the outcome of this experiment. The figure shows that the mAP rapidly decreases when reducing the number of dimensions for the transformed features. While such transformed features might be more indexable, the resulting quality would be too low to have any practical interest. Using a linear scan is not an option either as it is too slow.

Most modern image features (VLAD, CNN-based features, etc.) share with the T-embeddings this property of lying in *truly* high-dimensional spaces. They can therefore hardly be indexed using traditional approaches. The following experiments demonstrate that group testing strategies better handle dimensionality.

4.3 Even-Size Groups of Similar Vectors

The lessons learnt from studying the literature suggest that creating even-size groups of similar vectors is best for group testing approaches. We proposed in Section 3.1 to take control of the random k-d tree creation process to this aim. The experiment described now shows this indeed works as the resulting performances are better. The competitive group testing method we compare against is [18]. Its group construction uses a fully random assignment procedure to create even-size groups. This experiment uses a similar setting as the one defined in [18], i.e., n = 15, m = 2, and R=M=133,532.

The mAP when using the pure random group creation technique is 50.8. In contrast, the mAP we observe when taking control of the k-d tree reaches 51.6. Forming groups according to some similarity (even quite weak as we utilize higher levels of the k-d tree) improves quality, which is however slightly below the baseline (mAP=51.9).

4.4 Redundancy for Better Candidate Vectors

When discussing the design options to scale group testing, we highlighted the necessity to decrease the number of true similarity computations between the query and the candidate features. This is requirement **R2**. We also claimed this goal could be achieved by increasing the redundancy of features in groups, i.e., increasing the value for m. The experiments discussed now are evaluating the mAP for sGT, varying the values of m and R.

The resulting experiments, illustrated by the Figure 2, show the mAP achieved by sGT when m goes from 2 (low redundancy) to 15 (high redundancy) as well as when R goes from 10,000 (small value, 1% of the database) to 100,000 (large value, 10% of the database, same settings as in [18]). It can be observed that for a fixed value for R, a better mAP is reached if m is larger. In other words, it is worth increasing m which reduces R for a fixed mAP.

However, increasing m also increases M (see eq. (1)), the total number of groups. This has a direct impact on the costs of equations (3) and (4). It is possible to keep these costs under control thanks to the indexing of the group representatives, as demonstrated by the next experiment.

4.5 Indexing Group Representatives

Indexing the vectors that represent the groups is a way to meet the requirement **R1** defined above. It is indeed quite straightforward. We used the same settings as above, with m = 3. We then give the collection of vector representatives to FLANN instructed to automatically determine the best index thanks to its `AUTOTUNE` setting. When

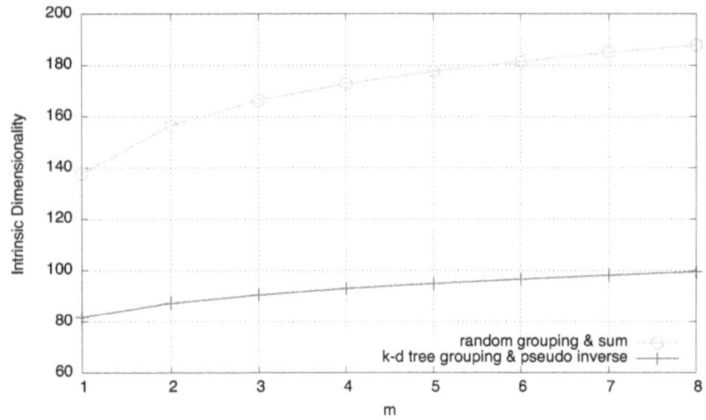

Figure 3: Intrinsic dimensionality varying m. Random and sum vs. k-d tree and pseudo-inverse group creation methods.

m = 3, there are 200,298 representatives corresponding to as many groups created with the taking control of the k-d tree process. FLANN finds that it is best to index that collection using a k-d tree which will provide a speed up of 39.26 compared to the linear scanning of all the representatives. Higher settings of m confirm significant speed up gains: FLANN estimates the speed up to be equal to 82.96 when $m = 4$ and 74.67 when $m = 8$. The scalability objective linked to **R1** is therefore achieved.

It is interesting to try to index group representatives when they result from the random construction process. Asking FLANN to determine the best index when fed with such 200,298 representatives fails: the library estimates that it is the linear scan that is the most competitive method when trying to identify the best representatives. Digging into the logs of FLANN shows that it is again the dimensionality of the group representatives which can explain this remarkable difference in behavior. While both k-d tree based representatives and random representatives have the same *representational* dimensionality (i.e. d =1,920), they have however a quite different *intrinsic* dimensionality.

With $m = 3$, k-d tree based group representatives have an estimated local intrinsic dimensionality of 90.6 ± 29.5 while random based group representatives have an intrinsic dimensionality of 166.4 ± 13.5. It is therefore much harder to index random based group vectors, and resorting on the linear scan is possibly the best strategy.

Indeed, blending randomly the features increases the entropy, explaining why the resulting intrinsic dimensionality is even higher than the one of the raw features. Such random group vectors are distributed all over the high-dimensional space, making it quite hard to distinguish the near neighbors from the most distant ones, as clearly stated in the seminal paper about neighbor meaningfulness [4]. Similar observations can be made for other values of m, as it is reported in Figure 3.

4.6 Overall Performance: Comparing Quality and Run Time

The last experiment compares the overall performance of sGT with (i) the performance of the k-d tree created by FLANN over all of the image features, as described in Section 4.2 and (ii) with the state-of-the-art group testing scheme by Shi et al. [18].

To measure the performance of the k-d tree of FLANN, we ask the library to return the top 1%, 2%, ..., 10% image features that are the most similar to the queries. This obviously impacts the response time as well as the resulting mAP. This is depicted by Figure 4 where a line that gives the performance of the FLANN index is plotted. This line shows that when an increasing number of features are considered, then the response time increases as does the mAP, as expected. It is possible to know the percentages of the most similar features that are considered at query time as it is specified along the line. For clarity, not all such percentages are indicated; the missing ones can easily be deduced.

The other series of lines display the performance of sGT. The parameter of utmost importance in this strategy is the redundancy, m, which we vary here. We therefore created 3 configurations of the groups for three specific values of that m parameter that are $m = 3$, $m = 4$ and $m = 8$. The Figure 4 therefore contains three other lines, each depicting the behavior of one group testing configuration for sGT.

To better understand the behavior of sGT, we have changed for each configuration the number of representatives that are identified to subsequently evaluate equations (3) and (4). One of the claims we make in this paper is that indexing the representatives is beneficial to performance because returning a particular number of them (k) among a total of M existing representatives is mostly independent of that M value while it boosts performance. We therefore instructed sGT to return the best k group representatives (with k ranging from 2,560 to 90,000) before identifying the R =50,000 best image features. We visualise along the sGT lines in Figure 4 some of these values for k. We explicitly give few such values to preserve the clarity of this figure. For example, the response times and the corresponding mAP obtained with the three configurations of sGT when $k \approx$10,000 are all three represented on the lines using a triangle pointing downward symbol. Similarly, the operating points are represented with the square symbol for $k \approx$50,000.

Using these symbols facilitates observing that indeed, the response times of sGT is mostly independent of M (which increases as m grows). When $m = 3$, then there are overall M =200,298 group vector representatives, while there are M =534,128 when $m = 8$. Despite these different values for M, retrieving the same number k of representatives takes roughly the same amount of time, between 160 and 180 seconds when $k \approx$90,000, see the circles on the figure. Furthermore, the order of these three circles on the time-line is not ruled by m, materializing the independence between M and the response time.

This figure also shows that the mAP improves as m increases, while the response time stays quasi identical thanks to having indexed the group representatives.

Finally, it is interesting to compare the response times and the mAP that Shi et al. [18] could achieve using the same parameters. Table 1 compares three configurations of the original group testing technique (based on random grouping and the use of the sum (2) to compute the representatives) to the same three configurations for sGT that we have described. Please note, however, that [18] uses *all* M representatives when evaluating equations (3) and (4) while we use only the $k \approx$90,000 best ones. The table shows that sGT is much faster than the original group testing proposal, while the quality does not differ significantly.

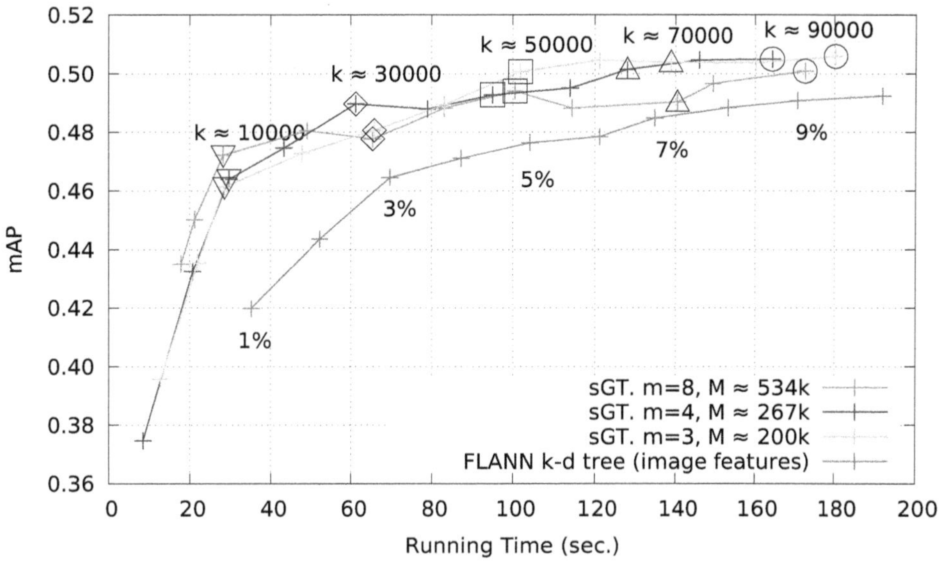

Figure 4: Response Times vs. mAP. FLANN k-d tree, several configuration for sGT.

	m=3		m=4		m=8	
	Time (s)	mAP	Time (s)	mAP	Time (s)	mAP
Random G.T. [18]	187	0.507	252	0.512	483	0.518
sGT [this paper]	180	0.505	164	0.504	172	0.500

Table 1: Comparing the search time of different group construction methods for group testing.

5. CONCLUSION

Drawing the lessons from the pioneer applications of group testing to similarity search [10, 18], we first propose a grouping strategy based on kd-trees. This ensures groups of even sizes comprising weakly similar features. An important byproduct of this approach is that the resulting representative vectors have small intrinsic dimensionality compared to the raw dataset features. This allows us to integrate an ANN search algorithm, such as FLANN, into the group testing framework. This is the keystone for freeing the total number of groups. We seize this opportunity to increase this number to compute more reliable scores. This in turn gives birth to a shorter list of candidates for the verification step. The overall construction improves the scalability of group testing similarity search while maintaining high search quality.

6. REFERENCES

[1] L. Amsaleg, O. Chelly, T. Furon, S. Girard, M. E. Houle, K. Kawarabayashi, and M. Nett. Estimating local intrinsic dimensionality. In *Proceedings of the 21th ACM SIGKDD International Conference on Knowledge Discovery and Data Mining*, pages 29–38. ACM, 2015.

[2] R. Arandjelovic and A. Zisserman. All about VLAD. In *Proceedings of the IEEE Conference on Computer Vision and Pattern Recognition*, June 2013.

[3] A. Babenko, A. Slesarev, A. Chigorin, and V. Lempitsky. Neural codes for image retrieval. In *Proceedings of the European Conference on Computer Vision*, 2014.

[4] K. Beyer, J. Goldstein, R. Ramakrishnan, and U. Shaft. When is nearest neighbor meaningful? In *Proceedings of the International Conference on Database Theory*, pages 217–235, August 1999.

[5] M. Datar, N. Immorlica, P. Indyk, and V. Mirrokni. Locality-sensitive hashing scheme based on p-stable distributions. In *Proceedings of the Symposium on Computational Geometry*, 2004.

[6] J. H. Friedman, J. L. Bentley, and R. A. Finkel. An algorithm for finding best matches in logarithmic expected time. *ACM Transaction on Mathematical Software*, 3(3):209–226, 1977.

[7] A. Gionis, P. Indyk, and R. Motwani. Similarity search in high dimension via hashing. In *Proceedings of the International Conference on Very Large DataBases*, pages 518–529, 1999.

[8] Y. Gong, L. Wang, R. Guo, and S. Lazebnik. Multi-scale orderless pooling of deep convolutional activation features. In *Proceedings of the European Conference on Computer Vision*, 2014.

[9] P. Indyk and R. Motwani. Approximate nearest neighbors: towards removing the curse of dimensionality. In *Proceedings of the ACM symposium on Theory of computing*, pages 604–613, 1998.

[10] A. Iscen, T. Furon, V. Gripon, M. Rabbat, and H. Jégou. Memory vectors for similarity search in high-dimensional spaces. *arXiv*, 2014.

[11] H. Jégou, M. Douze, and C. Schmid. Hamming embedding and weak geometric consistency for large scale image search. In *Proceedings of the European Conference on Computer Vision*, October 2008.

[12] H. Jégou and A. Zisserman. Triangulation embedding and democratic kernels for image search. In

Proceedings of the IEEE Conference on Computer Vision and Pattern Recognition, June 2014.

[13] Q. Lv, W. Josephson, Z. Wang, M. Charikar, and K. Li. Multi-probe LSH: Efficient indexing for high-dimensional similarity search. In *Proceedings of the International Conference on Very Large DataBases*, pages 950–961, 2007.

[14] M. Muja and D. G. Lowe. Scalable nearest neighbor algorithms for high dimensional data. *IEEE Transactions on Pattern Analysis and Machine Intelligence*, 36, 2014.

[15] F. Perronnin and C. R. Dance. Fisher kernels on visual vocabularies for image categorization. In *Proceedings of the IEEE Conference on Computer Vision and Pattern Recognition*, June 2007.

[16] J. Philbin, O. Chum, M. Isard, J. Sivic, and A. Zisserman. Object retrieval with large vocabularies and fast spatial matching. In *Proceedings of the IEEE Conference on Computer Vision and Pattern Recognition*, June 2007.

[17] C. R. Rao and S. K. Mitra. Generalized inverse of a matrix and its applications. In *Proceedings of the Sixth Berkeley Symposium on Mathematical Statistics and Probability, Volume 1: Theory of Statistics*, 1972.

[18] M. Shi, T. Furon, and H. Jégou. A group testing framework for similarity search in high-dimensional spaces. In *ACM International conference on Multimedia*, November 2014.

[19] R. Weber, H.-J. Schek, and S. Blott. A quantitative analysis and performance study for similarity-search methods in high-dimensional spaces. In *Proceedings of the International Conference on Very Large DataBases*, pages 194–205, 1998.

Vinereactor: Crowdsourced Spontaneous Facial Expression Data

Edward Kim
Department of Computing Sciences
Villanova University
800 E. Lancaster Ave, Villanova, PA
edward.kim@villanova.edu

Shruthika Vangala
Department of Computing Sciences
Villanova University
800 E. Lancaster Ave, Villanova, PA
svangal1@villanova.edu

ABSTRACT

Although machines are more pervasive in our everyday lives, we are still forced to interact with them through limited communication channels. Our overarching goal is to support new and complex interactions by teaching the computer to interpret the expressions of the user. Towards this goal, we present Vinereactor, a new labeled database for face analysis and affect recognition. Our dataset is one of the first to explore human expression recognition *in response to* a stimulus video, enabling a new facet of affect analysis research. Furthermore, our dataset is the largest of its kind, nearly a magnitude larger than its closest related work.

Keywords

affect recognition, emotion classification, face analysis, video database, crowdsourcing

1. INTRODUCTION

Basic face detection and recognition have made notable progress in the past couple years due to the advancements in machine learning, high resolution cameras, and availability of standard datasets. However, in order to further the communication capabilities between humans and machines, a computer must be able to incorporate affect recognition and understand how a person is feeling. Recognition and interpretation of human non-verbal communication cues can help inform a huge variety of computer aided applications, including pain medicine, online education, and marketing.

Towards this goal, we are researching novel ways to use computer vision algorithms to collect and analyze spontaneous facial expressions. In our application, we collected a random database of short internet video clips that have been categorized by genre (comedic, shocking, etc.) and have a high probability of eliciting an emotion response. We then play these "stimulus" videos for human observers and record their reactions, see Figure 1. This recording task was crowdsourced over Amazon Mechanical Turk and hundreds of gigabytes of video data were collected and analyzed using face analysis algorithms. Our spontaneous facial expression dataset has been annotated with facial landmark points and FACS labels (Facial Action Coding System). FACS are one of the most comprehensive methods of categorizing facial activity in a quantitative way [4]. The muscle activations in the face are labeled using action units (AUs) and the combination of certain AUs infer a particular emotion.

Our data contributes to two major objectives. First, our large annotated dataset can be used to improve face analysis and emotion classification algorithms. We are freely distributing the largest annotated databases of spontaneous facial expression data to date. Second, the recorded spontaneous reaction data is linked with a database of stimulus videos. This opens up a whole new avenue of research where one could use our data to begin looking at the interaction between general videos and human reactions. For example, if we can quantify the emotion displayed by a human

(a) Vine ex.a (b) Vine ex.b (c) Vine ex.c

(d) Reaction ex.a (e) Reaction ex.b (f) Reaction ex.c

Figure 1: A screenshot from three example stimulus videos are shown in (a)(b)(c). These videos are played to a set of crowdsourced observers whose reactions are recorded and analyzed (d)(e)(f).

ICMR'16, June 06 - 09, 2016, New York, NY, USA

ISBN 978-1-4503-4359-6/16/06... $15.00

DOI: http://dx.doi.org/10.1145/2911996.2912038

watching these videos, we can attempt to transfer the emotion classified from the observer to the video for indexing and retrieval. Furthermore, we can begin looking at general, non-face video emotion classification (stimulus videos) by knowing how people react. Currently, even given the state-of-the-art computer vision classification models, this idea of general video emotion classification is essentially an impossible problem to solve without the use of additional manual annotation. We hypothesize that our reaction data can provide the annotation data by just analyzing people's facial reactions instead of explicitly asking for their input.

2. BACKGROUND

A very large number of datasets for face analysis already exists. In this section, we will mention some of the most popular and most closely related datasets to our work in both image-based and video-based datasets.

2.1 Image & Video Datasets for Face Analysis

The CK+ dataset [10] - This popular dataset is fully FACS encoded with emotion labels and Active Appearance Models (AAMs) [2] face landmarks. The dataset contains 593 image sequences across 123 subjects.

The HELEN dataset [9] - The HELEN dataset consists of 2,000 training images and 330 test images with highly accurate, detailed and consistent annotations of facial components. This dataset is primarily an effort to build facial feature localization algorithms.

Multi-PIE dataset [5] - The Multi-PIE database is one of the largest databases, containing over 750,000 images with various camera angles, facial expressions, and illuminations. The data consists of 337 subjects with AAM style labels for 6,152 of the images. As a side note, this database is not freely available.

Labeled Faces in the Wild dataset [6] - This database contains 13,000 face photographs collected from the web. The faces contain a label of the name of the person pictured, which would be useful for unconstrained face recognition.

UNBC-McMaster (Pain AU) [11]- The UNBC-McMaster Shoulder Pain Archive (Pain AU) is one of the largest databases of AU coded videos of spontaneous facial expressions. There are 200 sequences across 25 subjects and all frames are FACS encoded with intensity labels.

YouTube Faces Database [13] - This dataset contains 3,425 videos of 1,595 different people. All the videos were downloaded from YouTube. An average of 2.15 videos are available for each subject.

BP4D [14] - The BP4D dataset is a 3D video database of spontaneous facial expressions in a diverse group of young adults. Well-validated emotion inductions were used to elicit expressions of emotion and paralinguistic communication.

UvA-NEMO [3] - This is a large-scale smile database which has 1240 smile videos (597 spontaneous and 643 posed) from 400 subjects. Ages of subjects vary from 8 to 76 years.

AM-FED [12] - This dataset contains 242 facial videos (168,359 frames) recorded in real world conditions. The data contains frame by frame FACS labels and 22 automatically detected landmark points. This work is the closest to ours where the data generated were people's responses to three internet advertisement videos.

This list is by no means comprehensive, but there are generalizations that we can highlight that differentiate our dataset from the existing image and video datasets for facial analysis. The first difference is that our dataset is the first to provide a database of stimulus videos *and* their associated human reactions. This combination is essential if we are to move beyond basic one-way analysis and begin analyzing complex interactions that humans have with machines and their environment. Second, our dataset is a magnitude larger than its closest related work, AM-FED, that has only three internet advertisements and 168,359 video frames. Our work has 200 general stimulus videos and over 1.3 million video response frames.

3. METHODOLOGY

Our process consisted of three major tasks. In the first task, we searched and downloaded random stimulus videos, known as vine videos. In our second task, we crowdsourced the collection of reactions to these videos, and in the final step, we analyzed the reaction videos to provide face landmark annotation and AU classifications.

3.1 Stimulus Videos

For the stimulus videos, we decided to use Vine videos because they were limited in size (maximum duration of 7 seconds) and manually categorized into different genres. We collected 200 random vine videos from the comedy vine.co[1] channel by scraping the featured videos from the website sporadically between May 2015 and September 2015. The videos have a duration range between 2 - 7 seconds and come with further associated meta data including url, number of likes, number of comments, and number of "revines".

3.2 Crowdsourced Reactions

Before the reaction data collection, we obtained ethics approval to conduct our research in the online crowdsourcing platform, Amazon Mechanical Turk. Each stimulus video was shown to a set of 30 unique viewers. The crowdsourcing task, HIT (human intelligence task), also asks for permission to activate the user's webcam and then instructs the user to center their face in the webcam's field of view. The worker can see their activated webcam (and face) next to an embedded video that requires an additional click to play the video. When they click to play the video, simultaneously, the stimulus video begins and their webcam begins to record their expressions. They are only able to watch the vine once, and for each 7-second vine video, we collected approximately 0.5 GB of total reaction video. After the video is complete, they are asked two questions. The first question is, how amusing is the video on a scale from 1-7, where 1 is not funny, 4 is fairly amusing, and 7 is extremely funny. The second question is related to giving consent to have their image, video, and likeness used for research purposes. This is a lengthy disclaimer describing our confidentiality procedures, and their rights as a participant in this study. It is explicitly stated that they do not have to give us permission to display and distribute their videos in order to be paid for the HIT. If permission is not granted, their data will not be released, distributed, or processed in any identifiable way. An optional comments section is available to the participant for providing any additional feedback. The workers are paid $0.10 USD for their participation. The total cost for data collection was $840.00 USD, which includes both the rewards and fees.

[1] https://vine.co/channels/comedy

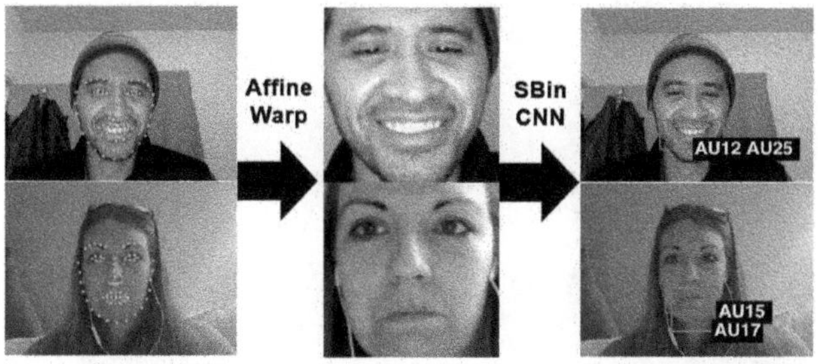

Figure 2: The face is first processed through a CLM [1] keypoint detection algorithm, then the cropped face area is affine warped to a base face shape and processed by the SBinCNN [8] algorithm to produce the AU activations.

3.3 Face Analysis

Keypoints - After collecting the reaction video, each reaction frame is processed to obtain the annotated 68 facial landmarks, see Figure 2. After an evaluation of several methods, we chose the CLM [1] framework which utilizes a constrained local neural field for landmark detection. In our experiments, it was the most robust in video annotation with variable lighting conditions, and had a relatively fast processing time ($<$ 0.5 seconds per frame on an Intel i7).

AU Labels - Given the 68 landmark annotations, we are able to move to the next step of our annotation process, i.e. action unit classification. For this process, we chose the SBinCNN [8] method as it had the highest f1 score in comparison to all the methods we tested. In the first step of this process, each face is aligned to a mean shape through an affine warp of the outer 27 keypoints of the face and 4 keypoints of the nose bridge. A full 68 keypoint warp was not used as it could distort the facial muscle activations. A contrast stretch is then applied to the image, and the resulting face is used for AU classification. This classification system is based upon a deep learning methodology. It uses a convolutional neural network training loss specific to AU intensity that utilizes a binned cross entropy method to fine-tune an existing network, e.g. CaffeNet [7]. The processing time for AU labeling is less than 5ms per image frame on a Tesla K40. The 10 AUs labeled in our dataset were the following, {1,2,4,6,7,12,15,17,25,26}. The most common AUs (and their approximate semantic meaning) that show up in our data are AU4 (brow lowering), AU12 (smile), AU15 (frown), AU17 (chin raised), and AU25 (lips apart).

4. RESULTS AND DATABASE STATISTICS

In this section, we present our analysis of the stimulus and reaction data, statistics of the video dataset, and failure cases which we will address in future work.

4.1 Stimulus and Reaction Videos

Stimulus Videos - We scraped 200 vine videos and used these videos as our stimulus to elicit reactions. The vine videos are stored in MP4 format and take up 280 MB of disk space. Each vine video has an associated XML file with the meta data from vine.co. Through our crowdsourcing process, we are also able to assign each video a numeric amusement value between 1-7 that corresponds to an average of 30 independent observers. The amusement values have an average standard deviation of 0.306 across all videos.

Reaction Videos-We collected 6,029 video responses from 343 unique mechanical turk workers in response to the 200 stimulus videos, with a minimum of 30 reaction videos per stimulus video. The total number of video frames in the database is 1,380,343 at a resolution of 320x240. All of the reactions are stored in JPG format and the total size of the reaction video data is 143 GB. See Figure 4 for an example of the stimulus video and processed reactions. Of the 6,029 video responses, 3455 (57.3%) of the reactions were approved to be used for research purposes and will be open and available for the community as long as the data is not redistributed or used for commercial applications. This public dataset includes 222 unique subjects with an average of 17.275 reactions per stimulus video.

4.2 Pitch, Yaw, Roll of Reactions

We further characterize the database by computing the distribution of the pitch, yaw, and roll of all the reaction faces and present them in Figure 3. The mean values for pitch, yaw, and roll are 6.23, -1.58, and 3.90 respectively. The variance is 35.26, 53.69, and 9.16, which shows more variability than datasets collected in controlled conditions. To put this in perspective, the UNBC-McMaster dataset [11] has variances of 23.58, 40.82, and 33.28.

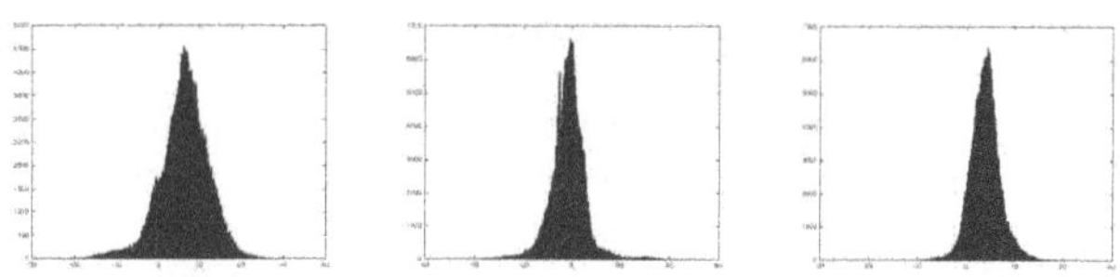

(a) Pitch (b) Yaw (c) Roll

Figure 3: The distribution of yaw, pitch, and roll in our dataset, where the measurements are in degrees.

4.3 Failure Cases

There are three typical failure cases with our post processing pipeline. The first failure case is the failure of the webcam to record; this produces a completely black sequence of images. This failure is rare, accounting for less than 0.3% of the total dataset. The second failure case was the missed detection of a face by our face detection cascade (which includes a fast matlab implementation, [15], [1]). In these cases, the faces were not visible or below a face detection threshold due to various lighting effects, occlusion, or perspective transformations. These two failure cases account for 5.2% of the total dataset and will be discarded in the public dataset.

The final failure case is an incorrect or mis-alignment of the facial keypoints. This is a much more difficult failure case to detect and we note that our future work will be research into both automatic and crowdsourced validation of the machine annotated labels in our dataset.

5. CONCLUSION

In summary, we present a new database for face analysis and affect recognition. Our database was collected "in the wild" and is fully labeled with 68 facial landmarks and AU classifications. Our contribution to the community is two fold. Our dataset is one of the first that addresses the complex problem of stimulus and reaction video. Furthermore,

(a) Input stimulus video - “grandma loves ping pong.” courtesy of Nico Anderson’s Vine

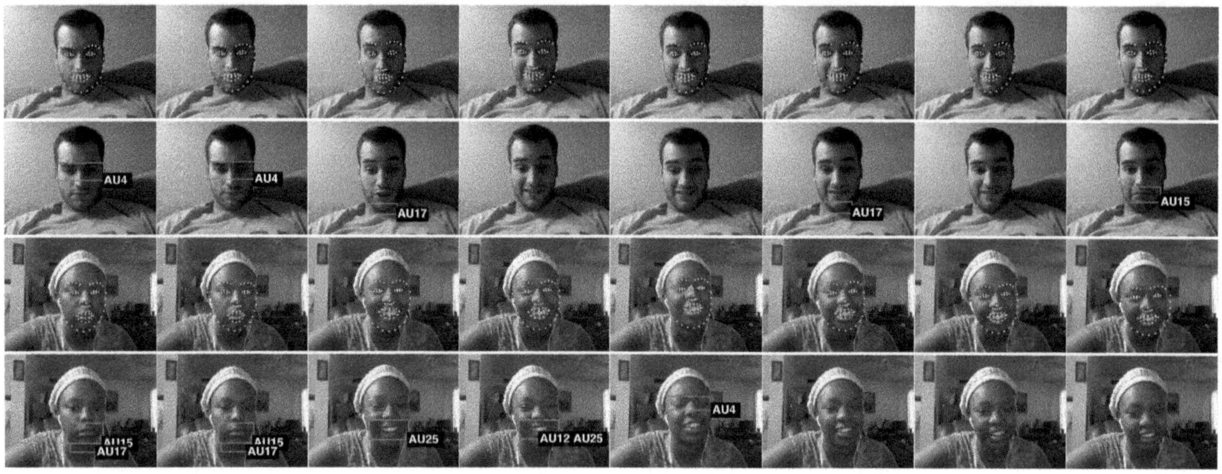

Figure 4: An example of an input stimulus video shown to crowdsourced workers (a) and a subset of responses to the video with the computed 68 facial landmarks annotated in green and AU activations boxed in red.

our dataset is the largest of its kind, nearly one magnitude larger than its closest related work. We plan to share the outcomes created during this project including the data, as well as the algorithms used to classify the reaction faces.

6. ACKNOWLEDGMENTS

We thank all of the mechanical turkers for their participation in this research project. This work was supported by an AWS in Education Grant award.

7. REFERENCES

[1] T. Baltrusaitis, P. Robinson, and L.-P. Morency. Constrained local neural fields for robust facial landmark detection in the wild. In *International Conference on Computer Vision Workshops*, pages 354–361, 2013.

[2] T. F. Cootes, G. J. Edwards, and C. J. Taylor. Active appearance models. *IEEE Transactions on Pattern Analysis & Machine Intelligence*, (6):681–685, 2001.

[3] H. Dibeklioğlu, A. A. Salah, and T. Gevers. Are you really smiling at me? spontaneous versus posed enjoyment smiles. In *ECCV*, pages 525–538. 2012.

[4] P. Ekman and E. Rosenberg. *What the face reveals: Basic and applied studies of spontaneous expression using the Facial Action Coding System (FACS).* Oxford University Press, 1997.

[5] R. Gross, I. Matthews, J. Cohn, T. Kanade, and S. Baker. Multi-pie. *Image and Vision Computing*, 28(5):807–813, 2010.

[6] G. B. Huang, M. Ramesh, T. Berg, and E. Learned-Miller. Labeled faces in the wild: A database for studying face recognition in unconstrained environments. Technical Report 07-49, University of Massachusetts, Amherst, October 2007.

[7] Y. Jia, E. Shelhamer, J. Donahue, S. Karayev, J. Long, R. Girshick, S. Guadarrama, and T. Darrell. Caffe: Convolutional architecture for fast feature embedding. In *ACM International Conference on Multimedia*, pages 675–678, 2014.

[8] E. Kim and S. Vangala. Deep action unit classification using a binned intensity loss and semantic context model. Technical report, Villanova University, 2016.

[9] V. Le, J. Brandt, Z. Lin, L. Bourdev, and T. S. Huang. Interactive facial feature localization. In *ECCV*, pages 679–692. 2012.

[10] P. Lucey, J. Cohn, T. Kanade, J. Saragih, Z. Ambadar, and I. Matthews. The extended cohn-kanade dataset (ck+): A complete dataset for action unit and emotion-specified expression. In *Computer Vision and Pattern Recognition Workshops*, pages 94–101, 2010.

[11] P. Lucey, J. Cohn, K. Prkachin, P. Solomon, and I. Matthews. Painful data: The unbc-mcmaster shoulder pain expression archive database. In *Automatic Face & Gesture Recognition and Workshops*, pages 57–64, 2011.

[12] D. McDuff, R. Kaliouby, and R. W. Picard. Crowdsourcing facial responses to online videos. *Affective Computing*, 3(4):456–468, 2012.

[13] L. Wolf, T. Hassner, and I. Maoz. Face recognition in unconstrained videos with matched background similarity. In *CVPR*, pages 529–534, 2011.

[14] X. Zhang, L. Yin, J. F. Cohn, S. Canavan, M. Reale, A. Horowitz, P. Liu, and J. M. Girard. Bp4d-spontaneous: a high-resolution spontaneous 3d dynamic facial expression database. *Image and Vision Computing*, 32(10):692–706, 2014.

[15] X. Zhu and D. Ramanan. Face detection, pose estimation, and landmark localization in the wild. In *CVPR*, pages 2879–2886, 2012.

Mirroring Facial Expressions: Evidence from Visual Analysis of Dyadic Interactions

Yuchi Huang
yhuang001@ets.org

Saad Khan
skhan002@ets.org

Educational Testing Service
660 Rosedale Rd
Princeton, NJ, 08541

ABSTRACT

We present results from a pilot study that explored evidence of non-conscious facial expression mirroring exhibited by human dyads in face-to-face interactions. We captured video data of study participants engaged in an online collaborative activity on science topics. The data was sub-sampled and organized into two sets: one consisting of time-synchronized video clips from dyad pairs and the other from unrelated nominal-dyads (or non-dyads). The videos were analyzed with an automated facial expression approach and distance between two video clips of each pair (from both two sets) was computed using a temporal pyramid matching strategy. By employing a two-sample t-test on these two populations, our results demonstrate a statistically significant convergence or mirroring of facial expressions between dyad pairs, which holds over a wide range of model parameter settings and extensive experimentation.

Keywords

Facial Expression Analysis, Temporal Pyramid Matching Kernel, Dyadic Interactions

1. BACKGROUND

Behavioral convergence refers to the unintentional imitation process of co-participants' behavior on a range of different time scales [4]. In literature it has been referred to by a variety of terms e.g., behavioral matching, mimicry, entrainment, etc [4] [6]. Social psychologists have postulated that behavioral convergence and mirroring presents an evolutionary component associated with the development of social bonds and empathy through cooperation [6]. In addition, studies have explored its impact on interpersonal skills, coordinated activity, negotiations, and how individuals influence the behaviors of others [2] [4]. As a complex activity that constitutes an interplay between cognitive processes, team work and collaboration are more effective when participants are engaged in the task and exhibit behaviors that facilitate interaction [10].

Recent research has explored the impact of behavioral mirroring and convergence of cognitive and non-cognitive behavior in interactive collaborative activity [3]. In particular, Luna Bazaldua et al. demonstrated a statistically significant convergence of cognitive and non-cognitive behavior between dyads engaged in online collaborative activity [3]. However, in their study participants were not able to see each other and only interacted over a text-based chat interface. In this paper we focus on mimicry and mirroring of facial expressions between dyad pairs during face-to-face conversation through a video conferencing system. Our hypothesis is that people engaged in collaborative activity demonstrate facial expression mirroring and that this effect can be measured as a similarity metric computed from automated facial expression analysis of video captured during such dyadic interactions.

ICMR '16, June 6–9, 2016, New York, NY, USA.
© 2016 ACM. ISBN 978-1-4503-4359-6/16/06... $15.00
DOI: http://dx.doi.org/10.1145/2911996.2912039

2. OUTLINE OF OUR METHOD

2.1 Preparation of Study Materials

Our study used an online collaboration assessment platform [9] [13] on which two participants in different locations were able to interact through video conference to solve a set of academic questions together, as shown in Figure 1. Twenty-six subjects participated in this study and were paired in thirteen dyads using random selection. At the time of the study, participants were graduate students or recently graduated from different universities. As mentioned earlier, the dyads were able to interact with each other over a videoconferencing interface. The video from each session was captured resulting in thirteen pairs of time aligned video recordings. Each dyad reviewed and responded to the same educational material and academic questions. The duration of dyad sessions varies from 36 minutes to 68 minutes, with an average length of about 52 minutes. This resulted in a total of 1,356 minutes of video data, which formed our core evidentiary dataset and was analyzed utilizing automated facial expression analysis as described in the following section.

2.2 Hypothesis and Experimental Protocol

As mentioned earlier, our hypothesis is that human dyads engaged in collaborative activity demonstrate facial expression mirroring, i.e., they will synchronize and exhibit facial expressions that convey similar emotions. To test our hypothesis, we analyzed the video data from thirteen dyad pairs engaged in online collaborative activity as described previously. We sub-sampled and divided this video corpus into two sets of video-clip pairs as described below:

Definition 1. Intra-Conversation Set: a set of video clip pairs from dyad face-to-face interaction videos. Each video clip pair has a predetermined fixed length and a randomly chosen start time (same for each pair) in the full duration of the dyadic interaction.

Definition 2. Inter-Conversation Set: a set of video clip pairs chosen from nominal dyad pairs, i.e., participants that have not in-

Table 1: Expression/attitude values of two participants in Figure 1 at Time 00:58 (first image pair). High level of Joy expression and Positive attitude are consistent with the image content.

	Joy	Anger	Surprise	Fear	Contempt	Disgust	Sadness	Neutral	Positive	Negative
Participant 1	**1.68**	-2.65	-1.58	-1.76	-2.26	-1.22	-2.87	-2.82	**1.68**	-1.2226
Participant 2	**1.93**	-3.84	-3.91	-1.31	-5.08	0.52	-5.10	-5.63	**1.93**	0.52

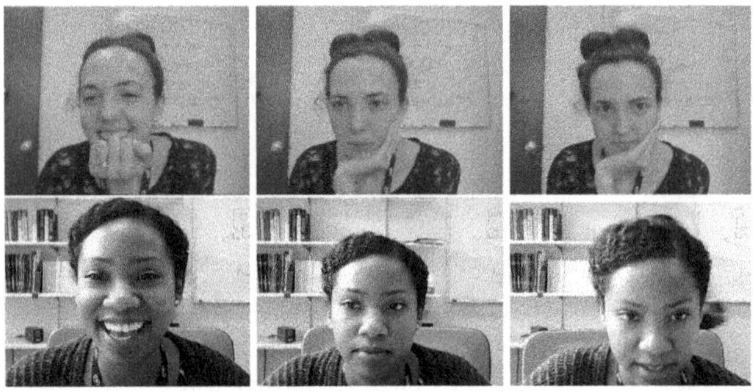

(a) (b) (c)

Figure 1: Two participants interacted through an online collaboration assessment platform. Cropped image pair (a), (b) and (c) shows the corresponding facial expressions at 00:58, 07:57 and 26:21 respectively.

teracted with each other. Each video clip pair has a predetermined fixed length and a randomly chosen start time (allowed to be different for each pair) in which two video clips of each pair were randomly sampled from the different conversation dyad, with a fixed length predefined.

For example, a video clip pair in the Intra-Conversation Set may be composed of a clip of 3 minutes which was sampled from the first video of the 7th dyad with a starting time of $32 : 00$, and another video clip of 3 minutes which was sampled from the second video of the 7th dyad with a starting time of $32 : 00$; one pair in an Inter-Conversation Set could be composed of one video clip of 3 minutes which was sampled from the first video of the 9th dyad with a starting time of $17 : 00$, and another video clip of 3 minutes which was sampled from the second video of the 11th dyad with a starting time of $41 : 00$.

Each video clip in the two sets was analyzed with an automated facial expression approach that results in a 10 dimensional per-frame facial expression descriptor. This descriptor contains seven basic expressions (Joy, Anger, Surprise, Fear, Contempt, Disgust, Sadness) and three comprehensive attitudes (Neutral, Positive and Negative). We then adopted a Bag-of-Words model [8] to represent the cumulative facial expression content of each video clip as a Cumulative Expression Histogram (CEH). Finally, in order to identify and measure the degree of facial expression mirroring between any two video clips, we developed a novel temporal pyramid matching approach that computed a similarity distance between their respective CEHs. This approach allowed us to capture mirroring not simply at the holistic global level but also at the local temporal level. Using this distance measure, we formed two populations of distance values over Intra-Conversation Set and Inter-Conversation Set, respectively. Without assuming two populations have equal variances, a one-tailed two-sample t-test was utilized on these two populations to verify that the mean distance value of Intra-Conversation Set is less than the mean distance value of Inter-Conversation Set, which demonstrated a statistically significant convergence or mirroring of facial expressions between dyad pairs. In the following sections we provide details of our technical approach and experimental results.

3. FEATURE REPRESENTATION

3.1 Per-frame Expression Descriptor

Based on the FACS system [5] of Paul Ekman, in this paper we utilize a per-frame expression descriptor with 10 dimensions, which contains seven basic expressions of human emotion (Joy, Anger, Surprise, Fear, Contempt, Disgust, Sadness) and three comprehensive emotional attitudes (Neutral, Positive and Negative). In our experiments we employed Emotient's Facet SDK [1] to compute element values of this expression descriptor. Each of these ten signals is assigned a numerical value called the Evidence number, which represents the odds, in logarithmic (base 10) scale, of a target expression/attitude being present. The evidence value can be transformed into the probability of an expression/attitude as follows:

$$P = \frac{1}{1 + 10^{-r}}. \quad (1)$$

Taking Joy as an example, a positive evidence value of r indicates that the observed expression is 10^{p} times more likely to be categorized by an expert human coder as joyful than not joyful; a negative evidence value of r indicates that the observed expression is 10^{-q} times more likely to be categorized by an expert human coder as not joyful than joyful. In table 1, we illustrate the expression/attitude values of two participants in a dyad in Figure 1 at Time 00:58. In practice positive values larger than 1 indicate that we have evidence for a meaningful expression/attitude effect, e.g., we can 'safely' bet that the person is showing a specific expression/attitude. Therefore, to extract valid features from video clips, we only consider those frames the per-frame expression descriptors of which contain at least one element larger than 1.

An individual's face can have a default appearance that resembles any of the emotional categories or the combination of them, even though he or she may be in a neutral state (e.g. a âĂIJnatural frownâĂİ). In order to remove this bias a calibration slide should be introduced to measure this default appearance. To reach optimal performance, we also used Emotient's Facet SDK [1] to obtain such a baseline expression descriptor at first. Before further computation, all measurements of the same person were processed by a simple subtraction using the baseline value.

3.2 Cumulative Expression Histogram

In information retrieval and computer vision, the Bag-of-Words model is widely used for feature representation, by mapping low level features into a pre-learned codebook to generate histograms of codewords for text documents or images. In this paper, we take per-frame expression descriptors as 'words' and sequences of frames as 'bags' to generate Cumulative Expression Histograms (CEH) for conversational video clips. For all the per-frame descriptors, we created a m-bin expression codebook by kâĂŞmeans clustering. We followed the method in [11] to obtain histograms by soft feature quantization, which was proven to provide remarkable improvement in object recognition [11]:

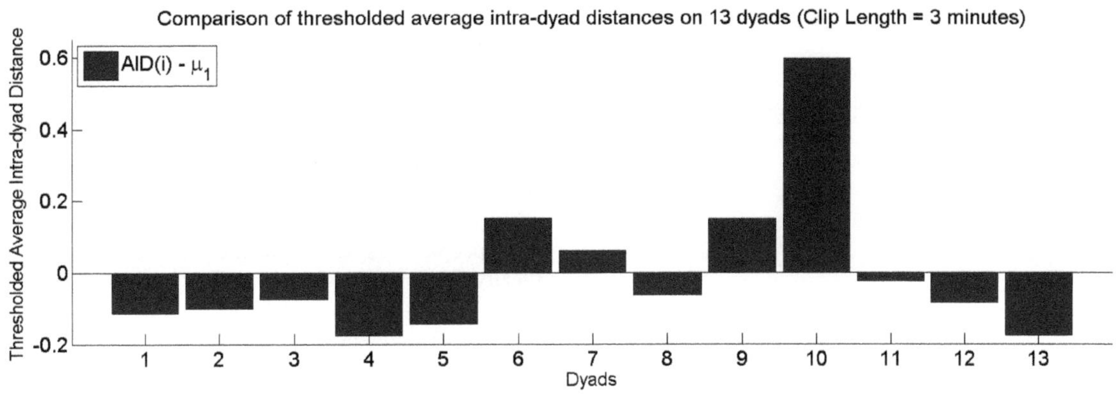

Figure 2: Comparison of thresholded Average Intra-dyad Distances (AID) over 13 dyads, by using μ_1 as the threshold (where μ_1 is the mean value of Population 1). Average Intra-dyad Distance (AID) of Dyad i was calculated as the mean distance of 100 intra-conversation pairs corresponding to Dyad i only.

$$CEH(w_f) = \frac{1}{n}\sum_{i=1}^{n} \frac{K_\sigma(D(w_f, f_i))}{\sum_{j=1}^{|V|} K_\sigma(D(v_j, f_i))}, \tag{2}$$

$$where\ K_\sigma(x) = \frac{1}{\sqrt{2\pi}\sigma} \exp\left(-\frac{1}{2}\frac{x^2}{\sigma^2}\right). \tag{3}$$

In Equation 2, n is the number of per-frame features in a video clip; f_i is the ith per-frame feature; $D(w_f, f_i)$ is the distance between a codeword w_f and the feature f_i; $CEH(w_f)$ is the histogram value on the codeword (bin) w. In practice we choose $m = 125$ and σ to be the average distance $\bar{D}(w_f, f_i)$ by cross-validation to achieve the best performance. Equation 2 distributes different probability mass to all relevant codewords (bins), where relevancy is determined by distances between an expression feature to all the codewords v in the vocabulary V.

3.3 Temporal Pyramid Matching Kernel

Intuitively, to measure the expression convergence between two video clips, we want to capture not only the global mirroring but also the local temporal coherence. That is, histogram matches in smaller temporal cells should be rewarded because two similar expressions (of two subjects) that come one after another are more likely to be engaged in a common topic and context, in contrast to those that take place with a large time lag. Putting all the pieces together, we propose a temporal pyramid matching approach based on [7] to calculate the similarity distance $Dis(i, j)$ between the cumulative expression histograms of two video clips $\{i, j\}$:

$$Dis(i,j) = \sum_{l=0}^{L} \frac{1}{\alpha^l} \sum_{p=1}^{m(l)} \beta_p^l \chi^2(CEH_p^l(i), CEH_p^l(j)). \tag{4}$$

In the above equation, $CEH_p^l(i)$ and $CEH_p^l(j)$ are two video clips' local cumulative expression histograms at the pth position of level l; α and β are two weighting parameters; $\chi^2(\cdot,\cdot)$ are the chi-square distance function used to measure the distance between two histograms. In this paper, we empirically chose ($L = 3$) levels of temporal pyramids for better results: $l = 0$ (Level of whole clip, $m(0) = 1$, $\beta_1^0 = 1$), $l = 1$ (Level of bipartition, $l = 1$, $m(1) = 2$, $\beta_1^1 \sim \beta_2^1 = \frac{1}{2}$), $l = 2$ (Level of quadripartition, $m(2) = 4$, $\beta_1^2 \sim \beta_4^2 = \frac{1}{4}$); $\alpha^l = 2^{L-l-1}$ for $l = 0, 1, 2$.

Table 2: Sample mean and standard error of Population 1 and Population 2 when clip length is 3 minutes.

	Population 1	Population 2
Number of Observation	1300	2600
Sample Mean	0.2410	0.2899
Sample STD	0.2769	0.2669
Significance level	0.05	
p-level	7.953×10^{-8}	
Critical value	-1.6495	
Confidence Interval	$[-\infty - 3.3564]$	

4. RESULTS

In our experiments we randomly sampled 100 pairs of video clips, each of 3 minute durations, from 13 dyads to form the Intra-Conversation Set containing 1300 pairs in all. To form the Inter-Conversation Set, first we randomly sampled 100 video clips (once again each of 3 minutes in length) for each of 26 participants. Then we paired each sample clip with a clip randomly selected from the conversation of a different dyad. In this way the Inter-Conversation Set contains 2600 nominal dyad pairs in total. The distance data in Population 1 (w.r.t. Intra-Conversation Set containing time-synced video clips from dyad pairs) and Population 2 (w.r.t. Inter-Conversation Set containing nominal dyad video clips) was computed according to Equation 4. The sample means and sample standard deviations of two populations are illustrated in Table 2.

Lower-tailed, two sample t-test on Population 1 and Population 2. Our original hypothesis that people engaged in face-to-face collaborative activity demonstrate a heightened degree of facial expression mirroring can now be tested using a lower-tailed, two sample t-test in which the null/alternative hypotheses is defined as H_0: $\mu_1 = \mu_2$ and H_α: $\mu_1 < \mu_2$ respectively, in which μ_1 (μ_2) represents the mean of Population 1 (Population 2). We adopted Matlab function *ttest2* to conduct this test in which Satterthwaite's approximation [12] was used for the case that equal variances of two data populations are not assumed. As shown in Table 2, at a significance level of 0.05, the computed upper-bound of the confidence interval (-3.3564) is less than the critical value (-1.6495); the computed p-value is 7.953×10^{-8}. So we accept the alternative hypothesis H_α ($\mu_1 < \mu_2$) at the 0.05 significance level, which concludes a sta-

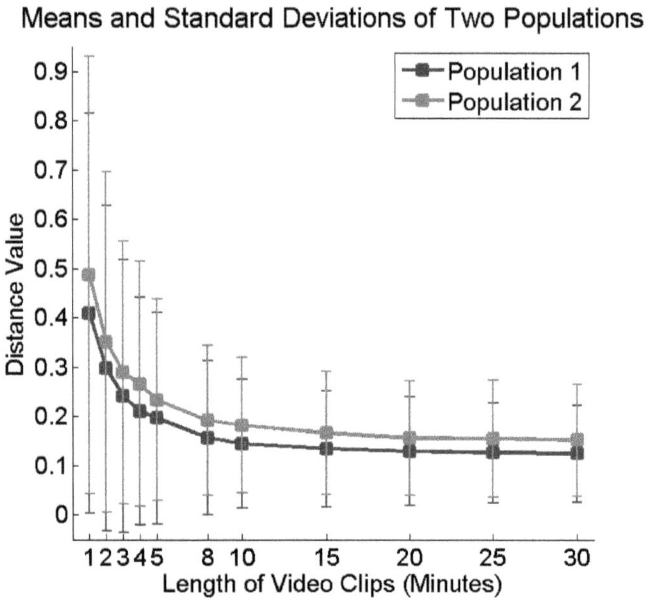

Figure 3: The means and standard deviations of two populations for different length of video clips. Both curves for Population 1 and Population 2 decrease monotonously w.r.t. length of video clips.

tistically significant mirroring effect in facial expressions between 3-minute dyad pairs.

Comparison on Level of expression mirroring w.r.t. different dyads. Intuitively, dyads should differ with each other on the level of expression mirroring. To measure this difference, in this experiment we employed μ_1 (the mean of Population 1) as the threshold to compute thresholded Average Intra-dyad Distances (AID) on 13 dyads. Average Intra-dyad Distance (AID) of Dyad i was calculated as the mean distance of 100 intra-conversation pairs corresponding to Dyad i only. Then for each Dyad i μ_1 was subtracted to obtain $thresholded\ AID(i)$. As illustrated in Figure 2, the thresholded AIDs of Dyad 1, 2, 3, 4, 5, 8, 11, 12, 13 (9 dyads out of the total 13 dyads) are distinctively less than 0, which suggests remarkable expression mirroring within these dyads. However, the thresholded AIDs of Dyad 6, 7, 9, 10 are evidently larger than 0, which demonstrates less facial expression convergence.

4.1 Results for varying video clip length

In addition to analyzing data at 3 minute clip durations, we also performed a sweep analysis over various lengths of video clips ranging from 1 minutes to 30 minutes. As shown in Figure 3, the means of Population 1 are consistently smaller than those of Population 2, with similar standard deviations for each length value. We employed a series of two sample t-tests for all the clip length and our hypothesis ($\mu_1 < \mu_2$) is always accepted at the 0.05 significance level.

As we can observe from Figure 3, both curves for Population 1 and Population 2 decrease monotonously w.r.t. length of video clips. This is reasonable because more similar expressions are available for matching when clip length increases.

5. DISCUSSION

In this paper we propose an approach to discover evidence of facial expression mirroring exhibited by human dyads in online face-to-face interactions. By utilizing a temporal pyramid matching approach on facial expression features from video of interacting dyads we were able to demonstrate a statistically significant facial expression mirroring effect. Further research on behavioral convergence needs to be conducted by using multi-modal features, including, but not limited to, body movement and non-verbal/verbal cues. It would also be meaningful to extend our study to the analysis on non-face-to-face dyads to test if our hypothesis still holds when people in the same dyad are not able to see each other's face. Finally, further research needs to be conducted to evaluate the impact of facial expression mirroring on the outcomes of collaborative activity, which might inform us on how to create appropriate affordances for improved outcomes.

6. REFERENCES

[1] Manual of emotient's facet sdk. *iMotions Inc.*, 2013.

[2] S. Barsade. The ripple effect: Emotional contagion and its influence on group behavior. *Administrative Science Quarterly*, 47:644–âĂŞ675, 2002.

[3] D. L. Bazaldua, S. Khan, A. von Davier, J. Hao, L. Liu, and Z. Wang. On convergence of cognitive and non-cognitive behavior in collaborative activity. In *The 8th International Conference on Educational Data Mining (EDM 2015).*

[4] S. Bilakhia, S. Petridis, and M. Pantic. Audiovisual detection of behavioural mimicry. In *IEEE Humaine Association Conference on Affective Computing and Intelligent Interaction*, Chicago, 2013.

[5] P. Ekman and W. Friesen. Facial action coding system: A technique for the measurement of facial movement. *Consulting Psychologists Press*, 1978.

[6] J. L. Lakin, V. E. Jefferis, C. M. Cheng, and T. L. Chartrand. The chameleon effect as social glue: Evidence for the evolutionary significance of nonconscious mimicry. *Journal of nonverbal behavior*, 27(3):145–162, 2003.

[7] S. Lazebnik, C. Schmid, and J. Ponce. Beyond bags of features: Spatial pyramid matching for recognizing natural scene categories. In *CVPR'06.*

[8] F.-F. Li and P. Perona. A bayesian hierarchical model for learning natural scene categories. In *CVPR'05*, Washington, DC, USA, 2005.

[9] L. Liu, J. Hao, A. von Davier, P. Kyllonen, and D. Zapata-Rivera. *A tough nut to crack: Measuring collaborative problem solving*. IGI-Global. In Press.

[10] A. A. Tawfik, L. Sanchez, and D. Saparova. The effects of case libraries in supporting collaborative problem-solving in an online learning environment. *Technology, Knowledge and Learning*, 19(3):337–358, 2014.

[11] J. van Gemert, J. Geusebroek, C. Veenman, and A. Smeulders. Kernel codebooks for scene categorization. In *ECCV'08.*

[12] B. L. Welch. The generalization of student's problem when several different population variances are involved. *Biometrika*, 34:28âĂŞ–35, 1947.

[13] D. Zapata-Rivera, T. Jackson, L. Liu, M. Bertling, M. Vezzu, and I. R. Katz. Assessing science inquiry skills using trialogues. *Intelligent Tutoring Systems*, 8474:625–âĂŞ626, 2014.

Video Description Generation using Audio and Visual Cues

Qin Jin
Multimedia Computing Lab, School of Information
Key Lab of Data Engineering and Knowledge Engineering
Renmin University of China
qjin@ruc.edu.cn

Junwei Liang
Language Technologies Institute
School of Computer Science
Carnegie Mellon University
junweil@andrew.cmu.edu

ABSTRACT
The recent advances in image captioning stimulate the research in generating natural language description for visual content, which can be widely applied in many applications such as assisting blind people. Video description generation is a more complex task than image caption. Most works of video description generation focus on visual information in the video. However, audio provides rich information for describing video contents as well. In this paper, we propose to generate video descriptions in natural sentences using both audio and visual cues. We use unified deep neural networks with both convolutional and recurrent structure. Experimental results on the Microsoft Research Video Description (MSVD) corpus prove that fusing audio information greatly improves the video description performance.

Keywords
video description; image caption; audio analysis; deep neural networks.

1. INTRODUCTION
Describing visual content automatically in natural language sentences is a challenging task. It can be widely applied in many applications such as assisting blind people. With the recent success in generating natural language sentence descriptions for images which is also called image caption [1-3], generation of natural descriptions for videos has also attracted more and more attention in the research community. However, it is a more complex problem than image caption. Although there have been successful examples in specific domains with a limited set of known actions and objects [4, 5], generating descriptions for open-domain videos such as YouTube videos remains an open challenge.

Many of the recent works for video description generation rely on Long-Short Term Memory networks (LSTMs) [6], a type of recurrent neural networks (RNNs), from the visual point of view only. Visual information in videos has been captured by video-level representations [7-8], or frames-level representations [9], or sub-sampling on a fixed number of input frames [10]. However, human verbalization of video contents may rely not only on the visual information but also on other content-related information such as audio content that is not directly present in the visual source. In this paper, we study utilizing audio cues in the video together with visual cues for creating a better description system. Our approach is inspired by the recent progress in image caption such as in [1]. We also utilize a LSTM-RNN to model sequence dynamics and connect it directly to a convolutional neural network (CNN) and an acoustic feature extraction module which process incoming video frames for visual and acoustic encoding.

The rest of the paper is organized as follows: section 2 summarizes related works. Section 3 describes the key components of our video description system using audio and visual information. Section 4 presents the experiments and case studies on the MSVD corpus. Section 5 concludes the paper.

2. RELATED WORK
Image caption, generating a natural language description for images, has received a lot of attention and achieved some exciting results recently. Many works have been proposed [1-3, 11-14]. Most of them rely on two networks: CNN and RNN in particular with LSTM. CNN is used to provide image encoding and LSTM-RNN is used to translate from images to sentences of flexible length. Some public datasets have been accumulated in the community such as the Flickr30k corpus [15] and the Microsoft COCO (MSCOCO) corpus [16] etc. There are also studies to emphasize the novelty of generated descriptions [17].

The task of video description generation has also attracted more and more interest lately [4-5, 7-10, 18]. We can generally categorize video description approaches into two types. The first type normally relies on action recognition, object detection, attributes recognition, or event recognition to extract the information needed to render the linguistic entities for sentence generation [19]. The second type normally relies on the end-to-end sequence-to-sequence model. Similar to image caption methods, they also rely on CNNs and LSTM-RNNs for video description. It has been shown that pre-training the LSTM-RNN network for image captioning and fine-tuning it to video description is beneficial [9]. Some work [20] also builds a 2-D and/or 3-D CNN for learning powerful video representation and the LSTM-RNN network for generating sentences and a joint embedding model for exploring the relationships between visual content and sentence semantics.

Most previous researches targeting the problem of generating natural language descriptions for videos rely on visual content only. However, acoustic information also plays an important

ICMR'16, June 06-09, 2016, New York, NY, USA
© 2016 ACM. ISBN 978-1-4503-4359-6/16/06…$15.00
DOI: http://dx.doi.org/10.1145/2911996.2912043.

role in explaining and understanding an event/action in videos. In semantic concept annotation and classification of videos, fusion of audio and visual cues has been demonstrated very helpful, such as in the TRECVID Multimedia Event Detection (MED), Multimedia Event Recounting (MER), Surveillance Event Detection (SED), and Semantic Indexing (SIN) Systems [21]. However, to the best of our knowledge, there hasn't been much work on video description based on deep models using acoustic information, although there are some works on video classification using deep models with both visual and acoustic cues [30]. Therefore, in this paper, we conduct a pilot study on utilizing acoustic information to improve the video description performance based on deep models using visual cues only.

3. SYSTEM DESCRIPTION

Our video description system relies on deep models such as CNN and LSTM-RNN, which is similar to what was proposed by Vinyals et al. in [1]. An illustration of our description system is shown in Figure 1. The visual-only description system shares the similar system structure with the audio-only system. The difference lies in the feature representation component. The visual-only system uses CNN for feature encoding while the audio-only uses bag-of-acoustic-words for feature encoding. There are two phases in the system execution: training phase and test phase. In the training phase, the LSTM-RNN model is trained using target domain training data or is pre-trained using related auxiliary data and fine-tuned on the target domain data. In the test phase, the trained LSTM-RNN is applied for sentence prediction. There are three key components: visual/acoustic feature representation, text sequence modeling.

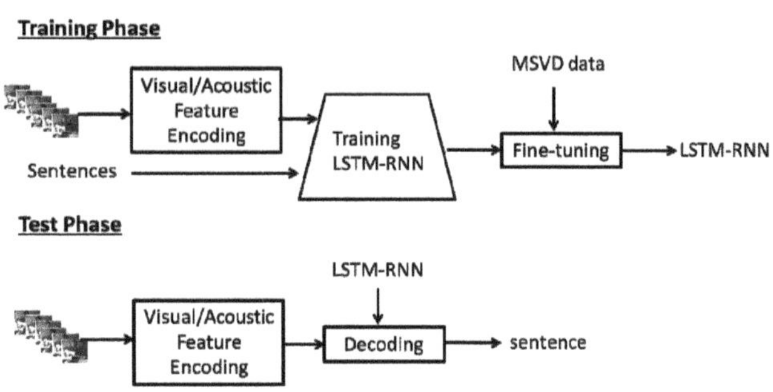

Figure 1: Illustration of video description system

3.1 Visual/Acoustic Feature Representation

A CNN is applied for visual feature representation. We use the pre-trained VGGNet [22] for visual feature extraction. A feature vector is extracted for each frame and mean pooling is applied to produce a video-level visual feature representation.

For acoustic feature representation, we first extract the single channel soundtrack from the video and re-sample it to 8kHz. We then apply feature extraction from the soundtrack. We use the Mel-frequency Cepstral Coefficients (MFCCs) [23] as our fundamental feature. The Fast Fourier Transformation (FFT) [24] is first applied over short-time window of 25ms with a 10ms shift. The spectrum of each window is warped to the Mel frequency scale, and the discrete cosine transform (DCT) [25] was applied over the log of these auditory spectra to compute MFCCs. Each video is then represented by a set of 39-dimensional MFCC feature vectors (13-dimensional MFCC + delta + delta delta). Finally, a bag-of-audio-words type of feature representation [26] is generated by applying an acoustic codebook to transform this set of MFCCs into a single fixed-dimension (4096) video-level feature representation.

3.2 Text Sequence Modeling

Standard RNNs learn to map a sequence of inputs ($X_1,...,X_N$) to a sequence of outputs ($Z_1,...,Z_N$) via a sequence of hidden states ($h_1,...,h_N$). The memory cell in LSTM model encodes, at every time step, the knowledge of the inputs that have been observed up to that step. The cell is modulated by gates that are all sigmoidal. The gates decide whether the LSTM keeps or discards the value from them. The recurrences for the LSTM are defined as:

$$i_t = \sigma(W_{xi}x_t + W_{hi}h_{t-1})$$
$$f_t = \sigma(W_{xf}x_t + W_{hf}h_{t-1})$$
$$o_t = \sigma(W_{xo}x_t + W_{ho}h_{t-1})$$
$$c_t = f_t \odot c_{t-1} + i_t \odot \phi(W_{xc}x_t + W_{hc}h_{t-1})$$
$$h_t = o_t \odot \phi(c_t)$$

where i, f, o, c, W represent the input gate, forget gate, output gate, memory cell and weight matrix respectively. σ is the sigmoidal non-linearity, ϕ is the tangent non-linearity, and $\odot$ is the product with the gate value. After we extract the visual/acoustic features, we train and/or fine-tune a LSTM-RNN network. We employ LSTM-RNN to encode the sentence description of the video, and decode a visual/acoustic feature representation of fixed length to generate natural language output. The encoding LSTM-RNN and decoding LSTM-RNN are shared.

4. EXPERIMENTS

4.1 Data Description

We conduct our experiments on the Microsoft Research Video Description (MSVD) Corpus [27]. The MSVD corpus contains 1970 YouTube clips with duration between 10 seconds to 25 seconds, mostly depicting a single activity. Each video was then used to elicit short sentence descriptions from annotators. There are multi-lingual human-generated descriptions for each video in the corpus. We only use the English descriptions which amount to about 40 sentences per video. We split the video dataset according to [9] into a training set, a validation set and a testing set which consists of 1200 videos for training, 100 for validation and 670 for testing. The training split contains about 48.7k text sentences; the validation split contains 4.3k text sentences and the testing split contains 27.7k text sentences. We apply simple preprocessing on the text data by converting all text to lower case, tokenizing the sentences and removing punctuation.

We also use the MSCOCO corpus [16], which is a new image recognition, segmentation, and captioning dataset, to pre-train the video description system based on visual information.

To pre-train the video description system based on audio information, we collect more audio data in-the-wild from freesound.org which contains user-collected recordings with descriptions and tags. In total, we collect over 10,000 audio files with a total duration of about 200 hours, covering a wide range of sound categories such as activities, locations, occasions, objects, scenes, and nature sounds etc. Each audio comes with tags and descriptions made by its uploader, but the format and quality of the descriptions differ greatly from each other. To ensure the quality of the data we use to train our model, we only keep the description sentences that match the tags to avoid unrelated descriptions. In the end, each audio comes with a description of one or two sentences.

4.2 Evaluation Metric

We use the METEOR [28] metric which was originally proposed to evaluate machine translation results for quantitative evaluation of the video description system. The METEOR score is computed based on the alignment between a given hypothesis sentence and a set of candidate reference sentences.

4.3 Baseline Results

For the visual-based video description system, we pre-train the LSTM-RNN on the MSCOCO dataset. We then fine-tune the model on the MSVD training set using a low learning rate. The system yields a METEOR score of 25.0% on the MSVD test set, which is comparable to the state-of-the-art description results as reported in [8-9]. The audio-based video description system achieves a METEOR score of 18.8% if we train the LSTM-RNN directly on MSVD training set. If the system is pre-trained on the freesound data as described in section 4.1 and then fine-tuned on the MSVD training data, the METEOR score is improved to 19.6%. The results show that visual-only system achieves better description performance than audio-only system.

As we look closely into the videos in the MSVD corpus, we find that some videos are post-edited with pure music. For the purpose of investigating how much additional information that audio content can contribute to the visual-only based description, we think such videos may not be useful for this purpose. We therefore filter out those videos that are post-edited with pure non-content-related music or with no soundtrack from the MSVD corpus. About 12% of the video data were filtered out and the remaining 1729 videos are used in the following experiments. A METEOR score of 23.70% and 20.21% is achieved respectively if the visual-only description system and audio-only description system are evaluated on the filtered test set. The performance of the audio-only system improves a bit but that of the visual-only system drops slightly which is not surprising since the filtering is biased towards audio. Although the visual-only system outperforms the audio-only system, from some detailed case analysis, we find that the audio-only system can provide complementary information that the visual-only system fails to capture. For example in Figure 2, the visual-only system predicts the description "A woman is exercising". While the audio-only system detects acoustic characteristics – the music playing in the room - and predicts the correct dancing activity and generates a better description "A girl is dancing".

4.4 Fusion of Audio and Visual Cues

As shown in the above example, audio and visual information are complementary and should be combined for a better description system. We therefore construct a video description system using both visual and acoustic cues. In this paper, we achieve the combination at the feature representation level by simply concatenating the video-level CNN visual features and the bag-of-audio-words acoustic features. We then train the LSTM-RNN model on the MSVD training set. To reduce the dimension of the simply concatenated audio+visual feature representation, we apply pca on the bag-of-audio-words feature to reduce its dimension to 400 before concatenation.

The description performance comparison in METEOR among the audio-only, visual-only and audio+visual combined systems is presented in Table 1. We can see that combining audio and visual cues together greatly improves the description performance over each single fine-tuned baseline.

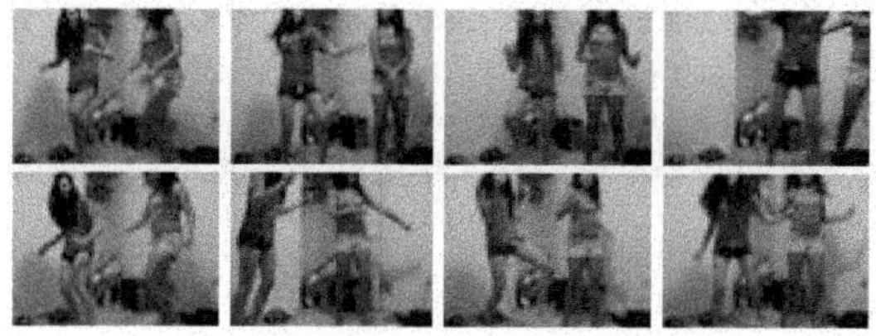

(a) Visual-only: A woman is excising
(b) Audio-only: A girl is dancing

Figure 2. An example description generated by the audio-only and visual-only system respectively

Table 1: Comparison among the audio-only, visual-only and combined description systems (METEOR in %)

System	Audio	Visual	Combined
METEOR	20.21	23.70	**26.17**

(a) Visual-only system: A woman is talking (35.06%)
(b) Combined system: A man is talking (100%)
(1)

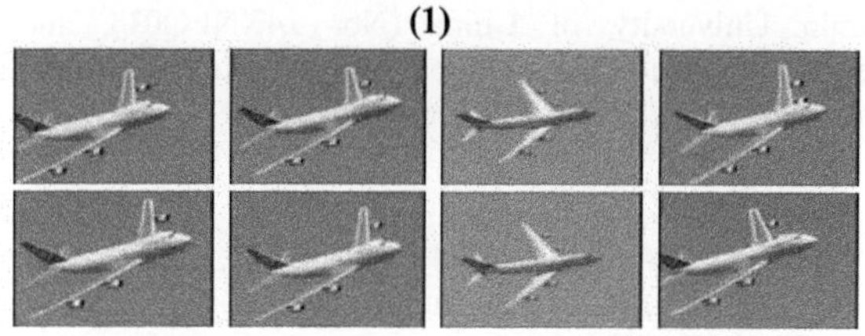

(a) Visual-only system: A car is running (9.04%)
(b) Combined system: A plane is flying (49.29%)
(2)

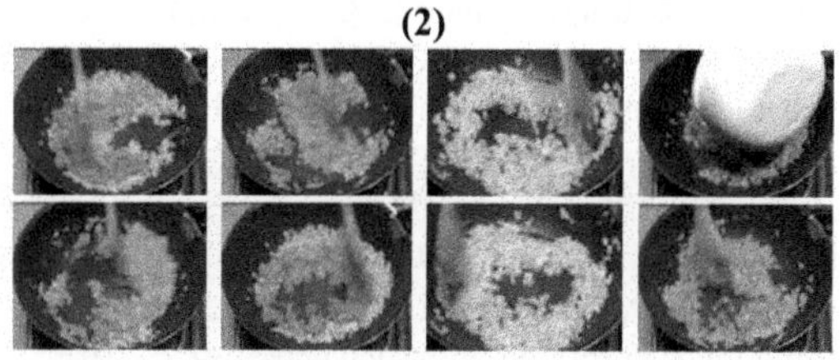

(a) Visual-only system: A person is cooking (25.24%)
(b) Combined system: A woman is cooking (49.29%)
(3)

Figure 3. Example descriptions from visual-only system vs. from combined system

In Figure 3, we showcase some video description examples from visual-only system vs. audio+visual combined system. On these examples, the combined system achieves higher METEOR score than the visual-only system. The METEOR score is shown in the brackets following each sentence. We observe that the combined system can provide more accurate description such as identifying the correct gender of the person by taking the acoustic cues into account, as shown in examples (1) and (3), or making correct object detection with the help of acoustic cues, as shown in example (2).

5. CONCLUSIONS

Generating natural language descriptions of video content is a challenging problem. Most works for video description generation focus only on visual information in the video. However, audio also provides rich information for describing video contents. In this paper, we investigate using acoustic information in addition to the visual information in the video for natural language description generation. Our system relies on CNN and LSTM-RNN two networks. We simply combine both acoustic and visual information at the video representation level. Experiments on the Microsoft Research Video Description corpus show that fusing audio information improves the description performance greatly. Case studies show that audio information can fix the acoustically related errors in the visual-only description output. Therefore, there is a lot of benefit to explore using acoustic information for video description prediction. In this work, the visual and acoustic information are both captured at holistic video representation level. In the future work, we will explore more powerful representation by taking into account the sequential aspect and synchronizing visual and acoustic information for joint modeling. We will look at larger video databases such as [29] as well.

6. ACKNOWLEDGEMENT

This work was partially supported by the Beijing Natural Science Foundation (No. 4142029), the Fundamental Research Funds for the Central Universities and the Research Funds of Renmin University of China (No. 14XNLQ01), and the Scientific Research Foundation for the Returned Overseas Chinese Scholars, State Education Ministry.

7. REFERENCES

[1] O. Vinyals, A. Toshev, S. Bengio, and D. Erhan. "Show and tell: A neural image caption generator". *arXiv:*1411.4555, 2014.

[2] J. Donahue, L. A. Hendricks, S. Guadarrama, M. Rohrbach, S. Venugopalan, K. Saenko, and T. Darrell. "Long-term recurrent convolutional networks for visual recognition and description". *CVPR,* 2015.

[3] J. Mao, W. Xu, Y. Yang, J.Wang, and A. L. Yuille. "Deep captioning with multimodal recurrent neural networks (m-rnn)". *arXiv:*1412.6632, 2014.

[4] H. Yu and J. M. Siskind. "Grounded language learning from videos described with sentences". *ACL*, 2013.

[5] P. Das, C. Xu, R. F. Doell, and J. J. Corso. "A thousand frames in just a few words: Lingual description of videos through latent topics and sparse object stitching". *CVPR*, 2013.

[6] S. Hochreiter and J. Schmidhuber. "Long short-term memory". *Neural Computation*, 1997.

[7] S. Guadarrama, et al. "Youtube2text: Recognizing and describing arbitrary activities using semantic hierarchies and zero-shoot recognition". *ICCV'13.*

[8] M. Rohrbach, et al. "Translating video content to natural language descriptions". *ICCV*'13.

[9] S. Venugopalan, et al. "Translating videos to natural language using deep recurrent neural networks". NAACL, 2015.

[10] L. Yao, et al. "Describing videos by exploiting temporal structure". *arXiv:1502.08029v4*, 2015.

[11] H. Fang, S. Gupta, et al. "From captions to visual concepts and back". *CVPR*, 2015.

[12] A. Karpathy, L. Fei-Fei. "Deep visual-semantic alignments for generating image descriptions". *CVPR*, 2015.

[13] R. Kiros, R. Salakhutdinov, R.S. Zemel. "Unifying visual-semantic embeddings with multimodal neural language models". *Trans. of ACL*, 2015.

[14] K. Xu, et al. "Show, attend and tell: Neural image caption generation with visual attention". *arXiv:1502.03044*, 2015.

[15] P. Young, et al. "From image descriptions to visual denotations: New similarity metrics for semantic inference over event descriptions". *Trans. of ACL,* 2014.

[16] T.-Y. Lin, et al. "Microsoft coco: Common objects in context". *arXiv:1405.0312*, 2014.

[17] J. Devlin, et al. "Language models for image captioning: The quirks and what works". *arXiv:1505.01809*, 2015.

[18] S. Venugopalan, M. Rohrbach, J. Donahue, R. J. Mooney, T. Darrell, and K. Saenko. "Sequence to Sequence - Video to Text". *arXiv: 1505.00487*, 2015.

[19] A. Barbu, et al. "Video In Sentence Out". UAI 2012.

[20] Y. Pan, et al. "Jointly modeling embedding and translation to bridge video and language". *arXiv:1505.01861*, 2015.

[21] L. Brown, et al. "IBM Research and Columbia University TRECVID-2013 MED, MER, SED, and SIN Systems". TRECVID 2013.

[22] K. Simonyan, A. Zisserman. "Very deep convolutional networks for large-scale image recognition". *arXiv:1409.1556*, 2014.

[23] S.B. Davis and P. Mermelstein . "Comparison of Parametric Representations for Monosyllabic Word Recognition in Continuously Spoken Sentences". *IEEE Trans. on Acoustics, Speech, and Signal Processing*, 28(4), 357–366, 1980.

[24] D.N. Rockmore, "The FFT: an algorithm the whole family can use". Computing in Science Engineering 2(1): 60-64, 2000.

[25] N. Ahmed, et al. "Discrete Cosine Transform". *IEEE Transactions on Computers* 23(1): 90-93, 1974.

[26] S. Pancoast, M. Akbacak. "Softening quantization in bag-of-audio-words", *ICASSP 2014*, 1370 - 1374.

[27] D. Chen, W. Dolan. "Collecting highly parallel data for paraphrase evaluation". *ACL,* 2011.

[28] S. Banerjee and A. Lavie. "Meteor: An automatic metric for MT evaluation with improved correlation with human judgments". *ACL Workshop on Intrinsic and Extrinsic Evaluation Measures for Machine Translation / Summarization*, 2005.

[29] T. Bart, B. Elizalde, D.A. Shamma, K. Ni, G. Friendland, D. Poland, D. Borth, L.J. Li. "YFCC100M: The new data in multimedia research". Communications of the ACM 59, No. 2 (2016): 64-73.

[30] Z. Wu, et al. "Exploring Inter-feature and inter-class relationships with deep neural networks for video classification". ACM Multimedia 2014.

Xplore-M-Ego: Contextual Media Retrieval Using Natural Language Queries

Sreyasi Nag Chowdhury Mateusz Malinowski Andreas Bulling Mario Fritz
Max Planck Institute for Informatics, Saarbrücken, Germany
sreyasi,mmalinowski,bulling,mfritz@mpi-inf.mpg.de

ABSTRACT

The widespread integration of cameras in hand-held and head-worn devices and the ability to share content online enables a large and diverse visual capture of the world that millions of users build up collectively every day. We envision these images as well as associated meta information, such as GPS coordinates and timestamps, to form a collective visual memory that can be queried while automatically taking the ever-changing context of mobile users into account. As a first step towards this vision, in this work we present *Xplore-M-Ego*: a novel media retrieval system that allows users to query a dynamic database of images using spatio-temporal natural language queries. We evaluate our system using a new dataset of real image queries as well as through a usability study. One key finding is that there is a considerable amount of inter-user variability in the resolution of spatial relations in natural language utterances. We show that our system can cope with this variability using personalisation through an online learning-based retrieval formulation.

What is there to the left of MPI-SWS?

What is there in front of bus terminal?

What is near MPI-INF?

What did this place look like in December?

Figure 1: Sample queries and retrieved images of our contextual media retrieval system Xplore-M-Ego.

1. INTRODUCTION

Due to the widespread deployment of visual sensors in consumer products and Internet sharing platforms, we have collectively achieved a detailed visual capture of the world in space and time over the years. In particular, mobile devices have changed the way we take pictures and new technology like life-logging devices will continue to do so. With efficient search engines, viewing images and videos of distant places is a few clicks away. But these search engines do not allow for complex natural language queries with spatio-temporal references. They also largely ignore the users' local context.

Similar to how mobile devices have changed the way we take pictures, we ask how media search should be transformed to make use of the rich context available at query time. What if we quickly want to know what is behind the building in front of us? What if we want to know what a particular cafe looks like to quickly locate it in a busy market area? What if we want to see what our new neighborhood looks like in winter? Our approach makes use of the user's ever-changing context to retrieve results of a spatio-temporal query on a mobile device. We have named our system *Xplore-M-Ego* (read *"Explore Amigo"*) – which stands for Exploration(Xplore) of Media(M) Egocentrically(Ego)".

ICMR'16, June 06 - 09, 2016, New York, NY, USA

ISBN 978-1-4503-4359-6/16/06...$15.00
DOI: http://dx.doi.org/10.1145/2911996.2912044

2. RELATED WORK

Spatio-temporal Media Retrieval: Previous work [17, 22, 20, 19] allow for browsing media in their geographic context, optionally at different points of time. In contrast, our approach implements egocentrism by taking users' context (geographical location and viewing direction) into account.

Natural Language Query Processing: Answering natural language questions by machines is often realizable by a semantic parser that transforms the question into its formal representation. Modern approaches to training a semantic parser [2, 10, 1] using question-answer pairs have replaced traditional ones using manual annotations [23, 21]. The subjective-ness of question-answering tasks has been pointed out in [13, 15]. Unlike existing work, we target a dynamic and egocentric environment instead of static data.

Media Retrieval Using Natural Language Queries: Previous research have matched queries to manual descriptions of images [11, 7, 6, 4]. Our work does not use human annotations. We extract media based on meta data such as geographical location (GPS coordinates). [18, 8] have used spatial relations in restricted queries. We lift restrictions such as fixed sentence structure or limited vocabulary.

To the best of our knowledge, no previous work venture into media retrieval with the user's context. The introduction of egocentrism for browsing large media collections opens an unexplored dimension and also aids in human interaction with the computer.

3. CONTEXTUAL MEDIA RETRIEVAL

Our contextual media retrieval system allows users to explore a collective media collection in a spatio-temporal context through natural language questions like those in Figure 1. The formulation of our architecture is shown below.

3.1 Learning - based, Contextual Media Retrieval by Semantic Parsing

In this section we describe a semantic parser architecture and its extension towards a contextual media retrieval task. The probabilistic model of our architecture is shown in Figure 2. A question x is mapped to a latent logical form z, which is evaluated with respect to a world w (database of facts), producing an answer y. The world w consists of w_s (a static database of geographic facts) and w_d (a dynamic database which stores user and media metadata). The logical forms z are represented as labeled trees and are induced automatically from question-answer (x, y) pairs.

3.1.1 Question-Answering with Semantic Parsing

Our approach is built on an existing framework for semantic parsing [10] that is able to answer questions about static facts. In the framework (left part of Figure 2 labeled **Semantic Parsing** and **Interpretation**), 'parsing' translates a question into its logical form z, and 'interpretation' executes z on the dataset of facts w producing its denotation $[\![z]\!]_w$ - an answer. Parameter θ is estimated solely on the training question-answer pairs (x, y) with an EM algorithm maximizing the following posterior distribution:

$$\theta^* := \arg\max_{\theta} \sum_{(x,y)\sim\mathcal{D}} \sum_{z} \underbrace{\mathbf{1}\{y = [\![z]\!]_w\}}_{Interpretation} \underbrace{p(z|x,\theta)}_{SemanticParsing} \tag{1}$$

where $\mathcal{D}$ denotes a training set, $\mathbf{1}\{a = b\}$ is 1 if a condition $a = b$ holds, and 0 otherwise. The posterior distribution marginalizes over a latent set of valid logical forms z. At test time, the answer is computed from the denotation $[\![z^*]\!]_w$ that maximizes the following posteriori:

$$z^* := \arg\max_{z} p(z|x, \theta^*) \tag{2}$$

The distribution over logical forms is modeled by a log linear distribution $p_\theta(z|x) \propto e^{\phi(x,z)^T\theta}$, where the feature vector ϕ measures compatibility between the question x and a logical form z. We perform a gradient descent scheme in order to optimize for parameters θ.

3.1.2 Static and Dynamic Worlds

Related existing work are based on a static environment [10, 1, 13]. In contrast, in our scenario an user (the source of the query - *user* in Figure 2) relocates herself in space and time in a continuously changing environment. The pool of media content (*Collective Visual Memory*) also grows as new media is added (crowd icon in Figure 2). Such an environment leads to decomposition of the world w into a static part w_s, which consists of geographical facts such as names of buildings and theirs GPS coordinates, and a dynamic part w_d. The dynamic world w_d breaks up into w_{d_m} that stores media metadata (timestamp, GPS coordinates) and is updated with continuously growing *Collective Visual Memory*, and w_{d_u} that models the user's context by storing her metadata (GPS coordinates, viewing direction). The latter is set anew for each query before it is fed into the semantic parser. Such representation renders the world $w = w_s + w_d$ static to the semantic parser although it is constantly changing.

3.1.3 Modelling User's Context

Understanding egocentric spatial relations in natural language forms a separate research area by itself [16, 8, 3, 14]. In our work, we approach ambiguity in the frame of reference [15] by defining predicates to resolve the spatial relations *front of, behind, left of, right of* based on the geomagnetic as well as the user-centric reference frames. Temporal references in questions (*what happened here five days ago?, how did this place look like in December?*) are modelled through predicates unifying the referenced time-stamp with those of the media files. The user's context is modelled by recording the GPS coordinates and viewing direction at query-time.

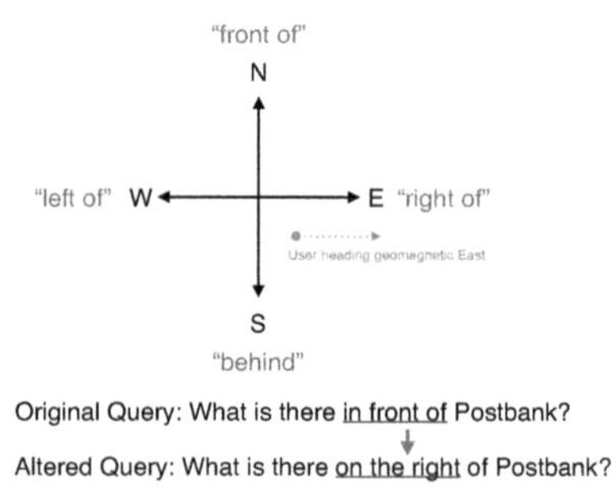

Figure 3: Modification of spatial reference in query for integrating *egocentrism* to media retrieval

However, it is hard to deduce the hidden intent for contextual questions since humans don't adhere to a consistent reference frame. They consider their own physical left or the *left side* of the geographic entity for *left of*. The prior requires an user-centric reference frame which is modelled by modifying the geomagnetic reference frame. Assuming that the user's viewing direction is the local north, the spatial reference in the query is modified in a pre-processing step. This is explained in Figure 3 – if the user faces east and queries for *What is there in front of postbank?*, the question is changed during pre-processing to *What is there on the right of postbank?*. The semantic parser predicts answer for the changed question. For simplicity we use only four basic heading directions - north, south, east and west.

3.1.4 Media Retrieval as Answers

In contrast to previous work on question answering [10, 13], we want to retrieve media instead of text as answers. This can be modeled by generating references to media files as denotations. For example, the question *What is there on the right of the campus center?* would predict the denotation (*image12, image58, ...*) which are references to relevant

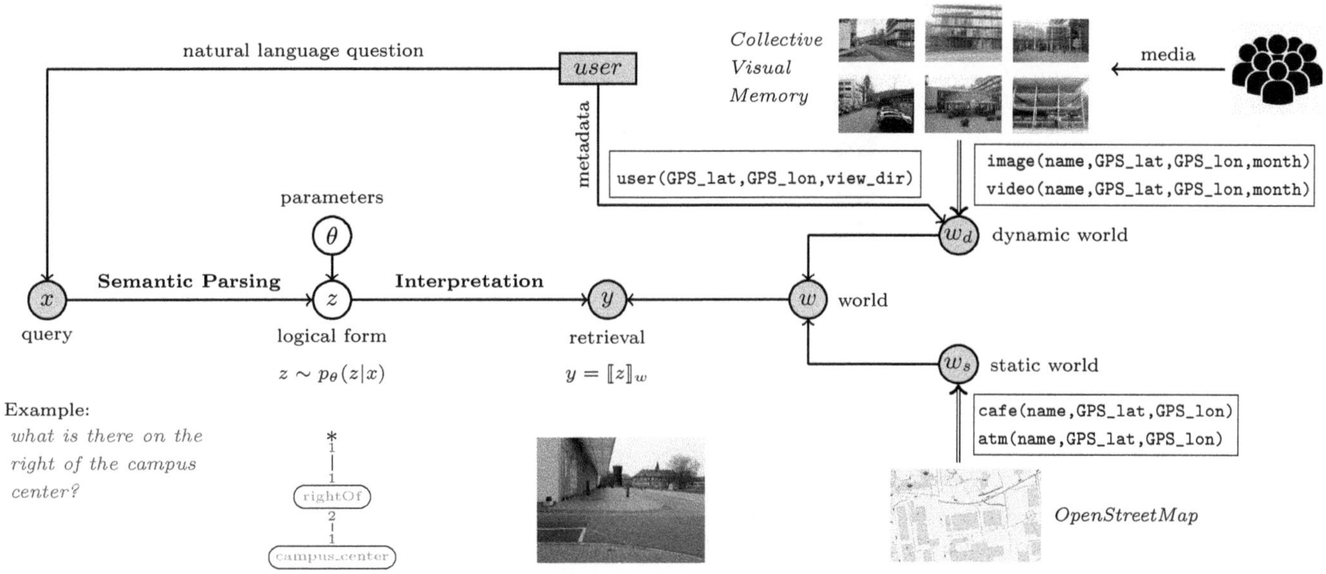

Figure 2: Our probabilistic graphical model: a question x in natural language is automatically mapped into a logical form z by the semantic parser. It is interpreted with respect to a world w to give retrievals y. The world w consists of a static part w_s (a database of geographical facts), and a dynamic part w_d (media content from *Collective Visual Memory* and the user's spatio-temporal context).

images. The actual images are then extracted from the *Collective Visual Memory* and returned to the user.

3.2 Data Collection

To enable spatio-temporal exploration of a geographic area we need a database which record physical features on the ground. To support media retrieval we need a database of images and videos rich with metadata. We also need natural language queries paired with corresponding media content as retrievals for training and testing our model. In the absence of a suitable benchmark, we record our own data set.

Geographical Facts: We extract the our geographic data from OpenStreetMap [5]. In our study, we restrict the spatial scope of our system to a university campus. We use information such as the type of the physical entity (*building, cafe, highway* etc.), their names, and their GPS coordinates.

Collective Visual Memory: Participants formulated questions and captured the photo(s)/video(s) that they expect as corresponding answers. 1000 questions-answer pairs with spatial references were collected. Question-answer pairs with temporal references were not collected because of the trivial infeasibility of capturing events from the past. The questions follow no particular template and contains a variety of spatial relations. The dataset was randomized and divided into 500 train and 500 test questions. To introduce sufficient amount of variations in natural language we chose participants from different cultural and linguistic background. Our instance of the *Collective Visual Memory* consists of 1025 images and 175 videos. The dataset is publicly available[1].

4. MODEL EVALUATION

Humans are inherently inconsistent in their perception of directions and idea of reference frames [9, 15]. The nature of speaking English questions also has variations based on a person's socio-cultural background. Hence, a system relying on fixed question templates and a particular set of rules to resolve spatial references does not guarantee high accuracy. To better understand these perceptual biases and efficiently analyze the system, a series of user studies were conducted.

4.1 Human Disagreements on Retrieved Results

The goal of this user study is to observe how accurate regular users find our system. Five users evaluated the retrieved results for 500 test questions as *relevant* or *irrelevant*. A canonical reference frame was used in this experiment to resolve spatial relations. According to this convention, *front of=north of*, *behind=south of*, *right of=east of* and *left of=west of*.

We observed that the opinions varied for each question. Based on this observation we divide the test questions into six groups – *(5,0)*, queries for which all five users agreed that the retrievals were relevant; *(4,1)*, queries for which four users found the retrievals relevant and one user found them irrelevant and likewise. Figure 4 depicts the result of this analysis. For 26.67% of the queries all five users deemed the retrievals relevant. However, if we consider the cases in which most of the users found the retrievals relevant, this number rises to 40%. The numbers in the middle region of the graph in Figure 4 point out the prominent difference in opinions among participants. This accounts for about 25% of all queries. We observed that the inter-user variability stems from the inherent inconsistencies with regards to reference frame resolution. This result also hints towards the difficulty of the problem at hand. From this observation we conjecture that the use of user-centric reference frames instead of geomagnetic reference frame could improve the performance of the system. In the deployment of the user-centric reference frame we mean to follow the user's physical egocentric directions – for example, her *right hand side* for *right of* etc.

[1]http://www.mpi-inf.mpg.de/xplore-m-ego

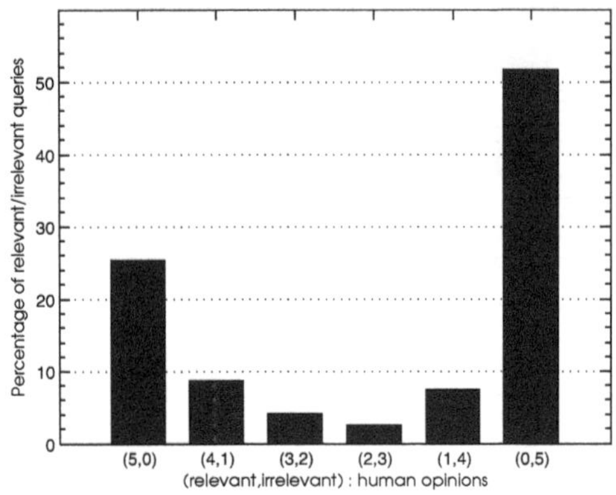

Figure 4: Inter-user variability in opinion

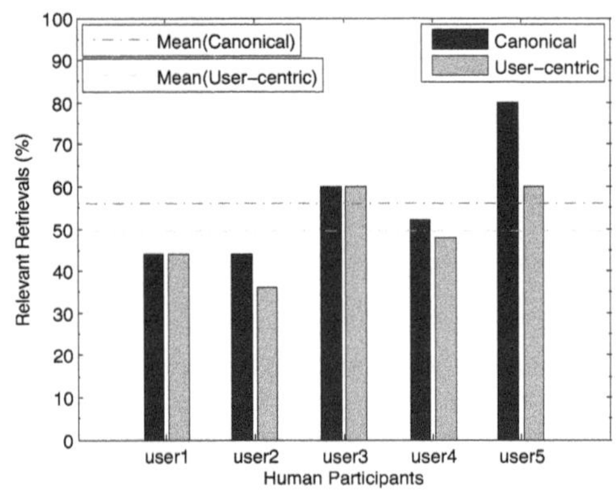

Figure 5: Difference in reference frame resolution among humans

4.2 Canonical and User-centric Reference Frame

The aim of this evaluation is to study the impact of using two different conventions of spatial relations resolution. Users were given two sets of retrieved results for each question – one set of media files retrieved according to the geomagnetic reference frame and the second set retrieved according to the user-centric reference frame. The experimental settings are similar to the previous user study.

Figure 5 shows the result of this user study. user1 and user3 remained neutral to the use of separate reference frames while the other users slightly preferred the canonical reference frame over the user-centric reference frame. This observation further highlights the subjectivity of the task.

4.3 Personalization of Xplore-M-Ego

Having observed this inter-person subjectivity, we hypothesize that personalization of our media retrieval system would increase its accuracy on a per user basis. By using an online relevance feedback mechanism, five users *(U1, U2, U3, U4, U5)* trained five different query-retrieval models *(M1, M2, M3, M4, M5)* with 500 questions. Every user was then asked to evaluate all five models keeping the identity of the models hidden.

The quantitative analysis of this study is shown in Figure 6. The diagonal shows the user-specific evaluation results and the rows depict inter-user evaluation results. It is clear from the figure that users deemed their own models more accurate than those trained by others. This observation leads us to believe that the query-retrieval model can be trained over time through relevance feedback to adapt

	$U1$	$U2$	$U3$	$U4$	$U5$
$M1$	25.36	8.84	14.84	12.21	15.79
$M2$	20.38	35.9	33.9	24.06	25.25
$M3$	15.66	13.25	37.33	15.06	28.59
$M4$	14.49	24.32	33.38	36.86	28.06
$M5$	8.58	11.34	23.53	17.48	37.84

Figure 6: Quantitative analysis of personalization of Xplore-M-Ego: F1-score

USE Questionnaire	Mean	SD
It is useful.	6.2	0.63
It saves me time when I use it.	6.1	0.73
It is easy to use.	6.3	0.48
I can use it without written instructions.	5.8	1.22
Both occasional and regular users would like it.	5.4	1.42
I learned to use it quickly.	6.5	0.52
I quickly became skillful with it.	6.1	0.99
I am satisfied with it.	5.5	0.52
It is fun to use.	6.3	0.82
I would recommend it to a friend.	5.9	0.73

Table 1: User Experience Evaluation: Mean Rating and Standard Deviation. The grades are between 1 ('strongly disagree') and 7 ('strongly agree').

to user-specific preferences of spatial relation resolution – hence, it should be personalized.

4.4 User Experience Evaluation

In this usability/desirability study, ten participants were given the Google Glass installed with our client-side application and asked to walk around in the university campus while making voice queries with spatio-temporal references. Afterward they were asked to fill in the USE Questionnaire [12]. This questionnaire has four groups of questions – Usefulness, Ease of Use, Ease of Learning and Satisfaction. Each question can be rated on a scale from 1 to 7, 1 meaning 'strongly disagree' and 7 meaning 'strongly agree'. Ten questions most representative of the entire questionnaire are chosen. The mean and standard deviation of the ratings of these questions are shown in Table 1.

The result of this evaluation shows that regular users find our application useful, easy to learn, and satisfying.

5. CONCLUSION

In this paper we propose *Xplore-M-Ego* – a novel system for media retrieval using spatio-temporal natural language queries in a dynamic setting. Our work brings forth a new direction to this paradigm by exploiting a user's current context. Our approach is based on a semantic parser that learns to infer interpretations of the natural language queries from question-answer pairs. We contribute several extensions which enable the user to dynamically refer to her context by spatial and temporal concepts. We analyze the system with various user studies that highlight the importance of our adaptive and personalized training approaches. For further details and discussions on our approach and observations we direct the readers to our technical report[2].

[2]http://arxiv.org/pdf/1602.04983.pdf

6. REFERENCES

[1] J. Berant and P. Liang. Semantic parsing via paraphrasing. In *Proceedings of ACL*, 2014.

[2] J. Clarke, D. Goldwasser, M.-W. Chang, and D. Roth. Driving semantic parsing from the world's response. In *Proceedings of the Fourteenth Conference on Computational Natural Language Learning*, pages 18–27. Association for Computational Linguistics, 2010.

[3] S. Guadarrama, L. Riano, D. Golland, D. Gouhring, Y. Jia, D. Klein, P. Abbeel, and T. Darrell. Grounding spatial relations for human-robot interaction. In *Intelligent Robots and Systems (IROS), 2013 IEEE/RSJ International Conference on*, pages 1640–1647. IEEE, 2013.

[4] A. Hakeem, M. W. Lee, O. Javed, and N. Haering. Semantic video search using natural language queries. pages 605–608, 2009.

[5] M. Haklay and P. Weber. Openstreetmap: User-generated street maps. *Pervasive Computing, IEEE*, 7(4):12–18, 2008.

[6] M. Hwang, H. Kong, S. Baek, and P. Kim. A method for processing the natural language query in ontology-based image retrieval system. In *Adaptive Multimedia Retrieval: User, Context, and Feedback*, pages 1–11. Springer, 2007.

[7] O. Kucuktunc, U. Güdükbay, and Ö. Ulusoy. A natural language-based interface for querying a video database. *IEEE MultiMedia*, 14(1):83–89, 2007.

[8] T. Lan, W. Yang, Y. Wang, and G. Mori. Image retrieval with structured object queries using latent ranking svm. In *Computer Vision–ECCV 2012*, pages 129–142. Springer, 2012.

[9] S. C. Levinson. *Space in language and cognition: Explorations in cognitive diversity*, volume 5. Cambridge University Press, 2003.

[10] P. Liang, M. I. Jordan, and D. Klein. Learning dependency-based compositional semantics. *Computational Linguistics*, 39(2):389–446, 2013.

[11] V. Lum and K.-c. K. Kim. Intelligent natural language processing for media data query. In *Proc. 2nd Int. Golden West Conf. on Intelligent Systems*, 1992.

[12] A. M. Lund. Measuring usability with the use questionnaire. *Usability interface*, 8(2):3–6, 2001.

[13] M. Malinowski and M. Fritz. A multi-world approach to question answering about real-world scenes based on uncertain input. In *Advances in Neural Information Processing Systems (NIPS)*, pages 1682–1690, 2014.

[14] M. Malinowski and M. Fritz. A pooling approach to modelling spatial relations for image retrieval and annotation. *arXiv:1411.5190 [cs.CV]*, November 2014.

[15] M. Malinowski and M. Fritz. Towards a visual turing challenge. In *NIPS Workshop on Learning Semantics*, 2014.

[16] T. Regier and L. A. Carlson. Grounding spatial language in perception: an empirical and computational investigation. *Journal of Experimental Psychology: General*, 130(2):273, 2001.

[17] N. Snavely, S. M. Seitz, and R. Szeliski. Photo tourism: exploring photo collections in 3d. *ACM transactions on graphics (TOG)*, 25(3):835–846, 2006.

[18] S. Tellex and D. Roy. Towards surveillance video search by natural language query. In *Proceedings of the ACM International Conference on Image and Video Retrieval*, page 38. ACM, 2009.

[19] J. Tompkin, K. I. Kim, J. Kautz, and C. Theobalt. Videoscapes: exploring sparse, unstructured video collections. *ACM Transactions on Graphics (TOG)*, 31(4):68, 2012.

[20] J. Tompkin, F. Pece, R. Shah, S. Izadi, J. Kautz, and C. Theobalt. Video collections in panoramic contexts. In *Proceedings of the 26th annual ACM symposium on User interface software and technology*, pages 131–140. ACM, 2013.

[21] Y. W. Wong and R. J. Mooney. Learning synchronous grammars for semantic parsing with lambda calculus. In *Annual Meeting-Association for computational Linguistics*, volume 45, page 960. Citeseer, 2007.

[22] F. Wu and M. Tory. Photoscope: visualizing spatiotemporal coverage of photos for construction management. pages 1103–1112, 2009.

[23] L. S. Zettlemoyer and M. Collins. Learning to map sentences to logical form: Structured classification with probabilistic categorial grammars. *arXiv preprint arXiv:1207.1420*, 2012.

Learning Music Embedding with Metadata for Context Aware Recommendation

Dongjing Wang[1,3], Shuiguang Deng*[1], Xin Zhang[2], Guandong Xu[3]

[1]College of Computer Science and Technology, Zhejiang University, Hangzhou, Zhejiang, China

[2]School of Computer Science and Technology, Shandong University, Jinan, Shandong, China

[3]Advanced Analytics Institute, University of Technology Sydney, Sydney, Australia

{tokyo1, dengsg}@zju.edu.cn; jiayou.zhangxin@163.com; Guandong.xu@uts.edu.au

ABSTRACT

Contextual factors can benefit music recommendation and retrieval tasks remarkably. However, how to acquire and utilize the contextual information still need to be studied. In this paper, we propose a context aware music recommendation approach, which can recommend music appropriate for users' contextual preference for music. In analogy to matrix factorization methods for collaborative filtering, the proposed approach does not require songs to be described by features beforehand, but it learns music pieces' embeddings (vectors in low-dimensional continuous space) from music playing records and corresponding metadata and infer users' general and contextual preference for music from their playing records with the learned embedding. Then, our approach can recommend appropriate music pieces. Experimental evaluations on a real world dataset show that the proposed approach outperforms baseline methods.

Categories and Subject Descriptors

H.2.8 [**Database Management**]: Database Applications—*Data Mining*

Keywords

Recommender Systems; Music Recommendation; Context Aware Recommendation; Embedding

1. INTRODUCTION

Nowadays, there are an enormous amount of musical contents available on the Internet. Therefore, it becomes more and more difficult for users to find the music that they enjoy. Therefore, recommender systems [1-4] have emerged to reduce search cost and offer only the relevant items from enormous amount of accessible data. Moreover, listening to music is a typical context-dependent behavior because people usually prefer different kinds of music under different contexts. It has been proven that contextual information like physical surroundings, emotional state, time, presence of other people can help recommender systems better understand and satisfy users' real-time requirements [5-7]. However, people can listen to music whenever and wherever they want, which makes the context of listening to music changeable and dynamic. Therefore, it becomes harder to acquire the real-time contexts directly.

Although the contextual factors may not be captured directly, they can be inferred from users' interactions with the system. More specifically, context is reflected in the sequence of music liked or listened to by the user in his/her current interaction with the system, such as recent playlists. For example, in Pandora[1], users create different playlists by choosing different track seeds or artists. Then, users can play each of these playlists based on his/her current preferences which can be influenced by different contexts. Therefore, the music recommender system should be able to infer the user's musical preference from given music pieces liked or listened to by him/her and then recommend appropriate music.

In this paper, we present a context aware music recommendation approach, which can infer the user's general and contextual preferences from his/her playing records and recommend music suitable for his/her current preferences. Specifically, the proposed approach learns music pieces' embeddings (feature vectors in low-dimensional continuous space) from music playing records and corresponding metadata, which is inspired by neural language models [8, 9]. As a result, music pieces that are played together in a music sequence have similar embeddings. Then, with the learned embeddings, our approach infers and models users' general and contextual preference from his/her complete playing history and his/her active interaction session (music sequence recently played by a user), respectively. Finally, music pieces, which conform to the user's general and contextual preference, are recommended to satisfy his/her real-time requirements. Experimental evaluations show that the proposed approach performs better than baseline approaches.

It is worthwhile to highlight the following three aspects of the proposed recommendation approach in this paper.

- We propose a music embedding model to learn the real-valued, low-dimensional representations of music pieces from music playing records and corresponding metadata.
- We propose a context aware music recommendation method, which can recommend appropriate music to satisfy users' real-time requirements.

* The corresponding author is Shuiguang Deng.

ICMR'16, June 06-09, 2016, New York, NY, USA

DOI: http://dx.doi.org/10.1145/2911996.2912045

[1] http://www.pandora.com

- We conduct extensive experiments to evaluate the proposed method on real world dataset, and the results show the effectiveness of our approach.

The remainder of this paper is structured as follows: Section 2 introduces the proposed approach in detail. Then, evaluations of the proposed approach are provided in section 3. Finally, the conclusion and future work are given in section 4.

2. RELATED WORK

In this section, we describe related works on context aware music recommendation, as well as neural language models that inspire our approach.

2.1 Context Aware Music Recommendation

Context aware music recommendation approaches are based on the fact that listening to music is a typical context-dependent behavior because people usually prefer different kinds of music under different contexts. The contexts include time [10, 7], location [5], activity [11], emotional state [6, 12] and so on. In [10], the authors incorporated temporal information in session-based collaborative filtering method to improve the performance of music recommendation. Negar et al. [13] adopted a LDA model to infer the topic probability distribution of songs with tags, and discovered pattern of topics in song sequence, which can be used as context to improve music recommendation performance. Han et al. [12] proposed a context-aware music recommendation system, in which music is recommended according to the user's current emotion state and music's influence on users' emotional changes.

2.2 Neural Language Models

Traditional language models suffer from dimensional disaster and data sparsity. Therefore, neural language models that induce low-dimensional and distributed embeddings of words by means of neural networks [8] have been proposed to solve these problems mentioned above. Besides, inefficient training of the neural network-based models has been successfully addressed by recent advances in the field, including highly scalable skip-gram (SG) and continuous bag-of-words (CBOW) language models [9] for learning word representations. These powerful, efficient models have shown very promising performance in many tasks, including sentences and paragraphs [14], relational entities [15], general text-based attributes [16], recommender systems [17, 18] and so on.

3. PROPOSED APPROACH

In this section, we describe the proposed approach for the task of context aware music recommendation, which considers both global music preference and contextual music preference. Formally, let $U = \{u_1, u_2, ..., u_{|U|}\}$ be a set of users and $M = \{m_1, m_2, ..., m_{|M|}\}$ represent a set of music pieces that users have listened to. For each user u, his/her historical playing sequence is a list of music records: $H^u = \{m_1^u, m_2^u, ..., m_{|H^u|}^u\}$, where each music record m_i^u ($m_i^u \in M$) is ordered according to its playing time. Therefore, the task becomes recommending music that user u would probably enjoy given his/her historical playing sequence H^u. To address this task, we first propose a music embedding model for learning the representations of each music piece, which is a feature vector in low-dimensional continuous space. Then we propose a context aware music recommendation approach, which can infer the user' general and contextual preference for music, and recommend appropriate music to satisfy his/her real-time requirements.

3.1 Learning Music Embedding

First of all, we propose the music embedding model (MEM) to learn the embeddings of music pieces from users' historical playing sequences and corresponding metadata. Here, each user's historical playing sequence is treated as a "sentence" and every record of music in the playing sequence is regarded as a "word", which are borrowed from natural language processing (NLP) domain.

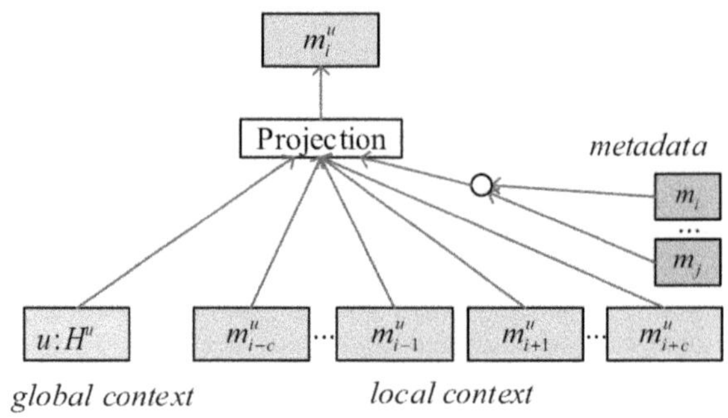

Figure 1. The music embedding model (MEM).

As shown in Figure 1, a sliding window is employed on the historical playing sequence of each user to generate the training data, where $2c+1$ is the length of the sliding window for playing sequences. Larger c results in more training examples, which leads to higher accuracy at the expense of more training time. In each sliding window, MEM aims to use local context music pieces $\{m_{i-c}^u : m_{i+c}^u\}$ to predict the central music piece m_i^u. Except for the local context, we also incorporate global context music pieces $u = H^u$ into our model. Therefore, the aim becomes predicting the central music piece m_i^u according to its local and global context music pieces. The corresponding probability function is defined as follows:

$$\Pr(m_i^u \mid m_{i-c}^u : m_{i+c}^u, u) = \exp(\overline{\mathbf{v}}^T \cdot \mathbf{v}'_{m_i^u}) \Big/ \sum_{m \in M} \exp(\overline{\mathbf{v}}^T \cdot \mathbf{v}'_m) \tag{1}$$

where $\mathbf{v}'_{m_i^u}$ is the output embedding of the central music piece m_i^u, and $\overline{\mathbf{v}}$ is the average input embedding of $u = H^u$ and $\{m_{i-c}^u : m_{i+c}^u\}$, which are the global and local context music pieces of m_i^u in u's historical playing sequence H^u, respectively. Formally, $\overline{\mathbf{v}}$ is defined as follows:

$$\overline{\mathbf{v}} = \frac{1}{2c+1}(\mathbf{v}_u + \sum_{-c \le j \le c, j \ne 0} \mathbf{v}_{m_{i+j}^u}) \tag{2}$$

where $\mathbf{v}_u$ is the average input embedding of all global context music pieces in u's historical playing sequence H^u. Specifically, $\mathbf{v}_u$ is defined as

$$\mathbf{v}_u = \sum_{1 \le i \le |H^u|} \mathbf{v}_{m_i^u} \Big/ |H^u| \tag{3}$$

where $|H^u|$ is the length of u's historical playing sequence H^u. Then, the log-likelihood objective function over the entire training data is defined as follows:

$$J = \sum_{u \in U, H^u \in H} \left(\sum_{m_i \in H^u} \log \Pr\left(m_i^u \mid m_{i-c}^u : m_{i+c}^u, u\right) \right) \quad (4)$$

Moreover, the embeddings of music pieces that belong to the same album or sung/played by the same musician should be close to each other. Let $s(m_i, m_j)$ be the similarity score between music pieces m_i and m_j. If m_i shares the same musician and the same album with m_j, their similarity is 1.0. If m_i only shares the same musician or the same album with m_j, their similarity becomes 0.5. Otherwise, their similarity is 0. Note that $s(m_i, m_j)$ is devised based on our experience, and if it is optimized on the dataset, the final performance can be further improved.

Then we encode the metadata, including album and musician information, using a regularization function R as

$$R = \sum_{m_i \in M} \sum_{m_j \in M} s(m_i, m_j) \cdot \exp(\mathbf{v}_{m_i}^T \cdot \mathbf{v}_{m_j}) \quad (5)$$

where the similarity score $s(m_i, m_j)$ serves as a weighting function.

Therefore, we get the final objective function of MEM, which incorporates metadata information into the music embedding learning process, as follows:

$$J_{MEM} = J + \beta R \quad (6)$$

where β is the combination coefficient. Our goal is to maximize the combined objective function J_{MME}.

In the learning phase, the complexity of computing the objective function is proportional to the total music set size $|M|$, which can easily reach several millions. In order to enhance the computing efficiency, we adopt negative sampling [9], which generates k noise samples for prediction, and k is a very small number compared with $|M|$. Therefore, the training time yields linear scale to the number of noise samples and becomes independent of the music set size $|M|$. Then stochastic gradient descent algorithm is used to maximize the optimized objective function J_{MME}.

Finally, the embedding of each music is learned, and similar music pieces lie nearby in the D-dimensional real-valued continuous space.

3.2 Context Aware Music Recommendation

Based on these learned embeddings, we can infer and model u's global and contextual preference for music. Specifically, u's global preference $\mathbf{p}_g^u$ is obtained by averaging the embeddings of music pieces in his/her historical playing sequence H^u, and his/her contextual music preference $\mathbf{p}_c^u$ is obtained by averaging the embeddings of music pieces in his/her recent music playing sequence (music sequence in his/her active interaction session).

Finally, a context aware music recommendation approach is proposed. Formally, given a user u and his/her global and contextual music preferences $\mathbf{p}_g^u$ and $\mathbf{p}_c^u$, the probability of u listening to a music piece m_i is defined as

$$p(m_i \mid \mathbf{p}_g^u, \mathbf{p}_c^u) = \cos(\mathbf{v}_{m_i}, \mathbf{p}_g^u) + \cos(\mathbf{v}_{m_i}, \mathbf{p}_c^u) \quad (7)$$

where $\mathbf{v}_{m_i}$ is the learned embedding of music piece m_i, and $\cos(\mathbf{v}, \mathbf{p})$ is the cosine similarity of vectors $\mathbf{v}$ and $\mathbf{p}$.

Finally, we rank candidate music pieces according to the probability defined above, and recommend the music pieces with high ranking scores to the target user.

4. EXPERIMENTS

In this section, we first introduce experimental design, including the dataset and evaluation metrics. Then, we illustrate the learned embedding in music embedding model (MEM) with an example, which is followed by a subsection on comparison between our method and baseline methods.

4.1 Experimental Design and Evaluation Metrics

In order to evaluate the performance of the proposed approach, we collect a real-world dataset from an online music service website named Xiami Music[2]. In detail, the dataset contains 4,284,000 music playing records of 361,861 music pieces by 4,284 users. We split the whole dataset into training sets and test sets according to the idea of 5-fold cross-validation. In each validation, we keep the complete playing sequences of 80% users and half of the remaining 20% users' historical playing sequences as the training set, and use the following half of the remaining 20% users' records as the test set.

The combination weight β used in MEM plays an important role in producing high quality music embedding. Finally, we set $\beta = 0.01$ empirically. Note that if the parameter is optimized on the validation set, the final performance can be further improved. Besides, it is also important to choose a proper dimension to balance accuracy performance and efficiency. Finally, we set the dimension of embedding as 200 based on our preliminary experiments.

Besides, four evaluation metrics are adopted, including precision, recall, F1 score, and hitrate [19]. Specifically, precision is the fraction of recommended music pieces that the target user actually listened to, and recall is the fraction of interested music of the target user that are recommended. F1 score is the harmonic mean of precision and recall. Hitrate is the fraction of hit, and a hit means the recommendation list contains at least one music pieces that the user actually listened to.

4.2 Illustrations of the Learned Embedding

In order to show what the learned embeddings look like, we provide a quantitative display of different music pieces. Figure 2 shows the visualization of similarity among music examples given in Table 1.

[2] http://www.xiami.com

Table 1. Basic information of corresponding music examples.

No	Song-Singer	Tags
1	Drowning-Backstreet Boys	pop, boy bands, ballad
2	As Long as You Love Me -Backstreet Boys	pop, 90s, boybands
3	Swear It Again-Westlife	pop, Irish, 90s
4	My Love-Westlife	pop, boy bands, Irish
5	Don't Cry-Guns N' Roses	classic rock, hard rock, ballad
6	Knockin' on Heaven's Door-Guns N' Roses	hard rock, rock, classic rock
7	Fade to Black-Metallica	thrash metal, heavy metal, rock
8	Summer-Joe Hisaishi	sound track, Japanese, anime, instrumental, classical
9	Moonlit Sea of Clouds-Joe Hisaishi	sound track, Japanese, anime, instrumental, classical
10	Canta Per Me-Yuki Kajiura	sound track, anime, Japanese
11	zero hour-Yuki Kajiura	sound track, anime, Japanese

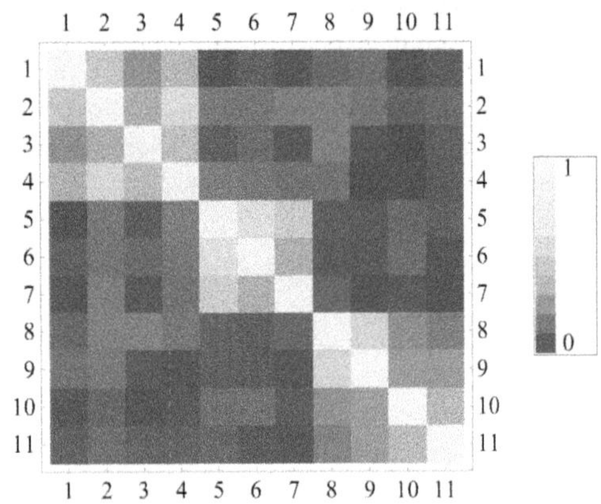

Figure 2. Similarity visualization of music examples

Firstly, music pieces with similar styles and genres indeed have similar embeddings. For example, the embeddings of the last four anime soundtrack music pieces (8-11) composed by Japanese artists in Table 1 are more similar to each other than the other music pieces. Secondly, the embeddings of music pieces sung/played by the same artists are usually closer to each other than the embedding of other pieces. Again, for the last four music pieces (8-11) in Table 1, the embeddings of the former two pieces are more similar to each other than the embeddings of the latter two pieces or the other pieces in Table 1. Therefore, the learned embedding can indeed capture the feature of the corresponding music pieces effectively.

In conclusion, the qualitative and quantitative analysis shows the effectiveness of our music embedding model in learning the embedding of music.

4.3 Comparison with Baselines

We further compare our methods with three state-of-the-art baseline methods, including Temporal Recommendation based on Injected Preference Fusion (IPF) [7], Bayesian Personalized Ranking (BPR) [2] and FISMauc (FISM) [1]. The performance results are shown in Figure 3, and we have two observations from the experimental results. (1) Our method has the best performance. Take the F1 score as an example. When compared with BPR, FISM, and IPF with the recommending number n=20, the relative performance improvements by MEM are around 96.4%, 69.7%, and 42.6%, respectively. The improvements show that our approach is more effective than baselines in contextual preference inferring and context aware music recommendation. Besides, they also indicate that users' contextual preferences play an important role in music recommendation. (2) IPF performs better than BPR and FISM, although it is not as good as our method. In our view, the reason is that IPF considers users' contextual preferences while BPR and FISM do not, which is quite important for users' interest prediction and music recommendation. Besides, it also shows our approach is more effective than IPF in acquiring and utilizing contextual information.

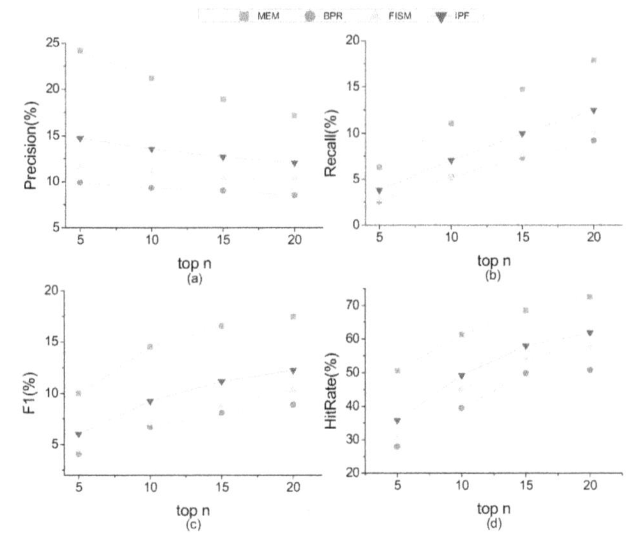

Figure 3. Performance comparison with baselines.

In conclusion, users' contextual preferences can indeed improve music recommendation. It also proves that our method can effectively learn music pieces' embedding as well as incorporate both users' general preferences and contextual preferences into music recommendation to satisfy their real-time requirements.

5. CONCLUSIONS AND FUTURE WORK

This paper presents an approach for context aware music recommendation, which can learn the embedding of music pieces, obtain users' general and contextual preference for music, and recommend appropriate music pieces that are in accordance with users' preference to users. Our work differs from prior works in two aspects: (1) the proposed approach depends on both playing sequences and user-item matrix to perform recommendation, and (2) the proposed approach incorporates both users' general and contextual musical preference into recommendation. Experimental evaluations on a real world dataset show the effectiveness of our approach.

Based on our current work, there are two possible future directions. First, we plan to adopt advanced recommending techniques, such as tensor factorization and factorization machine, to further improve the performance. Secondly, our approach is only evaluated by offline experiments in this work, and we will explore if users' satisfaction can be increased by online experiments.

Acknowledgement

This work was supported in part by the National Key Technology Research and Development Program of China under Grant 2014BAD10B02 and Australian Research Council (ARC) Linkage Project under No. LP140100937.

6. REFERENCES

[1] S. Kabbur, X. Ning, and G. Karypis, Fism: factored item similarity models for top-n recommender systems. In *Proceedings of the 19th ACM International Conference on Knowledge Discovery and Data Mining*, 659-667, 2013.

[2] S. Rendle, C. Freudenthaler, Z. Gantner, and L. Schmidt-Thieme, BPR: Bayesian personalized ranking from implicit feedback. In *Proceedings of the 25th Conference on Uncertainty in Artificial Intelligence*, 452-461, 2009.

[3] D. Wang, S. Deng, S. Liu, and G. Xu, Improving Music Recommendation Using Distributed Representation. In *Proceedings of the 25th International Conference Companion on World Wide Web*, 125-126, 2016.

[4] M. Yan, J. Sang, and C. Xu, Unified youtube video recommendation via cross-network collaboration. In *Proceedings of the 5th ACM on International Conference on Multimedia Retrieval*, 19-26, 2015.

[5] Z. Cheng and J. Shen, Just-for-me: An adaptive personalization system for location-aware social music recommendation. In *Proceedings of International Conference on Multimedia Retrieval*, 185, 2014.

[6] S. Deng, D. Wang, X. Li, and G. Xu. Exploring user emotion in microblogs for music recommendation. *Expert Systems with Applications*, 42, 23 (12/15/), 9284-9293, 2015.

[7] L. Xiang, Q. Yuan, S. Zhao, L. Chen, X. Zhang, Q. Yang, and J. Sun, Temporal recommendation on graphs via long- and short-term preference fusion. In *Proceedings of the 16th ACM SIGKDD International Conference on Knowledge Discovery and Data Mining*, 723-732, 2010.

[8] R. Collobert, J. Weston, L. Bottou, M. Karlen, K. Kavukcuoglu, and P. Kuksa. Natural language processing (almost) from scratch. *The Journal of Machine Learning Research*, 12, 2493-2537, 2011.

[9] T. Mikolov, I. Sutskever, K. Chen, G.S. Corrado, and J. Dean, Distributed representations of words and phrases and their compositionality. In *Advances in Neural Information Processing Systems*, 3111-3119, 2013.

[10] R. Dias and M.J. Fonseca, Improving music recommendation in session-based collaborative filtering by using temporal context. In *the 25th IEEE International Conference on Tools with Artificial Intelligence*, 783-788, 2013.

[11] X. Wang, D. Rosenblum, and Y. Wang, Context-aware mobile music recommendation for daily activities. In *Proceedings of the 20th ACM International Conference on Multimedia*, 99-108, 2012.

[12] B.-J. Han, S. Rho, S. Jun, and E. Hwang. Music emotion classification and context-based music recommendation. *Multimedia Tools and Applications*, 47, 3, 433-460, 2010.

[13] N. Hariri, B. Mobasher, and R. Burke, Context-aware music recommendation based on latenttopic sequential patterns. In *Proceedings of the 6th ACM Conference on Recommender Systems*, 131-138, 2012.

[14] Q.V. Le and T. Mikolov. Distributed representations of sentences and documents. *arXiv preprint arXiv:1405.4053*, 2014.

[15] R. Socher, D. Chen, C.D. Manning, and A. Ng, Reasoning with neural tensor networks for knowledge base completion. In *Advances in Neural Information Processing Systems*, 926-934, 2013.

[16] R. Kiros, R. Zemel, and R.R. Salakhutdinov, A multiplicative model for learning distributed text-based attribute representations. In *Advances in Neural Information Processing Systems*, 2348-2356, 2014.

[17]M. Grbovic, V. Radosavljevic, N. Djuric, N. Bhamidipati, J. Savla, V. Bhagwan, and D. Sharp, E-commerce in Your Inbox: Product Recommendations at Scale. In *Proceedings of the 21th ACM SIGKDD International Conference on Knowledge Discovery and Data Mining*, 1809-1818, 2015.

[18] P. Wang, J. Guo, Y. Lan, J. Xu, S. Wan, and X. Cheng, Learning Hierarchical Representation Model for NextBasket Recommendation. In *Proceedings of the 38th International Conference on Research and Development in Information Retrieval*, 403-412, 2015.

[19] P. Cremonesi, Y. Koren, and R. Turrin, Performance of recommender algorithms on top-n recommendation tasks. In *Proceedings of the Fourth ACM Conference on Recommender Systems*, 39-46, 2010.

Region Trajectories for Video Semantic Concept Detection

Yuancheng Ye[1], Xuejian Rong[2], Xiaodong Yang[3], and Yingli Tian[1,2]
[1]The Graduate Center, City University of New York
yye@gradcenter.cuny.edu

[2]The City College, City University of New York
{xrong, ytian}@ccny.cuny.edu

[3]NVIDIA Research
xiaodongy@nvidia.com

ABSTRACT

Recently, with the advent of the convolutional neural network (CNN), many CNN-based object detection algorithms have been proposed and achieved encouraging results. In this paper, we introduce an algorithm based on region trajectories to establish the connections between object localizations in individual frames and video sequences. To detect object regions in the individual frames of a video, we enhance the region-based convolutional neural network (R-CNN), by incorporating EdgeBox with the Selective Search to generate candidate region proposals and combining the GoogLeNet with the AlexNet to improve the discriminability of the feature representations. The DeepMatching algorithm is employed in our proposed region trajectory method to track the points in the detected object regions. The experiments are conducted on the validation split of the TRECVID 2015 Localization dataset. As demonstrated by the experimental results, our proposed approach improves the object detection accuracy in both temporal and spatial measurements.

Keywords

Object detection, convolutional neural network, region trajectory algorithm

1. INTRODUCTION

Nowadays, with the success of deep learning technologies, many computer vision areas including object detection have ushered a new era which has witnessed the significant improvements compared with previous methods [18, 17]. Inspired by region-based convolutional neural network (R-CNN) [5], many other approaches have been proposed to exploit the advantages of deep learning methods for object detection and achieved a great success. However, most of these approaches only focus on object detection at the image level, and few methods have been proposed to detect objects at the video level. In this paper, we propose a novel region trajectory algorithm to connect the object regions, localized by the imaged-based object detection algorithm, from the individual frames to generate object trajectories in videos.

ICMR'16, June 06 - 09, 2016, New York, NY, USA

ISBN 978-1-4503-4359-6/16/06...$15.00

DOI: http://dx.doi.org/10.1145/2911996.2912046

1.1 Related Work

Since convolutional neural network (CNN) achieved the impressive image classification accuracy on the ImageNet Large Scale Visual Recognition Challenge (ILSVRC) 2012 [10, 8, 12], many approaches have tried to incorporate CNN to tackle the problem of object detection at the image level. Region-based convolutional neural network (R-CNN) is one of the first successful attempts, which utilizes one of the state-of-the-art region proposal algorithms and a simple technique (affine image warping) to resize each candidate object region to the uniform size required by the CNN model [5, 3]. Then discriminative features are extracted from the CNN model and fed into a linear SVM. Despite its straightforward structure, R-CNN enjoys a great success compared with the traditional object detection approaches [13, 1, 4, 2], which rely on the sliding windows and hand-crafted features.

Although the image-based object detection has attracted more and more interests, few methods have been proposed to tackle the object detection in videos [9, 21, 24, 11, 15]. Inspired by [6], our proposed method first detects the object regions in individual frames and then try to connect them in the temporal domain. However, the linking algorithm adopted by [6] makes an assumption that an action keeps being presented from the first frame to the end, which is usually not the case for object detection due to occlusion and viewpoint change. The approach developed in the paper [25, 26] is similar to our method, which keeps tracking the action regions localized by the image-based object detection algorithm. However, the tracking mechanism in [25] depends on the neighboring windows around the detected regions, and cannot handle the situation of large displacements of object motion which is common in wild videos.

1.2 Our Proposed System

To bridge the gap between image-based and video-based object detection, a novel region trajectory algorithm is presented in this paper. Moreover, two modifications are made to the standard R-CNN method to improve the performance of object detection at the image level. One is to combine the EdgeBox [28] with the Selective Search [22] to obtain a

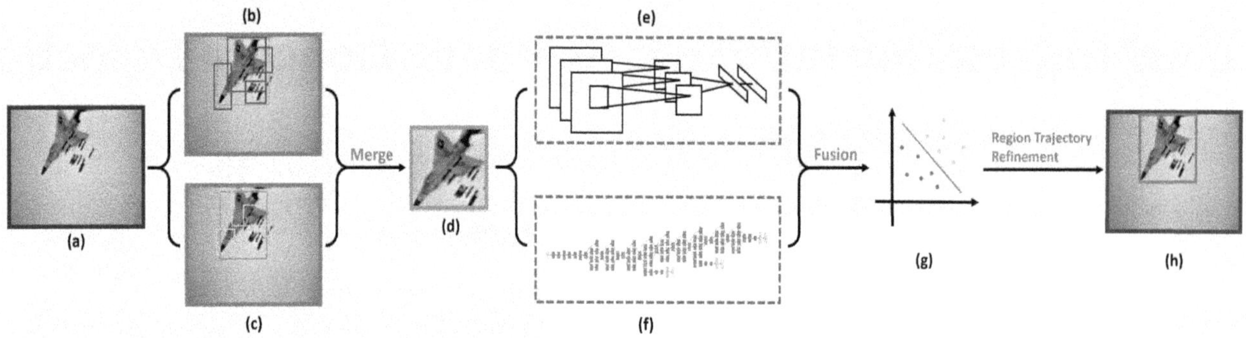

Figure 1: Overview of the Proposed System Structure. (a) Input image. (b) Region proposals by Selective Search. (c) Region proposals by EdgeBox. (d) Region proposals fused by (b) and (c). (e) Extracting features of region proposals by AlexNet. (f) Extracting features of region proposals by GoogLeNet. (g) Applying linear SVM classifier to the vector concatenating by the ℓ_2 normalization of (e) and (f). (h) Final region box obtained by the region trajectory algorithm.

higher coverage rate for the generated region proposals. Another is to incorporate the GoogLeNet [20] with the AlexNet [10], which is the only CNN model employed in the R-CNN, to produce a more discriminative feature representation of each region proposal.

To track the object locations detected by the image-based object detection method, the state-of-the-art point-matching algorithm, DeepMatching [27], is employed. After performing the tracking algorithm on the candidate object regions in different frames, several object region trajectories are produced. If the tracking process is based on a falsely detected object region, the obtained corresponding object region trajectory may also be incorrect. To prune these false trajectories, two thresholds are applied: the average SVM score of the regions in the trajectory and the ratio of the number of regions detected by R-CNN and the total number of the regions in the trajectory. The structure of our system is illustrated in Figure 1.

The rest of the paper is organized as follows. Section 2 presents the enhanced R-CNN method employed in our system. Section 3 introduces the details of our proposed region trajectory algorithm. In Section 4, experimental results on the validation split of TRECVID 2015 Localization dataset are presented, and an ablation study of the parameters in our region trajectory algorithm is also provided. Finally, our paper is concluded in Section 5.

2. ENHANCED R-CNN

R-CNN is one of the first successful algorithms that apply deep learning techniques to the object detection task. It decomposes the detection task into three aspects: 1) generating sufficient category-agnostic region proposals to cover as many objects as possible in the image; 2) applying a fine tuned convolutional neural network to extract a discriminative feature representation for each proposed region; 3) training a set of category-specific linear SVMs based on the extracted feature representation to classify those region proposals. In our implementation, two modifications are made when compared with the method described in [5] to further improve the object detection accuracy at the image level.

Selective Search [22] and EdgeBox [28] are combined in our implementation to generate region proposals [7], which can improve the coverage rate of the objects in the image. Another modification is that, in addition to the AlexNet [10], the GoogLeNet [20] is also employed in our method. By concatenating the ℓ_2 normalization of the features extracted from the last fully connected layers of these two models, a more discriminative feature representation can be generated. After applying the generated feature to the trained class-specific SVMs, the scores of the region for each class can be obtained. Given all scored regions in an image, a greedy non-maximum suppression is independently applied for each class to reject the regions which have a large overlap with the region with higher SVM score.

3. REGION TRAJECTORIES FOR OBJECT DETECTION

To extend the image-based object detection algorithm into the video domain, one important step is how to establish the connections among the object regions in different frames. In this paper, we propose the region trajectory algorithm based on the state-of-the-art point-matching algorithm, DeepMatching, to establish the object trajectories for the video-based object detection. Our region trajectory algorithm is illustrated in Figure 2.

Inspired by the dense trajectory method for action recognition [23], we propose the region trajectory algorithm to establish the temporal connections of object regions in different frames. For a set of frames $\{f_1, \dots, f_i, \dots, f_n\}$ in a video, suppose that R-CNN detects an object region b_i in the frame f_i, then an object trajectory, T_i, can be generated based this detected region b_i. The tracking procedure is performed both forwardly and backwardly to determine the start and end regions for the object trajectory T_i. In the following discussions, we only take the forward tracking procedure as the example to illustrate how our region trajectory algorithm works.

Firstly, a set of points $\{p_k\}$ in the region b_i can be computed by applying the DeepMatching algorithm, and a set of matched points, $\{p'_k\}$, is also generated in the frame f_{i+1}. Based on these two sets of matched points, $\{p_k\}$ and $\{p'_k\}$, an affine model can be acquired , which consists of a linear

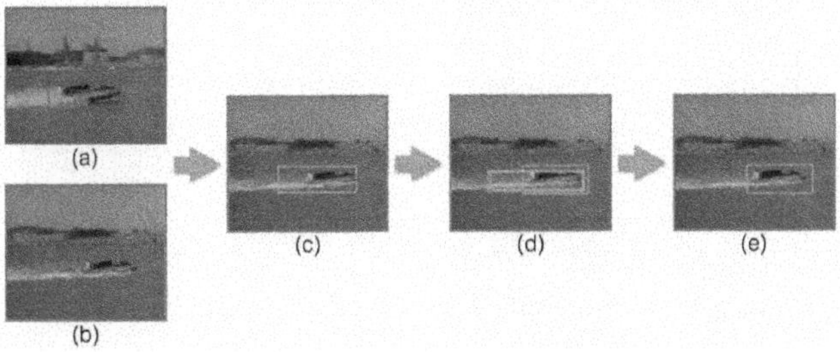

Figure 2: The illustration of the proposed region trajectory algorithm. (a) The first frame with the detected object region by R-CNN. The star marks are the matched points inside the localized object bounding box. (b) The second frame in which the R-CNN fails to locate the object region. (c) The second frame with the object region predicted by the affine model. (d) The bounding boxes with IOU values larger than 0.5 with the bounding box singled out in (c). (e) The bounding box with the highest SVM score from the set of boxes noted in (d).

transformation matrix, $A \in \mathbb{R}^{2\times 2}$, and a translation vector, $\vec{b} \in \mathbb{R}^{2\times 1}$. Then by applying the coordinates $(x_i^j, y_i^j)^T$ of each corner of the object region, b_i, into the affine model:

$$(x_{i+1}^j, y_{i+1}^j)^T = A(x_i^j, y_i^j)^T + \vec{b}, \tag{1}$$

the corresponding points of the four corners of b_i in the next frame can be obtained. However, these four locations, $\{(x_{i+1}^j, y_{i+1}^j)\}_{j=0,1,2,3}$, may be distorted or fall out of the image. To obtain the reasonable predicted object region, b'_{i+1}, in the frame f_{i+1}, a correction procedure should be applied, which is defined as:

$$\alpha_{i+1} = \max(0, \min_j(\{x_{i+1}^j\})), \tag{2}$$

$$\beta_{i+1} = \max(0, \min_j(\{y_{i+1}^j\})), \tag{3}$$

$$\mu_{i+1} = \min(width, \max_j(\{x_{i+1}^j\})), \tag{4}$$

$$\nu_{i+1} = \min(height, \max_j(\{y_{i+1}^j\})), \tag{5}$$

where $(\alpha_{i+1}, \beta_{i+1})$ and (μ_{i+1}, ν_{i+1}) stand for the coordinates of the upper-left corner and bottom-right corner of the predicted region respectively. *width* is the horizontal size of the image, and *height* is vertical size of the image.

Furthermore, to improve the spatial accuracy and reduce repeating tracking process, the predicted region, b'_{i+1}, is replaced by the object region, b_{i+1}, which is detected by the R-CNN algorithm in the frame f_{i+1}, if the value of intersection-over-union (IOU) is larger than a threshold (0.7 in our implementation).

If the region, b'_{i+1}, predicted by the affine model is not replaced by an object region detected by R-CNN, a set of bounding boxes, generated by Selective Search [22] and EdgeBox [28] algorithms, are selected if their IOU values with b'_{i+1} are larger than 0.5. Then the bounding box, b''_{i+1}, with the highest SVM score is chosen from the set of bounding boxes plus the region b'_{i+1} as the predicted object region. The SVM score of b''_{i+1} should then be compared with a threshold to determine whether this region is a reasonable object bounding box. Specifically, if the SVM score is smaller than a threshold, this region should not be assigned to the object trajectory T_i, and the tracking process should also be terminated on this direction.

After performing the tracking process in both forward and backward directions based on the algorithm described above, the object trajectory T_i can be obtained. However, if the object region, *e.g.* , b_i, is falsely detected by the R-CNN, the trajectory T_i which is generated based on b_i may also be incorrect. To prune these falsely produced object trajectories, two kinds of thresholds are applied: the average SVM score of the regions contained in the object trajectory and the ratio of the number of regions detected by R-CNN and the total number of the regions in the trajectory.

We observe that only using the average SVM score of the trajectory as the threshold cannot improve the performance. The reason is that some falsely detected regions have high SVM scores, which makes the average score of false trajectories higher than the average score of correct object trajectories. On the other hand, the value of the ratio of the number of regions detected by R-CNN and the total number of the regions in the trajectory can reflect how many regions in the trajectory are localized by the R-CNN algorithm and how many are inferred by the affine model, which implies that the higher ratio indicates a higher probability that the trajectory is correct.

The score function described in [6] is also employed in our approach to prune the plausible object trajectories. It measures the correctness of a trajectory based on both SVM scores and the IOU values of the regions. If the computed trajectory score, S_T, is below a threshold, the trajectory T will be deleted. Otherwise, this object trajectory can be considered as a reasonable one.

Run	iframe_fscore	mean_pixel_fscore
1	0.7447	0.4723
2	0.7682	0.4542
3	0.7309	0.5085
4	0.7661	0.4591
MediaMill*	0.7662	0.6557
PicSOM*	0.6643	0.3944
TokyoTech*	0.6699	0.6688
Trimps*	0.7357	0.4760

Table 1: The results of Mean_Per_Run for our four submitted runs in the TRECVID competition. * indicates the best results of other teams among all of their submitted runs.

4. EXPERIMENTAL RESULTS AND DISCUSSION

Our proposed video-based object detection system is evaluated on the TRECVID 2015 Localization dataset [16], which is comprised of ten concepts: airplane(1003), anchorperson(1005), boat_ship(1015), bridges(1017), bus(1019), computers(1031), motorcycle(1080), telephones(1117), flags(1261), and quadruped(1392). The numbers in the parentheses represent the code names of the corresponding concepts. There are four other teams submitted final results for this task: MediaMill (University of Amsterdam Qualcomm), PicSOM (Aalto University and University of Helsinki), TokyoTech (Tokyo Institute of Technology), Trimps (Third Research In-

Params	Metrics	1003	1005	1015	1017	1019	1031	1080	1117	1261	1392	Mean
pos_1.0_neg_0.0	iframe_fscore	0.7848	0.9991	0.6779	0.5788	0.6687	0.9051	0.6788	0.6843	0.8396	0.7775	0.7595
	mean_pixel_fscore	0.6671	0.9567	0.4692	0.4433	0.5643	0.8168	0.4698	0.5940	0.7331	0.7054	0.6420
pos_0.7_neg_0.1	iframe_fscore	0.8433	0.9991	0.7404	0.6349	0.6667	1.0000	0.6519	0.7634	0.8873	0.8184	0.8005
	mean_pixel_fscore	0.6203	0.9567	0.3980	0.4349	0.4815	0.8136	0.4054	0.4690	0.6419	0.6281	0.5849
fusion	iframe_fscore	0.8433	0.9991	0.7406	0.6298	0.6667	1.0000	0.6543	0.7634	0.8892	0.8188	0.8005
	mean_pixel_fscore	0.6292	0.9567	0.4220	0.4746	0.4816	0.8699	0.4202	0.4759	0.6603	0.6435	0.6034

Table 2: The results of the three sets of parameters for each concept detected by R-CNN.

Params	Methods	Metrics	Mean
pos_1.0_neg_0.0	without traj	iframe_fscore	0.7595
		mean_pixel_fscore	0.6420
	with traj	iframe_fscore	0.7926
		mean_pixel_fscore	0.6143
fusion	without traj	iframe_fscore	0.8005
		mean_pixel_fscore	0.6034
	with traj	iframe_fscore	0.8823
		mean_pixel_fscore	0.6348

Table 3: The comparison of the overall performance of the video-based object detection system with and without region trajectory algorithm.

System	Params	Metrics	Mean
TRECVID	pos_1.0_neg_0.0	iframe_fscore	0.7724
		mean_pixel_fscore	0.5926
	fusion	iframe_fscore	0.8110
		mean_pixel_fscore	0.5867
RegionTraj	pos_1.0_neg_0.0	iframe_fscore	0.7926
		mean_pixel_fscore	0.6143
	fusion	iframe_fscore	0.8823
		mean_pixel_fscore	0.6348

Table 4: The results of the two systems can achieve on the two sets of parameters with their own tracking algorithms for temporal and spatial measurements respectively.

stitute of the Ministry of Public Security, P.R. China). The overall results of the TRECVID 2015 Localization competition are shown in Table 2. Our team submitted four runs for this task, and the overall results of the TRECVID 2015 Localization competition are showed in Table 2. These results are obtained by another video-based object detection system, which will be compared with the one described in this paper in detail.

Since the ground truth of the testing data is not available, we report the results of the video-based object detection system described in this paper on the validation split of the training data.

The measurements of the results are in two folds. The first is the temporal accuracy, *iframe_fscore*, and the second is the spatial accuracy, *mean_pixel_fscore*. *fscore* is calculated by the formula:

$$fscore = \frac{2 \times Precision \times Recall}{Precision + Recall}, \tag{6}$$

where *Precision* is the ratio of the number of true positives detected by the system and the total number of positives in the test dataset, while *Recall* stands for the ratio of the number of true positives and the total number of positives both detected by the system.

The CNN models of AlexNet and GoogLeNet are both pre-trained on the PASCAL VOC 2012 detection dataset as well as the ImageNet dataset. In practice, we apply two sets of parameters to train the SVM. The first, denoted as pos_1.0_neg_0.0, only employs the ground truth as the positive training data and uses the regions which have no overlap with the ground truth as the negative data. The second set, denoted as pos_0.7_neg_0.1, employs not only the ground truth regions as the positive training data, but also the regions which have the IOU values larger than 0.7 with the ground truth. For the negative training data, it uses the regions with the IOU values smaller than 0.1 and larger than 0 with the ground truth. The results of these two sets of parameters are also fused to form a third set of results, which is denoted as fusion. The evaluation of these three sets of parameters is provided in Table 2.

After obtaining the object regions in individual frames, the object trajectories can then be generated by applying the region trajectory algorithm. The comparison of the results with and without region trajectory algorithm is provided in the Table 3.

The differences between the system submitted in the task of Localization of TRECVID 2015 and the one described in this paper are mainly in two aspects. Firstly, the Kanade-Lucas-Tomasi Feature Tracker (KLT) [14, 19] is employed as the tracking algorithm in previous system, while the DeepMatching algorithm is utilized in the second one. Secondly, in the previous system the object regions predicted by the affine model are not replaced by the object regions detected by R-CNN, even if they have large IOU values. The comparison of these two systems is presented in Table 4.

5. CONCLUSION

In this paper, we have presented a video-based object detection algorithm, which is based on the image-based R-CNN method and the state-of-the-art point-matching algorithm, DeepMatching. Specifically, a novel region trajectory algorithm is proposed to generate object trajectories in the videos based on the object regions detected in individual frames. Then these object trajectories are pruned according the confidence scores associated with them. The experiments demonstrate that our proposed video-based object detection algorithm can robustly and effectively locate the object regions in the video both in the temporal and spatial domain.

6. ACKNOWLEDGEMENT

This work was supported in part by NSF grants EFRI-1137172, IIP-1343402, and IIS-1400802.

7. REFERENCES

[1] B. E. Boser, I. M. Guyon, and V. N. Vapnik. A training algorithm for optimal margin classifiers. In *Proceedings of the fifth annual workshop on Computational learning theory*, pages 144–152. ACM, 1992.

[2] N. Dalal and B. Triggs. Histograms of oriented gradients for human detection. In *Computer Vision and Pattern Recognition (CVPR)*, volume 1, pages 886–893. IEEE, 2005.

[3] M. Everingham, L. Van Gool, C. K. Williams, J. Winn, and A. Zisserman. The pascal visual object classes (voc) challenge. *International Journal of Computer Vision (IJCV)*, 88(2):303–338, 2010.

[4] P. F. Felzenszwalb, R. B. Girshick, D. McAllester, and D. Ramanan. Object detection with discriminatively trained part-based models. *Pattern Analysis and Machine Intelligence (PAMI)*, 32(9):1627–1645, 2010.

[5] R. Girshick, J. Donahue, T. Darrell, and J. Malik. Rich feature hierarchies for accurate object detection and semantic segmentation. In *Computer Vision and Pattern Recognition (CVPR)*, pages 580–587. IEEE, 2014.

[6] G. Gkioxari and J. Malik. Finding action tubes. In *Computer Vision and Pattern Recognition (CVPR)*. IEEE, 2015.

[7] J. Hosang, R. Benenson, P. Dollár, and B. Schiele. What makes for effective detection proposals? *arXiv preprint arXiv:1502.05082*, 2015.

[8] Y. Jia, E. Shelhamer, J. Donahue, S. Karayev, J. Long, R. Girshick, S. Guadarrama, and T. Darrell. Caffe: Convolutional architecture for fast feature embedding. *arXiv preprint arXiv:1408.5093*, 2014.

[9] A. Klaser, M. Marszałek, and C. Schmid. A spatio-temporal descriptor based on 3d-gradients. In *British Machine Vision Conference (BMVC)*, pages 275–1. British Machine Vision Association, 2008.

[10] A. Krizhevsky, I. Sutskever, and G. E. Hinton. Imagenet classification with deep convolutional neural networks. In *Advances in neural information processing systems*, pages 1097–1105, 2012.

[11] I. Laptev and P. Pérez. Retrieving actions in movies. In *IEEE Intenational Conference on Computer Vision (ICCV)*, pages 1–8. IEEE, 2007.

[12] Y. LeCun, L. Bottou, Y. Bengio, and P. Haffner. Gradient-based learning applied to document recognition. *Proceedings of the IEEE*, 86(11):2278–2324, 1998.

[13] D. G. Lowe. Object recognition from local scale-invariant features. In *The IEEE International Conference on Computer Vision (ICCV)*, pages 1150–1157, 1999.

[14] B. D. Lucas, T. Kanade, et al. An iterative image registration technique with an application to stereo vision. In *International Joint Conference on Artificial Intelligence (IJCAI)*, volume 81, pages 674–679, 1981.

[15] D. Oneata, J. Verbeek, and C. Schmid. Efficient action localization with approximately normalized fisher vectors. In *Computer Vision and Pattern Recognition (CVPR)*, pages 2545–2552. IEEE, 2014.

[16] P. Over, G. Awad, M. Michel, J. Fiscus, W. Kraaij, A. F. Smeaton, G. QuÃl'enot, and R. Ordelman. Trecvid 2015 – an overview of the goals, tasks, data, evaluation mechanisms and metrics. In *Proceedings of TRECVID 2015*. NIST, USA, 2015.

[17] S. Ren, K. He, R. Girshick, and J. Sun. Faster r-cnn: Towards real-time object detection with region proposal networks. In *Advances in Neural Information Processing Systems (NIPS)*, pages 91–99, 2015.

[18] P. Sermanet, D. Eigen, X. Zhang, M. Mathieu, R. Fergus, and Y. LeCun. Overfeat: Integrated recognition, localization and detection using convolutional networks. *International Conference on Learning Representations (ICLR)*, 2013.

[19] J. Shi and C. Tomasi. Good features to track. In *Computer Vision and Pattern Recognition (CVPR)*, pages 593–600. IEEE, 1994.

[20] C. Szegedy, W. Liu, Y. Jia, P. Sermanet, S. Reed, D. Anguelov, D. Erhan, V. Vanhoucke, and A. Rabinovich. Going deeper with convolutions. *Computer Vision and Pattern Recognition (CVPR)*, 2015.

[21] Y. Tian, R. Sukthankar, and M. Shah. Spatiotemporal deformable part models for action detection. In *Computer Vision and Pattern Recognition (CVPR)*, pages 2642–2649. IEEE, 2013.

[22] J. R. Uijlings, K. E. van de Sande, T. Gevers, and A. W. Smeulders. Selective search for object recognition. *International Journal of Computer Vision (IJCV)*, 104(2):154–171, 2013.

[23] H. Wang, A. Kläser, C. Schmid, and C.-L. Liu. Action Recognition by Dense Trajectories. In *Computer Vision and Pattern Recognition (CVPR)*, pages 3169–3176, Colorado Springs, United States, June 2011.

[24] L. Wang, Y. Qiao, and X. Tang. Video action detection with relational dynamic-poselets. In *European Conference on Computer Vision (ECCV)*, pages 565–580. Springer, 2014.

[25] P. Weinzaepfel, Z. Harchaoui, and C. Schmid. Learning to track for spatio-temporal action localization. June 2015.

[26] P. Weinzaepfel, J. Revaud, Z. Harchaoui, and C. Schmid. DeepFlow: Large displacement optical flow with deep matching. In *IEEE Intenational Conference on Computer Vision (ICCV)*, Sydney, Australia, Dec. 2013.

[27] P. Weinzaepfel, J. Revaud, Z. Harchaoui, and C. Schmid. DeepFlow: Large displacement optical flow with deep matching. In *IEEE Intenational Conference on Computer Vision (ICCV)*, 2013.

[28] C. L. Zitnick and P. Dollár. Edge boxes: Locating object proposals from edges. In *Computer Vision–ECCV 2014*, pages 391–405. Springer, 2014.

Audiovisual Summarization of Lectures and Meetings Using a Segment Similarity Graph

Chidansh Bhatt*
FX Palo Alto Laboratory, Inc.
3174 Porter Drive
Palo Alto, CA, USA 94304
bhatt@fxpal.com

Andrei Popescu-Belis
Idiap Research Institute
Rue Marconi 19, CP 592
Martigny, Switzerland 1920
apbelis@idiap.ch

Matthew Cooper
FX Palo Alto Laboratory, Inc.
3174 Porter Drive
Palo Alto, CA, USA 94304
cooper@fxpal.com

ABSTRACT

We propose a method for extractive summarization of audiovisual recordings focusing on topic-level segments. We first build a content similarity graph between all segments across the collection, using word vectors from the transcripts, and then select the most central segments for the summaries. We evaluate the method quantitatively on the AMI Meeting Corpus using gold standard reference summaries and the ROUGE metric, and qualitatively on lecture recordings using a novel two-tiered approach with human judges. The results show that our method compares favorably with others in terms of ROUGE, and outperforms the baselines for human scores, thus also validating our evaluation protocol.

Keywords

Multimedia summarization, task-based evaluation, content-based similarity

1. INTRODUCTION

Audiovisual summarization is a key technique for efficient, large scale video retrieval. It uses structural characterizations of multimedia to generate proxies for longer streams that represent the essence of the original content with minimal redundancy. In this paper, we propose an approach to generate summaries of lectures or meetings from large repositories. We use speech transcripts and topic-level segments, and design a graph-based method, which builds a content-based segment similarity graph and selects the most connected segments for inclusion in summaries. A first evaluation using ground-truth extractive summaries from the AMI Meeting Corpus shows that our method outperforms two state-of-the-art methods. A second evaluation uses an innovative two-tiered protocol which relies on subjects writing summaries based on the automatic audiovisual summaries of lectures, and human judges rating their written summaries only. The results show that our method outperforms two baselines, and validate the protocol.

*Work performed at the Idiap Research Institute and at the FX Palo Alto Laboratory, Inc.

ICMR'16, June 06-09, 2016, New York, NY, USA

© 2016 ACM. ISBN 978-1-4503-4359-6/16/06...$15.00

DOI: http://dx.doi.org/10.1145/2911996.2912047

2. RELATED WORK

Existing methods for A/V summarization can be categorized based on the modalities they use: text, audio, video, or a combination. Surveys are available for individual modalities, e.g. for text [14] or video summarization [13]. The style and extent to which various modalities are used within summaries varies greatly. Here we focus on extractive video summarization based on text speech transcripts, leveraging automatically detected topic structure.

To generate extractive summaries based on speech transcripts, several methods exist to rank sentences according to relevance metrics. In supervised approaches, a classifier is trained on sentence features such as keywords, sentence length, and position. Unsupervised approaches like Maximal Marginal Relevance [17] typically create a term vector per sentence.

Graph-based methods include eigenvector centrality approaches such as TextRank [12] and LexRank [5]. Extensions to such approaches include ClusterRank [6], which segments the transcript by subject. Like ClusterRank, our approach relies on topic-coherent segments; however, excerpts are selected with a different criterion.

3. TopS SUMMARIZATION METHOD

The proposed summarization method, named *TopS*, proceeds in three stages: topic segmentation of the ASR transcripts, computation of a content similarity graph relating all segments of the collection, and selection of the most connected segments as the summary of each recording. Finally, to create viewable audiovisual summaries, we sort the segments by order of occurrence in the recording, and append them together separated by fading effects for smooth transitions, to enhance the viewing experience.

3.1 Topic Segmentation

Most previous work on extractive summarization has focused on ranking *sentences*, but here, to avoid separating sentences from their contexts, we obtain *topic-level segments* of each lecture or meeting, using transcripts from automatic speech recognition (ASR) [7]. We use TextTiling [8] as implemented in the NLTK toolkit [2], for its robustness and simplicity. In TextTiling, topic shifts are determined from lexical co-occurrence patterns, computed here from 20-word pseudo-sentences. Topic similarity scores are computed at sentence gaps using block comparison. Boundaries are set at peak differences between scores, adjusted to the closest speech segment breaks.

3.2 Centrality-based Summarization

We create a word-vector representation of each segment, after conversion to lower-case, tokenization, and stop word removal. We consider only unigrams, with a vocabulary size of 20,000 words. Each topic-level segment is indexed in the word-vector space with tf-idf weights for its words. Given the corpus C with a total of M segments, we consider the segment-indexed feature vectors $S = \{\mathbf{s}_i : i = 1, \ldots, M\}$. The similarity between segments $\mathbf{s_i}$ and $\mathbf{s_j}$ is computed as the cosine similarity between their word-vectors. We thus generate an M-by-M segment similarity score matrix, where each row corresponds to a segment and the cells of the row represent its similarity scores to the other ones. The matrix can be seen as a segment similarity graph, with a node for each segment and edges represented by the matrix entries and can be used for recommendation or hyperlinking tasks as well [1].

Graph centrality is an established criterion for extractive summarization [15], typically at the sentence level. Intuitively, the central segments of the graph, i.e. those that are strongly related to other segments in the collection (multiple document relations) or within the document (single document relations), should be preferred for inclusion in a summary of the lecture or meeting from which they originate. We propose a summarizer that maximizes centrality relative to either a single document or the entire collection.

We compute a global relevance score for each segment $\mathbf{s_i}$ as the sum of its similarity scores with all other segments in the graph: $Global(s_i) = 1/M \sum_{j=1}^{M} \mathrm{sim}(\mathbf{s_i}, \mathbf{s_j})$. Similarly, a local relevance score for each segment $\mathbf{s_i}$ is computed as the summation of its similarity scores over the nodes in the sub-graph of its document, divided into segments s_p to s_r as explained in Section 3.1, as $Local(s_i) = 1/(r-p) \sum_{j=p}^{r} \mathrm{sim}(\mathbf{s_i}, \mathbf{s_j})$.

To build the summary of a recording, its segments are sorted by decreasing relevance scores (either *Global* or *Local*), and the top scoring ones are added to the summary, until the desired duration is reached. Typically, this duration is a proportion of the original recording. For instance, as indicated by Mani et al. [11] in the case of written material, summaries as short as 17% of the full text's length speed up decision-making by a factor of two.

Unlike previous graph-based approaches to summarization, our method does not consider sentences but larger topic-level segments, to improve the local coherence of the summary. Moreover, while many graph-based approaches ignore edges with very low weights, we use all edges to determine the most important segments within a recording.

3.3 Hybrid Summarization

Hybrid approaches combine the *Local* and *Global* relevance scores and domain-specific features. For instance, we consider the sum (or product) of *Local* and *Global* to enforce both properties during segment selection. Or, we can consider *Local–Global* (or even *Local/Global*) to select segments having high similarity within the document and low similarity within the corpus as in discriminative key-frame selection approach [4].

Table 1: Scores of *TopS* and two other methods.

Method	ROUGE 1 P	ROUGE 1 R	ROUGE 1 F	ROUGE 2 P	ROUGE 2 R	ROUGE 2 F
TopS(Global)	**.66**	**.70**	**.65**	**.42**	**.43**	**.41**
TextRank	.30	.21	.24	.05	.03	.04
ClusterRank	.32	.26	.28	.05	.04	.04

TopS can be combined with genre-specific features for multi-party meetings. The first one is the *number of unique speakers* in each topic segment, e.g., a speaker sequence of A-A-A-C-D has 3 unique speakers. The second one is the *number of speaker changes* (or turns) in each topic segment, e.g., 2 in the example above. We hypothesize that segments with more unique speakers and with more speaker changes are more active and thus more relevant to a summary. These features can be used with the *Global* and *Local* scores in *TopS*, noted as *TopS*(Global + Change + Unique).

4. REFERENCE-BASED EVALUATION

For evaluation, we use all available reference extractive summaries for meetings of the AMI Meeting Corpus [3]. Each meting has an ASR transcript of 3000–7000 words, and topic segmentation generates an average of 50 segments per meeting. The reference summaries contain utterances selected by human judges as best representing each meeting's content. We measure the overlap between these reference summaries and those found by *TopS*(Global) using ROUGE [10], a metric that counts the number of overlapping n-grams (up to $n = 4$). ROUGE-1 was argued to be the most relevant version for meeting summarization [16].

The length of the *TopS* summaries is set at 17% of each meeting's length. We compare the ROUGE scores of *TopS* with those obtained by TextRank and ClusterRank, using respectively the scores from [12] and [6].

Table 1 shows that *TopS* (Global) outperforms TextRank and ClusterRank for both levels of ROUGE (n=1 and n=2) for which TextRank and ClusterRank scores are available, with more than 110% improvement in terms of average score. Another approach using lexical and prosodic features [9] achieves a ROUGE-1 F-score of 0.59, still below the *TopS* F-score of 0.65. As for n=3 and n=4, ROUGE F-scores of *TopS*(Global) are 0.26 and 0.22 respectively, with slightly higher precision scores (0.30 and 0.26 respectively).

Fig. 1 represents the performance of several variants of our approach. *TopS* using *Global* similarity marginally outperforms *Local* similarity (and hence their sum), a result related to the 80% overlap between the summary segments of *Global* and *Local*. The use of *Local–Global* similarity to create summaries with more locally unique segments leads to higher precision but lower recall and F1 scores. The domain-specific features (Speaker Change and Unique Speaker) score below the graph-based ones, especially in terms of recall, and their combination with *TopS* does not improve performance. In sum, we conclude that *TopS* summarization outperforms other existing methods in our evaluation.

5. SUBJECTIVE EVALUATION

While there is a growing consensus on evaluating meeting summarization, other genres lack widely accepted evaluation protocols. We now describe an efficient and broadly applicable approach to evaluating audiovisual summaries of

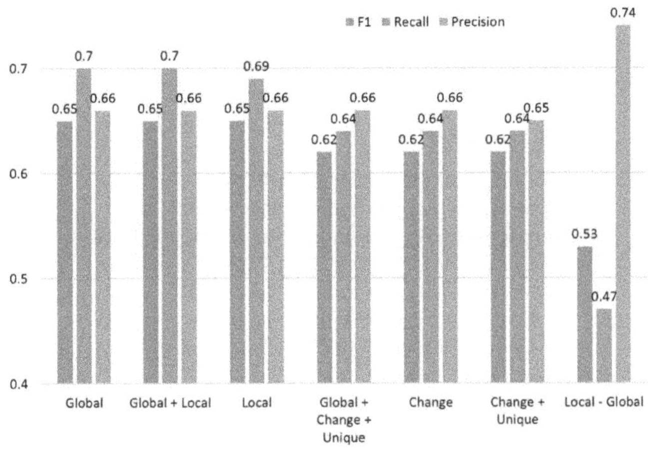

Figure 1: Performance of TopS and hybrid combinations according to the ROUGE-1 metric.

recordings of university lectures and scientific conferences, and apply it to the *TopS* method.

5.1 Evaluation Protocol

We consider 169 recordings with ASR transcripts lectures recorded and distributed by Klewel (www.klewel.com). As human-generated extractive summaries are not available to compute ROUGE, we propose a two-tiered evaluation protocol involving human subjects. This task-based protocol avoids requiring judges to rate summaries by comparison with the entire recording, or to define reference ones.

The task we have in mind is the production by a human of a *written summary* of a recording after watching the *automatically created audiovisual summary*. The written summaries are then rated by judges who view the entire recording—but only once for potentially multiple summaries, methods and/or human subjects. The judges can thus easily compare multiple summaries, and we propose two dimensions for this comparison, to be rated on 5-point scales: *fidelity*, i.e. how much of the original content is rendered in the summary, and *fluency*, i.e. how correct is the English used in the summary. These are distinguished in order not to penalize subjects who render correctly the content of lecture but do not write English fluently. The evaluation protocol consists of the following steps:

1. Subjects watch an A/V summary online, possibly multiple times with play/pause/rewind.
2. Subjects write summaries of the lectures, using their own words as much as possible.
3. Judges watch the original A/V recording and rate one or more summaries in terms of fidelity and fluency.
4. The ratings are averaged over recordings, subjects and judges into one score for each summarization method.

Our hypothesis is that better summarization methods lead to better written summaries and higher scores. This evaluation protocol is efficient because subjects (writers) only have to watch short A/V summaries, while judges, who must view an entire recording, can then rate an arbitrary number of written summaries. Subjects must not watch different summaries of the same recording, to avoid learning effects. Such effects are a potential drawback of traditional subjective evaluation of summaries, in which each judge watches the original recording as well as different summaries before they provide their judgment. In the experiments below, we show that this evaluation method can accommodate variability across recordings, subjects, and judges to provide conclusive results.

We conducted two evaluations based on this protocol: a pilot and a full study. Their main goal is to compare *TopS* with two common baseline methods: either display an excerpt from the very beginning of a recording (a method noted as *First*), or select several random segments (noted *Random*). As we use topical segments from TextTiling, this likely improves the coherence of *Random* compared to using uniform segments. For all methods, summaries are again 17% of the ASR transcript's length.

5.2 Pilot Study

In the pilot study, we selected three video lectures from Klewel and generated A/V summaries for each of them using the three methods above. We showed to three subjects one summary of each video, each from a different method (3x3 Latin square design), instructing them to write a summary of at most 100 words. The nine resulting summaries were rated by two judges each. On average, users spent 10 minutes to watch each A/V summary and to write their textual summary. The average summary length was 72 words. *TopS* resulted in the highest fidelity scores from both judges, while *Random* was second and *First* was third.

5.3 Full Study

In the full study, we selected six lecture recordings from Klewel (not used in the pilot study) and generated A/V summaries using the same automatic methods: *First*, *Random* and *TopS*. We showed to each of the six subjects (English-speaking PhD students at our institution who were paid for their participation) one summary of each video, distributed evenly over the methods—hence each subject saw two summaries from each method, without knowledge of the method, but never more than one summary of the same video. Conversely, each of the three summaries of each video was seen by two subjects, to measure agreement. Finally, all 36 written summaries were rated by three different judges (English-speaking researchers in the field) who saw the videos in full before rating the written summaries.

Subjects spent on average 12 minutes to watch each A/V summary and write their textual summary, again a reasonable duration given that lectures lasted between 30 and 60 minutes. The average summary length was 84 words.

The fidelity scores for each summarization method when averaging over lectures and judges (but not subjects) appear in Table 2. For 5 of the 6 subjects, the fidelity is highest for *TopS*. The differences between *TopS* and, respectively, *Random* and *First* represent consistent trends at the 90% level (paired t-test across subjects, $p < 0.1$), while the difference between *Random* and *First* is not significant.

Table 3 shows the fidelity scores per method. This time we keep the lectures separate, as opposed to the different subjects, and we average over the two subjects seeing each A/V summary and the three judges rating the written summaries. The results indicate that for four lectures out of six (lectures 3 to 6), fidelity is highest for *TopS*. On average, *TopS* significantly outperforms *Random* (paired t-test across subjects, $p < 0.01$), though not *First*. Still, *TopS* also outperforms *First* if we exclude the first two lectures, which

Table 2: **Fidelity of human written summaries based on three A/V summarization methods, for six subjects, *averaged over lectures and judges.***

Subject	*First*	*Random*	*TopS*
1	3.00	3.17	**4.33**
2	2.83	2.50	**3.67**
3	3.17	**3.75**	2.75
4	3.17	1.75	**3.33**
5	2.08	1.75	**2.58**
6	2.58	1.92	**3.50**
Average	2.81	2.47	**3.36**

happen to start with an overview that actually provides a summary, which explains the good results of *First*. These two lectures are courses in software engineering, while the other four are short non-technical conference presentations.

Table 3: **Fidelity of human written summaries based on three different A/V summarization methods, for six lectures, *averaged over subjects and judges.***

Lecture	*First*	*Random*	*TopS*
1	**2.92**	2.25	2.58
2	**3.33**	2.83	3.25
3	1.67	3.08	**3.92**
4	2.83	1.42	**3.08**
5	2.83	2.67	**3.67**
6	3.25	2.58	**3.67**
Average	2.81	2.47	**3.36**

Although less marked, there are differences in fluency as well. The average fluency per method is 4.21 vs. 4.06 vs. 3.82 respectively for *TopS*, *First*, and *Random*. *TopS* significantly outperforms *First* ($p < 0.05$) but not *Random* (despite the larger difference). As expected, the average fluency per subject varies quite a lot (the values are: 4.72, 4.25, 4.28, 3.31, 3.47, and 4.14). However, when looking at fluency per lecture, no significant differences appear across the three methods, as the values are closer because they are averaged over the same subjects.

6. CONCLUSION

We have presented *TopS*, a graph-based method for extractive summarization of audiovisual lecture recordings. *TopS* leverages topic segmentation and content-based similarity at the collection level to provide a simple yet effective approach to summarization. *TopS* is computationally efficient and compares favorably with state-of-the-art methods. Our experiments validate *TopS* using gold-standard summaries from the AMI Meeting Corpus and the ROUGE metric, but also, when no reference summary was available, using a task-based approach which considers audiovisual extractive summaries as a means for producing human-written summaries of lectures. In the future, we aim to enrich content-similarity with visual features and extend the content-similarity graph using collaborative filtering and per-segment view count information, in order to integrate user behavior and preferences.

7. ACKNOWLEDGMENTS

We are grateful to the Swiss National Science Foundation for its support (AROLES project n. 51NF40-144627).

8. REFERENCES

[1] C. Bhatt, N. Pappas, M. Habibi, and A. Popescu-Belis. Multimodal reranking of content-based recommendations for hyperlinking video snippets. In *Proc. of Int. Conf. on Multimedia Retrieval (ICMR)*, pages 225–232, 2014.

[2] S. Bird. NLTK: the Natural Language Toolkit. In *Proc. of the COLING/ACL Interactive Presentation Sessions*, 2006.

[3] J. Carletta. Unleashing the killer corpus: experiences in creating the multi-everything AMI Meeting Corpus. *Lang. Resources & Evaluation*, 41(2):181–190, 2007.

[4] M. Cooper and J. Foote. Discriminative techniques for keyframe selection. In *IEEE International Conference on Multimedia and Expo (ICME)*, 2005.

[5] G. Erkan and D. R. Radev. LexRank: Graph-based lexical centrality as salience in text summarization. *Journal of Artificial Intelligence Research*, 2004.

[6] N. Garg, B. Favre, et al. ClusterRank: a graph based method for meeting summarization. In *Proc. INTERSPEECH*, 2009.

[7] T. Hain et al. Transcribing meetings with the AMIDA systems. *IEEE Trans. on Audio, Speech, and Language Processing*, 20(2):486–498, 2012.

[8] M. A. Hearst. TextTiling: Segmenting text into multi-paragraph subtopic passages. *Computational Linguistics*, 23(1):33–64, 1997.

[9] C. Lai and S. Renals. Incorporating lexical and prosodic information at different levels for meeting summarization. In *Proc. of Interspeech*, 2014.

[10] C.-Y. Lin and E. Hovy. Automatic evaluation of summaries using n-gram co-occurrence statistics. In *Proc. of NAACL-HLT*, 2003.

[11] I. Mani, G. Klein, D. House, L. Hirschman, T. Firmin, and B. Sundheim. SUMMAC: A text summarization evaluation. *Natural Lang. Eng.*, 8(1):43–68, 2002.

[12] R. Mihalcea and P. Tarau. TextRank: bringing order into texts. In *Empirical Methods in Natural Language Processing (EMNLP)*, 2004.

[13] A. G. Money and H. Agius. Video summarisation: A conceptual framework and survey of the state of the art. *Journal of Visual Communication and Image Representation*, 19(2):121–143, 2008.

[14] A. Nenkova and K. McKeown. A survey of text summarization techniques. In *Mining Text Data*. 2012.

[15] R. Ribeiro and D. M. de Matos. Revisiting centrality-as-relevance: Support sets and similarity as geometric proximity. *Journal of Artificial Intelligence Research*, 42:275–308, 2011.

[16] K. Riedhammer, B. Favre, et al. Long story short–global unsupervised models for keyphrase based meeting summarization. *Speech Communication*, 2010.

[17] D. Wang, S. Zhu, T. Li, and Y. Gong. Comparative document summarization via discriminative sentence selection. *ACM Transactions on Knowledge Discovery from Data (TKDD)*, 7(1):2, 2013.

Recurrent Support Vector Machines for Audio-Based Multimedia Event Detection

Yun Wang, Florian Metze
Language Technologies Institute
Carnegie Mellon University
Pittsburgh, PA 15213, USA
{yunwang, fmetze}@cs.cmu.edu

ABSTRACT

Multimedia event detection (MED) is the task of detecting given events (*e.g.* parade, birthday party) in a large collection of video clips. While the most useful information comes from visual features and speech recognition, a lot can also be inferred from the non-speech audio content, either alone or in conjunction with visual and speech cues. This paper studies MED with non-speech audio information only.

MED is usually performed in two stages. The first stage generates a representation for each clip in the form of either a single vector or a sequence of vectors, often by aggregating frame-level features; the second stage performs binary or multi-class classification to decide whether each target event occurs in each clip. Common classifiers used for the second stage include support vector machines (SVMs), feed-forward deep neural networks (DNNs), and recurrent neural networks (RNNs).

In this paper, we propose to classify clips for events using "recurrent SVMs". These models combine the kernel mapping and the large-margin optimization criterion of SVMs, and the ability to process sequences of variable lengths of RNNs. Reinforced with data augmentation, recurrent SVMs have achieved higher mean average precision (MAP) on the TRECVID 2011 MED task than both SVMs and RNNs.

Keywords

Multimedia event detection (MED); noisemes; support vector machines (SVMs); recurrent neural networks (RNNs); kernel mapping; large margin; hinge loss; data augmentation

1. INTRODUCTION

Multimedia event detection (MED) is the task of detecting given events happening in a video clip, and can be used to index video clips in large collections such as YouTube for efficient retrieval. While it is obvious that the visual and speech information in the video clips is useful for event detection, non-speech audio information can also be important: some non-speech sounds may directly reveal the event happening, such as the distinct clatter of a bowling ball hitting the pins; other sounds indicate the environment in which events happen, such as the buzz of machines in a factory. Some of this audio information may not even be present in the visual content. As a result, a number of systems have been designed to perform event detection with non-speech audio information only (see below).

MED systems usually consist of two stages. In the first stage, a clip-level representation is generated for each video clip. Such representations usually come in the form of a vector or a sequence of vectors, and are often an aggregation of frame-level features. In the second stage, binary or multi-class classifiers are built for the target events, taking the clip-level representations as inputs.

The methods to generate clip-level representations may be classified into three types. The first type, inspired by speaker identification, models each video clip as a GMM supervector [1, 2] or an "i-vector" [3, 4, 5]. The second type, inspired by topic classification, first learns a "vocabulary" of frame-level acoustic features by vector quantization, and then represents each video clip with a bag-of-audio-words (BoAW) vector [6]. In both approaches above, the frame-level features are treated as mutually independent, and their order is ignored altogether. As a remedy to this loss of information, semantically meaningful short audio segments have been proposed as the units of the third type of clip-level representation. These units may be either learnt in an unsupervised fashion [7, 8] or defined by humans [9]. The semantic units can be detected with either hidden Markov models (HMMs) or recurrent neural networks (RNNs) [10, 11, 12, 13, 14]. In this paper, we adopt sequences of "noiseme confidence vectors" [15] generated with a bidirectional RNN [16] as the representation of video clips.

The clip-level representations may be classified in various ways. BoAW vectors can be modeled with latent Dirichlet allocation (LDA) [17], treating each event as a topic; alternatively, all types of clip-level representations can be classified with general-purpose classifiers such as support vector machines (SVMs) [2, 18], random forests [15], feed-forward DNNs [13, 14], and recurrent neural networks [16].

In [16], the authors report a mean average precision (MAP) of 4.6% on the TRECVID 2011 MED task [19]. This number is rather low considering the usually amazing ability of RNNs to process sequential data, and actually falls behind an SVM implemented as in [18] on the same clip-level representation (7.1%, see Sec. 3). In this paper, we propose "recurrent SVMs" to combine the merits of SVMs and RNNs. We start by grafting elements of SVMs on

ICMR'16, June 06-09, 2016, New York, NY, USA

DOI: http://dx.doi.org/10.1145/2911996.2912048

to a feed-forward neural network: first, we implement the implicit kernel mapping of SVMs explicitly as a frontend of the network; then, we replace the cross-entropy loss function of the neural network with a squared hinge loss as is common in SVMs. At this step, the model is essentially an SVM with a non-linear hidden layer. The recurrent SVM is finally constructed by making the hidden layer recurrent, and it achieves a higher MAP than both SVMs and RNNs.

2. THE TRECVID 2011 MULTIMEDIA EVENT DETECTION TASK

In this section, we introduce the data and the evaluation criterion of the TRECVID 2011 MED task [19], and the representation of video clips used in this paper.

The TRECVID 2011 MED corpus has been used in a number of papers [2, 17, 15, 20, 21]. It consists of 3,104 training video clips and 6,642 test video clips. These video clips are "user-generated content posted to Internet video hosting sites", and exhibit a diversity of quality and duration. The median duration of the clips is 82 seconds; the mode is around 30 seconds. Some of the clips are labeled with one out of 15 events[1]; others are background clips. The goal is to train one or multiple models that would produce a confidence score given a test clip and an event. The scores can be used to make binary predictions about whether an event occurs in a test clip, or to form a ranked list of the test clips for each event.

We adopt the mean average precision (MAP) as the evaluation metric, as is done in [15] and [20]. For each event, the *average precision* measures the quality of the ranked list produced by a model. Sort the test clips by their confidence scores in descending order, and suppose the i-th positive instance is ranked at the r_i-th position (we break ties by ranking negative instances higher). The average precision is defined as $\text{AP} = \frac{1}{n}\sum_{i=1}^{n} i/r_i$, where n is the total number of positive test instances. The mean of the AP across all events is called the *mean average precision* (MAP).

The representation of video clips used in this paper, as well as in [16], is sequences of "noiseme confidence vectors" (NCVs), proposed in [15]. A *noiseme* is an audio segment that has an interpretable and descriptive meaning, such as "music", "cheer", and "engine". 42 types of noisemes are defined in [9] (the corpus actually contains 48 distinct noiseme labels); we manually merged some rare noisemes into semantically close ones, ending up with 17 noisemes (plus a "background" class). We form the NCV sequence with the following steps:

1. Extract low-level acoustic features (*e.g.* MFCC, F_0) with the OpenSMILE toolkit [22], and compute various statistics of these features (*e.g.* mean, variance) using sliding windows of 2 s moving 100 ms at a time;
2. From the 6,669 dimensions of features produced above, select 983 dimensions using the information gain criterion, as done in [15];
3. Predict the probability of each noiseme occurring at each frame using a bidirectional recurrent neural network (BRNN) trained in [16], resulting in a 18-dimensional NCV sequence.

[1]See [16] for a complete list of the 15 events; note that the names of the events E004 and E005 were reversed by mistake in that paper.

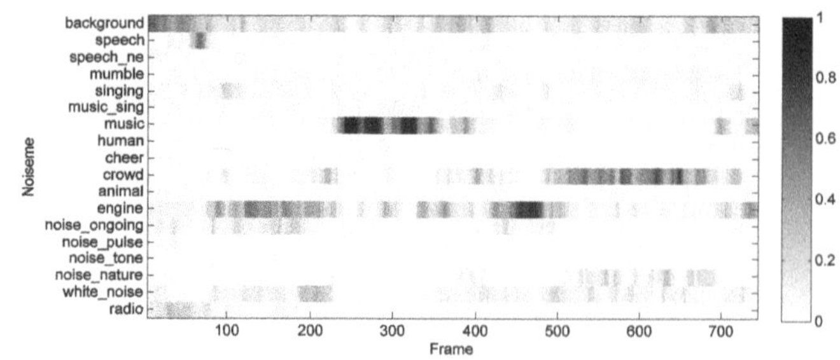

Figure 1: *An example noiseme confidence vector sequence.*

Fig. 1 shows an example of a clip represented as an NCV sequence.

For the non-recurrent SVM model and the feed-forward neural networks discussed in Section 3, the input to the model is the average of the NCVs across all the frames. For the recurrent SVM models discussed in Section 4, in theory the NCV sequences could be used directly as the input. However, the sequences are often very long. In order to save computation time, we first shorten all sequences whose length l is greater than 50 to $m = \sqrt{50l}$ frames, by dividing the original sequence evenly into m segments and taking the average within each segment. The resultant sequences, with a median length of 203 frames, are still too long to train a recurrent model reliably. So we further shorten each sequence of length m to m^β frames, with $\beta \in \{0.3, 0.5, 0.6, 0.7\}$. We choose non-linear functions because they have a larger compressing effect on longer sequences.

3. MIMICKING AN SVM WITH A FEED-FORWARD NEURAL NETWORK

In [18], support vector machines (SVMs) were employed for event detection. One separate SVM was built for each event, using the χ^2-RBF kernel and a hinge loss function. By applying these SVM models to the NCV representation introduced in Sec. 2, we obtained a MAP of 7.1%. On the other hand, the authors of [16] report a MAP of 4.0% for a feed-forward DNN, and a MAP of 4.6% for a recurrent neural network using long short-term memory (LSTM) cells. In our experiments (see Sec. 3.4), we obtained a MAP of 3.6% with a feed-forward neural network with a single hidden layer of 1,000 rectified linear units (ReLUs). To bridge the gap between the neural network and the SVMs, we enhance the neural network by grafting elements of SVMs one at a time.

3.1 Explicit Kernel Mapping

By inspecting the predictions made by the feed-forward neural network, the first problem we realized was that the model did not have enough resolution in the low-dimensional input space. The neural network always assigned similar scores to instances whose features fell close in the input space, while the SVMs were able to single out many positive instances. Therefore we decided to map the 18-dimensional NCVs to high-dimensional vectors using the kernel mapping of the SVMs, which is a composition of the χ^2 kernel and the RBF kernel.

The χ^2 kernel has been found to work well with histogram data (*e.g.* in [17]). NCVs, being L_1-normalized, are histograms, so the χ^2 kernel is suitable for them as well. For two D-dimensional histograms $\mathbf{x} = [x_1, \ldots, x_D]$ and

$\mathbf{y} = [y_1, \ldots, y_D]$, the χ^2 kernel is defined as:

$$k_{\chi^2}(\mathbf{x}, \mathbf{y}) = \sum_{i=1}^{D} \frac{2x_i y_i}{x_i + y_i} \quad (1)$$

and a distance measure can be derived from the kernel:

$$d_{\chi^2}^2(\mathbf{x}, \mathbf{y}) = k_{\chi^2}(\mathbf{x}, \mathbf{x}) + k_{\chi^2}(\mathbf{y}, \mathbf{y}) - 2k_{\chi^2}(\mathbf{x}, \mathbf{y}) = \sum_{i=1}^{D} \frac{(x_i - y_i)^2}{x_i + y_i} \quad (2)$$

The χ^2 kernel falls in the range of $[0, 1]$, and the χ^2 distance lies in $[0, \sqrt{2}]$.

The radial basis function (RBF) kernel is a kernel that depends only on the distance between the two arguments:

$$k_{\text{RBF}}(\mathbf{x}, \mathbf{y}) = \exp[-\gamma d^2(\mathbf{x}, \mathbf{y})] \quad (3)$$

Plugging the χ^2 distance $d_{\chi^2}(\mathbf{x}, \mathbf{y})$ into the RBF kernel, we get the χ^2-RBF kernel. The SVMs in [18] use $\gamma = 4$.

A kernel $k(\mathbf{x}, \mathbf{y})$ can be understood as the inner product of the two input arguments mapped into a high-dimensional feature space via a feature mapping function $\Phi(\cdot)$:

$$k(\mathbf{x}, \mathbf{y}) = \langle \Phi(\mathbf{x}), \Phi(\mathbf{y}) \rangle \quad (4)$$

Because SVMs can be solved in the dual space, it is enough to know the formula of the kernel $k(\cdot, \cdot)$, and the mapping function $\Phi(\cdot)$ can be kept implicit. To use kernels in neural networks, however, $\Phi(\cdot)$ must be implemented explicitly.

Following [23], we construct an approximation of the χ^2 mapping function, which is a 306-dimensional real vector consisting of the following elements ($D = 18, \Delta = 2\pi/17$):

$$\begin{aligned}\Phi_{\chi^2}(\mathbf{x}) = [&\sqrt{\Delta \cdot x_i}, \sqrt{2\Delta \cdot x_i \text{sech}(\pi\omega)} \cos(\omega \log x_i), \\ &\sqrt{2\Delta \cdot x_i \text{sech}(\pi\omega)} \sin(\omega \log x_i)] \\ &(i = 1 \ldots D, \omega = \Delta \ldots 8\Delta) \quad (5)\end{aligned}$$

And using the method in [24], we approximate the RBF mapping function as follows:

$$\begin{aligned}\Phi_{\text{RBF}}(\mathbf{x}) = [&\cos\langle \boldsymbol{\omega}_1, \mathbf{x} \rangle, \ldots, \cos\langle \boldsymbol{\omega}_N, \mathbf{x} \rangle, \\ &\sin\langle \boldsymbol{\omega}_1, \mathbf{x} \rangle, \ldots, \sin\langle \boldsymbol{\omega}_N, \mathbf{x} \rangle] \quad (6)\end{aligned}$$

where $\boldsymbol{\omega}_1, \ldots, \boldsymbol{\omega}_N$ are 306-dimensional real vectors sampled from the Gaussian distribution $\mathcal{N}(0, 2\gamma I)$. We choose $N = 5,000$, resulting in 10,000-dimensional feature vectors.

3.2 Squared Hinge Loss

The second problem we found with the feed-forward neural network lies with the loss function. The network had 15 sigmoid output nodes, one for each event, whose values stood for the probabilities of each event occurring in the clip. The traditional cross-entropy loss function was chosen as the objective of the optimization. In the face of a highly unbalanced training corpus (on average only 3% positive instances), the network spent most of its effort driving the scores of the negative instances very close to zero, instead of trying to boost the scores of the few positive instances. This is because the cross-entropy loss still has a non-zero gradient no matter how close the outputs are already to the target. On the contrary, the hinge loss in SVMs has a value of zero as long as an instance is correctly classified and far enough from the decision boundary. Even though the training data are highly unbalanced, the loss function only takes contribution from the few instances falling within the margin.

We replace the sigmoid output nodes of the neural network with linear output nodes, and apply the hinge loss function.

Model	MAP (%)
Feed-forward NN	3.6
+ χ^2 kernel	4.2
+ RBF kernel	5.8
+ Squared hinge loss	6.9
+ Data augmentation	7.2
SVM	7.1

Table 1: *Mean average precision (MAP) after every modification made to the feed-forward neural network inspired by SVMs.*

An instance having class label $t \in \{-1, +1\}$ and an output $y \in \mathbb{R}$ will incur a hinge loss of

$$\text{hinge}(yt) = \max(0, 1 - yt) \quad (7)$$

Some previous works [25, 26] investigating the hinge loss on neural networks used the squared hinge loss. The squared hinge loss is also used in the LibLINEAR toolkit [27]. In our experiments, we have also found the squared hinge loss to work better than the hinge loss.

3.3 Data Augmentation

To further deal with the problem of data imbalance, we performed augmentation on the training data. We perturb the NCVs of the positive class to produce new positive training instances. However, simply adding Gaussian noise is not feasible, because the NCVs must be kept non-negative and L_1-normalized. To comply with this constraint, we generate a perturbed NCV $\mathbf{y}$ from an existing NCV $\mathbf{x}$ by sampling from a Dirichlet distribution $D(\alpha x_1, \ldots, \alpha x_D)$ [28, p. 594]. The mean of this Dirichlet distribution is equal to $\mathbf{x}$, and the parameter α controls its degree of concentration. For each training clip in which at least one of the target events occurs, we generate 9 extra training instances with $\alpha = 10,000$.

3.4 Experiments

We implemented neural networks with the Theano toolkit [29]. Our initial feed-forward neural network had 18 input nodes, one hidden layer of 1,000 ReLU units, and 15 sigmoid output nodes. The network was optimized for the cross-entropy loss, using the gradient descent algorithm with a Nesterov momentum coefficient [30] of 0.9. We adopted the adaptive learning rate schedule as in [16]. The best initial learning rate was selected using 5-fold cross validation.

Starting from this initial model, we made the following incremental modifications one by one:

1. Transform the input into 306-dimensional real vectors using the χ^2 kernel mapping;
2. Transform the input into 10,000-dimensional real vectors using the χ^2-RBF kernel mapping;
3. Replace the sigmoid output nodes with linear units, and the cross-entropy loss with a squared hinge loss;
4. Perform data augmentation on the training instances.

For each setup, Table 1 shows the average MAP obtained with 4 neural networks trained with different random initializations. It can be seen that each modification made a little contribution, and finally the neural network matched the performance of the SVMs.

4. RECURRENT SUPPORT VECTOR MACHINES

The model we have constructed so far is essentially an SVM with an extra hidden layer. Although its performance doesn't yet exceed that of conventional SVMs, the extra hidden layer opens up the possibility of recurrence. By making the hidden layer recurrent, the model will be able to process NCV sequences of variable lengths. And we call such a recurrent model a *recurrent SVM*.

A similar model with the same name has been proposed in [31], where the output of an RNN is used as the input of an SVM. Our model differs from [31] in two points: first, the kernel mapping in our model is applied *before* the recurrent layer, while in [31] the kernel mapping is a part of the SVM, *i.e.* applied *after* the recurrent layer; second, we train our model with the stochastic gradient descent (SGD) algorithm, while a genetic algorithm is used in [31].

In this section, we explore four setups of recurrence: the hidden units may be either ReLU units or LSTM cells [32]; the hidden layer may be either unidirectional (one chain going forward) or bidirectional (one chain going forward and one chain going backward). In the two unidirectional setups, the 15 linear output nodes are only connected to the hidden units of the last frame; in the two bidirectional setups, the output nodes are connected to the last frame of both chains (note that the last frame of the backward chain actually corresponds to the first frame of the clip).

We trained all the four types of recurrent SVMs with 500 hidden units in each chain. The input sequences were shortened from m frames to m^β frames, where $\beta \in \{0.3, 0.5, 0.6, 0.7\}$. This is because training tended to diverge if the input sequences were too long. We used the stochastic gradient descent algorithm with a batch size of 15,000 frames, and the same adaptive learning rate schedule as in Sec. 3. Nesterov momentum was not applied. The initial learning rate was selected using 5-fold cross validation.

With the capacity brought by the recurrence, all the recurrent SVM models demonstrated overfitting to the training data. The models were able to produce scores larger than $+1$ for almost all the positive instances and scores smaller than -1 for almost all the negative instances, thereby achieving a MAP of nearly 100%. On the other hand, the MAP on the test data started to degenerate after reaching a peak. We resorted to early stopping by monitoring the 5-fold cross-validation MAP at each epoch; if the maximum cross-validation MAP didn't get updated for 5 successive epochs, we stopped the training and took the result of the epoch with the highest cross-validation MAP as the final result.

Table 2 compares the MAP obtained with different types of recurrence and input sequence lengths. For each combination, four recurrent SVMs were trained with different random initializations. The numbers in the table are the average MAP of the four runs (or three if one of the runs diverged). "Divergent" means at least two of the four runs diverged.

We can see that all the recurrent SVMs are able to outperform non-recurrent models by a remarkable margin. Bidirectional models generally achieve higher MAPs than unidirectional models. LSTM cells are able to make use of slightly longer sequences ($\beta = 0.5$) than ReLU units ($\beta = 0.3$), but unfortunately their performance falls short.

We experimented with a number of other techniques in the hope of boosting the performance of recurrent SVMs with LSTM cells. We tried to make the state of the models at every time step contribute to the loss function (instead of only the last time step); we also tried to train the models for longer sequences using models for shorter sequences as a starting point, as done in [16]. Nevertheless, neither of these techniques made a significant difference.

β	0.3	0.5	0.6	0.7
Median sequence length	5	14	24	41
Unidirectional ReLU	8.4	5.7	2.8	Divergent
Bidirectional ReLU	8.8	6.4	6.1	Divergent
Unidirectional LSTM	7.5	7.8	6.0	Divergent
Bidirectional LSTM	8.0	8.2	6.4	6.5

Table 2: *Mean average precision (MAP) of recurrent SVMs with different setups and different input lengths.*

An inspection at the average precision of each event individually reveals that the improvement from the feed-forward neural network to the recurrent SVM mainly comes from the events on which the baseline SVMs already perform well. That is, recurrent SVMs are good at detecting the "easier" events better. As for the "difficult" events where the baseline SVMs exhibit poor performance ($< 3\%$ AP), the recurrent SVM made a small improvement on some, and performed as poorly as the baseline SVM on others. This may indicate that the current feature set does not contain the necessary information for detecting these events.

5. CONCLUSION

In this paper, we studied the task of audio-based event detection using sequences of "noiseme confidence vectors" as input features. We contrasted a feed-forward neural network with SVMs, and pointed out the elements that made SVMs suitable for the task: the χ^2-RBF kernel mapping, and the squared hinge loss function. By grafting these elements onto the feed-forward neural network, and with the help of data augmentation, we were able to make it match the performance of SVMs; by further making the hidden layer recurrent, we constructed recurrent SVMs that outperformed the baseline SVMs. The excellent performance of recurrent SVMs is attributed to the improved ability of detecting the "easier" events.

The best recurrent SVM we built used bidirectional chains of ReLU units. LSTM cells, being able to keep a longer memory, should be able to outperform simple ReLU units in theory, but we weren't able to observe this in our experiments. It remains a direction for future research to make recurrent SVMs with LSTM cells reach the performance they deserve.

6. ACKNOWLEDGMENTS

This work used the Extreme Science and Engineering Discovery Environment (XSEDE), which is supported by NSF grant number OCI-1053575.

This work was partially funded by Facebook, Inc. The views and conclusions contained herein are those of the authors and should not be interpreted as necessarily representing the official policies or endorsements, either expressed or implied, of Facebook, Inc.

This work has also been supported by a gift award from Robert Bosch GmbH.

7. REFERENCES

[1] W. M. Campbell, D. E. Sturim, and D. A. Reynolds. Support vector machines using GMM supervectors for speaker verification. *Signal Processing Letters, IEEE*, 13(5):308–311, 2006.

[2] Q. Jin, P. F. Schulam, S. Rawat, S. Burger, D. Ding, and F. Metze. Event-based video retrieval using audio. In *Proceedings of INTERSPEECH*, page 2085, 2012.

[3] N. Dehak, P. Kenny, R. Dehak, P. Dumouchel, and P. Ouellet. Front-end factor analysis for speaker verification. *Audio, Speech, and Language Processing, IEEE Transactions on*, 19(4):788–798, 2011.

[4] X. Zhuang, S. Tsakalidis, S. Wu, P. Natarajan, R. Prasad, and P. Natarajan. Compact audio representation for event detection in consumer media. In *Thirteenth Annual Conference of the International Speech Communication Association*, 2012.

[5] B. Elizalde, H. Lei, and G. Friedland. An i-vector representation of acoustic environments for audio-based video event detection on user generated content. In *Multimedia (ISM), International Symposium on*, pages 114–117. IEEE, 2013.

[6] S. Pancoast and M. Akbacak. Bag-of-audio-words approach for multimedia event classification. In *Interspeech*, pages 2105–2108, 2012.

[7] B. Byun, I. Kim, S. M. Siniscalchi, and C.-H. Lee. Consumer-level multimedia event detection through unsupervised audio signal modeling. In *INTERSPEECH*, pages 2081–2084, 2012.

[8] S. Chaudhuri, M. Harvilla, and B. Raj. Unsupervised learning of acoustic unit descriptors for audio content representation and classification. In *Interspeech*, pages 2265–2268, 2011.

[9] S. Burger, Q. Jin, P. F. Schulam, and F. Metze. Noisemes: Manual annotation of environmental noise in audio streams. 2012.

[10] Z. Kons and O. Toledo-Ronen. Audio event classification using deep neural networks. In *INTERSPEECH*, pages 1482–1486, 2013.

[11] O. Gencoglu, T. Virtanen, and H. Huttunen. Recognition of acoustic events using deep neural networks. In *Signal Processing Conference (EUSIPCO), 2014 Proceedings of the 22nd European*, pages 506–510. IEEE, 2014.

[12] E. Cakir, T. Heittola, H. Huttunen, and T. Virtanen. Polyphonic sound event detection using multi label deep neural networks. In *Neural Networks (IJCNN), 2015 International Joint Conference on*, pages 1–7. IEEE, 2015.

[13] M. Ravanelli, B. Elizalde, K. Ni, and G. Friedland. Audio concept classification with hierarchical deep neural networks. In *Signal Processing Conference (EUSIPCO), 2014 Proceedings of the 22nd European*, pages 606–610. IEEE, 2014.

[14] K. Ashraf et al. Audio-based multimedia event detection with DNNs and sparse sampling. In *Proceedings of the 5th ACM on International Conference on Multimedia Retrieval*, pages 611–614. ACM, 2015.

[15] Y. Wang, S. Rawat, and F. Metze. Exploring audio semantic concepts for event-based video retrieval. In *Acoustics, Speech and Signal Processing (ICASSP), 2014 IEEE International Conference on*, pages 1360–1364. IEEE, 2014.

[16] Y. Wang and F. Metze. Audio-based multimedia event detection using deep recurrent neural networks. In *Acoustics, Speech and Signal Processing (ICASSP), 2016 IEEE International Conference on*. IEEE, 2016.

[17] S. Rawat, P. F. Schulam, S. Burger, D. Ding, Y. Wang, and F. Metze. Robust audio-codebooks for large-scale event detection in consumer videos. 2013.

[18] L. Bao et al. Infomedia @ TRECVID 2011. In *Proceedings of TREC Video Retrieval Evaluation*.

[19] NIST. TRECVID multimedia event detection evaluation plan. [Online] http://www.nist.gov/itl/iad/mig/upload/MED11-EvalPlan-V03-20110801a.pdf, 2011.

[20] F. Metze, S. Rawat, and Y. Wang. Improved audio features for large-scale multimedia event detection. In *Multimedia and Expo (ICME), 2014 IEEE International Conference on*, pages 1–6. IEEE, 2014.

[21] Y. Yan, Y. Yang, D. Meng, G. Liu, W. Tong, A. G. Hauptmann, and N. Sebe. Event oriented dictionary learning for complex event detection. *Image Processing, IEEE Transactions on*, 24(6):1867–1878, 2015.

[22] F. Eyben, F. Weninger, F. Gross, and B. Schuller. Recent developments in opensmile, the munich open-source multimedia feature extractor. In *Proceedings of the 21st ACM international conference on Multimedia*, pages 835–838. ACM, 2013.

[23] A. Vedaldi and A. Zisserman. Efficient additive kernels via explicit feature maps. *Pattern Analysis and Machine Intelligence, IEEE Transactions on*, 34(3):480–492, 2012.

[24] A. Rahimi and B. Recht. Random features for large-scale kernel machines. In *Advances in neural information processing systems*, pages 1177–1184, 2007.

[25] Y. Tang. Deep learning using linear support vector machines. *arXiv preprint arXiv:1306.0239*, 2013.

[26] S. Chen and Y. Wang. Convolutional neural network and convex optimization. *Dept. of Elect. and Comput. Eng., Univ. of California at San Diego, San Diego, CA, USA, Tech. Rep*, 2014.

[27] R.-E. Fan et al. LIBLINEAR: A library for large linear classification. *The Journal of Machine Learning Research*, 9:1871–1874, 2008.

[28] L. Devroye. *Non-Uniform Random Variate Generation.* Springer-Verlag, 1986.

[29] J. Bergstra et al. Theano: a CPU and GPU math expression compiler. In *Proceedings of the Python for scientific computing conference (SciPy)*, volume 4, page 3. Austin, TX, 2010.

[30] Y. Nesterov. A method of solving a convex programming problem with convergence rate O(1/sqr(k)). In *Soviet Mathematics Doklady*, volume 27, pages 372–376, 1983.

[31] J. Schmidhuber, M. Gagliolo, D. Wierstra, and F. Gomez. Evolino for recurrent support vector machines. *arXiv preprint cs/0512062*, 2005.

[32] S. Hochreiter and J. Schmidhuber. Long short-term memory. *Neural computation*, 9(8):1735–1780, 1997.

Adding Chinese Captions to Images

Xirong Li[†] Weiyu Lan[†] Jianfeng Dong[‡] Hailong Liu[§]
[†]Key Lab of Data Engineering and Knowledge Engineering, Renmin University of China
[‡]College of Computer Science and Technology, Zhejiang University
[§]Pattern Recognition Center, WeChat Department, Tencent

ABSTRACT

This paper extends research on automated image captioning in the dimension of language, studying how to generate Chinese sentence descriptions for unlabeled images. To evaluate image captioning in this novel context, we present Flickr8k-CN, a bilingual extension of the popular Flickr8k set. The new multimedia dataset can be used to quantitatively assess the performance of Chinese captioning and English-Chinese machine translation. The possibility of re-using existing English data and models via machine translation is investigated. Our study reveals to some extent that a computer can master two distinct languages, English and Chinese, at a similar level for describing the visual world. Data is publicly available at http://tinyurl.com/flickr8kcn.

Keywords

Image captioning, Bilingual dataset, Chinese language

1. INTRODUCTION

This paper studies Image Captioning – automatically generating a natural language description for a given image. Different from the ongoing research that focuses on improving computational models for image captioning [2, 6, 12], which is undoubtedly important, we consider a new dimension of the problem: *Language*. While current works are on English, we study the possibility of captioning images in another language. In particular, we consider *Chinese*, the most spoken language in the world.

Extending along the language dimension is not just engineering efforts such as constructing a dataset in another language and applying existing models. We argue that this line of research is scientifically interesting in multiple aspects. An image caption is intended to provide clear descriptions of salient entities and events present in the image. The perception of saliency, however, could be culture dependent. Consider for instance the image shown in the first row of Table 1. While both English and Chinese annotators capture the event of taking a photo, they use distinct qualifiers for the word 'woman': 'Asian' in the English sentence and 中年 (middle-aged) in the Chinese sentence. Asian faces are probably too common to be visually salient from a Chinese point of view. By contrast, in the Chinese caption of the second image, the little girl is qualified with 金色头发 (blonde-haired). Research on multilingual captioning helps reveal how people from culturally and linguistically diverse backgrounds describe the visual world. Further, the divergence may provide complementary information to each of the languages and thus mutually boost the performance of individual language models. More fundamentally, while it remains controversial whether English or Chinese is the harder language to learn for human, it will be interesting to investigate if a computer can master the two languages at the same level for describing images. Towards answering the above questions, image captioning in a bilingual setting is a good starting point.

To build a Chinese-captioning model, an intuitive and inexpensive solution is to employ machine translation. Either in an early stage to automatically translate all the training text from English to Chinese, or in a late stage to translate the output of a pretrained English model. While the use of web-scale data has substantially improved translation quality, machine translation remains unreliable. A relatively simple sentence as 'A young girl in pigtails plays in the water' is translated to 一位年轻的女孩辫子起着水 by Google and 在发挥水的辫子姑娘 by Baidu. Neither of the translation makes sense. Given translation unreliability, questions arise as is machine translation still usable, which translation to use, and in what stage?

In this paper we present a pilot study for Chinese captioning of images. We extending the widely used Flickr8k dataset [5] to a bilingual version, with both machine translated and human written Chinese sentences. The new dataset can be used to assess the accuracy of Chinese captioning and the quality of machine translation. To the best of our knowledge, datasets of this kind do not exist in the public literature. We investigate the possibility of re-using existing English captions and models via machine translation. Three solutions are proposed and evaluated on the new bilingual dataset. Consequently, we identify good strategies for building a Chinese-captioning model.

2. PROGRESS ON IMAGE CAPTIONING

The state-of-the-art follows an image-encoding and sentence-decoding pipeline. A popular implementation, as developed in [3, 6, 12], is to encode an image with a pretrained deep

ICMR'16, June 06 - 09, 2016, New York, NY, USA

ISBN 978-1-4503-4359-6/16/06... $15.00

DOI: http://dx.doi.org/10.1145/2911996.2912049

Table 1: Some examples of Flickr8K-CN, a bilingual multimedia dataset for image captioning.

Image	English caption	Google translation	Baidu translation	Human translation	Chinese caption
	An Asian woman is taking a photograph outside a white columned building	一个亚洲女子走的是一条白色的圆柱状建筑外的照片	一个亚洲女人是白色圆柱的大楼外拍照	一个亚洲女人在一个白色圆柱大楼外拍照	一个中年女人正在拿着照相机准备拍照
	The little girl is running and laughing	这个小女孩奔跑着，欢笑着	小女孩在奔跑和欢笑	小女孩奔跑着，笑着	金色头发的小女孩
	A furry black and white dog jumps over a bar during an agility test	一个毛茸茸的黑色和白色的狗跳在一个酒吧的敏捷性测试中	一个毛茸茸的黑色和白色的敏捷测试过程中在一个酒吧的狗跳	一只毛茸茸的黑白相间的狗在敏捷性测试中跨栏	一只狗在跨栏
	A group of basketball players wearing yellow and green reach for a ball	A组篮球运动员身穿黄色和绿色端起一球	一群穿着黄色和绿色的篮球运动员	一群穿着黄色和绿色球服的篮球运动员在抢球	篮球比赛的现场

Convolutional Neural Networks (CNN), and then feed the image embedding to a Recurrent Neural Network (RNN), which eventually outputs a sequence of words as the caption. As for the RNN architecture, a bidirectional RNN is adopted in [6], while Long Short-Term Memory (LSTM) is utilized in [12]. Different from a one-layer word embedding [6, 12], Mao *et al.* incorporate a two-layer word embedding in their network [3]. LSTM based solutions have been ranked top in recent benchmark evaluations [1, 4, 7].

Besides the good progress on models, novel datasets are continuously developed, e.g., Flickr8k [5], Flickr30k [13] and MSCOCO [8], increasing the number of captioned images from a few thousands to hundreds of thousands. However, all the text is English. More recently, a bilingual dataset on the base of MSCOCO is introduced for answering questions about the content of an image [3]. A sample question-answer pair is 'what is there in yellow?' and 'Banana'. Questions are not captions. They are written in a different motivation. Datasets suited for studying image captioning in a bilingual setting remains to be established.

3. A BILINGUAL MULTIMEDIA DATASET

For captioning images in Chinese, we need a set of images accompanied with Chinese descriptions. For cross-language analysis, we choose to depart from an existing dataset wherein each image is already associated with some English captions. In particular, we employ Flickr8k [5], as it is well recognized in the literature [6,9,12] and its relatively small size is more suited for a pilot study. Given the data partition from [6], Flickr8k consists of 8,000 images, where 6,000 images are used for training, 1,000 images for validation, and the remaining 1,000 images for test. Each image has five English sentences collected via Amazon's Mechanical Turk. Written by US residents, these sentences were meant for briefly describing main objects and scenes in the image.

To make Flickr8k bilingual, a straightforward solution is to translate each sentence from English to Chinese by machine translation. We employ English-Chinese translation services provided by Google and Baidu, respectively. Some examples are given in Table 1. We observe that machine translation does not perform well as sentences become longer and contain ambiguous words.

Even though the translated sentences would have been perfect, they do not necessarily reflect how a Chinese describes the same image. In order to acquire sentences that better match with Chinese conventions, we recruited a local crowdsourcing service. The annotation was performed by a number of native speakers of Chinese, where they were asked to write sentences describing salient objects and scenes in every image, from their own point of views. Apart from this, we do not specify any rules on wording, intending to gather sentences written in a free style. Each image in Flickr8k receives five manually written Chinese sentences.

We compare sentences written in the two languages in terms of the most common words, see Table 2. For the ease of analysis, each word is manually assigned to one of four visual classes, i.e., objects, scenes, actions and colors. A noticeable difference is that the Chinese sentences contain much less words related to colors. For instance, the word 'black' is used 3,832 times in the English sentences, while the corresponding Chinese word 黑色 appears 116 times only. One reason is that color–object combinations such as 黑狗 (*black dog*) and 黑衣服 (*black clothes*) are valid and common words in Chinese. Such a convention makes the color-related words underestimated. Unsurprisingly, as the sentences were contributed by multiple persons, we observe that distinct words are used to express the same meaning, e.g., 水里 and 水中 to describe something in water, 跑 and 奔跑 for verb 'run' and 玩 and 玩耍 for verb 'play'.

Table 2: The most common words in the bilingual dataset, shown in four classes, i.e., objects, scenes, actions, and colors. Next to each Chinese word is its English translation, provided for non-Chinese readers.

Objects				Scenes				Actions				Colors			
English		Chinese		English		Chinese		English		Chinese		English		Chinese	
word	count	word	count	word	count	word	count	word	count	word	count	word	count	word	count
dog	8,136	人 *person*	7,841	grass	1,622	草地 *grass*	1,532	wearing	3,062	玩 *play*	2,363	white	3,940	黑狗 *black dog*	424
man	7,266	狗 *dog*	6,541	snow	1,492	雪地 *snow*	942	running	2,073	奔跑 *run*	1,739	black	3,832	白狗 *white dog*	126
boy	3,581	男人 *man*	4,564	field	1,280	水中 *in water*	901	playing	2,008	玩耍 *play*	1,726	red	2,672	红色 *red*	121
woman	3,403	小孩 *kid*	3,195	air	1,058	海边 *seaside*	570	standing	1,789	坐在 *sit on*	1,324	brown	2,563	黑色 *black*	116
girl	3,328	女人 *woman*	2,583	beach	1,046	草坪 *lawn*	526	jumping	1,472	骑 *ride*	1,046	blue	2,268	黄狗 *yellow dog*	115
people	2,887	男子 *man*	1,917	street	943	水里 *in water*	512	sitting	1368	站 *stand*	989	green	1,225	白色 *white*	111
dogs	2,125	孩子 *kid*	1,505	outside	791	沙滩 *beach*	425	holding	1324	拿 *hold*	896	yellow	1,213	黄色 *yellow*	65
ball	1,779	自行车 *bicycle*	1,126	pool	691	街道 *street*	412	walking	1,165	穿着 *wear*	742	orange	741	黑 *black*	51
child	1,545	小狗 *puppy*	1,117	wall	556	地上 *on ground*	361	jumps	979	跑 *run*	681	pink	735	粉色 *pink*	43
person	1,542	小女孩 *little girl*	1,079	mountain	554	路上 *on road*	276	runs	925	滑雪 *ski*	655	colorful	217	红 *red*	31

We may learn Chinese models either from the machine translated text or from the human written text. Due to the divergence between speakers of English and speakers of Chinese in describing images, it is unfair to evaluate models learned from machine translation using the crowdsourced ground truth. To faithfully describe English sentences in Chinese, we generate human translation for the test set.

As aforementioned, the test set is comprised of 1,000 images, each associated with five English sentences. Although these sentences are relatively simple in terms of words and structures, properly translating them into Chinese is non-trivial. We hired seven students in our university. Being native speakers of Chinese, they are fluent in English. Examples of human translation are shown in the fifth column of Table 1. On average a human translated sentence contains 15.9 words, almost double the number of a crowdsourced sentence (which is 7.5 words).

Putting all the above together, we have augmented Flickr8k with Chinese sentences generated by machine translation and crowdsourcing, respectively. Moreover, we provide human translation of the 5,000 English sentences in the test set. All this allows us to assess varied approaches to learning Chinese-captioning models.

4. CHINESE-CAPTIONING MODEL

For a novel image I, we aim to automatically predict a Chinese sentence S that describes in brief the visual content of the image. Naturally, the sentence is a sequence of n Chinese words, $S = \{w_1, \ldots, w_n\}$. One way to acquire S is to employ a pre-trained English-captioning model and translate its output from English to Chinese by machine translation. In contrast to such a Late Translation strategy, we discuss in this section how to build a Chinese model directly from a Chinese multimedia corpus, denoted as $\mathcal{C} = \{(I_i, S_{i,1}, \ldots, S_{i,m_i})\}$, where the i-th training image is accompanied with m_i sentences.

In this work we investigate the Neural Image Captioning (NIC) model for generating Chinese sentences, as shown in Fig. 1. NIC is a probabilistic model that uses an LSTM neural network to compute the posterior probability of a sentence given an input image. Consequently, the image will be annotated with the sentence that yields the maximal probability. Given θ as the model parameters, the probability is expressed as $p(S|I;\theta)$. Applying the chain rule together with log probability for the ease of computation, we have

$$\log p(S|I;\theta) = \sum_{t=0}^{n+1} \log p(w_t|I, w_0, \ldots, w_{t-1};\theta), \quad (1)$$

where w_0 = START and w_{n+1} = END are two special tokens indicating the beginning and the end of the sentence.

Conditional probabilities in Eq (1) are estimated by the LSTM network in an iterative manner. The network maintains a cell vector c and a hidden state vector h to adaptively memorize the information fed to it. The embedding vector of an image, obtained by applying an affine transformation on its visual feature vector, is fed to the network to initialize the two memory vectors. In the t-th iteration, new probabilities p_t over each candidate word are re-estimated given the current chosen words. The word with the maximum probability is picked up, and fed to LSTM in the next iteration. The recurrent connections of LSTM carry on previous context. Following [6,12], per iteration we apply beam search to maintain k best candidate sentences. The iteration stops once the END token is selected. To express the above process in a more formal way, we write

$$x_{-1} := W_e \cdot CNN(I), \quad (2)$$

$$x_t := W_s \cdot \mathbf{w}_t, \quad t = 0, 1, \ldots, \quad (3)$$

$$p_0, c_0, h_0 \leftarrow \text{LSTM}(x_{-1}, \mathbf{0}, \mathbf{0}), \quad (4)$$

$$p_{t+1}, c_{t+1}, h_{t+1} \leftarrow \text{LSTM}(x_t, c_t, h_t). \quad (5)$$

The parameter set θ consists of W_e, W_s, and affine transformations inside LSTM. While DeViSE directly takes a pre-trained word2vec model to construct W_s, NIC optimizes W_e and W_s simultaneously via maximum-likelihood estimation:

$$\max_{\theta} \sum_{(I,S)\in\mathcal{C}} \log p(S|I;\theta). \quad (6)$$

We use ET-NIC and CS-NIC to indicate models respectively learned from machine translated and crowdsourced Chinese sentences. LT-NIC refers to the use of machine translation in a late stage.

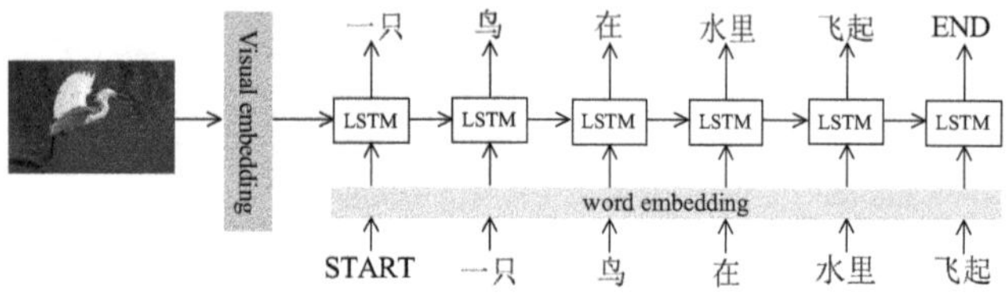

Figure 1: The Chinese-captioning model.

5. EVALUATION

5.1 Setup

Preprocessing. Unlike an English sentence that has spaces as explicit word boundary markers, a Chinese sentence lacks such markers. In order to tokenize a Chinese sentence into a list of meaningful words, we employ Jieba[1], an open-source software for Chinese text segmentation.

For the CNN feature, we employ the pool5 layer of a pre-trained GoogLeNet [11]. For all models the size of the visual and word embeddings is set to be 512.

Concerning the choice of machine translation services, we find that Baidu yields higher BLEU scores than Google for English-to-Chinese and Chinese-to-English translation. So Baidu translation is used in the following experiments.

Evaluation criteria. We adopt BLEU [10], originally developed for automatic evaluation of machine translation and now widely used to evaluate image captioning. To better understand the cross-language influence, we report BLEU with and without the corpus-level brevity penalty

5.2 Experiments

Experiment 1. Which Model for Chinese Captioning? With crowdsourced sentences as references, CS-NIC performs the best, see Table 3. When using human translated sentences as references, ET-NIC is the best, see Table 4. This is largely due to the divergence between crowdsourced sentences and human/machine translated sentences. For instance, as the former is shorter, sentences generated by CS-NIC tend to be shorter than those from ET-NIC and LT-NIC. This also explains why the brevity penalty does not affect BLEU scores of ET-NIC and LT-NIC when evaluating on crowdsourced references. Since machine translated sentences are on average one word shorter than human translation, the penalty causes decreases in BLEU scores when evaluating on human translated references. CS-NIC has a more dramatic decrease. The result also shows the importance of the brevity penalty for cross-corpus evaluation.

As for the two machine translation based models, ET-NIC surpasses LT-NIC. English-to-Chinese translation is error-prone, with BLEU-1 of 65.8 and BLEU-2 of 47.7. The superior performance of ET-NIC implies that the LSTM network has a sort of ability to tolerate the translation error.

Given what we have observed, the answer to the question of which model is more suited for Chinese captioning depends on what ground truth is in use. Nevertheless, we consider ET-NIC more appealing as it performs relatively well and requires no any extra manual annotation.

Experiment 2. Which Language is More Difficult to Learn? For a cross-language comparison, Table 5 shows the performance of the English model. Recall that NIC, ET-NIC and CS-NIC share the same model architecture, except that NIC is trained on English text, while the other two are trained on Chinese text. Moreover, they are tested on the same image set except for the reference sentences. So their comparison gives us a brief idea of how the machine masters each language to describe images.

[1]https://github.com/fxsjy/jieba/

Table 3: Performance of Chinese-captioning models, using crowdsourced sentences as references.

Model	BLEU-1	BLEU-2	BLEU-3
ET-NIC	45.8 (45.8)	22.8 (22.8)	10.5 (10.5)
LT-NIC	41.1 (41.1)	18.4 (18.4)	7.2 (7.2)
CS-NIC	**63.4** (61.1)	**41.6** (40.1)	**22.1** (21.3)

Table 4: Performance of Chinese-captioning models, using Human translated sentences as references.

Model	BLEU-1	BLEU-2	BLEU-3
ET-NIC	62.9 (53.9)	**37.4** (32.1)	**19.6** (16.8)
LT-NIC	56.8 (46.8)	30.1 (24.8)	13.5 (11.2)
CS-NIC	**63.3** (34.8)	31.3 (17.2)	7.2 (3.9)

Table 5: Performance of English-captioning models.

Model	BLEU-1	BLEU-2	BLEU-3
NIC	**63.4** (57.9)	**40.5** (37.0)	**19.8** (18.1)

For NIC, it obtains BLEU-1 at 57.9 and BLEU-2 at 37.0 (with the brevity penalty). The corresponding numbers for ET-NIC are 53.9 and 32.1, and 61.1 and 40.1 for CS-NIC. The better performance of CS-NIC is presumably because crowdsourced sentences generally contain less words, and shorter text is in principle easier to reconstruct. The relative lower performance of ET-NIC is not only because the length of the reference sentences has doubled, but also because the training text is machine translated (which has BLEU-1 at 62.7 after the brevity penalty). Interestingly, the averaged performance of the two Chinese models, with BLEU-1 at 57.5 and BLUE-2 at 36.1, is on par with the English model. The result suggests that the LSTM network has the capability to learn the two languages at a similar level.

6. CONCLUSIONS

Given image captioning experiments in a bilingual setting, our conclusions are as follows. In spite of its unreliability, machine translation can be used, in particular in an early stage in advance to model learning, for building a Chinese-captioning model. Baidu translation is preferred to Google translation. Which model is more suited for Chinese captioning depends on what ground truth is used. We consider ET-NIC promising as it performs relatively well and requires no extra manual annotation. Our evaluation suggests that the NIC model has the capability to learn both English and Chinese at a similar level for describing images.

Acknowledgements. This research was supported by the Fundamental Research Funds for the Central Universities and the Research Funds of Renmin University of China (No. 16XNQ013).

7. REFERENCES

[1] MS COCO Captioning Challenge. http://mscoco.org/dataset/#captions-challenge2015.

[2] H. Fang, S. Gupta, F. Iandola, R. Srivastava, L. Deng, P. Dollar, J. Gao, X. He, M. Mitchell, J. Platt, L. Zitnick, and G. Zweig. From captions to visual concepts and back. In *Proc. of CVPR*, 2015.

[3] H. Gao, J. Mao, J. Zhou, Z. Huang, L. Wang, and W. Xu. Are you talking to a machine? Dataset and methods for multilingual image question answering. In *Proc. of NIPS*, 2015.

[4] A. Gilbert, L. Piras, J. Wang, F. Yan, E. Dellandrea, R. Gaizauskas, M. Villegas, and K. Mikolajczyk. Overview of the ImageCLEF 2015 Scalable Image Annotation, Localization and Sentence Generation task. In *CLEF working notes*, 2015.

[5] M. Hodosh, P. Young, and J. Hockenmaier. Framing image description as a ranking task: Data, models and evaluation metrics. *J. Artif. Int. Res.*, 47(1):853–899, 2013.

[6] A. Karpathy and L. Fei-Fei. Deep visual-semantic alignments for generating image descriptions. In *Proc. of CVPR*, 2015.

[7] X. Li, Q. Jin, S. Liao, J. Liang, X. He, Y. Huo, W. Lan, B. Xiao, Y. Lu, and J. Xu. RUC-Tencent at ImageCLEF 2015: Concept detection, localization and sentence generation. In *CLEF working notes*, 2015.

[8] T. Lin, M. Maire, S. Belongie, L. Bourdev, R. Girshick, J. Hays, P. Perona, D. Ramanan, P. Dollár, and C. Zitnick. Microsoft COCO: Common objects in context. *CoRR*, abs/1405.0312, 2014.

[9] J. Mao, W. Xu, Y. Yang, J. Wang, Z. Huang, and A. Yuille. Deep captioning with multimodal recurrent neural networks (m-RNN). In *Proc. of ICLR*, 2015.

[10] K. Papineni, S. Roukos, T. Ward, and W. Zhu. BLEU: A method for automatic evaluation of machine translation. In *Proc. of ACL*, 2002.

[11] C. Szegedy, W. Liu, Y. Jia, P. Sermanet, S. Reed, D. Anguelov, D. Erhan, V. Vanhoucke, and A. Rabinovich. Going deeper with convolutions. In *Proc. of CVPR*, 2015.

[12] O. Vinyals, A. Toshev, S. Bengio, and D. Erhan. Show and tell: A neural image caption generator. In *Proc. of CVPR*, 2015.

[13] P. Young, A. Lai, M. Hodosh, and J. Hockenmaier. From image descriptions to visual denotations: New similarity metrics for semantic inference over event descriptions. *TACL*, 2:67–78, 2014.

Emotion Recognition from EEG Signals Enhanced by User's Profile

Tanfang Chen, Shangfei Wang*, Zhen Gao, Chongliang Wu
University of Science and Technology of China
Hefei, Anhui, P.R.China, 230027
tanfang@mail.ustc.edu.cn, sfwang@ustc.edu.cn
gzgqllxh@mail.ustc.edu.cn, clwzkd@mail.ustc.edu.cn

ABSTRACT

The main stream of current research of emotion recognition from electroencephalogram (EEG) signals infers users' emotion directly from EEG signals, without considering users' profile, which carries crucial information for emotion recognition. To address this, we propose a novel approach of emotion recognition from EEG signals enhanced by users' profile, which is only required during training. Specifically, we propose to use discriminative Restricted Boltzmann Machine (DRBM) to capture the inherent relationships among users' profile, EEG signals and emotion labels. During training, the proposed RBM classifier learns the mapping function from EEG signals and users' profile to emotion labels through discriminative learning algorithm. During testing, users' emotion can be recognized from EEG signals through marginalizing over users' profile, since RBM is a generative model. Experimental results on three benchmark databases, i.e. the DEAP database, the MAHNOB-HCI database and the USTC-ERVS database, demonstrate the effectiveness of the proposed approach in leveraging users' profile for enhancing emotion recognition from EEG signals and the superior emotion recognition performance of the proposed approach over existing approaches.

Keywords

Emotion Recognition; EEG; Discriminative Restricted Boltzmann Machine

1. INTRODUCTION

Recent years there have been increasing attention of emotion recognition in both academia and industry. Emotions can be detected from multiple channels, including facial expressions, speeches, and physiological signals. Among them, the electroencephalogram (EEG) signal provides important cue of human emotions, since it records electrical activity of the brain, where emotional activities evoke. Therefore, emotion recognition from EEG signals is of great interest.

Current emotion recognition from EEG signals consists of two steps: feature extraction and emotion classification. Frequency features, such as power spectrum density (PSD), are often employed to describe EEG signals and classifiers, such as K-nearest Neighbors (kNN), Bayesian network, Logistic regression, artificial neural network and Support Vector Machine (SVM), are widely used to recognize emotions. The mainstream of current research infers users' emotion directly from EEG signals, without considering users' profile, which carries crucial information for emotion recognition, since emotion is subjective and person-dependent.

Therefore, in this paper, we propose to use discriminative Restricted Boltzmann Machine (DRBM) to integrate EEG features and users' profile in training procedure to model the patterns embedded in users' EEG signals and users' profile. Specifically, during training, the proposed RBM classifier learns the mapping function from EEG signals and users' profile to emotion labels through discriminative learning algorithm. During testing, users' emotion can be recognized from EEG signals through marginalizing over users' profile, since RBM is a generative model.

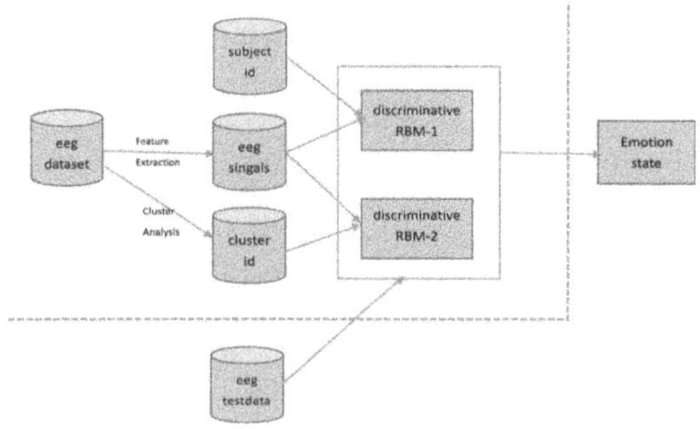

Figure 1: The framework of our method

2. EMOTION RECOGNITION WITH THE HELP OF USERS' PROFILE

The framework of our proposed approach is summarized in Figure 1. First, we extract EEG features from EEG signals. In the training stage, we train the DRBM using EEG features as well as the subject id or cluster id as user profile information. In the test stage, our model can predict the emotion state with only EEG features. The subject/cluster id is only available during training. Our model can tackle

*This is the corresponding author (Telephone: +86-551-3602824)

ICMR'16, June 06-09, 2016, New York, NY, USA
© 2016 ACM. ISBN 978-1-4503-4359-6/16/06...$15.00
DOI: http://dx.doi.org/10.1145/2911996.2912050

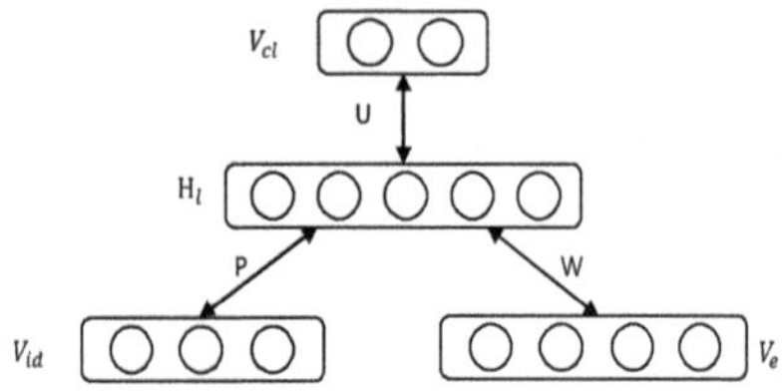

Figure 2: The Discriminative RBM

this information asymmetry and exploit the additional information during training to improve the performance for emotion recognition.

2.1 EEG Feature Extraction

First, we process the denoising to the original EEG signals. We eliminate and mitigate the HEGO and VEOG from EEG signals, then we apply a bandpass filter to acquire the frequency period between 0.3Hz and 45Hz[6, 4]. Second, we extract EEG features from five frequency sub-bands for 32 electrodes from delta(0-4Hz), theta(4-8 Hz), alpha(8-13 Hz), beta(13-30 Hz) and gamma(30-45 Hz) [3]. We calculate the power spectrum(PS) and the PS asymmetry between 14 pairs of electrodes from these sub-bands. The features are defined as the ratio of the power in each sub-band to the overall power. Finally, we extract 216 EEG features.

2.2 Analysis of User's Profile

We adopt subject id as one kind of user's profile information. Furthermore, we group subjects into several clusters using K-Means from EEG features. The cluster id obtained by K-Means is used as another kind of user's profile information.

2.3 The Discriminative Restricted Boltzmann Machine

DRBM is an extended RBM for classification. It exploits the hidden layer to capture the relationships between the features and the target labels to construct a non-linear binary classifier.

Figure 2 illustrates the structure of our DRBM. The visible nodes consist of three parts: V_e represents EEG features, V_{id} acts on behalf of the subject/cluster id and V_{cl} indicates the emotional labels. H_l represents the hidden layer on purpose of modeling the latent relations among the visible nodes. V_e is set as the Gaussian nodes since EEG features are continuous, while V_{cl}, V_{id} and H_l are binary nodes. The energy of our DRBM is defined as follows:

$$\begin{aligned} E(V_e, V_{id}, V_{cl}, H_l|\Theta) &= p_v(\mathbf{V_e} - \mathbf{b_e})^T(\mathbf{V_e} - \mathbf{b_e}) \\ &- \mathbf{b_{cl}}^T\mathbf{V_{cl}} - \mathbf{b_{id}}^T\mathbf{V_{id}} - \mathbf{b_l}^T\mathbf{H_l} - \mathbf{H_l}^T\mathbf{W}\mathbf{V_e} - \\ &\mathbf{H_l}^T\mathbf{U}\mathbf{V_{cl}} - \mathbf{H_l}^T\mathbf{P}\mathbf{V_{id}} \end{aligned} \tag{1}$$

where $\Theta = (\mathbf{b}, \mathbf{p}, \mathbf{W}, \mathbf{U}, \mathbf{P})$ are the parameters of our model.

The joint probability over V_e, V_{id}, V_{cl} and H_l are defined as following:

$$p(V_e, V_{id}, V_{cl}, H_l|\Theta) = \frac{1}{Z(\Theta)} exp(-E(V_e, V_{id}, V_{cl}, H_l|\Theta)) \tag{2}$$

where $Z(\Theta)$ is used for normalization.

Observed the states of hidden nodes, each visible node is independent of each other. Hence, the conditional probability can be factorized. The conditional probability for V_e, V_{cl}, V_{id} is defined as Equation 3,4,5.

We assume that unit node in V_e is independent of each other, and each of them obeys the Gaussian distribution $N(\mu, \sigma)$ with the mean value 0 and the variance 1 as follows:

$$p(V_e|H) = \prod_{i=1}^{D_e} p(V_{e(i)}|H) = \prod_{i=1}^{D_e} N(b_{e(i)} + \sum_{l=1}^{D_H} W_{il}h_l, 1) \tag{3}$$

where $b_{e(i)}$ is the bias of the ith node in V_e.

We first normalize the EEG features with mean value as 0 and variance as 1. Hence, we fix the variance as 1 during training for simplicity as shown in Equation 3.

We assume that nodes in V_{id} and V_{cl} are binary unit, they are independent of each other, and each of them are defined as follow:

$$p(V_{id}|H) = \prod_{j=1}^{D_{id}} p(V_{id(j)}|H) = \prod_{j=1}^{D_{id}} \sigma(b_{id(j)} + \sum_{l=1}^{D_H} P_{jl}h_l) \tag{4}$$

$$p(V_{cl}|H) = \prod_{k=1}^{D_{cl}} p(V_{cl(k)}|H) = \prod_{k=1}^{D_{cl}} \sigma(b_{cl(k)} + \sum_{l=1}^{D_H} U_{kl}h_l) \tag{5}$$

where the $\sigma()$ is the sigmoid function as $\sigma(x) = \frac{1}{1+exp(-x)}$ and $b_{id(j)}$ is the bias of the jth node in V_{id} and $b_{cl(k)}$ is the bias of the kth node in V_{cl}.

Observed the visible nodes, the condition probability of the hidden nodes can also be factorized as follows:

$$\begin{aligned} p(H_l|V_e, V_{cl}, V_{id}) &= \prod_{k=1}^{D_H} p(H_{l(k)})|V_e, V_{cl}, V_{id}) \\ &= \prod_{k=1}^{D_H} \sigma(b_{l(k)} + \sum_{i=1}^{D_e} V_{e(i)}W_{ik} + \sum_{i=1}^{D_{cl}} V_{cl(i)}U_{ik} + \sum_{i=1}^{D_{id}} V_{id(i)}P_{ik}) \end{aligned} \tag{6}$$

Given the training set $D_{train} = \{T^1, T^2, ..., T^n\}$, where n is the number of training samples and the superscript i indicates the ith examples $(V_e^i, V_{cl}^i, V_{id}^i)$, the negative conditional log-likelihood is defined as follows:

$$L_{disc}(D_{train}) = -\sum_{i=1}^{|D_{train}|} log\ p(V_{cl}^i|V_e^i, V_{id}^i) \tag{7}$$

We need to compute the following conditional distribution:

$$p(V_{cl}|V_e, V_{id}) = \frac{p(V_{cl}, V_e, V_{id})}{p(V_e, V_{id})} = \frac{\sum_H p(V, H)}{\sum_H \sum_{V_{cl}} p(V, H)} \tag{8}$$

We try to learn the parameters Θ of our model by minimizing the L_{disc}. The gradient of L_{disc} is calculated as:

$$\frac{\partial L_{disc}}{\partial \theta} = < \frac{\partial -E}{\partial \theta} >_{p(V_{id}, H_l|V_e, V_{cl})} - < \frac{\partial -E}{\partial \theta} >_{p(V_{cl}, V_{id}, H_l|V_e)} \tag{9}$$

We adopt the effective Contrastive Divergence Algorithm[2] to train our model, as shown in Algorithm 1 .

Algorithm 1 Training Algorithm for DRBM over $(V_e, V_{id}, V_{cl}, H_l)$

Input: training pair $(V_e^i, V_{id}^i, V_{cl}^i)$ and learning rate λ
Output: $\Theta = (\mathbf{b}, \mathbf{p}, \mathbf{W}, \mathbf{U}, \mathbf{P})$
%Notation:$x \leftarrow y$ means x is set to value y
% $x \backsim q$ means x is sampled from q

% Positive Phase
$V_e \leftarrow V_e^i,\ \ V_{cl} \leftarrow V_{cl}^i,\ \ V_{id} \leftarrow V_{id}^i$
$\widehat{H}_l \leftarrow \sigma(b_H + V_e^i W + V_{cl}^i U + V_{id}^i P)$

% Negative Phase
$H_l \backsim p(H_l|V_e, V_{id}, V_{cl}),\ V_e^{'} \backsim p(V_e|V_{id}, V_{cl}, H_l)$
$V_{cl}^{'} \backsim p(V_{cl}|V_e, V_{id}, H_l),\ V_{id}^{'} \backsim p(V_{id}|V_e, V_{cl}, H_l)$
$\widehat{H}_l^{'} \leftarrow \sigma(b_H + V_e W + V_{cl}^{'} U + V_{id}^{'} P)$

%Update
for $\theta \in \Theta$ **do**
$\theta \leftarrow \theta$ -$\lambda(\frac{\partial}{\partial\theta}E(V_e, V_{id}, V_{cl}, \widehat{H}_l)$-$\frac{\partial}{\partial\theta}E(V_e^{'}, V_{id}^{'}, V_{cl}^{'}, \widehat{H}_l^{'}))$
end for

2.4 Emotion Recognition

In the test phase, the EEG features are the only information available. The posterior probability given EEG features is obtained by Equation 8 marginalizing over the user information. We use the state of the nodes representing label with the maximum probability as our prediction as follows:

$$V_{cl} = \arg\max_{V_{cl}} p(V_{cl}|V_e) = \arg\max_{V_{cl}} \sum_{V_{id}} p(V_{cl}, V_{id}|V_e) \quad (10)$$

3. EXPERIMENT

3.1 Experimental Conditions

To validate the proposed approach, experiments are conducted on three benchmark databases, the MAHNOB-HCI[7], USTC-ERVS[8] and DEAP databases[5].

The MAHNOB-HCI database records 533 EEG segments from 27 participants during their watching of 20 videos. The self-report valence and arousal ratings are in nine scale from 1 to 9. The DEAP database consists of 1216 EEG segments from 32 participants during their watching of 38 videos. The self-report valence and arousal ratings are also in nine scale from 1 to 9. The USTC-ERVS database contains 197 EEG segments from 28 subjects during their watching of 92 videos. The self-report valence and arousal ratings are in five scale from -2 to 2. We changed the ratings into positive and negative for valence and arousal based on whether it is larger than the mean of ratings. Thus, for valence, we get 289 positive samples and 244 negative samples, 672 positive samples and 544 negative samples, 77 positive samples and 120 negative samples on the MAHNOB-HCI database, the DEAP database and the USTC-ERVS database respectively. For arousal, there are 268 positive samples and 265 negative samples, 726 positive samples and 490 negative samples, 149 positive samples and 48 negative samples on the MAHNOB-HCI database, the DEAP database and the USTC-ERVS database respectively.

Three emotion recognition experiments are conducted: emotion recognition from EEG signals only, emotion recognition enhanced by subject id, and emotion recognition enhanced by cluster id. Since the USTC-ERVS database does not provide subject id, we do not conduct the experiment of emotion recognition enhanced by subject id on this database. Leave-one-video-out cross-validation is adopted, and accuracy and F1 score are used as the metrics.

Table 1: Experimental results in valence recognition

		features only		with subject id		with cluster id	
		pos	neg	pos	neg	pos	neg
DEAP	pos	376	296	449	223	388	284
	neg	278	266	265	279	212	332
	acc	52.80%		59.87%		59.21%	
	F1	0.481		0.533		0.572	
MAHNOB-HCI	pos	184	105	160	129	180	109
	neg	120	124	75	169	90	154
	acc	57.78%		62.66%		64.35%	
	F1	0.524		0.607		0.634	
USTC-ERVS	pos	45	32			46	31
	neg	51	69			29	91
	acc	57.87%				69.54%	
	F1	0.520				0.605	

Table 2: Experimental results in arousal recognition

		features only		with subject id		with cluster id	
		pos	neg	pos	neg	pos	neg
DEAP	pos	371	355	444	282	453	273
	neg	201	289	203	287	180	310
	acc	54.28%		60.12%		62.75%	
	F1	0.509		0.542		0.577	
MAHNOB-HCI	pos	194	74	187	81	180	88
	neg	129	136	94	171	97	168
	acc	61.91%		67.17%		65.29%	
	F1	0.572		0.661		0.645	
USTC-ERVS	pos	123	26			107	42
	neg	29	19			14	34
	acc	72.08%				75.13%	
	F1	0.408				0.601	

3.2 Experimental Results and Analysis

The experimental results for valence and arousal recognition are shown in Table 1 and Table 2 respectively, where 'pos' means positive and 'neg' means negative. In Table 1 and Table 2, we give out confusion matrix, accuracy and F1-score.

For valence recognition, compared to the method merely using EEG signals, the method with subject id increases accuracy by 7.07% and 4.88% and F1-score by 0.052 and 0.083 on the DEAP and MAHNOB-HCI databases respectively; the method using cluster id improves the accuracy and F1-score by 6.41% and 0.091 on the DEAP database, and 6.57% and 0.11 on the MAHNOB-HCI database as well as 11.67% and 0.085 on the USTC-ERVS database respectively. Using cluster id as users' profile achieves better performance than using the subject id, since it improves the evaluation metrics of all results except the accuracy decreases by 0.66% slightly on the DEAP database.

For arousal recognition, compared to the method merely using EEG signals, accuracy and F1-score are improved

Table 3: **Related Works[1] on the MAHNOB-HCI database**

	Valence		Arousal	
	pos	neg	pos	neg
pos	164	125	170	98
neg	105	139	99	166
acc	56.9%		63.0%	
F1	0.547		0.628	

with the method using subject id by 5.84% and 0.033 on the DEAP database as well as 5.26% and 0.089 on the MAHNOB-HCI database; the method using cluster id improves the accuracy by 8.47%, 3.38% and 3.05% while F1-score is improved by 0.068, 0.073 and 0.193 on the DEAP, MAHNOB-HCI and USTC-ERVS databases respectively. Using cluster id achieves better performance than using subject id on the DEAP database while using subject id has better performance on the MAHNOB-HCI database.

From these two tables, we can find that using the user information available during training can improve the prediction result a lot; compared with the way merely using EEG features, the recognition results of our model is unbiased in all cases, especially for the USTC-ERVS database whose data is significant unbalanced, demonstrating our model has better robustness; the improvement is higher for valence than for arousal, which indicates valence recognition can be easier to be modeled; the results obtained by the method using cluster id are comparable with using subject id. Cluster id is obtained by unsurpervised learning based on the variousness across different subjects in EEG signals. Compared with using subject id, the method using cluster id has better generalization performance, since it does not require subject id explicitly.

3.3 Comparison with Related Work

On the MAHNOB-HCI[7] database, we compare our work with Gao et al[1]. They adopted the hierarchical Bayesian Network exploiting specificity of different subjects and generality among subjects to help the emotion recognition. Their experiments are on the same condition as ours. Compared to our method, their model is a generative model and requires the subject id as privileged information. The results are displayed in Table 3. Our work outperforms theirs in both the valence and arousal space. The results demonstrate that our DRBM with hidden layers captures more reliable relations among the EEG features, the user information and targets, hence achieves better performance.

For DEAP[5] database, we compare our work with Koelstra et al.[5] as well as Gao et al.[1]. Table 4 displays the results. As described in [5], we adopt the F1-score*, which means average F1-score, as our evaluation metrics. In both valence and arousal space, our method outperforms both of them. Compared with [5] using the user information both during training and testing, our model only use user information during training. The results further demonstrate the effectiveness of our method.

4. CONCLUSIONS

In this paper, we propose a novel method for emotion recognition using the DRBM with the user's profile during training. The results on the USTC-ERVS, DEAP and

Table 4: **Related Works on the DEAP database**

	Valence		Arousal	
Method	Accuracy	F1 score*	Accuracy	F1 score*
DEAP[5]	57.60%	0.563	62.00%	0.583
Gao[1]	58.00%	0.578	58.40%	0.569
Ours	59.87%	0.590	60.12%	0.594

MAHNOB-HCI databases show that our model enhanced by user's profile outperforms the methods merely using EEG features and the results with the cluster id obtained from EEG features by unsupervised learning are comparable with subject id without adding the extra user information.

5. ACKNOWLEDGEMENTS

This work has been supported by the National Science Foundation of China (Grant No. 61175037, 61228304, 61473270), and the project from Anhui Science and Technology Agency (1106c0805008).

6. REFERENCES

[1] Z. Gao and S. Wang. Emotion recognition from eeg signals using hierarchical bayesian network with privileged information. In *Proceedings of the 5th ACM on International Conference on Multimedia Retrieval*, pages 579–582. ACM, 2015.

[2] G. Hinton. A practical guide to training restricted boltzmann machines. *Momentum*, 9(1):926, 2010.

[3] Z. Ji and S. Qin. Detection of eeg basic rhythm feature by using band relative intensity ratio (brir). In *Acoustics, Speech, and Signal Processing, 2003. Proceedings.(ICASSP'03). 2003 IEEE International Conference on*, volume 6, pages VI–429. IEEE, 2003.

[4] S. Koelstra, C. Mühl, and I. Patras. Eeg analysis for implicit tagging of video data. In *Affective Computing and Intelligent Interaction and Workshops, 2009. ACII 2009. 3rd International Conference on*, pages 1–6. IEEE, 2009.

[5] S. Koelstra, C. Mühl, M. Soleymani, J.-S. Lee, A. Yazdani, T. Ebrahimi, T. Pun, A. Nijholt, and I. Patras. Deap: A database for emotion analysis; using physiological signals. *Affective Computing, IEEE Transactions on*, 3(1):18–31, 2012.

[6] S. Koelstra, A. Yazdani, M. Soleymani, C. Mühl, J.-S. Lee, A. Nijholt, T. Pun, T. Ebrahimi, and I. Patras. Single trial classification of eeg and peripheral physiological signals for recognition of emotions induced by music videos. In *Brain informatics*, pages 89–100. Springer, 2010.

[7] M. Soleymani, J. Lichtenauer, T. Pun, and M. Pantic. A multimodal database for affect recognition and implicit tagging. *Affective Computing, IEEE Transactions on*, 3(1):42–55, 2012.

[8] S. Wang, Y. Zhu, G. Wu, and Q. Ji. Hybrid video emotional tagging using usersâĂŹ eeg and video content. *Multimedia tools and applications*, 72(2):1257–1283, 2014.

Multimodal Deep Convolutional Neural Network for Audio-Visual Emotion Recognition

Shiqing Zhang[1,2], Shiliang Zhang[1], Tiejun Huang[1], Wen Gao[1]
[1]School of EE&CS, Peking University, Beijing, China
[2]Institute of Intelligent Information Processing, Taizhou University, Taizhou, China
tzczsq@pku.edu.cn, slzhang.jdl@pku.edu.cn, tjhuang@pku.edu.cn, wgao@pku.edu.cn

ABSTRACT

Emotion recognition is a challenging task because of the emotional gap between subjective emotion and the low-level audio-visual features. Inspired by the recent success of deep learning in bridging the semantic gap, this paper proposes to bridge the emotional gap based on a multimodal Deep Convolution Neural Network (DCNN), which fuses the audio and visual cues in a deep model. This multimodal DCNN is trained with two stages. First, two DCNN models pre-trained on large-scale image data are fine-tuned to perform audio and visual emotion recognition tasks respectively on the corresponding labeled speech and face data. Second, the outputs of these two DCNNs are integrated in a fusion network constructed by a number of fully-connected layers. The fusion network is trained to obtain a joint audio-visual feature representation for emotion recognition. Experimental results on the RML audio-visual database demonstrates the promising performance of the proposed method. To the best of our knowledge, this is an early work fusing audio and visual cues in DCNN for emotion recognition. Its success guarantees further research in this direction.

Keywords

Emotion recognition; Multimodal deep learning; Deep convolution neural network

1. INTRODUCTION

Emotion plays a significant role in social interaction, human intelligence, perception, etc [12]. Speech signal and facial expression are two most natural and effective ways of expressing emotions. During the last decade, integrating speech and facial expression for human emotion recognition has attracted extensive attentions. However, for computers, emotion recognition is still a challenging task.

Feature extraction, as the first step of distinguishing emotion, heavily affects recognition performance. So far there has been a substantial number of work [11, 6, 13, 14, 2] on low-level hand-crafted feature extraction for audio-visual emotion recognition. Wang et al. [11] extracted prosodic, Mel-frequency Cepstral Coefficient (MFCC), and formants from speech signals, and Gabor wavelet features from facial images, respectively. Then they concatenated these two streams of features for audio-visual emotion recognition. Mansoorizadeh et al.[6] adopted the statistical moments of energy and pitch contours of the speech signal as audio features, and the collected motion parameters of head, eyebrows, eyes and mouth as facial features. Then emotion classification was performed by face and speech independently and the final classification scores were fused at decision level. Nevertheless, due to the emotional gap between subjective emotion and low-level hand-crafted features, these features can not sufficiently and efficiently discriminate high-level emotions.

In recent years, some works [4, 8] start to employ deep leaning [3] for audio-visual emotion recognition due to its promising unsupervised feature learning ability. Kim et al.,[4] used Deep Belief Network (DBN) to learn high-level audio-visual features from the extracted low-level features, including audio prosodic and spectral, and Facial Animation Parameters (FAP). Pang et al.[8] employed Deep Bolzmann Machine (DBM) to learn a joint density model for emotion recognition over the space of multimodal inputs, including face, speech, and text modalities. Although having shown promising performance, most of these works still use hand-crafted features as input for DBN and DBM, thus they still suffer from the low discriminative power of low-level features.

As another representative deep learning model, Deep Convolutional Neural Network (DCNN)[5] is mainly composed of convolutional layers and fully connected layers, where convolutional layers learn a discriminative multi-level feature representation from raw input and the fully connected layers can be regarded as a non-linear classifier. Due to the large-scale available training data and the effective training strategies introduced in recent works, DCNN has exhibited significant success in various visual tasks like object detect and recognition [5, 1, 7].

Motivated by the capability of automatic feature learning and the flexible network configuration of DCNN, we propose to use DCNN to learn a joint audio-visual feature representation for emotion classification. Figure 1 illustrates the structure of our proposed multimodal DCNN. Our multimodal DCNN training consists of two steps: (1) We convert the raw 1-D audio signals into 3-D images as DCNN input. Two individual DCNN models pre-trained on large-scale im-

ICMR '16, June 06-09, 2016, New York, NY, USA
© 2016 ACM. ISBN 978-1-4503-4359-6/16/06...$15.00
DOI: http://dx.doi.org/10.1145/2911996.2912051

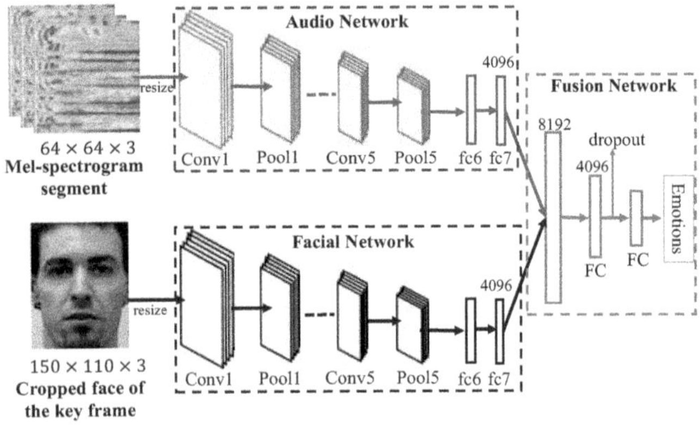

Figure 1: The structure of our multimodal deep Convolutional Neural Network.

age classification tasks are hence fine-tuned to perform audio and visual emotion recognition tasks, respectively. (2) The audio and visual features learned by these two DCNNs are integrated in a fusion network, which is trained to predict correct emotion labels. After these two stages of training, we use the output of fully connected layers in fusion network as the joint audio-visual feature, which is finally feeded into Support Vector Machine (SVM) for classification.

Affective feature learning is one of key steps in bridging the emotional gap. Previous work mainly extract hand-crafted low-level features, which are not discriminative enough to high-level emotions. Different from previous works, this work automatically learns an audio-visual feature representation from raw audio and visual cues using a multi-modal DCNN. Experimental results show that our learned features yield promising emotion recognition performance. This clearly exhibits our contributions. The success of this work also guarantees further investigation in this direction.

2. OUR METHOD

As shown in Figure 1, our multimodal DCNN is composed of two individual streams, *i.e.*, the audio network processing audio signals and the facial network processing visual data. The outputs of fully connected layers of these two networks are fused in a fusion network.

Because of the limited amount of annotated data, we leverage the pre-trained DCNN on large-scale image classification to initialize multimodal DCNN, then use the labeled emotion data for fine-tuning. In our current setting, we use the AlexNet [5] for network initialization because of its promising performance and generalization ability in various vision tasks. The AlexNet model [5] contains five convolutional (Conv.) layers, three of which are followed by max-pooling (Pool.) layers, and three fully connected (FC) layers. The first two FC layers (fc6, fc7) consist of 4096 units, respectively, and the last FC layer (fc8) has 1000 dimension corresponding to class labels. Similarly, both the audio and facial networks have five Conv. layers and two FC layers, whose initial parameters are copied from AlexNet.

In the followings, we introduce how the DCNN inputs are generated, and how this multimodal DCNN is trained.

2.1 Generation of DCNN Input

Because video samples for emotion classification may show different time of duration, we divided each of them into overlapping segments and learn audio-visual features from each segment. This also augments the DCNN training data. Specifically, we first extract the whole log Mel-spectrogram from audio signals, then divide the spectrogram into overlapping segments using a context widow with a fixed length. The central video frame in this context window is selected as the key frame of visual data. In this way, for each video segment, we can get its Mel-spectrogram and the corresponding key frame facial image. Then, we present how these audio and visual cues are processed.

1)Audio input generation: To transform the 1-D speech signals into suitable input for DCNN, which is commonly feeded with 2-D or 3-D images, we extract three channels of log Mel-spectrogram segment, *i.e.*, the *static*, *delta* and *delta*^{2}, respectively. In detail, for an utterance, we adopte 64 Mel-filter banks from 20 to 8000 Hz to obtain the whole log Mel-spectrogram using 25ms Hamming window with a 10ms overlapping. Then, a context window of 64 frames with 30 frames of overlap is applied to the whole log Mel-spectrogram to extract the *static* 2-D Mel-spectrogram segments with size: 64×64. To capture the temporal information in Mel-spectrogram, after extracting the static 2-D Mel-spectrogram segment, we compute its first-order (*delta*) and second-order (*delta*^{2}) frame-to-frame time derivatives. As a result, we can obtain three channels of Mel-spectrogram segment with size: $64 \times 64 \times 3$.

We initialize the audio network with the AlexNet [5], which has the input size $227 \times 227 \times 3$. Therefore, we resize the original spectrogram with size $64 \times 64 \times 3$ into a new size: $227 \times 227 \times 3$ with bilinear interpolation. In this way, the extracted three channels of Mel-spectrogram can be regarded as a RGB image representation illustrated in Fig. 1. In the followings, we denote the audio input as a.

2)Visual input generation: After dividing the video sample into segments, we take the central frame in each segment as the key frame for emotion recognition. Then on the key frame, we run face detection, estimate the eye distance, and finally crop a RGB face image with size $150 \times 110 \times 3$ referring to the methods in [10, 15]. Similar to the input for the audio network, the face image is resized to $227 \times 227 \times 3$. We denote the visual input as v.

2.2 Network Training

Given audio-visual data $X = \{(a_i, v_i, y_i)\}_{i=1,2,\cdots,K}$, where i is the index of the audio-visual segment, a_i and v_i represent the audio data and face data, respectively, and y_i denotes the corresponding class label. Let $\Upsilon^A(a_i; \theta^A)$ denote the 4096-D output of the second FC layer (fc7) in audio network (denoted as A) with network parameters θ^A. Similarly, $\Upsilon^V(v_i; \theta^V)$ represents the 4096-D visual feature (fc7) of the facial network (denoted as V) with network parameters θ^V. During network training, we first train the audio and facial networks respectively in the first stage, then jointly train the fusion network in the second stage.

1)Training audio and facial networks: We first train the audio and facial networks individually. This is conducted by connecting their fc7 layers with a new fully connected layer similar to the fc8 layer in AlexNet, respectively. Different from the one in AlexNet, our fc8 layer corresponds to the emotional class labels in the target dataset. For example, if there are 6 emotional labels, fc8 produces 6 outputs. Therefore, we predict the emotional labels with audio and facial networks, respectively, then compute the prediction errors and finally update the network parameters to minimize the negative log likelihood L over the training data.

On audio training data, we solve the following minimization problem to update the audio network A with back propagation:

$$\min_{W^A,\theta^A} \sum_{i=1}^{K} L(\mathrm{softmax}(W^A \cdot \Upsilon^A(a_i;\theta^A)), y_i) \quad (1)$$

where W^A represents the parameters of the fc8 layer, and the softmax log-loss is calculated by

$$L(A, y) = -\sum_{j=1}^{l} y_j \log(y_j^A) \quad (2)$$

where y_j is the j-th value of the ground truth label, y_j^A denotes the j-th output of the softmax layer for the network A, and l denotes the total number of class labels.

Similarly, on face training data a minimization problem is solved to update the facial network V. Therefore, the prediction error of V can be minimized. The stage-1 training updates the parameters in audio network and facial network, respectively to learn more discriminative audio and visual features, *i.e.*, $\Upsilon^A(a_i;\theta^A)$ and $\Upsilon^V(v_i;\theta^V)$. To fuse the audio and visual features, we proceed to introduce the training of our fusion network.

2) Training fusion network: After training the audio and facial networks, we discard their fc8 layers and connect their fc7 layers to the fusion network illustrated in Figure 1. In this way, two 4096-D features *i.e.*, $\Upsilon^A(a_i;\theta^A)$ and $\Upsilon^V(v_i;\theta^V)$ are concatenated to form a 8192-D feature as the input of the fusion network $f([\Upsilon^A(a_i;\theta^A), \Upsilon^V(v_i;\theta^V)];\theta^F)$ with network parameters θ^F. This fusion network contains two FC layers and a softmax layer, as depicted in Figure 1. Additionally, the dropout method is adopted to reduce over-fitting. Let $\Upsilon^A = \Upsilon^A(a_i;\theta^A)$ and $\Upsilon^V = \Upsilon^V(v_i;\theta^V)$, we train the fusion network by optimizing the following minimizing problem with back propagation, *i.e.*,

$$\min_{W^F,\theta^F} \sum_{i=1}^{K} L(\mathrm{softmax}(W^F \cdot f([\Upsilon^A, \Upsilon^V];\theta^F)), y_i) \quad (3)$$

Note that, we fix the parameters in A and V during the stage-2 training. During the training, the parameters of fusion network are updated to produce more accurate emotional predictions, which corresponds to a more optimal feature fusion strategy.

2.3 Emotion Classification

Once finish training the fusion network, we can obtain a 4096-D joint feature representation for each video segment. Because each audio-visual sample has a variant number of segments, for each sample, we apply average pooling on its segment features to acquire its final global feature representation. We have tested different pooling strategies including average pooling and max pooling. Experimental results show average pooling generally gets the best performance. Based on the global feature representation, emotion prediction can be easily implemented with classifiers such as the linear SVM classifier.

3. EXPERIMENTS

In this section, we will present experimental results and analysis on the RML audio-visual database [11].

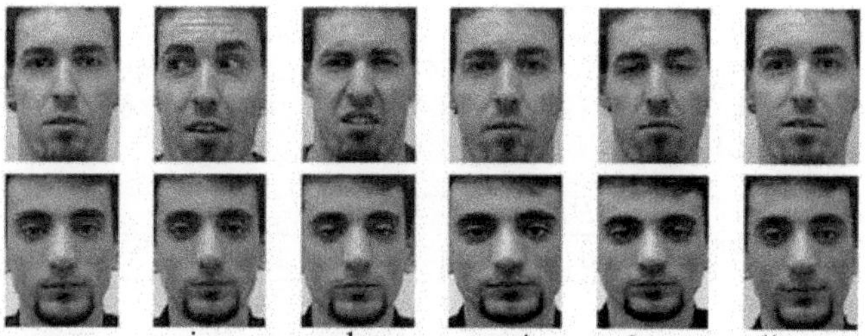

Figure 2: The cropped key frame facial images on the RML database.

3.1 Experimental Setup

To testify our multimodal DCNN and the joint audio-visual feature representation, we use the RML audio-visual database [11] for experiments. The RML database contains 720 utterances from eight subjects with six emotions: anger, disgust, fear, joy, sadness, and surprise. The audio signals are recorded at a sampling rate of 22,050 Hz with 16-bit resolution. The average duration of each audio file is around 5 seconds. Figure 2 shows some samples of cropped facial images with different emotions on this database.

Our DCNN model is trained using a mini-batch size of 30, and a stochastic gradient descent with a momentum of 0.9. The number of epochs and learning rate are set as 300 and 0.001, respectively for fine-tuning. During the fusion network training, the dropout parameter is set to 0.3. We perform experiments with MATLAB2014 and MatConvNet package [1] on a NVIDIA GTX TITAN X GPU. For SVM, we employed the LIBSVM [2] with the linear kernel. To evaluate the performance, we use the average leave-one-speaker-out(LOSO) accuracy suggested in [9], *i.e.*, use the samples of one subject for testing and the samples from others for training.

3.2 Experimental Results

In this section, we first show the performance of a baseline using linear SVM and low-level hand-crafted features. The 1582-D acoustic LLD feature extracted from the utterance [9] is used as audio feature. The typical LBP feature [10, 15] is employed as visual feature. Specifically, a 2478-D LBP feature is extracted from each key frame with similar settings in [10, 15]. Then, average-pooling is used over all key frames to produce the final visual feature.

We also test the performance of features extracted by the original AlexNet. This is conducted by feeding our audio and visual inputs into AlexNet, taking its FC7 layer outputs as audio and visual features, respectively, and finally performing classification with methods introduced in Sec. 2.3.

To show the benefits of our DCNN based feature fusion, We also implement two commonly used fusion strategies, *i.e.*, *Early Fusion* (*EF*) and *Late Fusion* (*LF*). *EF* is obtained by concatenating audio and visual features before classification. *LF* is achieved by voting multiple classification results of divided segments from an sample.

Table 1 presents the performance of baselines on RML database. The results show that fusing the two features gets better performance than using each feature individually. It is also clear that, although AlexNet is trained on an independent image dataset,

[1] available at http://www.vlfeat.org/matconvnet/
[2] available at https://www.csie.ntu.edu.tw/ cjlin/libsvm/

Table 1: Performance of Baselines. $Alex_{Audio}$ **and** $Alex_{Visual}$ **are audio and visual features extracted by AlexNet, respectively.** $EF_{LLD+LBP}$ **denotes early fusion of LLD and LBP features.**

Methods	LLD	LBP	$Alex_{Audio}$	$Alex_{Visual}$	$EF_{LLD+LBP}$
Acc. (%)	61.86	56.9	59.46	54.49	70.62

Table 2: Performance of our methods. $Anet$, $Vnet$, **and** $Fnet$ **are the features of audio network, facial network, and fusion network, respectively.** LF **and** EF **denote late fusion and early fusion, respectively.**

Methods	$Anet$	$Vnet$	$Fnet$	$LF_{Anet+Vnet}$	$EF_{Anet+Vnet}$
Acc. (%)	66.17	60.79	**74.32**	57.45	72.18

it shows comparable performance with hand-crafted features on emotion classification tasks. Therefore, it is reasonable to use AlexNet for network initialization.

To show the performance of our methods, we first test the features of the audio and facial networks in Figure 1, *i.e.*, the outputs of their FC7 layers. As shown in Table 2, the features learned by DCNNs outperform the hand-crafted features in Table 1. It also can be concluded that, our training strategy significantly improves the performance of AlexNet on emotion classification task, *i.e.*, improving its accuracies from 59.46% to 66.17% and 54.49% to 60.79%, respectively.

Table 1 also shows the performance of the joint audio-visual feature representation learned by our fusion network. It is clear that $Fnet$ significantly outperforms the features of audio and facial networks. Moreover, it also performs better than both the early fusion and late fusion methods. This clearly show that our DCNN model jointly learns a discriminative audio-visual feature representation, which performs better than previous hand-crafted features and fusion methods.

Figure 3 shows our classification confusion matrix on different emotions. It is interesting to find that "joy" and "sadness" are more difficult to be identified than "anger" and "surprise". This might be because their audio-visual cues are not distinct enough.

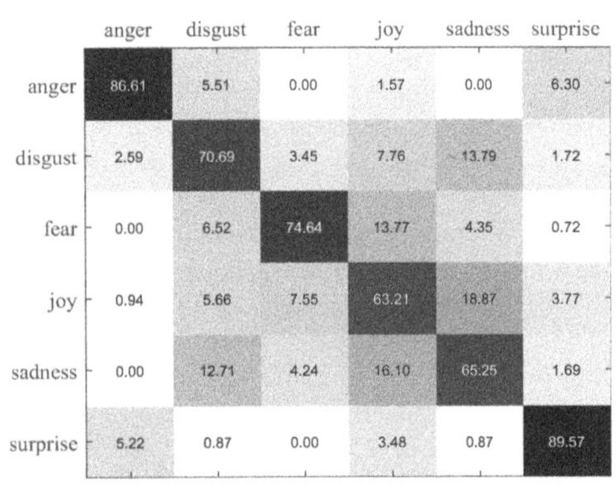

Figure 3: Classification confusion matrix of our method

4. CONCLUSIONS

This paper presents a new method for audio-visual emotion recognition with a multimodal DCNN. The outputs of audio and facial networks are connected with a fusion network. To learn a joint feature representation, this network is trained with two stages: 1) the audio and visual networks are initialized with AlexNet for fine-tunning, and 2) the fusion network is trained on the target emotion classification dataset. Experimental results on the RML database show that our DCNN model jointly learns a discriminative audio-visual feature representation, which performs better than previous hand-crafted features and fusion methods in emotion recognition tasks. In our future work, we will investigate more strategies to further improve the performance of our multimodal DCNN.

5. ACKNOWLEDGEMENTS

This work is supported by National Science Foundation of China (NSFC) under Grant No.61203257, and Zhejiang Provincial NSFC under Grant No.LY16F020011, and is also supported in part to Dr. Shiliang Zhang by NSFC under Grant No.61572050 and No.91538111.

6. REFERENCES

[1] Y. Cao, Y. Chen, and D. Khosla. Spiking deep convolutional neural networks for energy-efficient object recognition. *Int. J. Comput. Vis.*, 113(1):54–66, 2015.

[2] A. Hanjalic and L. Xu. Affective video content representation and modeling. *IEEE Trans. Multimed.*, 7(1):143–154, 2005.

[3] G. E. Hinton and R. R. Salakhutdinov. Reducing the dimensionality of data with neural networks. *Science*, 313(5786):504–507, 2006.

[4] Y. Kim, H. Lee, and E. M. Provost. Deep learning for robust feature generation in audiovisual emotion recognition. In *ICASSP*, 2013.

[5] A. Krizhevsky, I. Sutskever, and G. E. Hinton. Imagenet classification with deep convolutional neural networks. In *NIPS*, 2012.

[6] M. Mansoorizadeh and N. M. Charkari. Multimodal information fusion application to human emotion recognition from face and speech. *Multimed. Tool. Appl.*, 49(2):277–297, 2010.

[7] W. Ouyang, X. Wang, X. Zeng, S. Qiu, P. Luo, Y. Tian, H. Li, S. Yang, Z. Wang, C.-C. Loy, et al. Deepid-net: Deformable deep convolutional neural networks for object detection. In *CVPR*, 2015.

[8] L. Pang and C.-W. Ngo. Multimodal learning with deep boltzmann machine for emotion prediction in user generated videos. In *ICMR*, 2015.

[9] B. Schuller, S. Steidl, A. Batliner, F. Burkhardt, L. Devillers, C. A. Müller, and S. S. Narayanan. The interspeech 2010 paralinguistic challenge. In *INTERSPEECH*, 2010.

[10] C. Shan, S. Gong, and P. W. McOwan. Facial expression recognition based on local binary patterns: A comprehensive study. *Image Vis. Comput.*, 27(6):803–816, 2009.

[11] Y. Wang and L. Guan. Recognizing human emotional state from audiovisual signals. *IEEE Trans. Multimed.*, 10(5):936–946, 2008.

[12] Z. Zeng, M. Pantic, G. Roisman, T. S. Huang, et al. A survey of affect recognition methods: Audio, visual, and spontaneous expressions. *IEEE Trans. Pattern Anal. Mach. Intell.*, 31(1):39–58, 2009.

[13] S. Zhang, Q. Huang, S. Jiang, W. Gao, and Q. Tian. Affective visualization and retrieval for music video. *IEEE Trans. Multimed.*, 12(6):510–522, 2010.

[14] S. Zhang, Q. Huang, Q. Tian, S. Jiang, and W. Gao. i. mtv: an integrated system for mtv affective analysis. In *ACM MM*, 2008.

[15] X. Zhao and S. Zhang. Facial expression recognition using local binary patterns and discriminant kernel locally linear embedding. *EURASIP J. Adv. Signal Process.*, 2012(1):1–9, 2012.

Large-Scale E-Commerce Image Retrieval with Top-Weighted Convolutional Neural Networks

Shichao Zhao[1], Youjiang Xu[1], Yahong Han[1,2]
[1]School of Computer Science and Technology, Tianjin University, Tianjin, China
[2]Tianjin Key Lab. of Cognitive Computing & Application, Tianjin University, Tianjin, China
{zhaoshichao, yjxu, yahong}@tju.edu.cn

ABSTRACT

Several recent researches have shown that image features produced by Convolutional Neural Networks (CNNs) provide the state-of-the-art performance for image classification and retrieval. Moreover, some researchers have found that the features extracted from the deep convolutional layers of CNNs perform better than that from the fully-connected layers. Features extracted from the convolutional layers have a natural interpretation: descriptors of local image regions correspond well to the receptive fields of the particular features. In order to obtain both representative and discriminative descriptors for large-scale e-commerce image retrieval, we come up with a new feature extraction framework. At first, we propose the Top-Weight method to detect the interesting area of e-commerce images automatically. With the estimated weight, we then aggregate local deep features and produce high-quality global representation for e-commerce image retrieval. We have conducted experiments on an e-commerce dataset ALISC [1] released by Alibaba Group. Experimental results show that our method outperforms other deep learning based methods.

Keywords

Image Features, CNNs, Top-Weight

1. INTRODUCTION

With the rapid progress of digital techniques, the amount of digital images is increasing explosively. This trend makes image retrieval an important and challenging research topic nowadays. Especially, the task of e-commerce image retrieval has bright prospect and great commercial value.

For much of the past decade, bag-of-features methods were considered to be the state-of-the-art [9], especially when built on top of locally invariant features like SIFT [8]. In recent years, deep convolutional neural networks have attracted much attention in visual recognition, largely due to their good performance. It has been discovered that the activations of CNNs pretrained on a large dataset, such as ImageNet [4], can be employed as a generalized image representation. And this representation could be adapted to many visual problems which delivers impressive performance. At first, researchers tried to utilize the fully-connected layers of deep networks as global image representation [3]. With the evolution of deep representations, research attention has shifted from the fully-connected layers to the deep convolutional layers of CNNs. For example, local convolutional descriptors are extracted from deep convolutional layers. How to aggregate a set of local descriptors into a global one has been studied extensively [5]. The best known aggregation approaches which have been used on SIFT are VLAD [7] and Fisher Vectors [10]. However, as the differences between deep convolutional features and hand-crafted features like dense SIFT, it was shown that the preliminary embedding step is not necessary for deep convolutional features because of their higher discriminative ability and different distribution property. So for deep convolutional features, usually only aggregation step is performed. What is more, SPoC [2] proposed a method named center prior based on priori-knowledge which achieves good performance on benchmark datasets. However, this descriptor aggregation approach has a strong hypothesis that the interesting object lies in the center of image. In many applications, such a hypothesis usually turns out to be a constraint that burdens the performance. Especially for the e-commerce images, which are different with the scene images, the target objects of the e-commerce images are very important for retrieval. Thus, the crux of the problem is to find the target object accurately.

Motivated by the above discussions, we put forward a more effective feature representation for e-commerce image retrieval. In this framework, we propose a new concept named Top-Weight, which pools the top convolutional layer by channel using average pooling. Figure 1 illustrated the flowchart of extracting the Top-Weight. And we can see that the Top-Weight exhibits high correlation with the target areas. Thus, we can get more discriminative image features with Top-Weight. We first calculate the Top-Weight from the top convolutional layer. Then we multiply the calculated Top-Weight by the features extracted from various convolutional layers varying from the shallow layer to the deep layer of the CNNs. Our goal is get both low-level and high-level information. Finally, we aggregate a set of local convolutional descriptors into a final feature representation for image retrieval. Based on the proposed method, we report the experimental results on an e-commerce dataset sampled from ALISC and the results demonstrate the effectiveness of our method compared with other CNNs method.

ICMR'16, June 06-09, 2016, New York, NY, USA

DOI: http://dx.doi.org/10.1145/2911996.2912052

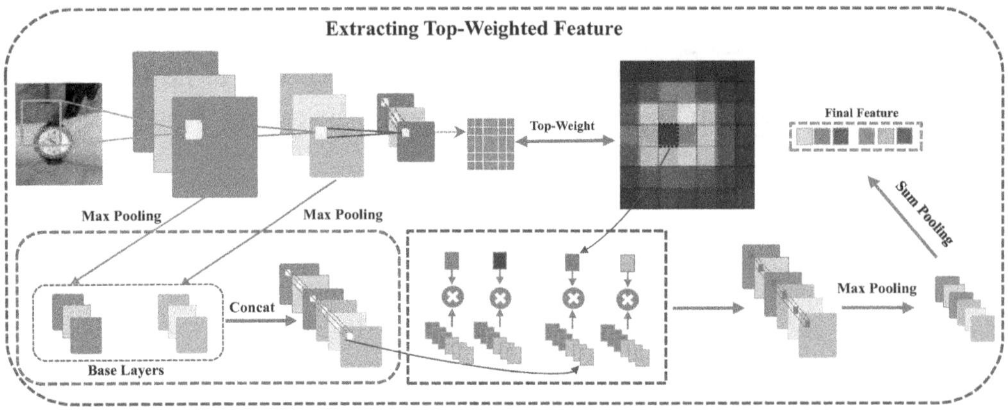

Figure 1: The flowchart of the proposed framework.

2. THE PROPOSED FRAMEWORK

Figure 1 depicts our framework based on Top-Weight approach for image representation learning. In the first stage, we extract Top-Weight from the top convolutional layer by averaging the channels. Then we pool the feature maps of different convolutional layers and concatenate them. Thus, the size of pooled feature maps are the same to the top convolutional layer. Next, we multiply Top-Weight by pooled feature maps in order to obtain the weighted feature maps. And the final representation is obtained by pooling aggregation. Lastly, we use Euclidean distance to measure the similarity of different images.

2.1 Top-Weight

The Convolutional Neural Networks are deep networks stacked by several convolutional and full-connected layers. The convolutional layers use sliding filters to generate feature maps. The well-known feature maps involve not only the strength of the responses, but also their spatial positions. From SPP-net [6], we know that a filter can be activated by some semantic content. Different filters will be activated by different shapes such as circle shape or other shapes. In order to get all kinds of interesting shapes, we average the feature maps produced by different filters. Additionally, from deeper layer features we can get an effective representation containing more semantic information than low layer features. Motivated by above discussions, we propose the Top-Weight approach.

The construction of Top-Weight starts with the average pooling on the channels of top convolution layer's feature maps. The Top-Weight can be computed as:

$$W = \frac{1}{N}\sum_{c=1}^{N} T(c), \tag{1}$$

where N is the number of channels on this convolution layer and $T(c)$ is the c-th channel feature map of the top convolution layer.

2.2 Different Weight-Stacking Methods

Center prior [2]. For most image retrieval datasets, objects of interest tend to be located close to the geometrical center of an image. The convolutional layers can be modified to incorporate such centering prior via a simple weighting heuristic. This heuristic assigns larger weights to the features from the center of the feature map stack, the formula is as follows:

$$L1_{(x,y)} = \alpha_{(x,y)} L_{(x,y)}, \tag{2}$$

$L_{(x,y)}$ denotes the feature corresponding to the spatial position (x, y) in the map stack produced by the convolutional layer. Coefficients $\alpha_{(x,y)}$ depend only on the spatial coordinates x and y. In particular, center prior uses the Gaussian weighting scheme:

$$\alpha_{(x,y)} = exp\{-\frac{(y-\frac{H}{2})^2 + (x-\frac{W}{2})^2}{2\sigma^2}\}, \tag{3}$$

where σ is set to be one third of the minimum value between W and H as default. H and W are the height and width of the convolutional feature maps respectively.

Top-Weight. Different from center prior, Top-Weight does not rely on some prior knowledge and can break the limitation that the object lies in the center of the image. It can detect interesting points from the image automatically. As we discussed in section 2.1, the Top-weight is extracted from top convolutional layer and the values on the spatial coordinates (x, y) can be used to measure the importance of corresponding neighborhood. We calculate the weighted feature maps using Top-Weight as follows:

$$L2_{(x,y)} = \alpha_{(x,y)} L_{(x,y)}, \tag{4}$$

$L_{(x,y)}$ and $\alpha_{(x,y)}$ are the same as used in formula 2.

$$\alpha_{(x,y)} = \frac{1}{N}\sum_{c=1}^{N} T_{(x,y)}(c), \tag{5}$$

$T_{(x,y)}$ means the local feature on the spatial position (x, y) of top convolutional layer. N is the number of channels on the top convolutional layer.

2.3 Pooling Strategy

After getting the weighted feature maps, we pool the maps on the fixed size by max pooling. There are two reasons for max pooling: on one hand, max pooling can enhance translation invariant; on the other hand, max pooling can keep the key information and remove noise. We fix the size of the pooled maps S.

In order to get the final image representation, we aggregate the pooled feature maps by sum pooling. And the size of pooling region is $S \times S$.

3. EXPERIMENTS

3.1 Datasets

We sample an e-commerce dataset from ALISC [1], which comprises 248,512 images. And ALISC is an open challenge for everyone. This dataset is split into two parts: query set and evaluation set. The query set contains 1,417 images which are real-world images taken by typical phone cameras. The evaluation dataset contains 154,523 noisy images and 92,572 images which are the target images of query images. The task of ALISC is to find the same or similar product from a large product image dataset for a set of query images and return the top 20 relevant results from evaluation set, which will be used for performance evaluation. The performance is measured using mean average precision (mAP@20) over all queries. With the influence of distortion and noise from phone cameras image, the query images are quite different from evaluation images. It is a very difficult task that retrieval on the dataset.

Figure 2: Sample images from datasets.

3.2 Experimental Setup

We extract CNN features using GoogLeNet [11] trained on ImageNet. We utilize the widely-used Caffe package for CNNs. For this architecture, the Top-Weight is extract on the last convolutional layer named inception (5b) by averaging channels. All images are resized to size 224×224 in advance to pass through the network. As a result, the size of the top convolutional maps is $W \times H = 7 \times 7$. We pool the low layer feature maps to the same size as the top convolutional layer (7×7). After stacking weight on the feature maps, we pool the feature maps to the size of 3×3 by max pooling. The region of max pooling is 3×3 and the stride is set to 2. Finally, we get final feature by sum pooling.

3.3 Experimental Results

The performance comparison of different layers of CNNs is shown in Table 1. We can see that the fully-connected layers (loss1, loss2, loss3) perform not so well compared with convolutional layers (inception). The reason is that the fully-connected layers are feature vectors which lack local and regional information.

In Table 2, we compare the performance of different pooling methods on the convolutional layers of CNNs. From the results, we can conclude that sum pooling performs significantly better than max pooling for aggregating the convolutional feature.

Table 1: Performance of full-connecting Layer and convolutional layer which is pooled a vector.

Layer	mAP@20
loss1/classifier	0.152
loss2/classifier	0.180
loss3/classifier	0.206
inception(3a)	0.160
inception(3b)	0.208
inception(4a)	0.258
inception(4e)	0.298
inception(5b)	0.274

Table 2: Comparison of different pooling.

Base Layer	Max-pooling	Sum-pooling
inception(3a)	0.124	0.160
inception(3b)	0.158	0.208
inception(4a)	0.191	0.258
inception(4e)	0.225	0.298
inception(5b)	0.259	0.274

We compare three weighting strategies for aggregating the image descriptors: the first one is the original feature maps for aggregating without any weight; the second one is the center prior strategy which utilizes the Gaussian weighting scheme in order to enhance the center area of image; the last one is the proposed Top-Weight on the convolutional maps to get the final feature. All results are presented in Table 3.

Table 3: Comparison of the different weight stacking on convolutional layer.

Base Layer	original	center-prior	Top-weight
inception(3a)	0.160	0.204	0.223
inception(3b)	0.208	0.263	0.281
inception(4a)	0.258	0.307	0.331
inception(4e)	0.298	0.327	0.337
3a+3b+4a+4e	0.310	0.375	0.384

From Table 3, we can see that the performance of center-prior is higher than the original. The result demonstrates that most objects in the images agree with the center prior assumption in the dataset. However, Top-Weight can further improve the performance compared with center prior. The result proved that Top-Weight is more effective than the others, mainly because Top-Weight adapts the object weights not only in the center but also other locations automatically and adaptively.

Table 4 shows the performance that using inception (3a) as a base layer and different layers as weighted layers. We can discover that using deeper layers as weighted layer can

Figure 3: Retrieval examples on the E-Commerce dataset. In each row, leftmost image is query image and the rest are top10 relevant results. Red color marks false positives and green color marks true positives.

Table 4: With inception(3a) as a base layer, performance of different layer as weight layer.

Weight-Layer	mAP@20
inception(3b)	0.159
inception(4a)	0.163
inception(4e)	0.182
inception(5b)	0.223

achieve better results than the lower layers. The reason is that deeper layers can get more accurate information and locate points of interest effectively. So we choose the top layer as the weighted layer and produce Top-Weight approach in our framework.

In Figure 3, we can see that the target images are similar to the query image. However, some similar images are false positives because the task of retrieval in the e-commence data is to get the same style images. This is a more difficult and different task compared with the traditional image retrieval tasks.

Top-Weight visualization. The extracted Top-Weight of sample images in the dataset are shown in Figure 4. From these examples, we see that the Top-Weight exhibits high correlation with the target areas.

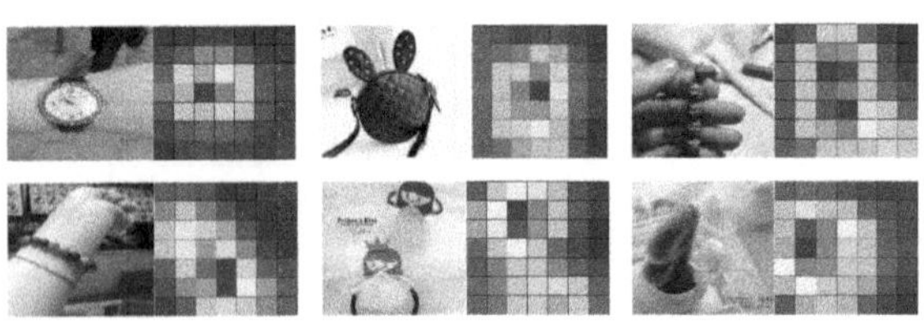

Figure 4: Top-Weight visualization.

4. CONCLUSIONS

In this paper, we propose an effective image presentation for image retrieval by using Top-Weight, which can detect the interesting areas and evaluate the weight of areas automatically. The advantages of this strategy is that Top-Weight is produced from deep feature maps automatically. And it is a learned weight that does not rely on any prior knowledge. The Top-Weight strategy is used to aggregate local convolutional features maps into final image feature representations. Our feature representation achieves superior performance compared with other methods on the task of e-commerce image retrieval.

5. ACKNOWLEDGMENTS

This work is supported by the NSFC (under Grant U1509206, 61472276). The datasets are provided by Alibaba Group.

6. REFERENCES

[1] Alisc. https://tianchi.aliyun.com/competition/introduction.htm?spm=5176.100066.333.11.da8UHF&raceId=231510&_lang=en_US, 2015.

[2] A. Babenko and V. Lempitsky. Aggregating local deep features for image retrieval. In *CVPR*, pages 1269–1277, 2015.

[3] A. Babenko, A. Slesarev, A. Chigorin, and V. Lempitsky. Neural codes for image retrieval. In *ECCV*, pages 584–599. Springer, 2014.

[4] J. Deng, W. Dong, R. Socher, L.-J. Li, K. Li, and L. Fei-Fei. Imagenet: A large-scale hierarchical image database. In *CVPR*, pages 248–255, 2009.

[5] Y. Han, Y. Yang, F. Wu, and R. Hong. Compact and discriminative descriptor inference using multi-cues. *Image Processing, IEEE Transactions on*, 24(12):5114–5126, 2015.

[6] K. He, X. Zhang, S. Ren, and J. Sun. Spatial pyramid pooling in deep convolutional networks for visual recognition. *PAMI*, 37(9):1904–1916, 2015.

[7] H. Jégou, M. Douze, C. Schmid, and P. Pérez. Aggregating local descriptors into a compact image representation. In *CVPR*, pages 3304–3311, 2010.

[8] D. G. Lowe. Distinctive image features from scale-invariant keypoints. *IJCV*, 60(2):91–110, 2004.

[9] F. Perronnin and C. Dance. Fisher kernels on visual vocabularies for image categorization. In *CVPR*, pages 1–8, 2007.

[10] F. Perronnin, Y. Liu, J. Sánchez, and H. Poirier. Large-scale image retrieval with compressed fisher vectors. In *CVPR*, pages 3384–3391, 2010.

[11] C. Szegedy, W. Liu, Y. Jia, P. Sermanet, S. Reed, D. Anguelov, D. Erhan, V. Vanhoucke, and A. Rabinovich. Going deeper with convolutions. In *CVPR*, pages 1–9, 2015.

Web Video Popularity Prediction using Sentiment and Content Visual Features

Giulia Fontanini*, Marco Bertini†, Alberto Del Bimbo
MICC, Università degli Studi di Firenze
Viale Morgagni 65 - 50134 Firenze, Italy
{*name.surname*}@unifi.it

ABSTRACT

Hundreds of hours of videos are uploaded every minute on YouTube and other video sharing sites: some will be viewed by millions of people and other will go unnoticed by all but the uploader. In this paper we propose to use visual sentiment and content features to predict the popularity of web videos. The proposed approach outperforms current state-of-the-art methods on two publicly available datasets.

Keywords

Video popularity; social networks; visual sentiment; affective computing

1. INTRODUCTION

Video accounts for the largest percentage of internet traffic and this figure is going to increase in the next few years, from 64% in 2014 up to 80% in 2019 [1]. Among US digital video viewers the two most popular sites are YouTube and Facebook [2]; YouTube reports to have 1 billion users and every minute hundreds of hours of videos are uploaded. However not all these videos receive the same attention from the viewers: some will be viewed billion of times, getting tens of millions of views in the very first days[1], while the vast majority will go unnoticed by all but the uploader.

In this context the ability to predict video popularity, i.e. the number of views of a video, is important to guide the design of technical services for video streaming and distribution, and to support economical decision-making processes. Advertisers, online social networks, content providers and content delivery networks are interested in predicting how many views an individual video may obtain, since this impacts on their business. For advertising, the popularity count is associated to the effectiveness of an advertising campaign; for social networks it may impact the algorithm that creates a personalized timeline of the users, as for Facebook; for content providers it is associated with ad revenues, and for content distribution networks, the prediction of access patterns improves the consumption of resources needed to distribute video content [10, 20]. Studying video content popularity can be also useful to help content producers to design new popular content. For these reasons there have been several studies on popularity prediction, typically considering earlier views of a video as predictor of its future views [3, 6, 11, 12, 16, 19], or analyzing characteristics of social networks that lead to video propagation and discovery [15, 18]. However, all these works do not consider the visual content of videos.

In this paper we propose to take into account both content and visual sentiment of videos to predict their popularity; we also propose to improve models based on the number of past views by taking into account different types of view patterns. The proposed approach has been tested on two standard datasets and improves over previous state-of-the-art methods in predicting the popularity of a video, based on the early days view patterns.

*giulia.fonta@gmail.com
†Corresponding author

[1]`http://youtube-trends.blogspot.it/2015/10/adeles-new-single-played-over-1m.html`

ICMR'16, June 06-09, 2016, New York, NY, USA
 ISBN 978-1-4503-4359-6/16/06...$15.00
DOI: http://dx.doi.org/10.1145/2911996.2912053

Figure 1: Frames of popular videos, from left to right: movie trailer, children performance in a talent show, cartoon.

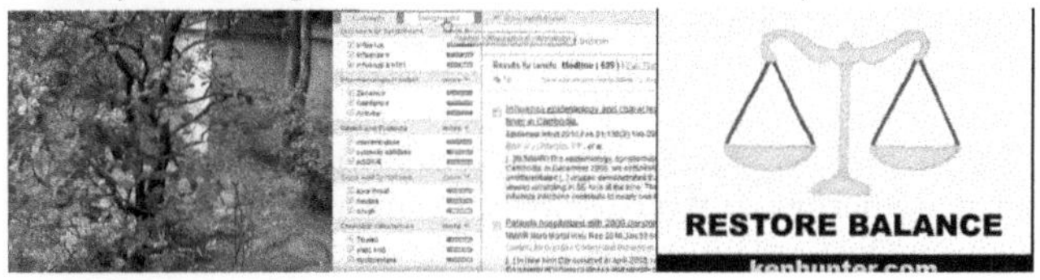

Figure 2: Frames of unpopular videos, from left to right: shooting of nature, presentation of a search engine, political propaganda.

2. PREVIOUS WORK

Crane and Sornette [9, 17] have analyzed the patterns of popularity evolution of YouTube videos, identifying four main classes: the majority of videos, that have no peak in popularity, belong to a "memoryless" class, while those that experience a peak of popularity are classified in "junk" (i.e. those that have a burst but do not spread through the social network), "viral" (i.e. slow increase of popularity, a burst due to word-of-mouth and then slow decrease) and "quality" (i.e. those characterized by a very sudden peak, due to external events such as being featured in the first page of YouTube, followed by slow decay as the video is shared by users).

Szabo and Huberman [19] have proposed three models to predict popularity based on the number of previous views of YouTube videos, observing that log-transformed long term popularity is strongly correlated to early popularity. The best performing model simply states that future popularity, in terms of video views, at target time t_t is related to the number of views at a reference time t_r (with $t_r < t_t$) by a constant factor α that depends only on target and reference dates, and can be fitted by linear regression.

Figuereido *et al.* [12] have analyzed how the popularity of individual videos evolves since the video's upload time, characterizing the types of the referrers that most often attracted users to each video (e.g. searching or external linking). Analysis has been performed on three datasets of YouTube videos, that have been made publicly available. In [11] Figuereido has proposed the use of K-spectral clustering applied to the time series of video views to predict the popularity patterns of YouTube videos, according to the four classes of [9,17].

Pinto *et al.* [16] have proposed two models for video popularity prediction: a Multivariate Linear (ML) model that extends the Szabo-Huberman (S-H) model sampling the number of views at regular intervals up to t_r; the ML model is then expanded considering video similarity evaluated using RBFs computed on the same feature vectors of ML (MRBF model). Experiments performed on the [12] datasets show that MRBF outperforms both S-H and ML.

Borghol *et al.* [3] have analyzed the impact of content-agnostic characteristics, finding that for "young" videos user characteristics and keywords become relatively important w.r.t. previous views pattern.

Li *et al.* [15] have addressed the problem of popularity prediction in social networks, analyzing the propagation of videos shared by users. Brodersen *et al.* [5] have shown that social sharing broadens the geographic reach of YouTube videos. Roy *et al.* [18] have proposed a method that uses knowledge from social streams to better predict videos with sudden bursts of popularity.

All these methods do not consider visual data of videos. Conversely, Khosla *et al.* [14] have shown that visual content is a useful feature to better predict the popularity of social image. Gelli *et al.* [13] have shown that adding visual sentiment analysis further improves popularity prediction of social images.

3. THE PROPOSED METHOD

In the proposed method specific prediction models for different popularity trend models are learned, differently from previous approaches [16, 19] that use only one model. Another novelty is the inclusion of visual content in the popularity prediction model. The goal is to forecast the number of views at target time t_t using the information available at reference time t_r, that may be the first day of the video upload, or one of the following days. In particular the goal of the method is to predict the early pattern of popularity, i.e. during the first days of video upload, in which the information related to the number of past views is still very limited or not available.

3.1 Popularity trends model

In the first step of the method is learned a classifier for the 4 different classes of video popularity trends $P_i \in \{P_1, \ldots, P_4\}$ identified in [9,17], using a variation of the method proposed in [11]. Firstly, a feature vector s_v that contains the number of views over time is used to cluster the videos of the training set, using the K-Spectral Clustering algorithm [21]. For each reference day t_r a model for the prediction of the popularity trend, based on Extremely Randomized Trees is learned, using video metadata (e.g. video category, upload date, etc.) and view features (e.g. # of views and # of comments, etc.); differently from [11] no referrer features are used since it is assumed that at the moment of video uploading these are not yet available.

3.2 The popularity prediction model

For each of the reference day t_r and each class of popularity trends $P_i \in \{P_1, \ldots, P_4\}$, a popularity prediction model is learned, combining both video content and early view information.

Visual content representation. Videos are subsampled extracting a frame every two seconds. Each frame is processed to obtain both content and sentiment features using CNNs. Regarding the former we have used the VGG-M-128 network [7], pre-trained on ImageNet dataset, using the 128-D features of the FC7 layer. For the latter descriptor we have used the DeepSentiBank network [8], using the 2089-D vector of the probabilities of visual sentiments expressed as couples of adjective-noun pairs, that are part of the Visual-Sentiment Ontology (VSO) developed in [4]; PCA is applied to this vector to reduce it to 131-D. Finally, the two feature vectors are combined together to represent the frame.

To represent the whole video, the frame feature vector are combined together using Fisher Vector encoding, and performing then a step of dimensionality reduction with PCA. This allows to evaluate visual similarity of videos of different duration and with different order of similar scenes.

Number of previous visualizations. Similarly to [16] we represent the number of previous views of a video at time t_r as a vector of the number of views for each day up to t_r; let $x_i(v)$ be the number of views of video v at day i, the feature vector is $X_{t_r} = (x_1(v), x_2(v), \ldots, x_{t_r}(v))$.

The model. We extend the MRBF model by learning for a specific popularity trend P_i, determined at the previous step of Sect. 3.1, the following model for popularity prediction:

$$\hat{N}_{P_i}(v, t_r, t_t) = \Theta_{(t_r,t_t)} \cdot X_{t_r}(v) + \sum_{v_c \in C} \omega_{v_c} \cdot RBF_{v_c}(v)$$

where $RBF_{v_c}(v)$ is a Gaussian radial basis function that captures the similarity of video v from some training video v_c of the video collection C: $RBF_{v_c} = e^{\left(-\frac{\|\hat{X}(v)-\hat{X}(v_c)\|^2}{2\cdot\sigma^2}\right)}$. $\Theta_{(t_r,t_t)}$ and ω_{v_c} are the parameters to be learned. The first part of the model extends the Szabo-Huberman (S-H) model, where the popularity of a video v at time t_t based on the number of views at time t_r (i.e. $N(v, t_r)$) is $\hat{N}(v, t_r, t_t) = \alpha_{t_r,t_t} \cdot N(v, t_r)$, by evaluating the differences of number of views over different days up to t_r. The second part exploits the similarity of the video to be analyzed based on a number of "training videos". In our model $\hat{X}$ is Fisher Vector representing visual content, as described above, and v_c videos are selected through k-means clustering, to select visually representative videos from the collection C. In [16] instead $\hat{X} = X_{t_r}$, i.e. the number of previous views, without considering visual content, and v_c videos are randomly selected. The model can be rewritten as:

$$\hat{N}_{P_i}(v, t_r, t_t) = \Theta^*_{(t_r,t_t)} \cdot X^*_{t_r}(v)$$

where Θ^* is the concatenation of Θ with ω_i and X^* is the concatenation of X_{t_r} with the RBF features. The model can be trained with linear or ridge regression. In the following we will refer to this model as PMRBFV, where P is related to the first step of popularity trend prediction and V is related to the use of visual features.

4. EXPERIMENTAL RESULTS

Dataset. For the evaluation, we have used the publicly available Top and Random datasets [12], that contain videos from all world-wide top lists provided by YouTube and random sample of YouTube videos, respectively. For each dataset, we removed videos no longer available in the platform, as well as videos with missing or inconsistent statistical information. We also discarded videos that were in the system for less than 30 days, since we have followed the experimental setup of [16,19], that requires to evaluate popularity prediction on the 30th day. After this skimming, our Top and Random datasets consist of 4,840 and 13,144 videos, respectively.

Experimental setup. The results were obtained using 4-fold cross validation: each dataset was randomly partitioned into 4 complementary and equal-sized subsets. The analysis was then performed using 3 folds as training set and the other one as test set. To reduce variability, the process was repeated 4 times, using a different fold as test set in each round and averaging the results over the rounds.

We used grid search to optimize the four main parameters that are defined for each model:

- the number of Gaussians $\in [16, 32, 64]$, used in the Fisher Vector encoding;
- the number of centroids $\in [10, 50, 100, 200, 500]$, used in the Fisher Vector clustering, i.e. the number of v_c videos used in the RBF features computation;
- the σ values $\in [1, 10, 50, 100, 1000]$, used in RBF features computation;
- the type of regression $\in [linear, ridge]$, used when fitting the models.

Popularity trends prediction. In this experiment we evaluate the performance of the classifier used to predict the pattern of popularity trend, used in the first step of the proposed method.

Table 1 shows average F_1 score performances, for different reference days and for each dataset, resulting in 0.70 and 0.55 F_1 scores, at 7th day, for Top and Random dataset, respectively. It is possible to notice that performances on Random dataset are slightly lower, probably due to the fact that Random videos have an higher variability of patterns, compared to Top videos one, resulting in a more difficult classification.

	Day						
Dataset	**1**	**2**	**3**	**4**	**5**	**6**	**7**
Top	0.57	0.60	0.63	0.66	0.69	0.70	0.70
Random	0.38	0.47	0.50	0.51	0.53	0.54	0.55

Table 1: F_1 score performances, in average on the four patterns, of popularity trends prediction task.

Video popularity and comparison. The proposed method has been compared to the method of Szabo and Huberman (S-H) [19], and the ML and MRBF methods of Pinto *et al.* [16]. Our method has three principal variants, based on the type of visual feature that is used for Fisher Vector encoding: Content and Sentiment models take into account just the corresponding visual content feature type, while Mixed model uses as video content feature the concatenation of the both. Performance is evaluated using mean Relative Squared Error (mRSE), as in [16,19], computed as the arithmetic mean of RSE values for all videos of a collection, where:

$$RSE = \left(\frac{\hat{N}(v, t_r, t_t)}{N(v, t_t)} - 1 \right)^2$$

with $N(v, t_t)$ is the total number of views video v receives up to day t_t ($N(v, 0) = 0$), and $\hat{N}(v, t_r, t_t)$ is the total number of views predicted for v at target date t_t based on data from the first t_r days. Following the experimental setup of [16,19] $t_t = 30$, while $t_r \in \{1, \ldots, 7\}$.

Table 2 shows performances, in terms of mRSE, for the MRBF model [16] and our PMRBFV visual models, for Top and Random dataset respectively. The proposed visual models always outperform the MRBF baseline model: in particular, for Top dataset, visual sentiment features lead to significant decreases in error, w.r.t. the baseline MRBF model, reaching up to **4.33%** reduction on average on the first 7 days, while, for Random dataset, Mixed model decreases in error on average of **7.79%**.

Day	MRBF	Content	Sentiment	Mixed
1	0.5071	0.3980	**0.3965**	0.3998
2	0.3831	0.3139	**0.3133**	**0.3133**
3	0.2985	0.2587	**0.2570**	0.2604
4	0.2411	0.2153	0.2143	**0.2126**
5	0.2052	0.1825	**0.1821**	**0.1821**
6	0.1810	**0.1620**	0.1641	0.1635
7	0.1599	0.1453	0.1454	**0.1452**
Mean	*0.2823*	*0.2394*	***0.2390***	*0.2396*

Day	MRBF	Content	Sentiment	Mixed
1	0.4329	0.2854	0.2846	**0.2845**
2	0.3606	0.2454	**0.2439**	0.2442
3	0.2963	0.2157	0.2161	**0.2151**
4	0.2461	0.1808	**0.1796**	0.1808
5	0.2093	0.1570	0.1571	**0.1564**
6	0.1847	0.1405	0.1407	**0.1400**
7	0.1614	0.1256	0.1250	**0.1249**
Mean	*0.2702*	*0.1929*	*0.1924*	***0.1923***

Table 2: Mean Relative Squared Error performances of visual predictive models with respect to the baseline MRBF model [16], for the first 7 days: *top)* Top dataset, *bottom)* Random dataset. The lower the figure, the better the performance.

Full comparisons to all the other models are reported in Figure 3 and 4, for Top and Random datasets respectively. For further information, we have performed additional comparisons with two new models, namely PML and PMRBF, which refer to the implementation of the ML and the MRBF models trained for each of the trends types, predicted using the first step of our method. In all the cases the proposed method outperforms the other state-of-the-art ML and MRBF methods.

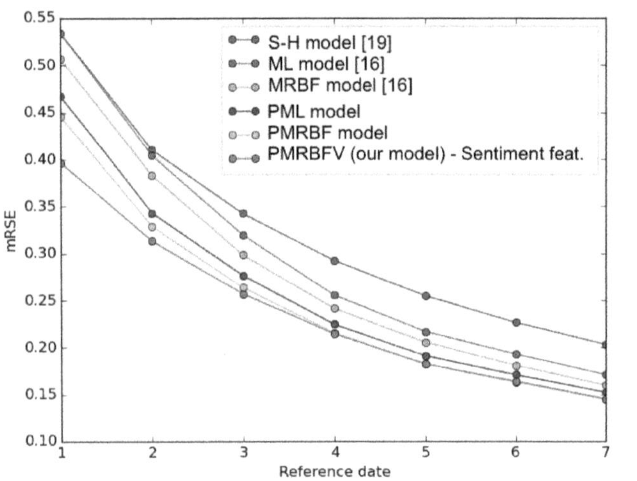

Figure 3: Comparison of all methods performances, in terms of mRSE, for Top dataset.

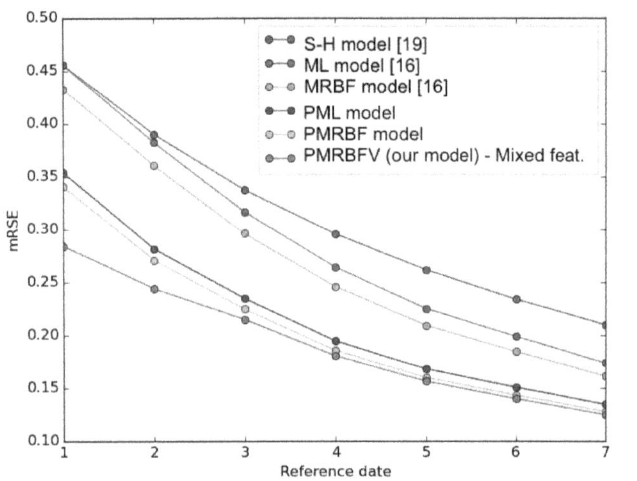

Figure 4: Comparison of all methods performances, in terms of mRSE, for Random dataset.

As the reference date t_r increases, both extensions of ML and MRBF models are improved by the additional steps of popularity trend prediction, as shown by the values obtained by PML and PMRBF. While the value of t_r increases the PMRBF tend to align with the visual PMRBFV models, for both datasets, showing the importance of the first step of our method. Despite this, the PMRBFV visual models remain the best in terms of performance, especially regarding the first few days after the uploading, in which visual features, as expected, are more important than the number of views, that can not provide yet much information.

Acknowledgments. This work is partially supported by the "Social Museum and Smart Tourism" MIUR project (CTN01_00034_231545).

5. REFERENCES

[1] Cisco visual networking index: Forecast and methodology, 2014–2019. Technical report, Cisco, 2015.

[2] Cross-platform video trends roundup. Technical report, eMarketer, 2015.

[3] Y. Borghol, S. Ardon, N. Carlsson, D. Eager, and A. Mahanti. The untold story of the clones: Content-agnostic factors that impact YouTube video popularity. In *Proc. of KDD*, 2012.

[4] D. Borth, R. Ji, T. Chen, T. Breuel, and S.-F. Chang. Large-scale visual sentiment ontology and detectors using adjective noun pairs. In *Proc. of ACM MM*, 2013.

[5] A. Brodersen, S. Scellato, and M. Wattenhofer. YouTube around the world: geographic popularity of videos. In *Proc. of WWW*, 2012.

[6] M. Cha, H. Kwak, P. Rodriguez, Y.-Y. Ahn, and S. Moon. Analyzing the video popularity characteristics of large-scale user generated content systems. *IEEE/ACM Transactions on Networking*, 17(5):1357–1370, 2009.

[7] K. Chatfield, K. Simonyan, A. Vedaldi, and A. Zisserman. Return of the devil in the details: Delving deep into convolutional nets. In *Proc. of BMVC*, 2014.

[8] T. Chen, D. Borth, T. Darrell, and S.-F. Chang. DeepSentiBank: Visual sentiment concept classification with deep convolutional neural networks. *arXiv preprint arXiv:1410.8586*, 2014.

[9] R. Crane and D. Sornette. Viral, quality, and junk videos on YouTube: Separating content from noise in an information-rich environment. In *Proc. of AAAI Spring Symposium: Social Information Processing*, 2008.

[10] J. Famaey, T. Wauters, and F. De Turck. On the merits of popularity prediction in multimedia content caching. In *Proc. of IEEE IM*, 2011.

[11] F. Figueiredo. On the prediction of popularity of trends and hits for user generated videos. In *Proc. of ACM WSDM*, 2013.

[12] F. Figueiredo, F. Benevenuto, and J. M. Almeida. The Tube over time: Characterizing popularity growth of YouTube videos. In *Proc. of ACM WSDM*, 2011.

[13] F. Gelli, T. Uricchio, M. Bertini, A. Del Bimbo, and S. F. Chang. Image popularity prediction in social media using sentiment and context features. In *Proc. of ACM MM*, 2015.

[14] A. Khosla, A. Das Sarma, and R. Hamid. What makes an image popular? In *Proc. of WWW*, 2014.

[15] H. Li, X. Ma, F. Wang, J. Liu, and K. Xu. On popularity prediction of videos shared in online social networks. In *Proc. of CIKM*, 2013.

[16] H. Pinto, J. M. Almeida, and M. A. Gonçalves. Using early view patterns to predict the popularity of YouTube videos. In *Proc. of ACM WSDM*, 2013.

[17] C. Riley and D. Sornette. Robust dynamic classes revealed by measuring the response function of a social system. In *Proc. of the National Academy of Sciences*, 2008.

[18] S. D. Roy, T. Mei, W. Zeng, and S. Li. Towards cross-domain learning for social video popularity prediction. *IEEE Transactions on Multimedia*, 15(6):1255–1267, 2013.

[19] G. Szabo and B. A. Huberman. Predicting the popularity of online content. *Communications of the ACM*, 53(8):80–88, 2010.

[20] Z. Wang, W. Zhu, X. Chen, L. Sun, J. Liu, M. Chen, P. Cui, and S. Yang. Propagation-based social-aware multimedia content distribution. *ACM Transactions on Multimedia Computing, Communications, and Applications (TOMM)*, 9(1s):52:1–52:20, Oct. 2013.

[21] J. Yang and J. Leskovec. Patterns of temporal variation in online media. In *Proc. of WSDM*, 2011.

Accurate Aggregation of Local Features by using K-sparse Autoencoder for 3D Model Retrieval

Takahiko Furuya
University of Yamanashi
4-3-11 Takeda, Kofu-shi
Yamanashi-ken, 400-8511, Japan
+81-55-220-8570
takahikof AT yamanashi.ac.jp

Ryutarou Ohbuchi
University of Yamanashi
4-3-11 Takeda, Kofu-shi
Yamanashi-ken, 400-8511, Japan
+81-55-220-8570
ohbuchi AT yamanashi.ac.jp

ABSTRACT

Aggregating a set of local features has been used widely to realize recognition or retrieval of multimedia data including 2D images and 3D models. A number of feature aggregation algorithms (e.g., Bag-of-Features [5], Locality-constrained Linear coding [26], or Fisher Vector coding [23]) have been proposed. They first learn a codebook, or a set of codewords, by clustering the local features and then encode these local features by using the learned codebook. Despite the great success of these feature aggregation algorithms, we argue that they are not necessarily optimal in terms of accuracy since their codebook learning and feature encoding are computed separately. In this paper, we propose two novel feature aggregation algorithms based on *k*-Sparse Autoencoder (*k*SA) [20] that realize more accurate local feature aggregation. Our proposed algorithms, called *Database-adaptive kSA (DkSA)* aggregation and *Per-data-adaptive kSA (PkSA)* aggregation, *jointly* optimize codebook learning and feature encoding. In addition, the *k*SA-based feature encoding enhances saliency of local features due to *k*-sparseness constraints and non-negativity constraints. Of the two proposed algorithms, the P*k*SA aggregation exploits reconstruction error of a local feature derived from the *k*SA for more accurate aggregated feature. Experimental evaluation using a shape-based 3D model retrieval scenario showed that the retrieval accuracy of our proposed algorithms are superior to the existing feature aggregation algorithms we have compared against.

Keywords

Feature aggregation, feature encoding, autoencoder, sparse coding, local feature, bag-of-features, content-based retrieval, 3D shape.

1. INTRODUCTION

Aggregation of local features is an important technological component for effective and efficient comparison among multimedia data objects, including 2D images, 3D models, etc. Recently, for the task of classification or retrieval of 2D images, "end-to-end" deep learning has achieved higher accuracy than the conventional approach which combines hand-crafted local features and their aggregation. On the other hand, recent studies (e.g., [10]) have shown that aggregating features derived from a deep neural network is also effective for 2D image retrieval. Also, for shape-based 3D model retrieval (3DMR) on which we focus in this paper, extracting local features from a 3D model and aggregating them per 3D model remains as one of the most promising approaches. We thus think that improving feature aggregation is still quite meaningful for progress of multimedia information retrieval.

Goal of local feature aggregation is to generate a feature vector that reflects, as well as possible, distribution of local features in their feature space. Feature aggregation generally consists of two steps, i.e., *encoding* and *pooling*. A set of codewords are chosen, typically, by clustering the set of local features. A local feature is encoded by using codewords around the feature and statistics associated with the codewords. Such statistics as density, mean, and/or variance, can be used for the encoding. For pooling, encoded local features are accumulated into a single feature per 3D model. For efficient inter-feature comparison, aggregated feature better be compact.

Many algorithms for feature aggregation have been proposed [12]. They can be roughly classified into two groups; sparse coding (SC)-based approach and higher-order statistics (HS)-based approach. The SC-based approach (e.g., [5][19][26]) sparsely encodes a local feature by using weighted linear sum of its neighboring codewords. Locality-constrained Linear (LL) coding [26] is one of the most representative SC-based methods. Bag-of-Features (BF) [5] is a special case of the SC-based approach in which a local feature is assigned to its nearest single codeword by vector quantization. On the other hand, the HS-based approach (e.g., [14][23][27]) tries to encode local features by using higher-order statistics around the codewords. Fisher Vector (FV) coding [23] employs mean and variance of local features around the codeword. Vector of Locally Aggregated Descriptor (VLAD) [14] approximates the FV by using only mean around the codeword.

These feature aggregation algorithms described above have been successfully utilized for recognition or retrieval of 2D images or 3D models. However, they are not necessarily optimal in terms of accuracy since the codebook learning and the feature encoding steps are processed separately. That is, as a pre-processing, a codebook (i.e., a set of codewords) is first learned by clustering the set of local features. Then, each local feature is encoded by using the learned codebook. This "greedy" framework is adopted by most of the feature aggregation algorithms including BF, LL[1], FV, VLAD, and Triangular Encoding (TE) [4]. The greedy approach could reduce expressive power of the aggregated features.

[1] Although joint optimization framework is proposed in [26], LL is typically used along with a codebook learned by *k*-means clustering in the literature.

ICMR'16, June 06-09, 2016, New York, NY, USA
© 2016 ACM. ISBN 978-1-4503-4359-6/16/06...$15.00
DOI: http://dx.doi.org/10.1145/2911996.2912054

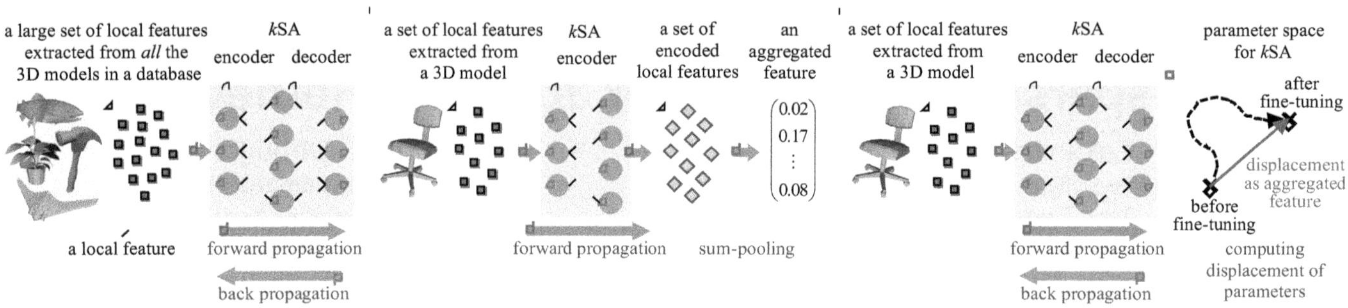

(a) training *k*SA (pre-processing). (b) D*k*SA aggregation. (c) P*k*SA aggregation.

Figure 1. Overview of the proposed feature aggregation algorithms using *k*-Sparse Autoencoder.

In this paper, aiming for more accurate aggregation of local features, we propose a pair of novel SC-based feature aggregation algorithms. The algorithm is based on *k*-Sparse Autoencoder (*k*SA) proposed by Makhzani et al. [20]. A *k*SA-based feature aggregation can be more accurate than the existing ones for two reasons. Firstly, *k*SA can jointly optimize codebook learning and feature encoding as *k*SA is trained by alternating encoding of local features and updating of codewords (i.e., updating of connection weights of *k*SA neurons) so that reconstruction error of the local features is minimized. Similar joint optimization framework is employed by Sparse Autoencoder (SA) [21] and KSVD [2], which are popular sparse coding algorithms. Secondly, feature encoding by *k*SA could enhance saliency of local features since the *k*SA has two constraints considered to aid accurate feature encoding, that are, *k*-sparseness and non-negativity. *K*-sparseness constrains feature encoding to use a small number (k) of codewords correlated to the local feature. Non-negativity forces coefficients weighting the codewords to be non-negative. Several state-of-the-art SC-based algorithms, e.g., LL coding and Localized Soft-assignment (LS) coding [19], showed these constraints improve accuracy of encoded features.

Our two *k*SA-based feature aggregation algorithms are called *Database-adaptive kSA* (*DkSA*) aggregation and *Per-data-adaptive kSA* (*PkSA*) aggregation. D*k*SA (Figure 1b) is a straight-forward approach for feature aggregation using *k*SA. As a pre-processing (Figure 1a), *k*SA is trained by using numerous and diverse local features sampled from the database (hence *database-adaptive*). After training, each of a set local features extracted from a 3D model is encoded by using the database-adapted *k*SA. The set of encoded local features are accumulated into a single feature vector per 3D model by sum-pooling for efficient comparison. P*k*SA (Figure 1c), on the other hand, aims at generating aggregated features more expressive than D*k*SA by exploiting *reconstruction error* of local features derived from the *k*SA. *k*SA is first trained in the same manner as D*k*SA (Figure 1a). Then, the database-adapted *k*SA is additionally trained, or *fine-tuned,* by using a set of local features extracted from each 3D model (hence *per-data-adaptive*). An aggregated feature for the 3D model is a set of displacements of parameters, or weights, caused by the fine-tuning. Table 1 compares characteristics of SC-based feature aggregation algorithms we will evaluate in the experimental section. The D*k*SA and the P*k*SA have potential to yield expressive aggregated features since both of them satisfy all the criteria essential for accurate feature aggregation, i.e., joint optimization of codebook and feature encoding, *k*-sparse constraint, and non-negative constraint. Exploiting reconstruction error of local features for P*k*SA is novel for the group of SC-based feature aggregation algorithms.

Table 1. Comparison of sparse coding-based feature aggregation algorithms.

algorithms	*k*-sparseness	non-negativity	joint optimization of codebook and encoding	exploiting reconstruction error
SA [21]	No	**Yes**	**Yes**	No
TE [4]	No	**Yes**	No	No
KSVD [2]	**Yes**	No	**Yes**	No
LL [26]	**Yes**	**Yes**	No[1]	No
D*k*SA (ours)	**Yes**	**Yes**	**Yes**	No
P*k*SA (ours)	**Yes**	**Yes**	**Yes**	**Yes**

Experimental evaluation under a 3DMR scenario shows that the proposed *k*SA-based feature aggregation algorithms significantly outperform existing SC-based and HS-based counterparts.

Contributions of this paper can be summarized as follows.

- Proposition of two *k*-Sparse Autoencoder based feature aggregation algorithms, that are, D*k*SA and P*k*SA, for more accurate aggregation of local features.
- Quantitative evaluation of D*k*SA and P*k*SA using multiple local features and multiple benchmark datasets for 3DMR.

2. PROPOSED ALGORITHM

2.1 Database-adaptive *k*SA Aggregation

As with the previous feature aggregation methods, D*k*SA (Figure 1b) aggregation consists of two processing steps, that are, encoding and pooling of local features. At the encoding stage, a set of local features extracted from a 3D model is first normalized by using ZCA-whitening [3] so that local features have zero means and all the pair of dimensions are uncorrelated. Then, each whitened local feature is fed into the trained *k*SA to obtain unit activations in the hidden layer. Feature encoding is performed as $\mathbf{h} = \sigma(\mathbf{y}) = \sigma(\mathbf{x}\mathbf{W}_e)$, where $\mathbf{h}$ is an encoded local feature (or unit activation in the hidden layer), $\mathbf{x}$ is a input (whitened) local feature, $\mathbf{W}_e$ is a weight matrix for encoder, and σ is a non-linear activation function. By using hidden layer with n units, d-dimensional local feature $\mathbf{x}$ is encoded into n-dimensional feature ($n > d$). Note that our *k*SA includes bias terms for both encoder and decoder, although the bias term is omitted from the equation for notation simplicity.

Activation function σ strongly influences saliency of encoded local features. Our activation function consists of Rectified Linear Units (ReLU) [16] and *k*-largest value selection. Specifically, y_i, which is i-th element of $\mathbf{y}$, is first rectified by using ReLU, i.e., $z_i = \max(0, y_i)$. ReLU ensures non-negativity of feature encoding. Then, k largest elements in $\{z_i \mid i = 1, \ldots, n\}$ are kept while the rest is set to 0.

At the pooling stage, the set of encoded local features is aggregated into a single feature vector per 3D model by summing. Therefore, the number of dimensions for aggregated feature is also n. Finally, the aggregated feature vector is normalized by using power normalization followed by L2 normalization as with [23]. Cosine similarity is used to compare a pair of D*k*SA-aggregated features.

D*k*SA has two hyper-parameters that require manual tuning, i.e., the number of units in the hidden layer n and the number of non-zero elements in the hidden layer k. In the experiments, n is typically set to 8,000 and small k (e.g.,k=3) is used.

Training of the *k*SA is performed as follows. The *k*SA is trained by minimizing mean squared reconstruction error of local features. We use T=250k local features randomly sampled from the database for training. We use Stochastic Gradient Descent (SGD) with mini-batch. Each mini-batch contains 200 local features randomly selected from the set of T training local features. To adaptively assign a learning rate to each parameter (i.e., each connection weight between neurons), we use AdaGrad algorithm [6] with an initial learning rate = 0.2. Training is regularized with weight decay coefficient $\lambda = 10^{-4}$. The optimization is iterated for 50 epochs.

2.2 Per-data-adaptive *k*SA Aggregation

P*k*SA (Figure 1c) aims at generating more accurate aggregated features than D*k*SA by exploiting reconstruction error of local features. For pre-processing, *k*SA is trained in the same manner as D*k*SA except for the initial learning rate = 0.05 for AdaGrad. We use this initial learning rate since it yielded slightly higher retrieval accuracy in the preliminary experiments.

To aggregate a set of local features extracted from a 3D model M, the database-adapted *k*SA is additionally trained, or fine-tuned, by using the local features of the 3D model M. The *k*SA parameters $\mathbf{W}_e$ for encoder and $\mathbf{W}_d$ for decoder are fine-tuned to reconstruct the local features of the 3D model M well. Then, we compute displacement, or differential, of parameters due to fine-tuning as $\Delta\mathbf{W}_d = \mathbf{W}^*_d - \mathbf{W}_d$, where $\mathbf{W}^*_d$ and $\mathbf{W}_d$ indicate weight matrices of the decoder after and before fine-tuning, respectively. The displacement matrix $\Delta\mathbf{W}_d$ is then vectorized to form a P*k*SA-aggregated feature for the 3D model M. The P*k*SA-aggregated feature vector has $D=(n+1)\times d$ dimensions where "+1" means that our *k*SA has bias terms. We can also use parameter displacement of the encoder, i.e., $\Delta\mathbf{W}_e = \mathbf{W}^*_e - \mathbf{W}_e$, for aggregation. However, preliminary experiments showed that decoder displacement $\Delta\mathbf{W}_d$ consistently outperformed encoder displacement $\Delta\mathbf{W}_e$.

Note that fine-tuning for P*k*SA aggregation is performed per 3D model. That is, the database-adapted *k*SA is duplicated for each 3D model, and each duplicated *k*SA is fine-tuned by using the set of local features extracted from the 3D model. For fine-tuning, we employ Steepest Descent (SD) algorithm; all the local features of the 3D model are used to compute gradients of the parameters. We use SD instead of SGD (with mini-batch) so as to exclude randomness from the result of fine-tuning. We use AdaGrad with initial learning rate = 0.05 and fine-tuning is iterated for 50 epochs.

Since P*k*SA aggregation produces higher-dimensional aggregated feature vectors than D*k*SA aggregation, we perform dimension reduction of the P*k*SA-aggregated features for efficient inter-feature comparison. We use Sparse Random Projection (SRP) [1] algorithm to compress the P*k*SA-aggregated features down to 8,000 dimensions. Preliminary experiments showed that the SRP down to 8,000 dimensions did not degrade retrieval accuracy. Comparison among the dimension-reduced P*k*SA-aggregated feature vectors is done in a manner identical to that of D*k*SA; aggregated features are power-normalized and then L2-normalized for Cosine similarity.

P*k*SA has the same hyper-parameters as D*k*SA, i.e., the number of units in the hidden layer n and the number of non-zero elements in the hidden layer k. In the experiments, n is to 500 and k is set to around 10, which is slightly larger than k for D*k*SA.

3. EXPERIMENTS AND RESULTS

3.1 Experimental Setup

To validate efficacy of the proposed feature aggregation algorithms, we use four benchmark databases for 3DMR; the Princeton Shape Benchmark (PSB) [24], the Engineering Shape Benchmark (ESB) [13], the SHREC 2011 Non-Rigid watertight meshes dataset (SH11NR) [17], and the SHREC 2014 Large-scale Comprehensive 3D shape retrieval dataset (SH14LC) [18]. For all the benchmarks, one of 3D models in the database is used as a query and remaining 3D models are used as retrieval targets. We use Mean Average Precision (MAP) [%] as an index of retrieval accuracy. Since optimization of the proposed algorithms using SGD have randomness, all the experiments for D*k*SA and P*k*SA are performed three times and their average MAP are reported. Table 2 summarizes the number of non-zero units k used for D*k*SA and P*k*SA aggregation. For another hyper-parameter, i.e., the number of hidden units, we use n=8,000 for D*k*SA and n=500 for P*k*SA unless otherwise stated.

Table 2. Number of non-zero units *k* used for experiments.

	POD	LSF	SI	RoPS	DSIFT	MO1SIFT
D*k*SA	3	3	3	3	1	3
P*k*SA	20	10	10	20	5	20

We compare the proposed feature aggregation algorithms against six existing feature aggregation algorithms, i.e., BF [5], LL [26], FV [23], VLAD (VL) [14], SV [27], and DM [9]. We also apply three sparse coding algorithms to local feature aggregation, i.e., Sparse Autoencoder (SA) [21], Triangular Encoding (TE) [4], and KSVD [2]. For sparse coding-based aggregation methods including BF, LL, SA, TE, and KSVD, we learn 8k codewords. On the other hand, for higher-order statistics-based methods including VL, FV, and SV, the number of codewords are determined so that dimensionality of aggregated feature vector becomes about 300k. For DM, we use 250k local features to generate a manifold graph for aggregation. All the aggregated feature vectors are power-normalized and are then L2-normalized. We use Cosine similarity for comparison among feature vectors.

We use six local features for 3DMR, i.e., Position and Orientation Distribution (POD) [9], Spin Image (SI) [15], Local Statistical Feature (LSF) [22], Rotational Projection Statistics (RoPS) [10], Dense SIFT (DSIFT) [7], and Multi-Orientation One SIFT (MO1SIFT) [8]. They are classified into two groups; local 3D geometric feature including POD, SI, LSF, RoPS, and local 2D visual feature including DSIFT and MO1SIFT. Each local feature extraction method has hyper-parameters, e.g., the number of local features per 3D model or the number of rendering views. In this paper, we follow the experimental settings by Furuya et al. [9].

3.2 Experimental Results

3.2.1 Comparison with Other Feature Aggregation Algorithms

Table 3 compares the proposed feature aggregation algorithms against the other feature aggregation algorithms for the PSB dataset. Part of the table is due to [9]. Table 3 shows our *k*SA-based feature aggregation algorithms outperform the existing SC-based methods, i.e., BF, SA, TE, KSVD, and LL. We try to explain the results by using Table 1. TE has non-negativity but it lacks *k*-sparseness for feature encoding. KSVD has *k*-sparseness (we used k=5 for the experiment) and it learns codebook and feature encoding jointly. However, feature encoding by KSVD could produce negative coefficients. LL has both *k*-sparseness (we used k=15) and non-negativity. But feature encoding would be not optimal because it uses a codebook learned by k-means clustering. In comparison, the DkSA and PkSA satisfy both k-sparseness and non-negativity of feature encoding. Also, DkSA and PkSA jointly optimize codebook learning and feature encoding. PkSA outperforms DkSA for five out of six features in Table 3 as the former exploits reconstruction error of local features for aggregation.

Table 3 also shows DkSA and PkSA outperform the state-of-the-art HS-based aggregation methods for most cases. Joint optimization framework of the proposed algorithms would produce more accurate aggregated features than the "greedy" approach adopted by the HS-based methods in Table 3.

Table 3. Comparison of MAP [%] (PSB dataset).

	POD	DSIFT	MO1SIFT	LSF	SI	RoPS
BF	47.8	54.0	51.9	33.0	38.1	40.5
SA	37.2	46.9	42.3			
TE	40.2	45.5	41.3			
KSVD	50.0	55.7	57.4			
LL	53.1	57.6	56.5	33.8	41.0	46.4
FV	52.9	61.7	54.2	36.7	44.9	46.3
VL	52.9	60.9	50.6	38.3	45.5	42.7
SV	55.3	63.8	53.2	40.2	49.6	48.4
DM	60.1	64.7	61.1	41.4	47.3	50.4
DkSA	57.1	56.7	63.7	35.3	37.4	52.1
PkSA	61.5	63.8	62.7	43.0	48.8	55.1

Figure 2 plots retrieval accuracies against the number of dimensions for aggregated features. We extracted POD features from the 3D models. Both DkSA and PkSA show higher retrieval accuracy than the state-of-the-art feature aggregation methods including LL, VL, FV, and SV. Also, PkSA significantly outperforms the DM which is one of the most accurate feature aggregation algorithm for 3DMR [9].

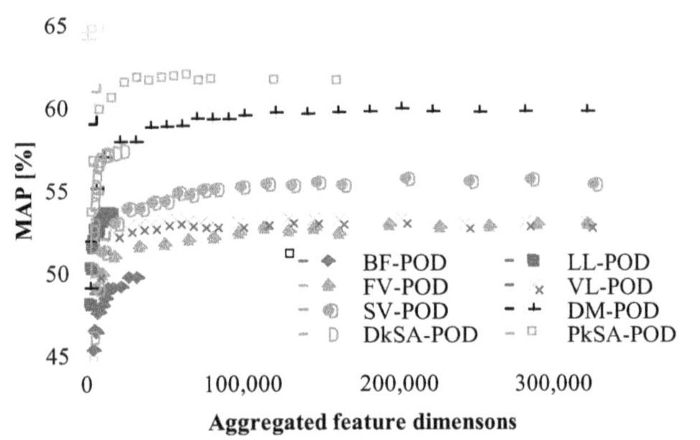

Figure 2. Comparison of feature aggregation methods (PSB).

In the experiments above, we used the only one benchmark database, i.e., the PSB. Table 4 shows generalization capability of the proposed algorithms for a variety of 3D model databases described in Section 3.1. We use POD local feature for the experiment. Table 4 shows the PkSA aggregation performs well, but not always the best, among the previous state-of-the-art feature aggregation algorithms.

3.2.2 Efficiency

We evaluate efficiency of the proposed kSA-based feature aggregation algorithms. We use a PC having two *Intel Xeon E5-2650V2* CPUs, 256GB DRAM, and a *GeForce GTX 980* GPU. Implementations of VL and SV are based on the VLFeat library [25]. They employ parallel computing on the multi-core CPUs for

Table 4. Comparison of MAP [%] (POD feature).

algorithms	PSB	ESB	SH11NR	SH14LC
BF	47.8	52.1	87.3	39.6
LL	53.1	53.0	94.7	44.7
FV	52.9	54.4	96.7	44.8
VL	52.9	49.8	95.9	44.0
SV	55.3	54.0	96.5	45.3
DM	60.1	57.2	95.8	50.7
DkSA	57.1	57.4	96.0	47.7
PkSA	61.5	59.4	96.4	50.9

Table 5. Computation time [s] for feature aggregation.

algorithms	pre-processing	feature aggregation per 3D model
VL	41.5	0.04
SV	342.6	0.08
DkSA	798.6	0.29
PkSA	226.9	0.75

both codebook learning and feature encoding. Computations of DkSA and PkSA are accelerated by using a GPU. We use our own implementations based on the CUDA library for DkSA and PkSA.

Table 5 compares efficiency of feature aggregation algorithms. In the table, pre-processing for VL and SV mean learning a codebook with 3k codewords. Meanwhile, pre-processing for DkSA and PkSA includes whitening of local features and training kSA. Number of hidden units n for DkSA and PkSA are set to 8k and 500 respectively. As for feature aggregation, we measured computation time for aggregating 3k POD features per 3D model. DkSA and PkSA are slower than VL and SV in aggregating local features. PkSA is the slowest among the four algorithms since it requires fine-tuning of kSA for aggregation. However, by the help of GPU, computation time of aggregation for both DkSA and PkSA are within 1 second, which is acceptable for 3DMR.

Querying a 3D model database by using the proposed algorithms is also efficient. We measured computation time per query for the SH14LC database which includes 8,987 3D models. A retrieval consists of three processes, i.e., extracting local features from the given query 3D model, aggregating the local features of the query, and computing similarities among the query and the 3D models in the database. 3DMR using DkSA took 0.61s per query and 3DMR using PkSA took 1.12s per query.

4. CONCLUSION AND FUTURE WORK

In this paper, for more accurate aggregation of local features, we proposed two novel feature aggregation algorithms DkSA and PkSA that employ k-Sparse Autoencoder (kSA). These algorithms jointly optimize codebook learning and feature encoding. Also, feature encoding using the kSA can enhance saliency of local features due to two constraints, i.e., k-sparseness and non-negativity, on unit activation in the hidden layer of the kSA. Furthermore, PkSA aggregation exploits reconstruction error of local features per data object for better retrieval accuracy.

Quantitative evaluation using multiple local features and multiple benchmarks for 3DMR showed that our proposed algorithms perform equal or better than existing state-of-the-art feature aggregation algorithms. As a future work, we will evaluate effectiveness of the kSA-based aggregation under 2D image retrieval or recognition setting.

5. ACKNOWLEDGMENTS

This research is supported by *JSPS Grant-in-Aid for Young Scientists (B)* #16K16055 and *JSPS Grant-in-Aid for Scientific Research on Innovative Areas* #26120517.

6. REFERENCES

[1] Achlioptas, D. 2003. Database-friendly random projections: Johnson-Lindenstrauss with binary coins. *Journal of Computer and System Sciences*, **66**(4), 671–687.

[2] Aharon, M., Elad, M., Bruckstein, A. 2006. K-SVD: An Algorithm for Designing Overcomplete Dictionaries for Sparse Representation. *IEEE Transactions on Signal Processing*, **54**(11), 4311–4322.

[3] Bell, A., Sejnowski, T.J. 1996. Edges are the `Independent Components' of Natural Scenes. *Proc. NIPS 1996.*

[4] Coates, A., Ng, A.Y., Lee, H. 2011. An analysis of single-layer networks in unsupervised feature learning. *Proc. AISTATS 2011*, 215–223.

[5] Csurka, G. et al. 2004. Visual Categorization with Bags of Keypoints, *Proc. ECCV 2004 workshop on Statistical Learning in Computer Vision*, 59–74.

[6] Duchi, J., Hazan, E., Singer, Y. 2011. Adaptive subgradient methods for online learning and stochastic optimization. *The Journal of Machine Learning Research*, **12**, 2121–2159.

[7] Furuya T., Ohbuchi. R. 2009, Dense sampling and fast encoding for 3D model retrieval using bag-of-visual features, *Proc. ACM CIVR* 2009, Article No. 26.

[8] Furuya, T., Ohbuchi, R. 2014. Fusing Multiple Features for Shape-based 3D Model Retrieval, *Proc. BMVC 2014.*

[9] Furuya, T., Ohbuchi, R. 2015. Diffusion-on-Manifold Aggregation of Local Features for Shape-based 3D Model Retrieval. *Proc. ICMR 2015*, 171–178.

[10] Gong, Y., Wang, L., Guo, R., Lazebnik, S. 2014. Multi-Scale Orderless Pooling of Deep Convolutional Activation Features. *Proc. ECCV 2014*, 392–407

[11] Guo, Y. et al. 2013. Rotational Projection Statistics for 3D Local Surface Description and Object Recognition, *IJCV*, **105**(1), 63–86.

[12] Huang, Y., Wu, Z., Wang, L., Tan, T. 2014. Feature Coding in Image Classification, A Comprehensive Study. *IEEE TPAMI*, **36**(3), 493–506.

[13] Jayanti, S., Kalyanaraman, Y., Iyer, N., Ramani, K. 2006. Developing an engineering shape benchmark for CAD models, *Proc CAD*, **38**(9), 939–953.

[14] Jégou, H., Douze, M., Schmid, C., P. Perez. 2010. Aggregating local descriptors into a compact image representation, *Proc. CVPR 2010*, 3304–3311.

[15] Johnson, A.E., Hebert, M. 1999. Using spin images for efficient object recognition in cluttered 3D scenes, *Pattern Analysis and Machine Intelligence*, **21**(5), 433–449.

[16] Krizhevsky, A., Sutskever, I., Hinton, G.E. 2012. ImageNet Classification with Deep Convolutional Neural Networks. *Proc. NIPS 2012*, 1097–1105.

[17] Lian, Z. et al. 2011. SHREC'11 Track: Shape Retrieval on Non-rigid 3D Watertight Meshes, *Proc. EG 3DOR 2011*, 79–88.

[18] Li, B. et al. 2014. Large Scale Comprehensive 3D Shape Retrieval, *Proc. EG 3DOR 2014*, 131–140.

[19] Liu, L., Wang, L., Liu, X. 2011. In defense of soft-assignment coding, *Proc. ICCV 2011*, 2486–2493.

[20] Makhzani, A., Frey B. 2012. *k*-Sparse Autoencoders, arXiv:1312.5663.

[21] Ng, A.Y. 2011. Sparse auto-encoder. CS294A Lecture notes.

[22] Ohkita, Y., Ohishi, Y., Furuya, T., Ohbuchi, R. 2012. Non-rigid 3D Model Retrieval Using Set of Local Statistical Features, *Proc. ICME 2012 Workshop on Hot Topics in 3D Multimedia*, 593–598.

[23] Perronnin, F., Sánchez, J., Mensink, T. 2010. Improving the fisher kernel for large-scale image classification, *Proc. ECCV 2010*, Part IV, 143–156.

[24] Shilane, P., Min, P., Kazhdan, M., Funkhouser, T. 2004. The Princeton Shape Benchmark, *Proc. SMI 2004*, 167–178.

[25] Vedaldi, A., Fulkerson, B. 2010. Vlfeat: an open and portable library of computer vision algorithms. *Proc. ACM MM 2010*, 1469–1472.

[26] Wang, J. et al. 2010, Locality-constrained Linear Coding for Image Classification, *Proc. CVPR 2010*, 3360–3367.

[27] Zhou, X., Yu, K., Zhang, T., Huang, T.S. 2010. Image Classification using Super-Vector Coding of Local Image Descriptors, *Proc. ECCV* 2010, 141–154.

Image Annotation using Multi-scale Hypergraph Heat Diffusion Framework

Venkatesh N. Murthy[1], Avinash Sharma[2], Visesh Chari[3], R Manmatha[1]
[1] {venk,manmatha}@cs.umass.edu
[1] School of Computer Science, University of Massachusetts, Amherst, MA, USA.
[2] asharma@iiit.ac.in [3] visesh@gmail.com
[2 3] Centre for Visual Information Technology, IIIT Hyderabad, Hyderabad, India.

ABSTRACT

The task of automatic image annotation involves assigning relevant multiple labels/tags to query images based on their visual content. One of the key challenge in multi-label image annotation task is the class imbalance problem where frequently occurring labels suppress the participation of rarely occurring labels. In this paper, we propose to exploit the multi-scale behavior in hypergraph heat diffusion framework for the automatic image annotation task. The proposed novel technique enables to model the higher order relationship among images in the feature space and provides a multi-scale label diffusion mechanism to address the class imbalance problem in the data.

General Terms

Algorithms, Experimentation, Measurement

Keywords

Image annotation, hypergraph, Deep learning, heat kernel

1. INTRODUCTION

The task of automatic image annotation involves assigning relevant labels/tags to query images based on their visual content [8]. However, it is difficult to extract variety of visual concepts embedded into an arbitrary image. The traditional techniques extract a set of low-level and/or high-level features on both training and testing images and subsequently apply fusion of various classifiers on these features to achieve automatic image annotation. In particular, nearest neighbor techniques with metric learning have reported best performance among all [17]. Nevertheless, these methods do not exploit the global structure of the underlying data domain well as they only focus on the local neighborhood structure (with a certain risk of overfitting).

One of the key challenge faced by existing techniques is the presence of severe class imbalance problem in real datasets.The class imbalance phenomenon is attributed to skewed distribution of labels in practical scenarios where a subset of over-represented labels (frequently occurring labels) dominate.It is common to exploit this dominance for achieving better performance (F-score) by focusing on retrieval of over-representend labels. Fortunately, the idea of reporting unique number of labels used in annotating test data (i.e., $N+$) keeps a good check on this trend. Thus, traditionally used datasets of moderate size are still relevant (challenging enough and unsaturated) to the task of automatic image annotation. One obvious solution to class imbalance problem is to give higher importance to under-representend labels (although by not loosing too much accuracy on over-represented labels).

In this paper, we propose to solve the automatic image annotation task using the novel multi-scale hypergraph heat diffusion framework. This would enable us to first capture the higher order similarity among multiple images in the feature space and subsequently exploit the topology of the underlying hypergraph. Such topological analysis enables us to perform simultaneous diffusion of the training labels at multiple scales in the transductive setup thereby addressing the key problem of class imbalance (by diffusing the under-represented labels at relatively large scale).

Firstly, we model the higher order feature similarity among images using the nearest-neighbour hypergraph modelling. Here, we use Convolutional Neural Networks (CNN) features that are proven to be more powerful for recognition kind of vision tasks as compared to the traditional array of low and high level features [13]. *Secondly,* we compute the spectrum of the associated hypergraph Laplacian matrix and use it to derive the hypergraph heat-kernel matrix. *Thirdly,* we diffuse the training image labels using the heat-kernel matrix at multiple scales and infer the test labels. *Finally,* we show the empirical validation of the proposed technique and demonstrate superior performance in comparison to many of the existing techniques that use multiple features.

2. LITERATURE SURVEY

Substantial research efforts have been made to solve the inherently difficult task of automatic image annotation in the past decade. At one hand, generative methods based on topic and mixture model exist where each image sample is modeled as a mixture of topics over visual features and labels [21, 2]. On the other hand, discriminative methods try to learn label specific discriminative models [19, 18]. Some of the recent methods proposed to combine both generative and discriminative [10].

Interestingly, recent data-driven techniques that are based

ICMR'16, June 06-09, 2016, New York, NY, USA

DOI: http://dx.doi.org/10.1145/2911996.2912055

on the combination of either generative or discriminative method coupled with nearest-neighbor (NN) approach have reported better results. These methods find visually similar training images for a given test image and transfer labels from those images. JEC [8] proposed to consider equal contributions from different features (mean of distances) while transferring annotations from NN to the test image. TagProp [4] proposed to combine large number of features via metric learning along with label-specific models in the NN setup. 2PKNN [17] exploits the semantic neighborhoods besides metric learning and learns weights for combining different features. Recently proposed NMF-KNN approach in [6] fused multiple features using weighted multi-view non-negative matrix factorization in conjunction with NN approach. Overall, the NN based approaches mainly exploit the local structure of the underlying data domain. However, this data domain seems to be non-Euclidean due to multiple labels and visual concepts assigned per image.

The graph-based transductive learning have recently became popular in the semi-supervised learning community [23]. These methods facilitates: 1) a natural representation of underlying non-Euclidean data domains as graphs and 2) an intuitive notion of scale dependent diffusion of class labels over graph neighbourhood for classification or labelling tasks. However, the simple graph based techniques suffers from the problem of finding the best similarity kernel parameters in the feature space. Another classical limitation is that each edge can only represent a dyadic relationship, thereby losing the higher order relationships among images in the feature space.

Hypergraph learning [22] have been proposed to address shortcomings of the simple graph techniques. It models the higher-order relationships among more than two data points (images) by using the concept of *hyperedge*. An adaptive hypergraph learning method for transductive image classification was proposed in [20], where the hyperedges were generated by linking images and their nearest neighbors (for varying size of neighborhood). Nevertheless, this method was used for predicting single class label per test image and only considered a fix scale spectral representation of graphs.

3. PROPOSED METHOD

In this section, we provide details of key steps of the novel multi-scale hypergraph heat diffusion (HHD) framework.

3.1 Feature Extraction

Given an image, we resize it to 224×224 irrespective of their aspect ratio in order to make it compatible with pre-trained CNN (VGG-16), followed by extracting a 4096-dimensional feature vector using a pre-trained CNN on ILSVRC-2014 dataset by VGG team as described in [1][11]. ILSVRC-2014 consists of 1.2 million images which are manually annotated with the presence/absence of 1000 categories. The VGG network was designed to classify these categories. Features are computed by forward propagating a mean-subtracted 224×224 RGB image through eight convolutional layers and three fully connected layers using Caffe software [5].

Let $\mathbf{x}_i$ be the 4096-dimensional feature vector representing i^{th} image, the entire dataset consisting of n images (including both training and testing sets) can be represented as:

$$\mathbf{X} = [\mathbf{x}_1, \ldots, \mathbf{x}_n].$$

We can separately represent training set of images with $\mathbf{X}^{train}$ and test set of images with $\mathbf{X}^{test}$ such that:

$$\mathbf{X} = \{\mathbf{X}^{train} \cup \mathbf{X}^{test}\}.$$

3.2 Hypergraph Construction

Hypergraph modelling enables capturing more information by employing the hyperedges that can link multiple nodes. We adopted hypergraph construction from [20] where each image is modelled as a node. Each node has one (or multiple) corresponding hyperedge(s) which connects k NN nodes in the feature space (for varying values of k). Let,

$$\mathbf{\Pi} = [\mathbf{he}_1, \ldots, \mathbf{he}_p] \tag{1}$$

be the incidence matrix of the NN hypergraph induced on the image feature set $\mathbf{X}$. Here, each hyperedge $\mathbf{he}_i = [he_i^1, \ldots, he_i^n]^T$ is an indicator vector of size n where each element $he_i^j = 1$ if node $\mathbf{x}_j$ participate in hyperedge $\mathbf{he}_i$ or else zero. Thus, multiple 1's suggest that respective nodes contribute to the same hyperedge. The total number of hyperedges i.e., p is multiple of n depending on if we induce one or multiple hyperedges per node.

3.3 Hypergraph Heat Diffusion (HHD) Framework

The heat-kernel is a symmetric, non-linear (exponential) family of kernel (analogous to Gaussian kernel) for non-Euclidean spaces represented as graphs and is used as a diffusion tool for multi-scale label or information diffusion on graphs [15]. In case of dyadic graphs, it is derived from the spectra (constituted by both eigenvalues & eigenvectors) of the graph Laplacian matrix [14]. Interestingly, the Laplacian for hypergraph was derived in [22] where it was shown to be analogous to simple graph Laplacian.

The Hypergraph Heat Diffusion (HHD) framework enables multi-scale (topological) analysis of hypergraphs and we propose to exploit this for addressing the class imbalance property in the image annotation task. Using the definition of hypergraph incidence matrix in Eq.1, the hypergraph Laplacian is subsequently defined as:

$$\mathbf{L} = \mathbf{I} - \left(\mathbf{D}_v^{-\frac{1}{2}} \mathbf{\Pi} \mathbf{W}_{he} \mathbf{D}_{he}^{-1} \mathbf{\Pi}^T \mathbf{D}_v^{-\frac{1}{2}}\right) \tag{2}$$

where, $\mathbf{\Pi}$ is incidence matrix of the hypergraph, $\mathbf{D}_v$ is degree matrix of nodes (defined as $\mathbf{D}_v = diag(\sum \mathbf{\Pi})$), $\mathbf{D}_{he}$ is the degree matrix of the hyperedges defined as $\mathbf{D}_{he} = diag(\sum \mathbf{\Pi}^T)$ and $\mathbf{W}_{he}$ is the hyperedge weight matrix defined as $\mathbf{W}_{he} = diag(w_1, \ldots, w_p)$.

The $\mathbf{W}_{he}$ matrix can be used to enforce the relative significance of certain hyperedges over others by setting a larger values. The eigen-decomposition of the hypergraph Laplacian matrix $\mathbf{L}$ is written as: $\mathbf{L} = \mathbf{U}\mathbf{\Lambda}\mathbf{U}^T$ where, $\mathbf{U} = [\mathbf{u}_1, \ldots, \mathbf{u}_n]$ be the matrix formed by the eigenvectors of $\mathbf{L}$ matrix and, $\mathbf{\Lambda} = diag(\lambda_1, \ldots, \lambda_n)$ be the diagonal eigenvalue matrix, together defines the Laplacian spectra.

The hypergraph heat diffusion framework can be derived using the associated Laplacian spectra. The $n \times n$ heat-kernel matrix for hypergraph can be computed as:

$$\mathbf{H}(t) = \mathbf{U} \exp(-\mathbf{\Lambda} t) \mathbf{U}^T \tag{3}$$

where, t act as the scale parameter which govern the heat diffusion. It is straightforward to show that the $\mathbf{H}(t)$ matrix is indeed a kernel matrix as it satisfies Mercer's kernel property, i.e., it is a real, positive semi-definite matrix with

Method	Feature Visual	Corel-5K				ESP Game				IAPRTC-12			
		P	R	F	N+	P	R	F	N+	P	R	F	N+
JEC [8]	HC	27	32	29	139	22	25	23	224	28	29	29	250
CCD [12]	HC	36	41	38	159	36	24	29	232	44	29	35	251
KSVM-VT [18]	HC	32	42	36	179	33	32	33	259	47	29	36	268
MBRM [3]	HC	24	25	25	122	18	19	19	209	24	23	24	223
TagProp(σML) [4]	HC	33	42	37	160	39	27	32	239	46	35	40	266
FastTag [2]	HC	33	43	37	166	46	22	30	247	47	26	34	280
2PKNN+ML [17]	HC	44	46	45	191	53	27	35.7	252	54	37	44	278
SVM-DMBRM [10]	HC	36	48	41	197	55	25	34	259	56	29	38	283
NMF-KNN*	HC	22	32	26	150	29	23	26	268	-	-	-	-
JEC	VGG-16	31	32	32	141	26	22	24	234	28	21	24	237
TagProp (σ)	VGG-16	30	35	32	149	31	28	30	246	38	30	34	260
2PKNN	VGG-16	33	30	32	160	40	23	29	250	38	23	29	261
HHD	VGG-16	31	49	38	194	35	36	34	257	32	44	36	280

Table 1: Results comparison. P: Average Precision, R: Average Recall, N+: Number of distinct labels that are correctly assigned to at least one test image. HC: bunch of hand-crafted/engineered features, VGG-16: CNN or deep learning feature.

real and positive eigenvalues ($\exp(-\mathbf{\Lambda}t)$ for $t \geq 0$) (see [22] for details).

3.4 Multi-scale Label Diffusion & Inference

An explicit control over the scale of diffusion allow one to diffuse over-represented and under-represented labels separately, thereby addressing the prevalent class imbalance scenario in real data. In case of HDD framework, the scale of diffusion is governed by the parameter t (see Eq. 3). The value of t can vary from 0 to ∞. A small scale diffusion (t closer to zero) would enforce the label diffusion in the smaller neighbourhood while a large scale diffusion (t closer to infinity) would enforce the label diffusion in a very large neighbourhood.

Let, the ground truth labels for both training and test labels can be represented as:

$$\mathbf{Y} = [\mathbf{y}_1, \ldots, \mathbf{y}_m]$$

where each $\mathbf{y}_i$ is an n-dimensional indicator vector (0's and 1's) for the multi-label annotation setup with label vocabulary of size m. Let $\mathbf{Y}^{train} \subset \mathbf{Y}$ be the set of known labels (training set) and $\mathbf{Y}^{test}$ be the complementary set of unknown labels (testing set). Thus, a scale dependent label diffusion can be accomplished as:

$$\mathbf{Y}_t = \mathbf{H}(t)\mathbf{Y}. \tag{4}$$

Let $\mathbf{Y}^{OR} \subset \mathbf{Y}$ be the subset of labels from over-represented class and $\mathbf{Y}^{UR}$ be the complementary set of under-represented class labels. The multi-scale (ms) diffusion to address the class imbalance problem can be achieved by diffusing over-represented labels at t_{small} and under-represented labels at t_{large} as:

$$\mathbf{Y}^{OR}_{t_{small}} = \mathbf{H}(t_{small})\mathbf{Y}^{OR}, \tag{5}$$

$$\mathbf{Y}^{UR}_{t_{large}} = \mathbf{H}(t_{large})\mathbf{Y}^{UR}, \tag{6}$$

These diffused label matrices can further be combined to

$$\mathbf{Y}_{ms} = \mathbf{Y}^{OR}_{t_{small}} \bigcup \mathbf{Y}^{UR}_{t_{large}}$$

.

Finally, we select the subset of multi-scale diffused labels for test set images (i.e., $\mathbf{Y}^{test}_{ms} \subset \mathbf{Y}_{ms}$) apply multi-label inference by taking the q largest entries of each row of $\mathbf{Y}^{test}_{ms}$ for inferring q labels for each test image. However, before inferring test image labels, we propose to normalize $\mathbf{Y}^{test}_{ms}$ with $L1$-normalization using $\mathbf{Y}^{train}_{ms}$. This type of normalization further helps in addressing the class imbalance problem.

4. EXPERIMENTS & RESULTS

In order to have a fair comparison to the previous methods, we use the same train and test split provided in [4] for the three datasets. Each test image is annotated with a fixed number of five labels, this makes it almost impossible to get perfect precision and recall score on these three datasets because each image has highly varying number of labels associated with it.

4.1 Dataset and Evaluation

We evaluate on four standard publicly available image annotation datasets - Corel-5k, ESP-Game, IAPRTC-12 and MIRFLICKR-25K. These datasets contain a variety of images like natural scene, game, sketches, transportation vehicles, personal photos and so on, thus making it a challenging task.We follow the standard evaluation metrics as reported in most of the previous work [10, 9, 17, 8, 3, 7].

4.2 Results

We evaluate the performance of the proposed method using CNN features on image annotation task and compare it with some of the existing methods in the literature. In addition, we also provide the effectiveness of using CNN features as opposed to 15 engineered/hand-crafted (HC) features (including both local and global features) in some of the existing methods like 2PKNN, TagProp and JEC. Experimental results provided in Table 1 are obtained using the standard evaluation metric [10].

We did not fully exploit the formulation by setting $W_{he} = I$, i.e., giving equal importance to all hyperedges. This was done intentionally, because we wanted to report generalized results and therefore a tuning which can be regarded as overfitting to datasets was avoided. Instead of using all eigenvectors of the Laplacian matrix, we used only 10% of the smallest eigenvectors for constructing a low rank heat kernel matrix for computation efficiency reasons. The scale parameters were empirically chosen for each dataset.

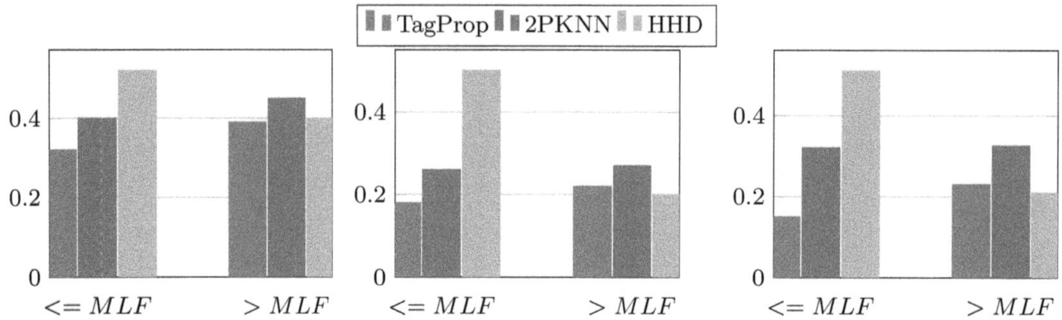

Figure 1: Annotation performance in terms of mean recall of labels in Corel 5k, ESP Game and IAPR TC12. On the Horizontal axis, the labels are grouped based on their frequency. The first bin corresponds to the 50% under represented labels and the second bin corresponds to the 50% over represented labels. *MLF*: Mean label frequency in the dataset.

For reporting the results of using CNN features in the existing methods, we implemented JEC method as described in [8] and for 2PKNN [17], we made use of the code provided by the authors (reported results are obtained using the following parameter values, $k = 4$ and $w = 1$). NMF-KNN* results are recomputed using the metric of computing mean recall and mean precision over all the words instead of just non-zero recall words (as originally reported in the paper [6]). Recomputed values are obtained as follows: $P_{new} = (P_{old} * (N+))/V_{size}$,, $R_{new} = (R_{old} * (N+))/V_{size}$ and $F_{new} = (2 * P_{new} * R_{new})/(P_{new} + R_{new})$.

Results on Corel-5k: From Table 1, we can clearly infer that the proposed method performs better than most of the existing methods when used with single CNN feature. Interestingly, the CNN features used in JEC, TagProp and 2PKNN methods performs better than some of the existing methods with HC features. However, their performance is poor in terms of both F and N+ measures when compared to our proposed method. This demonstrates that the improvement in the performance is attributed to our novel HHD framework and not just the feature alone.

We have also listed performance of existing methods on 15 HC features too though it does not amount to a fair comparison as these methods uses many features. For instance, our F and N+ measures are greater than the strong baseline TagProp(σML) method. Though our method underperformed slightly than the current state-of-the-art 2PKNN+ML method in terms of F measure, it is significantly better in terms of N+ measure (number of distinct labels used for annotation). Both 2PKNN+ML and TagProp(σML) methods are based on nearest neighbor approach employing metric learning to find an optimal combination of HC features. In terms of N+, it clearly indicates that our method provides a good generalization as opposed to metric learning techniques. For reporting the results using TagProp, we made use of the code provided by the authors [4].

Results on ESP-Game and IAPRTC-12: On both datasets, HHD provides a significant improvement over existing methods (JEC, 2PKNN) using a single CNN feature. In case of 15 HC features, we can observe that our HHD method performs almost similar to state-of-the-art 2PKNN method in terms of F measure and outperforms in N+ measure for ESP-Game. This demonstrates that our method effectively handles the imbalance data and the poor labeling problems. In case of IAPRTC-12, our method performance is competitive to TagProp(σML) and slightly lower compared to 2PKNN+ML in terms of F measure, but when it comes to N+ HHD method performs better than both the other methods. This suggests that hypergraph heat diffusion framework with the CNN feature is able to provide an effective solution for the image annotation task.

Results on MIRFLICKR: From Table 2, we can clearly see that proposed HHD method significantly outperforms both TagProp and SVM models in terms of **AP** measure. **AP** was computed as described in [16] per label. This clearly indicate that given a label our method is able to accurately retrieve most of the images which makes it suitable for real world applications and this is also indicates that the proposed method generalizes well compared to others.

Method	AP (Average Precision)
TagProp-Rank [16]	46.9
TagProp-Distance [16]	45.9
SVM [16]	52.0
HHD	**75.0**

Table 2: Experimental results of our proposed method with previously reported best scores on MIRFLICKR-25K.

4.2.1 *Impact on Class Imbalance*

Figure 1 demonstrates the performance of automatic annotation for both most frequent (>MLF) and least frequent labels ($\leq$MLF). Here, the performance is measured in terms of mean recall. For all three datasets, we can see that HHD method provides significant improvement for rare labels (under-represented label class)as compared to 2PKNN+ML & TagProp(σML) and with slight performance degradation for most frequent labels. This clearly indicates that multi-scale diffusion in the hypergraph helps in striking the balance between retrieving the rare words and the most frequent words.

5. CONCLUSION & FUTURE WORK

The proposed novel image annotation technique exploits the multi-scale diffusion to address class imbalance problem and outperforms the majority of existing techniques through empirical evaluation on standard image annotation datasets.

As part of the future work, it will be interesting to explore how to exploit the label based semantic similarity among images in conjunction with visual similarity in the proposed HHD framework. One can also explore the adaptive techniques for finding optimal parameters in HHD framework.

6. REFERENCES

[1] K. Chatfield, K. Simonyan, A. Vedaldi, and A. Zisserman. Return of the devil in the details: Delving deep into convolutional nets. In *British Machine Vision Conference*, 2014.

[2] M. Chen, A. X. Zheng, and K. Q. Weinberger. Fast image tagging. In *International Conference on Machine Learning*, pages 1274–1282, 2013.

[3] S. L. Feng, R. Manmatha, and V. Lavrenko. Multiple bernoulli relevance models for image and video annotation. In *Proceedings of the 2004 IEEE Computer Society Conference on Computer Vision and Pattern Recognition*, CVPR'04, pages 1002–1009, 2004.

[4] M. Guillaumin, T. Mensink, J. Verbeek, and C. Schmid. Tagprop: Discriminative metric learning in nearest neighbor models for image auto-annotation. In *International Conference on Computer Vision*, pages 309–316, 2009.

[5] Y. Jia, E. Shelhamer, J. Donahue, S. Karayev, J. Long, R. Girshick, S. Guadarrama, and T. Darrell. Caffe: Convolutional architecture for fast feature embedding. In *Proceedings of the ACM International Conference on Multimedia*, pages 675–678. ACM, 2014.

[6] M. M. Kalayeh, H. Idrees, and M. Shah. NMF-KNN: image annotation using weighted multi-view non-negative matrix factorization. In *Computer Vision and Pattern Recognition*, pages 184–191, 2014.

[7] V. Lavrenko, R. Manmatha, and J. Jeon. A model for learning the semantics of pictures. In *in NIPS*. MIT Press, 2003.

[8] A. Makadia, V. Pavlovic, and S. Kumar. A new baseline for image annotation. In *European Conference on Computer VisionI*, pages 316–329, 2008.

[9] S. Moran and V. Lavrenko. A sparse kernel relevance model for automatic image annotation. *International Journal of Multimedia Information Retrieval*, 3(4):209–229, 2014.

[10] V. N. Murthy, E. F. Can, and R. Manmatha. A hybrid model for automatic image annotation. In *Proceedings of International Conference on Multimedia Retrieval*, pages 369:369–369:376, 2014.

[11] V. N. Murthy, S. Maji, and R. Manmatha. Automatic image annotation using deep learning representations. In *Proceedings of the 5th ACM on International Conference on Multimedia Retrieval*, pages 603–606. ACM, 2015.

[12] H. Nakayama. *Linear distance metric Learning for large-scale generic image recognition.* PhD thesis, The University of Tokyo, Japan, 2011.

[13] A. Sharif Razavian, H. Azizpour, J. Sullivan, and S. Carlsson. Cnn features off-the-shelf : An astounding baseline for recognition. In *Computer Vision and Patter Recognition*, pages –, 2014.

[14] A. Sharma. *Representation, Segmentation and Matching of 3D Visual Shapes using Graph Laplacian and Heat-Kernel.* PhD thesis, 2012.

[15] A. D. Szlam, M. Maggioni, and R. R. Coifman. Regularization on graphs with function-adapted diffusion processes. *Journal of Machine Learning Research*, 9:1711–1739, 2008.

[16] J. Verbeek, M. Guillaumin, T. Mensink, and C. Schmid. Image annotation with tagprop on the mirflickr set. In *Proceedings of the international conference on Multimedia information retrieval*, pages 537–546. ACM, 2010.

[17] Y. Verma and C. V. Jawahar. Image annotation using metric learning in semantic neighborhoods. In *Proceedings of the 12th European Conference on Computer Vision - Volume Part III*, ECCV'12, pages 836–849, Berlin, Heidelberg, 2012. Springer-Verlag.

[18] Y. Verma and C. V. Jawahar. Exploring SVM for image annotation in presence of confusing labels. In *British Machine Vision Conference*, 2013.

[19] X. Xu, A. Shimada, and R.-i. Taniguchi. Image annotation by learning label-specific distance metrics. In *Image Analysis and Processing âĂŞ ICIAP 2013*, volume 8156, pages 101–110, 2013.

[20] J. Yu, D. Tao, and M. Wang. Adaptive hypergraph learning and its application in image classification. *Transactions on Image Processing*, 21(7):3262–3272, 2012.

[21] S. Zhang, J. Huang, Y. Huang, Y. Yu, H. Li, and D. N. Metaxas. Automatic image annotation using group sparsity. In *CVPR*, pages 3312–3319, 2010.

[22] D. Zhou, J. Huang, and B. Schölkopf. Learning with hypergraphs: Clustering, classification, and embedding. In *Advances in Neural Information Processing Systems*, pages –, 2006.

[23] X. Zhu, A. B. Goldberg, R. Brachman, and T. Dietterich. *Introduction to Semi-Supervised Learning.* Morgan and Claypool Publishers, 2009.

Discriminant Cross-modal Hashing

Xing Xu
University of Electronic Science and Technology of China
Chengdu, China
xing.xu@uestc.edu.cn

Fumin Shen
University of Electronic Science and Technology of China
Chengdu, China
fumin.shen@gmail.com

Yang Yang
University of Electronic Science and Technology of China
Chengdu, China
dlyyang@gmail.com

Heng Tao Shen
University of Electronic Science and Technology of China
Chengdu, China
The University of Queensland
Brisbane, Australia
shenhengtao@hotmail.com

ABSTRACT

Hashing based methods have attracted considerable attention for efficient cross-modal retrieval on large-scale multimedia data. The core problem of cross-modal hashing is how to effectively integrate heterogeneous features from different modalities to learn hash functions using available supervising information, e.g., class labels. Existing hashing based methods generally project heterogeneous features to a common space for hash codes generation, and the supervising information is incrementally used for improving performance. However, these methods may produce ineffective hash codes, due to the failure to explore the discriminative property of supervising information and to effectively bridge the semantic gap between different modalities. To address these challenges, we propose a novel hashing based method in a linear classification framework, in which the proposed method learns modality-specific hash functions for generating unified binary codes, and these binary codes are viewed as representative features for discriminative classification with class labels. An effective optimization algorithm is developed for the proposed method to jointly learn the modality-specific hash function, the unified binary codes and a linear classifier. Extensive experiments on three benchmark datasets highlight the advantage of the proposed method and show that it achieves the state-of-the-art performance.

CCS Concepts

•Information systems → Multimedia and multimodal retrieval;

ICMR'16, June 06-09, 2016, New York, NY, USA

DOI: http://dx.doi.org/10.1145/2911996.2912056

Keywords

Cross-modal retrieval; cross-modal hashing; discriminant analysis

1. INTRODUCTION

Nowadays, the fast growth of multimedia data on the Internet has significantly increased the demand for more sophisticated multimedia indexing [10] and retrieval technologies [11, 6]. Especially, the cross-modal retrieval problem [1, 9] that aims at matching one modal data to the other modal data, has gained much attentions due to the heterogeneous source of the multimedia data, i.e., texts, images and videos. However, different modal data cannot be directly matched due to the intrinsic diversity in different modalities.

To tackle this problem, several hashing-based approaches [7, 13, 15, 3] have garnered considerable interest and shown promising performance on cross-modal retrieval problem. These hashing based methods find the linear projections to embed the heterogeneous data into a common Hamming space, where the multi-modal features are indexed as binary codes. These methods can handle large-scale data with both low memory cost and computational cost, because the learned hash codes can be compactly stored and Hamming distance can be fast calculated with bit-wise XOR operations. Nevertheless, these methods are generally unsupervised since the valuable class label information has not been leveraged yet.

Indeed, utilizing the class label information has been found helpful to construct the correlations across different modalities, e.g., reducing the semantic gap between the low-level visual features and high level semantic descriptions [8]. Several recent studies [2, 14, 4] leverage supervising information like class labels or semantic affinities of training data incrementally to further improve retrieval performance. These supervised approaches can often achieve higher accuracy than the aforementioned unsupervised ones. However, one limitation of these supervised approaches is that the discrimination of supervising information is implicitly captured for hash function learning. It may inhibit these methods from learning effective hash codes that well capture the correlations of different modalities and incorporate the discrimination of supervising information.

To address the above challenges, we propose a novel cross-modal hashing method that learns unified binary codes from different modalities more effectively by explicitly capturing the discrimination of class labels. In the proposed method, the unified binary codes are produced by the modality-specific hash functions for one instance consisting of different modalities. The modality-specific hash functions are proposed to account the unique structure of each modality. With the help of class labels as the supervising information, the resulting binary codes are designed to be the optimal representation of the multi-modal data for classification. Unlike previous works [4, 14, 15] that utilize the class labels to generate semantic affinities for approximating hash codes or to cast independently learning each bit of hash codes to binary classification problem, the class label information is naturally leveraged in the unified binary codes learning process of the proposed method. Due to the NP-hard optimization problem in the proposed method, an efficient approximation algorithm is developed to iteratively obtain the quasi-optimal binary codes under the classification framework.

The main contributions of our work can be summarized as follows: 1) We propose a novel hashing method for cross-modal retrieval, in which the unified binary codes and a linear classifier are jointly learned with the modality-specific hash functions. 2) An efficient algorithm is developed for the proposed method to iteratively obtain the approximate optimized solution. 3) The proposed method is extensively evaluated on three benchmark dataset and the results show its superiority to several other state-of-the-art methods.

The remainder of this paper is organized as follows. Section 2 presents the details of the proposed method. Extensive experiments on three cross-modal datasets are depicted in Section 3. Lastly, the conclusions are made in Section 4.

2. PROPOSED METHOD

2.1 Problem Formulation

Suppose that we have a set of n multi-modal training instances $\mathcal{X} = \{x_i\}_{i=1}^n$, and each instance $x_i = (v_i, t_i)$ has a class label vector $y_i \in \mathbb{R}^{c\times 1}$; $v_i \in \mathbb{R}^{m\times 1}$ is the image feature vector, and $t_i \in \mathbb{R}^{d\times 1}$ is the text feature vector. Here we denote $V = \{v_i\}_{n=1}^m \in \mathbb{R}^{m\times n}$, $T = \{t_i\}_{i=1}^d \in \mathbb{R}^{d\times n}$ and $Y = \{y_i\}_{i=1}^c \in \mathbb{R}^{c\times n}$ as the image, text and label matrices of $\mathcal{X}$. We aim to learn binary codes matrix $B = \{b_i\}_{i=1}^n \in \{-1,1\}^{L\times n}$, where b_i is the unified L-bits hash codes for instance x_i.

In our work, we introduce the modality-specific hash functions $F_V(\cdot)$ and $F_T(\cdot)$ for image and text modalities, respectively. Specifically, given the multi-modal feature vectors v_i and t_i of the i-th instance, these two hash functions are correspondingly defined as:

$$F_V(v_i) = P_V^\top v_i, \quad F_T(t_i) = P_T^\top t_i, \tag{1}$$

where $P_V \in \mathbb{R}^{m\times L}$ and $P_T \in \mathbb{R}^{m\times L}$ are the linear projection matrices that map the original feature representations of v_i and t_i onto the low-dimensional latent spaces.

Furthermore, we consider that one instance x_i consisting of two modalities has unified binary codes b_i. Similar to [5], to leverage the supervised label information, b_i is expected to be ideal feature vector to represent original multi-modal data for classification. Given the binary codes b_i and label vector y_i for x_i , we import the simple linear classification form with binary constraints on b_i as in [5]:

$$\min_B \sum_{i=1}^n \|y_i - W^\top b_i\|^2 + \lambda\|W\|^2, \quad s.t. \;\; b_i \in \{-1,1\}^L. \tag{2}$$

Here $W \in \mathbb{R}^{L\times c}$ is the linear classifier, $\|\cdot\|$ is the L_2 norm for vectors and Frobenius norm for matrices, and λ is the regularization parameter.

Moreover, b_i is also desired to bridge the semantic gap between original data v_i and t_i of instance x_i. Thus we assume that the projected spaces of $F_V(v_i)$ and $F_T(t_i)$ are commonly shared as the Hamming space, where the unified binary codes b_i can be generated. We follow the discrete optimization scheme in [5] to preserve the binary constraints on b_i and to fit the errors of binary codes b_i with $F_V(v_i)$ as $\|b_i - F_V(v_i)\|$, with $F_T(t_i)$ as $\|b_i - F_T(t_i)\|$, respectively.

Finally, the optimization problem in the proposed method is formulated by jointly learning the modality-specific hash functions, unified binary codes and a linear classifiers, as:

$$\min_{B,W,F_V,F_T} \sum_{i=1}^n \|y_i - W^\top b_i\|^2 + \mu_V \sum_{i=1}^n \|b_i - F_V(v_i)\|^2 \tag{3}$$
$$+ \mu_T \sum_{i=1}^n \|b_i - F_T(t_i)\|^2 + \lambda\|W\|^2, \quad s.t. \;\; b_i \in \{-1,1\}^L,$$

where μ_V and μ_T are the penalty parameters. From Eq. 3 it can be learned that the first term demands good binary codes for supervised classification to preserve the discrimination, and the last two terms ensure the modality-specific hash functions are simultaneously optimized to fit the binary codes with less errors.

2.2 Optimization Algorithm

To make the derivation more intuitive, Eq. 3 can be rewritten in matrix form as follows:

$$\min_{B,W,F_V,F_T} \|Y - W^\top B\|^2 + \mu_V\|B - F_V(V)\|^2 \tag{4}$$
$$+ \mu_T\|B - F_T(T)\|^2 + \lambda\|W\|^2, \quad s.t. \;\; B \in \{-1,1\}^{L\times n}.$$

The optimization problem in Eq. 4 is non-convex with respect to matrices variables B, W, F_V and F_T and difficult to solve. However, it is convex with respect to any one of the four variable while fixing the other three. Therefore, Eq. 4 can be solved by an iterative framework with the following steps until convergency is reached.

Step1: Learn projection matrices P_V and P_T by fixing other variables, the problem in Eq. 4 becomes

$$\min_{F_V} \mu_V\|B - F_V(V)\|^2 = \min_{P_V} \mu_V\|B - P_V V\|^2,$$
$$\min_{F_T} \mu_T\|B - F_T(T)\|^2 = \min_{P_T} \mu_T\|B - P_T T\|^2, \tag{5}$$

respectively, which can be computed by regression as:

$$P_V = (VV^\top)^{-1}VB^\top,$$
$$P_T = (TT^\top)^{-1}TB^\top. \tag{6}$$

Step2: Learn classification matrix W by fixing other variables, the problem in Eq. 4 becomes

$$\min_W \|Y - W^\top B\|^2 + \lambda\|W\|^2, \;\; s.t. \;\; B \in \{-1,1\}^{L\times n}, \tag{7}$$

which is a simple regularized least squares problem. Thus the closed-form solution of W can be derived as:

$$W = (BB^\top + \lambda I)^{-1} BY^\top. \quad (8)$$

Step3: Learn binary codes matrix B by fixing other variables, the problem in Eq. 4 becomes:

$$\min_{W} \|Y - W^\top B\|^2 + \mu_V \|B - F_V(V)\|^2 + \mu_T \|B - F_T(T)\|^2,$$
$$s.t. \quad B \in \{-1, 1\}^{L \times n}. \quad (9)$$

The problem in Eq. 9 is NP-hard for directly optimizing the optimal binary codes B. However, we can solve a relaxed problem through discarding the discrete constraints in Eq. 9, then the gradient regarding to B can be derived as:

$$g(B) = W(Y - W^\top B) + \mu_V(B - P_V V) + \mu_T(B - P_T T). \quad (10)$$

After setting $g(B)$ to zero, we can get the continuous closed-form solution of B, which is:

$$B = [WW^\top + (\mu_V + \mu_T)I]^{-1}(WY + \mu_V P_V V + \mu_T P_T T). \quad (11)$$

Finally, the approximate binary codes for the training instances can be obtained by quantization, as $sgn(B)$.

2.3 Discussion

In each iteration of the training phase described above, the time complexity is about $\mathcal{O}(k^2 n)$, where $k = \max\{m, d, L\}$. Thus the training time of the proposed method is linear to the size of training set, hence is very efficient and scalable for large-scale training data.

During the test phase, given a new query instance x', generating its hash codes b' relying on its components. Specifically, when x' only contains data of one modality, i.e. $x' = (v',)$ or $x' = (t',)$, its hash codes can be computed as $b' = sgn(F_V(v'))$ or $b' = sgn(F_T(t'))$; when x' consists of data of two modalities, i.e. $x' = (v', t')$, its hash codes is computed as the quantization of Eq. 11.

3. EXPERIMENT

3.1 Experimental Settings

To verify the effectiveness of the proposed method, we conduct experiments on three real-world datasets: Wiki, MIRFlickr and NUS-WIDE, for cross-modal retrieval problem. All these datasets consist of both image and text modalities, for cross-modal retrieval. Some general statistics of these datasets and the query/retrieval splits in our experiments are illustrated in Table 1. dataset Regarding the

	Wiki	MIRFlickr	NUS-WIDE
Retrieval Size	2,173	15,902	184,711
Training Set	2,173	5,000	5,000
Query Set	693	836	1,866
Labels	10	24	10

Table 1: General statistics of three datasets.

feature representations of image and text modalities, for each instance on Wiki dataset, its image is represented by a 128-dimension SIFT feature vector and its text as a 10-dimension topic vector generated by latent Dirichlet allocation (LDA); on MIRFlickr dataset, its image is represented by 150-dimensional edge histogram, and its text as a 500-dimensional feature vector generated from PCA on its index tagging vector; on NUS-WIDE dataset, its image is represented by a 500-dimension SIFT feature vector and its text as an index vector of selected top 1,000 tags.

Furthermore, like the setting in [4], to reduce the computational cost on large-scale datasets MIRFlickr and NUS-WIDE, we randomly select 5,000 instances from their retrieval database to train hash functions, and then these hash functions are applied to the other instances in the databases to generate hash codes for them; for Wiki dataset, we take the entire retrieval set as the training data because of its small size. Moreover, for query instances, we follow the scheme in Section 2.3 to generate unified hash codes for these out-of-sample instances.

We compare the proposed methods with various state-of-the-art cross-modal hashing methods, including unsupervised ones IMH [7], LSSH [15], CMFH [3] and supervised ones CMSSH [2], CRH [14], SCM$_{Seq}$ [12], SePH$_{km}$ [4]. We use the codes and suggested parameters published by the respective authors. We perform 10 runs for all these methods and take the average performance for comparison. All the experiments are performed on Matlab platform installed in a desktop which has 4-core 3.2GHz CPUs with 16GB RAM.

Two types of cross-modal retrieval tasks are conducted in our experiments: 1) *Text2Img* that uses text as query to search similar images and 2) *Img2Text* that uses images as query to search similar texts. The retrieval performance is evaluated by the widely-used *mean average precision* (mAP), which is an overall metric on a set of queries. Note that a larger mAP indicates better performance that relevant ones have high rank in the retrieved instances.

3.2 Parameter Sensitive Analysis

The parameters μ_V and μ_T in the proposed method control the error of the learned binary codes of different modalities, in this subsection we analyze their effects on the qualities of the learned hash codes during training. By prefixing the code length as 16 bits, we vary both μ_V and μ_T in $\{10^{-6}, 10^{-5}, ..., 1\}$ and assess their qualities with two retrieval tasks on the training set of Wiki and MIRFlickr datasets. Figure 1 shows the average mAP of *Img2Text* and *Text2Img* tasks under different settings of μ_V and μ_T on the two datasets. It can be observed that the proposed method can achieve stable performance under a wide range of values of μ_V and μ_T when they are considerably large and comparable, e.g., μ_V and μ_T are from the range $[10^{-2}, 1]$. Therefore, to make comprehensive comparison with other baselines, for the proposed method, we empirically set λ to 1, μ_V and μ_T both to 10^{-1} in the following experiments.

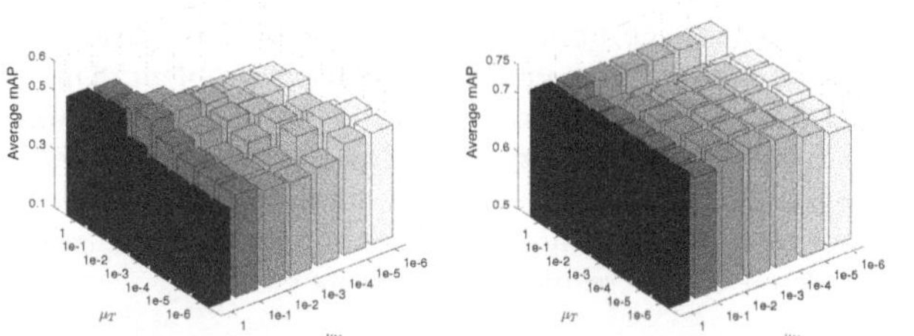

(a) On Wiki (b) On MIRFlickr

Figure 1: The average mAP under different settings of the parameters μ_V and μ_T.

Table 2: Overall comparison of mAP values on the three datasets. The top panel is the performance for Img2Text task and the bottom panel is for Text2Img task.

Method	Wiki				MIRFlickr				NUS-WIDE			
	16 bits	32 bits	64 bits	128 bits	16 bits	32 bits	64 bits	128 bits	16 bits	32 bits	64 bits	128 bits
CMSSH [2]	0.1976	0.1999	0.1889	0.1907	0.5520	0.5539	0.5506	0.5559	0.4686	0.4768	0.4741	0.4637
IMH [7]	0.1869	0.1938	0.1873	0.1834	0.6088	0.6063	0.5977	0.5857	0.4543	0.4469	0.4371	0.4285
LSSH [15]	0.2141	0.2216	0.2218	0.2211	0.5784	0.5804	0.5797	0.5816	0.3900	0.3924	0.3962	0.3966
CMFH [3]	0.2403	0.2474	0.2533	0.2572	0.6273	0.6343	0.6410	0.6451	0.5150	0.5208	0.5256	0.5285
CRH [14]	0.2031	0.1966	0.1982	0.1943	0.5826	0.5745	0.5726	0.5718	0.5136	0.5079	0.4996	0.5013
SCM_{Seq} [12]	0.2210	0.2337	0.2442	0.2596	0.6237	0.6343	0.6448	0.6489	0.4842	0.4941	0.4947	0.4965
$SePH_{km}$ [4]	0.2787	0.2956	0.3064	0.3134	**0.6723**	0.6771	0.6783	0.6817	**0.5421**	0.5499	0.5537	0.5601
Proposed	**0.3253**	**0.3340**	**0.3443**	**0.3558**	0.6687	**0.6911**	**0.7015**	**0.6992**	0.5292	**0.5595**	**0.5622**	**0.5643**
CMSSH [2]	0.2495	0.2360	0.2348	0.2382	0.6010	0.6048	0.6029	0.6041	0.4635	0.4685	0.4594	0.4556
IMH [7]	0.3731	0.3967	0.3720	0.3519	0.5996	0.5999	0.5914	0.5824	0.4546	0.4497	0.4415	0.4304
LSSH [15]	0.5031	0.5224	0.5293	0.5346	0.5898	0.5927	0.5932	0.5932	0.4286	0.4248	0.4248	0.4175
CMFH [3]	0.5705	0.5909	0.6022	0.6110	0.6095	0.6134	0.6184	0.6199	0.5952	0.6133	0.6282	0.6283
CRH [14]	0.2634	0.2622	0.2631	0.2625	0.5944	0.5913	0.5838	0.5811	0.5273	0.5114	0.5033	0.4977
SCM_{Seq} [12]	0.2134	0.2366	0.2479	0.2573	0.6133	0.6209	0.6295	0.6340	0.4536	0.4620	0.4630	0.4644
$SePH_{km}$ [4]	0.6318	0.6577	0.6646	0.6709	0.7197	0.7271	0.7309	0.7354	0.6302	0.6425	0.6506	0.6580
Proposed	**0.7014**	**0.7002**	**0.7165**	**0.7231**	**0.7542**	**0.7753**	**0.7968**	**0.7991**	**0.6555**	**0.6742**	**0.6773**	**0.6796**

3.3 Overall Comparison with Baselines

For the proposed two methods and all baselines, we report their cross-modal retrieval performance on the three dataset in Table 2 with code length ranging from 16-bit to 128-bit. Note that since we use the same experimental settings as in $SePH_{km}$ [4], here we refer to the experimental results of LSSH, SCM_{Seq} and $SePH_{km}$ in [4]. From Table 2, we have the following observations: 1) On all three datasets, in most cases the proposed method significantly outperforms all baselines with different hash code length on different retrieval tasks and achieves the state-of-the-art performance, which well demonstrates its effectiveness. The superiority of the proposed method can be attributed to its advantaged hashing framework that integrates unified hash code generation and classifier training. The generated hash codes well incorporate the correlation between different modalities and preserve the discrimination of the class label information; 2) Generally, the mAP scores of the proposed method consistently increase when the code length becomes longer. It also indicates that they can encode more discriminative information and better preserve the semantic relations between different modalities by utilizing longer hash codes.

4. CONCLUSION

In this paper, we proposed a novel supervised hashing method for cross-modal retrieval. The proposed method was formulated in a linear classification framework, where the supervised label information was naturally leveraged to preserve the discrimination during the unified binary code learning process. In this framework, the modality-specific hash functions, the unified binary codes and a linear classifier were learned in a joint optimization problem. Due to the intractability of the optimization problem in the proposed method, we proposed an efficient approximate algorithm to obtain the quasi-optimal solution. The proposed method was validated on three benchmark datasets, where the state-of-the-art results validated its efficacy.

Acknowledgements

This work was supported in part by the National Natural Science Foundation of China under Project 61502081 and Project 61572108, and the Fundamental Research Funds for the Central Universities under Project ZYGX2014Z007.

5. REFERENCES

[1] L. Ballan, T. Uricchio, L. Seidenari, and A. Del Bimbo. A cross-media model for automatic image annotation. In *ACM International Conference on Multimedia Retrieval*, 2014.

[2] M. Bronstein, A. Bronstein, F. Michel, and N. Paragios. Data fusion through cross-modality metric learning using similarity-sensitive hashing. In *IEEE Conference on Computer Vision and Pattern Recognition*, pages 3594–3601, 2010.

[3] G. Ding, Y. Guo, and J. Zhou. Collective matrix factorization hashing for multimodal data. In *IEEE Conference on Computer Vision and Pattern Recognition*, 2014.

[4] Z. Lin, G. , M. Hu, and J. Wang. Semantics-preserving hashing for cross-view retrieval. In *IEEE Conference on Computer Vision and Pattern Recognition*, 2015.

[5] F. Shen, C. Shen, W. Liu, and H. T. Shen. Supervised Discrete Hashing. In *IEEE Conference on Computer Vision and Pattern Recognition*, 2015.

[6] F. Shen, C. Shen, Q. Shi, A. Van Den Hengel, and Z. Tang. Inductive hashing on manifolds. In *IEEE Conference on Computer Vision and Pattern Recognition*, 2013.

[7] J. Song, Y. Yang, Y. Yang, Z. Huang, and H. T. Shen. Inter-media hashing for large-scale retrieval from heterogeneous data sources. In *Proceedings of the 2013 ACM SIGMOD International Conference on Management of Data*, pages 785–796, 2013.

[8] J. Wang, S. Kumar, and S.-F. Chang. Semi-supervised hashing for scalable image retrieval. In *IEEE Conference on Computer Vision and Pattern Recognition*, pages 3424–3431, 2010.

[9] X. Xu, Y. Yang, A. Shimada, R.-i. Taniguchi, and L. He. Semi-supervised coupled dictionary learning for cross-modal retrieval in internet images and texts. In *Proceedings of the 23rd ACM International Conference on Multimedia*, pages 847–850, 2015.

[10] Y. Yang, Z.-J. Zha, Y. Gao, X. Zhu, and T.-S. Chua. Exploiting web images for semantic video indexing via robust sample-specific loss. *IEEE Transation on Multimedia*, 16:1677–1689, 2014.

[11] Y. Yang, H. Zhang, M. Zhang, F. Shen, and X. Li. Visual coding in a semantic hierarchy. In *Proceedings of the 23rd ACM International Conference on Multimedia*, pages 59–68, 2015.

[12] D. Zhang and W.-J. Li. Large-scale supervised multimodal hashing with semantic correlation maximization. In *AAAI Conference on Artificial Intelligence*, 2014.

[13] D. Zhang, F. Wang, and L. Si. Composite hashing with multiple information sources. In *Proceedings of the 34th International ACM SIGIR Conference on Research and Development in Information Retrieval (SIGIR)*, SIGIR '11, pages 225–234, 2011.

[14] Y. Zhen and D.-Y. Yeung. Co-regularized hashing for multimodal data. In *Advances in neural information processing systems*, pages 1385–1393, 2012.

[15] J. Zhou. Latent Semantic Sparse Hashing for Cross-Modal Similarity Search. *Proceedings of the 37th International ACM SIGIR Conference on Research & Development in Information Retrieval*, pages 415–424, 2014.

CNN-based Style Vector for Style Image Retrieval

Shin Matsuo Keiji Yanai
Department of Informatics,
The University of Electro-Communications
Chofu, Tokyo 182-8585 JAPAN
{matsuo-s,yanai}@mm.inf.uec.ac.jp

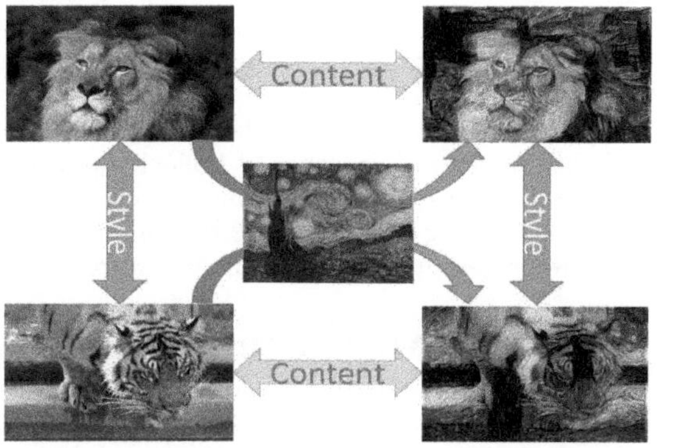

Figure 1: (Left) Original (content) images, (center) Style image, (right) Images synthesized by style transfer method.

ABSTRACT

In this paper, we have examined the effectiveness of "style matrix" which is used in the works on style transfer and texture synthesis by Gatys et al. [2, 3] in the context of image retrieval as image features. A style matrix is presented by Gram matrix of the feature maps in a deep convolutional neural network. We proposed a style vector which are generated from a style matrix with PCA dimension reduction. In the experiments, we evaluate image retrieval performance using artistic images downloaded from Wikiarts.org regarding both artistic styles ans artists. We have obtained 40.64% and 70.40% average precision for style search and artist search, respectively, both of which outperformed the results by common CNN features. In addition, we found PCA-compression boosted the performance.

1. INTRODUCTION

Figure 1 shows a lion image, a tiger image and the images the styles of which are modified using the style of Gogh's Starry Night by the style transfer method proposed by Gatys et al. [2]. In this figure, the images in the right and the left have common contents, while the image in the top and the bottom have common styles. When we classify them in terms of object categories, the images in the top are classified as "lion", and the images in the bottom are classified as "tiger". However, we sometimes classify images in terms of their styles. In such case, the images in the left are classified as "photo", while the images in the right are classified as "drawing".

Classifying images in terms of their styles is expected to help various kinds of applications such as style analysis of images/videos, and style-based image search. However, in the computer vision community, recognition of image contents is paid much more attention to than styles. After Deep Convolutional Neural Network (DCNN) [6] won ImageNet Large Scale Visual Recognition Challenge (ILSVRC) in 2012, image recognition employing CNN becomes very common to achieve high performance. Although the performance of CNN for 1000-class object category classification have already outperformed human [4], style classification has not been explored extensively except [5]. In object classification where classifying object categories regardless of image styles is important, CNN is regarded as the best architecture at present, while it is not confirmed if CNN is the best in style recognition of images where classifying styles regardless of contents is needed.

In 2014, Karayev et al. [5] proposed the method on image style recognition employing CNN-based image features and showed CNN features outperformed the conventional features such as color histogram and GIST with a large margin. However, the classification rates on style classification are not as high as the rates on object categorization. Therefore, style recognition is regarded as more challenging task than object classification.

Recently, Gatys et al. proposed an algorithm on artistic style transfer [2] which synthesis an image which has the style of a given style image and the contents of a given content image. This method replaces the information which are degraded while the signal of the content image goes forward through CNN layers with style information extracted the style image, and reconstructs a new image which has the same content as a given content images and the same style as a given style image as shown in Figure 1. In this method, they introduced "style matrix" which was presented by Gram matrix of the feature maps, that is, correlation matrix between feature maps in a deep convolutional neural network (DCNN). Originally, a style matrix was introduced in texture synthesis with DCNN by the same authors [3].

Then, in this paper, we introduce style vectors which is transformed from style matrix, and examine its effectiveness when using it as image features for image retrieval. By the experiments, we confirmed style matrix is more effective

ICMR'16, June 06-09, 2016, New York, NY, USA

DOI: http://dx.doi.org/10.1145/2911996.2912057

than common CNN activation features in image retrieval tasks. In addition, we found PCA-compression boosted the performance.

2. RELATED WORKS

Although the number of works on image style analysis is not so large, several works have been published so far. Most of them are related to aesthetic analysis of images.

Datta et al. estimates aesthetic rating of images employing various visual features such as color saturation and hue, exposure of light and colorfulness, and wavelet-based texture co-efficients. Marchesotti et al. [7] also proposed a method to evaluate aesthetic rating using Aesthetic Visual Analysis (AVA) dataset [8].

Keren [1] proposed a method to classify artistic styles and achieved classification of drawings of Pollock and Dali using local features. As a recent work, Karayev et al. [5] classified style images using CNN activation features, and showed CNN feature outperformed conventional features greatly.

3. PROPOSED METHOD: STYLE VECTOR

Style matrix is used as an representation of image style in the work on style transfer by Gatys et al. [2], which is computed as Gram matrix of feature maps in the specific layer of CNN. In their method, the style of a given style image is transferred into a synthesized image by minimizing the Euclidean loss between the style matrix of both images with back propagation. Because style matrix contains style information of an image, we propose to use style vectors which is transformed from style matrix as image representation of image retrieval.

Style matrix G is a set of correlation values between feature maps in the specific layer l. Style matrix $G^l \in R^{M_l \times M_l}$ is represented as

$$G^l = F^l(F^l)^T \tag{1}$$

where $F^l \in R^{M_l \times N_l}$ is a feature map in the layer l.

In this paper, we transform a style matrix in each layer into a feature vector. Because a style matrix is a symmetrical matrix, the number of independent elements are $(M_l)(M_l+1)/2$ where M_l is the number of the feature maps in the layer l. We define a style vector V^l as follows:

$$V^l = [{G^l}_{1,1}, {G^l}_{2,1}, ..., {G^l}_{M_l,1}, {G^l}_{M_l,2}, ..., {G^l}_{M_l,M_l}] \tag{2}$$

We L2-normalize V^l without/with signed square root before using a raw style vector as a feature vector. We represent L2-normalized of V^l without/with signed square root as $S^{l_{L2}}$ and $S^{l_{sgnsqrt}}$, respectively. They are calculated as follows:

$$S^{l_{L2}} = \frac{V^l}{\|V^l\|} \tag{3}$$

$$S^{l_{sgnsqrt}} = \frac{\mathrm{sgn}(V^l)\sqrt{|V^l|}}{\|\mathrm{sgn}(V^l)\sqrt{|V^l|}\|} \tag{4}$$

4. EXPERIMENTS

For experiments, we prepared an artistic pictorial image dataset which contains metadata on image style and artists by gathering them from Wikiart.org, and classified them with style vectors extracted from five intermediate layers (conv1_1, conv2_1, conv3_1, conv4_1, and conv5_1) of the VGG-16 network [9]. In addition, we also examined the combined style vectors of all the five layers as well. Finally, we compared performance with Karayev et al. [5] using the same dataset.

Figure 2: Images in "Style Dataset".

Figure 3: Images in "Artist Dataset".

4.1 Dataset

We created two kinds of datasets by gathering images from Wikiart.org which was used as the data source in the work by Karayev et al. [5]. The first one is "Style dataset", and the other is "Artist dataset".

"Style dataset" contains 100 images of each of 25 style categories which are officially defined in Wikiart.org. That is, it contains 2500 images in total. We selected 25 style categories each of which contains more than 100 images among all the style categories in Wikiart.org. Figure 2 shows some examples in "Style dataset".

"Artist dataset" contains 1000 images of the top 10 artists regarding the number of images in Wikiart.org. We prepared this dataset for examining if the style vector is effective for classifying artist drawing styles. Figure 3 shows some examples in "Artist dataset".

4.2 Evaluation of Style Vector

To search for an image which has similar style to a given query images, we use nearest neighbor search with respect to the style vector. In the experiments, to evaluate the effectiveness of a style vector for image style search, we examine if the nearest image to a query image belongs to the same style as the given query image. This is equivalent to nearest neighbor classification. In section 4.5, we used SVM as a classifier as well for comparison to the existing work.

4.3 Style Estimation for Two Datasets

We made experiments with two datasets by 5-fold classification with the nearest neighbor classifier. As a metric, we used standard Euclidean distance.

The convolutional neural network (CNN) we used in the experiments was 16-layered very deep convolutional neural network, VGG-16 [9], pre-trained with the ILSVRC-2012 1000-class dataset. We extracted style vectors from the layer conv1_1, conv2_1, conv3_1, conv4_1 and conv5_1. We used them as single features and concatenation of them as combined features. In addition, we extracted fc6 and fc7 from VGG-16, and fc6 from the standard Alexnet [6]. We use them as visual features with raw, L2-normalization and L2-normalization signed square root. Table 1 shows the results for Style and Artist dataset.

The style vector which was the most effective for both Style dataset and Artist dataset was the one extracted from conv5_1 with signed square root and L2 normalization. Therefore, this experimental result revealed that style vectors outperformed conventional CNN features regarding style-based image search. Especially, signed square root and L2 normalization of style vectors is significant to obtain the best performance. Note that in the rest part we use signed square root L2 normalization for all the style vectors.

Table 2 shows average precision on each category in Style dataset. The categories in which style vectors outperform CNN features were "Art Nouveau", "Modern", "High Renaissance", "Post-Impressionism", and "Symbolism". Among them, the accuracy of "Nouveau Modern" was the highest, which outperformed CNN features by 0.13. This is because the images of "Art Nouveau Modern" tends to expose very unique style but to have common scenes and objects as motifs. For example, as shown in Figure 4 which depicts two person with unique patterns, CNN features capture persons, while style vectors are expected to represent patterns.

Conversely, the categories where CNN features is better than style vectors were "Color Field Painting", "Mannerism Late Renaissance", and "Minimalism". Especially, the accuracy of "Color Field Painting" were better than style vectors by 0.2. Figure 5 shows a sample of "Color Field Painting" the nearest neighbor of which was an image of "Abstract Art" in case of style vectors. This is because style vectors reflect local patterns rather than whole image structures.

Style_all which is an aggregation of the style vectors extracted from five layers tends to be inferior to Style_conv5_1. Exceptionally, in "Ukiyo-e" it achieved the best performance among all the features. This is because "Ukiyo-e" includes various scales of unique patterns.

Regarding the results for "Artist dataset', in the categories of "Chagall", "Konchalovsky", and "Gogh", style vectors clearly outperformed CNN features as shown in Figure 6. In their drawings, common motifs were drawn with unique pattern and touch. This is the similar tendency to Style dataset. Although "Picasso" also have unique style, the performance was almost the same in case of style vector and CNN features. Since "Pissaro" and "Monet" are similar to each other in terms of their motifs and styles, they tended to be confused with each other using any of style vectors or CNN features. The images in the category of "Piranesi" was correctly classified using any features we used in the experiments.

4.4 Dimensionality reduction with PCA

Although the most effective style vector was S^{conv5_1} in the previous experiment, its dimension was very high, $131,328$ ($= 512 \times (512+1)/2$), which is 32 times as many as the dimension of CNN features, 4096. To resolve high dimensionality, we applied PCA to style vectors for dimension reduction. With PCA compression, we obtained 128-d, 256-d, 512-d, 1024-d, 2048-d, and 4096-d style vectors, and made the same experiments as the previous ones. Table 3 shows the results for both Style Dataset and Artist Database.

For Style dataset, 2048-d style vectors achieved the best performance, while 4096-d vectors was the best for Artist dataset. Surprisingly, both the results exceeded the results with raw style vectors with large margin by 3.44 and 5.1, respectively. From these results, PCA is helpful not only for dimension reduction but also boosting of the classification performance.

Figure 4: Similar images to a sample of "Art Nouveau Modern" by a style vector and a CNN feature.

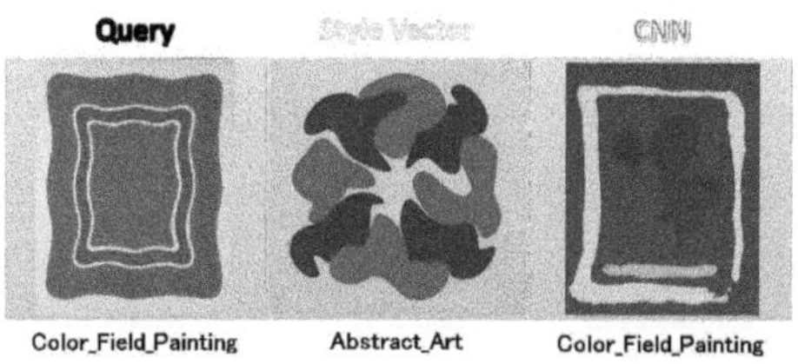

Figure 5: Similar images to a sample of "Color Field Painting" by a style vector and a CNN feature.

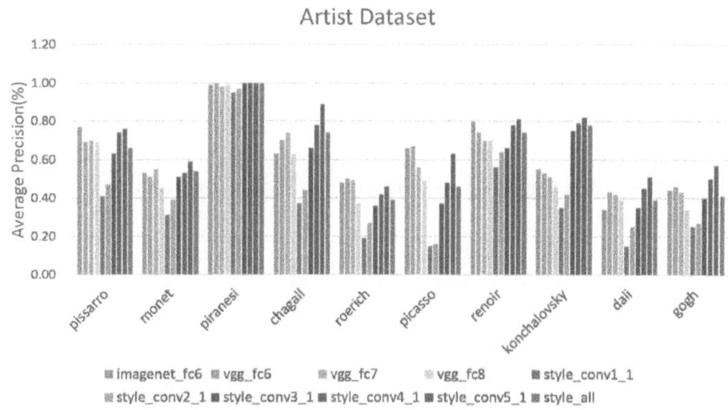

Figure 6: All per-category APs on "Artist dataset".

4.5 Comparison with the previous work

We made experiments with the same image data as Karayev et al. [5] for comparison. We used PCA-compressed Style_conv5_5 (1024d, 2048d and 4096d) as style vectors and fc6 and fc7 as CNN features. For style features, we used SVM as a classifier as well as a nearest neighbor classifier. Table 4 shows the results including the results in [5]. As a result, style vectors outperformed [5] greatly, which proved the effectiveness of the style vector.

Table 1: Mean APs on two datasets

		Alex fc6	VGG fc6	VGG fc7	Style_conv1_1	Style_conv2_1	Style_conv3_1	Style_conv4_1	Style_conv5_1	Style_all
Style	raw	36.28	33.68	32.04	15.40	19.20	25.48	31.20	34.08	25.72
	L2norm	39.28	39.44	36.04	17.36	21.36	28.56	34.48	39.60	27.36
	sgnsqrt	38.00	39.36	36.28	20.20	21.16	29.92	35.04	**40.64**	33.08
Artist	raw	61.70	59.3	56.7	34.00	40.90	52.80	60.70	64.70	51.90
	L2norm	61.00	62.9	61.1	32.60	42.80	56.00	63.80	68.80	52.20
	sgnsqrt	61.90	62.3	60.8	36.90	42.80	56.90	64.70	**70.40**	61.10

Table 2: All per-category APs on the Style dataset

	Abstract Art	Abstract Expressionism	Art Informel	Art Nouveau Modern	Baroque	Color Field Painting	Cubism	Early Renaissance	Expressionism	High Renaissance	Impressionism	Magic Realism
imagenet_fc6	0.26	0.47	**0.34**	0.45	0.38	0.73	0.28	0.61	0.26	0.29	0.26	0.37
vgg_fc6	0.33	0.54	0.33	0.45	0.43	0.73	0.28	**0.66**	0.24	0.22	0.27	0.41
vgg_fc7	**0.36**	0.50	0.30	0.42	0.40	**0.77**	0.24	0.65	0.17	0.21	0.25	0.43
style_conv1_1	0.05	0.24	0.20	0.42	0.26	0.33	0.12	0.32	0.13	0.21	0.13	0.27
style_conv2_1	0.08	0.22	0.17	0.38	0.24	0.40	0.20	0.34	0.17	0.15	0.13	0.24
style_conv3_1	0.17	0.32	0.27	0.46	0.32	0.52	0.23	0.48	0.22	0.19	0.29	0.34
style_conv4_1	0.21	0.38	0.31	0.52	0.45	0.55	0.24	0.53	0.22	0.23	**0.33**	0.41
style_conv5_1	0.31	**0.46**	0.30	**0.58**	**0.49**	0.61	**0.35**	0.65	**0.27**	**0.36**	0.26	**0.47**
style_all	0.21	0.36	0.30	0.50	0.39	0.55	0.28	0.53	0.21	0.19	0.29	0.37

Mannerism Late Renaissance	Minimalism	Naive Art Primitivism	Neoclassicism	Northern Renaissance	Pop Art	Post Impressionism	Realism	Rococo	Romanticism	Surrealism	Symbolism	Ukiyo-e
0.42	0.50	0.38	**0.60**	**0.44**	0.23	0.26	0.19	0.42	**0.27**	0.20	0.19	0.70
0.55	0.55	0.34	0.52	0.31	0.29	0.28	**0.27**	**0.45**	0.24	**0.21**	0.21	0.73
0.53	**0.56**	0.30	0.41	0.30	0.24	0.23	**0.27**	0.37	0.23	0.16	0.22	0.55
0.20	0.27	0.15	0.28	0.23	0.12	0.17	0.13	0.16	0.09	0.06	0.10	0.41
0.19	0.33	0.18	0.30	0.28	0.16	0.18	0.09	0.15	0.12	0.04	0.11	0.44
0.32	0.38	0.33	0.43	0.31	0.20	0.18	0.18	0.29	0.14	0.10	0.12	0.69
0.44	0.36	0.31	0.54	0.34	0.32	0.31	0.14	0.35	0.24	0.11	0.18	0.74
0.45	0.47	**0.42**	0.59	0.41	**0.33**	**0.35**	0.21	0.42	0.25	0.16	**0.29**	0.70
0.39	0.38	0.37	0.51	0.32	0.26	0.26	0.15	0.28	0.15	0.11	0.15	**0.76**

Table 3: APs and features' dimension on each dataset.

		128	256	512	1024	2048	4096	original
Style	conv1_1	23.52	24.24	24.68	24.80	24.92	19.20	20.20
	conv2_1	27.80	28.48	29.16	29.60	29.88	30.12	21.16
	conv3_1	33.60	34.28	35.28	35.80	36.32	36.80	29.92
	conv4_1	38.52	39.28	40.36	41.32	41.32	40.88	35.04
	conv5_1	41.92	43.20	43.08	43.24	**44.08**	43.36	40.64
Artist	conv1_1	44.1	44.7	44.8	45.0	45.2	36.8	36.9
	conv2_1	50.8	52.6	53.6	54.2	54.1	54.0	42.8
	conv3_1	62.8	65.1	65.7	66.1	66.0	65.2	56.9
	conv4_1	71.6	71.8	73.3	73.1	73.9	73.5	64.7
	conv5_1	72.4	74.2	75.0	75.0	74.5	**75.5**	70.4

Table 4: Comparison with previous work.

[5]	style_1024	style_2048	style_4096	fc6	fc7
47.30	53.98	**54.27**	**54.27**	45.72	41.35
SVM ⇒	54.94	56.26	**57.00**	—	—

5. CONCLUSIONS

In this paper, we have proposed style vectors which is based on style matrices used in neural style transfer by Gatys et al. [2], and have proved that style vectors is more effective than DCNN features for style classification using the same dataset as Karayev et al. [5] as well as two datasets gathered from Wikiart.org. Especially, they were so effective for the images which depict common object and scenes with unique styles or touches. In addition, it was shown that the performance was boosted by using PCA dimension reduction to several thousand dimension. In comparison with Karayev et al. [5], we achieved about 9.7 point improvements using a 4096-d PCA-compressed style vector.

Since image style is different from image content, style vectors which are effective as style representation of images can be applied for many tasks such as style image search and image style analysis. We believe the results of our work is significant and helpful.

We have several future works: (1) we will apply style vectors for other domains than artistic drawings, and (2) we need to improve processing time to extract style vectors. Regarding extraction speed, we expect it can be reduced much with efficient GPU implementation. Once extracting style vectors and applying PCA dimension reduction, style vectors can be used in the same way as common visual features.

Acknowledgement: This work was supported by JSPS KAKENHI Grant Number 15H05915 (Grant-in-Aid for Scientific Research on Innovative Areas "Innovative SHITSUKSAN Science and Technology").

6. REFERENCES

[1] K. D. Painter identification using local features and naive bayes. In *Proc. of IAPR International Conference on Pattern Recognition*, 2002.

[2] L. A. Gatys, A. S. Ecker, and M. Bethge. A neural algorithm of artistic style. In *arXiv:1508.06576*, 2015.

[3] L. A. Gatys, A. S. Ecker, and M. Bethge. Texture synthesis and the controlled generation of natural stimuli using convolutional neural networks. In *Advances in Neural Information Processing Systems*, 2015.

[4] K. He, X. Zhang, S. Ren, and J. Sun. Delving deep into rectifiers: Surpassing human-level performance on imagenet classification. In *Proc. of IEEE International Conference on Computer Vision*, 2015.

[5] S. Karayev, M. Trentacoste, H. Han, A. Agarwala, A. Darrell, T. Hertzmann, and H. Winnemoeller. Recognizing image style. In *Proc. of British Machine Vision Conference*, 2014.

[6] A. Krizhevsky, I. Sutskever, and G. E. Hinton. Imagenet classification with deep convolutional neural networks. In *Advances in Neural Information Processing Systems*, 2012.

[7] L. Marchesotti and F. Perronnin. Learning beautiful (and ugly) attributes. In *Proc. of British Machine Vision Conference*, 2013.

[8] N. Murray, D. Barcelona, L. Marchesotti, and F. Perronnin. Ava: A large-scale database for aesthetic visual analysis. In *Proc. of IEEE Computer Vision and Pattern Recognition*, 2012.

[9] K. Simonyan and A. Zisserman. Very deep convolutional networks for large-scale image recognition. In *Proc. of International Conference on Learning Representation*, 2015.

MVC: A Dataset for View-Invariant Clothing Retrieval and Attribute Prediction

Kuan-Hsien Liu
Academia Sinica
128, Sec. 2, Academia Rd.
Taipei, Taiwan
liukh@iis.sinica.edu.tw

Ting-Yen Chen
Academia Sinica
128, Sec. 2, Academia Rd.
Taipei, Taiwan
timh20022002
@iis.sinica.edu.tw

Chu-Song Chen
Academia Sinica
128, Sec. 2, Academia Rd.
Taipei, Taiwan
song@iis.sinica.edu.tw

ABSTRACT

Clothing retrieval and clothing style recognition are important and practical problems. They have drawn a lot of attention in recent years. However, the clothing photos collected in existing datasets are mostly of front- or near-front view. There are no datasets designed to study the influences of different viewing angles on clothing retrieval performance. To address view-invariant clothing retrieval problem properly, we construct a challenge clothing dataset, called Multi-View Clothing dataset. This dataset not only has four different views for each clothing item, but also provides 264 attributes for describing clothing appearance. We adopt a state-of-the-art deep learning method to present baseline results for the attribute prediction and clothing retrieval performance. We also evaluate the method on a more difficult setting, cross-view exact clothing item retrieval. Our dataset will be made publicly available for further studies towards view-invariant clothing retrieval.

CCS Concepts

•Information systems → Retrieval models and ranking;

Keywords

Clothing retrieval; multi-view clothing; view-invariant clothing retrieval; cross-view clothing retrieval

1. INTRODUCTION

View invariant object recognition and cross-view object retrieval are important topics in computer vision and content-based image search. However, due to the lack of large-scale datasets, progress toward this direction is still limited. In this paper, we tackle the problem in the clothing retrieval domain. We introduce a dataset containing multi-view clothing images for each item collected in the dataset. This dataset, termed as the Multi-View Clothing (MVC), is organized with a regular setting and abounding attributes. Each item contains four views in the MVC dataset, and the attributes are arranged in a coarse-to-fine hierarchy such as *Women -> Shirts & Tops -> T Shirts -> Colors/Patterns.* With these attributes, one can verify the performance of a multi-view retrieval algorithm, finding the key attributes appropriate for view-invariant recognition, or facilitating the attribute search of clothing images in arbitrary views.

Figure 1: Some sample multiview clothing images from MVC dataset.

Compared to the existing datasets, MVC has a unique feature as it provides multiple views for a clothing item as shown in Figure 1. Besides, the amount of annotated images (161,260) is also large. Most publicly available datasets (eg., Clothing Attribute dataset[2], Colorful-Fashion dataset[12]) have only thousands of images. Apparel Style dataset [1] has more ($> 80,000$), but the image resolution is low. The MVC dataset that contains more images and a well-annotated hierarchy of attributes could be more suitable for learning fundamental feature representations for clothing retrieval.

We evaluate the performance of a recent successful deep CNN model, VGG [19], on the proposed MVC dataset with two different criteria. The first is attributed-based, where the cross-view image retrieval is considered having higher precision score if more attributes are matched. The second is item-based, which deals with a more difficult setting that the retrieval is treated correct if exactly the same item is found. The experimental results serve as baseline performance for further study and comparison.

This paper is organized as follows. In Section 2, we review the related work. In Section 3, the construction of the Multi-View Clothing (MVC) Dataset is introduced. We conduct experiments and provide discussion in Section 4. Finally, the concluding remarks are given in Section 5.

2. RELATED WORK

We first give a brief review on clothing retrieval/recognition approaches. Then, we review publicly available datasets for clothing retrieval and related research.

ICMR'16, June 06-09, 2016, New York, NY, USA
© 2016 ACM. ISBN 978-1-4503-4359-6/16/06. . . $15.00
DOI: http://dx.doi.org/10.1145/2911996.2912058

2.1 Clothing Retrieval

Clothing related studies can be roughly divided into the following categories: clothing modeling [3, 16], segmentation [7, 20], recognition [21], recommendation [13], people describing [4], classification [1], and retrieval [9, 2, 14, 6, 12]. They are summarized according to the feature types employed as follows.

Formula-Based: One of the formula-based studies is proposed by Chen *et al.* [3], where a context-based And-Or graph is introduced to deal with the wide variability of clothes configurations. Hasan *et al.* [7] built a prior shape model by a Markov Random Field (MRF) formulation for clothing segmentation.

Traditional Features Learning: These methods usually use hand-craft features combined with machine learning methods. Wang *et al.* [20] use clothing shapes to build a Bayesian model to segment clothes. Another similar work [21] adopts gender, age, skin, color and texture to train a linear SVM for clothing recognition. Recently, Chen *et al.* [2] use low-level features such as HOG [5] and SIFT [15] to learn attribute classifiers. Liu *et al.* [14] extract HOG, LBP [17], color moment, color histogram, and skin descriptor features from human parts with a nearest neighbor search to solve a cross-scenario clothing retrieval problem. Di *et al.* [6] also use 5 different low-level features to learn linear SVMs for clothing style recognition and retrieval.

Deep Features Learning: In past years, some deep learning based approaches have been introduced to deal with clothing retrieval. Chen *et al.* [4] built an Online Shopping dataset containing 341,021 images for the problem of describing people based on fine-grained clothing attributes. They designed a double-path deep convolutional neural network for the problem. Lin *et al.* [11] use the AlexNet [10] with an additional latent layer to learn effective hash bits, and perform a hierarchical deep search on a large dataset containing 161,234 images for clothing retrieval.

Although the above two datasets are large, they are not publicly available and thus the results cannot be further refined or compared by others. In following section, we review some publicly available datasets.

2.2 Datasets Publicly Available

Most datasets focus on the problem of clothing category or attribute classification and clothing retrieval.

Clothing Attribute dataset [2] constructed by Chen *et al.* [2] is designed for the attribute classification. This dataset contains only 1,856 images and 26 attributes in total. The image size for most clothes is around 260×400 to 500×750 pixels, where the resolution is somewhat insufficient for analyzing detailed information.

Colorful-Fashion dataset [12] is a good source for fashion data analysis. It consists of 2,682 images in total, and all the pixels in the images are annotated with color and category labels, where 13 colors and 23 categories are involved. The image resolution of this dataset is 400×600 pixels.

Apparel Style dataset [1] is another publicly available dataset used in two tasks: clothing type classification and attribute detection. For type classification, the authors collected a dataset defining 15 clothing types and consisting of over 80,000 images. For atribute detection, another dataset with 25,002 images is constructed with 78 attributes. The image resolution for most clothes is lower than 200×300 pixels. Although the size of this dataset is much larger than previous two datasets, its resolution is the lowest. We summarized some information of these three dataset in Table 1.

Table 1: Comparison of clothing datasets

Datasets	images	attributes	resolution
Clothing Attribute [2]	1,856	26	$\leq 500 \times 750$
Apparel Style [1]	25,002	78	$\leq 200 \times 300$
Colorful-Fashion [12]	2,682	36	400×600
MVC [ours]	161,638	264	1920×2240

In this paper, we introduce a dataset having more images and attributes of a higher resolution, and it supports view-invariant retrieval that is overlooked by previous studies.

3. MULTI-VIEW CLOTHING DATASET

In this section, we introduce the MVC dataset, which is made publicly available[1]. Existing clothing datasets do not take different viewing directions of clothes into account; they often have front views only, which are unsuitable for evaluating cross-view clothing classification and retrieval tasks. We introduce a new dataset containing four viewing angles for each clothing item.

3.1 Data Collection

We collect the MVC dataset by crawling images from several online shopping websites, such as Amazon.com, Zappos.com or Shopbop.com. The challenge in constructing the dataset is to gather complete four different views (front, back, left, and right views) for each clothing item, as there may be only two or three views available for some clothes.

In current stage, the MVC dataset consists of 37,499 items and 161,638 clothing images, where most items have at least four views. Most of the image resolutions are 1920×2240 pixels, which thus offers sufficient details for various clothing related studies such as clothing attribute localization and type classification. Some sample images with four different viewing directions are shown in Figure 1.

3.2 Clothing Attributes and Categories

To measure the clothing retrieval accuracy, we propose to use clothing attributes to establish the relevance between two images. We collect the ground truth attributes from the websites and manually select 264 attributes for similarity evaluation.

These 264 attributes are organized into a three-layer hierarchy. The first layer enforces the gender of clothes, which contains two attributes, Men and Women. There are eight categories for Men's clothes and nine categories for Women's clothes, where most of them overlap, as shown in Figure 2. The third layer contains more detailed attributes. Eg., in the branch "Women->Shirts & Tops", there are type, color, pattern and style attributes. Type includes Blouses, Button Up Shirts, T Shirts and Tank Tops. Color involves blue, brown, green, ... etc. Horizontal stripes, floral print are some attributes belonged to Pattern. Style contains attributes like short-sleeve, round-neckline, long-dress.

The attributes in the first two layers are disjoint, i.e, each image belongs to a single attribute in the first and second layers, respectively. The third layer is non-disjoint, where an image could have multiple attributes in this layer. Combining the three layers forms a multi-label dataset. Some basic statistics of MVC are summarized in Table 1.

[1] http://mvc-datasets.github.io/MVC/

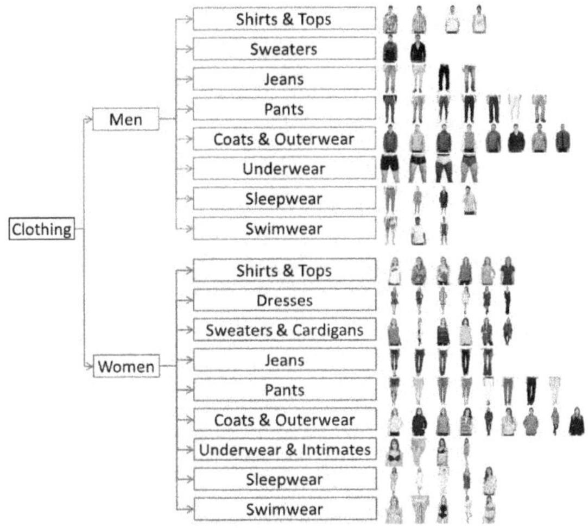

Figure 2: The clothing categories of the first two layers of the MVC dataset with some sample images.

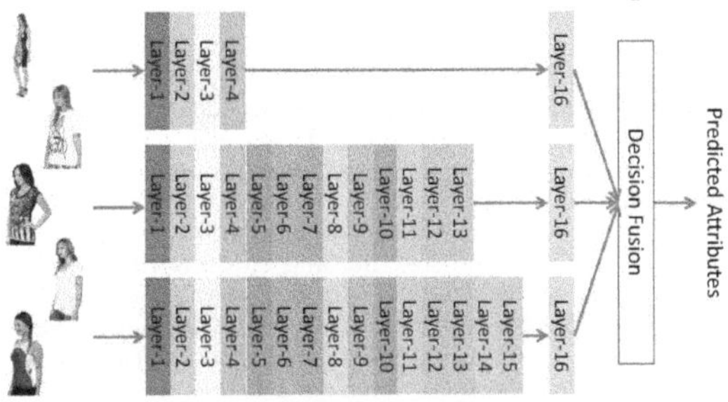

Figure 3: The proposed cross-view clothing retrieval approach. The outputs of three layers of VGG model are late-fused for attribute prediction.

4. EXPERIMENTS

In this section, we first describe our method and experimental settings, and then show experimental results on attribute prediction, clothing retrieval and exact match.

4.1 Method

Considering the recent success of deep learning approaches, we choose a popular deep CNN model, VGG [19], for clothing retrieval. In our experiment, the 16-layer VGG model is selected because it offers similar performance as the 19-layer VGG model but has fewer parameters.

The 16-layer VGG model pre-trained on the ImageNet is fine-tuned on the MVC datasets by Caffe [8] for better fitting the multi-view clothing domain. The soft-max loss function (adopted for single-label classification) in the original VGG model is modified to the sigmoid cross-entropy loss for multi-label training on our problem. The final layer of the VGG model is replaced with 264 outputs.

A deep model consists of multiple feature extractors in different layers. Generally, lower layers extract features preserving local characteristics, and higher layers capture more global features with semantic information. Our approach fuses different layers to predict the clothes attributes. As it is time consuming to evaluate the performance of all layers, we simply choose three layers of VGG-16: 4-th (conv3-128), 13-th (conv3-512), and 15-th layers (FC-4096) in this work. To avoid the high dimensionality of the feature space, we choose not to fuse the extracted features directly, but late-fuse the attributes predicted by the three networks, as shown in Figure 3. The final prediction is then determined by a decision-fusion rule that is introduced below.

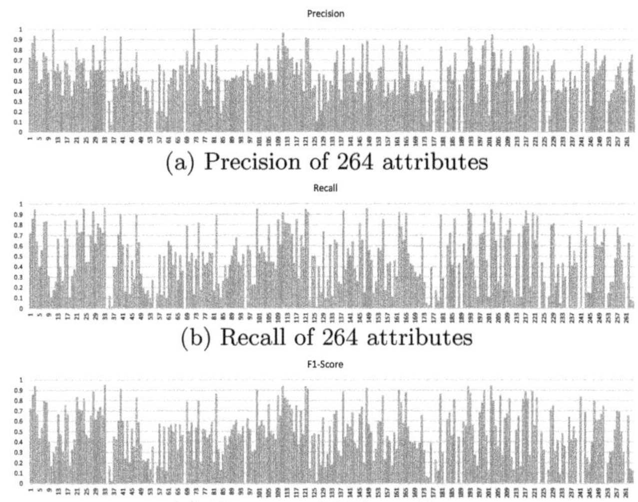

(a) Precision of 264 attributes

(b) Recall of 264 attributes

(c) F_1-score of 264 attributes

Figure 4: The precision, recall, and F_1-score of 264 attributes for the fusion system.

4.2 Experimental setting

We conduct several experiments on MVC dataset with the following setting. First, we randomly select one image for each clothing item to form the training set. We then randomly select another image of a different view-angle from the rest images of each clothing item to built the validation set. Finally, all the remaining images serve as the test set.

The validation set is used in deep CNN training to choose a stopping time on the Caffe package [8]. It is also used for building the decision-fusion rule. First, we get three attribute-prediction results via the three deep networks, respectively, based on the validation set; three F_1-scores are accordingly computed per attribute. Then, for each attribute, the network with the highest F_1-score on the validation set is chosen as the winner for this attribute on the test set. Eg., if attribute 1 has F_1-scores 0.55, 0.68, 0.47 with L4, L13, L15 networks, respectively on the validation set, then the L13 prediction results are chosen for attribute 1 in the test stage.

4.3 Results

Attribute recognition. We use *precision*, *recall*, and F_1-*score* to evaluate the attribute recognition performance. Because each image is predicted as being with/without each of the 264 attribute labels, the prediction accuracy per attribute can be computed by comparing the predicted labels with ground truth labels, as shown in Figure 4.

Among them, 35 attributes are predicted over 80% accuracy (in F_1-score), such as Bras, Snow Pants, Short Sleeves. They can be termed as the clothing attributes easier to recognize; 93 attributes are within the accuracy between 50% and 80%, including V-neck, Fringe, Scalloped, and so on. These attributes are termed with middle-level difficulty. 136 attributes are recognized below the accuracy 50%, such as Ultra Low Rise, Unlined, Wide Leg, referred to as the difficult attributes in MVC dataset. The results may be explained as follows. If the attributes (e.g., Short Sleeves) clearly show their distinction on clothing images for human eyes, they would be recognized better than those (e.g., Unlined) that are uneasy to be examined by human eyes.

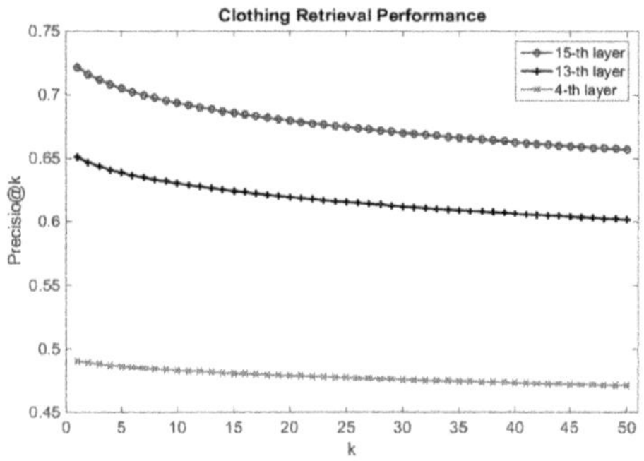

Figure 5: ***precision@k*** **curve of clothing retrieval.**

Table 2: Accuracy for top-1, top-5, top-10 and top-20 exact clothing match

Method	top-1	top-5	top-10	top-20
Layer-4	0.32 %	1.28 %	2.20 %	3.57 %
Layer-13	2.96 %	8.72 %	12.92 %	18.46 %
Layer-15	5.28 %	13.95 %	19.70 %	26.78 %
Fusion	5.31 %	14.01 %	19.74 %	26.81 %

Clothing retrieval. We treat each network's outputs as a feature vector of 264 dimension, and perform retrieval by using Euclidean distance in the feature space. We investigate the impact of different layers of the network in this experiment as well.

The retrieval performance is measured by the multi-attribute precision calculation suggested in [18]. Given a test image t, the retrieval procedure will assign a rank to all images in the dataset (here, the training set). A top-k retrieval precision with respect to a test image t is,

$$Precision(k) = \frac{\sum_{i=1}^{k} R(i)}{N}, \quad (1)$$

where $R(i)$ is the relevance between t and the ith ranked image, and N is a constant making the precision score 1. Details can be found in [18]. Figure 5 shows the retrieval results with different networks. It can be observed that higher layers perform more favorably than lower layers for all k.

These results provide baseline performance for future studies and comparisons on the cross-view clothes retrieval problem introduced in this paper.

Exact match. The exact clothing match considers a retrieval result correct if one of the item in the top-k retrieved images is the same as that of the query image. We list top-1, top-5, top-10 and top-20 exact match results in Table 2. As can be seen, higher layers perform better than lower layers in this setting too, and the fusion system offers the highest matching accuracy. The results also reveal that finding exactly matched clothing item is more difficult than retrieving similar items.

5. CONCLUSIONS

We introduce a new dataset *MVC* with abundant attributes, and investigate a practically challenging problem, view-invariant clothing retrieval/match. *MVC* has 37,499 items and 161,638 clothing images with 264 attributes. We present a modified VGG-16 deep CNN network for multi-labels prediction to evaluate the performance. Our solution serves as a baseline in attribute recognition and cross-view clothing retrieval. In the future, we plan to enrich the dataset regarding *attribute*, *size*, *view* and *application*, and offer more results on the problem.

6. REFERENCES

[1] L. Bossard, M. Dantone, C. Leistner, C. Wengert, T. Quack, and L. Van Gool. Apparel classification with style. In *Computer Vision–ACCV 2012*, pages 321–335. Springer, 2013.

[2] H. Chen, A. Gallagher, and B. Girod. Describing clothing by semantic attributes. In *Computer Vision–ECCV 2012*, pages 609–623. Springer, 2012.

[3] H. Chen, Z. J. Xu, Z. Q. Liu, and S. C. Zhu. Composite templates for cloth modeling and sketching. In *Computer Vision and Pattern Recognition, 2006 IEEE Computer Society Conference on*, volume 1, pages 943–950. IEEE, 2006.

[4] Q. Chen, J. Huang, R. Feris, L. M. Brown, J. Dong, and S. Yan. Deep domain adaptation for describing people based on fine-grained clothing attributes. In *Proceedings of the IEEE Conference on Computer Vision and Pattern Recognition*, pages 5315–5324, 2015.

[5] N. Dalal and B. Triggs. Histograms of oriented gradients for human detection. In *Computer Vision and Pattern Recognition, 2005. CVPR 2005. IEEE Computer Society Conference on*, volume 1, pages 886–893. IEEE, 2005.

[6] W. Di, C. Wah, A. Bhardwaj, R. Piramuthu, and N. Sundaresan. Style finder: Fine-grained clothing style detection and retrieval. In *Computer Vision and Pattern Recognition Workshops (CVPRW), 2013 IEEE Conference on*, pages 8–13. IEEE, 2013.

[7] B. Hasan and D. Hogg. Segmentation using deformable spatial priors with application to clothing. In *BMVC*, pages 1–11, 2010.

[8] Y. Jia, E. Shelhamer, J. Donahue, S. Karayev, J. Long, R. Girshick, S. Guadarrama, and T. Darrell. Caffe: Convolutional architecture for fast feature embedding. *arXiv preprint arXiv:1408.5093*, 2014.

[9] I. King and T. K. Lau. A feature-based image retrieval database for the fashion, textile, and clothing industry in hong kong. In *Proc. of International Symposium Multi-Technology Information Processing*, volume 96, pages 233–240, 1996.

[10] A. Krizhevsky, I. Sutskever, and G. E. Hinton. Imagenet classification with deep convolutional neural networks. In *Advances in neural information processing systems*, pages 1097–1105, 2012.

[11] K. Lin, H.-F. Yang, K.-H. Liu, J.-H. Hsiao, and C.-S. Chen. Rapid clothing retrieval via deep learning of binary codes and hierarchical search. In *Proceedings of the 5th ACM on International Conference on Multimedia Retrieval*, pages 499–502. ACM, 2015.

[12] S. Liu, J. Feng, C. Domokos, H. Xu, J. Huang, Z. Hu, and S. Yan. Fashion parsing with weak color-category labels. *Multimedia, IEEE Transactions on*, 16(1):253–265, 2014.

[13] S. Liu, J. Feng, Z. Song, T. Zhang, H. Lu, C. Xu, and S. Yan. Hi, magic closet, tell me what to wear! In *Proceedings of the 20th ACM international conference on Multimedia*, pages 619–628. ACM, 2012.

[14] S. Liu, Z. Song, G. Liu, C. Xu, H. Lu, and S. Yan. Street-to-shop: Cross-scenario clothing retrieval via parts alignment and auxiliary set. In *Computer Vision and Pattern Recognition (CVPR), 2012 IEEE Conference on*, pages 3330–3337. IEEE, 2012.

[15] D. G. Lowe. Distinctive image features from scale-invariant keypoints. *International journal of computer vision*, 60(2):91–110, 2004.

[16] H. N. Ng and R. L. Grimsdale. Computer graphics techniques for modeling cloth. *Computer Graphics and Applications, IEEE*, 16(5):28–41, 1996.

[17] T. Ojala, M. Pietikäinen, and T. Mäenpää. Multiresolution gray-scale and rotation invariant texture classification with local binary patterns. *Pattern Analysis and Machine Intelligence, IEEE Transactions on*, 24(7):971–987, 2002.

[18] B. Siddiquie, R. S. Feris, and L. S. Davis. Image ranking and retrieval based on multi-attribute queries. In *Computer Vision and Pattern Recognition (CVPR), 2011 IEEE Conference on*, pages 801–808. IEEE, 2011.

[19] K. Simonyan and A. Zisserman. Very deep convolutional networks for large-scale image recognition. *arXiv preprint arXiv:1409.1556*, 2014.

[20] N. Wang and H. Ai. Who blocks who: Simultaneous clothing segmentation for grouping images. In *Computer Vision (ICCV), 2011 IEEE International Conference on*, pages 1535–1542. IEEE, 2011.

[21] M. Yang and K. Yu. Real-time clothing recognition in surveillance videos. In *Image Processing (ICIP), 18th IEEE International Conference on*, pages 2937–2940. IEEE, 2011.

A Quality Adaptive Multimodal Affect Recognition System for User-Centric Multimedia Indexing

Rishabh Gupta * [1,2], Mojtaba Khomami Abadi * [1,3],
Jesús Alejandro Cárdenes Cabré [1], Fabio Morreale [3], Tiago H. Falk [2], Nicu Sebe [3]
[1] Sensaura Inc., Montréal, Canada
[2] INRS-EMT, University of Quebec, Montréal, Canada
[3] Department of Information Engineering and Computer Science, University of Trento, Italy
rishabh.gupta@emt.inrs.ca, khomamiabadi@disi.unitn.it,
jesus.cardenes@sensauratech.com, morreale@disi.unitn.it, falk@emt.inrs.ca,
sebe@disi.unitn.it

ABSTRACT

The recent increase in interest for online multimedia streaming platforms has availed massive amounts of multimedia information that need to be indexed to be searchable and retrievable. User-centric implicit affective indexing employing emotion detection based on psycho-physiological signals, such as electrocardiography (ECG), galvanic skin response (GSR), electroencephalography (EEG) and face tracking, has recently gained attention. However, real world psycho-physiological signals obtained from wearable devices and facial trackers are contaminated by various noise sources that can result in spurious emotion detection. Therefore, in this paper we propose the development of psycho-physiological signal quality estimators for unimodal affect recognition systems. The presented systems perform adequately in classifying users affect however, they resulted in high failure rates due to rejection of bad quality samples. Thus, to reduce the affect recognition failure rate, a quality adaptive multimodal fusion scheme is proposed. The proposed scheme yields no failure, while at the same time classify the users' arousal/valence and liking with significantly above chance weighted F1-scores in a cross-user experiment. Another finding of this study is that head movements encode liking perception of users in response to music snippets. This work also includes the release of the employed dataset including psycho-physiological signals, their quality annotations, and users' affective self-assessments.

Keywords

Affective Computing; Multimedia Indexing; Cross-User; User-Centric; Implicit Affective Tagging; Psycho-Physiological Signals; Signal Quality; Multimodal Interaction; Decision Fusion

*these authors contributed equally to the implementation of this work.

ICMR'16, June 06-09, 2016, New York, NY, USA

DOI: http://dx.doi.org/10.1145/2911996.2912059

1. INTRODUCTION

The burgeoning number of platforms for online multimedia streaming/storage (e.g. YouTube, Netflix) has resulted in generation of a huge database of multimedia content online. In 2015, approximately 400 hours of videos were uploaded every minute on YouTube[1]. This enormous amount of data is not limited to the online realm, the availability of portable devices storing thousands of music tracks and pictures has brought massive amounts of multimedia information in our pockets. However, the huge amount of generated multimedia information needs to be indexed to be searchable and retrievable by the users.

Multimedia retrieval systems that rely on user-generated labels for indexing are potentially biased by subjective judgements and/or intentions[11]. Moreover, manual tagging of multimedia content interrupts the user experience process. Therefore, it is necessary to automate the process of multimedia indexing through implicit tagging. The classical multimedia indexing relies on cognitive indexing procedures which are based on concepts to characterize the multimedia content, such as locations, objects, and events. Whereas, a recent approach, the so-called affective indexing, depends on the emotions generated by the multimedia content [15]. The implicit affective indexing technique is expected to provide more detailed and meaningful information regarding users experience with multimedia [11, 5]. Previously, affective tags have been used for indexing multimedia content for improving information retrieval and recommendation systems [14, 5].

This work presents a multimodal approach on a hard implicit affective-indexing problem. We tackled cross-user and user-centric implicit affective-tagging of (weakly-affective) and short music snippets when the information sources are damaged by various noise artifacts. We achieved significantly above chance results for classification of user perceptions on affective music snippets and we also found that head movements encode *liking* perception in response to music snippets. We made the dataset publicly available for research community so that other researcher can improve our methods.

2. RELATED WORK

Two general approaches of generating affective tags for multimedia content are (i) using the information content of multimedia [3] and (ii) using the human affective perception (via detecting users' emotions) to tag the perceived content (implicit user-centric approach [4]). Certainly a hybrid approach [6, 8] could be success-

[1] www.reelseo.com/hours-minute-uploaded-youtube/

Table 1: **Features used for quality estimation and affect recognition for each modality.**

Modality	Quality Estimation	Affect Recognition
NeuroSky EEG	Statistical measures (such as, mean, median, skewness, kurtosis) for EEG data, power spectral features in ranges (0-1, 0-4, 4-8, 8-12, 12-30, 30-50, 58-62 Hz)	Band powers for δ, θ, α, β and γ bands, statistical measures for cognitive measures provided by NeuroSky
ECG	Statistical measures for heart rate and heart rate variability, power spectral features from ECG for ranges (5-15, 5-40, 0-40, 1-40 Hz) and their ratios	Wavelet based power spectral features over ECG and HRV, statistical measures for the spectral features and Poincare features
GSR	Statistical measures for raw GSR signal, and GSR signal band-passed between ranges (0-0.08, 0.08-0.2, 1-2, 1-2, 10-20, 20-30 Hz)	Power spectral features, rise time, fall time and zero crossing rate for very low frequency (≤ 0.08 Hz) and low frequency ($0.08 - 0.2$ Hz) components of the signal
Face/Head-pose	Features encoding information regarding lips thickness, ratios, such as upper lip to lower lip thickness, eye brows width to lips width	Statistical measures, rise time, drop time and zero crossing rate for head's pitch, yaw and roll

fully utilized. This work follows the second approach in a multi-modal scheme.

Affective computing techniques have been successfully utilized for detection of users' emotions in response to multimedia content [17, 6, 8, 15] by leveraging the information of a plethora of modalities including facial expressions, gestures, body postures, voice, heart activities, electrodermal signals, and brain responses.

Since many of the underlying affective patterns in the above mentioned modalities are highly subjective (i.e. they significantly vary from one user to another), most of the state of the art user-centric emotion recognition studies focus on subject-based emotion recognition when the training and the test data for evaluation of a scheme comes from the same user [6, 8, 15]. However, a scalable implicit affective indexing system should be able to classify human emotions for any *unseen* user. Such framework where the test data is from unseen users is called *cross-user*.

A multimodal system for affect recognition is expected to perform better than a unimodal system, as reported in previous studies [6, 2, 8, 15], which can be attributed to the fusion of complimentary information provided by each modality.

However, the signals from the above mentioned modalities are often contaminated with various sources of noise [13], that significantly hinders the task of affect recognition. Particularly, in real-world biomedical signals, for e.g. signals obtained from wearable devices, the problem of noise contamination is more exaggerated.

This paper presents the first steps towards the validation and development of a user-centric multi-modal quality adaptive affect recognition system for cross-user implicit affective indexing of multimedia content.

3. MATERIALS AND METHODS

3.1 Experimental Setup

We recruited a total of thirty-three participants (with age distribution of 29.7 ± 5.4 years, 21 males) for the study. The participants were asked to listen to music excerpts, originally generated by *Robin* [10], an algorithmic composer that generates western classical-like music with affective connotation in real time. The stimuli are weakly affective being evident from the fact that facial expressions in the dataset are negligible if not absent.

The participants experienced music excerpts using a AKG K512 headphone inside a silent room at the University of Trento, Italy. At the beginning of the experiment, four training excerpts were played to the participants to make the subjects familiar with the task. During the experiment, participants were presented with twenty thirty-two seconds long music excerpts in random order. While experiencing the music excerpts, participants' physiological signals, including electrocardiography (ECG), galvanic skin response (GSR), frontal electroencephalography (EEG), and facial videos were recorded. The ECG and GSR signals were recorded using the Shimmer sensors, whereas for recording EEG, we used a NeuroSky Mindwave headset. Moreover, participants' facial videos were recorded using an A4Tech webcam at a resolution of 640 X 480 pixels and the SDM face alignment method[16] is employed to detect users' head poses and facial landmark tracks. All the recordings are available online via the dataset website[2].

In order to measure valence, arousal and liking, participants were asked to rate them on three seven-point semantic differential scales, from 1 (negative, relaxing or unlike) to 7 (positive, exciting or like). To record the levels of arousal, valence and liking, participants were asked to type in numbers between 1-7 on a keyboard after listening to each excerpt. Moreover, to reduce emotional bias, a sequence of randomly generated notes were played, from a set of five 15 second long pre-recorded snippets, between each music excerpt. The obtained subjective scores showed substantial inter-rater agreement as measured using intra-class correlation (ICC), where ICC for arousal, valence and liking was 0.79, 0.63 and 0.81, respectively.

3.2 Signal Quality Estimator Development

Towards developing a quality adaptive affect recognition system signal quality estimators (SQEs) were developed for each modality. In order to realize the SQEs, first, the quality of the signals was assessed by two expert annotators, forming the ground truth. We employed the Cohen's kappa to measure inter-rater agreement over the annotations of the experts and measures of 0.96, 0.98, 0.94, 0.73 were observed over the quality annotations for EEG, Facial detections, ECG, GSR, respectively. The first three are indicating *almost perfect agreement* (≥ 0.9) and the agreement on GSR quality is *substantial* (≥ 0.7). The marginal disagreement on the GSR quality could be due to two issues: (i) GSR has a slow response so that the structures of GSR signals sometimes are not recognizable over short recordings, and (ii) noise artifacts that are present on the signal sometimes induce patterns that are similar to the structure of GSR responses. In cases of disagreement between the two annotators, the annotation of the second expert is employed. Features listed in Table 1 were extracted, as they encode signal quality information for each modality. Finally, a bagging classifier with decision trees as a base estimator was implemented to differentiate between good/bad quality signals for each modality. The classification performance was validated using a leave-one-subject-out cross-validation i.e., the classifier was trained on samples from all the subjects except the one used for testing. Moreover, the performance of the SQEs was assessed using a weighted F1-score [12], as it accurately measures the classifier performance for a highly imbalanced classification problem.

3.3 Affect Classifier Development

As a next step, features (listed in Table 1, column labeled 'Affect recognition') that encode affect [6], were extracted. The affect en-

[2]mhug.disi.unitn.it/wp-content/QAMAF/QAMAF.html

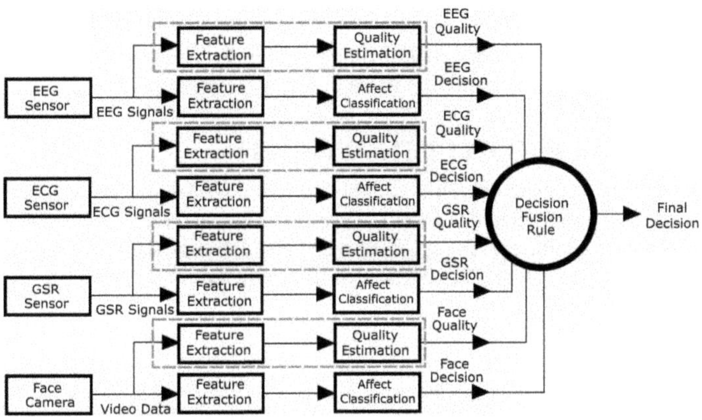

Figure 1: Quality adaptive multimodal decision level fusion schema.

coding features were then employed with linear support vector machine (SVM, C = 1.0) and Naive Bayes (NB) classifiers for three binary classification problems of differentiation between high/low valence, arousal and liking, respectively. For validation of the developed classifiers, a cross-subject classification approach was adopted using a leave-one-subject-out cross-validation [1]. Due to high intra-variability among human signal patterns, cross-subject affect recognition is a *harder*, but more *generalizable*, problem than subject specific affect recognition (as used in [6]). In this study we validated our results using cross-subject cross-validation.

In our proposed quality adaptive affect recognition scheme, during the development of affect binary classifiers, good quality samples form the train data and SQEs are applied to assess the quality of the test samples. The SQEs provided the reliability of the predictions thus, assisting in rejecting the bad quality samples. For accurate measurement of classifier performance for an imbalanced classification problem, we computed weighted F1-scores [12]. The performance of each classifier developed above was tested for significance against random voting using a paired *t-test.*

3.4 Quality Adaptive Multimodal Fusion

The quality adaptive multimodal decision fusion affect recognition system in this study is developed by modifying the decision fusion scheme presented in [9]. In our study, we used a decision fusion classifier for multimodal fusion as depicted in Fig. 1. In decision level fusion, a linear combination of the individual unimodal classifiers' outputs is calculated as the output. The decision fusion can be implemented (i) using an equal weight scheme i.e., all modalities used for affect recognition being given equal weights or (ii) using an optimal weight scheme i.e., the weight for each modality can be optimised given a set of training data [9]. The weights indeed encode the relative importance of the unimodal classifiers in calculation of the final output. The formulation and implementation of the fusion scheme that is employed in this study are described below.

3.4.1 Formulation

For the decision level fusion scheme, the fusion classification probability $p_0^x \in [0,1]$ for each class $x \in \{1,2\}$ can be denoted by

$$p_0^x = \sum_{i=1}^{N} \alpha_i p_i^x q_i t_i \tag{1}$$

where, i is the index of a particular modality used for affect recognition, N is the number of modalities used, α_i are the weights corresponding to each modality ($\sum_{i=1}^{N} \alpha_i = 1$), q_i [3] corresponds

[3] $q_i \in \{1,0\}$: i.e. good or bad according to the output of the SQE binary classification for the ith modality

to the quality of the respective modality and t_i is the normalized training set performance for a particular modality, such that the fusion probabilities for all classes sum up to 1, and is given by

$$t_i = \frac{F_i}{\sum_{i=1}^{N} \alpha_i q_i F_i} \tag{2}$$

where, F_i is the F1-score obtained on the training set using a particular modality and $F_i \in [0,1]$. Then, it can be shown that,

$$p_0^1 + p_0^2 = \sum_{i=1}^{N} \alpha_i q_i t_i = \sum_{i=1}^{N} \left(\frac{\alpha_i q_i F_i}{\sum_{i=1}^{N} \alpha_i q_i F_i} \right) = 1 \tag{3}$$

3.4.2 Implementation

The quality adaptive fusion scheme described above was implemented using equal weights for EEG, ECG, GSR and head pose. Therefore, the weights used for fusion were $\alpha_i = 0.25$ and the class probabilities from each single modality is given by,

$$p_Q^x = 0.25 \times (p_{ee}^x q_{ee} t_{ee} + p_{ec}^x q_{ec} t_{ec} + p_{gs}^x q_{gs} t_{gs} + p_{hp}^x q_{hp} t_{hp}) \tag{4}$$

where subscripted 'Q' denotes quality adaptive system, abbreviations ee, ec, gs and hp denote EEG, ECG, GSR and head pose, respectively. Whereas, for non-adaptive multimodal fusion was developed using similar decision rule while excluding the quality term 'q_i' from the equation resulting in,

$$p_{nQ}^x = 0.25 \times (p_{ee}^x t_{ee} + p_{ec}^x t_{ec} + p_{gs}^x t_{gs} + p_{hp}^x t_{hp}) \tag{5}$$

where subscripted 'nQ' denotes non-adaptive system for multimodal fusion.

4. RESULTS

The SQEs for each modality performed adequately for each modality, as the weighted F1-scores were as follows: EEG - 0.93, ECG - 0.95, Face/headpose - 0.86 and GSR - 0.78, while the weighted F1-score for random voting for each modality was 0.62. Moreover, the performance of the affect classifiers (both, quality adaptive and non-adaptive) are reported in Table 2, which can be compared to the baseline weighted F1-score of 0.50, obtained from random voting for valence, arousal and liking. It was observed that, using the quality adaptive affect recognition system, for arousal, all the modalities performed significantly better than chance. Moreover, for valence EEG, ECG and face/headpose produced significant results whereas, for liking only face/headpose using a SVM classifier performed significantly better than chance. The non-adaptive affect recognition systems resulted in very few significant results. However, it should be noted that *uni-modal* quality adaptive systems had higher failure rate due to sample rejections. The non-adaptive multimodal decision fusion produced significantly better than chance classification performance for the three subjective dimensions of valence, arousal and liking, using the NB classifier whereas, no significant results were obtained using SVM classifier. Furthermore, the quality adaptive multimodal decision fusion also produced significantly better than chance classification performance for valence, arousal and liking, using the NB classifier whereas, using SVM classifier significant results were observed only for valence classification. Moreover, the sample rejection rate was brought down significantly, to 0%, using the quality adaptive multimodal fusion.

5. DISCUSSION AND CONCLUSION

The developed SQEs performed well for each modality (weighted F1-score of about 0.90). However, for GSR the obtained weighted F1-score was relatively lower than the other modalities

Table 2: Classification results for the self-assessment of valence (V), arousal (A) and liking (L) using a leave-one-subject-out cross-validation schema. The weighted F1-scores significantly higher than chance level (0.50) are highlighted (superscripted $* : p < 0.05$). The table also lists the percentage of samples rejected in quality adaptive schema for each modality.

Modality	Classifier	Quality Adaptive				Non-Adaptive		
		A	V	L	Rejections	A	V	L
NeuroSky EEG	SVM	**0.57***	0.53	0.54	22.58%	0.52	0.50	0.51
	NB	**0.56***	**0.57***	0.53		0.52	0.50	0.51
ECG	SVM	**0.59***	**0.57***	0.53	18.33%	0.57*	0.52	0.50
	NB	0.54	**0.57***	0.54		0.55	0.55*	0.51
GSR	SVM	0.52	0.52	0.46	13.79%	0.51	0.52	0.52
	NB	**0.55***	0.48	0.54		0.54	0.52	0.53
Headpose	SVM	0.55*	**0.58***	**0.58***	5.76%	**0.56***	0.54	**0.58***
	NB	0.50	0.55*	0.53		0.53	0.52	0.55
Decision Fusion	SVM	**0.60***	**0.59***	**0.58***	**0%**	0.57*	0.54	**0.58***
	NB	**0.57***	**0.58***	**0.56***		0.56*	0.56*	0.55*

suggesting that better features could aid in improving the GSR signal quality estimation. Moreover, the advantage of using a quality adaptive affect recognizer is evident from Table 2, where the quality adaptive affect recognizer produced more number of significant results compared to a non-adaptive affect recognizer. However, a higher percentage of sample rejections for *uni-modal* quality adaptive systems resulted in their higher failure rate. The efficacy of multi-modal fusion techniques, both quality adaptive and non-adaptive, is evident as both techniques produced significant results for all three affective dimensions. The quality adaptive multimodal fusion has an added advantage of decreasing the failure rate resulting from quality adaptive uni-modal systems and achieving slightly higher performances. Moreover, the results reported in Table 2 validate the performance of our approach for *cross-user* affect recognition in noisy recordings (e.g. due to noise in environment) for multimedia implicit affective indexing.

Furthermore, it is worth noting that quality adaptive arousal and valence classifiers performed significantly above chance on all the modalities except on valence recognition using GSR that is in corroboration with the finding in [7]. It is worthy to mention that low unimodal performances on GSR could be due to the fact that GSR responses are slow. Therefore, GSR is an unsuitable modality for an experiment with short recordings like ours.

According to the observed results, a link between participants' head-pose (e.g. following the rhythm of music) and the likeability of a music excerpt was observed as the liking classifiers developed using head-pose features performed significantly above chance. Head-pose also significantly encodes valence and arousal perceptions.

In the study presented here, we developed a quality adaptive multimodal affect recognition system for cross-user and user-centric implicit mutlimedia indexing. The multimodal system was developed using data from four different modalities of EEG, ECG, GSR and face/headpose videos while users experienced affective music generated by an algorithmic composer, *Robin*. The signal quality for each modality was estimated first using a bagging classifier, which was followed by affect recognition. The quality adaptive uni-modal affect recognition performed better than chance however, these systems resulted in high failure rate due to bad quality sample rejection. Towards decreasing the failure rate of the uni-modal affect recognition systems, we proposed a quality adaptive multimodal decision fusion rule, giving equal weights to each modality, which performed adequately for affect recognition while lowering the failure rate. However, to improve the classification performance, quality adaptive modality weight optimisation should be explored in future studies. We release the dataset for the community, so that researchers in the community would improve our baseline results employing more innovative signal-quality adaptive methods.

6. ACKNOWLEDGEMENTS

This research was funded and supported by Sensaura Inc. The dataset was collected at the University of Trento, Italy and we acknowledge the great support we received during the data collection. We do also acknowledge Mr. Jean-Philip R. Poulin for his support at Sensaura Inc.

7. REFERENCES

[1] M. Esterman, B. J. Tamber-Rosenau, Y.-C. Chiu, and S. Yantis. Avoiding non-independence in fmri data analysis: leave one subject out. *Neuroimage*, 50(2):572–576, 2010.

[2] R. Gupta, K. ur Rehman Laghari, and T. H. Falk. Relevance vector classifier decision fusion and eeg graph-theoretic features for automatic affective state characterization. *Neurocomputing*, 174(PB):875–884, Jan. 2016.

[3] A. Hanjalic and L.-Q. Xu. Affective video content representation and modeling. *IEEE Transactions on Multimedia*, 7(1):143–154, 2005.

[4] M. Khomami Abadi, S. M. Kia, R. Subramanian, P. Avesani, and N. Sebe. User-centric affective video tagging from meg and peripheral physiological responses. In *ACII*, 2013.

[5] M. Khomami Abadi, J. Staiano, A. Cappelletti, M. Zancanaro, and N. Sebe. Multimodal engagement classification for affective cinema. In *ACII*, 2013.

[6] M. Khomami Abadi, R. Subramanian, S. M. Kia, P. Avesani, I. Patras, and N. Sebe. Decaf: Meg-based multimodal database for decoding affective physiological responses. *IEEE Transactions on Affective Computing*, 6(3):209–222, July 2015.

[7] J. Kim and E. AndrÕ. Emotion recognition based on physiological changes in music listening. *IEEE Transactions on Pattern Analysis and Machine Intelligence*, 30(12):2067–2083, Dec 2008.

[8] S. Koelstra, C. Muhl, M. Soleymani, J. S. Lee, A. Yazdani, T. Ebrahimi, T. Pun, A. Nijholt, and I. Patras. Deap: A database for emotion analysis ;using physiological signals. *IEEE Transactions on Affective Computing*, 3(1):18–31, Jan 2012.

[9] S. Koelstra and I. Patras. Fusion of facial expressions and {EEG} for implicit affective tagging. *Image and Vision Computing*, 31(2):164 – 174, 2013.

[10] F. Morreale, R. Masu, and A. De Angeli. Robin: an algorithmic composer for interactive scenarios. *Proceedings of 10th Sound and Music Comp.*, 2013.

[11] M. Pantic and A. Vinciarelli. Implicit human-centered tagging [social sciences]. *IEEE Signal Processing Magazine*, 26(6):173–180, November 2009.

[12] F. Pedregosa, G. Varoquaux, A. Gramfort, V. Michel, B. Thirion, O. Grisel, M. Blondel, P. Prettenhofer, R. Weiss, V. Dubourg, J. Vanderplas, A. Passos, D. Cournapeau, M. Brucher, M. Perrot, and E. Duchesnay. Scikit-learn: Machine learning in python. *Journal of Machine Learning Research*, 12:2825–2830, Nov. 2011.

[13] T. Penzel, B. Kemp, G. Klosch, A. Schlogl, J. Hasan, A. Varri, and I. Korhonen. Acquisition of biomedical signals databases. *IEEE Engineering in Medicine and Biology Magazine*, 20(3):25–32, May 2001.

[14] M.-K. Shan, F.-F. Kuo, M.-F. Chiang, and S.-Y. Lee. Emotion-based music recommendation by affinity discovery from film music. *Expert Systems with Applications*, 2009.

[15] M. Soleymani, J. Lichtenauer, T. Pun, and M. Pantic. A multimodal database for affect recognition and implicit tagging. *IEEE Transactions on Affective Computing*, 3(1):42–55, Jan 2012.

[16] X. Xiong and F. De la Torre. Supervised descent method and its applications to face alignment. In *CVPR*, 2013.

[17] Z. Zeng, M. Pantic, G. I. Roisman, and T. S. Huang. A survey of affect recognition methods: Audio, visual, and spontaneous expressions. *IEEE Transactions on Pattern Analysis and Machine Intelligence*, 31(1):39–58, Jan 2009.

Rank Diffusion for Context-Based Image Retrieval

Daniel Carlos Guimarães Pedronette
Dept. of Statistic, Applied Math. and Computing
Universidade Estadual Paulista (UNESP)
Rio Claro, Brazil
daniel@rc.unesp.br

Ricardo da S. Torres
Recod Lab - Institute of Computing
University of Campinas (UNICAMP)
Campinas, Brazil
rtorres@ic.unicamp.br

ABSTRACT

This paper presents an efficient diffusion-based re-ranking approach. The proposed method propagates contextual information defined in terms of top-ranked objects of ranked lists in a diffusion process. That makes the method suitable for large scale real-world collections. Experiments were conducted considering public image collections, several descriptors, and comparisons with state-of-the-art methods. Experimental results demonstrate that the proposed method provides high effectiveness gains with low computational costs.

Keywords

content-based image retrieval; unsupervised distance learning; rank diffusion process

1. INTRODUCTION

A relevant change can be observed in the multimedia content generation, since common users are not long mere consumers and have become active producers. As a result, huge amounts of visual content have been accumulated daily, generated from a large variety of digital sources. The Content-Based Image Retrieval (CBIR) systems are considered a promising solution in this scenario, supporting searches capable of taking into account the visual properties of digital images.

The development of CBIR systems has been mainly supported by the creation of various visual features (based on shape, color, and texture properties) and different distance measures. However, more recently, research initiatives have focused on other stages of the retrieval process, which are not directly related to low-level feature extraction procedures. In several computer vision and image retrieval applications, capturing and exploiting the intrinsic manifold structure becomes a central problem for different vision, learning, and retrieval tasks [14].

Diverse methods also have been proposed in order to improve the effectiveness of distance measures in image retrieval tasks, specially based on diffusion approaches [14, 15, 39, 40]. In general, these post-processing methods aims at replacing pairwise distances by more global affinity measures capable of considering the dataset manifold [40]. Although indispensable for improving the effectiveness of retrieval, the wide use of post-processing methods on large-scale real-world applications also depends on efficiency and scalability aspects [24]. More recently, due to the high computational costs associated with diffusion-based approaches, other methods have emerged. Mainly based on rank analysis, such contextual rank measures [2, 26] can be efficiently computed.

In this paper, we propose a novel hybrid approach, named Rank Diffusion, which is based on a diffusion process defined in terms of ranking information. This method establishes a relationship between diffusion approaches and contextual rank measures in the sense it spreads ranking information, taking into account the dataset structure. A relevant contribution of the proposed approach is given in terms of efficiency aspects. Despite the use of a diffusion strategy, since only rank information is considered, low computational efforts are required.

An experimental evaluation was conducted, considering public datasets and several image descriptors, including global, local, and convolution-neural-network-based descriptors. Experiments were conducted on different retrieval tasks. The proposed method achieved significant effectiveness gains, yielding better results in terms of effectiveness performance than state-of-the-art approaches. For example, an accuracy score of 100% and a N-S score of 3.94 were achieved on the well-known MPEG-7 [17] and UKBench [22] datasets.

2. RELATED WORK

In various multimedia and learning applications, objects are often modeled as high dimensional points in an Euclidean space. For retrieval or classification purposes, the distance between two objects is computed often considering the Euclidean distance. However, once pairwise distance measures define relationships only between pairs of images, the global structure of the dataset and the context wherein the query is computed are ignored. Therefore, how to capture and exploit the intrinsic manifold structure becomes a central problem in the vision and retrieval applications [14]. In this scenario, many approaches have been proposed [6, 9, 12, 14, 26, 28, 38, 39] to improve the effectiveness of image retrieval tasks. Such methods take into account the dataset manifold and the global relationships among images, without the need of any user intervention. Some of the most important diffusion- and rank-based methods.

ICMR'16, June 06-09, 2016, New York, NY, USA
© 2016 ACM. ISBN 978-1-4503-4359-6/16/06...$15.00
DOI: http://dx.doi.org/10.1145/2911996.2912060

Diffusion-based approaches [7] rely on the definition of a global measure, which describes the relationship between pairs of points in terms of their connectivity. In general, diffusion processes consider as input a pairwise affinity matrix W, which can be interpreted as a graph that encodes the relationships among objects [9]. Let $G = (V, E)$ be a graph, such as the nodes $v_i \in V$ are associated with dataset objects and edges $e_{ij} \in E$ indicate the existence of relationships among them. Edge weights, in turn, are defined by the affinity values w_{ij}. The matrix W is often computed by applying a Gaussian kernel to a distance matrix computed by an image descriptor [14]. Giving the edge weights [9] defined by the matrix W, the diffusion processes spread the affinities through the graph. In general, a walk in the graph occurs more likely through the edges with larger weights.

Several methods based on diffusion approaches have been proposed [9, 14, 38, 39]. The diffusion-based algorithms have been achieving significant improvements on retrieval performance although they are very expensive to compute, specially when the size of datasets becomes larger [2, 27].

Recently, various contextual rank-based approaches [2, 6, 26, 27, 29] have yielded very significant gains on retrieval effectiveness. Additionally, since the most relevant information of rankings is found at top positions, the rank-based approaches can significantly reduce the computational efforts required by exploiting indexing structures [24]. Therefore, other important requirements, such as efficiency and scalability [2, 24], are met.

In this paper, a novel hybrid re-ranking approach, which is based on a diffusion process defined in terms of ranking information, is presented. An advantage of the proposed method when compared with other approaches rely on its efficiency. As the diffusion process is based o rank information, only the top-ranked images can be considered.

3. FORMAL PROBLEM DEFINITION

This section formally defines the image retrieval and ranking model. Let $\mathcal{C}=\{img_1, img_2, \ldots, img_n\}$ be an image collection. The notation $\rho(i,j)$ denotes the distance between two images img_i and img_j according to a given descriptor. Let img_q be a query image. A ranked list τ_q can be computed in response to img_q based on the distance function ρ. The ranked list $\sigma_q=(img_1, img_2, \ldots, img_n)$ can be defined as a permutation of the collection $\mathcal{C}$. A permutation σ_q is a bijection from the set $\mathcal{C}$ onto the set $[N] = \{1, 2, \ldots, n\}$. For a permutation σ_q, we interpret $\sigma_q(i)$ as the position (or rank) of image img_i in the ranked list σ_q.

The top positions of ranked lists are expected to contain the most similar images to the query image. Additionally, σ_q is expensive to compute, specially when n is high. Therefore, the computed ranked lists can consider only a sub-set of the images. Let τ_q be a ranked list that contains only the L most similar images to img_q, where $L \ll n$. Formally, let $\mathcal{C}_L$ be a sub-set of of the collection $\mathcal{C}$, such that $\mathcal{C}_L \subset \mathcal{C}$ and $|\mathcal{C}_L| = L$. The ranked list τ_q can be defined as a bijection from the set $\mathcal{C}_L$ onto the set $[N] = \{1, 2, \ldots, L\}$. Every image $img_i \in \mathcal{C}$ can be taken as a query image img_q. A set of ranked lists $\mathcal{T} = \{\tau_1, \tau_2, \ldots, \tau_n\}$ can also be obtained, with a ranked list for each image in the collection $\mathcal{C}$.

Our goal is to exploit the similarity information encoded in the set $\mathcal{T}$, with the aim of computing a more effective set $\mathcal{T}_r$. In fact, a more effective distance function ρ_r is defined, giving rise to a new set of ranked lists. Additionally, the fusion problem is also considered, in which different sets of ranked lists $\{\mathcal{T}_1, \mathcal{T}_2, \ldots, \mathcal{T}_d\}$ are taken as input aiming at computing a more effective set $\mathcal{T}_r$.

4. RANK DIFFUSION PROCESS

This section discusses and defines the proposed rank diffusion process, presenting each step involved in the method, until the computation of the rank-diffusion distance.

4.1 Rank Similarity Matrix

Many diffusion-based algorithms use the distance information for defining a similarity matrix W. A Gaussian kernel is often considered, such that $w_{ij} = exp(\frac{-\rho^2(i,j)}{2\sigma^2})$, where σ is a parameter to be defined. Therefore, some strategies are required to define a suitable value for the parameter, also considering that the distance distribution may vary among different descriptors.

In this work, a rank similarity matrix W is proposed based only on rank information. The rank modeling of similarity information allows an uniform representation, independent of distance scores. The similarity score w_{ij} varies linearly according to the position of img_j in the ranked list τ_i. Additionally, the score considers only a neighborhood set, which is defined by the size of ranked lists.

Let m denote the size of ranked lists and, therefore the neighborhood considered. Let $\mathcal{N}(i, m)$ be the neighborhood set, which is formally defined as follows:

$$\mathcal{N}(i,m) = \{\mathcal{R} \subseteq \mathcal{C}, |\mathcal{R}| = m \wedge \forall x \in \mathcal{R}, y \in \mathcal{C} - \mathcal{R} : \rho(i,x) \leqslant \rho(i,y)\}. \quad (1)$$

The similarity rank matrix W_m is defined as:

$$w_{m_{ij}} = \begin{cases} m - \tau_i(j) + 1 & if\ img_j \in \mathcal{N}(i,m) \\ 0 & otherwise. \end{cases} \quad (2)$$

The size of the ranked list can assume different values depending on the desired analysis. In the proposed method, the matrix W is defined assuming $m \leq k$, for a local neighborhood analysis, and $m = L$ for a more comprehensive collection sub-set. Notice that, since the matrix W has dimension of $n \times n$, both k and L values are much smaller than n, i.e, $k, L \ll n$. Therefore, the matrix W is very sparse. This property is exploited for defining an efficient algorithm, which computes operations that are equivalent to a matrix multiplication considering W.

4.2 Reciprocal Rank Normalization

While most of similarity pairwise measures are symmetric, the same does not occur for rank measures. In other words, an image img_i well ranked for a query img_j does not imply that img_j is well ranked for query img_i. However, the benefits of improving the symmetry of the k-neighborhood relationship are remarkable in image retrieval applications [12]. Thus, a simple rank normalization procedure is conducted before the rank diffusion process. The reciprocal references among all ranked lists at top-L positions are considered, such $m = L$. For this, the similarity matrix W_L is used and its asymmetry is exploited. The value of w_{ij} is defined considering the position of img_j in the ranked list τ_i, while w_{ji} considers the position of img_i in τ_j. Therefore, a normalized rank similarity matrix $\bar{R_L}$ can be defined as the sum of the original matrix W with its transposed:

$$\bar{R} = W_L + W_L^T. \quad (3)$$

Based on the matrix $\bar{R}$, a rank normalized distance $\bar{\rho}$ is defined as:

$$\bar{\rho}(i,j) = \frac{1}{1+\bar{r}_{ij}}, \quad (4)$$

where $\bar{r}_{ij} \in \bar{R}$.

In the following, all the ranked lists are updated according to the normalized distance, using a stable sorting algorithm. In this way, all similarity scores defined as 0 in the matrix $\bar{R}$ have their distance changed to 1. In these cases, after the execution of the stable sorting algorithm, the previous order of ranked lists are maintained.

This update gives rise to a new set of ranked lists $\bar{\mathcal{T}}$, used as input for the next steps of the proposed algorithm.

4.3 Iterative Rank Diffusion

The proposed rank diffusion approach is defined by an iterative update of similarity information encoded into a matrix P. The update at each iteration is computed according to a rank similarity matrix W of increasing neighborhood size. The central idea consists in spreading the similarity information through P considering initially a small neighborhood, which is gradually expanded over iterations. Therefore, the number of iterations is defined proportionally to the neighborhood size.

Formally, let $^{(t)}$ denote the current iteration and let s be a constant value, which defines the initial neighborhood size. The rank similarity matrix at a given iteration t is defined as:

$$W^{(t)} = W_{s+t}. \quad (5)$$

where the size of ranked lists $m = (s+t)$. The value of $s = 2$ can be used as a default starting value, or s can be manually defined. The initialization of matrix P is defined considering $t = 0$, and therefore:

$$P^{(0)} = W_s. \quad (6)$$

Given the asymmetry rank relationships, a normalization similarity value is computed proportionally to the accumulated rank similarity of each image. The normalization is defined for matrices W and P, respectively as

$$\bar{W_{ij}}^{(t)} = \frac{W_{ij}^{(t)}}{\sum_{c=1}^{n} W_{jc}^{(t)}}, \quad (7)$$

and

$$\bar{P}_{ij}^{(t)} = \frac{P_{ij}^{(t)}}{\sum_{c=1}^{n} P_{jc}^{(t)}}. \quad (8)$$

The iterative diffusion step is defined in terms of the multiplication of the normalized matrices $\bar{P}$ and $\bar{W}$. At each iteration, a larger neighborhood is considered in $\bar{W}$ and disseminated along P:

$$P^{(t+i)} = \bar{P}^{(t)} \bar{W^{(t)}}^{T}, \quad (9)$$

where i indicates the increment (its default value is 1). The process is iteratively executed while $t \leq (k-s)$, where k is a parameter that defines the size of the neighborhood considered.

4.4 Reciprocal Rank Diffusion

The diffusion step defined in Equation 9 considers the transposed matrix $\bar{W^{(t)}}^{T}$. In this way, the similarity of a given image img_i to other images is updated according to the ranked list τ_i and is encoded in the similarity matrix.

However, the reciprocal similarity information should also be considered. With this purpose, after the iterative rank diffusion, a self-diffusion step is defined as:

$$P_r = \bar{P}^{(k-s)} \bar{P}^{(k-s)}, \quad (10)$$

where $\bar{P}^{(k-s)}$ represents the last matrix computed by the iterative diffusion after normalization.

4.5 Rank Diffused Distance

Finally, a new rank diffused distance ρ_d is computed inversely proportional to the reciprocal similarity matrix P_r:

$$\rho_r(i,j) = \frac{1}{1+P_{r_{ij}}} \quad (11)$$

Based on the distance ρ_r, the new and more effective set of ranked lists $\mathcal{T}_r$ is computed using a stable sorting algorithm. As for the rank normalization step, images, which present similarity values equal to 0, maintain the previous order in the ranked lists.

5. RANK AGGREGATION

Different features often encode distinct and complementary visual information extracted from images. Therefore, if a feature produces effective rankings by itself and is complementary (heterogeneous) to other features, then it is expected that a higher search accuracy can be achieved by combining them [42].

In this work, a rank aggregation approach is presented for combining different rankings using the proposed rank diffusion process. The rank diffusion is performed in two stages: first, for each descriptor in isolation and in the next, considering a fused set of ranked lists.

Let $\mathcal{D} = \{D_1, D_2, \ldots, D_d\}$ be a set of different image descriptors and let $\{\mathcal{T}_1, \mathcal{T}_2, \ldots, \mathcal{T}_d\}$ be their respective set of ranked lists. The rank diffusion process is computed for each set $\mathcal{T}_i$, in order to compute a matrix P_r (Equation 10). In the following, a fused matrix P_f is defined as:

$$P_f = \sum_{j \in \mathcal{D}} P_{r_j}. \quad (12)$$

Based on P_f, a new distance ρ_f is computed:

$$\rho_f(i,j) = \frac{1}{1+P_{f_{ij}}}. \quad (13)$$

A fused set of ranked lists $\mathcal{T}_f$ is computed using the distance ρ_f. Finally, we aim at exploiting the contextual information of the fused set of ranked lists $\mathcal{T}_f$. Once the set $\mathcal{T}_f$ presents the same structure of a set obtained for a single descriptor, it is submitted to the regular rank diffusion process, giving rising to a final set $\mathcal{T}_r$.

6. EXPERIMENTAL EVALUATION

The proposed method was evaluated on shape and natural image retrieval tasks, considering the MPEG-7 [17] and UKBench [22] datasets, which are commonly used as benchmark for image retrieval and post-processing methods. All images of each dataset are used as query images. Regarding parameters, we used s=5, i=5, and k=20 for the MPEG-7 [17] dataset and s=2, i=2, and k=6 for the UKBench [22] dataset, due to the small number of images per class.

6.1 Shape Retrieval

The shape retrieval experiments were condcuted on the MPEG-7 [17], which is a well-known shape dataset, composed of 1400 shapes divided into 70 classes. Six shape descriptors were considered and the *Mean Average Precision* (MAP) was used as effectiveness measure.

Table 1 presents the experimental results for shape retrieval experiments. Statistical paired t-tests were conducted comparing the results before and after the use of the proposed algorithm. Different values of L are considered: $L = 400$ and the whole ranked list. Positive gains with statistical significance can be observed for all descriptors, reaching high effectiveness gains up to +40.72%. The effectiveness results obtained for partial and the entire ranked lists are very similar, demonstrating that only a sub-set of ranked lists is enough to obtain high effectiveness gains.

Results for rank aggregation tasks are also presented considering the combination of the three best descriptors. The relative gains are computed based on the descriptor with the lowest MAP score. As it can be observed, high effective results are also obtained, reaching 99.78% for CFD+AIR.

Table 1: Rank Diffusion for shape retrieval tasks (MAP as score).

Descriptor	Orig. MAP	$L = 400$			*Full L*		
		Rank Diff.	**Gain**	**Stat. Sig.**	**Rank Diff.**	**Gain**	**Stat. Sig.**
SS [8]	37.67%	52.17%	+38.49%	•	53.01%	+40.72%	•
BAS [1]	71.52%	82.36%	+15.16%	•	83.03%	+16.09%	•
IDSC [18]	81.70%	90.89%	+11.25%	•	91.09%	+11.49%	•
CFD [25]	80.71%	93.75%	+16.16%	•	94.17%	+16.68%	•
ASC [19]	85.28%	92.98%	+9.03%	•	93.07%	+9.13%	•
AIR [10]	89.39%	97.98%	+9.61%	•	97.97%	+9.60%	•
CFD+ASC	-	99.29%	+23.02%	•	99.25%	+22.97%	•
ASC+AIR	-	99.57%	+16.76%	•	99.58%	+16.77%	•
CFD+AIR	-	99.78%	+23.63%	•	99.79%	+23.64%	•

6.2 Natural Image Retrieval

We evaluate the proposed method in natural image retrieval tasks considering the University of Kentucky Recognition Benchmark – UKBench [22]. The UKBench dataset has a total of 10,200 images, composed of 2,550 objects or scenes, where each object/scene is captured 4 times from different viewpoints. The small number of images per class constitutes a challenging scenario for unsupervised learning approaches. Various distinct features are used, including color and color/texture features available on LIRE framework [20]. Local features are considered based on Vocabulary Tree (VOC) [36]. Convolution neural networks (CNN) features based on Caffe [13] framework are also considered.

Table 2 presents the effectiveness results considering the UKBench [22] dataset. The N-S score is used as effectiveness measure, varying between 1 and 4. This score corresponds to the number of relevant images among the first four image returned (the highest achievable score is 4). We can observe significant improvements for N-S scores. Notice, for example, the Caffe [13] convolutional neural network, which is improved from 3.31 to 3.61. The results are even more impressive considering the rank aggregation tasks.

6.3 Comparison with Other Approaches

The proposed method is also evaluated in comparison with various other state-of-the-art approaches and recently proposed retrieval approaches. Table 3 presents the results of Rank Diffusion method on the UKBench [22] dataset in comparison with recent retrieval approaches. Table 4 presents the obtained results on the MPEG-7 [17] dataset in comparison with various other state-of-the-art post-processing methods. The bull's eye score, which counts the matching shapes within the top-40 ranked images, is used as evaluation measure. As it can be observed, the effectiveness results of the proposed method compares favorably with the recent retrieval approaches.

Table 2: Rank Diffusion on the UKBench [22] dataset.

Descriptor	**Original N-S**	**Rank Diffusion**
CEED-SPy [4, 20]	2.81	3.10
FCTH-SPy [5, 20]	2.91	3.19
SCD [21]	3.15	3.35
ACC-SPy [11, 20]	3.25	3.51
CNN-Caffe [13]	3.31	3.61
ACC [20]	3.36	3.60
VOC [36]	3.54	3.72
VOC+ACC	-	3.90
VOC+CNN	-	3.90
ACC+CNN	-	3.87
VOC+ACC+CNN	-	**3.94**

Table 3: Retrieval comparison on the UKBench [22] dataset.

N-S scores for recent retrieval methods					
Zheng *et al.* [43]	Qin *et al.* [28]	Wang *et al.* [34]	Zhang *et al.* [41]	Zheng *et al.* [42]	Xie *et al.* [37]
3.57	3.67	3.68	3.83	3.84	3.89

N-S scores for the Rank Diffusion method			
Rank Diff.: ACC+CNN	Rank Diff. VOC+CNN	Rank Diff. VOC+ACC	Rank Diff. VOC+ACC+CNN
3.88	3.90	3.90	**3.94**

Table 4: Comparison on the MPEG-7 [17] dataset.

Shape Descriptors		
CFD [25]	-	84.43%
IDSC [18]	-	85.40%
ASC [19]	-	88.39%
AIR [10]	-	93.67%
Post-Processing Methods		
Algorithm	**Descriptor(s)**	**Score**
Graph Transduction [38]	IDSC	91.00%
Locally C. Diffusion Process [39]	IDSC	93.32%
Shortest Path Propagation [35]	IDSC	93.35%
Locally C. Diffusion Process [39]	ASC	95.96%
Rank Diffusion	**CFD**	**96.19%**
Tensor Product Graph [40]	AIR	99.99%
Generic Diffusion Process [9]	AIR	100%
Neighbor Set Similarity [2]	AIR	100%
Rank Diffusion	**AIR**	**100%**

7. CONCLUSIONS

Post-processing procedures based on unsupervised learning approaches have been established as indispensable tools for improving the effectiveness of CBIR systems. Since diffusion process methods require high computational efforts, rank-based approaches attracted a lot of research attention recently to circumvent their limitations. In this paper, a novel rank diffusion method is proposed exploiting characteristics of both diffusion and rank-based approaches. A rigorous experimental evaluation demonstrated the effectiveness of the proposed approach. Future work focuses on the deep investigation of contextual information encoded in the rank similarity matrix.

8. ACKNOWLEDGMENTS

The authors are grateful to FAPESP (grants 2013/08645-0 and 2013/50169-1), CNPq (grants 306580/2012-8 and 484254/2012-0), CAPES, AMD, and Microsoft Research.

9. REFERENCES

[1] N. Arica and F. T. Y. Vural. BAS: a perceptual shape descriptor based on the beam angle statistics. *Pattern Recognition Letters*, 24(9-10):1627–1639, 2003.

[2] X. Bai, S. Bai, and X. Wang. Beyond diffusion process: Neighbor set similarity for fast re-ranking. *Information Sciences*, 325:342 – 354, 2015.

[3] P. Brodatz. *Textures: A Photographic Album for Artists and Designers*. Dover, 1966.

[4] S. A. Chatzichristofis and Y. S. Boutalis. Cedd: color and edge directivity descriptor: a compact descriptor for image indexing and retrieval. In *ICVS*, pages 312–322, 2008.

[5] S. A. Chatzichristofis and Y. S. Boutalis. Fcth: Fuzzy color and texture histogram - a low level feature for accurate image retrieval. In *WIAMIS*, pages 191–196, 2008.

[6] Y. Chen, X. Li, A. Dick, and R. Hill. Ranking consistency for image matching and object retrieval. *Pattern Recognition*, 47(3):1349 – 1360, 2014.

[7] R. R. Coifman and S. Lafon. Diffusion maps. *Applied and Computational Harmonic Analysis*, 21(1):5 – 30, 2006.

[8] R. da S. Torres and A. X. Falcão. Contour Salience Descriptors for Effective Image Retrieval and Analysis. *Image and Vision Computing*, 25(1):3–13, 2007.

[9] M. Donoser and H. Bischof. Diffusion Processes for Retrieval Revisited. In *CVPR*, pages 1320–1327, 2013.

[10] R. Gopalan, P. Turaga, and R. Chellappa. Articulation-invariant representation of non-planar shapes. In *ECCV*, volume 3, pages 286–299, 2010.

[11] J. Huang, S. R. Kumar, M. Mitra, W.-J. Zhu, and R. Zabih. Image indexing using color correlograms. In *CVPR*, pages 762–768, 1997.

[12] H. Jegou, C. Schmid, H. Harzallah, and J. Verbeek. Accurate image search using the contextual dissimilarity measure. *IEEE TPAMI*, 32(1):2–11, 2010.

[13] Y. Jia, E. Shelhamer, J. Donahue, S. Karayev, J. Long, R. Girshick, S. Guadarrama, and T. Darrell. Caffe: Convolutional architecture for fast feature embedding. *arXiv preprint arXiv:1408.5093*, 2014.

[14] J. Jiang, B. Wang, and Z. Tu. Unsupervised metric learning by self-smoothing operator. In *ICCV*, pages 794–801, 2011.

[15] P. Kontschieder, M. Donoser, and H. Bischof. Beyond pairwise shape similarity analysis. In *ACCV*, pages 655–666, 2009.

[16] V. Kovalev and S. Volmer. Color co-occurence descriptors for querying-by-example. In *ICMM*, page 32, 1998.

[17] L. J. Latecki, R. Lakmper, and U. Eckhardt. Shape descriptors for non-rigid shapes with a single closed contour. In *CVPR*, pages 424–429, 2000.

[18] H. Ling and D. W. Jacobs. Shape classification using the inner-distance. *IEEE TPAMI*, 29(2):286–299, 2007.

[19] H. Ling, X. Yang, and L. J. Latecki. Balancing deformability and discriminability for shape matching. In *ECCV*, volume 3, pages 411–424, 2010.

[20] M. Lux. Content based image retrieval with LIRe. In *ACM MM '11*, 2011.

[21] B. Manjunath, J.-R. Ohm, V. Vasudevan, and A. Yamada. Color and texture descriptors. *IEEE Transactions on Circuits and Systems for Video Technology*, 11(6):703–715, 2001.

[22] D. Nistér and H. Stewénius. Scalable recognition with a vocabulary tree. In *CVPR*, volume 2, pages 2161–2168, 2006.

[23] T. Ojala, M. Pietikäinen, and T. Mäenpää. Multiresolution gray-scale and rotation invariant texture classification with local binary patterns. *IEEE TPAMI*, 24(7):971–987, 2002.

[24] D. C. G. Pedronette, J. Almeida, and R. da S. Torres. A scalable re-ranking method for content-based image retrieval. *Information Sciences*, 265(1):91–104, 2014.

[25] D. C. G. Pedronette and R. da S. Torres. Shape retrieval using contour features and distance optmization. In *VISAPP*, volume 1, pages 197 – 202, 2010.

[26] D. C. G. Pedronette and R. da S. Torres. Image re-ranking and rank aggregation based on similarity of ranked lists. *Pattern Recognition*, 46(8):2350–2360, 2013.

[27] D. C. G. Pedronette and R. da S. Torres. Unsupervised manifold learning using reciprocal knn graphs in image re-ranking and rank aggregation tasks. *Image and Vision Computing*, 32(2):120–130, 2014.

[28] D. Qin, S. Gammeter, L. Bossard, T. Quack, and L. van Gool. Hello neighbor: Accurate object retrieval with k-reciprocal nearest neighbors. In *CVPR*, pages 777 –784, june 2011.

[29] X. Shen, Z. Lin, J. Brandt, S. Avidan, and Y. Wu. Object retrieval and localization with spatially-constrained similarity measure and k-nn re-ranking. In *CVPR*, pages 3013 –3020, june 2012.

[30] R. O. Stehling, M. A. Nascimento, and A. X. Falcão. A compact and efficient image retrieval approach based on border/interior pixel classification. In *CIKM*, pages 102–109, 2002.

[31] M. J. Swain and D. H. Ballard. Color indexing. *International Journal on Computer Vision*, 7(1):11–32, 1991.

[32] B. Tao and B. W. Dickinson. Texture recognition and image retrieval using gradient indexing. *JVCIR*, 11(3):327–342, 2000.

[33] J. van de Weijer and C. Schmid. Coloring local feature extraction. In *ECCV*, pages 334–348, 2006.

[34] B. Wang, J. Jiang, W. Wang, Z.-H. Zhou, and Z. Tu. Unsupervised metric fusion by cross diffusion. In *CVPR*, pages 3013 –3020, 2012.

[35] J. Wang, Y. Li, X. Bai, Y. Zhang, C. Wang, and N. Tang. Learning context-sensitive similarity by shortest path propagation. *Pattern Recognition*, 44(10-11):2367–2374, 2011.

[36] X. Wang, M. Yang, T. Cour, S. Zhu, K. Yu, and T. Han. Contextual weighting for vocabulary tree based image retrieval. In *ICCV'2011*, pages 209–216, Nov 2011.

[37] L. Xie, R. Hong, B. Zhang, and Q. Tian. Image classification and retrieval are one. In *ACM ICMR '15*, pages 3–10, 2015.

[38] X. Yang, X. Bai, L. J. Latecki, and Z. Tu. Improving shape retrieval by learning graph transduction. In *ECCV*, volume 4, pages 788–801, 2008.

[39] X. Yang, S. Koknar-Tezel, and L. J. Latecki. Locally constrained diffusion process on locally densified distance spaces with applications to shape retrieval. In *CVPR*, pages 357–364, 2009.

[40] X. Yang, L. Prasad, and L. Latecki. Affinity learning with diffusion on tensor product graph. *IEEE TPAMI*, 35(1):28–38, 2013.

[41] S. Zhang, M. Yang, T. Cour, K. Yu, and D. Metaxas. Query specific rank fusion for image retrieval. *IEEE TPAMI*, 37(4):803–815, April 2015.

[42] L. Zheng, S. Wang, L. Tian, F. He, Z. Liu, and Q. Tian. Query-adaptive late fusion for image search and person re-identification. In *CVPR'2015*, 2015.

[43] L. Zheng, S. Wang, and Q. Tian. Lp-norm IDF for scalable image retrieval. *IEEE TIP*, 23(8):3604–3617, Aug 2014.

Bags of Local Convolutional Features for Scalable Instance Search

Eva Mohedano*, Kevin McGuinness and Noel E. O'Connor
Insight Center for Data Analytics
Dublin City University
Dublin, Ireland
eva.mohedano@insight-centre.org

Amaia Salvador*, Ferran Marqués, and Xavier Giró-i-Nieto
Image Processing Group
Universitat Politecnica de Catalunya
Barcelona, Catalonia/Spain
{amaia.salvador, xavier.giro}@upc.edu

ABSTRACT

This work proposes a simple instance retrieval pipeline based on encoding the convolutional features of CNN using the bag of words aggregation scheme (BoW). Assigning each local array of activations in a convolutional layer to a visual word produces an *assignment map*, a compact representation that relates regions of an image with a visual word. We use the assignment map for fast spatial reranking, obtaining object localizations that are used for query expansion. We demonstrate the suitability of the BoW representation based on local CNN features for instance retrieval, achieving competitive performance on the Oxford and Paris buildings benchmarks. We show that our proposed system for CNN feature aggregation with BoW outperforms state-of-the-art techniques using sum pooling at a subset of the challenging TRECVid INS benchmark.

Keywords

Instance Retrieval, Convolutional Neural Networks, Bag of Words

1. INTRODUCTION

Convolutional neural networks (CNNs) have been demonstrated to produce global representations that effectively capture the semantics in images. Such CNN-based representations [2, 3, 15, 16, 20, 21] have improved upon the state-of-the-art for instance retrieval.

Despite CNN-based descriptors performing remarkably well in retrieval benchmarks like Oxford and Paris Buildings, state-of-the-art solutions for more challenging datasets such as TRECVid Instance Search (INS) have not yet adopted pipelines that depend solely on CNN features. Current INS systems [11, 22, 23, 24] are still based on aggregating local hand-crafted features using bag of words (BoW) encoding [18] to produce very high-dimensional sparse image representations. Such high-dimensional sparse representations are more likely to be linearly separable, while having relatively few non-zero elements makes them efficient both in terms of storage and computation.

Many successful image retrieval engines combine an initial highly-scalable ranking mechanism on the full image database with a more computational demanding yet higher-precision reranking mechanism (e.g. geometric verification) applied to the top retrieved items.

Inspired by advances in CNN-based descriptors for image retrieval, yet still focusing on instance search, we revisit the BoW encoding scheme using local features from convolutional layers of a CNN. This work presents three contributions:

- We propose a sparse visual descriptor based on a Bag of Local Convolutional Features (BLCF), which allows fast image retrieval by means of an inverted index.
- We introduce the assignment map as a new compact representation of the image, which maps pixels in the image to their corresponding visual words, allowing the fast composition of a BoW descriptor for any region of the image.
- We take advantage of the scalability properties of the assignment map to perform a local analysis of multiple image regions for reranking, followed by a query expansion stage using the obtained object localizations.

Using this approach, we present a retrieval system that achieves state-of-the-art performance in several instance re-

Figure 1: Examples of the top generated rankings for queries of three different datasets: Oxford (top), Paris (middle), TRECVid INS 2013 (bottom).

*denotes equal contribution.

ICMR'16, June 06-09, 2016, New York, NY, USA

DOI: http://dx.doi.org/10.1145/2911996.2912061

trieval benchmarks. Figure 1 illustrates some of the rankings produced by our system on several datasets.

2. RELATED WORK

Many works in the literature have proposed CNN-based representations for image retrieval. Early works [3, 15] focused on replacing traditional hand-crafted descriptors with features from fully connected layers of a CNN pre-trained for image classification. A second generation of works reported significant gains in performance when switching from fully connected to either sum [2, 7] or max [16, 20] pooled convolutional features. Our work shares similarities with all the former in that we use convolutional features extracted from a pre-trained CNN. Unlike these approaches, however, we propose using a sparse, high-dimensional encoding that better represents local image features.

Several works have tried to exploit local information in images by passing multiple image sub patches through a CNN to obtain local features from either fully connected [15, 9] or convolutional [4] layers, which are in turn aggregated using techniques like average pooling [15], BoW [9], or VLAD [4]. Although many of these methods perform well in retrieval benchmarks, they require CNN feature extraction from many image patches, which slows down indexing and feature extraction at retrieval time. Instead, other works [10, 1] treat the activations of the different neuron arrays across all feature maps in a convolutional layer as local features. This way, a single forward pass of the entire image through the CNN is enough to obtain the activations of its local patches, which are then encoded using VLAD. Our approach is similar to the ones in [10, 1] in that we also treat the features in a convolutional layer as local features. We, however, use BoW encoding instead of VLAD to take advantage of sparse representations for fast retrieval in large-scale databases.

Some of the approaches cited above propose systems that are based or partially based on spatial search over multiple regions of the image. Razavian et al. [16] achieve a remarkable increase in performance by applying a spatial search strategy over an arbitrary grid of windows at different scales. Although they report high performance in several retrieval benchmarks, their proposed approach is very computationally costly and does not scale well to larger datasets and real-time search scenarios. Tolias et al. [20] introduce a local analysis of multiple image patches, which is only applied to the top elements of an initial ranking. They propose an efficient workaround for sub patch feature pooling based on integral images, which allows them to quickly evaluate many image windows. Their approach improves their baseline ranking and also provides approximate object localizations. In this direction, our work proposes using the assignment map to quickly build the BoW representation of any image patch, which allows us to apply a spatial search for reranking. Unlike [20], we use the object localizations obtained with spatial search to mask out the activations of the background and perform query expansion using the detected object location.

3. BAG OF WORDS FRAMEWORK

The proposed pipeline for feature extraction uses the activations at different locations of a convolutional layer in a pre-trained CNN as local features. Similar to [20, 7], we discard the softmax and fully connected layers of the original network while keeping the original image aspect ratio. Each convolutional layer in the network has D different $N \times M$ feature maps, which can be viewed as $N \times M$ local descriptors of dimension D.

We propose to use bag of words encode the local convolutional features of an image into a single vector. Although more elaborate aggregation strategies have been shown to outperform BoW-based approaches for some tasks in the literature [5, 12], Bag of words encodings produce sparse high-dimensional codes that can be stored in inverted indices, which are beneficial for fast retrieval. Moreover, BoW-based representations are more compact, faster to compute and easier to interpret.

Bag of words models require constructing a visual codebook to map vectors to their nearest centroid. We use k-means on local CNN features to fit this codebook. Each local CNN feature in the convolutional layer is then assigned its closest visual word in the learned codebook. This procedure generates the *assignment map*, i.e. a 2D array of size $N \times M$ that relates each local CNN feature with a visual word. The assignment map is therefore a compact representation of the image which relates each pixel of the original image with its visual word with a precision of $(\frac{W}{N}, \frac{H}{M})$ pixels, where W and H are the width and height of the original image. This property allows us to quickly generate the BoW vectors of not only the full image, but also its parts. We describe the use of this property in our work in Section 4.

Figure 2 shows the pipeline of the proposed approach, which encodes the image into a sparse high dimensional descriptor to be used for instance retrieval.

4. IMAGE RETRIEVAL

This section describes the image retrieval pipeline, which consists of an initial ranking stage, followed by a spatial reranking, and query expansion.

(a) Initial search: The initial ranking is computed using the cosine similarity between the BoW vector of the query image and the BoW vectors of the full images in the database. We use a sparse matrix based inverted index and GPU-based sparse matrix multiplications to allow fast retrieval. The image list is then sorted based on the cosine similarity of its elements to the query. We use two types of image search based on the query information that is used:

- Global search (GS): The BoW vector of the query is built with the visual words of all the local CNN features in the convolutional layer extracted for the query image.
- Local search (LS): The BoW vector of the query contains only the visual words of the local CNN features that fall inside the query bounding box.

(b) Local reranking (R): After the initial search, the top T images in the ranking are reranked based on a localization score. We choose windows of all possible combinations of width $w \in \{W, \frac{W}{2}, \frac{W}{4}\}$ and height $h \in \{H, \frac{H}{2}, \frac{H}{4}\}$, where W and H are the width and height of the assignment map. We use a sliding window strategy directly on the assignment map with 50% of overlap in both directions.

We additionally perform a simple filtering strategy to discard those windows whose aspect ratio is too different to the aspect ratio of the query. Let the aspect ratio of the query bounding box be $AR_q = \frac{W_q}{H_q}$ and $AR_w = \frac{W_w}{H_w}$ be the aspect ratio of the window. The score for window w

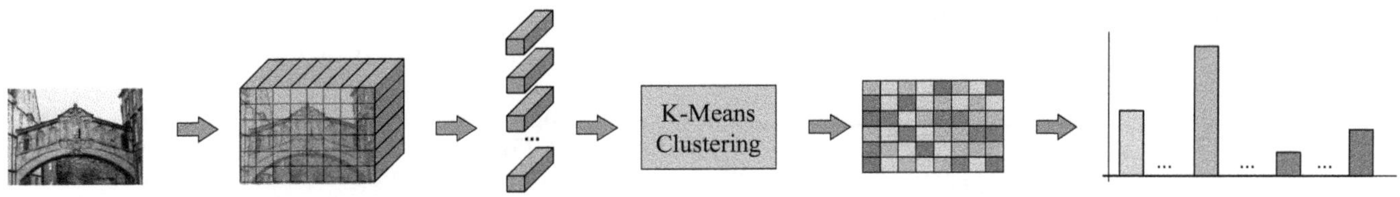

Figure 2: The Bag of Local Convolutional Features pipeline (BLCF).

is defined as $score_w = \frac{min(AR_w, AR_q)}{max(AR_w, AR_q)}$. All windows with a score lower than a threshold th are discarded.

For each of the remaining windows, we construct the BoW vector representation and compare it with the query representation using cosine similarity. The window with the highest cosine similarity is picked as the object localization and its score is kept for the image. We also enhance the BoW window representation with spatial pyramid matching [8] with $L = 2$ resolution levels (i.e. the full window and its 4 sub regions). We construct the BoW representation of all sub regions at the 2 levels, and weight their contribution to the similarity score with inverse proportion to the resolution level of the region. The cosine similarity of a sub region r to the corresponding query sub region is therefore weighted by $w_r = \frac{1}{2^{(L-l_r)}}$, where l_r is the resolution level of the region r. With this procedure, the top T elements of the ranking are sorted based on the cosine similarity of their regions to the query's, and also provides the region with the highest score as a rough localization of the object.

(c) Query expansion We investigate two query expansion strategies based on global and local BoW descriptors:

- Global query expansion (GQE): The BoW vectors of the N images at the top of the ranking are averaged together with the BoW of the query to form the new representation for the query.
- Local query expansion (LQE): Locations obtained in the local reranking step are used to mask out the background and build the BoW descriptor of only the region of interest of the N-top images in the ranking. These BoW vectors are averaged together with the BoW of the query bounding box to perform a second search.

5. EXPERIMENTS

5.1 Preliminary experiments

We experiment with three different instance retrieval benchmarks to evaluate the performance of our approach: Oxford Buildings [13], Paris Buildings [14] and a subset of TRECVid Instance Search 2013 (INS 23k) [19] containing only those keyframes that are relevant to at least one of the queries. For the Paris and Oxford datasets, we also test the performance when adding 100,000 distractor images collected from Flickr to the original datasets (resulting in the Oxford 105k and Paris 106k datasets, respectively).

Feature extraction was performed using *Caffe* [6] and the VGG16 pre-trained network [17]. We extracted features from the last three convolutional layers (conv5_1, conv5_2 and conv5_3) and compared their performance on the Oxford 5k dataset. We experimented on different image input sizes: 1/3 and 2/3 of the original image. Following several other authors [2, 7], we l_2-normalize all local features, followed by PCA, whitening, and a second round of l_2-normalization. The PCA models were fit on the same dataset as the test data in all cases. Unless stated otherwise, all experiments used a visual codebook of 25,000 centroids fit using the (L^2-PCA-L^2 transformed) local CNN features of all images in the same dataset.

We apply bilinear interpolation on the convolutional layers to obtain higher resolution maps as a workaround of using bigger input size image. We find this strategy to be beneficial for all layers tested, achieving the best results when using conv5_1. Inspired by the boost in performance of the Gaussian center prior in SPoC features [2], we apply a weighting scheme on the visual words to provide more importance to those belonging to the center of the image.

Table 1: mAP on Oxford 5k and Paris 6k for the different stages in the pipeline introduced in Section 4.

		Baseline	+R	+GQE	+R +GQE	+R +LQE
Oxford	GS	0.653	0.701	0.702	0.771	**0.782**
	LS	0.738	0.734	0.773	0.769	**0.788**
Paris	GS	0.699	0.719	0.774	0.801	**0.835**
	LS	0.820	0.815	0.814	0.807	**0.848**

5.2 Reranking and query expansion

We apply the local reranking (R) stage on the top-100 images in the initial ranking, using the sliding window approach described in Section 4. The presented aspect ratio filtering is applied with a threshold $th = 0.4$, which was chosen based on a visual inspection of results on a subset of Oxford 5k. Query expansion is later applied considering the top-10 images of the resulting ranking. Table 1 contains the results for the different stages in the pipeline.

The results indicate that the local reranking is significantly beneficial only when applied to a ranking obtained from a search using the global BoW descriptor of the query image (GS). This is consistent with the work by Tolias et al. [20], who also apply a spatial reranking followed by query expansion to a ranking obtained with a search using descriptors of full images. They achieve a mAP of 0.66 in Oxford 5k, which is increased to 0.77 after spatial reranking and query expansion, while we reach similar results (e.g. from 0.652 to 0.769). However, our results indicate that a ranking originating from a local search (LS) does not benefit from local reranking. Since the BoW representation allows us to effectively perform a local search (LS) in a database of full indexed images, we find the local reranking stage applied to LS to be redundant in terms of the achieved quality of the ranking. However, the local reranking stage does provide with a rough localization of the object in the images of the

Table 2: Comparison to state-of-the-art CNN representations (mAP). Results in the lower section consider reranking and/or query expansion.

	Oxford		Paris	
	5k	105k	6k	106k
Ng *et al.* [10]	0.649	-	0.694	-
Razavian *et al.* [16]	**0.844**	-	**0.853**	-
SPoC [2]	0.657	0.642	-	-
R-MAC [20]	0.668	0.616	0.830	**0.757**
CroW [7]	0.682	**0.632**	0.796	0.710
uCroW [7]	0.666	0.629	0.767	0.695
GS	0.652	0.510	0.698	0.421
LS	0.739	0.593	0.820	0.648
CroW + GQE [7]	0.722	0.678	0.855	0.797
R-MAC + R + GQE [20]	0.770	**0.726**	**0.877**	**0.817**
LS + GQE	0.773	0.602	0.814	0.632
LS + R + LQE	**0.788**	0.651	0.848	0.641

ranking, as depicted in Figure 1. We use this information to perform query expansion based on local features (LQE).

Results indicate that query expansion stages greatly improve performance in Oxford 5k. We do not observe significant gains after reranking and QE in the Paris 6k dataset, although we achieve our best result with LS + R + LQE.

5.3 Comparison with the state-of-the-art

We compare our approach with other CNN-based representations that make use of features from convolutional layers on the Oxford and Paris datasets. Table 2 includes the best result for each approach in the literature. Our performance using global search is comparable to that of Ng et al. [10], which is the one that most resembles our approach. However, they achieve this result using VLAD features, which are more expensive to compute and, being a dense high-dimensional representation, do not scale as well to larger datasets. Similarly, Razavian et al. [16] achieve the highest performance of all approaches in both the Oxford and Paris benchmarks by applying a spatial search at different scales for all images in the database. Such approach is prohibitively costly when dealing with larger datasets, especially for real-time search scenarios. Our BoW-based representation is highly sparse, allowing for fast retrieval using inverted indices, and achieves consistently high mAP in all tested datasets.

We also compare our local reranking and query expansion results with similar approaches in the state-of-the-art. The authors of R-MAC [20] apply a spatial search for reranking, followed by a query expansion stage, while the authors of CroW [7] only apply query expansion after the initial search. Our proposed approach also achieves competitive results in this section, achieving the best result for Oxford 5k.

5.4 Experiments on TRECVid INS

In this section, we compare the Bag of Local Convolutional Features (BLCF) with the sum pooled convolutional features proposed in several works in the literature. We use our own implementation of the *uCroW* descriptor from [7] and compare it with BLCF for the TRECVid INS subset. For the sake of comparison, we test our implementation of sum pooling using both our chosen CNN layer and input size (conv5_1 and 1/3 image size), and the ones reported in [7] (pool5 and full image resolution). For the BoW representation, we train the codebook using 3M local CNN features chosen randomly from the INS subset. In this case, we do not apply center prior to the feature to avoid down weighting local features from image areas where the objects might appear. Table 3 compares sum pooling with BoW in Oxford, Paris, and TRECVid subset datasets. As stated in earlier sections, sum pooling and BoW have similar performance in Oxford and Paris datasets. For the TRECVid INS subset, however, Bag of Words significantly outperforms sum pooling, which demonstrates its suitability for challenging instance search datasets, in which queries are not centered and have variable size and appearance. We also observe a different behavior when using the provided query object locations (LS) to search, which was highly beneficial in Oxford and Paris datasets, but does not provide any gain in TRECVid INS. We hypothesize that the fact that the size of the instances is much smaller in TRECVid than in Paris and Oxford datasets causes this drop in performance. Global search (GS) achieves better results on TRECVid INS, which suggests that query instances are in many cases correctly retrieved due to their context.

Table 3: mAP of sum pooling and BoW aggregation techniques in Oxford, Paris and TRECVid INS subset.

		Oxford 5k	Paris 6k	INS 23k
BoW	GS	0.650	0.698	**0.323**
	LS	**0.739**	**0.819**	0.295
Sum pooling (as ours)	GS	0.606	0.712	0.156
	LS	0.583	0.742	0.097
Sum pooling (as in [7])	GS	0.672	0.774	0.139
	LS	0.683	0.763	0.120

6. CONCLUSION

We proposed an aggregation strategy based on Bag of Words to encode features from convolutional neural networks into a sparse representations for instance search. We achieved competitive performance with respect to other CNN-based representations in Oxford and Paris benchmarks, while being more scalable in terms of index size, cost of indexing, and search time. We also compared our BoW encoding scheme with sum pooling of CNN features in the far more challenging TRECVid instance search task, and demonstrated that our method consistently and significantly performs better. Our method does, however, appear to be more sensitive to large numbers of distractor images than methods based on sum and max pooling. We speculate that this may be because the distractor images are drawn from a different distribution to the original dataset, and may therefore require a larger codebook to better represent the diversity in the visual words. Future work will investigate this further.

Acknowledgements

This publication has emanated from research conducted with the financial support of Science Foundation Ireland (SFI) under grant number SFI/12/RC/2289, project BigGraph TEC2013-43935-R, funded by the Spanish Ministerio de Economía y Competitividad and the European Regional Development Fund (ERDF), as well as the donation of a GeForce GTX Titan X from NVIDIA Corporation.

7. REFERENCES

[1] R. Arandjelović, P. Gronat, A. Torii, T. Pajdla, and J. Sivic. NetVLAD: CNN architecture for weakly supervised place recognition. *arXiv:1511.07247*, 2015.

[2] A. Babenko and V. Lempitsky. Aggregating local deep features for image retrieval. In *International Conference on Computer Vision (ICCV)*, December 2015.

[3] A. Babenko, A. Slesarev, A. Chigorin, and V. Lempitsky. Neural codes for image retrieval. In *Computer Vision–ECCV 2014*. 2014.

[4] Y. Gong, L. Wang, R. Guo, and S. Lazebnik. Multi-scale orderless pooling of deep convolutional activation features. In *Computer Vision–ECCV 2014*. 2014.

[5] H. Jégou, M. Douze, C. Schmid, and P. Pérez. Aggregating local descriptors into a compact image representation. In *Computer Vision and Pattern Recognition (CVPR)*, 2010.

[6] Y. Jia, E. Shelhamer, J. Donahue, S. Karayev, J. Long, R. Girshick, S. Guadarrama, and T. Darrell. Caffe: Convolutional architecture for fast feature embedding. In *ACM Multimedia*, 2014.

[7] Y. Kalantidis, C. Mellina, and S. Osindero. Cross-dimensional weighting for aggregated deep convolutional features. *arXiv:1512.04065*, 2015.

[8] S. Lazebnik, C. Schmid, and J. Ponce. Beyond bags of features: Spatial pyramid matching for recognizing natural scene categories. In *Computer Vision and Pattern Recognition (CVPR)*, 2006.

[9] Y. Liu, Y. Guo, S. Wu, and M. S. Lew. Deepindex for accurate and efficient image retrieval. In *International Conference on Multimedia Retrieval (ICMR)*, 2015.

[10] J. Ng, F. Yang, and L. Davis. Exploiting local features from deep networks for image retrieval. In *Computer Vision and Pattern Recognition Workshops (CVPRW)*, 2015.

[11] V.-T. Nguyen, D.-L. Nguyen, M.-T. Tran, D.-D. Le, D. A. Duong, and S. Satoh. Query-adaptive late fusion with neural network for instance search. In *International Workshop on Multimedia Signal Processing (MMSP)*, 2015.

[12] F. Perronnin, Y. Liu, J. Sánchez, and H. Poirier. Large-scale image retrieval with compressed fisher vectors. In *Computer Vision and Pattern Recognition (CVPR)*, 2010.

[13] J. Philbin, O. Chum, M. Isard, J. Sivic, and A. Zisserman. Object retrieval with large vocabularies and fast spatial matching. In *Computer Vision and Pattern Recognition (CVPR)*, 2007.

[14] J. Philbin, O. Chum, M. Isard, J. Sivic, and A. Zisserman. Lost in quantization: Improving particular object retrieval in large scale image databases. In *Computer Vision and Pattern Recognition (CVPR)*, 2008.

[15] A. S. Razavian, H. Azizpour, J. Sullivan, and S. Carlsson. CNN features off-the-shelf: an astounding baseline for recognition. In *Computer Vision and Pattern Recognition Workshops (CVPRW)*, 2014.

[16] A. Sharif Razavian, J. Sullivan, A. Maki, and S. Carlsson. A baseline for visual instance retrieval with deep convolutional networks. In *International Conference on Learning Representations*. ICLR, 2015.

[17] K. Simonyan and A. Zisserman. Very deep convolutional networks for large-scale image recognition. *arXiv preprint arXiv:1409.1556*, 2014.

[18] J. Sivic and A. Zisserman. Efficient visual search of videos cast as text retrieval. *IEEE Transactions on Pattern Analysis and Machine Intelligence*, 31(4), 2009.

[19] A. F. Smeaton, P. Over, and W. Kraaij. Evaluation campaigns and trecvid. In *International Workshop on Multimedia Information Retrieval (MIR)*, 2006.

[20] G. Tolias, R. Sicre, and H. Jégou. Particular object retrieval with integral max-pooling of CNN activations. *arXiv preprint arXiv:1511.05879*, 2015.

[21] L. Xie, Q. Tian, R. Hong, and B. Zhang. Image classification and retrieval are one. In *International Conference on Multimedia Retrieval (ICMR)*, 2015.

[22] W. Zhang and C.-W. Ngo. Topological spatial verification for instance search. *IEEE Transactions on Multimedia*, 17(8), 2015.

[23] X. Zhou, C.-Z. Zhu, Q. Zhu, S. Satoh, and Y.-T. Guo. A practical spatial re-ranking method for instance search from videos. In *International Conference on Image Processing (ICIP)*, 2014.

[24] C.-Z. Zhu and S. Satoh. Large vocabulary quantization for searching instances from videos. In *International Conference on Multimedia Retrieval (ICMR)*, 2012.

Interactive Multimodal Learning on 100 Million Images

Jan Zahálka[1], Stevan Rudinac[1], Björn Þór Jónsson[1,2],
Dennis C. Koelma[1], and Marcel Worring[1]
[1]Informatics Institute, University of Amsterdam, The Netherlands
[2]School of Computer Science, Reyjkavik University, Iceland
{j.zahalka, s.rudinac, d.c.koelma, m.worring}@uva.nl, bjorn@ru.is

ABSTRACT

This paper presents Blackthorn, an efficient interactive multimodal learning approach facilitating analysis of multimedia collections of 100 million items on a single high-end workstation. This is achieved by efficient data compression and optimizations to the interactive learning process. The compressed ι-I64 data representation costs tens of bytes per item yet preserves most of the visual and textual semantic information. The optimized interactive learning model scores the ι-I64-compressed data directly, greatly reducing the computational requirements. The experiments show that Blackthorn is up to 105x faster than the conventional relevance feedback baseline. Blackthorn is shown to vastly outperform the baseline with respect to recall over time. Blackthorn reaches up to 92% of the precision achieved by the baseline, validating the efficacy of the ι-I64 representation. On the YFCC100M dataset, Blackthorn performes one complete interaction round in 0.7 seconds. Blackthorn thus opens multimedia collections comprising 100 million items to learning-based analysis in fully interactive time.

Keywords

Interactive multimodal learning; multimedia analytics; data compression; YFCC100M

1. INTRODUCTION

Multimedia collections are becoming the central information resource for a growing number of domains, such as physics, forensics, and marketing. This increases the need for methods for fast and insightful analysis of the data. Often, the analysts need to progress from the dataset to insight in hours or few days at most. For example, a journalist discovering stories about the Brussels terrorist attack in the ensuing flood of social media content cannot wait weeks before publishing the story; she needs at least preliminary insights right away. An essential ingredient of insight gain in multimedia analytics in any knowledge domain is *interaction* [17, 28]. Currently, multimedia collections can easily reach millions of items, and even larger datasets are common. Behemoths such as the Yahoo Flickr Creative Commons 100M (YFCC100M) dataset [21] were not so long ago considered inconceivable challenges, yet to truly advance large-scale multimedia analytics, techniques for analyzing such large datasets are needed. How can interactivity in multimedia analytics be assured facing the rapid growth of collection size?

Interactive learning techniques, such as relevance feedback or active learning, are a good fit for multimedia analytics, as they elicit training data labels from the user directly and train the model based on them [9]. This paradigm aligns well with insight, the goal of multimedia analytics. Insight is iteratively built by the analyst through interaction with all or most of the data in the collection and application of the analyst's domain knowledge [17, 28]. Since interactive learning trains its model online based on the user's interactions, the analysis is timely. How to enable interactive and multimodal learning to support large-scale multimedia analytics using modest computational resources (standard high-end workstation with 64 GB RAM and 16-core CPU) is the research question addressed in this work.

In this paper we introduce Blackthorn, an efficient interactive multimodal learning approach for collections of 100 million multimedia items.[1] The architecture of Blackthorn is depicted in Figure 1. Blackthorn brings three main contributions: a multimedia content compression method allowing to fit billions of items into 64 GB of RAM; optimizations to the interactive learning process; and opening up the possibility of analytics on a collection of 100M multimedia items in interactive time (under 1 second per interaction round). To the best of our knowledge, no work has yet addressed fully interactive-learning-based exploration of an image dataset with 100 million items on a single workstation.

2. RELATED WORK

In response to the rapid growth of digital collections, a number of approaches facilitating more efficient search and exploration have been proposed. Interactive learning (e.g., relevance feedback) has been proven invaluable for improving multimedia information retrieval [9], and benchmarks such as the Video Browser Showdown were introduced [19]. However, the collections considered in these benchmarks are much smaller than the one considered in this work. In addition, most of current approaches employ entire computa-

ICMR'16, June 06-09, 2016, New York, NY, USA
© 2016 ACM. ISBN 978-1-4503-4359-6/16/06...$15.00
DOI: http://dx.doi.org/10.1145/2911996.2912062

[1]As this paper focuses on *efficiency* of interactive learning, the name is inspired by the efficiency of the blackthorn shrub: as fire wood, it yields much heat with little smoke.

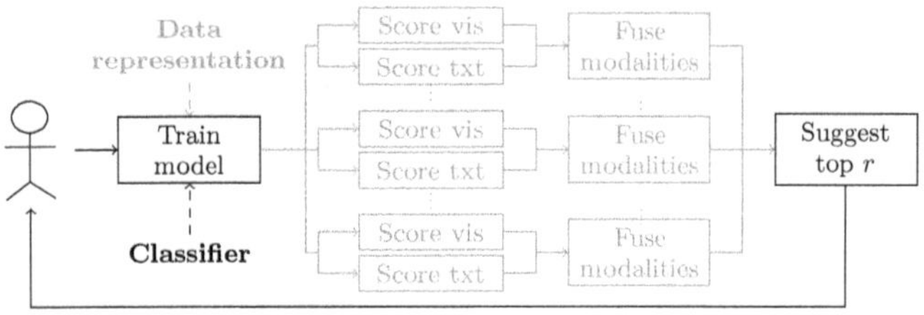

Figure 1: Interactive learning with Blackthorn. The components of interactive learning innovated by Blackthorn are marked orange.

tional clusters to facilitate analysis of the data in interactive time [6, 12]. The algorithmic efficiency component often boils down to reducing the number of items for which the similarity is computed, reducing the dimensionality of data representation, or simplifying the similarity computation.

Early work demonstrated that exact k-nn search techniques suffer from the curse of dimensionality [2], paving the way for approximate methods. Several recent works from the multimedia and computer vision communities rely on embedding visual features in binary space to compress the data and reduce the distance computation time [4, 8, 11, 15, 16, 24, 29]. LSH is a well-known scalar-based indexing technique [1]. The NV-tree is a scalar-based method, which has been shown to significantly outperform LSH while requiring about 6 bytes per descriptor [14]. Product quantization is a family of vector-based quantization schemes producing compact code-words by indexing low-dimensional subspaces independently [10, 13, 26].

While these approaches for scaling up image retrieval were proven effective in k-nn search, their applicability in analytic tasks remains limited for at least two reasons. First, binary hashes are not suited for classification, which is an essential component of most analytic platforms. Moreover, in many analytic tasks search and exploration are alternately performed, which requires updating, summarizing and repartitioning of the collection based on user interactions [28]. Such operations require preservation of the original vectors or a significant portion of information contained in them. Novel approaches are needed for building such representations for efficient deployment in analytic tasks.

3. DATA REPRESENTATION

In the interactive learning setting, it is desirable that the user understands the data representation. Hence, we focus on representations carrying semantic meaning. However, in case the collection comprises 100 million items, the memory requirements of such representations are prohibitive. Indeed, assuming 1000 visual concepts, 100 text topics, and 8 bytes (B) as the size of one floating-point number, the semantic representation of a 100M collection requires roughly 880 GB of RAM. We address this issue by introducing a data compression method that greatly reduces the representation size with only a modest information loss.

Semantic representations such as visual concept scores output by a convolutional neural network [20] or LDA topics in the text domain [3] are *sparse*, allowing the design of an efficient representation following the established sparse representation practices [25]. Thus, in each modality, most of the information contained in a feature vector with n_f features can be preserved by encoding only the top t_f features in compact bit fields, since $t_f \ll n_f$. For the k-th feature, $1 \leqslant k \leqslant t_f$, we need to encode the feature ID (denoted i_k) and the respective score (denoted s_k). The bit cost for encoding the ID (denoted b_i) is $\lceil \log_2 n_f \rceil$. The bit cost for encoding the score (denoted b_s) is $\lceil p \cdot \log_2 10 \rceil$, where p denotes the decimal precision. Further, we encode the number of features actually encoded for item I (denoted e_I), as due to sparsity, e_I could be smaller than t_f. The bit cost of this encoding (denoted b_e) is $\lceil \log_2 f \rceil$. Obtaining the bit field compressing the feature IDs of item I in each modality (denoted $\mathcal{I}$) is defined by Equation 1. Obtaining the bit field compressing the scores, $\mathcal{S}$, is defined in Equation 2. Here, $\vee$ denotes the binary OR operation, $\ll$ the left bit shift operation, and $[\cdot]$ the rounding function.

$$\mathcal{I} \quad = \quad e_I \vee \bigvee_{k=0}^{e_I - 1} i_k \ll (k \cdot b_i + b_e) \qquad (1)$$

$$\mathcal{S} \quad = \quad e_I \vee \bigvee_{k=0}^{e_I - 1} [10^p \cdot s_k] \ll (k \cdot b_s + b_e) \qquad (2)$$

The memory bit requirements for $\mathcal{I}_I$ and $\mathcal{S}_I$, $b_{\mathcal{I}}$ and $b_{\mathcal{S}}$, are then equal to $e_I \cdot b_i + b_e$ and $e_I \cdot b_s + b_e$, respectively. $\mathcal{I}$ and $\mathcal{S}$ can be decompressed to obtain the encoded features, setting the features outside the top t_f to 0. Let $\wedge$ denote the bitwise AND operation and $\gg$ the right arithmetic bit shift operation. Equation 3 describes the decompression of the number of encoded features (e_I), Equation 4 describes the decompression of the k-th feature ID, and Equation 5 describes the decompression of the respective feature score.

$$e_I \quad = \quad \mathcal{I} \wedge \left(2^{b_e} - 1\right) \qquad (3)$$

$$\delta(\mathcal{I}, k) \quad = \quad (\mathcal{I} \gg (k \cdot b_i + b_e)) \wedge \left(2^{b_i} - 1\right) \qquad (4)$$

$$\delta(\mathcal{S}, k) \quad = \quad \frac{(\mathcal{S} \gg (k \cdot b_s + b_e)) \wedge \left(2^{b_s} - 1\right)}{10^p} \qquad (5)$$

Since most current machines are 64-bit, it is desirable to choose t_f and p so that $\mathcal{I}$ and $\mathcal{S}$ align with the 64-bit architecture. Given a semantic representation with less than 1024 relevant visual concepts and text topics and $p = 3$, we can encode $\mathcal{I}$ and $\mathcal{S}$ each in ι 64-bit integers, keeping the top 6ι features. This setting enables a trade-off between minimizing memory and computational requirements (low ι) on the one hand and information loss on the other (high ι).

The resulting memory-efficient **ι-integer (ι-I64) representation** only requires $4\iota + 1$ 64-bit integers per item: 2ι for $\mathcal{I}$ and $\mathcal{S}$ per modality, as well as an additional integer for the item ID. With $\iota = 1$, the representation is 220x smaller than the uncompressed representation and allows fitting 1.5 billion items into 60 GB of memory. This makes ι-I64 representation suitable for large-scale interactive multimodal learning.

4. INTERACTIVE LEARNING

Each interactive multimodal learning session consists of a number of *interaction rounds*, each with 3 steps. Firstly, a classifier is trained for each modality on the user-provided examples. Secondly, the unlabelled items in the collection are scored. Thirdly, the rankings per modality are aggregated and the top r results are returned to the user. A user

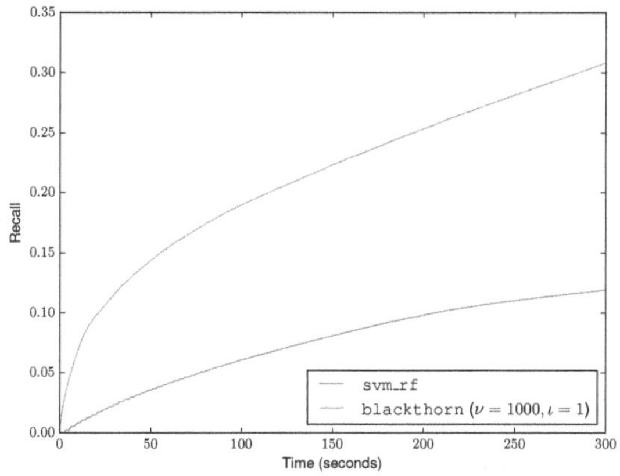

Figure 2: Recall over time (YFCC100M-California).

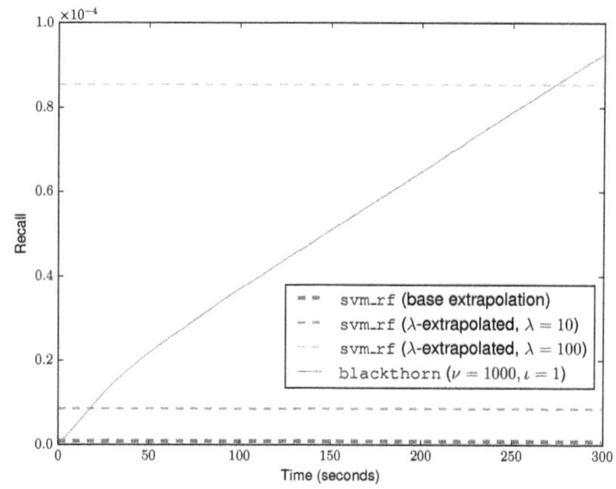

Figure 3: Recall over time (YFCC100M). The baseline values are extrapolated from YFCC100M-California, with λ further multiplying the extrapolated performance.

Table 1: Precision and time per interaction round (YFCC100M-California).

Algorithm	Precision	Time
`svm_rf`	0.48	3.16 s
`blackthorn` ($\nu = 1000$, $\iota = 1$)	0.44 (92%)	0.07 s (45x faster)
`blackthorn` ($\nu = 200$, $\iota = 1$)	0.35 (73%)	0.03 s (105x faster)

typically provides at most tens of examples per interaction round, regardless of the collection size. However, the time cost of steps 2 and 3 increases dramatically as the collection grows larger. We have alleviated this issue somewhat by data compression and an efficient parallel implementation in C, but this does not solve the issue. In this section, we address Blackthorn's algorithmic optimizations.

Blackthorn utilizes a linear SVM classifier. To improve the classifier's efficiency, we design a custom SVM scoring function that operates directly in ι-I64-compressed space. The SVM scoring function σ performs a vector multiplication of the model's weight vector $\mathbf{w}$ with the feature vector $\mathbf{x}$, adding bias b to the result. This costs $2n_f + 1$ mathematical operations (multiplications and additions) per item and modality. In the ι-I64 representation, only the 6ι encoded features carry any value. Hence, we can obtain the SVM score by multiplying only the decompressed feature values by the corresponding values of the model's weight vector $\mathbf{w}$:

$$\sigma_c(I) = \sum_{j=0}^{\iota-1} \sum_{k=0}^{e_I-1} \left(w_{\delta(\mathcal{I},6j+k)} \cdot \delta(\mathcal{S}, 6j+k) \right) + b \qquad (6)$$

This computation costs $42\iota + 1$ mathematical operations per item and modality. Since $\iota \ll n_f$, this amounts to a considerable speedup: for example, in a setting with $\iota = 1$ and $n_f = 1000$ (for instance, 1000 visual concepts), the number of mathematical operations is reduced 46.5x.

Late modality fusion is another aspect requiring attention with respect to algorithmic complexity. With a straightforward implementation, this requires $O(N \log N)$ time, which is higher than the $O(N)$ complexity of scoring. To reduce fusion complexity to $O(N)$, we follow the protocol of top-d rank aggregation [7] in order to obtain the top r relevant results. For each modality, the top-scoring ν ($r \leqslant \nu \ll n$) results in that modality are nominated to the final ranking in $O(N)$ time. The multimodal ranking is obtained by performing rank aggregations on the nominated items ($O(\nu \log \nu)$ time). Because $\nu \ll N$, modality fusion is essentially computed in linear time. Optimized modality fusion in combination with efficient scoring ensures that all stages of interactive learning complete in $O(N)$ time.

5. EXPERIMENTAL SETUP

To gauge Blackthorn's analytic performance and scalability, we report three evaluation measures: recall over time, precision, and time per interaction round. We compare our approach (`blackthorn`) with the standard linear-SVM-based relevance feedback approach (`svm_rf`) [9]. Both algorithms use 1000 ILSVRC ImageNet concepts [18] extracted by GoogLeNet [20] as visual features and 100 LDA topics [3] extracted using Gensim [23] from the tags, title, and description of each image. Both `blackthorn` and `svm_rf` are implemented in C and use the VLFeat SVM library [22]. Two datasets are used in the experiments. The first one is the YFCC100M dataset itself, which is too big to be handled by `svm_rf`. To allow for direct comparison of `blackthorn` and `svm_rf`, we use a custom second dataset, YFCC100M-California, which contains all items in YFCC100M tagged with the *california* tag. This dataset has 1,221,608 items.

To evaluate YFCC100M in an interactive setting, we perform a task inspired by the MediaEval Placing task [5]. The evaluation task is to retrieve items pertaining to a large city based *solely* on visual and text content. Note that this is a very difficult task. However, it is suitable the sake of providing a comparison between approaches. This task is performed by artificial users (*actors*), each corresponding to one city in the top 50 cities with the highest number of items. The geo information is discarded for evaluation purposes. Each actor conducts 50 sessions, initializing each with 100 uniform random samples from its city as positives and 200 uniform random samples from the collection as negatives. In each interaction round, 25 items are suggested.

6. RESULTS ON YFCC100M-CALIFORNIA

The precision and time per interaction round are reported in Table 1. The development of recall in the time period of

Figure 4: Example items involved in the first interaction round performed on the YFCC100M dataset by the actor interested in items from Prague. None of the suggestions are regarded as relevant for our evaluation task, despite the semantically similar content.

5 minutes is depicted in Figure 2. For all three evaluation measures, we compare `svm_rf` with the best-scoring ν, ι configuration of `blackthorn`. We have tested `blackthorn` with $\nu \in \{100, 200, \ldots, 1000\}$ and $\iota \in \{1, 2, 3\}$. Varying ν has some impact on precision, with $\nu = 100$ reaching roughly 75% of the precison of $\nu = 1000$. Increasing ν impacts the time per interaction round: $\nu = 1000$ costs roughly twice the time of the $\nu = 100$. Regarding recall over time, low ν tends to outperform the higher values due to the lower time per interaction round. Regarding ι, we observe that increasing its value brings very minimal precision and recall gain, but has a negative impact on the time per interaction round. We believe that the low precision and recall gain is caused by insufficient decimal precision of the compressed values. We aim to investigate this further. Overall, we recommend choosing $\iota = 1$ in all cases, higher ν for maximum precision, and lower ν for maximum recall over time and speed.

The experiments clearly show that computational speed and efficiency are `blackthorn`'s forte. One interaction round of `blackthorn` on YFCC100M-California takes 0.05 ± 0.01 seconds on average across all evaluated ν values, and the fastest configuration is 105x faster than `svm_rf`. The information loss incurred by the ι-I64 representation turns out to be affordable. The highest-precision configuration of `blackthorn` keeps 92% of the average precision with a speed-up of 45. The recall over time plot (Figure 2) clearly shows that `blackthorn` dramatically surpasses `svm_rf`.

7. RESULTS ON YFCC100M

Our approach succeeded in the test of interactivity on the large dataset: on average across all ν values, `blackthorn` takes 0.69 ± 0.01 seconds per interaction round. Figure 3 shows the development of recall over time on YFCC100M. Given the dataset's prohibitive size, `svm_rf` is infeasible. In order to compare the approaches, we extrapolate `svm_rf`'s results on YFCC100M-California. Since `svm_rf`'s computational cost is $O(N)$, the 3.16 second performance on 1.2M becomes roughly 4.3 minutes. Hence, only the first interaction round needs to be considered. The base extrapolation is twice the recall value of `blackthorn`'s recall in the first interaction round, following the trend observed on YFCC100M-California. In addition, we report two λ-extrapolated `svm_rf` baselines, where $\lambda \in \{10, 100\}$ further multiplies the base extrapolation. We believe this more than compensates for any potential unverifiable factors influencing the true recall scalability. The results clearly show `blackthorn`'s efficiency with respect to recall gain over time: it is able to surpass all three interpolations in the first 5 minutes of the analysis.

The precision per interaction round on the YFCC100M dataset, averaged over all ν values, is 0.003 ± 0.0001. Note that the low values are influenced by two important factors. Firstly, the size of the dataset brings an increase in noise and lower discriminative power of feature vectors. Secondly, the evaluation task is extremely difficult. Indeed, there are cases where the algorithm's suggestions are evaluated as irrelevant, despite their semantic similarity to the provided positives. This is demonstrated in Figure 4. In a less strict setting, these suggestions could be easily deemed relevant. Despite the low values of precision, `blackthorn` does provide relevant suggestions even on the large dataset.

8. CONCLUSION

In this paper, we have presented Blackthorn, an efficient interactive multimodal learning framework which enables full interactive-learning-based analysis of a collection with 100M multimedia items. The data compression method of Blackthorn, ι-I64, is shown to reduce the size of multimodal features by a factor of 220 *and* preserve most of the information contained in the original features. Blackthorn yields a massive 105x speed-up in comparison to the classic relevance feedback paradigm. The experiments further show that Blackthorn is suitable for the analysis of the entire YFCC100M dataset. It is able to learn on the fly from the user-provided training samples, and one interaction round on the entire 100M collection takes less than a second. Its high efficiency and low resource cost would also support multi-category exploration with proactive suggestions by the system. The analysis can be performed on a single standard high-end workstation with 64 GB RAM and 16 CPU cores. In order to foster further research on YFCC100M, the Blackthorn software package has been made available as an open-source tool [27]. In conclusion, Blackthorn is a step forward towards fully harnessing the wealth of information contained in large-scale multimedia collections.

9. REFERENCES

[1] A. Andoni and P. Indyk. Near-optimal hashing algorithms for approximate nearest neighbor in high dimensions. *Commun. ACM*, 51(1):117–122, 2008.

[2] K. S. Beyer, J. Goldstein, R. Ramakrishnan, and U. Shaft. When is 'nearest neighbor' meaningful? In *ICDT*, 1999.

[3] D. M. Blei, A. Y. Ng, and M. I. Jordan. Latent dirichlet allocation. *JMLR*, 3:993–1022, 2003.

[4] S. Bondugula, V. Manjunatha, L. S. Davis, and D. Doermann. Shoe: Sibling hashing with output embeddings. In *ACM MM*, pages 823–826, 2015.

[5] J. Choi, C. Hauff, O. V. Laere, and B. Thomee. The Placing task at MediaEval 2015. In *MediaEval*, 2015.

[6] O. de Rooij and M. Worring. Active bucket categorization for high recall video retrieval. *IEEE TMM*, 15(4):898–907, June 2013.

[7] C. Dwork, R. Kumar, M. Naor, and D. Sivakumar. Rank aggregation methods for the web. In *WWW*, pages 613–622, 2001.

[8] A. Gordo, F. Perronnin, Y. Gong, and S. Lazebnik. Asymmetric distances for binary embeddings. *IEEE TPAMI*, 36(1):33–47, 2014.

[9] T. Huang, C. Dagli, S. Rajaram, E. Chang, M. Mandel, G. E. Poliner, and D. Ellis. Active learning for interactive multimedia retrieval. *Proc. IEEE*, 96(4):648–667, 2008.

[10] H. Jégou, M. Douze, and C. Schmid. Product quantization for nearest neighbor search. *IEEE TPAMI*, 33(1), 2011.

[11] H. Jégou, F. Perronnin, M. Douze, J. Sánchez, P. Pérez, and C. Schmid. Aggregating local image descriptors into compact codes. *IEEE TPAMI*, 34(9):1704–1716, 2012.

[12] L. Jiang, S.-I. Yu, D. Meng, Y. Yang, T. Mitamura, and A. G. Hauptmann. Fast and accurate content-based semantic search in 100M internet videos. In *ACM MM*, pages 49–58, 2015.

[13] Y. S. Kalantidis and Y. Avrithis. Locally optimized product quantization for approximate nearest neighbor search. In *IEEE CVPR*, 2014.

[14] H. Lejsek, B. T. Jónsson, and L. Amsaleg. NV-Tree: nearest neighbors at the billion scale. In *ICMR*, 2011.

[15] P. Li, M. Wang, J. Cheng, C. Xu, and H. Lu. Spectral hashing with semantically consistent graph for image indexing. *IEEE TMM*, 15(1):141–152, 2013.

[16] M. Norouzi, A. Punjani, and D. Fleet. Fast search in hamming space with multi-index hashing. In *CVPR*, pages 3108–3115, 2012.

[17] C. North. Towards measuring visualization insight. *IEEE TCGA*, 26(3):6–9, 2006.

[18] O. Russakovsky, J. Deng, H. Su, J. Krause, S. Satheesh, S. Ma, Z. Huang, A. Karpathy, A. Khosla, M. Bernstein, A. C. Berg, and L. Fei-Fei. Imagenet large scale visual recognition challenge. *IJCV*, 115(3):211–252, 2015.

[19] K. Schoeffmann. A user-centric media retrieval competition: The video browser showdown 2012-2014. *IEEE MM*, 21(4):8–13, 2014.

[20] C. Szegedy, W. Liu, Y. Jia, P. Sermanet, S. Reed, D. Anguelov, D. Erhan, V. Vanhoucke, and A. Rabinovich. Going deeper with convolutions. *CVPR*, 2015.

[21] B. Thomee, B. Elizalde, D. A. Shamma, K. Ni, G. Friedland, D. Poland, D. Borth, and L.-J. Li. YFCC100M: The new data in multimedia research. *Commun. ACM*, 59(2):64–73, 2016.

[22] A. Vedaldi and B. Fulkerson. VLFeat: An open and portable library of computer vision algorithms. http://www.vlfeat.org/, 2008.

[23] R. Řehůřek and P. Sojka. Software framework for topic modelling with large corpora. In *LREC*, pages 45–50, 2010.

[24] J. Wang, H. T. Shen, S. Yan, N. Yu, S. Li, and J. Wang. Optimized distances for binary code ranking. In *ACM MM*, pages 517–526, 2014.

[25] J. Wright, Y. Ma, J. Mairal, G. Sapiro, T. S. Huang, and S. Yan. Sparse representation for computer vision and pattern recognition. *Proceedings of the IEEE*, 98(6):1031–1044, 2010.

[26] E. S. Xioufis, S. Papadopoulos, Y. Kompatsiaris, G. Tsoumakas, and I. P. Vlahavas. A comprehensive study over VLAD and product quantization in large-scale image retrieval. *IEEE TMM*, 16(6), 2014.

[27] J. Zahálka. Blackthorn. http://staff.fnwi.uva.nl/j.zahalka/blackthorn.html, 2016.

[28] J. Zahálka and M. Worring. Towards interactive, intelligent, and integrated multimedia analytics. In *IEEE VAST*, pages 3–12, 2014.

[29] L. Zhang, Y. Zhang, J. Tang, X. Gu, J. Li, and Q. Tian. Topology preserving hashing for similarity search. In *ACM MM*, pages 123–132, 2013.

Combining Holistic and Part-based Deep Representations for Computational Painting Categorization

Rao Muhammad Anwer
Department of Computer Science
Aalto University, Finland
rao.anwer@aalto.fi

Fahad Shahbaz Khan
Computer Vision Laboratory
Linköping University, Sweden
fahad.khan@liu.se

Joost van de Weijer
Computer Vision Center
CS Dept. Universitat Autonoma de Barcelona, Spain
joost@cvc.uab.es

Jorma Laaksonen
Department of Computer Science
Aalto University, Finland
jorma.laaksonen@aalto.fi

ABSTRACT

Automatic analysis of visual art, such as paintings, is a challenging inter-disciplinary research problem. Conventional approaches only rely on global scene characteristics by encoding holistic information for computational painting categorization. We argue that such approaches are sub-optimal and that discriminative common visual structures provide complementary information for painting classification.

We present an approach that encodes both the global scene layout and discriminative latent common structures for computational painting categorization. The region of interests are automatically extracted, without any manual part labeling, by training class-specific deformable part-based models. Both holistic and region-of-interests are then described using multi-scale dense convolutional features. These features are pooled separately using Fisher vector encoding and concatenated afterwards in a single image representation. Experiments are performed on a challenging dataset with 91 different painters and 13 diverse painting styles. Our approach outperforms the standard method, which only employs the global scene characteristics. Furthermore, our method achieves state-of-the-art results outperforming a recent multi-scale deep features based approach [11] by 6.4% and 3.8% respectively on artist and style classification.

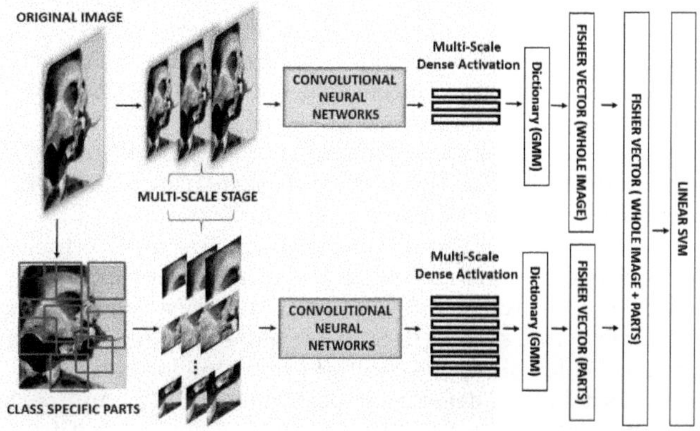

Figure 1: An overview of our approach for painting categorization problem. Both holistic and part-based information are encoded in our method. The discriminative parts are automatically captured, without any manual part labeling, by training a class-specific DPM detector. The holistic and class-specific parts are then described using multi-scale dense convolutional features from a pre-trained CNN. The two sets of features are later pooled separately using the Fisher vector encoding and concatenated afterwards in a single image representation.

1. INTRODUCTION

Digital analysis of art, such as paintings, is a challenging cross-disciplinary research problem. It has gained much attention recently [8, 2] due to the emergence of significant amount of visual artistic data on the web. Computational techniques to manage online large digital art data have several applications, such as, e.g. art recommendation systems in the tourism industry, analysis and labeling tools for experts in museums and detection systems to identify art forgery. In this paper, we investigate the task of automatically categorizing a painting to its artist and style.

The artist classification task involves associating a painting image to its respective painter. The style categorization problem tackles inferring artist paintings with respect to a school of art or art movement, e.g. renaissance, impressionism and modernism. Both these tasks are challenging due to large amount of inter-class and intra-class variations. For instance, Picasso's paintings span multiple styles such as cubism and surrealism. Other factors, such as stroke patterns, choice of color palette, scene composition and line styles, influence the art work making the problem of computational painting categorization further complicated.

ICMR'16, June 06-09, 2016, New York, NY, USA

DOI: http://dx.doi.org/10.1145/2911996.2912063

Most existing approaches [6, 2] tackle the problem of painting categorization using different low-level features such as appearance, texture and color. These low-level features are further used within the bag-of-words framework to obtain histogram-based image representations. Within the bag-of-words framework, several encoding schemes, e.g. hard assignment [6] and Fisher vector [8] have been employed for painting classification. Recently, deep features based representations, extracted from the Convolutional Neural Network (CNNs), have been applied for painting categorization [11, 10]. The CNNs are trained using raw image pixels and consist of a series of convolution and pooling operations followed by one or more fully connected (FC) layers. The deep features, trained using large amount of labeled data (e.g. ImageNet), are known to be generic and applied for many vision applications. Generally, the deep features are extracted using the activations from some FC layers of the network for the classification task.

In the context of object and texture recognition, it has been shown that activations from the last convolutional layers are more discriminative and provide superior performance compared to standard features from the FC layers of the network [3]. The convolutional layers mitigate the requirement of fine-tuning for a specific dataset. The activations from the convolutional layers can be further used as dense local features encoded using Fisher vectors. In this work, we also employ activations from the convolutional layer as dense local features and pool them using Fisher vectors for computational painting categorization.

Beside holistic image representations, intermediate image parts have often serve as region of interests that capture key object or scene regions. Typically, parts are extracted using object detectors such as deformable part-based models [4] or poselets [1] for object recognition. In a standard object detection settings, a deformable part-model (DPM) approach is trained using the positive examples annotated with the bounding box locations of the corresponding object class. The parts in the DPM framework are learned using a latent SVM (LSVM) formulation. Each object is then modeled as a deformable collection of parts with a root model at its center. The DPMs are also employed to capture latent common structures within a scene for scene recognition [9]. In such a case, no bounding box information is available for training and the root filter corresponds to the whole image with moveable parts representing the important scene regions. In the context of action recognition, class-specific action detectors [7] have shown to provide promising results. Here, we propose to employ DPMs to automatically capture latent common structures as region of interests within paintings for computational painting categorization tasks.

1.1 Contribution

We propose an approach that encodes both the global layout and the region of interests (ROI's) in digital paintings. Multi-scale dense convolutional features are computed over the entire image to capture the global scene characteristics. These multi-scale local convolutional features are pooled using the Fisher vector encoding [13] to obtain a single image representation. The ROI's are obtained automatically without any manual part labeling by training a class-specific DPM detector. The class-specific parts are then described similarly by using multi-scale dense convolutional features later pooled using the Fisher vector encoding. Both part-based and image-level deep Fisher vectors are then contacted into a single representation. Figure 1 shows an overview of our approach. Experiments are performed on the challenging painting-91 dataset [6] with two tasks: artist and style classification. On both artist and style classification tasks our approach improves the mean classification accuracy by 2.7% and 4.7% respectively, compared to using only the global scene characteristics. Further, our approach achieves state-of-the-art results on both tasks, outperforming a recent CNN-based approach [11].

1.2 Relation to Prior Works

Existing approaches [6, 2, 11] either employ low-level features or deep features for painting categorization. The ones [11, 10] based on deep features employ activations from the FC layers for the painting classification. Other than painting classification, it has been shown recently that activations from deeper convolutional layers provide superior results for object and texture recognition [3]. Typically, dense multi-scale convolutional features are extracted over an entire image. These features are then pooled using Fisher vector encoding to obtain an image representation.

In the context of fine-grained and scene recognition [12, 9, 15], part-based information is often exploited to capture the semantic content and composition of the integral regions in an image. Quattoni and Torralba [12] propose to incorporate part based information by using manually labeled data for scene recognition. The work of [9] uses a DPM framework to automatically capture part information for scene recognition. To the best of our knowledge, we are the first to incorporate part-based information in a multi-scale convolutional features based framework for painting categorization problem. Our approach goes beyond the conventional deep features based painting classification methods [11, 10] by capturing both the holistic and part-based information.

2. OUR APPROACH

Inspired by the recent success of CNNs, we base our approach on deep features and employ it for both components: holistic and part-based representations. We use the VGG-16 network [14][1] pre-trained on the ImageNet. In this network, the input images employ small 3×3 convolution filters per pixel. The stride is set to 1 pixel. The network comprises of several max-pooling layers that perform spatial pooling at a stride of 2 pixels over 2×2 pixel windows. At the end, the network contains 3 fully connected (FC) layers. The width of the network starts with 64 feature maps and goes to 512 feature maps at its widest. We refer to [14] for more details. Next, we describe our deep features based holistic and part-based representations.

2.1 Holistic Representation

As discussed earlier, most deep features based methods employ activations from the FC layer for computational painting classification [11, 10]. Instead, we employ activations from the last convolutional layer of the network since it was recently shown to provide superior results for object and texture recognition tasks [3]. The convolutional layer returns dense activations of 512 dimensions, computed over the entire image. We employ multi-scale strategy by rescal-

[1]The deep network models available at: http://www.robots.ox.ac.uk/~vgg/research/very_deep/

ing each image over a range of scales and pass them through the network to obtain dense convolutional activations. The use of convolutional layer also mitigates the need of resizing the original image to a fixed size. The number of local convolutional patches depend on the size of the input image.

As in [3], a visual vocabulary is constructed over the multi-scale dense local patches by using a Gaussian mixture model (GMM). The multi-scale features are then pooled in a single image representation via Fisher encoding scheme [13]. Our holistic representation can be seen as analogous to the recently introduced Fisher vector CNN (FVCNN) approach [3].

2.2 Part Representation

The DPM framework [4] is previously employed to automatically extract parts for fine-grained [15] and scene classification [9] tasks. Here, we employ the DPM framework [4] to obtain region of interests in digital paintings. The DPM framework consists of a root filter and a deformable collection of moveable parts. The deformation parameters are employed to penalize the movements of parts from their default locations relative to the root. In DPMs, both the root and parts are represented by a dense grid of non-overlapping cells and Latent SVM (LSVM) formulation is used for learning. A 31-dimensional HOG histogram is constructed for each cell. The detection score for each window is computed by concatenating the root filter, the part filters and the configuration deformation cost of all parts.

The standard DPM framework assumes bounding box information to be available at training time and the part locations are treated as latent information. Since no bounding box information is available in our case, the root filter surrounds the whole image. As in [9], we restrict the root filter to have at least 40% overlap with the image. A class-specific DPM is trained using instances from all other classes as negative samples. During the training, the root filter weights are initialized to cover the entire training images, whereas part filters are initialized same as in [4]. Each class-specific DPM is trained using a single mixture component and eight parts. Figure 2 shows a visualization of three style models together with five sample images for each respective style class. The root filter is shown in red, whereas the parts are visualized in blue.

To obtain part locations, the trained class-specific models are then applied on all images. The discriminative part regions are cropped from an image and rescaled over a range of scales before passing through the deep network. As described in Section 2.1, dense activations from the last convolutional layer of the network are extracted and a single GMM-based vocabulary is constructed for all parts. The multi-scale part based local features are then pooled together in a single representation via the Fisher encoding scheme. Finally, the holistic and part-based image representations are concatenated before input to a classifier.

3. EXPERIMENTS

We evaluate our approach on the challenging Painting-91 dataset [6] for both artist and style classification tasks. The dataset consists of 4266 paintings of 91 painters, such as Picasso, Ruben and Warhol. For style classification, the dataset contains 13 artistic styles such as Baroque, Cubbism and Realism. The train/test split is provided by the respective authors [6]. For multi-scale settings, we use 3 scales: 0.5, 1.0, 1.5. For both holistic and part-based vocabularies, we use a GMM with 16 components. For classification, we use one-vs-all linear SVMs using LibLinear package.For evaluation, we employ the same protocol as provided with the dataset [6]. Each test image is assigned the label of the classifier giving the highest confidence. The final performance is evaluated as the mean recognition rate.

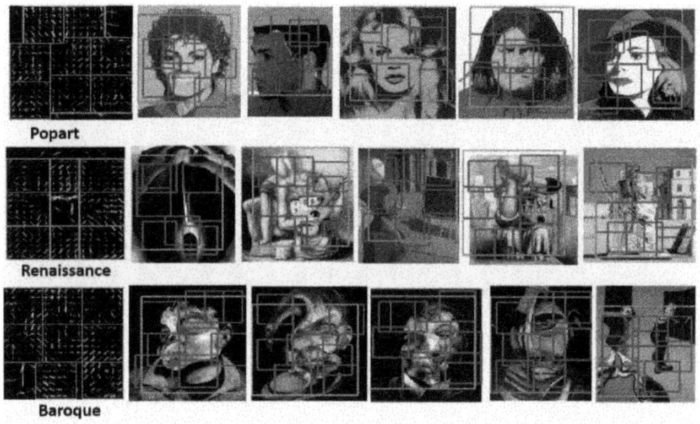

Figure 2: Style models for classes: popart, renaissance and baroque. Example images with root (red) and part locations (blue) are shown for each respective class. The visualizations show that the parts are able to capture latent common structures in a class.

Method	VGG-16 FC [14]	MOP [5]	Holistic [3]	Ours
Artist	51.7	59.7	61.8	**64.5**
Style	67.2	68.8	70.1	**74.8**

Table 1: Comparison (in average classification rates) of standard deep features (FC), the MOP approach, the baseline holistic alone, and our proposed approach combining the holistic and part-based deep representations. Our approach yields consistent improvements for both tasks.

Baseline experiment: We first compare our approach with different baseline methods on the Painting-91 dataset. Note that all approaches employ the same VGG-16 network. The VGG-16 FC method corresponds to using standard deep features with 4096 dimensions from FC layer of the network [14]. The multi-scale orderless pooling (MOP) approach [5] employs FC activations at three levels: 4096-D activations over the entire image, 128×128 of 4096-D pooled using VLAD encoding with 100 words and similar encoding with 64×64 image patches. The three levels are concatenated into a single image representation. Table 1 shows the comparisons on both artist and style classification tasks. On the artist classification task, the standard FC activation based method [14] achieves an average classification score of 51.7%. The MOP approach [5] obtains a mean classification accuracy of 59.7%. A mean classification score of 61.8% is obtained by using the holistic representation alone. Our approach that combines the holistic and part-based representations significantly improves the performance with a classification score of 64.5%. Similarly, on the style classification task, our combined approach improves the performance by 4.7% compared to the holistic alone method [3].

Figure 3 shows comparison on classes where our approach achieves maximum gain in performance, compared to the standard holistic alone approach. A significant gain in performance is achieved especially for Jacques David (+20%), Jean Ingres (+16%), and Arshille Gorky (+12.5%), compared to holistic only representation.

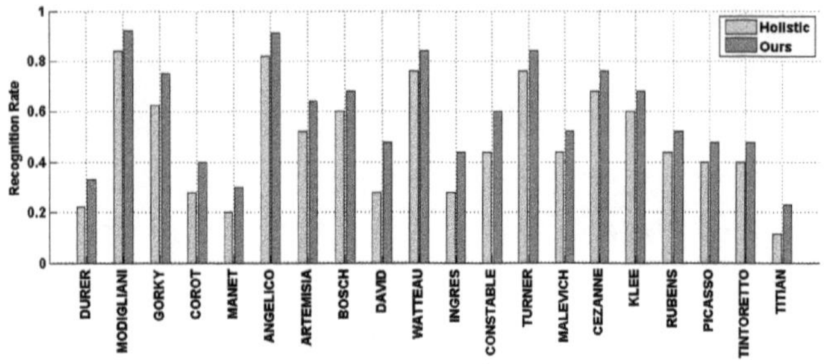

Figure 3: Average classification rates for 20 classes where maximum improvement is obtained with our approach, compared to the standard holistic method [3].

Num. of parts	0	2	4	6	8	10	12
Style	70.1	70.9	72.2	73.1	**74.8**	74.6	74.5

Table 2: Results when varying the number of parts for style classification. The first entry (0) corresponds to using holistic alone with no parts. The best results are obtained with 8 parts in combination with the holistic approach.

Number of part filters: As discussed in Section 2.2, we employ 8 parts for each DPM model. To further validate the impact of number of parts, we perform an experiment by varying the number of parts. Table 2 shows the results for the style classification task. The performance improves marginally with only 2 parts. The best results are obtained when using 8 parts and the performance starts to saturate when this number exceeds.

State-of-the-art comparison: Table 3 shows a comparison of our approach with state-of-the-art methods for both artist and style classification. For artist classification, the cross-layer CNN approach (CL-CNN) [10] based features from multiple CNN layers, achieves a mean accuracy of 56.4%. The multi-scale CNN approach (MS-CNN) [11] employs a multi-scale strategy for CNN features and obtains a mean accuracy of 58.1%. Our approach achieves a considerable gain of 6.4% in mean accuracy, compared to MS-CNN approach [11]. Similarly, our approach outperforms the state-of-the-art results for style classification, achieving a mean classification rate of 74.8%.

4. CONCLUSIONS

We have proposed an approach based on exploiting both holistic and part-based information for painting categorization. Our method automatically extracts discriminative part by training class-specific DPMs. Both holistic and part-based regions are described using multi-scale convolutional features. Experiments show that our approach outperforms the baseline methods, leading to the state-of-the-art results.

5. ACKNOWLEDGMENTS

This work has been funded by the grant 251170 of the Academy of Finland, VR (EMC^2), the projects TIN2013-41751 and of the Spanish Ministry of Science and the Catalan project 2014 SGR 221. The calculations were performed using computer resources within the Aalto University School of Science "Science-IT" project. We also acknowledge the support from Nvidia and NSC.

Method	MF [6]	CL-CNN [10]	MS-MCNN [11]	Ours
Artist	53.1	56.4	58.1	**64.5**
Style	62.2	69.2	71.0	**74.8**

Table 3: Comparison of our approach with state-of-the-art methods. Our approach achieves the best results compared to existing methods based on deep features.

6. REFERENCES

[1] L. Bourdev, S. Maji, and J. Malik. Describing people: A poselet-based approach to attribute classification. In *ICCV*, 2011.

[2] G. Carneiro, N. Silva, A. Bue, and J. Costeira. Artistic image classification: An analysis on the printart database. In *ECCV*, 2012.

[3] M. Cimpoi, S. Maji, and A. Vedaldi. Deep filter banks for texture recognition and segmentation. In *CVPR*, 2015.

[4] P. Felzenszwalb, R. Girshick, D. McAllester, and D. Ramanan. Object detection with discriminatively trained part-based models. *PAMI*, 32(9):1627–1645, 2010.

[5] Y. Gong, L. Wang, R. Guo, and S. Lazebnik. Multi-scale orderless pooling of deep convolutional activation features. In *ECCV*, 2014.

[6] F. S. Khan, S. Beigpour, J. van de Weijer, and M. Felsberg. Painting-91: a large scale database for computational painting categorization. *MVA*, 25(6):1385–1397, 2014.

[7] F. S. Khan, J. Xu, J. van de Weijer, A. Bagdanov, R. M. Anwer, and A. Lopez. Recognizing actions through action-specific person detection. *TIP*, 24(11):4422–4432, 2015.

[8] T. Mensink and J. Gemert. The rijksmuseum challenge: Museum-centered visual recognition. In *ICMR*, 2014.

[9] M. Pandey and S. Lazebnik. Scene recognition and weakly supervised object localization with deformable part-based models. In *ICCV*, 2011.

[10] K.-C. Peng and T. Chen. Cross-layer features in convolutional neural networks for generic classification tasks. In *ICIP*, 2015.

[11] K.-C. Peng and T. Chen. A framework of extracting multi-scale features using multiple convolutional neural networks. In *ICME*, 2015.

[12] A. Quattoni and A. Torralba. Recognizing indoor scenes. In *CVPR*, 2009.

[13] J. Sanchez, F. Perronnin, T. Mensink, and J. Verbeek. Image classification with the fisher vector: Theory and practice. *IJCV*, 105(3):222–245, 2013.

[14] K. Simonyan and A. Zisserman. Very deep convolutional networks for large-scale image recognition. In *ICLR*, 2015.

[15] N. Zhang, R. Farrell, F. Iandola, and T. Darrell. Deformable part descriptors for fine-grained recognition and attribute prediction. In *ICCV*, 2013.

Bidirectional Joint Representation Learning with Symmetrical Deep Neural Networks for Multimodal and Crossmodal Applications

Vedran Vukotić
INSA Rennes
IRISA & INRIA Rennes
Rennes, France
vedran.vukotic@irisa.fr

Christian Raymond
INSA Rennes
IRISA & INRIA Rennes
Rennes, France
christian.raymond@irisa.fr

Guillaume Gravier
CNRS
IRISA & INRIA Rennes
Rennes, France
guillaume.gravier@irisa.fr

ABSTRACT

Common approaches to problems involving multiple modalities (classification, retrieval, hyperlinking, etc.) are early fusion of the initial modalities and crossmodal translation from one modality to the other. Recently, deep neural networks, especially deep autoencoders, have proven promising both for crossmodal translation and for early fusion via multimodal embedding. In this work, we propose a flexible crossmodal deep neural network architecture for multimodal and crossmodal representation. By tying the weights of two deep neural networks, symmetry is enforced in central hidden layers thus yielding a multimodal representation space common to the two original representation spaces. The proposed architecture is evaluated in multimodal query expansion and multimodal retrieval tasks within the context of video hyperlinking. Our method demonstrates improved crossmodal translation capabilities and produces a multimodal embedding that significantly outperforms multimodal embeddings obtained by deep autoencoders, resulting in an absolute increase of 14.14 in precision at 10 on a video hyperlinking task ($\alpha = 10^{-4}$).

Keywords

neural networks; deep learning; representation; embedding; multimodal; crossmodal; retrieval; video retrieval; video hyperlinking; image and text; autoencoder; bidirectional learning; tied weights; shared weights

1. INTRODUCTION

Deep neural networks have been long know to produce meaningful data representations [5], either as deep belief networks, autoencoders or a combination of both. More recently, deep neural networks have been successfully deployed in tasks requiring consideration of multiple modalities. These tasks vary from retrieval [4, 9, 6], ranking [10] and classification tasks [2, 8] to generative tasks [9]. Data often consist of bimodal pairs such as images and tags [2], images and speech [4, 6], audio and video [8], but the systems exploiting them are not necessary bounded to those pairs.

ICMR'16, June 06 - 09, 2016, New York, NY, USA

ISBN 978-1-4503-4359-6/16/06...$15.00

DOI: http://dx.doi.org/10.1145/2911996.2912064

In all generality, methods for fusing modalities are often required when working with multimodal data. The most common approach consists in creating a joint multimodal representation by embedding every single-modal representations into a common representation space. There are two main groups of such approaches:

1. *Multimodal approaches* create a joint representation of the initially disjoint modalities or otherwise merge the initial modalities without necessarily providing a bidirectional mapping of the initial representation spaces to the new representation space and back. These approaches are typically used in retrieval and classification tasks where translating back from the multimodal representation to the single-modal ones is not required.

2. *Crossmodal approaches* focus on bidirectional mapping of the initial representations [4], often by also creating a joint representation space in the process of doing so. They are able to map from one modality to another and back, as well as representing them in a joint representation space. These approaches can be used where crossmodal translation is required (e.g., multimodal query expansion, crossmodal retrieval) in addition to classification tasks.

In this work, we present a novel deep neural network architecture for crossmodal mapping and multimodal embedding. The seminal idea of the approach is to keep separate deep neural networks for each modality while tying the weights of the middle layers between the neural networks so as to yield a common multimodal representation. In this setting, the common middle layer acts as a common multimodal representation space that is attainable from either one of the modalities and from which we can attain either one of the modalities. As a proof of concept, experimental evidence of the benefits of the architecture is given by multimodal query expansion and multimodal retrieval tasks within the context of video hyperlinking. Extensions to other multimodal and crossmodal tasks remains straightforward.

2. METHODOLOGY

In this section, we analyze two methods for creating joint multimodal representations: multimodal autoencoders and

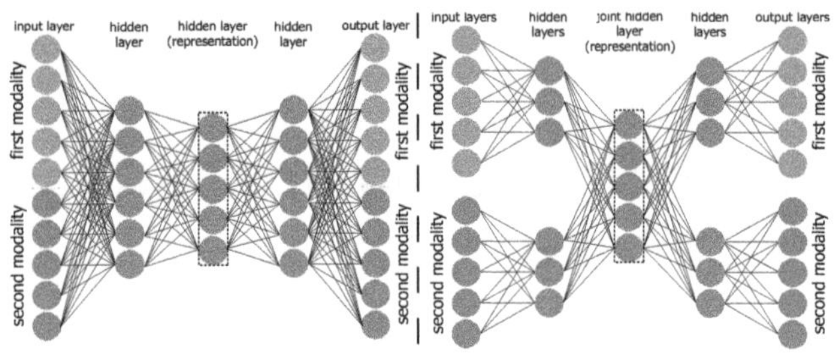

Figure 1: Two typical autoencoder architectures: left - concatenated representations at input and output, all hidden layers are joint; right - separated inputs, outputs and hidden layers, one hidden layer in common

our proposed method, i.e., bidirectional learning with deep neural networks with forced symmetry. Both approaches can do both crossmodal translation and provide a joint multimodal embedding. Autoencoders are one of the most commonly used methods for obtaining multimodal representations. Single-modal autoencoders often include forced symmetry and are used for dimensionality reduction. Our method is based on the idea of learning crossmodal mappings in both directions while applying restrictions to force symmetry in deep neural networks in order to form a common multimodal embedding space that is common to the two crossmodal mappings.

2.1 Multimodal Autoencoders

Two typical autoencoders are shown in Figure 1. The first (left) one illustrates a common approach that consists in concatenating the representations [8, 6] of the two modalities and training the autoencoder to reconstruct the data presented as input. The hidden layer in the middle is then used to obtain a joint multimodal representation (multimodal embedding).

The second (right) architecture is quite similar but has separate inputs and outputs (one for each modality) and separate hidden layers. One hidden layer in common is used for creating a joint multimodal representation. Sometimes, one modality is sporadically removed from the input to make the autoencoder learn to represent both modalities from one. The activations of the hidden layer are used as a multimodal joint representation. This enables autoencoders to also provide crossmodal mapping [8] in addition to a joint representation.

2.2 Bidirectional Representation Learning - Deep Neural Networks with Tied Weights

Previously described multimodal autoencoders include fully connected hidden layers that interact with both modalities. In other terms, the two modalities are available on the input and/or the two are reconstructed. The middle hidden layer represents a multimodal embedding and crossmodal translation is possible through this layer. However, mixing modalities is less optimal than directly mapping from one modality to another and back.

We propose a variation of the second autoencoder that implements a deep neural network translating from one modality to the other and back. Learning is performed in both directions: one modality is presented as an input and the other as the expected output while at the same time the second one is presented as input and the first one as expected

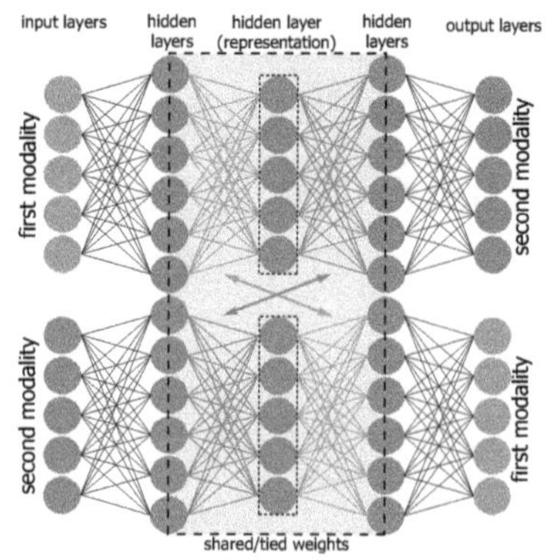

Figure 2: Proposed architecture: training is done in both directions; a shared representation is created by tying the weights (sharing the variables) and enforcing symmetry in the central part

output. This is equivalent to using two separate deep neural networks and tying them (sharing specific weight variables) to make them symmetrical, as illustrated in Figure 2. Implementation-wise the variables representing the weights are shared across the two networks and are in fact the same variables. Learning of the two crossmodal mappings is then performed simultaneously and they are forced to be as close as possible to each other's inverses by the symmetric architecture in the middle.

A joint representation in the middle of the two crossmodal mappings is also formed while learning.

Formally, let $\mathbf{h_i^{(j)}}$ denote (the activation of) a hidden layer at depth j in network i ($i = 1, 2$; one for each modality), $\mathbf{x_{m_i}}$ the feature vector for modality i and $\mathbf{o_i}$ the output of the network for modality i. In turn, for each network, $\mathbf{W_i^{(j)}}$ denotes the weight matrix of layer j and $\mathbf{b_i^{(j)}}$ the bias vector. Finally, we assume that each layer admits f as an activation function. The architecture is then defined by:

$$\begin{aligned}
\mathbf{h_1^{(1)}} &= f(\mathbf{W_1^{(1)}} \times \mathbf{x_{m_1}} + \mathbf{b_1^{(1)}}) \\
\mathbf{h_2^{(1)}} &= f(\mathbf{W_2^{(1)}} \times \mathbf{x_{m_2}} + \mathbf{b_2^{(1)}}) \\[4pt]
\mathbf{h_1^{(2)}} &= f(\mathbf{W^{(2)}} \times \mathbf{h_1^{(1)}} + \mathbf{b_1^{(2)}}) \\
\mathbf{h_2^{(2)}} &= f(\mathbf{W^{(3)}}^{\mathbf{T}} \times \mathbf{h_2^{(1)}} + \mathbf{b_2^{(2)}}) \\[4pt]
\mathbf{h_1^{(3)}} &= f(\mathbf{W^{(3)}} \times \mathbf{h_1^{(2)}} + \mathbf{b_1^{(3)}}) \\
\mathbf{h_2^{(3)}} &= f(\mathbf{W^{(2)}}^{\mathbf{T}} \times \mathbf{h_2^{(2)}} + \mathbf{b_2^{(3)}}) \\[4pt]
\mathbf{o_1} &= f(\mathbf{W_1^{(4)}} \times \mathbf{h_1^{(3)}} + \mathbf{b_1^{(4)}}) \\
\mathbf{o_2} &= f(\mathbf{W_2^{(4)}} \times \mathbf{h_2^{(3)}} + \mathbf{b_2^{(4)}})
\end{aligned}$$

It is important to note that in the above equations, the weight matrices $\mathbf{W^{(3)}}$ and $\mathbf{W^{(2)}}$ are used twice due to weight tying, for computing $\mathbf{h_1^{(2)}}$, $\mathbf{h_2^{(3)}}$ and $\mathbf{h_2^{(2)}}$, $\mathbf{h_1^{(3)}}$ respectively. Training is performed by applying gradient descent to minimize the mean squared error of $(\mathbf{o_1}, \mathbf{x_{m_2}})$ and $(\mathbf{o_2}, \mathbf{x_{m_1}})$ thus effectively minimizing the reconstruction error in both directions and creating a joint representation in the middle, where both representations are projected.

Given such an architecture, crossmodal translation is done straightforwardly by presenting the first modality as $\mathbf{x_{m_i}}$ and obtaining the output in the representation space of the second modality as $\mathbf{o_i}$. A multimodal embedding is obtained by presenting one or both modalities ($\mathbf{x_{m_1}}$ and/or $\mathbf{x_{m_2}}$) at their respective inputs and reading the central hidden layers

Table 1: Available modalities for anchor/target pairs

Anchors		Targets: Both	Targets: Transcripts	Targets: Visual c.	Targets: None
Anchors	Both	10,525	236	528	11
	Transcripts	0	0	0	0
	Visual c.	957	15	68	0
	None	0	0	0	0

$\mathbf{h}_1^{(2)}$ and/or $\mathbf{h}_1^{(2)}$. If both modalities are available, a concatenation of their embedding is used. If only one modality is available its embedding is duplicated. This allows for easy comparison, independently of modality availability.

3. EXPERIMENTS

3.1 Dataset and Initial Representations

We tested the symmetric bidirectional architecture within the framework of the video hyperlinking task using the MediaEval 2014 dataset and the respective groundtruth that was collected as part of the challenge [3]. In this task, there are two main concepts: anchors and targets. Anchors represent segments of interest within videos that a user would like to know more about. Targets represent potential segments of interests that might or might not be related with a specific anchor. The goal is to hyperlink relevant targets for each anchor by using multimodal approaches. For each video, multiple data and modalities are available. In this work, we used two modalities: the automatic transcripts of the audio track and KU Leuven visual concepts. In practice, targets are not given and have to be defined automatically before assessing their relevance to each of the 30 anchors provided. Evaluation of the relevance is thus done post hoc on Amazon Mechanical Turk (AMT). In this paper, we consider a set of targets made of the top-10 targets that each participating team proposed for each anchor, along with the relevance judgments from AMT. In total, the dataset consists of 30 anchors, 10,809 targets and a ground truth with 12,340 anchor-target pairs (either related or unrelated). Interestingly, among the anchor and target segments, not all have both transcripts and visual concepts available. Table 1 illustrates the different cases of modality availability within the dataset. The task consists of using multimodal information to rank the targets by relevance for each anchor and comparing their relevance with the previously established groundtruth.

We chose to represent the transcripts and visual concepts of each anchor and target with a *Word2Vec* skip-gram model with hierarchical sampling [7], a representation size of 100 and a window size of 5. The visual concepts were sorted previous to learning and the representations of the words and concepts found within a segment were averaged [1]. This option worked best for our task (see Table 2) and additionally, our work is focused on cross-modality and joint multimodal representations, thus the choice of the input representations is not crucial. A standard cosine distance is used in all the experiments.

We implemented the two autoencoders described in Section 2.1 in *Keras*[1] and our proposed bidirectional symmetrical deep neural network in *Lasagne*[2]. All embeddings have a dimension of 100 as larger dimensions did not bring any significant improvement. The autoencoders we tested had architectures with 200-100-200 hidden layers, as had the symmetrical bidirectional networks. Other sizes were also tested but performed worse or not better and were not included in the comparison. Since this is unsupervised learning, the learning was performed on the part of the dataset that contains both transcripts and visual concepts and tested on the whole dataset.

[1]http://keras.io

[2]https://github.com/Lasagne/Lasagne

Table 2: Comparison of initial (single-modal) representations. Precision at 10 (%) obtained with TF-IDF, Word2Vec and Paragraph Vectors

Representation	Transcripts	Visual concepts
LSI & TF-IDF	23.67	18.33
Avg. Word2Vec	**58.67**	**50.00**
PV-DM	45.00	45.33
PV-DBOW	41.67	48.33

Table 3: Comparison of the tested methods: precision at 10 (%) and standard deviation

Method	P@10	σ
Baseline		
Only transcripts	58.67	-
Only visual concepts	50.00	-
Linear combination	61.32	3.1
Autoencoders		
Embedded tran. and v. c. with AE #1	57.40	1.24
Embedded tran. and v. c. with AE #2	59.60	0.65
Bidirectional DNNs with tied weights		
Embedded transcripts	70.43	0.46
Embedded visual concepts	54.92	0.99
Embedded transcripts and visual c.	**73.74**	**0.82**
Expanded transcripts	58.16	0.24
Expanded visual concepts	55.75	0.13
Expanded transcripts and visual c.	62.35	0.25

Table 3 reports the performance of the different methods. Using only transcripts yields a precision at 10 (P@10) of 58.67 % while using only visual concepts yields 50.00 %. Combining the two modalities in different linear combinations yields an improved P@10 to 61.32 %.

3.2 Crossmodal Query Expansion

Bidirectional symmetrical architectures enable crossmodal expansion where a missing modality is filled in by translating from the other one. If the transcript is not available for a segment, it is generated from the visual concepts and conversely. Using query expansion so that all segments have all modalities, we obtain 55.75 % for the visual concepts and 58.16 % for the transcripts. The first difference is significant ($\alpha = 0.001$) improvement, while the second is not. This is due to the relatively small number of samples with one missing modality, so filling the missing modalities does not have a big influence.

3.3 Multimodal Embedding

A multimodal representation created with the two autoencoders (AE) of Sec. 2.1 yields 57.40 % (left part of Fig. 1) and 59.60 % (right part of Fig. 1). With symmetrical bidirectional networks, the two modalities are handled in the

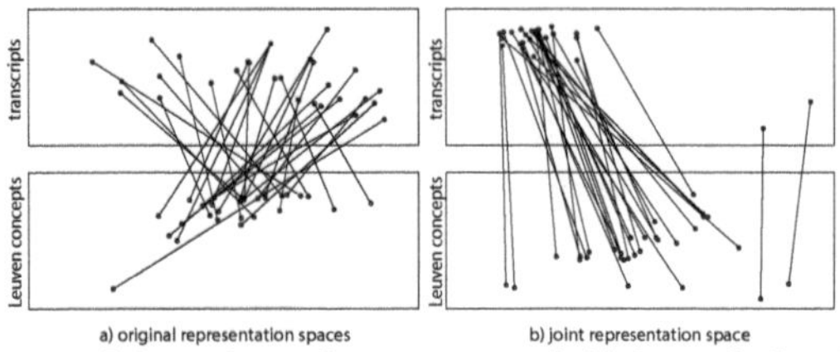

Figure 3: Mapping the two modalities of the 30 anchors (first two components): a) in the original representation spaces b) after embedding them

following manner to generate a multimodal embedding: 1) the modalities are both present for both the target and the anchor: all four representations are projected into the new multimodal representation space 2) one segment (anchor or target) has just one modality while the other has both: everything is projected into the new multimodal representation space, the one available modality of one segment being compared against the two modalities of the other 3) segments have only one modality: both modalities are projected into the new multimodal representation space.

When embedding only the transcripts to the new joint multimodal representation space with our proposed architecture, we obtain a P@10 of 70.43 %. Embedding only the visual concepts yields 54.92 %. The biggest improvement is achieved when embedding the two modalities, which yields 73.74 %, a significant ($\alpha = 10^{-4}$) improvement over autoencoders of 14.14 in P@10.

Figure 3 illustrates the first two principal components of the two modalities, in their original representation spaces (left) and the first two principal components of their representation in the joint embedding space. The 30 anchors that are shown display a more ordered structure in the embedding space then in their original space, indicating that projections to a common representation space are successful.

Figure 4 shows a comparison of the two possible usage of bidirectional symmetrical architectures: for multimodal expansion (as a crossmodal translator) and as a multimodal embedder that translates the two modalities to a joint representation space that has been trained in a bidirectional way and that represents a common space for the crossmodal translation. The graph shows P@10 values for 10k training iterations. For reference, also the three baseline values are included (original transcripts, visual concepts and their linear combination). Multimodal query expansion improves P@10, not by a large margin due to the small number of samples missing one modality but it proves successful crossmodal translation. Embedding into the new joint representation space improves P@10 with a bigger margin.

4. CONCLUSIONS

Our proposed deep neural network architecture with tied weights is trained bidirectionally from the first modality to the second and from the second modality to the first and creates a crossmodal mapping between the two representation spaces that can be successfully used in multimodal query expansion. Due to its enforced symmetry, a joint multimodal embedding is also created that further improves multimodal data representation. We have shown that projecting into this space is significantly better than translating between the initial spaces, even when using only one modality. Projecting both modalities into the joint multimodal representation space yields the best results on our task. We expect that this architecture may provide similar improvements for

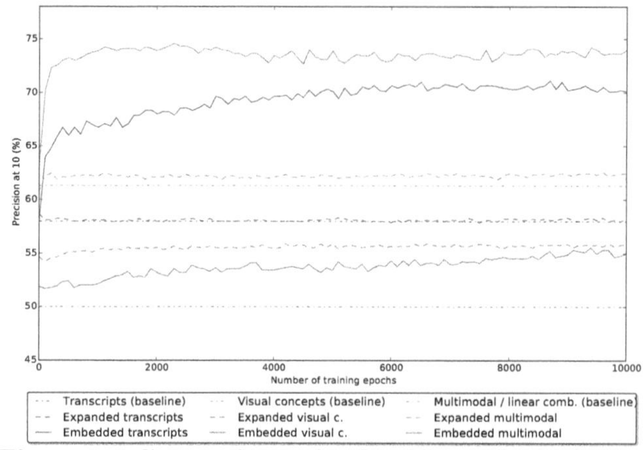

Figure 4: Comparison of P@10 for different training epochs (averages across multiple runs) and the baseline (original representations)

other tasks that would be the subject of future works.

5. ACKNOWLEDGMENTS

Partially funded via the CominLabs excellence laboratory financed by the National Research Agency under reference ANR-10-LABX-07-01.

6. REFERENCES

[1] M. Campr and K. Ježek. Comparing semantic models for evaluating automatic document summarization. In *Text, Speech, and Dialogue*, 2015.

[2] M. Cha, Y. Gwon, and H. T. Kung. Multimodal sparse representation learning and applications. *CoRR*, abs/1511.06238, 2015.

[3] M. Eskevich, R. Aly, D. N. Racca, R. Ordelman, S. Chen, and G. J. Jones. The search and hyperlinking task at MediaEval 2014. In *Working Notes MediaEval Workshop*, 2014.

[4] F. Feng, X. Wang, and R. Li. Cross-modal retrieval with correspondence autoencoder. In *ACM Intl. Conf. on Multimedia*, pages 7–16, 2014.

[5] G. E. Hinton and R. R. Salakhutdinov. Reducing the dimensionality of data with neural networks. *Science*, 313(5786):504–507, 2006.

[6] H. Lu, Y. Liou, H. Lee, and L. Lee. Semantic retrieval of personal photos using a deep autoencoder fusing visual features with speech annotations represented as word/paragraph vectors. In *Annual Conf. of the Intl. Speech Communication Association*, 2015.

[7] T. Mikolov, I. Sutskever, K. Chen, G. S. Corrado, and J. Dean. Distributed representations of words and phrases and their compositionality. In *Advances in Neural Information Processing Systems*, 2013.

[8] J. Ngiam, A. Khosla, M. Kim, J. Nam, H. Lee, and A. Y. Ng. Multimodal deep learning. In *Intl. Conf. on Machine Learning*, 2011.

[9] N. Srivastava and R. Salakhutdinov. Learning representations for multimodal data with deep belief nets. In *Intl. Conf. on Machine Learning*, 2012.

[10] J. Weston, S. Bengio, and N. Usunier. Large scale image annotation: learning to rank with joint word-image embeddings. *Machine learning*, 81(1):21–35, 2010.

SSD Technology Enables Dynamic Maintenance of Persistent High-Dimensional Indexes

Björn Þór Jónsson
School of Computer Science
Reykjavik University, Iceland
bjorn@ru.is

Laurent Amsaleg
CNRS–IRISA
Rennes, France
laurent.amsaleg@irisa.fr

Herwig Lejsek
Videntifier Technologies
Reykjavík, Iceland
herwig@videntifier.com

ABSTRACT

In today's world of ever-increasing multimedia collections, dynamically and persistently maintaining high-dimensional indexes is imperative for industrial applications. Since HDD performance is the main bottleneck in index maintenance, we investigate the impact of SSD technology. We use the NV-tree to drive our analysis, as the only high-dimensional index in the literature which has seriously addressed updates. Our simulation model indicates that an index of 1.5 billion descriptors can be built dynamically on a high-end SSD in just over four hours of disk time, which is more than 500x faster than using a high-end HDD. Relatively small investment in the new SSD technology can thus make dynamic and persistent high-dimensional indexes very feasible.

Keywords

High-dimensional index; Index maintenance; SSDs; NV-tree.

1. INTRODUCTION

Multimedia collections are getting increasingly large. As a result, there has been significant interest in the scalability of k-NN search [6, 1, 4, 2, 5, 3, 8]. But nearly all of this work has ignored the effect of the *growth* of the collections, effectively ignoring the need to perform updates on the collection and the resulting index structure.

A prototypical multimedia retrieval system works as follows: First, each media item is described using one or more high-dimensional features. For large-scale collections, the resulting feature collection is much too large to fit in main memory and must be made persistent on disk. Then the high-dimensional features are somehow compressed into a smaller representation, sometimes only a few bytes, and inserted into an indexing structure for efficient searches. In some cases, the final representation of the features may depend on the index and thus vary based on, for example, the distribution in the high-dimensional space.

In an industry setting with specific response time requirements, it is necessary to maintain a persistent index of the entire collection. For example, it is not acceptable to keep a list of the newly added features, which is scanned sequentially in addition to searching the high-dimensional index, and then re-index the entire collection offline once in a while. First, the list of new features will grow steadily and with it the retrieval time, so performance will quickly become unacceptable. Second, full re-indexing will be a very time- and resource-consuming process, which cannot be done frequently. Furthermore, in case of crashes, the persistent index allows resuming the service immediately. The only way to achieve industry-standard service levels is to maintain a dynamic and persistent high-dimensional index!

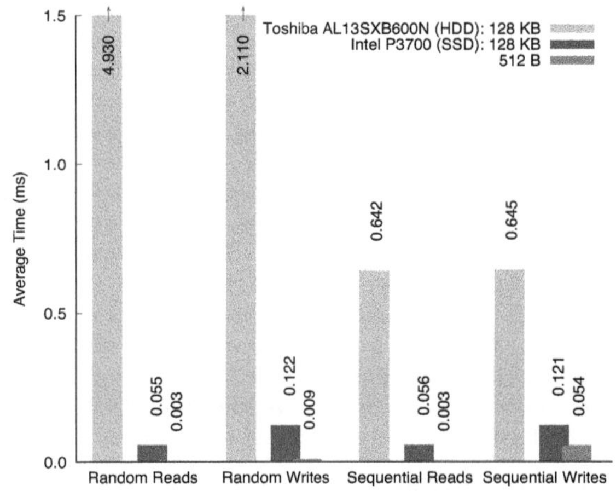

Figure 1: Performance comparison of a high-end HDD (600 GB, $360) and a high-end SSD (400 GB, $900). The y-axis (truncated) shows the time for each of the operations on the x-axis, in milliseconds. The numbers show that SSDs are faster than HDDs by a factor of 5x to 1000x, depending on operation and data quantity. See Section 2.5 for more details.

1.1 Costs of Index Maintenance

In the short term, new features may be accommodated by inserting them into the appropriate index cell of the existing structure. While standard logging techniques can be used to reduce cost, the changes must eventually be made persistent on disk. When the index fits in memory, a single write suffices; otherwise it may be necessary to read the corresponding cell from disk and then write it back. Reading

ICMR'16, June 06-09, 2016, New York, NY, USA

 ISBN 978-1-4503-4359-6/16/06...$15.00

DOI: http://dx.doi.org/10.1145/2911996.2912065

and writing single cells results in random disk operations, which are costly using traditional hard-disk drives (HDDs).

In the long term, inserting into existing cells leads to excessively large cells which can negatively impact both retrieval time and result quality. Index structure maintenance will therefore be required in order to split these cells and redistribute their contents. And again, those changes must be made persistent leading to disk reads and writes.

If the final representation of features depends on the index structure, further costs are incurred as the original features must be retrieved to compute a new representation against the modified index. Since the feature collection on disk is not aligned with the index, the original features of a single cell can be located anywhere in the feature collection and unlikely in close proximity to each other. Therefore, reading the features from disk can be a costly process of multiple random disk reads. This is particularly true with traditional HDDs which do not support small random reads well.

Recently, however, solid-state disks (SSDs) have appeared which have very different characteristics, as Figure 1 clearly demonstrates (see Section 2.5 for details of the figure). First, because they have no moving parts they are much faster than HDDs (particularly high-end SSDs). Second, again since they have no moving parts, the size of the IO impacts the performance much more than with HDDs, which in turn means that random reads become quite efficient, and in particular small random reads become very efficient. It is therefore of interest to observe the impact of SSDs on update performance of high-dimensional indexes.

1.2 Contributions

One of the most scalable high-dimensional indexing methods in the literature is the NV-tree [4, 5]. It has been used for large-scale experiments and is currently the backbone of a professional copy-detection service indexing more than 150 thousand hours of video. It is also the only scalable high-dimensional index in the literature, as far as we know, where update performance has been seriously studied [4, 7]. We therefore use the NV-tree as the vehicle of our study.

In this paper we make the following contributions. We first review the NV-tree and identify the impact points of SSD technology on the performance of persistent and dynamic index maintenance. We then present simulation results which show that using a high-end SSD enables the insertion of 1.5 billion high-dimensional descriptors in just over four hours of disk time, which is more than 500x faster than using HDD technology. Moreover, the results show that for the NV-tree in particular, SSD technology allows a much simpler implementation of index maintenance than HDD technology, again due to its performance characteristics. We conclude that by using SSD technology, it is now very feasible to dynamically and persistently maintain high-dimensional indexes at a large scale.

2. THE NV-TREE

Overall, an NV-tree is a tree index consisting of: a) a hierarchy of small *inner nodes*, which are kept in memory during query processing and guide the vector search to the appropriate leaf node; and b) larger *leaf nodes*, which are stored on disk and contain references to the actual features. In this section, we give describe the algorithms of the NV-tree for index construction, retrieval and maintenance. This description is brief and simplified; refer to [5] for details.

2.1 Index Creation

When the tree construction starts, all features from the collection are first projected onto a single projection line through the high-dimensional space. The projected values are then partitioned based on their position on the projection line, thus partitioning the root node of the tree. To build subsequent levels of the NV-tree, this process of projecting and partitioning is repeated for each and every partition using a new projection line at each level, thus creating the hierarchy of partitions that are represented by inner nodes. The process stops when the number of vectors in a partition falls below a limit designed to be disk I/O friendly. A new projection line is then used to order the vector identifiers in each final partition and the ordered identifiers are written to the leaf node on disk. Each feature is represented by a 4 byte identifier and, since the leaves are on average about 2/3 full, a total of 6 bytes are required per feature.

Two partitioning strategies co-exist inside the NV-tree. The first partitioning strategy is such that the distance between partition boundaries at each level of the tree is equal. As the inner products between a set of high-dimensional vectors and a projection line typically form a normal distribution, the resulting partitions usually have very different cardinalities and dense areas are partitioned deeper than sparse areas. This first partitioning strategy is used at the upper levels of the NV-tree. The second partitioning strategy is used at the lowest levels of the tree: when a partition fits into a disk I/O, then data is partitioned according to an equal cardinality criterion (instead of an equal distance criterion). This switch to balanced partitioning occurs when a partition fit within 6×6 leaves, creating balanced *leaf groups* of up to 6 nodes containing up to 6 leaves each. The goal of this latter partitioning strategy is to enable efficient search in nearby leaves, as described below.

2.2 Nearest Neighbor Retrieval

The search first traverses the hierarchy of inner nodes of the NV-tree. At each level of the tree, the query vector is projected to the projection line associated with the current node. The search is then directed to the sub-partition with center-point closest to the projection of the query vector. This process of projection and choosing the right sub-partition is repeated until the search reaches a leaf group.

At each level of the leaf-group, the two nearest branches are considered, or up to four leaves, and the nearest vectors along the projection lines are merged to form the final set of approximate nearest neighbors. As only two adjacent leaves are read at each level, at most four leaves will be read with this method. As these leaves are organized together on disk, they will span at most 12 pages, and can thus (with high likelihood) be read in a single disk read.

2.3 Index Maintenance

Insertion to NV-tree leaves proceeds as follows. When the correct leaf node is found, using the exact same process as during search, the position within the leaf node is calculated and the identifier is inserted in the designated position. During index creation, leaf nodes are not filled completely in order to leave space for such insertions. Once a leaf node is filled, however, it must be split in order to provide more storage capacity within the tree.

A basic method to split a node is very similar to the index construction process. A new internal node is created with two new leaf nodes as children. A projection line is then assigned to the internal node using the same method as during index construction. The contents of the full leaf node are projected along the projection line and inserted to the appropriate leaf. Each leaf is then also assigned a projection line and the contents of the leaf ordered based on the projection to that line.

Using this basic method, however, the index would quickly become very deep, as each leaf would always be split into two leaves and all the new internal nodes would have only two children. A better method is to consider a group of l leaves together, and re-distribute their contents to $l + \Delta$ leaves. The NV-tree goes one step further, and considers the leaf groups described above as the unit of splits; when that group exceeds $6 \times 6 = 36$ leaves, the group is split into 4 to 8 new leaf groups, depending on the distribution of the high-dimensional vectors in the original leaf group.

2.4 Re-Projection of Features

In order to project the contents of a filled leaf group, it is necessary to use the original features, as a) a new projection line is (most likely) chosen for the internal nodes, and b) each new leaf also has a new projection line. Leaf nodes only contain feature identifiers, so the features themselves must be retrieved from disk. The features of the leaf group are randomly distributed over the whole feature collection, however, so their retrieval is a costly operation.

Three methods can be used to retrieve the features of a leaf group from the feature collection. First, it is possible to sequentially scan the entire collection. Second, it is possible to randomly read only the required features. Both are simple to implement, but neither is efficient using HDDs: the first methods reads too much data, while the second requires expensive random accesses.

A third method, proposed in [7], is to maintain an independent feature database for each NV-tree—called partition files—which is organized in the same manner as the leaf groups. With this last method, only a small number of sequential disk reads are required to retrieve the features of the leaf group. When using HDDs, this method has been shown to be the most efficient [7], even though the redundant partition files must also be maintained during splits.

2.5 Expected Impact of SSDs

As mentioned above, Figure 1 compares two high-end disks from each category: HDD and SSD. Prices are obtained from allhdd.com and amazon.com, respectively. The performance of the SSD is obtained with actual performance measurements using the fio benchmark. The performance of the HDD, on the other hand, is extrapolated from [9] as follows: the average sequential throughput is used directly to calculate the cost of sequential operations and read/write access times is used as the cost of random operations. Based on Figure 1, we make the following observations:

- For the HDD, sequential operations are ~10x faster than random operations. Random writes are faster than random reads due to buffering, as the disk buffers writes temporarily to improve performance. Small operations (not shown) take roughly the same time as larger operations.
- The SSD, in contrast, shows no difference between random and sequential operations. Reads are twice as fast as writes, due to properties of the storage medium.
- For the SSD, small operations are ~10x faster than large operations, due to the absence of movable parts.
- Overall, the SSD is 5–10x faster than the HDD for sequential operations and 10–100x faster for random operations.
- For small disk reads, however, the SSD is ~1000x faster than the HDD. This is particularly beneficial for the re-projection of features during splits.

Overall, the expected impact of using SSDs on NV-tree maintenance is two-fold. First, due to the overall performance improvement, we expect the index maintenance to be significantly faster, making it feasible to dynamically maintain persistent indexes. Second, due to the capacity for very fast small random reads, we expect that reading the features to re-project randomly from the large collection will be more efficient than maintaining the redundant feature database.

3. PERFORMANCE EVALUATION

In this section, we study the performance of NV-tree maintenance with both HDD and SSD technology. We first describe our simulation model, which is similar to the one in [7], and then present the results.

3.1 Modeling NV-tree Maintenance

Assume that the feature collection consists of N_F features in S_F blocks of 128 KB. We assume each feature is 132 bytes (128 dimensions) and that the NV-tree requires 6 bytes per feature. The NV-tree consists of N_L leaves organized into N_G leaf groups. Each leaf is at most 4 KB, so each leaf group is at most $36 \times 4 = 144$ KB. We assume that each leaf-group is stored in a contiguous chunk of space on disk and can be read or written with a single IO operation.

If partition files are maintained, there are also N_G partition files. The size of the partition file depends on the number of features it stores but overall, partition files are about 20 times larger than leaves. Since they also can be organized in a contiguous manner, reading or writing a partition file requires a number of sequential operations.

At insertion time, a system buffer is maintained which is organized the same way as the NV-tree. This system buffer contains feature identifiers and projected values, and in the case of partition files, also the feature itself. If the buffer fills up, it is flushed by sequentially reading all partitions and writing out with the added feature identifiers. For each partition file represented in the buffers, the end of the partition file is read, appended to and written again.

When a leaf is split, one random read is first performed to read the leaf group. The cost of a random read of a leaf group is termed C^L_{RR} and given in Figure 1; we assume that each such read is 128 KB. Then a random write of the leaf group is required to persist the change (C^L_{RW}). When the entire leaf group is full and is split into four leaf groups, the writing phase consists of four leaf-group sized random writes ($4C^L_{RW}$). Note that when a partition is split, its features are removed from the buffers. If partition files are maintained, similar operations must be performed; since partition files are about 20 times larger, however, the costs are higher.

The cost of re-projection of features during split of a leaf group G depends on the method used. As described in the previous section, there are three alternatives which we explore: The first alternative is that of sequentially scanning then entire collection of features; this costs $S_F \times C^L_{SR}$. The

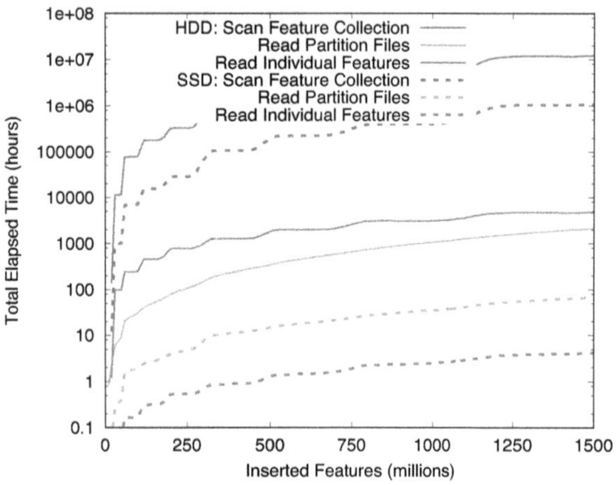

Figure 2: A comparison of total elapsed disk time for index maintenance using the high-end HDD (solid lines) and high-end SSD (dashed lines).

second alternative is to retrieve all the features from the feature collection; this costs $S_G C_{RR}^F$, where C_{RR}^F is the cost of a small random read and S_G is the number of features in the leaf group. Finally, if partition files are maintained, they can be read, which costs between C_{SR}^L and $20C_{SR}^L$, depending on the size of the given partition file.

Initially, the NV-tree consists of 50 million descriptors. A total of 1.5 billion descriptors are then inserted, one by one, keeping track of the total elapsed time, as measured by the estimated IO time.

3.2 Simulation Results

Figure 2 shows the total elapsed time for both the HDD and the SSD from Figure 1. Let us focus first on the HDD (solid lines). As expected, the figure shows that scanning the collection (red) is the slowest method, while maintaining the partition files (yellow) is faster than reading individual features (green). Note that even though the reduced cost of reading partition files during leaf splits is partially offset by the cost of maintaining them during leaf-group splits, the maintenance cost is much smaller than the time savings. In total, however, inserting the 1.5 billion descriptors requires more than 2,000 hours of disk time, which is infeasible.

Turning to the SSD performance in Figure 2 (dashed lines) we first observe that the maintenance time is significantly reduced compared to the HDD. In fact, for both full collection scan (red) and partition file scan (yellow), which are dominated by large sequential reads, the SSD is more than 10x faster, as sequential reads are $\sim$10x faster with the SSD. Reading the individual features (green), however, which is dominated by small random reads, is more than 1000x faster. Again, this is as expected, as the SSD is $\sim$1000x faster for such reads. The most efficient method using the SSD—reading individual features—takes just over 4 hours, which is more than 500x faster than using partition files on the HDD. Four hours of disk time for 1.5 billion descriptors is very feasible, even in demanding industry settings.

4. CONCLUSIONS

We have argued that the performance of high-dimensional index maintenance is a very worthy subject of investigation in today's world of large-scale and ever-increasing multimedia collections: in order to offer industry-strength solutions with reliable retrieval performance, it is necessary to maintain a dynamic and persistent copy of the high-dimensional index on disk. Since HDD performance is the bottleneck in such index maintenance, we have investigated the impact of SSD technology on the implementation of index maintenance. We have used the NV-tree to drive our analysis, as it is the only high-dimensional index in the literature which has seriously addressed updates.

Our results show that using SSD technology 1.5 billion can be inserted into the index in a matter of just over four hours. Furthermore, while a redundant copy of the entire feature collection was needed when using HDDs, a straightforward method of reading the required features randomly is by far the best solution using SSDs. These results mean that a very modest investment in the new SSD technology can simplify index maintenance and allow the dynamic and persistent maintenance of even large-scale high-dimensional indexes.

5. ACKNOWLEDGMENTS

The authors wish to cordially thank Philippe Bonnet, Ivan Luiz Picoli, Max Enroth and Carla Villegas Pasco of the IT University of Copenhagen for their performance measurements of the Intel P3700 SSD card and related discussions.

6. REFERENCES

[1] M. Douze, H. Jégou, H. Sandhawalia, L. Amsaleg, and C. Schmid. Evaluation of GIST descriptors for web-scale image search. In *Proc. CIVR*, Santorini, Greece, 2009.

[2] H. Jégou, M. Douze, and C. Schmid. Product quantization for nearest neighbor search. *TPAMI*, 33(1), 2011.

[3] H. Jégou, F. Perronnin, M. Douze, J. Sánchez, P. Pérez, and C. Schmid. Aggregating local image descriptors into compact codes. *TPAMI*, 34(9), 2012.

[4] H. Lejsek, F. H. Ásmundsson, B. T. Jónsson, and L. Amsaleg. NV-Tree: An efficient disk-based index for approximate search in very large high-dimensional collections. *TPAMI*, 31(5), 2009.

[5] H. Lejsek, B. T. Jónsson, and L. Amsaleg. NV-Tree: nearest neighbors at the billion scale. In *Proc. ICMR*, Trento, Italy, 2011.

[6] T. Liu, C. Rosenberg, and H. Rowley. Clustering billions of images with large scale nearest neighbor search. In *Proc. IEEE WACV*, Austin, TX, USA, 2007.

[7] A. Ólafsson, B. T. Jónsson, L. Amsaleg, and H. Lejsek. Dynamic behavior of balanced NV-trees. *Multimedia Systems*, 17(2), 2011.

[8] X. Sun, C. Wang, C. Xu, and L. Zhang. Indexing billions of images for sketch-based retrieval. In *Proc. ACM MM*, Barcelona, Spain, 2013.

[9] Tom's Hardware. All enterprise HDD charts. http://www.tomshardware.com/charts/enterprise-hdd-charts/benchmarks,156.html, accessed Feb 3, 2016.

Item-Based Video Recommendation: an Hybrid Approach considering Human Factors

Andrea Ferracani, Daniele Pezzatini, Marco Bertini, Alberto Del Bimbo
Università degli Studi di Firenze - MICC
Firenze, Italy
[name.surname]@unifi.it

ABSTRACT

In this paper we propose a method for video recommendation in Social Networks based on crowdsourced and automatic video annotations of salient frames. We show how two human factors, users' self-expression in user profiles and perception of visual saliency in videos, can be exploited in order to stimulate annotations and to obtain an efficient representation of video content features. Results are assessed through experiments conducted on a prototype of social network for video sharing. Several baseline approaches are evaluated and we show how the proposed method improves over them.

Keywords

Video tagging, crowdsourcing, automatic video tagging, item-based video recommendation, user profiles, visual saliency

1. INTRODUCTION AND RELATED WORK

Collaborative Filtering (CF) is a technique often used by Recommender Systems (RSs) which aims at predicting interesting items to a user based on the preferences, explicit and implicit, of other users. A standard item-based video RS builds its prediction model considering user preferences for videos, expressed according to ratings, and suggests potential videos of interests comparing their distributions. Hybrid approaches in RSs have been proved to give best results [5]. These approaches combine CF with content-based techniques and reduce issues related to the large amount of data to be annotated and data sparsity. Recommending relevant videos can help users to find the most pertinent content according to their view habits or preferences. As shown in [21], recommendation is a powerful force in driving users to watch other videos, much more than direct search of new videos. Hybrid approaches presented in the literature typically exploit textual video metadata, sometimes complemented by multimedia content analysis [19], user profiling, social features and User-Generated Content (UGC) [1, 4, 8]. Crowdsourced data is usable information that can be leveraged to improve different online services. In [3] crowdsourced annotations are used to create video previews that are more related to the queries of the users, to improve video retrieval. In [14] the performance of a video retrieval system based on crowdsourced annotations of sport videos shows that despite the heterogeneity and poor quality of the annotations, they are close to ground-truth. Time accurate annotations of social videos, based on user comments and temporal, personalised topic modelling, has been proposed in [17]. In [18] a large crowdsourcing experiment has been carried out to analyse the differences between "timed" tags (i.e. added to a specific timecode in a video) *versus* "timeless" tags. The authors observed that most of the visually-related tags are relevant for short segments of the video, i.e. people tend to tag when something is "flashed" in the video.

We build on top of these studies and propose the adoption of an hybrid approach in which a brief and comprehensive representation of video content can improve the performance of a standard recommender based on CF (i.e. using only ratings). The approach relies on content-based features gathered both through crowdsourced and CNN-based classifiers annotations. The dataset has been collected through a prototype of a Social Network (SN). Annotations collection is improved exploiting two human factors: *i)* user profile interfaces and *ii)* video frames visual saliency. The main goals are: *i)* to increase the number of crowdsourced annotations, that provide an enrichment of automatic video annotations; *ii)* to improve the quality of video recommenders through video content analysis.

The paper is organised as follows: in Sect. 2 the social network architecture and modules are described. Experimental results are presented in Sect. 3 to show the influence of user profiles and visual saliency on the collection of user annotations of videos. Evidence is given that systems featuring a user profile interface stimulates user activity, increasing the number of annotations. We also show that frames with an high visual saliency are more likely to be annotated; this can be used as a criterion *i)* to suggest to users relevant frames; *ii)* to filter relevant frames for automatic annotation. The recommender is evaluated in Sect. 3.3.

2. THE SYSTEM

The item-based RS has been implemented in a prototype of a SN[1]. The idea behind the SN is to exploit user profiling techniques to propose to the user targeted recommendations of videos, exploiting suggestions of topics of interest

[1]`http://fiona.micc.unifi.it/intime`

ICMR'16, June 06-09, 2016, New York, NY, USA
© 2016 ACM. ISBN 978-1-4503-4359-6/16/06...$15.00
DOI: http://dx.doi.org/10.1145/2911996.2912066

and similar users. This is achieved tracking user's activities on the SN, such as comments, number of video views, click-through data and video ratings. Users can comment videos at frame level tagging concepts derived from Wikipedia. All the concepts manually added are clustered in 54 categories using Fuzzy K-Means and classified using a semantic distance [9] with a kNN approach. Categorised resources in videos are used to build a vector describing video content, then exploited in the RS. The SN also allows users to build a public personal profile of resources of interest from those extracted from comments or added by the SN users. The profile module is exposed relying on the hypothesis that self-expression and *self-esteem* can be exploited to engage the user in the annotation process, in this way easing the collection of crowdsourced annotations. Salient frames of each video are extracted and related users activity on them is monitored in order to verify if visual saliency can affect user engagement with the system. The positive correlation, verified in Sec. 3.2, is exploited at the interface level for easing the annotation process proposing a widget of most salient frames above each video. Automatic video annotations are then extracted using a CNN-classifier on the more salient frames.

User profile interface. As noted in [20], profile curation is inherent to the use of SNs since management of personal content is integrated with its generation. The content that people choose to share online has to do with how they curate their self-image and present themselves to others. In a 2013 survey, participants ranked their relational identities as most important to them when sharing content on social media [11]. SNs such as Facebook and LinkedIn, for example, are commonly regarded as a space for personal self-expression and self-promotion [15]: users shape their identities in order to gain popularity and reach more and more recognition and connectedness. Our prototype system provides users with a public profile that can be curated in a semiautomatic way. The profile shows user's last comments and annotations as well as annotated video frames and tagged Wikipedia resources with thumbnails. A profiling algorithm categorizes annotations and automatically proposes inferred user interests. Each user can present himself with a set of categories that are visually shown on his profile. Resources annotated by SN users, automatically categorised, are suggested as items that users can drag and promote in their public profile for each detected user interest, as shown in Fig. 1.

Many factors influence users' continued intention to use SNs such as social interactions, knowledge expansion and targeted recommendations [7]. The users' desire of social interactions has been demonstrated to increase the number of *likes* and comments in [6]. The assessment of users engagement with content gives the opportunity to improve targeted services and recommendation. User propulsion at showing knowledge for self-promotion is used, for example, by platforms such as LinkedIn (Q&A) and StackOverflow as a mean to increase the quality and number of crowdsourced annotations but, to the best of our knowledge, there is not a study in the literature which confirms that user profile interfaces affect and improve user activity in SNs. In 3.1 we have conducted a controlled experiment to show how the user's effort to shape his public identity can be exploited

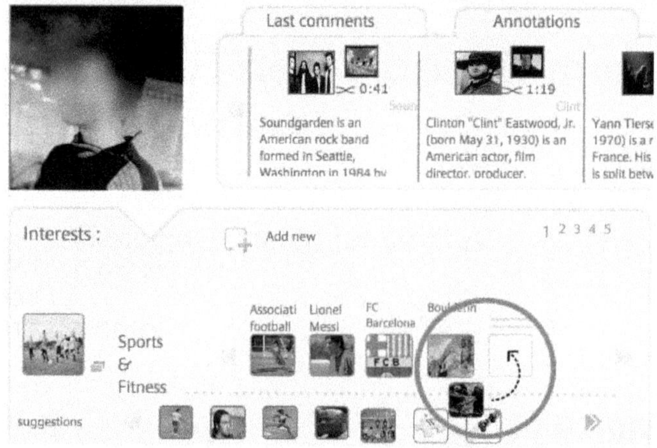

Figure 1: User profile interface: the user can publish resources of interest dragging suggestions from the below to the above carousel.

to increase user's activity and production of crowdsourced annotations.

Visual saliency. We propose the use of visual saliency in SN systems and interfaces at two levels: *i)* at the automatic annotation level to reduce the computational cost of processing all the frames; *ii)* at the interface level to propose to the users possible frames of interest. The SN prototype also features a salient frames carousel above each video to ease the addition of crowdsourced comments. Videos are preprocessed to eliminate letterboxing (i.e. black bars in videos). Then, visual saliency maps are extracted for all the video frames. Maps are defined by a visual attention model which uses a dynamic neural network on multiscale image features computed with the iLab Neuromorphic Toolkit [12]. Salient frames in the video carousel are selected by identifying the peaks of saliency using the crest detection algorithm proposed in [16]. Automatic annotation is performed on frames selected computing the average saliency of the video and choosing those above the average, to have a dense sampling of video content.

Crowdsourced annotations. Users can comment videos at frame level and add semantic references to Wikipedia entities using an autosuggest widget, as shown in Fig. 2. Wikipedia entities are also extracted automatically using entities detection.

A carousel of the most salient frames is also shown above the video player as a video summary. This facilitates fast and accurate annotations at exact timecodes, since users are more likely to interact with salient frames rather than with the less visually interesting ones. A vector of categories C, with the same dimensionality of the SN categories taxonomy, is used to represent video content. Each category in C is assigned with a weight defined by the average of the semantic distance of each annotation to the categories' taxonomy. This semantic relatedness between the terms is obtained using the Wikipedia Link-based Measure [9].

Visual features. Automatic annotation of all the frames of the videos in a SN is a time-consuming task which requires a lot of resources. In the proposed SN video frames are

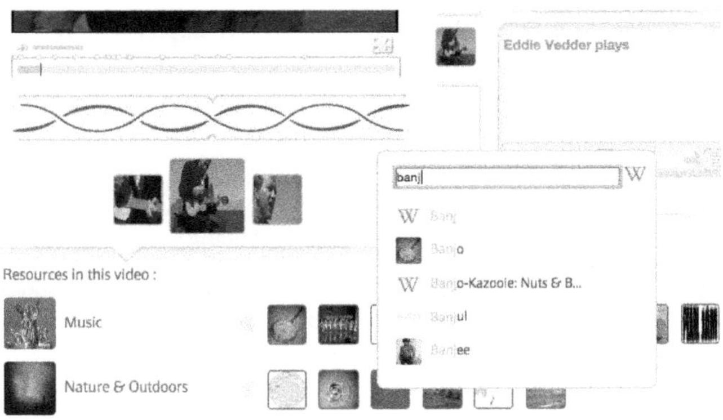

Figure 2: Wikipedia annotation in video frame-level comments.

subsampled according to their visual saliency, allowing the system to scale while maintaining a reasonably dense sampling of video content. The convolutional network used was trained on the ImageNet ILSVRC 2014 dataset to detect 1000 synsets. A very deep CNN with 16 layers [2] was used to extract the final output layer for each frame, containing 1,000 object probabilities. Video content is represented using a Bag-of-Words (BoW) approach. The features vector is computed using the frequency of occurrence of detected concepts with a probability above a threshold, then also complemented by crowdsourced annotations.

The Recommender. Compared to user-based CF approaches, item-based recommenders minimise the sparse item ratings issue, are scalable and in general perform better than user-based recommenders [13]. The proposed hybrid RS adopts a solution that combines a semantic pre-filtering of content with an item-based algorithm. Videos are represented using a feature vector that concatenates the histogram of the categories of the crowdsourced comments and the BoW description obtained using the CNN classifier. User's rating on a video is computed combining explicit and implicit activity. Users can explicitly vote a video on a 5 point scale with a visual widget. Number of visualizations, frame browsing and annotations are also taken into account. In order to reduce the dimensionality of the item-item matrix used by the algorithm, a pre-filtering on the set of possible videos to suggest is performed. Given a user u, we extract a set F_u of videos for which u generated a rating. For each video v_i contained in F_u, the system selects the top-N similar videos creating a subset of similar videos S_i. The set of videos that will be used for the item-based recommender for user u is then composed by the union of all the subsets S_i, namely:

$$R_u = \bigcup_{i=1}^{|F_u|} S_i. \tag{1}$$

The set of video $R_u \cup F_u$ is used to create the item-item matrix used for recommendation. This set is significantly smaller than the whole collection of videos contained in the system. The pre-filtering step uses several approaches in order to infer the top-N similar videos. These approaches, reported in Sect. 3.3, exploit automatic and crowdsourced annotations as well as visual saliency, and use distance measures to compute the overlap between histograms distributions.

3. EXPERIMENTAL RESULTS

Recommendation is a prediction problem: the system should be able to predict the user's level of interest in specific items (e.g. videos) and rank these according to their predicted values [10]. In order to evaluate the accuracy of the prediction, a percentage of the collected data, represented by users ratings on videos, is extracted and used as test data, not used to train the RS. The RS produces rating predictions for the missing test data, that are compared to the actual values in order to evaluate the accuracy. The performance is evaluated using Root Mean Square Error (RMSE). The more accurately the RS predicts user ratings, the lower the RMSE will result. The SN dataset is composed by 632 videos, of which 468 have been annotated with 1956 comments and 1802 annotations. 613 videos were rated by 950 of the 1108 users of the prototype SN.

3.1 User profile interface

An A/B test experiment was conducted at the interface level to test the user profile influence on users' comments activity. The experiment was run on all the active users of the prototype SN for three months. Users were exposed to one of two variants of the SN, featuring (i.e. the variant) or not (i.e. the control) the profile curation interface. The variant was introduced in the third month, so that the number of users exposed to the variant is smaller than that of the control interface. Users who logged into the system and commented on videos since the third month were assigned to the variant (group B), whilst the others were assigned to the control group (group A). In this period of time there were 464 active users (321 in group A and 143 in group B) with a conversion rate of 3.75 and 5.81 average comments. User annotation average increased by a factor of 2.06. The result was statistically significant and validated by a t-test that gave a t-difference = -2.684. Minimum sample size for the evaluation criterion validity was calculated and resulted in 127 for both group A and group B with an optimum allocation ratio of 3.42. Results show a positive correlation between the use of the user profile interface and the increment in user annotations, and suggest that modules for profile curation can be effective in improving conversion rate in user online activity (e.g. videos annotations).

3.2 Visual saliency and manual annotations

The impact of the visual saliency of video frames on user comment activity has also been tested. In the experiment were considered: *i)* the number of comments added without using the most salient frames carousel and *ii)* all the comments, i.e. adding also those coming from a click in the carousel. Results of case i show that 53.5% of user comments are on frames with a saliency above the average saliency of the videos, and that the percentage of frames above the average saliency is 46.5%. Therefore, salient frames receive more attention by users, although not considerably. Results improve consistently considering also carousel driven annotations as in case *ii*: in fact the percentage of comments increases to 65.24%. Percentage of comments carousel driven is 24.01% of the overall dataset, showing that one out of four comments are added using the carousel: it is an high percentage considering threaded comments, added by users in response to others. So, it can be said that salient frames suggestion can be useful if proposed in a web interface as to visually capture the user's attention and help in the annotation tasks.

3.3 Recommendation

The RS is evaluated, in terms of RMSE, comparing it to several baselines: *i)* standard item-based RS, that considers users ratings of all the videos; *ii)* RS working on a selection of videos, based on similarity computed using system categories only (no BoW content description); *iii)* RS working on a selection of videos, based on content similarity (i.e. automatic annotations) computed on n randomly selected frames; *iv)* RS working on a selection of videos, based on content similarity computed on n frames with visual saliency above the average; *v)* RS working on a selection of videos, based on content similarity computed on *a)* frames with visual saliency score above the average and *b)* crowdsourced annotations.

Results are reported in Fig. 3 and show how the proposed *v)* approach results in a lower RMSE value than all the other approaches. In particular, it can be observed that video representation using salient frames improves over random selection, and that the addition of semantics extracted from manual annotations provides another improvement. In this experiment the threshold used to select the confidence scores of the classifiers is 0.85. In a second experiment we have evaluated the effect of the confidence of the classifier, using a threshold of 1. In this case the RMSE is further improved from 0.97 to 0.86.

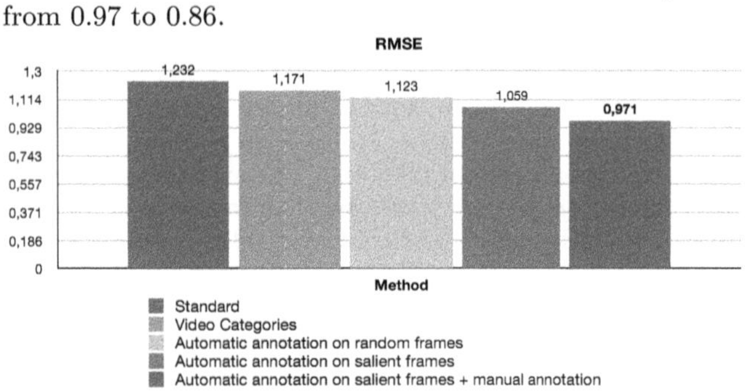

Figure 3: Comparison of the proposed recommender (rightmost result) w.r.t. baselines in terms of RMSE.

4. CONCLUSIONS

In this paper we presented a system to improve an item-based video RS. The RS uses a reduced item-item matrix, computed from content based description of videos obtained from crowdsourced and automatic annotations. User engagement through profile curation and visual saliency has been used *i)* to increase the number of crowdsourced annotations, presenting the most relevant frames to users, and *ii)* to address system scalability in terms of automatic annotation, reducing the number of frames to be processed. The effectiveness of exploiting human factors for user engagement (i.e. self-esteem in user profile interfaces and visual saliency) is evaluated by user experiments on a SN prototype. Experiments show also that the proposed RS improves over the standard implementation of an item-based algorithm, and that the combination of manual and automatic annotations is more effective than the use of a single type of annotations. A positive correlation of the two human factors with the performance of the RS is not yet fully demonstrated, but it can be hypothesized and it is worth of further investigation.

Acknowledgments. This work is partially supported by the "Social Museum and Smart Tourism" MIUR project (CTN01_00034_231545).

References

[1] M. Bertini, A. Del Bimbo, A. Ferracani, F. Gelli, D. Maddaluno, and D. Pezzatini. Socially-aware video recommendation using users' profiles and crowdsourced annotations. In *Proc. of WSAM*, 2013.

[2] K. Chatfield, K. Simonyan, A. Vedaldi, and A. Zisserman. Return of the devil in the details: Delving deep into convolutional nets. In *Proc. of BMVC*, 2014.

[3] B. Craggs, M. Kilgallon Scott, and J. Alexander. ThumbReels: Query sensitive web video previews based on temporal, crowdsourced, semantic tagging. In *Proc. of CHI*, 2014.

[4] P. Cui, Z. Wang, and Z. Su. What videos are similar with you?: Learning a common attributed representation for video recommendation. In *Proc. of ACM MM*, 2014.

[5] A. Felfernig, M. Jeran, G. Ninaus, F. Reinfrank, S. Reiterer, and M. Stettinger. Basic approaches in recommendation systems. In *Recommendation Systems in Software Engineering*, pages 15–37. Springer, 2014.

[6] F.-H. Huang. Motivations of Facebook users for responding to posts on a community page. In *Proc. of OCSC*, 2013.

[7] K.-Y. Lin and H.-P. Lu. Intention to continue using Facebook fan pages from the perspective of social capital theory. *Cyberpsychology, Behavior, and Social Networking*, 14(10):565–570, 2011.

[8] X. Ma, H. Wang, H. Li, J. Liu, and H. Jiang. Exploring sharing patterns for video recommendation on YouTube-like social media. *Multimedia Systems*, 2013.

[9] D. Milne and I. H. Witten. Learning to link with Wikipedia. In *Proc. of ACM CIKM*, 2008.

[10] B. Mobasher. Data mining for web personalization. *The adaptive web*, 2007.

[11] R. Morris. Identity salience and identity importance in identity theory. *Current Research in Social Psychology*, 21(8):23–36, 2013.

[12] V. Navalpakkam and L. Itti. Modeling the influence of task on attention. *Vision Research*, 45(2), 2005.

[13] B. Sarwar, G. Karypis, J. Konstan, and J. Riedl. Item-based collaborative filtering recommendation algorithms. In *Proc. of WWW*, 2001.

[14] F. Sulser, I. Giangreco, and H. Schuldt. Crowd-based semantic event detection and video annotation for sports videos. In *Proc. of CrowdMM*, 2014.

[15] J. Van Dijck. 'You have one identity': performing the self on Facebook and LinkedIn. *Media, Culture & Society*, 35(2):199–215, 2013.

[16] Z. Wang, J. Yu, Y. He, and T. Guan. Affection arousal based highlight extraction for soccer video. *Multimedia Tools and Applications*, 73(1), 2014.

[17] B. Wu, E. Zhong, B. Tan, A. Horner, and Q. Yang. Crowdsourced time-sync video tagging using temporal and personalized topic modeling. In *Proc. of ACM KDD*, 2014.

[18] P. Xu and M. Larson. Users tagging visual moments: Timed tags in social video. In *Proc. of CrowdMM*, 2014.

[19] B. Yang, T. Mei, X.-S. Hua, L. Yang, S.-Q. Yang, and M. Li. Online video recommendation based on multimodal fusion and relevance feedback. In *Proc. of ACM CIVR*, 2007.

[20] X. Zhao and S. E. Lindley. Curation through use: Understanding the personal value of social media. In *Proc. of CHI*, 2014.

[21] R. Zhou, S. Khemmarat, L. Gao, and H. Wang. Boosting video popularity through recommendation systems. In *Proc. of DBSocial*, 2011.

Human's Scene Sketch Understanding

Yuxiang Ye
Texas State University
y_y13@txstate.edu

Yijuan Lu
Texas State University
lu@txstate.edu

Hao Jiang
Boston College
hjiang@cs.bc.edu

ABSTRACT

Human's sketch understanding is important. It has many applications in human computer interaction, multimedia, and computer vision. Recognizing human sketches is also challenging. Previous methods focus on single-object sketch recognition. Understanding human's scene sketch that involves multiple objects and their complex interactions has not been explored. In this paper, we tackle this new problem. We create the first scene sketch dataset "Scene250" and propose a deep learning method to understand human scene sketches. We propose "Scene-Net", a new deep convolutional neural network (CNN) structure, based on which we build a novel scene sketch recognition system. Our system has been tested on the collected scene sketch dataset and compared with other state-of-the-art CNNs and sketch recognition approaches. Our experimental results demonstrate that our method achieves the state of art.

Categories and Subject Descriptors

I.5 [**Pattern Recognition**]: Miscellaneous

Keywords

Sketch understanding; scene sketch; deep learning

1. MOTIVATION

Since prehistoric times, sketching has been a unique way to visually render human's mind. In nowadays, with the increasing popularity of devices with touch screens (e.g., touch pads and smart phones), sketching has become one of the most natural means of human-computer interaction. Sketching on the a scene of a smart phone has been used to provide the input to an image retrieval system. It can be used as a frontal end for generating full 3D models. Sketching also provides an attractive interface for children, especially pre-school kids, to interact with computers. Teaching computers to understand hand-drawn sketches is thus valuable. Sketch understanding has received more and more interests recently.

Sketch understanding is also quite challenging. The difficulty is mainly because a sketch only contains lines and lacks color, texture, and enough visual cues compared to color images. Human sketches also often depict complex high-level concept. Current sketch-related methods mainly focus on recognizing sketches that contain only one single object [1, 9] in each image. However, these single-object sketches are very different from the sketches that people usually draw. In a human drawn sketch, we often see complete scenes or even a depicted story (Fig. 1). Without the information of object regions and segmentations, understanding a scene sketch with multiple objects is more challenging than recognizing single-object sketch. Another factor that complicates scene sketch recognition is the possible variation of rotation, scale and view point as shown in Fig. 2. There is also an uncertainly about the drawing style. One thousand people may sketch the same scene in one thousand different ways. When sketching the same scene, different people tend to choose different set of objects (Fig. 2: Desert). The sketches of "River" can be either several strokes to depict the river shape or a portrait with fine details of plants along the river (Fig. 2: River). So far, there is a lack of a comprehensive study of how human's scene sketches can be well understood by computers.

In this paper, we study scene sketch understanding. We create the first scene sketch dataset Scene250 and explore deep learning approach to scene sketch understanding. We propose a new deep CNN structure and build a novel scene sketch understanding system based on this model. The performance of our system has been tested on the collected scene sketch dataset and compared with other state-of-the-art sketch recognition approaches. Our methods give much better results than these previous methods.

To our best knowledge, this work is the first attempt to explore scene sketch understanding and to construct a deep learning CNN to solve the problem. Our main contributions introduced in this paper are highlighted as follows:

- The first scene sketch dataset is created and open to public. It contains 250 scene sketches in 10 categories. The sketches include common indoor and outdoor scenes.
- A new scene sketch deep CNN structure is proposed to target the scene sketch recognition task.
- Comprehensive experiments have been conducted to evaluate the state-of-the-art sketch recognition approaches on human's scene sketch recognition.

ICMR '16, June 6–9, 2016, New York, NY, USA.

DOI: http://dx.doi.org/10.1145/2911996.2912067

- Our proposed scene sketch recognition method provides enabling technique for different sketch-based applications.

Figure 1: Example scene sketches of our Scene250 dataset (one example per category)

2. RELATED WORK

In scene sketch recognition, we classify the input into different scene categories. In the following, we first review current public domain sketch datasets, and then we discuss previous sketch recognition approaches.

(1) Dataset. Early sketch datasets such as the artistic drawing dataset [7] and the structure sketch dataset [6] are either small or restricted to a specific domain. The more recent TU Berlin dataset [1] is larger. It contains 20,000 single-object sketches in 250 daily object categories. In contrast to the TU Berlin dataset, in this paper, we deal with scene sketches that involve multiple objects and complex interaction among these objects. We have constructed a new dataset Scene250 that contains 250 sketches in ten categories.

(2) Sketch recognition. Early sketch recognition methods [2, 8] have been used to enhance the human computer interaction experience. They use direct inputs from drawings on touch screens or mouses. Such inputs are often noise free. Nowadays, sketch recognition methods have been developed to handle line drawings in noisy scanned or photographed images. Different hand-crafted features, such as stroke length, stroke order and stroke orientation have been used in sketch recognition. Eitz et al. [4] proposed to use sHOG and bag-of-word methods for sketch understanding. Even though this method gave a promising correct classification rate of 56% on the TU Berlin sketch dataset, designing effective hand-crafted features is a challenging task. It requires extensive knowledge on drawing. And, there is also no guide line about how to construct the optimal features. More flexible sketch recognition approach needs to be designed.

Deep learning, which tackles learning the features and classifiers simultaneously, is a promising framework to tacking the problem. Convolution Neural Networks (CNNs) have shown remarkable results in many vision tasks of different domains. With the introduction of rectifier linear (ReLU) [5], max-pooling, local response normalization (LRN) [4], and dropout regularization units [3], CNNs become less likely to overfit. They generalize well on unseen data. Yu et al. [9] designed a sketch-oriented deep CNN model "Sketch-a-Net" for sketch recognition task and achieved the accuracy of 74.9% on TU Berlin dataset.

Most previous works only focus on single-object sketch recognition. However, in realistic world, people usually draw a sketch with multiple objects, i.e., a scene sketch, rather than a simple single-object sketch. Compared with single-object sketch recognition, scene sketch understanding is more challenging. Some examples are shown in Fig. 2.

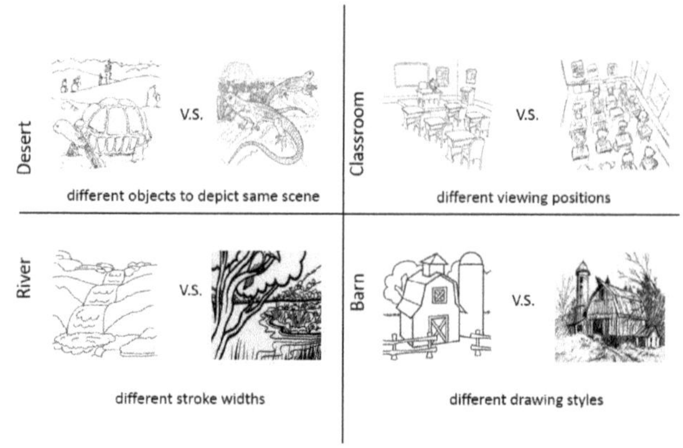

Figure 2: Examples to demonstrate scene sketch recognition challenges

3. METHOD

3.1 A deep CNN model

We propose a novel scene sketch oriented deep CNN model "Scene-Net". Its architecture is illustrated in Fig. 3, while more detailed parameters can be found in Table 1. As shown in Fig. 3, our Scene-Net CNN contains five convolutional layers (L1~L5) followed by three fully-connected layers (L6~L8). Each layer has a ReLU unit except for the layer L8. LRN units are appended to the layers L1 and L2 while max pooling units are appended to the layers L1, L2 and L5. We apply dropout units to the first two fully connected layers (L6 and L7). The third fully connected layer (L8), which is appended by a softmax loss layered, is the last layer of our CNN model. The output size of the last layer is 10, which corresponds to the 10 scene categories.

3.2 Smaller Input Size

Setting the input size of a CNN is critical, since all the following layers depend on the input layer. Many modern deep CNNs [4, 9] use large input size around 225×225. However, we find that smaller input size is more appropriate for scene sketch recognition. The major reason is that scene sketches usually contain multiple objects within one image. Smaller input size combined with random data augmentation can capture more sophisticated features. To this end, input size of 193×193 is used in our Scene-Net.

3.3 Local Response Normalization

Local Response Normalization (LRN) performs a kind of "lateral inhibition" by normalizing inputs in local regions. In this paper, we denote the size of local region as n, the scaling parameter as α, and the exponent as β in Table 1.

3.4 Dropout

Dropout reduces complex co-adaptations of neurons by randomly setting unit activation to zero. The "dropped out" neurons do not participate in the forward pass and back-propagation. In our Scene-Net, we set the dropout rate as

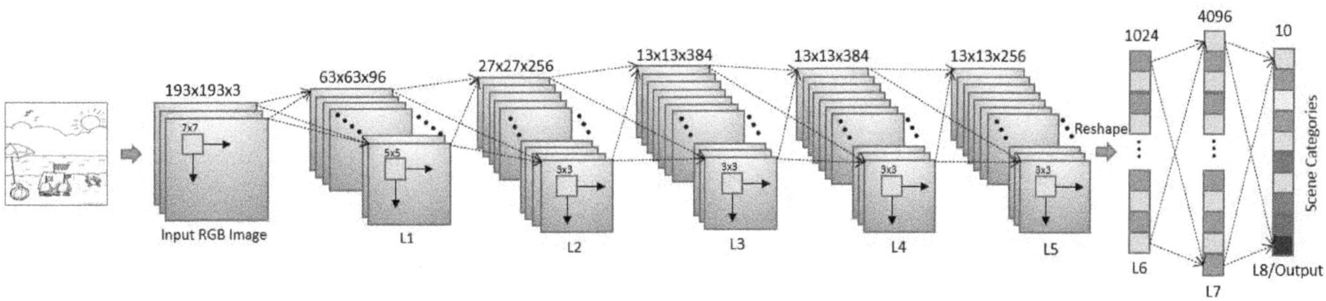

Figure 3: Overall architecture of Scene-Net model

0.5, which is a reasonable approximation. Dropout layers are appended to the first two fully connected layers.

3.5 Fine-tuning

We use fine-tuning to deal with the small training dataset problem. Since our training dataset is very small, directly training the neural network with millions of parameters would make cause the overfit of the trained classier on the small dataset. We there first pre-trained Scene-Net model on the TU Berlin dataset and obtained the initial learning weights for the Scene-Net model. Then, we resumed the training process on the Scene250 dataset to fine tune Scene-Net model for scene sketch recognition task. In our experiments, we find applying fine-tuning significantly increases the recognition accuracy and prevents the overfitting problem.

4. EXPERIMENTS AND DISCUSSIONS

4.1 Scene250 Dataset Collection

We create the scene sketch dataset "Scene250". Scene250 (Fig. 1) contains 250 scene sketches from the Internet. These sketches cover 10 different categories and each category includes 25 sketches. To construct the dataset, we searched for sketches via Google using different key words. We downloaded more than 100 sketches for each category and selected 25 representative ones. The following criteria are used when selecting the categories and scene sketches in each category.

- Completeness. Although the categories of Scene250 does not cover all the scene categories, the selected 10 categories represent the most common ones in the everyday life and contain both indoor and outdoor scenes.
- Unambiguous. Each selected sketches that can be classified into more than one category. For example, we don't select the sketches that can be classified as either "desert" or "river".
- Recognizable. Human observer should be able to recognize these selected sketches from their shape alone without other context information such as text.
- Diversity. Sketches in the same scene category should be diversified. We avoid selecting the sketches that are visually identical in order to guarantee the diversity.

We manually inspected the whole dataset by displaying sketches on a screen. All the scene sketches in the same category were displayed together, which allowed us to identify improper ones easily. We removed those sketches that are in the wrong category (e.g., a mountain scene in the bedroom category) or not subject to our selection constraints. We also rescaled the dataset to contain exactly 25 scene sketches per category yielding the final 250 scene sketches in the Scene250 dataset. Benefited from consistent size of each category, there is no need to correct for bias toward the categories with different size when performing training or testing.

4.2 Image Format

We rescaled all the images to 256 × 256 pixels and read the images as single channel or multiple channels, which depends on the architecture of CNNs.

4.3 Data Augmentation

We randomly perturb the data to generate a bigger set of training data to prevent overfitting. In our experiments, each image is perturbed randomly to generate 500 different inputs. Each image is randomly shifted in the x or/and y directions by 0-63 pixels. The result is further rotated randomly in 0-360 degrees and then flipped vertically with a 50% chance.

4.4 Comparison

We compared our Scene-Net model with two other deep CNN models: AlexNet [4] and Sketch-a-Net. Although AlexNet is a photo-oriented deep CNN model designed for ImageNet, it gives good results in many different applications (e.g., video, robotics, and bioinformatics). Sketch-a-Net is a sketch-oriented deep CNN model specifically designed for single-object sketch classification. It even beats human recognition accuracy by 1.8% on TU Berlin dataset. Both AlexNet and Sketch-a-Net have five convolutional layers followed by three fully-connected layers (last fully-connected layer is the output layer). Sketch-a-Net uses larger first layer filters (11 × 11), higher dropout rate (0.55), and overlapped pooling.

We compared our Scene-Net with the above CNN methods using our Scene250 dataset. Following the settings in previous works, we used 2/3 sketches per category for training and 1/3 for testing. In addition, since there are two types of scene sketches in Scene250: indoor scene (i.e., bedroom, classroom, kitchen, and library) and out-door scene (i.e., barn, beach, castle, desert, mountain, and river), we also tested these CNN models on in-door scene and out-door scene recognition individually. The comparison results are listed in Table 2 and 3. Our Scene-Net model not only beats AlexNet and Sketch-a-Net on overall recognition performance but also beats them on both in-door and out-door scene recognition task.

Table 1: Detailed architecture of Scene-Net

Index	Layer	Type	Filter Size	Filter Num	Stride	Pad	Output Size
0		Input	-	-	-	-	193×193
1	L1	Conv	7×7	96	3	0	63×63
2		ReLU	-	-	-	-	63×63
3		LRN($n = 5, \alpha = 10^{-4}, \beta = 0.75$)	-	-	-	-	63×63
4		Maxpool	3×3	-	2	0	31×31
6	L2	Conv	5×5	256	1	0	27×27
7		ReLU	-	-	-	-	27×27
8		LRN($n = 5, \alpha = 10^{-4}, \beta = 0.75$)	-	-	-	-	27×27
9		Maxpool	3×3	-	2	0	13×13
10	L3	Conv	3×3	384	1	1	13×13
11		ReLU	-	-	-	-	13×13
12	L4	Conv	3×3	384	1	1	13×13
13		ReLU	-	-	-	-	13×13
12	L5	Conv	3×3	256	1	1	13×13
13		ReLU	-	-	-	-	13×13
14		Maxpool	3×3	-	2	0	6×6
15	L6	Fully-connected	6×6	1024	1	0	1×1
16		ReLU	-	-	-	-	1×1
17		Dropout(0.5)	-	-	1	0	1×1
18	L7	Fully-connected	1×1	4096	1	0	1×1
19		ReLU	-	-	-	-	1×1
20		Dropout(0.5)	-	-	1	0	1×1
18	L8	Fully-connected	1×1	10	1	0	1×1
19		Softmax loss	-	-	-	-	1×1

4.5 Implementation details

We implemented Scene-Net model using Matlab and the MatConvNet toolbox. All the experiments were executed on a Linux machine with an 8-core 3.50GHz CPU and a GeForce GTX Titan X GPU. The pre-training time for our Scene-Net model on the TU Berlin dataset is approximately 8 hours on GPU, while fine-tuning with Scene250 dataset is about 3 hours on GPU.

Table 2: Scene sketch recognition performance comparison

Scene-Net	AlexNet	Sketch-a-Net
0.6000	0.5250	0.3875

Table 3: In-door/Out-door scene sketch recognition comparison

	Scene-Net	AlexNet	Sketch-a-Net
In-door	0.5000	0.4688	0.2500
Out-door	0.6667	0.5625	0.4792

5. CONCLUSIONS AND FUTURE WORK

Scene sketch understanding is a challenging research problem. In this work, we make the first attempt to recognize human's scene sketches. We build the first scene sketch dataset "Scene250" and open it to public. We propose, implement, and test a novel deep CNN model "Scene-Net" on scene sketch recognition. We perform fine-tuning to reduce overfitting and improve robustness of our "Scene-Net" model. The experiment results show that Scene-Net outperforms other two deep CNN models (AlexNet and Sketch-a-Net) by 7.50% and 21.25% on scene recognition respectively. Future work include collecting a large-scale scene sketches dataset, optimizing Scene-Net architecture to reduce the training time, and applying our method to sketch-based 3D model retrieval.

6. ACKNOWLEDGMENTS

This work is supported by Army Research Office grant W911NF-12-1-0057 and NSF CNS grant 1305302 to Dr. Yijuan Lu and NSF grant 1018641 to Dr. Hao Jiang.

7. REFERENCES

[1] M. Eitz, J. Hays, and M. Alexa. How do humans sketch objects? In *SIGGRAPH*, 2012.

[2] C. F. Herot. Graphical input through machine recognition of sketches. In *SIGGRAPH*, 1976.

[3] G. E. Hinton, N. Srivastava, A. Krizhevsky, I. Sutskever, and R. R. Salakhutdinov. Improving neural networks by preventing co-adaptation of feature detectors. In *arXiv:1207.0580*, 2012.

[4] A. Krizhevsky, I. Sutskever, and G. E. Hinton. Imagenet classification with deep convolutional neural networks. In *NIPS*, 2012.

[5] Y. LeCun, L. Bottou, G. B. Orr, and K. R. Müller. Neural networks: Tricks of the trade. In *Efficient BackProp*, pages 9–50. Springer, 2002.

[6] T. Y. Ouyang and R. Davis. Chemink: a natural real-time recognition system for chemical drawings. In *International Conference on Intelligent User Interfaces*, 2011.

[7] P. Sousa and M. J. Fonseca. Geometric matching for clip-art drawing retrieval. *Journal of Visual Communication and Image Representation*, 20(2):71–83, 2009.

[8] I. E. Sutherland. Sketch pad a man-machine graphical communication system. In *AFIPS*, 1964.

[9] Q. Yu, Y. Yang, Y.-Z. Song, T. Xiang, and T. Hospedales. Sketch-a-net that beats humans. In *arXiv:1501.07873*, 2015.

Retrieval of Multimedia Objects by Fusing Multiple Modalities

Ilias Gialampoukidis
ITI-CERTH
Thessaloniki, Greece
heliasgj@iti.gr

Anastasia Moumtzidou
ITI-CERTH
Thessaloniki, Greece
moumtzid@iti.gr

Theodora Tsikrika
ITI-CERTH
Thessaloniki, Greece
theodora.tsikrika@iti.gr

Stefanos Vrochidis
ITI-CERTH
Thessaloniki, Greece
stefanos@iti.gr

Ioannis Kompatsiaris
ITI-CERTH
Thessaloniki, Greece
ikom@iti.gr

ABSTRACT

Effective multimedia retrieval requires the combination of the heterogeneous media contained within multimedia objects and the features that can be extracted from them. To this end, we extend a unifying framework that integrates all well-known weighted, graph-based, and diffusion-based fusion techniques that combine two modalities (textual and visual similarities) to model the fusion of multiple modalities. We also provide a theoretical formula for the optimal number of documents that need to be initially selected, so that the memory cost in the case of multiple modalities remains the same as in the case of two modalities. Experiments using two test collections and three modalities (similarities based on visual descriptors, visual concepts, and textual concepts) indicate improvements in the effectiveness over bimodal fusion under the same memory complexity.

1. INTRODUCTION

Multimedia retrieval systems are becoming more and more popular as there is a need for effective and efficient access to very large and diverse collections of multimedia objects, such as videos (e.g. YouTube and Netflix) and images (e.g. Flickr). Searching in such collections is challenging due to the heterogeneous media that each item in the collection may contain (e.g. text, images, and videos). Therefore, these multiple media and the different features that can be extracted from them, e.g. low-level visual descriptors (based on color, shape, location, etc.), low-level textual features (image captions, video subtitles, etc.), high-level textual or visual features (named entities, concepts, etc.), or metadata (timestamps, tags, etc.), need to be combined to support various multimedia analysis tasks, such as retrieval, summarization, clustering, and classification; this combination of multiple modalities is referred to as *multimodal fusion.*

ICMR'16, June 06-09, 2016, New York, NY, USA

DOI: http://dx.doi.org/10.1145/2911996.2912068

Multimodal fusion has been widely investigated and is typically performed at the feature level (*early fusion*), at the decision level (*late fusion*), or in a *hybrid* manner; see [3] for a survey. This work focuses on the decision level or late fusion of multiple modalities for the multimedia retrieval task; to this end, several multimedia and cross-media approaches have been proposed. Metric fusion [13] is a random walk approach designed to fuse different "views" of the same modality, such as SIFT, GIST and LBP visual features; our focus though is on the combination of diverse modalities, such as textual and visual similarity scores. A recent video retrieval framework [9] proposes to fuse textual similarity scores based on video subtitles with visual similarity scores based on visual concepts in a simple non-linear way.

Other approaches have been motivated by Latent Dirichlet Allocation (LDA) and either generate a joint topic probability distribution for all modalities, or combine the topic distribution per modality [4]. Each query is related to a topic and the retrieved documents are assigned a topic distribution. If the topic distribution of a retrieved document is maximized at the query's topic, the document is considered to be relevant. Convolutional Neural Networks (CNN) have also been used to learn high-level features and combine two modalities (text-image pairs) for cross-modal retrieval [12]. A Partial Least Squares (PLS) based approach [10] that maps different modalities into a common latent space has also been used in an image retrieval task. Contrary to these approaches that require training, our focus is on unsupervised multimodal fusion. Furthermore, many of these approaches can only support monomodal queries, whereas our goal is to also cater for queries consisting of multiple modalities. It should be noted that multimedia search systems are often interactive and user feedback is incorporated for progressively refining the query (e.g. [14]); such relevance feedback approaches are beyond the scope of this work.

One unsupervised multimedia retrieval approach that has been recently proposed [2] combines textual and visual similarities by integrating into a unifying graph-based framework (i) a cross-media approach that not only considers the similarity of the query to the objects in the collection, but also the similarities among them [1] and (ii) a random walk approach for multimodal fusion, and in particular a video retrieval approach that links two objects (i.e. nodes in the graph) with a weighted edge if there exists a multimodal similarity between them [6]. To decrease the complexity, the framework assumes that the textual part of a multimodal query "is the main semantic source with regard to the user information" [2] and thus it first selects the top-l multimedia objects based on their textual similarity to the query, and then applies graph-based techniques only to these l selected items. This graph-based framework includes as special cases all well-known early, late, weighted, diffusion-based, as well as graph-based fusion models, does not require users' relevance feedback, and has been evaluated in the context of multimedia retrieval tasks. Thus far, though, this framework has only considered two modalities.

This work extends this unsupervised unifying framework to multiple modalities (Section 2) and performs experiments using two test collections for evaluating the effectiveness of merging three modalities, and in particular similarity scores based on low- and high-level textual and visual features, for the retrieval of multimodal documents relevant to multimodal queries (Section 3). Moreover, to account for the memory cost of introducing additional modalities, a complexity analysis is performed for estimating the number of top-l documents that can be considered in multimodal fusion so as to have the same memory cost as bimodal fusion.

2. METHODOLOGY

First, we briefly describe the graph-based framework proposed in [2] that supports the fusion of two modalities and, then, we present its extension to M modalities.

2.1 Background

As described above, the framework first selects the top-l multimedia documents based on their textual similarity to query q. All subsequent operations are performed on these l selected documents. First, the $1 \times l$ query-based similarity vectors on the textual and visual modalities, $s_t(q,.)$ and $s_v(q,.)$, respectively, are computed and are normalized so that their elements sum to one. Then, the $l \times l$ textual and visual similarity matrices, S_t and S_v, respectively, are computed for these documents and are normalized using: $(s(d,d') - \min s(d,.))/(\max s(d,.) - \min s(d,.))$, where $s(d,d')$ denotes the similarity between two documents d and d'. By denoting the regular matrix multiplication operation as "$\cdot$" and the (i,j) element of a matrix A as $A[i,j]$, this graph-based framework sets $x_{(0)} = s_t(q,.)$, $y_{(0)} = s_v(q,.)$, and defines the following update rule:

$$x_{(i)} \propto \mathbf{K}(x_{(i-1)},k)\cdot[(1-\gamma)D\cdot(\beta S_t+(1-\beta)S_v)+\gamma e\cdot s_t(q,.)]$$

$$y_{(i)} \propto \mathbf{K}(y_{(i-1)},k)\cdot[(1-\gamma)D\cdot(\beta S_v+(1-\beta)S_t)+\gamma e\cdot s_v(q,.)]$$

where D is the row-normalizing matrix, e is the $l \times 1$ vector of ones, and the operator $\mathbf{K}(x,k)$ takes as input a vector x and assigns a zero value to elements with score strictly lower than the k-th highest score in x. Following i iterations, the final ranking with respect to query q is given by the linear combination of $s_t, s_v, x_{(i)}$ and $y_{(i)}$:

$$score(q) = \alpha_t s_t(q,.) + \alpha_v s_v(q,.) + \alpha_{tv} x_{(i)} + \alpha_{vt} y_{(i)} \quad (1)$$

under the restriction that: $\alpha_t + \alpha_v + \alpha_{tv} + \alpha_{vt} = 1$.

This framework includes all well-known weighted, graph-based and diffusion-based fusion techniques, as special cases of its parameters. For $a_{tv} = a_{vt} = 0$, Equation (1) becomes the weighted mean fusion model. For $a_t = a_v = a_{vt} = 0, \gamma = 0$ and sufficiently large number of iterations i, the model is the random walk approach [6]. For $a_v = a_{tv} = 0, \beta = 0, \gamma = 0$, and $i = 1$, the model is the cross-media approach [1].

In the experiments reported in [2], $\beta = 0, \gamma = 0.3, i = 1$ and $k = 10$ are recommended as the default parameters when fusing the top-l ($l = 1000$) results returned by text-based search. The weights in the linear combination of $s_t, s_v, x_{(1)}$ and $y_{(1)}$ are tuned in $\{0.1, 0.2, \dots, 0.9\}$ and the best values are compared to the uniform weighting strategy ($\alpha_t = \alpha_v = \alpha_{tv} = \alpha_{vt} = 0.25$). The results show only an incremental increase in Mean Average Precision (MAP) in one dataset and no increase in the other datasets, indicating the potential effectiveness of this uniform weighting scheme.

2.2 Multimedia Retrieval Using M Modalities

Our aim is to extend the aforemonetioned graph-based framework to more than two modalities. Assuming that there are M modalities with corresponding $1 \times l$ query-based similarity vectors $s_m(q,.)$ and $l \times l$ similarity matrices S_m, $m = \{1, 2, \dots, M\}$, we compute the following contextual similarity matrix for each modality m:

$$C_m = \left(1 - \sum_{w=1}^{M-1} \beta_w\right) S_m + \sum_{w=1}^{M-1} \beta_w S_{w \neq m} \quad (2)$$

The matrices C_m of Equation (2) are row-normalized so as to obtain the corresponding row-stochastic transition probability matrices P_m with elements:

$$P_m[i,j] = \frac{C_m[i,j]}{\sum_{j=1}^{l} C_m[i,j]} \quad (3)$$

For all modalities m, we set $x^m_{(0)} = s_m(q,.), m = \{1, \dots, M\}$, and motivated by [2], we define the following update rule:

$$x^m_{(i)} \propto \mathbf{K}(x^m_{(i-1)},k) \cdot \left[\left(1 - \sum_{\substack{w=1 \\ w \neq m}}^{M} \gamma_w\right) P_m + \sum_{\substack{w=1 \\ w \neq m}}^{M} \gamma_w s_w(q,.)\right] \quad (4)$$

Inspired by the model of Equation (1), we finally propose the vector of relevance score in response to query q:

$$score(q) = \sum_{m=1}^{M} \alpha_m s_m(q,.) + \sum_{m=1}^{M} \alpha'_m x^m_{(i)} \quad (5)$$

where

$$\sum_{m=1}^{M} \alpha_m + \sum_{m=1}^{M} \alpha'_m = 1 \quad (6)$$

For three modalities, for example, Equation (2) becomes:

$$C_1 = (1 - \beta_1 - \beta_2)S_1 + \beta_1 S_2 + \beta_2 S_3$$
$$C_2 = (1 - \beta_1 - \beta_2)S_2 + \beta_1 S_1 + \beta_2 S_3$$
$$C_3 = (1 - \beta_1 - \beta_2)S_3 + \beta_1 S_1 + \beta_2 S_2$$

The contextual similarity matrices $C_m, m = \{1, 2, 3\}$ are row-normalized to obtain $P_m, m = \{1, 2, 3\}$ using Equation (3), and the update rule (Equation (4)) becomes:

$$x^1_{(i)} \propto \mathbf{K}(x^1_{(i-1)},k)\cdot[(1-\gamma_2-\gamma_3)P_1+\gamma_2 e\cdot s_2(q,.)+\gamma_3 e\cdot s_3(q,.)]$$

$$x^2_{(i)} \propto \mathbf{K}(x^2_{(i-1)},k)\cdot[(1-\gamma_1-\gamma_3)P_2+\gamma_1 e\cdot s_1(q,.)+\gamma_3 e\cdot s_3(q,.)]$$

$$x^3_{(i)} \propto \mathbf{K}(x^3_{(i-1)},k)\cdot[(1-\gamma_1-\gamma_2)P_3+\gamma_1 e\cdot s_1(q,.)+\gamma_2 e\cdot s_2(q,.)]$$

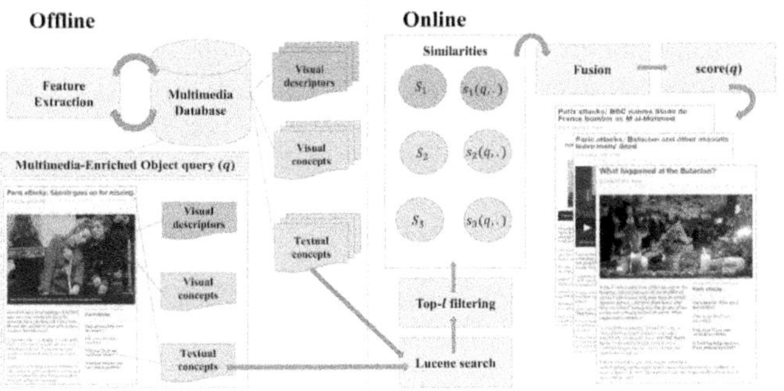

Figure 1: Our multimedia retrieval framework when fusing three modalities.

Finally, $score(q)$ is computed as in Equation (5), which linearly combines $s_m(q,.)$ and $x^m_{(i)}$ for $m = \{1, 2, 3\}$.

Figure 1 depicts our multimedia retrieval framework in the particular case of fusing three modalities, namely visual features, visual concepts and textual concepts. The top-l documents in the filtering step are obtained by using the textual concepts to index and retrieve each document in response to the q using the open-source Apache Lucene[1] system. Then, the $l \times l$ similarity matrices: S_1 on visual descriptors, S_2 on visual concepts and S_3 on textual concepts, and the corresponding $1 \times l$ query-based similarity vectors: $s_1(q,.)$ on visual descriptors, $s_2(q,.)$ on visual concepts and $s_3(q,.)$ on textual concepts are conputed. Finally, we fuse these similarity matrices and query-based similarity vectors to get a single relevance score vector w.r.t. query q: $score(q)$.

Memory Complexity. The memory complexity is $\mathcal{O}(l^2)$ for the computation of each similarity matrix S_m, $\mathcal{O}(l)$ for each similarity vector $s_m(q,.)$ and $\mathcal{O}(kl)$ for each $x^m_{(i)}, m = \{1, 2, \ldots, M\}$; therefore, the overall memory complexity is quadratic in l: $\mathcal{O}(Ml^2 + Mkl + Ml)$. In order to compare directly the baseline method with our retrieval framework with M modalities, under the same memory complexity, we seek the number of filtered documents l', such that $Ml'^2 + Mkl' + Ml' = 2l^2 + 2kl + 2l$. The non-negative solution is:

$$l' = \sqrt{\frac{(k+1)^2}{4} + \frac{2l^2 + 2kl + 2l}{M}} - \frac{k+1}{2} \tag{7}$$

For example, for $M = 3, k = 10, l = 1000$, we find $l' \cong 815$. We also observe that even for 15 modalities, the number of the top-l filtered documents remains > 300, hence a significant number of documents is involved in the fusion, even in the case of several modalities. We shall examine whether the fusion of three modalities in this framework outperforms the baseline approach, without additional memory cost.

3. EXPERIMENTS

In this section, we describe the datasets used for evaluation, the features extracted from their multimedia objects, the employed similarities, and the experimental results.

3.1 Evaluation Datasets

We evaluate our framework using two test collections: the IAPR-TC12[2] and the WIKI11[3], both created in the context of the ImageCLEF benchmarking activities. The IAPR-TC12 collection consists of (i) 20,000 images, each annotated with a title and a description, and also various metadata (e.g. date, location, etc.) not considered in this work and (ii) the 60 topics created in ImageCLEF 2007, each with a title and three image examples. The WIKI11 collection consists of (i) 237,434 images extracted from Wikipedia and their user-generated captions/descriptions and (ii) 50 topics, each with a title and one to five query images.

3.2 Features and Monomodal Similarities

We use the following state-of-the-art features and similarity functions for each modality in the documents and queries; it should be noted though that our method is capable of fusing any similarity score obtained by any kind of features. As visual descriptors (VD), we extract the scale-invariant local descriptors RGB-SIFT [11], which are then locally aggregated into one vector representation using VLAD encoding [7], and we employ a similarity function based on the Euclidean distance [5]. We also employ the 346 high-level visual concepts (VC) introduced in the TRECVID 2011 semantic indexing task[4], which are detected by multiple independent concept detectors that use the aforementioned visual descriptors as input to Logistic Regression classifiers that have their output averaged and further refined [8]. Finally, we use the title/caption of each image so as to extract textual concepts (TC) using the DBpedia Spotlight[5] annotation tool. For the cases of visual and textual concepts, similarities are computed based on Lucene's retrieval function.

3.3 Experimental Setup and Results

We evaluate the MAP of our framework that fuses three modalities against the baseline (Section 2.1) that fuses two modalities. As the baseline models all well-known weighted, graph-based and diffusion-based fusion techniques as special cases of its parameters α, β, and γ, the best performance among all these fusion techniques coincides with the best performance of the weight parameters α, β and γ. Therefore, we tune these parameters so as to present, in Table 1, the best MAP scores of the fusion using two modalities. First, we combine textual concepts with visual descriptors (TC & VD), and then, we combine textual with visual concepts (TC & VC); the combination of visual descriptors and concepts (VD & VC) is not considered as it reduces the problem to the classic image retrieval task and no initial filtering can be performed with respect to the textual modality. We adopt the default parameters reported in [2], i.e. $k = 10$, one iteration ($i = 1$) and uniform weights ($a_t = a_v = a_{tv} = a_{vt} = 1/4$).

To compare directly the baseline method with our framework with three modalities under the same memory complexity, we use $l' = 815$ (see Equation (7)). For $m = \{1, 2, 3\}$, we adopt a uniform weighting strategy ($\alpha_m = \alpha'_m = 1/6$) and we tune the parameters γ_m, while the parameters β_m are kept constant (and equal to 1/3); the results for different values of γ_m are reported in Table 1.

We observe that our framework outperforms the baseline method for several values of the parameters $\gamma_m, m = \{1, 2, 3\}$ under the same memory cost. In particular, MAP increases up to 13.44% for WIKI11 ($\gamma_1 = 0.5, \gamma_2 = 0.25, \gamma_3 = 0.25$) and up to 15.71% for IAPR-TC12 ($\gamma_1 = 0.25, \gamma_2 =$

[1] https://lucene.apache.org/core/
[2] http://imageclef.org/photodata
[3] http://www.imageclef.org/wikidata
[4] http://www-nlpir.nist.gov/projects/tv2011/tv11.sin.346.concepts.simple.txt
[5] http://dbpedia-spotlight.github.io/demo/

Table 1: **MAP values for both datasets; in bold the values which outperform the baselines.**

M	γ_1	γ_2	γ_3	WIKI11	IAPR
2	TC & VD (best α, β, γ)			0.3654	0.2769
2	TC & VC (best α, β, γ)			0.3472	0.2729
3	0.00	0.00	1.00	0.3637	**0.3065**
3	0.00	1.00	0.00	0.3433	**0.2858**
3	1.00	0.00	0.00	**0.3855**	0.2518
3	0.50	0.50	0.00	**0.4083**	**0.2912**
3	0.5	0.25	0.25	**0.4145**	**0.2970**
3	0.25	0.50	0.25	**0.4029**	**0.3136**
3	0.25	0.25	0.50	**0.4048**	**0.3204**
3	0.34	0.33	0.33	**0.4105**	**0.3148**

$0.25, \gamma_3 = 0.5$). We further tuned the parameters α_m, α'_m and $\beta_m, m = \{1,2,3\}$ and we did not observe any further increase in MAP, which implies that there is no other weighted, graph-based or diffusion-based fusion techniques that outperforms our framework. The small differences in MAP when employing the best parameters $\gamma_m, m = \{1,2,3\}$ compared to the uniform ones ($\gamma_m = 1/3$) allows for setting $\gamma_m = 1/3, m = \{1,2,3\}$, without significant decrease in MAP (less than 2%).

4. CONCLUSION

We presented an unsupervised graph-based framework that fuses M modalities for multimedia retrieval. In this work, we consider the fusion of three modalities (textual concepts, visual descriptors, and visual concepts), but the overall framework is directly applicable to any number of modalities. We also presented a theoretical formula which provides the optimal number of documents that need to be initially filtered, so that the memory cost in the case of M modalities remains the same as in the case of two modalities. The experiments have shown that the MAP improves in the case of three modalities (up to 15.71% in some cases). We also observed that the results of a uniform weighting strategy do not significantly differ from those obtained using the best weights. In the future, we plan to evaluate our framework in multilingual settings using language agnostic features, such as textual concepts either in the language of the query or mapped to a common language using multilingual ontologies.

5. ACKNOWLEDGMENTS

This work was partially supported by the European Commission by the projects MULTISENSOR (FP7-610411) and KRISTINA (H2020-645012).

6. REFERENCES

[1] J. Ah-Pine, S. Clinchant, and G. Csurka. Comparison of several combinations of multimodal and diversity seeking methods for multimedia retrieval. In *Multilingual Information Access Evaluation II. Multimedia Experiments: Proceedings of the 10th Workshop of the Cross-Language Evaluation Forum (CLEF)*, pages 124–132. Springer, 2009.

[2] J. Ah-Pine, G. Csurka, and S. Clinchant. Unsupervised visual and textual information fusion in cbmir using graph-based methods. *ACM Transactions on Information Systems (TOIS)*, 33(2):9, 2015.

[3] P. K. Atrey, M. A. Hossain, A. El Saddik, and M. S. Kankanhalli. Multimodal fusion for multimedia analysis: a survey. *Multimedia systems*, 16(6):345–379, 2010.

[4] J. Costa Pereira, E. Coviello, G. Doyle, N. Rasiwasia, G. R. Lanckriet, R. Levy, and N. Vasconcelos. On the role of correlation and abstraction in cross-modal multimedia retrieval. *Pattern Analysis and Machine Intelligence, IEEE Transactions on*, 36(3):521–535, 2014.

[5] J. Hafner, H. S. Sawhney, W. Equitz, M. Flickner, and W. Niblack. Efficient color histogram indexing for quadratic form distance functions. *Pattern Analysis and Machine Intelligence, IEEE Transactions on*, 17(7):729–736, 1995.

[6] W. H. Hsu, L. S. Kennedy, and S.-F. Chang. Video search reranking through random walk over document-level context graph. In *Proceedings of the 15th International Conference on Multimedia*, pages 971–980. ACM, 2007.

[7] H. Jégou, M. Douze, C. Schmid, and P. Pérez. Aggregating local descriptors into a compact image representation. In *Proceedings of the 2010 IEEE Conference on Computer Vision and Pattern Recognition (CVPR)*, pages 3304–3311. IEEE, 2010.

[8] B. Safadi and G. Quénot. Re-ranking by local re-scoring for video indexing and retrieval. In *Proceedings of the 20th ACM International Conference on Information and Knowledge Management (CIKM)*, pages 2081–2084. ACM, 2011.

[9] B. Safadi, M. Sahuguet, and B. Huet. When textual and visual information join forces for multimedia retrieval. In *Proceedings of the ACM International Conference on Multimedia Retrieval (ICMR)*, page 265. ACM, 2014.

[10] B. Siddiquie, B. White, A. Sharma, and L. S. Davis. Multi-modal image retrieval for complex queries using small codes. In *Proceedings of the ACM International Conference on Multimedia Retrieval (ICMR)*, page 321. ACM, 2014.

[11] K. E. Van De Sande, T. Gevers, and C. G. Snoek. Evaluating color descriptors for object and scene recognition. *Pattern Analysis and Machine Intelligence, IEEE Transactions on*, 32(9):1582–1596, 2010.

[12] J. Wang, Y. He, C. Kang, S. Xiang, and C. Pan. Image-text cross-modal retrieval via modality-specific feature learning. In *Proceedings of the 5th ACM International Conference on Multimedia Retrieval (ICMR)*, pages 347–354. ACM, 2015.

[13] Y. Wang, X. Lin, and Q. Zhang. Towards metric fusion on multi-view data: a cross-view based graph random walk approach. In *Proceedings of the 22nd ACM International Conference on Information and knowledge management (CIKM)*, pages 805–810. ACM, 2013.

[14] S. Xu, H. Li, X. Chang, S.-I. Yu, X. Du, X. Li, L. Jiang, Z. Mao, Z. Lan, S. Burger, et al. Incremental multimodal query construction for video search. In *Proceedings of the 5th ACM International Conference on Multimedia Retrieval (ICMR)*, pages 675–678. ACM, 2015.

Incremental Learning for Fine-Grained Image Recognition

Liangliang Cao
Yahoo Labs
New York, NY, USA
liangliang@yahoo-inc.com

Jenhao Hsiao
Yahoo Taiwan
Taipei, Taiwan
jenhaoh@yahoo-inc.com

Paloma de Juan
Yahoo Labs
New York, NY, USA
pdjuan@yahoo-inc.com

Yuncheng Li
University of Rochester
Rochester, NY, USA
yli@cs.rochester.edu

Bart Thomee
Yahoo Labs
San Francisco, CA, USA
bthomee@yahoo-inc.com

ABSTRACT

This paper considers the problem of fine-grained image recognition with a growing vocabulary. Since in many real world applications we often have to add a new object category or visual concept with just a few images to learn from, it is crucial to develop a method that is able to generalize the recognition model from existing classes to new classes. Deep convolutional neural networks are capable of constructing powerful image representations; however, these networks usually rely on a logistic loss function that cannot handle the incremental learning problem. In this paper, we present a new method that can efficiently learn a new class given only a limited number of training examples, which we evaluate on the problems of food and clothing recognition. To illustrate the performance of our proposed method on the task of recognizing different kinds of food, when using only 1.3% of training examples per category we achieved about 73% of the performance (as measured by F1-score) compared to when using all available training data.

Keywords

Incremental Learning; Dynamic Vocabulary; Deep Convolutional Neural Networks; Image Recognition

1. INTRODUCTION

Fine-grained image recognition is the task of recognizing specific object classes present in images, such as different breeds of dogs, species of birds, kinds of food, and types of clothing. In recent years there have been a number of studies on this topic [4, 9, 5], although all of them addressed the problem using a fixed vocabulary, i.e. the classes to detect were predefined. In realistic scenarios, however, it may be necessary to define new classes over time, as well as to redefine or remove existing classes. Consider for example the problem of clothing recognition (see Figure 1), where we may initially have defined a number of high-level categories (e.g. coat, shirt, pants, etc.), but later realize that we also need to recognize more specific subclasses of some of these categories (e.g. types of skirts: straight, mermaid, ruffed, etc.). Given an unseen example (e.g. a kilt), and with limited access to examples of the various clothing categories, we need to decide whether the new instance belongs to one of these existing categories, or to a new one. The same applies to the identification of specific colors or patterns. To address such scenarios, we propose a novel incremental learning strategy based on deep convolutional neural networks for handling the fine-grained recognition problem using a dynamic vocabulary, which only needs a limited number of training examples to accurately learn an object class.

ICMR'16, June 06-09, 2016, New York, NY, USA
© 2016 ACM. ISBN 978-1-4503-4359-6/16/06...$15.00
DOI: http://dx.doi.org/10.1145/2911996.2912069

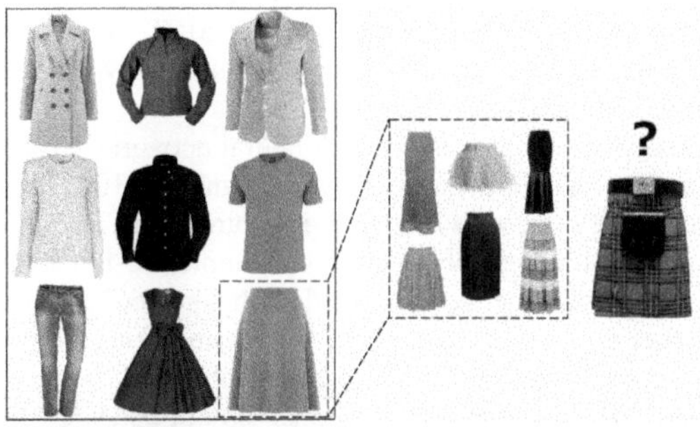

Figure 1: The problem of incremental learning. Based on a limited number of examples from multiple object classes, we need to determine whether a new example belongs to any of the existing classes, or to a new class.

How to learn fine-grained classes efficiently is a challenging problem, considering that the more specific a class is the fewer training examples of the class are available. However, the fine-grained image recognition problem enjoys the three following characteristics: (i) it follows strictly multiclass learning, where we know that any class is mutually exclusive with its sibling classes, as well as with all those from different branches if a class hierarchy is used, which we thus can use as negative examples, (ii) sibling classes are similar to each other in some sense, so we can employ a shared representation to facilitate the classification task, and (iii) each new class corresponds to a simple concept that has limited diversity, which can be learned with relatively few examples.

In this paper, we present an incremental learning method for fine-grained image recognition that exploits the three aforementioned characteristics. Since the fine-grained objects may share similar patterns, we can explore the models and examples for existing classes that can reduce the amount of training required. A surprising fact is that our method can learn a new class from just ten examples, while obtaining comparable accuracy to a model that uses all available data.

2. RELATED WORK

There have been a number of studies on image recognition using deep learning. Domain adaptation [1] focuses on predicting auxiliary problems based on the current features, while a never-ending learning frame [6, 7] was used to learn new visual concepts. More recently, context information from videos [8, 11] was also used for learning new concepts. A key difference between these works and our proposed method is that existing classes are mutually exclusive to any new classes that have to be modeled in fine-grained image recognition. Moreover, our method focuses on using as few examples as possible to learn a new (sub-)class.

The most closely related technique to our work is the k-nearest neighbor (k-NN) method that was extended to incremental learning [13, 16]. Since a k-NN method can easily separate a new category from the old categories, such a method can be applied to the fine-grained recognition problem. However, the two aforementioned methods are based on a histogram of SIFT words, which is not as efficient as the deep convolutional neural network representation we use in our work.

In recent years, deep convolutional neural networks have shown impressive results in large-scale image recognition [10, 12, 17, 18]. Borrowing a network with transferred features from a related task can greatly boost the performance. For example, off-the-shelf deep convolutional neural networks trained on ImageNet have been applied to other datasets, such as Caltech-256, and achieved good results [15]. Even better performance can be obtained by fine-tuning the network [9]. However, these studies did not consider the fine-grained recognition problem and can not be applied to the incremental learning scenario.

3. METHOD

Classic deep convolutional neural networks [10, 17, 18] use the cost function of logistic loss (also known as cross entropy), given by

$$C = -\sum_{i=1}^{N}\sum_{k=1}^{K} \mathbb{1}(y_i = k) \cdot \log p_k(\mathbf{x}_i),$$

where $i = 1, \cdots, N$ denotes the index of training examples, $k = 1, \cdots, K$ the index of class labels, y_i the label of example i and $\mathbf{x}_i$ the feature vector of example i, which in a neural network is the output of the penultimate layer; the indicator function $\mathbb{1}(\cdot)$ equals 1 if the condition is true or 0 otherwise, and $p_k(\cdot)$ is the prediction score of the neural network that satisfies

$$\sum_{k=1}^{K} p_k(\mathbf{x}) = 1, \ \forall \mathbf{x}. \tag{1}$$

In practice, $p_k(\cdot)$ is usually obtained by the output of a softmax layer.

The challenge of incremental learning lies in the fact that Equation (1) does not hold when a new class is added. Namely, when a new class $K + 1$ is introduced,

$$\sum_{k=1}^{K} p_k(\mathbf{x}) + p_{K+1}(\mathbf{x}) > 1.$$

To overcome this problem, we consider the softmax function

$$p_l(\mathbf{x}) = \frac{\exp(\mathbf{w}_l^T\mathbf{x})}{\sum_{k=1}^{K}\exp(\mathbf{w}_k^T\mathbf{x})},$$

where l and k are indexes of class labels, and $\mathbf{w}_l$ and $\mathbf{w}_k$ are the parameters corresponding to l and k, respectively[1]. We observe that this function can also be written as

$$\begin{aligned} p_l(\mathbf{x}) &= \frac{1}{\sum_{k=1}^{K}\exp((\mathbf{w}_k - \mathbf{w}_l)^T\mathbf{x})} \\ &= \frac{1}{1 + \sum_{k=1, k\neq l}^{K}\exp((\mathbf{w}_k - \mathbf{w}_l)^T\mathbf{x})}. \end{aligned}$$

Now it becomes clear that the prediction score is determined by the differences between $\mathbf{w}_k$ and $\mathbf{w}_l$. To emphasize this, we introduce a new function for incremental learning that we call the "softratio", given by

$$r_{k,l}(\mathbf{x}) = \exp((\mathbf{w}_k - \mathbf{w}_l)^T\mathbf{x}).$$

If the classifier successfully predicts that $\mathbf{x}$ belongs to the l-th class, then $\mathbf{w}_k^T\mathbf{x} - \mathbf{w}_l^T\mathbf{x} < 0$; this tends to be a large negative number, such that

$$r_{k,l}(\mathbf{x}) = \exp((\mathbf{w}_k - \mathbf{w}_l)^T\mathbf{x})) \approx 0. \tag{2}$$

Using the softratio function, we can now define the cost for an example from the new class ($l = K + 1$) as

$$\begin{aligned} C_l^+(\mathbf{x}) &= -\log\frac{1}{1 + \sum_{k=1}^{K} r_{k,l}(\mathbf{x})} \\ &= \log[1 + \sum_{k=1}^{K} r_{k,l}(\mathbf{x})], \end{aligned} \tag{3}$$

where the definition of this cost is no longer constrained by Equation (1). The cost for an example from one of the existing classes ($l \leq K$) is defined as

$$\begin{aligned} C_l^-(\mathbf{x}) &= \log[1 + \sum_{k=1, k\neq l}^{K+1} r_{k,l}(\mathbf{x})] \\ &= \log[1 + r_{K+1,l}(\mathbf{x}) + \sum_{k=1, k\neq l}^{K} r_{k,l}(\mathbf{x})] \\ &\approx \log[1 + r_{K+1,l}(\mathbf{x})], \end{aligned} \tag{4}$$

where $\approx$ holds following Equation (2). Our new cost function for incremental learning is then a combination of Equations (3) and (4), given by

$$C = \sum_{i=1}^{N} \mathbb{1}(y_i \leq K) C_{y_i}^-(\mathbf{x}_i) + \mathbb{1}(y_i = K+1) C_{y_i}^+(\mathbf{x}_i). \tag{5}$$

With this cost function, we can keep adding new classes into our model in an incremental manner. Given a network trained with K classes, we can add a new class $K+1$ by introducing new examples and then retrain the model using the cost function in Equation (5). We can simply repeat this process to add additional classes. In practice, for an incremental class $K + 1$, we only learn the parameter vector $\mathbf{w}_{K+1}$, while keeping the existing parameters fixed.

To ensure learning is balanced, we usually require every class (including classes $1, \cdots, K$) to have the same amount of training examples. Since our objective is to learn with a limited number of training examples, we cannot afford to adjust too many parameters as this will lead to significant overfitting.

To further reduce the requirement of training examples from existing classes, we can take the $\bar{\mathbf{x}}_k$ as the mean statistic of $\mathbf{x}$ in the

[1]For simplicity, we let $\mathbf{x} \leftarrow [\mathbf{x}, 1]$ so that $\mathbf{w}^T\mathbf{x}$ denotes a general linear function.

k-th existing class, i.e.

$$\bar{\mathbf{x}}_k = \frac{\sum_{i=1}^{N} \mathbb{1}(y_i = k)\mathbf{x}_i}{\sum_{i=1}^{N} \mathbb{1}(y_i = k)},$$

such that the new cost function becomes

$$C = \sum_{k=1}^{K} C_k^-(\bar{\mathbf{x}}_k) + \sum_{i=1}^{N} \mathbb{1}(y_i = K+1) C_{y_i}^+(\mathbf{x}_i). \quad (6)$$

Although we will show that the performance of Equation (6) is worse than that of Equation (5), it is particularly suitable for the scenario where we cannot access the examples of previously added classes, but only mean statistics of their features.

4. EXPERIMENTS

We evaluated our method using two datasets. In both datasets, our method can be viewed as a two-step process. First, we train a deep convolutional neural network on a number of predefined fine-grained classes, where each class has as many training examples as are available in the dataset. Second, we apply our incremental learning approach to learn new classes, where each class may only have a limited amount of training examples.

Food-101 [4] is a large-scale fine-grained public dataset containing 101 classes of food. Each class contains 750 training images and 250 test images. In this paper, we used the first 90 classes as the set of existing classes and the last 11 classes as the new classes for incremental learning.

Clothing-33 is a proprietary dataset containing 33 different clothing attributes, of which 23 refer to different colors (e.g. white, apricot, cream) and 10 to different patterns (e.g. floral, dotted, striped). The practice of clothing recommendation prefers a dynamic vocabulary in which a new color or a pattern may be added from time to time, a scenario for which incremental learning is very well suited. To learn color models, we randomly selected 19 colors as the existing classes and the remaining 4 colors as the new classes, while to learn pattern models, we randomly selected 7 patterns as the existing classes and the remaining 3 patterns as the new classes.

We split the datasets into training and test sets, each including all classes.

We initialized our deep convolutional neural network using a model trained on ImageNet [5], which is based on a million images annotated with 1,000 object classes, and then tailored it to either the food or clothing dataset using Nesterov stochastic gradient decent (SGD) [14]. We implemented the SGD using Theano [3] on K80 GPU cards, with the batch size fixed to 128 and the learning rate decreasing from 0.002, where we trained the network for 100 epochs over existing classes. Once the network was tailored to the dataset, we then started the process of incremental learning. During incremental learning, we found that stochastic optimization is less preferred, since there are only a limited amount of training examples. Instead, we placed all of training examples in memory and employed limited-memory BFGS [2], which can quickly converge to the solution in both smooth and non-smooth functions.

We first present our experiments on food recognition. We tailored the deep network to the Food-101 dataset using the first 90 classes, and then learned an incremental model for all the other 11 classes using the cost function given by Equation (5). In Figure 2 we see that the incremental model is able to learn well from a limited number of examples, achieving 73.18% of the average F_1 score (the harmonic mean of precision and recall) which is comparable with the result of using all 750 examples. In contrast, when

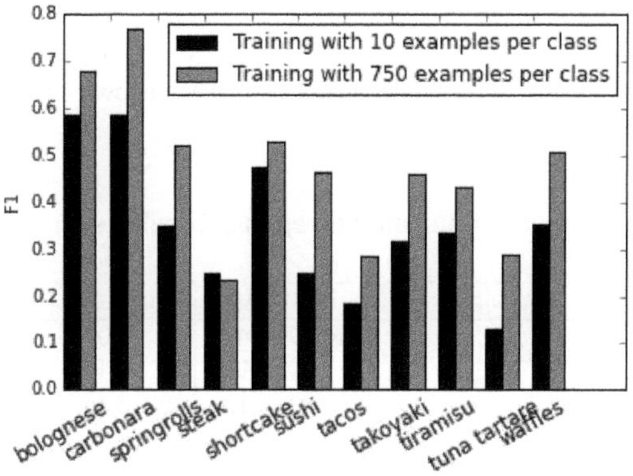

Figure 2: Measuring the F_1 score of incremental learning using the cost function in Equation (5) on the Food-101 dataset for different numbers of training examples per class.

we learned an incremental model using Equation (6) the average F_1 score dropped to 53.50% when we only use the mean statistics of the existing classes.

To illustrate why our incremental learning method is able to obtain a good performance with only a few training examples, in Figure 3 we show how the F_1 score, precision and recall change with additional examples for the class `bolognese` (class 91) of the Food-101 dataset. Although we intuitively would expect the performance to grow with more training data, the performance appears to plateau after only a small number of training examples. The reason is that our method is able to effectively utilize the representation from existing classes. As shown in Equation (5), we only need to learn $\mathbf{w}_{K+1}$, while we can keep reusing $\mathbf{w}_1, \cdots, \mathbf{w}_K$. By reducing the parameters to learn, we can reach a good performance with a limited number of training examples from every new class. For all classes, we found that the performance generally started to plateau after about 10 examples.

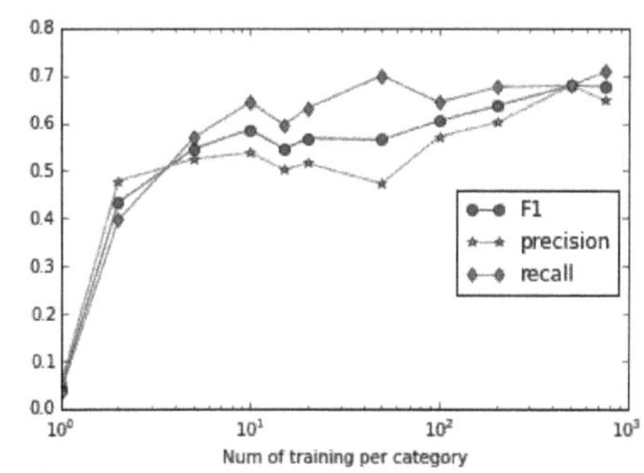

Figure 3: The performance of incremental learning using the cost function in Equation (5) for varying numbers of training examples for the `bolognese` class of the Food-101 dataset.

To further demonstrate the effectiveness of our method, Table 1 compares our incremental learning method with several baseline methods, namely the random forest discriminant components [4] (RFDC), the fine-tuned deep convolutional network [9] (FCNN), and the nearest neighbor-based incremental learning [16] (NNIL), where the latter uses the same deep features as FCNN. The methods in the "standard learning" group used all 750 examples per class, while the methods in the "incremental learning" group only used a few examples per class. For a fair comparison with the results reported in the RFDC and FCNN papers, we calculated the accuracy over the same data (25,250 test images, 101 classes). We can see that that our method significantly outperforms RFDC, and is also much better than NNIL. The performance of our method is close to that of FCNN, which is impressive since our own incremental method used less training examples.

Table 1: Comparing our method against baselines on the Food-101 dataset.

Setting	Methods	Accuracy (%)
Standard learning	RFDC [4]	50.76
	FCNN [9]	64.37
Incremental learning	NNIL [16]	45.93
	Our method	60.32

We now apply our method to incrementally learn clothing colors and patterns. In the Clothing-33 dataset there are 6K images with pattern labels and 32K images with color labels. We use 80% of the images for training and the other 20% for testing. We apply our method using the cost function given by Equation (5) to incrementally learn four colors (apricot, white, leopard print, cream) and three patterns (floral, dotted, stripe) from the Clothing-33 dataset. Figure 4 compares the performance when using only a few examples with when using all examples. Our incremental learning method again achieves a performance that is competitive for a number of classes. While the striped pattern and the white color were more difficult to capture using just a few examples, the performance of learning the dotted pattern and the cream color was comparable to learning them with all available examples.

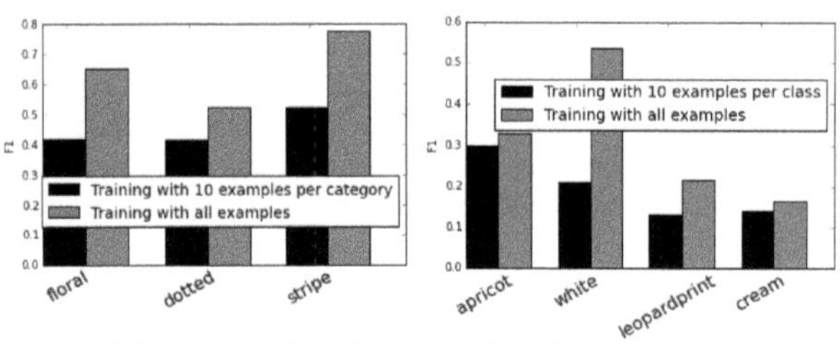

Figure 4: Measuring the F_1 score when incrementally learning clothing patterns (left) and colors (right).

Table 2 offers another view on how effective our method is using limited training examples. For the problem of incremental food recognition, when using only 1.3% of all available training examples per class, we can achieve about 73% of the performance (as measured by F_1 score) compared to when using all examples. The task of incrementally learning clothing patterns and colors appears to be more difficult than food recognition, but the relative performance obtained with incremental learning is nonetheless still about 65%.

Table 2: Comparing the sampling percentage and relative performance of using 10 examples per class versus using all examples per class.

Task	Avg. sampling %	Avg. F_1 %
Food	1.33%	73.18%
Clothes color	3.02%	64.48%
Clothes pattern	4.32%	65.00%

5. CONCLUSIONS

This paper considers the problem of incrementally learning a new category in fine-grained image recognition using only a few examples. Our solution benefits from the recent advances of deep convolutional networks, as well as from the fact that fine-grained image categories are correlated but mutually exclusive. We generalized the traditional softmax function to a new cost function, so it can be applied in an incremental learning scenario. The experimental results on food and clothing suggest that our method can learn a reliable model with only a few examples per class. In future work we aim to generalize our method to the YFCC100M dataset.

6. REFERENCES

[1] R. Ando and T. Zhang. A framework for learning predictive structures from multiple tasks and unlabeled data. In *JMLR*, pages 1817–1853, 2005.

[2] G. Andrew and J. Gao. Scalable training of L1-regularized log-linear models. In *ICML*, 2007.

[3] J. Bergstra, O. Breuleux, F. Bastien, P. Lamblin, R. Pascanu, G. Desjardins, J. Turian, D. Warde-Farley, and Y. Bengio. Theano: a CPU and GPU math expression compiler. In *SciPy*, 2010.

[4] L. Bossard, M. Guillaumin, and L. Van Gool. Food-101 – mining discriminative components with random forests. In *ECCV*, 2014.

[5] K. Chatfield, K. Simonyan, A. Vedaldi, and A. Zisserman. Return of the devil in the details: delving deep into convolutional nets. In *BMVC*, 2014.

[6] X. Chen, A. Shrivastava, and A. Gupta. NEIL: Extracting Visual Knowledge from Web Data. In *ICCV*, 2013.

[7] S. Guadarrama, E. Rodner, K. Saenko, N. Zhang, R. Farrell, J. Donahue, and T. Darrell. Open-vocabulary object retrieval. *Robotics: Science and Systems*, 2014.

[8] M. Hasan and A. Roy-Chowdhury. Incremental activity modeling and recognition in streaming videos. In *CVPR*, 2014.

[9] S. Karayev, M. Trentacoste, H. Han, A. Agarwala, T. Darrell, A. Hertzmann, and H. Winnemoeller. Recognizing image style. In *BMVC*, 2014.

[10] A. Krizhevsky, I. Sutskever, and G. Hinton. ImageNet classification with deep convolutional neural networks. In *NIPS*, 2012.

[11] A. Kuznetsova, S. Hwang, B. Rosenhahn, and L. Sigal. Expanding object detector's horizon: incremental learning framework for object detection in videos. In *CVPR*, 2015.

[12] M. Lin, Q. Chen, and S. Yan. Network in network. *ICLR*, 2013.

[13] T. Mensink, J. Verbeek, F. Perronnin, and G. Csurka. Distance-based image classification: Generalizing to new classes at near-zero cost. *TPAMI*, 35(11):2624–2637, 2013.

[14] Y. Nesterov. A method of solving a convex programming problem with convergence rate O(1/k2). *Soviet Mathematics Doklady*, 27(2):372–376, 1983.

[15] A. Razavian, H. Azizpour, J. Sullivan, and S. Carlsson. CNN features off-the-shelf: an astounding baseline for recognition. *CoRR*, abs/1403.6382, 2014.

[16] M. Ristin, M. Guillaumin, J. Gall, and L. Van Gool. Incremental learning of NCM forests for large-scale image classification. In *CVPR*, 2014.

[17] K. Simonyan and A. Zisserman. Very deep convolutional networks for large-scale image recognition. In *ICLR*, 2015.

[18] C. Szegedy, W. Liu, Y. Jia, P. Sermanet, S. Reed, D. Anguelov, D. Erhan, V. Vanhoucke, and A. Rabinovich. Going deeper with convolutions. In *CVPR*, 2015.

Spatially Localized Visual Dictionary Learning

Valentin Leveau
INA / INRIA Zenith, France
valentin.leveau@ina.fr

Alexis Joly
INRIA Zenith, France
alexis.joly@inria.fr

Olivier Buisson
INA, France
olivier.buisson@ina.fr

Patrick Valduriez
INRIA Zenith, France
patrick.valduriez@inria.fr

ABSTRACT

This paper addresses the challenge of devising new *representation learning algorithms* that overcome the lack of *interpretability* of classical visual models. Therefore, it introduces a new recursive visual patch selection technique built on top of a *Shared Nearest Neighbors* embedding method. The main contribution of the paper is to drastically reduce the high-dimensionality of such over-complete representation thanks to a recursive feature elimination method. We show that the number of *spatial atoms* of the representation can be reduced by up to two orders of magnitude without much degrading the encoded information. The resulting representations are shown to provide competitive image classification performance with the state-of-the-art while enabling to learn highly interpretable visual models.

1. INTRODUCTION

Over recent years, specialized image classification challenges such as plants, vehicles, buildings or logos recognition have received a lot of attention. Many supervised classification algorithms have shown very good performance on such datasets reducing more and more the gap between humans and machines. A very interesting and promising challenge would be to transfer the knowledge of these learning algorithms to humans so that we can gain insights into which part of the data is used by the learning algorithm to discriminate between different visual concepts. This would allow humans such as domain experts to (i) understand which visual patterns are discriminant or ambiguous from a concept to an other, (ii) detect some errors or limitations in the machine learning process, and (iii) improve their knowledge of the objects of interest by taking advantage of the machine to discover fine relevant details. However, the visual representations used in classical visual models are too abstract to fulfill these interpretability objectives. The learned *atoms* (*e.g.* latent variables in probabilistic models or *visual words* in codebook learning methods) do actually not have a uniquely defined and easily interpretable visual appearance. They can typically not be directly *visualizable* or mapped without any ambiguity onto localized visual contents in the training set. The challenge addressed in this paper is to devise new image representation learning algorithms that overcome this lack of *interpretability*. Therefore, we propose a supervised method for learning a compact vocabulary of *discriminant* and *spatially localized* visual patches to be used as atoms of a highly interpretable image representation. To do so, we introduce a recursive visual patch selection technique built on top of a recently introduced embedding scheme called Shared Nearest Neighbor match kernel [10]. The interesting property of such embedding is that it explicitly maps the visual content of a given image onto a potentially huge set of visual patches. So that the image can be represented through a very high-dimensional feature vector encoding its similarity to each visual patch in the training set. In this paper, we propose to drastically reduce the dimensionality of such brute-force and over-complete representations thanks to a recursive feature elimination method. We show that the number of *spatial atoms* of the representation can be reduced by up to two orders of magnitude without much degrading the encoded information. The resulting representations are shown to provide competitive image classification performance with the state-of-the-art while enabling to learn highly interpretable visual models.

ICMR'16, June 06-09, 2016, New York, NY, USA
© 2016 ACM. ISBN 978-1-4503-4359-6/16/06...$15.00
DOI: http://dx.doi.org/10.1145/2911996.2912070

2. RELATED WORKS

Codebook learning methods: One of the most popular *representation learning* algorithm is the so-called Bags-Of-Visual-Words paradigm (BoVW) [7]. It mainly consists in learning a visual vocabulary from a set of local feature vectors through an unsupervised learning algorithm (*e.g* KMeans or GMM). More effective *codebook learning methods* were proposed in the following years using aggregated-based methods such as the Fishers Vectors [13] and VLAD schemes [14] that do not only encode the number of occurrences of each visual word but also encode additional information about the distribution of the descriptors. Such very high-dimensional representations are effective for classification tasks but they are not adapted to our interpretability objectives. Sparse Coding and in particular the supervised dictionary learning method of Mairal *et al.* [9] are a way of learning much more compact visual representations. However, as discussed in the introduction, the atoms of the learned vocabularies do still not correspond to easily interpretative visual patterns. They do not have a uniquely defined visual representation and might embed different visual patterns in the same atom.

Spatially localized representations: In [5], the authors introduce an unsupervised scheme to learn a visual dictionary by randomly picking spatially localized local features selection and ranking them with an information gain criterion combined with a saliency score. Krapac et al proposed in [6] a alternative approach rather based on a prototype selection approach: local descriptors are all kept in their original form (without quantization) and a distance-adaptive prototype is trained for each of them in a supervised way. Our method is different in two main points: first, the elementary atoms of our representation are not individual local features but sets of spatially neighboring local features. This allows embedding much more information in a single *spatial atom*. Secondly, we use a *recursive* feature elimination approach that allows selecting a much better set of spatial atoms than one-shot approaches.

3. PROPOSED METHOD (RVPS)

We define a *spatially localized vocabulary* as a set $\mathcal{Z}$ of *spatial atoms* Z_j, $j \in [1, N]$, each uniquely corresponding to a spatial region R_j of an image in the training set. We define each *spatial atom* Z_j as being itself composed of a set of spatially localized d-dimensional feature vectors $\mathbf{z}_j^i$, $i \in [1, |Z_j|]$, extracted from R_j and representing its local visual content. Our aim is to automatically learn a *spatially localized vocabulary* $\mathcal{Z}$ that is as much compact as possible while still containing the most explanatory visual patterns of the labeled classes in the training set. We therefore introduce a new Recursive Visual Patch Selection algorithm (RVPS) that is summarized in **Algorithm 1**. Its principle is to progressively compress the *spatially localized vocabulary* $\mathcal{Z}$ by recursively eliminating the less discriminant atoms. Each recursion includes 3 main steps: (i) the computation of the SNN representation [10] of the images in the training set $\mathcal{X}$ (based on the current *spatially localized vocabulary* $\mathcal{Z}^{(t)}$), (ii) the learning of a multi-class support vector machine on top of the computed SNN representations and (iii), the elimination of the less discriminant spatial atoms $Z_j^{(t)}$ in $\mathcal{Z}^{(t)}$. These 3 steps are repeated T times. The main parameter of the algorithm is the filtering ratio s that fixes the percentage of non-eliminated atoms at each iteration (*e.g.* $s = 0.9$ means that 90% of the atoms are kept within the *SpatialAtomsFiltering* function). The initialization of the algorithm as well as the description of the different steps of each recursion are detailed hereafter.

Algorithm 1: *RecursivePatchSelection*

input : Vocabulary $\mathcal{Z}$, filtering ratio s, training set $\mathcal{X}$, image labels $\mathcal{Y}$, Number of iterations T
output: Filtered Vocabulary $\mathcal{Z}^{(T)}$

```
if (T>1)
    Z^(T-1)=RecursivePatchSelection(Z,s,X, Y, T-1);
else
    Z^(T-1)=Z;
Φ=ComputeSNN(X,Z^(T-1));
W=LearnSVM(Φ,Y);
Z^(T)=SpatialAtomsFiltering(Z^(T-1),W,s);
return Z^(T)
```

Initialialization: The initial vocabulary $\mathcal{Z}^{(0)}$ to be used as input of the *RecursivePatchSelection* algorithm is created by randomly picking N_0 spatial atoms within the images of the training set $\mathcal{X}$. When N_0 is very large (e.g. 1 million of potentially overlapping regions), this allows starting the vocabulary learning with an over-complete representation to be progressively reduced afterwards. More practically, we uniformly draw N_0 local features $\mathbf{z_j}$ from the raw set of all spatially localized local features extracted from the images (be they hand crafted such as SIFT features or off-the-shelf low level features learned through a convolutional neural network). The j-th spatial atom Z_j is then formed by $\mathbf{z_j}$ itself and by the set of its top-m spatially neighboring local features $\mathbf{z_j^i}$, $i \in [1, m]$.

SNN representations computation: The goal of this step is to compute intermediate representations of the images $X \in \mathcal{X}$ based on a *spatially localized vocabulary* $\mathcal{Z}$. Each image in X is supposed to be described by a set of d-dimensional spatially localized local features $X = \{\mathbf{x}\}$. To map these local features onto the N spatial atoms Z_j of the vocabulary $\mathcal{Z}$, we use the Shared Nearest Neighbor embedding method introduced in [10] and from which we can derive the following explicit embedding function:

$$\mathbf{\Phi}(X) = \sum_{j=1}^{N} \Phi_j(X).\vec{e_j} = \sum_{j=1}^{N} \frac{1}{|X|} \sum_{\mathbf{z} \in Z_j} \sum_{\mathbf{x} \in X} \varphi(r_{\mathbf{x}}(\mathbf{z})).\vec{e_j} \qquad (1)$$

where $r_{\mathbf{x}}(\mathbf{z}) : \mathbb{R}^d \rightarrow \mathbb{N}^+$ is a ranking function returning the rank of $\mathbf{z}$ according to its L_2 distance to $\mathbf{x}$. The function $\varphi(r)$ is a rank-based activation function that is decreasing while increasing r and that is close to zero when the rank r becomes sufficiently high (see [10] for more details). Intuitively, each component $\Phi_j(X)$ of the high-dimensional representation $\mathbf{\Phi}(X)$ quantifies how likely it is that the image X contains the same visual pattern than the one depicted by the spatial atom Z_j. In practice, because of scalability issues, it is not possible to compute the exact rankings $r_{\mathbf{x}}(\mathbf{z})$ for all $\mathbf{x} \in \mathcal{X}$ and all $\mathbf{z}$ belonging to all the atoms $Z_j \in \mathcal{Z}$. Therefore, an approximate nearest neighbor search method is used and only the approximate K nearest neighbors of each $\mathbf{x}$ are considered in the SNN embedding.
In [10], Leveau *et al.* propose a variant of the base SNN scheme for embedding rigid geometry constraints. This is done by multiplying the activation function $r_{\mathbf{x}}(\mathbf{z})$ by a geometry consistency indicator function $\delta_{\mathbf{x}}(\mathbf{z})$ equals to one if $\mathbf{z}$ is an inlier of a RANSAC-like algorithm estimating the best affine transformation between the image X containing $\mathbf{x}$ and the spatial atom Z_j containing $\mathbf{z}$ (and zero otherwise). In our experiments, we used this variant for the datasets that involve rigid objects, *i.e.* buildings and logos.

SVM learning and spatial atoms filtering: To select the most discriminant atoms for a given classification task, we adopt a SVM-based multi class feature selection strategy first proposed in Guyon *et al.* [4] and Chapelle *et al.* [12]. We therefore consider that each image in the training set $\mathcal{X}$ is associated to a class label $y \in [1, C]$. Now, the principle is to define a filtering criterion ρ_j for the j-th component Φ_j of the representation space by analyzing the weights w_{jk} with $k \in [1, C]$ across the C one-versus-all L_2 regularized Support Vector Machine (SVM) classifiers learned on the task. A very simple and theoretically elegant filtering criterion is the l_2 norm of the vector $\mathbf{w_j} = \sum_{k=1}^{C} w_{jk}\vec{e_k}$ so that the more optimal component j^* to remove is given by :

$$j^* =_j \sum_{k=1}^{c} w_{jk}^2 =_j |\mathbf{w_j}|_2^2 \quad (2)$$

The filtering score of an atom Z_j can then be computed as $\rho_j = |\mathbf{w_j}|_2^2$ and the filtering consists in ranking all the components thanks to ρ_j and keep only the top sN atoms (where N is the total number of atoms in $\mathcal{Z}$ and s the filtering ratio). Note that when an atom Z_j is pruned, all the local features $\mathbf{z_j^i}$ belonging to it are definitely removed from the vocabulary.

Discussion: We highlight the fact that our Recursive Visual Patch Selection algorithm (RVPS) is actually different from a classical Recursive Feature Elimination (RFE) [12]. The RFE method actually relies on a fixed representation space and attempts to find the optimal subspace by eliminating the less informative components. On the contrary, the representation space induced by our manifold learning method is evolving at each iteration. Not only some components atoms are removed from the vocabulary but the contribution of the remaining ones do evolve as well. This is mainly due to the rank-based activation function of the SNN embedding. When removing some atoms, the rank $r_{\mathbf{x}}(\mathbf{z})$ of the kept features can only decrease and, as a consequence, the contribution $\Phi_j(X)$ of the remaining atoms can only increase. So that the selected atoms do progressively increase their contribution to the representation of more and more pictures. In other words, we do progressively improve the encoding of the manifold structure of the data thanks to the selection of more and more contributive data items. If we did not recompute the SNN representations after each atom elimination step, we would select some discriminant atoms but we would not select the most generative ones.

4. EXPERIMENTS

To evaluate our method, we used three datasets of the literature: (i) **FlickrLogos32** [3] containing 2,240 images labeled with 32 logo classes (split into 1,280 training images and 960 test images without considering distractors of the original dataset), (ii) **Paris Buildings** [2] containing 6,392 photographs of labeled with 12 Parisian buildings (split into 3,199 training images and 3,193 test images, and (iii) **Oxford Flower** [8] containing 8,189 pictures labeled with 102 flower species (split into 2,040 training images and 6,149 test images). For the *FlickrLogos32* and *ParisBuildings* datasets, SIFT features were extracted around Harris-Hessian-Laplace interest points. For the OxfordFlower dataset, we rather used off-the-shelf CNN-based features learnt with the GoogleNet CNN architecture pre-trained on the ImageNet dataset [1]. Images were forwarded to the inception_3a layer output leading to 784 densely sampled 256-dimensional spatially localized features for each image. All descriptors were L_2-normalized to the unit ball and square rooted. For the SNN embedding computation, we used the same parameters as in [10] except for the knn quality search parameter α that we fixed to $\alpha = 40\%$ and the length b of the hash codes that was fixed to 128 bits for SIFT features and 256 bits for the CNN features. We used the spatially consistent variant of the SNN embedding only for the two datasets involving rigid objects, *i.e. FlickrLogos32* and *ParisBuildings*. The number N_0 of random spatial atoms in the initial vocabulary $\mathcal{Z}^{(0)}$ was fixed to $N_0 = 2^{20}$ the spatial neighborhoods size of of each atom was fixed to $m = 256$ local features.

Recursive filtering impact: To study the impact of the filtering ratio s of our RVPS algorithm, we ran it with five different values, *i.e.* $s = 0.5$, $s = 0.3$, $s = 0.1$ and $s = 0.01$. The recursively computed image representations were then used as input of a L_1 regularized logistic regression (with default regularization constant $C = 1$). Figure 2 displays the resulting classification accuracy on the *FlickrLogos32* dataset as a function of the number of spatial atoms in the learnt vocabulary. It shows that if the filtering ratio is too strong (*e.g.* $s = 0.1$ or $s = 0.01$), the classification performance quickly degrades. On the other side, with a reasonable filtering ratio of $s = 0.5$ or $s = 0.3$, the classification performance remains rather stable with up to two orders of magnitude less atoms in the vocabulary. When the vocabulary contains only 256 spatial atoms, the accuracy is still very acceptable meaning that they are highly informative for the classification task.

RVPS vs. RFE: To further study the effectiveness of our Recursive Visual Patch Selection algorithm (RVPS), we compared it with a classical Recursive Feature Elimination (RFE) computed on top of our initial SNN representations (*i.e.* the ones based on the initial vocabulary $\mathcal{Z}^{(0)}$). The results are provided in Table 1. They show that at constant dimensionality, the representations learned by RVPS are much more effective for the classification task than the ones learned by RFE. This is not sufficient to conclude that the selected spatial atoms are better in terms of interpretability (the generative aspect is probably even more important). But this proves that they do provide a better generalization ability which is a already an interesting criterion.

# atoms	256	1,024	4,096	16,384	65,536
RFE	12.19	15.94	39.2	75.6	81.32
RVPS	78.4	83.6	84.4	86.9	86.15

Table 1: RVPS vs. RFE classification accuracy

RVPS vs. CNN: we also compared the classification accuracy obtained from the RVPS representations to the one of the GoogleNet convolutional neural network [11], with or without pre-training on ImageNet (we respectively used a learning rate of 0.001 with local multipliers of 10 on the last fully connected layers and a learning rate of 0.01 without adding additional local multiplier). For both finetuning and no-finetuning, we used a weight decay parameter of 0.0005 and a momentum of 0.9. The results are provided in Table 2 for the three datasets. They show that the RVPS-based representations are quite competitive with the CNN ones with slightly lower performance than the network fine-tuned on ImageNet. But much better performance are obtained with our approach when considering CNN models learnt from the same data, *i.e* without fine-tuning on the ImgaNet dataset. Now, the main advantage of RVPS is to allow interpreting very easily which visual patterns of the training set were learnt. Indeed, each spatial atom of the spatially localized visual vocabulary has a uniquely defined visual representation.

Notre Dame | Guiness | Google | Arc de Triomphe | Daffodil | Hard-leaved pocket orchid

Figure 1: Learned Spatial Atoms for 6 classes

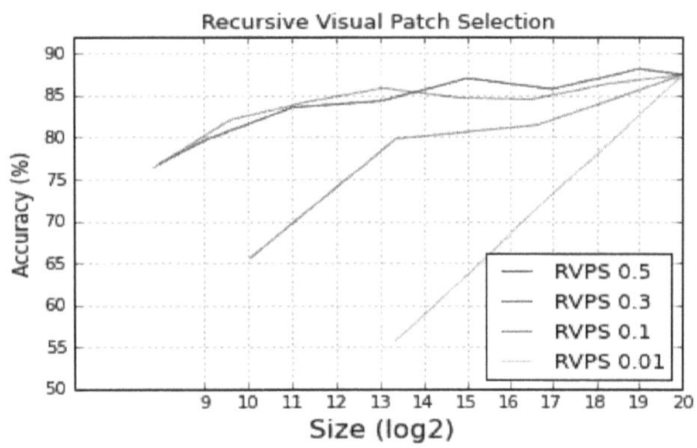

Figure 2: RVPS accuracy vs. number of spatial atoms

Method	*FlickersLogos*	*Paris*	*Flower*
GoogleNet FT	87.5	70.5	89.56
GoogleNet no FT	66.8	54.4	61.7
RVPS - $16,384$ atoms	86.9	73.2	86.43
RVPS - $4,096$ atoms	84.4	70.9	86.36
RVPS - $1,024$ atoms	83.6	67.6	84.31

Table 2: RVPS vs. CNN classification Accuracy

Interpretabilty of the learnt vocabulary: to qualitatively illustrate how interpretable the spatial atoms of our visual representations are, Figure 1 diplays the top-3 most contributive atoms of several classes based on a vocabulary of size 1024 atoms for each dataset. We therefore trained one-vs-all SVM's on top of our representations and ranked the atoms according to their class-wise weight w_{jk}. We see that for some domain such as logos, the chosen patches often correspond to variants of the same visual pattern or to the same visual pattern but under different view conditions. For more complex visual entities such as buildings or plants, the chosen patches rather correspond to different parts of the whole entity which might be very helpful for domain experts.

5. CONCLUSION AND PERSPECTIVES

This paper addressed the challenge of devising a new representation learning algorithm to overcome the lack of *interpretability* of classical visual models. We did show that the proposed Recursive Visual Patch Selection algorithm allows to learn highly discriminant and interpretable representations that maps the visual content of the images onto a vocabulary of uniquely defined and spatially localized visual atoms. In further works, we will attempt to devise innovative active learning methods allowing the experts to directly interact with the vocabulary.

6. REFERENCES

[1] A. Krizhevsky, et al. Imagenet classification with deep convolutional neural networks. In *NIPS'12*.

[2] J. Philbin et al. Lost in quantization: Improving particular object retrieval in large scale image databases. In *CVPR'08*.

[3] S. Romberg et al. Scalable logo recognition in real-world images. In *ICMR'11*.

[4] I. Guyon et al. Gene Selection for Cancer Classification Using SVM. In *Machine Learning Journal'02*.

[5] T. Urruty et al, Iterative Random Visual Word Selection. In *ICMR'14* .

[6] J. Krapac et al. Instance classification with prototype selection. In *ICMR'14*.

[7] G. Csurka et al. Visual categorization with bags of keypoints. In *ECCV04*.

[8] M-E. Nilsback and A. Zisserman. Automated Flower Classification over a Large Number of Classes. In *Indian Conference on Computer Vision, Graphics and Image'08*.

[9] J. Mairal et al. Supervised Dictionary Learning. In *NIPS'08*

[10] V. Leveau et al. Kernelizing Spatially Consistent Visual Matches for Fine-Grained Classification. In *ICMR 2015*.

[11] C. Szegedy et al. Going Deeper with Convolutions. In *CVPR'15*.

[12] O. Chapelle et al. Multi-class feature selection with svm. In Proceedings of the ASA.

[13] F. Perronnin and C. Dance. Fisher kernels on visual vocabularies for image categorization. In *CVPR'07*.

[14] H. Jegou et al. Aggregating local descriptors into a compact image representation. In *CVPR"10*.

Semantic Binary Codes

Sravanthi Bondugula
UMIACS, University of Maryland
College Park, MD, USA
sravb@umiacs.umd.edu

Larry S. Davis
UMIACS, University of Maryland
College Park, MD, USA
lsd@umiacs.umd.edu

ABSTRACT

Fast Image Retrieval is required for many applications like Image Search and Shopping, especially for large datasets. Hashing addresses this problem by learning compact binary codes for images and using them as direct addresses into hash tables. In practice, using binary codes as addresses does not guarantee fast retrieval, as similar images are not mapped to the same binary code(address). We address this problem by presenting an efficient supervised hashing method that aims to explicitly map all images from the same class to a unique binary code to obtain fast retrieval. We refer to the binary codes of the images as 'Semantic Binary Codes' and the unique code for all same class images as 'Class Binary Code'. We formulate this intuitive objective 'directly' by minimizing the squared error criterion between the semantic binary codes and the corresponding class binary codes. We further propose a Deep Semantic Binary Code model that utilizes the class binary codes and show that we significantly outperform the state-of-the-art. We also propose a new class-based Hamming metric that dramatically reduces the retrieval times for larger databases and also improves the performance of the method by large margins.

CCS Concepts

•Information systems → Image search;

Keywords

Hashing, Class/(Deep)Semantic Binary Codes

1. INTRODUCTION

Approximate Nearest Neighbor(ANN) search for image retrieval using compact binary codes has been extensively investigated for faster retrieval and efficient storage. Encoding images with short bit vectors offers great compression. Retrieval is faster predominantly because binary codes can be used as direct addresses into hash tables and ANN's in principal are identified with just a few lookups, compared to an exhaustive linear scan[19]. In practice, using binary codes as addresses does not guarantee fast ANN search, as similar images are not mapped to the same binary code(address). Instead, nearest neighbors must be discovered from examining binary codes within some Hamming radius around the query code. So, the number of lookups required grows exponentially with radius. State-of-the art hashing algorithms then resort to linear scan for large radius. Therefore, there is an explicit need for a hashing algorithm that learns to map similar images to the same binary code.

There exist supervised [12, 8, 2, 20] and unsupervised [1, 25, 14, 13] hashing algorithms for learning similarity preserving binary codes. Unsupervised hashing algorithms try to preserve Euclidean neighbors while supervised hashing algorithms try to preserve semantic neighbors. The notion of similarity is well defined for semantic neighbors compared to Euclidean neighbors as similarity values are discrete(1(same) or 0(different)) for the former and continuous for the latter. In this paper, we develop a new approach to supervised hashing, where we want to **learn both image and class binary codes such that all images from the same class are ideally assigned a unique binary code**. We refer to the image binary codes as 'Semantic Binary Codes' (SBC) and the unique binary code for a class as the 'Class Binary Code' (CBC). By learning both these codes, the performance of a hashing algorithm is naturally improved by retrieving more relevant neighbors within a smaller Hamming ball around the query code.

Only a handful of approaches [12, 16, 8, 2, 20] have been developed to learn a unique binary code for all images from the same class, but they do not formulate this directly into the objective. They instead, learn same binary codes for same class images and different binary codes for different class images. Further, their optimization is complex due to the pair-wise formulation which forces them to resort to a greedy iterative procedure of learning bit by bit which leads to a slow training process. In contrast to these approaches, we propose a simple and efficient supervised hashing algorithm with point-wise formulation of the objective. The first objective eliminates noise by learning projections of input features such that the projected vectors are highly correlated with class vectors. The second objective then minimizes the quantization error between semantic and class binary codes. We jointly optimize these two objectives to obtain the hash functions that meet our goal. Further, we propose a Deep Semantic Binary Code model that utilizes the CBC's.

The remainder of the paper is organized as follows. We first discuss related work in Section 2. We propose a novel

ICMR '16, June 6–9, 2016, New York, NY, USA.

ISBN 978-1-4503-4359-6/16/06...$15.00

DOI: http://dx.doi.org/10.1145/2911996.2912071

joint framework for dimensionality reduction and learning semantic and class binary codes and its deep learning model in Section 3. Retrieval experiments are carried out in Section 4. Finally, we conclude in Section 5.

2. RELATED WORK

Supervised hashing methods in [12, 8, 9, 16, 17, 2, 23] use pair-wise formulations that lead to complex optimization procedure. Recently, Supervised Discrete Hashing(SDH) [20] proposed an efficient optimization procedure using point-wise formulation and learns binary codes that are optimal for classification. While, our end goal is not specifically to learn better classification codes, we intend to learn both image and class binary codes. Recently, several Deep Supervised Hashing(DSH) Models [15, 11, 26, 27, 7, 10] have been proposed and showed superior performance over the shallow methods.The output of these neural networks yields a binary code by applying either a hyperbolic tangent or a sigmoid function to the output followed by a thresholding operation, leading to the final binary hash code. Some networks [15, 11] assume a hand crafted visual representation to learn binary codes and are limited by the performance of the assumed representation. Other networks in [26, 27, 7, 10] do not assume a specific feature representation and instead, learn both the features and hash functions. The latter methods have consequently shown better performance.

3. SEMANTIC BINARY CODES

Input features/labels: We are given a data set of n samples $\{(\boldsymbol{x_i}, y_i)\}_{i=1}^{n}$, where $\boldsymbol{x_i} \in \mathcal{R}^d$ is the input feature and $y_i \in \{1, 2, ..k\}$ denotes the class label of the ith sample. Let $Y \in \mathcal{R}^{k \times n}$ denote the class indicator matrix with one-of-k embeddings i.e $Y_{ij} = 1$ if the class of the jth sample is i and -1 otherwise. We apply the radial basis kernel features with m random sample points to obtain $\phi(x) : x \rightarrow \bar{x} \in \mathcal{R}^m$ as done commonly in[12, 20, 24].

Objective: We aim to jointly minimize both the dimensionality reduction error and quantization error between the image binary codes and the corresponding class binary codes.

Input Projections/Hash Projections: We want to learn semantic binary codes $\boldsymbol{b_i} \in \{-1, 1\}^l$ and the corresponding class binary codes $\boldsymbol{c_{y_i}} \in \{-1, 1\}^l$, both of length l for the ith sample, such that a unique binary code is learned for all same class images. We utilize the hash functions $\{h_j(\phi(\boldsymbol{x})) = sgn(\boldsymbol{u_j}^T \phi(\boldsymbol{x})\}_{j=1}^{l}$ to obtain l bits, where, sgn(.) is the sign function, which outputs +1 for positive number and -1 otherwise. $\boldsymbol{u_j} \in \mathcal{R}^m$ is a column vector that gives the bit b_{ij} for the ith sample. Let $U = [\boldsymbol{u_1}, \boldsymbol{u_2}, ..., \boldsymbol{u_l}] \in \mathcal{R}^{r \times l}$ which can be decomposed into two projection matrices V and W. Then, the corresponding hash functions are: $\{h_j(\phi(\boldsymbol{x})) = sgn(\boldsymbol{w_j}^T V^T \phi(\boldsymbol{x})\}_{j=1}^{l}$, where $V \in \mathcal{R}^{m \times r}$ are the input projections and $\boldsymbol{w_j} \in \mathcal{R}^r$ are the hash projections on the reduced features $V^T \phi(\boldsymbol{x})$. We solve the following joint formulation of the objective:

$$\min_{W,V,c} \sum_{i=1}^{n} \left\| V^T \phi(\boldsymbol{x_i}) - Y_i \right\|_2^2 + \sum_{i=1}^{n} \|\boldsymbol{b_i} - \boldsymbol{c_{y_i}}\|_2^2$$
$$b_i = sgn(W^T V^T \phi(x_i)) \quad (1)$$

where, $\|.\|_2^2$ is the L2-norm.

The first term of the objective eliminates noise by learning projections of input features such that the projected vectors are highly correlated with the class vectors. This is a least squares error formulation for dimensionality reduction and has been shown to be equivalent to CCA [21], with an appropriate form of class indicator matrix $((YY^T)^{-\frac{1}{2}} Y)$. Similarly, the second term of the objective decreases the quantization error between image and class binary codes. Relaxing the sign function in the objective, we get:

$$\min_{W,V,C} \left\| V^T \phi(X) - Y \right\|_F^2 + \left\| W^T V^T \phi(X) - C \right\|_F^2$$
$$B = sgn(W^T V^T \phi(X)) \quad (2)$$

where, $\|.\|_F^2$ is the Frobenius norm and $C \in \{-1, 1\}^{l \times n}$ with $C_i = c_{y_i}$ denote the corresponding class codes for all the samples. Solving this is an NP-Hard problem as there are many variables to learn. We therefore employ an iterative procedure, by solving for one variable at a time.

Solving for V***:*** Given the binary codes of classes C and the hash projections W, we can solve for the input projections V. Let $S = V^T \phi(X)$, we first learn S and then learn V. Expanding (2), we obtain:

$$tr(S^T(I + WW^T)S) - 2tr(S^T(WC + Y)) + nl + const$$

where tr(.) is the Trace function. Taking derivative of the above equation w.r.t.to S and equating to zero yields:

$$S = (WW^T + I)^{-1}(WC + Y) \quad (3)$$

Given the reduced features S, we then obtain the input projections V as: $V = (\phi(X)\phi(X)^T)^{-1}\phi(X)S^T$ (4)

Now, we can learn binary codes of images B and classes C independently from the dimensionality reduction step, by solving:

$$\min_{W,C} \left\| W^T S - C \right\|_F^2$$
$$s.t. \;\; B = sgn(W^T S) \quad (5)$$

Solving for W***:*** Given binary codes of classes C, we obtain the hash projections W on the reduced features S by taking the derivative of (5) and setting it to zero. We obtain the following closed form solution for W:

$$W = (SS^T)^{-1} SC^T \quad (6)$$

Utilizing the hash projections learned, we now obtain the binary codes for the images B by simply taking the sign of the projected vector $W^T S$, given as $B = sgn(W^T S)$.

Solving for C***:*** Given binary codes of the images B, we can learn the class binary codes without the relaxed formulation. We rewrite the objective in (5) with discrete constraints on binary codes, for each sample as:

$$\min_{\boldsymbol{c}} \sum_{i=1}^{n} \|\boldsymbol{b_i} - \boldsymbol{c_{y_i}}\|_2^2, \;\; s.t. \;\; \boldsymbol{c_{y_i}} \in \{-1, 1\}^l \quad (7)$$

It is easy to see that the objective is minimized when the class code is obtained by simply taking the sign of the sum

Set/Tr(t)	SBC(C)	SBC	SDH	ITQ	FastH	KSH⁻
Cifar100	44	44	378	**8**	739⁻	5800
Ilsvrc10	116	116	283	**81**	8580⁻	3e+4
Set/R(t)	SBC(C)	SBC	SDH	ITQ	FastH	KSH
Cifar100	**0.13**	2.9	2.9	2.7	4.8	2.9
Ilsvrc10	**0.94**	351	351	350	354	351

Table 1: We compare the training(Tr(t) in sec) and retrieval(R(t) in milli sec) times on Cifar-100(96 bits) and ILSVRC2010(256 bits). (C) denotes that, we use CHD.

of the bit vector of the class samples. Let $\mathcal{Y}_\kappa$ contain the indices of the samples belonging to class κ and $n_\kappa = |\mathcal{Y}_\kappa|$, the number of samples per class. We construct the class binary code by:

$$\boldsymbol{c}_\kappa = sgn(\sum_{j \in \mathcal{Y}_\kappa} \boldsymbol{b}_j), \quad \forall \kappa \tag{8}$$

We have now learned all the variables, one at a time. We do this iteratively until the objective converges or we reach a maximum number of iterations. We empirically observed that the whole algorithm converges very fast and typically takes fewer than 3 iterations to converge. In either case, we set the maximum number of iterations to be 5. We use initialization from CCA to learn the initial W and then obtain an initial B & C, using the initial solution of V as $(\phi(X)\phi(X)^T)^{-1}\phi(X)Y^T$.

3.1 Class Hamming Distance(CHD)

Most hyperplane hashing functions use Hamming Distance (HD) between the query code (b_q) and database codes (b_d) to compute nearest neighbors in the database for a query(q). Here, we propose a suitable metric: Class Hamming Distance(CHD) to retrieve using Class Binary Codes. Given binary codes for each class, CHD retrieves nearest neighbors for a query q in two steps: First, we compute the nearest class binary code $c_\kappa, \kappa = \arg\min_j HD(c_j, b_q)$. Second, we retrieve the nearest neighbors in the database to the closest class binary code c_κ (instead of the test binary code b_q). Note that, we do not use any labels of the database images when we rank the nearest neighbors in the database to the class binary code.The advantages of doing this are two fold: 1) For a correctly assigned class binary code, there is a high probability of obtaining the same class images as the top retrievals, but the same cannot be said for an incorrect assignment. We expect to reduce the overall error using this approximation. 2) Retrieval is much faster as we only need to compute Hamming distance to the class codes. For each class code, nearest neighbors in the database can be computed offline once and the ranking is stored. Nearest neighbors can now be returned with a single lookup. The total retrieval time is only $O(k)$ instead of $O(n)$, $k << n$.

3.2 Deep Semantic Binary Codes

Recently, Deep Supervised Hashing(DSH) methods[26, 10, 7] have been shown to improve hashing performance by large margins over shallow methods([12, 3]). The model of SBC is a single layer neural network and does not take advantage of the deep training procedure. We present a deep neural network method for SBC that also aims to learn a unique binary code for all same class images. We do so by training a deep network model using the Class Binary Codes learned to form the output layer. We retrain the AlexNet[5] model by replacing the 1000-dimensional output layer(i.e. fc8) with the Class Binary Codes(Equation (8)) of the images and use Sigmoid Cross Entropy Loss as the loss function for the output layer. For a new image, hash codes are obtained by thresholding the sigmoid activations of the output ($thr = 0.5$). We refer to this model as a Deep Semantic Binary Code model and the binary codes learned from the network as Deep Semantic Binary Codes(SBC-D).

4. EXPERIMENTS

We evaluate our proposed supervised hashing method(SBC) and its deep model(SBC-D) on Cifar-100[4] and ILSVRC2010 Train[18] datasets. We compare our approach to the state-of-the art supervised hashing techniques: SDH[20], FastHash [8], KSH[12], ITQ+CCA[3] and BRE[6]. We use their publicly available implementations and the suggested parameters to obtain their best performance. We compute 512-dim GIST features for Cifar-100 and fc7 CNN features of AlexNet for ILSVRC2010 Train datasets. We kernelize the features which take the form $\{\kappa(x, a_1), \kappa(x, a_2), ...\kappa(x, a_m)\}$ where κ is a radial basis kernel, and m is the cardinality of a subset of training sample, designated as 'anchor points' as done in [12, 20, 24]. All the features are unit normalized.

Train/Test Partitions: Cifar-100 contains images from 100 classes, with each class containing 600 samples. The entire dataset is split into a test set with 1000 samples(10 per class) and a retrieval set with all remaining samples. We report performance for methods trained with subsets of size 5000 and the whole retrieval set and construct kernelized features with anchor points of size 1000 and 3000. For the ILSVRC2010 Train dataset containing 1.2M images of 1000 categories, we randomly select 1000 queries and use the rest as the retrieval dataset. For training, we chose 50K samples(50 per class) from the retrieval set and again compute radial basis kernel with 3000 anchor points. For all the datasets, we construct the ground truth from class label information, required for supervised training. During retrieval, we do not use any class label information.

Evaluation metrics: We report the standard retrieval performance metrics: Precision@K(pre@K), Mean Average Precision(mAP) and Precision@Hamming radius(preH@r). pre@K gives the precision at top-K nearest neighbors retrieved. Here, we report for $K = 10$ for Cifar-100 dataset. mAP calculates the area under the precision-recall curve, thereby evaluating the performance of the method for all the ranked images. For Cifar-100, we report mAP and for ILSVRC2010 Train, we report mAP@10K. preH@r is the percentage of the number of images within a Hamming radius r of the query code that belong to the same class as the query. For $r = 0$, these are exact collisions i.e. images are mapped to the same code as the query code. We penalize the query when there are no retrievals within a Hamming radius r. We report Precision@Hamming radius 2 for Cifar-100 and radius 0 and 2 for ILSVRC2010 Train datasets. We show the performance of our method with both Hamming distance and Class-based Hamming distance (CHD). We append the notation (C) when CHD based performance is reported. For Cifar-100 and ImageNet datasets, we learn $\{8, 16, 32, 64, 96\}$ and $\{32, 64, 128, 256\}$ bits respectively.

4.1 Comparison with other methods

BRE and KSH incur high training times for large training samples. In our experiments, for efficiency reasons, we show performance of these methods for only $5K$ training samples for Cifar-100 dataset and $10K$ training samples for $1K$ anchor points on ILSVRC2010 datasets. For FastHash, we use 50K samples for training despite its high training time to report reasonable performance.Both, SDH and ITQ+CCA are scalable and efficient. They obtain the maximum performance with larger numbers of training samples and therefore, we show their performance when trained on the larger training set. For all the reported metrics, we significantly

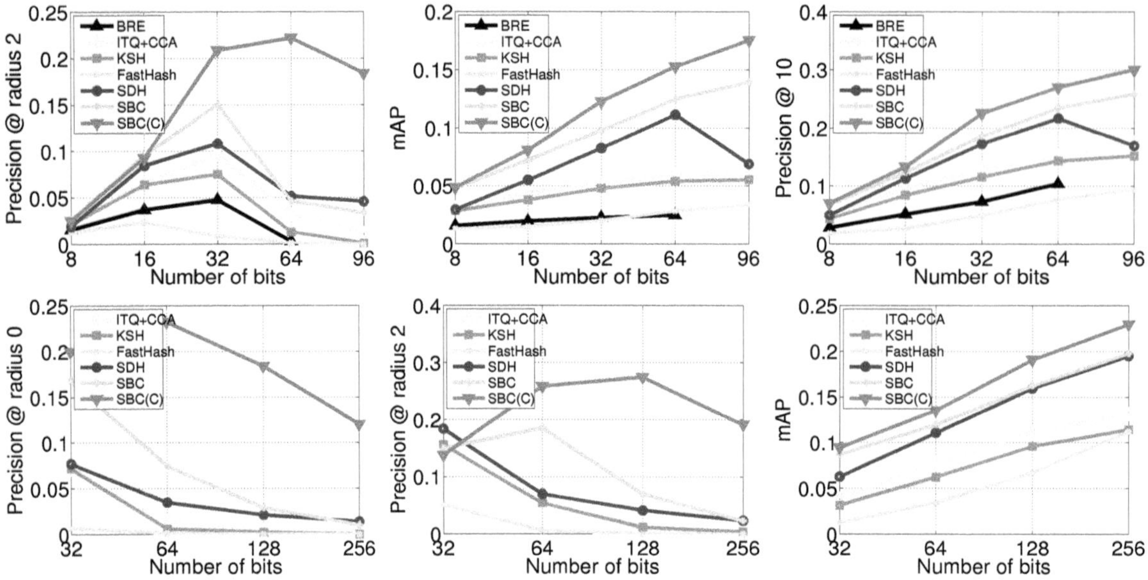

Figure 1: Performance of various metrics for varying numbers of bits on Cifar-100 (top row) and ILSVRC10 (bottom row) is shown.

Mthd	64 bits			96bits		
	mAP	pre@1	preH@0	mAP	pre@1	preH@0
SBC-D	**57.9**	**57.4**	**52.4**	**49.7**	**52.5**	**45.4**
DLH[10]	14.2	26.6	5.8	26.9	42.4	2.7

Table 2: Performance comparison of DSH methods for various metrics and various numbers of bits for Cifar-100 dataset.

outperform the state-of-the art methods by a large gap and we do this with very small training and retrieval times as indicated in Table 1. Figure 1 shows performance on the Cifar-100 and ILSVRC2010 Train datasets.The results show that SBC(C) generalizes better than the second best method SDH on all metrics. Here, we see that as we learn larger numbers of bits, SDH performs better than FastHash, KSH, ITQ+CCA and BRE but worse than both SBC and SBC(C). We also observe that the performance of both SBC (without the Hamming distance) and SDH converges for precision@radius 2 for 96 bits for Cifar-100 datasets. We report performance of BRE only up to 64 bits as it did not converge in 8 hours for more bits. Table 1 shows that the retrieval times of SBC with CHD is significantly faster than HD, as we only compute Hamming distance to the class binary codes.

Comparison Methods for SBC-D: It has been shown that the model proposed by Kevin et al (DLH) [10] outperforms the model of CNNH and its variants proposed by Xia et al [26] and other Deep Supervised Hashing methods([15], [11]). As training deep neural networks is computationally expensive, we here compare SBC-D with only the best baseline DLH and only on Cifar-100 dataset.

For training SBC-D 's, we use the AlexNet [7] architecture and replace the output layer with the learned Class Binary Codes in Section 3. For training the model of DLH, we use their publicly available code[1]. For Cifar-100, we use a batch size of 100 and we train two models for learning 64 and 96 bits. We train up to 50K iterations, so that training is completed in a reasonable amount of time. We report the mean average precision(mAP), precision@1(pre@1) and precision@radius 0(preH@0) for both the methods in Table 2 at 50K iterations. We see that our model SBC-D outperforms DLH for all the metrics for both 64 and 96 bits and has significantly improved over SBC. The high precision of exact collision binary codes(preH@0) of our method indicates that we achieve the goal of mapping all same class images to a unique binary code. We report a gain of 43.7% and 23% in mAP over DLH and a gain of 42% and 30.7% over SBC for 64 and 96 bits respectively. We have shown that by transforming the labels to the class binary code space and replacing the output layer with the binary codes, an efficient supervised deep hashing method can be learned. Although we should emphasize that the improvement in performance with the deep model comes with an increase in training time(10 hours to train each of the 64 and 96 models), compared to only few minutes for the SBC model.

[1]https://github.com/kevinlin311tw/caffe-cvprw15

5. CONCLUSION

The key idea in our paper is to address the practical aspects of faster retrieval using image binary codes as addresses. Our goal was to learn supervised hashing functions such that all same class images are mapped to a unique binary code. The proposed model jointly minimizes the dimensionality reduction error and quantization error between the image and class binary codes, by formulating independent objectives with a least squared criterion. A deep extension of the SBC model is also presented to take advantage of the deep training procedure. We also introduced Class Hamming Distance that utilizes the class binary codes and showed significant improvement in performance and retrieval times compared to instance-based Hamming Distance. Our experiments demonstrate the superiority of both the shallow and deep proposed methods over the state-of-the art.

6. REFERENCES

[1] M. Datar, N. Immorlica, P. Indyk, and V. S. Mirrokni. Locality-sensitive hashing scheme based on p-stable distributions.

[2] T. Ge, K. He, and J. Sun. Graph cuts for supervised binary coding. In *ECCV '14*.

[3] Y. Gong and S. Lazebnik. Iterative quantization: A procrustean approach to learning binary codes. In *CVPR'11*.

[4] A. Krizhevsky. Learning multiple layers of features from tiny images. Technical report, 2009.

[5] A. Krizhevsky, I. Sutskever, and G. E. Hinton. Imagenet classification with deep convolutional neural networks. In *NIPS*. 2012.

[6] B. Kulis and T. Darrell. Learning to hash with binary reconstructive embeddings. In *NIPS' 09*.

[7] H. Lai, Y. Pan, Y. Liu, and S. Yan. Simultaneous feature learning and hash coding with deep neural networks. In *CVPR*, 2015.

[8] G. Lin, C. Shen, Q. Shi, A. van den Hengel, and D. Suter. Fast supervised hashing with decision trees for high-dimensional data. In *CVPR' 14*.

[9] G. Lin, C. Shen, D. Suter, and A. van den Hengel. A general two-step approach to learning-based hashing. In *ICCV' 13*.

[10] K. Lin, H.-F. Yang, J.-H. Hsiao, and C.-S. Chen. Deep learning of binary hash codes for fast image retrieval. In *CVPR Workshops*, 2015.

[11] V. E. Liong, J. Lu, G. Wang, P. Moulin, and J. Zhou. Deep hashing for compact binary codes learning. In *CVPR*, 2015.

[12] W. Liu, J. W. 0006, R. Ji, Y.-G. Jiang, and S.-F. Chang. In *CVPR*, 2012.

[13] W. Liu, C. Mu, S. Kumar, and S.-F. Chang. Discrete graph hashing. In *NIPS*, 2014.

[14] W. Liu, J. Wang, and S. fu Chang. Hashing with graphs. In *In ICML*, 2011.

[15] J. Masci, A. M. Bronstein, M. M. Bronstein, P. Sprechmann, and G. Sapiro. Sparse similarity-preserving hashing. 2014.

[16] M. Norouzi and D. J. Fleet. Minimal loss hashing for compact binary codes. In *ICML'11*.

[17] M. Rastegari, A. Farhadi, and D. A. Forsyth. Attribute discovery via predictable discriminative binary codes. In *ECCV '12*.

[18] O. Russakovsky, J. Deng, H. Su, J. Krause, S. Satheesh, S. Ma, Z. Huang, A. Karpathy, A. Khosla, M. Bernstein, A. C. Berg, and L. Fei-Fei. ImageNet Large Scale Visual Recognition Challenge. *IJCV*, 2015.

[19] R. Salakhutdinov and G. Hinton. Semantic hashing. *Int. J. Approx. Reasoning*, 2009.

[20] F. Shen, C. Shen, W. Liu, and H. T. Shen. Supervised discrete hashing. *CVPR' 15*.

[21] L. Sun, S. Ji, and J. Ye. Canonical Correlation Analysis for Multilabel Classification: A Least-Squares Formulation, Extensions, and Analysis. *IEEE*, 2011.

[22] A. Torralba, R. Fergus, and W. T. Freeman. 80 million tiny images: A large data set for nonparametric object and scene recognition. *IEEE' 08*.

[23] Q. Wang, B. Shen, S. Wang, L. Li, and L. Si. Binary codes embedding for fast image tagging with incomplete labels. In *ECCV '14*.

[24] W. Wang and M. Á. Carreira-Perpiñán. The role of dimensionality reduction in classification. In *AAAI' 14*.

[25] Y. Weiss, A. Torralba, and R. Fergus. Spectral hashing. In *NIPS, 2009*.

[26] R. Xia, Y. Pan, H. Lai, C. Liu, and S. Yan. Supervised hashing for image retrieval via image representation learning. In *AAAI*, 2014.

[27] F. Zhao, Y. Huang, L. Wang, and T. Tan. Deep semantic ranking based hashing for multi-label image retrieval. *CVPR*, 2015.

On the Effects of Spam Filtering and Incremental Learning for Web-Supervised Visual Concept Classification

Matthias Springstein[1]
matthias.springstein@tib.eu
[1]German National Library of Science and Technology (TIB)
Hannover, Germany

Ralph Ewerth[1, 2]
ralph.ewerth@tib.eu
[2]Leibniz Universität Hannover, Faculty of Electrical Engineering and Computer Science
Hannover, Germany

ABSTRACT

Deep neural networks have been successfully applied to the task of visual concept classification. However, they require a large number of training examples for learning. Although pre-trained deep neural networks are available for some domains, they usually have to be fine-tuned for an envisaged target domain. Recently, some approaches have been suggested that are aimed at incrementally (or even endlessly) learning visual concepts based on Web data. Since tags of Web images are often noisy, normally some filtering mechanisms are employed in order to remove "spam" images that are not appropriate for training. In this paper, we investigate several aspects of a web-supervised system that has to be adapted to another target domain: 1.) the effect of incremental learning, 2.) the effect of spam filtering, and 3.) the behavior of particular concept classes with respect to 1.) and 2.). The experimental results provide some insights under which conditions incremental learning and spam filtering are useful.

Keywords

Deep convolutional neural network; visual concept classification; Web-supervised learning

1. INTRODUCTION

Current approaches for semantic image search usually rely on a lexicon of pre-defined visual concepts which have to be detected automatically. For example, deep neural networks [10] are successfully applied to the task of visual concept classification. However, these methods require a large number of positive training examples for each concept category which is a time-consuming and costly task. Common image datasets such as Pascal Visual Object Classes (VOC) [6] or ImageNet [14] have been created by hundreds of people who judged the presence of visual concepts and additionally labeled object locations. Not so long ago, training data creation has been a pure manual task. To solve this problem, it has been proposed to use web and social media. For example, some approaches [1, 15] exploit image search engines to gather images in order to train a concept classifier. Other sources of information, such as Flickr, provide more realistic images with natural background, but this kind of source also includes more noisy tags [2, 18, 16, 9]. Image tags or surrounding text information on websites such as Flickr can be incomplete, subjective, ironic, or simply wrong. Recently, images available in the web are also employed to train a detector for localizing the target concepts in an image [2, 3, 4]. Another kind of approaches uses incremental learning to iteratively optimize the concept model with additional images [3, 11] or to find new concepts in the downloaded data. In general, a further popular alternative is to use pre-trained models, e.g., pre-trained deep neural networks such as GoogleNet or Alexnet [5], but normally these models require fine-tuning based on additional training data for an envisaged target domain.

In this paper, we investigate some properties of a web-supervised learning system for visual concept classification. The envisaged scenario is to build an automatic classification system, which is only initialized with the concept names to be learned, for the target domain Flickr. The baseline system can be an (initially) untrained network as well as a pre-trained network based on ImageNet data. After it has been initialized, the system starts gathering images from Flickr with appropriate tags, i.e., the concept names, and iteratively refines the network model via incremental learning. A spam filtering step based on textual and visual information can precede the model update in each training iteration. The objective of the paper is to provide an insight into 1.) the effect of incrementally adding training data to the network, 2.) the usefulness of spam filtering based on textual and visual information, and 3.) it is investigated if concept classes behave differently with respect to incremental learning and spam filtering. Experimental results are presented for Pascal VOC 2012 data. The performance of the web-supervised system is also compared with a supervised version that is fine-tuned using Pascal VOC 2012 training data.

The remainder of the paper is organized as follows. In section 2, the web-supervised learning system is presented. Experimental results are discussed in section 3 and section 4 concludes the paper and outlines areas for future work.

2. WEB-SUPERVISED LEARNING

In this section, we describe the framework for web-supervised learning of visual concepts. The system consists of

ICMR'16 June 06-09, 2016, New York, NY, USA

ACM ISBN 978-1-4503-4359-6/16/06.
DOI: http://dx.doi.org/10.1145/2911996.2912072

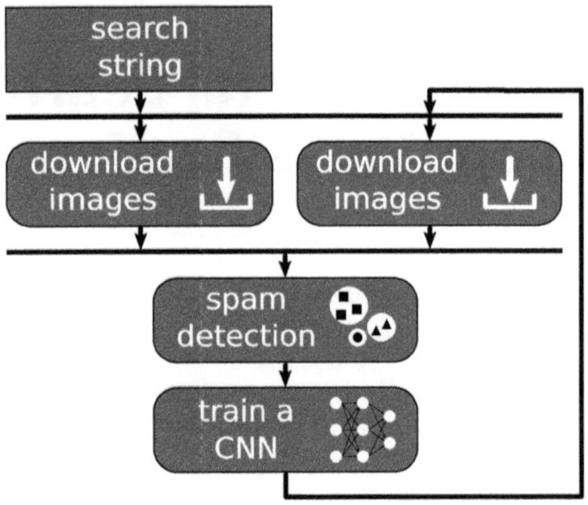

Figure 1: Iterative model of the system.

Figure 2: Example images from a non-spam (2 top rows) and a spam (2 bottom rows) cluster.

three components: crawling, spam detection, and concept learning using convolutional neural networks (CNN). The system is initialized only with the names of the target concepts. Then, our target domain Flickr is used to find positive training examples for all concepts. If an appropriate entry is found, the image and all related information are downloaded and stored. Search engines such as Google or Bing are not exploited since it has been shown that they tend to be biased towards "clear" iconic images [13, 12], i.e., images showing only one visual category. Textual and visual information are exploited to identify "good", i.e., positive training images and to filter out "spam" images from the downloaded content. An image is filtered out if one of the two filters (textual or visual) considers an image as spam. Spam detection based on textual information is described in previous work [7]. The crawling of web content and the spam detection steps are conducted separately for each specified target concept. The system learns in several iterations and is basically designed to learn endlessly. The system's workflow is illustrated in Figure 1.

2.1 Visual Spam Detection

This filter exploits the visual information of each image candidate in order to separate spam images from relevant images which are supposed to be useful for training. To describe an image, a feature vector is generated using a pre-trained CNN. The Caffe model BVLC GoogLeNet [17] is used which is trained on the ImageNet Large Scale Visual Recognition Challenge (ILSVRC) 2012 data [14]. The feature vector is computed using the last pooling layer of the GoogLeNet model. Then, the feature vectors are clustered using k-means algorithm. To estimate the best number of clusters, k is iterated from 2 to 20 clusters. The silhouette coefficient describing the homogeneity of clustering results is computed for each k. The clustering with the maximum silhouette coefficient is used in the next step.

Clusters consisting of a low number of images or having a silhouette coefficient below a threshold are discarded as spam. In the next step, the average distance of each cluster member to its cluster center is computed. These average distances are sorted in ascending order and the maximum of two successive pairs are computed. The maximum is used to split the sorted list into relevant and irrelevant clusters (images). All clusters below this threshold are used as training data while the other clusters are discarded as spam. Some examples of clustered images are shown in Figure 2.

2.2 Incremental Learning Process Using CNN

The clusters that remain after spam detection are used as positive training examples for the target concept. We consider two scenarios to train a CNN as classifier. In the first scenario we use CNN with randomly initialized weights, while a CNN pre-trained on ILSVRC 2012 training set is exploited in the second scenario.

The first deep neural network that we are using is the BVLC AlexNet [10] model from Caffe [8]. The system uses a stochastic gradient descent (SGD) learning algorithm with a momentum term of 0.9. In the first scenario, the network is initially trained with 450 000 iterations and a batch size of 256. We start with a learning rate α of 0.01 and after 100 000 iterations, the learning rate is dropped by a factor of 10. In the second scenario, only 100 000 iterations are used to train the network. Also an initial learning rate α of 0.001 is used, but it is increased in the last layer by a factor of 10. After 25 000 iterations, the learning rate is reduced by a factor of 10.

In addition, a pre-trained CNN GoogLeNet [17] model from Caffe [8] is used as a classifier and fine-tuned for the new task. This model has shown good performance on the ILSVRC 2014 [14]. A SGD learning algorithm is used for fine-tuning and the number of neurons in the last layer is set to the number of target concepts. Only 100 000 iterations with a batch size of 128 and a momentum term of 0.9 are used. The initial learning rate α is reduced by the factor 10 to 0.001, but the learning rate in the last layer is increased by the factor of 10. To increase the number of training examples, all images are scaled to a size of 256×256 and a region of size 224×224 pixels is cropped from the image. Additionally, the training examples are mirrored randomly.

For each incremental training step, 2500 images per target concept are used to optimize the CNN. As long as the system finds further (2500) training examples in the web, this process is repeated.

3. EXPERIMENTAL RESULTS

All experiments are based on an incremental learning setting. The deep neural networks are configured as described in the previous section. In each iteration, new training examples (2500 images per concept) gathered from the web are passed as additional input to the spam filter and the network. The validation set of Pascal VOC 2012 [6] is used to

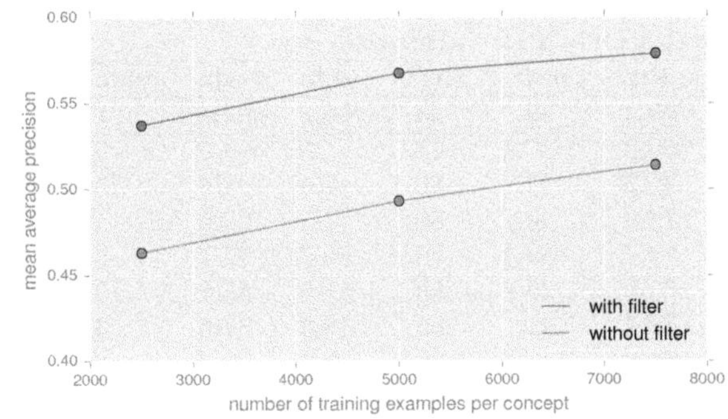

Figure 3: Effect of spam filtering for a CNN with randomly initialized weights.

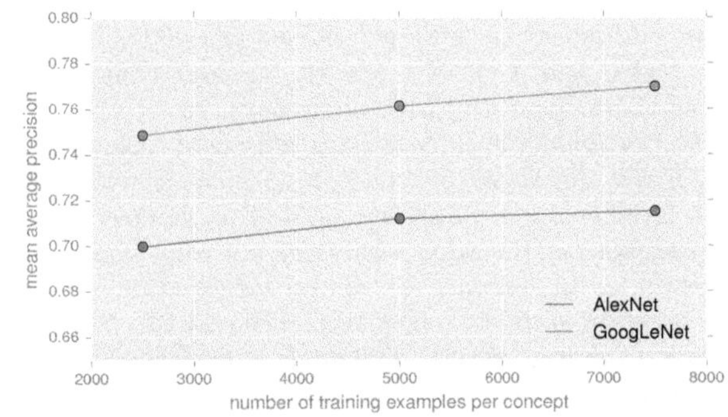

Figure 4: Incremental learning results for two CNNs pre-trained on ILSVRC 2012.

test and compare the performance of the models. This validation set is annotated with respect to 20 visual classes. The first experiment is conducted using 17 classes, since there were not enough training data available (at least 7500) at the time of this experiment for the concepts potted plant, dining table, and TV monitor. This effect was resolved by searching for synonyms as well, which has been employed in the subsequent experiments, i.e., results for the more comprehensive second experiment are reported for all 20 classes.

3.1 Validation of Spam Detection

In the first experiment, the impact of spam detection based on textual and visual information is evaluated. For this purpose, an untrained AlexNet with randomly initialized weights is used. Two AlexNet models are trained: The first model uses the raw image data captured from the Web, whereas the second model employs the spam filters.

Results in Figure 3 show that the mean average precision (MAP) is noticeably better for spam detection for all training iterations. This finding is confirmed in another experiment (described below) using GoogLeNet and 20 classes.

Based on this result, we have tested pre-trained versions of AlexNet and GoogLeNet in conjunction with the spam filtering process. The results displayed in Figure 4 show that the GoogLeNet outperforms the AlexNet network. Hence, a pre-trained GoogLeNet is used in the next experiment.

3.2 Incremental Learning Capability

In this experiment, the behavior of a pre-trained GoogLeNet is investigated for a larger number of eight iterations

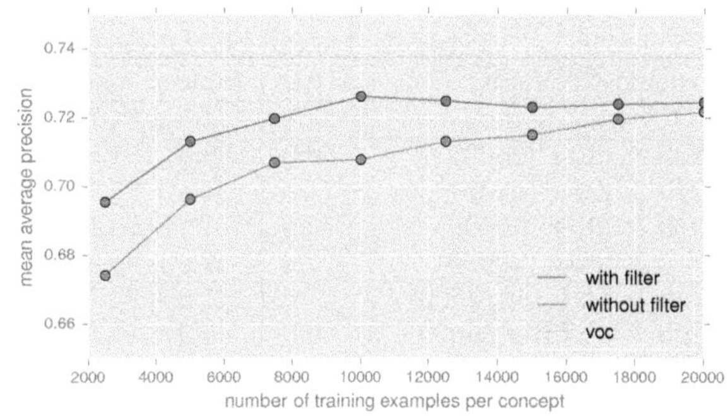

Figure 5: Results of a supervised (VOC training data) and two web-supervised versions, each version building on a CNN pre-trained on ILSVRC 2012.

for two conditions: with and without spam filtering. Again, in each iteration 2500 images per concept class are passed to the CNN and the (optional) spam filtering. That is, in the version without spam filtering 400 000 have been passed to the system. In addition a purely supervised CNN, i.e. without using any image data acquired from the web, is fine-tuned with the Pascal VOC 2012 training data in the same manner as described in section 2.2.

Figure 5 shows the trend of MAP for the eight iterations starting from 2500 up to 20 000 samples per target. The performance of the model using the filter system increases from 69.5 % to 72.4 %.

Also, it can be observed that spam filtering noticeably improves the MAP in the first iterations and MAP of both systems start to converge for 12 500 examples per concepts. Hence, it can be concluded that spam filtering is most helpful when using a smaller number of training examples. Although the web-supervised system version are slightly outperformed by the CNN using "clean" training data (73.7 %), they achieve (nearly) a similar performance – without any supervision and manual efforts for annotating training data.

3.3 Effects on Particular Concepts

The effects of incremental learning in conjunction with (and without) spam filtering can be observed in Table 1 for 10 out of 20 classes. The absolute improvement ranges from -0.7 % for dining table up to 7.6 % TV monitor when using spam filtering. Interestingly, for the system version without spam filtering this behavior is reversed. The absolute improvement ranges from -0.4 % for TV monitor up to 15.7 % for dining table. These concepts tend to be very sensitive to the spam filtering or incremental learning, respectively. Another interesting observation is that additional training examples beyond the size of 10 000 do not improve the system accuracy and the performance converges. From this point on, the learning process has to be modified, for example, by means of network parameters or training data selection.

4. CONCLUSIONS

In this paper, we have investigated the effect of spam filtering and incremental learning for a web-supervised deep learning framework for visual concept classification. A visual spam filter has been suggested which is used in conjunction with a textual filter in order to remove noisy images.

Several conclusions can be drawn. For a target domain

Table 1: Image classification results on Pascal VOC 2012 validation set.

Trained CNN with ...	MAP	table	dog	horse	mbike	person	pplant	sheep	sofa	train	monitor
VOC training data	73.7	61.5	84.7	77.7	83.2	76.4	40.0	83.7	56.2	91.4	71.5
Web & filter (2500)	69.5	48.3	85.6	81.7	84.1	69.3	37.6	78.3	45.6	89.5	32.3
Web & filter (5000)	71.3	51.5	85.0	87.7	84.1	70.3	42.5	80.1	47.4	91.4	38.0
Web & filter (10000)	72.6	51.2	86.1	90.9	83.6	72.9	40.2	80.6	47.5	92.0	49.0
Web & filter (20000)	72.4	47.6	86.8	91.2	84.4	73.1	39.4	80.1	50.7	92.1	39.9
Web & no filter (2500)	67.4	41.6	84.7	85.3	81.5	63.0	39.8	83.1	41.5	85.7	32.2
Web & no filter (5000)	69.6	45.9	84.5	88.3	82.0	62.1	42.1	85.5	48.8	87.6	33.6
Web & no filter (10000)	70.8	49.4	83.9	90.0	83.8	65.3	41.6	86.3	45.1	90.2	35.2
Web & no filter (20000)	72.2	57.3	84.6	89.5	83.1	66.7	45.5	88.7	48.3	90.7	31.8

such as Flickr, a purely web-supervised system based on a pre-trained CNN can achieve nearly the same performance as a system that is fine-tuned with manually annotated data. It has been further shown that the spam filter is useful for system with less training data, up to sample size of 10 000 per concept, or fewer training rounds. From this point on, the accuracy converges. Another insight is that a system without a spam filter can be on a par with the version using spam filter, when it used about twice as many training examples as the latter one. Finally, it has been demonstrated that there are some concept classes which are very sensitive to incremental learning or spam filtering, respectively.

In the future, we plan to investigate which system aspects such as self-validation, training data selection, or network layer modifications can prevent the system's performance from converging. For example, a self-evaluation component is needed that retains parts of a model structure (for particular concepts) which are superior to its own next generation.

5. REFERENCES

[1] K. Chatfield, R. Arandjelović, O. Parkhi, and A. Zisserman. On-the-fly learning for visual search of large-scale image and video datasets. *International Journal of Multimedia Information Retrieval*, 4(2):75–93, 2015.

[2] X. Chen and A. Gupta. Webly supervised learning of convolutional networks. *arXiv preprint arXiv:1505.01554*, 2015.

[3] X. Chen, A. Shrivastava, and A. Gupta. Neil: Extracting visual knowledge from web data. In *IEEE International Conference on Computer Vision (ICCV)*, pages 1409–1416. IEEE, 2013.

[4] S. K. Divvala, A. Farhadi, and C. Guestrin. Learning everything about anything: Webly-supervised visual concept learning. In *IEEE Conference on Computer Vision and Pattern Recognition (CVPR)*, pages 3270–3277. IEEE, 2014.

[5] J. Donahue, Y. Jia, O. Vinyals, J. Hoffman, N. Zhang, E. Tzeng, and T. Darrell. Decaf: A deep convolutional activation feature for generic visual recognition. *arXiv preprint arXiv:1310.1531*, 2013.

[6] M. Everingham, L. Van Gool, C. K. I. Williams, J. Winn, and A. Zisserman. The pascal visual object classes (voc) challenge. *International Journal of Computer Vision*, 88(2):303–338, June 2010.

[7] R. Ewerth, K. Ballafkir, M. Mühling, D. Seiler, and B. Freisleben. Long-term incremental web-supervised learning of visual concepts via random savannas. *IEEE Transactions on Multimedia*, 14(4):1008–1020, 2012.

[8] Y. Jia, E. Shelhamer, J. Donahue, S. Karayev, J. Long, R. Girshick, S. Guadarrama, and T. Darrell. Caffe: Convolutional architecture for fast feature embedding. *arXiv preprint arXiv:1408.5093*, 2014.

[9] P. Kakar and A. Y.-S. Chia. If you can't beat them, join them: Learning with noisy data. In *ACM International Conference on Multimedia*, pages 571–580. ACM, 2015.

[10] A. Krizhevsky, I. Sutskever, and G. E. Hinton. Imagenet classification with deep convolutional neural networks. In *Advances in neural information processing systems*, pages 1097–1105, 2012.

[11] L.-J. Li and L. Fei-Fei. Optimol: automatic online picture collection via incremental model learning. *International Journal of Computer Vision*, 88(2):147–168, 2010.

[12] T.-Y. Lin, M. Maire, S. Belongie, J. Hays, P. Perona, D. Ramanan, P. Dollár, and C. L. Zitnick. Microsoft coco: Common objects in context. In *Computer Vision–ECCV 2014*, pages 740–755. Springer, 2014.

[13] E. Mezuman and Y. Weiss. Learning about canonical views from internet image collections. In *Advances in Neural Information Processing Systems*, pages 719–727, 2012.

[14] O. Russakovsky, J. Deng, H. Su, J. Krause, S. Satheesh, S. Ma, Z. Huang, A. Karpathy, A. Khosla, M. Bernstein, A. C. Berg, and L. Fei-Fei. ImageNet Large Scale Visual Recognition Challenge. *International Journal of Computer Vision (IJCV)*, 115(3):211–252, 2015.

[15] F. Schroff, A. Criminisi, and A. Zisserman. Harvesting image databases from the web. *IEEE Transactions on Pattern Analysis and Machine Intelligence*, 33(4):754–766, 2011.

[16] C. Sun, C. Gan, and R. Nevatia. Automatic concept discovery from parallel text and visual corpora. In *IEEE International Conference on Computer Vision*, pages 2596–2604, 2015.

[17] C. Szegedy, W. Liu, Y. Jia, P. Sermanet, S. Reed, D. Anguelov, D. Erhan, V. Vanhoucke, and A. Rabinovich. Going deeper with convolutions. *arXiv preprint arXiv:1409.4842*, 2014.

[18] B. Zhou, V. Jagadeesh, and R. Piramuthu. Conceptlearner: Discovering visual concepts from weakly labeled image collections. In *IEEE Conference on Computer Vision and Pattern Recognition*, pages 1492–1500, 2015.

Semi-supervised Identification of Rarely Appearing Persons in Video by Correcting Weak Labels

Eric Müller[1,2]
eric.mueller@tib.eu
[1]German National Library of Science and Technology (TIB)
Hannover, Germany

Christian Otto[2]
christian.otto@eah-jena.de
[2]University of Applied Sciences Jena
Jena, Germany

Ralph Ewerth[1,3]
ralph.ewerth@tib.eu
[3]Leibniz Universität Hannover
Hannover, Germany

ABSTRACT

Some recent approaches for character identification in movies and TV broadcasts are realized in a semi-supervised manner by assigning transcripts and/or subtitles to the speakers. However, the labels obtained in this way achieve only an accuracy of $80\% - 90\%$ and the number of training examples for the different actors is unevenly distributed. In this paper, we propose a novel approach for person identification in video by correcting and extending the training data with reliable predictions to reduce the number of annotation errors. Furthermore, the intra-class diversity of rarely speaking characters is enhanced. To address the imbalance of training data per person, we suggest two complementary prediction scores. These scores are also used to recognize whether or not a face track belongs to a (supporting) character whose identity does not appear in the transcript etc. Experimental results demonstrate the feasibility of the proposed approach, outperforming the current state of the art.

Keywords

Face identification in video, semi-supervised learning.

1. INTRODUCTION

The challenging task of person identification in movies and TV broadcast is fundamental for a broad variety of multimedia applications, such as face retrieval, video recommendation, and automatic character labeling. While some approaches rely on manually annotated training data [7], many other proposals [4, 9, 1, 6] employ semi-supervised learning where the labels for training are directly extracted from the test video. For that purpose, it is necessary to link a speaker from subtitles and/or transcripts to the visual content of the current face tracks. This scenario bears a couple of challenges since the required speaker detection is a difficult problem itself. As a result, the accuracy of the extracted *weak labels* is typically between 80% and 90%. Besides, the gallery of persons obtained this way is often highly imbalanced with respect to the number of examples per individual. This is caused by the uneven speaker distribution in a video, where some face tracks even remain unlabeled. Hence, a special treatment of these *unknown* persons is required.

In this paper, we present a semi-supervised system for person identification in video that addresses these issues. An initial prediction step is executed to find highly reliable results by combining a k-nearest neighbor approach with a complementary score that considers the distribution of similarities. The highly reliable predicted tracks are added to the training dataset, which increases the amount of training data of rarely appearing persons. In a next step, this additional knowledge is used to correct the original set of weak labels in order to enhance their accuracy. Furthermore, a combined criterion is utilized to identify face tracks of (unknown) persons that do not belong to an individual of the gallery set, e.g., supporting actors. Experimental results show that the proposed approach noticeably reduces the error rate of character identification in video.

The remainder of the paper is organized as follows. Section 2 discusses recent advancements in the field of person recognition in video. The proposed approach is described in detail in section 3. Section 4 reports experimental results, while section 5 concludes the paper and outlines some areas for future work.

2. RELATED WORK

Person identification in video can be separated into two categories depending on the source of knowledge concerning the target characters. Supervised approaches, such as Ortiz et al. [7], rely on manually annotated training data for each identity. Even though they yield promising results, fully-automatic, semi-supervised approaches as introduced by Everingham et al. [4] are often more desirable. The authors suggest a method that combines textual and visual cues to generate so called weak labels for frontal face images, which has been extended by Sivic et al. [8] to half-profile and profile views. Cinbis et al. [3] exploit frames of the same face track to model intra-person variations and sequences of different persons acting together in a shot for extra-class relations. Tapaswi et al. [9] argue that constraints such as "the same person cannot appear twice in one frame" are very helpful for person identification. To make these rules more viable, they add clothing features in case that the face is not visible in the current frame. In a similar way, Bäuml et al. [1] model the appearances of characters in a multinomial logistic regression (MLR).

ICMR'16 June 06-09, 2016, New York, NY, USA

ACM ISBN 978-1-4503-4359-6/16/06.

DOI: http://dx.doi.org/10.1145/2911996.2912073

One main drawback of all aforementioned approaches is the usage of partially incorrect weak labels for classification. A detailed discussion of this problem is presented by Tapaswi et al. [10], incorporating both positive and negative constraints between and within tracks to enhance speaker assignment. In addition, the weakly labeled data is unevenly distributed for the different characters. To conquer this imbalance, Cherniavsky et al. [2] iteratively add the top 10% of their recognition results to the training data in order to learn facial attributes. The issue of identifying face tracks from *unknown* characters is addressed by Ortiz et al. [7] using classification based on sparse representation.

3. PERSON IDENTIFICATION IN VIDEO

The algorithm proposed in this paper follows a similar strategy as the approaches discussed above, but without adding any external data, constraints, or clothing features.

The input of our person recognition system are face tracks extracted from the given video and labels $\mathcal{Y} = \{1, \ldots, K\}$ generated by assigning one of $|\mathcal{Y}| = K$ different possible speakers based on lip movement detection. Face sequences labeled with an assigned speaker are called *supervised tracks* and are used for training, the remainders are called *unsupervised tracks*. All face tracks are represented by the features described in section 3.1. Based on the prediction step introduced in section 3.2, the original set of supervised tracks is extended (section 3.3) and corrected (section 3.4). Then, face tracks of unknown persons are recognized based on a criterion introduced in section 3.5. Finally, an identity is predicted for each given face track (supervised as well as unsupervised) utilizing the improved input data.

3.1 Feature Extraction

In a first step, face images are aligned according to [5] and cropped to a size of 100×100 pixels. Subsequently, they are represented by the descriptor of Vu [11] combining patterns of oriented edge magnitudes (POEM) with patterns of orientation difference (POD). The representations are further divided into 8×8 blocks for a histogram representation using local binary patterns (LBP). A maximum of $L = 30$ time-sampled faces per track are added to the dataset. In order to reduce dimensionality and to select the most prominent features, principal component analysis (PCA) is applied followed by a whitening process to improve the robustness and discriminative power as proved by [11]. The latter one is learned a priori on the aligned *Labeled Faces in the Wild* dataset provided by [12]. Each face track t consists of a feature vector set $\mathcal{F}_t = \{f_i\}_{i=1}^{L}$. They are used to generate the supervised set $\mathcal{X}_s = \{(\mathcal{F}, y) \mid y \; corresponds \; to \; \mathcal{F}\}$ of N speaking tracks with the corresponding labels y and an unsupervised set $\mathcal{X}_u = \{(\mathcal{F}, \emptyset)\}$ of M non-speaker tracks.

3.2 Prediction with Complementary Scores

Two feature vectors f_1 and f_2 are compared using the cosine similarity, which is measured by:

$$s_{cos}(f_1, f_2) = \frac{f_1 f_2}{\|f_1\| \, \|f_2\|}. \qquad (1)$$

The similarity between two track feature sets $s(\mathcal{F}_1, \mathcal{F}_2)$ is defined as the maximum of all (30×30 at most) scores of feature vector comparisons:

$$s(\mathcal{F}_1, \mathcal{F}_2) = \max\{s_{cos}(f_1, f_2) \mid f_1 \in \mathcal{F}_1 \land f_2 \in \mathcal{F}_2\}. \qquad (2)$$

In the next step, the similarities of a track t to all N supervised tracks are calculated, sorted in descending order, and then stored in $\mathcal{S}_t$ along with their associated labels:

$$\mathcal{S}_t = \{(s(\mathcal{F}_t, \mathcal{F}_x), y) \mid x \in \mathcal{X}_s \land y \; corresponds \; to \; \mathcal{F}_x\}. \quad (3)$$

This set is used as the input for the prediction step. Two different scores are suggested to recognize the identity $y_t \in \mathcal{Y}$ of track t. The first one determines the mean of the k highest similarity values regarding a certain character c:

$$p_t^{knn}(c) = \frac{1}{k} \sum_{i=1}^{k} s_i \,, s_i \in \mathcal{S}_t, y_{s_i} = c, k \in \mathbb{N}. \qquad (4)$$

This is problematic if the currently compared character c has a low number of training samples, due to the higher variance of the k similarity scores. The lack of diversity, regarding the intra-class variations (e.g., pose, illumination, expression), will most likely lead to a low similarity score. This effect can be reduced by choosing a low value for k. There are two drawbacks of this approach: 1.) Outliers (in particular, due to incorrect track labels) skew the result heavily, and 2.) overfitting, since actors with a large number of training examples have a higher chance to match the pose and expression conditions of the current face track.

We address this problem by introducing a second score which considers all similarities. Therefore, the normalized similarities $\overline{s}$ are quantized into Q segments. To build a score, a weighting system is added, which rates each segment $w \in \mathbb{N}_{>1}$ times higher than its predecessor. The final cumulative score is calculated via the following equation:

$$p_t^{dis}(c) = \frac{1}{N_c} \sum_{i=0}^{Q-1} w^i \left| \left\{ \overline{s} \mid \overline{s} > \frac{i}{Q} \land y_{\overline{s}} = c, \overline{s} \in \mathcal{S}_t \right\} \right|, \quad (5)$$

where N_c denotes the number of training images of character c and $y_{\overline{s}}$ is the corresponding label for $\overline{s}$ according to equation 3.

The final prediction score of character c is calculated using the normalized result of equation (4) and (5). The $|\mathcal{Y}|$ final scores can be also exploited in order to decide whether track t shows a known or an unknown person, respectively. The decision is made using the criteria introduced in section 3.5. If it is a known person, the final prediction label y_t is determined by equation 6:

$$y_t = \operatorname*{argmax}_{c \in \mathcal{Y}} \{\alpha \times \overline{p_t^{knn}(c)} + (1 - \alpha) \times \overline{p_t^{dis}(c)}\}, \qquad (6)$$

with $\alpha \in [0, 1]$ weighting the two scores. Overfitting of persons with a large number of training examples is avoided by evaluating the distribution of similarities and taking all possible intra-class variations into account. We argue that these two scores complement each other well, which leads to a better identification performance.

Regardless, if the ratio between the training data of different characters is extremely large, a correct prediction is very difficult. Hence, we introduce a procedure that allows us to extend the number of supervised tracks for all persons in a reliable manner.

3.3 Adding Training Data

Poor recognition performance can be observed for persons with fewer appearances or speaking roles due to the resulting uneven distribution of training data. For this reason, the weakly labeled data $\mathcal{X}_s$ and an initial prediction process (as described in 3.2) are employed to predict the unsupervised data $\mathcal{X}_u$. In order to only add reliable results, an additional ratio R is calculated for each track t, defined by dividing the second highest by the highest score according to equation (6). If this ratio fulfills the following confidence criterion;

$$1 - R \geq \tau_c, \tag{7}$$

with τ_c as a confidence threshold, then the face track and the corresponding predicted label is added to the (supervised) training data. These *extended supervised tracks* $\mathcal{X}_e$ not only enhance the prediction performance, but also open up the possibility for a robust *correction* of weak labels. This is essential to reduce the influence of outliers to the k-nearest neighbor classifier described in section 3.2.

3.4 Correcting Speaker Labels

As stated before (see also Bäuml et al. [1]), the assigned labels relying on speaker detection are typically noisy and therefore impair the recognition results. To tackle this problem, the extracted extended data $\mathcal{X}_e$ are used as a training set to correct them. For this purpose, another prediction process is conducted for each track in the original data $\mathcal{X}_s$ to predict a refined label y_t, replacing the original one. This step yields the *final supervised training dataset* $\mathcal{X}_f$.

3.5 Recognition of Unknown Persons

Bäuml et al. [1] annotate all background and supporting actors, detected during the speaker assignment process without an unique label in the subtitles or transcripts, as *unknown*. As a result, training data for an unknown person (and its related label) represents a variety of different persons, whereas the other labels always only denote exactly one individual. In contrast to Bäuml et al. [1], we claim that this variety makes it very challenging to assign the label *unknown* to the face track under consideration.

Based on this observation, we combine two conditions to detect if a track does not belong to a known identity ($y_t \notin \mathcal{Y}$). The first condition checks if the averaged k-nearest neighbor score from equation (4) is below a threshold τ_{knn}, while the second one checks if equation (7) is false. If both conditions are fulfilled, then the current face track t is labeled as $y_t = unknown$.

4. EXPERIMENTS

4.1 Experimental Setup

The dataset[1] of Bäuml et al. [1] is used in our experiments. It consists of the first six full episodes from season one of the TV sitcom *The Big Bang Theory* (*BBT-1* to *BBT-6*). The dataset contains 3,759 face tracks with a total of 11 identities and an additional label for unknown characters. In addition, 986 speaker labels are provided with an accuracy of 88.03%. The number of speaking tracks per character is shown in Table 1.

Our system is evaluated using the accuracy of identification according to [1], i.e., all face tracks are required to be labeled correctly, even if there are no training data available for an individual. The proposed approach is compared with Multinomial Logistic Regression + Markov Random Fields (MLR+MRF) of [1] and Mean Sequence Sparse Representation-based Classification (MSSRC) + Affinity of [6]. To the

[1]From: http://cvhci.anthropomatik.kit.edu/projects/mma

Table 1: Number of training tracks N_c and the corresponding identification accuracy *with respect to all 3,759 tracks*, per character c for the BBT dataset.

	#training tracks		accuracy [%]	
	original	final	original	final
Leonard	300	966	95.23	97.29
Sheldon	320	791	94.81	97.78
Penny	170	424	88.09	92.38
Howard	73	225	84.28	86.29
Raj	32	109	50.54	67.74
Mary	49	85	85.26	80.00
Leslie	11	47	57.14	80.95
Kurt	14	33	81.25	87.50
Gabelhauser	4	4	0.00	6.25
Doug	0	0	0.00	0.00
Summer	0	0	0.00	0.00
Unknown	13	13	71.33	75.90
All	986	2,697	—	—

Table 2: Number of training tracks and their corresponding label accuracy for the BBT dataset.

	#training tracks	accuracy [%]
original[1] $\mathcal{X}_s$	986	88.03
extended $\mathcal{X}_e$	2,697 (986 + 1,711)	93.59 (88.03 + 96.79)
final $\mathcal{X}_f$	2,697 (986 + 1,711)	96.52 (96.04 + 96.79)

best of our knowledge, the latter one is the best result on BBT data. It should be noted that Bäuml et al. [1] exploit additional clothing features and Ortiz [6] uses only the supervised images of the current investigated episode, except for *Raj* and *Howard*, where training data from all episodes are taken into account to handle the character imbalance.

In the experiments, the prediction step described in 3.2 is applied to all 3,759 face tracks (supervised as well as unsupervised tracks) of the BBT dataset. We estimate the parameters for the experiments using $\mathcal{X}_s$ by setting all tracks of *howard* in $\mathcal{X}_s$ to *unknown*. Apart from requiring the parameters to yield the maximum accuracy for the remaining known characters, an auxiliary condition of a minimum prediction rate of 50% for *unknown* tracks has to be fulfilled. The estimated parameter setting is as follows: $k = 4$, $Q = 10$, $w = 2$, $\alpha = 0.8$, $\tau_c = 0.1$ and $\tau_{knn} = 0.71$. Since solely reliable tracks should be added in the extension step, τ_c is doubled to 0.20. Consequently, the parameters are reestimated as described before, but assigning *howard* in $\mathcal{X}_f$ to *unknown* and requiring a minimum prediction rate of 75% for *unknown*, because the final data set contains more information and less incorrect labels. In this way, the parameter setting is obtained for the experiments with $\mathcal{X}_e$ and $\mathcal{X}_f$: $k = 3$, $Q = 10$, $w = 2$, $\alpha = 0.8$, $\tau_c = 0.2$ and $\tau_{knn} = 0.72$.

4.2 Results

The number of supervised face tracks and their related accuracy are displayed in Table 2. The extension of the training dataset improves the accuracy by 8.0% with respect to the original weak labels. The overall accuracy of the final label set X_f exceeds the baseline's accuracy by 8.5%. Besides, a total of 1711 tracks are additionally considered as training examples, which is spread over the different actors as shown

Table 3: Identification accuracy [%] for the BBT dataset.

	BBT-1	*BBT-2*	*BBT-3*	*BBT-4*	*BBT-5*	*BBT-6*	**AVG**
MLR+MRF [1]	95.18	94.16	77.81	79.35	79.93	75.85	**83.71**
MSSRC + Affinity [6]	95.19	90.53	86.00	84.21	83.11	85.91	**87.49**
Ours (original labels)	92.44	91.15	85.81	83.13	85.84	77.07	**85.91**
Ours (extended labels)	94.37	93.45	87.77	85.89	91.04	81.22	**88.96**
Ours (final labels)	96.30	94.87	89.23	87.09	92.47	81.59	**90.26**

in Table 1. It is obvious that the number of training tracks increases for each person except for *unknown* (which is intended) and for *Gabelhauser*. This can be explained by the very low number of four supervised tracks for *Gabelhauser* in the original training dataset, where only two of them have sufficient quality making it difficult to find additional training data. As a consequence, a prediction rate of only 6.3% for *Gabelhauser* is achieved.

Due to the higher number of training tracks, a gain in the identification accuracy can be observed for each known person (except mary) in Table 1. In particular, significant improvements for the characters *Raj*, *Leslie* and *Kurt* with less than 50 training tracks are achieved. It should be noted that no training material is available in the dataset for *Doug* and *Summer*, which explains the accuracy of 0%. Compared to the result of 13% reported by [1], the accuracy of predicting unknown persons is significantly increased to 75.9%, which is similar to the required value in the validation step.

The proposed system outperforms the results reported by Bäuml et al. [1], as displayed in Table 3, in each episode resulting in a higher prediction accuracy of 6.6% on the average. While only a slight improvement is achieved on *BBT-1* and *BBT-2*, more significant improvements can be observed on the remaining episodes. The reason is the higher number of *unknown* character occurrences in *BBT-3* to *BBT-6*, which proves the robustness of our treatment of *unknown* persons. Compared to Ortiz' system [6], the approach presented in this paper noticeably reduces the error rate from 12.5% to 9.7%, which is a relative improvement of 22.2%.

5. CONCLUSIONS

In this paper, we have presented a novel semi-supervised approach for automatically naming characters in TV broadcasts by extending and correcting weakly labeled training data. For this purpose, the combination of two complementary scores has been exploited. The common problem of an imbalanced number of training data and the handling of *unknown* persons have been addressed by the proposed approach as well. Experimental results have been reported on a benchmark test set of six episodes of the TV sitcom *The Big Bang Theory*. The system has achieved superior accuracy compared with two state of the art systems.

In future work, we plan to further enhance the identification process by weighting the scores depending on the number of training images per person. Another possibility for future research is to extract features using deep convolutional neural networks and to model them in a Joint Bayesian approach.

6. ACKNOWLEDGMENT

Part of this work is financially supported by the German Federal Ministry of Economic Affairs and Energy (BMWi, ZIM-KOOP, grant no. KF2135608KM3).

7. REFERENCES

[1] M. Bäuml, M. Tapaswi, and R. Stiefelhagen. Semi-supervised learning with constraints for person identification in multimedia data. In *IEEE Conference on Computer Vision and Pattern Recognition*, pages 3602–3609. IEEE, 2013.

[2] N. Cherniavsky, I. Laptev, J. Sivic, and A. Zisserman. Semi-supervised learning of facial attributes in video. In *Trends and Topics in Computer Vision*, pages 43–56. Springer, 2012.

[3] R. G. Cinbis, J. Verbeek, and C. Schmid. Unsupervised metric learning for face identification in tv video. In *IEEE International Conference on Computer Vision*, pages 1559–1566. IEEE, 2011.

[4] M. Everingham, J. Sivic, and A. Zisserman. "Hello! My name is... Buffy"–Automatic Naming of Characters in TV Video. In *British Machine Vision Conference*, pages 92.1–92.10, 2006.

[5] V. Kazemi and J. Sullivan. One millisecond face alignment with an ensemble of regression trees. In *IEEE Conference on Computer Vision and Pattern Recognition*, pages 1867–1874. IEEE, 2014.

[6] E. G. Ortiz. *Taming Wild Faces: Web-Scale, Open-Universe Face Identification in Still and Video Imagery*. PhD thesis, University of Central Florida Orlando, Florida, 2014.

[7] E. G. Ortiz, A. Wright, and M. Shah. Face recognition in movie trailers via mean sequence sparse representation-based classification. In *IEEE Conference on Computer Vision and Pattern Recognition*, pages 3531–3538. IEEE, 2013.

[8] J. Sivic, M. Everingham, and A. Zisserman. "Who are you?"-Learning person specific classifiers from video. In *IEEE Conference on Computer Vision and Pattern Recognition*, pages 1145–1152. IEEE, 2009.

[9] M. Tapaswi, M. Bäuml, and R. Stiefelhagen. "Knock! Knock! Who is it?" probabilistic person identification in TV-series. In *IEEE Conf. on Computer Vision and Pattern Recognition*, pages 2658–2665. IEEE, 2012.

[10] M. Tapaswi, M. Bäuml, and R. Stiefelhagen. Improved weak labels using contextual cues for person identification in videos. In *IEEE International Conference and Workshops on Automatic Face and Gesture Recognition*, volume 1, pages 1–8. IEEE, 2015.

[11] N.-S. Vu. Exploring patterns of gradient orientations and magnitudes for face recognition. *IEEE Trans. on Inform. Forensics and Security*, 8(2):295–304, 2013.

[12] L. Wolf, T. Hassner, and Y. Taigman. Effective unconstrained face recognition by combining multiple descriptors and learned background statistics. *IEEE Transactions on Pattern Analysis and Machine Intelligence*, 33(10):1978–1990, 2011.

Introducing Concept And Syntax Transition Networks for Image Captioning

Philipp Blandfort
University of Kaiserslautern
Kaiserslautern, Germany.
philipp.blandfort@dfki.de

Tushar Karayil
University of Kaiserslautern
Kaiserslautern, Germany.
tushar.karayil@dfki.de

Damian Borth
German Research Center for Artificial Intelligence (DFKI)
Kaiserslautern, Germany.
damian.borth@dfki.de

Andreas Dengel
University of Kaiserslautern
German Research Center for Artificial Intelligence (DFKI)
Kaiserslautern, Germany.
andreas.dengel@dfki.de

ABSTRACT

The area of image captioning i.e. the automatic generation of short textual descriptions of images has experienced much progress recently. However, image captioning approaches often only focus on describing the content of the image without any emotional or sentimental dimension which is common in human captions. This paper presents an approach for image captioning designed specifically to incorporate emotions and feelings into the caption generation process. The presented approach consists of a Deep Convolutional Neural Network (CNN) for detecting Adjective Noun Pairs in the image and a novel graphical network architecture called "Concept And Syntax Transition (CAST)" network for generating sentences from these detected concepts.

Keywords

Auto Caption, Image Captioning

1. INTRODUCTION

With its exponential growth in the last two decades, the Internet has become a major source of information exchange across the world. Powered by new technologies and increased computational resources, web sites have become more visual and animated. Moreover, the world wide web is flooded with new images everyday, e.g. Instagram has reported an average of 80 million photo uploads a day.[1] Most of these images come with titles which can be generic (e.g. IMG_123), descriptive or give additional information that can not be directly seen in the image.

Recently, there have been significant advances in generating descriptive image captions ([7],[8],[9]) but so far, the focus was on generating factual descriptive image captions like Microsoft COCO [3]. These datasets provide a rich textual description of images. However, these descriptions might not be representative for natural image captioning since human subjects were given clear instructions on writing the captions [3]. Such descriptions, although informative, constitute only a small subset of the different styles of captioning.

In contrast, large real-world datasets such as "Yahoo Flickr Creative Commom 100 Million" (YFCC100M [12]) displays a huge variety of captioning styles but these titles can only be considered to be weak labels (cf. [13]): Here, captions can be descriptive, emotional or mention information that is not visible in the image.

Humans often tend to associate a sentiment with an image and express that in the caption. One such method is by using an emoji.[2] A richer use of text would be another way to express the associated sentiment with the caption.

It was shown by [1] that adjectives can add an emotional component to nouns and the resulting Adjective Noun Pairs can express the visual contents in the image. Hence we assume that incorporating adjectives into machine generated captions is one feasible way of adding an emotional component to the caption. To this end, we describe a model that is capable of generating subjective image captions and thereby going beyond factual image descriptions. We train and test our model on the YFCC100M database.

2. RELATED WORK

The available methods in linking images to text can be classified broadly into three categories.

The first set of methods is used to detect a triplet (eg. <*object,action,scene*>) of scene elements in the image and convert them into sentences. Triplets provide a holistic idea of what is most important in the image and they are combined using various techniques to generate captions. [4], [8]

[1]https://www.instagram.com/press/

[2]http://instagram-engineering.tumblr.com/post/117889701472/emojineering-part-1-machine-learning-for-emoji

ICMR'16, June 06 - 09, 2016, New York, NY, USA

ISBN 978-1-4503-4359-6/16/06...15.00

DOI: http://dx.doi.org/10.1145/2911996.2930060

use this approach and a template based system to generate the sentences after identifying the objects.

The second set of methods bring the images and sentences into a single multi dimensional space by converting each of them into vectors. Thereafter a set of distance measures are used to find the closest matching description of a given image ([5], [11]). [11] uses neural networks to map images and sentences into the same vector space. Although the above mentioned methods have shown promising results they cannot be used for generating novel descriptions. Hence the performance of these methods drop when there are new compositions of objects in a given image (even though individual objects have been observed during training).

The third set of methods which have shown the most promising results use a combination of Deep Convolutional Neural Networks (DCNN) for feature extraction and a Multimodal Recurrent Neural Networks (RNN) on top of it for text generation from the extracted features [14].

However, despite the promising results, approaches of the third kind suffer from several shortcomings:

- **Robustness**: RNNs heavily rely on suitable ground truth information. We argue that training an RNN on the YFCC100M would require expensive preprocessing since there are too many images with titles that can not be learned with current methods (e.g. because the relation to the visual content is not straight-forward) and could therefore disturb the training.

- **Transparency**: It is hardly possible to interpret what exactly is happening inside the RNN. The problem we see with this lack of transparency is that it forces you to treat the whole sentence generation part as single task that can not readily be broken down into distinct parts. This makes it hard to gain new insights about human language processing from the performance of the system or to incorporate new insights into the model. As a result, the performance depends heavily on the training data and modifications often have to be done by trial and error.

We apply *DeepSentiBank* as fixed visual concept extraction and generate captions from the features with the novel CAST network architecture instead of RNN in order to address the aforementioned shortcomings. This combination is quite robust and you can follow and influence all the steps from detected concepts to final sentence, giving you much more control and allowing for easier future changes of the architecture.

3. PRESENTED APPROACH

The presented system follows a pipeline approach consisting of the following steps:

1. **Visual concept extraction**: We process the image with *DeepSentiBank* to extract concepts including emotional cues.

2. **CAST network**: Generate ranked sentences from the detected concepts.

3. **Templates**: If the rankings from the network are below a threshold, we use a template-based approach to create sentences.

3.1 Data Preparation

The YFCC100M dataset contains user captioned Flickr images. Users' captions/tags often do not provide the appropriate data required to train classifiers and generate graphical language models. For example, the images often contain camera generated captions, generic titles, single word captions, locations as reported in [6]. Therefore it was important to extract the relevant Image-Caption pairs useful for model training.

We filter and remove all images with titles that are generic (e.g. IMG_1234.jpg), have less than 2 words or contain one or more non-English words.

After applying the filter, we end up with a training set consisting of 9.6 million images and a validation set consisting of 1.2 million images where the split into train and validation set is based on the user identifier present in the image meta-data. The cleaned up set still contains captions that are not directly related to the image, often providing extra information. But as this is natural in human image captioning, we deliberately keep this kind of data.

We build our graph (including word2vec model) on this data only, showing that our method works well with noisy real-world data without any sophisticated preprocessing.[3]

3.2 Visual Concept Extraction

To generate human like caption, the first step is to capture the emotional and visual contents from the image. The work published in [1], introduced Adjective Noun Pair (ANP) concepts able to describe images beyond visual content (e.g. "dog") by capturing positive or negative polarity (e.g. "cute dog" or "scary dog"). The resulting set of ANPs as trained by a deep convolution neural network is called *DeepSentiBank* and was published by [2]. This pairing of adjectives and nouns does also provide an insight into the general emotion associated with an analyzed image.

Processing the image with *DeepSentiBank* gives us a feature vector where each element corresponds to one ANP from a list of 2089 ANPs.

These 2089 ANPs contain 231 distinct adjectives and 424 nouns. This size is quite small when we want to generate different styles of sentences. To increase the size of vocabulary we generated a word2vec [10] model from all the training titles. (See next point.)

3.3 Concept And Syntax Transition (CAST) Network

The CAST network is a multi-directed graph where each node in the network represents a concept (i.e. noun, adjective, verb or adverb) connected to other concepts. It is generated in the following steps:

1. **Nodes**: For each content word with occurrence count greater than 40 in the training titles, we create a node. This leads to a vocabulary of over 21000 words.

   Additionally, we add a START and an END node.

2. **Similarity edges**: We train a word2vec model on all training sentences. word2vec maps words to a vector space of a given dimension (200 in our case) where words that are used in similar contexts are mapped to vectors that are close together in the target space.

[3] In principle it would be possible to train the visual concept detector on the YFCC100M data as well.

Under the assumption that semantically similar words are used similarly, this makes it possible to compute semantic distances between words.

For each node we add similarity edges to all nodes that have a word2vec similarity above some fixed threshold. This accounts for the possibility of replacing words by semantically similar words in the sentence generation process.

3. **Syntax edge**: For each sentence in the training titles we check how content words are connected. For each such connection that does not use another content word, a directed edge is created between the corresponding concept nodes. The connecting string (usually consisting of propositions, articles, etc.) is used as edge label and the total number of connection occurrences is annotated as edge weight.

   These edges contain information about the syntax of the language and are used to connect different concepts.

The whole graph generation was done in less than 40h and the model can be used without any further training.

In CAST networks generating a sentence from a set of concepts is reduced to the problem of finding a path from the start to the end node through a set of activated nodes. Computing a list of such paths is done in a heuristic way and this list is then ranked by considering the weights of the included edges. The path with the highest score is then converted to a sentence in a straight-forward way, where similarity edges are used to substitute words. An illustration of a simple CAST network can be found in Figure 1.

In general, CAST networks provide a new possibility for the challenging task of generating sentences from an arbitrary sets of words. By using word similarity in the sentence generation process, they display a high degree of creativity, effectively extending the vocabulary. They do all this in a simple and transparent way which makes it easy to find the source of mistakes, allowing for systematic improvements or customization of the system in the future.

3.4 Template-based Approach

The idea of this approach is to use different templates of the kind "HUMAN with PROPERTY doing VERB on EVENT in LOCATION" to form sentences from a set of visual concepts that have been tagged by according category and are detected in the image.

For this we need:

- **Category tags**: We manually assigned category tags (e.g. "HUMAN" or "LOCATION") to all nouns that occur in any ANPs.

- **Templates**: A few (5) templates based on these category tags were created manually. From that we automatically generated different template variations by removing parts of the template. (E.g. the variations of the above template would include "HUMAN doing VERB in LOCATION" and "HUMAN with PROPERTY on EVENT in LOCATION".)

Sentences are now generated in the following steps:

1. **Input**: Given ANP scores from *DeepSentiBank*, we consider all ANPs that have a score above a fixed threshold to create sentences from all suitable template variations. (If no score exceeds the threshold we take the ANP with highest confidence and return it as caption.)

2. **Ranking**: We rank all resulting sentences based on a scalar rating score that is computed for each sentence individually, using for the computation the *DeepSentiBank* scores of all ANPs that are present in the sentence.

3. **Output**: The sentence with the highest score is given as caption.

4. RESULTS

In order to evaluate the *humanness* factor of the generated caption, we selected 200 random images from our test set. These images were assigned two captions: The original caption present in the YFCC100M dataset and the caption generated by our method. Without informing the individual about the source of the two captions, we asked human subjects to choose one among the two captions which they thought were generated by a human. To compensate for the subjective bias in human evaluation, each image was shown to three different individuals and the opinion of the majority was decided as the final result for that image.

We report that 31.5% of the captions generated by our method were reported as more human-like in comparison to the original caption by at least two subjects. In 62.5% of images at least one subject chose our caption over the original one. These results are encouraging. The generated captions often read naturally and convey emotions. The creativity and subjectivity that is displayed in some of the captions is very entertaining. Figure 2 shows a small selection of titles generated by our method.

5. CONCLUSIONS

We presented an approach of combining the top Adjective Noun Pairs detected in an image with a graphical model to form captions that are not only descriptive but also carry subjective meaning. A human evaluation of our method on a subset of the YFCC100M dataset we often obtain natural image captions.

To improve the existing model and to get the caption quality closer to human levels we are planning to extend our work by incorporating the following points: The grammar of the whole sentence needs to be given more weight. We are currently working on an additional ranking mechanism to take that into account.

Also, so far the confidences of the detector are only respected in the thresholding and then discarded. We plan to either modify the network traversing algorithm such that it also respects the concept scores or respect the scores in the final ranking of the proposed sentences. We also want to use additional concept detectors to get more different sentences from the network and optimize the whole network on more data.

6. ACKNOWLEDGMENTS

This work was partially funded by the BMBF project Multimedia Opinion Mining (MOM: 01WI15002).

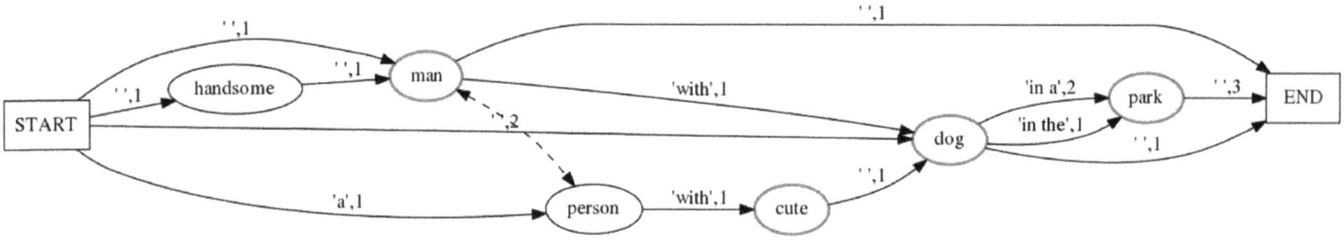

Figure 1: Example of a CAST network generated from the titles "handsome man", "a person with cute dog", "dog in a park", "dog in the park" and "man with dog in a park". The dashed line indicates a similarity edge (and is in this toy example not generated from the given sentences). If the red nodes denote the activated concepts, the resulting sentence would be "person with cute dog in a park". (Substituting "man" by "person" because a similarity edge was traversed.)

Figure 2: Qualitative results of our approach for images of the YFCC100M dataset. The captions in black are the ground truth titles, in blue we have captions produced by the combination of *DeepSentiBank* and CAST. The "X" marks indicate which caption the majority of people in our evaluation experiment believed to be created by a human.

7. REFERENCES

[1] D. Borth, R. Ji, T. Chen, T. Breuel, and S.-F. Chang. Large-scale Visual Sentiment Ontology and Detectors Using Adjective Noun Pairs. In *ACM Int. Conf. on Multimedia (ACM MM)*, 2013.

[2] T. Chen, D. Borth, T. Darrell, and S.-F. Chang. Deepsentibank: Visual sentiment concept classification with deep convolutional neural networks. *arXiv preprint arXiv:1410.8586*, 2014.

[3] X. Chen, H. Fang, T. Lin, R. Vedantam, S. Gupta, P. Dollár, and C. L. Zitnick. Microsoft coco captions: Data collection and evaluation server. *arXiv:1504.00325*, 2015.

[4] A. Farhadi, M. Hejrati, M. A. Sadeghi, P. Young, C. Rashtchian, J. Hockenmaier, and D. Forsyth. Every picture tells a story: Generating sentences from images. In *Computer Vision–ECCV 2010*, pages 15–29. Springer, 2010.

[5] M. Hodosh, P. Young, and J. Hockenmaier. Framing image description as a ranking task: Data, models and evaluation metrics. *Journal of Artificial Intelligence Research*, pages 853–899, 2013.

[6] S. Kalkowski, C. Schulze, A. Dengel, and D. Borth. Real-time analysis and visualization of the yfcc100m dataset. In *MM COMMOMS Workshop*, 2015.

[7] A. Karpathy and L. Fei-Fei. Deep visual-semantic alignments for generating image descriptions. In *Proceedings of the IEEE Conference on Computer Vision and Pattern Recognition*, pages 3128–3137, 2015.

[8] S. Li, G. Kulkarni, T. L. Berg, A. C. Berg, and Y. Choi. Composing simple image descriptions using web-scale n-grams. In *Proceedings of the Fifteenth Conference on Computational Natural Language Learning*, pages 220–228. ACL, 2011.

[9] J. Mao, W. Xu, Y. Yang, J. Wang, and A. L. Yuille. Explain images with multimodal recurrent neural networks. *arXiv preprint arXiv:1410.1090*, 2014.

[10] T. Mikolov, I. Sutskever, K. Chen, G. Corrado, and J. Dean. Distributed representations of words and phrases and their compositionality. *CoRR*, abs/1310.4546, 2013.

[11] R. Socher, A. Karpathy, Q. V. Le, C. D. Manning, and A. Y. Ng. Grounded compositional semantics for finding and describing images with sentences. *Transactions of the ACL*, 2:207–218, 2014.

[12] B. Thomee, B. Elizalde, D. A. Shamma, K. Ni, G. Friedland, D. Poland, D. Borth, and L.-J. Li. Yfcc100m: The new data in multimedia research. *Communications of the ACM*, 59(2):64–73, 2016.

[13] A. Ulges, D. Borth, and T. M. Breuel. Visual concept learning from weakly labeled web videos. In *Video Search and Mining*, pages 203–232. Springer, 2010.

[14] O. Vinyals, A. Toshev, S. Bengio, and D. Erhan. Show and tell: A neural image caption generator. *arXiv preprint arXiv:1411.4555*, 2014.

SentiCart: Cartography and Geo-contextualization for Multilingual Visual Sentiment

Brendan Jou*
Electrical Engineering
Columbia University
New York, NY 10027
bjou@ee.columbia.edu

Margaret Yuying Qian*
Computer Science
Columbia University
New York, NY 10027
margaret.qian@columbia.edu

Shih-Fu Chang
Electrical Engineering
Columbia University
New York, NY 10027
sfchang@ee.columbia.edu

ABSTRACT

Where in the world are pictures of cute animals or ancient architecture most shared from? And are they equally sentimentally perceived across different languages? We demonstrate a series of visualization tools, that we collectively call `SentiCart`, for answering such questions and navigating the landscape of how sentiment-biased images are shared around the world in multiple languages. We present visualizations using a large-scale, self-gathered geodata corpus of >1.54M geo-references coming from over 235 countries mined from >15K visual concepts over 12 languages. We also highlight several compelling data-driven findings about multilingual visual sentiment in geo-social interactions.

CCS Concepts

•Information systems → Geographic information systems; Multimedia databases; Data mining; Web interfaces; •Human-centered computing → Visualization; •Applied computing → *Psychology; Sociology;*

Keywords

affective computing; geodata; multilingual; visual affect; sentiment; ontology; visualization; GIS

1. INTRODUCTION

How geographically diverse are our sentiments in social multimedia? And specifically, how diverse (or localized) are our sentiments in the images and concepts we use everyday along linguistic and geographical lines? Following trends of other fields, the advent of high-volume and weakly-supervised data are driving increased interest in *large-scale* sentiment studies in affective computing. These two data properties, sometimes referred to as "volume" and "veracity" respectively, are key elements of any Big Data problem.

*Denotes equal contribution.

ICMR'16, June 6–9, 2016, New York, NY, USA
© 2016 ACM. ISBN 978-1-4503-4359-6/16/06...$15.00
DOI: http://dx.doi.org/10.1145/2911996.2912022

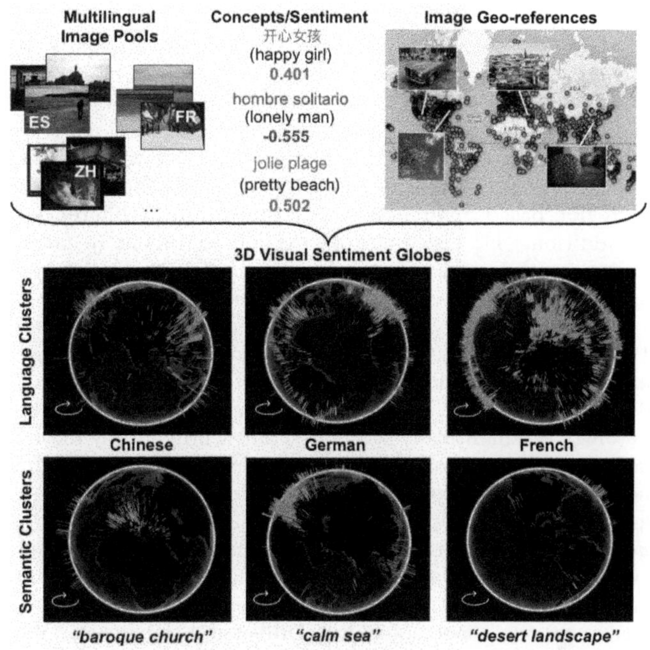

Figure 1: Example globe visualizations of geographical data from sentiment-biased images around the world in `SentiCart` by language and semantics.

In this work, we focus on unpacking another tenant of "Big Affective Computing" that deals with the multi-faceted or multimodal nature of visual affect data (i.e. "variety"). We build on the recent work of [6] which presented a Multilingual Visual Sentiment Ontology (MVSO) consisting of >15K sentiment-biased visual bi-concepts and >7.3M images over 12 different languages. Though it is only a small sampling of web image content, it represents the largest affect-biased unconstrained image dataset from multiple languages to date. The goal of [6] was to expand affective variety by introducing cultural diversity, accomplishing this via language diversity. We believe that *language is only one of many signals to capture multicultural visual sentiment*; and geographical data (geodata) is another signal not previously explored for visual sentiment understanding, to the best of our knowledge. Since any one language may be spoken across a multitude of countries and with varying density, to truly understand visual sentiment around the world, geodata is a necessary complement to the language dimension. Here, to assist the study of visual sentiment variety in geodata, we developed a visualization system called SentiCart to chart the landscape of multilingual visual sentiment around the world.

Contextualizing social multimedia with explicit location or implicit geographical metadata has been a topic of research interest for over a decade [1][5][7]. Among the first for digital photography, [10] presented several frameworks for location tag acquisition, geo-referencing and image media browsing interfaces. In computer vision, [12] used geotagged photos to assist visual landmark detection over about 20M images. In [4] and [8], Twitter posts are used to study geographic sentiment and music preference differences, respectively, while in [9], Twitter and Flickr posts are analyzed spatiotemporally to map out social visual interests. These geographical information systems (GIS) each lack a multilingual, visual grounding, or sentiment biasing component we seek here.

One close relative to our system is [11] where a large-scale collection of >1.5M facial expression videos sourcing from over 94 countries was presented. Subjects were shown one of about 8K online videos as stimuli and their reactions were captured via a web camera. Although there is a wide variety in originating locations of subjects, this study focuses more on region-based differences rather than cultural differences. In addition, [11] also relies on explicit sentiment in facial expression videos as a form of sentiment feedback while we use weakly supervised semantic cues for sentiment.

In [6], an ontology of 15,630 visual concepts coming from 12 different languages was presented along with accompanying social photos and metadata called Multilingual Visual Sentiment Ontology (MVSO). Each visual concept in the ontology is semantically structured and sentimentally biased using a construct called adjective-noun pairs (ANPs). The noun component provides a visual grounding to the concept and the adjective defines a sentimental attribute, e.g. *fluffy dog* or *abandoned railroad*. MVSO aimed at gathering culturally diverse visual concepts for studying sentiment and emotion in social multimedia; however, the ontology only strikes at one aspect of cultural diversity: language. We augment the work in [6] by also incorporating geographical data signals toward multicultural affect research.

The contributions of our work include: (1) an intuitive, interactive and fluid browsing visualization system called SentiCart for uncovering geographical insights in visual sentiment data, (2) an implementation using large-scale visual sentiment geographical data with over 1.54M geo-references covering 237 countries, and (3) the public release of this geographical data over a multilingual ontology.

2. GEODATA ACQUISITION

In order to collect geo-localization data for social photos, we use a combination of two multi-source methods – one with high reliability, but low coverage and another with lower reliability, but higher coverage. We root our geodata collection and analysis on top of MVSO [6] because of publicly available auxiliary data streams that can be mined from the same social media platform, i.e. Flickr. The multilingual nature of the data also lends itself toward being geographically spread, and the large-scale nature of over 7.3M images maximizes our opportunity to also study language and culture together on a significant geographic scale.

2.1 GPS Coordinate Data

Global positioning system (GPS) geo-localization provides highly reliable latitude-longitude coordinates (usually within several meters worst-case depending on satellite-receiver precision) and may be encoded in image headers of some digital photos. In November 2015, we queried the Flickr API[1] over the entire MVSO corpus [6] of 7,368,364 images and acquired GPS coordinate data for 1,410,892 images. The remaining images were either not GPS-tagged or privacy permissions were not granted for public querying. The top three languages with GPS-tagged images in order are: Persian (32.24%), French (25.35%) and Italian (24.40%). Although the largest language by image count is English (4,049,507), it only had a 17.48% coverage in GPS-tagged images.

Language	*#ANPs*	*#Georefs*	*Language*	*#ANPs*	*#Georefs*
Arabic	22	99	Italian	3,184	206,315
Chinese	395	11,553	Persian	10	92
Dutch	315	16,292	Polish	67	3,873
English	4,407	707,846	Russian	95	2,014
French	2,241	163,193	Spanish	3,241	259,138
German	717	38,544	Turkish	137	1,933

Table 1: Number of GPS-based geo-references (georefs) collected from MVSO [6] images by language. Since not every visual concept (ANP) had images with GPS data, we also show the number of remaining ANPs with at least one geo-referenced image.

2.2 Metadata-inferred Location Data

In most social media platforms, including our setting on Flickr, users can and do often provide image title and descriptions to add additional context for their media posts. Locations are commonly found in these user metadata because they provided a concrete grounding for *where* an event or memory took place. For geo-localization though, this data can often be very uninformative, e.g. user input text like "our new house," as well as arbitrary, e.g. "Little Rock" could refer to a literal small rock in the image content or a town in Arkansas, USA. These two streams of user text from title and description offer greater coverage of images than depending on the presence of GPS data, but introduces noise is less reliable in localizing. As result, when GPS data is available, we always use it to geo-localize a given image regardless of user-provided metadata. Otherwise, we prefer automatically extracted locations in the image title over those in descriptions.

Using image metadata streams, we extracted location fields by performing named entity recognition (NER) [2] on user-provided text. We translated all text into English[2] and used only English NER models. We note that translation allowed us to get a higher recall of tagged locations compared to native-language NER models due to the frequency at which users posted descriptions with mixed languages, e.g. an image title "Small Alley in 香港". We extracted metadata-inferred locations for all languages with under 100K GPS-tagged images to bolster their geo-reference count.

We applied NER-tagged locations as queries to Google Maps' Geocoding API[3] to retrieve latitude-longitude coordinates as well as to filter incorrect NER detections or ambiguous locations. Since geocoding queries can be region-biased, we performed multiple searches over all relevant country

[1] https://www.flickr.com/services/api
[2] https://translate.google.com
[3] https://developers.google.com/maps

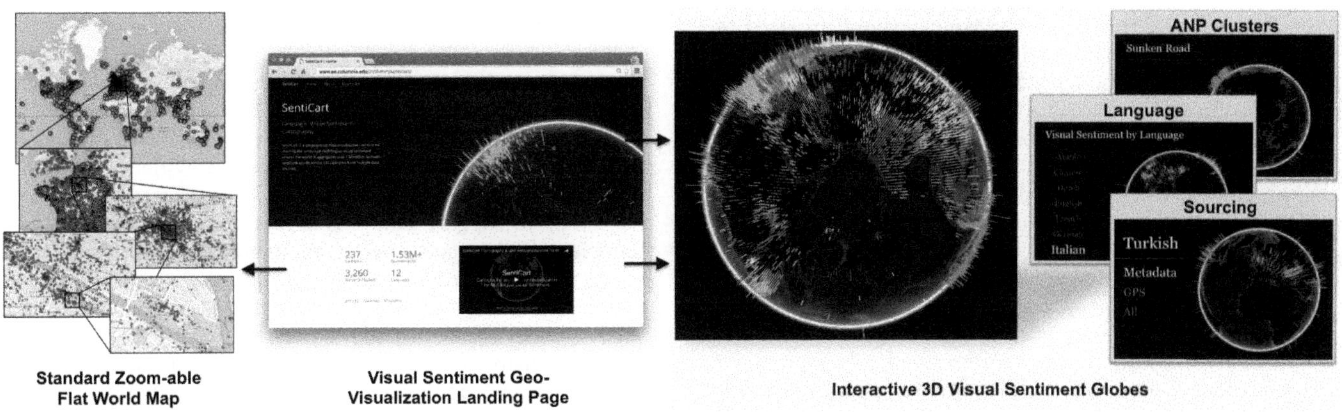

Figure 2: Example visualizations in `SentiCart` of multilingual visual sentiment around the world show the main landing page along with a classic flat world map view, here on the French sub-corpus, and 3D globe visualizations of visual sentiment. The colorful globe shows country-colored sentiment for the English sub-corpus and adjacent cards show additional display modes in `SentiCart` along source, semantics and language.

code top-level domains (ccTLDs) per language according to official ICANN listings, e.g. `.pl` for Polish was included, `.ir` for Persian, `.ru` for Russian, etc. This increased the likelihood that matches were found in regions that speak the target language and also gave queries as many chances to succeed overall as there were ccTLDs per language, e.g. "Main Street"; for example, we queried across over 10 different ccTLDs for Arabic given the diversity of regions it is spoken in. When multiple named locations were detected by NER, we queried for geocodes in descending string length order taking the first query that succeeded. And when multiple geocoding results matched, e.g. the query "Gulf Coast" can match to "Gulf Coast Airport, Tivoli, TX", "Gulf Coast, Missouri City, TX" and "Gulf Coast, Naples, FL", we selected one at random only if all matches came from the same country, and otherwise, omitted the query result altogether for its ambiguity. We also ruled out geo-references to continents, e.g. "South America," and large bodies of water, e.g. "Mediterranean Sea," for being too broad for our setting. If all queries failed to geocode an image, we determined that the image lacked sufficient information needed to localize.

Language	*#Locs*(T)	*#Georefs*(T)	*#Locs*(D)	*#Georefs*(D)
Arabic	318	102	1,317	137
Chinese	27,631	9,110	179,407	28,579
Dutch	8,537	3,344	73,315	13,848
German	23,867	13,947	207,630	52,159
Persian	124	49	545	140
Polish	4,048	854	23,222	2,721
Russian	2,731	1,168	20,586	3,539
Turkish	4,235	734	28,890	2,781

Table 2: Number of named locations (locs) recognized and geo-references (georefs) coded from user-provided title (T) and description (D) metadata in MVSO [6] images by language. Only *new* geo-references counts are given, i.e. #Georefs columns are mutually exclusive with each other and also mutually exclusive to GPS-tagged images in Table 1.

On the subset of eight languages we extracted metadata-inferred geo-references for, a total of 133,212 new geodata points were extracted compared to 74,400 GPS coordinates (i.e. in relative, 79.05% greater image coverage). The combination of GPS and metadata-inferred geodata accounted for 20.96% of the total 7,368,364 images in the MVSO [6] image dataset.

The geographical data we collected and web visualizations can be accessed at http://www.ee.columbia.edu/ln/dvmm/senticart and a video showcasing the functionality of **`SentiCart`** can be accessed at https://youtu.be/cI-2llSErSo.

3. VISUAL AFFECT GEOVISUALIZATION

In order to better understand visual sentiment around the world in **`SentiCart`**, we developed two interactive visualizations. One visualization is a flat, point-wise, low-interaction view of geodata points. The lower interactivity in this visualization allowed for batch processing and thus precise localization to geodata points at our large input scale. The other visualization is a three-dimensional, fluid, high-interaction globe of geo-references. This visualization allowed us to quickly and easily compare across data modalities and also gives us an additional dimension along which to interact with the geodata. The two modes of visualization provide a trade-off in exploring geographical distributions of visual sentiment. In Figure 2, we show examples from our visualizations. For the flat world map view, our interface matches many other canonical map interfaces but scales to hundreds of thousands of geodata points by linking with Google Fusion Tables [3]. The interface allows for a zoomable, albeit flat view of the data and can render elements like political borders without burdening usability.

For the 3D globe view, we enable fast and fluid browser-based rendering using WebGL and a base globe library[4]. To maintain low-latency interaction in this rendering, we reduced the resolution of the geo-references by performing geohashing, where latitude-longitude coordinates are hashed into geodesic spatial bins and where hash lengths, or precisions, correspond directly to geographical distances. In our visualization and scale of 1,544,104 geo-references, we found that quantizing coordinates to within 19.55 km (or 12.14 mi), which corresponds to 10 hash bits for both latitude and longitude, provided the best latency-to-resolution visualization trade-off on most modern browsers and machines. The

[4]https://www.chromeexperiments.com/globe

added dimension of the 3D globe visualization compared to the flat world map, also allowed us to visualize the sentiment magnitudes at given geo-localization points. Since we perform geohashing, to aggregate sentiment in a given spatial bin, we take the weighted average of the image sentiment values from adjective-noun pairs.

In the globe view, we provide multiple slice views of the ontology and geodata we collected. We can visualize sentiment by language around the world and easily compare regional differences. On the surface of the globe, bar heights correspond to sentiment strengths scaled $[0, h \in \mathbb{R}]$ where colors represent positive or negative (usually red/"hot" and blue/"cool"). In addition, since we had multiple sources for our geodata, we can visualize each source's geographical origins to compare localization consistency. We also enable visualization along ANP clusters using the ontology structure in MVSO [6] where ANPs were gathered into semantically coherent groups, e.g. we can visualize geodata and sentiment of images in the multilingual cluster "old town square."

Given our geodata visualizations, we highlight several preliminary insights from the geo-social data we collected using Multilingual Visual Sentiment Ontology [6] imagery. One striking, but in retrospect, intuitive phenomena we observed about geodata in [6] is that despite its focus on multilingual breadth, most language's geodata were not as geographically constrained as we expected. In fact, while there were indeed geo-references that originated from countries where the primary language was the same as the corresponding language source, there were also a sizable number of geo-references that originated from regions outside. We hypothesize that because MVSO collected its imagery from a social multimedia platform, the phenomena is due to photo tourism – that is, photos are geographically tagged in countries that users are just visiting and when posting on social media, they unsurprisingly still use their native tongue to describe the image. As an example, many images from the Chinese ontology branch actually geo-localized to locations in Japan with ANP tags such as 古建築 (*ancient architecture*)[5]. Yet, it is unclear how pervasive this tourism phenomena is in [6] and whether it is stronger in some languages than others, e.g. geo-references for the Spanish ANP for *tropical landscape* (*paisaje tropical*) mostly localized to places in Mexico, Brazil, Spain and Colombia as one might expect.

In general, we found that geo-localizations for many multilingual ANP clusters and their sentiments coincided with intuition. For example, clusters referring to bodies of water like seas and lagoons did mostly geo-localize along coastlines and were composed of positive sentiment ANPs. Some weather-related clusters like *rainy day* and *cloudy landscape* tended to be geographically diverse and overwhelmingly negative in sentiment across languages. In some cases, where geo-references *did not* occur was also telling, e.g. the ANP cluster *stray cat* had fewer points in Asia than Western countries, likely owing to more domesticated cats in the West.

4. CONCLUSIONS

We presented a fluid and interactive visualization system called **SentiCart** for visual sentiment geodata, implemented with 1.54M latitude-longitude points over more than 235 countries originating from visual concepts across 12 languages. We aggregated geodata from multiple sources including native GPS tagging as well as automatically extracted geo-references from image metadata using natural language processing and geocoding. Two modes of visualization were demonstrated in **SentiCart**: a flat world map view and a 3D globe view. We also presented evidence that the multilingual ontology presented in [6] is affected by photo tourism, and suggest that this is consistent with social multimedia and language usage phenomena. Overall, **SentiCart** has provided concrete visual confirmation that multicultural visual sentiment is a deeply geographic-dependent entity as much as it is a semantically-dependent one.

In the future, we seek to expand our geo-reference coverage by training our own or applying higher fidelity native language NER models and incorporate implicit signals from user profiles to better localize social photos. We also plan to make our sentiment scores more fine-grained and accurate. In addition, we will investigate using geodata for regularizing the training of models for culture and language prediction.

[5]Despite these two cultures sharing character sets, we verified from image metadata text that users did use Chinese.

5. ACKNOWLEDGMENTS

We would like to thank Miriam Redi, Mercan Topkara, Nikolaos Pappas and Tao Chen from the MVSO team for their support and insightful discussions. We especially thank Nikolaos Pappas for providing English metadata translations for our implicit location extraction.

6. REFERENCES

[1] L. Backstrom, E. Sun, and C. Marlow. Find me if you can: Improving geographical prediction with social and spatial proximity. In *WWW*, 2010.

[2] J. R. Finkel, T. Grenager, and C. Manning. Incorporating non-local information into information extraction systems by gibbs sampling. In *ACL*, 2005.

[3] H. Gonzalez, A. Halevy, C. S. Jensen, A. Langen, J. Madhavan, R. Shapley, and W. Shen. Google Fusion Tables: Data management, integration, and collaboration in the cloud. In *ACM SOCC*, 2010.

[4] M. Hao, C. Rohrdantz, H. Janetzko, U. Dayal, D. A. Keim, L.-E. Haug, and M.-C. Hsu. Visual sentiment analysis on Twitter data streams. In *IEEE VAST*, 2011.

[5] R. Ji, Y. Gao, W. Liu, X. Xie, Q. Tian, and X. Li. When location meets social multimedia: A survey on vision-based recognition and mining for geo-social multimedia analytics. *ACM TIST*, 6(1), 2015.

[6] B. Jou*, T. Chen*, N. Pappas*, M. Redi*, M. Topkara*, and S.-F. Chang. Visual affect around the world: A large-scale multilingual visual sentiment ontology. In *ACM MM*, 2015.

[7] J. Luo, D. Joshi, J. Yu, and A. Gallagher. Geotagging in multimedia and computer vision - A survey. *Multimedia Tools and Applications*, 51(1), 2011.

[8] J. L. Moore, T. Joachims, and D. Turnbull. Taste space versus the world: An embedding analysis of listening habits and geography. In *ISMIR*, 2014.

[9] V. K. Singh, M. Gao, and R. Jain. Social pixels: Genesis and evaluation. In *ACM MM*, 2010.

[10] K. Toyama, R. Logan, A. Roseway, and P. Anandan. Geographic location tags on digital images. In *ACM MM*, 2003.

[11] T. Vandal, D. McDuff, and R. E. Kaliouby. Event detection: Ultra large-scale clustering of facial expressions. In *FG*, 2015.

[12] Y.-T. Zheng, M. Zhao, Y. Song, H. Adam, U. Buddemeier, A. Bissacco, F. Brucher, T.-S. Chua, and H. Neven. Tour the world: Building a web-scale landmark recognition engine. In *CVPR*, 2009.

Personalized Retrieval and Browsing of Classical Music and Supporting Multimedia Material

Marko Tkalčič
Free University of Bolzano
Faculty of Computer Science
Piazza Domenicani 3
Bolzano, Italy
marko.tkalcic@unibz.it

Markus Schedl
Johannes Kepler University
Department of Computational Perception
Altenbergerstrasse 69
Linz, Austria
markus.schedl@jku.at

Cynthia C. S. Liem and Mark S. Melenhorst
Delft University of Technology
Mekelweg 4
Delft, The Netherlands
c.c.s.liem@tudelft.nl
m.s.melenhorst@tudelft.nl

ABSTRACT

This paper reports on three demonstrators developed to provide personalized, enhanced experiences of classical music, within the EU FP7 project "Performances as Highly Enriched aNd Interactive Concert eXperiences" (PHENICX)[1]: (i) an interface for accessing supplemental multimodal material about music items, (ii) a recommender system for visualizations of classical music, and (iii) a recommender system for tagging. The personalization in all three demos is achieved through modeling users' personality and musical sophistication. The links to the web interfaces are provided as well as the outcomes of quantitative and qualitative evaluations.

CCS Concepts

•**Human-centered computing** → *HCI design and evaluation methods; Interactive systems and tools; Collaborative filtering; Social tagging;*

Keywords

classical music ; personalization ; visualization ; tagging

1. INTRODUCTION

Classical music consumption, especially live performances, did not change much over the recent decades, despite the development of new technologies. The share of consumption on mobile devices and the buzz on social media is very limited [14]. In order to provide the listeners of classical music an with an enhanced experience that new technologies can offer (such as additional information and personalization) and lower the barriers for engagement with classical music [9], we performed a series of studies and implemented a set of demonstrators, presented here. These demonstrators are also targeted at attracting new audiences to classical music.

2. RELATED WORK

In order to implement personalized applications, such as adaptation of user interfaces [10], for end users the system should be able to acquire the user preferences. Implicit acquisition of such data in the domain of classical music has shown to be hard as users hardly leave any traces on their preferences about classical music on social media [14]. However, related work suggests that preferences are related to two proxy constructs, personality and music sophistication. Several studies have shown that preferences for music are correlated with user's personalities in terms of the five factor model (FFM) [13]. The FFM is a well-known model of personlity that takes into account individual differences in many areas [7]. Furthermore, algorithms for the implicit acquisition of personality from social media have been proposed [2]. The concept of music sophistication has been presented recently and it has shown good correlation with music preferences [11]. In an earlier study we have shown that both personality and music sophistication are correlated with the user preferences for supporting multimodal material for classical music [15].

3. DEMONSTRATORS

We present three demonstrators: (i) a personalized interface for accessing supplemental multimodal material, (ii) a recommender system for the visualization of classical music and (iii) a recommender system for tagging of classical music.

The PHENICX project's long-term goal was to develop services that acquire the user characteristics (personality and music sophistication) in an unobtrusive way, which appears to be supported by related work [2]. However, for the demonstrators shown here we acquired these characteristics through questionnaires. As the questionnaires used are lenghty (10 questions used in the TIPI (Ten Items Personality Questionnaire [4]) personality questionnaire, 44 questions used in the BFI (Big Five Inventory [7]) personality questionnaire and 38 questions used in the MSI (Music Sophistication Index [12]) questionnaire), we performed a set of initial studies where we identified the questionnaire items (i.e., questions) that are most informative. We set the number of these questions to two or three, in accordance to user

[1]http://phenicx.upf.edu

ICMR'16, June 06 - 09, 2016, New York, NY, USA

ISBN 978-1-4503-4359-6/16/06...$15.00

DOI: http://dx.doi.org/10.1145/2911996.2912023

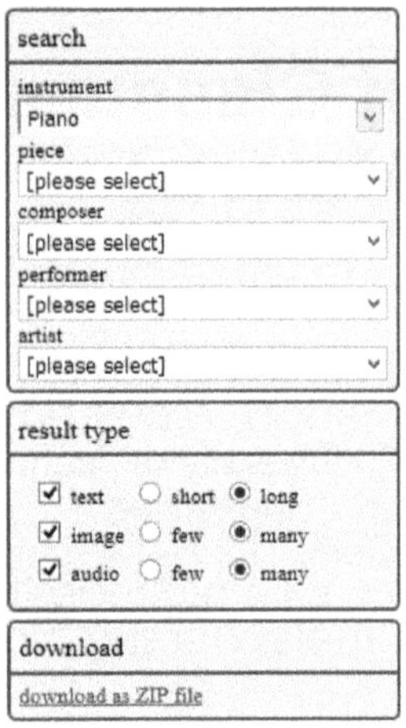

Figure 1: Part of the personalized user interface for the retrieval of supporting material.

experience guidelines. The choice of the questions is described in the following subsections on a per-demonstrator basis.

3.1 Access to Supplemental Multimodal Material

This demonstrator is a web interface[2] that allows to retrieve supporting information about the composers, pieces, instruments and performers of a classical performance. The results of a query are presented in the form of text, images and audio.

The query is defined through a set of dropdown menus, as shown in Fig. 1. The search query itself (the upper frame of the user interface) is not personalized. The personalization affects the result type preferences (the result type frame in the user interface). More specifically, for the two multimodal types analyzed (i.e. text and image) the personalization affects the length and amount of the results. Some users prefer long text over short and some prefer many images over few. For example, people who score high on openness, agreeableness, conscientiousness and extraversion tend to show a positive correlation with consumption, interestingness and novelty, hence meaning that they prefer to consume more of the material, find it interesting and novel.

The choice of the two questions was done by observing how the user answers to the music sophistication and personality questions correlate with the preferences for the content. We observe that among the music sophistication questions the one with the highest absolute value of the correlation was *How many classical concerts do you attend per year?*. Among the personality questions the one with the highest absolute correlation was *I myself as someone who is reserved, quiet.*

In order to personalize the web interface for the supporting multimedia material, we implemented a recommender system that adapts the result types (i.e. the length of the text and the number of the images shown) to the end user. The personalization is done by recommending the result types that are most popular in the cluster of users the active user belongs to, where clusters are created by categorizing users according to their answers to the two selected questions.

In order to evaluate the satisfaction of users with the recommended settings, we performed a user study. The users were asked to rate the personalized interface through the question *I like the way the material is presented.* In the next step, the participants were shown a random snapshot of the interface and were asked to provide a rating. In the final step the participants were shown both snapshots next to each other and were asked to select the one they preferred. In total we recruited 96 participants through Amazon Mechanical Turk.

The results have shown that in 63 (out of 96) of the cases the participants preferred the personalized snapshot, which corresponds to 66%. The higher preference for the personalized interface was confirmed also in the comparison of the ratings given to the two snapshots. The mean rating for the personalized snapshot was 3.29 (on a scale from 1 to 5, where 1 was the lowest and 5 the highest score) compared to the mean rating for the random snapshot of 2.92. The Wilcoxon signed-rank test [3] showed that the mean difference was significant ($p = 0.01$).

3.2 Recommendation of Visualizations

This demonstrator[3] recommends a music visualization to the user in the form of a streamed video within the web browser. In order to enable users to get additional insight into music, a set of music visualizations (called Score Follower, Structure Layout and Orchestra Layout) have been developed within the PHENICX project. The visualizations are depicted in Figs. 2, 3 and 4, respectively. In the initial user study we observed that people with different personalities tend to prefer (in terms of pragmatic quality (PQ) scores, as defined by [5]) different visualizations.

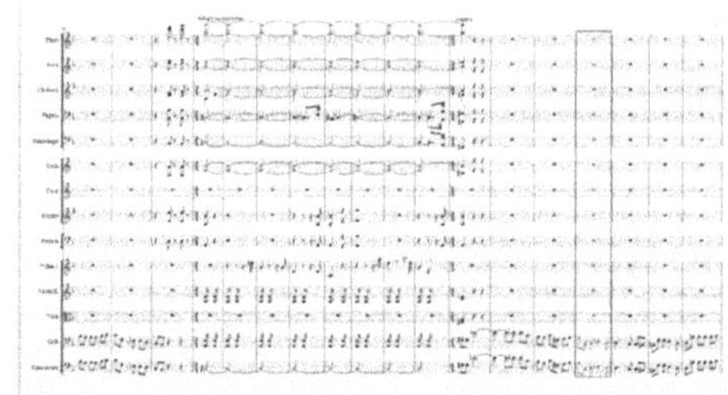

Figure 2: The *Score Follower* visualization.

Similarly to the first demonstrator, we recommended to each user the visualization that has the highest average rating among the users that are in the same cluster. To this end we (i) choose the BFI questions for user clustering and (ii) ranked the visualizations within each user cluster.

The two BFI questions that account for most of the variance in the sample of users from the initial study were *I see myself as someone who is helpful and unselfish with others* and *I see myself as someone who tends to be disorganized.* We clustered the users into four clusters based on the median value along each variable.

After answering the two initial questions the user is shown a page where the three visualizations are presented in such

[2]http://bird.cp.jku.at/phenicx_mmsupp

[3]http://bird.cp.jku.at/phenicx_visrecsys

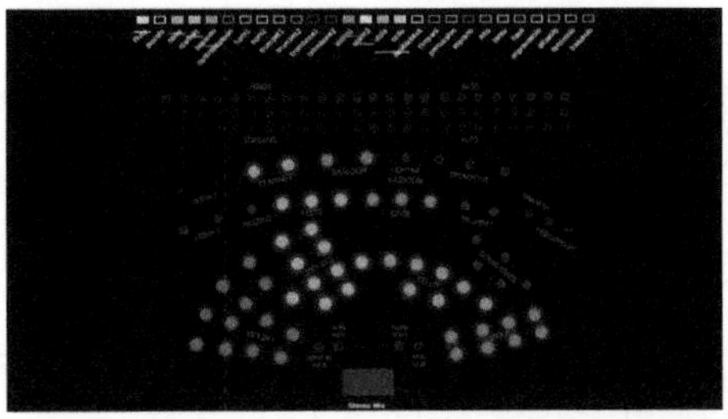

Figure 3: The *Orchestra Layout* visualization.

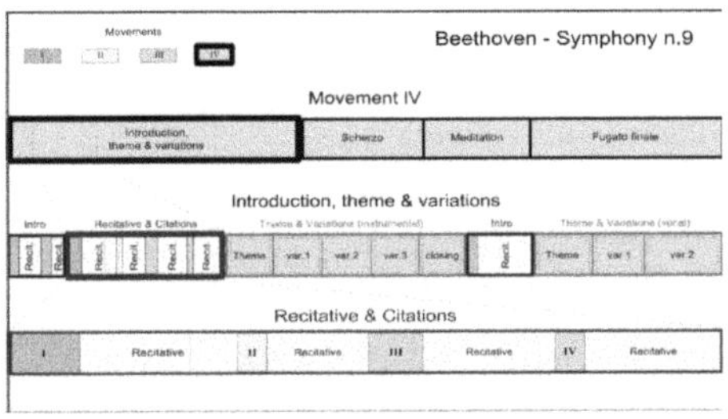

Figure 4: The *Structure visualization.*

a way that the top-ranked is in the central position and the other two are rendered smaller at the bottom of the interface (see Fig. 5). The user can switch from the recommended visualization to any of the other two.

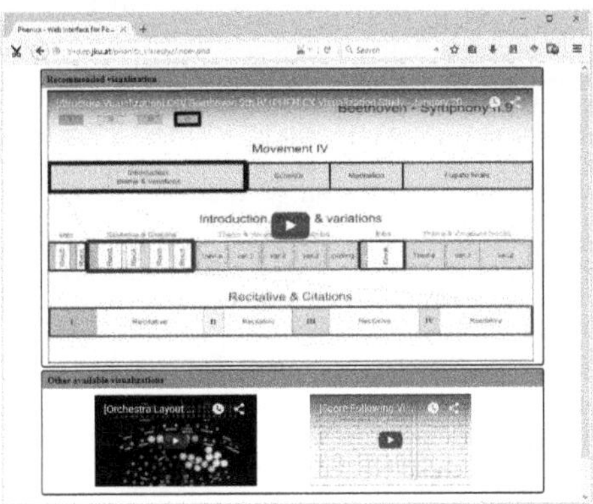

Figure 5: Rendering of the visualizations with the top ranked visualization bigger and positioned on top. The second ranked is positioned bottom-left and the third ranked is bottom-right.

We performed the evaluation of the recommender system for visualization through a user study. In total we had 79 participants recruited through Amazon Mechanical Turk. The participants were shown the snapshots of the three visualizations in a row next to each other. The order was randomly assigned for each participant. Then the participants were instructed to watch each visualization for at least 20 seconds. Finally, the participants were asked to rank the visualizations according to their preferences.

We computed the normalized discounted cumulative gain (NDCG) to assess the quality of the personalized rankings. We compared the mean NDCG of the recommended visualization rankings (*ndcg_rec*) to the mean NDCG of randomly ranked visualizations (*ndcg_rand*). The obtained values were $ndcg\_rec = 0.87$ and $ndcg\_rand = 0.82$. The independent t-test showed that the difference of the means was significant ($p = 0.03$). The significant difference means that our system's better average NDCG metric was not due to chance, but due to a systematically better prediction of the personalized recommender for visualization.

3.3 Tag Recommender System

The idea in this demonstrator[4] is to allow the user to capture certain moments by tagging the music during or after the concert. These tags represent the personal impressions of the users and it is possible to share them. The sharing is done through a recommender system that suggests the tags of similar users.

Tag recommender systems are popular in social media. The most widely used approach is to recommend tags that similar users have provided [8]. Various user similarity measures are used in the related work, depending on the domain and data available [8, 6]. We employ a variant of the classic K-nearest neighbors (K-NN) approach (see also [1]) for collaborative filtering to recommend tags similar users have provided, where similarity is computed based on personality.

The steps of the recommender system are to (1) compute the likelihood that a user would enter a tag at a given time in the piece, (2) rank these tags and (3) present them to the user.

In the initial study we choose two questions from the BFI questionnaire that correlate best with the *active engagement* factor of music sophistication. Two two top ranked questions were *I see myself as someone who is sophisticated in art, music, or literature* and *I see myself as someone who has an assertive personality.* Again, we clustered the users into four clusters based on the median value along each of the two variables. The likelihood of a user generating a tag at a given time is calculated by taking into account the tags that similar users have given around the same time. The user similarity measure is a binary function that returns one if the users are in the same cluster, zero otherwise. We set the time window to 20 seconds.

The top three recommended tags are shown as clickable buttons in the user interface. The user can, at any given time, submit a tag either by entering it through the textbox (and press Enter) or click on a button with a recommended tag. The recommended tags change through time as the music piece progresses.

In order to evaluate the tag recommender system, we performed a user study in two steps. In the first step we collected free-form tags. In the second step these tags were used as a basis for the recommendations. In the first step the participants were shown the textbox only, without any recommendations. In total we had 22 participants recruited through Amazon Mechanical Turk. We choose a 2-minute-long segment of the Eroica streamed from YouTube.[5] Each participant had to enter at least 5 tags. After data cleaning there were 128 valid tags (5.8 tags per user on average).

A qualitative analysis of the tags showed that the participants gave either (a) tags related to the performance or (b)

[4] http://bird.cp.jku.at/phenicx_tagrecsys
[5] https://www.youtube.com/embed/gr2Hrq_GE68?enablejsapi=1&vq=hd1080

Figure 6: The interface for tagging classical music is composed of the video of the classical music piece (top) and the tagging interface (bottom) with the textbox for freetext tagging and the recommended tags.

tags related to the participant's perception.

In the second step we enabled the recommendations. The participants (not the same as in the previous step) were divided into two groups. The first group received recommended tags according to the presented algorithm, while the second (control) group received random recommendations from the pool of all tags collected in step one. In total we recruited 31 participants for the first group and 26 participants for the control group.

The results show that the average satisfaction was higher in the first group that received tags recommended by our system (3.81) than in the second (3.26). The t-test showed that the difference was significant ($p = 0.008$).

Furthermore we analyzed the shares of the number of tags given through the textbox (custom tags) and those given through a button (recommended tags). Interestingly, in the first group, which was given recommended tags, this share is higher (46%) than in the second group, which was given random tags (37%). It seems that the recommended tags inspired participants to come up with additional tags.

We investigated whether the position of the button plays a role in the preferences. In the first group (recommended tags) the distribution of clicks for the left, mid and right buttons was 46, 40 and 27, respectively, while for the second group (control group) it was 57, 41 and 35, respectively. This suggests that the location of the recommended items plays a role.

Finally, we carried out a qualitative analysis of the tags in the first group (recommended tags) to see what was the relation between the participants' personality and the type of tags they were giving. We coded each tag as *performance-related* or as *perception-related*. Among all users the *performance-related* tags account for 80%, while this figure is different for each user cluster, which indicates that users with different personalities tend to prefer different kinds of tags.

4. CONCLUSION

In this paper, we have presented three demonstrators that show how to personalize different aspects of classical music-related information to the user requirements. The demos have also been evaluated through a set of user studies that confirmed the benefit of the personalized systems over non-personalized ones, from the user experience perspective.

5. ACKNOWLEDGMENTS

This research is supported by the EU-FP7 project no. 601166 ("PHENICX") and the Austrian Science Fund (FWF): P25655.

6. REFERENCES

[1] C. Desrosiers and G. Karypis. A Comprehensive Survey of Neighborhood-based Recommendation Methods. In F. Ricci, L. Rokach, B. Shapira, and P. B. Kantor, editors, *Recommender Systems Handbook*, pages 107–144. Springer US, Boston, MA, 2011.

[2] G. Farnadi, G. Sitaraman, S. Sushmita, F. Celli, M. Kosinski, D. J. Stillwell, S. Davalos, M.-F. Moens, and M. D. Cock. Computational Personality Recognition in Social Media. *User Modeling and User-Adapted Interaction: The Journal of Personalization Research (UMUAI)*, (Special Issue on Personality in Personalized Systems), 2016.

[3] A. Field, J. Miles, and Z. Field. *Discovering Statistics Using R.* Sage Publications, 2012.

[4] S. D. Gosling, P. J. Rentfrow, and W. B. Swann. A very brief measure of the Big-Five personality domains. *Journal of Research in Personality*, 37(6):504–528, dec 2003.

[5] M. Hassenzahl. The Interplay of Beauty, Goodness, and Usability in Interactive Products. *Human-Computer Interaction*, 19(4):319–349, dec 2004.

[6] R. Jäschke, L. Marinho, A. Hotho, L. Schmidt-Thieme, and G. Stumme. Tag Recommendations in Folksonomies. *Proceedings of the 11th European Conference on Principles and Practice of Knowledge Discovery in Databases (PKDD'07)*, 4702:506–514, 2007.

[7] O. John and S. Srivastava. The Big Five trait taxonomy: History, measurement, and theoretical perspectives. In L. A. Pervin and O. P. John, editors, *Handbook of personality: Theory and research*, volume 2, pages 102–138. Guilford Press, New York, second edition, 1999.

[8] L. B. Marinho, A. Nanopoulos, L. Schmidt-Thieme, R. Jäschke, A. Hotho, G. Stumme, and P. Symeonidis. Social Tagging Recommender Systems. In F. Ricci, L. Rokach, B. Shapira, and P. B. Kantor, editors, *Recommender Systems Handbook*, pages 615–644. Springer US, Boston, MA, 2011.

[9] M. S. Melenhorst and C. C. S. Liem. Put the Concert Attendee in the Spotlight. A User-Centered Design and Development Approach for Classical Concert Applications. *ISMIR 2015*, pages 800–806, 2015.

[10] V. G. Motti and J. Vanderdonckt. A computational framework for context-aware adaptation of user interfaces. In *IEEE 7th International Conference on Research Challenges in Information Science (RCIS)*, pages 1–12. IEEE, may 2013.

[11] D. Müllensiefen, B. Gingras, J. Musil, and L. Stewart. The musicality of non-musicians: an index for assessing musical sophistication in the general population. *PloS one*, 9(2):e89642, jan 2014.

[12] D. Müllensiefen, B. Gingras, L. Stewart, and J. Ji. Goldsmiths Musical Sophistication Index (Gold-MSI) v1.0: Technical Report and Documentation Revision 0.3. Technical report, University of London Goldsmiths, 2013.

[13] P. J. Rentfrow and S. D. Gosling. The do re mi's of everyday life: The structure and personality correlates of music preferences. *Journal of Personality and Social Psychology*, 84(6):1236–1256, 2003.

[14] M. Schedl and M. Tkalčič. Genre-based Analysis of Social Media Data on Music Listening Behavior. In R. Zimmerman and Y. Yu, editors, *Proceedings of the First International Workshop on Internet-Scale Multimedia Management - WISMM '14*, pages 9–13, New York, New York, USA, 2014. ACM Press.

[15] M. Tkalčič, B. Ferwerda, D. Hauger, and M. Schedl. Personality Correlates for Digital Concert Program Notes. In *UMAP 2015, Lecture Notes On Computer Science 9146*, volume 9146, pages 364–369. 2015.

The Social Picture

Sebastiano Battiato‡, Giovanni M. Farinella‡, Filippo L.M. Milotta‡, Alessandro Ortis‡
Luca Addesso†, Antonino Casella†, Valeria D'Amico†, Giovanni Torrisi†
‡Universitá degli Studi di Catania, Viale A. Doria 6, 95125 - Catania, Italy
†JOL WAVE - Telecom Italia, Viale A. Doria 6, 95125
{battiato, gfarinella, milotta, ortis}@dmi.unict.it
{luca.addesso, antonino.casella, valeria1.damico, giovanni.torrisi}@telecomitalia.it

ABSTRACT

We present *The Social Picture*, a framework to collect and explore huge amount of crowdsourced social images about public events, cultural heritage sites and other customized private events. *The Social Picture* aims to create social communities of users that contribute to the creation of image collections about common interests. The collections can be explored through a number of advanced Computer Vision and Machine Learning algorithms, able to capture the visual content of images in order to organize them in a semantic way. The interfaces of *The Social Picture* allow the users to create customized collections by exploiting semantic filters based on visual features, social network tags, geolocation, and other information related to the images.

Keywords

Social Media, Crowdsourcing, Multimedia, Image Collections, Image Understanding

1. INTRODUCTION

Images and videos have become one of the most popular media by which users express their emotions and share their experiences in the social networks. Nowadays, the diffusion of social networks plays a crucial role in collecting information about people opinion and trends. The proliferation of mobile devices and the diffusion of social media, have changed the communication paradigm of people that share multimedia data, by allowing new interaction models (e.g., social networks). In social events (e.g., concerts), the audience typically produces and share a lot of multimedia data with mobile devices (e.g., images, videos, geolocation, tags, etc.) related to what has captured their interest. The redundancy in these data can be exploited to infer social information about the attitude of the attending people. For example, systems such as RECfusion [6] can be exploited to understand if there are groups of people interested to specific scenes. In the context of big social data, Machine Learning and Computer Vision algorithms can be used to develop new advanced analysis systems to automatically infer knowledge from large scale visual data [9], and other multimedia information gathered by multiple sources.

In this paper we introduce a framework called *The Social Picture* (TSP) to collect, analyze and organize huge flows of visual data, and to allow users the navigation of image collections generated by the community. We designed the system to be applied on three main scenarios: public events, cultural heritage sites, private events. TSP is a social framework populated by images uploaded by users or collected from other social media. The social peculiarities of such collections can be exploited not only by the people who participate to an event. Indeed each collection has two kind of users: the event organizer and the event partecipant. Imagine an art-gallery manager who leases a famous Picasso's painting with the aim to include it in a event exhibition, together with other famous and expensive artworks. How does he know he did a good investment? Which was the more attractive artwork? From which position of the hall have people taken the most number of pictures?

These information can be inferred by analysing the multimedia audience activity (i.e., uploaded images) of the organized event in *The Social Picture*. The collection of the uploaded images of an event, gives the sources analysed in TSP to answer the aforementioned questions. The obtained information can be then exploited by the event organizers for the event evaluation and further planning.

On the other hand, from the user point of view, the collection of an event can be exploited in a visualization tool which uses Computer Vision and Machine Learning algorithms to organize images by visual content. In this way, the "social picture" of the event can be captured and shared among users.

In Figure 1, an example of visual output produced by the proposed framework is shown. It is computed by considering images automatically gathered from social media related to the cultural heritage site of Teatro Massimo in Catania. As detailed in the following sections, the interaction with a heat map interface allows the users to explore in a smart way all the images belonging to the involved cultural heritage site collection.

2. ARCHITECTURE

The architecture of the developed framework is shown in Figure 2. Users can add an image to an event's collection by using a mobile application that gives access to *The Social Picture* repository (TSP). The new images can be uploaded

ICMR'16, June 06-09, 2016, New York, NY, USA
© 2016 ACM. ISBN 978-1-4503-4359-6/16/06...$15.00
DOI: http://dx.doi.org/10.1145/2911996.2912024

Figure 1: Heat map visualization.

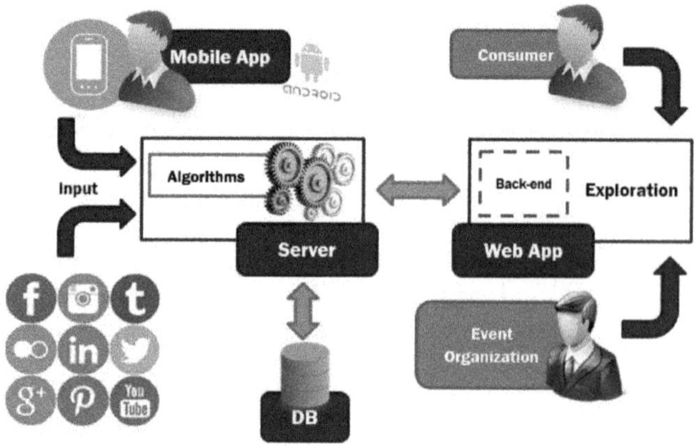

Figure 2: The Social Picture's architecture.

in TSP by using a mobile camera or by selecting images from the most common social networks for images (e.g. Flickr, Panoramio, Instagram). Once an image is uploaded, it is analysed by a set of Computer Vision and Machine Learning algorithms, and then stored in the database, together with the extracted features and the inferred high level attributes (e.g., type of scene recognized by the algorithm). These information are exploited in TSP to create smart interfaces for the users, which can be used during the exploration of the images related to an event's collection. The framework collects all the data uploaded by the users of an event, and exploits this crowdsourced multimedia flow of pictures to infer social behavioural information about the event (e.g., by considering the popularity of the uploaded scenes [6]).

The collections can be explored from smartphones, tablet or desktop computers via a web application, which exhibits a range of filtering tools to better explore the huge amount of data (see Figure 3). The web application shows different interfaces depending on the specific user and the event in which he has joined after an invitation from the event manager (the person who created the event). To join an event's collection, the user must upload at least one picture related to that event. Collections can be explored by several data visualization enviroments, which are selected by the event manager. Anyone registered to *The Social Picture* can become an event manager and start a social collection: this follows the "prosumer" paradigm, where the users are both producers and consumers of a service. The developed framework is characterized by a modular architecture: new visualization interfaces, as well as new semantic filters can be independently created and futher added to the system. Thus, when an event manager creates a new collection, he is allowed to specify several options to customize the image gathering, the social analysis to be performed, and the visualization tools to be shown for the users of that collection. The event manager is also allowed to set a range of statistics, which will be available after the analysis of the collected images. These statistics helps organizers to extract useful social information from the crowdsourced pictures [5]. For example, what is the most popular artwork of a museum? What is the least considered? From which perspective these pictures were taken? These information could be exploited, for example, to perform aimed investments. The system can suggest what is the better subject to use for the advertising campaign of the event, or which of the attractions it worth to mainly reproduce in the souvenir shop products, to support merchandising strategies. Feedback about what is the most interesting part (i.e., the most photo captured) of a landmark building can help on taking decisions about renovating some parts rather than others as first investment.

The connotation of importance is achieved by the crowd who generated "the social picture" for that building by uploading related images.

The several exploration tools are based on both visual and textual data. The system exploits information such as Exif data (camera model, geolocalization, acquisition details, JPEG compression, and others) when available, and a number of ad-hoc extracted visual features.

The visual analysis module of the system feds all the images into two different CNNs [3, 10], in order to extract the classification labels and image representations. To attach semantic labels to the visual content of the images, we used *AlexNet* [3] and *Places205-AlexNet* [10]. The CNN used in [3] consists of seven internal layers with a final 1000-way softmax which produces a distribution over the 1000 predefined classes of the ImageNet dataset [7].We considered the feature activations induced at the last hidden layer, which consists of 4096 dimensional feature (fc-7 feature), as an image representation to be further used with t-SNE algorithm [8] for visualization purposes. We also fed the images to the *Places205-AlexNet* CNN [10]. This CNN has the same architecture of *AlexNet* CNN, but it was trained on 205 scene categories related to places learned by using the database *Places205-AlexNet* composed by 2.5 million images.

3. USER EXPERIENCE

An event manager (i.e., a user of *The Social Picture* which starts a new collection) creates a new event by selecting among three possible types of event: public event (e.g., a concert), cultural heritage site (e.g., a museum) or private event (e.g., a wedding). The available event categorization can be further extended to include other customized categories. We considered these three categories to better focus the aims of the specific analysis, as well as the inferred information that an organizator wants to extract. The data gathering from users can be performed within a specific time window. The manager is allowed to control the image acquisition by selecting fine-grained criteria such as filtering media by hashtag, associated text or geolocalization distance. After creating the event and its acquisition settings, the manager can select the statistics that the system have to compute by exploiting the collection of multimedia data gathered for that event.

The pictures can be grouped by hierarchical categories depending on the combination of two or more of the extracted visual features, this allows us to create several taxonomies in the image collection (panoramic pictures versus

Figure 3: Example of exploration interface. It is composed by three main areas: the map area (upper-right) shows the positions where the images have been taken from. This gives the positions of the users during the event and some hints about the most interesting parts of the site. The interaction with this map allows the users to know more details by selecting the images from their positions. The gallery (bottom) shows the collection organized by using t-SNE algorithm and considering the selected filters. The area upper-left of the interface shows the details of a picture selected from the gallery and presents the available filters. From this interface, the user can launch the t-SNE algorithm on a subset of images obtained applying one or more filters, and to know more about the statistics performed by the system on the subset of images.

close-ups, natural versus artificial, indoor or outdoor, the presence or absence of crowds, selfies versus not selfies, and others). Specific image categorizations help users to better handle huge amount of crowdsourced pictures, this kind of grouping can be exploited as a pre-processing stage before performing an image based visual search. Given a seed image, the system selects a set of similar pictures. The system provides different exploration tools. There is a tool for the exploration of outdoor collections such as cultural sites. One more tool can be exploited to better navigate any huge image collection. These exploration tools together with other advanced tools are described in the next subsections. A video of the demo is available at the following link: http://iplab.dmi.unict.it/TSP

3.1 Heat Map Exploration

In a cultural heritage site, people usually take pictures from different points of view and consider different details and parts related to famous and appreciated attractions and artworks. The heat map exploration tool of *The Social Picture* aims to infer the "interest" of people with respect to the different parts of a site. An example of heat map generated from data in *The Social Picture* is shown in Figure 1. Through this visualization tool, an organizer of a collection will be able to know which parts of the site captures people's interests. On the other hand, users can explore the collection related to a site in a very simple and intuitive way. So, to highlight the "interest" of people related to parts of a site, the proposed system creates an heat map by aligning images in *The Social Picture* with respect to panoramic images of the site of interest [4].

The heat map is a visualization used to depict the intensity of images at spatial points. The heat map consists of a colored overlay applied to the original image. Areas of higher intensity will be colored red, and areas of lower intensity will appear blue. The intensity of the heat map is related to the number of collected pictures that contain that visual area. By clicking on a point of the heat map, the user can retrieve and visualize the images that contribuited to generate the map intensity at that point. This set of pictures can be further refined by selecting one of them to ask the system to search similar pictures, or use the image subset as a starting point for furhter analysis. In other words, the heat map visualization gives the possibility to understand the behaviour of the people. Also it can be considered as a powerful and intuitive image retrieval tool for the collections related to cultural heritage sites.

3.2 t-SNE Exploration

We exploit the *fc7* feature extracted with the *AlexNet* architecture [3] for each image and use the t-SNE embedding algorithm [8] to compute a 2D embedding that respects the pairwise distances between visual features, forcing to fit a grid layout (Figure 4). The t-SNE (t-Distribuited Stochastic Neighbour Embedding) is a technique for feature space dimensionality reduction that is particularly well suited for the visualization of high dimensional image datasets. Note that images with the same subject are automatically arranged nearby (see Figure 4). Moreover, the system arranges very close those images which are not the same but have a similar visual content. It is also important to highlight that the employed CNN [3] has been trained using a different dataset concerning 1000 classes of objects, but the *fc7* features resulted expressive and representative enough to be applied succesfully to a generic event collection.

With this exploration tool, the user can apply a translation or a zooming to all the viewed images, just clicking and dragging the mouse along the desidered direction and

Figure 4: t-SNE visualization. The images are forced to fit a grid layout. Images of an event are automatically organized by visual content. Images close in the 2D layout are also close in terms of visual content.

by using the scroll wheel respectively. This helps the user to better explore the image distribution in a custom level of detail. Furthermore, the user can choose a subset of images and compute the t-SNE embedding of them directly on the browser (see Figure 4).

3.3 Other Advanced Tools

Among the tools included in *The Social Picture*, there is the one useful to generate automatic subsets of images from a specific photo collection. This tool allows the user to set the number of images to obtain as output for a collection in TSP, and automatically generates the subset of images taking into account visual features as well as EXIF information related to the images composing the photo collection (e.g., GPS location, TAGS, day, time, etc). In this way, the user can have some representative image prototypes related to the collection to be used for different purposes (e.g., printing the most significative pictures of paintings of a museum for a specific social group). For this tool CNN representation used in [10] is employed.

One more feature included in *The Social Picture* is the automatic image captioning, as described in [2]. With the aim to help the user to include a description to an uploaded image, *The Social Picture* automatically generates and suggests a description to the user that can then refine it. The descriptions of images can be used for text based query performed by the user.

Finally, to allow a more advanced exploration of the collections, we have included the Visual Question and Answer functionality exploiting the algorithms described in [1]. The user is allowed to ask natural language questions about a collection (e.g., is there a building in the image?) and get back the subset of images which have got a positive answer. This tool also allows *The Social Picture* to assist visually impaired people while interacting with a collection.

4. ACKNOWLEDGMENTS

This work has been performed in collaboration with Telecom Italia | TIM - JOL WAVE in the project FIR2014-UNICT-DFA17D.

5. REFERENCES

[1] S. Antol, A. Agrawal, J. Lu, M. Mitchell, D. Batra, C. L. Zitnick, and D. Parikh. VQA: Visual question answering. In *International Conference on Computer Vision*, 2015.

[2] A. Karpathy and L. Fei-Fei. Deep visual-semantic alignment for generating image descriptions. In *Computer Vision and Pattern Recognition*, 2015.

[3] A. Krizhevsky, I. Sutskever, and G. E. Hinton. Imagenet classification with deep convolutional neural networks. In *Advances in neural information processing systems*, pages 1097–1105, 2012.

[4] A. Mikulík, F. Radenović, O. Chum, and J. Matas. *Asian Conference on Computer Vision*, chapter Efficient Image Detail Mining, pages 118–132. 2015.

[5] F. L. M. Milotta, S. Battiato, F. Stanco, V. D'Amico, G. Torrisi, and L. Addesso. RECfusion: Automatic scene clustering and tracking in video from multiple sources. In *IS&T Electronic Imaging*. IS&T, 2016.

[6] A. Ortis, M. Farinella, Giovanni, V. D'Amico, L. Addesso, G. Torrisi, and S. Battiato. Recfusion: Automatic video curation driven by visual content popularity. In *ACM Multimedia*, 2015.

[7] O. Russakovsky, J. Deng, H. Su, J. Krause, S. Satheesh, S. Ma, Z. Huang, A. Karpathy, A. Khosla, M. Bernstein, A. C. Berg, and L. Fei-Fei. ImageNet Large Scale Visual Recognition Challenge. *International Journal of Computer Vision*, 115(3):211–252, 2015.

[8] L. Van der Maaten and G. Hinton. Visualizing data using t-sne. *Journal of Machine Learning Research*, 9(2579-2605):85, 2008.

[9] T. Weyand and B. Leibe. Visual landmark recognition from internet photo collections: A large-scale evaluation. *Computer Vision and Image Understanding*, 135:1–15, 2015.

[10] B. Zhou, A. Lapedriza, J. Xiao, A. Torralba, and A. Oliva. Learning deep features for scene recognition using places database. In *Advances in Neural Information Processing Systems*, pages 487–495, 2014.

Watching What and How Politicians Discuss Various Topics - A Large-Scale Video Analytics UI

Emily Song, Joseph G. Ellis, Hongzhi Li and Shih-Fu Chang
Columbia University
{emily.song, jge2105, hongzhi.li, sc250}@columbia.edu

ABSTRACT

Accurately gauging the political atmosphere is especially difficult in this day and age, as individuals have access to a constantly growing collection of written and audiovisual news sources. This is especially true with regards to the U.S. presidential election, as there are numerous candidates, countless stories, and opinion articles discussing the merits of each particular candidate. It is therefore challenging for people to make an accurate assessment of what each candidate represents and how they would act if they were elected into office. To address this problem, we present a large-scale dataset comprised of videos of politicians speaking organized by the topics they are speaking about, and a user interface for exploring this interesting dataset. Our interface links people and events to relevant pieces of audiovisual media, and presents the desired information in a meaningful and intuitive manner. Our approach is unique by direct linking to actual speaking by politicians about specific topics, rather than links to textual quotes only. We describe the larger underlying infrastructure, a novel automated system that crawls thousands of internet news sources and 100 television news channels daily, and automatically discovers entities and indexes the content into events and topics. We examine how our user interface provides helpful and unique insights to its users, and give an example of the type of large scale trend analysis that can be performed with our system. Our online demo can be accessed at:
http://www.ee.columbia.edu/dvmm/PoliticialSpeakerDemo

Keywords

Multimedia Application, Topic Linking, User Interface, Visualization Platform, Person Naming, Event Detection

1. INTRODUCTION

In the world today, we are exposed to politics through a wide variety of sources. With evening newscasts, talk

ICMR '16, June 06–09, 2016, New York, New York USA

ISBN 978-1-4503-4359-6/16/06...$15.00
DOI: http://dx.doi.org/10.1145/2911996.2912025

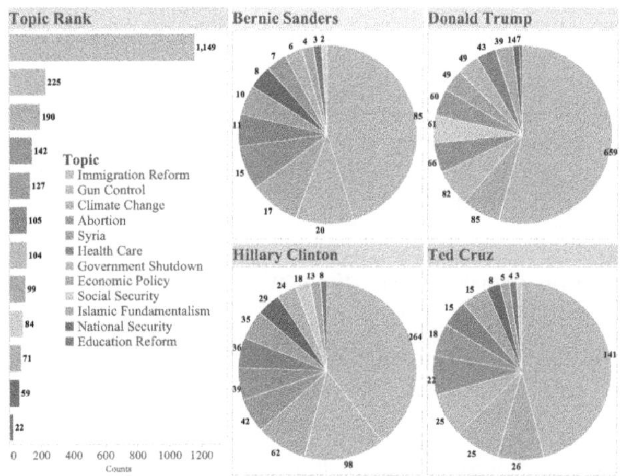

Figure 1: Breakdown of the political topics covered by different politicians and the aggregate statistics of the whole dataset broken down by topic.

shows, newspaper articles, and other forms of digital media all around us, we have greater access to news on this subject matter than ever before. We are subjected to a constant stream of stories and opinions, skewed in one way or another, to the point where we are unsure of how to make sense of it all. In this environment it is difficult to make well-founded judgments about important issues, and where candidates stand on them.

Political awareness is crucial to understanding the most pressing matters of today, but it is difficult to achieve, considering the abundance of news available. This is especially true with regards to the political election, where extensive media coverage has resulted in an overflow of information. Given that the presidential election is arguably the most important political event in the nation, there is an urgent need for a system that organizes this wealth of material in a coherent manner.

With so many candidates, and so many stories, people are overwhelmed and struggle to see the complete picture. How can individuals keep track of what different candidates are saying, what stories are trending, and how their statements on these topics changed over time or vary in comparison to one another? To address this problem, we built a user interface that allows a user to search and display the actual presidential candidates talking about different political topics in videos, rather than text quotes only. We automatically discover from raw television news streams when a politician appears and link what they are talking about to important political topics that take place in this election. Our system allows a user to search our video database by political candidates and topics, and to view the desired information on a well-organized timeline.

'A simple search with this tool leads to valuable and unique insights. For instance, users will quickly find that some candidates speak more on certain topics than others, and that clusters of speaker segments indicate trending topics. In addition, users can take advantage of the scalable timeline feature in order to analyze how individuals have changed their opinions over time, or how individuals have experienced surges in popularity at certain moments in time.

The contributions of our work can be summarized as follows:

- Using our automated video processing pipeline, we have generated a large collection of video political speech segments from the U.S. presidential candidates in the 2016 presidential election.
- Our system automatically detects and links video political speech to specific news events, and broad political topics.
- We demonstrate an interesting data analysis study that can be done with the massive collection of speech segments.
- Our video collection is fully searchable, and we provide a novel user interface for analyzing politicians' views over time and compared to one another.

1.1 Related Work

Political analysis using multimedia information is an interesting research topic. Many works from interdisciplinary researchers focus on this area. The automatic tools developed in the data mining, machine learning, and computer vision community play an important role in political science. Stewart [4] analyzed and provided a set of natural language processing tools for political scientists. Information extraction from "big data" [1], event detection, linking and coreference techniques discussed in [9] and [11] are useful components in building a political analysis system. In this paper, we discuss how we leverage state-of-the-art techniques to build a fully automatic data collection, analysis and representation system that explores information regarding political candidates and topics.

2. SYSTEM OVERVIEW

In this section we detail our video processing and recording pipeline that has enabled the creation of our archival political demo. The system architecture is shown in Figure 2.

2.1 Recording Infrastructure

Our system has access to over 100 US news channels. Our infrastructure can record and process 12 channels simultaneously in real-time. We record both broadcast and cable television news programs, examples of the programs that are collected are: *CNN Newsroom*, *The Today Show*, *ABC World News*, *NBC Nightly News*, *News 4 New York at 5*, and *The Situation Room*. Our system automatically tunes a digital TV tuner to record any news programs that are available at given points in time, based on the information provided by an Electronic Program Guide. Each of the chosen programs are recorded in their full digital transport stream (.ts), and then transcoded down to a more compact format (.mp4) to conserve space on our storage servers and allow for display in all browsers, which support this format.

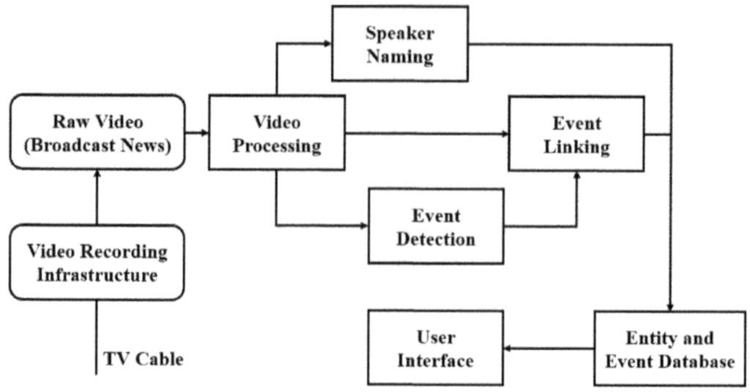

Figure 2: System Architecture

Once the videos are fully recorded we then begin processing each video by performing automatic speech recognition on the audio track within the video using the CMU sphinx library [7]. We extract the closed caption text that accompanies each video program, and then time-align the closed caption transcipt to the generated speech transcript from ASR. The closed caption text tends to be more accurate, but is shifted from what is actually being said on screen. By combining the two sources we are able to obtain a time-aligned accurate transcript of the speech on screen. Across one news program many different topics are covered, we want to separate each story, so that we can accurately search and determine what each politician is speaking about. To accomplish this we segment the news program into distinct "story segments", which are portions of the news program in which only one topic is covered. To accomplish this we utilize a variety of multimodal cues, such as closed caption special characters, black screen detection, shot boundary detection, consistent visual logos, and more to detect commercials in the news program and change of segments across the program. For more information on the algorithms used in this work to perform story segmentation and commercial detection, please refer to [5], [6], and comskip [1] .

2.2 Event Detection and Person Detection

Once we have separated the full news program into separate news stories we then attempt to detect when breaking news or important news events have been generated. To perform this operation we have developed a data mining algorithm for finding breaking news events. The details of the algorithm can be found in [6] and [8].

A unique aspect of our system is the ability to detect and find speakers from our collected and recorded news stories. Politicians are of particular interest in news, and our system is able to automatically detect who is talking on-screen with a precision of 86%. We employ two algorithms for speaker detection, which are documented and described here [6] and

[1]comskip: http://www.kaashoek.com/comskip/

[3]. Due to space considerations, we have omitted the details of our speaker detection algorithms from this paper. We encourage the reader to explore the algorithms in the cited works.

2.3 Political Topic Linking

To allow a user to browse through the broader political topics that are shaping the 2016 political election we assign each political speaker segment to its appropriate political topics. First, we have developed a crawler to automatically monitor the topics and content that are aggregated by Google News. We download new articles and Google news topics every 5-10 minutes. To date, we have found 45,000 distinct news topics and 25 million articles that are linked to those topics.

To discover broader political categories we have manually defined 12 distinct topics that are prevalent in coverage of the 2016 presidential election. Examples of these topics are *Immigration Reform*, *Gun Control*, and *Abortion*, and a complete list can be seen in Table 2. To link each speech segment to a political topic we extracted the closed caption from a given segment, and used n-gram similarity to find the closest political topic. A more detailed look at our topic linking algorithm can be seen in [8] and [6].

3. STATISTICAL ANALYSIS

Using our video political speech dataset one can extract insightful observations, examples of which are summarized in the included Tables 1 and 2 and Figures 1 and 3. Upon examining the number of videos per speaker and the number of videos per topic, we find that media coverage of the presidential election is far from balanced. This finding strongly suggests the presence of media bias, which in earlier studies has been found to greatly influence voter opinion and election outcome [2]. For example, Donald Trump and Hillary Clinton have so far dominated the media coverage in their respective parties, and not surprisingly at the time of publication they are both the odds-on favorites for the primary nominations. Interestingly, Ted Cruz at the time of writing has performed second to Donald Trump in an aggregation of national polls[2], and we have found that Ted Cruz is in the top three in total speech segments for republicans in our dataset. Conversely, Jeb Bush appears the second most often in the dataset, but is currently more than 10% behind Ted Cruz[2]. It is obvious that their is a correlation between performance in national polls and media coverage, whether it is a causal relationship is unclear. We hope that further analysis with our video dataset could be enlightening as to the causal nature of this relationship.

Furthermore, upon examining the breakdown of the topics discussed by each speaker, we discover noticeable fluctuations of the topics covered over time in Figure 3. What candidates are talking about is altered by when particular events happen, and the overall interests of the media shift and change.

Our comprehensive presidential candidate speaking set is useful in that it allows us to highlight disparities in media coverage and to pinpoint trends in political discussion, thereby allowing us to present a more complete picture of the speakers and topics. For example, if we look at Figure 1 we see that Immigration Reform is popular, but Donald Trump speaks about immigration reform proportionally more than any of the other leading candidates. This information may give us insight into the demographics and geographic portions of America that are more likely to vote for him. In the world of biased news reporting and a constantly changing political climate, this large scale data analysis can be very enlightening to expose biases or a candidate's tendencies. The patterns discovered here speak volumes about the issues most important to the candidates and their party affiliations [10].

[2]fivethirtyeight.com

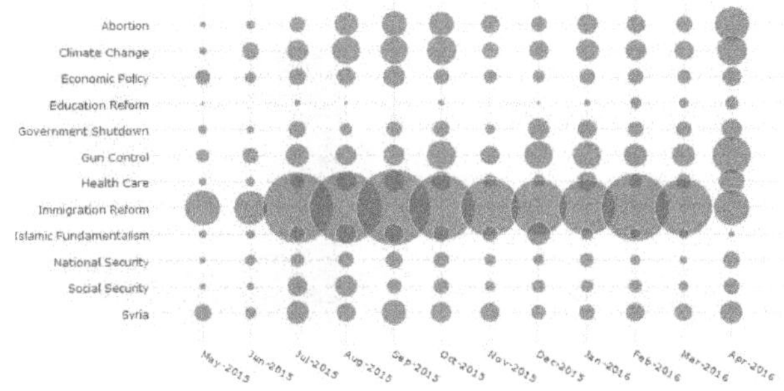

Figure 3: The amount of video story segments for each topic over time.

Table 1: Breakdown by Speaker

Speaker	Number of Segments
Jeb Bush (R)	817
Ben Carson (R)	67
Chris Christie (R)	109
Ted Cruz (R)	520
Carly Fiorina (R)	44
John Kasich (R)	111
Rand Paul (R)	143
Marco Rubio (R)	224
Rick Santorum (R)	76
Donald Trump (R)	1950
Hillary Clinton (D)	1143
Bernie Sanders (D)	321

4. USER INTERFACE

Our user interface exhibits a scalable timeline to represent the desired political candidate and topic the viewer is interested in. The visualization demo initially prompts the user to select multiple speakers and one topic from two separate drop down menus, and this search query then determines what speaker segments appear on the generated timeline.

The timeline has several notable features: (1) The timeline is scalable, allowing for easy comparison of statements over time. (2) Each speaker segment is an item on the timeline, flagged with a photo of the speaker and a title for the video. (3) Clicking on an item on the timeline generates the video, along with its date, title, and speech transcript.

The design of the timeline allows for accurate snap judgments, but also for careful exploration of the timeline content. An accurate snap judgment may occur when a user sees a clustering of videos around a certain date - this immediately suggests a trending event. An instance where

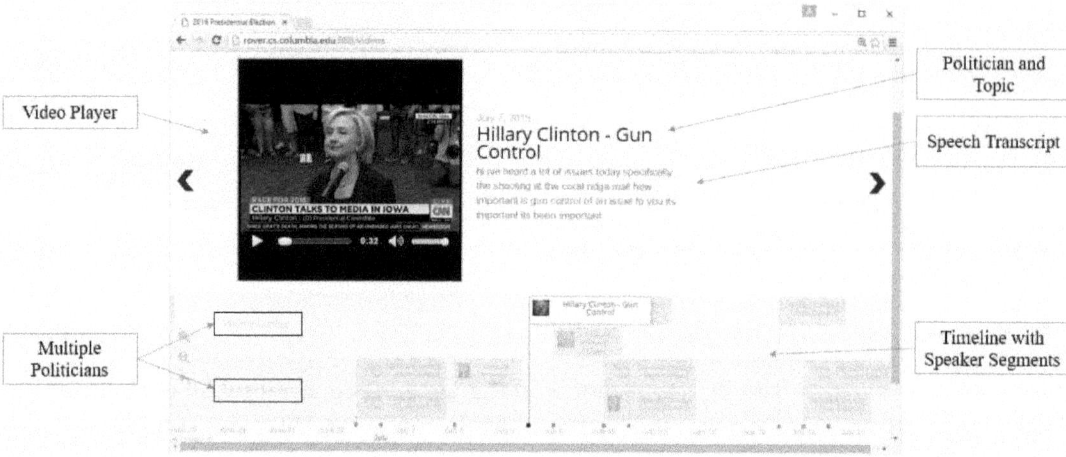

Figure 4: Topic linking user interface: Scalable timeline allows a user to easily navigate through the videos temporally. Videos can be viewed in time sequence, allowing for direct comparison of two speakers discussing the same event.

Table 2: Breakdown by Topic

Topic	Number of Segments
Islamic Fundamentalism	124
Syria	195
Health Care	153
Climate Change	268
Government Shutdown	138
Immigration Reform	1729
Gun Control	315
Social Security	113
National Security	100
Education Reform	28
Economic Policy	142
Abortion	221

careful exploration of the timeline content may be helpful is when someone wants to directly compare several candidates - systematically going through videos of different candidates speaking on the same days allows the user to find differences between their responses to the same event.

5. CONCLUSION

We have presented an automated video processing system and user interface that allows a user to search and watch videos of political candidates by political topics. This visualization demo aims to illuminate political attitudes in the presidential election with an intuitive timeline populated with relevant speaker segments. Our platform is notable for the following reasons: (1) Using our automated video processing pipeline, we have generated a large collection of video political speech segments from the U.S. presidential candidates. (2) Using this data, we have demonstrated interesting data analysis studies that can be performed. (3) Selecting people and topics with this tool can lead to meaningful realizations regarding the presidential election, enabling the voting public to be more well-informed. The demo website is live so that others can benefit from its usefulness. This material is based upon work supported by the National Science Foundation Graduate Research Fellowship under Grant No. DGE-11-44155.

6. REFERENCES

[1] K. Arceneaux, M. Johnson, R. Lindstädt, and R. J. Wielen. The influence of news media on political elites: Investigating strategic responsiveness in congress. *American Journal of Political Science*, 2016.

[2] D. D'Alessio and M. Allen. Media bias in presidential elections: a meta-analysis. *Journ. of Comm.*, 2000.

[3] J. G. Ellis, B. Jou, and S.-F. Chang. Why we watch the news: A dataset for exploring sentiment in broadcast video news. In *ICMI*, 2014.

[4] J. Grimmer and B. M. Stewart. Text as data: The promise and pitfalls of automatic content analysis methods for political texts. *Political Analysis*, 2013.

[5] W. Hsu, L. Kennedy, C.-W. Huang, S.-F. Chang, C.-Y. Lin, and G. Iyengar. News video story segmentation using fusion of multi-level multi-modal features in trecvid 2003. In *ICASSP*, 2004.

[6] B. Jou, H. Li, J. G. Ellis, D. Morozoff-Abegauz, and S.-F. Chang. Structured exploration of who, what, when, and where in heterogeneous multimedia news sources. In *ACM MM*, 2013.

[7] P. Lamere, P. Kwok, E. Gouvea, B. Raj, R. Singh, W. Walker, M. Warmuth, and P. Wolf. The cmu sphinx-4 speech recognition system. In *ICASSP*, 2003.

[8] H. Li, B. Jou, J. G. Ellis, D. Morozoff, and S.-F. Chang. News rover: Exploring topical structures and serendipity in heterogeneous multimedia news. In *ACM MM*, 2013.

[9] R. Li, K. H. Lei, R. Khadiwala, and K. C.-C. Chang. Tedas: A twitter-based event detection and analysis system. In *IEEE ICDE*, 2012.

[10] B. Yu, S. Kaufmann, and D. Diermeier. Classifying party affiliation from political speech. *Journal of Information Technology & Politics*, 2008.

[11] T. Zhang, H. Li, H. Ji, and S.-F. Chang. Cross-document event coreference resolution based on cross-media features. In *EMNLP*, 2015.

Object-aware Deep Network for Commodity Image Retrieval

Zhiwei Fang[1] Jing Liu[1] Yuhang Wang[1]
Yong Li[1] Hang Song[1] Jinhui Tang[2] Hanqing Lu[1]
[1]National Lab of Pattern Recognition, CASIA, Beijing 100190, China
[2]School of Computer Science and Engineering, Nanjing University of Science and Technology, China
{zhiwei.fang, jliu}@nlpr.ia.ac.cn jinhuitang@njust.edu.cn

ABSTRACT
Recent years, with the development of e-commerce and population of mobile phones, image-based commodity retrieval has attracted much attention. This paper proposed a deep framework for commodity image retrieval(CMIR) from the view that they are same designed commodities. Our framework can catch as many design details as possible by exploring object detection and ranking sensitive feature learning, while the former is performed based on Faster R-CNN, and the later is learned with a multi-task Siamese Network. Besides, we refine the processing speed of the framework to make it a live system. Our framework is implemented on an android application based on Client/Server structure model whose server response time is about 150 ms per query.

Keywords
Deep Network, Commodity Retrieval, Object Detection

1. INTRODUCTION
With the prosperity of electronic commerce, the demand of commodity retrieval has been growing. Traditional commodity retrieval systems are mainly based on text information. However, text data has a limited ability to describe a commodity comprehensively. In contrast, image-based commodity retrieval technique is a solution to overcome the limitation in that image can provide much more information of a commodity, such as its texture, color, style and so on, which is becoming a trend in e-commerce.

Commodity image retrieval (CMIR) is a task to search images containing the same commodity instance as the query image, whose typical application is Pailitao in Taobao.com. From the view of searching objective, CMIR is different from traditional content-based image retrieval (CBIR), in which visually similar images within the same semantic category to a given query image are the required searching results. Such a difference can be understood more easily with the illustration in Fig. 1, i.e., images including white mugs are correct for CBIR, while only the mugs with the same design are required in CMIR. Therefore, CMIR is a more challenging and semantically fine-grained task than CBIR, and how to access the same-design characteristic is an essential problem in CMIR.

ICMR'16, June 06-09, 2016, New York, NY, USA
© 2016 ACM. ISBN 978-1-4503-4359-6/16/06...$15.00
DOI: http://dx.doi.org/10.1145/2911996.2912027

Figure 1: Comparison between CMIR and CBIR, in which the former is a more semantically fine-grained task than the later.

Besides, the peculiarities of commodity images intensify the challenge in CMIR. As shown in Fig. 2, there are three peculiarities. First, commodity instance may occur more than once in an image, thus making it looks not visually the same as the query from the whole image perspective though they contain the same instance. Second, the same commodity instances are possibly surrounded with other objects or diverse backgrounds, which may mislead the system about the user's intention. Third, many kinds of commodities like coats, dress and pants are dressed on human body and seriously affected by the diversity of human pose.

Considering the above challenges, we design an object-aware feature learning framework for CMIR, which includes three steps: object detection, feature extraction for the most possibly object region, image hashing and ranking. First, we adopt Faster R-CNN[9] for object detection. Considering the high cost of obtaining images with object bounding boxes for training Faster R-CNN, in order to fully utilize images with image-level labels(e.g., coat, shoes, cosmetic etc. as the main categories of commodity, are almost freely available in e-commence), an image classification CNN is trained on large-scale commodity images to learn a base discrimination for commodity objects. Then we use the classification CNN to initialize both RPN and Fast R-CNN, making them

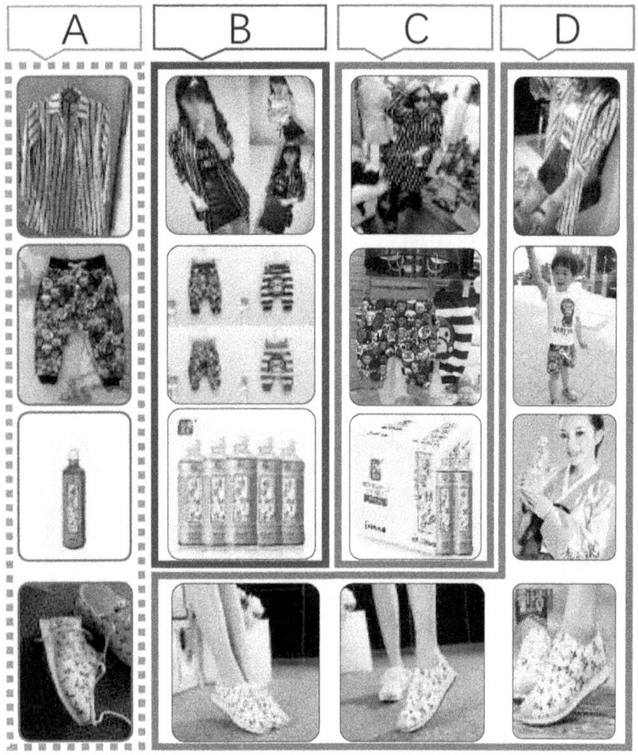

Figure 2: The peculiarities of commodity images. Box A for query and each row stands for a query and its true recalls; Box B for instances reoccurring; Box C for complex background; Box D for pose diversity.

obtain a nearly cost-free image classification in testing. Second, we design a multi-task fine-tuned Siamese[3] network to learn a ranking-sensitive feature representation. Besides, model ensemble techniques are used to reflect the same-design characteristic in CMIR as good as possible. Third, we adopt typical hashing approach, i.e, Local sensitive hashing (LSH)[6], and Hamming distance to perform efficient feature indexing and ranking. Jointly exploring above steps, we build a mobile app to demonstrate our CMIR system, which indexes about 3 millions of commodity images provided by Alibaba and can complete a search process within 150ms on average. The retrieval performance has a rise of 2.73 percentage points to Alibaba's baseline.

2. DATASET

The dataset in this work consists of four parts of subsets: training set, evaluation set, validation set and test set. Training set consists of 1,950,988 images which are divided into 10 categorise: accessory, coat, skirt, snacks, pants, luggage, furniture, drink, cosmetic and shoes. It is also divided into 676 more fine-grained sub-categorise. Each image in training set has a category tag and a sub-categorise tag as its image-level label, with noise. Evaluation set, which is the base dataset of our system, consists of 3,195,334 images without any label. Validation set consists of 1417 query images and their ground truth, totally 93989 images. Test set consists of 3567 query images without ground truth. The dataset is provided by Alibaba Large-scale Image Search Challenge 2015(ALISC2015).

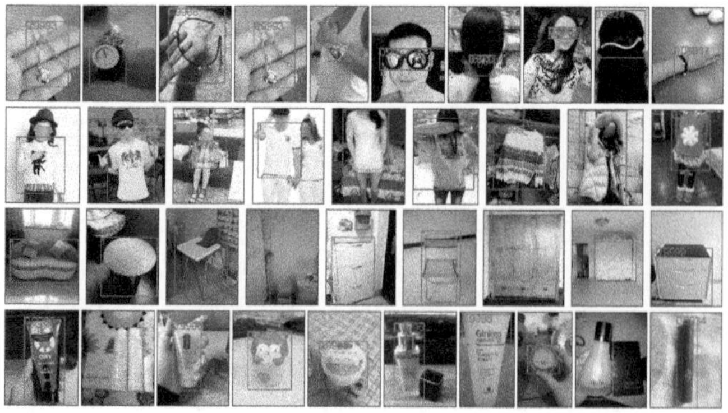

Figure 4: Demonstration of the results of our Object Detection Module. From top row to bottom are accessory, coat, furniture and cosmetic.

3. SYSTEM OVERVIEW

Fig. 3 shows the overall framework of our commodity image retrieval system which includes three modules: object detection, feature extraction as well as hashing and ranking.

3.1 Object Detection

Since object detection is the primary task which directly influences the system, we must make sure the object detection module works excellently in performance. The challenge is how to train an excellent object detection model on commodity images whose category labels are usually freely obtained and enough while box-level labels are rare and obtained with high cost. To address this challenge, we designed a training pipeline to make full use of the labeled data step by step. First, we train an initial classifier CNN on the training set over 10 main categories based on Alexnet[8]. This is important because the initial classifier CNN model has strong discriminative ability in 10 categories of commodity, and can be used as a pre-trained model for object detection. Second, we adopt a typical model of Faster R-CNN[9] for object detection, which is trained based on limited box-level labeled images. Both the RPN and the Fast R-CNN are initialized from the classifier CNN model. After this step, we can train a satisfactory Faster R-CNN more easily. However, the Faster R-CNN will detect all categories of commodities in images no matter whether they are the main commodity(see the query image in Fig. 3). So in the third step, we reconstruct a classifier to determine the main commodity category in an image. We add one max-pooling layer and two fully-connected layers upon the conv5 layer of Faster R-CNN and train it on the whole training set again, during which, we fix the parameters of shared convolutional layers and only update the added layers to make sure that the performance of Faster R-CNN is not affected. Besides, the sharing of convolutional layers makes the judgement of main category nearly cost-free in testing stage.

When given an image, the classification part gives the image a main category label to point out what kind of commodity the main object is. At the same time, the object-detection part detects all commodity instances with bounding boxes regardless of what category they belong to and give the boxes their box-level label. Finally, we only select boxes whose box-level label is the same as its image-level label. In order to train the object detection model, we man-

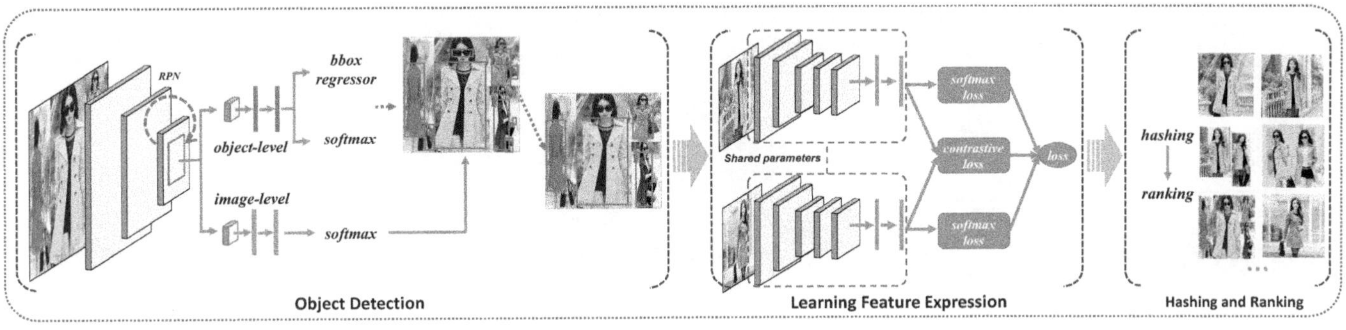

Figure 3: Overall Framework

ually annotated 10,000 images, i.e., 0.51% of the training set, with bounding boxes. Fig. 4 shows some examples of the object detection module. After this module, the images are instead by their selected regions and the following work is how to embed the regions into a better feature space.

3.2 Feature Extraction

We design a Multi-task Siamese Network[3] (MSN, shown in Fig. 3) to learn features with both a primary discrimination among different commodities and a relative correlation in same-designed commodities, i.e., in the learned feature space, the same-designed commodity instances are much closer than the different-designed instances. MSN is builded on VGG_CNN_S[1] with three loss layers: two softmax loss and a contrastive loss. The contrastive loss is defined as

$$L_c(x_p, x_q) = \begin{cases} ||x_p - x_q||^2 & positive \\ max(0, m^2 - ||x_p - x_q||^2) & negetive \end{cases} \quad (1)$$

where m is the margin, x_p and x_q are positive pair when the belong to the same sub-category, or negative pair when in other cases. Since the sub-category reflects more information about commodity's attributes and design details, contrastive loss with such selected pairs makes the model more sensitive to the commodity's differences of design. Softmax loss which is also defined on sub-categories, not only improves the speed of the convergence process but also enhance the ability of image feature expression. The VGG_CNN_S we used is pre-trained on ImageNet[4], and m is set to 0.2. If we choose the output of pool5 as the feature, the dimension is 512 x 6 x 6 = 18432, which is too long! So we add a new max-pooling layer called pool6_33 whose kernel size is 3 x 3 with stride 1. The reduced feature dimension is 512 x 4 x 4 = 8192.

Besides, considering that model ensemble technique is usually effective, we choose an Inception-BN Network[7] pre-trained on full ImageNet dataset with 14,197,087 images in 21,841 classes as the second model, whose last max-pooling layer's output is selected as the second feature, called inception feature, whose dimension is 1024. Since the model is per-trained on a different and more general image dataset, its feature is complementary to VGG_CNN_S feature. The model ensemble increases our online MAP@20 by 3.39%.

3.3 Hashing and Ranking

Quickly finding the most similar top K relevant images among 3 million samples is a challenge itself. There are two time-consuming steps in this module. Step 1, compare the query feature with each of the all features in dataset

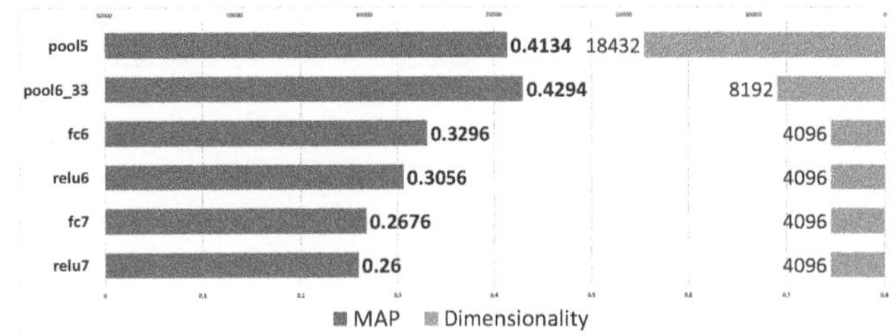

Figure 6: The comparison of features from different CNN layers.

and compute their distance. Step2, find the most smallest top K distances and return their indexing numbers. We use local-sensitive hashing(LSH)[6] to accelerate step 1 and a Hamming-distance-based ranking algorithm[2] whose complexity is just $O(n + k)$(finding top k in n numbers) to accelerate step 2.

Our tests show that cosine distance is a better choice to measure the distance between two features than Euclidean distance. We define the distance between features as

$$D_{cos}(x_1, x_2) = 1 - \frac{x_1 \cdot x_2}{||x_1|| \, ||x_2||} \quad (2)$$

where x_1 and x_2 are features of two images. As saying above, directly computing cosine distance 3 million times is not computation efficient. We use LSH to transform the raw features to binary codes and compute Hamming distance instead of cosine distance in parallel, which reduces the time consumption of step 1 from 556 ms to 83 ms. Then we adopt the Hamming-distance-based sorting algorithm to decrease step 2 from 100 ms to less than 1 ms. At last, we can complete a query procedure with 150 ms in which 83 ms for ranking.

4. EXPERIMENTS

We build an android application based on Client/Server structure model to demonstrate our commodity image retrieval system. Our system indexes all the images in evaluation set as introduced in Section 2. The evaluation metric is Mean Average Precision at top 20 recalls(MAP@20). The official baseline of ALISC2015 is 0.436. Our experiments was did on a server with 16 GB memory, whose GPU is Titan-Black and CPU is Intel(R)Core(TM)i7@3.6GHz with 8 Cores.

In CNNs, compared with features of higher layers, features

Figure 5: Final result demonstration. The top images are query images and the rest are search results. Images with red border are false search results.

Table 1: Comparison among different models and acceleration methods.

Model & Method	Dimension	MAP@20
VGG_CNN_S	8192	42.94 %
Inception-BN	1024	36.57 %
Model Ensemble	9216	46.33 %

of lower layers keep more details of the image[5], which is important for the retrieval problem.As shown in Fig. 6, the performance of different layers are variant, and pool6_33 operates better than any other layer, which is the reason we finally choose pool6_33 as feature extraction layer.

Tab. 1 shows the comparison among different models and acceleration methods, where model ensemble reaches the highest MAP, 2.73 % higher than official baseline, which demonstrate that combining models of great diversity often yields better features. Fig. 5 shows some examples of the demo where images with red border are false results.

5. CONCLUSION

In this paper, we proposed a framework to search commodity images which are in the same design. In order to ensure the framework's performance, we designed tree modules to catch the commodity's design details and accelerate the system. An android application was built to demonstrate our framework and the results show that our system can achieve a high MAP@20 which is 2.73 percentage points higher than the official baseline, whose response time is only about 150 ms on average.

6. ACKNOWLEDGEMENT

This work was supported by 973 Program (2012CB316304) and National Natural Science Foundation of China (61332016, 61272329, and 61472422).

The dataset used in this work is from Alibaba Group and rewarded by Alibaba Large-scale Image Search Challenge 2015(ALISC2015).

7. REFERENCES

[1] K. Chatfield, K. Simonyan, A. Vedaldi, and A. Zisserman. Return of the devil in the details: Delving deep into convolutional nets. In *British Machine Vision Conference*, 2014.

[2] J. Cheng, C. Leng, J. Wu, H. Cui, H. Lu, et al. Fast and accurate image matching with cascade hashing for 3d reconstruction. *CVPR. IEEE*, 2014.

[3] S. Chopra, R. Hadsell, and Y. LeCun. Learning a similarity metric discriminatively, with application to face verification. In *Computer Vision and Pattern Recognition, 2005. CVPR 2005. IEEE Computer Society Conference on*, volume 1, pages 539–546 vol. 1, June 2005.

[4] J. Deng, W. Dong, R. Socher, L.-J. Li, K. Li, and L. Fei-Fei. Imagenet: A large-scale hierarchical image database. In *Computer Vision and Pattern Recognition, 2009. CVPR 2009. IEEE Conference on*, pages 248–255, June 2009.

[5] A. Dosovitskiy and T. Brox. Inverting convolutional networks with convolutional networks. *arXiv preprint arXiv:1506.02753*, 2015.

[6] A. Gionis, P. Indyk, R. Motwani, et al. Similarity search in high dimensions via hashing. In *VLDB*, volume 99, pages 518–529, 1999.

[7] S. Ioffe and C. Szegedy. Batch normalization: Accelerating deep network training by reducing internal covariate shift. *arXiv preprint arXiv:1502.03167*, 2015.

[8] A. Krizhevsky, I. Sutskever, and G. E. Hinton. Imagenet classification with deep convolutional neural networks. In *Advances in neural information processing systems*, pages 1097–1105, 2012.

[9] S. Ren, K. He, R. B. Girshick, and J. Sun. Faster R-CNN: towards real-time object detection with region proposal networks. *CoRR*, abs/1506.01497, 2015.

An Automated End-To-End Pipeline for Fine-Grained Video Annotation using Deep Neural Networks

Baptist Vandersmissen[1] Lucas Sterckx[3] Thomas Demeester[3]

Azarakhsh Jalalvand[1] Wesley De Neve[1,2] Rik Van de Walle[1]

{firstname.lastname}@ugent.be

[1] Data Science Lab, ELIS, Ghent University – iMinds, Ghent, Belgium
[2] Image and Video Systems Lab, KAIST, Daejeon, South Korea
[3] Internet Based Communication Networks and Services, INTEC, Ghent University – iMinds, Ghent, Belgium

ABSTRACT

The searchability of video content is often limited to the descriptions authors and/or annotators care to provide. The level of description can range from absolutely nothing to fine-grained annotations at the level of frames. Based on these annotations, certain parts of the video content are more searchable than others.

Within the context of the STEAMER project, we developed an innovative end-to-end system that attempts to tackle the problem of unsupervised retrieval of news video content, leveraging multiple information streams and deep neural networks. In particular, we extracted keyphrases and named entities from transcripts, subsequently refining these keyphrases and named entities based on their visual appearance in the news video content. Moreover, to allow for fine-grained frame-level annotations, we temporally located high-confidence keyphrases in the news video content. To that end, we had to tackle challenges such as the automatic construction of training sets and the automatic assessment of keyphrase imageability.

In this paper, we discuss the main components of our end-to-end system, capable of transforming textual and visual information into fine-grained video annotations.

Keywords

deep neural networks, fine-grained video annotation, video retrieval

1. INTRODUCTION

Fully automated metadata generation for multimedia content is the holy grail of information retrieval, given that fine-grained annotation enables more accurate searchability in multimedia archives. In this paper, we present a fully automated end-to-end system for generating metadata for news video content. Indeed, television broadcasters have a great need for accurate annotations, so to ensure future searchability and monetization of their video content.

The system discussed in this paper was developed within the context of the STEAMER project[1], a collaborative research project funded by both industry and the Flemish government. Our system extracts relevant keyphrases and candidate persons from information residing in transcripts. To cope with the different nature of keyphrases (concept detection) and candidate persons (face recognition), our systems processes the two types of information differently. The relevance of a subset of keyphrases is reassessed based on the presence of visual elements linked to the core concepts of each specific keyphrase. Candidate persons (discovered via named entity extraction) are visually matched based on deep face features to increase the relevance and ranking of these annotations. Both types of information are processed by making use of state-of-the-art deep learning techniques, for example to extract effective features.

Furthermore, the system discussed in this paper supports the learning and recognition of an infinite number of concepts, thus making it possible to move away from a limited semantic coverage. To do so, we developed methods to automatically construct training sets and to automatically assess the visual representativeness of keyphrases. In addition, our system allows for fine-grained annotation of news video content with both general and specific concepts (via keyphrases), as well as with the presence of noteworthy persons (via named entity detection), thus greatly increasing the searchability of the news video content in question.

After a brief review of related work in Section 2, we describe the main components of our system in Section 3. Next, we discuss both quantitave and qualitative results in Section 4. Finally, we conclude our work in Section 5, also giving some hints for future improvements.

2. RELATED WORK

The problem of automatic multimedia enrichment has been tackled by many projects before. In this section, we dis-

ICMR'16, June 06-09, 2016, New York, NY, USA

DOI: http://dx.doi.org/10.1145/2911996.2912028

[1] http://www.iminds.be/en/projects/2014/07/12/steamer

cuss two recent projects that are of interest, namely AXES [10] and LinkedTV [8]. The AXES project[2] attempted to develop tools that provide various types of users with new ways to interact with audiovisual libraries. Specifically, information sources such as audio streams and blogs were used to increase the overall explorability of audiovisual content. LinkedTV[3] is a similar project that uses semi-automatic audiovisual analysis of television content to generate links to relevant web content.

The essential difference between these projects and the system proposed in this paper is the fact that our system attempts to enrich the video in an unconstrained manner without any human interference. This means that our sytem considers every possible relevant keyphrase, introducing challenges such as the automatic building and cleaning of training sets, as well as the assessment of the visual representativeness of a keyphrase. Regarding the automatic building of training sets, the authors of [2, 3, 5, 6] introduced novel ideas to collect and increase the overall relevancy of both the positive and negative training samples, whereas the authors of [9] provided an in-depth analysis of the concept of visual representativeness.

3. METHODOLOGY

In this section, we describe the overall architecture of the proposed system and we explain the different components built. Figure 1 provides a visual overview of these components. As depicted, a video segment and an accompanying transcript are used as inputs. Next, after processing, the extracted transcript information is matched against the visual content, making it possible to adjust the relevance of keyphrases and candidate persons.

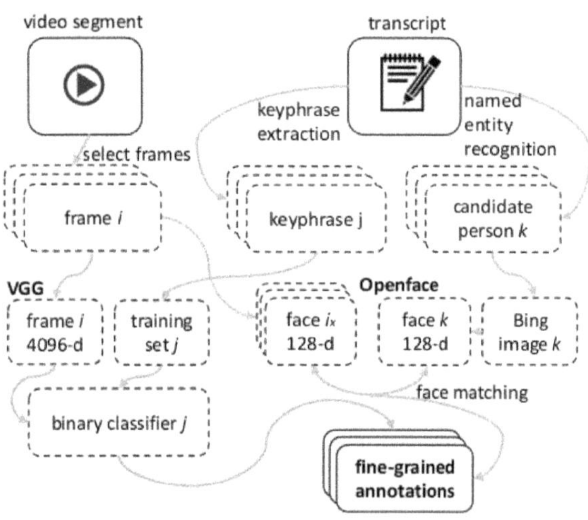

Figure 1: Simplified overview of our system.

In what follows, we describe the general flow of our system in more detail, outlining the role and functioning of the different components.

3.1 Transcript Information

Transcript information is reduced to extracted keyphrases and candidate persons.

[2]http://www.axes-project.eu/
[3]http://www.linkedtv.eu/

3.1.1 Keyphrase Extraction

Candidate keyphrases are extracted by Part-Of-Speech (PoS) tagging the transcript and by filtering sequences of words with tags satisfying a regular expression that takes the form of <JJ>*<NN.*>+. The PoS tag JJ refers to an adjective, while NN refers to a noun. Keyphrases are then ranked according to a supervised model trained on annotated documents provided by the VRT, a Flemish broadcaster and one of the project partners. In particular, 1,250 documents were annotated with keyphrases by 300 users instructed to select the most prominent phrases in the document. Each document was assigned six keyphrases on average, and where these keyphrases were used as positively labeled training samples; candidates not in this set were assigned a negative label. For each candidate, the following features were extracted: (i) keyphrase frequency; (ii) number of tokens in the keyphrase; (iii) length of the longest term in the keyphrase; (iv) a binary feature indicating whether the keyphrase contains a named entity; (v) PoS tags; (vi) relative position of the first and last occurrence; (vii) span (relative last occurrence minus relative first occurrence); and (viii) TF*IDF score. The supervised model was trained by means of a binary classifier using logistic regression.

3.1.2 Collection of Images

Since we aim for a fully automated system with support for an unlimited number of keyphrases, several challenging steps are introduced. This includes filtering of keyphrases based on their visual relevance (imageability) and the automatic construction of training sets. The top j ranked keyphrases are taken into account as possible accurate descriptors for the linked video segment under consideration. Each of these keyphrase is then automatically translated from Dutch to English using Google Translate. Next, a set of representative images is collected using several commercial and social image search engines (that is, Bing Images, Google Images and Flickr). Challenges like wrongly translated, ambiguous or rare keyphrases increase the degree of difficulty to obtain representative images.

3.1.3 Imageability of a Keyphrase

A key difficulty is the assessment of the visual nature of a keyphrase (i.e., the imageability of a keyphrase). Tag imageability or representativeness can be defined as the extent to which a tag is able to effectively describe the visual content of a set of images annotated by that tag [9]. In this context, a tag is imageable if images annotated with that tag share similar concepts (that is, objects, scenes and actions).[4]

Assessing the imageability of a keyphrase is an important step as numerous keyphrases do not depict a single concept that is clearly visual in nature. Examples are abstract concepts like *"thoughts"* and *"interests"*, *feelings* and *notions of time*. These examples are nonvisual in nature, thus making it difficult or merely impossible to recognize these examples in video content. Therefore, we developed an algorithm to evaluate the imageabilty of a keyphrase.

This algorithm analyses a number of properties of the collected set of images: (i) the average Euclidean distance between all images based on a feature representation (cf. Section 3.1.4); (ii) the number of outliers in the image set; and

[4]The concept of imageability comes with a dubious interpretation. However, we consider a more detailed treatment of this topic to be out-of-scope for this demo paper.

(iii) the number of clusters based on a hierarchical clustering algorithm. A Support Vector Machine (SVM) model is trained based on a set of 200 keyphrases annotated with a binary label.

3.1.4 Training of a Visual Model

To accurately recognize a keyphrase in a video segment, a visual model for each keyphrase is trained. To train such a model, a training set is automatically collected. Positive samples are collected via aforementioned search engines and filtered for outliers. An outlier image is identified based on its overall distance to all other images in the set. Negative samples are collected by randomly selecting the same number of samples from a fixed collection of images (depicting typical news content) and images originating from previously collected and differing keyphrases.

Next, for each image, an effective feature representation is computed based on recently developed deep convolutional neural networks. In that regard, we use the popular framework Caffe [4] to extract the activations of layer FC_7 from the state-of-the-art Visual Geometry Group (VGG) 16-layer network [7] trained on the ImageNet Challenge dataset[5]. Each image is preprocessed (i.e., resized, cropped and mean subtracted) and feed forwarded through the network, resulting in a 4096-dimensional feature vector.

Finally, a model based on a linear SVM is trained using the extracted feature vectors as input, combined with a dedicated target indicating whether the image is either positive or negative with respect to the target keyphrase. This model is used as an indicator for the visual presence of a keyphrase in a video segment at a specific timestamp.

3.1.5 Candidate Persons

Named entities, and candidate persons in particular, are extracted from transcripts using software developed by the company Zeticon[6], also a STEAMER project partner. Five representative images are downloaded for each candidate person using the top results of the above described search engines (by filtering on portrait images only). The face in each image is detected and aligned. Next, a 128-dimensional representation is obtained using the activations of the last layer of the Openface deep neural network [1]. This representation contains different core characteristics of a face, enabling a cross-age comparison between multiple representations. Two faces are matched based on the L_2 distance between their face representations. This implies a candidate person is deemed to be visually present in the video if its representative face has been matched to one or more detected faces in the video content.

3.2 Video Segments

The video segments used as an input to our system are part of daily television news broadcast episodes. They contain in-studio news announcements, interviews, debates and reports.To be able to process video segments in a reasonable amount of time, the video is downsampled to one frame every second, thus discarding temporal information (cf. Section 5 for future work). Following the approach previously described in Section 3.1.4, for each of these frames, the activations of the FC_7 layer of the VGG deep convolutional neural network are extracted and used as a representation.

[5]http://www.image-net.org/challenges/LSVRC/
[6]http://www.zeticon.com/

3.3 Workflow

To automatically enrich a video segment with fine-grained annotations, the representation of each frame is fed as an input to all keyphrase classifiers separately. The output of each keyphrase classifier is a measure as to what extent the keyphrase is visually present in the video content. Further, all outcomes are aggregated over all frames to generate a final score per keyphrase, denoting its visual presence.

Regarding the recognition of candidate persons in a video segment, all face patches are first detected per selected frame. This is done by applying a combination of the Viola-Jones algorithm [11] (detection) and a deep convolutional neural network (confirmation). For each detected and aligned face patch, the corresponding face representation is then compared to all representations retrieved for the candidate persons. Depending on a threshold, video segment face patches are linked to candidate persons.

The final output of our system consists of a video segment with both coarse- and fine-grained textual keyphrase annotations, filtered and reranked based on their visual presence in the video. In addition, the video segment in question has been annotated with visually occurring persons on a frame-level basis.

(a) (b)

Figure 2: Example metadata generation for keyphrases "Tomorrowland" and "Appeal Trial".

4. RESULTS

To evaluate the overall performance of the proposed system, we need frame-level annotations for all considered keyphrases and candidate persons. Due to the current absence of such a dataset, we mainly provide a qualitative evaluation of the different functionalities of the proposed system.

4.1 Keyphrases

For each video segment, the top-k best scoring keyphrases are taken into consideration as possible video enrichments.

4.1.1 Imageability

We assess the correctness of the imageability scores attached to a number of keyphrases based on a constructed test set. Specifically, we randomly selected 100 keyphrases originating from a large set of transcript files, having these annotated by at least five different annotators. Given a clear definition of imageability, each keyphrase is assigned a label $\in$ {"*Yes*", "*Mostly Yes*", "*Mostly No*", "*No*"}. These labels are subsequently transformed into a weight $\in \{1.0, 0.67, 0.33, 0\}$ and averaged over all annotators resulting in one imageability score per keyphrase. The annotator agreement is measured by averaging the F_1 scores over all annotators (leaving the remaining annotators as ground truth), resulting in a score of 69%. Our predictor achieves a precision of 47% and a recall of 64% on this test set, resulting in an F_1 score of 55%. Considering the challenging nature of this task, we state that the difference between both F_1 scores (annotator versus algorithm) is reasonably small, showing the effectiveness of our approach.

4.1.2 *Fine-grained Enrichments*

The examplary Figure 2(a) shows the correct identification of the keyphrase "Tomorrowland". However, going from transcript data to relevant and imageable keyphrases introduces many hazards. Most mistakes are due to keyphrases depicting concepts that are either too general or too specific, resulting in a training set primarily consisting of noisy and diverse images. This is something that can be observed in Figure 2(b). In this example, the keyphrase "appeal trial" is to be recognized. Whereas the concept of a "trial" itself depicts a clear visual concept, the addition of "appeal" greatly increases the abstract nature of this keyphrase.

4.2 Candidate Persons

The recognition of faces and thus the presence of certain people in video content is challenging. This is primarily due to the large variation of representative images, the different styles, and the different age people can have in video segments. The main difficulties are a lack of online representative images for unknown persons and candidate persons being matched to lookalikes in the video. An example of such conflict is shown in Figure 3. The system correctly identifies "Amanda Knox" in Figure 3(a) but generates a false positive by assuming "Deanna Knox" to be her sister in Figure 3(b).

(a) Correct. (b) Incorrect.

Figure 3: Metadata generated for "Amanda Knoxx".

5. CONCLUSIONS & FUTURE RESEARCH

In this paper, we have introduced a fully automated end-to-end pipeline for generating fine-grained metadata for news broadcast video segments. Our discussion mainly focussed on the automatic construction of training sets and the automatic assessment of the visual representativeness of a keyphrase. In that regard, we have trained a linear SVM-based classifier for each keyphrase, leveraging features extracted from a deep convolutional neural network. Some qualitative evaluation of our system indicates that the proposed system could greatly aid broadcasters in organizing their content, increasing its overall searchability and monetization.

In future research, we will focus on an extensive quantitative analysis of the effectiveness of our system. In addition, we plan to investigate methods to improve the automatic construction of training sets, given that empirical evidence has shown this to be a crucial step in our pipeline. Furthermore, we will improve the accuracy of our algorithm for tag imageability assessment. Finally, we will study several aggregation methods in more detail, as well as the inclusion of temporal information, so to facilitate more effective keyphrase models.

6. ACKNOWLEDGEMENTS

The research presented in this article relates to STEAMER, a MiX-ICON project facilitated by iMinds Media and funded by IWT and Innoviris.

7. REFERENCES

[1] B. Amos, B. Ludwiczuk, J. Harkes, P. Pillai, K. Elgazzar, and M. Satyanarayanan. OpenFace: Face Recognition with Deep Neural Networks. http://github.com/cmusatyalab/openface.

[2] K. Chatfield, R. Arandjelović, O. M. Parkhi, and A. Zisserman. On-the-fly learning for visual search of large-scale image and video datasets. *International Journal of Multimedia Information Retrieval*, 2015.

[3] N. Ikizler-Cinbis, R. Cinbis, and S. Sclaroff. Learning actions from the web. In *12th International Conference on Computer Vision IEEE*, pages 995–1002, 2009.

[4] Y. Jia, E. Shelhamer, J. Donahue, S. Karayev, J. Long, R. Girshick, S. Guadarrama, and T. Darrell. Caffe: Convolutional architecture for fast feature embedding. *arXiv preprint arXiv:1408.5093*, 2014.

[5] S. Kordumova, X. Li, and C. G. M. Snoek. Best practices for learning video concept detectors from social media examples. *Multimedia Tools and Applications*, pages 1291–1315, 2014.

[6] X. Li, C. Snoek, M. Worring, D. Koelma, and A. Smeulders. Bootstrapping visual categorization with relevant negatives. *IEEE Transactions on Multimedia*, pages 933–945, 2013.

[7] K. Simonyan and A. Zisserman. Very deep convolutional networks for large-scale image recognition. *CoRR*, 2014.

[8] D. Stein, E. Apostolidis, V. Mezaris, N. de Abreu Pereira, and J. Müller. Semi-automatic video analysis for linking television to the web. In *FutureTV Workshop*, pages 1–8, 2012.

[9] A. Sun and S. Bhowmick. Quantifying visual-representativeness of social image tags using image tag clarity. In *Social Media Modeling and Computing*, pages 3–23. 2011.

[10] P. Van Der Kreeft, K. Macquarrie, M. Kemman, M. Kleppe, and K. McGuinness. Axes-research 2014; a user-oriented tool for enhanced multimodal search and retrieval in audiovisual libraries. In *12th International Workshop on Content-Based Multimedia Indexing*, pages 1–4, 2014.

[11] P. Viola and M. Jones. Rapid object detection using a boosted cascade of simple features. In *Proceedings of the IEEE Computer Society Conference on Computer Vision and Pattern Recognition.*, pages 511–518, 2001.

Serendipity-driven Celebrity Video Hyperlinking

Shujun Yang[1], Lei Pang[1], Chong-Wah Ngo[1], Benoit Huet[2]
[1]Department of Computer Science, City University of Hong Kong, Hong Kong, China
[2]EURECOM, Sophia Antipolis, France
{xingguinvwu, cactuslei}@gmail.com, cscwngo@cityu.edu.hk, Benoit.Huet@eurecom.fr

ABSTRACT

This demo showcases the utility of video hyperlinks with celebrities as the link anchors and their social circles as targets, aiming to help users quickly explore the *aboutness* of a celebrity by link traversal. Through content analysis, our system embeds hyperlinks into videos such that users can click-and-jump between celebrity faces in different videos to get-to-know their social circles. One peculiar feature is the ability of the system in providing links that maximize users' chance encounter, or serendipitous experience, beyond information need. Our system is enabled by two key components, name-face association and diversity-based ranking, for the *aboutness* and *serendipity* features respectively in hyperlinking. The former component assigns names video faces while mining celebrity social networks. The latter performs topic modeling so as to rank videos based on topic diversity.

CCS Concepts

•Human-centered computing → Hypertext / hypermedia;

Keywords

Video hyperlinking; Face naming; Serendipity

1. INTRODUCTION

Making searchers happy beyond supplying relevant information is a problem seldom being addressed in the field of multimedia retrieval. Video hyperlinking is one such effort initiated by MediaEval [9] and TRECVID [15] for embedding links into videos so as to enable efficient and on-the-fly content navigation between video segments. One usage scenario is detail-on-demand [1, 8, 12, 14], where similar to HTML web pages, a user clicks on an anchor text and the browser leads user to a new page with additional information about the subject of interest.

This paper presents a system for hyperlinking celebrities in videos. Celebrity is picked as the subject of exploration in this demo, due to the fact that the majority of queries and significant amount of video uploads on social sharing platforms concern famous people. According to YouTube trends map, around 80% of popular videos are people related, and among them around 75% are about celebrities. The application scenario is that a user may want to know the social circle of a celebrity. Hyperlinks allow the user quickly learns the circle by listing socially connected celebrities along with their related videos for exploration. Connecting videos based on featuring celebrities will enhance the accessibility of web videos for nonlinear interactive browsing/navigation hence improving user experience.

Our system emphasizes *aboutness* [1] and *serendipity* [13] when recommending videos for hyperlinking. Different from *relevancy* which seeks for similar videos, *aboutness* provides summary along with links to other videos for detailing or explaining the subject of interest. *Serendipity* refers to unexpected but delightful chance encounters, by referring user to additional information that is previously unknown and could potentially "surprise" viewers. Our system models *serendipity* as content diversity, by recommending videos based on topic diversity or novelty. Ideally, the first few ranked videos should cover different perspectives of a subject. By doing so, users quickly grasp new knowledge and hence enhance the chance of experiencing serendipitous browsing. Figure 1 illustrates our system. While a video showing Barack Obama is playing, the user may hover with the mouse or tap on him to expose his social circle composed of Michelle Obama, Jinping Xi, David Cameron, etc. Each celebrity in the circle is linked to a list of videos ranked based on diversity. When selecting Jinping Xi from Obama's social circle, the top-3 videos shown on the right end side highlight different content topic-wise. Specifically, both v_1 and v_3 report meetings between Barack Obama and Jinping Xi in different occasions, and v_2 is about the nuclear problem in North Korea that involves both political leaders.

Existing research efforts mostly treat video hyperlinking as a retrieval task. Concretely, given a query (or link anchor), the task is to recommend videos (or link targets) that will potentially interest users based on relevancy between anchor and target. Examples of approaches include ranking videos by low-level textual-visual features [3, 4, 7, 11], visual concept classifiers [17] and query expansion through linked data [10]. A major drawback of these approaches is that similar or sometimes redundant videos are recommended, rather than the videos that could supplement the anchor for detail-on-demand browsing. Furthermore, these approaches use to return a long list of candidate videos, re-

ICMR'16, June 06-09, 2016, New York, NY, USA
© 2016 ACM. ISBN 978-1-4503-4359-6/16/06. . . $15.00
DOI: http://dx.doi.org/10.1145/2911996.2912029

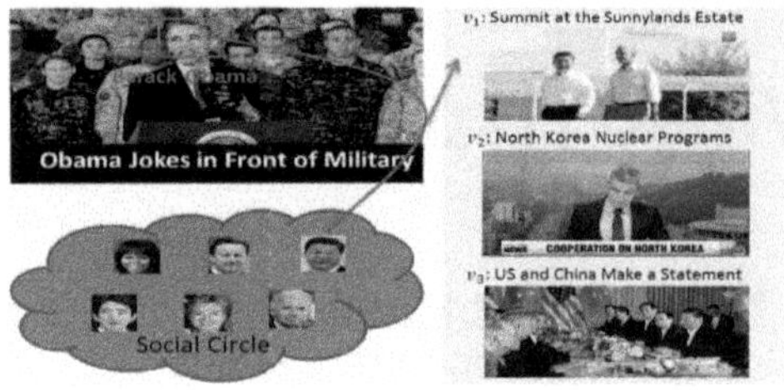

Figure 1: An example of linking Obama to his social circle. Each celebrity (e.g., Jinping Xi) in the circle is further linked to diverse videos elaborating different perspectives of the relationship with Obama.

sulting in the problem of "link explosion" as mentioned by [1]. One exception is the work by [18], which emphasizes serendipity in hyperlinking, by constructing a deep topical structure of 10 hierarchies for weighting the contribution of videos based on topic specificity. Therefore, videos of different granularities in topics could be selectively recommended, which effectively controls the number of videos for serendipitous hyperlinking. Our demo is similar in spirit to [18], specifically to recommend limited but diverse videos useful for exploration, but operates in the domain of social circles. Potentially there are rich information (e.g., anecdote, event, rumor, opinion) to be exploited for hyperlinking in this domain, which are yet to be studied. Particularly, concerning the utility of hyperlinks for helping users navigate in large scale media collections.

2. SYSTEM ARCHITECTURE

We developed two key modules for enabling celebrity hyperlinking; face naming and diversity-based ranking. For practical consideration, face-name corresponding is learned from weakly tagged images crawled from the Web (sections 2.1-2.2). LDA (Latent Dirichlet Allocation) is performed to discover fine-grained topics underlying within the video corpus for novelty ranking (sections 2.3-2.4).

2.1 Name-face association

We employ CRF (Conditional Random Field) for name-face association based on our prior work [16]. CRF considers a rich set of relationships including name-to-face unary energy and multiple face-to-face pairwise energies. This results in a network of faces and names as vertices and energies as edges for name inferencing. Based on person names given in the video metadata, weakly tagged web images are crawled and used for face model training. By these models, unary potential estimates the likelihood of a detected face belonging to a mentioned name in the video metadata. Pairwise potential considers similarities between faces appearing in different shots. In addition, multiple constraints including spatial-temporal proximity of faces and restriction that no two faces in a frame should be labeled the same name are incorporated for pairwise energy modeling. The inference of names is performed by LBP (loopy belief propagation) algorithm, allowing null assignment of names.

2.2 Deep face feature

As in [16], CRF is sensitive to the underlying facial feature representation, especially when the faces undergo moderate to large changes in visual appearance. Different from [16] which represents face with local features extracted from 13 facial regions, deep face feature is employed in our system. We employ the deep model in [2] due to its greater representational efficiency, which achieves state-of-art face recognition performance using only 128-bytes per face. The input to the model is a cropped frontal face which is rectified by Dlib's real-time pose estimation with OpenCV's affine transformation. The deep network is based on NN4 of GoogLeNet style Inception models where the input face resolution is 96×96. The facial feature is extracted from the layer corresponding to face embedding, which is the layer after the deep CNN and L2 normalization. The feature is encoded as a vector in 128 dimension. Different from [16] which employs GMM (Gaussian Mixture Model) for learning, SVM classifiers are trained for each celebrity face model.

2.3 Corpus-wise topic modeling

As in [18], topic modeling is performed so as to measure video similarity based on topic distribution rather than BoW (bag-of-words) representation. As empirically studied in [18], using latent topics has a better chance to retrieve videos with diverse content potentially useful for serendipitous hyperlinking. This is in opposition to BoW modeling where very often only highly similar videos are returned. In the implementation, LDA is performed on the video metadata, or specifically words pooled from title, tag and user description. The number of latent topics is empirically set to be 50, and each topic is modeled as a probability distribution over a set of words. In such a way, each video is represented as a vector of 50 dimensions, where each dimension specifies the likelihood of a video belonging to a topic. Similarity between two videos can thus be straightforwardly measured by cosine similarity.

2.4 Novelty Ranking

As videos are recommended based on celebrity relationship, the first step is to model celebrity co-occurrence in the video corpus. Our system performs person name extraction from metadata and verifies each name against Wikipedia. Basically names without the category tag "birth year" in the Wikipedia pages are removed from processing. The relationship between two names is then calculated by Dice coefficient based on the frequency of two names being tagged in videos. By doing so, the system maintains a sparse graph with celebrities as vertices and edges as closeness between two vertices. This sparse graph is represented as an inverted index. Each entry in the index corresponds to a celebrity linking to his or her social circle, followed by the sets of videos where both celebrities appear.

Using this inverted index, each named face in a video can be quickly hyperlinked with the related celebrities based on co-occurrence. Furthermore, the set of relevant videos can also be easily retrieved for hyperlinking. To limit the number of videos while not linking to redundant videos, we experiment two different methods, based on greedy search and clustering respectively, for diversifying the recommended videos for hyperlinking.

2.4.1 MMR-based greedy search

Inspired by MMR [5], maximal diversity (MD) is used as the criterion for selecting diverse videos. Denote R as the set of all videos having both celebrities, and $S \subset R$ is the subset already selected by the algorithm. Thus, $R \setminus S$ is the

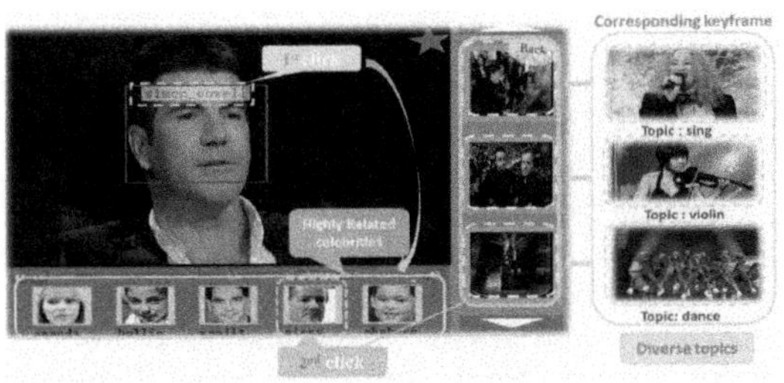

Figure 2: System interface showing how users can explore "Simon Cowell" and his social circle through interacting with hyperlinks for video navigation.

subset of as yet unselected videos. The next video $v_i \in R \backslash S$ to be included in S is selected based on MD, defined as

$$Arg \min_{v_i \in R \backslash S} \max_{v_j \in S} sim(v_i, v_j) \quad (1)$$

At each iteration, $v_i \in R \backslash S$ is compared against every video in S, and its similarity with S is determined based on the highest similarity score. The video to be included into S is the most dissimilar one, i.e., with minimal relevance score, so as to maximally diversify the topics of existing videos in S. The process starts by picking a video from $R \setminus S$ as the first video. The second selected video is the one most diverse from the first video. The remaining videos are then greedily included into S until the desired number of videos is reached. Here, we only select $K = \min(5, N * 0.5)$ videos for hyperlinking, where N is number of videos. We repeat this process by picking every video $v_i \in R$ as the first video. This ends up with N different numbers of lists. The list which has the minimum average similarity of K videos is picked as the recommended list for hyperlinking. Note that if the value of N is large, the process is only repeated for a subset of videos randomly picked. Finally, we match the K selected videos with the remaining $N - K$ videos based on their similarities. In other words, each of the remaining videos is matched to the closest one in the K selected videos. The K videos in the recommended list is ranked based on the number of matches. Similarity between videos is computed using cosine similarity between their 50 dimensional topic vectors (section 2.3).

2.4.2 K-medoids clustering

The second method is based on video clustering by K-medoids, which is a variant of Kmeans algorithm and is more robust to outliers. By clustering on 50 dimension vector resulting from LDA, similar videos are grouped and the idea is to pick one video per group for ranking. We set the number of medoids as $K = \min(5, N * 0.5)$, where N equals to number of videos, and select the most centrally located video (i.e., medoids) of each cluster for hyperlinking. The ranking of videos is based on the size of their clusters.

3. DEMONSTRATION

The demonstration focuses on showcasing the utility of hyperlinks on a dataset consisting of 2,583 videos crawled from YouTube where 141 celebrities have been identified. The average length of a video is about 4 minutes. Figure 2 shows our system's interface which offers three panels users can use for efficient navigation and exploration of celebrity relationships in video collections. The first panel displays a video, and a "star" on the top right corner hints about the availability of a hyperlink. By mouse hovering on the face, the corresponding name "Simon Cowell" is prompted. Further clicking the name shows a list of frequently co-occurring celebrities in the second panel. In Figure 2, the celebrity "Piers Morgan" is selected and the recommended videos are displayed on the third panel based on K-medoids clustering. Each of the videos has a different theme, respectively, "singing", "violin show" and "dancing", where "Simon Cowell" and "Piers Morgan" are both judges for these TV shows. Through these videos, users quickly know the kinds of performances that both celebrities once judged. The ranking of videos also inherently gives the clue that most frequent performances are about "singing".

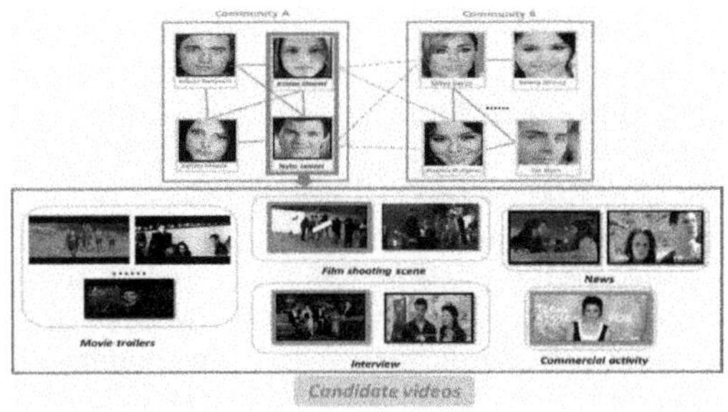

Figure 3: Example of candidate videos (manually grouped into clusters) to be selected and linked for elaborating the relationship between "Kristen Stewart" and "Taylor Lautner". Potentially serendipitous targets are highlighted with red boxes.

4. EVALUATION

This section gives insights about the performance of our system. We first introduce the video dataset used for demonstration, followed by the experimental results for celebrity naming and diversity ranking.

4.1 Dataset

The video corpus is WebV-Cele [6], which consists of 2,583 YouTube videos. A total of 141 celebrities are labeled for 19,240 frontal faces in the dataset. The celebrities altogether form 12 social communities. Figure 3 shows a snapshot of few celebrities in two networks. Take "Kristen Stewart" and "Taylor Lautner" as examples, our system retrieves 12 videos which are relevant to them. When asking a user watching these videos, three videos were picked and regarded as "surprise". Interestingly, while most candidate videos are movie trailers, the selected videos are a raw footage not screening in the film "twilight" and an interview that both celebrities talked about their personal lives. For this example, our system is able to pick two out of the three "surprise" videos as link targets.

4.2 Celebrity Naming

Around 4,000 web images are crawled for training face models for 141 celebrities. Images with more than one face detected are excluded from learning. We employ accuracy, which counts the number of faces correctly labeled, to measure the performance of name-face association. Using deep features for training SVM classifiers, we achieve an accuracy of 52.1%. Further using CRF for probabilistic labeling, the accuracy is boosted to 59.3%, versus 58.4% as reported in [16] using hand-crafted local features and GMM.

4.3 Serendipitous Hyperlinking

We measure serendipity based on video diversity. In the dataset, there are 199 celebrity pairs detected by our system. We rank the celebrity pairs in descending order of their video frequency, and select the top 13 pairs for evaluation. The number of candidates for hyperlinking video to these pairs ranges from 6 to 53. The evaluation is to measure the degree of diversity for top K videos recommended by the system, where $K = \min(5, N * 0.5)$ and N is the number of candidate videos. To generate ground-truth for experiment, an evaluator was recruited to manually group topic-wise similar videos into clusters. The evaluator took 2 days to complete the process, and the number of clusters ranges from 3 to 5 for 13 celebrity pairs. In addition, we asked the evaluator to pick serendipitous videos from each celebrity pair. A total of 26 videos are picked for 13 pairs. We employ cluster recall (CR) to measure the diversity, defined as

$$CR(K) = \frac{clusters(K)}{tc} \tag{2}$$

where $clusters(K)$ is the number of different clusters encountered up to and including the Kth ranked video, and tc is the total number of clusters in the ground-truth. The perfect value for CR is 1.0 when the top K videos cover all the clusters. Our result shows that K-medoids (CR=0.74) outperforms MMR (CR=0.66). Using K-medoids, for 6 out of 13 celebrity pairs, our system is able to recommend serendipitous videos picked by the evaluator.

5. CONCLUSION

We have presented a system allowing users to navigate in video collections by following hyperlinks created based on celebrity circles. Our analysis, shows that our approach, using face-naming and topic diversity modeling is able to effectively select serendipitous videos. It was noticed that the evaluator favored amusing or unexpected video (e.g., two celebrities introducing a cute cat). Recommending such videos is beyond the capability of the current system. Future work will include online learning of personal interest and analysis of emotional and semantic cues in videos for serendipitous videos detection.

6. ACKNOWLEDGEMENT

The work described in this paper was fully supported by a grant from the Research Grants Council of the Hong Kong Special Administrative Region, China (CityU 11210514), and a grant from the National Hi-Tech Research and Development Program (863 Program) of China under Grant 2014AA015102.

7. REFERENCES

[1] R. Aly, R. J. Ordelman, M. Eskevich, G. J. Jones, and S. Chen. Linking inside a video collection: What and how to measure? In *WWW*, 2013.

[2] B. Amos, B. Ludwiczuk, J. Harkes, P. Pillai, K. Elgazzar, and M. Satyanarayanan. OpenFace: Face Recognition with Deep Neural Networks. http://github.com/cmusatyalab/openface.

[3] W. Bailer, M. Lokaj, and H. Stiegler. Context in video search: Is close-by good enough when using linking? In *ICMR*, 2014.

[4] C. A. Bhatt, N. Pappas, M. Habibi, and A. Popescu-Belis. Multimodal reranking of content-based recommendations for hyperlinking video snippets. In *ICMR*, 2014.

[5] J. Carbonell and J. Goldstein. The use of mmr, diversity-based reranking for reordering documents and producing summaries. In *SIGIR*, 1998.

[6] Z. Chen, C.-W. Ngo, W. Zhang, J. Cao, and Y.-G. Jiang. Name-face association in web videos: A large-scale dataset, baselines, and open issues. *JCST*, 29(5):785–798, 2014.

[7] Z. Cheng, X. Li, J. Shen, and A. Hauptmann. Cmu-smu@ trecvid 2015: Video hyperlinking. 2015.

[8] J. Doherty, A. Girgensohn, J. Helfman, F. Shipman, and L. Wilcox. Detail-on-demand hypervideo. In *ACM MM*. ACM, 2003.

[9] M. Eskevich, R. Aly, D. Racca, R. Ordelman, S. Chen, and G. Jones. The search and hyperlinking task at mediaeval 2014. In *Working Notes Proceedings of the MediaEval 2014 Multimedia Benchmark Workshop*, 2014.

[10] M. Eskevich, G. J. Jones, R. Aly, R. J. Ordelman, S. Chen, D. Nadeem, C. Guinaudeau, G. Gravier, P. Sébillot, T. de Nies, P. Debevere, R. Van de Walle, P. Galuscakova, P. Pecina, and M. Larson. Multimedia information seeking through search and hyperlinking. In *ICMR*, 2013.

[11] M. Eskevich, G. J. F. Jones, C. Wartena, M. Larson, R. Aly, T. Verschoor, and R. Ordelman. Comparing retrieval effectiveness of alternative content segmentation methods for internet video search. In *CBMI*, 2012.

[12] M. Eskevich, H. Nguyen, M. Sahuguet, and B. Huet. Hyper video browser: Search and hyperlinking in broadcast media. In *ACM MM*, 2015.

[13] A. Foster and N. Ford. Serendipity and information seeking: an empirical study. *Journal of Documentation*, 59(3):321–340, 2003.

[14] A. Girgensohn, L. Wilcox, F. Shipman, and S. Bly. Designing affordances for the navigation of detail-on-demand hypervideo. In *AVI*, 2004.

[15] P. Over, G. Awad, M. Michel, J. Fiscus, W. Kraaij, A. F. Smeaton, G. Quénot, and R. Ordelman. Trecvid 2015 – an overview of the goals, tasks, data, evaluation mechanisms and metrics. In *TRECVID*, 2015.

[16] L. Pang and C.-W. Ngo. Unsupervised celebrity face naming in web videos. *IEEE Transactions on Multimedia*, 17(6):854–866, 2015.

[17] B. Safadi, M. Sahuguet, and B. Huet. When textual and visual information join forces for multimedia retrieval. In *ICMR*, 2014.

[18] A.-R. Simon, R. Bois, G. Gravier, P. Sébillot, E. Morin, and S. Moens. Hierarchical topic models for language-based video hyperlinking. In *Workshop on Speech, Language and Audio in ACM Multimedia*, 2015.

Complura: Exploring and Leveraging a Large-scale Multilingual Visual Sentiment Ontology

Hongyi Liu[*†], Brendan Jou[*†], Tao Chen[*†], Mercan Topkara[*‡], Nikolaos Pappas[*§], Miriam Redi[*¶], Shih-Fu Chang[†]

†Columbia University, New York, NY USA
‡JW Player, New York, NY USA
§Idiap Research Institute/EPFL, Martigny, Switzerland
¶Yahoo, London, UK

ABSTRACT

What would someone from another culture think of this photograph I just took? Would they think my picture of this 'wilted flower' was also sentimentally positive or would they perceive it negatively instead? Or what if I wanted to find other photographs that are semantically related to my image as well as sentimentally sensitive, but from other cultures? In fact, this cultural and sentimental relevancy are features that we would expect of any recommender system and query expansion engine, respectively. Motivated by this, we present an online demonstration of a system called **Complura**. Our system implements three major functions: an interactive multilingual ontology browser, a cross-lingual image-based sentiment analyzer, and a culturally-coherent, sentiment-aware image query expansion engine. We ground our system on a multilingual visual sentiment ontology, containing over 10k sentiment-polarized visual concepts over 12 languages and over 7.3M images.

CCS Concepts

•Information systems → Multimedia databases; Recommender systems; Sentiment analysis; •Human-centered computing → Information visualization; Visualization toolkits;

Keywords

Multilingual; Culture; Ontology; Browsing Interfaces; Sentiment Analysis; Query Expansion

1. INTRODUCTION

The uniqueness and intertwining of culture, language and sentiment are some of the things that make our world so diverse and beautiful. Amidst the tremendous amount of social multimedia content shared around world each day, how images in various languages are used to express language-specific concepts, as well as how these concepts connect to emotion and sentiment remain open questions. Recently, a large-scale multilingual visual sentiment ontology (MVSO), consisting of over 15,000 sentiment- and emotion-polarized visual bi-concepts called adjective-noun pairs (ANP) over 12 languages, was proposed for language-dependent content analysis [6]. The adjective-noun pair semantic structure used in the ontology is a powerful construct where the noun component defines a visually grounded, and hopefully machine-detectable object or concept, and the adjective contributes a sentiment or emotion attachment. This multilingual visual sentiment ontology provides researchers a rich information source for analyzing cultural connections and characteristics of visual sentiment across language lines. In

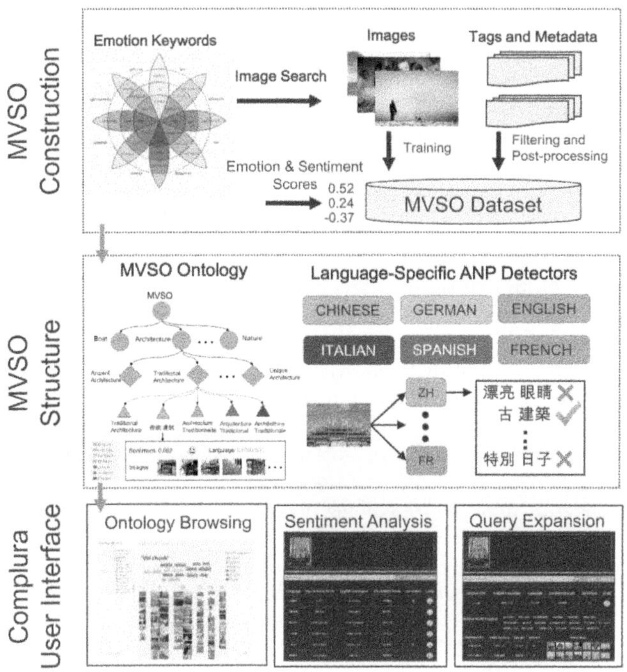

Figure 1: *Complura* System Architecture Overview. The Multilingual Visual Sentiment Ontology [6] (MVSO) forms the basis of *Complura*'s backend.

[*]Denotes equal contribution.

ICMR'16, June 06-09, 2016, New York, NY, USA

DOI: http://dx.doi.org/10.1145/2911996.2912030

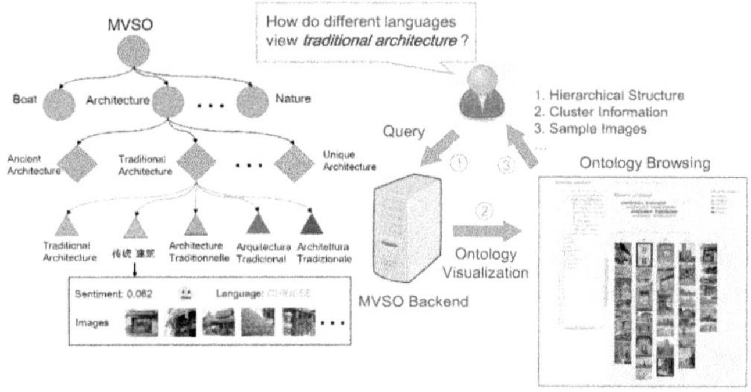

Figure 2: Workflow of *Complura*'s Ontology Browser. A researcher with a question or hypothesis about how visual affective concepts are understood across languages or sentimentally portrayed can explore the MVSO corpus by querying Complura and exploring the ontology. *Complura* visualizes the hierarchical structure, cluster information and shows related sample images in mined from Flickr to help users to answer their research questions about multilingual visual sentiment.

addition, it carries the potential for novel augmentations to retrieval and recommendation tasks in social media.

In order to explore hierarchically structured information, a number of systems have been proposed in the past [2]. For example, a node-link paradigm is utilized by many systems [9, 5, 10] for visualization, while others like *CropCircles* [14] use concentric circles to represent hierarchical ontology. And some hybrid works like *Knoocks* [7], *OntoTrix* [1] and *NodeTrix* [4] combine node-link, nested blocks and adjacency matrix representations. These systems provide deep insights into the visualization of their respective ontologies, but they seldom provide integrated functions that allow users to leverage the ontology for other purposes.

In this work, we aim to answer the question of how to understand and leverage the cultural influence given the massive number of images shared in social media expressing strong sentiments and emotions. Our prior work [6] focused on the construction and analysis of the MVSO dataset, but it did not provide an intuitive system for individuals to explore and leverage this ontology. We present an integrated system called **Complura**[1], that allows users to formulate and verify hypothesis by interactively browsing and exploring the ontology, examine the image sentiment of different languages, and perform cultural-coherently expanded image query through leveraging the MVSO dataset.

Our proposed system provides three major functions: (1) an interactive ontology browsing interface for a multilingual visual sentiment ontology; (2) a language-specific image-based sentiment analyzer; and (3) a culturally-coherent image query expansion engine with sentiment-aware sensitivity. To the best of our knowledge, **Complura** is the first system to explore and utilize the hierarchical structure of such a large-scale multilingual visual sentiment ontology.

2. ONTOLOGY ORGANIZATION

We develop **Complura** on top the Multilingual Visual Sentiment Ontology (MVSO) [6] and its accompanying image dataset because of its rich structured cross-cultural information with visual sentiment in different languages. This makes it possible for us to both evaluate the sentiment of visual content and create novel applications in a multicultural context. The development of the MVSO in [6] can be summarized in two major stages: a data aggregation and a ontology construction stage.

Table 1: Summary Statistics of the Multilingual Visual Sentiment Ontology (MVSO) Dataset [6].

#Languages	12
Total #ANPs	15,630
Total #Images	7,368,364
Average #Images/ANP	471

2.1 Data Aggregation

The data aggregation stage of MVSO dataset begins with a set of emotion seed keywords selected from Plutchik's Wheel of Emotions [12]. These seed keywords, inspired by psychology theory, including *joy, trust, fear*, and so on, are translated by native speakers of 12 different languages: Arabic, Chinese, Dutch, English, French, German, Italian, Persian, Polish, Russian, Spanish and Turkish. These keywords are used to query for images along with their tags and metadata on the social multimedia platform, Flickr[2]. Part-of-speech labelling and adjective-noun combinations are performed to generate semantic structures called adjective-noun pairs (ANPs), such as *young children*, *smiling face* and *nice car*. The final ANP set is obtained through a course-to-fine filtering process on candidate ANPs based on language, semantics, sentiment, frequency and diversity. Sentiment and emotion scores are also calculated and crowdsourced for each ANP. A set of 15,630 ANPs are ultimately used to also create a multilingual image dataset of over 7.3M social images. And the images are used in [6] to train convolutional neural network (CNN)-based, language-specific visual concept detectors of ANPs [8] on a subset of six major languages cover over 10k of the ANPs. The classification performance of the ANP detectors range from ~10.1% for English on 4,342 ANPs to ~30.1% for German on 275 ANPs. A more detailed explanation can be found in [6].

2.2 Ontology Construction

The construction of hierarchically structured ANPs in the MVSO follows a bottom-up strategy, including exact matching, noun-based grouping and synonym-based group merging. In particular, we first group ANPs of different languages that share the same English translation together. For example, 传统 建筑 (ZH), *architecture traditionnelle* (FR), *architettura tradizionale* (ES), *traditional architecture* (EN) are grouped together as they all have the same English translation (*traditional architecture*). Then all the groups, or clusters, represented by English translation of ANPs, are further grouped by noun. English translations like *ancient architecture, beautiful architecture, traditional architecture* are grouped as they share the same noun (*architecture*). And finally, noun groups that are synonyms, such as *clothes* and *dress* are merged together to enhance the compactness and diversity of the ontology.

[1]http://mvso.cs.columbia.edu/complura

[2]https://www.flickr.com

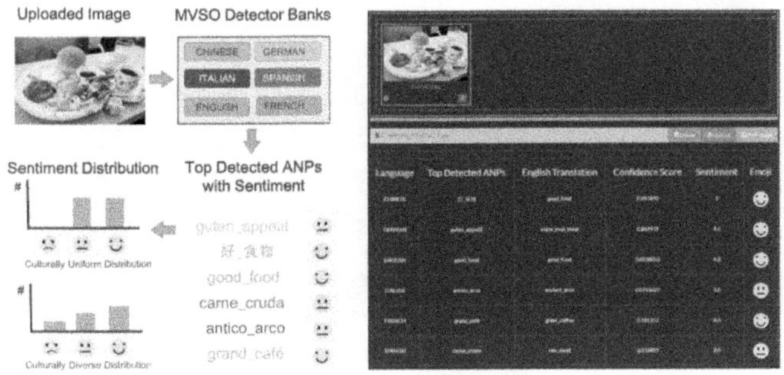

Figure 3: *Left*: Three-stage workflow of image sentiment analysis across languages. Given an input image, top detected ANPs of different languages with corresponding sentiment scores are returned. *Right*: Screenshot of interface for image sentiment analysis.

3. SYSTEM OVERVIEW

As shown in Figure 1, our system **Complura** builds on two main aspects of MVSO: the ontology and language-specific ANP detectors. The ontology refers to the hierarchical structure of the ANPs, and is valuable for capturing mid-level, sentiment-biased semantic information across languages, where each ANP is associated with a sentiment value and related images. There are also six ANP detector banks trained in [6] capable of detecting the presence of ANPs from Chinese, German, English, Italian, Spanish and French in images. The goal of **Complura** is to assist users in exploring and leveraging the ontology for semantic analysis of visual content across multiple languages. We implement three major features: ontology browsing, sentiment analysis and multilingual image-based query expansion.

3.1 Ontology Browsing

We focus on high interaction browsing of the Multilingual Visual Sentiment Ontology in **Complura**. The ontology browser enables users to formulate hypothesis, choose controlled categories, and visualize image differences tagged with different languages. Given a scenario like the one shown in Figure 2, if a user wants to research the cultural difference of the visual concept *traditional architecture*, they need only use the ontology browser in our system which visualizes MVSO in a succinct, intuitive and interactive browser interface. In the web interface, as shown in the bottom-right of Figure 2, the ontology browser consists of three main panels: the ontology-structure panel (left), word cloud panel (top-right) and image comparison panel (bottom-right).

The hierarchical structure is visualized using an interactive tree library[3], which provides folder-like expansion interactions for the user to navigate through the ontology. This approach offers a top-down view of the whole ontology. For non-leaf nodes in the ontology, the word cloud panel allows user to intuitively grasp the content of certain node. When a user mouses over a word cloud item, a hover box is shown and displays additional contextual information for that item like English translations and number of child nodes. As shown in the Figure 2, each column of the visualization page (right side) show a maximum of eight images related to specific ANP, and a language may occupy multiple columns, depending on the number of ANPs that appear in this group. All the ANPs in a group share the same English translation, which generally corresponds to their semantic coherence. This column-based panel allows users to compare both inter- and intra-language connections and discrepancies of a certain ANP, all at the same time.

Consider again the scenario where a researcher wants to explore the cross-cultural differences of a visual concept like *traditional architecture*, they can directly compare the visual difference of sample images of *traditional architecture* between different languages on a single page in **Complura**. In addition, they can easily navigate to the siblings of the target node, such as *ancient architecture*, *modern architecture* and so on. Without this ontology visualizer, users may have had to manually find the translations of *traditional architecture* in different languages, and then perform text- or tag-based image query on search engines like Google Images or Flickr, which is tedious and inconvenient.

3.2 Ontology Applications

Here, we utilize the unique ontological structure and the language-specific ANP detectors of MVSO to implement two novel applications: language-specific image sentiment analysis and culturally-coherent image query expansion.

3.2.1 Multilingual Image Sentiment Analysis

In our ontology, each ANP is associated with a sentiment score, which is calculated using SentiStrength [13] and SentiWordnet [3], and verified by crowdsourcing validation [11]. Using these scores, we seek to perform multilingual sentiment analysis for a given image using the MVSO ANP detector banks [6] as a proxy.

Imagine a scenario where a Chinese businessperson is designing a website to advertise *good food* or *modern art* but wants to expand to markets of different languages. In this case, it critical that they pick the culturally-sensitive images to use in these other markets. One solution that **Complura** provides is an application mode where users can check if an image is appropriate. A user can choose and upload an image to find if the image is suitable for foreign markets. We run our ANP detector banks from various languages on it and given the top detected ANP in each language, and the user can make a judgment on its cultural sensitivity, e.g. based on the sentiment of the top detected ANP. In **Complura**, we enable an option for the user to also find more images of the detected ANPs in foreign languages. By checking the sentiment distribution of the detected ANPs across different languages, the user can determine whether their image is uniformly perceived in sentiment across cultures. This multilingual sentiment analysis process is shown in Figure 3.

3.2.2 Multicultural Image Query Expansion

Another application of MVSO and feature in **Complura** is an image query expansion engine with cultural and sentiment coherence using the semantic structure and detectors in [6]. As illustrated in the Figure 4, users begin by choosing a specified ANP detector of certain language and upload an image to the server. The system then detects ANPs in specified language, and ANPs with culturally-coherent semantics are retrieved through traversing a related sub-tree in the ontology. Some results are then pruned by ANP detector confidence scores as well as sentiment scores of re-

[3]https://www.jstree.com

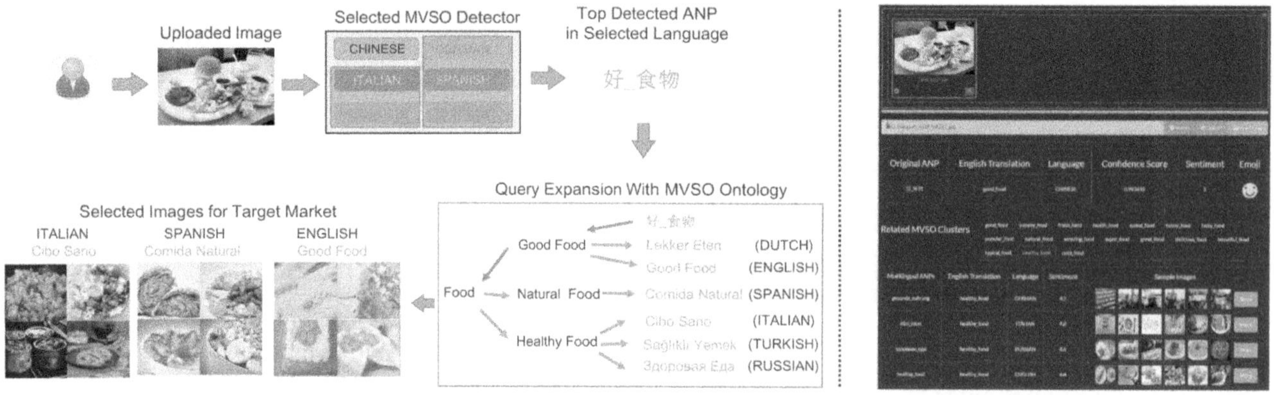

Figure 4: *Left:* Workflow of sentiment sensitive image query expansion across languages. Given an image and selected language, the top detected ANP using detectors of that language is applied toward query expansion by discovering related ANPs in the hierarchical structure of the ontology. Sample images and related ANPs are returned to user for further comparison and selection. *Right:* Screenshot of interface for query expansion.

trieved ANPs. Thus, our system is able to return ANPs of the specified language, together with other ANPs that are semantically- and sentimentally-coherent in other languages. Image query expansion is then achieved by simply returning images associated with the retrieved multilingual ANPs.

Following the same scenario in Section 3.2.1, the Chinese businessperson can also perform image query expansion using **Complura**. After uploading a target image and selecting the origin language, i.e. Chinese in this case, **Complura** will then run the Chinese ANP detectors on the image. The system maps the detected Chinese ANPs to the top MVSO clusters that elicit distinct and uniform semantics. From each of these mapped MVSO clusters, the user can then view the English translated meanings and the sentiment of the retrieved multilingual ANPs. We also show sample images related to retrieved ANPs from the other languages. Compared with the image sentiment analysis application, which focuses on checking the "correctness" of visual content across languages, **Complura**'s image query expansion aims to provide the user with images that have semantic and sentimental coherence across multiple languages. Thus, users are able to pick suitable images that are associated with relevant ANPs for each foreign market.

4. CONCLUSIONS & FUTURE WORK

We have presented a web-based system called **Complura** for exploring and leveraging a Multilingual Visual Sentiment Ontology [6]. **Complura** is built on hierarchically organized sentiment-biased visual concepts and language-specific adjective-noun pair detectors. **Complura** implements three major functions: an interactive multilingual ontology browser, a cross-lingual image-based sentiment analyzer and a culturally-coherent, sentiment-sensitive image query expansion engine. We provided corresponding usage scenarios for each function to show that it is a convenient tool that facilitates multilingual content analysis for researchers and illustrated its potential business value.

In the future, we plan to enhance our system along two major dimensions. The first is to enlarge the coverage in [6] to include more comprehensive entities, e.g. more ANPs across more languages. In addition, we want to explore other human factors such as gender and age to add more diversity.

5. REFERENCES

[1] B. Bach, G. Legostaev, and E. Pietriga. Visualizing populated ontologies with OntoTrix. In *Intl Journ. on Semantic Web & Info. Sys.*, 2010.

[2] N. Bikakis and T. Sellis. Exploration and visualization in the web of big linked data: A survey of the state of the art. *arXiv preprint arXiv:1601.08059*, 2016.

[3] A. Esuli and F. Sebastiani. SentiWordnet: A publicly available lexical resource for opinion mining. In *Language Resources and Evaluation Conf. (LREC)*, volume 6, 2006.

[4] N. Henry, J.-D. Fekete, and M. J. McGuffin. Nodetrix: A hybrid visualization of social networks. *IEEE Trans. on Vis. and Comp. Graphics*, 13(6), 2007.

[5] W. Hop, S. de Ridder, F. Frasincar, and F. Hogenboom. Using hierarchical edge bundles to visualize complex ontologies in GLOW. In *ACM Symp. on Applied Computing (SAC)*, 2012.

[6] B. Jou*, T. Chen*, N. Pappas*, M. Redi*, M. Topkara*, and S.-F. Chang. Visual affect around the world: A large-scale multilingual visual sentiment ontology. In *ACM Intl Conf. on Multimedia (MM)*, 2015.

[7] S. Kriglstein and R. Motschnig-Pitrik. Knoocks: New visualization approach for ontologies. In *Intl Conf. on Info. Vis. (InfoVis)*, 2008.

[8] A. Krizhevsky, I. Sutskever, and G. E. Hinton. ImageNet classification with deep convolutional neural networks. In *Adv. in Neural Info. Processing Sys. (NIPS)*, 2012.

[9] S. Lohmann, S. Negru, F. Haag, and T. Ertl. Visualizing ontologies with VOWL. *Semantic Web*.

[10] E. Motta, P. Mulholland, S. Peroni, M. d'Aquin, J. M. Gomez-Perez, V. Mendez, and F. Zablith. A novel approach to visualizing and navigating ontologies. In *Intl Conf. on the Semantic Web (ISWC)*. Springer, 2011.

[11] N. Pappas, M. Redi, M. Topkara, B. Jou, H. Liu, T. Chen, and S.-F. Chang. Multilingual visual sentiment concept matching. In *ACM Intl Conf. on Multimedia Retrieval (ICMR)*, 2016.

[12] R. Plutchik. *Emotion: A Psychoevolutionary Synthesis.* Harper & Row, 1980.

[13] M. Thelwall, K. Buckley, G. Paltoglou, D. Cai, and A. Kappas. Sentiment strength detection in short informal text. *Journ. of Ameri. Soci. for Info. Sci. and Tech.*, 61(12), 2010.

[14] T. D. Wang and B. Parsia. *CropCircles: Topology Sensitive Visualization of OWL Class Hierarchies.* Springer, 2006.

Multimodal Event Detection and Summarization in Large Scale Image Collections

Manos Schinas
CERTH-ITI
Thessaloniki, Greece
manosetro@iti.gr

Symeon Papadopoulos
CERTH-ITI
Thessaloniki, Greece
papadop@iti.gr

Georgios Petkos
CERTH-ITI
Thessaloniki, Greece
gpetkos@iti.gr

Yiannis Kompatsiaris
CERTH-ITI
Thessaloniki, Greece
ikom@iti.gr

Pericles A. Mitkas
Aristotle University of
Thessaloniki, Greece
mitkas@eng.auth.gr

ABSTRACT

This paper describes a multimodal graph-based approach to address the problem of event detection and summarization in large scale image collections. A first version of our system was presented in the Yahoo-Flickr Event Summarization Challenge of ACM Multimedia 2015 [6]. The objective of the approach is to automatically detect events within millions of photos and summarizing them efficiently for user consumption. The presented approach uses a moving time window over the collection of multimedia items to build a same-event image graph and applies graph clustering to detect events. In addition, it makes use of a graph-based diversity-oriented ranking algorithm to summarize instances of the detected events. A demo of the system is online at http://mklab.iti.gr/acmmm2015-gc/.

Keywords

Event Detection, Clustering, Event Summarization

1. INTRODUCTION

Due to the wide use of media sharing platforms, increasing amounts of diverse multimedia content become available online. Therefore, there is a great need for information systems that can effectively organize such content. As real-world events are key parts of social life, the organization of content around them is an obvious, yet effective, way for navigating and searching large multimedia collections.

In this paper, we describe a prototype system aiming at the detection and summarization of events from a set of about 100 million images [7]. To handle the massive scale of the collection, we opted for an incremental approach that uses a sliding time-window. During this procedure, a graph of images is constructed, and a graph clustering algorithm is applied to detect events. To keep track of evolving events the system merges newly detected into previously detected events. To perform summarization, a graph-based ranking algorithm is applied per event to produce a diverse set of images, ranked by their importance.

ICMR'16, June 06 - 09, 2016, New York, NY, USA

ISBN 978-1-4503-4359-6/16/06...$15.00

DOI: http://dx.doi.org/10.1145/2911996.2912031

2. SYSTEM OVERVIEW

The presented system consists of three components: event detection and tracking, event summarization, and event presentation. The detection and tracking component identifies events per timeslot and keeps track of their evolution across timeslots. The summarization component genarates a summary per event by calculating a score for each image in it. Finally, event presentation is the online component of the system, used to present the detected events to end users.

2.1 Event Detection and Tracking

The system uses a sliding time-window to detect and keep track of events. As the window moves forwards, new images are inserted into the window while others are removed. For images within a given timeslot we test whether they are related to the same event by use of the Same Event Model (SEM) [3]. This takes as input the set of per modality similarities between two images and predicts how likely it is that they belong to the same event. More details on SEM can be found in [4]. A graph of images $\mathcal{G}_I$ is constructed, in which the existence of an edge between a pair of images denotes the positive prediction of the SEM. Subsequently, a graph-based clustering algorithm is applied on $\mathcal{G}_I$ to obtain a full clustering. Finally, the method either merges these clusters into events from previous timeslots or creates new events.

As the time-window moves forward, new images are inserted into the image graph $\mathcal{G}_I$. At the same time, the out-of-window images and the corresponding edges are removed. For the newly inserted images, edges between them and im-

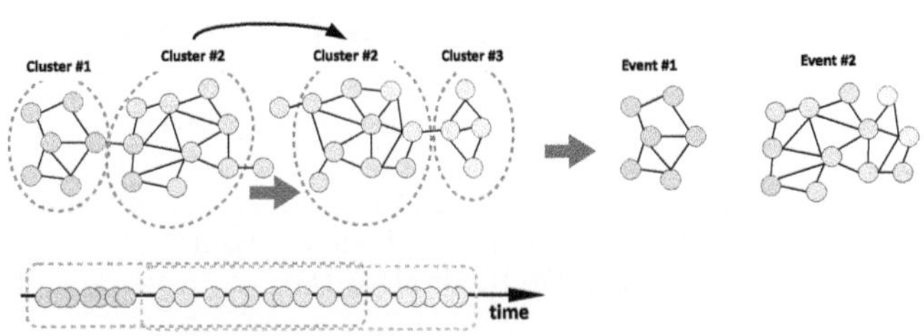

Figure 1: Event tracking in successive timeslots.

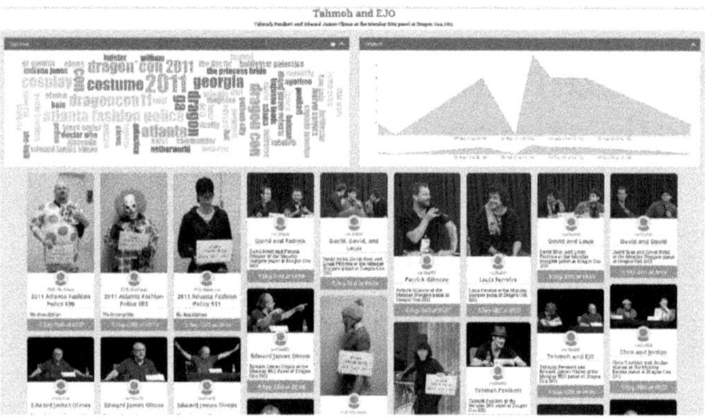

Figure 3: Example of event summary.

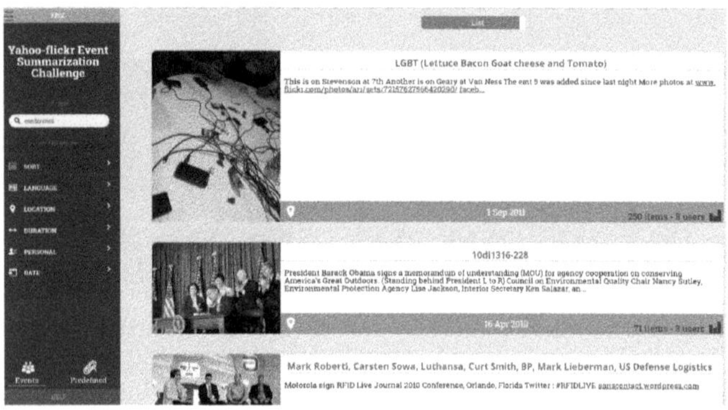

Figure 2: A view of the system that depicts a list of detected events.

ages already in the graph are calculated based on the SEM. To limit the number of SEM evaluations and improve scalability, we follow an approximate k-nearest neighbor graph construction approach, by using an algorithm named NN-Descent [1]. To detect the events in a time window we used the Structural Clustering Algorithm for Networks (SCAN) [8]. We apply SCAN on $\mathcal{G}_I$ to identify dense sub-graphs of images that represent the events in this timeslot.

As new events are detected, the system attempts to associate them with events from previous timeslots. To identify that two clusters are referring to the same event we use the structural similarity between the underlying sub-graphs, expressed as the Jaccard coefficient of their edges. If this similarity exceeds a certain threshold (0.6), we assume that the later sub-graph is arising from the previous one and therefore we merge them into a single event. In addition, we check for *inactive* events, which are the events having no new inserted images for the last three timeslots.

2.2 Event Summarization and Presentation

Our goal is to generate a concise summary of a selected event e for an arbitrary time-frame. To support this at retrieval time, we calculate a significance score for each event image according to its position on the event sub-graph. This calculation is based on the *MGraph* summarization method [5], which utilizes the DivRank algorithm [2], a variant of PageRank that aims at diversity. In our case, we create segments corresponding to one-day timeslots, and apply scoring in the same way as [5]. At the end of this process, for an event lasting D timeslots, we have a rank of the images within each time-slot $t_i, i = 1...D$. At retrieval time, we use the DivRank scores to generate a summary of arbitrary length. To achieve this, we iterate over the event timeslots and keep the top scored images using a greedy approach.

To facilitate event retrieval, we added a set of filters that supports exploration of the events (Figure 2). These include time-, location- and user-based filtering. More specifically, for each event we calculate whether it is *local*, *regional* or *global*. Also, events with images from a single user are tagged as *personal* and event that last only one day are tagged as single-day events. Regarding the event view (Figure 3), the end user can select a summary of the event or retrieve all the images related to it ordered by recency or relevance.

3. ACKNOWLEDGMENTS

This work was supported by the REVEAL project, partially funded by the European Commission, under contract number FP7-610928.

4. REFERENCES

[1] W. Dong, C. Moses, and K. Li. Efficient k-nearest neighbor graph construction for generic similarity measures. In *Proceedings of the 20th international conference on World wide web*, pages 577–586. ACM, 2011.

[2] Q. Mei, J. Guo, and D. Radev. Divrank: The interplay of prestige and diversity in information networks. In *Proceedings of the 16th ACM SIGKDD International Conference on Knowledge Discovery and Data Mining*, KDD '10, pages 1009–1018, NY, USA, 2010. ACM.

[3] G. Petkos, S. Papadopoulos, and Y. Kompatsiaris. Social event detection using multimodal clustering and integrating supervisory signals. In *Proceedings of the 2nd ACM International Conference on Multimedia Retrieval*, ICMR '12, pages 23:1–23:8, New York, NY, USA, 2012. ACM.

[4] G. Petkos, S. Papadopoulos, E. Schinas, and Y. Kompatsiaris. Graph-based multimodal clustering for social event detection in large collections of images. In *Proceedings of the 20th Anniversary International Conference on MultiMedia Modeling - Volume 8325*, MMM 2014, pages 146–158, New York, NY, USA, 2014. Springer-Verlag New York, Inc.

[5] M. Schinas, S. Papadopoulos, Y. Kompatsiaris, and P. Mitkas A. Visual event summarization on social media using topic modelling and graph-based ranking algorithms. In *Proceedings of the ACM International Conference on Multimedia Retrieval*, ICMR 2015, 2015.

[6] M. Schinas, S. Papadopoulos, G. Petkos, Y. Kompatsiaris, and P. A. Mitkas. Multimodal graph-based event detection and summarization in social media streams. In *Proceedings of the 23rd Annual ACM Conference on Multimedia Conference*, pages 189–192. ACM, 2015.

[7] B. Thomee, D. A. Shamma, G. Friedland, B. Elizalde, K. Ni, D. Poland, D. Borth, and L.-J. Li. The new data and new challenges in multimedia research. *arXiv preprint arXiv:1503.01817*, 2015.

[8] X. Xu, N. Yuruk, Z. Feng, and T. A. J. Schweiger. Scan: A structural clustering algorithm for networks. In *Proceedings of the 13th ACM SIGKDD International Conference on Knowledge Discovery and Data Mining*, KDD '07, pages 824–833, New York, NY, USA, 2007. ACM.

Multimodal Analysis of User-Generated Content in Support of Social Media Applications

Rajiv Ratn Shah
School of Computing, National University of Singapore, Singapore
rajiv@comp.nus.edu.sg

ABSTRACT

The number of user-generated multimedia content (UGC) online has increased rapidly in recent years due to the ubiquitous availability of smartphones, cameras, and affordable network infrastructures. Thus, it attracts companies to provide diverse multimedia-related services such as preference-aware multimedia recommendations, multimedia-based e–learning, and event summarization from a large collection of multimedia content. However, a real-world UGC is complex and extracting semantics from only multimedia content is difficult because suitable concepts may be exhibited in different representations. Modern devices capture contextual information in conjunction with a multimedia content, which greatly facilitates in the semantics understanding of the multimedia content. Thus, it is beneficial to analyse UGC from multiple modalities such as multimedia content and contextual information (*e.g.*, spatial and temporal information). This doctoral research studies the multimodal analysis of UGC in support of above-mentioned social media problems. We present our proposed approaches, results, and works in progress on these problems.

Keywords

Multimodal analysis; UGC; Social media applications

1. INTRODUCTION AND MOTIVATION

Due to advancements in technologies, capturing UGC such as user-generated images (UGIs) and user-generated videos (UGVs) anytime and anywhere, and then instantly sharing them on social media platforms has become a very popular activity. Therefore, it necessities social media companies to understand the semantics and sentics of UGC in order to provide diverse multimedia-related services. However, it is very challenging due to the following reasons: (i) the difficulty in capturing the semantics of UGC, (ii) the existence of noise in available metadata, (iii) the difficulty in handling big size datasets, (iv) the difficulty in learning user preferences, and (v) the insufficient accessibility and searchability

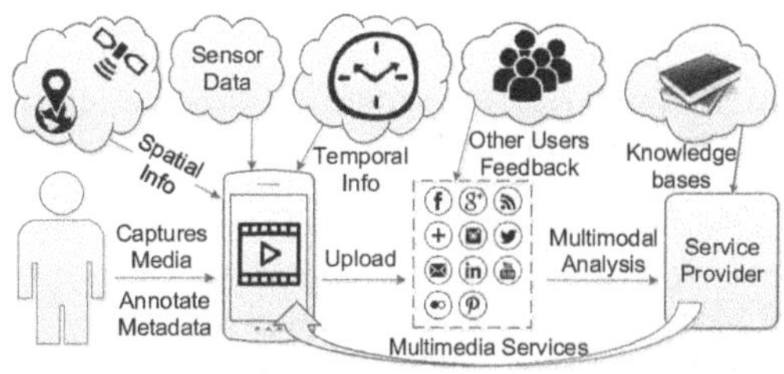

Figure 1: Overview of our approach.

of video content. Since multimodal information augments knowledge bases by inferring semantics and sentics from unstructured multimedia content and contextual information, we leverage it in our proposed approaches to the following three social media problems. First, we answer the automatic soundtrack recommendation task for UGVs [16, 17]. Next, we work on the task of automatic lecture video segmentation [14, 15]. Finally, we address the automatic event summarization task from a large collection of UGIs [13].

Sound is a very important aspect that contributes greatly to the appeal of a UGV when it is being viewed. However, many outdoor UGVs lack a certain appeal because their soundtracks consist mostly of ambient background noise (*e.g.*, environmental sounds such as cars passing by). Thus, it entails to replace the background noise of the UGV with a matching soundtrack that matches with scenes, locations, and users' preferences by exploiting both content and contextual information. However, generating soundtracks for the UGV is not easy in mobile environment due to the following reasons: (i) traditionally it is tedious and time-consuming for a user to add a custom soundtrack to the UGV and (ii) an important aspect is that a good soundtrack should match and enhance the overall mood of the UGV. We present a fast and effective heuristic ranking approach based on heterogeneous late fusion by jointly considering three aspects: venue categories, visual scenes, and the listening history of the user. First, we predict scene moods from a real-world video dataset that was collected from the user's daily outdoor activities. Second, we perform heuristic rankings to fuse the predicted confidence score of multiple models. Finally, we customize the video soundtrack recommendation functionality to make it compatible with mobile devices. Further, we consider other areas such as eduction where UGVs have a significant impact on society.

Due to rapid growth in digital lecture videos online, a multimedia-based e–learning system such as MIT OpenCourseWare[1] has become an important learning environ-

ICMR'16, June 06-09, 2016, New York, NY, USA
© 2016 ACM. ISBN 978-1-4503-4359-6/16/06. . . $15.00
DOI: http://dx.doi.org/10.1145/2911996.2912032

[1] www.ocw.mit.edu/

ment which uses electronic educational technologies as a platform for teaching and learning activities. Since a specific topic of interest is often discussed in only a few minutes of a long lecture video recording, it is often relatively easy to find relevant videos in an archive but difficult to find proper positions within the videos. Websites such as VideoLectures.NET enable students to access different topics within lecture videos. However they determine the topics based on the manual annotation of segment boundaries, which is a very time consuming, subjective, error prone, and costly process. Thus, it necessities a video segmentation system that can automatically determine segment boundaries accurately from a lecture video despite its quality is not sufficiently high. We argue that the presence of contextual information in conjunction with UGVs assists in an effective temporal segmentation. Thus, we present the ATLAS and TRACE systems that leverage multimodal information and late fusion techniques in our solutions. Specifically, we combine confidence scores produced by models constructed from visual, transcriptional, and Wikipedia features in the late fusion. Additionally, we consider areas where UGIs are exploited to provide multimedia-related services.

We present the EventBuilder system to efficiently obtain the multimedia summary of an event from a large collection of UGIs aggregated in social media platforms. It has three novel characteristics: (i) leveraging Wikipedia as event background knowledge to obtain additional contextual information about the event during event detection, (ii) visualizing the event on Google Map in real-time with a diverse set of social media activities, and (iii) solving an optimization problem to produce text summaries for the event.

In this doctoral research we aim to exploit both the content and contextual information of UGC in the support of the three problems discussed above. Figure 1 shows an overview of our approach. Moreover, we exploit knowledge bases for a better semantics and sentics understanding of UGC. In our work in progress, we mainly focus on sentics determination from the multimedia content leveraging the fusion of multimodal information.

2. STATE OF THE ART

The area of music recommendation for UGC is largely unexplored. Earlier works [8, 21] add soundtracks to the slideshow of UGIs. There exist a few approaches [6,20,22] to recognize emotions from videos but the field of video soundtrack recommendation for UGVs [4,24] is largely unexplored. Multi-feature late fusion techniques have been advocated in various applications such as video event detection and object recognition [23]. Moreover, Lu *et al.* [10] used heuristic approaches for querying desired songs from a music database by humming a tune. Such earlier works inspired us to build the ADVISOR system [16] by performing heterogeneous late fusion to recognize moods and retrieve a ranked list of songs using a heuristic approach for UGVs.

Due to the high cost and rapidly growing sizes of databases, it is not feasible to manually determine segment boundaries of lecture videos. Earlier approaches [7, 9, 14] attempted to segment videos automatically by exploiting visual, audio, and linguistic features. However, these approaches fail when the quality of a lecture video is not sufficiently high. This motivates us to leverage knowledge bases such as Wikipedia and other contextual information in conjunction with the content of the lecture video in our multimodal approach for temporal segmentation [15].

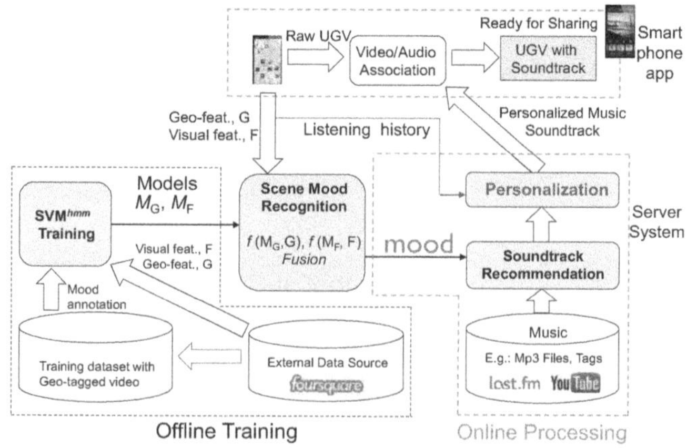

Figure 2: System overview of soundtrack recommendations for UGVs with ADVISOR [16].

Significant works [3, 11] have been done in the area of event modeling, detection, understanding, and summarization from multimedia over the past few years. Fabro *et al.* [5] presented an algorithm for the summarization of real-life events based on community-contributed multimedia content using photos from Flickr and videos from YouTube. In our novel event summarization system [13], we leverage multimodal information of UGIs and knowledge bases such as Wikipedia in event detection and summarization.

In our earlier work [12] we have shown that multimodal information is useful in uploading videos over adaptive middleboxes to news servers in weak network infrastructures. Moreover, we presented a system [18,19] for SMS-based FAQ retrieval by performing a match between SMS queries and FAQ database. In the future, we want to extend this concept to build an SMS-based news retrieval system leveraging information from multiple modalities.

3. PROPOSED APPROACH

As discussed in the previous sections, there are several multimdia-related problems which emerged after rapid growth in UGC online. Some problems are not addressed yet, and rest need efficient solutions after more contextual information is available. To the best of our knowledge, our work (**OBJ-1**) is the first attempt to recommend soundtracks for outdoor UGVs that correlates preference-aware activities from different behavioral signals of individual users, *e.g.*, online listening activities and physical activities. Furthermore, our work (**OBJ-2**) is the first attempt to compute segment boundaries from lecture videos leveraging knowledge bases such as Wikipedia. Finally, we present a novel event summarization and visualization system (**OBJ-3**) for a large collection of UGIs. The following is more details about our approaches for above three objectives.

OBJ-1. Figure 2 shows the architecture of our proposed music video generation system, called ADVISOR [16]. It consists of two parts: an offline training and an online processing component. The online processing is further divided into two modules: a smartphone app and a server backend system. This app allows users to capture sensor-annotated videos. Geographic contextual information (*i.e.*, geo-categories such as *Park* and *Lake* derived from Foursquare[2]) for a UGV serves as an important dimension to represent valuable semantics information while its video

[2]www.foursquare.com

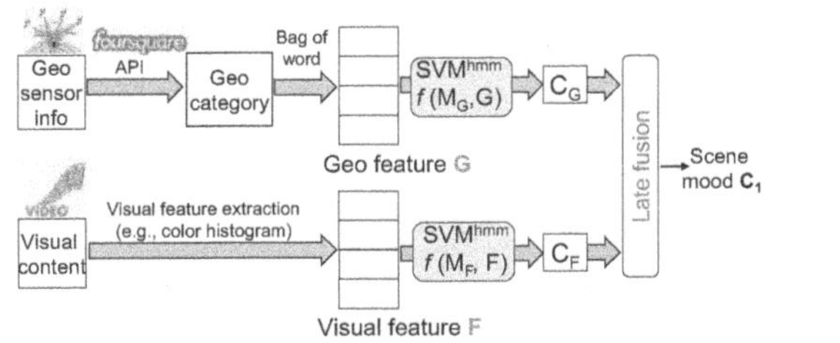

Figure 3: Mood recognition from UGVs [16].

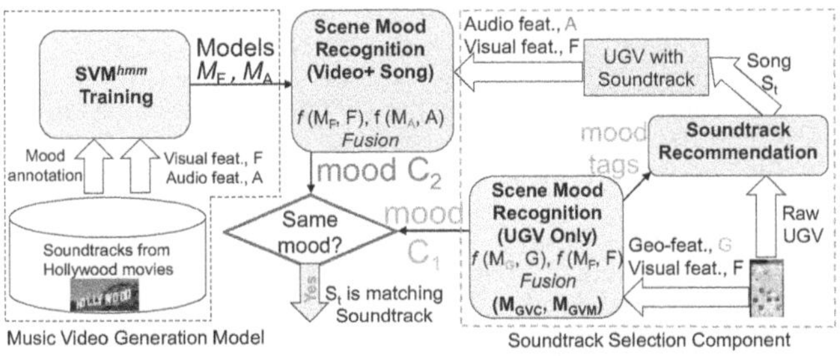

Figure 4: Soundtrack selection process in [16].

frame content is often used in scene understanding. During offline processing, models M_G and M_F are trained by exploiting geo- and visual features (G and F) to predict geo- and visual aware mood tags (C_G and C_F), respectively, using a SVM^{hmm} technique from a dataset with geo-tagged videos. Next C_G and C_F are fused, and mood tags with high likelihoods are regarded as scene moods C_1 of the UGV (see Figure 3). Then, songs matching the scene moods are recommended. Among them, the songs matching a user's listening history are considered as user preference-aware songs.

We propose a heuristic music retrieval method to recommend a list of songs for input scene moods. We calculate the total score of each song based on the likelihood of predicted mood tags for a UGV and then retrieve a ranked list of soundtracks. Further, our system extracts audio features including MFCC and pitch from a user's frequently listened audio tracks. We re-rank the retrieved list by correlating it with the computed audio features, and then recommending a list of user preference-aware songs. Next, the soundtrack selection component automatically chooses the most appropriately matching song from this list and attaches it as the soundtrack to the UGV (see Figure 4). We leverage the soundtrack of Hollywood movies to select an appropriate song for UGV since such soundtrack is generated by professionals and ensures a good harmony with the movie content. We learn from the experience of such experts using their *professional soundtracks* of Hollywood movies through a SVM^{hmm} learning model. We construct this model based on heterogeneous late fusion of SVM^{hmm} models constructed from visual features such as a color histogram and audio features such as MFCC, mel-spectrum, and pitch. The soundtrack selection process consists of two components. First a music video generation model that maps visual features F and audio features A of the UGV with a soundtrack S_t to mood tags C_2 based on the late fusion of F and A. Second, a soundtrack selection component that attaches S_t to the UGV if C_2 is similar to C_1 (mood tags predicted based on geo- and visual features).

OBJ-2. The proposed temporal segmentation system [15] has the following main contributions: (i) the extraction of

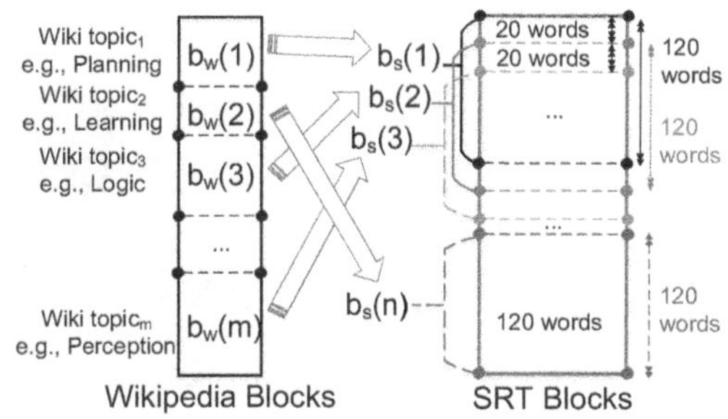

Figure 5: Architecture for segment boundary detection using SRT and Wikipedia [15].

a novel linguistic-based Wikipedia feature which is useful in finding segment boundaries of low quality videos, (ii) a SVM^{hmm} model which learns temporal transition cues from visual features, and (iii) the investigation of the late fusion of video segmentations derived from state-of-the-art methods. Figure 5 shows the architecture of segment boundaries detection from SRT using the proposed linguistic-based method. It leverages Wikipedia texts of subjects which lecture videos belong. We assume that the subject (say, *Artificial Intelligence*) of a lecture video is known. We use the Wikipedia API to find related Wikipedia articles and texts of different topics. Say, b_w is the block of texts corresponding to a Wikipedia topic. We determine POS tags for Wikipedia texts and SRT of the lecture video. Next, we find a block b_s of 120 words from SRT which matches closely with the Wikipedia block b_w for each topic in Wikipedia texts. Specifically, first we create linguistic feature vectors based on noun phrases in the entire Wikipedia texts. Next, we compute cosine similarities between a Wikipedia block b_w and all SRT blocks b_s. In this way determine the closest matching SRT block corresponding to each Wikipedia block, hence segment boundaries for the lecture video. Next, we compute temporal transitions derived from other modalities such as visual content and SRT using state-of-the-arts, and investigate the effect of their fusion with boundaries determined leveraging Wikipedia. We fuse segment boundaries by replacing two transitions less than ten seconds apart by their average transition times and keeping rest transitions as the final temporal transitions for the lecture video [14].

OBJ-3. Figure 6 shows the architecture of EventBuilder. It detects events from UGIs by computing the relevance score $u(p, e)$ of a UGI p for a given event e. It is computed by combining confidence scores from different modalities as follows: $u(p,e) = w_1\ \xi + w_2\ \lambda + w_3\ \gamma + w_4\ \mu + w_5\ \rho$, where $w_{i=1}^{5}$ are weights for different modalities such that $\sum_{i=1}^{5} w_i = 1$, and ξ, λ, γ, μ, and ρ are similarity functions for the given p and e with respect to event name, temporal information, spatial information, keywords, and camera model, respectively, as described in EventBuilder [13]. EventBuilder also produces text summaries from UGIs and Wikipedia articles of e. First, it determines important *concepts* (*e.g.*, *kid-play-holi* for the event named *holi*) from available texts. Next, it solves an optimization problem by selecting the minimal number of sentences which cover the maximal number of important *concepts* from matrix constructed by the available texts and the extracted concepts. Finally, EventBuilder presents an interactive visualization of the event on Google Maps from a representative set of UGIs for e.

Work in progress. Sentiments are very useful in personalized search, retrieval, and recommendation systems [1].

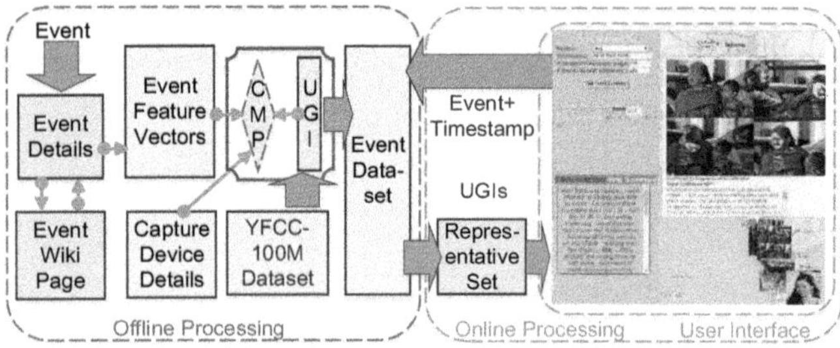

Figure 6: System framework of EventBuilder [13].

We determine sentiments for a photo by leveraging concepts determined from its visual content and contextual information. Further we use SenticNet-3 knowledge base [2] which bridges the conceptual and affective gap between word-level natural language data and the concept-level sentiments conveyed by them. We perform sentiment analysis to determine mood tags associated with photos, and subsequently provide sentics based multimedia services to users.

4. RESULTS

To evaluate **OBJ-1** we utilized 402 soundtracks from Hollywood movies, 1213 sensor-annotated videos, 729 songs from ISMIR, and 20 most frequent mood tags from Last.fm [16,17]. Next, we used 133 lecture videos with several metadata from the VideoLectures.NET and NPTEL[3] to evaluate **OBJ-2** [14, 15]. Finally, we evaluate **OBJ-3** on the YFCC100M dataset, a collection of 100 million photos and videos from Flickr [13].

5. CONCLUSIONS

This doctoral research addressed the following three problems leveraging multimodal analysis and knowledge bases: (i) the soundtrack recommendation for outdoor UGVs, (ii) temporal segmentations of lecture videos, and (iii) multimedia event summarization from a large collection of UGIs. Experimental results confirm that our approaches worked well in semantics understanding from multimedia content. Currently, we are working on sentics understanding from UGC using multimodal information access.

ACKNOWLEDGMENTS

This research has been supported in part by Singapore's Ministry of Education (MOE) Academic Research Fund Tier 1, grant number T1 251RES1415.

6. REFERENCES

[1] E. Cambria, J. Fu, F. Bisio, and S. Poria. AffectiveSpace 2: Enabling Affective Intuition for Concept-Level Sentiment Analysis. In *AAAI Conference on Artificial Intelligence*, pages 508–514, 2015.

[2] E. Cambria, D. Olsher, and D. Rajagopal. SenticNet 3: A Common and Common-Sense Knowledge Base for Cognition-Driven Sentiment Analysis. In *AAAI Conference on Artificial Intelligence*, pages 1515–1521, 2014.

[3] J. Choi, E. Kim, M. Larson, G. Friedland, and A. Hanjalic. Evento 360: Social Event Discovery from Web-scale Multimedia Collection. In *ACM MM*, pages 193–196, 2015.

[4] M. Cristani, A. Pesarin, C. Drioli, V. Murino, A. Rodà, M. Grapulin, and N. Sebe. Toward an Automatically Generated Soundtrack from Low-level Cross-modal Correlations for Automotive Scenarios. In *ACM MM*, pages 551–560, 2010.

[5] M. Del Fabro, A. Sobe, and L. Böszörmenyi. Summarization of Real-life Events based on Community-contributed Content. In *MMEDIA*, pages 119–126, 2012.

[6] A. Hanjalic and L.-Q. Xu. Affective Video Content Representation and Modeling. *In IEEE Transactions on Multimedia*, 7(1):143–154, 2005.

[7] A. Haubold and J. R. Kender. Augmented Segmentation and Visualization for Presentation Videos. In *ACM MM*, pages 51–60, 2005.

[8] C. T. Li and M. K. Shan. Emotion-based Impressionism Slideshow with Automatic Music Accompaniment. In *ACM MM*, pages 839–842, 2007.

[9] M. Lin, M. Chau, J. Cao, and J. F. Nunamaker Jr. Automated Video Segmentation for Lecture Videos: A Linguistics-based Approach. *In IJTHI*, 1(2):27-45, 2005.

[10] L. Lu, H. You, and H. Zhang. A New Approach to Query by Humming in Music Retrieval. In *IEEE ICME*, pages 22–25, 2001.

[11] V. Mezaris, A. Scherp, R. Jain, and M. S. Kankanhalli. Real-life Events in Multimedia: Detection, Representation, Retrieval, and Applications. *In Springer MTAP*, 70(1):1–6, 2014.

[12] R. R. Shah, M. Hefeeda, R. Zimmermann, K. Harras, C.-H. Hsu, and Y. Yu. NEWSMAN: Uploading Videos over Adaptive Middleboxes to News Servers in Weak Network Infrastructures. In *Springer MMM*, pages 100–113, 2016.

[13] R. R. Shah, A. D. Shaikh, Y. Yu, W. Geng, R. Zimmermann, and G. Wu. EventBuilder: Real-time Multimedia Event Summarization by Visualizing Social Media. In *ACM MM*, pages 185–188, 2015.

[14] R. R. Shah, Y. Yu, A. D. Shaikh, S. Tang, and R. Zimmermann. ATLAS: Automatic Temporal Segmentation and Annotation of Lecture Videos Based on Modelling Transition Time. In *ACM MM*, pages 209–212, 2014.

[15] R. R. Shah, Y. Yu, A. D. Shaikh, and R. Zimmermann. TRACE: A Linguistic-based Approach for Automatic Lecture Video Segmentation Leveraging Wikipedia Texts. In *IEEE ISM*, pages 217–220, 2015.

[16] R. R. Shah, Y. Yu, and R. Zimmermann. ADVISOR: Personalized Video Soundtrack Recommendation by Late Fusion with Heuristic Rankings. In *ACM MM*, pages 607–616, 2014.

[17] R. R. Shah, Y. Yu, and R. Zimmermann. User Preference-Aware Music Video Generation Based on Modeling Scene Moods. In *ACM MMSys*, pages 156–159, 2014.

[18] A. D. Shaikh, M. Jain, M. Rawat, R. R. Shah, and M. Kumar. Improving Accuracy of SMS Based FAQ Retrieval System. In *Springer Multilingual Information Access in South Asian Languages*, pages 142–156. 2013.

[19] A. D. Shaikh, R. R. Shah, and R. Shaikh. SMS based FAQ Retrieval for Hindi, English and Malayalam. In *ACM FIRE*, page 9, 2013.

[20] M. Soleymani, J. J. M. Kierkels, G. Chanel, and T. Pun. A Bayesian Framework for Video Affective Representation. In *IEEE ACII*, pages 1–7, 2009.

[21] A. Stupar and S. Michel. Picasso: Automated Soundtrack Suggestion for Multi-modal Data. In *ACM CIKM*, pages 2589–2592, 2011.

[22] H. L. Wang and L. F. Cheong. Affective Understanding in Film. *In IEEE TCSVT*, 16(6):689–704, 2006.

[23] G. Ye, D. Liu, I.-H. Jhuo, and S.-F. Chang. Robust Late Fusion with Rank Minimization. In *IEEE CVPR*, pages 3021–3028, 2012.

[24] Y. Yu, Z. Shen, and R. Zimmermann. Automatic Music Soundtrack Generation for Outdoor Videos from Contextual Sensor Information. In *ACM MM*, pages 1377–1378, 2012.

[3] www.nptel.ac.in/

Multimodal Visual Pattern Mining with Convolutional Neural Networks

Hongzhi Li
Department of Computer Science
Columbia University
hongzhi.li@columbia.edu

ABSTRACT

In this paper we describe a novel framework and algorithms for discovering image patch patterns from a large corpus of weakly supervised image-caption pairs generated from news events. Current pattern mining techniques attempt to find patterns that are representative and discriminative, we stipulate that our discovered patterns must also be recognizable by humans and preferably with meaningful names. We propose a new multimodal pattern mining approach that leverages the descriptive captions often accompanying news images to learn *semantically meaningful* image patch patterns. The mutltimodal patterns are then named using words mined from the associated image captions for each pattern. Our methods also discover named patterns beyond those covered by the existing image datasets like ImageNet. To the best of our knowledge this is the first algorithm developed to automatically mine image patch patterns that have strong semantic meaning specific to high-level news events, and then evaluate these patterns based on that criteria.

Keywords

Multimodal, Pattern Mining, Convolutional Neural Network

1. INTRODUCTION

With recent advances in the capabilities of computer vision systems, researchers have been able to demonstrate performance at near-human level capabilities in difficult tasks such as image recognition. These advances have been made possible by the pervasiveness of deep learning network architectures that utilize vast amounts of supervised image information. Image classification and recognition performance on supervised datasets will continue to improve, and because of this rapid improvement technologies are quickly being integrated into production level products such as Google Photos with tremendous public approval. Now that we can perform supervised image classification and recognition tasks with great accuracy we propose to utilize the developed technologies to attempt tasks that may not be as straightforward. We propose one such problem: how can we discover semantically meaningful image patches from a large set of unstructured image and caption pairs? In addition, how do we discover meaningful patterns specific to high-level events such as "Baltimore Protest".

ICMR'16, June 06 - 09, 2016, New York, NY, USA

ISBN 978-1-4503-4359-6/16/06...$15.00

DOI: http://dx.doi.org/10.1145/2911996.2912033

Recently, [7] and [4] proposed using image patches as a feature for classification instead of low-level visual bag of words features (BoW). Visual patterns have also been used to summarize image collections by [9]. Traditionally, the desired visual patterns must be *representative* and *discriminative* to perform well on image classification or summarization. *Representative* refers to the tendency of this patch to appear in many of the images for a target class, and *discriminative* refers to the fact that it should be unique and not appear frequently in images outside of the target category. Insuring that the patterns found are representative and discriminative leads to patterns that are useful for image classification, but does not imply that they are meaningful on their own or useful for other high level information extraction tasks. Unique but often meaningless local texture-based image patches are usually discovered using traditional pattern mining methods. If image patterns are semantically meaningful they can be used for tasks beyond just image classification. For example, the image patches can be used to automatically understand the possible actors and actions in a collection of images from a specific scenario or event. This information can actually be mined from the data, eliminating the need for expensive supervised bounding box based training data for learning. Our goal in this paper is to discover image patches that are not only discriminative and representative, but also contain high-level semantic meaning and are not simply a particular texture or part of a larger object. We establish a third important characteristic of our image patches, that our discovered patches must be *informative*. We define a *semantic visual pattern* as the patterns that are recognizable to a human and can be explained or named by a word or collection of words.

To accomplish this goal we have created an image-caption pair dataset with categories that are news related events such as a *demonstration* or *election*, which can be visually diverse. This visual diversity of news events allows us to discover higher level concepts with our image patches compared to previous pattern mining works which operate on datasets for scene classification or image recognition with lower level categories. For example, in our dataset we are able to find image patches that represent concepts like air strike, press conference, or award ceremony. Contrast this with the state of the art on the MIT Indoor scene recognition dataset [4], where the discovered patterns correspond to a chair, ceiling or other very concrete lower level concepts. To generate image patch patterns that are informative we propose a new multimodal pattern mining algorithm, which will be shown to generate patterns that are more semantically meaningful than visual-only methods in Sec. 4.1. Due to the fact that we utilize image captions we are also able to name our discovered image patch patterns. To the best of our knowledge, no other related works address the issue or evaluate whether their discovered image patch patterns are informative. Other researchers use the discovered patterns to build a mid-level representation of images and test the new features on image classification tasks. These evaluations demonstrate that the mid-level visual patterns are certainly useful, but in our opinion these evaluations don't address the fundamental question of pattern mining, what is the pattern? We argue that the current evaluation procedures are not sufficient to evaluate the quality of discovered patterns. In this paper, we propose a set of new subjective methods in conjunction with the objective methods to evaluate the performance of visual pattern mining.

2. RELATED WORK

Visual pattern mining is an important task in Computer Vision community. [2] and [9] use low level features and a hashing approach to mine visual patterns from image collections. [8] utilizes a spatial random partition to develop a fast image matching approach to discover visual patterns. All of these methods obtain image patches from the original image collection either by random sampling or salient/objectness detection and utilize image matching or clustering to detect similar patches to create visual patterns. These methods are computationally intense, because they have to examine possibly hundreds or thousands of image patches from each image. These methods rely heavily on low level image features, and therefore do not often produce image patches that exhibit high level semantic meaning. The generated image patterns are usual visually duplicated or near-duplicated image patches.

Convolutional neural networks (CNN) have achieved great success in many research areas [6], [3]. Recently, [4] combined the image representation from a CNN and association rule mining technology to effectively mine visual patterns. They first randomly sampled image patches from the original image and extracted the fully connected layer response as features for each image patch utilized in an association rule mining framework. This approach is able to find consistent visual patterns, but cannot guarantee the discovered visual patterns are semantically meaningful. Most of the existing visual pattern mining work focuses on how to find visually consistent patterns. To the best of our knowledge, our paper is the first attempt to find high level semantically meaningful visual patterns.

3. MULTIMODAL PATTERN MINING

3.1 Weakly Supervised Event Dataset Collection

We believe that by using weakly supervised image data from target categories that are sufficiently broad we can automatically discover meaningful and recongizable image patch patterns. To accomplish this task we collect a set of image caption pairs from a variety of types of news event categories. We begin by crawling the complete Twitter feeds of four prominent news agencies, the Associated Press, Al Jazeera, Reuters, and CNN. Each of these agencies have a prominent twitter presence, and tweet links to their articles multiple times a day. We collect the links to the articles and then download the html file from each extracted link. The article links span the time frame from 2007-2015, and cover a variety of different topics. We then parse the raw html file and find the image and caption pairs from the downloaded news articles. Through this process we are able to collect approximately 280k image-caption pairs.

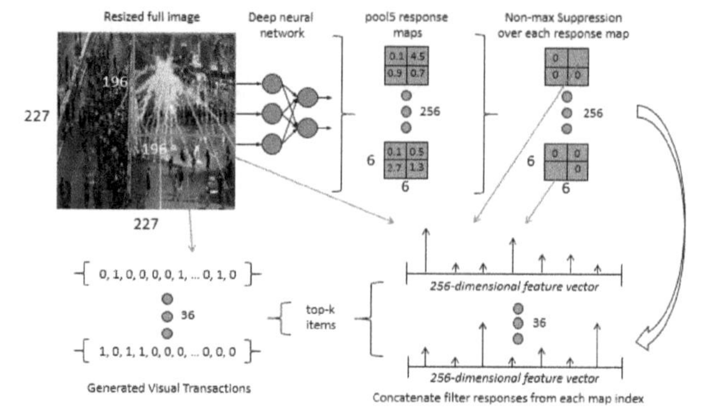

Figure 1: Generate Visual transaction using the feature maps from the last convolutional layer of CNN

3.1.1 *Using CNN Pool5 Features for Transaction Generation from Images*

Certain portions of a CNN are only activated by a smaller region of interest (ROI) within the original image. The last layer in which the particular neurons do not correspond to the entire image is the output of the final convolutional and pooling layer for [3]. Based on this observation, for each image we find the maximum magnitude response from a particular feature map from the pool5 layer of the CNN defined by [3]. The pool5 layer of this network consists of 256 filters, and the response of each of the filters over a 6×6 mapping of the image. The corresponding ROI from the original image in which all the pixels in that region contribute to the response of a particular neuron in the pool5 layer is a 196×196 image patch from the 227×227 resized image. These 196×196 image patches come from a zero-padded representation of the image with zero-padding around the image edges of 64 pixels and a stride of 32. Using this approach we are able to use the current existing architecture and computational power of the CNN for image patch mining without actually changing the network structure. This idea allows us to extract image patch patterns in a way that is much more efficient than current state of the art methods.

We use the pre-trained CNN model from [3] that was trained using the ImageNet dataset to extract the pool5 features for the news event images. For each image, we find the maximum response over the 6×6 feature map for all 256 filters, resulting in a 256 dimensional feature vector representation for each image patch. It has been shown in [4] that most of the information is carried by the top k magnitude dimensions of the feature vector, and the magnitude response of these dimensions is not particularly important.

Thus, we follow their suggestion and set the top k magnitude dimensions of the CNN vector to 1 and the others to 0, creating a binary representation of which filters are activated for each image patch. We use these sparse binarized features to build *transactions* for each image patch, where the non-zero dimensions are the items in our transaction.

3.1.2 Generating Transactions from Captions

We begin by cleaning each of the image captions by removing stopwords and other ancillary words that should not appear (html tags or urls). We then tokenize each of the captions and find all of the words that appear in at least 10 captions in our dataset. Once we find these words we use the skip-gram model proposed in [5] that was trained on a corpus of Google News articles to map each word to a 300 dimensional embedded space. The skip-gram model works well in our context because words with similar uses end up being embedded close to each other in the feature space. Words such as "religious clergy", "priest", and "pastor" all end up close in euclidean distance after embedding and far away from words that are not similar. We cluster the words using K-means clustering to generate 1000 word clusters.

To generate transactions for each caption we map each word back to its corresponding cluster, then include that cluster index in the transaction set. We remove patterns that contain cluster indices that are associated with commonly used words by having a high confidence score threshold. The cluster indices that frequently appear in captions from a particular event category but rarely for other categories are found through our association rule mining framework.

We require our discovered patterns to contain items from both the visual and text transactions. By requiring words with similar meaning to appear in all captions of a visual pattern we are able to discard patterns that may be visually similar but semantically incoherent. The skip-gram based algorithm is able to handle differences in word choice and structure between captions to effectively encode meaning into our multimodal transactions.

3.2 Mining the Patterns

We add the event category of each image as an additional item in the generated transaction for each of the image caption pairs. Inspired by [4], we use the popular apriori algorithm [1] to find patterns within the transactions that predict which event category the image belongs to. We only find the association rules which have a confidence higher than 0.8, and calculate the support threshold that insure that the at least 30 image patches exhibit a found pattern. Finally, we also remove any rules which only contain items generated from the image or caption transactions, insuring that we only retain truly multimodal patterns.

3.3 Naming the patterns

If we can name the generated patterns we can use them for higher level information extraction tasks. We leverage the fact that we have captions associated with each of the images to generate names for each pattern.

We begin the process of name generation by removing the stop words from captions. And than we sum the tf-idf vector representations of each word in all of the captions associated with a particular pattern. We then take the argument max over the summed tf-idf representations to obtain the name

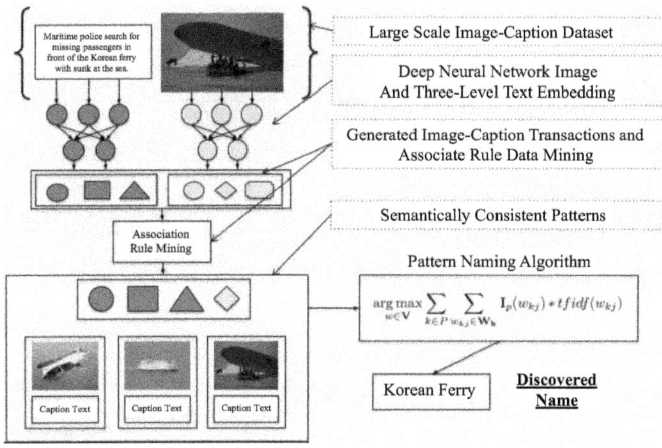

Figure 2: Our full pattern discovery and naming pipeline

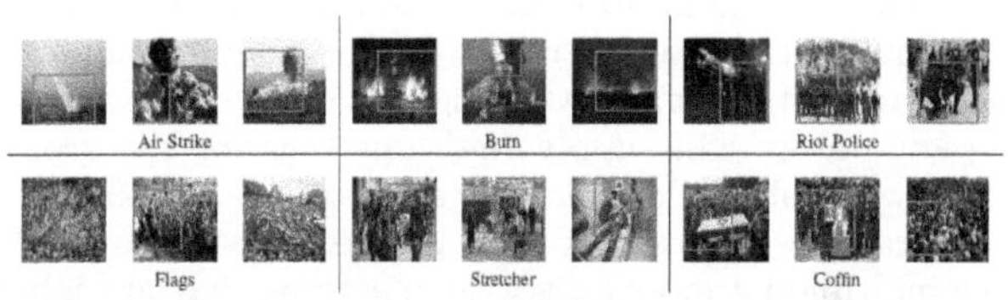

Figure 3: Examples of image patches and names discovered by the proposed multimodal approach.

for this pattern. Once the names are found, we remove any name that appears in more than 10% of the captions of a particular event. This is important because for particular events like "injure", words such as *injure* and *wounded* appear across many captions, and may lead to poor naming. Some examples of discovered patterns and the names that we have assigned to them can be seen in Fig 3. Our full pattern naming algorithm and pipeline can be seen in Fig 2.

4. EVALUATION

We believe that the pattern mining algorithm that we have developed can be used for more than image classification performance. To prove this we have developed an evaluation to determine the percentage of our patterns that are semantically meaningful as well as if we are able to accurately name the patterns that we have found.

4.1 Semantic Relevance of Patterns

To accomplish this task we built an Amazon Mechanical Turk (AMT) interface, which we used to gather annotations. To generate the patterns for inspection we randomly sampled patterns from the event categories of *Attack*, *Demonstrate*, *Transport*, *Injure*, and *Elect*, and *Meet* for a total of 99 randomly sampled patterns. These samples were taken from our multimodal pattern mining algorithm and a visual-only version of the algorithm, which is the same as the multimodal algorithm without using any text transactions. We then randomly sample up to 16 of the image patches from a given pattern to represent the pattern and show them to the annotator. The annotator is asked to decide whether

Table 1: Subjective Evaluation of semantic consistency.

Method	Accuracy
% of Semantically Consistent Patterns	
Multimodal	**82.0%**
visual-only	72.6%
% of Tag Agreement Among Subjects	
Multimodal	**49.5%**
visual-only	39.2%

the group of images exhibit similar and consistent semantic content. If the annotator agrees that the images exhibit consistent semantics then we ask them to supply up to 3 tags that could be applied to this group of images. We choose to have the annotators provide three tags (which can be synonyms), so that we have three words from each annotator to compare to each other given that different annotators may choose different tags with similar semantic meaning. We analyze the inter-annotator tag agreement to determine if the patterns are semantically relevant. Our assumption is that if the image patches exhibit strong semantic consistency then the annotators will supply the same tags for the group of images. We obtained at least 4 annotations per pattern.

We can see the results from this experiment in Table 1. Our multimodal model discovers patterns that are labelled by the annotators to be more semantically consistent than the visual-only patterns. The annotators answered that a pattern generated by our multimodal method was semantically consistent 82% of the time compared to 72.6% for visual-only. We believe that because humans have a strong capability for reasoning they may "find" semantic meaning in a group of images that could be spurious. For this reason we also checked the agreement between the annotator provided tags. If a pattern received tags from at least 3 annotators (annotators could say the patterns were not semantically consistent and choose not to provide tags), and *at least* half of the annotators provided the same tag for a pattern we decided that this pattern had "tag agreement". In this metric our multimodal approach greatly outperformed the visual-only approach with the percentage of patterns exhibiting tag agreement for multimodal at **49.5%** and visual-only at 39.2%. Our method outperforms the visual-only pipeline in all of our subjective tests, in particular we demonstrate that the agreement across a group of people of our image patches increases by **26.2%** over the state of the art visual model. The multimodal pipeline outperforms the visual-only model because the visual transaction pipeline can discover similar "looking" image patches across our image dataset, but these group of patches that "look" similar do not necessarily represent a similar semantic concept. However, by adding our caption transaction generation to this pipeline we are able to discover image patches with consistent semantics. For example, in the visual model pipeline we have patches taken from images of forest fires and explosions, because each pattern exhibits the similar visual components of smoke. Our multimodal pipeline separates these images in a meaningful way, because a forest fire and explosion are semantically different concepts that may have little overlap in their text captions. The multimodal information is particularly important in datasets like the one we have created because there is a high level of semantic and visual variance across the data.

4.2 Evaluation of automatic pattern naming

We test how well we are able to name the patterns. To accomplish this task we utilize AMT to analyze whether our applied names are reasonable or not. To generate the test data we utilized all of the patterns that were tested in Sec. 4.1. To evaluate our naming algorithm on an image patch level we asked an annotator to decide if the name that we supplied to the pattern described the semantic content. From the 100 patterns we obtained 776 images. We used 3 annotators per image-patch and name pair and took the majority vote to determine if that name aptly described the content in the image. The annotation revealed that we had correctly applied names to 434 images and incorrectly to 353 images, for a total naming accuracy of **54.5%**. We remind the reader that this accuracy comes using *no* supervised data. Our model is also able to learn patterns that are not contained in current supervised image datasets. Using our naming algorithm we applied 246 unique names to our patterns (some names apply to many patterns), but only 100 (40.6%) of these names are part of the current ImageNet ontology. Examples of our mined semantic visual patterns and their applied names are shown in Fig. 3.

5. REFERENCES

[1] R. Agrawal, R. Srikant, et al. Fast algorithms for mining association rules. In *Proc. 20th int. conf. very large data bases, VLDB*, volume 1215, pages 487–499, 1994.

[2] J. Han, J. Pei, and Y. Yin. Mining frequent patterns without candidate generation. In *ACM Sigmod Record*, volume 29, pages 1–12. ACM, 2000.

[3] A. Krizhevsky, I. Sutskever, and G. E. Hinton. Imagenet classification with deep convolutional neural networks. In *Advances in neural information processing systems*, pages 1097–1105, 2012.

[4] Y. Li, L. Liu, C. Shen, and A. van den Hengel. Mid-level deep pattern mining. In *Computer Vision and Pattern Recognition (CVPR), 2015 IEEE Conference on*, pages 971–980. IEEE, 2015.

[5] T. Mikolov, I. Sutskever, K. Chen, G. S. Corrado, and J. Dean. Distributed representations of words and phrases and their compositionality. In *Advances in neural information processing systems*, pages 3111–3119, 2013.

[6] K. Simonyan and A. Zisserman. Very deep convolutional networks for large-scale image recognition. *arXiv preprint arXiv:1409.1556*, 2014.

[7] S. Singh, A. Gupta, and A. Efros. Unsupervised discovery of mid-level discriminative patches. *Computer Vision–ECCV 2012*, pages 73–86, 2012.

[8] J. Yuan and Y. Wu. Spatial random partition for common visual pattern discovery. In *Computer Vision, 2007. ICCV 2007. IEEE 11th International Conference on*, pages 1–8. IEEE, 2007.

[9] W. Zhang, H. Li, C.-W. Ngo, and S.-F. Chang. Scalable visual instance mining with threads of features. In *Proceedings of the ACM International Conference on Multimedia*, pages 297–306. ACM, 2014.

Facial Landmark Detection and Tracking for Facial Behavior Analysis

Yue Wu
Rensselaer Polytechnic Institute
110 8th street, Troy, NY, USA
wuy9@rpi.edu

ABSTRACT

The face is the most dominant and distinct communication tool of human beings. Automatic analysis of facial behavior allows machines to understand and interpret a human's states and needs for natural interactions. This research focuses on developing advanced computer vision techniques to process and analyze facial images for the recognition of various facial behaviors.

Specifically, this research consists of two parts: automatic facial landmark detection and tracking, and facial behavior analysis and recognition using the tracked facial landmark points. In the first part, we develop several facial landmark detection and tracking algorithms on facial images with varying conditions, such as varying facial expressions, head poses and facial occlusions. First, to handle facial expression and head pose variations, we introduce a hierarchical probabilistic face shape model and a discriminative deep face shape model to capture the spatial relationships among facial landmark points under different facial expressions and face poses to improve facial landmark detection. Second, to handle facial occlusion, we improve upon the effective cascade regression framework and propose the robust cascade regression framework for facial landmark detection, which iteratively predicts the landmark visibility probabilities and landmark locations.

The second part of this research applies our facial landmark detection and tracking algorithms to facial behavior analysis, including facial action recognition and face pose estimation. For facial action recognition, we introduce a novel regression framework for joint facial landmark detection and facial action recognition. For head pose estimation, we are working on a robust algorithm that can perform head pose estimation under facial occlusion.

CCS Concepts

•Computing methodologies → Activity recognition and understanding; Interest point and salient region detections; *Object detection; Tracking;*

ICMR'16, June 06 - 09, 2016, New York, NY, USA

ISBN 978-1-4503-4359-6/16/06...$15.00

DOI: http://dx.doi.org/10.1145/2911996.2912034

Keywords

Facial behavior analysis; Facial landmark detection and tracking; Probabilistic graphical model

1. INTRODUCTION

Humans communicate through multiple channels, including visual, auditory, olfactory, and tactile. The face plays an important role in visual communication. For example, humans can automatically extract many nonverbal messages by visualizing and analyzing facial behavior. In particular, facial behavior includes the facial deformations caused by facial expressions, head movements, and eye movements. Facial behavior reflects a human's emotion, focus of attention, and mental state. Facial behavior has been applied to multiple application areas, including human and computer interaction, entertainment, and medical applications.

In computer vision, there are a few major facial behavior analysis tasks (see Figure 1). First, given the facial images or videos as visual inputs, face detection/tracking techniques are performed to locate the face. Given the location of the face, facial landmark detection and tracking techniques are used to locate the fiducial facial key points, such as eye corners and eye centers. The facial landmark locations are used to perform advanced tasks such as facial expression and action recognition, head pose estimation, eye movement and gaze estimation, etc.

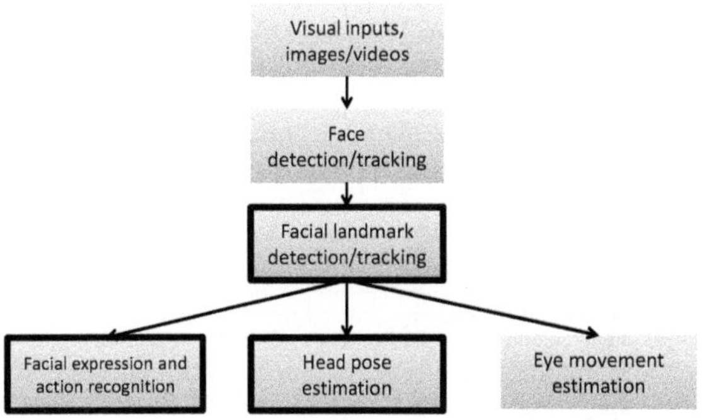

Figure 1: Major facial behavior analysis tasks in computer vision. The bold boxes highlight the topics covered in this research.

As highlighted in Figure 1, the major facial behavior analysis topics covered in this research include facial landmark detection/tracking, facial expression and action recognition, and head pose estimation. In particular, the first part of the research focuses on facial landmark detection in the wild, which refers to the landmark detection on images with varying facial expressions, head poses, and facial occlusion. In the second part of this research, we apply robust facial landmark detection and tracking methods for facial expression and action unit recognition and head pose estimation. In particular, our work extends the existing research and contributes in the following aspects:

1. For facial landmark detection under varying facial expressions and head poses, we improve upon the CLM by proposing two effective facial shape models.

2. For facial landmark detection under facial occlusion, we improve upon the general cascade regression methods and propose a robust cascade regression method, which iteratively predicts facial landmark locations and facial occlusions.

3. To improve the facial expression and facial action unit recognition, we propose the joint cascade regression framework for simultaneous facial action recognition and facial landmark detection.

4. We are working on a robust method to improve head pose estimation under facial occlusion.

The remaining part of this manuscript is organized as follows: In section 2, we introduce the facial landmark detection algorithms. In section 3, we introduce the facial action unit recognition method. In section 4, we introduce the robust head pose estimation method. We summarize this manuscript in section 5.

2. FACIAL LANDMARK DETECTION AND TRACKING

2.1 Overview

Facial landmarks refer to the fiducial facial key points around the facial components and contour, as shown in Figure 2. They are usually with unique local facial appearance, and they are utilized as anchor points on the face. The goal of facial landmark detection and tracking techniques is to estimate the 2D coordinates of the facial landmarks on facial images or videos. Estimation of facial landmark locations is important, since these locations can jointly represent the face shape, which is usually required by facial behavior analysis tasks as shown in the flowchart in Figure 1.

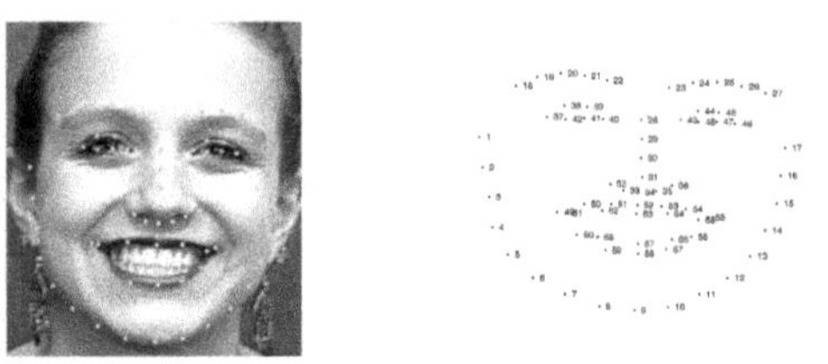

Figure 2: Facial landmark on a sample image.

In general, the facial landmark detection and tracking algorithms can be classified into three major categories depending on how the algorithm captures the facial appearance and facial shape information. These categories include holistic methods [1], Constrained Local Methods (CLM) [2], and regression-based methods[13]. Holistic methods explicitly build appearance and shape prior models to capture the global appearance and shape variations of facial images during training. CLMs build global face shape models and local appearance models for each facial landmark independently. The regression-based methods use appearance and shape information implicitly, and they do not explicitly build any appearance or shape model.

The limitation of the existing methods is that there is lack of robust algorithms that can handle facial images with "in-the-wild" conditions with significant facial expressions, head poses, facial occlusions, etc. This is mainly due to the following reasons:

- There is no effective model that can capture the face shape variations caused by the significant facial expression and head pose, which are coupled together to generate the 2D face shape. The existing algorithms usually rely on the simple linear Active Shape Model, which may not be effective for such a difficult task.

- There is no systematic way to handle facial occlusions caused by extreme head poses and object occlusions. Most of the existing facial landmark detection and tracking algorithms would assume that all the facial landmarks are visible and consider them equally. Thus, they tend to fail on images with facial occlusions.

To tackle these limitations and facilitate facial landmark detection and tracking in real-life conditions, we propose several facial landmark detection and tracking methods as discussed in the following sections.

2.2 Facial landmark detection and tracking under varying facial expressions and head poses

We propose two face shape models [11][12][7] to handle facial expression and head pose variations for robust facial landmark detection. The first face shape model is a directed hierarchical probabilistic face shape model [12]. The model incorporates two levels of information with the explicit help of the facial expression and head pose information. In the lower level, the model captures the facial shape variations of each facial component. In the higher level, the model automatically exploits the relationships among facial components, facial expression, and head pose through automatic model structure learning and parameter learning. Model structure learning and parameter learning are non-trivial due to the existence of latent variables. To alleviate this problem, we designed effective learning algorithms based on Structural EM algorithm [4].

Although the proposed hierarchical probabilistic face shape model is effective at improving the performance of facial landmark detection algorithms, its training requires the explicit annotations of the facial expression and head pose for each training image, which limits its application areas. To solve this problem, we propose the second face shape model, which is an undirected discriminative deep face shape model based on the factored three-way Restricted Boltzmann Machine model and deep learning techniques [11][7]. Instead of explicitly utilizing the expression and head pose labels,

Table 1: List of a selection of facial action units.

AU id	1	7	27
Description	Inner Brow Raiser	Outer Brow Raiser	Lid Tightener
Example image		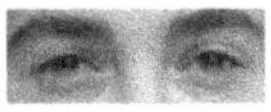	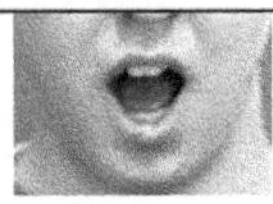

the second model implicitly decouples the face shape variations into expression-related parts and head pose-related parts with the help of additional frontal training images. Effective algorithms are proposed to facilitate model learning with incomplete data and model inference for the prediction of facial landmark locations.

We evaluated the proposed two probabilistic face shape models on both controlled images and general "in-the-wild" facial images. The experiments show the effectiveness of the proposed probabilistic face shape models for facial landmark detection comparing to state-of-the-art works [11][12][7].

2.3 Facial landmark detection under facial occlusion

To perform facial landmark detection under facial occlusion, we improve upon the cascade regression framework and propose an improved robust cascade regression method [8] [9]. The proposed method iteratively predicts the facial landmark locations and facial landmark visibility probabilities. Unlike existing methods, which use local appearance information from all facial landmarks to predict landmark locations, the proposed method relies on visible landmarks rather than the occluded landmarks based on their visibility probabilities. When predicting landmark occlusions, we explicitly learn the occlusion pattern with the Auto-Encoder (AE) model and embed it as a constraint to aid prediction. By considering the facial occlusion caused by extreme head poses as a special case of object occlusion, the proposed model can handle facial images with both object occlusions and extreme head poses, outperforming the existing methods, which can only handle one of them. Experiments on benchmark databases with object occlusion and extreme head poses demonstrate the state-of-the-art performance of the proposed method.

3. FACIAL ACTION UNIT RECOGNITION

3.1 Overview

Facial expression refers to the global facial deformation caused by different emotions. Typical facial expressions include anger, sadness, disgust, happiness, surprise, and fear. In contrast to the global facial expressions, the facial Action Units (AUs) defined in the Facial Action Coding System (FACS) [3] are more local and they characterize the local facial muscle movements. For example, Table 1 shows some typical AUs, their descriptions, and sample images. The goal of AU recognition is to detect the activation of particular AUs on facial images.

Facial action unit recognition methods contain two sequential steps: feature extraction and facial action recognition. For the first step, effective features such as the appearance features, the geometric features, or their combinations are extracted to represent the facial images. In the estimation step, the methods recognize AU based on the features [5][6]. Early AU recognition methods consider each AU independently, while recent works focus on joint AU recognition by exploiting the relationships among AUs.

Even though facial action unit recognition has been studied for a few decades, a fully automatic system has not been developed. The existing facial action unit recognition algorithms suffer from the following limitations:

- Facial action unit recognition relies on the location of facial landmarks. In existing works, facial landmark detection is usually performed before facial action analysis. This sequential approach is suboptimal, as it ignores the interactions and joint relationships among facial action units and face shape.
- It is difficult for the existing algorithms to handle facial action unit recognition on facial images with spontaneous and natural movements. This is partially due to the failure of the facial landmark detection algorithms in those challenging cases.

To tackle these limitations of existing AU recognition algorithms, we propose a robust method that jointly performs facial landmark detection and action recognition, which we further discuss in the following section.

3.2 Joint facial landmark detection and facial action recognition

We propose the constrained joint cascade regression framework to improve facial action unit recognition [10]. Unlike existing methods which perform facial landmark detection and facial action unit recognition sequentially, the proposed method performs them simultaneously and jointly. The model first learns the relationship among facial action units and face shape as a constraint. It then iteratively updates the facial landmark locations and the AU activation probabilities until convergence. The experimental results on benchmark posed and spontaneous databases show that the proposed method can improve the performance of both facial landmark detection and facial action unit recognition.

4. HEAD POSE ESTIMATION

4.1 Overview

In computer vision, head pose estimation refers to the prediction of the head orientation and position with respect to the camera coordinate system. The orientation of head pose can be characterized by the pitch, yaw, and roll angles. In this research, we classify head pose estimation methods into *learning-based methods* and *model-based methods*. Learning-based methods utilize pattern recognition and machine learning techniques to estimate the head pose from facial data. Model-based methods utilize 3D computer vision techniques and projection models to estimate head pose, and they usually require facial landmark location information.

The existing head pose estimation methods still suffer from the following limitations:

- The existing head pose estimation algorithms have difficulty to handle facial occlusion. Existing methods usually rely on the holistic facial appearance or the detected facial landmark locations for all points, while ignoring the fact that the facial appearance and the detected facial landmark locations on the occluded facial part are unreliable.

- Since the rigid head movements and the non-rigid facial motion are coupled together to generate the 2D facial images, non-rigid facial motion may affect accuracy of head pose estimation for existing methods. The field currently lacks an effective method to decouple the non-rigid motion before head pose estimation.

- The existing head pose estimation methods are either learning-based or model-based methods. There is no effective way to combine them to boost the performance of head pose estimation.

To tackle these limitations of existing automatic head pose estimation methods, we propose a robust landmark-based head pose estimation method, which is further discussed in the following section.

4.2 Robust head pose estimation

We are currently working on a robust algorithm that can perform head pose estimation under facial occlusion. The method is based on the previous work in [14], which uses linear and nonlinear methods to decouple rigid head motion from non-rigid facial motion and estimates the head poses based on the detected 2D facial landmark points. We propose to add landmark occlusion/confidence information to improve the robustness of the head pose estimation algorithm. The decoupled non-rigid facial motion information can also be used for facial expression recognition. In addition, we propose to combine the learning-based and model-based methods to improve the robustness and accuracy of head pose estimation, which is rarely exploited in the literature.

5. CONCLUSION

In this research, we proposed several robust and accurate algorithms for facial behavior analysis. We focused on three major research topics: facial landmark detection and tracking, facial action recognition, and head pose estimation. In the first part of the research, we proposed two probabilistic face shape models, including the hierarchical probabilistic face shape model and the discriminative deep face shape model to handle facial expressions and head poses for facial landmark detection. We also proposed a robust cascade regression framework for facial landmark detection under facial occlusion. In the second part of this research, we applied the landmark detection algorithms for facial action recognition and head pose estimation. In particular, we proposed a constrained joint cascade regression framework for simultaneous facial action recognition and facial landmark detection. We are working on a robust head pose estimation algorithm to handle facial occlusion.

In the future, the goal is to extend the proposed algorithms and models for other applications and research areas. Some potential research topics include: automatic facial landmark detection in the wild, vision-based human behavior analysis, human event and action recognition, and probabilistic graphical model based applications.

6. REFERENCES

[1] T. F. Cootes, G. J. Edwards, and C. J. Taylor. Active appearance models. *IEEE Transactions on Pattern Analysis and Machine Intelligence*, 23(6):681–685, jun 2001.

[2] D. Cristinacce and T. F. Cootes. Feature detection and tracking with constrained local models. In *Proceedings of the British Machine Vision Conference*, 2006.

[3] P. Ekman and E. L. Rosenberg, editors. *What the face reveals: basic and applied studies of spontaneous expression using the facial action coding system(FACS)*. Series in affective science. Oxford University Press, first edition, 1997.

[4] N. Friedman. Learning belief networks in the presence of missing values and hidden variables. In *Proceedings of the Fourteenth International Conference on Machine Learning*, pages 125–133, 1997.

[5] B. Jiang, M. Valstar, and M. Pantic. Action unit detection using sparse appearance descriptors in space-time video volumes. In *Automatic Face Gesture Recognition and Workshops (FG 2011), 2011 IEEE International Conference on*, pages 314–321, March 2011.

[6] Z. Wang, Y. Li, S. Wang, and Q. Ji. Capturing global semantic relationships for facial action unit recognition. In *Computer Vision (ICCV), 2013 IEEE International Conference on*, pages 3304–3311, Dec 2013.

[7] Y. Wu and Q. Ji. Discriminative deep face shape model for facial point detection. *International Journal of Computer Vision*, 113(1):37–53, 2015.

[8] Y. Wu and Q. Ji. Robust facial landmark detection under significant head poses and occlusion. In *The IEEE International Conference on Computer Vision (ICCV)*, December 2015.

[9] Y. Wu and Q. Ji. Shape augmented regression method for face alignment. In *The IEEE International Conference on Computer Vision (ICCV) Workshops*, December 2015.

[10] Y. Wu and Q. Ji. Constrained joint cascade regression framework for simultaneous facial action unit recognition and facial landmark detection. In *Computer Vision and Pattern Recognition (CVPR), 2016 IEEE Conference on*, 2016.

[11] Y. Wu, Z. Wang, and Q. Ji. Facial feature tracking under varying facial expressions and face poses based on restricted boltzmann machines. In *Proceedings of the 2013 IEEE Conference on Computer Vision and Pattern Recognition*, pages 3452–3459, 2013.

[12] Y. Wu, Z. Wang, and Q. Ji. A hierarchical probabilistic model for facial feature detection. In *Computer Vision and Pattern Recognition (CVPR), 2014 IEEE Conference on*, pages 1781–1788, June 2014.

[13] X. Xiong and F. De la Torre Frade. Supervised descent method and its applications to face alignment. In *IEEE International Conference on Computer Vision and Pattern Recognition (CVPR)*, May 2013.

[14] Z. Zhu and Q. Ji. Robust real-time face pose and facial expression recovery. In *Computer Vision and Pattern Recognition, 2006 IEEE Computer Society Conference on*, volume 1, pages 681–688. IEEE, 2006.

Author Index

Addesso, Luca 397
Amsaleg, Laurent 213, 347
Andersen, Kristina 95
Anwer, Rao Muhammad 339
Baraldi, Lorenzo 23
Battiato, Sebastiano 397
Bertini, Marco 289, 351
Bhatt, Chidansh 261
Blandfort, Philipp 385
Bondugula, Sravanthi 371
Borth, Damian 385
Buisson, Olivier 367
Bulling, Andreas 243
Cao, Liangliang 39, 363
Cao, Yue 197
Cárdenes Cabré, Jesús Alejandro 317
Casella, Antonino 397
Chakraborty, Prithwi Raj 55
Chandran, Vinod 55
Chang, Shih-Fu..5, 151, 389, 401, 417
Chari, Visesh 299
Chen, Chu-Song 313
Chen, Tanfang 277
Chen, Tao 151, 417
Chen, Ting-Yen 313
Cooper, Matthew 261
Cucchiara, Rita 23
D'Amico, Valeria 397
Davis, Larry S. 371
de Boer, Maaike 127
de Juan, Paloma 47, 363
De Neve, Wesley 409
Del Bimbo, Alberto 289, 351
Demeester, Thomas 409
Deng, Cheng 167
Deng, Shuiguang 249
Dengel, Andreas 385
Dong, Jianfeng 271
Eguchi, Koji 229
Ellis, Joseph G. 401
Ewerth, Ralph 377, 381
Falk, Tiago H. 317
Fang, Zhiwei 405
Farinella, Giovanni M. 397
Feng, Ranran 3
Ferracani, Andrea 351
Fontanini, Giulia 289
Fritz, Mario 243
Fu, Yanwei 15
Furon, Teddy 213
Furuya, Takahiko 293
Gao, Jiyang 31
Gao, Wen 281
Gao, Zhen 277
Gialampoukidis, Ilias 359
Giró-i-Nieto, Xavier 327
Grana, Costantino 23
Gravier, Guillaume 343
Gupta, Rishabh 317
Han, Yahong 285
Hang, Song 405
Hao, Yangyang 111
Hsiao, Jenhao 363
Huang, Tiejun 281
Huang, Yuchi 225
Hudelot, Céline 63
Huet, Benoit 413
Iscen, Ahmet 213
Jaimes, Alejandro 47
Jain, Prateek 189
Jain, Ramesh 1, 87
Jalali, Laleh 87
Jalalvand, Azarakhsh 409
Jawahar, C. V. 189
Jiang, Hao 355
Jiang, Yu-Gang 7, 15
Jin, Qin 239
Joly, Alexis 367
Jónsson, Björn Þór 333, 347
Jou, Brendan 151, 389, 417
Karayil, Tushar 385
Ke, Zi-Yi 235
Khan, Fahad Shahbaz 339
Khan, Saad 225
Khomami Abadi, Mojtaba 317
Kim, Edward 221
Knees, Peter 95
Koelma, Dennis C. 175, 333
Kompatsiaris, Ioannis 359
Kompatsiaris, Yiannis 71, 421
Kordumova, Svetlana 143
Laaksonen, Jorma 339
Lan, Weiyu 271
Le Borgne, Hervé 63, 119
Lejsek, Herwig 347
Leveau, Valentin 367
Li, Boyang 15
Li, Hongzhi 401, 427
Li, Qing 159
Li, Xirong 271
Li, Yong 405
Li, Yucheng 39
Li, Yuncheng 363
Liang, Junwei 239
Liem, Cynthia C. S. 393
Lin, Shilun 135
Lin, Weiyao 167
Lin, Xiao 111
Liu, Hailong 271
Liu, Hongyi 151, 417
Liu, Jing 405
Liu, Kuan-Hsien 313
Liu, Zhengguang 183
Long, Guoping 39
Long, Mingsheng 197
Lu, Hanqing 405
Lu, Yi-Jie 127
Lu, Yijuan 355
Luo, Jiebo 159
Ma, Lizhuang 111
Ma, Wenjing 39
Malinowski, Mateusz 243
Manmatha, R. 299
Marqués, Ferran 327
Matsuo, Shin 309
McGuinness, Kevin 327
Mei, Tao 159
Melenhorst, Mark S. 393
Mensink, Thomas 143
Mettes, Pascal 175
Metze, Florian 265
Milotta, Filippo L. M. 397
Mitkas, Pericles A. 421
Mohedano, Eva 327
Morreale, Fabio 317
Moumtzidou, Anastasia 359
Müller, Eric 381
Murthy, Venkatesh N. 299
Nag Chowdhury, Sreyasi 243
Nevatia, Ram 31
Ngo, Chong-Wah 127, 413
O'Connor, Noel E. 327
Ohbuchi, Ryutarou 293

Ortis, Alessandro 397
Otto, Christian 381
Palomaki, Jussi 79
Pang, Lei 413
Papadopoulos, Symeon 71, 421
Pappas, Nikolaos 151, 417
Pedronette, Daniel Carlos Guimarães 321
Petkos, Georgios 421
Pezzatini, Daniele 351
Pongpaichet, Siripen 1, 87
Popescu, Adrian 71, 119
Popescu-Belis, Andrei 261
Prabhakaran, Balakrishnan 3
Qian, Margaret Yuying 389
Qiu, Zhaofan 159
Rao, Vidyadhar 189
Raymond, Christian 343
Redi, Miriam 151, 417
Robinson, Peter 79
Rong, Xuejian 255
Rudinac, Stevan 333
Rui, Yong 159
Salvador, Amaia 327
Schedl, Markus 103, 393
Schinas, Manos 421
Sebs, Nicu 317
Shah, Rajiv Ratn 423
Shan, Zhenyu 183
Sharma, Avinash 299
Shen, Fumin 305
Shen, Heng Tao 305
Sheng, Bin 111
Sigal, Leonid 15
Singh, Vivek K. 1
Snoek, Cees G. M. 143, 175
Song, Emily 401
Song, Yale 47
Springstein, Matthias 377
Spyromitros-Xioufis, Eleftherios 71
Sterckx, Lucas 409
Su, Fei 135
Sun, Chen 31
Sun, Zhenfeng 7
Tamaazousti, Youssef 63, 119
Tang, Jinhui 405
Tang, Mengfan 87
Thomee, Bart 363
Tian, YIngli 255
Tjondronegoro, Dian 55
Tkalčič, Marko 393
Topkara, Mercan 151, 417
Torres, Ricardo da S. 321
Torrisi, Giovanni 397
Tsikrika, Theodora 359
Valduriez, Patrick 367
Van de Walle, Rik 409
van de Weijer, Joost 339
Vandersmissen, Baptist 409
Vangala, Shruthika 221
Vrochidis, Stefanos 359
Vukotić, Vedran 343
Wang, Dongjing 249
Wang, Jianmin 197
Wang, Ronggang 205
Wang, Shangfei 277
Wang, Wenmin 205
Wang, Xi 7
Wang, Yuhang 405
Wang, Yun 265
Wei, Xingjie 79
Worring, Marcel 333
Wu, Chongliang 277
Wu, Yue 431
Xia, Yingjie 183
Xu, Baohan 15
Xu, Guandong 249
Xu, Xing 305
Xu, Youjiang 285
Xue, Jianfei 229
Yan, Jeff 79
Yan, Junchi 167
Yanai, Keiji 309
Yang, Shujun 413
Yang, Xiaodong 255, 167
Yang, Yang 305
Yao, Ting 159
Yao, Yiyang 183
Ye, Yuancheng 255
Ye, Yuxiang 355
Yeh, Mei-Chen 235
Yin, Xu-Cheng 167
Yu, Lei 39
Zahálka, Jan 333
Zen, Gloria 47
Zha, Hongyuan 167
Zhang, Hao 127
Zhang, Ligang 55
Zhang, Shiliang 281
Zhang, Shiqing 281
Zhang, Wenqiang 7
Zhang, Xin 249
Zhao, Shichao 285
Zhao, Zhicheng 135
Zhen, Mingmin 205
Zhou, Yu 7
Zhu, Han 197
Zhu, Hengliang 111

www.ingramcontent.com/pod-product-compliance
Ingram Content Group UK Ltd.
Pitfield, Milton Keynes, MK11 3LW, UK
UKHW051412290926
15471UKWH00009B/1563

9 781450 345996